SIXTH EDITION
ACCOUNTING 1

GEORGE SYME, B. Com., C.A.

TIM IRELAND, B.P.E.
Eric Hamber Secondary School, Vancouver

PEARSON

Prentice
Hall

Toronto

National Library of Canada Cataloguing in Publication Data
Syme, G. E.
  Accounting 1

6th ed.
Includes index.
ISBN 0-13-092332-X

1. Accounting.   I. Ireland, T. W.   II. Title.

HF5635.S98 2002   657'.042   C2001-903861-5

The publisher has taken care to meet or exceed industry specifications for the manufacturing of textbooks. The spine and the endpapers of this sewn book have been reinforced with special fabric for extra binding strength. The cover is a premium, polymer-reinforced material designed to provide long life and withstand rugged use. Mylar gloss lamination has been applied for further durability.

ISBN: 0-13-092332-X

PUBLISHER: Reid McAlpine
EDITOR: Susan Cox
PRODUCTION COORDINATORS: Helen Luxton, Denise Wake
COVER DESIGN: Alex Li
COVER IMAGE: © Peter Griffith/Masterfile
INTERIOR DESIGN: ArtPlus Limited
PAGE LAYOUT: Heather Brunton, Ruth Nicho!son/ArtPlus Limited

Printed and bound in Canada

8   TCP   08 07

Table of Contents

Preface

In 1970, Prentice-Hall published the first edition of *Accounting 1*. More than 25 years later, the text has retained the features that made it so successful, while keeping pace by adding new material on current accounting practices and procedures. At the same time, new features have also been incorporated in response to requests and suggestions from accounting teachers. We are now proud to introduce the sixth edition on *Accounting 1*, a blend of the best of the old and the new.

We are especially indebted to Mary Watson of ACCPAC International for her expert advice on the new versions of *Simply Accounting*. We would also like to thank ACCPAC International for permission to reproduce screens from the Simply Accounting programs. Thanks also go to Microsoft Corporation for the use of *Microsoft Excel* spreadsheet screens.

Since the teaching of accounting is fundamental to business education, the accounting teacher is a key person in communicating to young people what success in today's business world really requires. We are grateful to all the teachers who have taken the time to share their knowledge and expertise in this area with us. A special thanks is due to those teachers who participated as reviewers and focus group members for this project. We acknowledge the work of Fred Voytek, Kevin Dillion, John Lewicki, Graham Murray, and Janet Smith-Mathiasen who contributed case studies. We would also like to thank the students in Mr. Ireland's class who worked out the exercises to provide answers—Karry Lai, Michelle Lee, Roberta Lei, and Fanny Leung.

GEORGE SYME   TIM IRELAND

Reviewers for Accounting 1, Sixth Edition

Sam Liota
Notre Dame Secondary School
Welland, ON

Diane Minichello
Killarney Secondary School
Vancouver, BC

Fred Masters
Resurrection Catholic Secondary School
Kitchener, ON

Emanuele Nasello
Lakeshore Collegiate Institute
Toronto, ON

Kathleen Ross
Iona Secondary School
Mississauga, ON

Welcome to Accounting 1, Sixth Edition.

This latest edition has been revised to reflect both the new curriculum requirements as well as changes in accounting practices in the business world.

Key Features of this Edition

Clear explanations are easy to read and understand, to ensure ease of student access.

Concepts grouped by sections with exercises and applications immediately after to reinforce concepts.

Realistic exercises, case studies, computer applications, and career profiles provide real-world examples.

New table of contents sequence ensures presentation of topics in a logical order.

Highly visual text that includes a variety of charts, graphs, tables, and screen illustrations to aid understanding.

Increased emphasis on the use of computers in accounting with background information and activities integrated throughout each chapter. Concepts are introduced in two ways: first, using a manual accounting system, and then using software applications (including spreadsheet and accounting software packages) to accomplish the same task.

Summary exercises at the end of the text are designed to reinforce concepts and provide a culminating activity for the course.

Web site icons throughout the text indicate a link to a site that will provide text updates and enhanced student content.

Chapter Overview

Each chapter is organized in the following order:

Chapter Opener — provides overview of chapter content

Chapter Topic — breaks chapter content into sections

Section Exercises — contains a series of short-answer questions and reinforcement activities to follow each section topic.

Computers in Accounting — provides additional topic information using a computer accounting system to complete the required tasks.

Chapter Summary and Review Exercises — includes a summary of key points from chapter, short-answer questions, exercises, case studies, and career profile. Some chapters contain additional computer applications as well.

1

Accounting and Business

As a student just beginning the study of accounting, you would naturally like to know exactly what accounting is. There is no simple definition. **Accounting** is a system of dealing with financial information that provides information for decision-making.

1.1 | What Is Accounting?

There are five main activities involved in accounting. These are:

1. **gathering financial information** about the activities of a business or other organization;
2. **preparing and collecting permanent records**. Records provide evidence of purchase, proof of payment, details of payroll, and so on. They also serve as the basis for dealings with other companies;
3. **rearranging, summarizing, and classifying** financial information into a more useable form;
4. **preparing information reports and summaries** for the following purposes:
   a. to help management reach decisions;

b. to serve the needs of groups outside the business, such as bankers and investors;

c. to measure the profitability of the business;

5. **establishing controls to promote accuracy and honesty among employees.** As businesses grow, owners can no longer look after everything alone. They have to hire others to help them. As soon as employees are hired, accounting controls become essential.

Accounting—An Information System

By enabling financial information to be gathered and prepared, a good accounting system provides the answers to many questions. For example, owners and managers might seek answers to questions such as the following:

- Is the business earning enough profit?
- Are the selling prices of the products high enough?
- How much does ABC Company owe the business?
- How much does the business owe to XYZ Company?
- What is the value of all of the goods for sale?
- Do any of the goods for sale need to be restocked?
- To whom was cheque No. 502 issued?
- How much does it cost to produce product X?
- How much did John Smith earn last year?
- Are our customers paying their bills on time?
- Do we have enough money to meet our needs?
- Can we finance a business expansion?

Accounting provides financial information so that decisions can be made.

Other persons, companies, or organizations might seek answers to the following questions:

- Should I lend money to this business? *(a banker)*
- Should I buy into this business? *(a potential investor)*
- Should I sell this business? *(an owner)*
- Is the business well run? *(an absentee owner)*
- Is the company growing satisfactorily? *(an absentee owner)*
- Can the business afford to pay more to its employees? *(a labour union)*
- Is the business paying the proper amount of income tax? *(the government)*

1.2 | Why Study Accounting?

A knowledge of accounting can be very useful to the student in several ways.

Accounting on the Job

Those of you who decide to enter the business world will find employment more easily if you have a background in accounting. A large number of jobs require accounting and clerical skills. The higher levels require more training and experience but they also offer higher salaries.

Accounting in Daily Life

A working knowledge of accounting is an advantage in daily life. An accounting background will help you with the language of business as well as accounting concepts. You will be better able to handle your personal business affairs, such as preparing a personal budget, keeping personal financial records, and preparing your income tax return. With an improved grasp of financial matters, you will be in a better position to take advantage of business opportunities or to understand the operation of the organization where you work.

An income tax return is a detailed report to the government to determine the amount of tax a person or company should have paid in the previous year

Owning Your Own Business

Many people want to own their own business. In fact, small business is the fastest-growing segment of our economy. If you achieve this goal, you will soon find yourself faced with accounting tasks such as:

- banking;
- keeping track of the amounts owed by customers;
- keeping accounting records for the government;
- producing an income statement for income tax purposes;
- possibly, preparing payrolls and making payroll deductions.

Clearly, a knowledge of accounting is helpful in small business. If a business is to be successful, the owner must be able to make sound management decisions based on good financial records.

Accounting as a Profession

Some of you may choose accounting as a profession. This requires several years of serious study and practice. By completing the requirements of one of the three professional organizations of accountants in Canada, you can become a Chartered Accountant (CA), a Certified General Accountant (CGA), or a Certified Management Accountant (CMA). Qualified professional accountants have the right to practise as public accountants.

A **public accountant** serves the general public for a fee in the same way as a doctor or a lawyer does. The main type of work done by public accountants is auditing. **Auditing** is the examination and testing of the books, records, and procedures of a business in order to be able to express an opinion about its financial statements. Public accountants also work as management consultants and tax advisors.

Professional accountants may choose industrial or institutional accounting rather than public accounting. *Industrial accountants* work for large companies such as IBM or Stelco. *Institutional accountants* work for the government, banks, large insurance companies, and similar organizations. Many of the senior management positions require one of the accounting designations (CA, CMA, CGA) as a qualification.

Complexity of Business

There are many laws laid down by the government concerning fair business practices, income taxes, and so on. However, the laws have become so numerous and complex that only experts can thoroughly understand them. Fully qualified accountants know these laws, so business owners, managers, and professionals (such as dentists, lawyers, etc.) often seek their advice. The increasing complexity of government regulations is a major reason why accounting is such an important profession.

Career Profiles and Activities

At the end of most chapters, you will find a profile of a person who has used accounting knowledge to build a career, as well as questions, information, or suggestions to help you think about your own future.

1.3 | Characteristics of Business

Types of Business

Businesses are the economic framework upon which our society is built. But, what is a business? Generally, *a business involves the manufacture and/or sale of goods or services in order to earn a profit.*

Most businesses fall within one of the following four main categories:

1. The Service Business

A **service business** sells a service to the public; it does not make or sell a product as its main activity. To picture a service business, think of a hairdressing salon, a tutoring service, or a dental clinic.

2. The Merchandising Business

A **merchandising business** buys goods and resells them at a higher price for a profit. To picture a merchandising business, think of a clothing store, a music store, or a supermarket.

(Note: Sometimes a service business sells some products; for example, a hairdressing salon will carry a line of shampoos. But the sale of shampoos is only a sideline, not the main business, which is the service of hairdressing. Similarly, a merchandising business, such as a clothing store, may provide some services, such as repairs and alterations. But these are only add-ons to the main business, which is selling goods.)

3. The Manufacturing or Producing Business

A **manufacturing business** buys raw materials, converts them into a new product, and sells these products to earn a profit. To picture a manufacturing business, think of a construction company, a paper mill, or a steel plant. Another type of business, closely related to manufacturing, is the **producing business**. A farm, for example, produces milk, grain, and other foods. Other activities of producing businesses include oil extraction, mining, forestry, hunting, and fishing.

4. The Non-Profit Organization

A **non-profit organization** may carry on activities to meet social needs and not for a financial profit. To picture these organizations, think of a church, a service club (such as the Rotary Club), an organization (such as the Cancer Society), or a recreational club (such as a community hockey league). Such organizations hope that their work will provide a social benefit. They are required to keep accounting records, especially if they receive funds or a tax-deductible status from the government.

Forms of Business Ownership

There are three main forms of business ownership. If you take a walk down any commercial street, you can see examples of each one.

1. You might notice a sign that reads "J. Wouk, Carpenter." This sign indicates that J. Wouk is in business for himself. He may work alone or others may work for him. This type of business is known as a **sole proprietorship**. The owner is a sole proprietor.
2. You might come across a sign that reads "Fogle, Silver, and Zimmerman, Accountants." This sign suggests that three persons share in the ownership and operation of an accounting business. A business of this type, involving more than one owner, is known as a **partnership**.
3. You might find a sign that reads "Red River Homes Limited." This sign tells you that the business is a limited company or a corporation. A **limited company** or **corporation** is a special form of business that is owned by shareholders. Almost all large business operations are corporations, and some have several thousand shareholders.

Most of the businesses we study in this text are sole proprietorships. Partnerships and corporations are introduced in Chapter 13.

1.4 | The Nature of Accounting

The accounting department of a business includes a wide variety of functions. In a small business, one or two people may do all of the necessary accounting work. In a large business, the accounting work may be divided into several departments, each of which may have many people working in it.

Categories of Accounting Work

Accounting work can be divided into three categories:

1. Routine Daily Activities

These activities occur in the same way nearly every day of the year. They include processing bills, preparing cheques, daily banking, recording transactions, preparing business papers, and so on.

2. Periodic Accounting Activities

These activities occur at regular intervals. Pay cheques are prepared every week or two. The bank accounts are checked every month. The financial reports are prepared each month and every year. Also, the income tax return is prepared every year, as required by government regulation.

3. Miscellaneous Activities

Some accounting activities cannot be predicted. For example, if an accounting employee resigns, the position must be filled quickly. An advertisement is prepared, interviews are conducted, and a selection is made. Or a bank manager may call expressing concern over the size of the bank loan, and a visit to the bank to discuss the matter may become necessary. A salesperson may call about a new machine that she claims will reduce office costs. Time may be taken to see a demonstration of the equipment. In addition, professional accountants take part in meetings and activities put on by their associations.

The Accounting Cycle

Accounting is thought of as occurring in cycles. Accounting activities are performed in relation to equal periods of time known as fiscal periods. The usual length for a fiscal period is one year. The **accounting cycle** can be thought of as the recurring set of accounting procedures carried out during each fiscal period. These accounting activities are carried out repeatedly, period after period. Figure 1.1 below shows the recurring nature of accounting activity.

The accounting cycle really consists of two separate cycles. Figure 1.1 shows these with an inner and an outer ring. Some of the activities shown on the outer ring occur every day. Others occur only once a month. If a computer accounting package is used, steps 2, 3, and 4 are automated and will occur at virtually the same time. The activities on the inner ring normally occur once a year and are based on data provided by the activities of the outer ring.

It must be understood, however, that each cycle is built upon the cumulative results of previous cycles. The business does not have a fresh start each fiscal period.

FIGURE 1.1

The accounting cycle. The terms used here will be explained later in the book.

Over the following eight chapters you will learn to do each of these essential accounting activities.

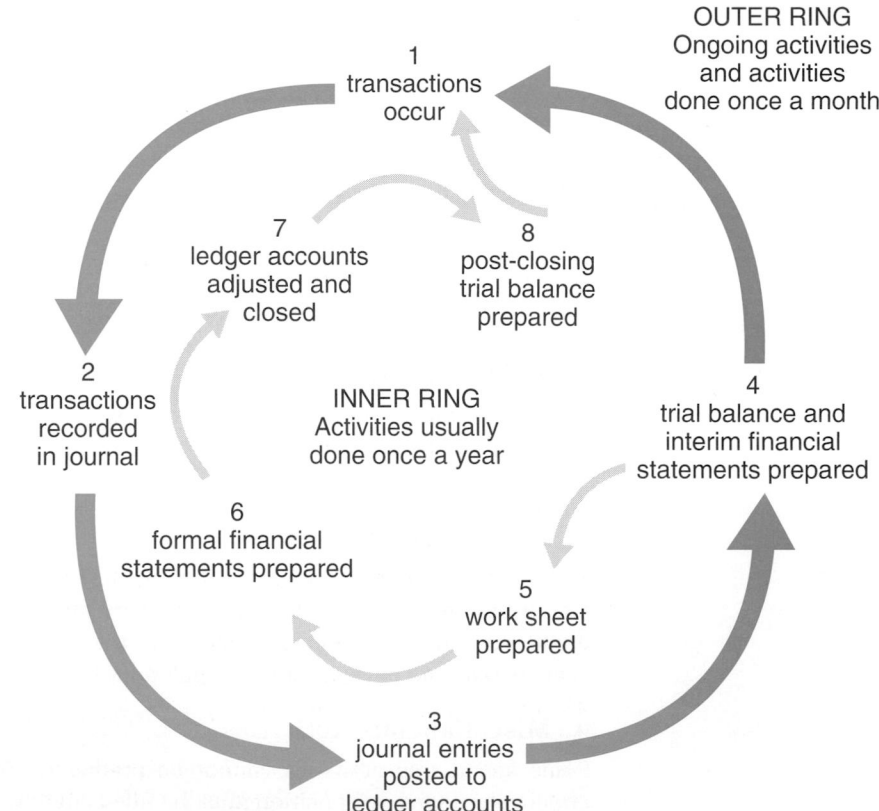

OUTER RING
Ongoing activities and activities done once a month

1 transactions occur

7 ledger accounts adjusted and closed

8 post-closing trial balance prepared

2 transactions recorded in journal

INNER RING
Activities usually done once a year

4 trial balance and interim financial statements prepared

6 formal financial statements prepared

5 work sheet prepared

3 journal entries posted to ledger accounts

1.5 | Becoming a Professional Accountant

A great many accounting jobs exist in our society. Some are entry-level positions with small firms and require only basic accounting skills. Others are high-level positions requiring exceptional competence and training. Between these two extremes, there lies a vast range of accounting occupations in business. Filling these positions are many persons with different backgrounds and abilities. Some may have little or no formal training. Others may have studied at an advanced level for a number of years.

Accountants get their formal training in high school, at college or university, or from a professional organization. In addition to formal studies in accounting, on-the-job experience is important. You are not really prepared to do professional accountancy until you have practical experience along with your formal training.

Most colleges and universities offer diplomas or degree courses in business. The study of accounting is included as part of the curricula of these courses.

Professional Accounting Organizations

To be a fully qualified accountant, you must complete the course prescribed by one of the three national professional accounting organizations:

Certified General Accountants Association
Members' professional designation: CGA (Certified General Accountant)
www.cga-canada.org

Society of Management Accountants of Canada
Members' professional designation: CMA (Certified Management Accountant)
www.cma-canada.org

Canadian Institute of Chartered Accountants (CICA)
Members' professional designation: CA (Chartered Accountant)
www.cica.ca

Each of these national associations has provincial associations working within provincial requirements. The members of all three of these organizations are highly respected professional accountants.

Training To Be a Professional Accountant

To qualify as a professional accountant, you will need further education after secondary school. You should carefully examine the course requirements of each of the three accounting organizations before you enroll. Each organization has its own requirements, which are outlined at their websites. Regardless of which organization you choose, plan on at least six years of post-secondary study and work. This is because the CGA, CMA, and CA organizations generally require their applicants to acquire a university degree and to complete 2 to 2 1/2 years of specialized courses and work experience. (A few non-degree routes to professional accounting designations exist, so interested applicants should use the Internet as a starting point in order to stay informed.)

The CGA program includes a wide range of finance and accounting courses. Students can tailor their careers by following one of four options: corporations/small-medium enterprise; information technology; government/not-for-profit, or public practice. The CGA association is well known for its distance education, which allows students to remain employed while they study to earn course credits towards a CGA designation.

The Society of Management Accountants place their emphasis on management accounting, and most of their graduates take management positions in business and industry, rather than in public practice. CMAs are regarded as experts in cost accounting and industrial accounting.

The CAs represent the longest-standing body in the profession. The Canadian Institute of Chartered Accountants is highly regarded, due in part to its publication of the *CICA Handbook*. The *CICA Handbook* sets accounting rules and standards and is accepted by the other accounting organizations. To enrol as a CA, you must be admitted to a university in a specific program prescribed by the Institute.

The practical experience for CA students is 30 months long and must be completed at an office that has received a training designation from CICA. At the end of the program, students must pass CICA's Uniform Final Exam (UFE), which is a demanding four-day national exam. Once qualified, CAs are especially well prepared to become auditors; however, they may choose careers in any area of accounting.

1.6 Roles of Accounting

Many people confuse "accounting" and "bookkeeping." Accounting and bookkeeping are different, although each is essential to the successful operation of a business. The terms "bookkeeper" and "accounting clerk" describe the same job, but accounting clerk is becoming the more popular designation.

The Accounting Clerk

The work of an **accounting clerk** is clerical in nature and for the most part it is concerned with routine matters. Some of the jobs of an accounting clerk are:

1. ensuring that transactions are properly recorded and that the necessary supporting documents are present and correct;
2. recording the accounting entries in the books of account and balancing the ledger as necessary;
3. making the payroll calculations and preparing the payroll cheques and other payroll records;
4. carrying out all necessary banking transactions.

The Accountant

The work of an **accountant**, on the other hand, is broader in scope and requires more education and experience. A professional accountant is usually responsible for maintaining the entire accounting system. Some of the things an accountant is concerned with are:

1. developing a system to ensure that correct data are entered into the accounting system;
2. ensuring that generally accepted accounting standards are met;
3. interpreting the data produced by the accounting system;
4. preparing reports based on the data output from the system;
5. participating in management meetings and assisting in making business decisions;
6. supervising the work of all accounting employees.

A professional accountant has a high-level position. Key people in many large corporations are professional accountants.

1.7 | How Accountants Use Computers

Computers are ideal for use in an accounting environment. Some of the "number-crunching" activities that computers do very well are recording, sorting, calculating, summarizing, storing, displaying, and printing. Accountants who work effectively with computers are better able to meet the demands of their careers.

All three national accounting organizations recognize the impact technology has on the profession. For example, students in the CGA program acquire "hands-on" computer experience beginning in the first year. Course content is delivered on a CD-ROM with a direct link to CGA websites. To help students gain the required computer knowledge, the association offers three computer tutorials covering spreadsheets, accounting software, and Windows® applications.

Since different businesses use different programs, accounting students must have exposure to a wide variety of computer software. Not only will such exposure make them more employable for clerical positions, but it will also better enable them to perform auditing and consulting functions in the future. Fortunately, once a student learns a few accounting and spreadsheet programs, new ones are mastered quite easily.

While computers are important, it should be stressed that they are merely tools for accountants. They do not make accounting skills unnecessary. For example, read the following job advertisement for a senior cost accountant in a manufacturing firm:

Career Opportunity

The senior cost accountant prepares forecasts, assists in the preparation of annual and long-term plans, and undertakes special studies on request. Specific duties include the maintenance of our product-costing system and the analysis of our monthly results.

Applicants must have superior analytical and problem-solving skills. Communication skills are also essential. Accounting experience in a manufacturing environment and familiarity with the use of computers are key for candidates for this position.

Notice that the important qualifications in this advertisement are listed first: "Applicants must have superior analytical and problem-solving skills." The ability to effectively *communicate* the results of analyses and problem-solving is also an essential requirement.

As you study accounting, keep in mind that developing computer skills along with financial analysis, problem-solving, and communication skills will qualify you for a wide variety of career options.

CHAPTER 1   Summary

CHAPTER HIGHLIGHTS

Now that you have completed Chapter 1, you should:

- have a broad understanding of the objectives of accounting;
- know the four main kinds of businesses and the three forms of business ownership;
- know the benefits to be gained by having a background in accounting;
- know what is meant by *professional accountant* and *public accountant*;
- know the type of work performed by an accounting department;
- understand what is meant by the accounting cycle;
- know the different ways that you can become an accountant;
- know the names of the three national professional accounting organizations;
- understand the value of computer skills to an accountant.

ACCOUNTING TERMS

accountant	corporation	producing business
accounting	limited company	public accountant
accounting clerk	manufacturing business	service business
accounting cycle	merchandising business	sole proprietorship
auditing	non-profit organization	
bookkeeper	partnership	

CHAPTER 1   Review Questions

1. List the five main activities involved in accounting.
2. Give three questions for which the accounting system can provide answers.
3. Identify the two groups that benefit from the information provided by the accounting system.
4. Describe how a knowledge of accounting can help you with respect to employment.
5. Explain how a knowledge of accounting can help people who own their own business.
6. Describe the work of a public accountant.
7. Explain what "auditing" is.
8. Identify three kinds of business besides the service business.
9. List the three forms of business ownership.
10. Give examples of a routine accounting activity and a periodic accounting activity.
11. Define the "accounting cycle."
12. Name the three professional accounting organizations.
13. On average, how long does it take, after enrollment, to become a qualified professional accountant?
14. Why is the Canadian Institute of Chartered Accountants highly regarded?

15. What length of work experience does the Canadian Institute of Chartered Accountants require?
16. Describe briefly the nature of an accounting clerk's work.
17. Describe the scope of an accountant's work.
18. Explain why computer studies are part of the curricula of accounting courses.
19. What computer tutorials do CGA students learn?
20. The computer is merely a tool of accountants. Comment on this statement.

CHAPTER 1 Review Exercises

Using Your Knowledge

1 A list of accounting terms is given below. **In your Workbook, write down the term that matches the statement.**

a. The professional accounting organization that is well-known for distance education.
b. The professional accounting organization that emphasizes management accounting.
c. The professional accounting organization that publishes a handbook of Canadian accounting rules and standards.
d. Formal accounting data, prepared at least once a year.
e. An organization whose main aim is to provide a social benefit, usually at little or no cost to the user.
f. The recurring set of accounting procedures carried out during each fiscal period.
g. A business that buys goods and resells them at a higher price for profit.
h. The owner of a business who is in business alone.
i. A special form of business that is owned by a number of persons called shareholders.
j. Professional persons who offer their services as accountants to the general public.
k. The examining and testing of the books, records, and procedures of a business in order to be able to express an opinion about the financial statements.
l. A business that sells a service to the public and does not make or sell a product.
m. A business that buys raw materials, converts them into a new product, and sells that product to earn a profit.

List of Words or Phrases

accounting cycle
auditing
Certified General Accountants
    Association
corporation
financial statements
Canadian Institute of Chartered
    Accountants (CICA)

manufacturing business
merchandising business
non-profit business
public accountants
service business
Society of Management Accountants
sole proprietor

2 Each of the statements below can be completed by filling in the blank(s) with one or more of the following: *accountant, accounting, accounting clerk.*

In your Workbook, supply the correct term in each of these statements.

a. The work of an _____ is clerical in nature.

b. The work of an _____ is concerned with routine matters.

c. An _____ ensures that the supporting documents are present and correct for every transaction.

d. An _____ ensures that generally accepted accounting principles are followed.

e. An _____ records the accounting entries in the books of account.

f. An _____ makes the payroll calculations.

g. An _____ prepares reports based on the data produced by the accounting system.

h. An _____ carries out all the necessary banking transactions.

i. An _____ participates in management meetings.

j. A professional _____ has a high-level position.

k. For centuries, all _____ was handwritten.

l. Some small businesses still do their _____ by hand.

3 **This exercise also appears in your Workbook.**

1. Which of the following statements does not fit the job title?
   a. An accounting clerk verifies source documents.
   b. An accounting clerk ensures that the ledger balances.
   c. An accounting clerk works neatly to guard against errors.
   d. An accounting clerk studies tax bulletins to keep up to date.

2. Which of the following statements does not fit the job title?
   a. An accounting clerk works out accounting entries.
   b. An accounting clerk, together with the owner, compares this year's and last year's income statements.
   c. An accounting clerk records accounting entries in the books.
   d. An accounting clerk inquires about a suspected error made by the bank.

3. Which of the following statements does not fit the job title?
   a. An accountant is a professional person.
   b. An accountant has a broad knowledge of accounting.
   c. An accountant ensures the accuracy of the payroll deductions.
   d. An accountant discusses the business's "cash flow" with the owners.

4. Which of the following statements does not fit the job title?
   a. An accountant talks about revising a spreadsheet model.
   b. An accountant investigates the credit rating of a new customer.
   c. An accountant is promoted to vice-president.
   d. An accountant is ill; a meeting with the bank manager has to be cancelled.

5. Which of the following statements does not fit the facts about computers?
   a. The computer is an ideal machine for use in an accounting environment.
   b. The computer can handle large quantities of data.
   c. The computer produces better profit figures.
   d. The computer can provide information for management very quickly.

4 **A.** Arrange a brief interview with a professional accountant. Your best sources are relatives and family friends. You may prefer to use the Yellow Pages under "accountants" or to contact the person in charge of the accounting department of a local business. On a sheet of paper, fill in the data for headings below. Be prepared to read your findings to the class.

Name	Professional Designation
Relation to You	General Job Description
Employer	List of Yesterday's On-The-Job Activities This category will give you a glimpse of an accountant's typical day.
Job Title	

B. Did the person you interviewed seem satisfied with the rewards of his or her employment? Would the on-the-job activities be appealing to you in a future career?

Optional

C. Repeat the above for an accounting clerk.

5 To get an idea of what computer software is being used in accounting, find ten job advertisements for accounting positions that mention a particular brand of software. You may use the career pages in a newspaper or online classified ads on the Internet. (To find online classified ads, go to any search engine and use words like "Accounting, Ads, Canada" as your key search words.) Summarize your findings in a table similar to the following:

		Simply Accounting	ACCPAC Pro	QuickBooks	Excel	Lotus 1-2-3	MS Office	Other
1 Company **Position** **Salary Offered**	Homby Real Estate General Accountant n/a		✔					
2 Company **Position** **Salary Offered**	Cottage Construction Office Manager $42 000	✔			✔		✔	
3 Company **Position** **Salary Offered**	Aaron Ong Graphics Payroll Administrator $37 000			✔		✔		WordPerfect
etc.								

(Note: The software names listed above are registered trademarks. MS Office includes Excel, Word, and Access. In advertisements, Simply Accounting usually refers to software made by ACCPAC International, Inc. for small businesses; ACCPAC Pro usually refers to software made by ACCPAC International, Inc. for larger businesses.)

After your table is complete, tally the results and summarize your findings in a one-page report; attach the original job advertisements.

Career

Tom Andrews / Student

Tom Andrews is now in his final year at Swift Current Comprehensive High School in Swift Current, Saskatchewan. His future plans are to obtain a Bachelor of Commerce degree at the University of Regina and then to enroll in the Canadian Institute of Chartered Accountants program.

During his last two years in high school, Tom has been studying accounting and computer concepts to prepare for a responsible position in the business world. He has enjoyed his accounting courses, and his grades have been very good in this area.

Because he had taken accounting courses, Tom was able to get a summer job in the accounting department of Agri-Farm Freight Company, which specializes in the shipping of wheat and other locally produced grains.

Agri-Farm Freight uses a computer system for accounts receivable. Accounts receivable is the money that customers owe to the business. Tom studied computer systems in high school, and was excited to gain practical experience. He handled all customer accounts, coded all sales for computer entry, prepared forms to enter these payments in the computer, and printed all weekly and monthly accounts receivable balances.

Each month, he also printed and issued monthly computer-produced customer statements.

Because he controlled the paper flow of a wide variety of tasks within an accounting office, Tom realizes that organization, neatness, and accuracy are extremely important.

The accounting courses and work experience provide Tom with a good base for further study. He finds it easier to concentrate on the concepts of accounting because he has already mastered the practical aspects.

Tom is very pleased with the work he has done for Agri-Farm Freight during the summer months. His employers are so impressed with his work that they would like him to return during the summer while he studies at university. They want him to accept a highly responsible position with the company once he has completed his education.

Discussion

1. The company that Tom works for, Agri-Farm Freight Company, ships grain for its customers. Would you describe this as a service business, a merchandising business, a manufacturing business, or a producing business, on the basis of what you have read in Chapter 1 about types of businesses?
2. Make a list of three different types of summer job for which accounting and business courses would make a student more eligible.
3. "Tom realizes that organization, neatness, and accuracy are extremely important." Why should these skills be important today, when computers are used extensively in most businesses?

The Balance Sheet

2.1 | Financial Position

One of the most important uses of accounting data is to show the *financial position* of a person or a business or other organization. In fact, the concept of **financial position** is basic to the whole system of accounting.

The concept of financial position is simple and straightforward. If you wanted to determine your own financial position, how would you go about it?

You would likely decide that the following three steps were necessary:

Step 1 **List and total the things that you own that have dollar values**. These are called **assets**.

Step 2 **List and total your debts**. These are called **liabilities**.

Step 3 **Calculate the difference between total assets and total liabilities**. This difference is called the **capital** or the **owner's equity** (or just equity). A less commonly used term is **net worth**.

Example:
Let us follow the three steps given above to work out the financial position of Chris Turner, a student, on July 15, 20–.

Step 1   List and total the things of value that Chris owns. These *assets* might be as follows:

Cash	$ 55.00
Bank Balance	215.50
Bicycle	185.00
Stereo	250.00
Ski Equipment	300.00
Total Assets	$1 005.50

Step 2   List and total Chris's debts. These *liabilities* might be as follows:

Owed to brother Philip	$ 80.00
Owed to Dad	200.00
Overdue Fines	12.50
Total Liabilities	$292.50

Step 3   Calculate the difference between total assets and total liabilities. The calculation is as follows

Total Assets	$1 005.50
Total Liabilities	292.50
Difference	$ 713.00

This difference of $713.00 is the amount that Chris is worth. It is known as his *capital*, his *equity*, or his *net worth*.

The analysis just completed shows that three steps are needed to work out a person's financial position. These same three steps are needed to work out the financial position of a business or other organization.

The Fundamental Accounting Equation

The previous section showed that the total assets minus the total liabilities is equal to the capital or equity. This relationship is always true and can be written in the form of an equation.

This **fundamental accounting equation** may be stated in this way:

$$A - L = OE \quad (\text{Assets} - \text{Liabilities} = \text{Owner's Equity})$$

The equation may also be stated in another way:

$$A = L + OE \quad (\text{Assets} = \text{Liabilities} + \text{Owner's Equity})$$

Now let us use the figures for Chris Turner to see the fundamental accounting equation at work:

$$
\begin{array}{ccccc}
A & - & L & = & OE \\
\$1\ 005.50 & - & \$292.50 & = & \$713.00
\end{array}
$$

or

$$
\begin{array}{ccccc}
A & = & L & + & OE \\
\$1\ 005.50 & = & \$292.50 & + & \$713.00
\end{array}
$$

The fundamental accounting equation is extremely important in the study of accounting. As you will soon see, it is the basis on which accounting theory is built.

Section 2.1   **Review Questions**

1. Explain how to calculate a person's financial position.
2. Define "asset."
3. Define "liability."
4. Define "owner's equity."
5. What is another term that means the same thing as "equity"?
6. Give two forms of the fundamental accounting equation.

Section 2.1   **Exercises**

1. **Classify each of the following as an asset or a liability:**

   office furniture   an amount loaned to R. Jonas
   land   mortgage payable
   bank loan   automobile
   house and lot   a Canada Savings Bond
   an unpaid heating bill

2. **Karen Lipka has assets of $150 000 and liabilities of $65 000. What is her equity?**

3. **If the total assets of a business are $37 486.49 and the total liabilities are $11 547.80, calculate the owner's equity.**

4. On December 31, 20–1, A. Lower's accounting equation was as follows:

   Assets ($150 000) − Liabilities ($70 000) = Equity ($80 000)

   If during 20–2 the assets increase by $70 000 and the liabilities decrease by $20 000, calculate the owner's equity at December 31, 20–2.

5. Claude Pineau, a factory worker in Hull, Quebec, asks you to help him find out how much he is worth. From a discussion with him you find out the following facts:

   a. His bank balance is $754.
   b. He owns a home valued at $82 500 which has a mortgage on it of $12 500.
   c. He owns furniture and household equipment valued at $16 000.
   d. He owns a summer property valued at $65 000 which he bought entirely with money borrowed from the bank. Since the time of purchase he has paid back $20 000 of the loan.
   e. He has unpaid bills amounting to $1 560.
   f. He owes his father-in-law, M. Dupuis, the sum of $10 000 which he borrowed interest-free several years ago at the time he bought his home.

   List Claude Pineau's assets in one column, his liabilities in another, and calculate his net worth.

6. Paul Silva's assets and liabilities are listed below in random order.
Bank balance, $856.25; Bank loan, $5 000.00; House and lot, $185 000.00; Cash on hand, $85.35; Amount owed to Imperial Oil, $135.60; Amount owed to Weston Hydro, $85.50; Miscellaneous equipment, $1 850.00; Mortgage on house and lot, $90 000.00; Household furniture and furnishings, $4 800.00; Amount loaned to Phil Silva, $2 000.00.

   A. List the assets in one column and total them.
   B. List the liabilities in another column and total them.
   C. Calculate Paul Silva's equity.

2.2 | The Balance Sheet

The formal way of presenting financial position is by means of a statement called a balance sheet. A **balance sheet** is a statement showing the financial position of a person, business, or other organization. You can see a balance sheet in Figure 2.1 below. This balance sheet shows the financial position of Chris Turner, whom you met on page 15.

FIGURE 2.1

A personal balance sheet.

Chris Turner					
Balance Sheet					
July 15, 20—					
Assets			*Liabilities*		
Cash	$	5 5 00	Owed to Philip	$	8 0 00
Bank Balance		2 1 5 50	Owed to Dad		2 0 0 00
Bicycle		1 8 5 00	Overdue Fines		1 2 50
Stereo		2 5 0 00	Total Liabilities	$	2 9 2 50
Ski Equipment		3 0 0 00			
			Owner's Equity		
			Chris Turner, Capital		7 1 3 00
Total Assets	$ 1 0 0 5 50		Total Liabilities and Equity	$ 1 0 0 5 50	

All balance sheets have the same general format. The balance sheet that appears in Figure 2.2 is for a small business.

Important Features of the Balance Sheet

Examine the two balance sheets carefully. In particular, observe the following:

1. The balance sheet is set up in the form of the fundamental accounting equation: A = L + OE. The assets appear on the left side, and the liabilities and the owner's equity appear on the right side.
2. A three-line heading is used. The heading tells:
   WHO?—the name of the individual, business, or other organization;
   WHAT?—the name of the financial statement (in this case, the balance sheet);
   WHEN?— the date on which the financial position is determined.

FIGURE 2.2

The balance sheet of a small business.

Easy Rent-Alls								
Balance Sheet								
September 30, 20—								
Assets				*Liabilities*				
Cash on Hand	$	4 0 20		Accounts Payable				
Bank Balance		7 1 0 00		– Arrow Supply	$	1 9 5 0 40		
Accounts Receivable				– Best Repairs		1 2 5 0 00		
– W. Boa		1 3 1 50		Bank Loan		15 0 0 0 00		
– T. Burns		3 5 0 00		Mortgage Payable		65 2 0 0 00		
Supplies		9 6 5 00		Total Liabilities		$83 4 0 0 40		
Land	48 0 0 0 00							
Buildings	114 0 0 0 00			*Owner's Equity*				
Rental Equipment	75 3 6 4 70			J. Salas, Capital		156 1 6 1 00		
Total Assets	$239 5 6 1 40			Total Liabilities and Equity		$239 5 6 1 40		

There is no uniform order in which long-lasting assets are listed on balance sheets. Many accountants show Land and Buildings before items such as Equipment because the former hold their value well upon liquidation. Others prefer to list these assets from the ones of least permanence to those of most permanence. This text usually shows Land and Buildings first.

3. The assets are generally listed in the order of their *liquidity*. **Liquidity** means the order in which the assets are converted into cash. Cash on Hand and Bank Balance, being cash already, are the most liquid and are listed first. Long-lasting assets such as equipment and buildings are listed later because normally they are not converted into cash but are used in the operation of the business.

4. The liabilities are generally listed in the order in which they are normally paid.

5. The financial details of any item are fully disclosed on a balance sheet. For example, on the balance sheet for Easy Rent-Alls, the Land and Buildings are listed in the Assets section at their respective values of $48 000 and $114 000. The amount that is owed against the property, the Mortgage Payable of $65 200, is listed in the Liabilities section. This is a more informative presentation than if, for example, Land and Buildings had just been shown as a total of $96 800 ($48 000 + $114 000 – $65 200).

6. The two final totals, one on each side of the balance sheet, are recorded on the same line and underlined with a double line.

Accounts Receivable and Accounts Payable

On the balance sheet of Easy Rent-Alls above, you will also see the items Accounts Receivable and Accounts Payable. These two items are explained as follows:

Accounts Receivable   The customers of a business often buy goods or services from a business with the understanding that they will pay for them later. These customers then owe money to the business. They are in debt to the business. The debts owed represent a dollar value to the business, so the business is right to include them among its assets on the balance sheet.

These debts of customers are known as **accounts receivable** (sometimes abbreviated A/R). Each of the customers who owes money to the business is one of its debtors. A **debtor** is anyone who owes money to the business.

Accounts Payable   Similarly, a business often purchases goods and services from its suppliers with the understanding that payment will be made later. The business is in debt to its suppliers. These debts to suppliers represent a dollar obligation of the business. The business is right to include them among its liabilities.

Debts owed by the business are referred to as **accounts payable** (sometimes abbreviated A/P). Each of the suppliers owed money by the business is one of its creditors. A **creditor** is anyone to whom the business owes money.

Preparing a Balance Sheet

The steps in preparing a simple balance sheet are shown in the following illustrations. The balance sheet of Easy Rent-Alls is used in the example.

Step 1   Write in the statement heading on columnar paper as shown in Figure 2.3 below. The heading must indicate the name of the business, the name of the statement, and the date of the statement.

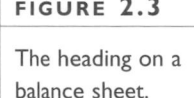

FIGURE 2.3

The heading on a balance sheet.

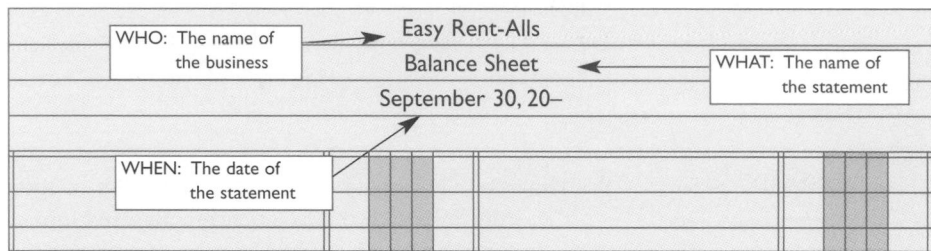

Step 2   Write in the sub-heading "Assets" at the top of the left-side column. Underline the sub-heading. Then write in the assets on the left side as shown in Figure 2.4 below.

FIGURE 2.4

The assets listed on a balance sheet.

Assets are generally listed in the order in which they can be converted to cash.

Since supplies are used fairly quickly, they are listed before items such as Land and Equipment.

Easy Rent-Alls		
Balance Sheet		
September 30, 20–		
Assets		
Cash on Hand	4 0	20
Bank Balance	7 1 0	00
Accounts Receivable		
– W. Boa	1 3 1	50
– T. Burns	3 5 0	00
Supplies	9 6 5	00
Land	48 0 0 0	00
Buildings	114 0 0 0	00
Rental Equipment	75 3 6 4	70

Sub-heading

Amounts in money column

Do not enter total assets figure at this time.

The assets are generally listed in the order of their liquidity. Cash and bank balance, being the most liquid, are listed first. Accounts receivable are listed next because they are usually collected within 30 days. The names of the customers are usually given in alphabetical order. Supplies and long-lasting assets are listed later because normally they are not converted into cash.

Step 3   Write in the sub-heading "Liabilities" at the top of the right-side column. Underline the sub-heading. Then write in the liabilities on the right side as shown in Figure 2.5 below. The liabilities are listed in the order in which they will be paid. Suppliers' names are usually placed in alphabetical order.

Draw a line below the last liability to indicate that you are adding up the figures above the line. Then write in "Total Liabilities" and the total.

FIGURE 2.5

The liabilities listed on a balance sheet.

Liabilities are listed in the order in which they must be paid. On page 26 you will see another location for "Bank Loan."

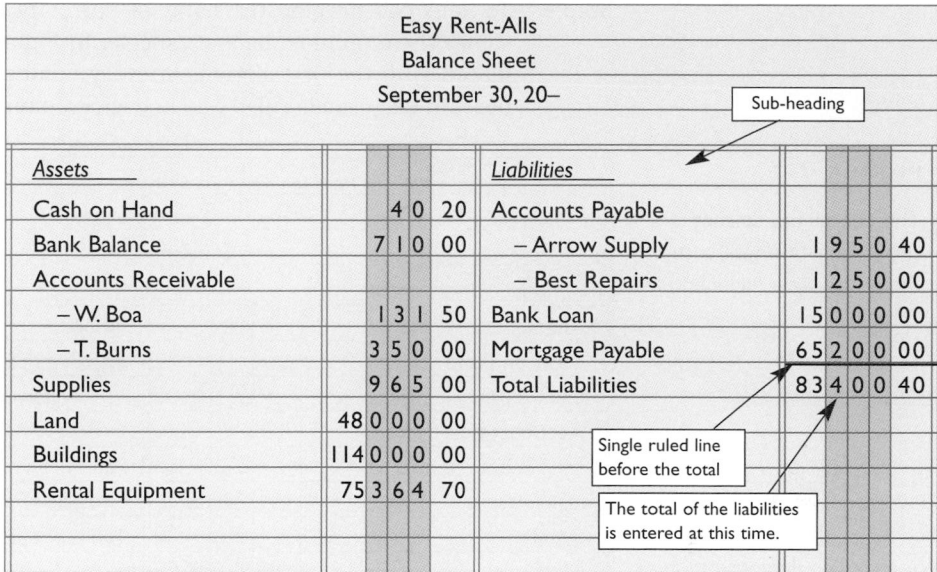

Step 4   Beneath the liabilities, write in the sub-heading "Owner's Equity." Underline the sub-heading. Then write in the owner's name plus the word "Capital" and the equity figure, as shown in Figure 2.6 below. As you know, this figure is the difference between the total assets and the total liabilities. You have to know the total assets figure to calculate the equity, but do not write it in until step 5 on page 22.

FIGURE 2.6

The owner's equity recorded on a balance sheet.

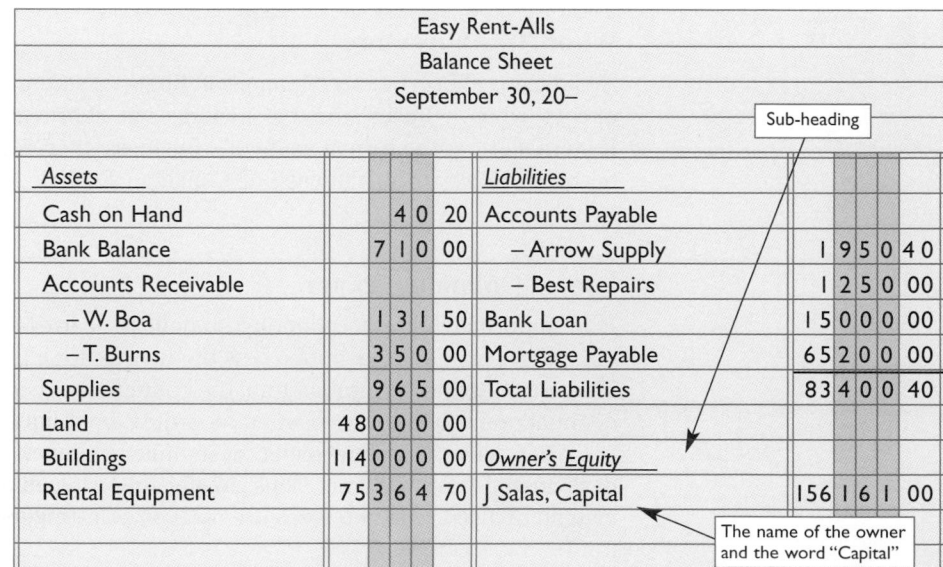

Step 5   Complete the balance sheet by writing in the final totals as shown in Figure 2.7. These totals are written on the first fully open line.

On this line, write in "Total Assets" on the left side and "Total Liabilities and Equity" on the right side. Write in the totals. The two totals must be on the same line and must agree. Place a single ruled line above and a double ruled line below each of the two totals.

Step 6   To help you develop the habit of correctly using dollar signs, this text shows them on most balance sheets. In Figure 2.7, notice a dollar sign is placed with the first amount in every column. A dollar sign is also used beneath each single-ruled line in each column.

FIGURE 2.7

The completed balance sheet for a business, with the dollar signs included.

For an online demonstration of the steps to follow to create a balance sheet, visit www.pearsoned.ca/accounting1

					Easy Rent-Alls						
					Balance Sheet						
					September 30, 20–						
Assets					*Liabilities*						
Cash on Hand	$		4	0 20	Accounts Payable						
Bank Balance		7	1	0 00	– Arrow Supply	$	1	9	5	0	40
Accounts Receivable					– Best Repairs		1	2	5	0	00
– W. Boa		1	3	1 50	Bank Loan		15	0	0	0	00
– T. Burns		3	5	0 00	Mortgage Payable		65	2	0	0	00
Supplies		9	6	5 00	Total Liabilities	$	83	4	0	0	40
Land	48	0	0	0 00							
Buildings	114	0	0	0 00	*Owner's Equity*						
Rental Equipment	75	3	6	4 70	J. Salas, Capital		156	1	6	1	00
Total Assets	$239	5	6	1 40	Total Liabilities and Equity	$239	5	6	1	40	

Basic Recordkeeping Practices

When To Abbreviate

Avoid using abbreviations of names on financial statements, such as balance sheets, except when a business name includes an abbreviation. For example, General Bakeries Ltd. is the formal name of a business; therefore, the abbreviation Ltd. can be used. However, in the case of Canadian Electric Company, do not abbreviate "Company" to "Co."

Use of Columnar Paper

It is important for an accounting student to learn to use columnar paper. When columnar paper is used, notice how the figures are placed carefully in the columns. This is to help the accountant total the columns correctly. Observe that commas and decimal points are not used when recording amounts of money in columns.

When using columnar paper, even-dollar amounts may be shown by placing a dash in the cents column. Thus, in the following illustration, 12— may be used instead of 12.00. The two zeros are used on printed reports.

```
     5 0 6 2 1
 1 0 0 0  –
       5 1 2 0
     1 2  –
```

Use of Ruled Lines

If a column of figures is to be totalled (added or subtracted), a single line is drawn beneath the column and the total is placed beneath this single line as shown below:

```
 1 3 1 1 0
   1 4 1 1
   3 1 0 5
 1 7 6 2 6
```

If a total happens to be a final total, such as the last amounts on the balance sheet, a double ruled line is drawn immediately beneath the total as shown below:

```
   1 4 6 2
 1 9 4 7 5
   3 0 0 0
   1 2 6 5
 2 5 2 0 2
```

On most balance sheets, in order to place the two final totals on the same line, it is necessary to leave one or more blank lines between the figures in a column and the column total. When this is done, the single ruled line is placed close to the "total" figure and not immediately beneath the figures in the column. The following examples show this.

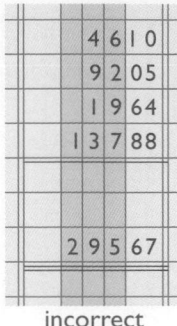
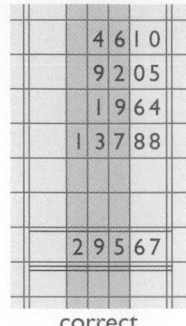

incorrect   correct

Neatness

It is most important that an accountant's work be neat and perfectly legible. This is necessary so that no one misinterprets the writing or the numbers. Although the work should never be untidy, it is not necessary for it to be beautiful—only neat and legible.

From the beginning, you should make it a habit to strive for neatness, accuracy, and clarity in all of your exercises. Be sure to use your ruler to rule lines beneath headings and in the columns.

Section 2.2   Review Questions

1. What is a balance sheet?
2. Where does the name of a business appear in the heading of a balance sheet?
3. On which side of a balance sheet are the assets listed? The liabilities?
4. How is an automobile that is not fully paid for listed on a balance sheet?
5. Give two rules for placing dollar signs on balance sheets.
6. On which side of a balance sheet does a creditor appear?
7. What is meant by a single ruled line drawn beneath a column of figures?
8. Why is it important for an accountant's work to be neat?
9. When is a double ruled line drawn beneath a total?
10. When can short forms or abbreviations be used on financial statements?
11. Which is the most liquid asset? Why?
12. In what order are liabilities listed on a balance sheet?
13. In what order are assets listed on a balance sheet?
14. What are accounts receivable?
15. What are accounts payable?
16. What term describes any supplier to whom the business owes money?
17. What term describes any company or person who owes money to the business?

Section 2.2   Exercises

1. Kate Kramer is the owner and operator of The Kramer Company located in Kingston, Ontario. On September 30, 20—, The Kramer Company had the following assets and liabilities.

A. **Prepare the September 30 balance sheet for The Kramer Company.**

The terms debtor and creditor are placed in brackets to help you identify them. Do not write these terms on your balance sheet.

Assets

Cash on Hand	$ 106
Bank Balance	1 530
J. Crothers (debtor)	1 100
R. Zack (debtor)	370
Supplies	1 200
Furniture and Equipment	14 700
Delivery Equipment	20 100

Liabilities

Able Supply Company (creditor)	740
C.P. Gregg (creditor)	3 000
Bank Loan	10 000

B. If the Kramer Company were a retailing business, it would list an asset named "Merchandise Inventory." **What do you suppose Merchandise Inventory is? After which asset on the balance sheet would you place Merchandise Inventory? Explain why you would choose this location.**

2. The New Western Company in Fort Frances, Ontario, owned by Guy Albrecht, had the following assets and liabilities on March 31, 20—. **Prepare a balance sheet for the company as of that date.**

Bank	$ 1 896
Tasty Beverages (debtor)	750
Food Haven (debtor)	400
Metro Mall (debtor)	1 235
Supplies	850
Furniture and Equipment	75 840
Trucks	35 000
Land	50 000
Building	140 000
Household Finance Company (creditor)	19 345
General Trading Company (creditor)	2 356
Lightning Electronics (creditor)	3 378
Bank Loan	10 000
Mortgage Payable	75 000

3. Michael Travis, the owner of Travis and Company located in Moncton, New Brunswick, gave the following list of assets and liabilities to a public accountant and asked him to prepare a balance sheet as of March 31, 20—. **Prepare the balance sheet as if you were the public accountant.**

Amounts owed to Travis and Company:

— G. Fordham	$ 1 042.16
— W. Gaines	743.86
— D. Samuelson	1 346.95

Amounts owed by Travis and Company to suppliers:

— Beacon Company	1 567.25
— Empire Insurance	150.00
— Gem Finance	1 236.45
— General Supply	15 540.00
— Raymond and Company	125.00

Office Supplies	326.40
Bank Balance	4 946.03
Office Equipment	11 960.00
Shop Equipment	3 535.00
Delivery Equipment	14 240.00
Bank Loan	25 000.00
Mortgage Payable	52 000.00
Building	135 000.00
Land	46 000.00

2.3 | Claims against the Assets

In the previous section, you saw that a business lists the assets it owns on the left side of a balance sheet. Who is entitled to these assets? The answer is shown on the right side of the balance sheet. That is, both the creditors and the owner have a claim on the assets.

Why do the creditors and owner have a claim on the assets? Part of the answer is that they have either provided the funds used to acquire the assets, or they have provided the assets themselves. The balance sheet of Paramount Design, owed by Janet Korey, shown in Figure 2.8 below, shows clearly who has a claim against the assets of her business.

FIGURE 2.8

The balance sheet of Paramount Design showing the claims against the assets.

In this text and in business, you will see some balance sheets showing Bank Loan before Accounts Payable. This is because the loan is repayable on demand, which gives the bank the right "call" in the loan at any time. This means the loan could be due before accounts payable, and so it is listed before accounts payable on the balance sheet. (In reality, a bank will only call a demand loan when the business is in financial trouble. Under normal circumstances, the loans have no set due date; businesses pay demand loans down when they want to reduce interest costs.)

Paramount Design							
Balance Sheet							
December 30, 20–							
Assets			*Liabilities*				
Cash	$ 1 407 10		Bank Loan		$ 9 000 00		
Accounts Receivable			Accounts Payable				
– R. Mason	350 00		– Modern Art Store		1 905 00		
– H. Morgan	1 706 00		– Oakes Supply		750 00		
Supplies	1 250 00		Total Liabilities		$11 655 00		
Furniture	970 00						
Equipment	10 000 00		*Owner's Equity*				
Automobile	19 350 00		Janet Korey, Capital		32 108 10		
Total Assets	$43 763 10		Total Liabilities and Equity		$43 763 10		

Claims of the creditors

Claim of the owner

As shown on the left side of the balance sheet, Janet's business assets are $43 763.10. The right side of the balance sheet shows that these assets, or the funds to obtain them, were provided by the bank, $9 000; the other creditors, $1 905 and $750; and Janet herself, $32 108.10.

Expressed in another way, according to the fundamental accounting equation:

$$\underbrace{\$43\ 763.10}_{\text{Assets}} = \underbrace{\$9\ 000 + \$1\ 905 + \$750}_{\substack{\text{Creditors' claims} \\ \text{against the assets}}} + \underbrace{\$32\ 108.10}_{\substack{\text{Owner's claim} \\ \text{against the assets}}}$$

Creditors' Claims First

If a business is closed down, to whom do the assets belong? They still belong to the owners and creditors. But the claims of the creditors are settled first, followed by the claim of the owner. This means that the owner has to accept any losses that might occur from selling off any assets. On the other hand, the owner benefits from any profits that might occur. The owner always gets what is left after the claims of the creditors have been paid.

Selling the assets of a business for cash is called **liquidation**.

Suppose that Janet Korey closed down the business and, in the process, suffered a loss of $7 200 when selling off the assets. The equation shown above would not remain the same, but would show the loss of $7 200 as follows:

$$\$36\ 563.10\ =\ \$9\ 000 + \$1\ 905 + \$750\ +\ \$24\ 908.10$$

Assets (now all cash) down $7 200	Creditors' claims remain the same	Owner's claim down $7 200

Section 2.3   **Review Questions**

1. Give two reasons why creditors have claims against the assets of a business.
2. How can you quickly find out who has a claim against the assets of a business?
3. Who has first claim against the assets of a business?
4. Who benefits from gains made in closing down a business?
5. Who (primarily) suffers from losses incurred in closing down a business?

Section 2.3   **Exercises**

1. Joseph Litz is the owner of Bayliner Boat Charters, a business in Truro, Nova Scotia, that has six sailboats for hire. Mr. Litz has been able to make a comfortable living from renting out these boats during the sailing season.

BAYLINER BOAT CHARTERS
BALANCE SHEET
OCTOBER 31, 20—

Assets			Liabilities	
Bank	$	900	Bank Loan	$ 18 000
Accounts Receivable		1 050	Accounts Payable	3 740
Supplies		1 250	Mortgage Payable	80 000
Property		175 000	Total Liabilities	$101 740
Equipment		4 390	Owner's Equity	
Boats		32 850	J. Litz, Capital	113 700
Total Assets		$215 440	Total Liabilities and Equity	$215 440

Mr. Litz is past retirement age and is finding the business more than he can comfortably handle. He has attempted to sell it intact, but has been unsuccessful. He has decided, therefore, to sell the assets for cash and pay off the claims of the creditors. In this way, he can get his equity out of the business.

Mr. Litz hires a liquidator to help him. Through this person's services, the accounts receivable are collected in full. The supplies are sold for $500; the equipment is sold for $2 000; the boats are sold for $20 350; and the property is sold for $180 000. The liquidator charges $1 500.

A. Prepare a detailed calculation showing how much Mr. Litz will receive as a result of his claim against the assets.

B. Why would the owner prefer to sell the business itself rather than the assets?

---

2. Carla Mann is the owner of Carla's Interior Design in London, Ontario. A new firm has come to town and Carla has accepted a position with them. Carla is closing down her own business and is in the process of selling the assets.

Just before she accepted her new position, the balance sheet of Carla's Interior Design was as follows:

CARLA'S INTERIOR DESIGN
BALANCE SHEET
JUNE 30, 20—

Assets		Liabilities	
Cash	$ 1 500	Bank Loan	$ 9 500
Accounts Receivable	7 870	Accounts Payable	1 250
Supplies	1 520	Total Liabilities	$10 750
Equipment	3 740	Owner's Equity	
Automobile	17 500	Carla Mann, Capital	21 380
Total Assets	$32 130	Total Liabilities and Equity	$32 130

Carla was successful in selling the supplies for $1 200 cash and the equipment for $2 200 cash. She was also able to collect in cash all of the accounts receivable except for $870, which was considered to be uncollectable.

A. Prepare a simple balance sheet as of July 31, after disposing of the three assets mentioned above.

B. Suggest the simplest way to dispose of the remaining assets and thus complete the closing of the business.

2.4 Generally Accepted Accounting Principles

In performing their work, accountants follow a set of rules or standards known as generally accepted accounting principles (GAAPs). GAAPs include a number of specific rules, practices, and procedures. Some are formal regulations and others set out what has become common practice over the years.

The Canadian Institute of Chartered Accountants (CICA) is the professional accounting organization that establishes the standards for accountants in Canada. The complete body of accounting knowledge and opinion is contained in the *CICA Handbook*. The handbook is prepared in looseleaf form so that it can be updated regularly. This is done by issuing revised pages with new information or to replace information that has become incorrect.

Three GAAPs are introduced below. Others are introduced at appropriate places throughout the text. A list of GAAPs is given in the Appendix.

GAAP—The Business Entity Concept

> The business entity concept **provides that the accounting for a business organization must be kept separate from the personal affairs of its owner, or from any other business or organization.**

This means that the owner of the business should not place any personal assets, such as the family home, on the business balance sheet. The balance sheet of the business must reflect the financial position of the business alone. Also, when transactions of the business are recorded, any personal expenditures of the owner are charged to the owner. They are not allowed to affect the operating results of the business.

The balance sheet of Easy Rent-Alls in Figure 2.2 on page 19 complies with the business entity concept. The balance sheet reflects the affairs of the business only. No personal assets or liabilities are included.

GAAP—The Continuing Concern Concept

> The continuing concern concept **assumes that a business will continue to operate unless it is known that it will not. This is also known as the** going concern concept.

The dollar values associated with a business that is alive and well are straightforward. For example, a supply of envelopes with the company's name printed on them would be valued at their cost price. This would not be the case if the company were going out of business. In that case, the envelopes would be difficult to sell because the company's name is on them. The values of such assets often cannot be determined until they are actually sold. When a company is going out of business, the values of the assets usually suffer because they have to be sold under unfavourable circumstances. But sometimes the values improve. For example, if a business had bought land in downtown Toronto in 1955, the land would undoubtedly sell for more than the value on the balance sheet if the business were to be closed down.

GAAP—The Principle of Conservatism

> The principle of conservatism **provides that accounting for a business should be fair and reasonable.**

In their work, accountants are required to make evaluations and estimates, to deliver opinions, and to select procedures. They should do this in such a way that assets or profits are neither overstated nor understated when uncertainty exists.

Section 2.4   Review Questions

1. Over the years, what has the Canadian Institute of Chartered Accountants established?
2. In what publication are most of the rules of accounting found?
3. What does GAAP stand for?
4. Explain the business entity concept.
5. Explain the continuing concern concept.
6. Explain the principle of conservatism.

Section 2.4   Exercises

1. **This exercise also appears in your Workbook.**

   Kevin Kaghee is the owner of Central Paving Company in Charlottetown, Prince Edward Island. His personal and business assets and liabilities are listed below and on page 31.

   A. Separate the list below into the two columns provided.

   B. Calculate the total assets and the total liabilities in each column.

   C. Calculate Kevin Kaghee's personal net worth and his equity in Central Paving Company.

Assets	Amount	Business	Personal
Accounts Receivable	$ 27 460		
Boat and Motor	16 520		
Business Bank Balance	1 852		
Business Automobiles	48 054		
Furniture and Appliances	6 528		
Government Bonds of Owner	20 000		
House and Lot	99 600		
Office Furniture and Equipment	18 324		
Office Supplies	3 545		
Owner's Automobiles	18 657		
Paving Materials	55 326		
Personal Bank Balance	1 258		
Plant Property and Buildings	125 358		
Summer Cottage	65 874		
Trucks and Equipment	285 657		
Total Assets			

Liabilities				
Accounts Payable	$ 3 500			
Business Bank Loan	56 000			
Mortgage on Plant Property	75 000			
Mortgage on House and Lot	60 000			
Mortgage on Summer Cottage	22 300			
Owed to Finance Co.—Business Equipment	136 522			
Total Liabilities				
Owner's Equity/Personal Net Worth				

Cases for Further Thought

Briefly answer the following questions.

1. A customer who owes $500 to the business has recently died. The lawyers for the customer's estate have told the business that there is only one chance in four of the debt being paid.
   a. Should the amount be included on the balance sheet of the business?
   b. Which GAAP(s) affect this situation? Explain.
2. A contracting company is involved in a dispute over its bill to a customer. The bill for $500 000 was recently reduced to $400 000 by a decision of the courts. The company is now appealing the decision.
   a. Which amount should be taken into the accounts (recognized)?
   b. Which GAAP(s) affect this situation? Explain.
3. Six months ago, you closed out your business. Now, a person has expressed an interest in acquiring the business. The potential buyer requests a current balance sheet, but you provide her with the one that was prepared just prior to closing.
   a. Will the balance sheet be accepted by the buyer and her accountant?
   b. Which GAAP(s) affect this situation? Explain.
4. Martha Higgins is currently trying to borrow some money from the bank. She has listed her personal automobile ($25 000) on the business balance sheet to make the statement look more attractive to the banker.
   a. Is this a reasonable thing to do?
   b. Which GAAP(s) affect this situation? Explain.
5. The manager of a business has heard that the business might be sold and that he might lose his job as a result. When preparing a balance sheet for the owner, the manager values everything as low as possible in order to discourage the prospective buyer. He claims that this practice is allowed by the principle of conservatism.
   a. Is the manager correct in his claim?
   b. Which GAAP(s) affect this situation? Explain.
6. A figure of $25 000 for computerized office equipment appears on a company balance sheet. Recently, better quality equipment has been developed and put on the market. However, the existing equipment still does an adequate job for the company, and the company has no intention of replacing it.
   a. Should the equipment figure be eliminated because it represents obsolete equipment?
   b. Which GAAP(s) affect this situation? Explain.

2.5 | Using a Computer:
A Spreadsheet for Personal Balance Sheets

Balance sheets present the financial position of a person, business, or organization in a formal way. To ensure the presentation is both accurate and attractive, accountants use computer systems and business software. Two popular types of software are spreadsheet and accounting programs. This section introduces you to spreadsheet software.

Spreadsheets are software programs designed for a large assortment of mathematical tasks, including calculating, organizing, and presenting data. They are arranged in a grid-like pattern. That is, they have columns and rows. In Figure 2.9, the vertical columns are identified by the letters of the alphabet, and the horizontal rows are identified by numbers. Each rectangle in the grid is known as a **cell**. Cells are formed by the intersection of the columns and the rows. This is why the cells are identified as A1, A2, B5, C8, and so on.

FIGURE 2.9

A Microsoft® Excel spreadsheet.

Cell Pointer

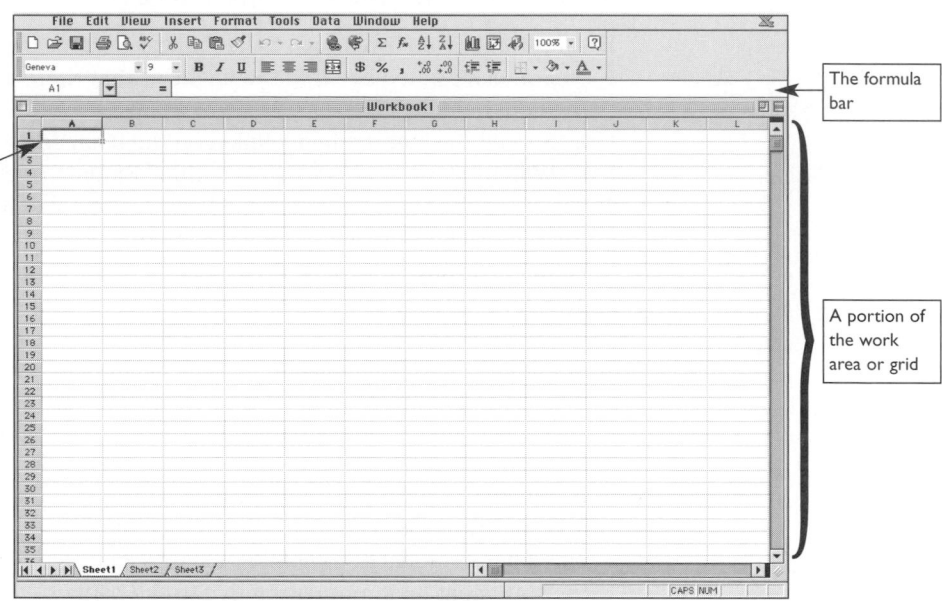

The formula bar

A portion of the work area or grid

Preparing a Personal Balance Sheet

Amy Beck is a high school student who needs to prepare a personal balance sheet to provide a picture of her financial position. You can now work along with the text to prepare a balance sheet for her. If you do not have access to a computer at this time, continue to read so you can identify the major components of a spreadsheet.

Labels

Load spreadsheet software into your computer. When you reach the grid, you will discover that it is much larger than what you can see on your screen at any one time. You can move the cell pointer around by using the mouse or pressing the Arrow, Tab, and Return Keys.

Amy has made a list of what she owns and owes. In spreadsheet terms, words are called **labels**. **Type the labels shown in Figure 2.10 into the cell locations indicated.** *(Note: If you make a mistake as you key, use the Backspace key. If you notice a mistake after you press the Return key, go back to the cell and re-key the label.)*

Values

Amy has estimated the original cost values of her possessions. These amounts, along with her liability figures, are shown in Figure 2.11 below. In spreadsheet terms, numerical amounts are referred to as **values**. Unlike labels, values can be manipulated mathematically.

Enter the values displayed in Figure 2.11 into your spreadsheet. Be sure to enter the information into the correct cells. For instance, in this spreadsheet, the first asset amount (for Cash) is 340. It must be entered at C6. Continue entering values into the correct cells, as shown in Figure 2.11.

FIGURE 2.10

The labels for Amy Beck's balance sheet.

If a label is longer than the width of a cell, it will "spill over" into the next cell — as long as the next cell is blank.

	A	B	C	D	E	F
1			Amy Beck			
2			Balance Sheet			
3			November 30, 20-			
4						
5	Assets			Liabilities		
6	Cash			Owed to Sister		
7	Clothes			Owed to Mom		
8	CD Collection			Total Liabilities		
9	CD Player					
10	Books			Owner's Equity		
11	Computer			A. Beck, Capital		
12	Jewellery					
13	Miscellaneous					
14				Total Liabilities		
15	Total Assets			and Equity		
16						

FIGURE 2.11

The values for Amy Beck's balance sheet.

	A	B	C	D	E	F
1			Amy Beck			
2			Balance Sheet			
3			November 30, 20-			
4						
5	Assets			Liabilities		
6	Cash		340	Owed to Sister		100
7	Clothes		1250	Owed to Mom		50
8	CD Collection		200	Total Liabilities		
9	CD Player		350			
10	Books		300	Owner's Equity		
11	Computer		1400	A. Beck, Capital		
12	Jewellery		375			
13	Miscellaneous		200			
14				Total Liabilities		
15	Total Assets			and Equity		

Cell Contents

As you typed labels and values, they were shown in a section above the grid that is called the **formula bar** by some programs (see Figure 2.9 on page 32). When you pressed the Return key, that label or value was entered into the grid. (The grid may also be called the *work sheet area*.)

Move the cursor to cell C2. Notice that the label "Balance Sheet" is shown in both the formula bar and the work sheet area. The formula bar is showing the *contents* of the cell. Whatever you actually typed is the cell's contents.

Now you will learn how to use the computer spreadsheet to add up the balance sheet. You will see that cell contents may differ from what is shown in the work sheet area when you create formulas and functions.

Formulas

Spreadsheet **formulas** perform mathematical operations. Cell contents may be added, subtracted, multiplied, and divided. An example of a formula is =A3+A4. This formula instructs the spreadsheet to add the contents of A3 to the contents of A4.

The equals sign in =A3+A4 is a prefix symbol that helps the spreadsheet identify the cell contents as a formula. If no prefix symbol were typed, the spreadsheet might interpret A3+A4 as a label. Different spreadsheets use different prefixes. The = and the + signs are common prefixes.

In Figure 2.12 below, the appearance of the spreadsheet has been changed in order to show you three formulas in column F. **Enter these formulas now.** Notice what happens in the work sheet area when you enter the formulas. Do not be concerned that two of the formulas will temporarily produce incorrect results. *Note: This textbook shows the formula prefix used by Microsoft® Excel which is the equal sign.*

FIGURE 2.12

The spreadsheet model, showing three formulas in column F and one function in column C.

Instead of typing cell reference in formulas, try "pointing" to them with the mouse. For example, to calculate TOTAL LIABILITIES, press the equal sign, click cell F6, press the plus sign, and click cell F7.

	A	B	C	D	E	F
1			Amy Beck			
2			Balance Sheet			
3			November 30, 20–			
4						
5	Assets			Liabilities		
6	Cash		340	Owed to Sister		100
7	Clothes		1250	Owed to Mom		50
8	CD Collection		200	Total Liabilities		=F6+F7
9	CD Player		350			
10	Books		300	Owner's Equity		
11	Computer		1400	A. Beck, Capital		=C15–F8
12	Jewellery		375			
13	Miscellaneous		200			
14				Total Liabilities		
15	Total Assets		=SUM(C6:C13)	and Equity		=F8+F11

Functions

If you were going to add up the assets using a formula, you would have to type in =C6+C7+C8+C9+C10+C11+C12+C13. But there is an easier way. You can use a function. **Functions** are detailed formulas built into spreadsheet programs, but they are expressed in a way that makes them simple to use. To calculate the total of Amy's assets, you will enter a function at C15. The built-in function for adding things up is the sum function.

Move the cell pointer to C15. Key =sum(C6:C13). Press ENTER and the amount of the total assets will appear in cell C15.

Changing Spreadsheet Amounts

Is a spreadsheet really any better than a calculator? A big advantage of spreadsheets over calculators is that formulas and functions can instantly update figures. For example, suppose Amy Beck forgot to include a $200 deposit when she calculated her cash total. The revised amount should be $540, not $340. **Enter the new total of 540 at cell C6** and observe what happens.

In response to the one change in the cash amount, three other figures were updated automatically: Total Assets; A. Beck, Capital; and Total Liabilities and Equity. The reason these three cells change is that each contain either a function or a formula. In a more complex spreadsheet hundreds of figures can be updated in response to a change in one cell.

Saving Your Work

You have just created a spreadsheet model. But it is stored only in the temporary memory of your computer and will be erased when you leave the program. Your teacher can instruct you on how and where to save this model. Use AMY as the file name.

Section 2.5   # Review Questions

1. In a spreadsheet, what is formed by the intersection of columns and rows?
2. How would you identify a cell in row 52 and in column C?
3. What is the spreadsheet term for words and titles?
4. Identify the differences between labels and values.
5. What are the "contents" of a cell and in what area of a spreadsheet are they seen?
6. Many spreadsheet programs require prefix symbols to be typed when entering formulas and functions. What would happen if you forgot to enter a prefix symbol when typing a *SUM* function into one of these programs?
7. Explain how the contents of a cell could be different than what is displayed in the work sheet area for that cell.
8. What does =sum(B3:B50) instruct a spreadsheet to do?
9. What does =A7–A5 instruct a spreadsheet to do?
10. Describe a main advantage of spreadsheets.

Section 2.5   # Exercises

1. A. Load the spreadsheet model you created for Amy Beck into your computer.
   B. Choose File, Save As and change the name of the file to AMY2. *(Note: Changing the name creates a second file on your disk, which ensures that data in the original AMY file will not be changed.)*
   C. Change the date at C3 to December 31, 20-3.
   D. Because it is one month later, you also need to make other changes. The new values to be entered are:
   Cash, 305; Clothes, 1 425; Owed to sister, 80; and Owed to Mom, 40.
   E. New totals are calculated as soon as you enter the above changes. Has Amy's financial position improved? Explain your answer.

2. You can change the appearance or format of a spreadsheet model. The improved format for the file AMY2 is shown below:

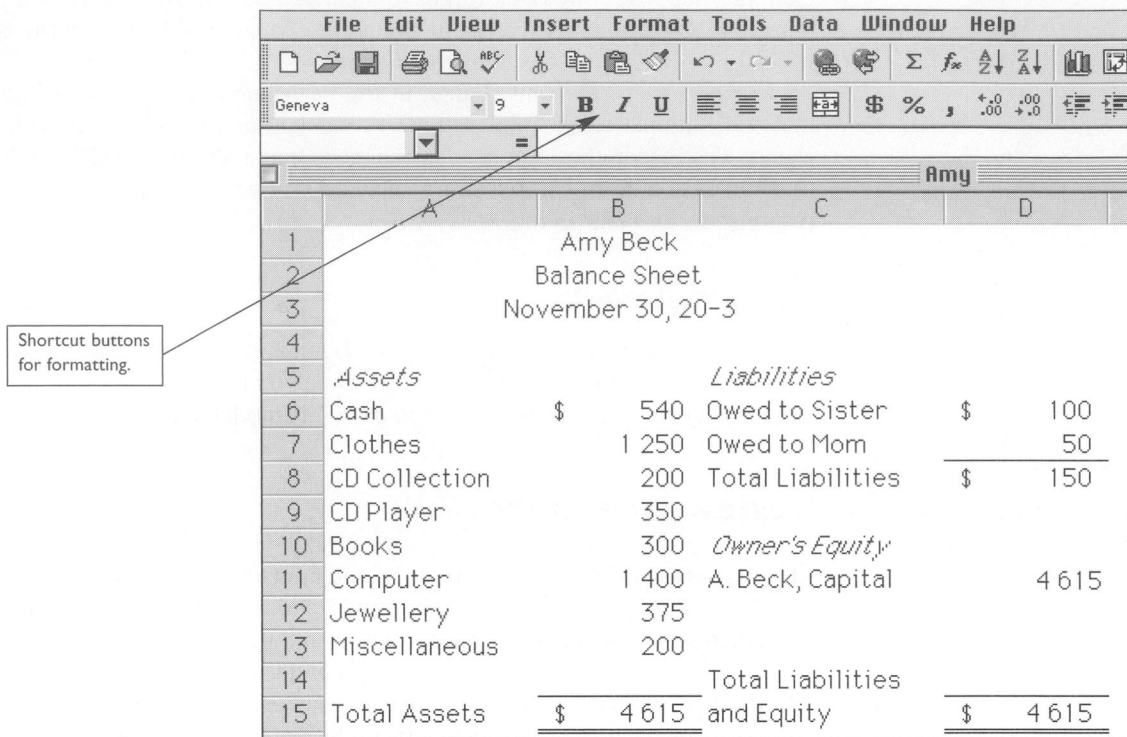

Shortcut buttons for formatting.

Here is a summary of the format changes:

- The empty columns between the balance sheet labels and amounts were deleted (columns B and E from Figure 2.12).
- Columns A and C were widened.
- The balance sheet heading was centred.
- Sub-headings were italicized.
- Dollar signs were added to some amounts. (And these amounts were formatted to show no decimal points.)
- Single and double rules were applied.
- Cell gridlines were removed from view.

Spreadsheet programs usually provide more than one method for completing a single task. For example, you can use menu selections or choose from a number of shortcuts.

A. Explore and use your spreadsheet software. Try to make all of the seven changes noted above. Hint: If you are using Microsoft® Excel, four of the seven changes can be done by selecting the shortcut buttons that appear above the Formula bar. To highlight an entire column, click the letter of the column. Removing the gridlines may require some investigation of the Tools menu.

| Section 2.5 | **Extending Your Computer Skills** |

1. Apply your knowledge of spreadsheets to create a personal balance sheet of your own. Use original cost values to estimate the value of your possessions. Your spreadsheet model should have at least one sum function. If you have some liabilities, your model will also have three formulas. Format the spreadsheet model so that it is attractive.

| Section 2.5 | **Communicate It** |

Amy Beck wants to join relatives on a five-day ski holiday. Her parents agree, on condition that she contribute $350 toward the costs.

Load Amy's December 31 balance sheet back into your computer and change the file's name from AMY2 to AMY3. Examine Amy's financial position and write a short paragraph to explain to her how she could raise the $350 without having to sell any assets. Include comments about the impact the ski trip will have on her financial position.

Type the paragraph directly below the balance sheet.

Update the spreadsheet by typing in the numbers that follow your recommendations.

| Section 2.5 | **Computer Terms** |

cell	function
cell contents	label
formula	spreadsheet
formula bar	value

CHAPTER 2 Summary

CHAPTER HIGHLIGHTS

Now that you have completed Chapter 2, you should:

- understand what is meant by the financial position of a person or a business;
- be able to prepare a simple balance sheet in proper form for an individual, a family, or a business;
- know the meaning of accounts receivable and accounts payable;
- understand the fundamental accounting equation;
- understand the meaning of claims against the assets;
- be able to use basic recordkeeping practices;
- understand the concept of liquidity;
- know three generally accepted accounting principles: the business entity concept, the continuing concern concept, and the principle of conservatism;
- understand the basic operations of a computer spreadsheet.

ACCOUNTING TERMS

accounts payable	fundamental accounting equation
accounts receivable	GAAP
asset	generally accepted accounting principles
balance sheet	going concern concept
business entity concept	liability
capital	liquidation
continuing concern concept	liquidity
creditor	net worth
debtor	owner's equity
financial position	principle of conservatism

CHAPTER 2 Review Exercises

Using Your Knowledge

1 For each of the following questions, write in your Workbook the letter that represents the best possible answer.

A. The financial position of a business is:
  a. the difference between total assets and total liabilities.
  b. represented by the assets, the liabilities, and the capital.
  c. the same as the net worth of the business.

B. If the total assets increase by \$10 000 and the total liabilities decrease by \$10 000, the capital will:
  a. increase by \$20 000.
  b. be unchanged.
  c. decrease by \$20 000.

C. Which one of the following is not true?
  a. A − E = L b. A − L = E
  c. A + L = E d. A = L + E

D. A balance sheet shows:
  a. all of the owner's assets and liabilities.
  b. a financial picture of the business on a certain date.
  c. the progress of the business over a period of time.

E. Which one of the following is not true?
  a. The heading of a balance sheet shows the date as of which it was prepared.
  b. Assets are listed in the order of their liquidity.
  c. Accounts receivable are considered to be a liquid asset.
  d. Personal assets have no place on the business balance sheet.
  e. A truck that cost $10 000 and for which $6 000 is owed is listed on the balance sheet at $4 000.

F. Abbreviations may be used on financial statements:
  a. when it is necessary to crowd things to conserve space.
  b. to save time in preparing the statements.
  c. in a company name if the abbreviation is a formal part of the name.

G. Which one of the following is least true? Columnar paper helps the accountant to:
  a. add columns more accurately.
  b. make records easier to read.
  c. make the records more appealing.
  d. make recordkeeping go more quickly.

H. Which one of the following is not true? Ruled lines are:
  a. used to underline headings.
  b. used to indicate that columns of numbers are to be totalled.
  c. necessary to separate sections of the balance sheet.
  d. doubled to indicate a final total.

I. Before a business is closed down, the equation for it is:

Assets ($125 000) = Liabilities ($37 000) + Equity ($88 000)

If assets of $70 000 are sold for $20 000, assets of $50 000 are sold for $90 000, and the remaining assets stay the same, the equation will become:
  a. $55 000   = $37 000 + $18 000
  b. $115 000 = $37 000 + $78 000
  c. $75 000   = $37 000 + $38 000
  d. $135 000 = $47 000 + $88 000
  e. $115 000 = $27 000 + $88 000

J. Which of the following is not true?
  a. In the liability section on a balance sheet, accounts payable may be listed first.
  b. On a balance sheet, there are three main totals.
  c. On a balance sheet, the owner's name appears only in the heading.
  d. On a balance sheet, the final totals are always on the same line.

2 If, over the course of the year, the equity increases by $42 000 and the assets increase by $26 000, what change has occurred in the liabilities?

3 If total assets increase by $10 000 and the equity increases by $3 000, what change has occurred in the liabilities?

Hint: Exercises 2, 3, and 4 are unrelated to each other

4 If the liabilities increase by $15 000 and the equity decreases by $5 000, what change has occurred in the assets?

5 Carmen Ing is a graphic designer who creates web pages for various businesses. She prepared a balance sheet for Carmen's Web Creations, which is shown below:

Carmen's Web Creations				
September 30, 20–				
Balance Sheet				
Accounts Receivable		*Liabilities*		
– Tse Networks	$ 1 7 8 0 .00	Drive Computer Co.	$ 6 7 6 .98	
– Nina's Creations	4 6 0 .50	Wilson's Supply	1 0 0 .90	
Cash	3 6 5 2 .80	Zip Software	4 1 2 .00	
equipment	6 5 0 0 .30	Bank Loan	3 5 0 0 .00	
supplies	9 0 0 .25	Total Liabilities	$ 4 6 8 9 .88	
		Owner's Equity		
Total Assets	13 2 9 3 .85	Carmen's Web Creations	8 6 0 3 .97	
		Total Liabilities and Equity	$13 2 9 3 .85	

A. List the errors that Carmen made when she prepared the balance sheet. (You should be able to find more than 10 errors.)

B. Prepare a new balance sheet for Carmen's Web Creations.

6 Shown below is the balance sheet of S. Magbool.
On the basis of the limited information given, would you say that Magbool has any kind of financial problem? Explain.

S. MAGBOOL			
BALANCE SHEET			
JANUARY 31, 20—			
Assets		*Liabilities*	
Cash	$ 6 000	Accounts Payable	$ 35 000
Accounts Receivable	14 000	Mortgage Payable	60 000
Land	40 000	Total Liabilities	$ 95 000
Buildings	95 000	*Owner's Equity*	
Equipment	25 000	S. Magbool, Capital	85 000
Total Assets	$180 000	Total Liabilities and Equity	$180 000

7 On December 31, 20—, you present your balance sheet, shown below, to the manager of the local bank with the hope of obtaining a small bank loan.

BALANCE SHEET
DECEMBER 31, 20—

Assets		Liabilities	
Cash	$ 5 000	Accounts Payable	$17 000
Accounts Receivable	25 000	Mortgage Payable	35 000
Land	10 000	Total Liabilities	$52 000
Building	30 000		
Equipment	20 000	Owner's Equity	38 000
Total Assets	$90 000	Total Liabilities and Equity	$90 000

During your conversation with the manager, certain facts are brought out:

a. About $8 000 owing from customers is considerably overdue.
b. A mortgage payment of $4 000 is due on January 31.
c. All creditors' accounts are due within 30 days.
d. The average earnings of the business for the past five years have been very good.

A. Would the bank manager grant the loan? Why?

B. What concerns might the manager have? Why?

Questions for Further Thought

Briefly answer the following questions.

1. The balance sheet is thought of as being a "snapshot" of the business. Explain this statement.

2. Assets and liabilities can be thought of as things that can be touched or seen. For example, you can go into the parking lot and touch the automobile, or you can see the signed bank loan at the bank. The equity is not like this. Explain.

3. Give reasons why business persons sell on credit when there is a chance that they will not be able to collect the debt.

4. Work out another acceptable definition of a balance sheet besides the one given in the textbook.

5. In three words, state what information is contained in the heading of a balance sheet.

6. If a bank were to lend funds to a business, the bank would become a "secured" creditor. What does this mean? How does the bank accomplish this? Why do other creditors not do the same?

7. Why is the CICA *Handbook* published in looseleaf form?

8. Given what you have learned so far, explain how the earnings of a business can be determined from its balance sheets if you know that the owner neither contributed nor withdrew any funds or other assets.

9. There is a saying in accounting: "Anticipate no profits and account for all possible losses." To which GAAP does this saying relate?

Case Studies

Is Money Better?

Hannah and Aysha are school friends of yours at Vanier High School. The two girls happen to be discussing their personal fortunes at the moment. Hannah is feeling rich because she has $2 000 in a personal bank account. A distant aunt who died recently left her the money.

Aysha feels pretty well off, too. She has less money but she does have some valuable possessions, including fashionable clothes and jewellery, as well as some shares that were left to her by her grandmother. For reasons that she cannot explain, she feels that she is just as well off as Hannah.

You get into the conversation at lunch break. You suggest to the two girls that they each prepare a personal balance sheet. You explain how to go about it and how to estimate the value of non-cash items. The balance sheets, you say, will show who is better off financially.

The girls prepare their balance sheets according to your directions and come up with the following:

HANNAH'S BALANCE SHEET SEPTEMBER 30, 20–	
Assets	
Bank Balance	$2 000
Clothes	1 500
Total Assets	$3 500
Liabilities and Equity	
Debts Owing	nil
Hannah's Capital	$3 500
Total Liabilities and Equity	$3 500

AYSHA'S BALANCE SHEET SEPTEMBER 30, 20–	
Assets	
Bank Balance	$ 10
CD Player	500
Jewellery	1 000
IBM Shares	1 100
Clothes	1 200
Total Assets	$ 3 810
Liabilities and Equity	
Debts Owing	$ 200
Aysha's Capital	3 610
Total Liabilities and Equity	$ 3 810

When the two girls get together to compare balance sheets, they still cannot agree. Hannah thinks that she is better off because she has more cash and clothes. Aysha disagrees because she has greater capital.

1. In a paragraph, discuss these balance sheets with Hannah and Aysha. Explain to them how to measure a person's equity.

CASE 2

Can You Spend the Equity?

Raj Singh is a young man who has just inherited a business from his father. Raj has little business experience but is anxious to learn and willing to work hard.

The business has not been operating very profitably lately because it badly needs to replace outdated equipment. This will cost $35 000.

The latest balance sheet of the business shows the following:

BANNAGER'S CLEANERS
BALANCE SHEET
APRIL 30, 20–

Assets		Liabilities	
Cash	$ 3 000	Accounts Payable	$ 5 000
Accounts Receivable	17 000	Bank Loan	30 000
Land	30 000	Mortgage Payable	50 000
Building	50 000	Total Liabilities	$ 85 000
Equipment	20 000		
Total Assets	$120 000	Owner's Equity	
		V. Singh, Capital	35 000
		Total Liabilities and Equity	$120 000

After examining the balance sheet, Raj believes that he sees the solution to the problem. He wants to use the equity to purchase the new equipment. The accountant hastens to point out to Raj that this is not possible. Raj demands an explanation.

1. What explanation will the accountant give?

CASE 3

Challenge

Are the Assets Always Worth What the Balance Sheet Says?

Hilda Lahti is the owner of Custom-Made Products in Ottawa, Ontario. Originally, Custom-Made Products was a machine shop that produced a variety of custom work. In the last few years, the company has developed and patented a line of scaffolding equipment for contractors and builders. The scaffolding equipment produced by the company is better than that of its competitors. As a result, the company has had great success with the new product. At the same time, the custom machine shop division of the business has been doing poorly. There is a lot of competition from other machine shops in the community. In the last year, the company earned $135 000. Of this, $110 000 was from the sale of scaffolding equipment and only $25 000 was from the machine shop.

Recently, Hilda has decided to make a major change in the company operations. In particular, she has decided to get out of machine shop work. She intends to concentrate all of the energies of the company on expanding the markets for scaffolding and developing new products of this type. The change in policy has been made official, and the customers of the company have been notified.

The most recent balance sheet for the company, prepared at the request of the company's bank, provides the following information:

Assets	
Cash	$ 1 500
Accounts Receivable	20 540
Supplies	1 821
Land and Building	102 500
Machinery and Equipment	205 365
Automotive Equipment	65 385
Total Assets	$397 111
Liabilities	
Bank Loan	$105 000
Accounts Payable	11 850
Mortgage Payable	85 000
Total Liabilities	$201 850
Owner's Equity	
H. Lahti, Capital	195 261
Total Liabilities and Equity	$397 111

The bank manager who receives the above balance sheet notices that no adjustment has been made to show the company's decision to quit custom machine shop work. Inquiries reveal that the company has $155 000 of specialized machine shop equipment included in the Machinery and Equipment figure of $205 365 on the balance sheet. It is generally agreed that the market for this type of equipment is quite poor. The company's equipment is outdated, and most other machine shops have already acquired modern computer-controlled equipment.

1. On the basis of the preceding statement, why would the bank manager be concerned about the repayment of the bank loan?
2. What additional information would help the bank manager to evaluate the company's loan?
3. What needs to be done regarding the above balance sheet?
4. Assuming that a buyer is found for the machine shop equipment who pays $35 000, what changes should be made on the balance sheet?
5. Prepare a simple balance sheet to show the changes.
6. What GAAP influenced you in your thinking?

CASE 4

Co-operative
Learning

Should Your Friends Purchase This Business?

Your friends Joseph and Janice Dubois have recently inherited some money and want to use it to purchase a business of their own. They have come to you for advice regarding the possible purchase of a sand and gravel business. They learned about the sale of the sand and gravel business through an advertisement in the newspaper.

The business is being sold by K. Vako, who has owned it for 20 years and wants a change because of failing health. The business has been profitable over the years, earning an average of $50 000 per year over the last 10 years.

The balance sheet below has been prepared by Mr. Vako personally.

VAKO SAND AND GRAVEL
BALANCE SHEET
DECEMBER 31, 20-

Assets		Liabilities	
Bank	$ 500	Bank Loan	$ 30 000
Accounts Receivable	17 400	Accounts Payable	22 740
Supplies	1 100	Mortgage Payable	50 000
Equipment	67 600	Total Liabilities	$102 740
Gravel Deposits	200 000		
Land	40 700	Owner's Equity	
Buildings	38 000	K. Vako, Capital	262 560
Total Assets	$365 300	Total Liabilities and Equity	$365 300

Mr. Vako is asking $250 000 for the business. This seems to be a very good price. It is less than his capital figure as shown on the balance sheet.

1. Work in a small group to help Joseph and Janice decide if they should buy the sand and gravel business. Prepare a list of questions that need to be answered and be ready to present your list to the class. To help you, a first question is already given below:

What condition is the equipment in and is it really worth $67 600?

Career

Julia Stavreff, CA / Founder of Accounting Firm Gory & Stavreff Chartered Accountants

When Julia Stavreff started her first accounting job in 1975, it wasn't the first time she had worked in a service industry. As a young girl, she used to help her father at his restaurant during summer vacation and on weekends.

A lifelong Toronto resident, Julia attended York Memorial Collegiate Institute, and later Wexford Collegiate Institute. After she graduated from the University of Toronto with a Bachelor of Arts degree in 1975, she articled with a small Toronto CA firm. When the 1983 recession forced companies to lay people off, she had to either find a new job or start her own practice. So, she opted to start her own practice. In the beginning, she had about five clients. "I knew I'd have to build it up from there," she says.

Like most small business people, Julia had to be clever at keeping costs down while providing a quality service. In the beginning, she shared secretarial services with another CA firm. Sharing not only cut costs, but also ensured that enough staff were always on hand to answer the phone and greet customers.

> **Like most small business people, Julia had to be clever at keeping costs down while providing a quality service.**

Julia discovered that "network" meetings were an ideal place to meet people who needed her accounting services. At these breakfast, lunch, or dinner gatherings of business people with similar interests or goals, she could hear speeches, get new information about the industry, and make business contacts. As a result of those contacts, she acquired new clients through referrals (recommendations). "Clients who think you perform well often recommend you to their friends. They are the best form of advertising and the most important way to get more business."

In 1991, Julia bought out an accountant who was retiring. This means that Julia took over the clients of the other accountant. Julia now has a bookkeeper/secretary and, in addition, has taken on a junior partner. Currently, because of the additional clients, she is quite busy, but she says, "soon my function won't be so much to do the accounting."

Instead, she will deal with the clients. "I'll discuss their needs, financial planning, and the work my office has done or can do for them."

Most of Julia's clients are small, owner-managed businesses that don't need their own full-time accountant. Julia's company prepares their financial statements and gives them business advice. Income tax preparation and filing, as well as bookkeeping, are also offered. Sometimes a client needs special advice. For example, questions about the GST are frequent nowadays. Or, "we might tell the client that they need to hire a new employee in their marketing department, that they can't afford so many perks, or that someone on the staff seems to be helping himself or herself to company money," adds Julia.

> **"Good communication skills are essential for self-employment; you have to understand the quirks of clients and not expect things to go perfectly."**

Julia recommends that young people who think they might like to have their own accounting business should work in an established accounting firm for at least five years and learn as much as they can before setting out. A practical foundation of knowledge is needed to deal with clients. "Good communication skills are essential for self-employment; you have to understand the quirks of clients and not expect things to go perfectly."

In general, Julia is very happy about being the boss of her own company. "The flexibility it gave me was really great," she says. "Although I've put in many hours, I have the satisfaction of building a successful business." Julia confirms what most people say about establishing a business: "You do your hardest work at the beginning, but if you're successful, the rewards come later."

Discussion

1. What major economic event was a factor in Julia Stavreff's decision to open her own business?
2. What method did she adopt for keeping costs down? Are there other methods that a small business person might adopt for this purpose? Think of at least one other way that a small business might maintain a quality service while keeping costs down.
3. What advantages does Julia Stavreff feel that network meetings provide? How did they help her establish her business?
4. What particular advice does she have for the young person who would like to own an accounting business? Would this advice apply to other businesses as well? Explain.

Analyzing Changes in Financial Position

3.1 | Business Transactions

On any given day, many events occur that cause the financial position of a business to change. Each of these events is called a business transaction. A business transaction may be defined as a financial event that causes a change in financial position.

For example, suppose the business buys a new truck for which it pays $20 000 cash. This event is a transaction because it causes the financial position of the business to change. There would be an increase of $20 000 in the item Trucks. There would be a decrease of $20 000 in the item Cash.

Or suppose that the business owes $7 000 to City Finance and makes a payment of $1 000 against the debt. This event is also a transaction that causes the financial position to change. The amount owed to City Finance would be reduced by $1 000. The cash on hand would be reduced by $1 000.

On the other hand, suppose that the city plumbing inspector inspects the building and leaves a letter suggesting some improvements. This is not a business transaction because no assets or liabilities have changed as a result of the activity.

Source Documents

When an asset, liability, or equity item is recorded for accounting purposes, a business paper or document is required to verify the dollar amount. A **source document** is the name given to such a business paper. It is the original record of the transaction—"the source"—and it provides the accounting department with the information it needs related to the transaction.

Examples of source documents include hydro bills, telephone bills, cheque copies, store receipts, cash register summaries, and credit card slips. They provide proof of payment, proof of purchase, and reference. Depending on the size of the business, source documents may move from person to person and from department to department. They are eventually filed because owners, managers, auditors, and others may want to ask questions. In chapter 6, a full discussion is devoted to source documents, with illustrations. For now, remember:

1. accounting entries are made from business papers known as source documents;
2. source documents are kept on file for reference purposes and are proof of transactions.

GAAP—The Objectivity Principle

Objectivity is a generally accepted accounting principle related to source documents.

> **The objectivity principle states that accounting will be recorded on the basis of objective evidence.**

It means that different people looking at the evidence will arrive at the same values for the transaction. Simply put, this means that transactions will be recorded on fact, not on personal opinion or feelings.

The source document for a transaction is almost always the best objective evidence available. For example, the best objective evidence for the purchase of a new desk used in the business is the bill received from the retailer. The source document shows the amount agreed to by the buyer and the seller, who are usually independent of each other.

 Section 3.1   **Review Questions**

1. What is a business transaction?
2. Give an example of a transaction, other than the ones noted in this section.
3. Give an example of an event in a business, other than the one noted in this section, that is not a transaction.
4. What is a source document?
5. Give several examples of source documents.
6. What happens to source documents after the accounting entries have been completed?
7. State and explain the objectivity principle. Give an example.

 Section 3.1   **Exercises**

1. **Given that a transaction is a financial event that requires changing the statement of financial position, decide whether or not each of the following is a transaction.** The business is Best Consultants of Kenora, Ontario.

   A. The business pays $800 to Mercury Finance to reduce the amount owed to them.
   B. The owner, P. Dufour, withdraws $500 from the business for her personal use.

C. A new employee is needed in the payroll department. P. Dufour interviews Stan Martin for the job.
D. A $700 consulting service is provided for Rita Bertoli on credit.
E. The business pays the rent for the month, $500.
F. The employee in question C above is hired to start work next Monday at $400 per week.
G. The business purchases a new computer for cash at the price of $3 000.
H. The computer in question G above is defective and is replaced at no cost to the business.

2. **Given that a transaction is a financial event that requires changing the statement of financial position, decide whether or not each of the following is a transaction.** You are working for Ace Collection Agency of Cornwall, Ontario, owned by Ingrid Lencz.

A. Gasoline for the company automobile was purchased for $40 cash.
B. Ingrid Lencz paid $15 out of her own pocket for lunch.
C. Ingrid's personal car was damaged and needed a $500 repair job.
D. A $250 service was performed for a customer who paid cash.
E. A leased computer broke down and needed to be replaced at no cost to the business. The man who brought the replacement said that the new machine was a $2 500 model.
F. A customer who owed the business $1 200 made a partial payment of $300.
G. The business bank loan was reduced by a direct payment to the bank of $1 000.
H. A burglar broke into the office and stole the leased computer. The business has 100 per cent replacement insurance to cover breaking and entering and theft.

3. **Examine the source document below and answer the questions that follow, using what you know so far.**

CAMPBELL & ASSOCIATES	Suite 40 100 University Avenue, Toronto, Ontario M5J 2K4

```
                           Smokey Valley Ski Club
                           R.R. #1, Horseshoe Valley, Ont.
July 22, 20-               L3V 3B0
```

```
Our fee for professional services rendered,
auditing the records of the club for the
year ended April 15, 20-, preparing therefrom
financial statements as at that date, and
reporting thereon:

                                        $1 600.00
           Goods and Services Tax          112.00
                                        $1 712.00
```

A. Who issued the bill?
B. Who received the bill?
C. When was the bill issued?
D. For what service was the bill issued?
E. Does the bill represent good objective evidence? Why?

---

4. **Examine the source document below and answer the questions that follow, using what you know so far.**

Box 500, Horseshoe Valley, Ontario L3V 3B0

THE DAVEY COMPANY

TROPHIES   GIFTWARE   ENGRAVERS

Sold to: Smokey Valley Ski Club
R.R. #1
Horseshoe Valley,ON L3V 3B0
Date Dec. 5, 20–

PURCH. ORDER NO.	GST	PST	DELIVERY DATE	TERMS	SHIP VIA	
6506	10.36	11.84	12/5	30 days	CPX	

35	Name tags		148.00
		Taxes	22.20
			170.20

A. Who issued the bill?
B. Who received the bill?
C. When was the bill issued?
D. When were the goods delivered? How were they delivered?
E. When is this bill due for payment?
F. Why was this bill issued?
G. Was this a cash sale transaction?
H. Why does the bill represent good objective evidence?

5. The accountant for a business received a memorandum from the owner. The memorandum stated that a new office desk recently installed in the owner's office was acquired at a cost of $2 500 and that it was paid for in cash by the owner personally.

    A. Why is the memorandum not objective evidence?

    B. What is the best objective evidence in this case?

3.2 | Equation Analysis Sheet

Your next step in the study of accounting is to learn how various business transactions affect and change the financial position. To begin, look at the simplified balance sheet of Metropolitan Movers of Windsor, Ontario, shown below.

FIGURE 3.1

The balance sheet of Metropolitan Movers.

A/R is a short form for Accounts Receivable. A/P is a short form for Accounts Payable.

METROPOLITAN MOVERS BALANCE SHEET —DATE—			
Assets		*Liabilities*	
Cash	$13 500	Accounts Payable	
Accounts Receivable		– Central Supply	$ 1 750
– B. Cava	1 300	Loan Payable	
– K. Lincoln	2 500	– Mercury Finance	18 370
Equipment	11 500	Total Liabilities	$20 120
Trucks	24 500		
		Owner's Equity	
		J. Hofner, Capital	33 180
Total Assets	$53 300	Total Liabilities and Equity	$53 300

The balance sheet of Metropolitan Movers shows the values of the assets, liabilities, and capital on a particular date. As business transactions occur, there are changes in the values of assets, liabilities, and capital. The balance sheet is not a suitable type of record on which to record these changes. Therefore, let us arrange the balance sheet items in a different manner. We will transfer the assets, liabilities, and capital from the balance sheet onto what we will call an *equation analysis sheet*. This sheet is ideal for studying and recording changes in financial position. In Figure 3.2 below, you can see the balance sheet items for Metropolitan Movers entered on an equation analysis sheet. Note that this arrangement is in the form of the fundamental accounting equation.

FIGURE 3.2

Equation analysis sheet for Metropolitan Movers.

	ASSETS					LIABILITIES		OWNER'S EQUITY
	Cash	A/R		Equipment	Trucks	A/P	Loan Pay.	J. Hofner, Capital
		B. Cava	K. Lincoln			Central Supply	Mercury Finance	
Beginning balances	13 500	1 300	2 500	11 500	24 500	1 750	18 370	33 180
			53 300		=	20	120 +	33 180

Updating the Equation Analysis Sheet

Let us now examine how transactions affect financial position.

TRANSACTION 1 **Metropolitan Movers pays $1 200 cash to Mercury Finance.**

FIGURE 3.3

Equation analysis sheet after transaction 1.

After this payment is made, the financial position shown in Figure 3.2 on the previous page will no longer be correct. Two changes are necessary: Cash must be reduced by $1 200 and the amount owed to Mercury Finance must also be reduced by $1 200. These changes are recorded on the equation analysis sheet shown in Figure 3.3 below.

		ASSETS				LIABILITIES		OWNER'S EQUITY
	Cash	A/R		Equipment	Trucks	A/P	Loan Pay.	J. Hofner,
		B. Cava	K. Lincoln			Central Supply	Mercury Finance	Capital
Beginning balances	13 500	1 300	2 500	11 500	24 500	1 750	18 370	33 180
Transaction 1	−1 200						−1 200	
New balances	12 300	1 300	2 500	11 500	24 500	1 750	17 170	33 180
			52 100		=	18	920 +	33 180

In analyzing transaction 1, observe that:

1. The amounts for Cash and Mercury Finance are updated: Cash is decreased by $1 200 and the debt owed to Mercury Finance is decreased by $1 200.
2. The amounts for the other items remain unchanged.
3. After the changes are recorded and the new totals determined, the equation is still in balance.

TRANSACTION 2 **K. Lincoln, who owes Metropolitan Movers $2 500, pays $1 100 in partial payment of the debt.**

FIGURE 3.4

Equation analysis sheet after transaction 2.

Can you figure out the changes to be made on the equation analysis sheet? Try to do this mentally before looking at Figure 3.4 below.

		ASSETS				LIABILITIES		OWNER'S EQUITY
	Cash	A/R		Equipment	Trucks	A/P	Loan Pay.	J. Hofner,
		B. Cava	K. Lincoln			Central Supply	Mercury Finance	Capital
Beginning balances	13 500	1 300	2 500	11 500	24 500	1 750	18 370	33 180
Transaction 1	−1 200						−1 200	
New balances	12 300	1 300	2 500	11 500	24 500	1 750	17 170	33 180
Transaction 2	+1 100		−1 100					
New balances	13 400	1 300	1 400	11 500	24 500	1 750	17 170	33 180
			52 100		=	18	920 +	33 180

In analyzing transaction 2, observe that:

1. The figure for Cash is increased by the amount received, $1 100.
2. The figure for K. Lincoln is decreased by $1 100. But $1 400 is still owing on the debt.
3. After the changes are recorded, the equation is still in balance.

FIGURE 3.5

Equation analysis sheet after transaction 3.

TRANSACTION 3   Equipment costing $1 950 is purchased for cash.

Again, try to make the changes mentally before looking at the entries recorded in Figure 3.5 below.

	ASSETS					LIABILITIES		OWNER'S EQUITY
	Cash	A/R		Equipment	Trucks	A/P	Loan Pay.	J. Hofner, Capital
		B. Cava	K. Lincoln			Central Supply	Mercury Finance	
Beginning balances	13 500	1 300	2 500	11 500	24 500	1 750	18 370	33 180
Transaction 1	−1 200						−1 200	
New balances	12 300	1 300	2 500	11 500	24 500	1 750	17 170	33 180
Transaction 2	+1 100		−11 00					
New balances	13 400	1 300	1 400	11 500	24 500	1 750	17 170	33 180
Transaction 3	−1 950			+1 950				
New balances	1 1450	1 300	1 400	13 450	24 500	1 750	17 170	33 180
			52 100			=	18 920 +	33 180

In analyzing transaction 3, observe that:

1. Cash is decreased by the amount paid, $1 950.
2. Equipment is increased by the cost of the equipment acquired, $1 950.
3. After the changes are recorded, the equation is still in balance.

TRANSACTION 4   A new pick-up truck is purchased at a cost of $18 000. Metropolitan Movers pays $10 000 cash and arranges a loan from Mercury Finance to cover the balance of the purchase price. (Note: This is considered to be a single transaction. Mercury Finance will pay $8 000 directly to the truck dealer, who will be paid in full.)

Again, try to work out the changes mentally before looking at the equation analysis sheet in Figure 3.6.

In analyzing transaction 4, observe that:

1. Cash is decreased by the amount paid, $10 000.
2. Trucks is increased by the cost of the new truck, $18 000.
3. The liability to Mercury Finance is increased by the additional amount borrowed, $8 000.
4. After the changes are recorded, the equation is still in balance.

FIGURE 3.6

FIGURE 3.6

Equation analysis sheet after transaction 4.

		ASSETS				LIABILITIES		OWNER'S EQUITY
	Cash	A/R		Equipment	Trucks	A/P	Loan Pay.	J. Hofner,
		B. Cava	K. Lincoln			Central Supply	Mercury Finance	Capital
Beginning balances	13 500	1 300	2 500	11 500	24 500	1 750	18 370	33 180
Transaction 1	−1 200						−1 200	
New balances	12 300	1 300	2 500	11 500	24 500	1 750	17 170	33 180
Transaction 2	+1 100		−11 00					
New balances	13 400	1 300	1 400	11 500	24 500	1 750	17 170	33 180
Transaction 3	−1 950			+1 950				
New balances	1 1450	1 300	1 400	13 450	24 500	1 750	17 170	33 180
Transaction 4	−10 000				+18 000		+8 000	
New balances	1 450	1 300	1 400	13 450	42 500	1 750	25 170	33 180
			60 100		=	26 920	+	33 180

TRANSACTION 5 **Metropolitan Movers completes a storage service for B. Cava at a price of \$1 500. A bill is sent to Cava to indicate the additional amount that Cava owes.**

FIGURE 3.7

Equation analysis sheet after transaction 5.

Work out the changes necessary and compare them with the equation analysis sheet in Figure 3.7.

		ASSETS				LIABILITIES		OWNER'S EQUITY
	Cash	A/R		Equipment	Trucks	A/P	Loan Pay.	J. Hofner,
		B. Cava	K. Lincoln			Central Supply	Mercury Finance	Capital
Beginning balances	13 500	1 300	2 500	11 500	24 500	1 750	18 370	33 180
Transaction 1	−1 200						−1 200	
New balances	12 300	1 300	2 500	11 500	24 500	1 750	17 170	33 180
Transaction 2	+1 100		−1100					
New balances	13 400	1 300	1 400	11 500	24 500	1 750	17 170	33 180
Transaction 3	−1 950			+1 950				
New balances	11 450	1 300	1 400	13 450	24 500	1 750	17 170	33 180
Transaction 4	−10 000				+18 000		+8 000	
New balances	1 450	1 300	1 400	13 450	42 500	1 750	25 170	33 180
Transaction 5		+1 500						+1 500
New balances	1 450	2 800	1 400	13 450	42 500	1 750	25 170	34 680
			61 600		=	26 920	+	34 680

Transaction 5 is not as simple to understand as the previous four. But "understanding" is vital to becoming a good accountant. Transaction 5 may be explained as follows:

1. Cava owes $1 500 more to Metropolitan Movers and therefore the figure for Cava is increased by $1 500.
2. No other asset or liability is affected.
3. J. Hofner's capital is increased by $1 500.

There are two ways to explain this increase in capital. First, remember that Metropolitan Movers is in the business of providing a service to earn profit. When the service to Cava has been completed and Cava legally owes the $1 500, a gain has been made. Metropolitan Movers is then better off by the amount of this gain. This is recorded by increasing the capital of the owner, J. Hofner.

Second, the increase in capital can be shown by arithmetic. Remember that capital is the difference between the total assets and the total liabilities and that adding $1 500 to Owner's Equity is necessary to keep the equation in balance.

	assets		liabilities		capital
After transaction 5 (Figure 3.7)	$61 600	−	$26 920	=	$34 680
Before transaction 5 (Figure 3.6)	$60 100	−	$26 920	=	$33 180
			Increase in Capital	=	$ 1 500

Clearly, there is an increase in capital of $1 500, which must be recorded on the equation analysis sheet.

FIGURE 3.8

Equation analysis sheet after transaction 6.

TRANSACTION 6   J. Hofner, the owner, withdraws $500 for personal use.

Work out the necessary changes and then check your work against the equation analysis sheet in Figure 3.8 below.

		ASSETS				LIABILITIES		OWNER'S EQUITY
	Cash	A/R		Equipment	Trucks	A/P	Loan Pay.	J. Hofner, Capital
		B. Cava	K. Lincoln			Central Supply	Mercury Finance	
Beginning balances	13 500	1 300	2 500	11 500	24 500	1 750	18 370	33 180
Transaction 1	−1 200						−1 200	
New balances	12 300	1 300	2 500	11 500	24 500	1 750	17 170	33 180
Transaction 2	+1 100		−1 100					
New balances	13 400	1 300	1 400	11 500	24 500	1 750	17 170	33 180
Transaction 3	−1 950			+1 950				
New balances	11 450	1 300	1 400	13 450	24 500	1 750	17 170	33 180
Transaction 4	−10 000				+18 000		+8 000	
New balances	1 450	1 300	1 400	13 450	42 500	1 750	25 170	33 180
Transaction 5		+1 500						+1 500
New balances	1 450	2 800	1 400	13 450	42 500	1 750	25 170	34 680
Transaction 6	−500							−500
New balances	950	2 800	1 400	13 450	42 500	1 750	25 170	34 180
			61 100			=	26 920 +	34 180

In analyzing transaction 6, observe that:

1. Cash is decreased by $500, the amount withdrawn.
2. No other asset or liability is affected.
3. Capital is decreased by $500. After changing the cash figure, the difference between total assets and total liabilities is $34 180. This is $500 less than it was immediately before the transaction.
4. After the changes are recorded, the equation is still in balance.

TRANSACTION 7 **One of the trucks requires an engine adjustment costing $75. The repair is paid for in cash when the truck is picked up.**

Work out the necessary changes and then check your work against the equation analysis sheet in Figure 3.9 below.

FIGURE 3.9

Equation analysis sheet after transaction 7.

	ASSETS					LIABILITIES		OWNER'S EQUITY
	Cash	A/R		Equipment	Trucks	A/P	Loan Pay.	J. Hofner,
		B. Cava	K. Lincoln			Central Supply	Mercury Finance	Capital
Beginning balances	13 500	1 300	2 500	11 500	24 500	1 750	18 370	33 180
Transaction 1	−1 200						−1 200	
New balances	12 300	1 300	2 500	11 500	24 500	1 750	17 170	33 180
Transaction 2	+1 100		−1 100					
New balances	13 400	1 300	1 400	11 500	24 500	1 750	17 170	33 180
Transaction 3	−1 950			+1 950				
New balances	11 450	1 300	1 400	13 450	24 500	1 750	17 170	33 180
Transaction 4	−10 000				+18 000		+8 000	
New balances	1 450	1 300	1 400	13 450	42 500	1 750	25 170	33 180
Transaction 5		+1 500						+1 500
New balances	1 450	2 800	1 400	13 450	42 500	1 750	25 170	34 680
Transaction 6	−500							−500
New balances	950	2 800	1 400	13 450	42 500	1 750	25 170	34 180
Transaction 7	−75							−75
New balances	875	2 800	1 400	13 450	42 500	1 750	25 170	34 105
			61 025		=	26 920	+	34 105

For an online demonstration of how to record transactions on the equation analysis sheet, visit www.pearsoned.ca/accounting1

In analyzing transaction 7, observe that:

1. Cash is decreased by $75, the amount paid for the repair.
2. No other asset or liability is affected. The value of the truck on the equation analysis sheet is not increased because the engine was merely tuned up.
3. Capital is decreased by $75. After changing the cash figure, the difference between total assets and total liabilities is $34 105. This is $75 less than it was immediately before the transaction.
4. After the changes are recorded, the equation is still in balance.

Updating the Balance Sheet

The figures for an updated balance sheet for Metropolitan Movers are taken from the last line of the equation analysis sheet. Figure 3.10 below shows the new balance sheet.

METROPOLITAN MOVERS
BALANCE SHEET
—DATE—

Assets		Liabilities	
Cash	$ 875	Accounts Payable	
Accounts Receivable		– Central Supply	$ 1 750
– B. Cava	2 800	– Mercury Finance	25 170
– K. Lincoln	1 400	Total Liabilities	$26 920
Equipment	13 450	Owner's Equity	
Trucks	42 500	J. Hofner, Capital	34 105
Total Assets	$61 025	Total Liabilities and Equity	$61 025

Section 3.2   Review Questions

1. Name the form used in this chapter for analyzing transactions.
2. Explain how this form is related to the balance sheet.
3. Explain the mathematical way of telling if capital has increased after a business transaction.
4. How do you know if the changes for a transaction recorded on an equation analysis sheet were balanced?
5. Does a transaction always change both sides of a balance sheet? How do you know?

Section 3.2   Exercises

1. The opening financial position is shown here for Sheila's Interior Decorating of Sudbury, Ontario, owned by Sheila Kostiuk. **In your Workbook, or on columnar paper, record in the correct columns the changes required for the transactions below and on page 60. After each transaction, calculate the new totals and make sure that the equation balances.**

	ASSETS					LIABILITIES		OWNER'S EQUITY
	Cash	Accounts Receivable	Supplies	Office Furniture	Truck	Accounts Payable		S. Kostiuk Capital
		D. Murray				Ace Supply	Pine Motors	
Opening balances	1 000	50						1 050

TRANSACTIONS

1. Stationery and supplies are purchased from Ace Supply on credit for $75. They will be paid for within 30 days.
2. A new desk for the office is purchased for $450 cash.
3. D. Murray, a debtor, pays her debt in full.
4. A $100 service is performed for a customer who pays immediately in cash.
5. A used truck costing $6 500 is purchased from Pine Motors. A down payment of $500 is made. It is agreed that the remainder of the purchase price will be paid within three months.
6. Ace Supply, a creditor, is paid $75.
7. The owner, Sheila Kostiuk, withdraws $100 from the business for her own use.

---

2. The balance sheet of Triangle Real Estate of Tweed, Ontario, at the close of business on September 30, 20-, is as follows:

Accounts Receivable and Accounts Payable may be abbreviated A/R and A/P for now. You will learn the standard format for listing these terms in Chapter 8.

TRIANGLE REAL ESTATE
BALANCE SHEET
SEPTEMBER 30, 20—

Assets		Liabilities	
Cash	$ 216	A/P – Acme Supply	$ 1 562
A/R – P. Adams	375		
A/R – J. Singh	150		
A/R – N. Swartz	200		
Supplies	4 175	Owner's Equity	
Office Furniture	21 967	J. Morse, Capital	25 521
Total Assets	$27 083	Total Liabilities and Equity	$27 083

A. **Record the above balance sheet figures on the equation analysis sheet provided in your Workbook.**
B. **Analyze the transactions of October 1, listed below, and record the necessary changes on the equation analysis sheet. After each transaction, ensure that the equation is still in balance.**
C. **After completing transaction 5, prepare a new balance sheet.**

The term "Total Liabilities" has been omitted here for a reason. A Totals line is optional when only one item is listed.

TRANSACTIONS

October 1

1. Triangle Real Estate receives $100 cash from N. Swartz in partial payment of the amount owed by him.
2. Acme Supply is paid $200 cash in partial payment of the debt owed to them.
3. Supplies costing $95 are purchased for cash from the Standish Company.
4. Triangle Real Estate sells a home for A.J. Buhler. For this service, Triangle Real Estate receives a commission of $4 700 cash.
5. A new desk (Office Furniture) is purchased from Ideal Furniture for $950 cash.

3. Alliance Appliance Service in Renforth, Ontario, owned by Wayne Dalli, has the following assets and liabilities at the close of business on October 20, 20–:

Assets		Liabilities	
Cash	$ 1 395	Bank Loan	$ 5 000
A/R – N. Chang	100	Mortgage Payable	52 700
A/R – P. O'Neil	527		
Equipment	8 316		
Delivery Truck	19 750		
Land	40 000		
Building	80 000		

A. Record the above items on the equation analysis sheet in your Workbook. Do not forget to calculate and include the capital figure.
B. Analyze the transactions of October 21, listed below, and record the necessary changes on the equation analysis sheet.
C. After completing transaction 5, calculate the new totals and ensure that the equation is still in balance. Then prepare a new balance sheet.

TRANSACTIONS

October 21
1. The owner, in need of money for his personal use, draws $500 cash out of the business.
2. P. O'Neil pays her debt of $527.
3. A repair service is performed for a customer. The customer pays the full amount of the bill, $90, in cash.
4. A new electrical tester is purchased for $410 and paid for in cash.
5. The regular monthly mortgage payment of $900 in cash is made.

3.3 | Summary of Steps in Analyzing a Transaction

The following steps will help you to analyze any transaction.

Step 1   Identify all items (assets and liabilities) that must be changed and make all necessary changes.

When thinking about the transaction, try to be logical and use common sense.

- Carefully analyze the information given for any transaction.
- Classify each item affected as an asset or a liability.
- Decide whether each item affected is to be increased or decreased.

Step 2   See if the owner's equity has changed.

Remember the accounting equation. For example, if assets decrease and there is a corresponding liability decrease, the owner's equity will not change. But if assets decrease and liabilities are unchanged, the equation must be balanced by a decrease in owner's equity. Eventually, you will come to recognize whether or not owner's equity has changed. Generally, if a business is better off after a transaction, owner's equity has increased. If a business is worse off after a transaction, owner's equity has decreased.

Step 3 Make certain that at least two of the individual items have changed.

It is possible for several items — assets, liabilities, or owner's equity — to change, but there can never be only one change.

Step 4 Make sure that the equation is still in balance.

The fundamental accounting equation must be respected: assets must equal liabilities plus owner's equity.

Developing Good Work Habits

The first step in the accounting process is to analyze a transaction to determine the financial changes that result from it. You must recognize the importance of performing this step correctly. Accounting must be accurate. Therefore, you must be accurate.

You must also realize that the possible number of different transactions is very large. Do not think of trying to memorize all of the changes for all of the transactions. If you tried to rely on memory alone, you could not become a truly good accountant. Good accountants use their memory, of course, but they also rely on common sense, clear thinking, and a thorough understanding of accounting theory.

Section 3.3   Review Questions

1. What four steps should be used to analyze the changes caused by a transaction?
2. What do good accountants rely on besides their memory to keep track of the business's finances?
3. Why must accounting be done accurately?
4. What is a good clue as to whether capital has increased or decreased?
5. Assets increase by $10 000 with no corresponding change in liabilities. What change is there in capital?

Section 3.3   Exercises

1. To practise the steps outlined in this section, you will analyze the ten transactions listed in the following chart. (This chart also appears in your workbook.) For each transaction, do the following:

    a. Identify all Items (assets and liabilities) that must be changed. Record the names in the "Item" columns and the amounts in the "$ Change" columns. (Use a plus or minus sign before each amount.)
    b. Show what has happened to Owner's Equity by completing the appropriate column(s) in the EQUITY section.
    c. After each transaction, check that your dollar changes do not throw the accounting equation out of balance.

    The first three transactions have been done for you. Study them carefully so that you are sure you can complete the remaining seven.

| | STEP ONE | | | | STEP TWO | | | |
| | ASSETS | | LIABILITIES | | EQUITY | | | |
	Item	$ Change	Item	$ Change	Increase	Decrease	No Change	$Change
1. Bought $350 of supplies with cash.	Supplies	+350						
	Cash	−350					✓	
2. Paid telephone bill, $45 cash.	Cash	−45						
						✓		−45
3. Paid $500 to reduce the bank loan.	Cash	−500						
			Bank Loan	−500			✓	
4. Sold services for $1000 cash.								
5. An accounts receivable customer pays us $600.								
6. Paid wages, $800.								
7. Sold services for $2000 on credit.								
8. Paid an accounts payable vendor $750.								
9. Bought $4500 of equipment on credit.								
10. Furniture valued at $400 was destroyed.								
		A =	L		+		OE	

2. Examine the simple chart below, for which the scale is one unit to $100.

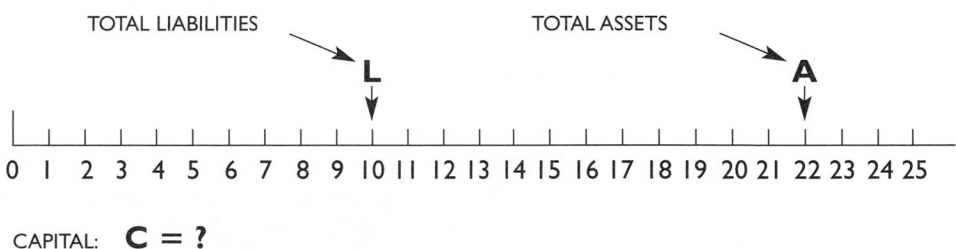

TOTAL LIABILITIES   TOTAL ASSETS

L   **A**

0 1 2 3 4 5 6 7 8 9 10 11 12 13 14 15 16 17 18 19 20 21 22 23 24 25

CAPITAL: **C = ?**

    A. What is the figure for total assets?
    B. What is the figure for total liabilities?
    C. Calculate the capital. How is it represented on the chart?

Now assume that a new desk is purchased for $200 cash.

D. Mentally calculate the new figure for total assets.
E. Mentally calculate the new figure for total liabilities.
F. Mentally place these new figures on the chart. Will the capital figure change and, if so, by how much? How does the chart show this?

---

3. Examine the chart below, for which the scale is one unit to $100.

CAPITAL: **C = ?**

A. What is the figure for total assets?
B. What is the figure for total liabilities?
C. Mentally calculate the capital. How is it represented on the chart?

Now assume that there is a loss by water damage of supplies worth $300 and that there is no insurance coverage on the supplies.

D. Mentally calculate the new figure for total assets.
E. Mentally calculate the new figure for total liabilities.
F. Mentally place these new figures on the chart. Will the capital figure change and, if so, by how much? How does the chart show this?

3.4 | # Using a Computer:
A Spreadsheet for Transaction Analysis

Spreadsheets were developed to give people easy access to the computer's extraordinary ability with numbers. Using spreadsheets, accountants can perform electronic calculations quickly and accurately without being experts at computer programming. The following example gives you an opportunity to gain more experience with transactions on an equation analysis sheet.

Business Background

Anna Antonelli runs a part-time business that provides clerical accounting services to small firms and charities. Recently, she developed a spreadsheet model to help new employees analyze transactions. Load that spreadsheet model into your computer. It is named ANNA and will look similar to Figure 3.11 on page 65.

The spreadsheet model for Antonelli's Accounting Services.

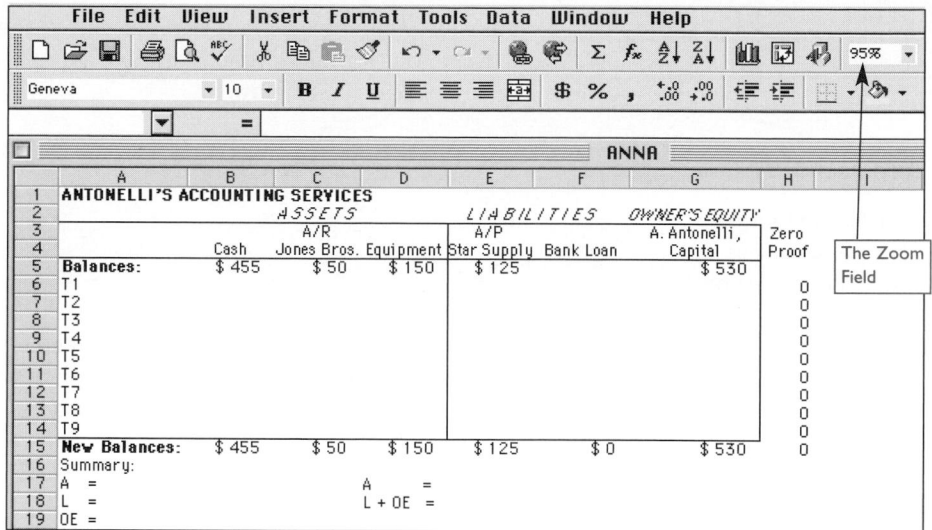

You may not be able to see the entire model shown above at one time because your monitor isn't large enough. If you are using Microsoft Excel, you can shrink or expand the appearance of the spreadsheet model by entering a percent value in the "zoom" field. In Figure 3.11 a value of 95% is entered in the zoom field.

Touring the Spreadsheet Model

Move the cell pointer around the model and observe the various cell contents that appear in the formula bar. The cells in column A contain labels, which, you will recall from Chapter 2, are words or symbols with no mathematical function. Move the cell pointer down to row 5. Many of the cells in row 5 have values that represent beginning balances. Row 15 has SUM functions to produce new totals. And the cells in column H contain more detailed entries that will be explained later.

Using Cell References

Reminder: The = sign is used by Microsoft® Excel as a prefix for formulas, functions, and cell references.

A summary of the accounting equation totals will be completed in the area starting at cell A16. The total assets and liabilities need to be calculated first. Enter a function for the assets and a formula for the liabilities as shown below. Instead of typing the entries below, try to use the "pointing" method explained to you in Chapter 2, page 34.

B17:   =*SUM(B15:D15)*
B18:   =*E15+F15*

At cell B19, the total owner's equity requires neither a formula nor a function. The owner's equity has only one item—A. Antonelli, Capital. The figure appears at cell G15. You simply need to be able to duplicate this figure at cell B19. To do this, you will use a cell reference.

Cell references are used to reproduce data from one cell to another. To enter a cell reference, simply type the = sign followed by the cell being referenced. For example, **at cell B19, type =G15.** A figure of $530 should be displayed.

Like formulas and functions, cell references offer the benefits of instant updates. When the total capital at cell G15 changes, cell B19 will be revised also.

To finish the summary section, **enter a cell reference and formula at cells E17 and E18.** Your formulas, functions, and cell references should be the same as those shown in Figure 3.12 below.

FIGURE 3.12

The function, formulas, and cell references for the Summary section.

	A	B	C	D	E
16	Summary:				
17	A =	=SUM(B15:D15)	A =		=B17
18	L =	=E15+F15	L + OE =		=B18+B19
19	OE =	=G15			

The totals produced by the formulas, functions, and cell references shown in Figure 3.12 are shown in Figure 3.13 below. These numbers will be updated instantly when you enter the first set of transactions for the business.

FIGURE 3.13

The numbers produced by the cell contents shown in Figure 3.12.

	A	B	C	D	E
16	Summary:				
17	A =	$ 655		A =	$ 655
18	L =	$ 125		L + OE =	$ 655
19	OE =	$ 530			

Entering Transactions

In the first transaction, *the business borrowed $3000 from the bank.* **Enter this transaction on row 6**. Your revised spreadsheet model should look like Figure 3.14 below.

FIGURE 3.14

The revised model after the first transaction is entered.

	A	B	C	D	E	F	G	H
1	ANTONELLI'S ACCOUNTING SERVICES							
2		ASSETS			LIABILITIES		OWNER'S EQUITY	
3			A/R		A/P		A. Antonelli,	Zero
4		Cash	Jones Bros.	Equipment	Star Supply	Bank Loan	Capital	Proof
5	Balances:	$455	$50	$150	$ 125		$ 530	
6	T1	3000				3000		0
7	T2							0
8	T3							0
9	T4							0
10	T5							0
11	T6							0
12	T7							0
13	T8							0
14	T9							0
15	New Balances:	$3 455	$ 50	$ 150	$ 125	$3 000	$ 530	0
16	Summary:							
17	A =	$3 655		A =	$3 655			
18	L =	$3 125		L + OE =	$3 655			
19	OE =	$ 530						

In response to the two values you entered, notice that six other cells have changed. This should give you a partial glimpse into the enormous mathematical power of a spreadsheet.

In the second transaction, *the business bought computer equipment for $2500 cash.* **Because cash is decreasing, make sure you enter –2500 at cell B7.** (Negative signs may be entered by pressing the hyphen key or the negative sign on the number pad.) **Also enter the $2500 increase to equipment. Use Figure 3.15 on page 67 to check your work.**

FIGURE 3.15

The entries for the
second transaction.

	A	B	C	D	E	F	G	H
1	ANTONELLI'S ACCOUNTING SERVICES							
2			*A S S E T S*		*L I A B I L I T I E S*		*OWNER'S EQUITY*	
3			A/R		A/P		A. Antonelli,	Zero
4		Cash	Jones Bros.	Equipment	Star Supply	Bank Loan	Capital	Proof
5	Balances:	$455	$50	$150	$ 125		$ 530	
6	T1	3000				3000		0
7	T2	(2500)		2500				0

Negative numbers
are often displayed in
brackets and red on
your monitor.

Checking Accuracy

To ensure that new employees do not record a transaction that causes the accounting equation to be out of balance, Anna Antonelli developed a formula for cells in
column H. **Move the cell pointer to H6.**

The formula reads $=sum(B6{:}D6)-sum(E6{:}G6)$. Notice that two functions are
being used in this formula. The formula instructs the spreadsheet to calculate all of
the changes in asset items and then subtract all of the changes in liability and equity
items. In a mathematical sense, the result of this formula is A$-$(L+OE). As you
know from your study of the fundamental accounting equation, the result must always
be zero. If it is not, the transaction has been analyzed or entered incorrectly.

Rows 6 through 15 in column H, the zero-proof column, have similar formulas.
This shows that spreadsheet models can be designed to improve accuracy. You have
already seen how quickly they perform calculations and how many cells can be
updated with just one change. Accuracy, speed, and numerical power are features
that make spreadsheets attractive to accountants.

Use the spreadsheet model to complete the transactions for Antonelli's
Accounting Services. These transactions appear in Computer Exercise 1 on page 68.

Section 3.4   Review Questions

1. In spreadsheets, what is the cursor usually called?
2. What is the purpose of entering a cell reference into a cell?
3. The figure for total assets is calculated at cell D22. If you also want this figure
   to be displayed at cell E30, what would you type? (Include the prefix symbol.)
4. What do cell references have in common with formulas and functions?
5. The text refers to the mathematical power of a spreadsheet. Explain what
   this means.
6. How are negative numbers entered into a spreadsheet?
7. Examine the zero-proof formula that appears in the cells of column H of the
   spreadsheet model named ANNA. Prove mathematically that this formula will
   produce a zero result if changes in assets totalled $25 000, liabilities totalled
   $8 000, and owner's equity totalled $17 000.
8. Identify three features of spreadsheets that make them attractive to accountants.

Section 3.4   Exercises

I. Update the spreadsheet file, ANNA, you worked on earlier.

A. Complete the transactions that follow.

TRANSACTIONS

Before you start, make sure you have done the first two transactions that are described on page 66.

3. Collected $50 from Jones Bros. in payment of their debt.
4. Purchased office equipment from Star Supply for $225. The bill is to be paid in 30 days.
5. Sold accounting services to Jones Bros. for $500. The amount is to be received at a later date.
6. Returned $80 of defective equipment to Star Supply. That company agreed to reduce the amount owed to them by $80.
7. Anna Antonelli withdrew $300 from the business for personal use.
8. Paid $600 to reduce the bank loan.
9. Sold more accounting services to Jones Bros. The total was $700, with $200 received now and the balance to be received in 30 days.

B. After all nine transactions are entered, check the zero-proof column (column H) for any cells that do not have a zero balance. If you find a balance that is not zero, you have made an error that must be found and corrected.

C. Check the *Summary* section of the spreadsheet model that begins at cell A16. If no errors were found in column H, the accounting equation will be in balance.

D. Save your work.

Section 3.4   Extending Your Computer Skills

I. Create a balance sheet for Antonelli's Accounting Services, starting near cell I25 of the ANNA spreadsheet model.

A. **Enter the labels first. Then, for each asset, liability, and owner's equity item, use a cell reference that will reproduce a number from row 15. Finally, use functions and formulas to calculate balance sheet totals.**

B. Assume a mistake was made with regard to transaction 4. Instead of $225, the bill for the office equipment was $252. **Make the necessary changes on row 9 of the spreadsheet model.**

C. **Check the balance sheet that you have created.** If you entered cell references, formulas, and functions properly, the balance sheet figures should have been automatically updated in response to the change in the office equipment bill.

D. **Save your work.**

2. **Load the spreadsheet file named MERRYMEN. Use this model to complete the transactions for Merrymen Window Washing that appear on page 72 of your text.**

Section 3.4   Communicate It

You and your sister are beginning accounting students and want to start a part-time landscaping business. She wants to use a manual equation analysis sheet similar to the one on page 58. You prefer to develop a spreadsheet model. Prepare a written explanation to defend your position, explaining why you think a spreadsheet would be better. Use the memo form found in the Skills Appendix.

CHAPTER 3 Summary

CHAPTER HIGHLIGHTS

Now that you have completed Chapter 3, you should:

- understand the factors that create changes in financial position;
- be able to define "business transaction";
- be able to work out the changes created in the assets, liabilities, or capital for any simple transaction;
- be able to record a series of transactions on an equation analysis sheet;
- be able to prepare a balance sheet from an equation analysis sheet;
- be able to state the four steps in analyzing a business transaction;
- know the purpose of source documents;
- understand the objectivity principle;
- be able to use labels, formulas, functions, and cell references in a simple spread-sheet model.

ACCOUNTING TERMS

business transaction   objectivity principle   source document

CHAPTER 3 Review Exercises

Using Your Knowledge

1 Shown below is an equation analysis sheet for the business of Brad Provost, a painter and decorator in Oakville, Ontario. **Examine the entries made on this sheet. Then prepare a list of five transactions that would have caused the changes in the financial position indicated by the entries.**

	ASSETS					LIABILITIES			OWNER'S EQUITY
	Cash	A/R C. Sully	A/R F. Vanweers	Supplies	Equipment	Bank Loan	A/P B. M. Co.	A/P Norpaints	B. Provost, Capital
	400	135	250	1 500	8 500	500	300		9 985
1.	+250		−250						
2.				+150				+150	
3.	+300								+300
4.		+115							+115
5.	−300						−300		
	650	250	⊘	1 650	8 500	500	⊘	150	10 400

② Shown below is an equation analysis sheet for the business of Brian Lee, an architect in Edmonton, Alberta. **After studying this sheet, prepare a list of five transactions that would have caused the changes in financial position shown.**

	Cash	A/R L. Swan	Supplies	Equipment	Auto	Bank Loan	A/P High Finance	B. Lee, Capital
			ASSETS			LIABILITIES		OWNER'S EQUITY
	500		1 300	7 000	17 000	4 000	5 000	16 800
1.	+500	+1 300						+1 800
2.	+1 500				−7 000		−5 000	−500
3.	−1 000				+20 000	+19 000		
4.	−1 50							−150
5.			−50					−50
	1 350	1 300	1 250	7 000	30 000	23 000	∅	17 900

③ At December 31, 20-0, Dowse Company had assets totalling $85 000. At December 31, 20-1, the assets totalled $115 000. During the same period, liabilities increased by $35 000. **If the equity at the end of the first year amounted to $60 000, what was the amount of the owner's equity at December 31 of the second year? Show how you arrive at your answer.**

④ **Describe four transactions that would cause the owner's equity to decrease.**

⑤ **Describe two transactions that would cause the owner's equity to increase.**

⑥ **Examine the source document below and answer the questions that follow on page 72.**

SMOKEY VALLEY SKI CLUB
R.R. #1, Horseshoe Valley, Ont. L3V 3B0

176

Nov. 12 20—

PAY TO THE ORDER OF   Mid-West Ski Lifts and Equipment $ 10 000.00

Ten Thousand   ------------------------ XX DOLLARS

THE COMMERCIAL BANK   Smokey Valley Ski Club

per   *A. Hart*
       R. Schwartz

⑈015⑈ ⑈11962⑈509⑈   7427⑈0⑈

A. What kind of source document is this?

B. Who issued the source document?

C. Who received the source document?

D. What do you think this source document is paying for?

E. As a result of this source document, two of the following are possible for the Smokey Valley Ski Club. Indicate which two are possible, and indicate which one of the two is more likely.

   a. An asset and a liability will both increase.
   b. An asset and a liability will both decrease.
   c. An asset will increase and another asset will decrease.
   d. An asset and equity will both decrease.

Challenge Exercise

7 Merrymen Window Washing is a business owned and operated by Carl Savich in Timmins, Ontario. On November 30, 20–, at the end of the day, the financial position of the business is as shown on the balance sheet below.

MERRYMEN WINDOW WASHING
BALANCE SHEET
NOVEMBER 30, 20—

Assets		Liabilities	
Cash	$ 2 750	A/P – Cleanall Co.	$ 124
A/R – Kwan	420	A/P – Hipp Co.	475
A/R – D. Pederson	75	Loan Payable	
Supplies	880	Simplex Finance	8 560
Truck	15 050	Total Liabilities	$ 9 159
Equipment	12 947	*Owner's Equity*	
		C. Savich, Capital	22 963
Total Assets	$32 122	Total Liabilities and Equity	$32 122

A. Set up the balance sheet items on an equation analysis sheet. Leave a blank column for a new account payable.

B. Analyze the transactions of December 1, listed on page 73, and record the necessary changes on the equation analysis sheet.

C. After completing the transactions, calculate the new totals, ensure that the equation is still in balance, and prepare a new balance sheet.

TRANSACTIONS

December 1

1. The regular monthly instalment payment of $800 is paid to Simplex Finance.
2. The company purchases but does not pay for $400 of supplies from Hipp Co.
3. The company receives $200 cash from T. Kwan in partial payment of his debt.
4. A new hoist is purchased from NRC Co. for $2 125. A cash down payment of $300 is made. The balance of the purchase price is to be paid at a later date.
5. The old hoist, included in the Equipment figure at $550, is sold for $100 cash.
6. A $500 window-washing service is performed for D. Pederson. Pederson pays $575, both for this service and to pay off the amount owed.
7. The truck was in a serious collision and is a write-off. The insurance company pays Merrymen Window Washing $14 500 cash.
8. The loan payable to Simplex Finance is paid off.
9. A new truck costing $23 000 is purchased. An $8 000 down payment is made. The balance is financed through Simplex Finance.
10. The amount owed to Hipp Co. is paid in full.
11. Supplies valued at $50 are taken out on a job and used up.

Questions for Further Thought

Briefly answer the following questions.

1. In your opinion, what is the difference between an account payable and a loan payable?

2. Explain why it is impossible for a balance sheet to be out of balance and to be correct.

3. Explain why it is possible for a balance sheet to be in balance and still be incorrect.

4. Explain why it is impossible for only a single item to change as a result of a business transaction.

5. Explain why an equation analysis sheet is better than a balance sheet for recording accounting changes.

6. Name a source document that would not originate in the accounting office.

7. Assume that your assets include a truck worth $7 000. Assume further that the truck represented by the $7 000 has recently been wrecked in an accident and that you are negotiating with your insurance company for a settlement. What financial changes (if any) will be recorded at this time?

8. One of your customers slips on your icy walkway and is injured. You receive a letter from the customer's lawyer to the effect that the customer wants $10 000 in damages. What financial changes (if any) will be recorded as a result of this letter?

Case Studies

CASE I

An Objective Balance Sheet?

Ted Roderiguez is very excited about starting his part-time gardening service. As a senior high school student, he has studied some accounting and has included the following two assets on his beginning balance sheet:

Lawn mowers	$ 160
Pick-up truck	$1 000

Ted purchased the two lawn mowers at a local flea market for $20 each but feels that he got a very good deal and that they are worth at least $80 each. The pick-up truck was a gift from his uncle. Ted thinks he has seen similar trucks advertised in the local newspapers for about $2 000. Ted would like his balance sheet to be accurate and to follow Generally Accepted Accounting Principles (GAAPs).

Questions

1. Has Ted violated any GAAPs on his balance sheet? Explain.
2. If he has made mistakes, how should he correct them?
3. How can an accurate balance sheet value for the truck be determined?
4. How would an overstatement of Ted's assets affect his capital on the balance sheet?

CASE 2

Checking Out a New Customer

Natalie Field, the owner of New Age Manufacturing, comes to you to arrange for the buying on credit of materials for her business. She advises you that the orders will amount to approximately $500 000 a year. This amount of new business could have a very beneficial effect on your company. You would even have to expand your own facilities to take advantage of it. You tell Ms. Field that you need time to consider the proposal.

When you approach your banker for a loan, she advises you to find out as much as you can about New Age Manufacturing. You go to a credit investigation bureau, which provides you with the following balance sheet totals for New Age Manufacturing.

Assets	$450 000
Liabilities	445 000
Equity	5 000

Questions

1. What conclusion would you draw from the balance sheet totals?
2. What dangers are there in dealing with New Age Manufacturing?
3. Would you do business with Ms. Field? Write a short memo to your banker, explaining your decision and giving a reason. Use the memo form given in the Skills Appendix.

CASE 3

The Balance Sheet Shuffle

Brandon Adams has recently opened a very successful dance club called "The Star-Lite" and has prepared the following balance sheet as at July 31, 20—:

THE STARLITE
BALANCE SHEET
JULY 31, 20–

Assets		Liabilities	
Cash	$ 4 000	Accounts Payable	$12 000
Accounts Receivable	3 000	Bank Loan Payable	30 000
Supplies	7 000	Total Liabilities	$42 000
Truck	8 000		
Dance Music CDs	10 000	Owner's Equity	
Stereo System	20 000	Brandon Adams, Capital	10 000
Total Assets	$52 000	Total Liabilities and Equity	$52 000

Brandon has recently applied for an additional bank loan, but has been turned down because his personal investment in the firm is too small. Brandon feels he can improve his capital balance by completing the three transactions below:

1. He will sell his truck to a friend for $8 000 because almost all of the club's supplies are delivered free.
2. He will borrow $10 000 from his brother, who will insist on signing a formal loan agreement.
3. He will use the cash from the first two transactions to reduce the accounts payable balance to zero.

Questions

1. What will be the revised amounts for total assets and total liabilities after the above three transactions?
2. Will Brandon's three transactions improve his capital on the balance sheet?
3. Will Brandon's chances for an additional bank loan be better or worse after the transactions?
4. Will Brandon's business be more healthy or less healthy as a result of his transactions? Why?

Career

Larry Lancefield CA, IFA, CFE / Forensic Accountant

Forensic medicine is a branch of medicine in which a physician provides evidence for the police or courts about someone's death or injury. Forensic accountant Larry Lancefield is called upon to give evidence in court too — except his evidence concerns accounting records rather than bodies.

"Say the word 'forensic,' and most people think of dead bodies," says Larry, who is Managing Director of Lancefield Inc., a business specializing in forensic accounting. "But *forensic* really means 'of or pertaining to law.'" A forensic accountant handles the accounting issues that are raised during legal cases and criminal investigations.

Forensic accountants are part of an investigative team that often includes lawyers and police officers investigating and prosecuting criminal cases. Although they take weeks, months, or even years to review documents, they often spend only a few days in court giving evidence. Those few days, however, can be the turning point in a trial. Larry notes that while criminal investigations make forensic accounting seem glamorous, the more common civil cases generate far more income for his firm. (In a civil case, no crime is being prosecuted; one person is suing another, claiming that the other person caused him or her a loss or injury.)

Forensic accounting began in the early 1970s, when police forces found that they were having difficulty supplying proof in fraud cases. The police began to recognize that specially trained forensic accountants could help them by condensing mountains of complex accounting transactions into a few simple accounting schedules for presentation to a judge or jury.

Larry got hooked on the forensic specialty early in his career. After graduating from the University of Toronto's Bachelor of Commerce program, and getting his CA designation, he left auditing to join Canada's largest forensic accounting firm in 1984. In 1995 he started Lancefield Inc. after a long career at KPMG. "My first forensic case seventeen years ago involved the investigation of Helmuth Buxbaum," he says. (Buxbaum, an Ontario businessman, was convicted of arranging the murder of his wife in 1985.) "The circumstances of this trial are an interesting example of how a forensic accountant can aid an investigation."

Larry was asked to determine if Buxbaum had a financial motive for the crime. That is, were his finances in such bad shape that the insurance on his wife's life would have been an obvious temptation? In addition, did a "financial trail" (a trail of transactions) exist that might implicate Buxbaum? Answering these questions wasn't a straightforward assignment — Buxbaum had 23 personal bank accounts, from which he withdrew a steady amount on a weekly basis. "We went back and reviewed all of his transactions for six months prior to the murder," says Larry. "We found that one week he withdrew $20 000, which turned out to be the cash for the 'hit.' The week of the murder, he withdrew another $20 000." The Forensic Group was able to amass evidence that supported a motive for murder.

Besides murder Larry has worked with the police on cases involving the tracing of organized crime monies which often cross international borders. Money launderers are known for trying to hide the proceeds of their criminal acts by investing in legitimate real estate transactions or cash-based businesses. They hope that investigators will give up tracing the money and fighting to unwind their subsequent business transactions.

What personal attributes make a good forensic accountant? "The bottom line with forensic accounting is that you can't afford to be wrong — you can't afford mistakes. This is why we usually don't bring people into the specialty unless they have their CA designation," says Larry. Recently the CICA has recognized the specialist designation of Investigative Forensic Accountant (IFA). A new diploma course in forensic accounting is offered at the University of Toronto and Larry is a member of faculty for this program.

On a personal note, he adds that he has a natural aptitude for detective work and "getting to the bottom of something." He is accustomed to dealing with lawyers and has learned to ask the right questions during an investigation. "If a company goes into receivership or is accused of financial wrongdoing, and something doesn't look right, I'm right in there digging up the dirt," says Larry, who has become quite comfortable investigating where people aren't happy to see him.

Are there many jobs opportunities for forensic accountants? Larry thinks that "as long as there are people who try to make money through financial wrongdoing, there will be a need for forensic accountants."

Discussion

1. What accounting designation does Larry Lancefield say is important in his work?
2. What other qualities are important to success as a forensic accountant?
3. According to the profile above, when and why did forensic accounting begin?
4. What specialized knowledge do you think accountants can bring to a complex financial situation that may involve a crime? Consider the importance of the correct analysis of transactions, which was the subject of this chapter. Where might the objectivity principle, which was also studied in this chapter, come in?
5. How important do you think the role of source documents is in Larry Lancefield's work? Explain.

4

The Simple Ledger

The purpose of Chapter 3 was to show you the effect that transactions have on financial position. In Chapter 3, you practised analyzing transactions and keeping a financial position up to date. The method used, the equation analysis sheet, was a very simple one. However, that method is not satisfactory when working with a complete business operation.

In an active business, many transactions occur each day. To be able to handle them all, accountants use a more complete system, based on the concepts presented in Chapter 3. While the system is more complex, it is also more efficient and orderly, and it is universally accepted.

4.1 | Ledger Accounts

In this chapter, you will be learning the system used to maintain an up-to-date financial position. For this purpose, accountants long ago developed the account and the ledger.

An **account** is a page specially designed to record the changes in each individual item affecting the financial position. There is one account for each such item. All the accounts together are called the ledger. A **ledger** is a group or file of accounts.

A ledger can be prepared in different ways. The accounts can be prepared on cards to form a card ledger. They can be prepared on looseleaf paper to form a looseleaf ledger. The accounts in a computer system are recorded on a disk. While all these methods may still be used, computer ledgers now dominate the business world.

FIGURE 4.1

Computer accounting ledger.

To research trends in the use of computers in accounting, visit the website www.pearsoned.ca/accounting1

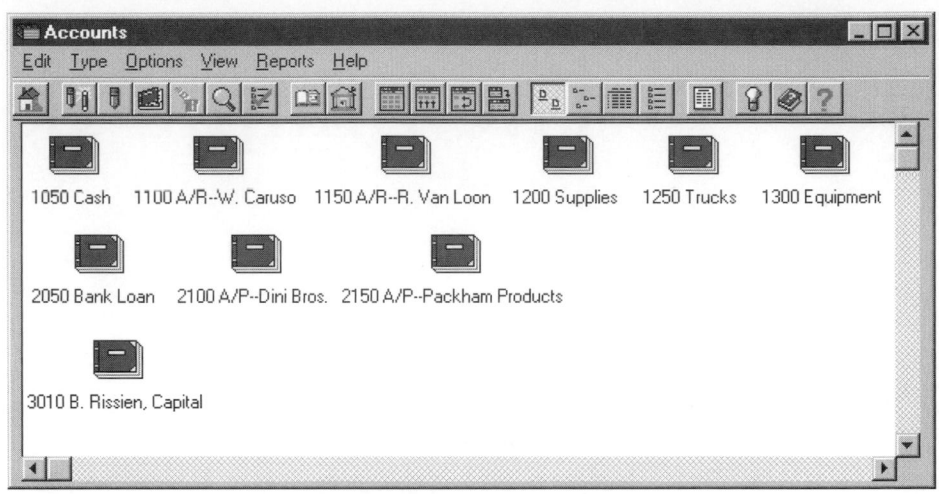

Let us begin our study of ledger accounts by referring to the records of Pacific Trucking, owned by Byron Rissien of Kelowna, British Columbia. The balance sheet of this business is shown in Figure 4.2 below.

FIGURE 4.2

The balance sheet of Pacific Trucking.

PACIFIC TRUCKING
BALANCE SHEET
JUNE 30, 20—

Assets		Liabilities	
Cash	$ 3 265	Bank Loan	$18 000
A/R – W. Caruso	150	A/P – Dini Bros.	1 516
A/R – R. Van Loon	620	A/P – Packham Products	3 946
Supplies	2 465	Total Liabilities	$23 462
Trucks	55 075	*Owner's Equity*	
Equipment	22 174	B. Rissien, Capital	60 287
Total Assets	$83 749	Total Liabilities and Equity	$83 749

The data from this balance sheet are used to set up the separate pages, called accounts. The dollar value for each item on the balance sheet gives the beginning value for that item's account.

Pacific Trucking will have 10 accounts, one account for each item on the balance sheet. These accounts are Cash; Accounts Receivable—W. Caruso; Accounts Receivable—R. Van Loon; Supplies; Trucks; Equipment; Bank Loan; Accounts Payable—Dini Bros.; Accounts Payable—Packham Products; and B. Rissien, Capital. All these accounts together form the ledger for Pacific Trucking.

FIGURE 4.3

The simple ledger accounts of Pacific Trucking.

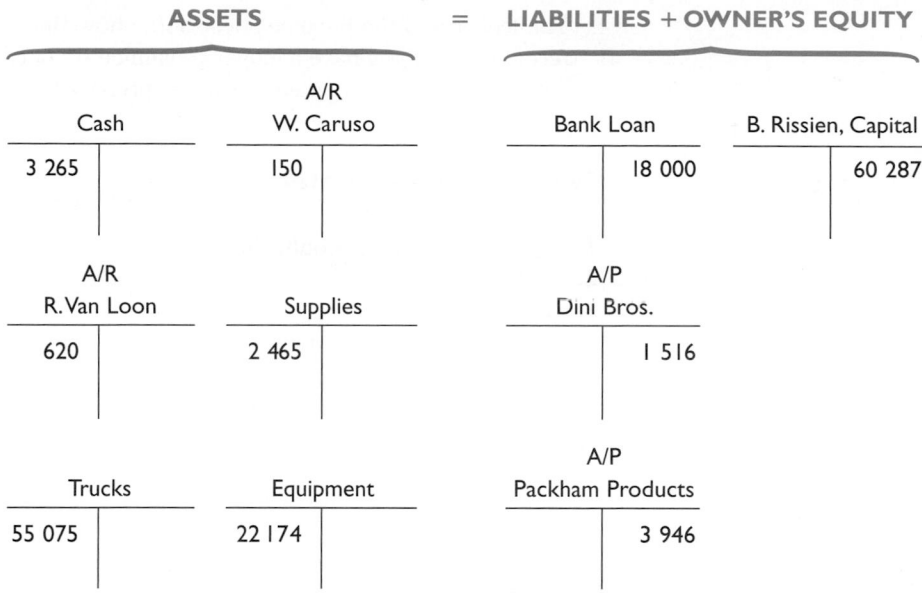

Figure 4.3 above shows the information from the balance sheet of Pacific Trucking presented as accounts in a ledger. These accounts are called T-accounts because, as you can see, each one looks like a T. The T-account is a simple type of account, used mainly to explain accounting theory. The formal account, the one actually used in business, will be introduced in a later chapter.

Important Features of Ledger Accounts

Using the ledger shown in Figure 4.3 above as a guide, let us look at four important features of all ledger accounts.

1. Each individual balance sheet item is given its own specially divided page with the name of the item at the top. (For now, think of each T as a page.) Each of these pages is called an account. In Figure 4.3, there are 10 accounts. You must learn to call them the Cash account, the R. Van Loon account, the Packham Products account, the Bank Loan account, and so on.
2. The dollar figure for each item is recorded in the account on the first line. This is the beginning value for the account.
3. It is especially important to record the dollar figure on the correct side of the account. For any item, the correct side is the side on which the item itself would appear on a simple balance sheet. Observe that for each of the *asset* accounts, the dollar amount is placed on the *left* side of the account page. For each of the *liability* accounts and the *owner's equity* account, the dollar amount is placed on the *right* side of the account page.

To determine an account's beginning value side, you can also think of the accounting equation. (Assets are on the **left** side of the equation, Liabilities and Equity are on the **right**.

Assets		=	Liabilities		+	Owner's Equity	
Beginning $ Value			Beginning $ Value			Beginning $ Value	
left	right		left	right		left	right

4. The ledger and the balance sheet both show financial position, although in different ways. If you have a ledger, a balance sheet can be prepared from it. If you have a balance sheet, a ledger can be prepared from it.

Section 4.1   Review Questions

1. Explain what an "account" is.
2. Define "ledger."
3. Name the different forms a ledger can take.
4. The accounting records are commonly referred to as the "books." Why would this name be used?
5. Why are the beginning amounts for a ledger usually taken from a balance sheet?
6. What is the principal use of T-accounts?
7. Explain where the dollar amounts in the accounts are placed when setting up the beginning amounts in a ledger.

Section 4.1   Exercises

1. The balance sheet for Stevens Woodworking is shown below.

STEVENS WOODWORKING
BALANCE SHEET
JUNE 30, 20—

Debits

Credits

Assets		Liabilities	
Cash	$ 2 000	Bank Loan	$ 20 000
A/R – A. Marks	375	A/P – Gem Lumber	2 500
A/R – C. Prentice	1 150	Mortgage Payable	55 000
Land	30 000	Total Liabilities	$ 77 500
Building	45 000		
Equipment	27 800	Owner's Equity	
Truck	14 500	T. Stevens, Capital	43 325
Total Assets	$120 825	Total Liabilities and Equity	$120 825

Set up the ledger for Stevens Woodworking in the T-accounts provided in your Workbook.

2. The balance sheet of Dr. Pauline Inaba is shown below.

DR. PAULINE INABA
BALANCE SHEET
MARCH 31, 20—

Assets			Liabilities		
Cash	$	500	A/P – A.B. Associates	$	1 200
A/R – P. Auul		350	A/P – Medico Supply		2 300
A/R – S. Wouke		1 250	Total Liabilities		$ 3 500
Supplies		3 900			
Furniture and Equipment		18 320	Owner's Equity		
Automobile		21 040	Pauline Inaba, Capital		41 860
Total Assets		$45 360	Total Liabilities and Equity		$45 360

Set up the ledger of Dr. Inaba in the T-accounts provided in your Workbook.

3. Shown below is the ledger of Lilly Wall, who operates an interior design business. The asset and liability account balances are given.

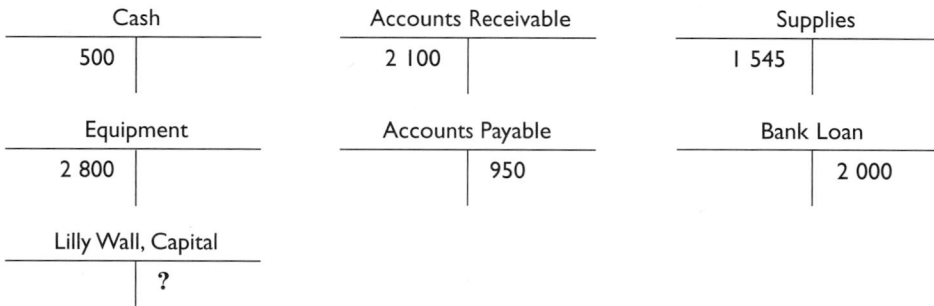

Show the fundamental accounting equation for Lilly Wall.

4.2 | Debit and Credit Theory

So far, you have learned that the idea that there is a "left side" and a "right side" is important in accounting. This is especially true when using ledger accounts. The theory of accounting using ledger accounts is based entirely on the understanding that every account page has these two distinct sides.

These two sides of an account page are described in the same way by accountants everywhere. **Debit** is the word associated with the left side of an account. **Credit** is the word associated with the right side of an account. In accounting terms, debit means "left," credit means "right."

Remember that the two new terms apply to every account, as shown on page 84.

Any Account

left side	right side
DEBIT	CREDIT
(short form DR or Dr)	(short form CR or Cr)

These two new words—debit and credit—are probably the two words you will use most often as you acquire accounting skills. Let us now begin to use these two new accounting terms ourselves. Looking back at the simple ledger in Figure 4.3 on page 81, you will notice that the beginning values of the assets were placed on the left side—the debit side—in each of their accounts. The values of the liabilities and of the capital were placed on the right side—the credit side—in each of their accounts. You may correctly conclude from this that asset accounts have debit values and that liability and capital accounts have credit values.

The Rules of Debit and Credit

You are familiar with the simple ledger and the terms *debit* and *credit*. You have discovered which side of the account to use to record the beginning value for each type of account. Now you are ready to learn how changes are recorded in the accounts. There is a simple set of rules for recording changes in accounts. *For each type of account, record increases on its beginning value side and decreases on the other side.* These rules are summarized, using the terms "debit" and "credit," in the chart below:

Types of Accounts	Beginning Value Side	Increases	Decreases
ASSET accounts	DEBIT	DEBIT	CREDIT
LIABILITY and OWNER'S EQUITY accounts	CREDIT	CREDIT	DEBIT

Applying the Rules of Debit and Credit

To give you practice in using the new rules of debit and credit, a number of transactions of Pacific Trucking are analyzed on the following pages. The ledger of Pacific Trucking was begun on page 81. In applying these rules to the transactions, you should try to do the analysis before reading the explanations. You must master the technique of analyzing transactions if you want to be a skilled accountant.

TRANSACTION 1 **The company purchases $200 worth of supplies from Packham Products, to be paid for later.**

Analysis When learning to analyze a transaction correctly, it is helpful to use a "transaction analysis sheet." This sheet, shown below, provides a place to organize your thoughts about the transaction. Proceed according to the following steps:

Step 1   In column (A), write down the names of the accounts that are affected by the transaction. In this example:

(A) Account Names	(B) Asset, Liability, or Owner's Equity	(C) Increase (+) or Decrease (−)	(D) Debit or Credit	(E) Amount
Supplies				
A/P − Packham Products				

Step 2   In column (B), write down whether each of these accounts is an asset, a liability, or the capital account. In this example:

(A) Account Names	(B) Asset, Liability, or Owner's Equity	(C) Increase (+) or Decrease (−)	(D) Debit or Credit	(E) Amount
Supplies	*Asset*			
A/P − Packham Products	*Liability*			

Step 3   In column (C), write down whether the accounts are to be increased or decreased. In this example:

(A) Account Names	(B) Asset, Liability, or Owner's Equity	(C) Increase (+) or Decrease (−)	(D) Debit or Credit	(E) Amount
Supplies	*Asset*	+		
A/P − Packham Products	*Liability*	+		

Step 4   In column (D), write down whether the accounts are to be debited or credited. Apply the rule given in the previous section: To increase an asset, you debit the account; to increase a liability, you credit the account. In this example:

(A) Account Names	(B) Asset, Liability, or Owner's Equity	(C) Increase (+) or Decrease (−)	(D) Debit or Credit	(E) Amount
Supplies	*Asset*	+	*DR*	
A/P − Packham Products	*Liability*	+	*CR*	

Step 5   In column (E), write in the amounts by which the accounts are increased or decreased. In this example:

To help you identify transactions, try placing encir-
cled numbers next to debit
and credit amounts, as
shown in these examples.

(A) Account Names	(B) Asset, Liability, or Owner's Equity	(C) Increase (+) or Decrease (−)	(D) Debit or Credit	(E) Amount
Supplies	Asset	+	DR	① 200–
A/P – Packham Products	Liability	+	CR	① 200–

This final step completes what is known as the *accounting entry* for the transaction. An **accounting entry** may be defined as all of the changes in the accounts
caused by one business transaction, expressed in terms of debits and credits.

For each type of account,
record increases on its
beginning value side and
decreases on the other side.

An accountant would express the accounting entry for transaction 1 in the following way: debit Supplies and credit A/P – Packham Products, $200. Notice that the
debited account is stated first. The credited account is stated second. After the
changes are recorded in the appropriate accounts, the two accounts affected appear
as shown below:

Supplies		A/P Packham Products	
2 465			3 946
① 200			200 ①

Notice that the transaction includes both a debit and a credit, and that the totals
of the debit and credit amounts are equal. This is the case with every transaction.

TRANSACTION 2   **The company pays $500 to Dini Bros. in partial payment
of the amount owed to them.**

Analysis This transaction is recorded on a transaction analysis sheet as follows:

(A) Account Names	(B) Asset, Liability, or Owner's Equity	(C) Increase (+) or Decrease (−)	(D) Debit or Credit	(E) Amount
A/P – Dini Bros.	Liability	−	DR	② 500–
Cash	Asset	−	CR	② 500–

An accountant would express the accounting entry as follows: debit A/P – Dini Bros.
and credit Cash, $500.

After the changes are recorded, the two accounts affected appear as shown below:

Cash		A/P Dini Bros.	
3 265	500 ②	② 500	1 516

TRANSACTION 3   The company receives $200 cash from R. Van Loon in partial payment of her debt.

Analysis   The accounting entry for this transaction is worked out on the transaction analysis sheet as follows:

To increase an asset, you debit the account; to increase a liability, you credit the account.

(A) Account Names	(B) Asset, Liability, or Owner's Equity	(C) Increase (+) or Decrease (−)	(D) Debit or Credit	(E) Amount
Cash	Asset	+	DR	③ 200–
A/R – R. Van Loon	Asset	−	CR	③ 200–

Read the changes as follows: debit Cash and credit A/R – R. Van Loon, $200.
     After the changes are recorded, the two accounts affected appear as shown below:

	Cash			A/R R. Van Loon	
3 265	500 ②		620	200 ③	
③ 200					

TRANSACTION 4   A delivery service is provided for a customer at a price of $400. The customer pays cash at the time the service is completed.

Analysis   The accounting entry for this transaction is worked out on the transaction analysis sheet as follows:

(A) Account Names	(B) Asset, Liability, or Owner's Equity	(C) Increase (+) or Decrease (−)	(D) Debit or Credit	(E) Amount
Cash	Asset	+	DR	④ 400–
B. Rissien, Capital	Owner's Equity	+	CR	④ 400–

Express these changes as follows: debit Cash and credit B. Rissien, Capital, $400.
     After the changes are recorded, the two accounts affected appear as shown below:

	Cash			B. Rissien, Capital	
3 265	500 ②			60 287	
③ 200				400 ④	
④ 400					

TRANSACTION 5 **A used truck costing $8 000 is purchased from Dini Bros. A cash down payment of $2 500 is made at the time of the purchase and the balance is to be paid at a later date.**

Analysis This transaction affects three accounts. The accounting entry for the transaction is worked out on the transaction analysis sheet as follows:

(A) Account Names	(B) Asset, Liability, or Owner's Equity	(C) Increase (+) or Decrease (−)	(D) Debit or Credit	(E) Amount
Trucks	Asset	+	DR	⑤ 8 000–
Cash	Asset	−	CR	⑤ 2 500–
A/P – Dini Bros.	Liability	+	CR	⑤ 5 500–

Read these changes: debit Trucks, $8 000; credit Cash, $2 500; credit A/P — Dini Bros., $5 500.

After the changes are recorded, the three accounts affected appear as shown below:

	Cash		Trucks			A/P Dini Bros.	
	3 265	500 ②	55 075		② 500	1 516	
③ 200	2 500 ⑤	⑤ 8 000			5 500 ⑤	
④ 400						

Notice that this transaction includes one debit but two credits. The total of the debit and the total of the credits are equal for the transaction.

TRANSACTION 6 **A delivery service is completed for R. Van Loon at a price of $350. Van Loon does not pay for the service at the time it is provided, but agrees to pay within 60 days.**

Analysis The accounting entry for this transaction is worked out on the transaction analysis sheet as follows:

(A) Account Names	(B) Asset, Liability, or Owner's Equity	(C) Increase (+) or Decrease (−)	(D) Debit or Credit	(E) Amount
A/R – R. Van Loon	Asset	+	DR	⑥ 350–
B. Rissien, Capital	Owner's Equity	+	CR	⑥ 350–

Read these changes: debit A/R — R. Van Loon and credit B. Rissien, Capital, $350.

After the changes are recorded, the two accounts affected appear as shown below:

	A/R R. Van Loon			B. Rissien, Capital	
	620	200 ③		60 287	
⑥ 350				400 ④	
				350 ⑥	

TRANSACTION 7 One of the lifting machines (part of Equipment) breaks down. The company spends $650 cash to have the machine repaired.

(Note: A common mistake made by students dealing with this type of transaction is to increase the Equipment account. To help you to avoid this mistake, here is a clue: the owner is worse off financially because the machine had to be repaired.)

Analysis This transaction is worked out on the transaction analysis sheet as follows:

(A) Account Names	(B) Asset, Liability, or Owner's Equity	(C) Increase (+) or Decrease (−)	(D) Debit or Credit	(E) Amount
Cash	Asset	−	CR	⑦ 650–
B. Rissien, Capital	Owner's Equity	−	DR	⑦ 650–

Read the changes: debit B. Rissien, Capital and credit Cash, $650.

After the changes are recorded, the two accounts affected appear as shown below:

Cash				B. Rissien, Capital		
	3 265	500	②	⑦　650	60 287	
③	200	2 500	⑤		400	④
④	400	650	⑦		350	⑥

Double-Entry System of Accounting

Whenever a transaction occurs, changes must be made in the accounts. For each transaction, all of the account changes together must balance. They are known as the accounting entry for the transaction.

In this chapter so far, there have been seven transactions. They are summarized in Figure 4.4 on page 90.

FIGURE 4.4

Seven accounting entries
for Pacific Trucking

The double-entry
system using debits
and credits is crucial
to your understanding
of accounting. If you
need to review this
system, go on-line at
www.pearsoned.ca/
accounting1 for a
demonstration.

Transaction	Account Names	Account Classifications A, L, OE	Debit or Credit	Amount
1	Supplies	A	DR	$ 200
	A/P – Packham Products	L	CR	$ 200
2	A/P – Dini Bros.	L	DR	$ 500
	Cash	A	CR	$ 500
3	Cash	A	DR	$ 200
	A/R – R. Van Loon	A	CR	$ 200
4	Cash	A	DR	$ 400
	B. Rissien, Capital	OE	CR	$ 400
5	Trucks	A	DR	$8 000
	Cash	A	CR	$2 500
	A/P – Dini Bros.	L	CR	$5 500
6	A/R – R. Van Loon	A	DR	$ 350
	B. Rissien, Capital	OE	CR	$ 350
7	B. Rissien, Capital	OE	DR	$ 650
	Cash	A	CR	$ 650

As you have noticed, each of the above seven transactions balances within itself. For each transaction, the total of the debit amounts equals the total of the credit amounts. This is basic to the whole accounting process and is true for every possible transaction. If you ever find an accounting entry that does not balance within itself, you can be certain that it is not correct. On the other hand, a balanced entry is not necessarily a correct entry. If the entry balances, that means that it is probably correct. If it does not balance, there is no chance that it is correct.

Now you can understand why the system you have been working with is known as the double-entry system of accounting. In the **double-entry system of accounting**, every transaction is recorded in the accounts in two steps. It is recorded first as a debit (or debits) and second as a credit (or credits), so that the total of the debit entries equals the total of the credit entries. The double-entry system of accounting is in general use throughout the business world.

Section 4.2   **Review Questions**

1. Explain the meaning of the words "debit" and "credit."
2. How is the beginning financial position in a ledger set up?
3. For what accounts does an increase mean "debit"?
4. For what accounts does a decrease mean "debit"?
5. For what accounts does an increase mean "credit"?
6. For what accounts does a decrease mean "credit"?
7. What is a transaction analysis sheet used for?
8. What is an accounting entry?
9. What must be true of every correct accounting entry?

10. What condition is true for an accounting entry that does not balance?

11. What condition is true for an accounting entry that does balance?

12. Explain the meaning of the double-entry system of accounting.

Section 4.2   Exercises

1. **Complete the following in your Workbook by writing either the word "increase" or the word "decrease" in the rectangles provided.**

ASSETS		=	LIABILITIES		+	OWNER'S EQUITY	
Debit	Credit		Debit	Credit		Debit	Credit

2. In the following list, there are four asset accounts, three liability accounts, and one capital account. In your workbook, write each title on a T-account, enter its beginning value on the proper side, and write a note to indicate the side on which the account increases and the side on which it decreases. The first one has been done for you.

```
         A/R—K Mak
    ─────────────────
     1 000  │
            │
            │
    Increases │ Decreases
```

Accounts

A/R—K. Mak	1 000
B. Chan, Capital	9 500
Bank Loan	9 000
Equipment	10 000
Supplies	5 000
A/P—Parry Supply Co.	500
Cash	6 000
A/P—Heiden Fashions	3 000

3. Flora Siska is the owner-operator of a fitness clinic. The ledger used in her business contains the following accounts:

Cash
Accounts Receivable (several)
Supplies
Furniture
Equipment
Automobile
Accounts Payable (several)
Flora Siska, Capital

Listed below are transactions of Flora's business. **Examine these transactions and record your analysis on the transaction analysis sheet provided in your Workbook and shown below**. To help you get a correct start, the first transaction has been done for you. **Be sure that each entry balances within itself.**

TRANSACTIONS

1. The business receives $300 cash from J. Parker, one of the accounts receivable.
2. The business purchases $200 worth of supplies for cash.
3. Little Bros., one of the accounts payable, is paid $100.
4. The owner withdraws $250 for her personal use.
5. A new piece of equipment costing $500 is purchased from Champion Sports. The business pays $125 cash at the time of purchase, with the balance of $375 to be paid within 30 days.
6. A new customer signs up for a fitness course. The $300 fee is paid in cash.

Transaction Analysis Sheet

Trans-action No.	Account Names	Asset, Liability, or Owner's Equity	Increase (+) or Decrease (−)	Debit or Credit	Amount
1	Cash	Asset	+	DR	300–
	A/R J. Parker	Asset	−	CR	300–

4. Crooks Garage is a small business operated by James Crooks. Shown below are 10 selected transactions of Crooks Garage. Analyze these transactions on pages 92 and 93 on the transaction analysis sheet in your Workbook. When performing your analysis, choose from the following accounts:

> Cash
> Accounts Receivable (several)
> Supplies
> Equipment
> Truck
> Bank Loan
> Accounts Payable (several)
> J. Crooks, Capital

TRANSACTIONS

1. A car is repaired for a customer who pays the $450 charge in cash.
2. The business purchases $170 of supplies for cash.
3. The business pays $125 to Rossi Co., an account payable.
4. The business receives $90 from G. Rawl, an account receivable.

5. A welding unit, included in the Equipment account at $500, is run over by a truck. It is so badly damaged that it has to be thrown away.
6. A new welding unit is purchased on credit from Bly Co. at a cost of $790.
7. For the repair of his car, F. Stefryk pays $100 cash and owes $250, the balance of the repair charge.
8. Arrangements are made with the bank to borrow $6 000. A promissory note for this amount is signed by Mr. Crooks for the bank, after which the bank provides the business with $6 000 cash.
9. Albert McCann, a mechanic employed by Crooks Garage, is paid wages of $375.
10. A towing service is performed for a customer for $40 cash.

4.3 Account Balances and Terminology

You started working with the accounts of Pacific Trucking on page 81. Then you worked out the accounting entries for seven transactions. After these accounting entries are entered in the accounts, the ledger appears as shown below in Figure 4.5.

FIGURE 4.5

The ledger of Pacific Trucking after recording the accounting entries for seven transactions.

ASSETS = LIABILITIES + EQUITY

Cash	
3 265	500 (2)
(3) 200	2 500 (5)
(4) 400	650 (7)

A/R W. Caruso	
150	

Bank Loan	
	18 000

B. Rissien, Capital	
(7) 650	60 287
	400 (4)
	350 (6)

A/R R. Van Loon	
620	200 (3)
(6) 350	

Supplies	
2 465	
(1) 200	

A/P Dini Bros.	
(2) 500	1 516
	5 500 (5)

Trucks	
55 075	
(5) 8 000	

Equipment	
22 174	

A/P Packham Products	
	3 946
	200 (1)

In the ledger of Pacific Trucking, there are 10 accounts. The following information is stored in each account:

1. the name of the account, which is written at the top;
2. the dollar value of the account and an indication of whether the value of the account is a debit or a credit.

Calculating the Balance of an Account

To calculate the balance of a T-account, two steps are performed. These two steps are shown in Figure 4.6 below, using accounts from the ledger of Pacific Trucking.

Step 1   Add the two sides of the account separately. Use tiny pencil figures to write down these two subtotals, one beneath the last item on each side. These tiny totals are called **pin totals** or **pencil footings**.

Step 2   a. Subtract the smaller total from the larger total.
          b. Write the result beside or beneath the larger of the two pin totals from Step 1. Circle this final amount.

FIGURE 4.6

Calculating the balance of a T-account.

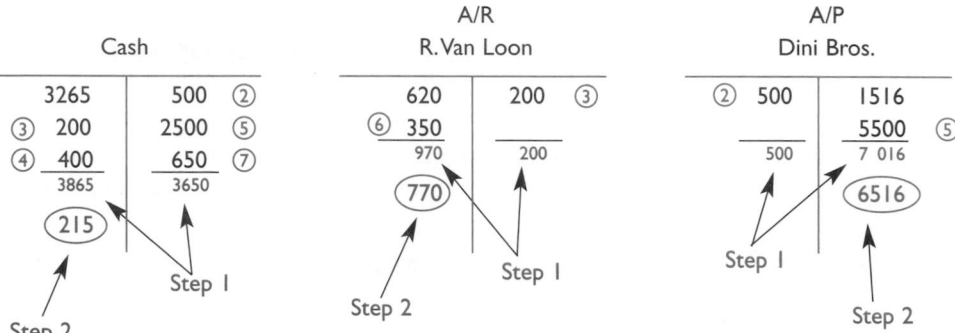

The circled amount is the dollar value of the account. The side on which it is recorded indicates which type of balance it is, debit or credit. Together, the two pieces of information represent the *account balance*. The **account balance** gives the dollar value of an account and shows whether it is a debit or credit value.

Interpreting the Balance of an Account

It is not enough simply to find the account balances. You must now learn to interpret the information stored in the accounts. They must mean something to you. Look at the accounts in Figure 4.6 above and see what you can learn from them.

It should be clear what the account balances are. The Cash account has a balance of $215, and it is a debit balance because it is entered on the left side. Similarly, the R. Van Loon account has a balance of $770, debit, and the Dini Bros. account has a balance of $6 516, credit.

So far, you are familiar with three types of accounts: assets, liabilities, and the capital. At this stage, all accounts fall into one of these categories. You already know that assets have debit balances and that liabilities and capital have credit balances.

It follows therefore that:

a. the Cash account is an asset because it has a debit balance;
b. the R. Van Loon account is an asset (an account receivable) because it has a debit balance;
c. the Dini Bros. account is a liability (an account payable) because it has a credit balance and is not the Capital account.

Exceptional Account Balances

Occasionally, an account that would normally have a debit balance ends up with a credit balance, or vice versa. Opposite balances are not necessarily the result of mistakes, although that possibility should certainly be checked out. There may be a good reason for an account to end up with a balance opposite to its normal one.

For example, suppose that Jack Evans, a customer, owes us $50. Suppose also that he sends a cheque for $55 in payment. His account will end up with a credit balance of $5, even though he is a customer and normally has a debit balance. The account balance is correct. It shows that the business owes Jack Evans $5. The account is temporarily a liability account.

A similar situation can affect the Bank account. For instance, we might temporarily spend more funds than we have in the bank (the bank would have to agree to this). Then we would end up with a credit balance in the Bank account. What does this credit balance mean? It means that the Bank account is temporarily in a liability position and that we are in debt to the bank.

Other transactions can bring about exceptional balances as well. Consider the following:

- you overpay an account payable;
- a customer with no account balance returns unsatisfactory merchandise for credit;
- you return goods for credit to a supplier with whom you have no account balance.

Exceptional balances do not last long. Ordinary business activity usually causes them to return quickly to normal.

The Bank Account

Business people rely heavily on the banking system. The most common ways to make payments are by cheque and electronic funds transfer. The storage of large quantities of cash on the premises is avoided, where possible. There is always the danger of theft or loss of the cash. Also, the business has a responsibility to its employees to avoid putting temptation in front of them.

After this, the account previously called "Cash" will be called "Bank."

The most important reason for businesses to use banking services is the convenience of making payments. It is much easier to send a cheque to someone than it is to deliver cash in person. This is especially true if the buyer and the seller are dealing with each other over a long distance. It is common practice to make all but very small payments by cheque.

As a result, you can expect to see an account called Bank in the ledger from now on, rather than one called Cash. When money is received or paid out, it is the Bank account, not Cash, that is increased or decreased.

The words "bank" and "cash" are often used interchangeably, however. When an accountant describes an item as bought for cash, this means that it is paid for at the time it is purchased. However, the payment is generally made by cheque and not by actual cash.

Cash and banking are discussed more fully in Chapter 10.

Buying and Selling on Credit

Businesses with good reputations are able to buy goods on short-term credit. This is a convenient way to do business. The purchaser is able to delay payment for a short period of time, usually 30 days. The purchaser thus has time to inspect or test the goods thoroughly before paying for them, and can refuse to pay for the goods if they are not satisfactory.

The buying and selling of goods on short-term credit is quite common in our society. Therefore, expect to see this type of transaction frequently in your exercises.

On Account

The term "on account" is used extensively in modern business. It is an essential part of business vocabulary. The term is used in four specific ways:

1. If an item is purchased on credit, this means that it is not paid for at the time of purchase. This is a purchase on account. A purchase on account is one that is not paid for at the time it is made.
2. When an item is sold on credit, it is not paid for at the time it is sold. This is a sale on account. A sale on account is a sale for which the money is not received at the time it is made.
3. If money is paid out to a creditor to decrease the amount owed to the creditor, it is a payment on account. A payment on account is money paid to a creditor to reduce the amount owed to that creditor.
4. When money is received from a debtor to reduce the amount owed, it is a receipt on account. A receipt on account is money received from a debtor to reduce the amount owed by that debtor.

 Section 4.3   **Review Questions**

1. What three pieces of information does an account contain?
2. Explain the two steps in calculating the balance of a T-account.
3. How do you know which type of balance (debit or credit) an account has?
4. What kind of account has a debit balance?
5. What kind of account has a credit balance?
6. What does it mean if an account has an exceptional balance?
7. Give two examples of situations that result in an exceptional balance.
8. Why do businesses prefer to make purchases on credit?
9. The term "on account" is used in four ways. What are these four ways?

 Section 4.3   **Exercises**

1. **The selected accounts on page 97 also appear in your Workbook. Calculate their balances. Remember to make your pencil footings in tiny figures and to circle the balance on the correct side of the account.**

Bank		A/R H. Devrie		A/P P. Helka		R. Smart, Capital	
250	190	25	175	30	75	150	3 140
1 210	48	150		45	40		
360	512	70			175		
29		35					

A. **What does the debit balance in the H. Devrie account mean?**
B. **What does the credit balance in the P. Helka account mean?**

---

2. The following three accounts have exceptional balances. **Examine them and answer the questions that follow.**

Bank		A/R P. Chu		A/P J. Reicher	
	500		100	300	

A. **For each account, explain what is unusual about the balance.**
B. **For each account, give a possible cause of the exceptional balance.**

---

3. A number of phrases appear below. To the right are two columns, one headed "Debit" and the other headed "Credit." **In your Workbook, indicate whether each phrase is best represented by the word "debit" or by the word "credit" by placing a check mark in the appropriate column.**

	Debit	Credit
a. The left side of an account.		
b. The balance of an account receivable.		
c. The balance of a supplier's account.		
d. A decrease in a liability.		
e. An exceptional balance in the Bank account.		
f. The balance in the Equipment account.		
g. The right side of an account.		
h. The balance in the Bank Loan account.		
i. An exceptional balance in an account payable.		
j. The larger side of a liability account.		
k. A creditor's account.		
l. A customer's account.		
m. An increase in an asset.		
n. A debtor's account.		
o. The effect on accounts receivable when we sell on account.		
p. The effect on accounts payable when we pay on account.		
q. The effect on account receivable when we have a receipt on account.		
r. The effect on accounts payable when we purchase on account.		

4.4 | Trial Balance

When setting up a ledger, as in Figure 4.3 on page 81, the information for the accounts is usually obtained from a balance sheet. This way, the ledger begins in a balanced position. The total of the accounts with debit balances equals the total of the accounts with credit balances.

The changes caused by business transactions are recorded in the ledger. These changes are all in the form of balanced accounting entries, that is, entries where debits equal credits. As a result, the ledger should be balanced after each full accounting entry. Just as a balance sheet must balance, a ledger must also balance.

Periodically, it is necessary to check the accuracy of the ledger. This is done by means of a trial balance. Taking off a trial balance is a simple procedure used to find out if the ledger is in balance. A **trial balance** is a listing of the account balances in a ledger. It is used to see if the dollar value of the accounts with debit balances is equal to the dollar value of the accounts with credit balances. To do this, you simply add up all of the debit balances, add up all of the credit balances, and see if the two totals are the same. If they agree, the ledger is said to be **in balance**. If they do not agree, the ledger is said to be **out of balance**. In manual accounting systems the whole process, called **taking off a trial balance**, was usually done at the end of each week or month. If you were to use a computerized accounting system, you could check the trial balance report as frequently as you wish. Accounting software updates the trial balance with each transaction and will display or print it on command.

The completed ledger for Pacific Trucking is shown in Figure 4.7 below. Let us now see if it is in balance by following the steps shown on page 99.

FIGURE 4.7

The completed ledger of Pacific Trucking.

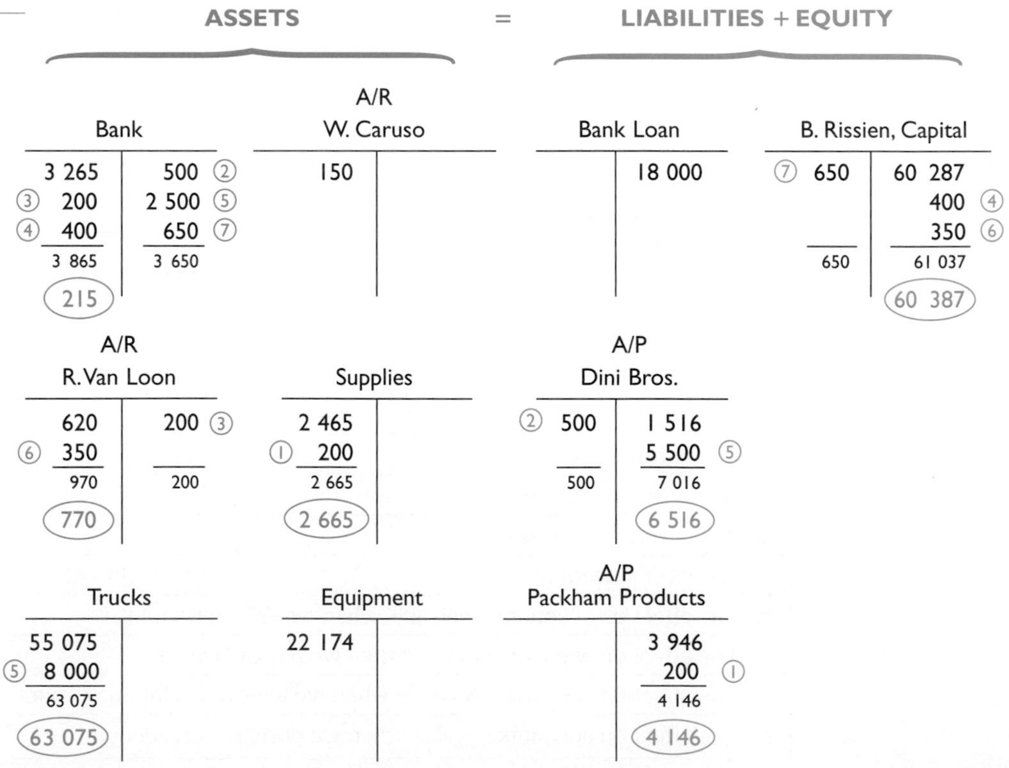

Methods of Taking Off a Trial Balance

To take off a trial balance, proceed as follows:

Step 1   List all the accounts and their balances. Leave room for a three-line heading.

Step 2   Place the debit balances in a debit column and the credit balances in a credit column.

Step 3   Add up the two columns.

Step 4   See if the two column totals are the same. Only if the two column totals are the same can you consider your ledger work to be correct.

Step 5   Write a heading at the top. A heading is necessary on the trial balance. It must show the name of the individual or business, the title "Trial Balance," and, very importantly, the date.

The completed trial balance for the ledger on page 98 is shown in Figure 4.8 below.

FIGURE 4.8

The trial balance for the ledger of Pacific Trucking.

PACIFIC TRUCKING TRIAL BALANCE JULY 2, 20–		
Accounts	DEBITS	CREDITS
Bank	2 1 5 –	
A/R – W. Caruso	1 5 0 –	
A/R – R. Van Loon	7 7 0 –	
Supplies	2 6 6 5 –	
Trucks	63 0 7 5 –	
Equipment	22 1 7 4 –	
Bank Loan		18 0 0 0 –
A/P – Dini Bros.		6 5 1 6 –
A/P – Packham Products		4 1 4 6 –
B. Rissien, Capital		60 3 8 7 –
	89 0 4 9 –	89 0 4 9 –

Heading: Who? What? When?

Account balances listed in correct columns.

Accounts listed in ledger order.

Column totals must agree.

Another way of taking off a trial balance is by using a printing calculator which shows the trial balance data on a paper tape.

     The procedure is as follows:

Step 1   Clear the machine by pressing the "total" button.

Step 2   Enter the balances in the machine in ledger order.
Make sure to enter the **debits** as + amounts and the **credits** as − amounts.

Step 3   Take off a total by depressing the "total" button. If your ledger work is correct, the sum of the + entries will be equal to the sum of the − entries. Therefore, the total should be 0.00.

The printing calculator method of taking off a trial balance is illustrated in Figure 4.9 below. Be certain that you understand the principle involved. Your work is arithmetically correct if you get zero for your tape total. Your work is incorrect if you do not get zero for your tape total. If your total is not zero, you must begin a search for the error (or errors).

FIGURE 4.9

Trial balance done on a printing calculator.

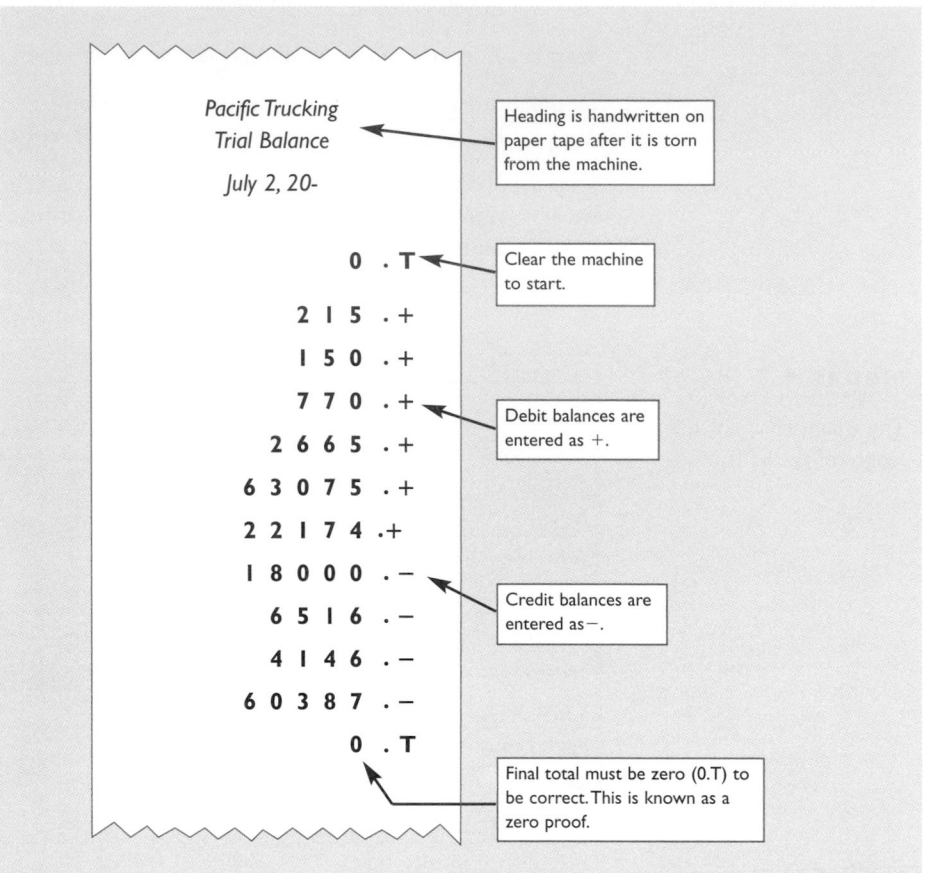

Importance of the Trial Balance

It is important to an accountant to have the ledger in balance. The work is not accurate if the ledger is not in balance. A ledger out of balance is a certain sign that at least one error has been made in the accounts. A good accountant does not rest until all errors are found and corrected.

Trial Balance out of Balance

Most of the time, trial balances do not work out on the first attempt. When the trial balance is out of balance, at least one error has been made in the accounting process. It is the accountant's job to find and correct these errors. The errors may have been caused by faulty addition, by entering an item on the wrong side, or by other mistakes.

Accounting software always produces trial balances that are mathematically correct; however, the accounting entries may still be incorrect.

Even if the ledger is in balance, it might still have errors in it. A ledger that is in balance may only be mechanically or mathematically correct. The accountant may have made incorrect entries that were balanced ones. Errors such as these are often the most difficult to find.

It takes a methodical approach to locate accounting errors because they are often quite difficult to detect. Skill in finding errors is a great advantage to an accountant.

For now, there is a four-step procedure to follow if you find a ledger that does not balance. This method is expanded in Chapter 7 (see pages 220 to 222). The four steps are:

Step 1   Re-add the trial balance columns.

Step 2   Check the figures from the ledger against those of the trial balance. Make sure that none are missing, none are on the wrong side, and none are for the wrong amount.

Step 3   Recalculate the account balances.

Step 4   Check that there is a balanced accounting entry in the accounts for each transaction.

You may be lucky enough to balance the ledger without having to go through all of these steps. In this event, your task is finished and you can file your trial balance.

On the other hand, you may have completed all of the steps and still not have balanced the ledger. When this happens, it means that you have made an error in one of the steps. You will have to go through the steps again, this time working more carefully. If all of the steps are done correctly, the errors will be found, and the ledger will be balanced.

Section 4.4   Review Questions

1. Give a mathematical explanation of why a ledger should always balance.
2. Describe the procedure for balancing a ledger.
3. Describe how one takes off a trial balance when using a printing calculator.
4. Why is it important to balance the ledger?
5. What happens to a completed trial balance?
6. What does it mean if you complete the procedure for balancing a ledger but the ledger is still not in balance?
7. What are the steps to be followed to balance a trial balance that is out of balance?

Section 4.4   Exercises

1. Mr. J. Strom is the owner of a hardware store in Shelburne, Nova Scotia. At the end of the year, he attempted to prepare a trial balance of the accounts in the general ledger. The trial balance appears on the next page. The balances themselves are correct. But Mr. Strom has no knowledge of double-entry bookkeeping, so he has made many errors in listing the balances.

   Find the errors and prepare a corrected trial balance.

```
                        J. STROM
                     TRIAL BALANCE
                   DECEMBER 31, 20—

                                        Debit        Credit
Bank                                 $    3 000
Land                                     50 000
A/R – Jones                                        $  10 940
Supplies                                  3 400
Office Equipment                         15 350
Automobile                                             21 200
Building                                140 000
A/P – Smith                               5 160
Bank Loan                                              52 000
J. Strom, Capital                                     108 230
Mortgage Payable                                       78 500

                                     $216 910        $270 870
```

2. The ledger for C. Hernandez, as of June 30, 20—, is given below.

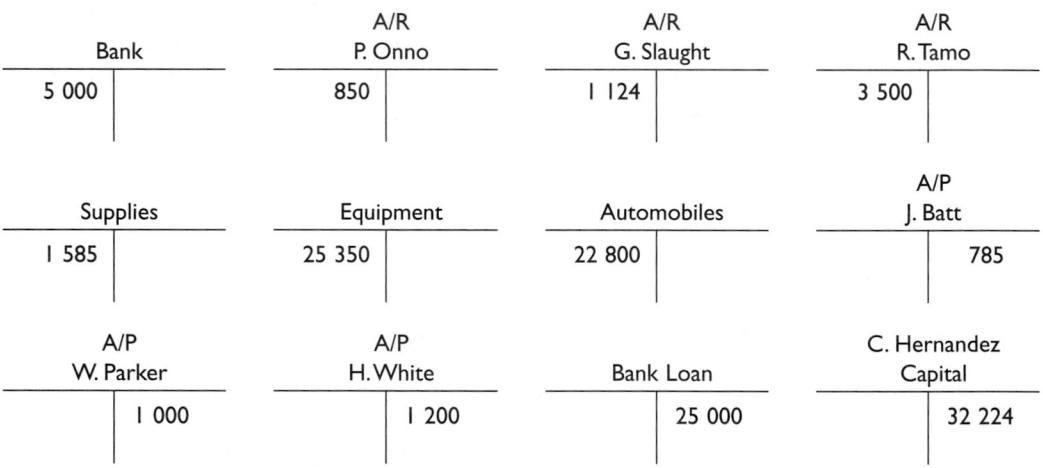

Prepare a trial balance for C. Hernandez as of June 30. Remember to write in the three-part heading.

3. The accounts and balances of Ceco Co. are arranged below in alphabetical order. **Prepare a trial balance of Ceco Co. with the accounts arranged in normal ledger order. Remember to write in the three-part heading. Date the trial balance June 30 of this year.**

Accounts	Balances
A/P — Jondahl Co.	1 350
A/P — P. Swartz	4 250
A/R — M. Legris	3 500
A/R — W. Nishi	850
Automobile	22 500
Bank	7 000
Bank Loan	10 000
C. Oke, Capital	27 471
Equipment	7 296
Supplies	1 925

4.5 | Accounting Software: Ledger Accounts and the Trial Balance

Even if you have no access to computers, read Section 4.5 and complete the Section Review Questions and the Section Exercise. By completing these activities, you will be able to make basic comparisons between computer and manual systems of accounting.

Now that you are familiar with T-accounts, the ledger, and the trial balance, you can begin to compare manual and computer methods of accounting. It is important for you to understand both systems. For instance, if you neglected pen and paper accounting, you would fail to appreciate how accounting software calculates totals and generates reports. If you ignored the computer's role, you would limit your potential for success in the accounting profession because it uses computer technology as a fundamental tool.

The accounting software shown most often in this text is Simply Accounting® for Windows® made by ACCPAC®INTERNATIONAL, INC. Be aware that your goal is not to become a trained expert in the current version of Simply Accounting. Rather, your aim is to skillfully use this software's capabilities, keeping in mind that other accounting programs share similar features. By acquiring skill in Simply Accounting now, you will be prepared to use its future versions, and you will approach other brands of accounting software with confidence.

The Home Window

The main menu of Simply Accounting is called the home window. There are several ways of loading the Simply Accounting program into your computer. Your teacher will inform you of the best method for your computer lab. One way is to double click the Simply Accounting file named *Sam's Softball City*. By doing so, you will eventually reach the home window for a business that you will work with at various points in this text. Although your monitor will look somewhat similar to Figure 4.10, you will notice some differences.

FIGURE 4.10

The home window of
Simply Accounting for
Windows

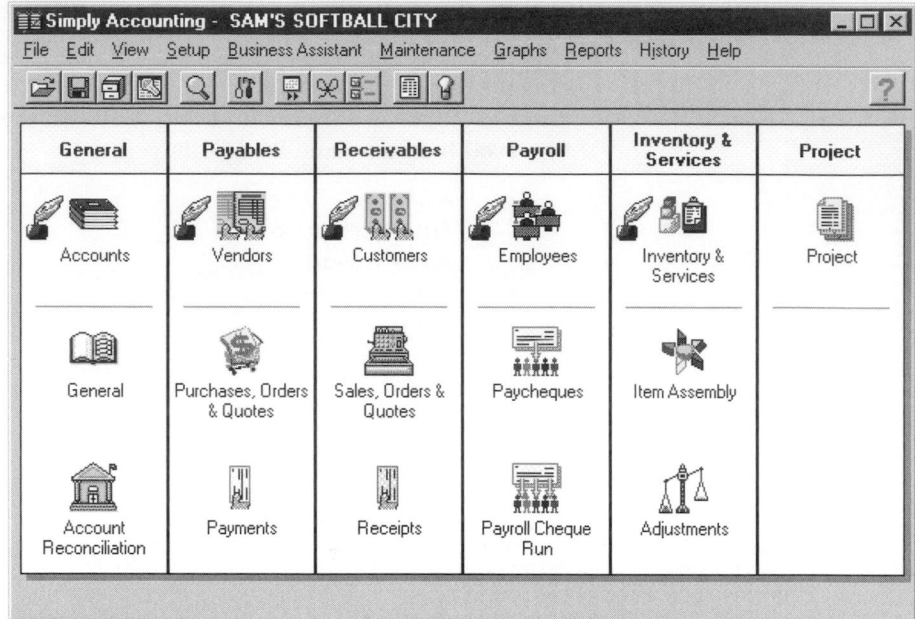

Figure 4.10 shows six major sections organized in columns. General, Payables, Receivables, Payroll, Inventory & Services, and Project. Each of these sections is called a module. In this text, you will have the opportunity to use each module. For now, however, it is easier to customize Simply Accounting by switching off modules that are not being used. Your monitor is actually closer in appearance to Figure 4.11 than it is to Figure 4.10 because this customization was made to your data file.

FIGURE 4.11

The home window
of Simply Accounting
with only the General
module showing.

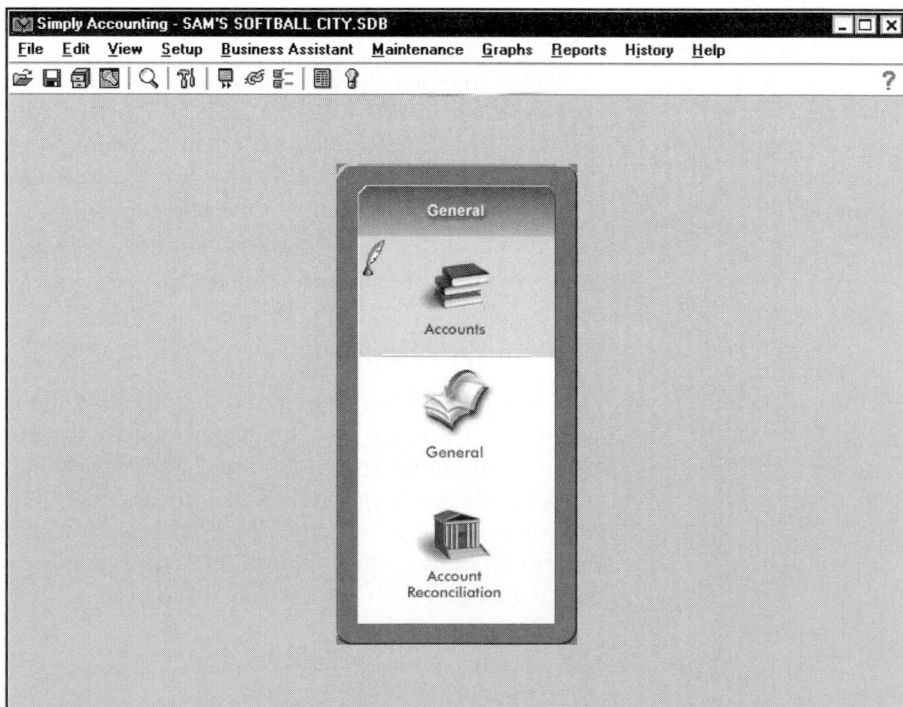

The General Module

The Ledger

The General module of Simply Accounting has three parts. Turn your attention to the top section, which shows a quill pen, a stack of three books, and the word Accounts. The picture of the three books is the icon for the **ledger** of Sam's Softball City. **Double-click the ledger icon to reveal the accounts for this business.** Your monitor will be appear like Figure 4.1 on page 80, which shows the Simply Accounting ledger for a different business named Pacific Trucking.

The Accounts

Close the window that shows the accounts in the ledger. **From the home window, choose Reports, Financials, and General Ledger. Enter the Start date as 4/01/01 and the Finish date as 4/30/01. Finally, select the Bank account and press the Enter key.** Your monitor will look like Figure 4.12.

FIGURE 4.12

The Bank account for Sam's Softball City.

General Ledger Report

File Options Help

4/1/01 to 4/30/01 — Debits, Credits, Balance

1010 Bank 0.00 Dr

Date	Description	Ref	J	Debits	Credits	Balance
4/1/01	Opening investment by the o...	DS001	J1	20,000.00	-	20,000.00 Dr
4/1/01	Bank loan repayable on demand	DS002	J2	35,000.00	-	55,000.00 Dr
4/1/01	Paid rent to Romeyn Propertie...	Chq 001	J3	-	4,500.00	50,500.00 Dr
4/2/01	Bought office and sports sup...	Chq 002	J4	-	5,000.00	45,500.00 Dr
4/30/01	Cash sales for the month	CS 001	J10	1,200.00	-	46,700.00 Dr
4/30/01	Service charges and interest	DM 430	J11	-	250.00	46,450.00 Dr
				56,200.00	9,750.00	

The Bank account shown in Figure 4.12 shows all the changes that happened to the business's cash in April, its first month of operation. The account shows more information than you are used to seeing in a typical T-account. However, if you exclude unfamiliar data, you should be able to visualize where a "T" could be drawn in Figure 4.12.

Close the window showing the details of the Bank account for April. Then, repeat the process of displaying account activity. **(Choose Reports, Financials, General Ledger, and enter the Start and Finish date.) This time, however, click the "Select All" button and press the Enter key.** Take the time to scroll through all the accounts of the business. Close the window when you are done.

The Trial Balance

Simply Accounting takes the effort out of preparing a trial balance. All you need to do is choose **Reports, Financials, Trial Balance, and press the Enter key.** Your monitor should look like Figure 4.13.

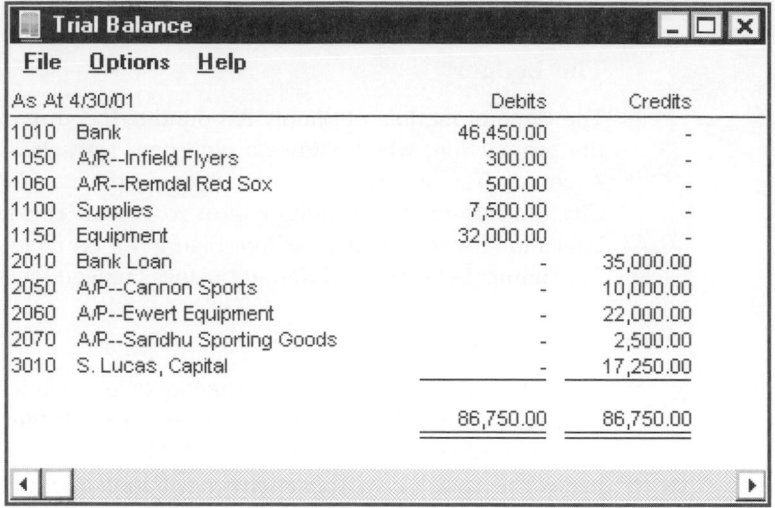

Trial Balance		
File Options Help		
As At 4/30/01	Debits	Credits
1010 Bank	46,450.00	-
1050 A/R--Infield Flyers	300.00	-
1060 A/R--Remdal Red Sox	500.00	-
1100 Supplies	7,500.00	-
1150 Equipment	32,000.00	-
2010 Bank Loan	-	35,000.00
2050 A/P--Cannon Sports	-	10,000.00
2060 A/P--Ewert Equipment	-	22,000.00
2070 A/P--Sandhu Sporting Goods	-	2,500.00
3010 S. Lucas, Capital	-	17,250.00
	86,750.00	86,750.00

When you produce a trial balance with Simply Accounting, there is no chance that it will be out of balance—the total of the debits will always equal the total of the credits. There are three reasons for this. First, when you record transactions in Simply Accounting, you are prevented from making an entry where debits and credits are unequal. Second, computers are very good at making calculations. And third, computers sort data extremely well. You can be sure that all ledger accounts are added correctly and that all final account balances are properly transferred to the trial balance.

Section 4.5   Review Questions

1. Given the tremendous growth in computer technology in recent years, it is no longer necessary to learn pen-and-paper bookkeeping. Comment on this statement.
2. What are two advantages of acquiring skill in one particular accounting software program, such as Simply Accounting?
3. Explain how the home window of Simply Accounting was customized for this chapter.
4. T-account data does not appear in the accounts produced by Simply Accounting. Comment on this statement.
5. Identify three mistakes that you might make along the way to producing a trial balance with pen and paper. (Hint: These would be three mistakes that Simply Accounting would not make.)

Section 4.5   **Exercises**

1. Comparing Manual Accounting to Computer Accounting

   A. Using T-accounts in your workbook, prepare account balances for the new
   business featured in this section—Sam's Softball City.

   TRANSACTIONS

   April
   1. Samuel Lucas, the owner, invested $20 000 in the business.
   2. Borrowed $35 000 from the bank, which was deposited in the business's
      bank account.
   3. Paid $4 500 to Romeyn Properties Ltd. for the monthly rent.
   4. Bought office and various sport supplies for $5 000 cash.
   5. Purchased $10 000 of bats, helmets, and other sports equipment from
      Cannon Sports on account. The amount is due in 30 days.
   6. Bought pitching machines from Ewert Equipment for $22 000 and have
      30 days in which to pay.
   7. Bought $2 500 of miscellaneous sports supplies on account from
      Sandhu Sporting Goods.
   8. Sold a one-month, team membership to the Infield Flyers for $300 on
      account. The amount is to be received in 15 days.
   9. Sold a two-month team membership to the Remdal Red Sox for $500 on
      account. The bill is due in 30 days.
   10. Cash sales for the month amounted to $1 200.
   11. Bank charges for services fees and interest amounted to $250, which
       was taken directly out of the business's bank account.

   B. Take off a trial balance dated April 30, 20-1. Estimate how long it takes you
   to prepare this trial balance. How much time do you suppose it took to prepare the trial balance shown in Figure 4.13?

   C. The T-account in your workbook for Sam's Softball City's Bank account has
   two columns. The Bank account produced by Simply Accounting in Figure
   4.12 on page 105 shows seven. Complete the following

   a. Write down what you think each column in Figure 4.12 represents.
   b. Which columns are most similar to the ones for the Bank account you
      just completed in your workbook?
   c. Two totals shown in Figure 4.12 are 56 200.00 and 9 750. What do these
      amounts represent? In a manual bookkeeping system, what would these
      two amounts be called?
   d. What feature of a Simply Accounting account (see Figure 4.12) would be
      the best addition to the T-accounts in your workbook?

| Section 4.5 | **Extending Your Computer Skills** |

Load the Simple Accounting files for Sam's Softball City into your computer. Try to make the right menu selections to produce the report shown below.

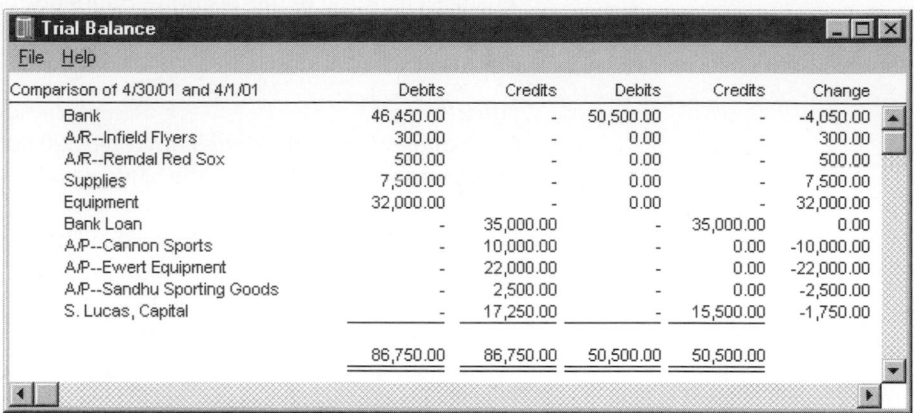

Comparison of 4/30/01 and 4/1/01	Debits	Credits	Debits	Credits	Change
Bank	46,450.00	-	50,500.00	-	-4,050.00
A/R--Infield Flyers	300.00	-	0.00	-	300.00
A/R--Remdal Red Sox	500.00	-	0.00	-	500.00
Supplies	7,500.00	-	0.00	-	7,500.00
Equipment	32,000.00	-	0.00	-	32,000.00
Bank Loan	-	35,000.00	-	35,000.00	0.00
A/P--Cannon Sports	-	10,000.00	-	0.00	-10,000.00
A/P--Ewert Equipment	-	22,000.00	-	0.00	-22,000.00
A/P--Sandhu Sporting Goods	-	2,500.00	-	0.00	-2,500.00
S. Lucas, Capital	-	17,250.00	-	15,500.00	-1,750.00
	86,750.00	86,750.00	50,500.00	50,500.00	

How might such a report be useful in the future? Notice that the mouse arrow changes into a magnifying glass when you move it around in the trial balance window. Experiment with the magnifying glass until you can explain the purpose of this feature. Why would such a feature be useful?

| Section 4.5 | **Communicate It** |

Compose a business letter to Samuel Lucas, owner of Sam's Softball City. Explain to him some of the differences between a manual accounting system and a computer accounting system. Give him some recommendations about which system he should choose. Support each of your recommendations.

CHAPTER 4 Summary

CHAPTER HIGHLIGHTS

Now that you have completed Chapter 4, you should:

- know what an account is and what a ledger is;
- know the rules of debit and credit as they apply to assets, liabilities, and capital;
- be able to record transactions in T-accounts and calculate an account balance;
- know what the balance in a T-account means;
- understand the concept of double-entry accounting;
- be able to take off a trial balance using both the handwritten method and the printing calculator method;
- understand the importance of the trial balance;
- be able to locate and correct errors in T-accounts;
- be able to use the term "on account" in the four customary ways;
- identify benefits that software provides to accountants.

ACCOUNTING TERMS

account	double-entry system	out of balance
account balance	of accounting	pencil footings
accounting entry	in balance	pin totals
credit	ledger	taking off a trial balance
debit	on account	trial balance

CHAPTER 4 Review Exercises

Using Your Knowledge

1 **Indicate whether each of the following statements is true or false by entering a "T" or an "F" in the space indicated in your Workbook. Explain the reason for each "F" response in the space provided.**

A. A number of individual balance sheet items may appear on one account page, as long as they are shown separately.

B. Many accountants use the equation analysis sheet instead of the ledger.

C. There is a page in the ledger for the total assets figure.

D. T-accounts are ideal for small businesses.

E. The first dollar amount recorded in an account is placed on the same side as it appears on a simple balance sheet.

F. There is no account for capital because it can always be found by subtracting the total assets from the total liabilities.

G. A transaction analysis sheet is a permanent accounting record.

H. For every transaction, there is always one debit amount and one credit amount, which are equal.

I. A balanced accounting entry is a correct accounting entry.

J. The balance of an account that is not zero must be either a debit or a credit.

K. The J.R. Dahl account in the ledger of C. Jacob is either an account payable or an account receivable.

L. Eric Lai's account has a credit balance. This means that he purchased our services on credit.

M. An exceptional balance is opposite to what would be normal.

N. A customer is given a refund because of unsatisfactory service. The account of this customer will now have an exceptional balance.

O. A ledger contains an exceptional balance. A trial balance cannot be taken until the exceptional item is transferred to another part of the ledger.

P. A trial balance that is in balance proves that there are no errors in the accounts.

Q. A trial balance is taken using a printing calculator. When the "total" key is pressed, the figure 89.00 comes up. This is the amount of the error.

R. The business buys supplies and pays cash. The accounting entry made in the accounts is Dr Bank and Cr Supplies. This causes the ledger to be out of balance.

---

② As a result of one error, the trial balance prepared by your company at the end of the month did not balance. In reviewing the entries for the month, the accountant noticed that one of the transactions, for the purchase of furniture and fixtures, was recorded as a debit to Furniture and Fixtures, $500, and a debit to Bank, $500.

Answer the following questions about this transaction:

A. Was the Bank account overstated, understated, or correctly stated on the trial balance? If overstated or understated, show by how much.

B. Was the total of the debit column of the trial balance overstated, understated, or correctly stated? If overstated or understated, show by how much.

C. Was the total of the credit column of the trial balance overstated, understated, or correctly stated? If overstated or understated, show by how much.

---

③ The accountant for M. Finney, owner of a janitorial service business in Whitehorse, Yukon Territory, prepared a trial balance at the end of December. When Ms. Finney examined the trial balance, she noticed that the S. Pearson Co. had a debit balance of $375. Ms. Finney remembered depositing a cheque received from Pearson for that amount. She wants to know why a debit balance still exists on the records.

Give three different explanations of how this could happen.

---

④ **State whether the following errors would cause a trial balance to be out of balance and, if so, by how much. Explain why or why not.**

A. The entry to record the purchase of delivery equipment for $1 500 was omitted from the Delivery Equipment account.

B. A new desk was purchased for cash. Bank was credited but Office Supplies was debited instead of Office Equipment. The cost of the desk was $400.

C. Cash of $100 was received from a client for services performed. Bank was debited for $100 and Capital was credited for $10.

D. Cash of $500 was borrowed from the bank. Bank was credited for $500 and Bank Loan was debited $500.

Comprehensive Exercises

5 A. Hoysted is a sign painter and truck letterer. Her business has the following assets and liabilities:

Assets		Liabilities	
Bank	$ 2 216	Bank Loan	$ 6 500
A/R – G. Anderson	357	A/P–Consumers' Supply	1 375
A/R–N. Ostrowski	402	A/P–Nu-Style Furniture	2 951
Office Supplies	2 980	Loan Payable, M. Hoysted	1 980
Painting Supplies	4 120		
Office Furniture	5 090		
Automobile	20 000		

A. **Set up A. Hoysted's financial position in the T-accounts provided in the Workbook. Include the equity account.**
B. **For the transactions listed below, record the accounting entries in T-accounts. If it is helpful for you, use a transaction analysis sheet.**

TRANSACTIONS

1. Received $200 cash from a customer for painting a sign.
2. Paid $500 to Consumers' Supply.
3. Received $402 cash from N. Ostrowski.
4. Sold an extra office desk (which is included in the Office Furniture figure at $450) to G. Brand at a price of $250. Brand paid $100 cash and owed the balance.
5. Reduced the bank loan by $1 000.
6. Paid the regular monthly bank loan payment, $500.
7. Paid the balance owing to Consumers' Supply.

C. **Calculate the account balances and balance the ledger by taking off a trial balance.**

---

6 Rainbow Real Estate is a business owned by Cathy Geraci. The accounts of the business are as follows:

Assets		Liabilities	
Bank	$ 1 056	Bank Loan	$ 19 000
Accounts Receivable		Accounts Payable	
D. Murray	1 351	Tuck Corporation	1 520
A. Niemi	2 516		
Office Supplies	1 115		
Furniture and Equipment	11 916		
Properties Owned	18 042	Equity	
Automobile	27 965	Cathy Geraci, Capital	

The financial position of Rainbow Real Estate is set up in T-accounts in the Workbook. **For the transactions listed on the following page, record the accounting entries in the T-accounts. Use a transaction analysis sheet if necessary. Calculate and record the balances in the accounts and take off a trial balance.**

TRANSACTIONS

a. Received $516 cash from A. Niemi.

b. Sold a home for V. Morris. For this service, Morris owes $4 150 to Rainbow Real Estate.

c. Paid $95 cash for office supplies.

d. Received $20 000 cash for sale of a property. (The property is included in the Properties Owned figure at $5 000.)

e. Paid $15 000 cash to the bank to reduce the amount of the bank loan.

f. Paid $520 cash to Tuck Corporation.

g. Paid $40 cash for a new headlight for the automobile.

h. Received $800 cash from D. Murray.

i. The owner withdrew $500 cash for her personal use.

j. Received $2 000 cash from V. Morris.

k. Paid the balance of the debt to Tuck Corporation in cash.

l. Purchased a new office desk at a cost of $600 from Pioneer Furniture but did not pay cash for it.

m. Sold a home for A. McIntosh. McIntosh paid Rainbow Real Estate $5 100 cash for the service.

Challenge Exercise

You will now create your own accounting exercise and share it with a partner.

1. Choose a type of service business and create a name for it. Make up a list of the titles for six asset accounts, three liability accounts, and one capital account. Write these titles on the T-accounts provided in your workbook.

2. In your workbook, write sentences to describe 12 transactions for your business.

   a) Make sure your sentences contain all the necessary information: Dollar amounts, names, whether cash or credit is used, and so on.

   b) Your **first** transaction must describe the **owner's initial investment of cash** into the business.

   c) Some of your transactions may have more than one debit or one credit. Be creative.

3. On a separate page in your workbook, prepare an answer key (T-accounts and trial balance).

4. Give a fellow student the page that has your list of accounts, transactions, and T-accounts. Ask him or her to complete the exercise you created and do the exercise that he or she created.

5. When both of you are finished, compare your results and mark each other's work.

Questions for Further Thought

Briefly answer the following questions.

1. A ledger account does not have the word "asset," "liability," or "equity" recorded on it. How can you tell if the account is an asset, a liability, or equity?

2. Assets, liabilities, and equity can each be thought of as having a natural side. What is the natural side for an asset? A liability? Equity?

3. Explain why the rules of debit and credit are identical for liabilities and equity.

4. Explain why you do not debit Automobiles when you pay to get a fender straightened out on your automobile.

5. Is the statement "For every debit there is a credit" perfectly true? Explain.

6. In a handwritten ledger what is the purpose of pin totals? Why are they written in pencil?

7. What assumption would you make if an account balance were given to you without your having been told if it is a debit or credit balance?

8. Suppose that you, an outsider to the business, were told that Sarah Jones had an account balance of $350. Can you tell if Sarah Jones is a debtor or a creditor?

9. What is an exceptional account balance? Would the word "unusual," "opposite," or "abnormal" be close to describing what "exceptional" means in this case?

10. The method of taking off a trial balance using a printing calculator is referred to as the "zero proof method." Explain why this is so.

Case Studies

CASE 1

Are Debits and Credits Confusing?

Grade 11 student Yolanda Fonagy sat in Mr. Voytek's accounting class, frustrated and confused. She felt certain that she knew the basics of debiting and crediting accounts. Furthermore, her textbook clearly showed that asset accounts, such as Bank, are increased by debiting. However, when she made her last bank deposit, she discovered that the teller had increased her bank balance by *crediting* her savings account!

She was certain that either the textbook, her teacher, or her bank teller had made a serious error.

Questions

1. Was Yolanda correct in assuming that an error had been made? Defend your position.
2. Check the passbook you have received from your bank. Has the bank also increased your bank balance by crediting your account?
3. Write a short paragraph explaining to Yolanda why her account was increased by a credit entry.

CASE 2

Property Value: A Matter of Opinion?

You are a loans officer with the Reliable Trust Company in Red Deer, Alberta. On March 30, 20—, a young businessman, Gary Marsden, comes to you in the hope of borrowing $75 000 for a business venture. When you inquire about his personal financial status, he presents you with the balance sheet shown below.

GARY MARSDEN
BALANCE SHEET
MARCH 20, 20—

Assets		Liabilities	
Bank	$ 2 000	Accounts Payable	$ 5 300
Accounts Receivable	1 500	Mortgage Payable	80 000
Furniture	9 000	Total Liabilities	$ 85 300
Supplies	1 300		
Truck	17 000	Owner's Equity	
Building Lot	175 000	Gary Marsden, Capital	120 500
Total Assets	$205 800	Total Liabilities and Equity	$205 800

When examining this statement, you become concerned about the item Building Lot for $175 000. You have lived in Red Deer for several years and you know that there are not many properties in town that are worth that much money.

Gary informs you that he bought the property one month ago for $80 000 and that he borrowed the entire sum from his father. This is shown properly on the statement as Mortgage Payable.

Your conversation with Gary indicates that he truly believes that the property will increase in value in the near future and that he has listed it at the amount he expects to sell it for. When you find out the location of the property, you realize that it is a piece of land that took over two years to sell.

Questions

1. What is your opinion about listing the property at $175 000? What GAAP is affected? (Hint: Refer to Chapter 2.)
2. Write out what you would say to Gary on this subject.
3. Would you lend Gary the money on the basis of only the financial data given to you? Compose a letter, using the letter format in the Skills Appendix, giving your answer and your reasons.

CASE 3

Challenge

Choosing between Two Companies

	Company A	Company B
Assets		
Bank	$ 21 500	$ 700
Accounts Receivable	3 000	59 500
Supplies	1 300	2 500
Equipment	15 600	42 400
Land and Building	54 000	150 000
Total Assets	$95 400	$255 100
Liabilities and Equity		
Accounts Payable	$22 800	$ 45 900
Mortgage Payable	22 000	128 000
Owner's Equity	50 600	81 200
Total Liabilities and Equity	$95 400	$255 100

Above are shown the balance sheets of two companies. Assume that each of the two companies has been forced out of business and must sell its assets for cash in order to pay its debts.

Questions

1. Are the values shown necessarily the values you could get? Explain.
2. Are there any problems associated with selling the assets? Explain any problems you see and why they occur.
3. Which company would be better to own? Write a short report (three to four paragraphs) explaining your position. Be prepared to give an oral report, if asked, based on your written report. See the Skills Appendix for advice on memo reports and oral reports.

Career

Melanie Appleyard /
Co-operative Education Student

Melanie Appleyard is a co-operative education student at Georgetown District High School. With the help of Betty Tamas, the co-op education teacher at her school, Melanie participated in the co-operative education program last year. The placement was a half-day every day for one semester. The hours of work varied depending on the day; in the mornings Melanie was at the business from 9:00–11:15 and in the afternoon from 1:00–4:00 or 4:30 depending on the amount of work there was to do. By the end of Melanie's co-op term she had worked approximately 240 hours and earned two Grade 11 Accounting credits.

The co-op placement was at the Chartered Accountants firm of Goebelle Macadam Alexander LLP. A variety of services are provided by this firm including auditing, accounting and bookkeeping, personal, corporate, and estate tax returns, financial planning, business valuations, management consulting, and computer consulting. Computers are used for most of the work done at this accounting firm.

Melanie enjoyed working at Goebelle Macadam Alexander and was given the opportunity to work on a variety of accounting tasks. "I created spreadsheets on the computer on Lotus, and rolled forward financial statements changing the new date and checking the addition on the statements. I also prepared bank statements as part of the bank reconciliation process. I had to verify that all cheques included on the statement were cashed and noted those that were still outstanding. I especially liked

completing the personal income tax return. I was given all the client's information and then had to complete the tax return first manually and then on the computer using a personal tax program."

After graduation, Melanie plans to attend Brock University to obtain her Bachelor of Accounting and she hopes to have another co-op placement while she is in the university program. After university she may continue her studies to become a Chartered Accountant.

Discussion

1. What are some of the advantages of taking part in a co-operative education program in accounting?
2. Why is it important for Melanie to have mastered the analysis of transactions when he uses the computer to input information?
3. a. List the steps in the accounting cycle that you have learned so far.
   b. "Computer use demands an understanding of the complete accounting cycle." Explain.
   c. Explain how the computer automatically completes many of the steps in the accounting cycle.
4. What are some of the businesses in your community that would welcome a co-operative education student in accounting?
5. In addition to the kinds of information mentioned in the career profile, what other accounting information may be stored permanently on file?

6. Explain why skill in communication will be important for future accountants.

Research and Writing Question

7. Research co-operative education programs in business and commerce offered through universities in your area. Write a couple of paragraphs about what is available. Answer the question, "Would co-operative education be a good option for a student in my position, with my goals?"

The Expanded Ledger: Revenue, Expense, and Drawings

5.1 **Expanding the Ledger**

5.2 **The Income Statement**

5.3 **Equity Relationships and the Balance Sheet**

5.4 **Simply Accounting, Spreadsheets and the Expanded Ledger**

In Chapter 4, you were introduced to a number of ledger accounts and to the basic system of debit and credit. In Chapter 5, new ledger accounts are introduced and the rules of debit and credit are expanded. The rules regarding the asset and liability accounts will not change. But the rules regarding the owner's equity account will be modified.

5.1 | Expanding the Ledger

To date, you have been accustomed to having a single account for owner's equity. Any change in the equity of the business was recorded in that one account, no matter what caused the change. Now you must become familiar with a system in which the ledger has a number of accounts in an equity section. Each of the new accounts reflects a particular kind of transaction that affects owner's equity. In the expanded equity section, you will see new accounts for:

revenues, which are related to the sale of goods or services;
expenses, which are the costs related to the revenues;
drawings, which are the owner's withdrawals for personal use.

Purpose of Expanding the System

The new accounts in the equity section of the ledger have one main purpose: to provide essential information about the progress of the business. This information is needed by managers and owners to see if the business is being run profitably and to help them make sound decisions. For example, imagine you are the accountant for Eve Boa, a lawyer in her first month of business. If you used the accounting skill you acquired in Chapter 4, her capital account and trial balance would look similar to what is shown in Figure 5.1.

FIGURE 5.1

The capital account and trial balance for Eve Boa, a lawyer. LLB stands for Bachelor of Laws.

	EVE BOA, LLB TRIAL BALANCE JANUARY 31, 20—	Dr.	Cr.
Bank		2 439	
A/R—H. Geroux		1 420	
A/R—J. Magill		757	
A/R—E. Parsons		1 395	
Supplies		2 316	
Office Equipment		7 550	
Automobile		16 800	
A/P—OK Supply			4 400
A/P—Computer Outlet			1 200
Bank Loan			940
E. Boa, Capital			26 137
		32 677	32 677

E. Boa, Capital

	21 878	Jan 1, 20—
3 950	7 290	
1 321	9 250	
615	7 120	
3 300		
385		
9 830		
19 401	45 538	
	26 137	Jan. 31, 20— → E. Boa, Capital

If the owner, Eve Boa, wanted to know how her legal firm performed in its first month, she might ask you the following questions:

How much money did the firm make in its first month?
How much was spent on advertising?
Are the wages fair?
Is the rent too high?
How much money did I withdraw from the business for personal expenses?

Could you answer Ms. Boa's questions by examining the financial records shown in Figure 5.1? The answer is no. The trial balance shows the assets and the claims on assets at the end of January, but it does not show what happened during the month.

Perhaps you could make some guesses about what happened during January from examining the *E. Boa, Capital* account. For instance, it is likely that three credits (7 290, 9 250, and 7 120) are increases in the owner's capital as a result of sales. But you cannot be sure. Also, which of the debits in the capital account represents advertising? Or rent? Or the money the owner withdrew for personal use? You cannot tell. And if you cannot answer these questions, you certainly cannot answer the most important question: How much profit was earned in January?

From a theoretical point of view, nothing is wrong with the accounting results presented in Figure 5.1. The credits are increases to the owner's equity and the debits are decreases. Yet the accounting system is deficient because it cannot provide the information the owner wants.

It is easy to provide more complete information. Simply remove January's transactions from *E. Boa, Capital* and place them in accounts with meaningful titles. Figure 5.2 shows what an expanded ledger for Eve Boa would look like:

FIGURE 5.2

The expanded ledger of Eve Boa, a lawyer, on January 31.

Assets	=	Liabilities	+	Owner's Equity

Bank

2 439 |

A/R – H. Geroux

1 420 |

A/R – J. Magill

757 |

A/R – E. Parsons

1 395 |

Supplies

2 316 |

Office Equipment

7 550 |

Automobile

16 800 |

A/P – OK Supply

| 4 400

A/P – Computer Outlet

| 1 200

Bank Loan

| 940

E. Boa, Capital

| 21 878

E. Boa, Drawings

3 950 |

Fees Earned

| 7 290
| 9 250
| 7 120
| 23 660

Advertising Expense

1 321 |

Car Expense

615 |

Rent Expense

3 300 |

Sundry Expense

385 |

Wages Expense

9 830 |

TOTAL ASSETS $32 677	=	TOTAL LIABILITIES $6 540	+	OWNER'S EQUITY $26 137

Some of the information in the new accounts is used to prepare an *income statement*, such as the simple one illustrated in Figure 5.3 on page 120. This statement is prepared from information found in the expanded ledger in Figure 5.2. As you can see from the illustration, the **income statement** shows in a detailed way whether the business is profitable or not. New equity accounts are organized to show the net income (or net loss) of the business for a given period of time.

EVE BOA, LLB
INCOME STATEMENT
MONTH ENDED JANUARY 31, 20–

Revenue		
Fees Earned		$23 660
Expenses		
Advertising Expense	$ 1 321	
Car Expense	615	
Rent Expense	3 300	
Sundry Expense	385	
Wages Expense	9 830	
Total Expenses		15 451
Net Income		$ 8 209

A lawyer earns revenue
from fees charged for
legal work done.

To summarize, the ledgers that you have worked with so far have had a single equity account—the Capital account. Any changes in the equity of a business were recorded in that one account. However, this does not provide sufficient information about changes in owner's equity. Now you must become familiar with a ledger that has a number of accounts in an equity section. These new accounts are used to gather the amounts that cause equity to change.

Revenue

Selling goods or services produces revenue. **Revenue** is an increase in equity resulting from the sale of goods or services in the usual course of business. Consider the following transaction:

> Eve Boa, a lawyer, draws up a legal agreement for J. Basso, a client, and for her services is paid a fee of $250 in cash.

Analysis
This transaction increases both Bank and equity by the amount of $250. Before, you would have debited Bank and credited E. Boa, Capital. Now, you will still debit Bank. But an increase in equity from business operations is revenue and must be credited to the Fees Earned account, not to E. Boa, Capital. The transaction is recorded as shown below.

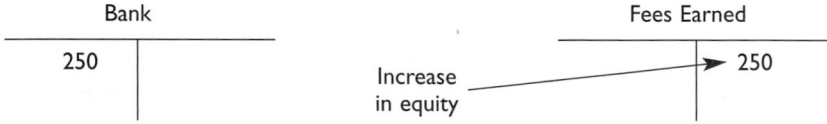

If the service performed for J. Basso was sold on credit, the transaction would be recorded as:

Revenue increases equity.

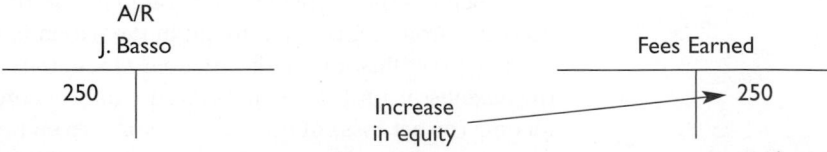

Think along the following lines:

1. Revenue represents an increase in equity.
2. An increase in equity requires a credit entry.
3. Therefore, the Fees Earned account is credited.

All similar transactions affecting fees revenue will be credited to the Fees Earned account. The account will have a credit balance. The account balance will be the total fees earned for the fiscal period to date.

Usually, a business has only one revenue account. It is given a name that identifies the source of the revenue. For example, a loan company earns its revenue in the form of interest. Its revenue account would likely be called Interest Revenue. A real estate company would have a revenue account called Commissions Earned. Some businesses may have more than one revenue account depending on the various aspects of their business. Suitable names for other revenue accounts might be Rental Revenue, Fees Revenue, Royalties, and so on.

GAAP—The Revenue Recognition Convention

> The **revenue recognition convention** states that revenue must be recorded in the accounts (recognized) at the time the transaction is completed.

Usually, this convention just means recording revenue when the bill for it is sent to the customer. If the transaction is for cash, the revenue is recorded when the sale is completed and the cash received.

Not every company can operate its revenue accounts in such a simple way. Think of the building of a large project such as an office tower. It takes a construction company a number of years to complete such a project. The company does not wait until the project is entirely completed before it sends its bill. Periodically, it bills for the amount of work completed and receives payments as the work progresses. Revenue is taken into the accounts on this periodic basis.

It is important to take revenue into the accounts correctly. If this is not done, the income statements of the company will be incorrect, and the readers of the financial statements will be misinformed.

Expense

There are costs associated with producing revenue—rent, wages, utilities, advertising, and so on. Each of these costs is known as an expense. An **expense** represents a decrease in equity resulting from the costs of producing the revenue. Consider the following transaction:

Eve Boa pays her secretary the regular weekly wage of $400 in cash.

Analysis
This transaction requires that both Bank and equity be decreased by $400. The decrease to Bank is handled as before, by a credit to the account. But a decrease in equity from business operations is an *expense*. It must be debited to an expense account. In this example, the Wages Expense account is debited. The transaction is recorded as follows:

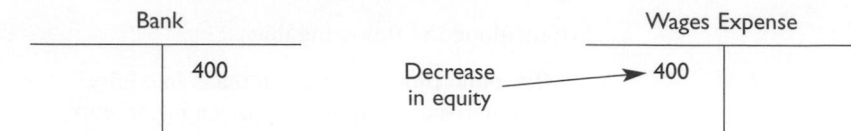

Expense decreases equity.

Think along the following lines:

1. Expense represents a decrease in equity.
2. A decrease in equity requires a debit entry.
3. Therefore, the Wages Expense account is debited.

The Wages Expense account, or any expense account for that matter, will normally receive debit entries. All wages will be accumulated in the one account. It will have a debit balance that is the total of the wages for the period to date.

There are many transactions that involve expenses. For example:

Eve Boa receives the monthly fuel bill for $195 from Municipal Gas. The bill is not paid immediately.

The transaction is recorded as follows:

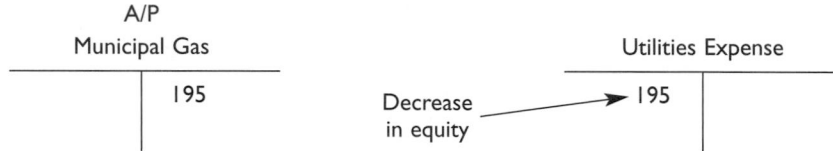

In any business, there are a number of expense accounts, each one representing a specific type of decrease in equity. The name of the account shows what type of decrease it is. Typical expense accounts are Rent Expense, Delivery Expense, Insurance Expense, Bank Charges, and Postage. Observe that the word "expense" is not always included in the account title; it may be omitted where there is no doubt that the item is an expense.

Not all expenditures are for expenses. The purchase of a long-lasting asset such as a new building, for example, would be debited to an asset account called Buildings. When you complete Chapter Nine, you will learn more about when to record an expenditure as an asset and when to record it as an expense.

Net Income or Net Loss

Revenues minus expenses equals net income or net loss.

It is from the revenue and expense accounts that a business can tell whether or not it has earned a net income (profit). Net income is the difference between the total revenues and the total expenses, where the revenues are greater than the expenses. If the expenses are greater than the revenues, the business has suffered a net loss.

Drawings

The owner usually looks to the profits of the business to provide a livelihood. In a healthy business, the owner will be able to take funds (generated by profits) out of the business on a regular basis, much like a salary. These withdrawals of funds by the owner are known as **drawings** and represent a decrease in equity. Drawings are *not* expenses. They have nothing to do with determining the net income or net loss.

Cash is the most common item withdrawn by an owner for personal use. For example:

Eve Boa, the owner of the business, withdraws $300 for her personal use.

Analysis

This transaction requires that both equity and Bank be decreased by $300. The decrease to Bank is handled in the usual way, as a credit to that account. But this particular decrease in equity is not an expense and must be charged to the owner. The transaction is recorded as follows:

Drawings decrease equity.

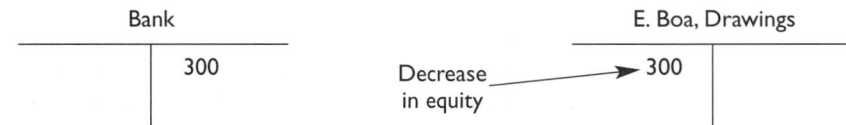

The Drawings account is also affected when the owner buys something for personal use but has the business pay for it. The owner may wish to take advantage of a special price that is offered to businesses but not to individuals. Or it may simply be that this form of payment is more convenient. In any event, when recording the transaction, the debit must be to Drawings.

For example, assume that Eve Boa purchases from Kitchen Plus a new coffee-maker through the business for personal use. A bill from Kitchen Plus for $85 for the coffee-maker arrives in the office. The $85 is not an expense of the business. It must be charged to Eve Boa. The transaction is recorded as follows:

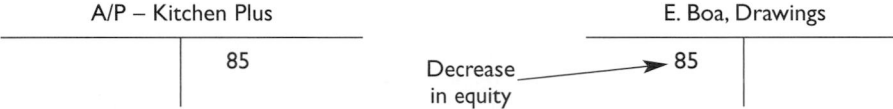

All entries affecting Drawings follow the rules of debit and credit. Drawings represents a decrease in equity, and decreases in equity require debit entries. Therefore, the Drawings account normally receives debit entries. All drawings will be gathered in this one account and it will have a debit balance.

Here are some other transactions that affect the Drawings account:

- the owner takes assets other than cash out of the business for personal use, for example, a computer, a table, or merchandise;
- the owner collects a debt from a customer and keeps the money for personal use.

The accounting clerks would have to be told of these transactions.

Equity Section Summary

There are four types of accounts in the equity section:

1. Capital: This account will now contain only the equity figure at the beginning of the fiscal period, plus new capital from the owner, if any.
2. Revenues: Increases in equity resulting from the sale of goods or services. A revenue account normally has a credit balance.
3. Expenses: Decreases in equity resulting from the costs of the materials or services used to produce the revenue. An expense account normally has a debit balance.

4. Drawings: Decreases in equity resulting from the owner's personal withdrawals. A drawings account normally has a debit balance. Drawings are not a factor when calculating net income or loss.

Revenue, expenses, and drawings show the changes in owner's equity from one period to the next.

Section 5.1   Review Questions

1. Name the new accounts in the equity section of the ledger.
2. What is the purpose of the Capital account in the expanded ledger?
3. What is the source of data for the income statement?
4. Define "revenue."
5. Define "expense."
6. Define "drawings."
7. Which accounts in the equity section affect the calculation of net income?
8. Give three examples of transactions that affect drawings.
9. Explain the revenue recognition convention.

Section 5.1   Exercises

1. The transactions for the first month of business for Spalding Consultants appear below:

    1. Borrowed $6 000 from the bank.
    2. Paid $1 500 for rent
    3. Alisha Dodds, the owner, invested $4 000 in the business.
    4. Purchased $800 of supplies on account from Percy's Office Outfitters.
    5. Sold services for $1 200 cash.
    6. Paid $160 for the monthly telephone charges.
    7. Sold services on account for $2 500 to Sarah McNeil.
    8. Paid wages, $1 800.
    9. Alisha Dodds, the owner, withdrew $1 400 for personal use.
    10. Received a hydro bill from Northern Utilities for $400, due in 15 days.

    A. Use T-accounts set up for you in your workbook for the above transactions. Record them in the same way you did in Chapter 4. In other words, record all equity transactions in the *A. Dodds, Capital* account.
    B. Calculate the final balances in the accounts. Show that the ledger balances by placing the total of the debits and credits in the spaces provided.
    C. To test your understanding of Section 5. 1, **duplicate the equity portions of the transactions** by transferring each amount in A. Dodds, Capital to the proper account in the *Expanded Ledger* section that appears in your workbook.
    D. In the *Expanded Ledger* section, subtract the debit account balances from credit account balances. Record the total in the space provided. What other amount does this total match?
    E. Calculate the net income or net loss for the first month. Label your amounts.

2. **This exercise also appears in your Workbook.**

A business has the beginning financial position recorded in the schedule below and in your Workbook. Ten simple transactions are listed in the left-side column. **Work out the revised totals for assets, liabilities, and owner's equity after each transaction. Enter these totals in your Workbook. Complete the last two columns of the chart by recording: a) the amount of change in equity (if any), and b) whether the change in equity represents revenue, expense, or drawings.**

	Total Assets	Total Liabilities	Owner's Equity	Change in Equity	Revenue? Expense? Drawings?
Beginning financial position	10 000	6 000	4 000		
Transactions					
1. Purchased $400 of supplies for future use and paid cash.					
2. Reduced bank loan by $1 000.					
3. Received $800 cash from a debtor.					
4. Sold services for $900 cash.					
5. Sold services on credit, $1 500.					
6. Paid hydro for month just ended, $125.					
7. Owner withdrew $750 cash for personal use.					
8. Paid employee's wages, $600.					
9. Purchased truck on credit, $20 000.					
10. Owner took supplies for personal use, $250.					

3. Eric Inahaba is in business for himself as a groundskeeper and gardener in Bathurst, New Brunswick. He cuts grass, weeds gardens, and trims trees and shrubs for a number of customers on a regular basis. The following accounts are in Eric Inahaba's ledger:

Bank	A/P—Pesticide Products
A/R—G. Hung	A/P—Pro Hardware
A/R—F. Sawchuck	E. Inahaba, Capital
A/R—W. Scott	E. Inahaba, Drawings
Chemical Supplies	Revenue
Equipment	Advertising Expense
Truck	Interest Expense
Bank Loan	Telephone Expense
A/P—Banner News	Truck Expense
	Wages Expense

Record the transactions shown below, using the chart provided in your workbook.

TRANSACTIONS

July
2   Received a bill from Pesticide Products regarding the purchase of $125 worth of chemical supplies on credit.
5   Received a bill from Pro Hardware for $150 for the purchase of a new ladder on credit.
6   Issued a cheque for $100 to W. Decorte for part-time wages.
10   Received $50 from a customer for services performed for cash.
13   Issued a bill to G. Hung for $100 for services sold on credit.
13   Received a bill from the *Banner News* regarding a $50 advertisement placed in the newspaper on credit.
16   Issued a cheque for $175 to E. Inahaba, the owner, for his personal use.
19   Received a notice from the bank stating that $90 had been taken by it from the business's bank account to pay for interest charges on the bank loan.
20   Received a memo from E. Inahaba, the owner, stating that he had received $100 from a cash customer. The money was not put in the bank as usual but was kept by Mr. Inahaba.

4. **In your Workbook, complete each of the following statements with either the word "debit" or the word "credit."**

   a. The Bank account normally has a _____ balance.
   b. A revenue account normally has a _____ balance.
   c. An expense account normally has a _____ balance.
   d. Paying a creditor involves a _____ entry to the creditor's account.
   e. The Drawings account receives a _____ entry when the owner withdraws money for personal use.
   f. A lawyer gives a cash refund to a customer. The Bank account will receive a _____ entry and the Revenue account will receive a _____ entry.
   g. Supplies are bought on credit. The Supplies account will receive a _____ entry and the supplier's account payable will receive a _____ entry.
   h. The Drawings account will not normally receive _____ entries.
   i. An increase in equity can be thought of as a _____ to the Capital account.
   j. Net income can be thought of as a _____ to the Capital account.
   k. Net loss can be thought of as a _____ to the Capital account.
   l. The owner takes a computer from the business for his personal (permanent) use. The Drawings account will receive a _____ entry.

5. A series of transactions for Ace Repair is given below. **A chart for the solutions is given in the Workbook. Show the effect of each of the transactions on assets, liabilities, and owner's equity by placing check marks in the appropriate columns of the chart.** The first transaction is done for you in the example below.

   TRANSACTIONS

   1. Performed a service for a customer for cash.
   2. Performed a service for a customer on credit.
   3. Sold a computer for cash for its value as shown in the accounts.
   4. Sold a fax machine for cash at less than its value as shown in the accounts.
   5. Purchased an automobile on credit.
   6. Paid cash to have the automobile repaired.
   7. The owner took out cash for his personal use.
   8. Paid an employee a weekly salary in cash.
   9. The owner took an automobile out of the business for his permanent personal use.
   10. Paid cash to the bank to reduce the bank loan.

Solutions Chart

No.	Asset Increase	Asset Decrease	Liability Decrease	Liability Increase	Revenue (Equity) (Increase)	Expense (Equity) (Decrease)	Drawings (Equity) (Decrease)
1	√				√		

5.2 | The Income Statement

You learned in the previous section that information was removed from the capital account and was classified as revenues, expenses, or drawings. You also learned that revenues and expenses together produce a net income or a net loss. For Eve Boa, a lawyer, you saw on page 120 that her revenues, expenses, and net income were summarized on the income statement. This is very important information because the income statement tells the owners and the managers how the business is doing (that is, whether or not it is profitable). These people will be keenly interested in this information because their livelihoods and the continuation of the business depend on profitability.

By definition, an **income statement** is a financial statement that summarizes the items of revenue and expense, and shows the net income or net loss of a business for a given period of time. The income statement of Basler Air Service is shown in Figure 5.4.

You should note carefully some important features of the formal income statement as shown in Figure 5.4 below. Explanations for the circled numbers follow the income statement.

FIGURE 5.4

The income statement for Basler Air Service showing a two-column presentation.

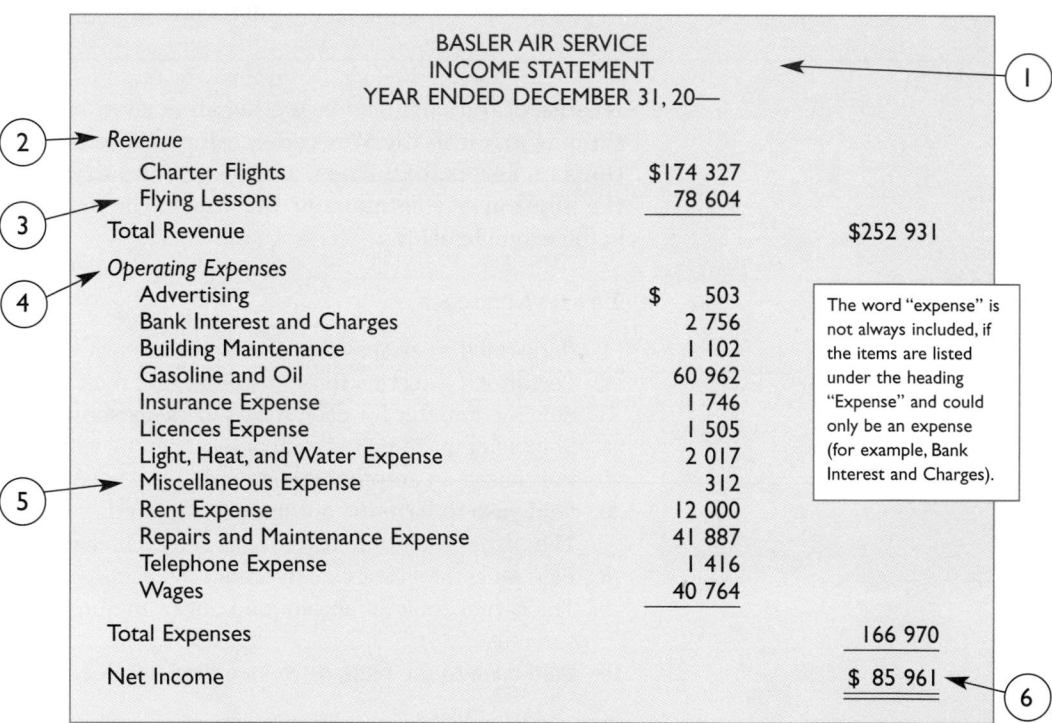

BASLER AIR SERVICE INCOME STATEMENT YEAR ENDED DECEMBER 31, 20—		
② Revenue		
Charter Flights	$174 327	
Flying Lessons	78 604	
③ Total Revenue		$252 931
④ Operating Expenses		
Advertising	$ 503	
Bank Interest and Charges	2 756	
Building Maintenance	1 102	
Gasoline and Oil	60 962	
Insurance Expense	1 746	
Licences Expense	1 505	
Light, Heat, and Water Expense	2 017	
⑤ Miscellaneous Expense	312	
Rent Expense	12 000	
Repairs and Maintenance Expense	41 887	
Telephone Expense	1 416	
Wages	40 764	
Total Expenses		166 970
Net Income		$ 85 961 ⑥

The word "expense" is not always included, if the items are listed under the heading "Expense" and could only be an expense (for example, Bank Interest and Charges).

① The **Heading** gives:
- name of business;
- name of statement;
- accounting period for which the figures have been accumulated.

② The **Revenue** section shows an increase in equity resulting from the proceeds of the sale of goods or services in the ordinary course of business.

③ Two types of revenue are shown in the statement for Basler Air Service.

④ The **Expense** section shows decreases in equity resulting from the cost of the goods or services used to produce the revenue.

⑤ Expenses are shown in detail.

⑥ The **Net Income** or **Net Loss** figure. Net Income is not cash. It is the difference between total revenues and total expenses, if the revenues are greater than the expenses. In this case a net income is the result.

Revenues	$ 252 931
Expenses	− 166 970
Net Income	$ 85 961

A net loss occurs if the expenses are greater than the revenues.

The Income Statement Put to Use

By Owners and Managers

The income statement is a very useful tool. It tells the owners or managers if their business is earning a profit and, if so, how much. The income statement is helpful to them in forming company goals and policies, and in making business decisions.

A business will not survive long if it does not earn a profit. All of the figures making up the profit or loss may be seen on the income statement. The figures for the current year may be compared with those for previous years. Unfavourable trends or problems may be seen quickly and can then be corrected. Successful business people make good use of the information on the income statement.

By Bankers

Bankers will want to see the financial statements of any business to which they loan money. Bankers need to know if the borrower will be able to repay the loan. Financial statements help inform bankers about the condition of a business.

By Income Tax Authorities

Every business is required by law to prepare an income statement once each year. The net income figure of a proprietorship must be included on the owner's income tax return. The income statement must be sent to the government along with the owner's income tax return.

The Fiscal Period

Net income is measured over a specific length of time, called the fiscal period. The **fiscal period** (also called the **accounting period**) is the period of time over which earnings are measured. All fiscal periods for an individual business are of the same length.

The earnings figure of a business does not mean anything if you do not know how long it took to produce those earnings. You would not be very informed about a business if all you knew about its net income was that it amounted to $8 000. You would not be favourably impressed if it took one year to earn that amount. On the other hand, if the $8 000 was earned in only one week, you would probably be quite impressed.

The fiscal period is the period of time over which earnings are measured.

In business today, the formal fiscal period is usually one year. The fiscal year does not have to be the same as the calendar year. It just has to run for 12 consecutive months. For example, a fiscal year could begin on July 1 and end on June 30 of the following year.

Half-yearly, quarterly, or monthly fiscal periods are used by some businesses. Managers can keep a close watch over their business by using short fiscal periods. Even when fiscal periods shorter than one year are used, it is still necessary to produce an annual income statement for income tax purposes.

GAAP—The Time Period Concept

> **The time period concept provides that accounting will take place over specific time periods known as fiscal periods.**

These fiscal periods are of equal length and are used when measuring the financial progress of a business.

GAAP—The Matching Principle

Separating revenues and expenses into specific fiscal periods challenges accountants to follow two important steps. In step one, they must be careful to record the proper amount of revenue in the proper period. In step two, they must subtract only those expenses that helped earn the revenue they recorded in step one.

For most transactions, recording the proper revenue is uncomplicated. Accountants simply follow the Revenue Recognition Convention that you read about on page 121. This means that they will record revenue when a transaction is completed (not necessarily when cash is received).

Recording expenses properly requires extra effort. Accountants keep in mind the following Generally Accepted Accounting Principle:

> **The matching principle states that each expense item related to revenue earned must be recorded in the same period as the revenue it helped to earn.**

Matching expenses with revenue in a fair manner is the goal. In some cases, reaching the goal is easy. For example, suppose a business purchases $30 000 of advertising on credit for a Boxing Day sale to be held on December 26, 2001. If the fiscal period ends December 31, 2001, the cost of the advertisement will be recorded in December, not in January 2002 when the bill is paid. Since the entire amount of the Boxing Day revenue was earned in the year 2001, the entire advertising expense must be recorded in 2001.

What if the situation were slightly different? Suppose the advertisement was published for a number of days to promote a two-week sale that started on December 26, 2001. The business's accountant would need to do more work. Since the advertisement now helps earn revenue in two different fiscal periods, a portion of the $30 000 advertising expense must be recorded in each year. If the accountant fails to do this, revenues and expenses will be mismatched. The impact of such a mismatch is that the net income (or net loss) will be inaccurate for both years—2001 and 2002.

Accountants follow the matching principle by making a number of mathematical adjustments in the accounts at the end of a fiscal year. You will learn how to do some of these adjustments when you study Chapter 9.

Chart of Accounts

To help organize the expanded ledger, it is customary to number the accounts in the ledger. These numbers are used for identification and reference, particularly in computer systems. The numbering system used in this text is the three-digit one shown below. You will use these numbers in later chapters.

Assets		100-199
Liabilities		200-299
	Capital	
	Drawings	300-399
Owner's		
Equity	Revenues	400-499
	Expenses	500-599

A **chart of accounts** is a list of the ledger accounts and their numbers arranged in ledger order. Most businesses have copies of their chart of accounts available for their employees, as well as for outsiders such as auditors. Eve Boa's chart of accounts is shown in Figure 5.5 below. It is taken from the ledger in Figure 5.2 on page 119. Notice the gaps left between account numbers in case new accounts need to be inserted.

For even greater flexibility inserting accounts, most accounting software programs now use four-digit systems. For example, instead of number 405, Fees Earned might be numbered 4050 in a four-digit system. Notice that in either system, the first digit—the number 4—identifies Fees Earned as a revenue account.

FIGURE 5.5

A chart of accounts for Eve Boa, LLB.

E. BOA, LLB
CHART OF ACCOUNTS

Assets	No.	Equity	No.
Bank	105	E. Boa, Capital	305
A/R – H. Geroux	110	E. Boa, Drawings	310
A/R – J. Magill	115		
A/R – E. Parsons	120	Fees Earned	405
Supplies	125	Advertising Expense	505
Office Equipment	130	Car Expense	510
Automobile	135	Rent Expense	515
		Sundry Expense	520
Liabilities		Wages Expense	525
A/P – OK Supply	205		
A/P – Computer Outlet	210		
Bank Loan	215		

Debit and Credit in the Expanded Ledger

The ledger is now expanded to include revenues, expenses, and drawings. Thus, the rules of debit and credit must now include these new items. The complete rules of debit and credit are as follows:

TYPE OF ACCOUNT		TO INCREASE	TO DECREASE
Assets		Debit	Credit
Liabilities		Credit	Debit
Equity	Capital	Credit	Debit
	Revenue	Credit	Debit
	Expense	Debit	Credit
	Drawings	Debit	Credit

Debit and Credit Balances

An accountant needs to understand thoroughly the account balances in a ledger. At this stage, it is not very difficult to tell whether an account is an asset or an expense, a liability or revenue. But it will not always be simple. Remember these rules:

1. Accounts with debit balances are normally assets, expenses, or drawings.
2. Accounts with credit balances are normally liabilities, capital, or revenue.

Trial Balance Procedure Unchanged

The new types of account do not change the trial balance procedure. Simply total the accounts with debit balances, total the accounts with credit balances, and see that the two totals agree. This is illustrated in Figure 5.6 on page 133 with the trial balance of Eve Boa's ledger.

FIGURE 5.6

Trial balance of Eve Boa, LLB's ledger.

EVE BOA, LLB TRIAL BALANCE JANUARY 31, 20—		
Account	DEBIT	CREDIT
Bank	2439 –	
A/R – H. Geroux	1420 –	
A/R – J. Magill	757 –	
A/R – E. Parsons	1395 –	
Supplies	2316 –	
Office Equipment	7550 –	
Automobile	16800 –	
A/P – OK Supply		4400 –
A/P – Computer Outlet		1200 –
Bank Loan		940 –
E. Boa, Capital		21878 –
E. Boa, Drawings	3950 –	
Fees Earned		23660 –
Advertising Expense	1321 –	
Car Expense	615 –	
Rent Expense	3300 –	
Sundry Expense	385 –	
Wages Expense	9830 –	
	52078 –	52078 –

The Equity accounts

The accounts needed for the income statement.

Section 5.2   Review Questions

1. What two classifications appear on the income statement?
2. How do you calculate net income? Net loss?
3. Name the three persons or groups who use the income statement.
4. Why are owners keenly interested in the income statement?
5. Why are bankers interested in seeing the income statement of a business to which the bank has loaned money?
6. Why must a business produce an income statement for the government?
7. Define the term "fiscal period."
8. Define the GAAP "time period concept."
9. How does the date on the income statement heading differ from that on the balance sheet?
10. Explain the "matching principle."
11. What is a chart of accounts?
12. Describe the account numbering system used in this text.
13. What types of account balances are normally found in an asset account? A liability account? A Revenue account? An Expense account? The Drawings account? The Capital account?

Section 5.2   Exercises

1. There are a number of errors in the annual income statement below for Mayfare Plumbing, owned by James Fare. **Examine the income statement, then complete the requirements below.**

	INCOME STATEMENT JAMES FARE DECEMBER 31, 20—	
Revenue		
Sales and Service		$107 416.00
Operating Expenses		
Advertising Expense	$ 1 150.50	
Bank Charges	1 750.00	
Car Expense	4 296.00	
Gas and Oil	4 935.00	
J. Fare, Drawings	18 076.09	
Utilities	3 975.12	
Materials Used	15 906.00	
Miscellaneous Expense	257.00	
Telephone Expense	250.00	
Total Expenses		55 095.71
Net Profit		$ 52 320.29

1. Identify the errors and list them in the space provided in your Workbook.
2. Prepare a corrected income statement in good form.

---

2. The ledger of Emily Stokaluk as at March 31, 20— is given below.

Bank	Accounts Receivable	Supplies
10 100	8 300	950

Land	Building	Equipment
35 000	110 000	22 000

Automobiles	Accounts Payable	Bank Loan
24 000	2 800	10 000

Mortgage Payable	E. Stokaluk, Capital	E. Stokaluk, Drawings
75 000	52 088	15 000

Fees Earned	Interest Earned	Advertising Expense
132 500	1 000	1 200

Bank Charges Expense	Building Maintenance Expense	Gas and Oil Expense
350	420	1 800

Utilities Expense	Miscellaneous Expense	Car Repair Expense
1 640	128	850

Wages Expense
41 650

A. **Prepare a trial balance in your Workbook.**
B. **Prepare a chart of accounts based on the numbering system used in the text and shown on page 131.**
C. **Prepare a simple income statement (one month).**

3. The ledger accounts of Express Air Service are shown below in alphabetical order.

Accounts Payable	Karen Koy, Capital
Accounts Receivable	Karen Koy, Drawings
Advertising Expense	Land
Airplanes	Legal Expense
Automobiles	Mortgage Payable
Bank	Revenue—Freight
Bank Charges Expense	Revenue—Passengers
Building	Salaries Expense
Building Repairs Expense	Supplies
Equipment	Supplies Expense
General Expense	Telephone Expense
Insurance Expense	Wages Expense

A. **Rearrange these accounts into the usual ledger order and prepare a chart of accounts using the numbering system on page 131 as a guide.**

4. **Shown below and in your Workbook is a chart for the rules of debit and credit. Complete the chart in your Workbook by writing the word "increase" or "decrease" in the appropriate spaces.**

Assets = Liabilities + Owner's Equity

Assets		Liabilities		Capital		Revenue	
DEBIT	CREDIT	DEBIT	CREDIT	DEBIT	CREDIT	DEBIT	CREDIT

				Drawings		Expense	
				DEBIT	CREDIT	DEBIT	CREDIT

5. The following information is for Atlas Associates for the month ended November 30, 20–.
Fees Earned, $31 700; Salaries Expense, $13 400; Rent Expense, $6 000; General Expense, $1 200; Advertising Expense, $600; Car Expense, $3 700; Utilities Expense, $3 500.

A. **Prepare an income statement for the month.**
B. The Salaries Expense of $13 400 included a $1 400 advance paid to an employee who desperately needed the money. The accounting clerk included the $1 400 in Salaries Expense because the employee was going to earn this amount of money in December. **What GAAP did the clerk violate when preparing the November expense figures? Explain why this was a violation**.
C. **Calculate the November net income if the GAAP you noted above had been followed.**
D. **Would the net for December be higher or lower if the GAAP was not followed?**

5.3 | Equity Relationships and the Balance Sheet

Understanding Equity Relationships

It is important to understand fully the equity section of the ledger. In Figure 5.7, the expanded ledger of Eve Boa is presented in a way that will help you to gain this understanding.

Study Figure 5.7 on page 137 and observe the following:

1. There are four types of accounts in the equity section of the ledger—capital, revenue, expense, and drawings.
2. The Capital account represents the beginning equity figure.
3. Changes in equity are recorded in the revenue, expense, and drawings accounts.
   - *Revenues* represent an increase in equity as a result of normal business activity. Because they represent an increase in equity, they are recorded as credits in the equity section.
   - *Expenses* represent a decrease in equity as a result of normal business activity. Because they represent a decrease in equity, they are recorded as debits in the equity section.
   - *Drawings* represent a decrease in equity as a result of the owner's personal withdrawals. Because they represent a decrease in equity, they are recorded as debits in the equity section.
4. The fundamental accounting equation is given at the bottom of the figure and shows that Eve Boa's ledger is in balance.
5. The difference between the total revenues and the total expenses is the net income or the net loss. *Net income* is the result if the revenues are greater than the expenses. *Net loss* is the result if the expenses are greater than the revenues. For Eve Boa, the net income is $8 209 (revenues of $23 660 less expenses of $15 451). The drawings have nothing to do with the calculation of net income or net loss.
6. The net income (or net loss) figure, together with the drawings figure, shows the increase or decrease in equity. For Eve Boa, there has been an increase in equity of $4 259 (increase from net income of $8 209 less a decrease from drawings of $3 950). If drawings are greater than net income, there will be an overall decrease in equity.
7. The following is the equity equation for Eve Boa:

Beginning Capital	+	Net Income	−	Net Loss	−	Drawings	=	Ending Capital
$21 878	+	$8 209	−	n/a	−	$3 950	=	$26 137

FIGURE 5.7

The expanded ledger of Eve Boa, LLB showing some important equity relationships.

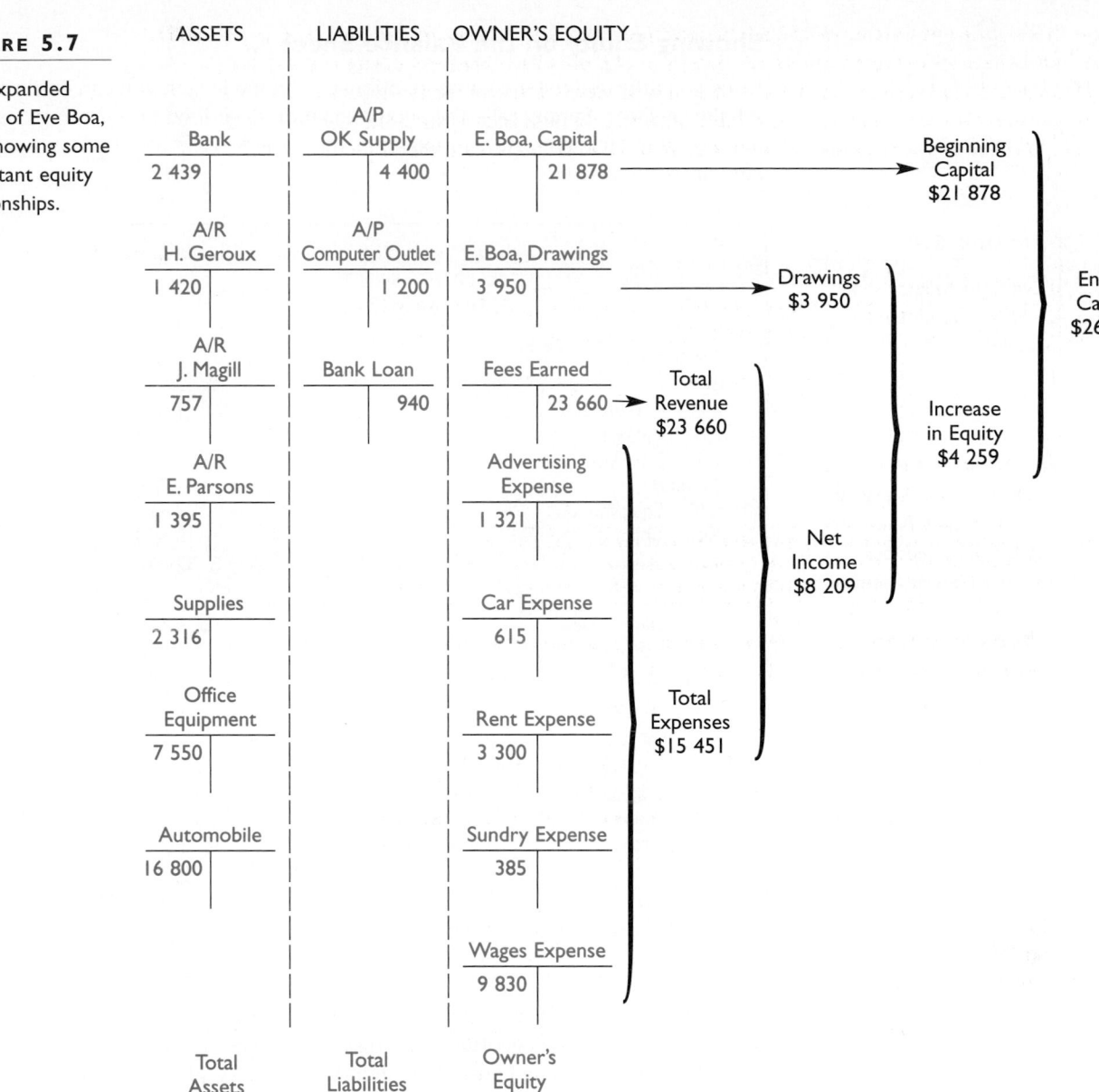

Showing Equity on the Balance Sheet

Once you fully understand equity relationships in the ledger, you can easily prepare a balance sheet. Simply take the equity equation described in point 7 on page 136 and present it in good form. For example, the balance sheet for Eve Boa would look similar to Figure 5.8.

FIGURE 5.8

Eve Boa's balance sheet with an expanded equity section.

For this balance sheet, the ASSETS section is placed on top of the LIABILITIES and EQUITY sections instead of beside them. This format is referred to as the *report form* of the balance sheet.

EVE BOA, LLB
BALANCE SHEET
JANUARY 31, 20—

Assets		
Bank		$ 2 439
A/R – H. Geroux		1 420
A/R – J. Magill		757
A/R – E. Parsons		1 395
Supplies		2 316
Office Equipment		7 550
Automobile		16 800
Total Assets		$ 32 677
Liabilities		
A/P – OK Supply		$ 4 400
A/P – Computer Outlet		1 200
Bank Loan		940
Total Liabilities		$6 540
Owner's Equity		
Eve Boa, Capital		
Balance January 1		$21 878
Net Income	$8 209	
Drawings	3 950	
Increase in Capital		4 259
Balance January 31		26 137
Total Liabilities and Owner's Equity		$ 32 677

The equity equation in balance sheet form.

Notice that the equity equation is seen on Eve Boa's balance sheet, and it clearly describes what happened during the month of January. She started the month with a claim on assets of $21 878. The net income in the month was greater than her drawings by $4 259, so her claim on assets increased to $26 137. Prior to expanding the ledger, all this information — including the income statement shown on page 120 — was hidden in the capital account.

Other Possible Changes to Equity

In Eve Boa's case, net income was greater than drawings. This caused an increase in equity. Consider two other cases that can describe what happens to equity over a fiscal period.

FIGURE 5.9

Two other equity sections showing how equity changes in a fiscal period.

Drawings greater than net income results in a decrease in capital.

Drawings greater than net income.

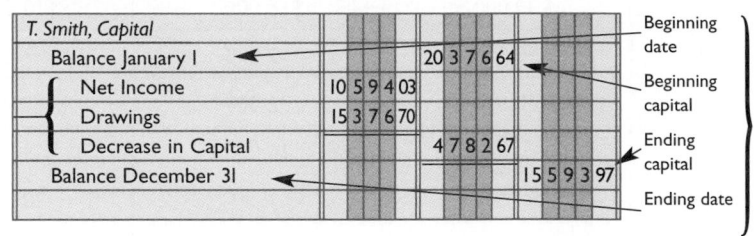

A loss results in a decrease in capital.

A net loss.

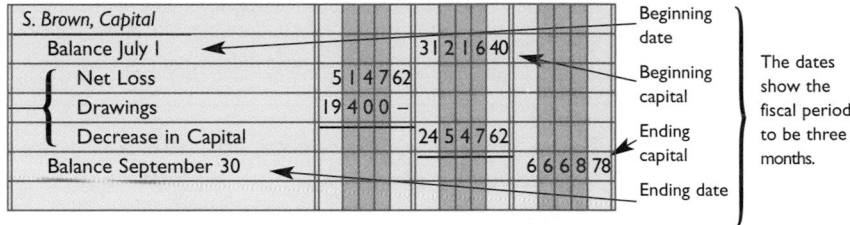

You should be aware that equity could increase in both cases shown in Figure 5.9. This would happen if the owners invested substantial additional personal funds in their businesses during the respective fiscal periods.

Section 5.3   Review Questions

1. State the equity equation.
2. Which account represents the beginning equity figure?
3. In which accounts are changes to equity recorded?
4. How do drawings affect the calculations of net income?
5. What will happen to equity if drawings are greater than net income?
6. Most of the time, a net loss will mean equity has decreased, even if the drawings are zero. True or False?
7. Give an example of when equity would increase if there was a net loss.

Section 5.3   Exercises

1. In your Workbook, complete the schedule below by filling in the blanks.

Items	Opening Capital	Net Income or Net Loss (−)	Drawings	Ending Capital
a.	$30 000	$15 000	$10 000	$
b.	50 000	−2 000	7 000	
c.	70 000	32 000		75 500
d.		16 000	19 500	33 200
e	56 000		30 000	40 000
f.	45 000		25 000	15 000
g.	22 000		10 000	28 000
h.		25 000	18 000	42 000
i.	120 000	42 000		112 000

2. In your Workbook, complete the following schedule by filling in the blanks for each of the five separate equity section relationships.

Financial Information	Company 1	Company 2	Company 3	Company 4	Company 5
Beginning capital	6 000	6 000	15 000		62 000
Total revenues	10 000		29 000		
Total expenses	8 000	11 000		30 000	35 000
Net income or loss (−)		14 000	11 000	20 000	− 5 000
Drawings	3 000	12 000		15 000	
Increase or decrease (−) in equity			− 6 000		− 10 000
Ending capital				10 000	

3. Prepare the equity section of the balance sheet from the data given for each case below.

Owner's name	G. Benvie	S. Robb	J. Bedford
Fiscal period	Year ended December 31, 20—	Three months ended March 31, 20—	Month ended May 31, 20—
Opening capital	$27 042.62	$19 641.25	$20 196.74
Net income (loss)	39 171.04	22 462.67	(3 750.20)
Drawings	35 000.00	25 575.00	10 047.17

5.4 | Simply Accounting, Spreadsheets, and the Expanded Ledger

In this section, you will see how the expanded ledger for Eve Boa's legal firm is handled by an accounting software program called Simply Accounting. It will be interesting for you to compare manual and electronic methods of preparing financial statements. In the Section 5.4 Exercises, you have the opportunity to use a spreadsheet to adjust the format of Simply Accounting's income statement and balance sheet.

Since the Simply Accounting portion of this section is brief, you do not need access to computers to understand it. Read the section material, study the illustrations carefully, and do the Section Review Questions. You will find the material useful later on in the course. To complete the Section Exercises, you will need a computer and spreadsheet software.

Chart of Accounts

Once the Simply Accounting home window is loaded for Eve Boa, LLB, by selecting the menu commands of **Reports, Lists, Chart of Accounts** you will produce a result similar to Figure 5.10.

FIGURE 5.10

Simply Accounting's Chart of Accounts for Eve Boa, LLB.

The H, G, T, and X are codes required by the software.

```
Chart of Accounts                      _ □ ✕
File   Help

ASSETS

1000  ------------------------------------------H
  1050  Bank --------------------------------- G
  1100  A/R--H. Geroux ----------------------- G
  1150  A/R--J. Magill ----------------------- G
  1200  A/R--E. Parsons ---------------------- G
  1250  Supplies ----------------------------- G
  1300  Office Equipment --------------------- G
  1350  Automobile --------------------------- G
1999  ------------------------------------------T

LIABILITIES

2000  ------------------------------------------H
  2050  A/P--OK Supply ----------------------- G
  2100  A/P--Computer Outlet ----------------- G
  2150  Bank Loan ---------------------------- G
2999  ------------------------------------------T

EQUITY

3000  ------------------------------------------H
  3050  E. Boa, Capital ---------------------- G
  3100  E. Boa, Drawings --------------------- G
  3600  Current Earnings --------------------- X
3999  ------------------------------------------T

REVENUE

4000  ------------------------------------------H
  4050  Fees Earned -------------------------- G
4999  ------------------------------------------T

EXPENSE

5000  ------------------------------------------H
  5050  Advertising Expense ------------------ G
  5100  Car Expense -------------------------- G
  5150  Rent Expense ------------------------- G
  5200  Sundry Expense ----------------------- G
  5250  Wages Expense ------------------------ G
5999  ------------------------------------------T
```

The main difference between Figure 5.10 and the chart of accounts presented in Chapter 5 is that four digits are used for account numbers. Notice that the first digit is still key to identifying the type of account. That is, all 1s are assets; 2s, liabilities; 3s, equity; 4s, revenue; and 5s expenses.

All the accounts listed in Eve Boa's ledger except one were created by her accountant. Account 3600, Current Earnings, was established automatically by the Simply Accounting software. If you cannot already guess, you will recognize the purpose for this account when you read about the balance sheet on page 143.

Income Statement

After transaction data is entered into Simply Accounting, an income statement is produced by choosing **Reports**, **Financials**, **Income Statement**. Then the fiscal period is entered into the appropriate fields. When the Return key is struck, an income statement like the one in Figure 5.11 will appear.

FIGURE 5.11

Simply Accounting's Income Statement for Eve Boa, LLB.

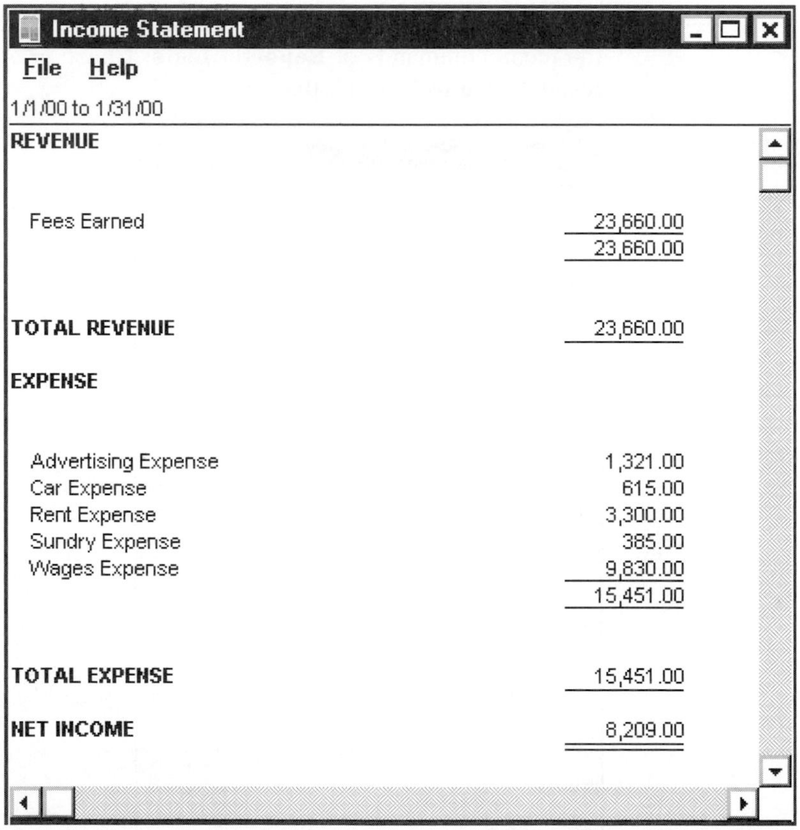

The software format for use of ruled lines for totals doesn't always conform to the guidelines given previously on pages 23–24.

Income Statement	
File Help	
1/1/00 to 1/31/00	
REVENUE	
Fees Earned	23,660.00
	23,660.00
TOTAL REVENUE	23,660.00
EXPENSE	
Advertising Expense	1,321.00
Car Expense	615.00
Rent Expense	3,300.00
Sundry Expense	385.00
Wages Expense	9,830.00
	15,451.00
TOTAL EXPENSE	15,451.00
NET INCOME	8,209.00

In the income statement above, the amounts are the same as the manual income statement on page 120. However, some differences in formatting exist. No dollar signs are used and the method for underlining is different. If a quick report of revenue and expenses is needed, the income statement in Figure 5.11 is sufficient. If a more formal presentation is needed, you can use a spreadsheet to do some re-formatting. You will have a chance to re-format the income statement shown in Figure 5.11 when you complete Exercise 1 on page 144.

Balance Sheet

The selections to produce a balance sheet are similar to those needed for an income statement. Choose **Reports**, **Financials**, **Balance Sheet**. Then, the date for the balance sheet is entered. For Eve Boa, LLB, the date to enter is January 31.

FIGURE 5.12

Simply Accounting's Balance Sheet for Eve Boa, LLB.

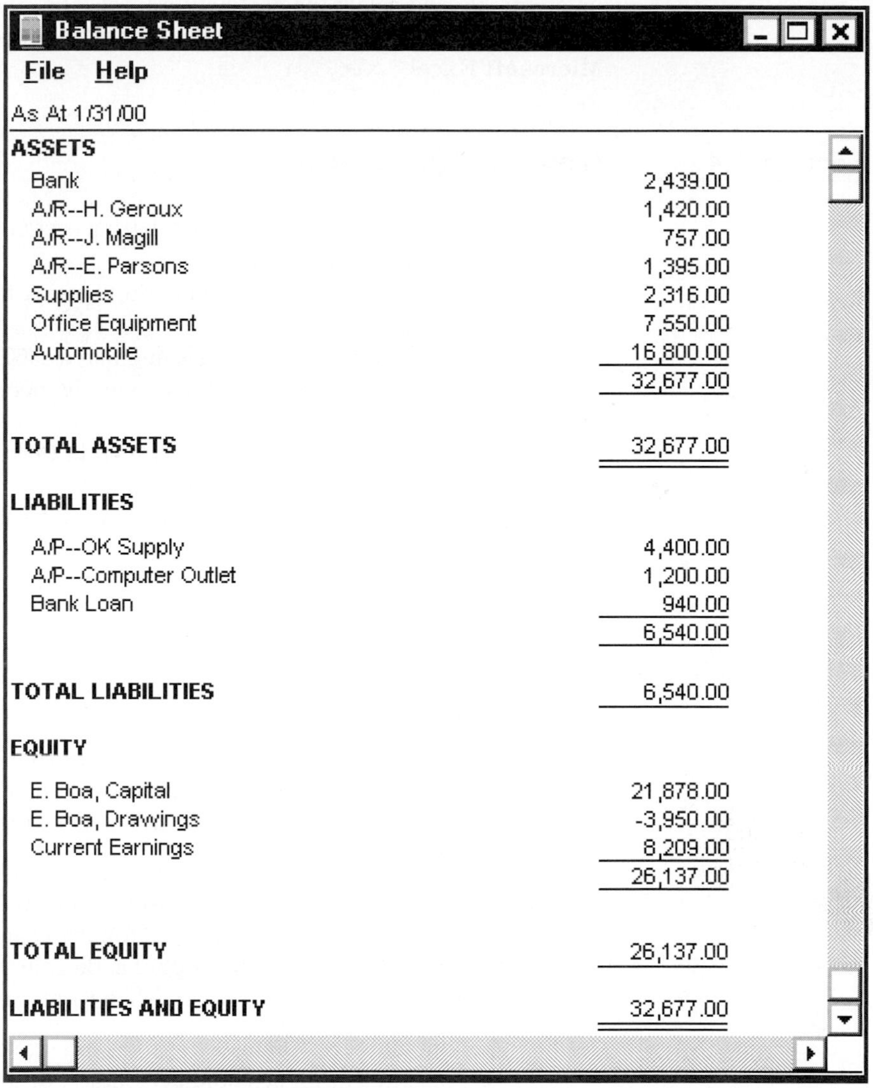

```
Balance Sheet                                   _ □ ×
 File   Help
As At 1/31/00
ASSETS                                                    ▲
  Bank                                         2,439.00
  A/R--H. Geroux                               1,420.00
  A/R--J. Magill                                 757.00
  A/R--E. Parsons                              1,395.00
  Supplies                                     2,316.00
  Office Equipment                             7,550.00
  Automobile                                  16,800.00
                                              32,677.00

TOTAL ASSETS                                  32,677.00

LIABILITIES

  A/P--OK Supply                               4,400.00
  A/P--Computer Outlet                         1,200.00
  Bank Loan                                      940.00
                                               6,540.00

TOTAL LIABILITIES                              6,540.00

EQUITY

  E. Boa, Capital                             21,878.00
  E. Boa, Drawings                            -3,950.00
  Current Earnings                             8,209.00
                                              26,137.00

TOTAL EQUITY                                  26,137.00

LIABILITIES AND EQUITY                        32,677.00    ▼
```

Take note of the Equity Section. The Current Earnings account contains the net income figure. Even though the format of Simply Accounting's Equity Section is unfamiliar to you, if you study the calculations, you will see that the equity equation you learned in this chapter still holds true.

Exporting Financial Statements

Exporting financial statement data is as simple as printing. And once you load the exported data into a spreadsheet program like Microsoft Excel, you can change the appearance of the report or statements. Each of the reports in Figures 5.10, 5.11, and 5.12 has a "File" menu near the top-left corner. Choosing File, Export, allows you to name the file and select the destination for saving (the drive and folder). You also identify the "type" of file you are saving. Using the drop-down menu you would select **Microsoft Excel *.xls**.

Section 5.4   # Review Questions

1. How does Simply Accounting's numbering system for accounts *differ* from the one presented on page 131?
2. How is Simply Accounting's numbering system for accounts *the same* as the one presented on page 131?
3. An account in Simply Accounting is numbered 5450. What type of account is this?
4. In what two ways does a Simply Accounting income statement differ from the one on page 120?
5. Write out the equity equation that is seen in Figure 5.12 on page 143. (Use the labels you learned in the text, not Simply Accounting's.)
6. Why would someone want to export a Simply Accounting financial statement to a spreadsheet program?

Section 5.4   # Exercises

Challenge Exercise

1. The spreadsheet model on page 145 was exported from Simply Accounting. The formatting is raw, and you have been asked to make a more formal presentation for Ms. Boa to take with her when she meets with the bank manager.

1. **Load the file named BoaIncome.xls.**
2. **Re-format the spreadsheet model so that it looks like the one shown in Figure 5.3 on page 120.** The following points are keyed to the illustration and refer to formatting options. Be able to show your teacher that you have used each of the features when formatting your model.

A. Font and Size: Changes the style and size of a font.
B. Font Effect: Applies boldface, italics, or underlining to the text.
C. Alignment Buttons: Positions data within a cell.
D. Currency and Comma Styles: Adjusts the appearance of numbers.
E. Decimal Selector: Increases or decreases the number of decimals displayed.
F. Indentation buttons: Increases or decreases the indentation within a cell.
G. Borders with drop-down menu: Applies various borders and underlining.
H. Column Width Adjustments: Changes column widths if the mouse pointer is placed on top of a column divider.
I. Colour: Applies colour to text and numbers.

You may want to delete a row or column. To delete a row, click the row number and choose **Edit**, **Delete**. Use the same procedure for columns. (To insert a row or column, make your selection and choose **Insert**, **Row** or **Insert**, **Column**.)

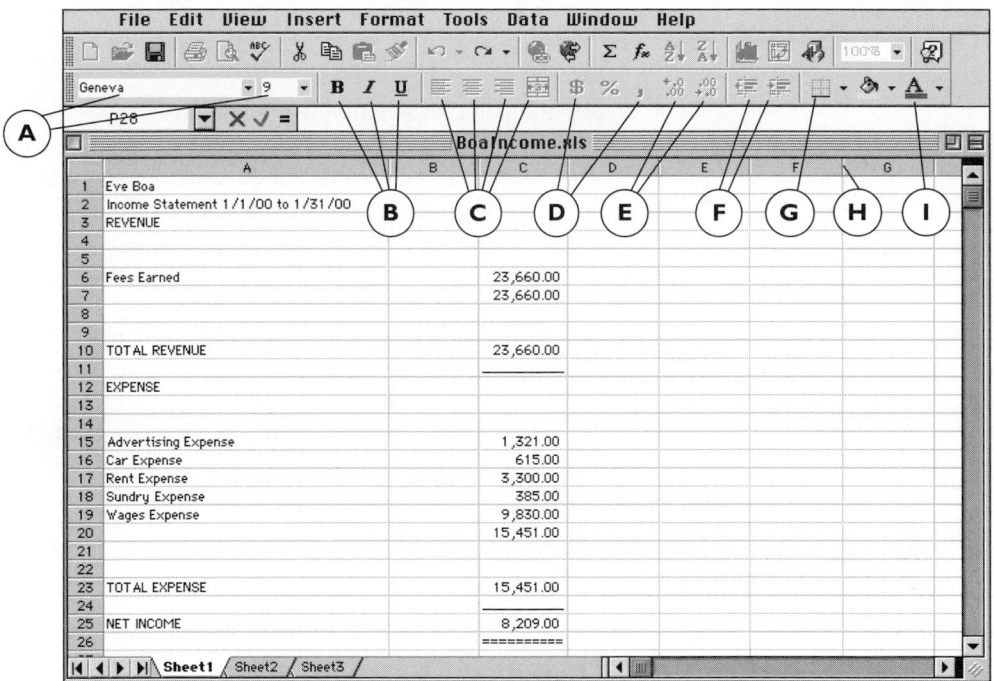

2. Load the file named BoaBal.xls, which was exported from Simply Accounting. Re-format this file so that it looks like the balance sheet shown in Figure 5.8 on page 138.

CHAPTER 5   Summary

CHAPTER HIGHLIGHTS

Now that you have completed Chapter 5, you should:

- realize the need for expanding the ledger;
- understand net income and net loss and be able to calculate both;
- be able to prepare an income statement from supplied figures;
- understand the importance of the income statement to owners, managers, and other interested parties;
- understand that the data for the income statement are accumulated in special accounts in the equity section of the ledger;
- be able to define revenue, expense, and drawings;
- know three new GAAPs: the time period concept, the revenue recognition convention, and the matching principle;
- be able to prepare an expanded equity section on a balance sheet.

ACCOUNTING TERMS

accounting period	matching principle
chart of accounts	net income
drawings	net loss
expense	revenue
fiscal period	revenue recognition convention
income statement	time period concept

CHAPTER 5   Review Exercises

Using Your Knowledge

1 Mrs. L. Bopara owns and operates a small florist shop in Gander, Newfoundland. She deposits all cash received in the bank and makes all payments by cheque. At the end of the last fiscal period, the Bank account showed a credit balance of $1 350 after all balances were found to be correct.

A. Assuming no errors, how is it possible for Bank, an asset account, to have a credit balance?

B. If, during the fiscal period, the revenue exceeded the expenses by $2 000 and the drawings amounted to $2 600, what is the net income figure for the period?

2 **Complete the following exercise in your Workbook.** A series of transactions is given below. **Using the list of debits and credits, show the effect of the accounting entry for each transaction.** The first transaction is done for you.

1.	Asset debit
2.	Asset credit
3.	Liability debit
4.	Liability credit
5.	Capital debit
6.	Capital credit
7.	Drawings debit
8.	Drawings credit
9.	Revenue debit
10.	Revenue credit
11.	Expense debit
12.	Expense credit

a. Purchase a new car on account.

b. Receive payment on account from a customer.

c. Owner withdraws cash for personal use.

d. Owner starts a new business by investing cash.

e. The car is repaired and paid for in cash immediately.

f. Perform a service for a customer for cash.

g. Perform a service for a customer on account.

h. Purchase supplies for cash.

i. Receive a bill for gas and oil for the car.

j. Pay a creditor on account.

k. Throw out some ruined supplies.

	DR	CR
a.	1	4
b.		
c.		
d.		
e.		
f.		
g.		
h.		
i.		
j.		
k.		

3 The income statement of Bianco Company is shown below.
Two errors were found in the books after the statement was prepared:

BIANCO COMPANY
INCOME STATEMENT
YEAR ENDED DECEMBER 31, 20—

Revenue		$47 416
Expenses		
Car Expense	$ 1 732	
Rent Expense	3 500	
Utilities Expense	1 075	
Wages Expense	23 072	29 379
Net Income		$18 037

A. A bill for $750 for automobile repairs had been incorrectly debited to Automobiles.

B. Owner's drawings of $5 000 had been incorrectly debited to Wages.

Prepare a corrected income statement.

④ The account balances in the ledger of Pamela Garside, a graphic designer, are shown below in the T-accounts and in your Workbook.

Pamela's auditor discovered the following errors when checking the records:

a. Cash revenue of $150 was credited incorrectly to the Capital account.
b. Owner's drawings of $500 was debited incorrectly to the Wages Expense account.
c. An automobile expense of $400 was debited incorrectly to the Automobiles account.
d. Equipment of $110 was debited incorrectly to Car Expense.

1. **In your Workbook, write out the changes to the accounts necessary to correct the above errors and make the entries in the accounts**.
2. The net income figure before the auditor's discoveries was determined to be $4 340. **What will the corrected net income figure be?**

Bank	A/R – P. Adler	A/R – A. Jackson	Supplies
1 745	50	70	610

Equipment	Automobiles	A/P–B & B Stone	A/P–Century Finance
5 000	7 900	110	5 500

P. Garside, Capital	P. Garside, Drawings	Revenue	Car Expense
5 625	200	11 920	500

Utilities Expense	Rent Expense	Wages Expense	
280	300	6 500	

⑤ With the expanded ledger, the accounting equation now appears as shown below. **In your Workbook, complete the schedule by filling in the rectangles with the correct figures for Penny Company over a four-year period.** (*Hint*: *Ending capital from one year becomes the beginning capital for the next year.*)

	Assets	=	Liabilities	+	Beginning Capital	+	Revenues	–	Expenses	–	Drawings
End of Year 1	100	=	20	+	70	+	60	–	45	–	5
End of Year 2	120	=	30	+	☐	+	90	–	60	–	☐
End of Year 3	130	=	☐	+	☐	+	105	–	80	–	20
End of Year 4	☐	=	30	+	☐	+	110	–	95	–	10

6 A partially completed summary of financial data is given below. The data pertain to the fundamental accounting equation for Dave Campos over a period of two years. **In your Workbook, fill in the missing figures, given that**:

1. revenues for 20-2 are $42 000;
2. expenses for 20-2 are $22 000;
3. drawings for 20-2 are $18 000;
4. the assets decreased by $5 000 from the end of 20-1 to the end of 20-2.

	Assets	Liabilities	Equity
End of 20–1		$27 400	
End of 20–2			$19 300

Comprehensive Exercise

7 N.A. James, a public accountant, decided to begin a business of his own on October 1, 20—. At that time, he invested in the business a bank balance of $5 000 and an automobile worth $18 000.

The accounts required are provided for you in the Workbook. Also, there is a ruled chart for you to write down the changes caused by the transactions.

A. **Work out the changes for the above transaction. Record these in the T-accounts provided in your Workbook.**

B. **For each of the transactions listed below, work out the changes for the transaction and record these changes in the T-accounts.**

N.A. James
Chart of Accounts

101	Bank	302	N.A. James, Drawings
110	A/R — Jenkins and Co.	401	Fees Earned
120	Office Supplies	505	Advertising Expense
125	Office Equipment	510	Car Expense
130	Automobile	515	Donations Expense
210	A/P — Office Supply Company	520	Miscellaneous Expense
301	N.A. James, Capital	525	Rent Expense

TRANSACTIONS

1. Purchased $300 of office supplies for cash. Issued a cheque in payment. (For now, when office supplies are purchased, debit Office Supplies instead of an expense account. You will learn more about handling supplies in Chapter 9.)

2. Issued a cheque for $50 for an advertisement in a local newspaper.

3. Received a bill from Office Supply Company for a desk, a chair, and a filing cabinet at a total cost of $1 100 on account.

4. Mr. James was hired by a client, Jenkins and Co. At the conclusion of the work, Mr. James charged Jenkins and Co. $900 and issued a bill for this service performed on account.

5. B. Masters, a client, paid $100 in cash for a bookkeeping service. W. Shields, another client, paid $75 in cash for having her tax return prepared. The total of $175 was deposited in the bank.

6. A cheque for $100 was sent as a donation to the Salvation Army.

7. A cheque for $300 was received from Jenkins and Co. on account.

8. A cheque was issued to Office Supply Company in full payment of the balance of its account.

9. Paid Louis's Service Station $120 for gasoline and repairs to the business automobile. A cheque was issued right away.

10. Performed an accounting service for T. Wu and received $200 cash in full payment. The owner, N.A. James, did not deposit this money in the bank, but kept it for his personal use.

11. Issued a cheque for $750 in payment of the rent for the month of October.

12. Purchased $120 of office supplies from Grand & Toy. The purchase was paid for by cheque.

13. Issued a cheque for $50 for an advertisement in a local newspaper.

14. Issued a bill for $600 to Jenkins and Co. for accounting services performed on account.

15. Issued a cheque for $70 for postage stamps. (*Note: Stamps are not considered to be supplies.*)

16. Issued a cheque for $500 to the owner for his personal use.

C. **Balance the ledger by means of a trial balance.**

D. **Prepare an income statement for the period, which is the month of October 20–.**

E. **Prepare a balance sheet with an expanded equity section. Use the one shown in Figure 5.8 on page 138 as your guide.**

Questions for Further Thought

Briefly answer the following questions.

1. In earlier chapters, there was no income statement to show the net income of a business. How can the owner calculate net income without producing an income statement?

2. The rules say that a credit entry is required to increase equity. Explain why an expense account, which is part of the equity, requires a debit entry to increase it.

3. Explain why there are usually only one or two revenue accounts but a number of expense accounts.

4. What information from the financial statements would be of particular interest to a banker for a business?

5. A company may have fiscal periods of any length as long as it produces an annual financial statement. Why does a company have to produce an annual statement?

6. Suppose that you were handed a ledger and asked to determine the equity. Describe two ways that this can be done.

7. Give appropriate names for the revenue account for the following businesses:
   a. a doctor;
   b. a loan company;
   c. a photographer;
   d. a real estate company;
   e. a hairdresser;
   f. a dry cleaning company.

8. You now know seven GAAPs. Name each and explain it briefly.

9. A business could be quite profitable and yet have a cash shortage. Give one reason why this might happen.

10. The text states that accounts with credit balances are liabilities, capital, or revenue. Still, it is possible for the Bank account to have a credit balance. Explain this apparent inconsistency.

11. Give three reasons why businesses prefer to make their purchases on credit.

12. Why is it just as important to control the expenses of a business as it is to increase the revenue?

13. John has earned $8 000 and Gary has earned $10 000. On the basis of this information, can you be sure who has the better earnings? Explain.

14. Bonanza Burger sells hamburgers for $1.49. Burger Giant sells them for $1.79. And yet, Bonanza Burger makes a larger profit. Give two reasons why this is possible.

Case Studies

CASE 1

"Timing Is Everything"

The owner and the accountant of the Arctic Lynx Snowmobile Company were busily preparing income statements for their important meeting with potential investors. The small snowmobile manufacturer badly needed additional investment in the firm in order to develop the new models for next year.

Two income statements were available to illustrate last year's performance. The first income statement, for the six-month period October 1 to March 31, showed a very healthy profit of $520 000. However, the second income statement, for the period April 1 to September 30, showed a loss of $100 000!

The owner, eager to please his new investors, argued with his accountant, telling her that she should show only the better income statement. He felt it didn't matter which time period they chose to measure the health of the business.

Questions

1. In a seasonal business such as this, what time period should the company choose for its income statements in order to obtain an accurate picture of its profitability?
2. Why was the period from October to March so profitable?
3. Calculate the true profit for last year's operations.
4. Did the firm's accountant have an obligation to reveal both income statements to the group of investors? What would you have done in this situation?

CASE 2

Pumping Profits

Doug Kurtz has just completed the income statement for his first month in business as the owner/operator of a new athletic club called Get In Shape! He had studied accounting in high school, so he felt confident enough to prepare his own income statement, summarized below:

GET IN SHAPE! FITNESS CLUB
INCOME STATEMENT
MONTH ENDED OCTOBER 31, 20—

Revenue	$25 000
Less: All expenses	8 000
Net Income	$17 000

The revenue figure includes 60 memberships at $300 each, which are good for one year. Most of these were sold on the first day of business. Doug is ecstatic with the high level of profits he has earned — but one of the club's members, a local accountant, has cautioned Doug to use all accounting principles properly, or serious errors could result.

Questions

1. Has Doug used any accounting principles improperly? If so, describe Doug's mistake.
2. Correct Doug's income statement, being sure to apply all accounting principles correctly.
3. What is Doug's obligation to the 60 signed members at this point?

CASE 3

Challenge

Revenue Roulette

Tom Lafleur, a university student living in northern Alberta, has created an interesting summer venture as a young entrepreneur. He has formed a firm called Tom's Tree Service, specializing in tree removal and pruning. He has been fortunate in securing a $10 000 contract to cut a large acreage of trees for a local golf course.

Tom estimates that it will take him from early June to the end of August to complete the job. The golf course owners have agreed to give Tom three progress payments on the dates indicated in the chart below:

	Progress payment amount	Tom's estimate of percentage of work completed each month
June 30	$ 3 000	40%
July 31	3 000	50%
August 31	4 000	10%
Totals	$10 000	100%

Tom would like to prepare monthly statements but cannot decide on the amount of revenue that should be recognized for each month of the contract. (**Note:** *For the purposes of this case, ignore expenses.*)

Questions

1. What inaccuracies would exist in the June and July income statements if Tom were to decide to recognize the full $10 000 as revenue on the August income statement?
2. Suggest two methods of revenue recognition that would allow Tom to recognize some revenue on the June and July income statements. (**Hint:** *You should consider the amounts of monthly progress payments received and the percentage of work completed in June and July.*)
3. How much revenue would Tom recognize in July, using each of the methods described in question 2? Which method do you prefer? Why?

CASE 4

Group Discussion

Perspective on Financial Statements

Neil Poje of Nolalu, Ontario, has an oil distribution business. The business has a $50 000 bank loan with a local bank. Following normal practice, the bank manager has requested a copy of the financial statements of the business for the latest year. Neil has provided her with audited financial statements. In simplified form, these statements appear below.

POJE FUELS
INCOME STATEMENT
YEAR ENDED JUNE 30, 20—

Revenues		$250 000
Expenses		
Cost of Oil	$150 000	
Other Expenses	65 000	
Total Expenses		215 000
Net Income		$ 35 000

POJE FUELS
BALANCE SHEET
JUNE 30, 20—

Assets	
Cash	$ 5 000
Accounts Receivable	14 000
Inventory of Oil	100 000
Other Assets	70 000
Total Assets	$189 000
Liabilities and Equity	
Bank Loan	$ 50 000
Accounts Payable	30 000
Total Liabilities	$ 80 000
Owner's Equity	109 000
Total Liabilities and Equity	$189 000

Questions

1. Why does a bank manager request financial statements?
2. In your opinion, should Neil Poje be satisfied with the net income figure?
3. Why might the bank manager be concerned about the bank loan?
4. Give an explanation for the business's being short of cash.
5. The inventory of oil is shown at $100 000. What could happen to make this figure higher or lower?
6. What could the bank manager require (if it has not already been done) to make the bank's position more secure?
7. The bank manager will probably compare these financial statements with those of previous years. Of what use would this be?
8. If you were the bank manager, what action would you take regarding this loan?

Career

Nicholas Schmidt / Sole Proprietor

In high school, Nicholas Schmidt of Thunder Bay, Ontario, took a number of business courses, including accounting. After graduation, he was hired as an accounting clerk for a branch office of the Global Service Corporation, an international corporation. Nicholas worked with cash receipts, accounts receivable, and accounts payable.

After two years, Nicholas decided to leave and start his own business. Following months of preparation, he opened Nicholas's Fabric Shoppe in a rented storefront on Thunder Bay's main street. The business has been extremely successful. Nicholas sells a high-quality selection of fabrics, wool, and needlepoint supplies. He enjoys the independence, variety, and contact with people that owning one's own store provides.

As the sole proprietor of a small business, Nicholas does all of his own accounting; his training and experience in this area have proven invaluable. Although he is very busy, Nicholas enrolled in an introductory accounting correspondence course at the university. This course acquainted him with some very important accounting principles and taught him some fundamental skills.

Today in his own business, Nicholas's accounting duties include keeping track of accounts receivable and accounts payable and reconciling his monthly bank statement. He also has to make sure that the correct amount of sales tax is sent to the provincial government. Further, he must be certain to have enough stock on hand to meet the demands of his customers.

Nicholas has recently approached his local bank for a loan of $10 000. He wants to purchase a point-of-sale terminal and computer equipment to help him manage his inventories. This will enable him to manage a larger stock. By buying in larger quantities, Nicholas hopes to take advantage of suppliers' discounts and increase his inventory. The loans manager, following standard procedure, has asked Nicholas to produce a balance sheet for his business. Nicholas's balance sheet contains the following assets, liabilities, and owner's equity.

Having prepared the balance sheet, Nicholas now sees that not all of the assets belong to him. If the loan is granted, the claims against the assets of Nicholas's Fabric Shoppe will total $14 000. Nonetheless, Nicholas is determined to expand his business. He feels that the risk is justified by the prospect of increased success for his business, made possible through the use of new microcomputer equipment.

NICHOLAS'S FABRIC SHOPPE
BALANCE SHEET
JUNE 30, 20—

Assets		Liabilities	
Bank Balance	$ 3 050.00	Accounts Payable	
Accounts Receivable		– Northcab Silk Co.	$ 1 800.00
– Bodley & Son	350.00	– H.A. Kidd Co.	2 200.00
– Lukes	200.00	Total Liabilities	$ 4 000.00
Merchandise Inventory	17 000.00		
Supplies	1 400.00		
Furniture & Fixtures	13 000.00	Owner's Equity	
Office Equipment	11 000.00	Nicholas Schmidt, Capital	42 000.00
Total Assets	$46 000.00	Total Liabilities and Equity	$46 000.00

Discussion

1. List some advantages and disadvantages of being a sole proprietor.
2. Discuss the types of merchandise inventory and supplies Nicholas would have in his store.
3. How have Nicholas's accounting courses helped him operate his business successfully?
4. Discuss how Nicholas would use the new equipment in his business.
5. Examine Nicholas's balance sheet. Can you see any reason why the bank manager might not grant the loan of $10 000?
6. Based on what you have learned in this chapter, what additional information might the bank manager want in order to grant this loan?
7. If Nicholas were denied the loan from the bank, discuss other approaches he could take in order to obtain the $10 000 for the purchase of the computer equipment he wants.
8. One thing that the bank manager might want to see from Nicholas is an updated business plan. Find out what a business plan is and write a paragraph explaining the concept and why the bank manager might want to see one.

chapter six

The Journal and Source Documents

6.1 | The Journal

In the last two chapters, you have practised analyzing transactions to determine what accounts were affected and whether the accounts should be debited or credited. You recorded the changes caused by transactions—referred to by accountants as *entries*—in ledger accounts called T-accounts.

However, ledger accounts alone do not satisfy all of the needs of accounting. As we have seen, each transaction requires two or more entries that must balance. In a ledger, each entry is recorded in a separate account. The accounts are on different pages. Therefore, as transactions mount up, the bits and pieces of the accounting entries become scattered through the ledger. The details for any one transaction become difficult to put back together. Yet this arrangement is often necessary. Therefore, accountants use another book, called a *journal*, to keep all of the entries together, transaction by transaction. The entries are actually recorded in the journal *before* they are recorded in the ledger accounts.

A **journal** is a book in which the accounting entries for all transactions are *first recorded*, before they are recorded in the ledger accounts. Each transaction is recorded separately. The transactions are recorded in the order of their occurrence. This is also known as chronological order. In this way, the journal provides an important continuous record of all transactions.

The Two-Column General Journal

There are several different types of journals used in accounting. The simplest one, which you will study in this chapter, is the two-column general journal. A page from a two-column general journal is shown in Figure 6.1 below. You will see that it has two money columns, one for the debit amounts and one for the credit amounts. There are also columns for Date, Particulars (account names and explanations), and P.R. (Posting Reference, explained on page 211).

FIGURE 6.1

A page from a two-column general journal.

General Journal Facts

GENERAL JOURNAL   PAGE 16

DATE		PARTICULARS	P.R.	DEBIT	CREDIT
Nov. 20	9	Supplies		135 –	
		Bank			135 –
		Letterhead and envelopes; cheque #40			
	12	Equipment		12 000 –	
		A/P – World Wide Fibre Optics			10 000 –
		Bank			2 000 –
		Network software installation; issued			
		cheque #41 with the balance due in 30 days			
	28	A/P – Internet Service Providers		750 –	
		Bank			750 –
		Partial payment; cheque #42			
Dec.	3	A/R – W. Hill		300 –	
		Fees Earned			300 –
		Service on account			
	17	Bank		5 000 –	
		Bank Loan			5 000 –
		Increase in bank loan			

Pages numbered consecutively.

Each journal entry balances.

Blank line, usually, between transactions.

A "compound entry" affects more than two accounts.

Account titles are capitalized.

Simple, brief explanations.

There are five transactions recorded in the journal shown in Figure 6.1 above. The transactions are separated by blank lines, making it easy to tell them apart. The accounting entries for the transactions are referred to as *journal entries*.

A **journal entry** is made up of all of the accounting changes for one transaction, in the form in which they are written up in the general journal. The transactions are recorded in the journal in a specific way. Notice that the debited account and amount are recorded first. The credited account and amount are recorded second and are indented. Notice that for each transaction there is at least one debit amount and one credit amount, and that the total of the debit amounts is equal to the total of the credit amounts. This is the case with every complete journal entry.

Journalizing is the process of recording accounting entries in the journal. The journal is known as a **book of original entry** because each balanced accounting entry is recorded there first. The basic process of recording transactions first in the journal and then in the ledger is shown in Figure 6.2 below.

FIGURE 6.2

The first three steps in the accounting cycle.

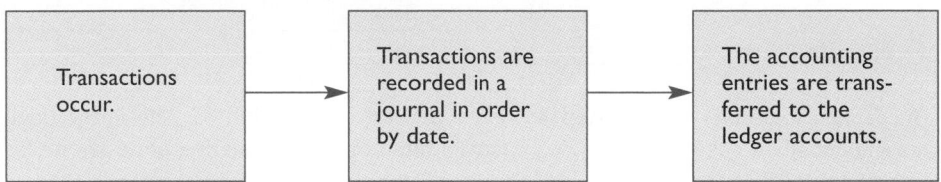

Journalizing in the Two-Column General Journal

Recording the Date

The following is the customary procedure for recording the date in the date column of a journal. Refer back to Figure 6.1 on page 158 as you read this.

1. **The year** Enter the year in small figures on the first line of each page. Do not repeat it for each entry. Enter a new year at the point on the page where it occurs.
2. **The month** Enter the month on the first line of each page. Do not repeat it for each entry. Enter a new month at the point where it occurs.
3. **The day** Enter the day on the first line of each journal entry. The day is repeated no matter how many transactions occur on any given day.

Steps in Recording a Journal Entry

There are four steps in recording a general journal entry. These are as follows:

Step 1   Enter the day in the date column; in this example, it is the 12th day.

GENERAL JOURNAL					PAGE 16	
DATE		PARTICULARS	P.R.	DEBIT	CREDIT	
Nov. 20—	9	Supplies		1 3 5 —		
		Bank			1 3 5 —	
		Letterhead and envelopes; cheque #40				
	12					

Transactions are recorded in a journal in order by date.

Step 2   Enter the names of the account(s) to be debited at the left side of the Particulars column. Enter the debit amounts in the Debit money column.

	12	Equipment		12 0 0 0 —			

Step 3   Enter the names of the account(s) to be credited. They are indented about 1.5 cm in the Particulars column. Enter the credit amounts in the Credit money column.

	12	Equipment	12 0 0 0 –	
		A/P – World Wide Fibre Optics		10 0 0 0 –
		Bank		2 0 0 0 –

The debited account(s) and amount(s) are recorded first. The credited account(s) and amount(s) are recorded second and are indented.

Step 4   Write a brief explanation for the entry beginning at the left side of the Particulars column on the line beneath the last credit item.

	12	Equipment	12 0 0 0 –	
		A/P – World Wide Fibre Optics		10 0 0 0 –
		Bank		2 0 0 0 –
		Network software installation; issued cheque #41		
		with the balance due in 30 days		

Usefulness of the General Journal

The chief purpose of the general journal is to provide a continuous record of the accounting entries in the order in which they occur. But this is not its only use.

The accounting clerk works out the accounting entries from the source documents and records them in the journal. The clerk can then see the work in an organized way. This is the time to check that each entry balances and generally that everything is in order. A job done well at this stage reduces errors and prevents problems from occurring later.

The journal is also useful for reference. It is often necessary to refer back to the journal to verify a transaction. This is particularly the case when balancing the ledger.

The Opening Entry

Every accounting entry is recorded first in the journal. This is done even for the first accounting entry, the one that sets up the financial position from a balance sheet. The journal entry that starts the books off, or "opens" them, is known as the **opening entry**.

For every complete journal entry, the total of the debit amounts equals the total of the credit amounts.

The opening entry for Shirley Cassar's photography business can be seen in Figure 6.3 below. The figures for this accounting entry came from a balance sheet prepared at the time.

FIGURE 6.3

The opening entry for a small business.

Oct.	30	Bank	1 4 0 0 –	
		Supplies	2 4 2 5 –	
		Equipment	8 7 1 5 –	
		Automobile	19 5 5 0 –	
		Bank Loan		10 0 0 0 –
		Shirley Cassar, Capital		22 0 9 0 –
		Opening financial position of Shirley Cassar		

Section 6.1   Review Questions

1. Explain what is meant by the statement, "the accounting entries become scattered through the ledger."
2. Why is a second book, the journal, necessary in accounting?
3. Define "journal."
4. What is a journal entry?
5. What is meant by "journalizing"?
6. Why is a journal known as a "book of original entry"?
7. Describe the appearance of a two-column general journal.
8. In the two-column general journal, how do you tell where one journal entry ends and another one begins?
9. Answer the following questions about the two-column general journal:
   a. Where is the year always entered?
   b. When do you re-enter the year?
   c. Where is the month always entered?
   d. When do you re-enter the month?
   e. What is the rule for recording the day of a transaction?
10. Which accounts are recorded first when recording a journal entry?
11. Which accounts are indented when recording a journal entry?
12. Describe how explanations are recorded in the journal.
13. Describe what is meant by the "opening entry."
14. What else does the journal provide besides a daily list of accounting entries?

Section 6.1   Exercises

1. Tony's Repair Shop is owned and operated by Tony Castillo. The chart of accounts for his business is given below.

> **TONY'S REPAIR SHOP**
> **CHART OF ACCOUNTS**
>
> | *Assets* | | | *Owner's Equity* | |
> |---|---|---|---|---|
> | 105 | Bank | | 305 | T. Castillo, Capital |
> | 110 | A/R – C. Jacobs | | 310 | T. Castillo, Drawings |
> | 115 | A/R – D. Steiger | | 405 | Repair Revenue |
> | 120 | Supplies | | 505 | Bank Charges Expense |
> | 125 | Equipment | | 510 | Light and Heat Expense |
> | | | | 515 | Miscellaneous Expense |
> | *Liabilities* | | | 520 | Rent Expense |
> | 205 | A/P – Ace Cartage | | 525 | Truck Expense |
> | 210 | A/P – Western Electric | | 530 | Wages Expense |

Journalize the following transactions for Tony's Repair Shop in the two-column general journal provided in the Workbook. Use page number 17.

TRANSACTIONS

20—

February

3   Paid the rent for February, $500 cash.
5   Paid $400 to Western Electric on account.
7   Performed a repair service for A. Abel for cash, $375.
10 The owner withdrew $200 cash for personal use.
11 Received $350 from C. Jacobs on account.
14 Paid $85 cash for repairs to the truck.
17 Paid $40 cash for gasoline for the truck.
24 Performed a repair service for D. Steiger on account, $275.
28 Paid $300 cash for wages for the month.

2. Paula Perna, a lawyer, has decided to open her own law office on June 1, 20—. On that date, she commenced business with the following assets and liabilities.

Assets		Liabilities	
Bank	$ 2 500	Acme Finance Company	$8 750
Law Library	3 500	The Stationery Store	3 250
Office Equipment	8 250		
Automobile	16 500		

A. **Prepare a balance sheet for Paula Perna as of June 1, 20—.**
B. **Record the beginning financial position of Paula Perna in a two-column general journal. Use page number 1. This is the opening entry.**
C. **Journalize the transactions for Paula Perna shown below and on page 163. Use the following chart of accounts.**

Chart of Accounts

Assets	*Owner's Equity*
Bank	P. Perna, Capital
A/R — R. Spooner	P. Perna, Drawings
A/R — T. & R. Builders	Fees Earned
Office Supplies	Car Expense
Law Library	General Expense
Automobile	Rent Expense
Office Equipment	Wages Expense

Liabilities
A/P — Acme Finance
A/P — The Stationery Store

TRANSACTIONS

June

1   Paid the rent for June, $500 cash.
2   Purchased typing and stationery supplies on account from The Stationery Store, $375.
3   Performed a legal service for cash, $200.

5   Performed a legal service on account for R. Spooner, $350.
8   Paid $1 000 cash to The Stationery Store on account.
10   Performed a legal service on account for T. & R. Builders, $1 100.
11   Received $350 on account from R. Spooner.
15   Paid $40 cash for gasoline for the business automobile.
20   Paid wages for part-time secretarial help, $250.
24   Paid $65 cash for postage.
24   Paid the regular monthly installment to Acme Finance, $320.
30   Paula withdrew $450. Of this, $400 was for personal use and $50 was for gasoline for the business automobile.

3. The general journal shown below contains a number of errors. **Study the journal and prepare a list describing these errors**.

DATE		PARTICULARS	P.R.	DEBIT	CREDIT
		GENERAL JOURNAL			PAGE
Feb	3	Bank		200 –	
		A/R – P. Simms			200 –
		Partial payment from customer			
Feb	7	Bank			50 –
		Supplies		50 –	
		Pencils, pens, and papers			
		purchased from Reingolds			
Feb	10	Bank		90 –	
		M. Farris, Capital		60 –	
		Equipment			250 –
		Sold equipment ($250) for $90 cash			
Feb	22	A/P – General Finance		315 –	
Feb	22	Bank			315 –
		A/R – N. Proulx		125 –	
		Fees Earned			125 –
		Service performed for cash			
Mar	3	Supplies			20 –
		A/P – Reingolds		20 –	
		Purchased folders on credit			

4. A number of journal entries are shown below without dates or explanations. These entries are for a beauty shop operated by Kelly Marshall in Stratford, Ontario. **Examine these entries and prepare a list of transactions that could have caused them**.

		DR	CR
a)	Bank	5 000	
	Kelly Marshall, Capital		5 000
b)	Supplies	530	
	Bank		530
c)	Kelly Marshall, Drawings	200	
	Bank		200
d)	A/R—Jan Vasko	220	
	Revenue		220
e)	Supplies	170	
	A/P—Fain Bros.		170

5. Rob D'Alvese begins business with the following assets and liabilities: Bank, $2 200; Land, $42 500; Building, $85 900; Office Equipment, $6 900; Account(s) Payable to Diamond Equipment, $350; Mortgage on Building, $32 560. **After calculating the equity figure, record the opening entry for Rob D'Alvese on August 1, 20— in a two-column general journal.**

6. Described below are a number of transactions of Clare Lehto Window Cleaning, located in Fredericton, New Brunswick. **In a two-column general journal, record the journal entries for these transactions. Use page number 14. Use the following accounts**:

Bank
A/R — (various debtors)
Cleaning Supplies
A/P — (various creditors)
C. Lehto, Capital
C. Lehto, Drawings
Revenue
Miscellaneous Expense
Telephone Expense
Wages Expense

TRANSACTIONS

20—
April
3   Received a cheque for $110 from P. Daniel on account.
6   Paid $300 to Walberg Bros. on account.
9   Purchased $500 of cleaning supplies from Merrick Products on account.
10   Performed a cleaning service for a customer and received $157 cash in payment.
15   Paid the telephone bill in cash, $24.50.
19   The owner withdrew $400 for her personal use.
20   Paid $450 for wages.
25   Corrected an error in the accounts. The Cleaning Supplies account had been debited $25 in error. The Miscellaneous Expense account should have been debited.

6.2 | **Source Documents**

As we have seen, transactions are first recorded by accounting personnel as journal entries. Where is the information about the transactions obtained? It is obtained from source documents. Source documents were briefly introduced in Chapter 3. In this chapter, they will be studied in detail.

A number of business transactions are started outside the accounting department. These transactions are initiated not by accounting personnel, but by the owner, sales-people, department supervisors, managers, and other authorized people.

The accounting department is informed of transactions by means of business papers that are sent to it. These business papers are called source documents. A **source document** is a business paper that shows the nature of a transaction and provides all of the information needed to account for it properly. The accounting department uses the source documents as the basis for recording the accounting entries. Almost every accounting entry is based on a source document.

For some transactions, there are no conventional source documents. The owner withdrawing money for personal use is an example. In such a case, the accounting entry must be supported by some other business paper or record. In this instance, a memorandum from the owner would be sufficient. In other cases, the supporting documents might be:

- detailed calculations prepared by the accounting department;
- a document drawn up years ago (for example, a long-term rental agreement), covering a series of transactions, including the current one.

A company is required to keep source documents on file. They will be used within the office for reference purposes, for locating errors, and so on. As well, source documents provide the factual evidence to verify transactions of the business. They provide proof that the accounting records have been prepared accurately and honestly.

Several basic source documents will be explained and illustrated in the next few pages. For each, the journal entries are given and explained. They are considered to be basic source documents because they are used in the most common business transactions. A company called Masthead Marine, owned by David Scott of Vancouver, B.C., is used to illustrate these source documents and their journal entries. Masthead Marine is in the business of selling boats, marine equipment, and boat parts and supplies. The revenue account for Masthead Marine is called Sales.

Cash Sales Slip

A **cash sales slip** is a business form showing the details of a transaction in which goods or services are sold to a customer for cash. Usually, there is an original and two copies. The features of a cash sales slip and the uses for the copies are shown in Figure 6.4 on page 166.

Journal Entry for a Cash Sales Slip

The accounting copy goes to the accounting department as the source document for the journal entry. For the above sales slip, the journal entry is:

	DR	CR
Bank	$35.90	
Sales		$35.90

A similar journal entry will be made for all cash sales slips.

FIGURE 6.4

Cash sales slip representing a sale of goods or services for cash.

If one of a business's prenumbered source documents is accidentally spoiled, it should be marked VOID and kept, so that all such documents can be accounted for.

This copy is sent to the accounting department to be used as the source document.

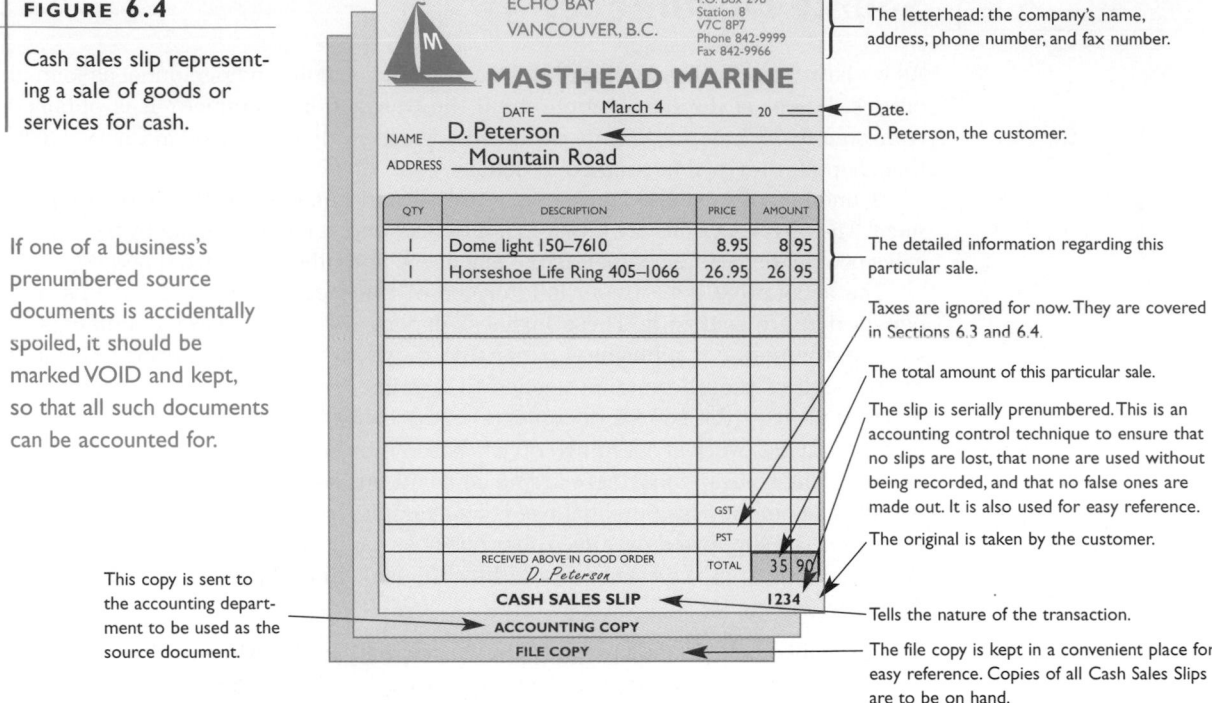

The letterhead: the company's name, address, phone number, and fax number.

Date.

D. Peterson, the customer.

The detailed information regarding this particular sale.

Taxes are ignored for now. They are covered in Sections 6.3 and 6.4.

The total amount of this particular sale.

The slip is serially prenumbered. This is an accounting control technique to ensure that no slips are lost, that none are used without being recorded, and that no false ones are made out. It is also used for easy reference.

The original is taken by the customer.

Tells the nature of the transaction.

The file copy is kept in a convenient place for easy reference. Copies of all Cash Sales Slips are to be on hand.

Sales Invoice

Many businesses do not deal with the general public and therefore normally do not have cash sales. Businesses of this type make nearly all their sales on account. For each sale on account, a sales invoice is issued to the customer. A **sales invoice** is a business form showing the details of a transaction in which goods or services are sold on account. Usually, there is an original and several copies. The features of a sales invoice and the uses for the copies are shown in Figure 6.5 below.

FIGURE 6.5

A sales invoice representing a sale of goods or services on account.

The shipping copy goes to the shipping department to tell what goods to send to the customer.

The file copy is kept in the reference file where all numbers are on hand.

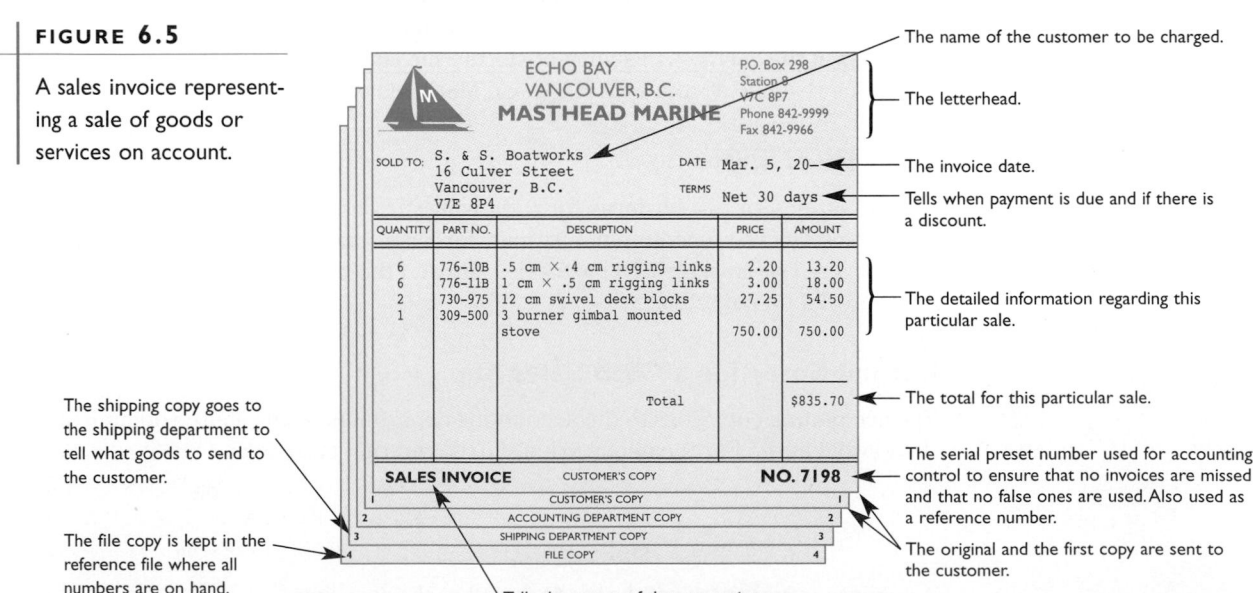

The name of the customer to be charged.

The letterhead.

The invoice date.

Tells when payment is due and if there is a discount.

The detailed information regarding this particular sale.

The total for this particular sale.

The serial preset number used for accounting control to ensure that no invoices are missed and that no false ones are used. Also used as a reference number.

The original and the first copy are sent to the customer.

Tells the nature of the transaction.

In any sales transaction, the party that sells is known as the *vendor* and the party that buys is known as the *purchaser*. In this case, Masthead Marine is the vendor and S. & S. Boatworks is the purchaser.

Journal Entry for a Sales Invoice

The accounting copy goes to the accounting department as the source document for the journal entry to record the sale. For this sales invoice, the journal entry is:

	DR	CR
A/R — S. & S. Boatworks	$835.70	
Sales		$835.70

A similar journal entry will be made for all sales invoices.

Point of Sale Summaries

Credit cards and debit cards are common forms of payment. A key piece of technology that makes them convenient is the point of sale terminal. A **point of sale (POS) terminal** is a computerized sales register that allows a business and its customers to exchange funds electronically. You will learn more about credit cards, debit cards, and POS terminals in Chapter 10. For now, you will concentrate on the journal entry required when credit and debit cards are used.

At the end of a business day, the accounting clerk will use the POS terminal to print at least two source documents. One is the Host Reconciliation/Card Summary shown in Figure 6.6.

```
         Host Reconciliation
            Card Summary
           October 30, 20—

Visa        7  Sale        412.50
            1  Return      −27.50
            0  Void

M/C         2  Sale         32.56
            0  Return
            0  Void

Debit       6  Sale        325.62
            0  Return
            0  Void
                         _____
                          743.18
```

You can see that this POS summary reveals the sales activities of three cards: Visa®, MasterCard®, and debit cards. It is referred to as a "host reconciliation" because the business (the host) will compare the total at the bottom ($743.18) to an amount that will appear on the bank statement. (Bank statements are prepared monthly by the business's financial institution.)

The other common POS summary is a report called a transaction log. A **transaction log** is a document generated by a point of sale terminal that contains detailed information about each transaction. This information includes each customer's name and card number. The transaction log is for reference and is especially useful when a customer disputes a transaction.

Journal Entry for POS Summaries

It is important for you to realize that credit and debit card transactions are treated as cash receipts from the business's point of view. This means that the total shown near the bottom of Figure 6.6 represents the net cash deposit for the credit and debit card transactions that occurred on October 30th. The journal entry for the source document in Figure 6.6 is:

	DR	CR
Bank	$734.18	
Sales		$734.18

Purchase Invoice

Masthead Marine is not always the vendor company. Often, it makes purchases from other companies. Then it is the purchaser company. When Masthead Marine makes a purchase on account from a supplier, the company supplying the goods issues a sales invoice to Masthead Marine. When the vendor's invoice arrives at the office of Masthead Marine, it becomes a purchase invoice. A **purchase invoice** is a business form representing a purchase of goods or services on account. It is the name used in the office of the purchaser to differentiate between its own sales invoices and those of its suppliers.

Two examples of purchase invoices are shown in Figures 6.7 and 6.8.

FIGURE 6.7

A purchase invoice for repairs to a lift truck.

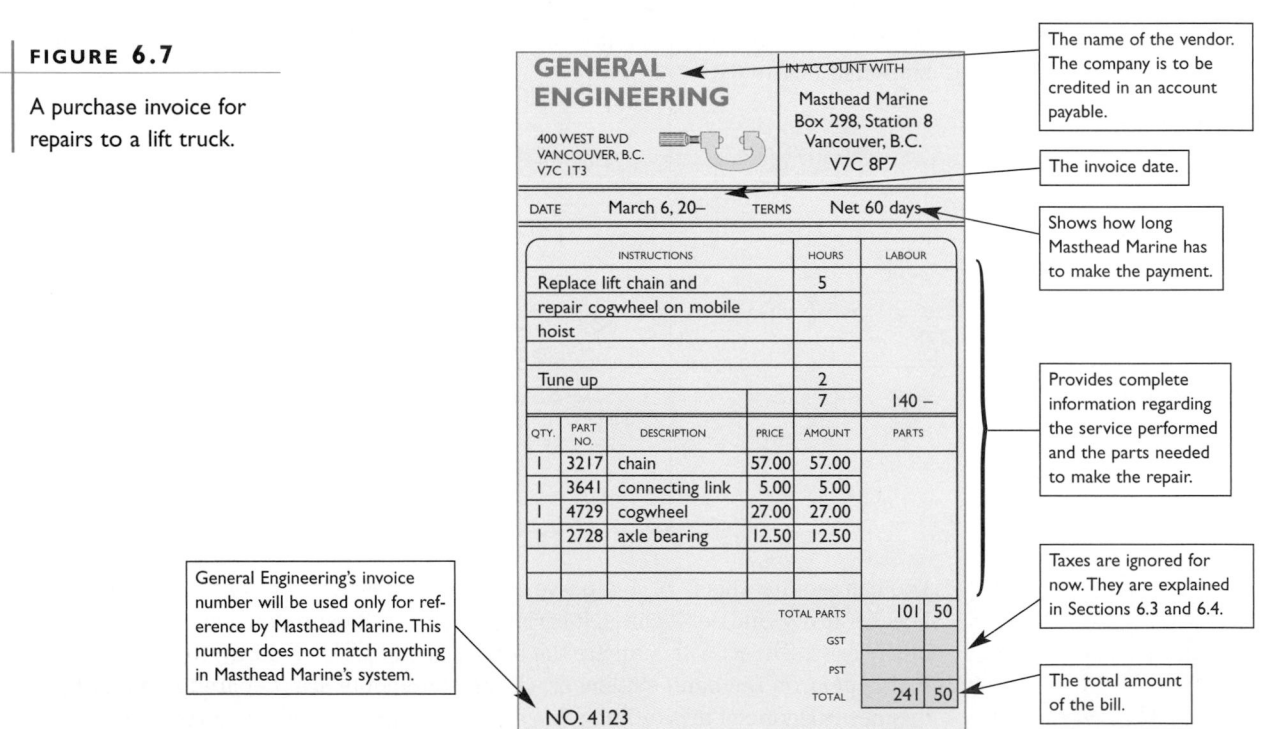

The name of the vendor. The company is to be credited in an account payable.

The invoice date.

Shows how long Masthead Marine has to make the payment.

Provides complete information regarding the service performed and the parts needed to make the repair.

General Engineering's invoice number will be used only for reference by Masthead Marine. This number does not match anything in Masthead Marine's system.

Taxes are ignored for now. They are explained in Sections 6.3 and 6.4.

The total amount of the bill.

FIGURE 6.8

A purchase invoice for advertising posters.

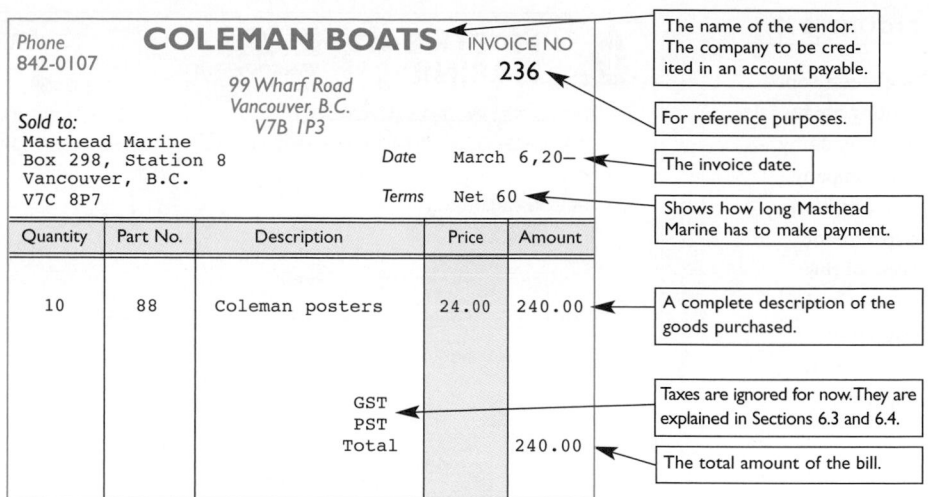

	COLEMAN BOATS	INVOICE NO	
Phone 842-0107		236	The name of the vendor. The company to be credited in an account payable.
	99 Wharf Road Vancouver, B.C. V7B 1P3		For reference purposes.
Sold to: Masthead Marine Box 298, Station 8 Vancouver, B.C. V7C 8P7	Date March 6, 20— Terms Net 60		The invoice date.
			Shows how long Masthead Marine has to make payment.

Quantity	Part No.	Description	Price	Amount	
10	88	Coleman posters	24.00	240.00	A complete description of the goods purchased.
		GST			Taxes are ignored for now. They are explained in Sections 6.3 and 6.4.
		PST			
		Total		240.00	The total amount of the bill.

Journal Entries for Purchase Invoices

Masthead Marine buys a variety of goods and services from numerous suppliers. No single journal entry will do for all of the different items purchased. The account debited will depend on what particular goods or services are purchased. The account credited will always be the same—accounts payable.

The journal entry for the purchase invoice in Figure 6.7 is:

	DR	CR
Equipment Repairs	$241.50	
A/P — General Engineering		$241.50

The journal entry for the purchase invoice in Figure 6.8 is:

	DR	CR
Advertising Expense	$240.00	
A/P — Coleman Boats		$240.00

The above two entries show clearly that:

- the account debited depends on the nature of the goods or services purchased;
- the account credited is always an account payable.

Cheque Copies

It has already been established that payments are normally made by cheque. The cheques themselves are sent out in the mail. A **cheque copy** is a document supporting the accounting entry for a payment by cheque.

Cheques may be issued for any number of reasons: cash purchases, wages, owner's withdrawals, payments on account, and so on. Most cheques are issued to pay for things previously bought on account and supported by purchase invoices on file. The purchase invoices being paid are summarized on the tear-off portion of the cheque. This is shown in Figure 6.9 on page 170.

A payment might be for a cash purchase, that is, a purchase paid for at the time it was made. In such a case, the cheque copy itself is not sufficient proof that the payment is proper. A bill or receipt is also needed to support the accounting entry for a cash purchase.

FIGURE 6.9

A cheque repre-
senting a pay-
ment made by
the company.
The accounting
department
copy of this
cheque is the
source docu-
ment for the
payment.

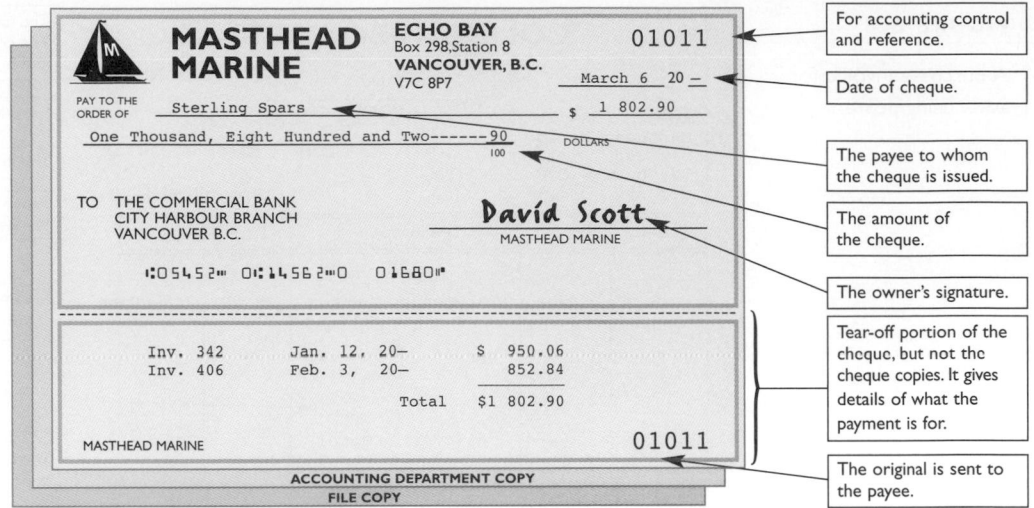

For some payments, no supporting voucher is needed. When the owner with-draws money from the business, the cashed cheque endorsed by the owner is suffi-cient proof of proper payment. For wages, the company's payroll records are the proof of proper payment.

Journal Entry for a Cheque Copy

The accounting department copy is sent to the accounting department where it is used as the source document for the transaction. The debit part of the journal entry depends on the nature of the transaction. The credit part of the journal entry is always to Bank. For this particular cheque copy, the journal entry is:

	DR	CR
A/P — Sterling Spars	$1 802.90	
Bank		$1 802.90

Cash Receipts Daily Summary

Each day in business, some cheques or cash are usually received from customers. These are referred to as the "cash receipts." The cheques themselves cannot be kept to support the accounting entries. The cheques must be deposited in the bank. Therefore, before making the deposit, a list of the cash receipts is prepared by the mail clerk or another employee.

The **cash receipts daily summary** is a business paper that lists the money com-ing in from customers. The cash receipts list is the source document for the accounting entries for cash receipts. This list shows the names of the customers, the dollar amounts, and what the amounts are paying for in each case. To help prepare this form, the clerk uses the information on the tear-off portions of cheques received, or remittance advices sent along with the cheques. A **remittance advice** is a form accompanying the cheque explaining the payment. Sometimes it is no more than a copy of the invoice.

A cash receipts daily summary is shown in Figure 6.10 on page 171.

FIGURE 6.10

A cash receipts daily summary.

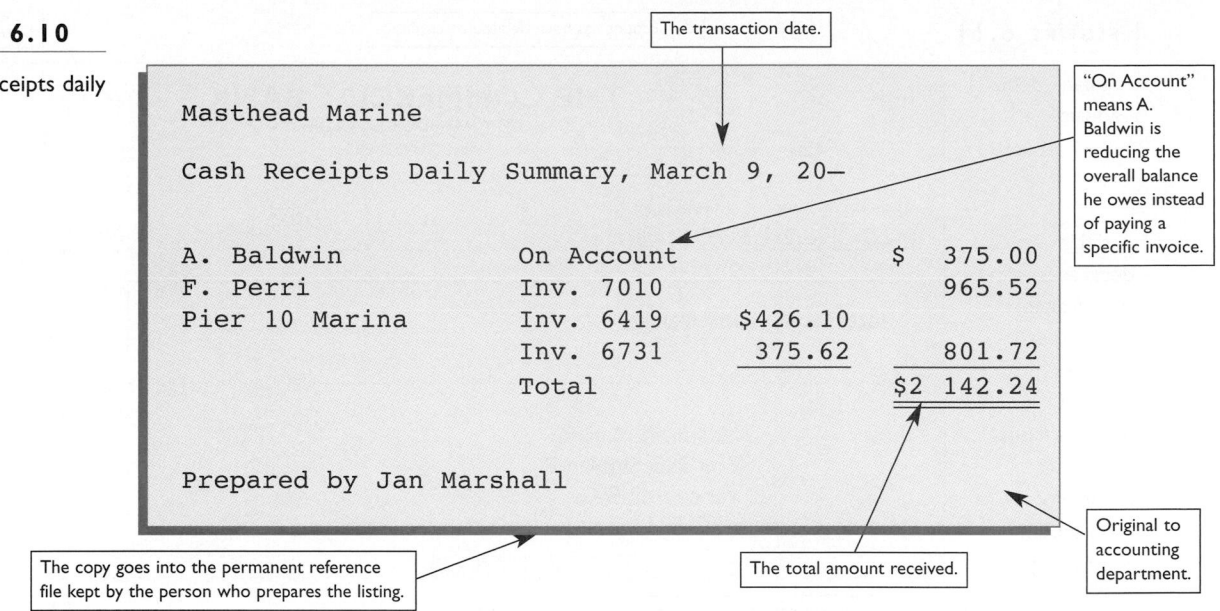

The transaction date.

"On Account" means A. Baldwin is reducing the overall balance he owes instead of paying a specific invoice.

```
Masthead Marine

Cash Receipts Daily Summary, March 9, 20—


A. Baldwin          On Account              $   375.00
F. Perri            Inv. 7010                   965.52
Pier 10 Marina      Inv. 6419     $426.10
                    Inv. 6731      375.62       801.72
                    Total                   $2 142.24



Prepared by Jan Marshall
```

The copy goes into the permanent reference file kept by the person who prepares the listing.

The total amount received.

Original to accounting department.

Journal Entry for a Cash Receipts Daily Summary

The original list goes to the accounting department as the source document for the accounting entry. For the cash receipts list above, the journal entry is:

	DR	CR
Bank	$2 142.24	
A/R — A. Baldwin		$375.00
A/R — F. Perri		$965.52
A/R — Pier 10 Marina		$801.72

Bank Advices

There are times when the bank itself initiates a change in the bank account of a business. The bank informs the business of such a transaction by means of a bank advice or bank memo. A **bank debit advice** is a bank document informing the business of a decrease made in the business's bank account. A **bank credit advice** is a bank document informing the business of an increase made in the business's bank account.

In Figure 6.11 on page 172, the Commercial Bank has sent a bank debit advice to Masthead Marine, telling them that their account was charged interest on a bank loan.

Journal Entry for a Bank Advice

The bank advice goes to the accounting department as the source document for the journal entry. In this case, the journal entry is:

	DR	CR
Bank Charges and Interest	$113.50	
Bank		$113.50

If the form had been a credit advice, the Bank account would have been debited and an appropriate account credited.

FIGURE 6.11

A bank debit advice.

A debit decreases the balance of Masthead Marine's account because from the bank's point of view, the account is a liability.

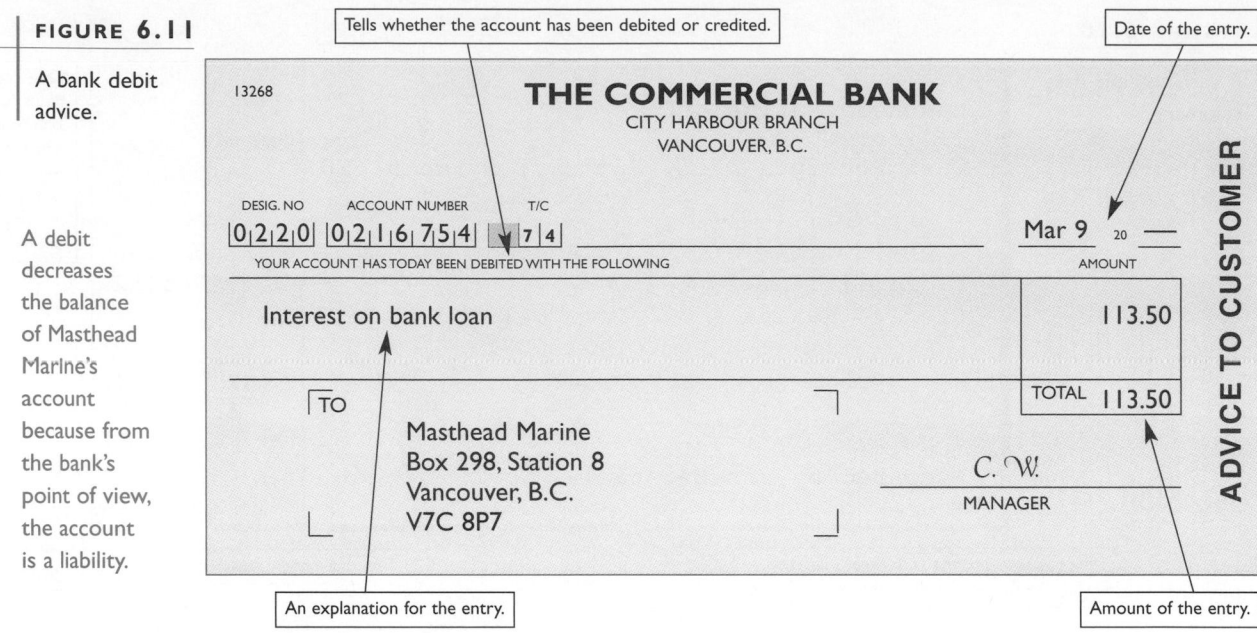

Tells whether the account has been debited or credited.

Date of the entry.

13268

THE COMMERCIAL BANK
CITY HARBOUR BRANCH
VANCOUVER, B.C.

DESIG. NO   ACCOUNT NUMBER   T/C
|0|2|2|0| |0|2|6|7|5|4| |7|4|

Mar 9 20 —

YOUR ACCOUNT HAS TODAY BEEN DEBITED WITH THE FOLLOWING

AMOUNT

Interest on bank loan

113.50

TO

Masthead Marine
Box 298, Station 8
Vancouver, B.C.
V7C 8P7

TOTAL 113.50

C. W.
MANAGER

ADVICE TO CUSTOMER

An explanation for the entry.

Amount of the entry.

Summary of Source Documents and Related Journal Entries

Source Document	Transaction Description	Journal Entries	
		Account(s) Debited	Account(s) Credited
Cash sales slip; POS Summaries	A sale of goods or services for cash	Bank	Sales or Revenue
Sales invoice	A sale of goods or services on account	Accounts Receivable	Sales or Revenue
Purchase invoice	A purchase of goods or services on account	1. An expense account such as Advertising 2. An asset account such as Supplies or Equipment	Accounts Payable
Cheque copy	1. Paying an account payable 2. Cash purchase of an asset * 3. Cash payment for an expense * 4. Owner draws out money for personal use	1. A liability account such as Accounts Payable 2. An asset account such as Automobiles 3. An expense account such as Car Expense 4. The Drawings account	Bank
Cash receipts daily summary	The cheques received from customers on account	Bank	Accounts Receivable
Bank debit advice	Bank account decrease	Interest Expense or other account	Bank
Bank credit advice	Bank account increase	Bank	Interest Earned or other account

* Must be accompanied by a bill or receipt.

Additional Supporting Documents

In addition to the source documents listed above, you may encounter the following:

- receipts, such as those for donations or postage;
- bills, such as hydro or telephone charges;
- e-mail invoices
- insurance endorsement certificates;
- written memos from the owner;
- bank statements;
- cash register tapes.

Number of Copies of Source Documents

There is no fixed number of required copies of business documents. Each business develops its own system to suit its own needs and preferences. Some owners and managers prefer a simple system, others a more elaborate one. The number of copies of any particular business document depends primarily on how elaborate the system is. Generally, the more elaborate the system, the greater the number of copies required to satisfy it.

GAAP—The Cost Principle

> The **cost principle** states that the accounting for purchases must be at the cost price to the purchaser.

In almost all cases, this is the figure that appears on the source document for the transaction. There is no place for guesswork or wishful thinking when accounting for purchases.

The value recorded in the accounts for an asset is not changed later if the market value for the asset changes. It would take an entirely new transaction based on new objective evidence to change the original value of an asset.

There are times when the objective evidence provided by a source document is not available. In those instances, the transaction is recorded at fair market value, which must be determined by independent means.

Section 6.2   Review Questions

1. Not all transactions requiring journal entries are initiated by the accounting staff. Explain.
2. How does the accounting department find out about all transactions?
3. What is a source document?
4. What is the principal use of source documents in the accounting department?
5. Give an example of a transaction for which there is no conventional source document.
6. Who else, besides the accounting department, may have reason to use the source documents on file?
7. What is the purpose of a cash sales slip?
8. Why is the cash sales slip regarded as less formal than the sales invoice?

9. Explain the essential difference between a sales invoice and a cash sales slip.
10. Explain who the "vendor" is.
11. What is a point of sale terminal?
12. When a customer uses a credit card to purchase an item, the business debits Accounts Receivable. True or False? Explain your answer.
13. What is a purchase invoice?
14. Explain why all journal entries for purchase invoices are not the same.
15. Why is a cheque not used as a source document?
16. What is the most common type of transaction for which a cheque is issued?
17. What supporting documents are needed for a cash purchase?
18. What is the supporting evidence for a payroll cheque?
19. Explain what cash receipts are.
20. Why is it necessary to prepare a cash receipts listing?
21. From what two sources does the clerk obtain the data to prepare the cash receipts listing?
22. Why do banks issue bank advices?
23. A bank debit memo requires a credit entry in the bank account of the business. Explain.
24. State the cost principle.
25. Why is an invoice regarded as an ideal source document?

Section 6.2   Exercises

1. **Answer the following questions related to the source document below**.

   a. What business document is it?
   b. What is the purpose of the document?
   c. Where does the information come from to prepare the list?
   d. Why is a list prepared?
   e. In the list, what does "on account" mean, compared to "Invoice 4502"?
   f. Give the journal entry that would be made as a result of the list.
   g. Who is G. Smalley?

SAYERS AND ASSOCIATES
CASH RECEIPTS DAILY SUMMARY
MARCH 14, 20—

Degagne Machine Shop	on account	$ 500.00
Kivella Bake Shop	Inv. 4502	315.43
Molner Paints	Inv. 3909	214.60
Robitaille Taxi	on account	200.00
G. Smalley	Total	$1 230.03

2. **Answer the following questions related to the source document below.**

   a. What business document is it?

   b. What is the purpose of the document?

   c. Who issued the document?

   d. Explain the purposes of the document number.

   e. Give the journal entry that would be made by the issuer of the document.

DAVIDSON TREE EXPERTS

Horseshoe Valley
Ontario, L4M 4Y8

Phone 321-8765
Fax 321-8862

Date   March 10   20–

NAME   F. Vailliant

ADDRESS   RR 1, Craighurst, ON L4M 4A7

QUANTITY	DESCRIPTION	PRICE	AMOUNT	
6	pruning of			
	mature trees,			
	removing dead			
	wood	30	180	–
2	cut down and			
	remove mature			
	trees	75	150	–
		GST		
		PST		
RECEIVED ABOVE IN GOOD ORDER		TOTAL	330	–
F. Vailliant				

CASH SALES SLIP   2651

3. Answer the following questions related to the source document below.

  a. What business document is it?
  b. Who is the sender of the document? Who is the receiver?
  c. To which business is this document the equivalent of a sales invoice? To which business is it a purchase invoice?
  d. Give the journal entry that would be made by the sender of the document.
  e. Give the journal entry that would be made by the receiver of the document.

Knutsen and Trebley is a legal firm.

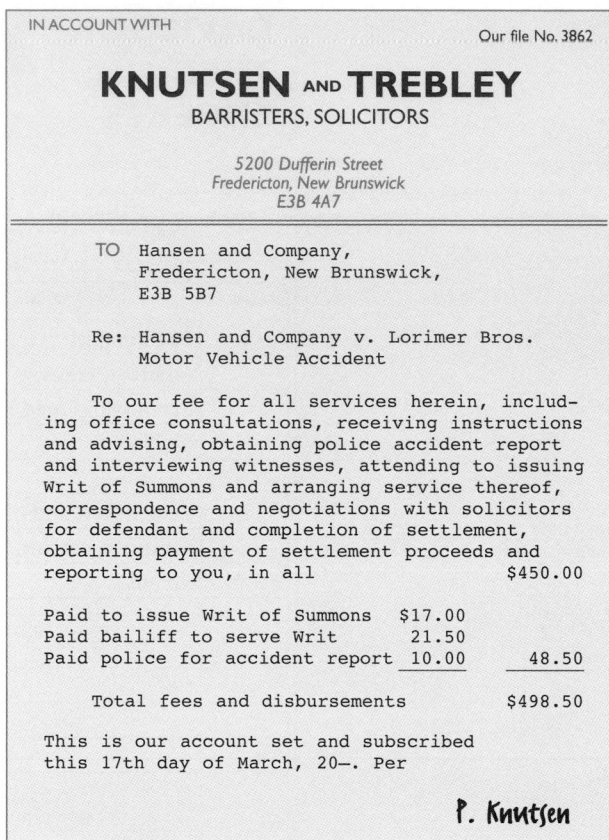

```
IN ACCOUNT WITH                                    Our file No. 3862


             KNUTSEN AND TREBLEY
                   BARRISTERS, SOLICITORS

                    5200 Dufferin Street
                  Fredericton, New Brunswick
                        E3B 4A7


     TO   Hansen and Company,
          Fredericton, New Brunswick,
          E3B 5B7

     Re: Hansen and Company v. Lorimer Bros.
         Motor Vehicle Accident

         To our fee for all services herein, includ-
     ing office consultations, receiving instructions
     and advising, obtaining police accident report
     and interviewing witnesses, attending to issuing
     Writ of Summons and arranging service thereof,
     correspondence and negotiations with solicitors
     for defendant and completion of settlement,
     obtaining payment of settlement proceeds and
     reporting to you, in all                 $450.00

     Paid to issue Writ of Summons   $17.00
     Paid bailiff to serve Writ       21.50
     Paid police for accident report  10.00      48.50

         Total fees and disbursements        $498.50

     This is our account set and subscribed
     this 17th day of March, 20—. Per

                                     P. Knutsen
```

4. The document on page 177 arrives at your place of business by mail. **Answer the following questions concerning it**.

  a. What business document is it?
  b. Whom do you work for?
  c. Why was this document sent to your company?
  d. What does the broken line on the document represent?
  e. Explain the information beneath the broken line.
  f. Give the journal entry that would be made in the books of your company to record the source document.
  g. What happens to the upper part of this document?

CARBIDE TOOLS LIMITED   4000 Essex Drive
Vancouver, B.C.
V7R 8S8   **No.1101**

May 10   20 —

PAY TO THE
ORDER OF   Presto-Can Company $ 1 368.30

One Thousand, Three Hundred and Sixty-Eight------------- $\frac{30}{100}$ **DOLLARS**

THE COMMERCIAL BANK
CITY HARBOUR BRANCH
VANCOUVER, B.C.

Marianne Mayo

CARBIDE TOOLS LIMITED

⑈030800 3⑈04⑈   004⑈⑈030800 3⑈

IN PAYMENT OF THE FOLLOWING

Invoice	Date	Amount
#6149	April 16	$ 217.02
#7002	April 30	400.12
#7109	May 7	751.16
	Total	$1 368.30

CARBIDE TOOLS LIMITED   1101

---

5. Answer the following questions related to the source document below.

    a. What business document is it?

    b. In whose books of account is a journal entry now necessary as a result of this source document?

    c. Give the journal entry that would be made as a result of the source document.

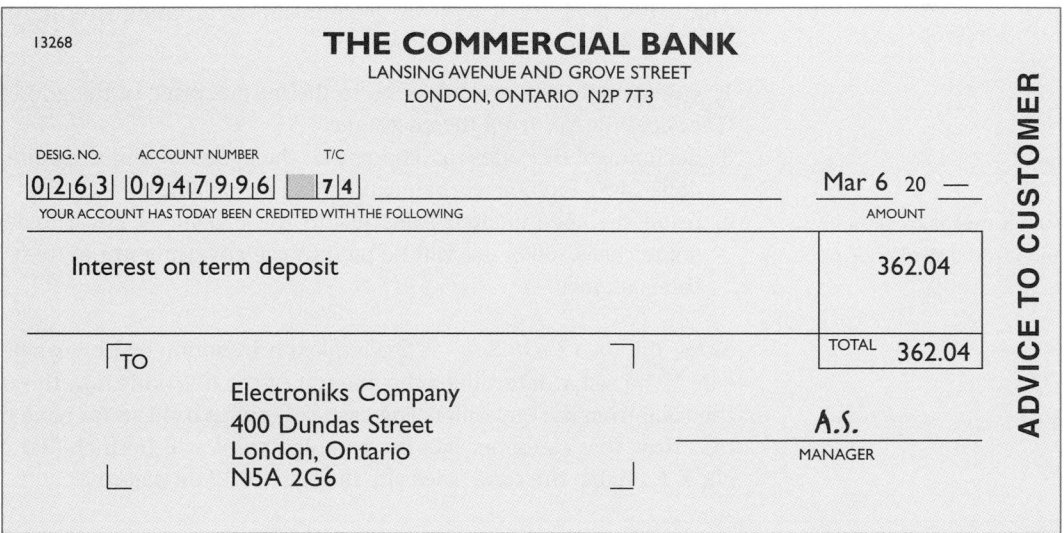

13268

THE COMMERCIAL BANK
LANSING AVENUE AND GROVE STREET
LONDON, ONTARIO N2P 7T3

DESIG. NO.   ACCOUNT NUMBER   T/C

|0|2|6|3| |0|9|4|7|9|6| |▧|7|4| Mar 6 20 —

YOUR ACCOUNT HAS TODAY BEEN CREDITED WITH THE FOLLOWING   AMOUNT

Interest on term deposit   362.04

TO   TOTAL   362.04

Electroniks Company
400 Dundas Street   *A.S.*
London, Ontario   MANAGER
N5A 2G6

ADVICE TO CUSTOMER

6.3 | Provincial Sales Tax

Sales tax is one way that provincial governments raise funds. There is a lot of detailed regulation associated with sales tax: which items are taxed, which items are not, what forms are necessary, and so on. Further, the rules can change whenever a provincial government passes new laws. A business involved in the selling of goods or services needs someone in the office to be familiar with sales tax regulations. Forms, regulations, and assistance may be obtained from government offices and on the Internet.

This text will not deal with sales tax in a detailed way. Sales tax will be explained in simple terms only, to provide a view of the basic concepts and procedures.

Retail Sales Tax

The current rate of provincial sales tax in Ontario is 8 per cent. That is the rate that will generally be used for calculations in this text.

A retail sales tax is charged by most provincial governments. A **retail sales tax** is a percentage tax based on the price of goods sold to a customer. The tax is added to the price and paid by the customer. The rates of tax are established by the provincial governments and vary from province to province and from time to time. The current practice in Canada is to tax the final consumer only. A sale from a wholesaler to a retailer is not normally subject to provincial sales tax. For the purposes of this discussion, the provincial retail sales tax will simply be called the "sales tax."

Accounting for Provincial Sales Tax

The Purchaser

The purchaser of goods does no accounting for provincial retail sales tax. The purchaser simply accounts for the transaction at the final figure on the sales slip or invoice. This final figure includes the sales tax and is part of the cost of goods or services.

The Seller

The seller is charged with the responsibility of administering the sales tax. The seller is obliged to do the following:

1. calculate the tax and add it on to the normal price of the goods;
2. collect the tax from the customer;
3. accumulate the sales tax charged to the customers in a special liability account, called PST Payable (Provincial Sales Tax Payable);
4. remit the accumulated sales tax to the provincial government periodically. In some cases, sales tax will be paid to the government before it is collected from the customer.

Remit means to send in money to a person or place.

Sales Tax on a Cash Sale   The simplest transaction involving sales tax is the "cash sale." The seller determines the amount of the tax, adds it to the price, and collects the total from the customer. The cash sales slips used so far have not included sales tax. Now that sales tax has been explained, it will be included on the cash sales slips. Examine the cash sales slip in Figure 6.12 on page 179.

FIGURE 6.12

A cash sales slip on which a sales tax has been added.

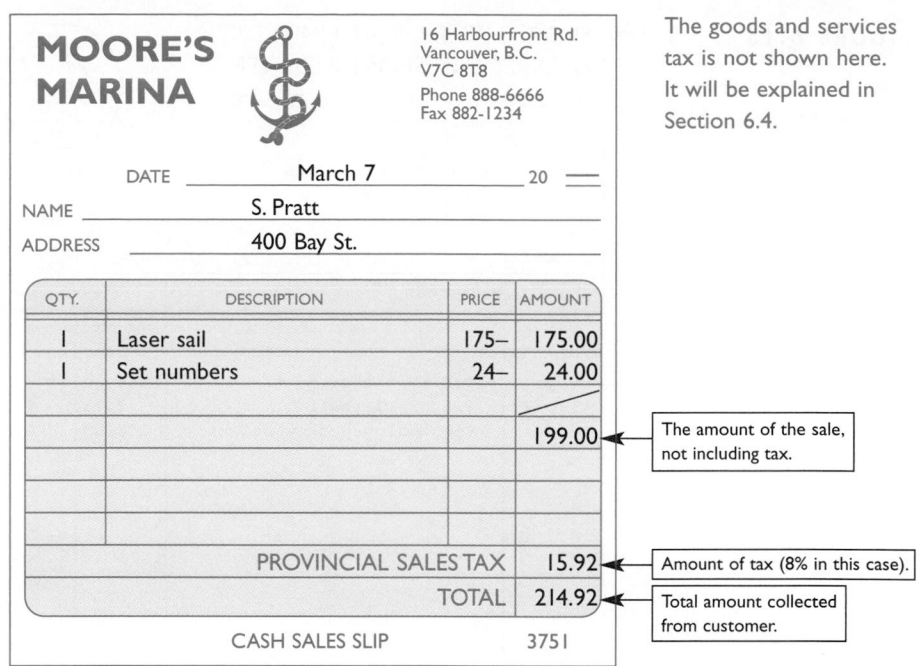

The goods and services tax is not shown here. It will be explained in Section 6.4.

MOORE'S MARINA

16 Harbourfront Rd.
Vancouver, B.C.
V7C 8T8
Phone 888-6666
Fax 882-1234

DATE _____ March 7 _____ 20 ___

NAME _____ S. Pratt _____

ADDRESS _____ 400 Bay St. _____

QTY.	DESCRIPTION	PRICE	AMOUNT
1	Laser sail	175–	175.00
1	Set numbers	24–	24.00
			199.00
	PROVINCIAL SALES TAX		15.92
	TOTAL		214.92

CASH SALES SLIP   3751

The amount of the sale, not including tax.

Amount of tax (8% in this case).

Total amount collected from customer.

Keep in mind that businesses do not immediately forward the tax they collect from customers every day. Sales tax must be remitted to the government periodically, and therefore represents a liability payable to the government. Businesses accumulate the tax they collect in the *PST Payable* account. For the sales slip in Figure 6.12 above, the journal entry is:

	DR	CR
Bank	$214.92	
Sales		$199.00
PST Payable		$15.92

Sales Tax on a Charge Sale   Sales tax is also added to a sale on account represented by a sales invoice. In Figure 6.13 on page 180, a sales invoice is shown that includes an 8 per cent sales tax. With a charge sale, the seller does not collect the tax at the time of the sale, but must wait until the customer pays his or her account. This is usually within 30 days.

The journal entry for the sales invoice in Figure 6.13 is:

	DR	CR
A/R — Marathon Recreation	$347.49	
Sales		$321.75
PST Payable		$25.74

FIGURE 6.13

Sales invoice on which a sales tax has been added.

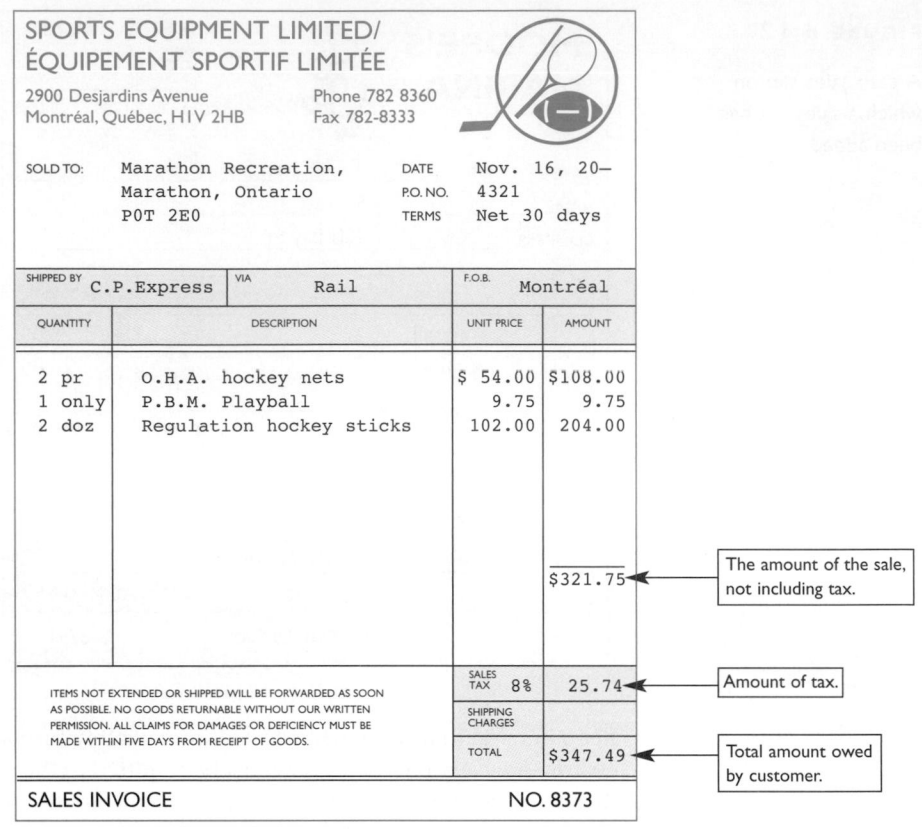

Remitting Sales Tax

Sales tax is collected for a month and is then remitted to the government. In most regions, the sales tax collected in any one month is to be remitted to the government by the 15th of the following month. Taxes collected in January are to be remitted by the 15th of February, and so on. From time to time, government auditors pay visits to businesses to check the accuracy of records, collections, and payments.

Assume that a total of $415.23 was recorded in the PST Payable account in the month of January. The T-account would appear as follows:

PST Payable	
	Jan. 415.23

The account represents a liability owed by the business to the government. When the balance is paid, the journal entry to record the payment is:

		DR	CR
Feb. 15	PST Payable	$415.23	
	Bank		$415.23

The payment will clear the January balance. In the meantime, the sales tax items for February will be gathering in the account.

Section 6.3   Review Questions

1. Why do governments apply sales taxes?
2. Where does one go to find out about sales tax rules and regulations?
3. What special accounting for sales tax is done by the purchaser of goods that have a tax added?
4. What four things is the seller of goods and services required to do regarding sales tax?
5. A cash sale of $100 is made. A sales tax of 7 per cent is applied. How much does the customer pay?
6. What kind of account is PST Payable?
7. Explain when sales tax is to be remitted to the government.
8. Explain how a business may be required to pay sales tax to the government before it has been collected from the customer.

Section 6.3   Exercises

1. A. A schedule for this exercise is provided in the Workbook. For each transaction given below, calculate the PST (at 8 percent) and calculate the total amount of the bill.

   B. Give the journal entry for each transaction in the books of the vendor.

   ### TRANSACTIONS

   a. A cash sale of goods at a price of $75.00.
   b. A cash sale of goods at a price of $120.00.
   c. A credit sale of goods at a price of $58.60.
   d. A credit sale of goods at a price of $98.00.
   e. A credit sale of goods at a price of $130.75.

2. The invoice below was issued by Masthead Marine.

   A. **Give the journal entry to be made in the books of the vendor.**

   B. **Give the journal entry to be made in the books of the purchaser, if the account to be debited is J. McCuaig, Drawings.**

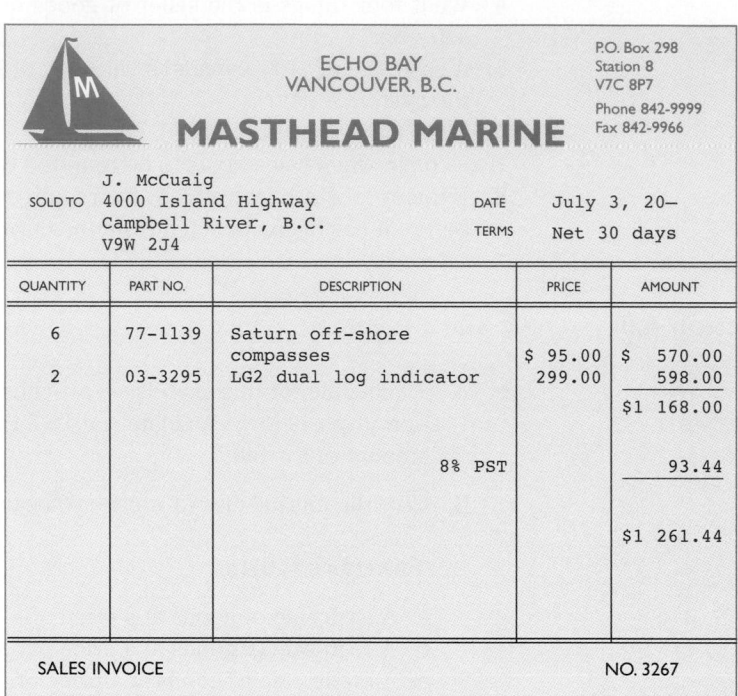

3. Jack Pritchard paid $330.96, including an 8 per cent sales tax, for some furniture.

   A. **Calculate the price of the goods before the sales tax is added.**

   B. **Calculate the sales tax on the goods.**

If a source document lists only a total price on a taxed item, use this formula to determine the tax to remit:

$$P \times 1.08 = \text{Total}$$

Therefore

$$P = \frac{\text{Total}}{1.08}$$

where P is the price and the tax rate is 8 per cent.

4. Examine the account information below and answer the questions that follow. (*Note: This is a formal account. The T-account is contained within it.*)

The BALANCE column at the far right shows the changes to the account as a result of each accounting entry. You will see more of these formal **balance column accounts** in Chapter 7.

ACCOUNT		Sales Tax Payable					No.	240	
20— DATE		PARTICULARS	P.R.	DEBIT	CREDIT	D/C	BALANCE		
Feb.	1	Forwarded account balance				Cr	4 7 6 30	
	15			4 7 6 30			Ø	
	28	Cash sales			2 4 2 95		2 4 2 95	
	28	Charge sales			3 1 6 20	Cr	5 5 9 15	
Mar.	15			5 5 9 15			Ø	
	31	Cash sales			2 5 1 86		2 5 1 86	
	31	Charge sales			3 0 1 19	Cr	5 5 3 05	

A. How much sales tax was accumulated in January?
B. How much sales tax was accumulated in February?
C. What does the account balance represent?
D. How much sales tax was accumulated in March?
E. When will the sales tax accumulated in March be paid?
F. Give the journal entry that will be made for the transaction of April 15.

---

5. On February 28, 20—, Moore's Marina sold the goods shown below to Valerie Miniaci of Bear Island, Alberta. The sale was a cash sale.

| 2 | Grumman canoes | @ | $1 950.00 each |
| 4 | Paddles | @ | $215.00 a pair |

A. **In your Workbook, write up the above sale on a cash sales slip. Sales tax at 8 per cent is to be added.**

B. **Give the journal entry in the vendor's books.**

6.4 | The Goods and Services Tax

GST is a tax applied by the Government of Canada.

The goods and services tax, usually called the GST, was put into effect by the federal government on January 1, 1991, replacing the federal sales tax. The **goods and services tax** is a tax on the sale of most goods and services. The seller of the goods or services is the one responsible for charging, collecting, and remitting the tax.

The GST is not a simple tax. There are many provisions and exceptions. No attempt is made in this text to present the GST fully. Only the basic rules are covered. Each business should have someone who understands the GST as it relates to that business.

Who Is Required To Register?

Any business with sales of taxable goods and services of more than $30 000 per year is required to complete a registration form and send it to Canada Customs and Revenue Agency (CCRA). Each registrant is assigned a special business number, such as 10 262 0110 RT000 1, for example, and is advised whether to report and remit the GST monthly, quarterly, or annually. The frequency of reporting depends on the value of annual sales or revenue. Only small businesses are permitted to report annually.

The GST — Two Aspects

Sales and the GST

The GST functions much like a provincial sales tax. The tax is added to the customer's invoice, collected from the customer, and remitted to the government. But the GST is a broader tax than the PST. With certain exceptions, it covers the sale of all goods, not just those sold by retailers to consumers. And it covers services as well.

Purchases and the GST

You should be aware of another important aspect of the GST. All businesses are entitled to recover the GST that they are charged by their suppliers. They are required to pay the tax to their suppliers, but are entitled to recover this tax from the government.

These two aspects of the GST require considerable recordkeeping by each business. By law, the tax payable (as a result of the company's sales) has to be accumulated. The tax recoverable (as a result of the company's purchases) has to be accumulated as well, both to comply with the law and in order to be reclaimed. You will now see how to account for both of these aspects of GST.

Accounting for the GST

The Accounts for GST

There are two accounts for GST in the ledger — GST Recoverable and GST Payable. These two accounts are shown in T-accounts below.

Both GST accounts appear in the Liabilities section of the ledger.

GST Recoverable No. 225		GST Payable No. 220	
$			$
$			$
$			$

A minus (or contra) liability account used to accumulate the GST **paid by** the business for the reporting period. It is deducted from the amount of the liability—GST Payable.

A liability account used to accumulate the GST amounts **charged to** customers during the reporting period.

The business remits the difference between these two account balances. If the GST Recoverable is greater than the GST Payable, the business will claim a refund.

In the Books of the Seller

The first step in accounting for GST is to calculate the tax on taxable goods or services sold and to add the tax to the sales invoice. You can see how this is done by examining the sales invoice of Custodial Services, shown below in Figure 6.14.

FIGURE 6.14

The sales invoice of Custodial Services showing the GST and the PST.

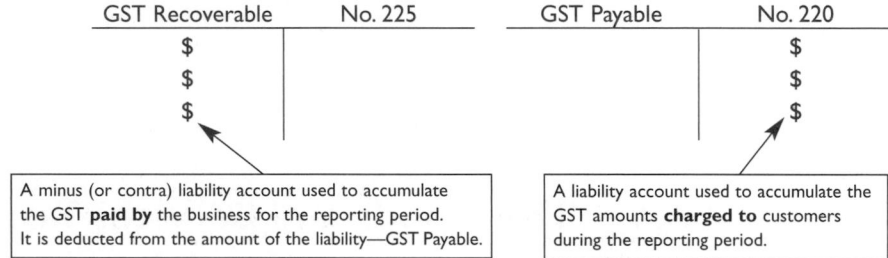

CUSTODIAL SERVICES

900 Lansdowne Avenue
Toronto, Ontario
M6K 2V7

INVOICE
NUMBER
941

Phone 416-767-8569   Fax 416-767-8533

GST No. 102620110	Terms Net 30	Date March 20, 20—

TO   M & R Publishing
      1900 Weston Road
      Toronto, Ontario
      M9N 1L4

FOR   Cleaning and maintenance
      service for month of February $1 500.00

GST 7%	$105.00
PST 8%	$120.00
TOTAL	$1 725.00

In Figure 6.14 above, observe that the company's GST number is entered on the invoice. This is a legal requirement. Note also that the goods and services tax (GST) and the provincial sales tax (PST) are shown separately and that the rates are 7 per cent and 8 per cent, respectively. Each of these taxes is calculated separately on the base amount of the invoice (in this case, $1 500).

The sales invoice is the source document for the accounting entries in the books of the seller. The invoice shown in Figure 6.14 is recorded in the books of Custodial Services as shown below:

		GENERAL JOURNAL			PAGE 16
DATE		PARTICULARS	P.R.	DEBIT	CREDIT
20-					
Mar.	20	A/R – M & R Publishing		1 7 2 5 00	
		Sales			1 5 0 0 00
		GST Payable			1 0 5 00
		PST Payable			1 2 0 00
		Sales Invoice #941			

In the T-accounts, the transaction appears as follows:

A/R–M&R Publishing	Sales	GST Payable	PST Payable
1 725	1 500	105	120

All sales of taxable goods and services are recorded in this way. Thus, the GST owed to the government is accumulated during the reporting period.

GST and PST are two separate taxes, payable to two different governments. They must be kept separate in the accounts. You are already familiar from Section 6.3 with the way PST is charged and remitted.

In the Books of the Purchaser

Custodial Services is not just a seller of goods. It also has to buy its goods and other items from wholesalers and manufacturers. So, in many of its transactions, Custodial Services is the purchasing company, receiving the sales invoices of other companies. As you know, in the hands of the purchaser, these are purchase invoices. A purchase invoice that Custodial Services received from one its suppliers, The Supply House, is shown in Figure 6.15.

FIGURE 6.15

A purchase invoice received by Custodial Services.

THE SUPPLY HOUSE

Box 2000
Sarnia, Ontario
N7S 5R6

INVOICE NUMBER
257

Phone 234-5678   Fax 234-5686

GST No. 113956554	Terms Net 60	Date March 24, 20—

TO   Custodial Services
       900 Lansdowne Avenue
       Toronto, Ontario
       M6K 2V7

FOR   20 pkgs Computer printing
       paper @ $30 each $600.00

       PST   48.00

                                            $648.00

GST 7%	$42.00
TOTAL	$690.00

Custodial Services is not entitled to recover the PST, so it becomes part of the total cost. It is, however, entitled to recover the GST.

In order to recover the GST added by the seller to the invoice shown in Figure 6.15 on page 185, the purchaser must account for it. The purchase invoice is the source document for the accounting entry. In the books of Custodial Services, the purchaser, it is recorded as shown below:

Custodial Services is entitled to recover the GST, so it keeps track of amounts paid in a separate account.

	GENERAL JOURNAL			PAGE 16	
DATE	PARTICULARS	P.R.	DEBIT	CREDIT	
20- Mar. 26	Office Supplies		6 4 8 00		
	GST Recoverable		4 2 00		
	A/P — The Supply House			6 9 0 00	
	Purchase Invoice #257				

In the T-accounts, the transaction appears as follows:

Office Supplies	GST Recoverable	A/P – The Supply House
648	42	690

All purchases involving GST are similarly recorded, which is the first step by the business to recover the GST it pays.

Remitting the GST

Most businesses are required to file monthly or quarterly and must remit the net tax owed within one month following the end of their reporting period. The remittance is accompanied by a tax return form — the *Goods and Services Harmonized Sales Tax (GST/HST) Return for Registrants*. The mail-in portion of this form is illustrated below in Figure 6.16.

FIGURE 6.16

The mail-in portion of the GST/HST Return for Registrants.

The remittance calculation is summarized on lines 105, 108, and 109. The government calls GST Recoverable "Input Tax Credits" (ITCs on line 108).

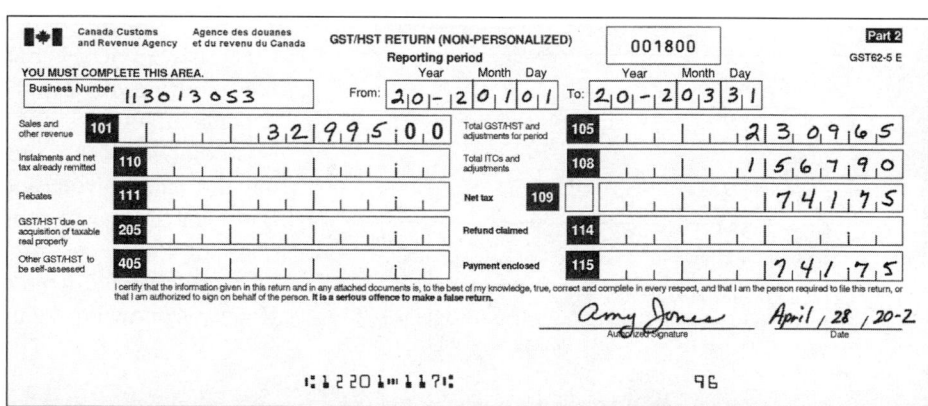

The figures entered on the form in Figure 6.16 are taken from the March 31 balances in the two T-accounts shown below:

GST Recoverable	GST Payable
1 567.90	2 309.65

Custodial Services will mail the form shown in Figure 6.16 along with a cheque for $741.75. Alternatively, it can take advantage of the electronic filing and remitting system established by the Canada Customs and Revenue Agency.

The journal entry to record the GST remittance for Custodial Services for the taxes for the month of March is as follows:

GENERAL JOURNAL   PAGE 16

DATE		PARTICULARS	P.R.	DEBIT	CREDIT
20— Apr.	28	GST Payable		2 3 0 9 65	
		GST Recoverable			1 5 6 7 90
		Bank			7 4 1 75

This journal entry has the effect of clearing out the balances in the two GST accounts for the reporting period and recording the payment of cash.

The Canada Customs and Revenue Agency (CCRA), charges interest and a penalty if the GST is not paid by the due date. Similarly, if a refund is claimed and not paid within 21 days after the tax return was filed, CCRA pays interest to the business.

GST on the Balance Sheet

The presentation of GST on the balance sheet is similar to what is reported to CCRA on the GST/HST Return For Registrants (see Figure 6.16). The smaller account balance is subtracted from the larger. If the difference is a credit, it is shown in the Liabilities section. If the difference is a debit, it may be shown in the Assets section. However, most computer-generated balance sheets will simply show a debit balance as a negative number in the Liabilities section. Figure 6.17 below shows you how it will usually appear.

FIGURE 6.17

The Liabilities section of a balance sheet, showing how to present GST.

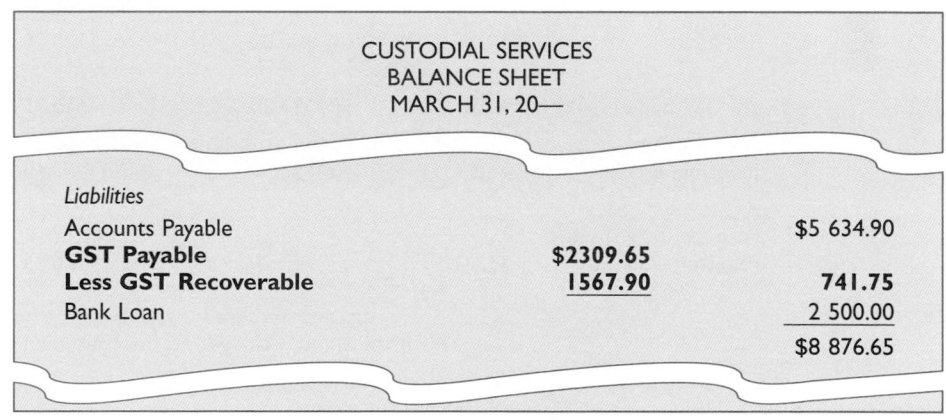

CUSTODIAL SERVICES
BALANCE SHEET
MARCH 31, 20—

Liabilities		
Accounts Payable		$5 634.90
GST Payable	$2309.65	
Less GST Recoverable	1567.90	
		741.75
Bank Loan		2 500.00
		$8 876.65

Other GST Facts

The following are extracts from the government booklet entitled *General Information for GST/HST Registrants*, which may be obtained from government offices or CCRA's website (www.ccra-adrc.gc.ca).

* The 7 per cent rate will be charged on almost all goods and services.

* A limited number of goods and services will be zero-rated under the GST. Even though no tax is charged on zero-rated goods and services, an input tax credit may be claimed on business purchases used to provide these goods and services. Examples of zero-rated goods and services are: basic groceries; agriculture and most fishery products; prescription drugs and dispensing fees; medical devices; exports.

* Certain goods and services have been designated as exempt and are not subject to the GST. The following is a list of some goods and services that are GST-exempt: previously owned or resale residential housing; long-term residential rents; most health, medical, and dental services. . .; educational services. . .; and most services provided by financial institutions.

* The **Quick Method** is available to most small businesses with annual sales and revenues of up to $200 000. This method simplifies remittance calculations by applying a certain percentage to overall sales. (The Quick Method is not used for transactions in this text.) In order to use this method, you must file an election with Canada Customs and Revenue Agency.

GST — A Value-Added Tax

The GST is known as a value-added tax. It is designed so that:

1. The government receives its money at each stage in the production/distribution chain, as value is added to the product.
2. Ultimately, only the final user pays for it.

You can see how a value-added tax works by studying the following chart. The example follows the process of converting a log into a chair and selling it to the final consumer.

	Logger sells to sawmill	Sawmill sells to chairmaker	Chairmaker sells to department store	Department store sells to consumer
Sale price	$50.00	$80.00	$225.00	$400.00
The sale 7% GST added	(a) $3.50	(a) $5.60	(a) $15.75	(a) $28.00
The purchase Input tax credit	(b) $0	(b) $3.50	(b) $5.60	(b) $15.75
Net tax remitted At each stage the tax remitted is (a − b)	$3.50	$2.10	$10.15	$12.25

Total tax remitted = $28.00
This is the amount charged to the consumer.

Variations in Taxation

As noted earlier, sales tax systems can be complex and subject to change. From studying Sections 6.3 and 6.4. you should be aware that retail sales taxes are paid to provincial governments. while the GST is paid to the federal government. In 1997, three provinces—New Brunswick, Nova Scotia, and Newfoundland—agreed to work together with the federal government to collect sales taxes. In these provinces, one tax is applied and is called the **Harmonized Sales Tax** (HST). The **HST** is a sales tax shared by the federal and provincial governments. It is charged to the same base of goods and services as the GST and has the same basic operating rules. The rate of 15% is the main difference. Of the percentage, 7% goes to the federal government and 8% to the province.

Other variations in sales taxes exist. For example, Alberta and the Territories have no retail sales taxes. In Quebec and Prince Edward Island, the PST is charged after the GST is added to the base amount. To understand the effect on the total tax charged, let's look at a $100 sale in Ontario. Presently, the GST is $7 ($100 × 7%) and the PST is $8 ($100 × 8%). If the regulations in Ontario were changed so that the PST is calculated after GST is added, the GST would still be $7 ($100 × 7%), but now the PST would increase to $8.56 ($107 × 8%).

The rates of various sales taxes at the time of printing are listed in the table below:

	PST	GST	HST
Alberta	0%	7%	–
British Columbia	7%	7%	–
Manitoba	7%	7%	–
New Brunswick	–	–	15%
Newfoundland and Labrador	–	–	15%
Northwest Territories	0%	7%	–
Nova Scotia	–	–	15%
Nunavut	0%	7%	–
Ontario	8%	7%	–
Prince Edward Island	10%	7%	–
Quebec	7.5%	7%	–
Saskatchewan	6%	7%	–
Yukon	0%	7%	–

Besides the different rates, a wide range of exemptions and rebates exist in the provinces. However, at this stage of your accounting studies, you should not be overwhelmed at the number of rules and the speed at which they change. Keep in mind the following points, which are constant:

1. Businesses collect money for governments. Since the money collected and deposited does not belong to the businesses, the funds are recorded in liability accounts (PST Payable, GST Payable, HST Payable, etc.). At some point, the businesses clear the liabilities by remitting the amounts owed to the governments.

2. Accountants specialize in understanding, explaining, and applying complex tax regulations. Being skilled in the area of taxation is another one of the reasons why accountants are so important to successful businesses.

Section 6.4 — Review Questions

1. Who is responsible for charging, collecting, and remitting the GST?
2. When is a business required to register for the GST?
3. How does one register for the GST?
4. The registrant obtains two things when registering. What are these?
5. Why is the purchaser of goods and services affected by the GST?
6. Name the two accounts used to account for the GST.
7. Explain how to calculate the amount of tax to be remitted.
8. What is the rate of the GST at the time of writing this book?
9. Why are GST and PST kept separately in the accounts?
10. Where does the purchaser of goods or services find the amount of GST that was charged?
11. How often is GST remitted?
12. Give the name of the remittance form that accompanies the tax.
13. What happens if a business is late in making its remittance for GST?
14. Who, ultimately, pays the GST?
15. What kind of tax is the GST?
16. What one sales tax do consumers pay in New Brunswick, Nova Scotia, and Newfoundland?
17. What does it mean to "charge PST on top of GST"?
18. If a consumer purchased $100 of CDs in Prince Edward Island, calculate the total amount of the bill. (Use percentage from the table on page 189).
19. Identify a skill that makes accountants important to business.

Section 6.4 — Exercises

1. **Complete the following schedule in your Workbook.**

End of Period	GST Recoverable	GST Payable	Amount of remittance	Refund claimed	Due date
March 31	$ 904.72	$1 507.20			
Sept. 30	$1 565.20	$2 074.21			
Dec. 31	$ 700.40	$ 608.32			
Aug. 31	$2 764.35	$1 964.32			
Jan. 31	$3 750.00	$4 209.64			

2. R. Sadco is the owner of Red Lake Campground. The sales of the business are on a cash basis. Goods and services are purchased by the business on credit. **In your Workbook, record the selected transactions of Red Lake Campground given below**. The business uses the standard method of accounting for GST. **Use the following accounts**:

Bank
A/P — Bell Canada
A/P — Corcoran Sod Farm
A/P — Highway Lumber
A/P — Municipality of Marmora
GST Payable
GST Recoverable
PST Payable
Sales
Property Taxes Expense
Maintenance and Repairs Expense
Telephone Expense

TRANSACTIONS

Source documents are shown in italics.

November

15 *Cash Sales*
Tickets for the week Nos. 160 to 169, $1 210 plus GST at 7 per cent and PST at 8 per cent.

17 *Property Tax Bill*
From the Municipality of Marmora, taxes for the period from July 1 to December 31, $500; PST and GST exempt.

18 *Purchase Invoice*
No. 707 from Highway Lumber, $874.80 (PST included) plus GST of $56.70, total $931.50, for materials used in trailer site repairs and maintenance.

19 *Purchase Invoice*
No. 292 from Corcoran Sod Farm, $604.80 (PST included) plus GST of $39.20, total $644, for sod used in trailer site repairs and maintenance.

20 *Purchase Invoice*
From Bell Canada, $79.92 (PST included) plus GST of $5.18, total $85.10, for telephone service for the month of October.

3. **A. In your Workbook, complete the preparation of the sales invoice for Custodial Services**. Both GST and PST apply to the sale.

CUSTODIAL SERVICES		
900 Lansdowne Avenue Toronto, Ontario M6K 2V7		INVOICE NUMBER 953
Phone 767-8569 Fax 767-8533		
GST No. 102620110	Terms Net 30	Date April 26, 20—

TO	Oakridge Ski Club Box 500, Medonte, Ontario L4M 4Y8		
FOR	2 #152 Floor Mops @ $12 6 gals. Floor Cleaner @ $15		$24.00 $90.00
		GST 7%	
		PST 8%	
		TOTAL	

B. Enter the journal entry to record the above invoice from Custodial Equipment and Supply. Date the entry April 26.

C. Enter the journal entry to record the above invoice to Oakridge Ski Club. Date the entry April 28.

4. Given on page 193 are some transactions for Jodry and Associates, which uses the standard method of accounting for GST. **Journalize these transactions in your Workbook**. The company records all of its business revenue in a Sales account. GST at 7 per cent and PST at 8 per cent are charged on all sales. **Ignore PST on purchases. Use the following accounts**:

A/R — Booker Industries
A/R — Genco Corporation
A/R — Hall Industries
A/R — Tocheri & Associates
Office Supplies
A/P — The Print Shop
A/P — Bell Canada
A/P — Great Stationers
GST Payable
GST Recoverable
PST Payable
Sales
Printing Expense
Telephone Expense

TRANSACTIONS

October

19   *Sales Invoice*
No. 459 to Booker Industries, for advertising services, $1 250 plus taxes.

19   *Sales Invoice*
No. 460 to Genco Corporation, for consulting services, $1 500 plus taxes.

19   *Sales Invoice*
No. 461 to Hall Industries, for advertising services, $2 700 plus taxes.

22   *Purchase Invoice*
From Bell Canada, $313.20 plus GST of $20.30, total $333.50, regular billing for the period ended October 15.

24   *Sales Invoice*
No. 462, to Tocheri & Associates, for marketing services, $1 750 plus taxes.

25   *Purchase Invoice*
From Great Stationers, No. 156; $826.20 plus GST of $53.55, total $879.75, for office supplies.

6.5 | Building Spreadsheet Models

The computer on the desk of an accountant or accounting clerk is on virtually all the time. And when the task at hand is something other than debits and credits, the software that is running is likely to be a spreadsheet. Therefore, being able to use spreadsheets efficiently is a skill you will want to develop.

Suppose the accounting clerk for a business was asked to prepare a table summarizing the monthly activity in the GST Payable and GST Recoverable accounts. The clerk can display that information, along with related data, in a table such as the one shown in Figure 6.18.

FIGURE 6.18

A summary report for various data related to GST.

		GST Payable	GST Recoverable	Remittance (Refund)	Total Sales	Total Purchases
1	January	690.25	340.89	349.36	9,860.71	4,869.86
2	February	700.09	360.55	339.54	10,001.29	5,150.71
3	March	809.55	425.36	384.19	11,565.00	6,076.57
4	April	795.66	412.81	382.85	11,366.57	5,897.29
5	May	856.39	439.62	416.77	12,234.14	6,280.29
6	June	800.66	405.88	394.78	11,438.00	5,798.29
7	July	598.36	298.66	299.70	8,548.00	4,266.57
8	August	412.89	450.33	(37.44)	5,898.43	6,433.29
9	September	722.99	359.14	363.85	10,328.43	5,130.57
10	October	877.85	430.95	446.90	12,540.71	6,156.43
11	November	945.62	470.45	475.17	13.508.86	6,720.71
12	December	998.25	505.96	492.29	14,260.71	7,228.00
	Totals	9,208.56	4,900.60	4,307.96	131,550.86	70,008.57

The above table appears to have taken a good deal of time and effort to prepare. Data were either keyed in spreadsheet cells or generated by formulas and functions. Then, an attractive format was applied to the entire model. But while the amount of work is impressive, the accounting clerk could have completed it quite quickly if he or she had used some of the features offered by spreadsheet software. You will now use Microsoft Excel to prepare the same table as the one shown in Figure 6.18.

Entering Data with AutoFill

Load your spreadsheet software into your computer. Save a new file as *GSTreport*. At cell A4, type 1; at A5, type 2. Instead of typing the remaining numbers in cells A6 to A15, you will use a feature called **AutoFill** to enter the remaining numbers automatically.

Use the mouse pointer to highlight cells A4 and A5. At the bottom right corner of the selection, you will see a small square commonly referred to as a handle. In this case, the handle is called the **fill handle**. Move the mouse pointer on top of the fill handle. You can tell the mouse pointer is directly over the fill handle when the pointer changes shape. The mouse pointer should now be a solid cross, as shown on the left side of Figure 6.19.

FIGURE 6.19

Using the AutoFill feature to enter numbers.

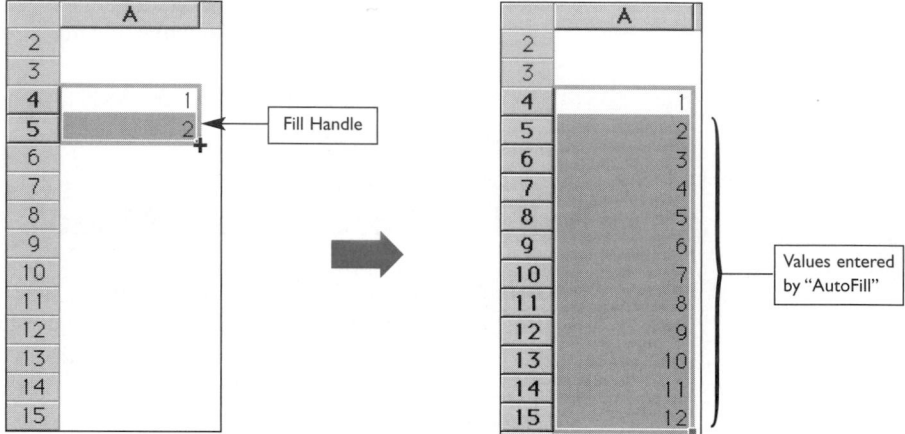

Click and drag the mouse pointer down to A15. When you release the mouse, the numbers 3 through 12 are "filled" into the cells, as shown on the right side of Figure 6.19. Microsoft® Excel needed two beginning cells—A4 and A5. It recognized that the data in A4 and A5 were values, and that the number in A5 was greater than the number in A4 by a value of 1. The AutoFill repeated this numerical pattern of increase throughout your highlighted selection.

The AutoFill feature works with other types of data. Sometimes, it does not even need two beginning cells to determine the pattern of change. For example, at cell B4, type **January**. Click on B4 to make sure the cell is highlighted. Then, drag the fill handle down to cell B15 and release the mouse. The months of the year are entered for you without keying them.

Entering Values and Labels

The accounting clerk needs to enter some data into the spreadsheet. He probably obtained the month-end balances for GST Payable and GST Recoverable by exporting data from an accounting software program like *Simply Accounting*. You, however, will have to key it. Using Figure 6.20 as your guide, key the GST account figures, as well as the labels shown in row 2, 3, and 16.

FIGURE 6.20

Labels and data for the spreadsheet model.

	A	B	C	D	E	F	G
1							
2			GST	GST	Remittance/	Total	Total
3			Payable	Recoverable	(Refund)	Sales	Purchases
4		1 January	690.25	340.89			
5		2 February	700.09	360.55			
6		3 March	809.55	425.36			
7		4 April	795.66	412.81			
8		5 May	856.39	439.62			
9		6 June	800.66	405.88			
10		7 July	598.36	298.66			
11		8 August	412.89	450.33			
12		9 September	722.99	359.14			
13		10 October	877.85	430.95			
14		11 November	945.62	470.45			
15		12 December	998.25	505.96			
16		Totals					

Copying with Relative Cell References

Instead of highlighting cells and choosing Edit, Fill, Down, you can use the AutoFill feature you just learned.

In column E, the amount of the remittance or refund for each month will be calculated. At cell, E4, type **=C4−D4**. (This subtracts the amounts of GST Recoverable from GST Payable.) The answer displayed at cell E4 is 349.36.

It would be time-consuming to type similar formulas for the remaining months. Fortunately, Microsoft Excel lets you copy the formula at E4 to other cells. Click on E4 and drag the mouse pointer to highlight from E4 to E15. (See the left side of Figure 6.21)

From the top-line menu, choose **Edit**, **Fill**, **Down**. The cells in column E will look like the right side of Figure 6.21.

FIGURE 6.21

Copying a formula in Microsoft® Excel.

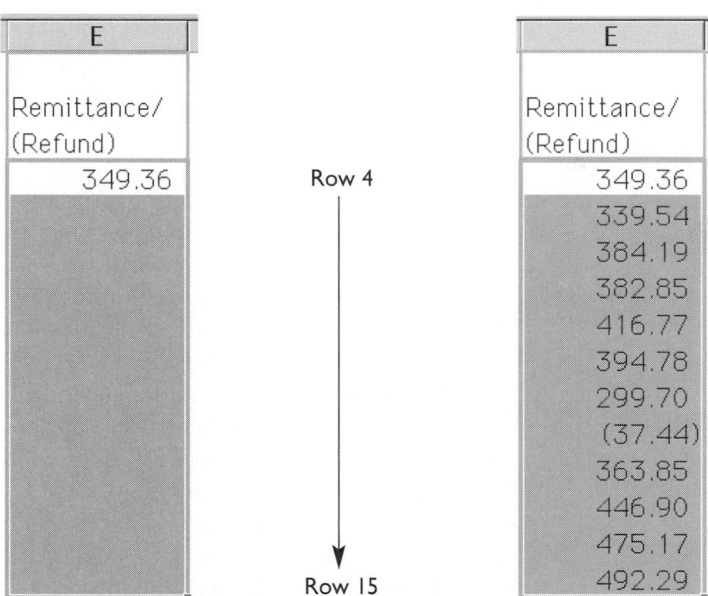

E		E
Remittance/ (Refund)		Remittance/ (Refund)
349.36	Row 4	349.36
		339.54
		384.19
		382.85
		416.77
		394.78
		299.70
		(37.44)
		363.85
		446.90
		475.17
	Row 15	492.29

Your original formula at cell E4 was **=C4−D4**. When it was copied down one row, it changed to **=C5−D5**; when it was copied down two rows, it changed to **=C6−D6**, and so on. The cell references in your original formula (C4 and D4) are called relative references. **Relative cell references** are ones that will change when they are copied to new locations.

Copying with Absolute Cell References

The accounting clerk wanted to include information about the total monthly sales and purchases on which GST Payable and Recoverable were based. Instead of going to the ledger accounts, he got the information he wanted by using a mathematical formula. In this case, January's GST Payable of $690.25 was 7% of Sales. Expressed as a formula, this is *$690.25 = Sales × .07*. To determine the Sales, the formula is adjusted algebraically to *Sales = 690.25/.07*.

You will now enter this formula in your spreadsheet. First enter **.07** (the divisor) at **H1**, a cell outside the table of data. Now, at cell F4, type **=C4/H1**. The answer is 9860.71429. To format this number, click *Comma Style* button (see Figure 6.23). Your answer should now be 9,860.71. Copy the formula at F4 down to row F15 using the same "Fill Down" procedures you learned for column E.

FIGURE 6.22

Copying cell F4 without, then with, absolute cell references.

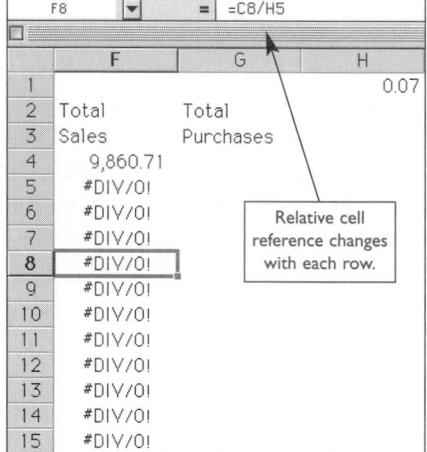
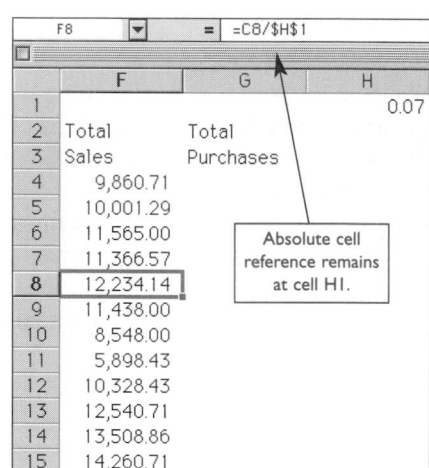

Instead of getting the data you expected, you got a number of error messages like those shown in the left side of Figure 6.22. Move the cell pointer to different "erroneous" cells in column F. You will observe that the numerator (a cell reference from column C) changes with each new row. This is what you want to happen. Unfortunately, the cell reference for the divisor also changes with each row. You do not want this number to change.

To make sure the divisor does not change from H1, the cell reference in the original formula must be made absolute. An **absolute cell reference** is one that will not change when copied to new locations. To correct the situation, type **=C4/$H$1** at cell F4. The dollar signs make cell H1 an absolute cell reference.

The answer at F4 stays the same (9,860.71). Now "fill" the formula at F4 down to F15. Your spreadsheet should look like the right side of Figure 6.22.

Check out the cells in column F. The divisor ($H$1) remains the same in each row because it is an absolute cell reference. The numerator (originally C4) changes with each row because it is relative.

Repeat this procedure for column G. Your starting formula at G4 is =D4/$H$1. Apply the *Comma Style* before you fill the formula down to row 15.

Completing the Spreadsheet Model

To finish the numerical calculations, move the cell pointer to cell C16. Click the *AutoSum* button (see Figure 6.23) and press the Enter key. Then click the *Comma Style* button. Make sure the cell pointer is at C16 because you will now copy its contents to new locations. Highlight from C16 to G16. From the top-line menu, choose **Edit, Fill, Right**. Do not be concerned if some cells fill up with the "#" sign. A column that contains such cells needs to be widened, but do not do that yet. Note: You can also use the AutoFill feature to copy.

FIGURE 6.23

Finalize the data for the GST report spreadsheet model.

For an on-line demonstration of this exercise, go to www.pearsoned.ca/accounting1

The total sales and purchases amounts at cells F16 and G16 are "off" by one cent. This is because the *Comma Style* button was selected instead of rounding the numbers in Columns F and G.

		GST Payable	GST Recoverable	Remittance/ (Refund)	Total Sales	Total Purchases
4	1 January	690.25	340.89	349.36	9,860.71	4,869.86
5	2 February	700.09	360.55	339.54	10,001.29	5,150.71
6	3 March	809.55	425.36	384.19	11,565.00	6,076.57
7	4 April	795.66	412.81	382.85	11,366.57	5,897.29
8	5 May	856.39	439.62	416.77	12,234.14	6,280.29
9	6 June	800.66	405.88	394.78	11,438.00	5,798.29
10	7 July	598.36	298.66	299.70	8,548.00	4,266.57
11	8 August	412.89	450.33	(37.44)	5,898.43	6,433.29
12	9 September	722.99	359.14	363.85	10,328.43	5,130.57
13	10 October	877.85	430.95	446.90	12,540.71	6,156.43
14	11 November	945.62	470.45	475.17	13,508.86	6,720.71
15	12 December	998.25	505.96	492.29	14,260.71	7,228.00
16	Totals	9,208.56	4,900.60	4,307.96	########	70,008.57

(AutoSum)

(Comma Style)

A wider column is needed to show the answer.

Polishing the final appearance of the spreadsheet model is very easy if you choose some of the preset formats offered by Microsoft Excel. First, highlight the table. (Drag from A2 to G16. Column H is not necessary.) Then, from the top-line menu, choose **Format**, **AutoFormat**. The AutoFormat chosen in Figure 6.18 on page 193 was named *List 2*. Scroll down until you can click that option. Reduce the width of column A, and your work will look as impressive as Figure 6.18. After saving your work, you may wish to experiment with some of the other automatic formats.

Section 6.5 — Review Questions

1. How many beginning cells does the AutoFill feature need in order to fill in a long list of numbers? Explain.
2. How many beginning cells does the AutoFill feature need to order to fill in a list of months?
3. What is a relative cell reference?
4. What is an absolute cell reference?
5. When copying a formula, what type of cell reference would you likely want for a numerator?
6. What does it mean if a cell fills up with the "#" sign?
7. Explain what Excel's AutoFormat feature does.

CHAPTER 6 Summary

CHAPTER HIGHLIGHTS

Now that you have completed Chapter 6, you should:

- understand why a journal and a ledger are both used in the accounting process;
- be able to record transactions in a two-column general journal;
- be able to work out an opening entry from a balance sheet;
- know the first three steps in the accounting cycle;
- be able to recognize a number of basic source documents and understand the uses for the various copies;
- know the journal entries for a number of source documents;
- understand that source documents are part of an overall accounting system for controlling and recording accounting transactions;
- understand the cost principle in recording transactions;
- know the purpose of retail sales tax and the GST levied by governments;
- be able to calculate sales tax and the GST and to include these in sales transactions;
- know the journal entries for source documents containing PST and GST;
- know the journal entries for remitting GST and PST to the government;
- be able to use various ways to create and copy cell data in spreadsheets;
- apply attractive formats to spreadsheet work.

ACCOUNTING TERMS

bank credit advice
bank debit advice
book of original entry
cash receipts daily summary
cash sales slip
cheque copy
cost principle
goods and services tax (GST)
harmonized sales tax (HST)
journal
journal entry

journalizing
opening entry
point of sale summary
point of sale terminal
provincial sales tax (PST)
purchase invoice
remittance advice
retail sales tax
sales invoice
source document
transaction log

CHAPTER 6 Review Exercises

Using Your Knowledge

1 The following exercise also appears in your Workbook.
Complete the following summary. Assume that there is GST and PST on all sales and that the business is PST exempt on purchases.

Nature of Transaction	Source Document or Documents	Required Journal Entry	
		Accounts Debited	Accounts Credited
Payment on account			
Sale on account			
Bank service charge			
Cash payment of phone bill			
Cash received on account			
Purchase of equipment on account			
Cash sale			

2 **The following exercise also appears in your Workbook.**
In the chart below, there is a list of numbered source documents to the left. To the right is a list of transactions. **You are to match the transactions with the source documents by writing the document number beside the transaction to which it relates.** Some transactions affect more than one source document. **If a transaction is supported by more than one source document, write in more than one document number.**

Source Document	Document Number
Bank credit memo	1
Bank debit memo	2
Cheque copy	3
Cash sales slip	4
Sales invoice	5
Purchase invoice	6
Cash receipts list	7
Owner's written memo	8
Bank statement	9

Transactions	Document Number(s)
1. Owner withdraws money.	
2. Purchase of equipment on account.	
3. Payment on account.	
4. Cash sale.	
5. Sale on account.	
6. Cheques received from customers on account.	
7. Increase bank loan.	
8. Owner invests additional money in the business.	
9. Bank service charge.	

3 This exercise also appears in your Workbook. Indicate whether each of the following statements is true or false by placing a "T" or an "F" in the space indicated. Explain the reason for each "F" response in the space provided.

A. Anyone in the business can initiate a business transaction.
B. Every journal entry is based on a source document.
C. The only purpose of source documents is to provide the basis for a journal entry.
D. A business that sells to its customers on a cash basis does not normally use a sales invoice.
E. Journal entries for all cash sales slips are essentially the same.
F. Sales invoices are used by businesses that make most of their sales on account.
G. For every sales invoice, there is a debit to an account receivable.
H. The transaction log that is produced by a POS terminal is used by an accounting clerk to record a debit to Bank and a credit to Sales.
I. Every sales invoice is also a purchase invoice.
J. The debit entry for every purchase invoice is always the same.
K. The supporting document for a payment on account is the tear-off portion of a cheque.
L. The credit entry for every cheque copy payment is always the same.
M. Cheques received are considered to be cash received.
N. The bank has no right to make deductions from the accounts of its customers.
O. We debit Bank when we receive a bank debit memo.
P. The cost principle states that every asset acquired is to be recorded at its cost price.
Q. The best objective evidence of a purchase is a purchase invoice received from an independent supplier.
R. Only provincial governments are allowed to levy sales taxes.
S. The purchaser of goods or services is required to make accounting entries for provincial sales tax.
T. The PST account is an expense account.

Comprehensive Exercises

4 The following exercise also appears in your workbook. Assume a purchase of $600 is made in each of the provinces listed. Fill in the blanks by calculating the PST, GST, HST, and total price of a $600 purchase. Refer to the table shown on page 189 to make your calculations.

$600 Purchase	PST	GST	HST	Total Price
Alberta				
Manitoba				
Newfoundland				
Ontario				
Quebec				
Saskatchewan				

5 Described below are source documents for Wayne Siebert, a professional photographer. **Journalize these transactions in a two-column general journal, using the accounts shown below**. The rate for PST is 8 per cent and for GST, 7 per cent. **Ignore PST on purchases.**

Bank
A/R — various debtors
Photo Supplies
Automobile
A/P — various creditors
GST Payable
GST Recoverable
PST Payable
W. Siebert, Capital
W. Siebert, Drawings
Fees Earned
Automobile Expense
Bank Charges Expense

TRANSACTIONS

November

4 *Sales Invoice*
No. 571, to R. Chevrier for photo services, $275.00 plus GST of $19.25 and PST of $22.00, total $316.25.

6 *Purchase Invoice*
Received from Black's Photo for photo supplies, $265.00 plus GST of $18.55, total $283.55.

9 *Purchase Invoice*
Received from Petro Canada for gasoline used in the company car, $165.00 plus GST of $11.55, total $176.55.

10 *Cheque Copy*
No. 652, issued to the owner for his own use, $325.00.

12 *Cash Sales Slip*
No. 214, for photo work performed, $145.00 plus GST of $10.15 and PST of $11.60, total $166.75.

15 *Bank Debit Memo*
From Commercial Bank for bank service charges, $35.50.

20 *Memorandum*
From the owner stating that he had taken $75.00 of photo supplies for his personal work at home.

22 *Cash Receipt*
Received $412.00 from H. Walker on account.

25 *Cheque Copy*
No. 653, paying for the supplies purchased above on November 6.

28 *Purchase Invoice*
Received from Oakley Motors for body repairs done on the business automobile, $750.00 plus GST of $52.50, total $802.50.

6 Champion Rent-All, a business in Brandon, Manitoba, rents out tools and equipment. The accounts for the business are as follows:

Bank	Frank N. Mazur, Drawings
A/R — various	Rental Revenue
Supplies	Bank Charges Expense
Rental Tools and Equipment	Delivery Expense
Truck	Utilities Expense
A/P — various	Miscellaneous Expense
GST Payable	Rent Expense
GST Recoverable	Telephone Expense
PST Payable	Wages Expense
Frank N. Mazur, Capital	

Journalize the transactions shown below in the two-column general journal provided in the Workbook. Calculate and add the GST and PST on all sales transactions. The rate for GST is 7 per cent. The rate for PST is 8 per cent. **Ignore PST on purchases.**

TRANSACTIONS

October

2 *Cash Sales Slip*
No. 409, to W. Franklin, $52.50 plus taxes.

4 *Charge Sales Slip*
No. 410, to G. Fairbridge, $87.50 plus taxes.

5 *Purchase Invoice*
From Vulcan Machinery, No. 3062 for one hydraulic jack, a rental tool, $315.00 plus GST of $22.05, total $337.05.

8 *Cheque Copy*
No. 1475, to Fair Supply Company on account, $215.90.

9 *Cash Sales Slip*
No. 411, to R. Gullett, $115.10 plus taxes.

11 *Cash Receipt*
From P. Mathers on account, $402.20.

15 *Cheque Copy*
No. 1476, to Municipal Hydro, for cash payment of hydro bill, $172.00 plus GST of $12.04, total $184.04.

17 *Cheque Copy*
No. 1477, to R. Klein for wages, $512.00.

17 *Cash Sales Slip*
No. 412, to A. Heisse, $90.00 plus taxes.

18 *Cheque Copy*
No. 1478, to the owner, Frank Mazur, for his own use, $350.00.

22 *Purchase Invoice*
From Husky Oil Company, for gas and oil used in the delivery truck, $209.00 plus GST of $14.63, total $223.63.

24 *Bank Debit Memo*
For bank service charge, $42.50.

25 *Cheque Copy*
No. 1479, to R. Klein for wages, $512.00.

7 Cheri Ohashi is in business as a commercial artist. The accounts for her business are as follows:

Bank	GST Payable	Car Expense
A/R — various	GST Recoverable	Utilities Expense
Art Supplies	PST Payable	Miscellaneous Expense
Equipment	Cheri Ohashi, Capital	Rent Expense
Automobile	Cheri Ohashi, Drawings	Telephone Expense
A/P — various	Fees Revenue	

A. **Journalize the following transactions in the two-column general journal in your Workbook. Calculate and add the GST and PST on all sales transactions**. The rate of GST is 7 per cent. The rate of PST is 8 per cent. **Ignore PST on purchases**.

TRANSACTIONS

March

3   *Sales Invoice*
No. 192, to Mountain Distributors, $175.00 plus taxes.

4   *Sales Invoice*
No. 193, to Old Fort Trading Co., $300.00 plus taxes.

4   *Cheque Copy*
No. 316, to Central Garage for the cash payment for repairs to the business automobile, $115.00 plus GST of $8.05, total $123.05.

6   *Cheque Copy*
No. 317, to Twin City Hydro for cash payment of the monthly hydro bill, $65.00 plus GST of $4.55, total $69.55.

10   *Purchase Invoice*
From C. & C. Equipment, No. 1401, for one large metal drawing table, $475.00 plus GST of $33.25, total $508.25.

10   *Cheque Copy*
No. 318, to Dejavu Art Supply for the cash payment for artist's supplies, $85.00 plus GST of $5.95, total $90.95.

13   *Cheque Copy*
No. 319, to the owner for her personal use, $350.00.

14   *Sales Invoice*
No. 194, to Display Design Company, $255.00 plus taxes.

14   *Cash Receipt*
From Victor Schilling on account, $150.00.

17   *Cheque Copy*
No. 320, to C. & C. Equipment, paying for the purchase made on March 10.

19   *Sales Invoice*
No. 195, to Scoville Sales, $235.00 plus taxes.

20   *Cheque Copy*
No. 321, to Fleming Properties, for the office rent for the month, $375.00 plus GST of $26.25, total $401.25.

23   *Purchase Invoice*
From Lougherys Limited, No. 634, for drafting and artist's equipment, $215.00 plus GST of $15.05, total $230.05.

25   *Cheque Copy*
No. 322, to Twin City Telephone, for cash payment of the monthly telephone bill, $28.50 plus GST of $2.00, total $30.50.

27 *Purchase Invoice*
From Esso, for the gas and oil used in the business automobile, $71.40 plus GST of $5.00, total $76.40.

31 *Cash Receipt*
From Old Fort Trading Co. on account, $300.00.

B. **Complete the GST/HST Return For Registrants** that appears in your Workbook. Sales for the month totalled $965.00. Ignore lines 110, 111, 205, and 405 on the form.

Questions for Further Thought

Briefly answer the following questions:

1. List three jobs in a secondary school that carry the right to make purchases.

2. Explain the term "source document."

3. Give an example other than owner's drawings of a transaction for which there would not usually be a source document.

4. In a period of rising prices, the assets on the balance sheet will be understated. Therefore, the balance sheet will be misleading. Comment on this.

5. Cash sales slips are prenumbered as a control feature. What would you tell your employees to do about cash sales slips that were spoiled and had to be redone?

6. Explain how an invoice can be both a "sales invoice" and a "purchase invoice."

7. Cash sales slips are usually loaded into a metal container for ease in preparation. What happens to the copies immediately after they are prepared?

8. Why can the invoice numbers on purchase invoices not be used for control purposes by the buyer?

9. The person who receives the mail, makes out the cash receipts list, and deposits the receipts in the bank is not normally an employee in the accounting department. Explain why.

10. The rule states that assets are debited when they are increased. However, the bank issues a "debit" memo when it decreases the bank account. Explain.

11. Once the cost of an asset is recorded in the accounts, it is not normally changed regardless of its market value. Give some reasons for this rule.

12. PST added to an invoice in March has to be paid by April 15. However, the invoice in question may not be collected until May. Express an opinion on this.

Cases for Further Thought

Comment briefly on each of the following mini-cases. Be prepared to present your comments to the class. Ignore GST and PST.

1. In the Truck account, there is a debit entry for a new truck in the amount of $45 000. You suspect that this figure is wrong. You find that the source document for the transaction is missing from the files when you look for it. How could you verify the amount?

2. Joan Nordquist purchased the property next to her business at a price of $55 000. She wanted the property for a much-needed expansion to the business premises. One week later, Joan received an independent offer to purchase the property for $75 000 but turned it down. However, she instructed her accountant to increase the value of the property in the accounts to $75 000. In her opinion, a new value for the property was established by the offer to purchase.

3. Fred Hebert purchased a new piece of equipment for his business. The normal selling price of this equipment was $22 000. Fred was given a special price of $18 000 because he was a close friend of the dealer. Fred wondered which value should be used to record the equipment in the accounts.

4. A company ran into serious long-term cash problems even though it was a consistently good money-maker. How could this happen?

5. The Colossimo Company ordered a new van at a cost of $23 000 on March 19. It was agreed that Colossimo Company would not take delivery of the van until July 31. Colossimo Company does not know if it should record the transaction now.

6. Sarah Tolp inherited a used automobile upon the death of a relative. She brought it into her business. She instructed the accountant to record the car at a value of $25 000 but provided no business papers to support that figure.

Case Studies

Accounting for a Package Deal

Ted Cyr is the owner of a large contracting company in Thompson, Manitoba. A competitor of Cyr's had gone bankrupt and his equipment was liquidated at a public auction. One particular lot attracted Cyr's attention. The lot included one bulldozer, two dump trucks, one crane, one pavement roller, and a property on which there was a good-sized construction building and a sand pit. Before the auction, Cyr obtained the services of a professional appraiser to help him evaluate the lot for sale. The appraiser estimated the values as follows:

Appraised Values	
Bulldozer	$ 60 000
Dump truck 1	12 000
Dump truck 2	6 000
Crane	120 000
Pavement roller	72 000
Land parcel	36 000
Construction building	30 000
Sand pit	24 000
Total	$360 000

Cyr decided in advance of the auction that he would bid as high as $300 000 for the lot. However, much to his satisfaction, he won the lot with a bid of only $234 000.

Cyr is a businessman who keeps proper books and records and complies with all accounting standards and conventions. He intends to set up the newly acquired assets properly in the accounts. He is not sure how to do this because they were acquired as a package. He is certain that the equipment and the land, at least, should be set up in separate accounts.

Cyr hires you, a public accountant, to prepare the accounting entries to record the new assets.

Questions

1. To set up the newly acquired assets, four asset accounts are used. What are these?
2. At what overall value should the newly acquired assets be set up in the accounts? What GAAP makes this necessary?
3. How can the appraised values be used to calculate cost values for the new assets?
4. Work out the cost values for the newly acquired assets, making sure that the total is equal to the auction price.
5. Give the journal entry to set up the assets and to record their payment.
6. Write a brief report outlining the steps in setting up the package of assets in the accounts. Use the memo report format shown in the Skills Appendix.

CASE 2

Group Discussion

Is a Profit Always a Profit?

In 1998, Marjorie Maepea, a dealer in small sailboats in Summerside, Prince Edward Island, had a profitable year. She ended the 1998 fiscal year with an extra $50 000 in cash and was looking for a good business opportunity. For some time, she had considered using the money to purchase a larger sailboat—to test the market in Summerside for larger boats. In particular, she looked at a 10-metre Tarzan selling for $50 000. However, she eventually abandoned the idea. Instead, she purchased a nearby piece of commercial property for $50 000.

At the end of 2001, Marjorie sold the land that she had purchased in 1998 for $80 000. She felt good about the deal. The profit of $30 000 looked good on the books and Marjorie again had cash available to pursue other interests. She again considered the move into larger sailboats and again looked at the new Tarzan 10, which was virtually unchanged from the 1998 model. She was shocked to learn that the price for a 2002 Tarzan 10 had risen to $74 000.

Questions

1. How much was the profit on the sale of the industrial property purchased in 1998?
2. Assuming that there is a special income tax (capital gains tax) of 20 per cent on this type of profit, calculate the amount of the tax and the amount of the profit after deducting the tax.
3. How much free cash does Marjorie have available as a result of the land transaction?
4. Is Marjorie in any better position now than she was in 1998 in respect to the purchase of the Tarzan 10? Explain, with figures.
5. Solely on the basis of the evidence presented in this case, determine whether Marjorie really made a profit on the sale of the commercial property. Explain in terms of straight dollars and in terms of purchasing power.
6. What word is used to explain the increase in the value of the property and the boat?
7. Could Marjorie's book profit be called a paper profit?

Career

Phil Quackenbush / President, Q.W. Page Associates

Phil Quackenbush, who along with co-worker Ronald Ward Benn spent five years developing the popular accounting software "NewViews™," is enjoying the rewards of hard work as the program gains popularity.

While completing his final year of a computer science degree at the University of Toronto, Phil decided to return to first year and take business courses in a Bachelor of Commerce program. (A Bachelor of Commerce or "B.Comm" is a business degree that focuses on accounting, economics, and commerce.) "Although I was primarily interested in computer programming, I wanted to have the business knowledge to actually run my own company or, at least, profit from the programs I intended to write." As it turned out, a business subject — accounting — was also to become Phil's main area of computer expertise.

Phil's first job after university was with a small firm that sold, installed, and supported software for offices.

"The accounting courses I had taken in university gave me a background in how accounting had evolved into almost a 'black art' over a 500-year period," he says. "Accounting practices were very convoluted, even when computerized."

Phil felt that there were too many disjointed programs on the market, given the advanced state of computer technology. He thought that one single piece of software could be designed to link customer files, supplier files, accounts receivable, accounts payable, the balance sheet, and the many other areas of accounting. In addition, software could be much more user-friendly and could allow faster access to subcategories of files. With this as their founding philosophy, Phil and Ronald Ward Benn formed Q.W. Page Associates in 1980 and got down to work designing the master program.

"My computer background, combined with my accounting knowledge, enabled me to look at an old problem from the perspective of a new technology," says Phil of the software that he and Ronald designed over a five-year period. Each of them often put in 60 to 70 hours a week. Their product,

NewViews, is designed for use by both small and large organizations.

Phil considers that the business world holds great rewards for people who have technical degrees, but only if they also have other skills — such as accounting and marketing.

NewViews, which won PC Magazine's Award for Technical Excellence — Application Software, is marketed internationally.

Phil considers that the business world holds great rewards for people who have technical degrees in areas such as computer science, engineering, and architecture, but only if they also have other skills — such as accounting and marketing — which ensure that they, and not others, "will get the value from their labour and brain power." He advises students to get business courses such as marketing and economics, in addition to a range of accounting courses, at the university level, regardless of the occupation they plan to follow later.

Phil believes that keeping track of finances has to be an issue for everyone involved in a business, not just its owners and accountants. "I like the technical people who work for me to not only understand their trade — such as engineering or computer science — I also want them to appreciate the financial, economic, and marketing ramifications of any project that we're discussing."

Discussion

1. Under what circumstances does Phil Quackenbush think that a person with a technical degree can succeed in business? What is your reaction to his view? Give reasons for your answer.
2. Phil wants his own technical staff to appreciate the financial, economic, and marketing issues of any project they are discussing. Why do you think that a company owner would want this? Do you think it would help a business if employees from different areas of expertise (accounting and computer programming, for example) were aware of each other's concerns? Can you think of any problems that might occur? How might they be handled?
3. In the interview above, Phil refers several times to marketing as an important aspect of business. Marketing is the area of business that seeks to identify the needs of customers. Market research is used for this purpose. What had Phil's research told him about the accounting programs on the market? How do you think he used this information to develop NewViews?
4. According to Phil, accounting evolved, over a period of 500 years, into "almost a 'black art'" (that is, a mysterious, magical art). Have you ever felt that way about accounting? Explain.

7

Posting

7.1 | Posting

In previous chapters, you were introduced to the ledger and the journal, the two important books in the accounting process. You are now ready to learn to use these books "formally," just as accountants do.

The Balance Column Account

So far, we have considered only the simple two-sided ledger account, showing debits on one side and credits on the other. However, a second style of ledger account, known as the balance column account, is actually more useful and convenient. In fact, it is the most commonly used account. The **balance column account** has three money columns: one for the debit amounts, one for the credit amounts, and a separate one for the balance. This method allows the balances to stand out more clearly. The T-account and the balance column account are compared in Figure 7.1 on page 210.

Opening an Account

An accounting entry often affects an item for which there is no existing account in the ledger. When this happens, it is necessary to open an account. **Opening an account** means preparing an account page and placing it in its proper place in the ledger. To open an account, proceed as follows:

Step 1 Obtain an unused account page.

Step 2 Write the name for the new account at the top of the page. The account name is known as the **account title** and will be written on the back of the page as well.

Step 3 Write in the account number.

Step 4 Insert the new account in its proper place in the ledger.

Both the front and the back of any account page are used for the same item.

FIGURE 7.1

Comparison of entries made in a T-account (top) and in a standard balance column account (bottom).

T-ACCOUNT

Bank	
5 000	350
700	1 750
200	960
450	
6350	*3060*
(3290)	

STANDARD ACCOUNT

The journal page number is shown.

The type of balance is indicated.

ACCOUNT Bank NO. 101

DATE		PARTICULARS	P.R.	DEBIT	CREDIT	DR/CR	BALANCE
July 20–	14		J4	5 000 –		DR	5 000 –
	17		J4	700 –		DR	5 700 –
	18		J5		350 –	DR	5 350 –
	18		J5		1 750 –	DR	3 600 –
	21		J6	200 –		DR	3 800 –
	23		J7	450 –		DR	4 250 –
	24		J7		960 –	DR	3 290 –

Each entry has its own line.

The date of each entry is shown.

Particulars column is not used until later.

Debit and credit columns form the core of the account.

The balance is shown after each entry.

Formal Posting

In the previous chapter, you learned that each accounting entry is first recorded in the journal. It is then transferred, or "posted," to the ledger. **Posting** is the process of transferring information from the journal to the ledger. Every individual amount recorded in the journal must be posted separately. The six-step procedure for posting is described below. Illustrations for posting an entire journal entry are given in Figures 7.2 through 7.5 on pages 211 through 213.

Six Steps in Posting

For each individual amount entered in the journal, you must perform the following six steps. Five of these steps are performed in the ledger; one of the steps is performed in the journal.

Five Steps in the Ledger

Step 1 Turn to the proper account in the ledger.

Step 2 Record the date. Use the next unused line in the account.

Step 3 Record the page number of the journal (where the transaction is journalized) in the posting reference (P.R.) column of the account. Write the letter J (for Journal) in front of this number (for example, J14). As you will see later, several journals may be used in accounting. Therefore, you must use a code to tell you which journal is being referred to. You can look ahead to see the journals to which these codes refer on page 549.

Step 4 Record the amount. Debit amounts are entered in the debit columns of the accounts. Credit amounts are entered in the credit columns of the accounts.

Step 5 Calculate and enter the new account balance in the balance column. Indicate whether it is a debit or a credit balance in the DR/CR column.

One Step in the Journal

Step 6 Record the account number to which the posting was made. Enter this in the posting reference (P.R.) column on the same line as the amount being posted.

Example

Shown below is a general journal entry to be posted. This is followed by a series of illustrations starting on this page and finishing on page 213, showing in detail how the postings are done.

FIGURE 7.2

A general journal entry to be posted.

FIGURE 7.3

This figure shows two steps: the debit item in the journal entry has been posted and cross-referenced to the Office Furniture account.

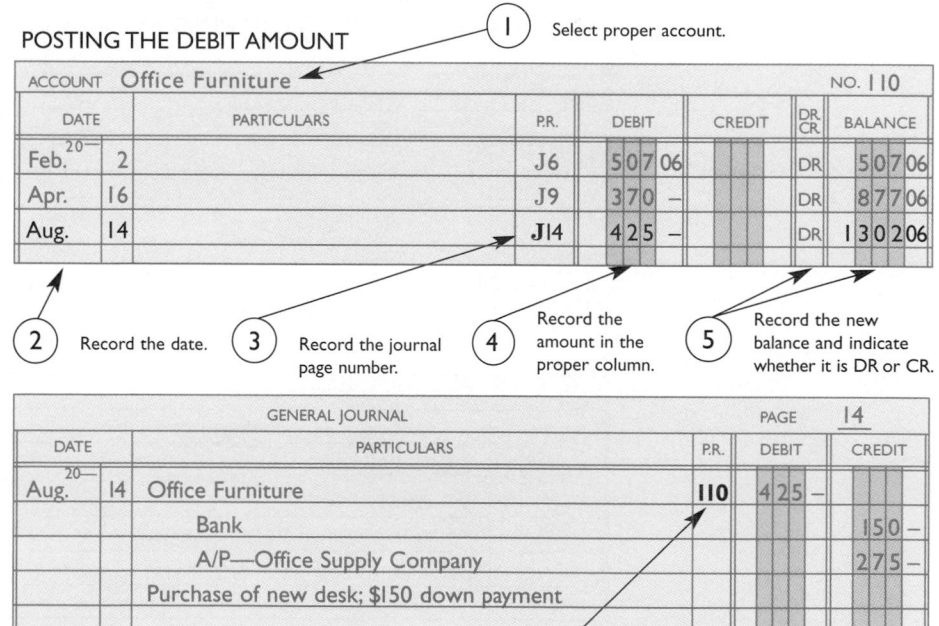

FIGURE 7.4

This figure shows that the first and second credit items in the journal entry have been posted and cross-referenced to Bank and Accounts Payable—Office Supply Company.

POSTING THE FIRST CREDIT AMOUNT

(1) Select proper account.

ACCOUNT **Bank**							NO. 101
DATE		PARTICULARS	P.R.	DEBIT	CREDIT	DR CR	BALANCE
Aug. 20–	3	Forwarded	–			DR	704 15
	9		J13	502 –		DR	1206 15
	14		**J14**		150 –	DR	1056 15

(2) Record the date. (3) Record the journal page number. (4) Record the amount in the proper column. (5) Record the new balance and indicate whether it is DR or CR.

GENERAL JOURNAL			PAGE 14		
DATE		PARTICULARS	P.R.	DEBIT	CREDIT
Aug. 20–	14	Office Furniture	110	425 –	
		Bank	**101**		150 –
		A/P—Office Supply Company			275 –
		Purchase of new desk; $150 down payment			

(6) Record the account number.

POSTING THE SECOND CREDIT AMOUNT

(1) Select proper account.

ACCOUNT **Accounts Payable—Office Supply Company**							NO. 212
DATE		PARTICULARS	P.R.	DEBIT	CREDIT	DR CR	BALANCE
May 20–	3		J10		386 –	CR	386 –
June	15		J10	386 –			Ø
Aug.	14		**J14**		275 –	**CR**	275 –

(2) Record the date. (3) Record the journal page number. (4) Record the amount in the proper column. (5) Record the new balance and indicate whether it is DR or CR.

GENERAL JOURNAL			PAGE 14		
DATE		PARTICULARS	P.R.	DEBIT	CREDIT
Aug. 20–	14	Office Furniture	110	425 –	
		Bank	101		150 –
		A/P — Office Supply Company	**212**		275 –
		Purchase of new desk; $150 down payment			

(6) Record the account number.

After the journal entry is completely posted, the general journal and the three accounts involved appear as shown below.

FIGURE 7.5

The journal and the ledger results from the six steps in the formal posting of a journal entry.

THE JOURNAL ENTRY BEING POSTED

GENERAL JOURNAL				PAGE	14	
DATE		PARTICULARS	P.R.	DEBIT	CREDIT	
Aug. 20–	14	Office Furniture	**110**	425 –		
		Bank	**101**		150 –	
		A/P—Office Supply Company	**212**		275 –	
		Purchase of new desk; $150 down payment				

⑥

THE THREE LEDGER ACCOUNTS AFFECTED BY THE JOURNAL ENTRY

①

ACCOUNT	Bank						NO.	101
DATE		PARTICULARS	P.R.	DEBIT	CREDIT	DR./CR.	BALANCE	
Aug. 20–	3	Forwarded	–			DR	704 15	
	9		J13	502 –		DR	1206 15	
	14		**J14**		150 –	**DR**	1056 15	

②   ③   ④   ⑤

①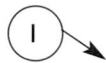

ACCOUNT	Office Furniture						NO.	110
DATE		PARTICULARS	P.R.	DEBIT	CREDIT	DR./CR.	BALANCE	
Feb. 20–	2		J6	507 06		DR	507 06	
Apr.	16		J9	370 –		DR	877 06	
Aug.	14		**J14**	425 –		**DR**	1302 06	

②   ③   ④   ⑤

①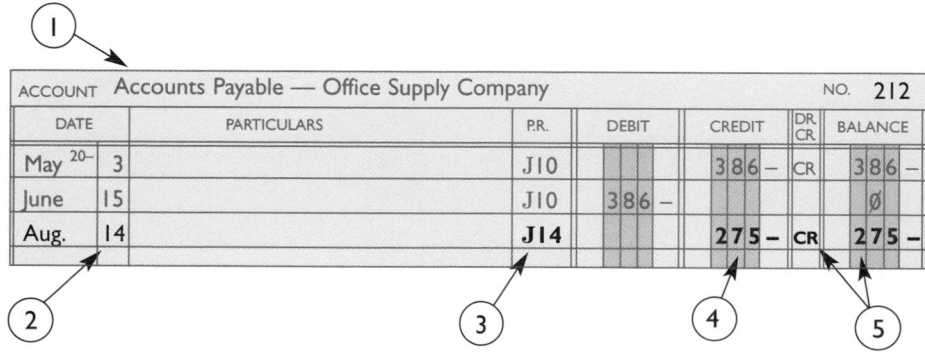

ACCOUNT	Accounts Payable — Office Supply Company						NO.	212
DATE		PARTICULARS	P.R.	DEBIT	CREDIT	DR./CR.	BALANCE	
May 20–	3		J10		386 –	CR	386 –	
June	15		J10	386 –			∅	
Aug.	14		**J14**		275 –	**CR**	275 –	

②   ③   ④   ⑤

Cross-Referencing

Steps 3 and 6 of the posting sequence illustrated in Figures 7.2 through 7.5 on pages 211 through 213 perform what is known as cross-referencing. **Cross-referencing** is the recording of the journal page number in the account and the recording of the account number in the journal. Cross-referencing is illustrated in Figure 7.6 below and on page 215.

FIGURE 7.6

Cross-referencing.

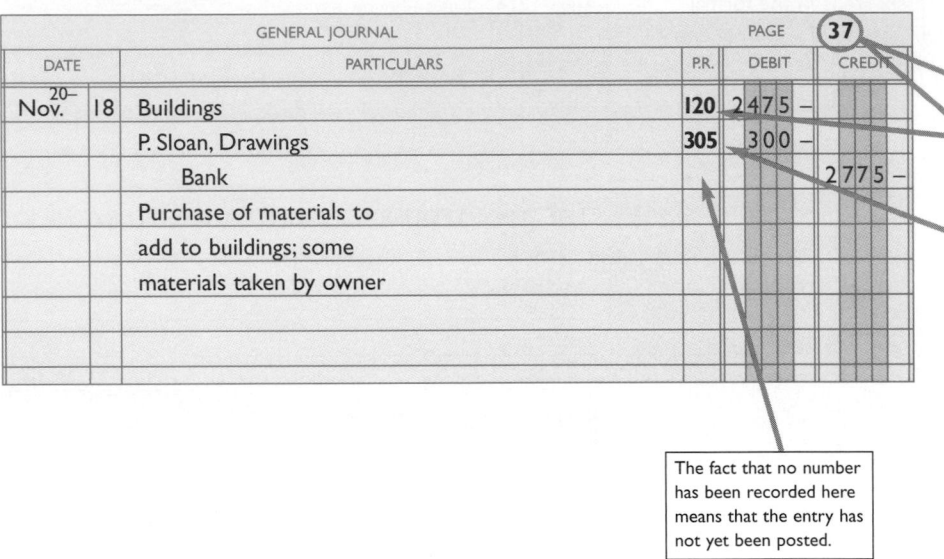

DATE		PARTICULARS	P.R.	DEBIT	CREDIT
20– Nov.	18	Buildings	120	2475 –	
		P. Sloan, Drawings	305	300 –	
		Bank			2775 –
		Purchase of materials to			
		add to buildings; some			
		materials taken by owner			

GENERAL JOURNAL   PAGE 37

The fact that no number has been recorded here means that the entry has not yet been posted.

There are three reasons for cross-referencing.

1. Entries in accounts can easily be traced back to their source in the general journal.
2. Entries in the journal can be followed through to the accounts where they have been posted.
3. If the posting process is interrupted, it is easy to tell where to begin again. Journal amounts that have been posted will have the account number entered.

LEDGER ACCOUNTS

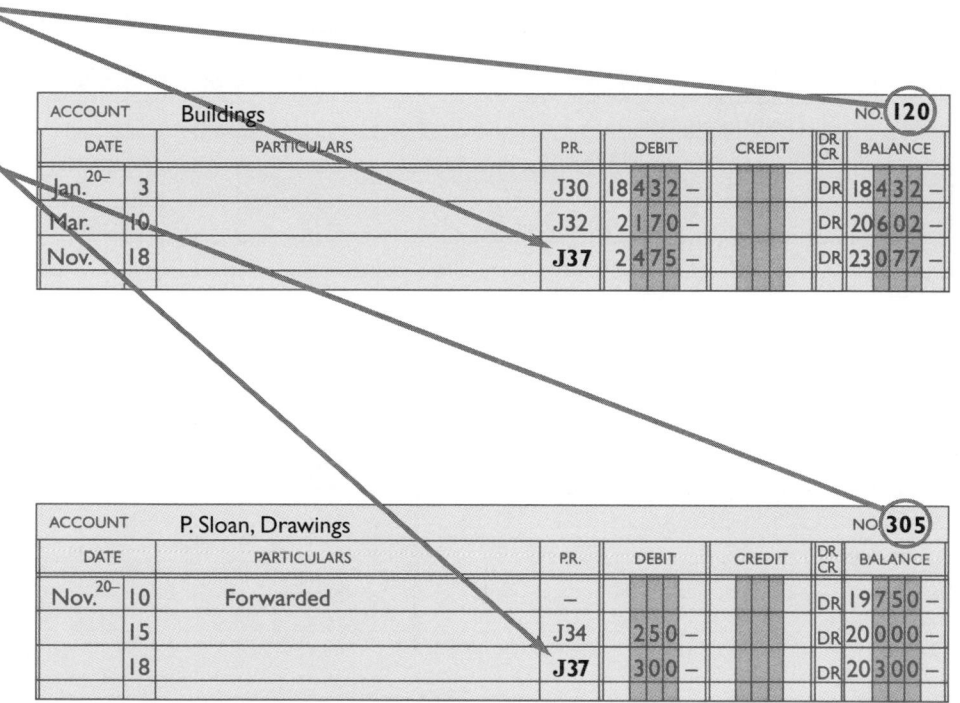

ACCOUNT **Bank**   NO. 101

DATE		PARTICULARS	P.R.	DEBIT	CREDIT	DR./CR.	BALANCE
Nov. 20–	15	Forwarded	–			DR	30 27 50
	17		J36	4 12 90		DR	34 40 40

ACCOUNT **Buildings**   NO. **120**

DATE		PARTICULARS	P.R.	DEBIT	CREDIT	DR./CR.	BALANCE
Jan. 20–	3		J30	18 4 32 –		DR	18 4 32 –
Mar.	10		J32	2 1 70 –		DR	20 6 02 –
Nov.	18		**J37**	2 4 75 –		DR	23 0 77 –

ACCOUNT **P. Sloan, Drawings**   NO. **305**

DATE		PARTICULARS	P.R.	DEBIT	CREDIT	DR./CR.	BALANCE
Nov. 20–	10	Forwarded	–			DR	1 9 7 50 –
	15		J34	2 50 –		DR	20 0 00 –
	18		**J37**	3 00 –		DR	20 3 00 –

Correcting Errors in the Books

Over the years, professional accountants have made it a rule not to erase. Erasures in the books might arouse the suspicions of the auditors, the official examiners of the books and records. Therefore, other methods are used for making corrections.

Errors Found Immediately

It is simple to correct an error that is found right away. Simply stroke neatly through the incorrect figures or letters and write in the correct ones immediately above. Figures 7.7 and 7.8 below show this type of correction:

FIGURE 7.7

Correcting a name in the journal.

An accounting clerk should learn to write small and neatly so that errors are easy to correct.

	GENERAL JOURNAL			Page 8
DATE	PARTICULARS	P.R.	DEBIT	CREDIT
Jun.²⁰⁻ 16	Bank		50 —	
	~~B. Martin~~ A/R – ~~A. Asscot~~			50 —
	Payment of account balance			

FIGURE 7.8

Correcting amounts in an account.

ACCOUNT	Bank					No. 101
DATE	PARTICULARS	P.R.	DEBIT	CREDIT	DR. CR.	BALANCE
Feb.²⁰⁻ 5		J3	64 10		DR	64 10
8		J6	~~131 75~~ 141 85		DR	~~195 85~~ 205 95

Errors Found Later

The accounting department may not learn of an error until quite some time has passed. In many cases, the error can be corrected by means of an accounting entry. For example, consider the following situation:

On July 5, an accounting clerk noticed that an invoice for $752 had been debited to the wrong account. The invoice was clearly for supplies but had been debited to the Equipment account. The error had been made on January 17, almost six months earlier.

The two accounts involved appear as shown in Figure 7.9 on page 217.

FIGURE 7.9

The two accounts affected by an incorrect posting.

Supplies

Date	Partcs	Dr	Cr	Balance	
Jan. 1	Forwarded			150 –	Dr
Feb. 12		370 –		520 –	Dr
20		110 –		630 –	Dr
Mar. 30		50 –		680 –	Dr
Apr. 19		225 –		905 –	Dr
May 12		70 –		975 –	Dr
28		125 –		1100 –	Dr
Jun. 25		45 –		1145 –	Dr

Equipment

Date	Partcs	Dr	Cr	Balance	
Jan. 1	Forwarded			7350 –	Dr
Jan. 17		752 –		8102 –	Dr
Jun. 5		1100 –		9202 –	Dr

The best way to correct an error of this type is by using a correcting journal entry. A **correcting journal entry** is an accounting entry that cancels the effect of an error. In the above case, the entry is needed to cancel the $752 in the Equipment account and set it up in the Supplies account. This journal entry is:

		DR	CR
July 5	Supplies	$752.00	
	Equipment		$752.00
	To correct posting error made on January 17th.		

This method makes it unnecessary to squeeze $752 into the Supplies account, to stroke through and change several dollar amounts, and to change several trial balances.

After correction, the two accounts appear as shown in Figure 7.10 below.

FIGURE 7.10

The two accounts after correction.

Supplies

Date	Partcs	Dr	Cr	Balance	
Jan. 1	Forwarded			150 –	Dr
Feb. 12		370 –		520 –	Dr
20		110 –		630 –	Dr
Mar. 30		50 –		680 –	Dr
Apr. 19		225 –		905 –	Dr
May 12		70 –		975 –	Dr
28		125 –		1100 –	Dr
Jun. 25		45 –		1145 –	Dr
Jul. 5		752 –		1897 –	Dr

Equipment

Date	Partcs	Dr	Cr	Balance	
Jan. 1	Forwarded			7350 –	Dr
Jan. 17		752 –		8102 –	Dr
Jun. 5		1100 –		9202 –	Dr
Jul. 5			752 –	8450 –	Dr

Forwarding Procedure

You may have noticed the word "Forwarded" written on the first line of many of the account pages you have seen, in the figures that illustrate posting. When an account page is full, the account must be continued on a new page. **Forwarding** is the process of continuing an account, or a journal, on a new page by carrying forward the date and the balance from the completed page. The process of forwarding is illustrated in Figure 7.11 below.

FIGURE 7.11

The finished account page after being forwarded (A.) and the new account page with the balance brought forward (B.).

The word "forwarded" is written in the particulars column of the account page that is full.

A.

ACCOUNT	A/R–T.J. Barker						NO. 112
DATE		PARTICULARS	P.R.	DEBIT	CREDIT	DR. CR.	BALANCE
Feb. 20– 7			J1	1 50 62		DR	1 50 62
9			J3	3 74 50		DR	5 25 12
11			J5		1 50 62	DR	3 74 50
12			J5	2 16 51		DR	5 91 01
16			J8	75 62		DR	6 66 63
18			J9		3 74 50	DR	2 92 13
19			J9	5 83 62		DR	8 75 75
21		Forwarded	J10		2 92 13	DR	5 83 62

B.

ACCOUNT	A/R–T.J. Barker						NO. 112
DATE		PARTICULARS	P.R.	DEBIT	CREDIT	DR. CR.	BALANCE
Feb. 20– 21		Forwarded				DR	5 83 62

Notice that nothing is written in the debit, credit, or P.R. columns because forwarding is not posting.

The Accounting Cycle

The total set of accounting procedures that must be carried out during each fiscal period is known as the **accounting cycle.** The steps in the accounting cycle are introduced gradually throughout the text. Figure 7.12 below shows the four steps in the accounting cycle that have been studied so far.

FIGURE 7.12

The first four steps in the accounting cycle.

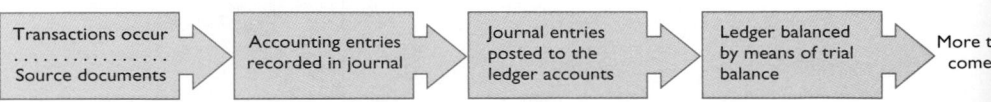

Transactions occur · · · · · · · · · · · · · · · Source documents → Accounting entries recorded in journal → Journal entries posted to the ledger accounts → Ledger balanced by means of trial balance → More t come

Section 7.1   **Review Questions**

1. Name the two important books in the accounting process.
2. Name the simple account that shows debit amounts on one side and credit amounts on the other.
3. Name the style of account most commonly used.
4. Why is the style of account referred to in question 3 considered useful?
5. Describe the steps in opening an account.
6. Where are accounting entries first recorded?
7. What is "posting"?
8. Give the five steps in posting that are performed in the ledger.
9. Give the one step in posting that is performed in the journal.
10. Describe "cross-referencing."
11. Give the three reasons for cross-referencing.
12. Why do we not make erasures in the books of account?
13. Describe the procedure for making a simple correction in the accounts or journal.
14. Describe the procedure for making a correction of an error found after some time has passed.
15. What is "forwarding"?
16. Name the first four steps in the accounting cycle.

 Section 7.1   **Exercises**

1. **Two partially completed accounts are given below and also in your Workbook. For each of these, complete the balance column by calculating and entering the balance after each entry. Be sure to indicate each time whether the balance is debit or credit.**

A.

Asset

Debit	Credit	Balance DR/CR	Amount
1 000 00			
250 00			
310 00			
	1 250 00		
200 00			
350 00			
	860 00		
850 00			
	1 000 00		
1 500 00			
200 00			

B.

Liability

Debit	Credit	Balance DR/CR	Amount
	3 500 00		
	1 600 00		
3 500 00			
1 000 00			
	2 000 00		
600 00			
2 000 00			
	450 00		
500 00			
	50 00		
	375 00		

2. **Workbook Exercise: Posting transactions.**

3. **Workbook Exercise: Forwarding an account balance.**

Trial Balance Out of Balance

As you have already learned, sometimes a trial balance prepared by hand does not balance. It is your job as accounting clerk or accountant to find and correct the errors. Skill in finding errors is important to an accountant.

Figure 7.13 on page 221 shows the sequence of five steps to be followed when a trial balance does not balance. Often, the error or errors will be detected before all of the steps are carried out. However, if you finish the five steps and the trial balance still does not balance, you did not do them correctly. You will have to go through the sequence again, this time working with more care.

Quick Tests for Detecting a Single Error

It may take a lot of time to go through the routine described in Figure 7.13. Experienced accountants try to avoid this whenever they can. They usually try one of four quick tests first.

The initial step in any of the quick tests is to calculate the *trial balance difference* — the amount by which the trial balance is out. Then, any of the following four tests may be applied:

1. **If the trial balance difference is a multiple of 10**, such as 10 cents, 1 dollar, and so on, an error in addition has likely been made. Therefore, re-add the trial balance columns. If this does not work, re-calculate the balance of each account.

2. **Check both the ledger and the journal to see if the trial balance difference is equal to an amount entered in the ledger or the journal.** Whenever you find such an amount, verify it to make sure that it has been handled correctly.

3. **Divide the trial balance difference by two.** Then search (1) the trial balance and (2) the ledger accounts for this divided amount. If an equivalent amount is found, check it carefully. In particular, look to see if a debit amount has been posted or transferred as a credit, or vice versa.

   An error of this type always produces a trial balance difference equal to twice the amount of the error. For example, consider the simplified trial balance shown. It contains a single error. The $30 item listed as a credit should have been listed as a debit. Notice that the difference between the totals is $60, twice the amount of the error.

TRIAL BALANCE

DR	CR
110	
40	
	30 ← Error
	55
	200
50	
25	
225	285

Trial balance difference: $60

FIGURE 7.13

Flowchart of the proce-
dure for balancing the
general ledger.

BALANCING THE GENERAL LEDGER

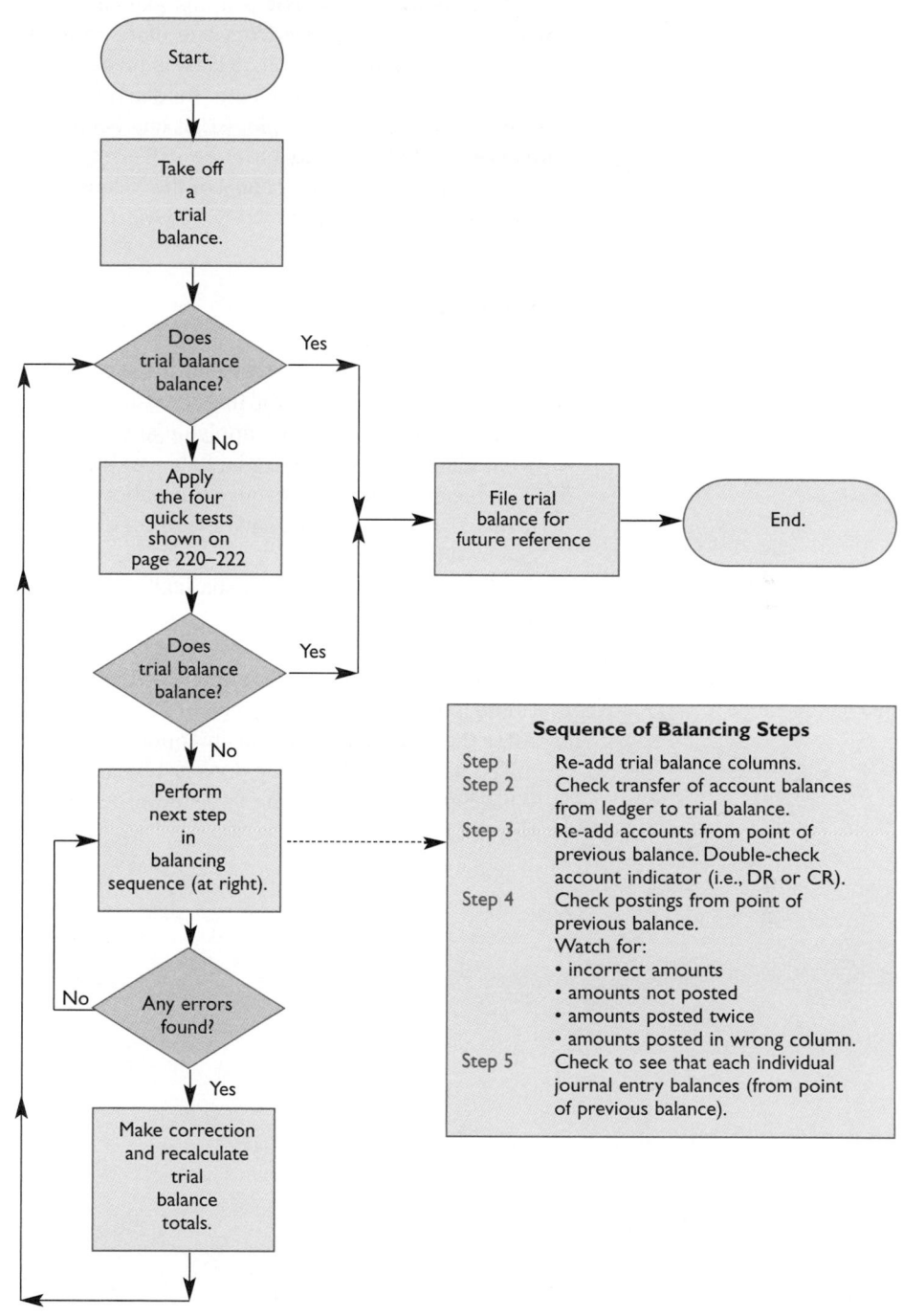

Sequence of Balancing Steps

Step 1 Re-add trial balance columns.
Step 2 Check transfer of account balances
        from ledger to trial balance.
Step 3 Re-add accounts from point of
        previous balance. Double-check
        account indicator (i.e., DR or CR).
Step 4 Check postings from point of
        previous balance.
        Watch for:
        • incorrect amounts
        • amounts not posted
        • amounts posted twice
        • amounts posted in wrong column.
Step 5 Check to see that each individual
        journal entry balances (from point
        of previous balance).

4. **If the trial balance difference is a multiple of 9**, it is likely that a transposition error or a decimal point error has occurred.

A **transposition error** is a mistake caused by changing the order of digits when transferring figures from one place to another. A transposition error has occurred when, for example, $35.60 is posted as $36.50. A decimal point error is a mistake caused by misplacing the decimal point. A **decimal point error** has occurred when, for example, $1.19 has been entered as $119.00. **Such errors always produce a trial balance difference that is exactly divisible by 9.** When this happens, steps 2 and 4 of the "Sequence of Balancing Steps" on page 221 should be performed first.

Section 7.2   Review Questions

1. Why is skill in locating errors important to an accountant?
2. List the four quick tests for finding a single error.
3. What must be done before applying any of the quick tests?
4. What kind of error does a trial balance difference of $10 suggest?
5. With regard to the error in question 4 above, what steps would be followed first?
6. If the trial balance difference is not an even amount, which of the quick tests can be eliminated?
7. Explain what happens mathematically when an amount is posted to the wrong side of an account.
8. What is a transposition error?
9. Could a trial balance difference of $270 be caused by a transposition error?
10. Could a trial balance difference of $2 430 be caused by a decimal point error?
11. After the quick tests have been applied, give the five-step procedure to be followed when a trial balance does not balance.
12. What has to be done if the five-step procedure is completed, but the ledger is still not balanced?

Section 7.2   **Exercises**

1. **Workbook Exercise: Locate and correct errors in a given journal, ledger, and trial balance.** This exercise has multiple errors, so use the five balancing steps from the flowchart on page 221 to guide you.

2. The four mini-exercises on pages 223 through 226 will give you practice at using the four quick tests for locating errors when a trial balance does not balance. **Each exercise has one error, which you are to find. For each mini-exercise, go through the four quick tests you learned in this section. When one of the quick tests works, make corrections so that trial balance is correct.**

1. **Why does it not balance?**

JOURNAL

DATE	PARTICULARS	DR	CR
Jan.²⁰⁻	Bank	4 500	
	Equipment	3 600	
	Capital		8 100
3	Supplies	73	
	Accounts Payable		73
6	Expense	47	
	Bank		47
10	Bank	195	
	Revenue		195
15	Drawings	100	
	Bank		100
19	Accounts Receivable	63	
	Revenue		63
24	Supplies	38	
	Bank		38

LEDGER

Bank
4 500	47
195	1 00
	38
4 695	185
(4 510)	

Accounts Receivable
| 63 | |

Supplies
73	
38	
(111)	

Equipment
| 3 600 | |

Accounts Payable
| | 73 |

Capital
| | 8 100 |

Drawings
| 1 00 | |

Revenue
	1 59
	63
	(222)

Expense
| 47 | |

TRIAL BALANCE

DR	CR
4 510	73
63	8 100
111	222
3 600	
100	
47	
8 431	8 395

2. **Why does it not balance?**

JOURNAL

DATE	PARTICULARS	DR	CR
Feb.3	Bank	3 000	
	Equipment	2 000	
	Capital		5 000
5	Supplies	490	
	Bank		490
9	Accounts Receivable	155	
	Revenue		155
15	Expense	56	
	Bank		56
25	Expense	72	
	Accounts Payable		72
28	Bank	312	
	Revenue		312
29	Drawings	97	
	Bank		97

LEDGER

Bank			Accounts Receivable	
3 000	490		155	
312	56			
	97			
3 312	643			
(2669)				

Supplies		Equipment	
490		2 000	

Accounts Payable		Capital	
	72		5 000

Drawings		Revenue	
97			155
			312
			(467)

Expense	
56	

TRIAL BALANCE

DR	CR
2 669	72
155	5 000
490	467
2 000	
97	
56	
5 467	5 539

3. **Why does it not balance?**

JOURNAL

DATE	PARTICULARS	DR	CR
Apr. 3	Bank	2 500	
	Equipment	7 000	
	Capital		9 500
4	Accounts Receivable	371	
	Revenue		371
8	Bank	269	
	Revenue		269
10	Supplies	53	
	Accounts Payable		53
11	Drawings	127	
	Bank		127
13	Expense	86	
	Bank		86
17	Expense	49	
	Accounts Payable		49

LEDGER

Bank			Accounts Receivable	
2 500	127		371	
269	86			
2769	213			
(2556)				

Supplies			Equipment	
53			7 000	

Accounts Payable			Capital	
	53			9 500
	49			
	(102)			

Drawings			Revenue	
127				371
				269
				(540)

Expense	
86	
49	
135	

TRIAL BALANCE

DR	CR
2 556	102
371	9 500
53	540
7 000	
127	
135	
10 242	10 142

4. **Why does it not balance?**

JOURNAL

DATE	PARTICULARS	DR	CR
Jul. 4	Bank	4 000	
	Equipment	3 000	
	Capital		7 000
5	Supplies	216	
	Accounts Payable		216
10	Accounts Receivable	321	
	Revenue		321
15	Expense	73	
	Bank		73
20	Expense	34	
	Accounts Payable		34
25	Drawings	41	
	Bank		41
30	Bank	150	
	Accounts Receivable		150

LEDGER

Bank
4 000	73
150	41
4 150	114
(4 036)	

Accounts Receivable
| 321 | 150 |
| (171) | |

Supplies
| 216 | |

Equipment
| 3 000 | |

Accounts Payable
	216
	34
	(250)

Capital
| | 7 000 |

Drawings
| 41 | |

Revenue
| | 321 |

Expense
73	
34	
(107)	

TRIAL BALANCE

DR	CR
4 036	250
171	7 000
216	41
3 000	321
107	
7 530	7 612

7.3 | Comparing Accounting Software Programs to Manual Accounting

In Chapter 4, you saw some of the components of Simply Accounting for Windows, an accounting software program. At that stage of your accounting studies, you were still recording transactions directly into T-accounts. Now, you have a better understanding of the accounting cycle. You can analyze source documents, record journal entries, post journal entries to the ledger, take off a trial balance, and prepare financial statements.

In this section, you will use Simply Accounting for Windows 8.0 to complete the parts of the accounting cycle that are familiar to you. Your experience with manual accounting will help you as you learn computerized accounting. Using software gives you the added benefit of reinforcing your understanding of all the important accounting procedures you have learned so far.

The main component of this section is an accounting exercise that is similar to exercises 7 and 8 on pages 240 and 243. To help you compare manual accounting to computer accounting, keep track of the time it takes you to complete each of these three exercises.

Sam's Softball City

Samuel Lucas wants to turn his passion for softball into a successful venture. He plans to develop an indoor/outdoor practice facility that individuals and teams will use to improve their skills, especially batting. Customers may rent the facilities on a cash basis, and credit will be granted to customers who become members.

The name of the business is *Sam's Softball City*. The ledger accounts have already been created in Simply Accounting. You will do the entries for April 2001, the first month of operation. The chart of accounts is shown in Figure 7.14 below.

FIGURE 7.14

The chart of accounts for Sam's Softball City.

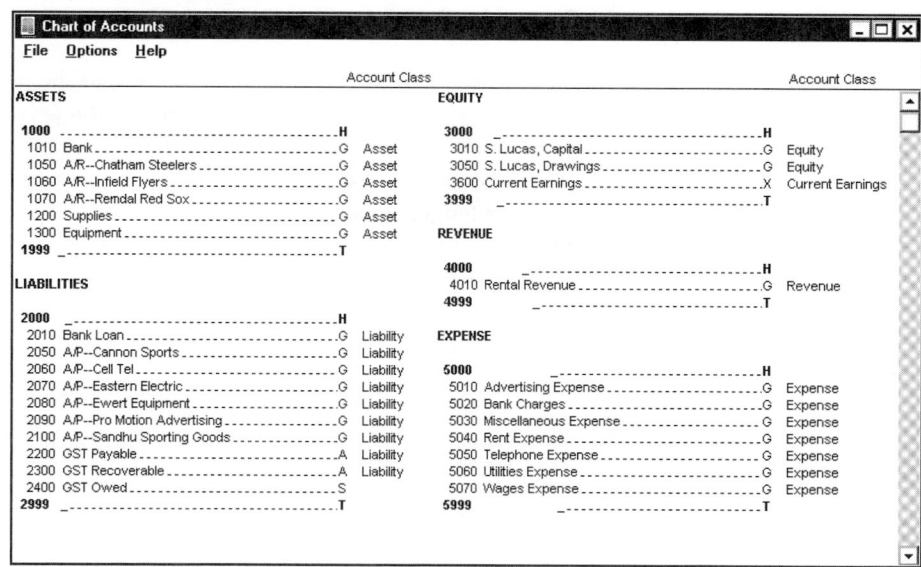

Loading the Account Files

When you load the Simply Accounting files for Sam's Softball City, you will be asked to confirm a "Session Date" of April 1, 2001. (The session date is normally the day when you enter transactions.) Click the OK button and you will see the home window of Simply Accounting, which will look similar to Figure 7.15

FIGURE 7.15

The home window for Sam's Softball City showing the General module.

Software instructions are shown for Simply Accounting for Windows 8.0. If you are using another version, visit www.pearsoned.ca/ accounting1 for other instructions.

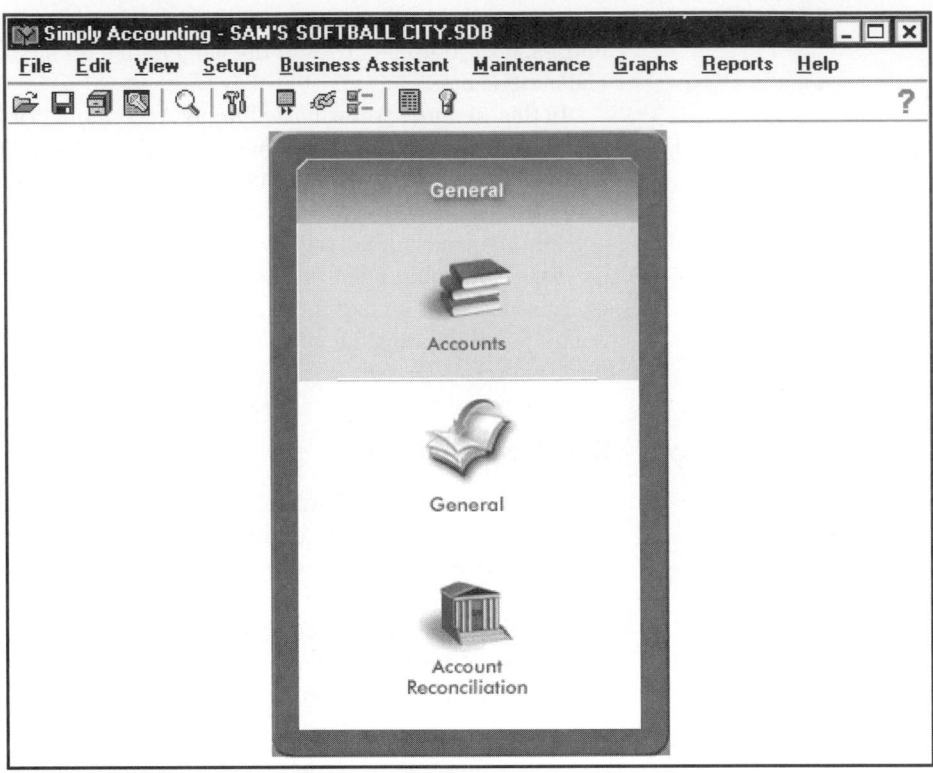

Simply Accounting has six modules for various accounting purposes. You will use all the modules as you progress through the text. For now, you need only the General module shown in Figure 7.15.

The icon near the top of the module is a stack of books, which represents the "books" or ledger accounts for Sam's Softball City. The icon showing the open book represents the general journal—the "book of original entry." Later on, you will discover the purpose of the Account Reconciliation icon near the bottom of the module.

Making Journal Entries

The first transaction for Sam's Softball City appears below. The first money column is for the base amount of the transaction plus PST, if any. When required, the GST will be calculated on the base amount before PST is added. The total amount of the transaction is shown in the last column.

TRANSACTION 1

| | Date | Transaction Details | Source Document Amounts | | |
			Base (+ PST)	GST	Total
#1	April 1	*Memorandum* The owner, Samuel Lucas, invested personal funds into the business.	20,000,00	—	20,000.00

To journalize this transaction in Simply Accounting, double click the general journal icon. In a moment, you will enter the data you see in Figure 7.16. Before you begin typing, be aware that the Source field is for source document numbers. If no source document number exists, type your initials.

When entering general journal data, many people prefer to use the Tab key to move from field to field. To make the bank and capital accounts appear, type their account numbers and press the Tab Key. You can now enter the data transaction shown below into the General Journal window on your screen. The debit item should be entered first.

FIGURE 7.16

The general journal data of the first transaction for Sam's Softball City.

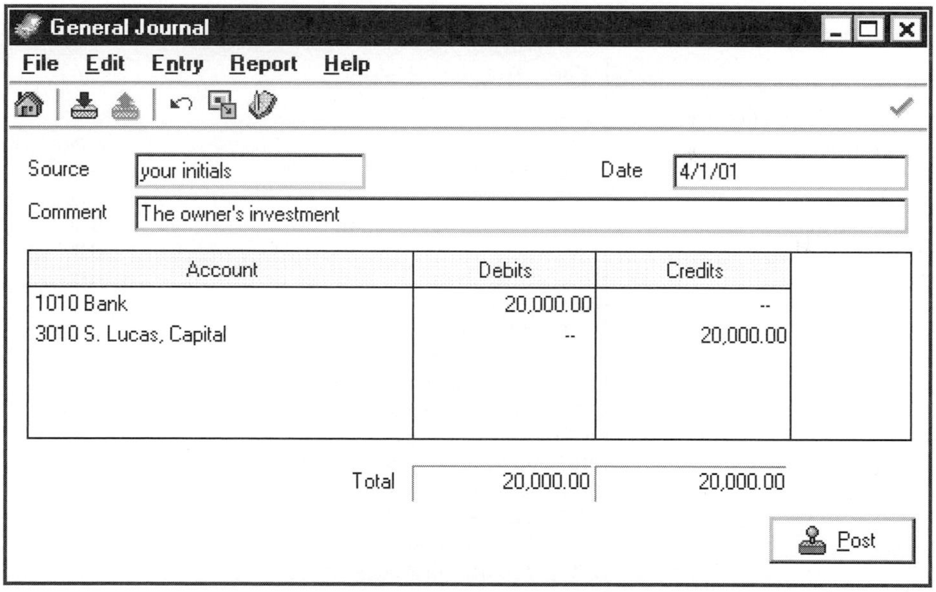

The Journal data are presented in a clear format in Figure 7.16. Yet, it looks different from what you saw in Chapter 6. To check your work in a more familiar format, choose **Report, Display General Journal Entry**. Your monitor should look like Figure 7.17.

FIGURE 7.17

The journal entry format for Transaction 1.

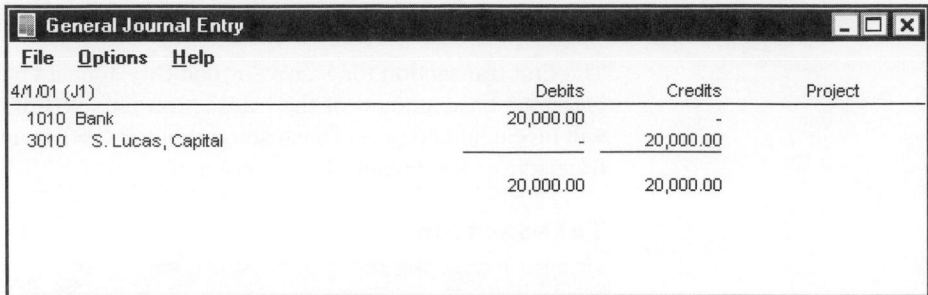

Checking your journal entries in the format shown in Figure 7.17 may help prevent errors. After you have displayed this journal entry and are satisfied that it is correct, close the window. You are now ready to post this transaction.

Posting

After you have returned to the general journal data entry screen (Figure 7.16), you may post your transaction. Simply click the Post button located near the bottom-right corner of the journal screen.

To check what Simply Accounting has done with your journal entry, return to the **Home** window and choose **Reports, Financials, Trial Balance** and click OK. Your monitor should look like Figure 7.18. Notice that the mouse pointer now looks like a small magnifying glass with a plus sign.

FIGURE 7.18

The trial balance after the first transaction has been posted.

Trial Balance			
File Options Help			
As At 4/1/01		Debits	Credits
1010	Bank	20,000.00	-
1050	A/R--Chatham Steelers	0.00	-
1060	A/R--Infield Flyers	0.00	-
1070	A/R--Remdal Red Sox	0.00	-
1200	Supplies	0.00	-
1300	Equipment	0.00	-
2010	Bank Loan	-	0.00
2050	A/P--Cannon Sports	-	0.00
2060	A/P--Cell Tel	-	0.00
2070	A/P--Eastern Electric	-	0.00
2080	A/P--Ewert Equipment	-	0.00
2090	A/P--Pro Motion Advertising	-	0.00
2100	A/P--Sandhu Sporting Goods	-	0.00
2200	GST Payable	-	0.00
2300	GST Recoverable	-	0.00
3010	S. Lucas, Capital	-	20,000.00
3050	S. Lucas, Drawings	-	0.00

The amounts in the first transaction have been posted to the Bank and S. Lucas, Capital accounts. The new balances in those accounts show up instantly on the trial balance.

Simply Accounting allows you to follow the "trail" of the first transaction. Move the mouse pointer (the magnifying glass) on top of the 20,000 debit to Bank. Double click the 20,000 and ledger account #1010 for Bank appears. Double click the 20,000 debit in the ledger account, and the original journal entry appears. From the trial balance report, Simply Accounting permits you to follow a number back to its originating journal entry. This ability is called the **drilldown** feature. Accountants find it very useful when they need to answer questions about the amounts that appear on financial statements.

You probably now have many windows open. Close them and return to the Simply Accounting home window.

TRANSACTION 2

Open the general journal and enter the second transaction, which appears below.

| | Date | Transaction Details | Source Document Amounts | | |
			Base (+ PST)	GST	Total
#2	April 1	*Credit Memo*			
		Borrowed funds from the bank;			
		repayable on demand	38,000.00	—	38,000.00

Note: If you do not know the account number for Bank Loan, you could flip back to the chart of accounts on page 131. However, there is a better way. When the cursor is in the Account field, press the Return or Enter key. A chart of accounts pops into view. You can select from this list by double clicking the account you want.

Post Transaction 2 when you are sure it is correct.

TRANSACTION 3 — CORRECTING ERRORS

A mistake has been made. The amount of the loan from the bank is $35 000, not $38 000. You might think the best way to approach this situation is to electronically delete Transaction 2 and start again. Accountants and auditors, however, like to see any changes that are made in the books of account. Therefore, instead of deleting the erroneous entry, you must make another journal entry (or entries) to adjust the totals in the accounts.

You could make two separate journal entries to fix the mistake. The first correcting journal entry could be the exact opposite of the error. In this case, you would debit Bank Loan for $38 000 and credit Bank for $38 000. When posted, these amounts would cancel the effects of the dollar amounts in Transaction 2. Then, you could simply redo Transaction 2 properly. Although two journal entries are required for this "undo/redo" method, you may prefer to use it for complex transactions.

Instead of making two journals entries, you could fix Transaction 2 with one journal entry. It is plain that the Bank and Bank Loan accounts were overstated by $3 000. Therefore, one journal entry to reduce both accounts to $35 000 will fix the error. Enter and post data shown in Figure 7.19. (Use your own initials in the Source field.)

FIGURE 7.19

The correcting journal entry for the loan from the bank.

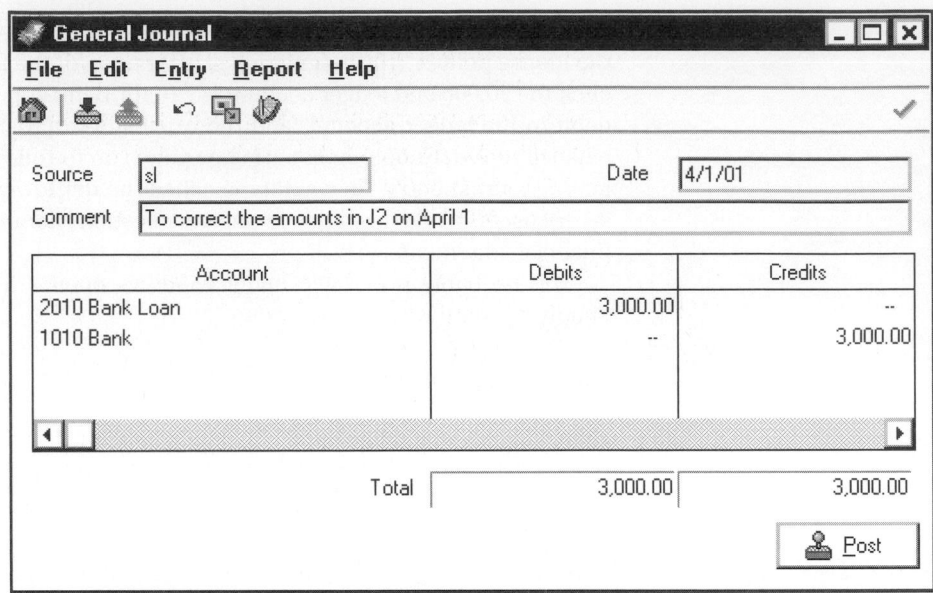

After posting, the results of the correcting entry in the Bank Loan account are shown in Figure 7.20. You can see from the final total in the Balance column that the amount of the loan is now correct.

FIGURE 7.20

The Bank Loan account after the correcting journal entry is posted.

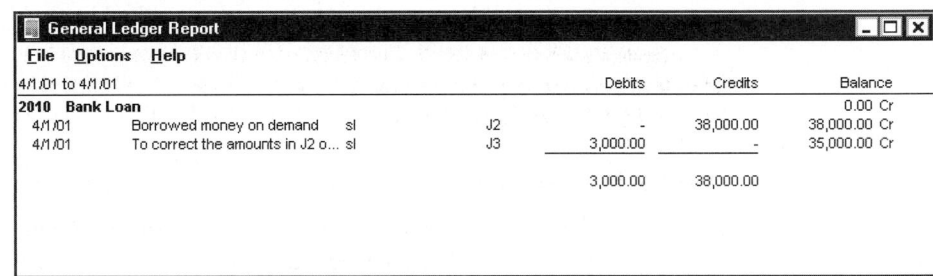

TRANSACTION 4 — CHANGING DEFAULT AMOUNTS

Transaction 4 is your first chance to work with GST in Simply Accounting. The details of transaction 4 are shown below.

| | Date | Transaction Details | Source Document Amounts | | |
			Base (+ PST)	GST	Total
#4	April 1	*Cheque Copy 001* Paid the monthly rent to Romeyn Properties Ltd.	4,500.00	315.00	4,815.00

Enter a portion of the rent payment data. Stop when your monitor looks like Figure 7.21.

FIGURE 7.21

A partial journal entry with incorrect GST results.

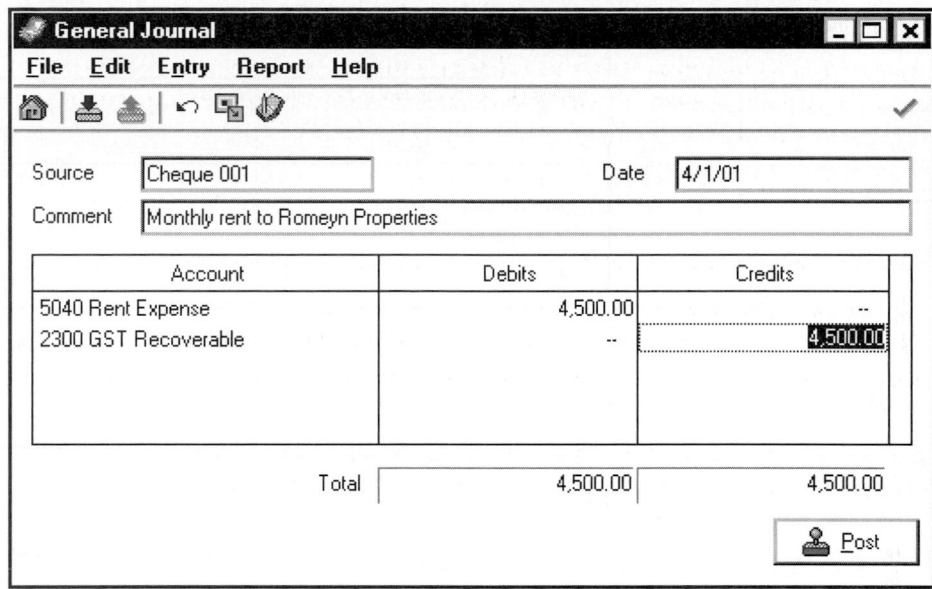

The $4 500 credit to GST Recoverable appeared by default, and it is not what you want. Simply Accounting anticipated that you wanted a credit entry of $4 500 because Rent Expense was debited $4 500. In most instances, the Simply Accounting defaults are correct, and they can save you a great deal of time and effort. However, the software cannot think for you. Occasionally, it guesses wrong.

From the transaction details on the previous page, you know the GST should be $315 ($4 500 × 7%). While the $4 500 credit to GST Recoverable is still highlighted, key –315 and press the Tab key. The negative sign transfers the $315 to the debit side because that is the decrease side of a liability account. (You can also use the Delete key, mouse, and keyboard to enter the $315 on the debit side.)

When you call up the Bank account, your monitor will look like Figure 7.22. Notice that the $4 815 credit to Bank appeared by default. This time, Simply Accounting guessed correctly. Post your entry when you are satisfied that it is correct.

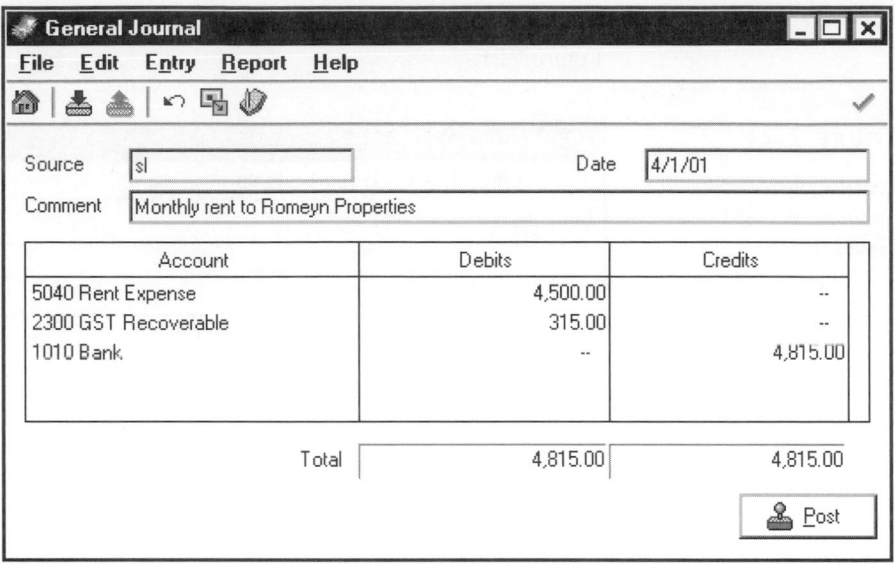

General Journal

File   Edit   Entry   Report   Help

Source   sl   Date   4/1/01

Comment   Monthly rent to Romeyn Properties

Account	Debits	Credits
5040 Rent Expense	4,500.00	--
2300 GST Recoverable	315.00	--
1010 Bank	--	4,815.00
Total	4,815.00	4,815.00

Post

Finishing the Journal Entries

Your background is now sufficient to complete the rest of the journal entries for the
first two months of business for Sam's Softball City.

The amounts in the GST
column may represent
either GST Recoverable
or GST Payable. You must
consider the details of
each transaction to make
the correct choice.

You don't need a PST
account for Sam's Softball
City for two reasons:
1) Although a business
is charged PST on pur-
chases, purchasers do
not keep an account
for PST payments, and
2) Sam's Softball City
sells services which
are PST exempt.

	Date	Transaction Details	Source Document Amounts		
			Base (+ PST)	GST	Total
#5	April 2	Cheque Copy 002 Purchased various supplies for the office and sports area.	4,995.00	323.75	5,318.75
#6	5	Purchase Invoice 03452 Purchased balls and bats from Cannon Sports Equipment; terms net 30 days.	9,996.48	647.92	10,644.40
#7	8	Purchase Invoice 771932 Purchased pitching machines from Ewert Equipment; terms net 30 days.	21,999.60	1,425.90	23,425.50
#8	9	Purchase Invoice 114A Bought supplies from Sandhu Sporting Goods; terms net 30 days.	2,484.00	161.00	2,645.00
#9	13	Cash Sales Summary CS001 Cash sales for the two weeks ended April 13.	525.00	36.75	561.75
#10	15	Cheque Copy 003 To employees for wages.	2,150.00	—	2,150.00
#11	15	Sales Invoice 001 Sold a 30-day membership to the Infield Flyers for $300; received $100, the balance to be paid in 30 days.	300.00	21.00	321.00

	Date	Transaction Details	Source Document Amounts		
			Base (+ PST)	GST	Total
#12	18	*Sales Invoice 002* Sold a 60-day membership to the Remdal Red Sox; terms net 30 days.	500.00	35.00	535.00
#13	23	*Purchase Invoice #98884* Hired Pro Motion Advertising to provide advertisements on public transit.	1,350.00	94.50	1,444.50
#14	27	*Cash Sales Summary CS002* Cash sales for the two weeks ended April 27.	675.00	47.25	722.25
#15	30	*Debit Memo* Funds were deducted from the business's bank account for interest and service charges.	250.00	—	250.00
#16	30	*Cheque Copy 004* To employees for wages.	2,150.00	—	2,150.00
#17	30	*Cheque Copy 005* To the owner for personal use.	3,000.00	—	3,000.00
#18	**May** 1	*Cheque Copy 006* Paid the monthly rent to Romeyn Properties Ltd.	4,500.00	315.00	4,815.00
#19	5	*Cheque Copy 007* Paid Cannon Sports Equipment the amount owed.	10,644.40	—	10,644.40
#20	6	*Telephone Bill 90384* Telephone bill for April received from Cell Tell. Due in two weeks.	168.00	11.76	179.76
#21	6	*Cheque Copy 008* To Ewert Equipment in partial payment of the amount owed to them.	11,000.00	—	11,000.00
#22	9	*Cheque Copy 009* Paid Sandhu Sporting Goods the amount owed.	2,645.00	—	2,645.00
#23	11	*Cash Sales Summary CS003* Cash sales for the two weeks ended May 11.	2,675.00	187.25	2,862.25
#24	15	*Cheque Copy 010* To employees for wages.	2,150.00	—	2,150.00
#25	17	*Remittance Slip 001* Received a cheque from the Infield Flyers to clear the amount owed.	221.00	—	221.00

	Date	Transaction Details	Source Document Amounts Base (+ PST)	GST	Total
#26	20	Cheque Copy 011 To reimburse the owner for the money spent to buy stamps for the business.	48.00	3.36	51.36
#27	20	Memorandum Cheque 002 written on April 2 was for equipment, not supplies, as previously recorded.	4,995.00	—	4,995.00
#28	20	Cheque Copy 012 Paid the telephone bill received from Cell Tell on May 6.	179.76	—	179.76
#29	24	Sales Invoice 003 Sold annual membership to the Chatham Steelers; terms net 30 days.	4,900.00	343.00	5,243.00
#30	May 25	Cash Sales Summary CS004 Cash sales for the two weeks ended May 25.	3,075.00	215.25	3,290.25
#31	31	Utilities Bill 840908 Received a bill from Eastern Electric for gas and electricity used; due in two weeks.	1,398.00	97.86	1,495.86
#32	31	Cheque Copy 013 To employees for wages.	2,150.00	—	2,150.00
#33	31	Cheque Copy 014 To the owner for personal use.	3,000.00	—	3,000.00
#34	31	Bank Statement Printout GST cash refund for April was electronically deposited into the business's bank account.	2,828.07	—	2,828.07

Hint: Check the trial balance for April 30 to help you analyze transaction #34.

Preparing to Print

Before you can print, you need to change two items. First, choose **Setup, Company Information** and type your name where indicated in the brackets. This ensures that your name will appear on printed reports.

Next, choose **Maintenance, Change Session Date**. Enter **05/31/01**. The Session date is normally the date when you enter transactions, so you could have done this step before you started entering transactions.

To enter dates, try the drop-down menus that appear next to the date fields.

Check with your teacher about which reports to print. When you wish to print a report, you must first view it on your monitor. Choosing Reports, Financials will allow you to make selections for an income statement and balance sheet. When choosing an income statement, you will enter the "start" and "end" dates for the first two months in which Sam's Softball City operated. The balance sheet is for one day only, so you will enter 05/31/01.

Once you see a financial report on your monitor, you can choose File, Print. If your teacher wants you to print journal entries, choose Reports, Journal Entries, All. Like the income statement, you must enter the start and end dates for the journal entries you want to see and print.

Section 7.3   Review Questions

1. Explain what the session date is in Simply Accounting.
2. In the home window of Simply Accounting, what does the stack of books represent?
3. What does the "drilldown" feature do?
4. A cash sale for $1000 was posted as a debit to Bank of $100 and a credit to Fees Earned of $100. Give the journal entry to correct this situation.
5. What is a software default and why is it beneficial?

Section 7.3   Exercises

1. Workbook Exercise for Simply Accounting—Kalley's Database Developments.

Section 7.3   Communicate It

For a better comparison, complete Chapter Exercises 7 and 8 manually before writing this letter.

Gary McKill enjoys the outdoors. Therefore, he is well suited to run his landscaping business, which has annual sales of approximately $80 000. However, he prefers to avoid technology. In fact, he does not even own a computer. His good grasp of accounting procedures enables him to do the bookkeeping himself, even though completing it by hand takes about 15 hours per week.

From the perspective of an accounting student, write him a letter that compares manual accounting to computerized accounting using Simply Accounting for Windows. Draw on the experience you gained from doing the exercises in this chapter. Try to use specific examples when making your comparisons. Finish your letter with a recommendation about which system he should use.

See the Skills Appendix for help in preparing the letter. The business is named Gary's GardenScapes and is located at 2749 Studer Drive, Kelowna, B.C., V8G 4K2.

CHAPTER 7 Summary

CHAPTER HIGHLIGHTS

Now that you have completed Chapter 7, you should:

- be able to post journal entries and balance them correctly;
- be able to work out an "opening entry" from a balance sheet and to "open" an account;
- understand why both a journal and a ledger are used in the accounting process;
- be able to use a balance column account correctly and with ease;
- understand the purpose of cross-referencing;
- know how to forward the balance of an account to a new page;
- know the first four steps in the accounting cycle;
- know how to make corrections in the journal and in the accounts, and how to make correcting journal entries;
- be able to use the quick tests correctly in locating trial balance errors;
- be able to use accounting software for the steps in the accounting cycle you have learned to this point;
- be able to compare manual and computer accounting methods.

ACCOUNTING TERMS

account title	cross-referencing	opening an account
balance column account	decimal point error	posting
correcting journal entry	forwarding	transposition error

CHAPTER 7 Review Exercises

Using Your Knowledge

This exercise also appears in the Workbook.

❶ Indicate whether each of the following statements is true or false by placing a "T" or an "F" in the space indicated. Explain the reason for each "F" response in the space provided.

A. The chief advantage of the balance-column account is that there is room for the account balance.

B. Both sides of an account page (front and back) are used for the same item (for example, Bank).

C. Entering the journal page number in the account is the sixth step in the posting process.

D. The step described in question c above is performed in the journal.

E. The process of setting up an account is known as "forwarding."

F. The fourth step in the accounting cycle, as we know it, is the taking off of a trial balance.

G. It is not possible for the ledger to be out of balance and also to be correct.

H. If the trial balance difference is an even amount, the error could not be a transposition error.

I. If the trial balance difference is zero, the ledger is correct.

J. Posting a debit item incorrectly as a credit produces a trial balance credit total that is smaller than the debit total by twice the amount of the error.
K. Very rarely does a transaction affect only one account.
L. Ledger accounts are arranged alphabetically to make them easier to find.
M. The presence of the account number in the journal indicates that the posting of an item has been completed.

2 **Complete the chart in the Workbook about the effect of errors on a trial balance.**

Error situations	Trial Balance will not balance		Trial Balance will balance but will not be correct
	Debits greater than credits by ($$)	Credits greater than debits by ($$)	
a. An entire journal entry is posted as $400 instead of $100.			
b. A debit of $200 is posted twice.			
c. A debit of $150 is posted as a credit.			
d. The Bank account is over-added by $80.			
e. The Drawings account balance of $5 500 is missed when preparing the trial balance.			
f. The Revenue account balance of $72 000 is listed on the trial balance as a debit.			
g. An entire general journal entry for $325 is not posted.			
h. An entire general journal entry for $50 is posted in reverse.			
i. A $40 debit is not posted.			
j. A $500 credit is posted as $50.			
k. A debit of $60 to Bank was posted to a customer's account instead of to Bank.			
l. A $40 debit is posted as $400.			

3 An accounting clerk prepares his trial balance as of June 30, 20— and determines that total debits equal total credits. He breathes a sigh of relief and informs his boss that his ledger is in balance and that therefore the accounts are correct. His boss, a chartered accountant, tells him that this is not necessarily the case. She asks him to prepare a list of four possible errors that could occur and yet not cause the trial balance to be out of balance. **Prepare this list as if you were the accounting clerk.**

4 An employee working on her first trial balance discovers that the Furniture and Equipment account has a credit balance of $5 000 and a customer's account has a credit balance of $200. **Has the accountant made a mistake in her records or is this situation possible? Explain.**

5 You have been employed by Wilson Building Depot as an accounting clerk. Your main duty is to record journal entries daily and post to the general ledger. Your procedure in posting is to post the entries by account order. For example, you first go through all of your journal entries and post all Bank entries. You then proceed to the second account, and so on. **Explain the advantage of this method.**

6 Dean Slovodnik posts from the journal to the ledger at the end of each week. Because he prepares a balance sheet once a year, he believes it is necessary to prepare a trial balance only once a year. **What are the disadvantages of taking a trial balance only once a year?**

Comprehensive Exercises

7 The accounts required for this exercise are shown in the chart of accounts below.

ROYAL CITY ENGINEERING CHART OF ACCOUNTS	
101 Bank	301 Pat Schelling, Capital
111 A/R — L. Pero	302 Pat Schelling, Drawings
113 A/R — K. Puna	401 Service Revenue
115 A/R — Spectrum Co.	505 Automobile Expense
117 A/R — W. J. Thomson	510 Bank Charges Expense
120 Supplies	515 General Expense
125 Equipment	520 Rent Expense
130 Automobiles	525 Telephone Expense
201 Bank Loan	530 Wages Expense
211 A/P — Imperial Garage	535 Loss on Sale of Equipment
213 A/P — Home Hardware	
220 GST Payable	
225 GST Recoverable	
230 PST Payable	

Pat Schelling began a business called Royal City Engineering. His beginning financial position is shown on the following balance sheet:

ROYAL CITY ENGINEERING
BALANCE SHEET
AUGUST 31, 20—

Assets		Liabilities	
Bank	$ 2 000	Bank Loan	$20 000
Supplies	1 450		
Equipment	14 732	Owner's Equity	
Automobiles	28 957	P. Schelling, Capital	27 139
Total Assets	$47 139	Total Liabilities and Equity	$47 139

A. Journalize the opening entry and post it in the accounts.

B. Journalize and post the transactions for September given below.
In working out the accounting entries, assume that 1) for the purposes of this exercise, the business is exempt from PST for its purchases, and 2) the business charges both GST and PST on all sales.

TRANSACTIONS

September
1 *Cheque Copy*
To Rosewell Investments for the rent for the month, $900.00 plus GST of $63.00, total $963.00.
3 *Purchase Invoice*
From Home Hardware for the purchase of supplies on account, $235.00 plus GST of $16.45, total $251.45.
5 *Sales Invoice*
To W. J. Thomson for services rendered on account, $3 500.00 plus GST of $245.00 and PST of $280.00, total $4 025.00.
5 *Sales Invoice*
To L. Pero for services rendered on account, $2 000.00 plus GST of $140.00 plus PST of $160.00, total $2 300.00.
9 *Cash Sales Slip*
Sold a piece of equipment for $500.00 cash (assume that this sale is not taxable). This piece of equipment had originally cost $1 200.00 and was included in the Equipment account at that figure. (Note: Although a sale has been made, this transaction does not affect the revenue account, which is used only for the normal revenue of the business.)
10 *Sales Invoice*
To Spectrum Co. for services rendered on account, $800.00 plus GST of $56.00 and PST of $64.00, total $920.00.
11 *Cheque Copy*
To the owner for personal use, $500.00.
12 *Cheque Copy*
To Home Hardware on account, $251.45.

15 *Purchase Invoice*

Received from Imperial Garage for gasoline and oil used in the business automobiles, $342.00 plus GST of $23.94, total $365.94.

16 *Cheque Copy*

Issued to the Marketplace for the cash purchase of supplies, $165.00 plus GST of $11.55, total $176.55.

18 *Cash Receipt*

Received a cheque from W. J. Thomson, in full payment of the account balance.

18 *Cheque Copy*

To the owner, reimbursement for out-of-pocket expenses: postage, $32.00 plus GST of $2.24; parking, $40 plus GST of $2.80; and gasoline and oil for business purposes, $78.00 plus GST of $5.46; total $160.50.

19 *Bank Debit Memo*

Received a memorandum from the bank stating that $250.00 had been deducted from the business bank account to pay for bank interest and charges.

19 *Cheque Copy*

To an employee for wages, $575.00.

19 *Sales Invoice*

To K. Puna for services rendered on account, $600.00 plus GST of $42.00 and PST of $48.00, total $690.00.

22 *Memorandum*

From the owner stating that the bank had acted on his instructions to reduce the bank loan by $2 000.00.

24 *Cheque Copy*

To Bell Canada in payment of the telephone bill, $58.00 plus GST of $4.06, total $62.06.

25 *Cash Receipt*

Received a cheque from L. Pero on account, $1 000.00.

26 *Sales Invoice*

To W. J. Thomson for services rendered on account, $400.00 plus GST of $28.00 and PST of $32.00, total $460.00.

26 *Cheque Copy*

To the owner for personal use, $450.00.

29 *Memorandum*

From the owner stating that 1) he had paid $190.00 plus GST of $13.30, total $203.30, out of his own pocket for supplies used for business purposes, and 2) his Drawings account is to be credited for the above.

30 *Cheque Copy*

To an employee for wages, $570.00.

30 *Cheque Copy*

To Imperial Garage, paying $365.94 on account.

30 *Purchase Invoice*

From Imperial Garage, charging for gasoline and oil used in the company automobiles; $312.00 plus GST of $21.84, total $333.84.

C. Balance the ledger by means of a trial balance.

D. Prepare an income statement for the month of September.

E. Prepare a balance sheet as at September 30. Use Figure 5.8 on page 138 as your guide.

---

8 **The accounts required for this exercise are set up in the Workbook.** The Harbour Golf Links, owned by Shirley Ng-A-Kien, operates a par-three golf course and a driving range. On September 30, 20—, the trial balance of the business is as shown below. Harbour Golf Links charges 7 per cent GST on all sales and rentals and 8 percent PST on certain prescribed items. **For the purposes of this exercise, assume that the business is PST-exempt on all purchases.**

HARBOUR GOLF LINKS
TRIAL BALANCE
SEPTEMBER 30, 20–

No.	Accounts	DR	CR
100	Bank	$ 3 750.20	
105	Supplies — Golf Course	10 236.00	
110	Supplies — Office	3 265.25	
115	Property	95 000.00	
120	Buildings	85 360.00	
125	Automotive Equipment	40 956.00	
130	Maintenance Equipment	22 650.60	
201	Bank Loan		$120 000.00
205	A/P — Blair's Automotive		
210	A/P — Main Supply		1 890.65
215	A/P — Pro Equipment		3 582.10
220	GST Payable		710.00
225	GST Recoverable	185.00	
230	PST Payable		250.50
240	Mortgage Payable		100 000.00
301	Shirley Ng-A-Kien, Capital		37 027.46
305	Shirley Ng-A-Kien, Drawings	18 000.00	
401	Revenue — Golf		52 655.00
405	Revenue — Food		9 250.50
500	Automotive Expense	5 963.01	
505	Bank Charges Expense	6 842.25	
515	Maintenance Expense	7 230.85	
520	Miscellaneous Expense	1 525.75	
525	Mortgage Interest Expense	4 500.00	
530	Telephone Expense	685.55	
510	Utilities Expense	2 850.45	
535	Wages Expense	16 365.30	
		$325 366.21	$325 366.21

A. Journalize and post the transactions below for the month of October. Use page 28 of the journal.

TRANSACTIONS

October

2 *Cheque Copy*
No. 652, cash purchase of miscellaneous expense item, $155.00 plus GST of $10.85, total $165.85.

4 *Purchase Invoice*
From Main Supply for fertilizer, $950.20 plus GST of $66.51, total $1 016.71.

5 *Bank Debit Memo*
Bank charges and loan interest for September, $1 250.00.

7 *Cheque Copy*
No. 653, for wages for the week, $650.00.

8 *Cash Receipts*
Cash receipts for previous week, golf $2 005.00, food $490.00, plus GST of $174.65 and PST of $74.40, total $2 744.05.

9 *Cheque Copy*
No. 654, to Main Supply, payment of debt owing, $1 890.65.

10 *Purchase Invoice*
From Blair's Automotive for truck repairs, $220.00 plus GST of $15.40, total $235.40.

11 *Purchase Invoice*
From Pro Equipment for golf supplies, $176.40 plus GST of $12.35, total $188.75.

13 *Cheque Copy*
No. 655, to the owner, for personal use, $1 500.00.

14 *Cheque Copy*
No. 656, for wages for the week, $700.00.

15 *Cash Receipts*
Cash receipts for previous week, golf $1 920.00, food $470.00, plus GST of $167.30 and PST of $91.20, total $2 648.50.

15 *Cheque Copy*
No. 657, to Provincial Treasurer, paying the PST for the previous month, $250.50.

17 *Purchase Invoice*
From Pro Equipment for repairs to lawnmowers, $400.00 plus GST of $28.00, total $428.00.

18 *Cheque Copy*
No. 658, to Axoil for the cash purchase of gasoline and oil for the business vehicles, $42.25 plus GST of $2.96, total $45.21.

20 *Cheque Copy*
No. 659, to Greco Investments, for mortgage payment, mortgage interest $750.00, loan reduction $1 000.00, total $1 750.00.

21 *Cheque Copy*
No. 660, for wages for the week, $680.00.

22 *Cash Receipts*
Cash receipts for the previous week, golf $2 200.00, food $500.00, plus GST of $189.00 and PST of $76.00, total $2 965.00.

23 *Cheque Copy*
No. 661, to Pro Equipment, for partial payment of debt owing, $2 000.00.

24 *Purchase Invoice*
From Main Supply, for office supplies, $95.00 plus GST of $6.65, total $101.65.

25 *Purchase Invoice*
From Blair's Automotive, for auto equipment repairs, $290.00 plus GST of $20.30, total $310.30.

26 *Cheque Copy*
No. 662, for the cash purchase of miscellaneous expense item, $85.00 plus GST of $5.95, total $90.95.

28 *Cheque Copy*
No. 663, for the wages for the week, $620.00.

29 *Cash Receipts*
Cash receipts for the previous week, golf $2 010.00, food $580.00, plus GST of $181.30 and PST of $77.20, total $2 848.50.

30 *Cheque Copy*
No. 664, cash payment for hydro for the month, $165.00 plus GST of $11.55, total $176.55.

31 *Cheque Copy*
No. 665, cash payment for telephone service for the month, $75.00 plus GST of $5.25, total $80.25.

31 *Cheque Copy*
No. 666, to the owner, for personal use, $1 500.00.

31 *Cheque Copy*
No. 667, to the Receiver General, paying the net GST for September, $525.00.

B. **Balance the ledger by means of a trial balance.**

C. **Prepare a simple income statement for the 10 months ended October 31.**

D. **Prepare a balance sheet for October 31.**

Questions for Further Thought

Briefly answer the following questions.

1. People who work in accounting departments often describe themselves as "accountants," regardless of how well qualified they are. Give your opinion of this practice, with reasons.

2. Is the person in charge of the payroll of a large business an important employee? Explain.

3. When cross-referencing, some accountants just use check marks. What are the advantages and disadvantages of this technique?

4. An accounting error that is found after quite some time would be corrected by a journal entry. Why would this method be used instead of stroking out incorrect figures and writing in the correct ones?

5. Some students prefer to look at the Teacher's Key when they have an exercise that does not balance. Why is this a bad habit?

6. Not long ago, you earned your accountant's qualification while employed by Superior Tire Manufacturing Company. You have recently taken a new position with the General Life Insurance Company. Your new position presents you with many new challenges directly related to the accounting function. Explain what differences you might encounter and why they would exist.

7. Your teacher asks you to give the accounting entry for the purchase of supplies for cash. You begin your response, "Credit Bank and————." Your teacher stops you, believing that your answer is incorrect. Why would the teacher think so?

8. A posting intended for Smith's account in the accounts receivable ledger was incorrectly made to Smythe's account. How would this error be detected?

9. If your ledger does not balance by $5 and you have been unable to find the error after a four-day search, is it all right simply to change one of the accounts to force it into balance? Justify your opinion.

Case Studies

CASE 1

A Stitch in Time . . . .

Karen Bulgarelli is a busy young woman. She works long days operating her used clothing shop, Second Debut. She also does much of the accounting work at home. In order to save time, Karen does not post her journal entries, which often number as many as 20 per day. When asked about her unusual accounting procedures, she replied, "My general journal is a complete record of all of my transactions, so I really don't need ledger accounts! Anyway, think of all the time I'm saving by not posting!"

Questions

1. Do you agree with Karen's comments? Explain.
2. What are the disadvantages of Karen's system?

CASE 2

Does the Order of Accounts Matter?

Randy Sandhu, owner of Randy's Car Care, journalizes and posts transactions with great care. But in order to save time in finding the ledger accounts, he has arranged them in alphabetical order, as shown in the recent trial balance below.

Randy feels that his procedure is acceptable because he has balanced the accounts.

RANDY'S CAR CARE TRIAL BALANCE OCTOBER 31, 20—		
Accounts Payable		$ 800.00
Advertising Expense	$ 91.00	
Car Care Equipment	8 600.00	
Cash	6 690.00	
Miscellaneous Expense	100.00	
Office Equipment	472.00	
Randy Sandhu, Capital		4 500.00
Rent Expense	350.00	
Sales		11 318.00
Supplies	315.00	
	$16 618.00	$16 618.00

Questions

1. What are the disadvantages of Randy's system?
2. Correct Randy's trial balance by placing the accounts in proper order.

CASE 3

Challenge

Frustration for the Auditor

Pera Painting of Montréal, Québec, has applied to the bank for a loan. The bank manager has some doubts about this customer. The owner of Pera Painting is Warren Simard, an aggressive young man with a reputation in the community for fast living. The records that Simard has submitted to the bank indicate that the business is quite profitable. However, Simard's recordkeeping techniques are unusual, and the bank manager is unsure about their accuracy. The bank manager asks Noel Des Roches, a public accountant, to audit the books.

Noel soon learns about Simard's methods. While at high school, Simard took an accounting course. Now he does his own bookkeeping. In order to save time, Simard does not use a journal but records all accounting entries directly in the accounts. In addition, he keeps a file of all business papers. He claims that he has never had a problem in checking back on a transaction.

Noel finds it a slow process trying to figure out which debits correspond to which credits in the ledger. He always seems to need Simard to explain things to him and Simard is usually out on a job. On the third day, Noel finds that he cannot proceed further until Simard explains some puzzling entries. Unfortunately, Simard is not available, having left for a week's skiing in Europe.

Shown below are the unverified entries in the accounts. (These are not all of the accounts and entries of the business, but only the ones that Noel has not yet figured out.)

Bank		A/R — P. Watt	Materials	Property
5 000	5 000	5 000	5 000	10 000
	10 000			

Automobile	A/P — C.P. Paints	City Loan Co.
10 000	5 000	5 000

Questions

1. From an office clerk, Noel learns the following:
   a. Simard bought either a car or an investment property from a customer. There was some talk of offsetting the customer's account balance against the cost price.
   b. Simard has a habit of taking some of the files home with him. Since there are no files or banking records in the office pertaining to the car or the property, Noel assumes that Simard has taken them home. Because Simard lives alone, these records are unavailable.

   Prepare a list of transactions that would explain the entries in the accounts.

2. Eventually, Noel realizes that he can't finish the audit until Simard returns from Europe, and he reports this to the bank manager. The bank manager asks Noel to write up a report for Simard. Noel is to explain the difficulties he has encountered with Simard's records and how these difficulties can be avoided by using conventional accounting procedures.

   Write this report as if you were Noel Des Roches. Use the business letter format that you will find in the Skills Appendix.

CASE 4

Group Discussion

To Fire or Not To Fire?

Sylvia Lomax is a recently qualified chartered accountant. Her first position after graduation has been as chief accountant with Mayflower Movers of Saskatoon. Shortly after taking this position, she placed an advertisement in a local newspaper for an experienced bookkeeper. She hired Steve Calquhon, one of several applicants for the job.

Steve's first task in his new position was to take off a trial balance. This task usually took about half a day to complete. Steve began work on the trial balance in the afternoon of his first day on the job. At the end of the day, the ledger was not yet balanced. Again, at the end of the second day, the ledger was not yet balanced.

Sylvia waited patiently for two more days for the task to be completed. When it was still not done at the day's end, she became concerned about Steve Calquhon.

Questions

1. Should a bookkeeper be able to balance any ledger?
2. Has Sylvia allowed enough time for Steve to balance the ledger?
3. Is Sylvia right to be concerned about Steve?
4. Who is at fault here: Steve, or Sylvia? Give reasons for your answer.
5. What should Sylvia do to correct this situation?
6. What might Steve and Sylvia each have done to avoid this situation?

Career

Fred Branch
Head of Information Systems, GLOBE, Global Business Excellence Nestlé SA

Say the name "Nestlé" and you probably think first of coffee, candy, or Quik. In fact, Nestlé is the largest food company in the world, and the Canadian corporation in among its top performers. Ever heard of Stouffer's frozen foods? Lean Cuisine? Fancy Feast? Kit Kat and Mirage? How about Good Start? They are all part of the Nestlé food family.

Frederick Branch has had an interesting career at Nestlé. The Corporate Controller at the Canadian operation for five and a half years until 1995, he was then given the very challenging position as Director of SAP implementation. Fred was responsible for implementing a company-wide software system to support "best in class" business processes. He now heads the Information Systems team for GLOBE, the Global Business Excellence Program at the Nestlé corporate offices in Vevey, Switzerland.

The sheer size of the company—spanning all five continents—means that he is never without a challenge. Nestlé's operations are autonomous in every country. The corporate headquarters sets strategic directions and operating performance targets to ensure long-term growth and profitability to maximize its return to shareholders. The GLOBE program is expected to help the company achieve its objectives and transform the company making the operations more flexible to help Nestlé quickly adapt to changing market conditions.

The GLOBE program has several key objectives designed to help Nestlé improve performance and operational efficiency worldwide. Two of these are the creation or adaptation of common business processes and practices. For example, the standardization of internal and external master data—using a single code for the same raw material—facilitates efficiencies in global purchasing. This will help position the company for effective use of "e" markets. A third area is the standardization of the information systems infrastructure. This provides for increased flexibility in responding to changes and reduces "hidden costs" of information systems. GLOBE will provide a menu of standard solutions that will be used world-wide throughout the company. A software business solution, mySAP.com, will support GLOBE. It is process-based rather than a system or a functional solution.

One of the biggest challenges faced by Fred in connection with the implementation of GLOBE was the design of the system and selection of the best tools to link the new software with the existing systems, which were unique to Nestlé, without disrupting business operations.

Fred says he got interested in business as a boy growing up in Barbados watching his mother—his first mentor—run a small grocery store. "I would watch her manage all of the operations—from planning which products would be stocked to over-the-counter sales and customer service—working seven days a week. I used to come into the store to help, but not until my homework was done and checked!"

When Fred graduated from high school in 1964, the local university only offered one business program, economics. "You could do anything in the arts, but I wanted to get into industry." He stayed in Barbados for five years, then immigrated to Canada and entered the CMA program in 1969. "I got my CMA in 1975 by working part time and going to school part time—you could enter without a university degree then." Already employed by Northern Telecom when he obtained his degree from the University of Toronto, Branch was subsequently offered a number of plum assignments, first as accountant for a Northern Telecom international field service project, then later as Financial Controller for the National Industrial Development Bank in Barbados.

Branch says he believes that his CMA background gave him an excellent perspective on business. An accountant is like the co-pilot of a plane and is involved in every facet of the business. Whether it is a capital investment decision or a new marketing and sales plan, a CMA is a key player in the mix. A key success factor is to acquire a broad, but in-depth, understanding of business, such as the processes and systems, the industry, and the entire demand and supply chain. When you know what makes the business tick, you become an invaluable asset to the company. Fred also believes that continuous training and skills development, such as his participation in a General Management Program at the Richard Ivy School of Business, is necessary for a successful and rewarding career.

Discussion

1. When and how did Fred Branch first become interested in business?
2. Fred is a Certified Management Accountant. Research this designation and the opportunities it offers.
3. Why is Nestlé implementing the GLOBE Business Excellence Program?
4. Fred identifies having a broad knowledge of business as being a key factor in his work. Why would this be true? Give examples from this profile. Research other examples from other industries.

8

The Work Sheet and Financial Statements

Financial statements are the main end-products of an accounting system. Significant business decisions are based on the information they provide. In this chapter, you will learn new methods for preparing and presenting financial statements. You will also explore how accountants use financial statements to successfully guide and direct businesses.

Financial statements are prepared from the information provided by the ledger accounts. You have already seen that accounting software can be used to prepare income statements and balance sheets on demand. However, at the end of a fiscal period, the preparation of formal financial statements requires extra care and is normally the work of senior accounting staff or professional accountants.

8.1 | The Six-Column Work Sheet

Purpose of the Work Sheet

When you prepared financial statements in Chapter 7, you obtained your data from a trial balance. Accountants prefer using a business form called a work sheet instead of relying on a trial balance alone. A **work sheet** is an informal business paper used to organize and plan the information for the financial statements. The work sheet is prepared on columnar accounting paper, usually in pencil, so that changes may be made easily. If a computer is used, spreadsheets are a good choice for preparing the worksheet because they can be changed easily, and they contain columns and rows, just like the work sheet.

Accountants normally use an eight-column work sheet in order to include additional information. The eight columns allow acountants to make adjustments required by certain GAAPs and to conveniently organize all the data needed for financial statements and year-end procedures. You will study the eight-column work sheet in Chapter 9. However, now we will use a six-column work sheet in order to present this new concept as simply as possible.

Control Accounts for Accounts Receivable and Accounts Payable

When you look at your first work sheet on page 253, you will see a difference in the way accounts receivable and accounts payable are handled. You will see that there are no debtors' names associated with the Accounts Receivable account or creditors' names associated with the Accounts Payable account. What you see on the work sheet are **control accounts**: the **Accounts Receivable control account** and the **Accounts Payable control account**. The Accounts Receivable control account represents the sum of the balances of all the individual Accounts Receivable accounts. The **Accounts Payable control account** represents the sum of the balances of all the individual Accounts Payable accounts.

Having two control accounts, instead of dozens or hundreds of individual debtors' and creditors' accounts, streamlines the work sheet. A single figure for accounts receivable and a single figure for accounts payable is shown. This is more efficient for preparing work sheets and provides a more effective presentation on the balance sheet.

The details about the accounts of individual debtors and creditors are kept in separate records. The formal procedure for maintaining control accounts and the separate records for debtors and creditors is one of the topics of Chapter 11.

Steps in Preparing a Work Sheet

Step 1   Write in the heading on the work sheet paper. Examine the heading in Figure 8.1 below carefully. Observe the precise way that the fiscal period is described.

FIGURE 8.1

Recording the heading on the work sheet.

Vulcan Rentalls		Work Sheet			Year Ended December 31, 20—		
ACCOUNTS	TRIAL BALANCE		INCOME STATEMENT		BALANCE SHEET		
	DR	CR	DR	CR	DR	CR	

Step 2   Enter all accounts with their balances in the first two columns, as shown in Figure 8.2 below. It is essential that the trial balance columns be correct before you continue. There is no hope of producing an accurate work sheet if the trial balance does not balance.

FIGURE 8.2

Recording the trial balance on a work sheet.

Vulcan Rentalls	Work Sheet		Year Ended December 31, 20—			
ACCOUNTS	TRIAL BALANCE		INCOME STATEMENT		BALANCE SHEET	
	DR	CR	DR	CR	DR	CR
Bank	3 457 15					
Accounts Receivable	19 402 50					
Supplies	1 240 —					
Equipment	20 400 —					
Automobiles	32 936 57					
Accounts Payable		5 296 10				
GST Payable		5 59 45				
GST Recoverable	3 51 12					
PST Payable		6 39 38				
Bank Loan		10 000 —				
R. Tessier, Capital		49 713 40				
R. Tessier, Drawings	24 000 —					
Sales		95 907 —				
Advertising Expense	7 56 —					
Bank Charges Expense	1 742 —					
Car Expense	6 575 80					
Miscellaneous Expense	1 75 —					
Rent Expense	12 000 —					
Telephone Expense	1 200 —					
Utilities Expense	1 370 —					
Wages Expense	36 509 19					
	162 115 33	162 115 33				

Step 3 Extend each of the amounts from the trial balance columns into one of the four columns to the right, as in Figure 8.3 below. The process is simple and logical. Revenue and expense items are extended into the Income Statement columns. These are the items that make up the net income or net loss. All other items—assets, liabilities, capital, and drawings—are extended into the Balance Sheet columns. Observe that the drawings are not a net income item and are not transferred to the Income Statement section.

Be careful to transfer amounts accurately and to record debit amounts in debit columns and credit amounts in credit columns. Be sure, too, that each account balance is transferred only once and that no item is missed.

FIGURE 8.3

Extending the amounts on a work sheet.

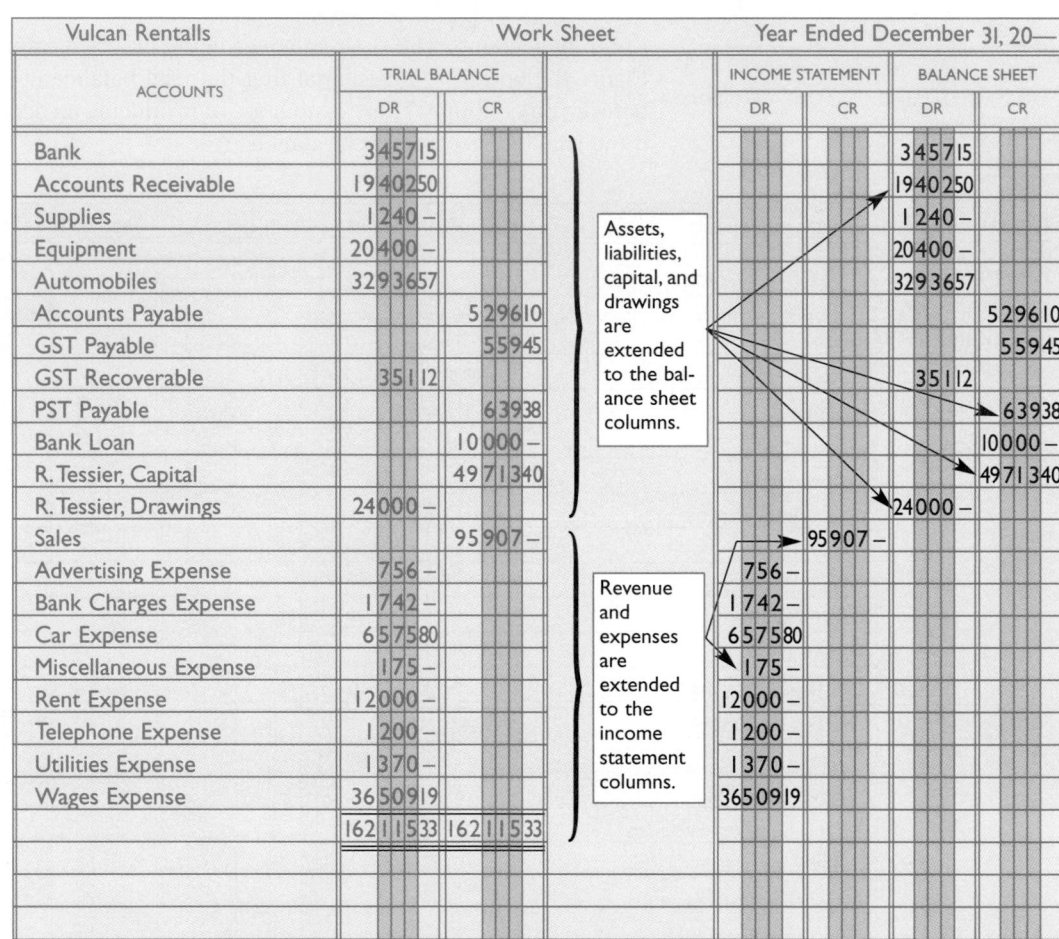

Vulcan Rentalls	Work Sheet				Year Ended December 31, 20—		
	TRIAL BALANCE				INCOME STATEMENT		BALANCE SHEET
ACCOUNTS	DR	CR			DR	CR	DR	CR
Bank	3 457 15						3 457 15	
Accounts Receivable	19 402 50						19 402 50	
Supplies	1 240 –						1 240 –	
Equipment	20 400 –						20 400 –	
Automobiles	32 93657						32 93657	
Accounts Payable		5 296 10						5 296 10
GST Payable		5 59 45						5 59 45
GST Recoverable	35 1 12						35 1 12	
PST Payable		6 39 38						6 39 38
Bank Loan		10 000 –						10 000 –
R. Tessier, Capital		49 713 40						49 713 40
R. Tessier, Drawings	24 000 –						24 000 –	
Sales		95 907 –				95 907 –		
Advertising Expense	7 56 –				7 56 –			
Bank Charges Expense	1 742 –				1 742 –			
Car Expense	6 575 80				6 575 80			
Miscellaneous Expense	1 75 –				1 75 –			
Rent Expense	12 000 –				12 000 –			
Telephone Expense	1 200 –				1 200 –			
Utilities Expense	1 370 –				1 370 –			
Wages Expense	36 509 19				36 509 19			
	162 111 533	162 111 533						

Assets, liabilities, capital, and drawings are extended to the balance sheet columns.

Revenue and expenses are extended to the income statement columns.

Step 4 Balance the work sheet, as shown in Figure 8.4 below. There are four steps in balancing the work sheet.

  a. Total each of the four right-hand money columns and write in the totals.
  b. Calculate the difference between the two Income Statement columns (in our example, $35 579.01), then the difference between the two Balance Sheet columns (again, $35 579.01), and see that the two differences are equal. If the differences are equal, this amount is called the balancing figure.

    If they are not the same, the work sheet does not balance. It is mathematically impossible for the work sheet to be correct if it does not balance. Therefore, you should not proceed to the preparation of the financial statements until all errors have been found and corrected.
  c. Record the balancing figure on the work sheet in two places, as shown in Figure 8.4 below. Because the revenues are greater than the expenses, the balancing figure represents a net income. Record the balancing figure on the debit side of the income statement columns and on the credit side of the balance sheet columns. The balancing figure appears on the credit side of the balance sheet section, because the net income represents an increase in the capital.

FIGURE 8.4

Balancing the work sheet (net income situation).

GST Recoverable is extended to the balance sheet section because it is a contra liability account.

Vulcan Rentalls	Work Sheet		Year Ended December 31, 20—			
ACCOUNTS	TRIAL BALANCE		INCOME STATEMENT		BALANCE SHEET	
	DR	CR	DR	CR	DR	CR
Bank	3 457 15				3 457 15	
Accounts Receivable	19 402 50				19 402 50	
Supplies	1 240 –				1 240 –	
Equipment	20 400 –				20 400 –	
Automobiles	32 936 57				32 936 57	
Accounts Payable		5 296 10				5 296 10
GST Payable		559 45				559 45
GST Recoverable	351 12				351 12	
PST Payable		639 38				639 38
Bank Loan		10 000 –				10 000 –
R. Tessier, Capital		49 713 40				49 713 40
R. Tessier, Drawings	24 000 –				24 000 –	
Sales		95 907 –		95 907 –		
Advertising Expense	756 –		756 –			
Bank Charges Expense	1 742 –		1 742 –			
Car Expense	6 575 80		6 575 80			
Miscellaneous Expense	175 –		175 –			
Rent Expense	12 000 –		12 000 –			
Telephone Expense	1 200 –		1 200 –			
Utilities Expense	1 370 –		1 370 –			
Wages Expense	36 509 19		36 509 19			
	162 115 33	162 115 33	60 327 99	95 907 –	101 787 34	66 208 33
Net Income			35 579 01			35 579 01
Balancing figure			95 907 –	95 907 –	101 787 34	101 787 34

Notice that the balancing figure ($35 579.01) is placed in two locations on the work sheet: in the outer two of the last four columns. This is normal when there is a profit.

d. Rule and show the final column totals, as shown in Figure 8.4 on page 255.

Net Income or Net Loss

The balancing figure on the work sheet indicates the net income or net loss for the fiscal period. A look at the Income Statement columns tells which of the two it is. A net income has been earned if the total revenues (credit column) are greater than the total expenses (debit column). A net loss has been incurred if the total expenses (debit column) are greater than the total revenues (credit column).

Finalizing the work sheet for a loss situation is done slightly differently than for a profit situation. The balancing figure is placed in the **inner two of the last four columns** when there is a loss. A balancing figure of $356.07 is shown in Figure 8.5 below.

FIGURE 8.5

Balancing the work sheet (net loss situation).

To review the steps required to complete a worksheet, visit www.pearsoned.ca/accounting1

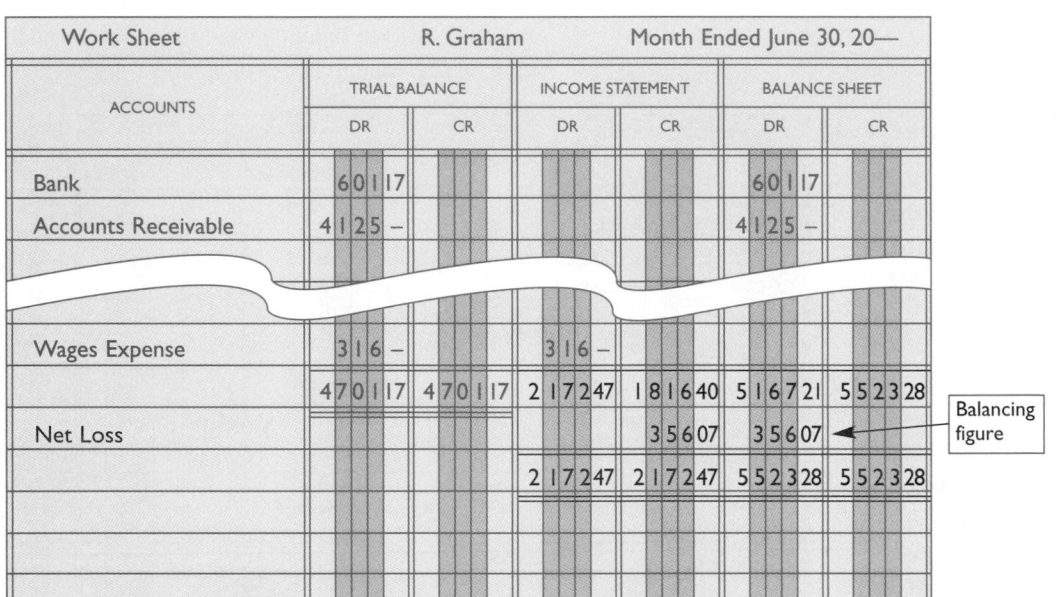

The Work Sheet and the Financial Statements

Owners and business executives rarely look at the raw data of actual financial records. They rely on the accounting department to maintain accurate records and to process the data into a more easily understood form. The owners and executives want to see finished accounting reports and financial statements. It is up to the accounting department to produce first-class reports and statements.

A completed work sheet contains all of the information needed to prepare the income statement and the balance sheet. Figures 8.6, 8.7, and 8.8 on pages 257 and 258 show how the income statement and the balance sheet of Vulcan Rentalls are prepared directly from the work sheet.

Vulcan Rentalls — Work Sheet — Year Ended December 31, 20—

ACCOUNTS	TRIAL BALANCE DR	TRIAL BALANCE CR	INCOME STATEMENT DR	INCOME STATEMENT CR	BALANCE SHEET DR	BALANCE SHEET CR
Bank	3 457 15				3 457 15	
Accounts Receivable	19 402 50				19 402 50	
Supplies	1 240 –				1 240 –	
Equipment	20 400 –				20 400 –	
Automobiles	32 936 57				32 936 57	
Accounts Payable		5 296 10				5 296 10
GST Payable		559 45				559 45
GST Recoverable	351 12				351 12	
PST Payable		639 38				639 38
Bank Loan		10 000 –				10 000 –
R. Tessier, Capital		49 713 40				49 713 40
R. Tessier, Drawings	24 000 –				24 000 –	
Sales		95 907 –		95 907 –		
Advertising Expense	756 –		756 –			
Bank Charges Expense	1 742 –		1 742 –			
Car Expense	6 575 80		6 575 80			
Miscellaneous Expense	175 –		175 –			
Rent Expense	12 000 –		12 000 –			
Telephone Expense	1 200 –		1 200 –			
Utilities Expense	1 370 –		1 370 –			
Wages Expense	36 509 19		36 509 19			
	162 115 33	162 115 33	60 327 99	95 907 –	101 787 34	66 208 33
Net Income			35 579 01			35 579 01
			95 907 –	95 907 –	101 787 34	101 787 34

The figures for the balance sheet are derived from these two columns of the work sheet.

Balancing figure

All of the figures for the income statement are derived from these two columns of the work sheet.

FIGURE 8.6

A six-column work sheet for Vulcan Rentalls, giving the information for the financial statements shown in Figure 8.7 and Figure 8.8.

FIGURE 8.7

The balance sheet, prepared from the amounts in the "balance sheet" columns of the work sheet.

The figures for the balance sheet are derived from these two columns of the work sheet.

Vulcan Rentalls				
Balance Sheet				
December 31, 20–				
Assets				
Bank			3457 15	
Accounts Receivable			19 402 50	
Supplies			1 240 –	24 099 65
Equipment			20 400 –	
Automobiles			32 936 57	53 336 57
Total Assets				77 436 22
Liabilities				
Accounts Payable			5 296 10	
GST Payable	559 45			
Less GST Recoverable	351 12	208 33		
PST Payable		639 38		
Bank Loan		10 000 –		16 143 81
R. Tessier, Capital				
Balance January 1		49 713 40		
Net Income	35 579 01			
Drawings	24 000 –			
Increase in Capital		11 579 01		
Balance December 31			61 292 41	
Total Liabilities and Owner's Equity				77 436 22

FIGURE 8.8

The income statement, prepared from the amounts in the "income statement" columns of the work sheet.

All of the figures for the income statement are derived from these two columns of the work sheet.

Vulcan Rentalls			
Income Statement			
Year Ended December 31, 20–			
Revenue			
Sales			95 907 –
Operating Expenses			
Advertising Expense		756 –	
Bank Charges Expense		1 742 –	
Car Expense		6 575 80	
Miscellaneous Expense		175 –	
Rent Expense	12 000 –		
Telephone Expense	1 200 –		
Utilities Expense	1 370 –		
Wages Expense	36 509 19		
Total Operating Expenses		60 327 99	
Net Income		35 579 01	

More on the Accounting Cycle

You have already learned that a certain set of procedures are to be followed during a fiscal period. Journalizing, posting, and balancing of the ledger are carried out by junior employees. The next two steps involve the preparation of the work sheet and the financial statements. These steps are carried out by senior people. All of the steps together constitute the accounting cycle to date.

The six steps of the accounting cycle studied so far are shown in Figure 8.9 below.

FIGURE 8.9

First six steps in the accounting cycle.

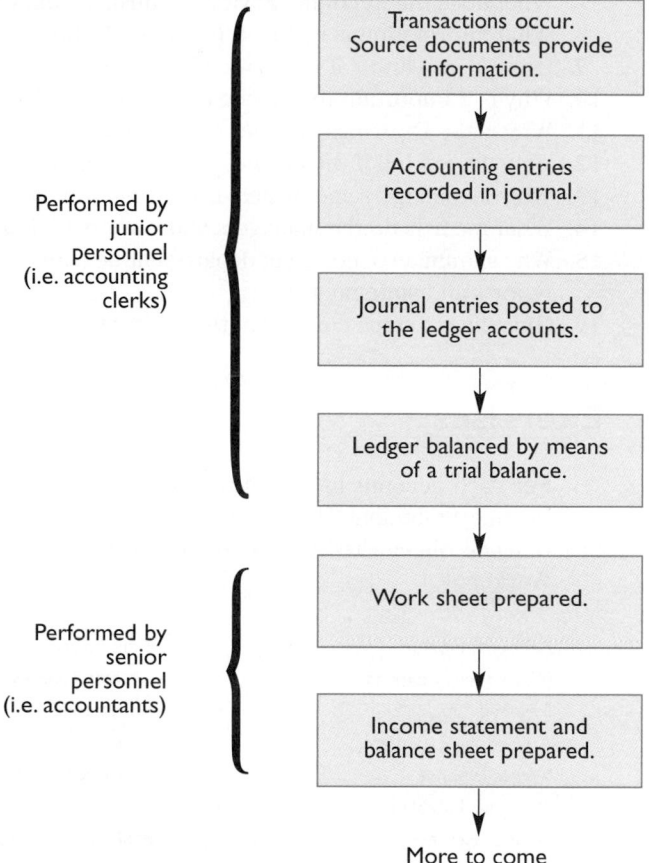

Performed by junior personnel (i.e. accounting clerks)

Transactions occur. Source documents provide information.

Accounting entries recorded in journal.

Journal entries posted to the ledger accounts.

Ledger balanced by means of a trial balance.

Performed by senior personnel (i.e. accountants)

Work sheet prepared.

Income statement and balance sheet prepared.

More to come

Section 8.1   Review Questions

1. When are financial statements prepared?
2. In the accounting department, who usually prepares the financial statements?
3. Name and describe the form used by accountants to help them prepare the financial statements.
4. Explain an important aspect of step 2 in completing a work sheet.
5. Which kinds of accounts are extended to the balance sheet columns?
6. What does the Accounts Receivable control account represent?
7. What does the Accounts Payable control account represent?
8. What information is included in the work sheet heading?
9. How do you know if the work sheet balances?
10. Why is it important to balance the work sheet?
11. Why is the Drawings account not extended to the Income Statement section?
12. How do you tell if the business has made a profit or suffered a loss?
13. Why do managers and owners usually not look at the actual accounting records?
14. What records do the managers and owners look at?
15. Why should an accounting department be concerned about producing first-rate reports and statements?
16. Give the six steps covered in the accounting cycle so far.

Section 8.1   Exercises

1. For each account listed below, indicate whether it would be extended to the Income Statement Debit, Income Statement Credit, Balance Sheet Debit, or Balance Sheet Credit column. (A chart for this exercise is provided in the Workbook.)

Accounts Payable	Bank Loan
Miscellaneous Expense	Accounts Receivable
Revenue	Automobile
Advertising Expense	Bank
Wages Expense	G. Rojek, Drawings
Mortgage Payable	Sales
Utilities Expense	Bank Charges Expense
Equipment	Rent Expense
G. Rojek, Capital	Supplies
Delivery Expense	Trucks
GST Recoverable	GST Payable

2. From the simplified data shown below, complete a work sheet for N. Foreman and Company for the month ended April 30, 20— (profit situation).

N. Foreman and Company
Trial Balance
April 30, 20—

Bank	$ 750.20	
Accounts Receivable	15 375.10	
Supplies	1 250.00	
Equipment	18 500.00	
Automobiles	29 300.88	
Bank Loan		$30 000.00
Accounts Payable		5 331.00
GST Payable		106.17
GST Recoverable	74.12	
PST Payable		121.33
N. Foreman, Capital		24 772.50
N. Foreman, Drawings	3 000.00	
Fees Revenue		18 200.00
Bank Charges Expense	250.00	
Car Expense	1 750.00	
Miscellaneous Expense	512.20	
Light and Heat Expense	746.00	
Rent Expense	1 100.00	
Telephone Expense	276.50	
Wages Expense	5 646.00	
	$78 531.00	$78 531.00

3. The trial balance for Collision Bodywork and Repairs for the year ended December 31, 20—, is given below.

Collision Bodywork and Repairs
Trial Balance
December 31, 20—

	DR	CR
Bank	$ 723.50	
Accounts Receivable	23 356.05	
Supplies	1 420.00	
Land	54 000.00	
Building	102 500.00	
Automobiles	35 256.20	
Equipment	25 750.00	
Bank Loan		$ 30 000.00
Accounts Payable		5 365.25
GST Payable		1 175.58
GST Recoverable	787.50	
PST Payable		1 340.00
B. Hughes, Capital		287 816.14
B. Hughes, Drawings	48 000.00	
Revenue — Bodywork		135 315.02
Revenue — Repairs		66 214.98
Advertising Expense	850.00	
Automobile Expense	4 569.33	
Bank Charges Expense	3 485.00	
General Expense	1 258.90	
Light and Heat Expense	2 585.00	
Materials Expense	36 750.25	
Telephone Expense	1 585.00	
Wages Expense	184 350.24	
	$527 226.97	$527 226.97

Prepare a six-column work sheet for the above (loss situation).

4. The simplified work sheet below contains a number of errors.

    A. **Locate the errors, make the necessary corrections, and balance the work sheet.** A work sheet for you to use has been provided in the Workbook. **Ignore GST and PST.**

    B. **State what the control account balances would be for accounts receivable and accounts payable.**

Work Sheet The Arthur Company Month Ended Oct. 31, 20—						
ACCOUNTS	TRIAL BALANCE DR	TRIAL BALANCE CR	INCOME STATEMENT DR	INCOME STATEMENT CR	BALANCE SHEET DR	BALANCE SHEET CR
Bank	1722.16				1722.16	
Accounts Receivable						
– H. Chan	116—				116—	
– M. Watson	72—				72—	
– J. Young	323—				323—	
Supplies	1255—				1255—	
Office Equipment	5863—				5863—	
Automobiles	13200—				13200—	
Accounts Payable						
– City Hydro		116.42				116.42
– O.K. Supply		421.72				421.72
– Slick Oil Co.		331.19				331.19
Bank Loan		10000—				10000—
P. Arthur, Capital		10504.82				10504.82
P. Arthur, Drawings	1000—		1000—			
Consulting Fees		4903.17		4903.17		
Advertising Expense	465.12		465.12			
Automobile Expense	270—				270—	
Bank Charges Expense	56.40		56.40			
Miscellaneous Expense	113.74		113.74			
Rent Expense	400—		400—			
Salaries Expense	1280—		1280—		1280—	
Telephone Expense	25.60		25.60			
Utilities Expense	115.30					
	26277.32	26277.32	2340.86	4903.17	12230.16	21074.15
Net Income			3562.31			8843.99
			5903.17	5903.17	12230.16	29918.14

8.2 | How Accountants use Income Statements

At this stage of your accounting studies, you have a good understanding of why financial statements are important. The balance sheet and income statement are essential documents a businessperson needs in order to evaluate the stability and growth of a business. To make it easier to extract meaningful information, accountants may use a variety of presentation and mathematical tools when preparing financial statements. You will explore some of these tools in the next two sections of the text.

Comparing Income Statements

When comparing income statements for two consecutive years, accountants often make the following two calculations for each item:

1. the dollar amount of the increase or decrease from the first year to the second;
2. the percentage amount of the increase or decrease from the first year to the second.

For example, consider the following item taken from an income statement:

Item	Year 1	Year 2
Car Expense	$50 250	$59 360

These figures, standing alone, are not as informative as the ones that follow, in which two more columns are included:

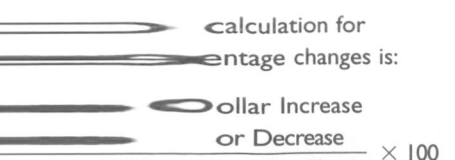

calculation for
entage changes is:

ollar Increase
or Decrease
ear One Total × 100

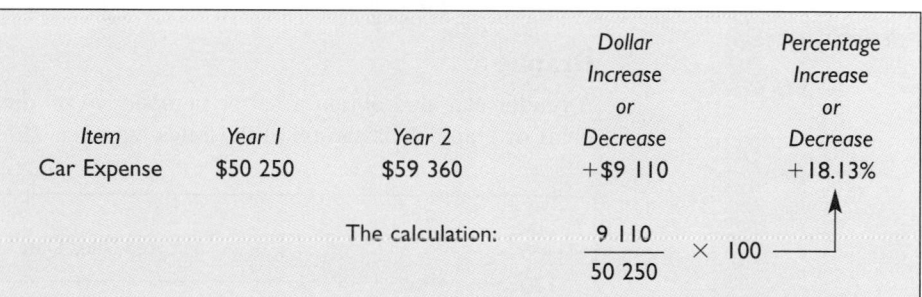

Item	Year 1	Year 2	Dollar Increase or Decrease	Percentage Increase or Decrease
Car Expense	$50 250	$59 360	+$9 110	+18.13%

The calculation: $\dfrac{9\ 110}{50\ 250} \times 100$

The information in the last two columns can be quite useful when analyzing any item on the income statement. It is studied carefully by owners and managers. For example, the owner or manager of a business will look for a reason for increased car expense. Is the sales force driving further and obtaining more orders? If so, Accounts Receivable or Sales Revenue (or both) should also show an increase. But if there is no increase in Accounts Receivable or Sales Revenue, it could be that some cars have become uneconomical and should be sold. Thus, the percentage analysis suggests an area for the owner or manager to investigate.

Trend Analysis

Another useful technique for examining
analysis shows financial data over a nun
following sales figures for a company:

	Year 1	Year 2	Ye
Sales	$55 000	$60 000	$75

It is not easy to interpret these figures jus
are changed to percentages or to a graph

Percentages

Converting the above data to percentag
interpret and discuss.

	Year 1	Year 2	
Sales	$55 000	$60 000	
Sales Percent	100.0%	109.1%	

Each of these percentages is calculated b
the sales figure for Year 1 and multiplyin
ure for Year 5 is calculated as follows:

$$\frac{105\ 000}{55\ 000} \times 100 =$$

Graphs

A reader can also obtain a better persp
chart or graph. A bar graph of the Sales f

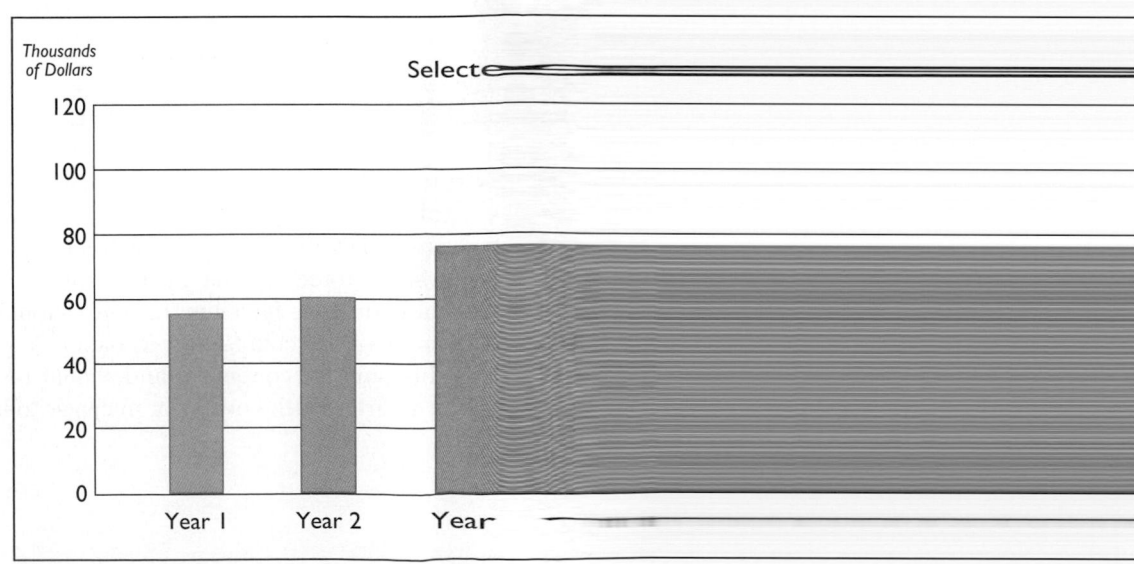

8.2 | How Accountants use Income Statements

At this stage of your accounting studies, you have a good understanding of why financial statements are important. The balance sheet and income statement are essential documents a businessperson needs in order to evaluate the stability and growth of a business. To make it easier to extract meaningful information, accountants may use a variety of presentation and mathematical tools when preparing financial statements. You will explore some of these tools in the next two sections of the text.

Comparing Income Statements

When comparing income statements for two consecutive years, accountants often make the following two calculations for each item:

1. the dollar amount of the increase or decrease from the first year to the second;
2. the percentage amount of the increase or decrease from the first year to the second.

For example, consider the following item taken from an income statement:

Item	Year 1	Year 2
Car Expense	$50 250	$59 360

These figures, standing alone, are not as informative as the ones that follow, in which two more columns are included:

The calculation for percentage changes is:

$$\frac{\text{Dollar Increase or Decrease}}{\text{Year One Total}} \times 100$$

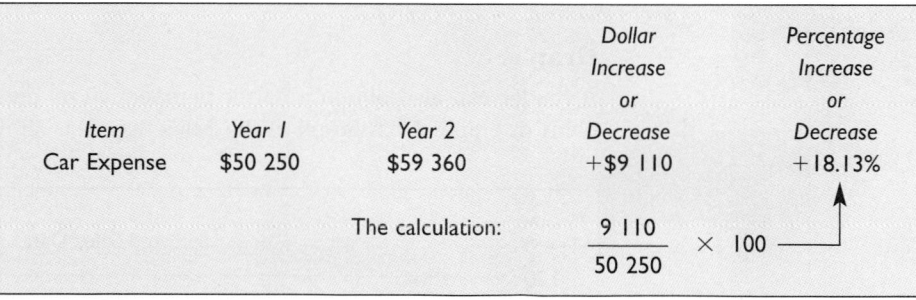

Item	Year 1	Year 2	Dollar Increase or Decrease	Percentage Increase or Decrease
Car Expense	$50 250	$59 360	+$9 110	+18.13%

The calculation: $\dfrac{9\ 110}{50\ 250} \times 100$

The information in the last two columns can be quite useful when analyzing any item on the income statement. It is studied carefully by owners and managers. For example, the owner or manager of a business will look for a reason for increased car expense. Is the sales force driving further and obtaining more orders? If so, Accounts Receivable or Sales Revenue (or both) should also show an increase. But if there is no increase in Accounts Receivable or Sales Revenue, it could be that some cars have become uneconomical and should be sold. Thus, the percentage analysis suggests an area for the owner or manager to investigate.

Trend Analysis

Another useful technique for examining financial data is trend analysis. A **trend analysis** shows financial data over a number of consecutive periods. Consider the following sales figures for a company:

	Year 1	Year 2	Year 3	Year 4	Year 5	Year 6
Sales	$55 000	$60 000	$75 000	$45 000	$105 000	$112 000

It is not easy to interpret these figures just by looking at them. But when the figures are changed to percentages or to a graph, they can be more easily analyzed.

Percentages

Converting the above data to percentages, as given below, makes them easier to interpret and discuss.

	Year 1	Year 2	Year 3	Year 4	Year 5	Year 6
Sales	$55 000	$60 000	$75 000	$45 000	$105 000	$112 000
Sales Percent	100.0%	109.1%	136.4%	81.8%	190.9%	203.6%

Each of these percentages is calculated by putting the sales figure for the year over the sales figure for Year 1 and multiplying by 100. For example, the percentage figure for Year 5 is calculated as follows:

$$\frac{105\ 000}{55\ 000} \times 100 = 190.9 \text{ (rounded off)}$$

Graphs

A reader can also obtain a better perspective on data if presented by means of a chart or graph. A bar graph of the Sales figures is shown below.

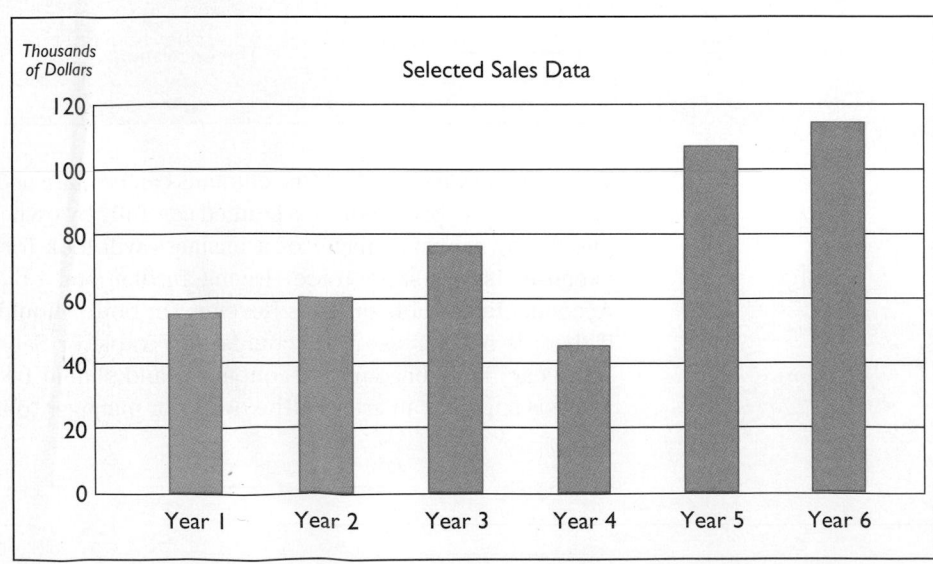

Suppose that, without giving any figures, the owner of this company claimed that "Sales have doubled in five years!" What does the trend analysis show you that the owner is overlooking? Clearly, there was a downturn in Year 4, about which you would want more information.

Common-size Income Statements

At times, it is necessary to compare the income statements of two different companies. But comparisons are not easy to make by just looking at the dollar figures alone, especially if the two companies differ greatly in size.

Consider the income statements below for two companies in the same line of business:

	INCOME STATEMENTS YEAR ENDED DECEMBER 31, 20–	
	Company A	Company B
Revenue		
Sales	$150 000	$450 000
Expenses		
Automotive Expense	$ 25 500	$ 54 000
Bank Interest Expense		18 000
Rent Expense	24 000	45 000
Wages Expense	60 000	270 000
Other Expenses	4 500	13 500
Total Expenses	$114 000	$400 500
Net Income	$ 36 000	$ 49 500

These two companies can be made to look the same size. This is done by converting each dollar amount to a percentage, using the sales figure as the base. The two income statements above, with two columns of percentages added in, appear again below. They are now in what is called common-size form.

	COMMON-SIZE INCOME STATEMENTS			
	Company A		Company B	
Revenue				
Sales	$150 000	100%	$450 000	100%
Expenses				
Automotive Expense	$ 25 500	17%	$ 54 000	12%
Bank Interest Expense			18 000	4%
Rent Expense	24 000	16%	45 000	10%
Wages Expense	60 000	40%	270 000	60%
Other Expenses	4 500	3%	13 500	3%
Total Expenses	$114 000	76%	$400 500	89%
Net Income	$ 36 000	24%	$ 49 500	11%

This calculation may be expressed as:

$$\frac{\text{Dollar Amount of Item}}{\text{Dollar Amount of Sales}} \times 100$$

To make each calculation, convert to a percentage. Put the dollar amount of the item over the dollar amount of sales and multiply by 100. For example, the calculation for Automotive Expense for Company A is:

$$\frac{25\ 500}{150\ 000} \times 100 = 17\%$$

Data in common-size form can be readily analyzed. For example, it can easily be seen that Company A earns more than twice as much as Company B, relative to sales. Similarly, Company B spends one and one-half times as much on wages as Company A.

Section 8.2 Review Questions

1. Why do accountants use a variety of presentation and mathematical tools?
2. Explain how to make the calculation for Percentage Increase or Decrease.
3. For a trend analysis of three years, which figure would you use for the divisor — Year 1, Year 2, or Year 3?
4. When comparing two different companies, what condition makes a common-size statement especially useful?
5. Which figure is the divisor when preparing a common-size income statement?

Section 8.2 Exercises

1. Shown on page 267 is an income statement for Professional Engineering and Consulting for 20-1 and 20-2. Study this income statement and complete the following:

A. **Complete the Dollar Increase or Decrease column in your Workbook.**

B. **Complete the Percentage Increase or Decrease column in your Workbook.**

C. **Identify the four expense accounts that show the greatest dollar change for the year.**

D. The owner, C. Haywood, is quite concerned about the dramatic decrease in net income from 20-1 to 20-2. **Prepare a brief report to Mr. Haywood explaining the factors causing this decrease.**

PROFESSIONAL ENGINEERING AND CONSULTING
INCOME STATEMENT
YEAR ENDED JUNE 30, 20-2 and 20-1

Revenues	20-2	20-1
Consulting	$ 62 250	$ 60 402
Construction	202 365	290 201
Designing	35 250	36 603
Total Revenue	$299 865	$387 206

Operating Expenses		
Advertising Expense	$ 3 520	$ 3 400
Automobiles Expense	25 025	16 350
Bank Charges Expense	15 850	11 200
Building Expense	4 200	3 700
Equipment Maintenance Expense	1 525	1 750
Insurance Expense	5 014	3 000
Light, Heat, and Water Expense	3 124	3 107
Miscellaneous Expense	312	250
Property Taxes Expense	1 215	950
Telephone Expense	1 507	904
Wages Expense	102 301	78 201
Total Expenses	$163 593	$122 812
Net Income	$136 272	$264 394

2. A. **In your Workbook, prepare a percentage trend analysis for the following sales data and complete the Workbook chart.**

	Year 1	Year 2	Year 3	Year 4	Year 5
Sales	$20 700	$22 356	$23 184	$23 805	$24 219

B. **Describe the sales performance that these data indicate.**

3. A. **For the data shown below, complete the percentage trend analysis in the space provided in your Workbook. Do your calculations to one decimal place.**

	Year 1	Year 2	Year 3	Year 4	Year 5
Sales	$57 000	$58 254	$58 767	$59 223	$59 451
Expenses	$35 000	$36 050	$36 575	$36 785	$37 520
Net Income	$22 000	$22 204	$22 192	$22 438	$21 931

B. **Briefly comment on the three aspects of this company's performance.**

4. A. **Prepare a bar graph for the following sales data for Soul Foods.**

	Year 1	Year 2	Year 3	Year 4	Year 5
Sales	$90 000	$99 000	$105 000	$95 000	$85 000

B. **Comment on the sales performance of this company.**

5. Given below are the income statements for two companies in the same line of business.

INCOME STATEMENTS
YEAR ENDED DECEMBER 31, 20–

	Company A	Company B
Revenue		
Sales	$197 000	$421 000
Expenses		
Automotive Expense	$ 40 200	$ 80 270
Bank Interest Expense	3 500	27 050
Rent Expense	12 000	30 000
Wages Expense	86 750	214 860
Other Expenses	1 800	10 900
Total Expenses	$144 250	$363 080
Net Income	$ 52 750	$ 57 920

A. **In your Workbook, convert the above statements to common-size form.**

B. Suppose that you are an investor interested in purchasing one of these two companies. **Evaluate the two companies, giving reasons. State which company appears to be the better buy.** What additional important data do you require before you can make a final decision?

6. Ace Cleaning is considering the purchase of Tip Top Cleaners, a smaller company in another town. Tip Top Cleaners has not been successful in recent years. The owners of Ace Cleaning feel confident that they can turn Tip Top Cleaners around. The income statements for the two companies are shown below.

INCOME STATEMENTS
YEAR ENDED DECEMBER 31, 20–

	Ace Cleaning	Tip Top Cleaners
Revenues	$294 325	$147 821
Operating Expenses		
Bank Charges Expense	$ 6 700	$ 7 100
Car Expense	28 070	11 190
Cleaning Supplies Expense	52 950	36 960
Insurance Expense	2 800	500
Utilities Expense	6 500	2 100
Miscellaneous Expense	1 800	750
Rent Expense	18 000	12 000
Telephone Expense	3 721	1 570
Wages Expense	100 971	75 360
Total Expenses	$221 512	$147 530
Net Income	$ 72 813	$ 291

A. **Complete the common-size income statements in your Workbook.**

B. **Identify areas of weakness in the operations of Tip Top Cleaners.**

C. In your opinion, can Ace Cleaning turn Tip Top Cleaners around? Should they proceed with the purchase? **Briefly give your reasons.**

8.3 | How Accountants Use Balance Sheets

Balance Sheet—Account Form and Report Form

The same methods used to analyze the income statement can also be applied to the balance sheet. The format of the balance sheets that you are going to work with in this chapter is different from the one you studied earlier. The previous balance sheets were shown in account form. The **account form of the balance sheet** is one on which the information is presented in a side-by-side, or horizontal, format.

In this chapter, you will use a style of balance sheet known as the report form. The **report form of the balance sheet** is one on which the information is presented in a one-above-the-other, or vertical format. The two styles are contrasted in Figure 8.11 below. The report form of the balance sheet is common because it uses standard-sized paper.

FIGURE 8.11

Two forms of the balance sheet.

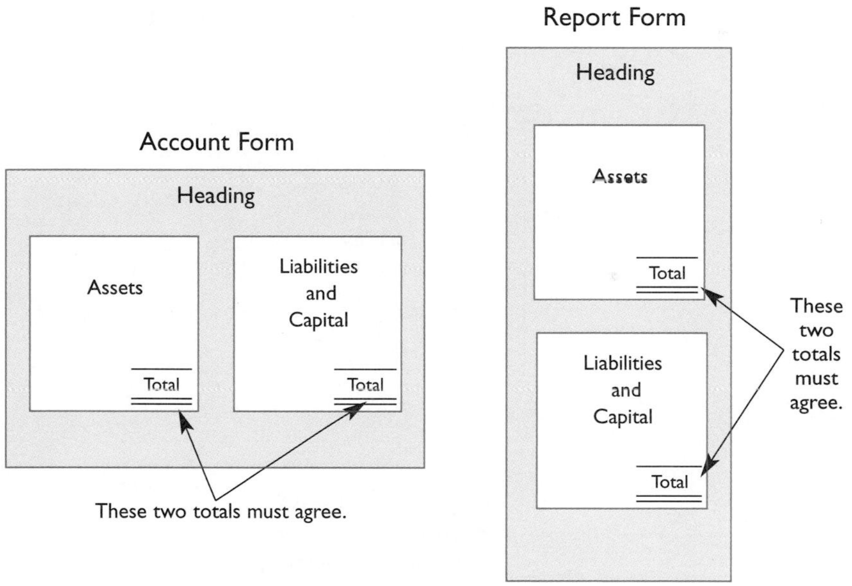

Classified Balance Sheet

Accountants prefer to organize balance sheet data in a format referred to as a classified balance sheet. A **classified balance sheet** has the data grouped according to major categories. This organization makes it easier to analyze the information on the balance sheet. A sample classified balance sheet is shown in Figure 8.12 on page 270. Observe the overall appearance of the balance sheet in Figure 8.12 carefully. Explanations for the circled numbers appear below the sample balance sheet and continue on page 271. In particular, note the meanings of the terms "current assets," "fixed assets," "current liabilities," and "long-term liabilities."

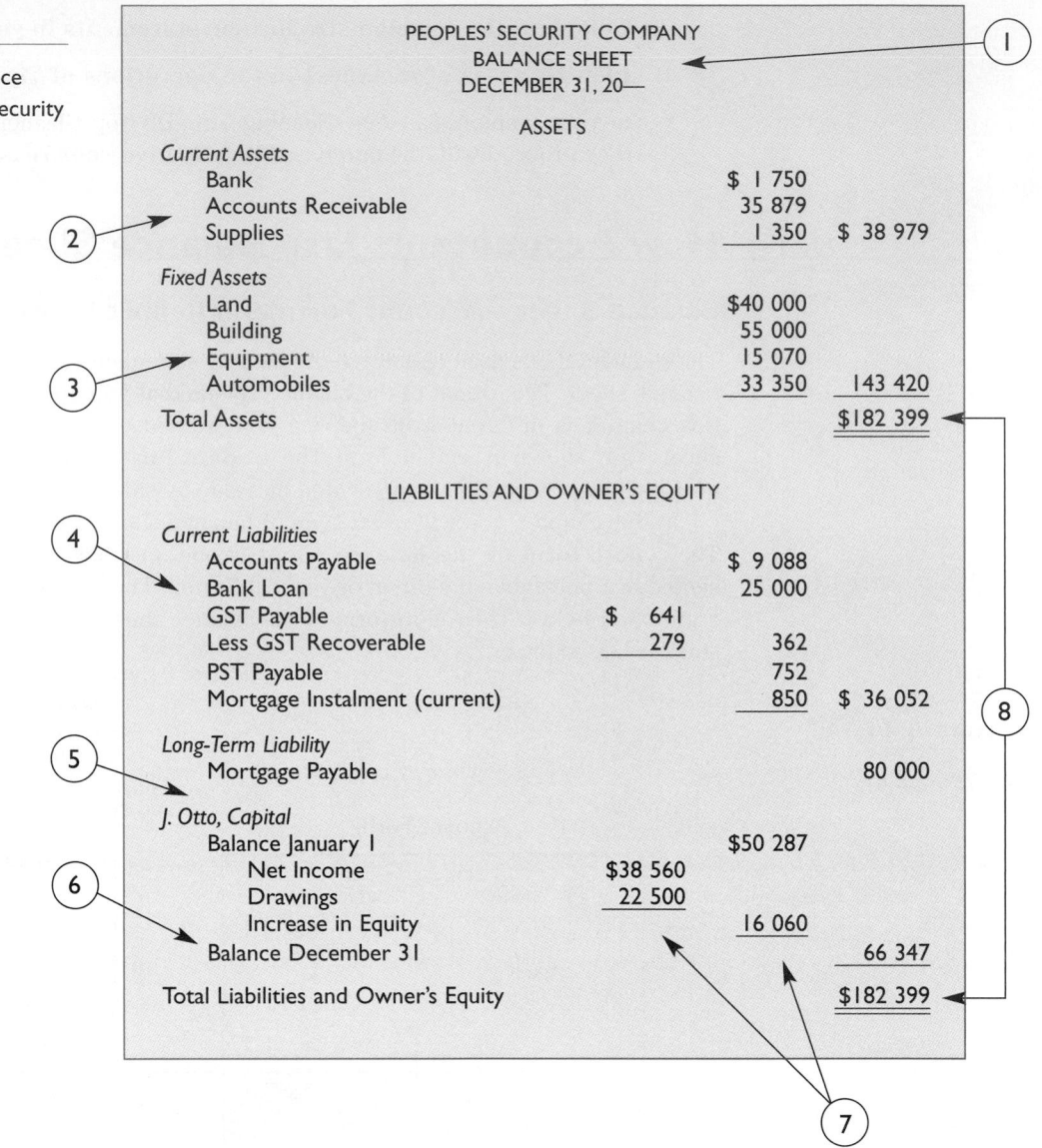

PEOPLES' SECURITY COMPANY
BALANCE SHEET
DECEMBER 31, 20—

ASSETS

Current Assets		
Bank	$ 1 750	
Accounts Receivable	35 879	
Supplies	1 350	$ 38 979
Fixed Assets		
Land	$40 000	
Building	55 000	
Equipment	15 070	
Automobiles	33 350	143 420
Total Assets		$182 399

LIABILITIES AND OWNER'S EQUITY

Current Liabilities			
Accounts Payable		$ 9 088	
Bank Loan		25 000	
GST Payable	$ 641		
Less GST Recoverable	279	362	
PST Payable		752	
Mortgage Instalment (current)		850	$ 36 052
Long-Term Liability			
Mortgage Payable			80 000
J. Otto, Capital			
Balance January 1		$50 287	
Net Income	$38 560		
Drawings	22 500		
Increase in Equity		16 060	
Balance December 31			66 347
Total Liabilities and Owner's Equity			$182 399

1. The **Heading** gives:
   - name of business;
   - name of statement;
   - date on which the balance is taken.

2. **Current assets:** assets that will be converted into cash (or used up) during the next year.

3. **Fixed assets (or plant and equipment):** long-term assets held for their usefulness in producing goods or services.

4. **Current liabilities:** short-term debts, payment of which is expected to occur within one year of the date of the balance sheet.

(5) **Long-term liabilities:** debts of the business that are not due within one year.

(6) **Capital:** the owner's claim on assets.
This section is organized to show clearly the beginning balance, the increase or decrease through profit or loss, the decrease through owner's withdrawals, and the ending balance.

(7) **Inner columns:** are used to list individual items building up to subtotals.

(8) The two **balancing totals:** total assets, and total liabilities plus owner's equity.

The classified balance sheet provides useful totals for comparison. For example, in Figure 8.12, the current assets of the People's Security Company are $38 979; the current liabilities are $36 052. These totals match up well because the time frame for both is one year or less. (The current assets amount mainly represents the assets that will be turned into cash within one year. The current liabilities amount shows the debts due within one year.)

The totals for current assets and current liabilities for People's Security Company are almost equal. Accountants use these two amounts to calculate "working capital." **Working capital** is the difference between the current assets and the current liabilities of a business. For example, for People's Security Company, the working capital is $2 927, that is $38 979 − $36 052. Obviously, the more working capital there is, the better off a business is. If People's Security Company had working capital of $20 000 instead of $2 927, they would be in a better position to pay their liabilities and would have more freedom to use their current assets for business improvements.

The fixed assets and long-term liabilities also match up well. The fixed assets for People's Security Company are $143 420, while the long-term liabilities are $80 000. This means the business has used debt to finance the purchase of fixed assets, and the amount of debt remaining is quite large (over half the total of fixed assets.) As you can see, accountants can draw many useful conclusions from studying the relationships of these key figures on a classified balance sheet.

Comparative Statements, Trend Analysis, and Common-Size Statements

In section 8.2, you worked with percentage changes, trend analysis, and common-size income statements. Accountants apply the same techniques when they analyze balance sheet data.

To display their calculations for changes in amounts and percentages, accountants prepare comparative financial statements. A **comparative financial statement** presents figures for successive years in side-by-side columns. Both income statements and balance sheets may be shown in comparative form. The comparative balance sheet for Apollo Printing is displayed in Figure 8.13.

FIGURE 8.13

A comparative balance sheet for Apollo Printing.

APOLLO PRINTING
COMPARATIVE BALANCE SHEET
DECEMBER 31, 2002 AND 2001

ASSETS	2002	2001	Increase (1) or Decrease (2)	Percent Change
Current Assets				
Bank	$ 9 270	$ 5 711	$ 3 559	62.3%
Accounts Receivable	42 100	17 500	24 600	140.6%
Printing Supplies	25 300	22 600	2 700	11.9%
Total Current Assets	$ 76 670	$ 45 811	$ 30 859	67.4%
Fixed Assets				
Land	$ 40 000	$ 40 000		0.0%
Buildings	57 500	60000	($2 500)	−4.2%
Equipment	104 650	109 400	(4 750)	−4.3%
Total Fixed Assets	$202 150	$209 400	($7 250)	−3.5%
Total Assets	$278 820	$255 211	$ 23 609	9.3%
LIABILITIES				
Current Liabilities				
Accounts Payable	$ 36 700	$ 19 050	$ 17 650	92.7%
Bank Loan	20 000	10 000	10 000	100.0%
Total Current Liabilities	$ 56 700	$ 29 050	27 650	95.2%
Long-Term Liabilities				
Mortgage Payable	$ 45 000	$ 50 000	($5 000)	
Total Liabilities	$101 700	$ 79 050	22 650	28.7%
OWNER'S EQUITY				
D. Fan, Capital	$177 120	$176 161	$ 959	0.5%
Total Liabilities and Equity	$278 820	$255 211	$ 23 609	9.3%

When analyzing comparative financial statements, first look for items showing unusual change. These could signal difficult situations. For example, accounts receivable grew by 140.6%. This could be a good sign if there was a corresponding increase in sales. However, if there had been a significant increase in sales, why did the business find it necessary to double its bank loan? More investigation is needed.

Perhaps the increase in accounts receivable was due to customers taking longer to pay. And if they took longer to pay, there might be insufficient cash for Apollo to pay its suppliers. This possibility seems supported by the fact that accounts payable increased by 92.7%.

Sometimes, little or no change should be flagged as a cause for concern. For instance, perhaps Apollo Printing spent a good deal of time and money trying to boost sales through advertising. Yet the equity grew by only 0.5%. Did the advertising really boost sales? Did factors other than sales limit the growth of equity? Should the advertising effort be continued?

Comparative financial statements are valuable not only for the answers they provide, but also for the questions they generate.

Trend Analysis

You saw in Section 8.2 that information from income statements is especially suited for trend analysis. Similarly, certain data obtained from the balance sheets also lend themselves to being presented over a number of consecutive periods.

The working capital for Apollo Printing is shown over a five-year period in Figure 8.14.

FIGURE 8.14

The trend analysis for the working capital of Apollo Printing.

To review how working capital is calculated, use amounts from Figure 8.13 to subtract Current Liabilities from Current Assets, and see if you can find your answers in Figure 8.14.

APOLLO PRINTING WORKING CAPITAL 1998 TO 2002				
1998	1999	2000	2001	2002
$19 626	$18 993	$20 584	$16 761	$19 970
100.0%	96.8%	104.9%	85.4%	101.8%

This trend analysis seems to point out problems with the sharp increase in working capital from 2001 to 2002. When the five years are analyzed, you can see that there has been minimal growth. In fact, even though the amount of working capital improved in 2002, it is still below the level reached in the year 2000.

Common-Size Statements

When constructing a common-size income statement, every figure is expressed as a percentage of sales. Therefore, if rent expense is 46 percent, one can say that for each dollar of sales, 46 cents goes to pay the rent. For common-size balance sheets, *every figure is expressed as a percentage of total assets.*

For example, the Accounts Receivable percentage is calculated as follows:

$$\frac{\text{Accounts Receivable 42 100}}{\text{Total Assets 278 820}} = 15\%$$

For Apollo Printing, the common size balance sheet appears in Figure 8.15.

FIGURE 8.15

The common-size balance sheet for Apollo Printing.

APOLLO PRINTING COMMON-SIZE BALANCE SHEET DECEMBER 31, 2001 AND 2002		
ASSETS		
Current Assets		
Bank	$ 9 270	3.3%
Accounts Receivable	42 100	15.1%
Printing Supplies	25 300	9.1%
Total Current Assets	$ 76 670	27.5%
Fixed Assets		
Land	$ 40 000	14.3%
Buildings (Net)	57 500	20.6%
Equipment (Net)	104 650	37.5%
Total Fixed Assets	$202 150	72.5%
Total Assets	$278 820	100.0%
LIABILITIES		
Current Liabilities		
Accounts Payable	$ 36 700	13.2%
Bank Loan	20 000	7.2%
Total Current Liabilities	$ 56 700	20.3%
Long-Term Liability		
Mortgage Payable	$ 45 000	16.1%
Total Liabilities	$101 700	36.5%
OWNER'S EQUITY		
D. Fan, Capital	$177 120	63.5%
Total Liabilities and Equity	$278 820	100.0%

Since every figure is divided by the total assets, accountants can communicate explanations in everyday language. For example, an accountant can point out most of Apollo Printing's assets consist of fixed assets — 72 and one-half cents out of every dollar, to be precise.

Common-size balance sheets become even more useful when comparing businesses of unequal size.

Section 8.3 **Review Questions**

1. What style was used to prepare the balance sheets in the early chapters of this text?
2. Describe the account form of the balance sheet.
3. Describe the report form of the balance sheet.
4. Give the meaning of the word "classified," as applied to financial statements.
5. Name the two asset classifications on the balance sheet in Figure 8.12 on page 270. Give an alternate name for one of these classifications.
6. Name the two liability classifications on the balance sheet in Figure 8.12.
7. The equity section of the balance sheet is made up from three figures on the work sheet. What are these three figures?
8. What is working capital?
9. What type of liabilities match up well with fixed assets?
10. What is the financial statement that presents figures for successive years in side-by-side columns?
11. What do you first look for when studying comparative financial statements?
12. What is the divisor for a common-size balance sheet?
13. On a common-size balance sheet, total liabilities are 75 percent. Explain what this means.

Section 8.3   **Exercises**

1. Shown below is the unclassified balance sheet for The Boat Repair Centre, owned by Anna Rodriguez of Halifax, Nova Scotia. **In your workbook do the following.**

   A. **Give the total of the current assets.**

   B. **Give the total of the fixed assets.**

   C. **Give the total of the current liabilities.**

   D. **Give the total of the long-term liabilities.**

   E. **Calculate the working capital.**

   F. **What is the total amount of the mortgage payable?**

THE BOAT REPAIR CENTRE
BALANCE SHEET
SEPTEMBER 30, 20-2

Assets

Bank		$ 2 125.00
Accounts Receivable		15 256.36
Office Supplies		1 500.00
Repair Supplies and Materials		15 236.00
Land		36 000.00
Building		48 000.00
Equipment		16 250.00
Truck		22 356.90
Total Assets		**$156 724.26**

Liabilities

Accounts Payable		$ 4 309.14
GST Payable	$ 520.02	
Less GST Recoverable	216.90	303.12
PST Payable		604.09
Bank Loan		10 000.00
Mortgage Instalment due within one year		2 000.00
Mortgage Payable		48 000.00
		$ 65 216.35

Owner's Equity

A. Rodriguez, Capital			
Balance October 1, 20-1		$80 356.00	
Net Income	$35 615.20		
Drawings	24 463.29		
Increase in Capital		11 151.91	
Balance September 30, 20-2			91 507.91
Total Liabilities and Owner's Equity			**$156 724.26**

2. Given below is a completed partial work sheet.
From this work sheet, prepare a classified balance sheet in report form in the space provided in your workbook.

Stanley Park Enterprises	Work Sheet	6 Months Ended June 30, 20—	
		Balance Sheet	
Accounts		Debit	Credit
Bank		3 050.15	
Accounts Receivable		26 750.85	
Supplies		3 500.00	
Equipment		75 352.00	
Automobiles		42 500.00	
Land		100 000.00	
Building		124 364.00	
Accounts Payable			3 900.95
GST Payable			460.50
GST Recoverable		235.90	
PST Payable			650.00
J. Hori, Capital			366 485.95
J. Hori, Drawings		56 000.00	
Commissions Earned			
Advertising Expense			
Car Expense			
Telephone Expense			
Utilities Expense			
Wages Expense			
		431 752.90	371 497.40
Net Income			60 255.50
		431 752.90	431 752.90

3. The current assets and the current liabilities of Goodenough Company for a five-year period are given below.

Goodenough Company
Balance Sheet Data

	Year 1	Year 2	Year 3	Year 4	Year 5
Current Assets	$50 000	$55 500	$59 500	$64 000	$68 500
Current Liabilities	35 000	38 000	40 000	42 500	45 000
Working Capital	?	?	?	?	?

In your workbook:

A. **Complete the above schedule by calculating the working capital figures for the five years.**

B. **Convert the above data into a Trend Analysis chart.**

C. **Show the above data in the form of a bar graph.**

4. The balance sheets for Neon Company and Radon Company as at December 31, 20 — are shown below.

    A. **Convert the two balance sheets into common-size form.**

    B. **Comment briefly on the ability of each of these companies to pay their accounts payable.**

    C. **Comment briefly on the total debt of each of these companies.**

BALANCE SHEETS DECEMBER 31, 20—	Neon Company	Radon Company
Assets		
Bank	$ 3 000	$14 500
Accounts Receivable	10 000	5 500
Plant and Equipment	132 000	53 000
Automobiles	38 000	26 000
Total Assets	$183 000	$99 000
Liabilities and Equity		
Accounts Payable	$ 19 000	$ 2 200
Mortgage Payable	92 500	18 000
Owner's Equity	71 500	78 800
Total Liabilities and Equity	$183 000	$99 000

5. Given below are the balance sheets for Leo Company and Capricorn Company.

    A. **Convert the two balance sheets into common-size form.**

    B. **Examine the financial positions shown by these balance sheets and discuss the positive and negative aspects of each company's position.**

BALANCE SHEETS DECEMBER 31, 20—	Leo Company	Capricorn Company
Assets		
Bank	$ 1 000	$ 31 000
Accounts Receivable	25 000	—
Plant and Equipment	150 000	160 000
Automobiles	50 000	29 000
Total Assets	$226 000	$220 000
Liabilities and Equity		
Accounts Payable	$ 25 000	$ 11 000
Loan Payable—Automobile	20 000	20 000
Mortgage Payable	—	150 000
Owner's Equity	181 000	39 000
Total Liabilities and Equity	$226 000	$220 000

6. Shown below is the partially completed comparative balance sheet for Playfair Company.

    A. Complete the statement for Playfair Company in your Workbook.

    B. Identify the four most significant changes. For each, say whether the change has been good or bad.

Playfair Company
Comparative Balance Sheet
December 31, 20-4 and 20-3

	20-4	20-3	Increase or Decrease (−)	% Change
ASSETS				
Current Assets				
Bank	$ 9 090	$ 5 500		
Accounts Receivable	65 220	35 700		
Supplies	70 636	45 600		
Total Current Assets	$144 946	$ 86 800		
Fixed Assets				
Land	$ 50 000	$ 50 000		
Buildings	135 000	138 000		
Equipment	141 000	160 000		
Automobiles	25 000	30 000		
Total Fixed Assets	$351 000	$378 000		
Total Assets	$495 946	$464 800		
LIABILITIES AND OWNER'S EQUITY				
Current Liabilities				
Accounts Payable	$ 97 936	$ 52 750		
Bank Loan	50 000	50 000		
Total Current Liabilities	$147 936	$102 750		
Long-Term Liability				
Mortgage Payable	$ 70 000	$ 75 000		
Total Liabilities	$217 936	$177 750		
T. Jennings, Capital				
Capital, January 1	$287 050	$277 700		
Net Income	90 960	84 350		
	$378 010	$362 050		
Drawings	100 000	75 000		
Capital, December 31	$278 010	$287 050		
Total Liabilities & Equity	$495 946	$464 800		

8.4 | Accountability

Accounting data is used in many ways. Perhaps the most important use is to provide the information for the financial statements. It is through the financial statements that managers of companies carry out an important function known as accountability. Accountability is the company officers' obligation to show how well they have been managing the company. Management must provide evidence of its performance. This is required by law, agreement, or custom.

Users of Financial Statements

The five groups who use financial statements most commonly are:

1. *Managers*   Managers probably use the financial statements more than any other group. They carefully study the statements in order to improve results and efficiency, and to eliminate weaknesses. The statements help managers make key business decisions.

2. *Owners*   Many owners are not directly involved in managing their companies. They use financial statements to evaluate the performance of the people who run the company for them, as well as to learn about company activities in general.

3. *Creditors*   Creditors, particularly bankers, ask for financial statements regularly. They use them to stay informed about a company's progress and its ability to meet its loan obligations. Bankers make sure that they are ready to act swiftly to protect their loans.

4. *Shareholders*   The law requires that corporations provide their shareholders with financial statements regularly. The shareholders are the real owners of an incorporated company. They must be made aware of its progress.

5. *Investors and brokers*   Shares of public corporations are traded by stockbrokers through stock exchanges. The employees of stock brokerage companies and potential investors stay informed about the affairs of corporations by reading their financial reports.

Quality of Financial Statements

As you can see, accounting statements are very important to various groups in business. Naturally, these groups will expect statements that are accurate, complete, up-to-date, and reliable. It is for this reason that the accounting profession has established the body of accounting standards known as generally accepted accounting principles (GAAPs). These standards play an important part in the accountability process. The reader of financial statements—absentee owner, banker, shareholder, or other—should be able to read the statements with confidence. To make sure that the standards are being met, most companies are required to have an independent audit. An **audit** is a critical review by a public accountant of the internal controls and accounting records of a company. The audit makes it possible to evaluate the fairness of a company's financial statements.

Before you can produce top-notch financial statements, there are GAAPs that you must learn in addition to the ones introduced in previous chapters.

GAAP—The Consistency Principle

> The **consistency principle** requires that a business must use the same accounting methods and procedures from period to period.

If there is a change in method from one period to another, the financial statements must clearly indicate the change. The readers of financial statements have the right to assume that consistency has been applied unless they are notified of some change in procedure.

The consistency principle prevents people from manipulating figures on financial statements by changing methods of accounting. For example, consider the case of a contracting company that records revenue when payments are received, not when invoices are issued. If the company had a bad year, it would be wrong to make the results look better by including some revenue for invoices issued but for which payment has not been received.

GAAP—The Materiality Principle

> The **materiality principle** requires accountants to include in a firm's financial statements any information that could be considered material (or important) to the users of that financial information.

For it to be acceptable not to include information in the financial statements, it must be such that neither the net income nor the financial position of the firm are impacted in any significant way. Excluding particular information must not lead statement users to make decisions different from what they would make were they to have that information.

For example, suppose a $50 invoicing error is discovered after a company's financial statements are printed, and this company had reported a $350 000 net income for the year. In this case, the information is not material to any decisions users might make using the firm's financial statements, because the $50 is not significant in relation to the net income figure of $350 000.

GAAP—The Full Disclosure Principle

> The **full disclosure principle** states that all information needed for a full understanding of the company's financial affairs must be included in the financial statements.

Some items that are necessary for an understanding of the company's financial affairs may not affect the ledger accounts directly. These would be included in the form of accompanying notes.

For example, suppose that a chemical company was being sued for millions of dollars by employees who claim that their health was ruined by working for the company, which had assured them that no danger existed. Assume also that the company would suffer seriously if it lost the lawsuit. This information would have to be revealed to the readers of the financial statements by means of an accompanying note.

Other examples of matters that might require an accompanying note are tax disputes and company takeovers.

Section 8.4   Review Questions

1. What is probably the most important use for accounting data?
2. What is meant by "accountability"?
3. Give reasons why managers require financial statements.
4. Name five groups of individuals who use financial statements.
5. Why would an absentee owner want financial statements for his or her business?
6. Why do bankers insist on financial statements from businesses to which they lend money?
7. Why do corporations provide their shareholders with financial reports?
8. Why do stockbrokers obtain copies of the financial reports of public companies?
9. Why should users of financial statements be able to rely on them?
10. Give another expression for "accounting standards."
11. What is an audit? What is its purpose?
12. Explain the consistency principle.
13. Explain the materiality principle.
14. Explain the full disclosure principle.

Section 8.4   Exercises

1. **Briefly answer the following questions.**

   A. Who is required by law to provide financial statements as evidence of accountability?
   B. Who would be required to provide financial statements as evidence of accountability even if not required to do so by law?
   C. Give three ways that management uses data from the financial statements. Do not include normal daily routines.
   D. What can an absentee owner do if he or she is not satisfied with the results of the business as shown on the financial statements?
   E. How else (besides reading the financial reports) could an absentee owner stay informed of company activities?
   F. Banks sometimes take swift action to protect a loan that they believe has gone bad. What action do you think that they would take?
   G. Usually banks obtain "security" before giving a loan. What does this mean?
   H. If a bank loan is secured, why is it sometimes still necessary to take swift action?
   I. What might banks insist on in order to be sure that they have been given reliable financial statements?
   J. What can a shareholder who is not happy with the progress of a corporation do about it?
   K. Compare what can be done in question 10 above with what can be done in question 4 above. Which individual, the absentee owner or the shareholder, has more power to change the situation?
   L. Assume that you lost a large sum of money in a business deal. Assume further that you relied on information from audited financial statements, some of which proved to be misleading. What might you do about this?

8.5 | Using Software for Analyzing Financial Statements

The developers of accounting and spreadsheet software know how useful comparative statements, common-size statements, and charts are to businesspeople. Therefore, they make certain their programs include these important tools for analyzing financial statements.

Financial Statement Options in Simply Accounting

You will now explore a few of the options for financial statements in Simply Accounting. Locate and load the Simply Accounting file named Sam's Softball City 8. (The "8" stands for Chapter 8, which should help you avoid confusion with the files you used in Chapter 7.) Accept the Session date of May 31, 2001.

From the Home window, choose Reports, Financials, and Balance Sheet. Check the box for the Comparative Balance Sheet option and enter the data for the "first" and "second" periods that appear in Figure 8.16. In the "Report On" field select "First Period vs. Second Period (with dollar difference)."

FIGURE 8.16

Data for creating a comparative balance sheet in Simply Accounting.

Balance Sheet Options   [X]

Report Type: ☑ Comparative Balance Sheet

First Period
As at: 5/31/01 ▼

Second Period
As at: 4/30/01 ▼

Report on: First Period vs. Second Period (with dollar difference) ▼

[Sort...]   [Filter...]   [OK]   [Cancel]

The first period asks for a May 31 balance sheet; the second period requests one for the end of the previous month. The "Report On" field at the bottom of Figure 8.16 designates the type of comparative statement desired. A two-period statement will be produced, and it will show the dollar difference between the two periods. When you enter the data in Figure 8.16 and press the Return key or select "OK," your monitor should look like Figure 8.17.

FIGURE 8.17

A comparative balance sheet for Sam's Softball City.

You may have to use the scroll bar to see all parts of the balance sheet shown in Figure 8.17 on your computer screen.

Balance Sheet						_ □ ×
File Options Help						
Comparative Balance Sheet		As At 5/31/01		As At 4/30/01		Change
ASSETS						
Current Assets						
Bank		11,266.30		38,700.25		-27,433.95
A/R--Chatham Steelers		5,243.00		0.00		5,243.00
A/R--Infield Flyers		0.00		221.00		-221.00
A/R--Remdal Red Sox		535.00		535.00		0.00
Supplies		2,484.00		7,479.00		-4,995.00
Total Current Assets		19,528.30		46,935.25		-27,406.95
Fixed Assets						
Equipment		36,991.08		31,996.08		4,995.00
Total Fixed Assets		36,991.08		31,996.08		4,995.00
TOTAL ASSETS		56,519.38		78,931.33		-22,411.95
LIABILITIES						
Current Liabilities						
Bank Loan		35,000.00		35,000.00		0.00
A/P--Cannon Sports		0.00		10,644.40		-10,644.40
A/P--Cell Tel		0.00		0.00		0.00
A/P--Eastern Electric		1,495.86		0.00		1,495.86
A/P--Ewert Equipment		12,425.50		23,425.50		-11,000.00
A/P--Pro Motion Advertising		1,444.50		1,444.50		0.00
A/P--Sandhu Sporting Goods		0.00		2,645.00		-2,645.00
GST Payable	745.50		140.00			605.50
GST Recoverable	-427.98		-2,968.07			2,540.09
GST Owed		317.52		-2,828.07		3,145.59
Total Current Liabilities		50,683.38		70,331.33		-19,647.95
TOTAL LIABILITIES						
		50,683.38		70,331.33		-19,647.95
EQUITY						
Samuel Lucas, Capital						
Opening Capital		20,000.00		20,000.00		0.00
S. Lucas, Drawings		-6,000.00		-3,000.00		-3,000.00
Current Earnings		-8,164.00		-8,400.00		236.00
Ending Capital		5,836.00		8,600.00		-2,764.00
TOTAL EQUITY		5,836.00		8,600.00		-2,764.00
LIABILITIES AND EQUITY		56,519.38		78,931.33		-22,411.95

The first glance at the cash figures on the comparative balance sheet in Figure 8.17 might alarm you. The cash balance declined by $27 433.95. However, the comparative statement also reveals that most of the money went to reduce accounts payable. And while the working capital is a negative number, the $236 change in current earnings means that the business had a net income in the second month of operations. This is a positive sign.

To gain more insight about the profit situation, you might want to examine the expenses more closely. From the Home window of Simply Accounting, choose Graphs, Expenses by Account. Your monitor should look like Figure 8.18.

FIGURE 8.18

Data for creating a pie chart
for Sam's Softball City.

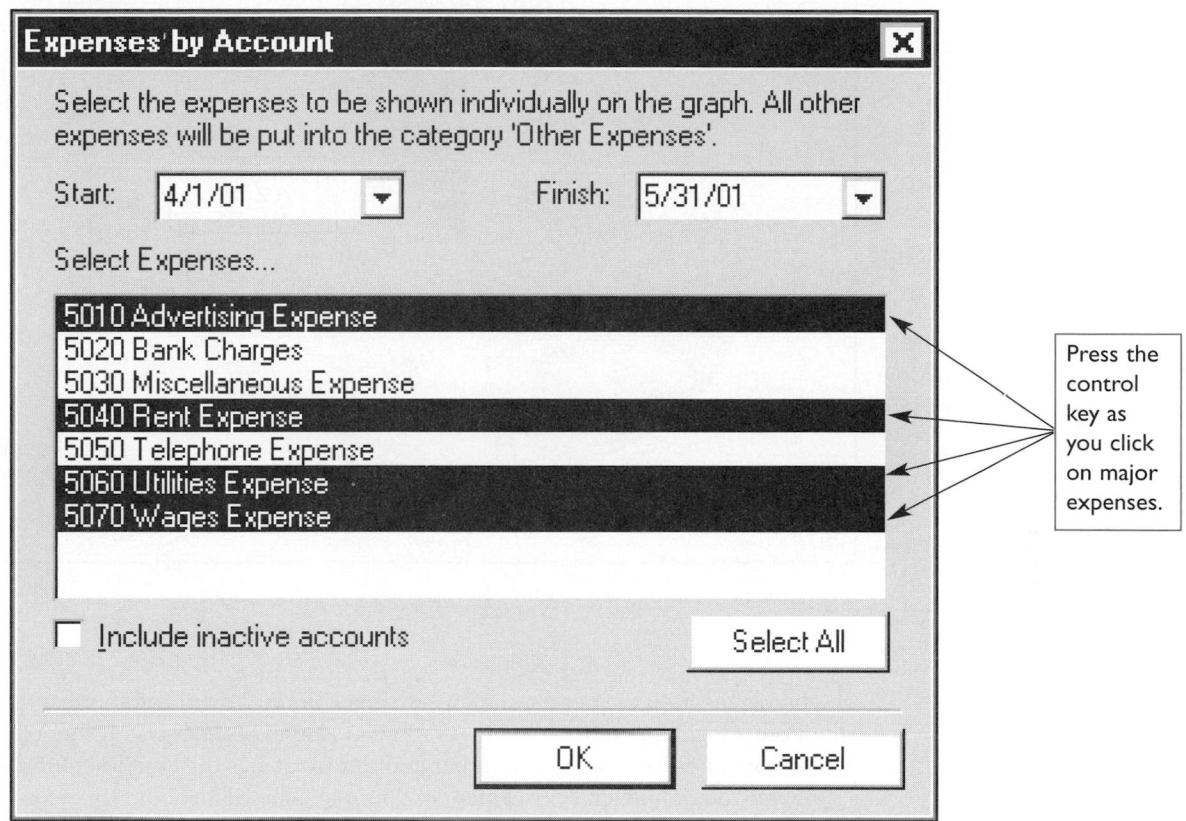

The sentence near the top of the computer screen in Figure 8.18 asks you to select
the expenses you want to show on the graph. Choosing all the expenses would display some very small pieces of pie. Instead, focus on the major items, the ones that
are highlighted. The minor expenses—Bank Charges, Miscellaneous Expense, and
Telephone Expense—will be combined into a category called "Other Expenses."

To make the same account selections as shown in Figure 8.18, press the Control
key as you click the major expenses. When you press the Return key or select "OK",
a pie chart like the one in Figure 8.19 on page 286 will appear.

FIGURE 8.19

A pie chart that displays expenses for the first two months.

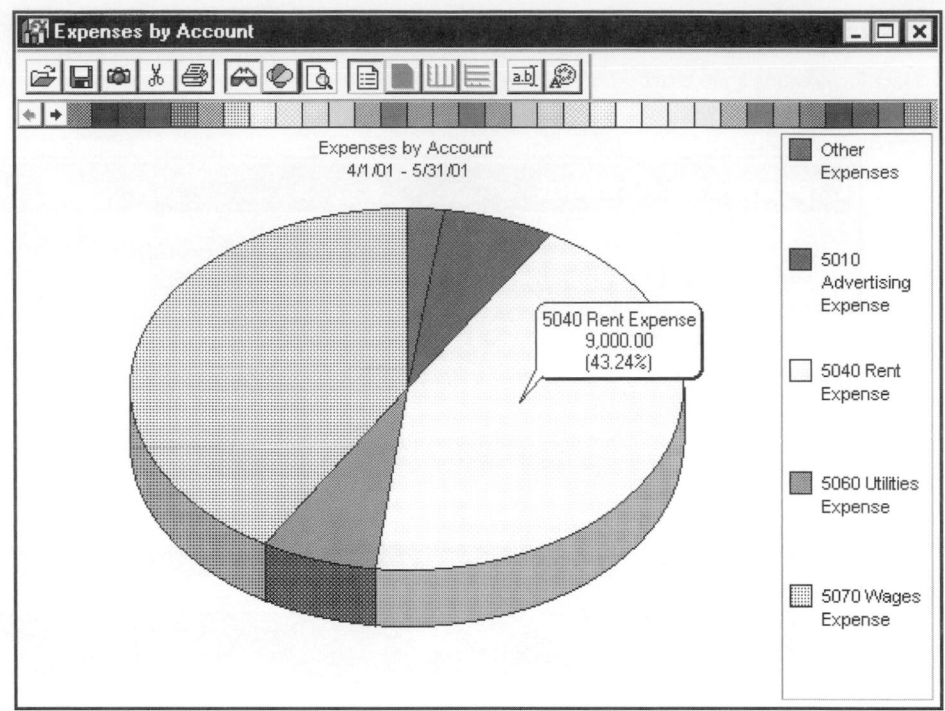

To change the look of your chart, you can drag colours from the colour bar and drop them onto segments of the pie chart. You can also experiment with the formatting icons that appear above the colour bar in order to change the location of the legend.

When you double-click a segment of your pie chart, data about that expense are shown. In Figure 8.19, Rent Expense has been double-clicked. The percentage shown was calculated by dividing Rent Expense by Total Expenses.

Financial Statement Options in Spreadsheets

By applying spreadsheet skills you have already acquired, you can present financial statements in formats that suit your needs and preferences. For example, from the Home window in Simply Accounting, choose Reports, Financials, and Income Statement. This displays the two-month income statement shown in Figure 8.20 on page 287.

FIGURE 8.20

The two-month income
statement for Sam's
Softball City.

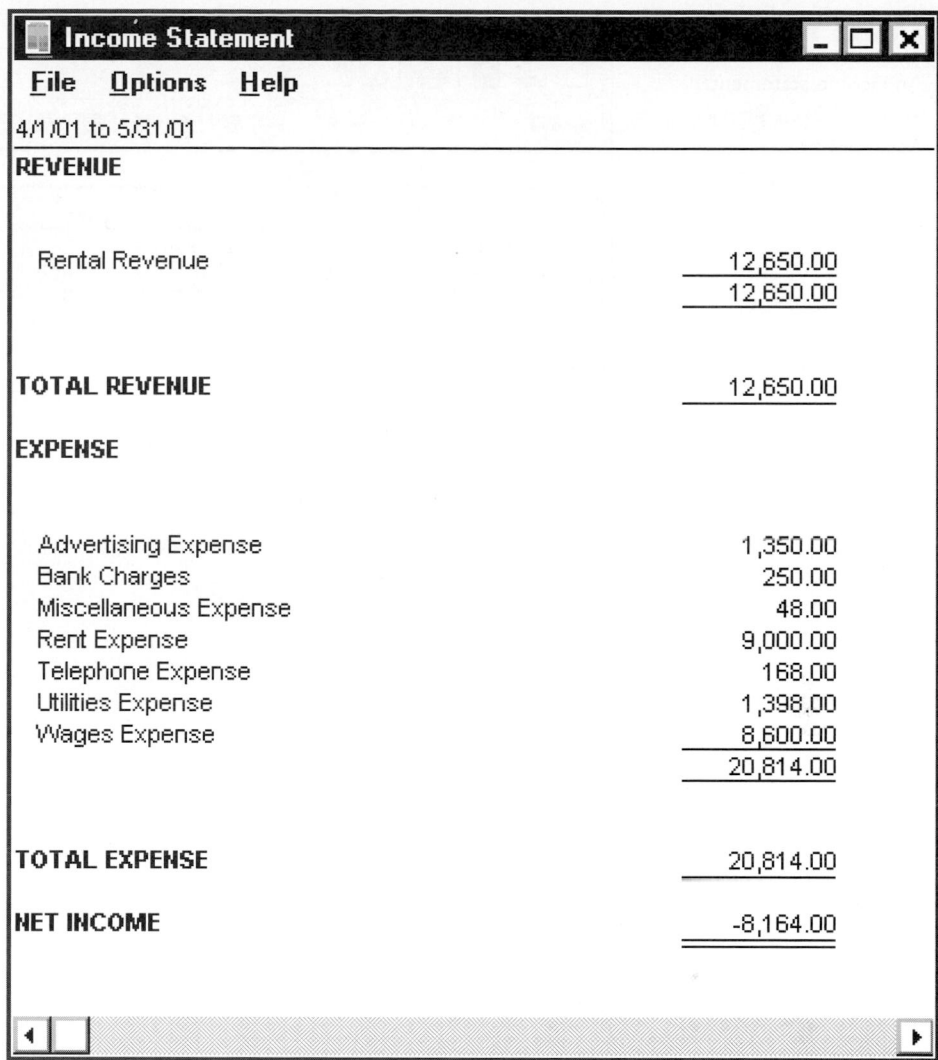

FIGURE 8.20

The two-month income statement for Sam's Softball City.

The destination of the exported file will be either a hard drive or floppy disc. Check with your teacher before exporting your file.

Suppose the format of the above statement does not suit your needs. You can modify this statement by exporting it to a spreadsheet and changing its appearance with that software. From the window shown in Figure 8-20, prepare to export the income statement by choosing File, Export. Then, after identifying the name and the destination of the file to be saved, choose a Microsoft® Excel format for the file. When you load the exported file in Microsoft® Excel, it will look similar to Figure 8.21.

FIGURE 8.21

An income statement exported from Simply Accounting to Microsoft Excel.

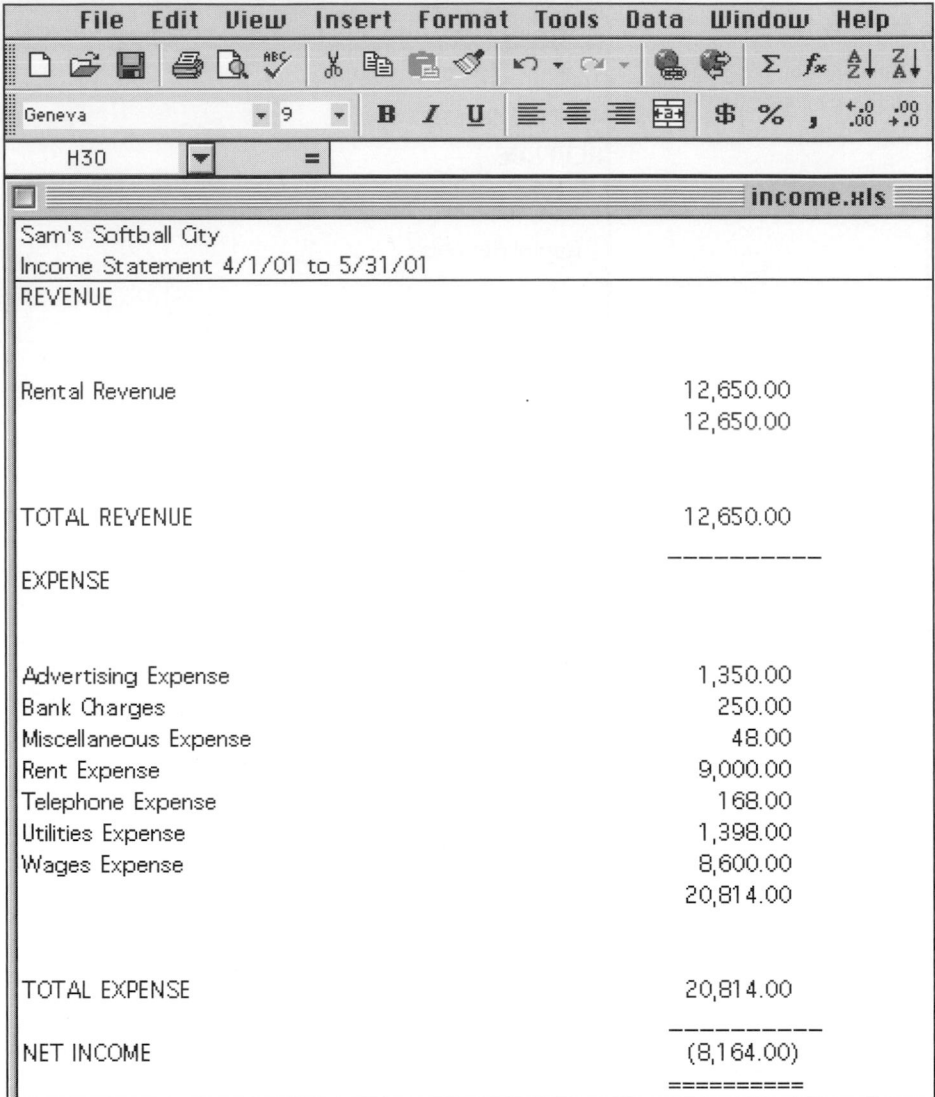

Before you start working on the statement in Microsoft Excel, follow this tip. Copy all the data into your "computer's clipboard." (Choose Edit, Select All followed by Edit, Copy.) Then open a new spreadsheet file, and paste the income statement into the new file. This procedure ensures you will not be thrown off track by Simply Accounting's default settings for exported statements.

Your goal is to produce a re-formatted income statement for Sam's Softball City with common-size percentages. For guidance, examine Figure 8.22 on page 289 and follow the advice that is given below the illustration.

FIGURE **8.22**

A common-size income statement for Sam's Softball City.

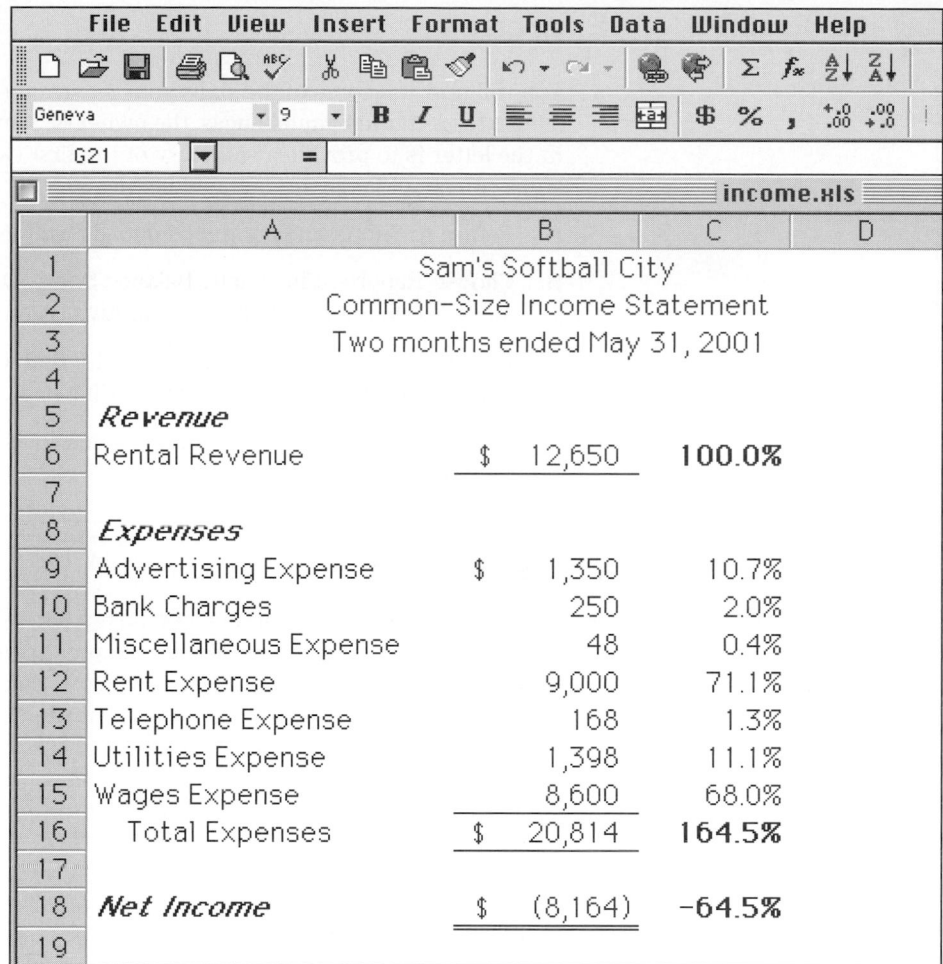

Most of the changes in Figure 8.22 are cosmetic. To achieve similar results on your spreadsheet model, delete some columns and rows, re-key headings, and apply different cell formats. The divisor for the common-size percentages is Rental Revenue (cell B6). In your first formula at C6, make the divisor an absolute cell reference (e.g., $B$6). Then, "fill" the formula down to C7 through C18. (Delete the unwanted results at C7, C8, and C17 because these rows contain no numbers.)

Section 8.5   Exercises

1. You will now use some of the skills you have acquired in this chapter to prepare a business letter to Samuel Lucas, the owner of Sam's Softball City. The purpose of the letter is to provide a summary of the first two months of operation. The steps you should take are outlined below:

   A. Return to Simply Accounting and load *Sam's Softball City 8.*

   B. Choose Reports, Financials, Balance Sheet. Display the balance sheet for May 31. (Do not check the Comparative Balance Sheet option.)

   C. Export the balance sheet to Microsoft Excel. Use steps similar to the ones you used for the income statement. (See pages 286–287.)

   D. Use Microsoft Excel to prepare a common-size balance sheet for Sam's Softball City.

Challenge Exercise

2. Create a word-processing file and compose a letter to Mr. Lucas. You can find the address for Sam's Softball City in Simply Accounting by choosing Setup, Company Information from the Home window. Enhance your letter by pasting in a pie chart, a common-size income statement, and a common-size balance sheet.

    To copy and paste a pie chart from Simply Accounting, display the chart and click the camera icon that is located above the colour bar. This will copy the pie chart. Open the word processing program on your computer. Open a file to begin your letter and paste in the pie chart.

    If you want to copy your financial statements from Microsoft Excel, highlight and copy the cells you desire, switch to Microsoft Word, choose Paste Special from the Edit menu, and select Microsoft Excel Worksheet Object. The pie chart and common-size statements can be re-sized by dragging the bottom-right corner of the object up and to the left.

    Suggestion: In your letter, refer to specific data revealed by the pie chart and financial statements. Incorporating visual objects into your letter makes sense only when you refer to their main points in the body of your letter. You may also want to use information revealed in the comparative balance sheet shown in Figure 8.17. For help setting up your letter, see the Skills Appendix.

CHAPTER 8   Summary

CHAPTER HIGHLIGHTS

Now that you have completed Chapter 8, you should:

- understand the purpose of a work sheet;
- be able to complete a six-column work sheet;
- know the two forms of the balance sheet, the account form and the report form;
- know the meaning of "classified" with respect to financial statements;
- be able to prepare a classified balance sheet;
- understand that the data for the financial statements come directly from the work sheet;
- know the first six steps in the accounting cycle;
- be able to analyze financial data using comparative statements, trend analysis, and common-size statements;
- know the meaning of accountability;
- use accounting and spreadsheet software to help analyze financial statements.

ACCOUNTING TERMS

accountability	fixed asset
balance sheet—account form	full disclosure principle
balance sheet—report form	long-term liability
classified balance sheet	materiality principle
common-size statements	plant and equipment
consistency principle	trend analysis
control accounts	work sheet
current asset	working capital
current liability	

CHAPTER 8   Review Exercises

Using Your Knowledge

1. Stacey Worrell, an accounting student, has discovered a slight variation in the procedure for balancing a work sheet. Her method is shown on page 292.

A. **Give your opinion of this method.**

B. **Explain why the balance sheet columns balance with the $112 net income figure included, but would not if the figure were excluded.**

Work Sheet	Morton Enterprises					Month Ended Dec. 31, 20–	
Accounts	Tr. Bal.		Inc. St.		Bal. Sht.	
	Dr	Cr	Dr	Cr	Dr	Cr
Bank	12 –				12 –	
Accounts Receivable	8 –				8 –	
Supplies	15 –				15 –	
Equipment	40 –				40 –	
Truck	120 –				120 –	
Accounts Payable		17 –				17 –
V. Maswich, Capital		141 –				141 –
V. Maswich, Drawings	75 –				75 –	
Revenue		300 –		300 –		
General Expense	10 –		10 –			
Utilities Expense	50 –		50 –			
Rent Expense	90 –		90 –			
Telephone Expense	8 –		8 –			
Wages Expense	30 –		30 –			
	458 –	458 –	188 –	300 –		
Net Income			112 –			112 –
			300 –	300 –	270 –	270 –

2 The trial balance figures of lawyer Ying Lo on June 30, 20-, after a fiscal period of six months, are as follows:

Bank	$ 516.20	
Accounts Receivable	9 255.50	
Office Supplies	1 525.00	
Office Equipment	10 356.00	
Automobile	19 255.65	
Professional Library	5 363.25	
Accounts Payable		$ 2 618.25
GST Payable		650.00
GST Recoverable	410.00	
Ying Lo, Capital		34 024.81
Ying Lo, Drawings	20 000.00	
Fees Earned		55 285.00
Car Expense	4 592.36	
Utilities Expense	589.25	
Miscellaneous Expense	1 254.85	
Rent Expense	7 200.00	
Salaries Expense	9 235.00	
Telephone Expense	3 025.00	
	$92 578.06	$92 578.06

Complete a six-column work sheet and prepare an income statement and classified balance sheet.

3 The trial balance figures of Star Delivery, owned by Danielle Nowak, on December 31, 20-, after a fiscal period of one year, are as follows:

Bank	$ 1 852.25	
Accounts Receivable	15 325.00	
Office Supplies	1 863.00	
Furniture and Equipment	7 258.36	
Land	45 500.00	
Buildings	52 365.50	
Automobile	9 255.65	
Trucks	36 252.95	
Accounts Payable		$ 3 579.25
GST Payable		730.00
GST Recoverable	450.00	
Bank Loan		25 000.00
Mortgage Payable		75 000.00
Danielle Nowak, Capital		58 099.98
Danielle Nowak, Drawings	32 000.00	
Fees Earned		125 254.00
Gas and Oil Expense	26 215.24	
Insurance Expense	2 657.25	
Miscellaneous Expense	1 526.85	
Telephone Expense	965.32	
Truck Repairs Expense	4 240.65	
Utilities Expense	1 575.65	
Wages Expense	48 359.56	
	$287 663.23	$287 663.23

Complete a six-column work sheet and prepare the financial statements.

---

4 **This exercise also appears in the Workbook.**
For each of the following, check off the most appropriate response in the space provided.

A. Financial statements are prepared:
  a. once a year.
  b. at the end of the fiscal period.
  c. whenever management requires them.
  d. all of the above.
  e. none of the above.

B. A work sheet is:
  a. one of the books of account.
  b. one of the financial statements.
  c. used instead of the financial statements.
  d. all of the above.
  e. none of the above.

C. Extending amounts on a work sheet means:
   a. adding to the amounts because of additional transactions.
   b. placing debit amounts in debit columns and credit amounts in credit columns.
   c. transferring amounts into the Balance Sheet section or the Income Statement section.
   d. all of the above.
   e. none of the above.

D. The process of balancing the work sheet involves:
   a. totalling the four right-hand money columns.
   b. calculating the difference between the two money columns in each of the last two sections.
   c. ensuring that the differences in b) above are equal to each other.
   d. all of the above.
   e. none of the above.

E. A work sheet will not balance if:
   a. the Telephone Expense amount is extended to the Balance Sheet section Debit column.
   b. the Drawings amount is extended to the Income Statement section Debit column.
   c. the Capital amount is extended to the Balance Sheet section Debit column.
   d. all of the above.
   e. none of the above.

F. You can tell what the net income or net loss figure is by:
   a. looking at the balancing figure in the Balance Sheet section of the work sheet.
   b. looking at the balancing figure in the Income Statement section of the work sheet.
   c. looking at the equity section of the completed balance sheet.
   d. all of the above.
   e. none of the above.

G. All of the following statements, except one, are false. Indicate which statement is true.
   a. The report form of balance sheet is the only style used in the real business world.
   b. The report form of balance sheet is common because it uses standard-sized paper.
   c. The report form of balance sheet is horizontal in form.

d. The style of the report form of balance sheet eliminates the need for "balancing" totals.
e. The report form of balance sheet is more difficult to understand.

H. All of the following statements, except one, are false. Indicate which statement is true. On a classified balance sheet:
   a. automobiles are not included in the Fixed Assets section because their value decreases over time.
   b. a mortgage payable is deducted from the asset, Building.
   c. supplies are not included as a current asset because they are normally converted into cash.
   d. a bank loan is included in long-term liabilities.
   e. the values shown for the fixed assets are not necessarily their true market value.

I. All of the following statements, except one, are true. Indicate which statement is false.
   a. The data in the books of account are considered to be "raw" data.
   b. Accountants are judged on the basis of the accounting statements and reports that they prepare. Therefore, their work should be first-class in form and content.
   c. All of the data necessary for the financial statements can be found on the work sheet.
   d. An overall decrease in capital can occur in two ways. An overall increase in capital can occur in only one way. Therefore, decreases in capital are more common.
   e. The beginning balance in the equity section of the balance sheet is not always that of January 1.

J. During a fiscal period, a business suffered a loss of $12 000, began the period with a capital balance of $20 000, and ended the period with a debit balance of $2 000. The drawings for the fiscal period were:
   a. $ 6 000
   b. $10 000
   c. $30 000
   d. $18 000
   e. $14 000

5 Evan Gordon is the owner of Fiesta Restaurant. The results of operation of the restaurant for the years 20-3 and 20-4 are shown below.

A. In your Workbook, complete the two additional columns for 1) Dollar Increase or Decrease and 2) Percentage Increase or Decrease.

B. Prepare a common-size income statement for both years.

C. Give your opinion on the Fiesta Restaurant's revenues and expenses. Pay particular attention to Mr. Gordon's ability to control expenses.

FIESTA RESTAURANT
INCOME STATEMENT
YEARS ENDED MARCH 31, 20-4 and 20-3

	20-4	20-3
Revenues		
Food and Dining	$163 595	$150 290
Liquor and Bar	197 492	181 410
Total Revenues	$361 087	$331 700
Operating Expenses		
Bank Charges Expense	$ 920	$ 1 520
Car Expense	3 516	3 725
Insurance Expense	1 800	1 800
Utilities Expense	1 610	1 570
Food and Liquor Expense	157 315	140 290
Miscellaneous Expense	920	950
Rent Expense	24 000	24 000
Telephone Expense	1 350	1 290
Wages Expense	49 316	51 374
Total Expenses	$240 747	$226 519
Net Income	$120 340	$105 181

Questions for Further Thought

Briefly answer each of the following questions.

1. The subtotals of the Balance Sheet columns of a worksheet are not equal. The difference between them is exactly the amount of the net income or net loss. Explain why this is so.

2. If the Equipment account balance in the Trial Balance section of the work sheet is extended incorrectly to the Income Statement debit column, the work sheet will still balance. Why is this so?

3. List three errors that would cause a work sheet to be out of balance.

4. Which form of the balance sheet—report form or account form—gives the better presentation of the financial statement? Give reasons for your answer.

Obtain a copy of a financial report of a public corporation and see what form is used.

5. Describe how columns are used efficiently in the preparation of financial statements.

6. What is probably the most significant observation that can be made from a classified balance sheet?

7. What can a public accountant do for the owner of a business to ensure that the accounting department does its work properly?

8. Is the owner's equity the amount that the owner would get from the sale of the business, or is it merely the amount of the owner's capital as shown by the books? Explain.

9. Explain why it is better to use a work sheet for the preparation of the financial statements rather than work directly from the ledger.

Case Studies

CASE 1

Can Net Income Be Increased?

Shown below are the results of operation for Dr. Tanis Tamo for a five-year period.

DR. TANIS TAMO OPERATING RESULTS (in thousands)	Year 1	Year 2	Year 3	Year 4	Year 5
Revenue					
Fees Earned	$143	$160	$184	$214	$239
Expenses					
Car Expense	$ 20	$ 22	$ 23	$ 25	$ 27
Insurance	8	8	9	12	13
Light and Heat	15	16	17	20	22
Office Expense	11	11	13	17	18
Rent	12	12	12	15	18
Telephone	5	5	6	7	8
Wages	20	22	28	30	33
Total Expenses	$ 91	$ 96	$108	$126	$139
Net Income	$ 52	$ 64	$ 76	$ 88	$100

Questions

1. On graph paper (provided in the Workbook), prepare a five-year line graph of 1) the revenue and 2) the total expenses.
2. Have total expenses increased as fast as revenue over the five years?
3. Does the graph tell anything about net income? Explain.
4. Determine which expense shows the greatest percentage increase over the five-year period.
5. Revenues are expected to rise by only 2 per cent in Year 6. This is because the workload is near its maximum. Dr. Tamo is anxious to increase her net income in Year 6 to $110 000. Write a memo to Dr. Tamo explaining what must be done in order to reach this goal. Use the memo format shown in the Skills Appendix.

CASE 2

Analyzing Business Data

Shown below in comparative form are the account balances of Metro Haulage Company for a number of years. The net income figures for Year 2 and Year 3 are also shown.

	Year 1	Year 2	Year 3	Year 4
Assets				
Cash	$ 500	$ 500	$ 500	$ 500
Accounts Receivable	10 000	11 000	12 000	12 000
Supplies	1 000	1 000	1 100	1 100
Land and Building		150 000	150 000	150 000
Equipment	4 000	5 000	5 000	10 000
Trucks	25 000	25 000	50 000	50 000
Total Assets	$40 500	$192 500	$218 600	$223 600
Liabilities and Equity				
Accounts Payable	$ 5 500	$ 6 000	$ 6 000	$ 10 000
Bank Loan	10 000	40 000	30 000	
Mortgage Payable		100 000	90 000	80 000
Owner's Equity	25 000	46 500	92 600	133 600
Total Liabilities and Equity	$40 500	$192 500	$218 600	$223 600
Net Income		$ 50 000	$ 81 000	

Questions

1. In Year 2:
   a. By how much did the total assets increase during the year?
   b. Make a list of the increases in the liabilities and the equity over the year.
   c. Explain in detail where the funds came from to pay for the increase in the assets.
   d. Calculate how much money the owner took out of the business.
2. In Year 3:
   a. By how much did the total assets increase during the year?
   b. In addition to the increase in assets, for what else did the business need funds?
   c. In detail, where did the funds come from to pay for the obligations of the business?
   d. Calculate how much money the owner took out of the business for the year.
3. In Year 4:
   a. By how much did the total assets increase?
   b. For what else was money needed in Year 4?
   c. Where did the money come from to pay for the obligations of the business?
   d. Calculate the profit of the company if the owner took $39 000 out of the business.

CASE 3

Why Doesn't Net Income Equal Cash?

Phil's Garage and Tune-Ups is owned by top-notch mechanic Phil Waggett. Phil is having some difficulty understanding his April income statement. The statement shows a net income of $4 000. Phil is satisfied with the income his business has earned, but he cannot understand why his bank balance has not increased by the same amount.

Phil directs this question to his accountant: "If my net income is $4 000 per month, why doesn't my bank balance also increase by $4 000? Instead, it has increased by only $500 during the month!"

Phil's accountant closely analyzes his financial statements to reveal the following information:

1. The balance sheet for the business at the beginning of the month showed the following:

ASSETS	
Cash	$2 200
Equipment	7 500
	$9 700
LIABILITIES AND OWNER'S EQUITY	
Accounts Payable	$3 000
P. Waggett, Capital	6 700
TOTAL LIABILITIES AND OWNER'S EQUITY	$9 700

2. Phil's drawings for the month were $3 000.
3. A bank loan for $1 500 was obtained during the month.
4. During April, Phil wrote cheques totalling $2 000 to cover several overdue accounts payable.
5. All of Phil's customers pay by cash or cheque.
6. No transactions affected equipment.

Questions

1. Prepare calculations showing the increases and decreases to Phil's bank account in order to explain the $500 increase in the bank balance.
2. Write an explanation that would help Phil understand that an increase in profit does not always result in a matching increase in cash.
3. Phil is talking about improving sales by extending credit to his customers. He wants to allow them 30 days to pay. Advise him of the possible effects on profits, accounts receivable, and cash flow (amount of money flowing into his bank account).

CASE 4

Interpreting Condensed Balance Sheets

Firewood Supply is a small business operated on a seasonal basis by Gerry Riel in St. Boniface, Manitoba. Comparative balance sheets for the business for the 20-1 and 20-2 seasons are shown below. These balance sheets are condensed; that is, only the information that is needed for the case is given.

FIREWOOD SUPPLY
BALANCE SHEET
DECEMBER 31, 20–2
(With comparative figures for 20–1)

	20-2	20-1
Assets		
Bank	$ 3 000	$ 2 000
Accounts Receivable	20 000	14 000
Equipment	15 000	15 000
Truck	29 000	15 000
Total Assets	$67 000	$46 000
Liabilities and Equity		
Accounts Payable	$20 000	$10 000
Bank Loan	14 000	14 000
Owner's Equity	33 000	22 000
Total Liabilities and Equity	$67 000	$46 000

Questions

1. Calculate the net income for 20-2 if the owner's drawings amounted to $15 000.
2. Explain how the accounts receivable would increase by $6 000.
3. Describe the business's ability to pay its debts.
4. The assets increased from $46 000 to $67 000. Explain in detail where the funds came from to acquire the assets.

CASE 5

Challenge

Could You Get Student Council out of the Hole?

At the beginning of the school year, the Riverview High School student council has inherited a bank balance that was overdrawn by $935. The council has no assets.

The members of the council executive are extremely concerned and have asked you, the treasurer, to examine the records of the council to find out the reasons for the poor financial position. They have also asked you to make recommendations for providing good management in the coming year.

As a result of your investigation, you find out that the previous council began its year with a positive bank balance of $200 and an inventory of 100 fully paid-for T-shirts, which had cost $5 each.

The bank book shows that the transactions shown below took place during the previous year:

	Cheques	Deposits	Balance
Beginning balance			$ 200
Sale of student cards (940 × $2.50)		$2 350	2 550
Cost of printing student cards	$ 350		2 200
Grant to drama club	1 000		1 200
Proceeds from dance (Nightmare)		2 000	3 200
Profit on refreshments (Nightmare)		70	3 270
Charge for musicians (Nightmare)	1 500		1 770
Grant to choir	1 000		770
Proceeds from sale of 100 T-shirts		375	1 145
Proceeds from variety show		140	1 285
Grant to athletic department	1 000		285
Proceeds from dance (Brainstorm)		300	585
Charge for musicians (Brainstorm)	1 600		−1 015
Profit on refreshments (Brainstorm)		80	−935

The previous student council had decided to have only top-notch entertainment at dances. Although this meant that the musical groups were expensive, a large profit was expected to be made on every dance. However, the "Brainstorm" dance fizzled because of bad weather and poor scheduling.

The T-shirts were sold at a bargain rate in order to promote school spirit. The three $1 000 grants were normal annual commitments made to the three school organizations.

Questions

1. Rearrange the above data to show more clearly how the bank balance dropped from $200 to negative $935.
2. Write a two-page report to the student council describing the factors that, in your opinion, contributed directly to the poor financial position. Use the memo report form shown in the Skills Appendix.
3. In your report, give recommendations for better management of the financial affairs of the student council in the future.
4. In particular, in your conclusion, suggest ways to remedy the negative bank balance.

Career

Lilian Goh / Director, Audit Operations Office of the Auditor General of Canada

An auditor ensures that an organization's accountants have done the accounting fairly, according to accepted methods, and that there has been no mishandling of funds. The federal government employs many auditors to ensure that taxpayers' money is collected and spent in the way that government policy directs. One of those auditors is Lilian Goh, who works with the Audit Operations Branch of the Office of the Auditor General of Canada (OAG).

The OAG's headquarters is based in Ottawa. It has 5 regional offices located in Halifax, Montreal, Winnipeg, Edmonton, and Vancouver. Provided that she has not gone on an assignment to various places across Canada, you will find Lilian at the Ottawa office. She says that the key to job satisfaction in audit operations is "liking lots of variety."

The daughter of an economist and journalist, Lilian grew up in Hong Kong and attended university in the United States and Canada. She graduated with a BA in economics from Whittier College in California and then obtained a MBA from the University of Toronto. She went on to get her first job in the Toronto office of international accounting firm Touche Ross. Her work at Touche Ross involved auditing private-sector companies and not-for-profit organizations.

"I enjoyed math right from the start, although I never enjoyed science," says Lilian. She describes herself as an organized thinker who likes to consider a problem carefully and then outline an approach to it. "I don't just tumble into a situation."

After a number of years in Toronto, Lilian transferred to Touche Ross's Halifax office and eventually the Ottawa office, where she worked as a senior consultant. While working there she obtained her CGA in 1983. In 1989, she decided that "working in the government would broaden my perspective." It wasn't long before she landed a job as an audit manager at the OAG with the responsibility to audit the Department of Indian Affairs and Northern Development (DIAND).

At Touche Ross, Lilian was known as an external auditor. Private-sector companies hire external auditors from accounting firms to check their books because they are considered impartial, unlike an internal auditor who works for the same organization that

produces the books. The results of an external audit tell senior management whether their financial statements have been done according to generally accepted accounting principles.

But in her job at the OAG, Lilian is an "external" auditor in the federal government environment. She manages a team of (usually) six people, including three who have professional accounting designations (CGA, CMA or CA) and two students who have completed their university training but are not yet designated professional accountants.

How does Lilian's team audit the DIAND? "We can't check the accounting records of every single branch in the DIAND," she explains. "So, early in the year, we pick a sample that we audit." Lilian's group must also determine the procedures that they will follow to conduct the audit of the department. If the audit team uncovers any evidence of irregular accounting or impropriety, they report the finding. In addition, they recommend procedures to prevent the irregularity from occurring again.

All federal departments, agencies, and most Crown corporations are audited by the OAG. Other than auditing the government's accounts and financial statements, the OAG also conducts value-for-money audits. These audits examine management practices, controls, and reporting systems to determine whether government programs are run economically and efficiently with due regard to the environmental effects, and whether the government has the means to measure the effectiveness of these programs. Lilian moved into value-for-money auditing in 1992 and has since been promoted to Director, Audit Operations in 1997. She audited issues that cut across government departments and agencies such as human resource management, service quality and performance reporting. She also conducts value-for-money audits of specific departments and agencies. For example, she is now auditing the Canada Customs and Revenue Agency.

The OAG produces the famous Auditor General's Report 2–3 times a year. The clearest examples of waste and mismanagement in the Auditor General's report are given wide media coverage. This report to the House of Commons is made public in order to inform Canadians how taxpayers' money was spent.

Lilian thinks that Native Canadians should consider careers in accounting, particularly in areas like hers that relate directly to their own lives. She notes that Native Canadians are attracted to law because law is important for understanding and establishing their rights. However, she points out, accounting is important too, because it is linked to economic development. Says Lilian, "If a society can find ways to prosper through careful money management, it can take advantage of so many different opportunities."

Research Questions

1. Use the Internet to research who the current Auditor General is and when the next Auditor General's report will come out. Or, if the report has been published recently, collect and read some of the information published in the media on its findings. Does any of the information available help you learn about the different types of auditing?

2. How does the information relate to the generally accepted accounting principles you have learned so far?

Completing the Accounting Cycle

In Chapter 8, you learned about the six-column work sheet and how financial statements are put to use. In this chapter, you will learn about adjusting entries and the important role they play in preparing financial statements. You will also use an expanded eight-column work sheet to make room for the adjusting entries and learn how to close the books at the end of the fiscal period.

9.1 | The Adjustment Process

In section 8.4, you saw that financial statements are used extensively to assist in making business decisions. Therefore, it is important for financial statements to be accurate, up-to-date, and consistent from year to year. The responsibility for these documents rests entirely with the company's accountants.

When preparing financial statements, the accountants must ensure that:

- all accounts are brought up to date;
- all late transactions are taken into account;
- all calculations have been made correctly;
- all GAAPs have been complied with.

Bringing the account data up-to-date at statement time is known as "making the adjustments." The accounting entries produced by this process are known as the adjusting entries. In most cases, an **adjusting entry** assigns amounts of revenue or expense to the appropriate accounting period before finalizing the books for the fiscal period.

One of the main GAAPs governing adjusting entries is the Matching Principle, which matches revenue for a fiscal period with the expenses that helped to produce that revenue.

Adjusting entries are necessary because the books of account are allowed to become inaccurate between statement dates. This means that certain things have been left undone because some accounts do not need to be perfectly accurate at the end of each business day. Leaving these things undone can save time, effort, and money. However, at statement time, the omissions must be accounted for. If the accounts are not adjusted at this time, a correct net income or net loss cannot be determined.

Adjusting Entries for Supplies

The Supplies account is an example of an account that requires an adjustment at the end of each accounting period. This is because the Supplies account is one of those accounts that is allowed to become inexact between statement dates.

The year-end balance of Supplies Expense should represent the total amount of supplies used, damaged, or stolen during a fiscal period.

When supplies are purchased, their cost is debited correctly to the Supplies account. But as supplies are used, which usually happens daily, no accounting entries are made to record the usage at the time. During the accounting period, the balance of the Supplies account represents the balance at the beginning of the period plus the cost of any new supplies purchased. And, the balance in the Supplies Expense account will be zero. Clearly, neither of these two balances is correct.

Consider the following accounts for Markell Company as at December 31, 20-2. In T-account form, the account balances are:

Supplies		Supplies Expense	
20-2		20-2	
Dec. 31 7 900		Dec. 31 0̸	

This practice is acceptable during the accounting period, but not at the end of the accounting period when statements are prepared. At that time, in accordance with the Matching Principle, the two account balances must be corrected. This is done by means of an adjusting journal entry.

The adjusting entry is simple to do. First, an inventory (or count of the remaining supplies) is taken. The value of the actual supplies on hand at December 31—in this example is $1 386. The difference between this amount, $1 386, and the balance in the Supplies account, $7 900 is the cost of the supplies used (or spoiled, or stolen), $6 514. The journal entry to correct the two accounts is:

20-2		DR.	CR.
Dec 31	Supplies Expense	6 514–	
	Supplies		6 514–

After this journal entry is recorded, the effect in the accounts is as shown below.

Supplies			Supplies Expense		
20-2			20-2		
Dec. 31	7 900		Dec. 31	0̶	
		6 514		6 514	
	1 386			6 514	

Now you see the effect of the adjusting entry. The two accounts now have the correct balances. In section 9.2, you will see how this adjusting entry is recorded on the work sheet.

Adjusting Entries for Prepaid Expenses

There are times in business when expense items are paid for in advance. This presents no special problem if the period covered by the expense item (rent, for example) falls entirely within the fiscal period. However, some items, such as insurance, may cover a length of time that affects the current fiscal period and the following fiscal period as well. Items of this nature are called prepaid expenses and require special accounting treatment at statement time.

A **prepaid expense** is an item paid for in advance, but one where the benefits extend into the future. Insurance is the most common prepaid expense. A business can purchase insurance to cover possible losses on automobiles, buildings, contents, crops, and so on. When you purchase insurance, you usually pay for one year's coverage in advance. Occasionally, an insurance company will provide businesses with insurance for a period longer than one year.

When prepaid expenses are purchased, they are usually debited to a prepaid expense account. For example, suppose Markell Company purchased a one-year automobile insurance policy on September 1, 20-2 at a cost of $1 800. At the time of purchase, the accounting clerk would make the following journal entry:

20-2		DR.	CR.
Sep 1	Prepaid Insurance	1 800–	
	Bank		1 800–

Prepaid expense accounts have value and are therefore classified as assets. To understand this classification, consider what would happen if Markell Company canceled the insurance policy a few days after buying it. If this were to happen, the business would get a full or partial cash refund. Clearly, prepaid expenses have value and belong in the asset category. On the balance sheet, they are usually listed in the current assets section because their value expires in a relatively short time (usually within one year from the date on the balance sheet.)

In regard to the previous transaction, the following two accounts affecting insurance would appear in simplified T-account form as shown below at December 31, 20-2.

Prepaid Insurance		Insurance Expense	
20-2		20-2	
Sept. 1 1 800		Dec. 31 ∅	

At Markell Company's year-end, neither of these two accounts is correct. If you think of the insurance as costing $5 a day, it should help you to understand that, as each day passes, $5 should be transferred from the Prepaid Insurance account to the Insurance Expense account. However, no such entries are made on a daily basis. This is another situation where the accounts are allowed to become inaccurate during the fiscal period and adjusted for at the year-end.

Since the insurance was purchased on September 1, four months of coverage have been used and eight months of coverage remain. The cost of the insurance used during the four months can be calculated as 1/3 of $1 800, which is $600. The cost of the insurance remaining is 2/3 of $1 800, which is $1200. With this calculation done, the adjusting entry can be made as follows:

20-2		DR.	CR.
Dec 31	Insurance Expense	600–	
	Prepaid Insurance		600–

The adjusted balances in T-account form are:

Prepaid Insurance		Insurance Expense	
20-2		20-2	
Dec. 31 1 800		Dec. 31 ∅	
	600	600	
1 200		600	

You will see how to record this adjustment on the work sheet in Section 9.2

Adjusting Entries for Late-Arriving Purchase Invoices

You have already seen a number of "accounting rules" (or GAAPs) used by accountants. You can now appreciate that an accountant must be on the watch for items that require special handling when the time comes to prepare financial statements. Among the items to which an accountant gives special attention are late-arriving invoices.

Goods and services are often bought and received toward the end of an accounting period. The bills for these items may not arrive until the subsequent fiscal period. Of course, that is the wrong fiscal period for them. The Matching Principle states that expenses are to be recognized in the same period as the revenue that they helped to earn. This means that the accounting department must see to it that all items are recorded in their proper accounting period in order to arrive at a proper determination of net income.

The financial statements are not usually prepared until two to three weeks after the fiscal year end. This time period should be sufficient for the late arrival of purchase invoices from suppliers. During this waiting period, the accounting department examines all purchase invoices in order to find those that affect the fiscal period that just ended. The ones that are set apart are summarized into an accounting entry which becomes the third adjusting entry to be studied.

For Markell Company, assume that the senior accountant has waited until January 15, 20-3 for late-arriving invoices. Assume further that two such invoices have arrived as follows: telephone, $212; utilities, $315. These invoices represent costs that helped the business earn revenue in the year 20-2 and must be recorded in that year. Therefore, an adjusting entry, as follows, is necessary.

20-2		DR.	CR.
Dec 31	Telephone Expense	212—	
	Utilities Expense	315—	
	Accounts Payable		527—

You will see how to record this adjusting entry on the work sheet in section 9.2.

For a demonstration of how to complete the three adjusting entries you have learned so far, visit www.pearsoned.ca/ accounting1

Review of Adjusting Entries

You now know how to prepare adjusting entries for three common year-end situations: supplies, insurance, and late-arriving invoices. Later in this chapter, you will be introduced to another item, depreciation, that also requires making an adjusting entry. Remember, no matter how complex an adjustment appears, you will be able to do it correctly if you use good common sense and follow the theory that you have learned so far.

Section 9.1   Review Questions

1. Define "adjusting entry."
2. Why are adjusting entries necessary?
3. Why are accounts allowed to become inexact between statement dates?
4. What is the main GAAP that governs adjusting entries?
5. What does the balance of the Supplies account represent during the accounting period?
6. What must be done at the end of the fiscal period to determine what the balance of the Supplies account should be?
7. What is the basic adjusting entry for supplies?
8. What is a prepaid expense?
9. What is the most common prepaid expense?
10. Where are prepaid expenses listed on the balance sheet?
11. Name the account that is debited when insurance is paid for in advance.
12. What must be done at the end of the fiscal period to determine what the balance of the Prepaid Insurance account should be?
13. What is the basic adjusting entry for insurance?
14. What is a late purchase invoice?
15. What does the Matching Principle state about expenses?
16. How are the late purchase invoices determined?
17. What account is credited when preparing the adjusting entry for late invoices?

Section 9.1 Exercises

1. Complete the following schedule in your Workbook.

Supplies	Trial Balance Figure	Supplies Closing Inventory Figure	Supplies Expense Figure
1.	$300.00	$100.00	
2.	$1 400.00	$650.00	
3.		$175.00	$250.00
4.	$950.00		$740.00
Prepaid Insurance	Trial Balance Figure	Prepaid Insurance Final Calculation	Insurance Expense Figure
1.	$875.00	$325.00	
2.	$9 600.00	$800.00	
3.	$925.00		$315.00
4.		$410.00	$375.00

2. The year-end trial balance dated December 31, 20-3, for Kareem Industries showed Supplies at $5 050 and Prepaid Insurance at $2 100. The senior accountant was given the following additional information:

A. An inventory of supplies revealed $1 450 to be on hand.

B. The Prepaid Insurance account consisted of one 12-month policy purchased on July 1, 20-3.

C. An invoice for advertising done in December arrived in January, 20-4. The amount of the invoice was $10 000.

Prepare the adjusting entries.

3. The Supplies account has a year end debit balance of $2 018. As part of the year-end procedures, the senior accountant asks the office staff to count the supplies. Their results are listed on the inventory sheet shown below. **In your Workbook complete the inventory sheet and make the adjusting entry in the T-accounts.**

Inventory Item	Quantity	Unit Price	Value	
Rubber bands	3 boxes	$ 1.50 per box		
Envelopes #8	10 boxes	32.00 per box		
Envelopes #10	4 1/2 boxes	36.00 per box		
Envelopes, manila	2 boxes	28.00 per box		
Printer Cartridges	2 boxes	31.20 per box		
Letterhead	10M sheets	22.50 per M		
Copy paper	4M sheets	10.00 per M		
File Folders	2 boxes	6.00 per box		
Paper clips	12 boxes	1.50 per box		
Staples	15 boxes	4.10 per box		
Pencils, regular	4 doz.	5.50 per doz.		
Pencils, red	2 doz.	6.10 per doz.		
		Total		

4. A one-year insurance policy was purchased on August 1, 20-1 for $648.

A. **Calculate the value of the prepaid insurance for this policy as of December 31, 20-1.**

B. **Calculate the portion of the cost of this insurance policy to be charged as an expense to each of the years ended December 31, 20-1 and 20-2.**

5. For each of the following insurance policies perform the required calculations:

A. **Calculate the value of the prepaid insurance at the year-end date shown.**

B. **Prepare the adjusting journal entry for the year end shown.**

Policy	a.	b.	c.
Purchase date	Oct. 1, 20–4	Oct. 1, 20–4	Oct. 1, 20–4
Year-end date	Dec. 31, 20–4	Dec. 31, 20–5	Oct. 31, 20–4
Term of policy	1 year	2 years	1 year
Premium	$360	$360	$456

Policy	d.	e.	f.
Purchase date	Mar. 1, 20–1	June 1, 20–6	July 1, 20–4
Year-end date	Dec. 31, 20–1	June 30, 20–6	Dec. 31, 20–5
Term of policy	1 year	1 year	2 years
Premium	$720	$900	$1080

6. **Use T-accounts to help you do this exercise in your Workbook.**
The Kaleido Glass Shop began business on October 1, 20-0. Its first fiscal year ended on September 30, 20-1. On January 1, 20-1, $720 was paid for a truck licence for the 20-1 calendar year.

A. **Give the accounting entry to record the above transaction.**

B. **Calculate the value for prepaid licences on September 30, 20-1.**

C. **Calculate the truck licence expense for the fiscal period ended September 30, 20-1.**

D. **Give the adjusting entry necessary at September 30, 20-1.**

On January 1, 20-2, $720 was paid for the truck licence for the 20-2 calendar year.

E. **Give the balance in the Prepaid Licences account after recording the above payment.**

F. **Calculate the value for prepaid licences on September 30, 20-2.**

G. **Calculate the truck licence expense for the fiscal period ended September 30, 20-2.**

9.2 | Adjusting Entries and the Work Sheet

In Section 9.1, you learned to analyze and record adjusting entries for supplies, pre-paid insurance and late invoices. Now that you are familiar with the adjustment process, you are ready to use a work sheet for adjustments.

The first place that adjusting entries are recorded is on the work sheet. As the work sheet is prepared, the adjusting entries are calculated and recorded in a section headed *Adjustments*. This section requires two additional columns on the work sheet, following the trial balance columns. The work sheet is balanced and finalized before any adjusting entries are recorded in the accounts. To show how this is done, a work sheet for Global Logistics is started in Figure 9.1 below. You will be shown how the adjusting entries are recorded on the work sheet as we proceed.

FIGURE 9.1

The trial balance of Global Logistics recorded on the work sheet.

Global Logistics	Work Sheet								Year Ended Dec. 31, 20-4	
ACCOUNTS	TRIAL BALANCE		ADJUSTMENTS		INCOME STATEMENT		BALANCE SHEET			
	DR	CR	DR	CR	DR	CR	DR	CR		
Bank	5 20 51									
Accounts Receivable	18 4 75 –									
Supplies	1 4 80 90									
Prepaid Insurance	6 5 64 –									
Furniture & Equipment	4 1 96 –									
Automotive Equipment	54 6 00 –									
Accounts Payable		2 5 10 –								
GST Payable		1 2 40 –								
GST Recoverable	7 20 –									
Bank Loan	25 0 00 –									
P. Marshall, Capital		28 8 95 42								
P. Marshall, Drawings	42 0 00 –									
Shipping Revenue		2138 21 –								
Bank Charges Expense	3 5 00 –									
Miscellaneous Expense	1 95 1 65									
Rent Expense	24 0 00 –									
Telephone Expense	1 8 00 –									
Truck Expense	41 95 1 16									
Utilities Expense	3 7 50 –									
Wages Expense	65 95 7 20									
	271 46 66 42	271 46 66 42								

Adjusting for Supplies

The Supplies figure on the trial balance for Global Logistics in Figure 9.1 is $1 480.90. This figure is inexact because supplies are used daily but not recorded. To discover what the Supplies figure should be, the accounting clerk of Global Logistics took a physical inventory and prepared the listing shown in Figure 9.2.

GLOBAL LOGISTICS
SUPPLIES INVENTORY
DECEMBER 31, 20–4

Description	Quantity		Cost	Value
Envelopes, #10, white	2	boxes	$ 29.00	$ 58.00
Envelopes, #8, white	3	boxes	23.50	70.50
Envelopes, manila	37		.25	9.25
Ball pens, blue	15		.22	3.30
Pencils, black, HB	75		.95	71.25
Pencils, red	32		.89	28.48
Pencils, auto .5	3		7.85	23.55
Scotch tape, 1 cm	12		4.50	54.00
Scotch tape, 2 cm	8		6.50	52.00
Paper clips, regular	16	boxes	1.89	30.24
Paper clips, jumbo	5	boxes	3.50	17.50
Printer Ink Cartridge	2	boxes	35.24	70.48
Gummed labels, #505	3	pkgs	6.50	19.50
Elastic bands	5	boxes	3.59	17.95
			Total	$526.00

When the adjustment process for Supplies is finished, the account balance should match the amount produced by the inventory listing ($526.00).

To change the balance in the Supplies account from what it is ($1 480.90) to what it should be ($526.00), calculate the difference between the figures and use this figure ($954.90) for your adjusting entry. The adjusting entry appears below:

20-4		DR.	CR.
Dec. 31	Supplies Expense	954.90	
	Supplies		954.90

The adjusting entry for supplies is not journalized at this time. It is only recorded in the Adjustments section of the work sheet, as shown in Figure 9.3 on page 312.

FIGURE 9.3

The supplies adjustment
recorded on the work sheet.

Numbering the
adjustments
with a small,
superscript
number will
help your
adjusting
entries be
organized.

Global Logistics	Work Sheet				Year Ended Dec. 31, 20-4							
ACCOUNTS	TRIAL BALANCE		ADJUSTMENTS								
	DR	CR	DR	CR							
Bank	5 2 0 51										
Accounts Receivable	18 4 7 5 —										
Supplies	1 4 8 0 90			① 9 5 4 90							
Prepaid Insurance	6 5 6 4 —										
Furniture & Equipment	4 1 9 6 —										
Automotive Equipment	54 6 0 0 —										
Accounts Payable		2 5 1 0 —									
GST Payable		1 2 4 0 —									
GST Recoverable	7 2 0 —										
Bank Loan		25 0 0 0 —									
P. Marshall, Capital		28 8 9 5 42									
P. Marshall, Drawings	42 0 0 0 —										
Shipping Revenue		213 8 2 1 —									
Bank Charges Expense	3 5 0 0 —										
Miscellaneous Expense	1 9 5 1 65										
Rent Expense	24 0 0 0 —										
Telephone Expense	1 8 0 0 —										
Truck Expense	41 9 5 1 16										
Utilities Expense	3 7 5 0 —										
Wages Expense	65 9 5 7 20										
	271 4 6 6 42	271 4 6 6 42									
Supplies Expense			① 9 5 4 90								

If an account name does not appear in the trial balance, it must be written in below.

Observe that Supplies Expense did not appear in the Accounts column on the work
sheet because the account balance on December 31 was zero. Therefore, you need
to write its title on the next available line of the work sheet, as shown in Figure 9.3
above. Also notice that the adjusting entry is referenced in Figure 9.3 with a circled
numeral "1."

Adjusting for Insurance Used

Working again with the example of Global Logistics, the trial balance shows a figure of $6 564 for prepaid insurance. This balance is out-of-date. The balance in the Prepaid Insurance account must be made equal to the total value remaining in all of the unexpired insurance policies at the statement date. This figure is calculated by means of an insurance listing such as the one shown in Figure 9.4 below:

FIGURE 9.4

A prepaid insurance listing.

	PREPAID INSURANCE LISTING					
	DECEMBER 31, 20–4					
Company	Policy Date	Term	Expiry Date	Premium	Unused Fraction	Value Remaining
Acme	Aug. 1, 20–4	1 yr	Jul. 31, 20–5	$1 824	7/12	$1 064
Fidelity	Aug. 1, 20–4	1 yr	Jul. 31, 20–5	1 248	7/12	728
Guarantee	Mar. 1, 20–4	1 yr	Feb. 28, 20–5	948	2/12	158
Blue Cross	Nov. 1, 20–4	1 yr	Oct. 31, 20–5	2 544	10/12	2 120
						$4 070

The out-of-date prepaid insurance figure on the trial balance shows $ 6 564. The prepaid insurance listing above shows a total value remaining of $4 070. This is the value of the insurance that belongs to a future period and is the amount that should appear on the balance sheet. The difference between the two figures, $2 494, is the dollar amount of the insurance used up. This is the figure used in the adjusting entry below:

20-4		DR.	CR.
Dec 31	Insurance Expense	2 494	
	Prepaid Insurance		2 494

The adjusting entry is not journalized at this time. It is entered in the Adjustments section of the work sheet, as shown in Figure 9.5 on page 314.

FIGURE 9.5

The insurance adjustment recorded on the work sheet.

Global Logistics			Work Sheet							Year Ended Dec. 31, 20-4			
ACCOUNTS	TRIAL BALANCE				ADJUSTMENTS								
	DR		CR		DR		CR						
Bank	520 51												
Accounts Receivable	18475 –												
Supplies	1480 90						① 954 90						
Prepaid Insurance	6564 –						② 2494 –						
Furniture & Equipment	4196 –												
Automotive Equipment	54600 –												
Accounts Payable			2510 –										
GST Payable			1240 –										
GST Recoverable	720 –												
Bank Loan			25000 –										
P. Marshall, Capital			28895 42										
P. Marshall, Drawings	42000 –												
Shipping Revenue			213821 –										
Bank Charges Expense	3500 –												
Miscellaneous Expense	1951 65												
Rent Expense	24000 –												
Telephone Expense	1800 –												
Truck Expense	41951 16												
Utilities Expense	3750 –												
Wages Expense	65957 20												
	271466 42		271466 42										
Supplies Expense					① 954 90								
Insurance Expense					② 2494 –								

Late Purchase Invoices

On January 15, 20-5, the accounting clerk for Global Logistics was instructed to send the senior accountant copies of all invoices received in the previous two weeks that covered expenses in the year 20-4. The clerk discovered three "late" purchase invoices that belonged to the 20-4 fiscal period.

Late Purchase Invoices

Telephone	$ 45
Truck repair	496
Printer repair	85
Total	$ 626

In order to record all expenses in the fiscal period in which they helped earn revenue the late invoices are summarized into an adjusting entry as follows:

20-4		DR.	CR.
Dec. 31	Telephone Expense	45	
	Truck Expense	496	
	Miscellaneous Expense	85	
	Accounts Payable		626

FIGURE 9.6

The adjustment for late purchase invoices recorded on the work sheet, and the adjustments columns balanced.

This adjusting entry is shown on the work sheet for Global Logistics in Figure 9.6 below. After the entry is made on the work sheet, the adjustments columns are totalled and ruled. The "late" purchase invoices are then absorbed into the regular accounting system to be checked, recorded, and eventually paid in the new fiscal period.

The adjustments columns must balance. If they do not, the figures should be checked and corrected before continuing.

Global Logistics	Work Sheet							Year Ended Dec. 31, 20-4	
ACCOUNTS	TRIAL BALANCE		ADJUSTMENTS		INCOME STATEMENT		BALANCE SHEET		
	DR	CR	DR	CR	DR	CR	DR	CR
Bank	5 20 51							
Accounts Receivable	18 4 75 –							
Supplies	1 4 80 90			① 9 54 90				
Prepaid Insurance	6 5 64 –			② 2 4 94 –				
Furniture & Equipment	4 1 96 –							
Automotive Equipment	54 6 00 –							
Accounts Payable		2 5 10 –		③ 6 26 –				
GST Payable		1 2 40 –						
GST Recoverable	7 20 –							
Bank Loan		25 0 00 –						
P. Marshall, Capital		28 8 95 42						
P. Marshall, Drawings	42 0 00 –							
Shipping Revenue		213 8 21 –						
Bank Charges Expense	3 5 00 –							
Miscellaneous Expense	1 9 51 65		③ 85 –					
Rent Expense	24 0 00 –							
Telephone Expense	1 8 00 –		③ 45 –					
Truck Expense	41 9 51 16		③ 4 96 –					
Utilities Expense	3 7 50 –							
Wages Expense	65 9 57 20							
	271 4 66 42	271 4 66 42						
Supplies Expense			① 9 54 90					
Insurance Expense			② 2 4 94 –					
			4 0 74 90	4 0 74 90				

Extending the Work Sheet

Each line of the work sheet must be extended to one of the last four columns. Extending is done as follows:

Step 1   Evaluate each item in the first four columns. You may have to add or subtract, depending on what is contained in the adjustments columns. The process will result in one number, together with an indication of whether that number is a debit or credit value.

Step 2   Transfer the value found in step 1 above to one of the last four columns of the work sheet. Each item belongs to either the Income Statement columns or the Balance Sheet columns. Debit values are transferred to debit columns and credit values are transferred to credit columns.

You can see this by looking at the partial work sheet shown in Figure 9.7 below.

FIGURE 9.7

A partial work sheet showing two items extended.

Global Logistics	Work Sheet						Year Ended Dec. 31, 20-4	
ACCOUNTS	TRIAL BALANCE		ADJUSTMENTS		INCOME STATEMENT		BALANCE SHEET	
	DR	CR	DR	CR	DR	CR	DR	CR
Supplies	1 480 90			① 954 90			526 —	
Accounts Payable		3 750 —		③ 626 —				4 376 —

For Supplies, the debit of $1 480.90 and the credit adjustment of $954.90, taken together, are worth $526.00 debit. Since Supplies is an asset, the $526.00 debit figure is carried over to the Balance Sheet section.

Look also at the Accounts Payable line. For Accounts Payable, the credit of $3 750.00 and the credit adjustment of $626.00 for late arriving purchase invoices, taken together, are worth $4 376.00 credit. Since Accounts Payable is a liability, the $4 376.00 credit is carried over to the Balance Sheet section.

Any item on the work sheet may be extended as soon as there are no more adjustments for that item. Most of the extending is done after all of the adjustments have been recorded.

For Global Logistics, all of the extended items can be seen in Figure 9.8 on page 317.

Balancing the Work Sheet for Global Logistics

The process of balancing the work sheet is the same as that shown in Chapter 8. This involves:

Step 1 totalling each of the last four columns;

Step 2 determining the difference between the two income statement columns ($66 836.09) and the difference between the two balance sheet columns ($66 836.09);

Step 3 ensuring that the two differences in step 2 above are the same. If they are not, the work sheet does not balance and contains one or more errors. These must be found and corrected before the financial statements are prepared.

FIGURE 9.8

The extended and balanced eight-column work sheet for Global Logistics.

Figure 9.8 below shows the balanced work sheet for Global Logistics. The difference between the two income statement columns is $66 836.09, and the difference between the two balance sheet columns is also $66 836.09. Therefore, the work sheet is balanced.

Global Logistics	Work Sheet						Year Ended Dec. 31, 20-4	
ACCOUNTS	**TRIAL BALANCE**		**ADJUSTMENTS**		**INCOME STATEMENT**		**BALANCE SHEET**	
	DR	CR	DR	CR	DR	CR	DR	CR
Bank	5 20 51						5 20 51	
Accounts Receivable	18 475 –						18 475 –	
Supplies	1 480 90			① 9 54 90			5 26 –	
Prepaid Insurance	6 564 –			② 2 494 –			4 070 –	
Furniture & Equipment	4 196 –						4 196 –	
Automotive Equipment	54 600 –						54 600 –	
Accounts Payable		2 510 –		③ 6 26 –				3 136 –
GST Payable		1 240 –						1 240 –
GST Recoverable	720 –						720 –	
Bank Loan		25 000 –						25 000 –
P. Marshall, Capital		28 895 42						28 895 42
P. Marshall, Drawings	42 000 –						42 000 –	
Shipping Revenue		213 821 –				213 821 –		
Bank Charges Expense	3 500 –				3 500 –			
Miscellaneous Expense	1 951 65		③ 85 –		2 036 65			
Rent Expense	24 000 –				24 000 –			
Telephone Expense	1 800 –		③ 45 –		1 845 –			
Truck Expense	41 951 16		③ 496 –		42 447 16			
Utilities Expense	3 750 –				3 750 –			
Wages Expense	65 957 20				65 957 20			
	271 466 42	271 466 42						
Supplies Expense			① 9 54 90		9 54 90			
Insurance Expense			② 2 494 –		2 494 –			
			4 074 90	4 074 90	146 984 91	213 821 –	125 107 51	58 271 42
Net Income					66 836 09			66 836 09
					213 821 –	213 821 –	125 107 51	125 107 51

Journalizing and Posting the Adjusting Entries

So far, the adjusting entries have been recorded only on the work sheet. Once the work sheet is completed, the adjusting entries must be recorded in the books of account.

Journalize and post all adjusting entries that appear in the adjustments section of the work sheet. This is no time for discovering new adjustments. The adjustment decision process took place when the work sheet was prepared. Now it is simply a matter of putting these adjustments into the accounts.

This journalizing and posting can be done by individual entries as shown in Figure 9.9 below, or in one grand entry, as is done by many accountants. The entries are usually dated on the last day of the fiscal period, and they are headed "adjusting entries."

FIGURE 9.9

The adjusting entries for Global Logistics.

		Adjusting Entries			
Dec.	31	Supplies Expense	9 5 4 90		
		Supplies		9 5 4 90	
	31	Insurance Expense	2 4 9 4 —		
		Prepaid Insurance		2 4 9 4 —	
	31	Miscellaneous Expense	8 5 —		
		Telephone Expense	4 5 —		
		Truck Expense	4 9 6 —		
		Accounts Payable		6 2 6 —	

FIGURE 9.10

The ledger of Global Logistics showing the effect of the adjusting entries.

When these adjusting entries have been journalized and posted, the ledger accounts will be updated. The updated ledger for Global Logistics is shown in Figure 9.10 below.

ASSETS	=	LIABILITIES	+	OWNER'S EQUITY
$82 387.51		$28 656.00		$53 731.51

Bank		Accounts Payable		P. Marshall, Capital		P. Marshall, Drawings	
520.51			2 510.00		28 894.42	42 000.00	
			626.00				
			⟨3 136.00⟩				

Accounts Receivable		GST Payable		Shipping Revenue		Bank Charges Expense	
18 475.00			1 240.00		213 821.00	3 500.00	

Supplies		GST Recoverable		Miscellaneous Expense		Rent Expense	
1 480.90	954.90	720.00		1 951.65		24 000.00	
⟨526.00⟩				85.00			
				⟨2 036.65⟩			

Prepaid Insurance		Bank Loan		Telephone Expense		Truck Expense	
6 564.00	2 494.00		25 000.00	1 800.00		41 951.16	
⟨4 070.00⟩				45.00		496.00	
				⟨1 845.00⟩		⟨42 447.16⟩	

Furniture & Equipment				Utilities Expense		Wages Expense	
4 196.00				3 750.00		65 957.20	

Automotive Equipment				Supplies Expense		Insurance Expense	
54 600.00				954.90		2 494.00	

Section 9.2   Review Questions

1. Where are adjusting entries first recorded?
2. What is the name of the new column on the work sheet?
3. Describe the process of extending the work sheet.
4. When are adjusting entries journalized and posted?
5. Why must adjusting entries be journalized and posted?
6. What date is used for journalizing the adjusting entries?

Section 9.2   Exercises

1. The simplified work sheet for P. Tang and Company, shown below with the trial balance figures already entered, is provided in the Workbook.

Work Sheet								
Work Sheet P. Tang and Company Year Ended Dec. 31, 20–4								
ACCOUNTS	TRIAL BALANCE		ADJUSTMENTS		INCOME STATEMENT		BALANCE SHEET	
	DR	CR	DR	CR	DR	CR	DR	CR
Bank	1 800 –							
Accounts Receivable	19 500 –							
Supplies	1 000 –							
Prepaid Insurance	1 750 –							
Equipment	22 000 –							
Automobile	21 000 –							
Accounts Payable		4 360 –						
P. Tang, Capital		54 040 –						
P. Tang, Drawings	15 000 –							
Fees Earned		60 300 –						
Car Expense	3 800 –							
General Expense	2 950 –							
Miscellaneous Expense	700 –							
Rent Expense	7 200 –							
Wages Expense	22 000 –							
	118 700 –	118 700 –						

A. Using the additional information given below, complete the eight-column work sheet.

B. Journalize the adjusting entries in a two-column general journal.

C. Post the adjusting entries to the T-account ledger provided in the Workbook and take off an adjusted trial balance.

Optional

D. Prepare an income statement and a classified balance sheet.

Additional Information

1. The value of the supplies on hand at the year-end amounted to $700.
2. The prepaid insurance at the year-end was calculated at $800.
3. Late-arriving invoices pertaining to the 20-4 fiscal period were:

Car Expense	$ 75
General Expense	100
Total	$175

2. The work sheet for Mission Marketing is shown below, with the trial balance figures already entered.

A. Using the additional information given below, complete an eight-column work sheet in your Workbook.

B. Journalize the adjusting entries in a two-column general journal.

C. Post the adjusting entries to the T-account ledger provided in the Workbook and take off an adjusted trial balance.

Work Sheet			Mission Marketing						Year Ended Dec. 31, 20–3	
ACCOUNTS	TRIAL BALANCE		ADJUSTMENTS		INCOME STATEMENT		BALANCE SHEET			
	DR	CR	DR	CR	DR	CR	DR	CR		
Bank	2490 –									
Accounts Receivable	21600 –									
Supplies	4250 –									
Prepaid Insurance	1254 –									
Equipment	19200 –									
Automobile	44200 –									
Accounts Payable		6565 –								
GST Payable		780 –								
GST Recoverable	510 –									
C. Ans, Capital		71275 –								
C. Ans, Drawings	40000 –									
Fees Earned		135700 –								
Car Expense	13214 –									
Miscellaneous Expense	1563 –									
Rent Expense	18000 –									
Utilities Expense	2800 –									
Wages Expense	45239 –									
	214320 –	214320 –								

Optional

D. Prepare an income statement and a classified balance sheet.

Additional Information

1. The value of the supplies on hand at the year-end was $950.
2. The prepaid insurance at the year-end was calculated to be $680.
3. Late-arriving invoices pertaining to the 20-3 fiscal period were for:

Car Expense	$150
Miscellaneous Expense	50
Utilities Expense	115
Total	$315

9.3   Closing Entries Concepts

In the previous section, you saw how adjusting entries are calculated and recorded on the work sheet for use in preparing the financial statements. These adjustments achieved one of the most important purposes of the accounting process. However, accounting is cyclical in nature. Remember the time period concept. It states that financial reporting, on net income in particular, is done in equal periods of time. The accounts must now be made ready for the next cycle.

The final stage of the accounting cycle is to prepare the accounts for the next fiscal period. To do this, you must understand which accounts have balances that continue from one period to the next and which do not.

Real Accounts and Nominal Accounts

Other names for real and nominal accounts are **permanent** and **temporary** accounts. These alternative terms help you remember which accounts will continue to have balances (permanent) and which will be closed out (temporary).

All asset and liability accounts, as well as the owner's capital account, are considered to be *real* accounts. **Real accounts** have balances that continue into the next fiscal period. Examples of real accounts are Bank, Trucks, and Accounts Payable.

On the other hand, Revenue, Expense, and Drawings accounts are known as *nominal* accounts. **Nominal accounts** have balances that do not continue into the next fiscal period. Nominal accounts, with the exception of the Drawings account, are related to the income statement, and the income statement deals only with a single fiscal period. All nominal accounts begin each fiscal period with a nil balance.

A special nominal account, called the *Income Summary account*, is used only during the closing entry process. The **Income Summary account** summarizes the revenues and expenses of the period. The temporary balance in this account represents either the amount of net income or the amount of net loss.

Closing Out the Nominal Accounts

Closing the accounts is sometimes called **clearing the accounts**.

Once the income statement for a period has been completed, the balances in the nominal accounts are no longer useful. These "old" balances in the nominal accounts must be removed to make the accounts "fresh" for the next accounting period. There must be no balance left in any nominal account to start off a new fiscal period. This process is known as *closing the accounts*. **Closing an account** means to cause it to have no balance. The nominal accounts are closed out at the end of every fiscal period, as explained in detail in the next section.

As you know, during any fiscal period, the total equity of a business is not contained in a single account. It is contained in a number of accounts in the equity section of the ledger. The Capital account shows the equity balance at the beginning of the period. Any changes in equity during the period are contained in Revenue, Expense, and Drawings accounts, which are the nominal accounts. Closing the *nominal* equity accounts involves moving the values collected in those accounts into the one *real* equity account, the Capital account. This is how the Capital account is updated to show the final equity figure at the end of each fiscal period.

End-of-Period Procedure

There are a number of things to be done at the end of each fiscal period:

Step 1 Bring the accounts up to date by journalizing and posting the adjusting entries. You will recall that some accounts were allowed to become inexact during the fiscal period. These were updated on the work sheet and on the financial statements, and later were journalized and posted to the ledger accounts.

Step 2 Close the nominal accounts to prepare them for the next fiscal period. This involves journalizing and posting the closing entries. This is done in two phases:

1. Transfer the balances of the revenue and expense accounts to the new Income Summary account.
2. Transfer the balances of the Income Summary and Drawings accounts to the Capital account.

When this is done all of the nominal accounts will have zero balances. But the Capital account, which continues to the next fiscal period, will have an updated balance. You will be shown how to do this in the next section.

Step 3 Take off a post-closing trial balance. There is a lot of potential for making errors in the process of journalizing and posting the adjusting and closing entries. A trial balance is taken off to ensure that the ledger is still in balance. A post-closing trial balance is taken as soon as the closing entries have been posted.

Complete Accounting Cycle

The post-closing trial balance is the final step in the accounting cycle. Figure 9.11 below shows the steps in the accounting cycle in its final form.

FIGURE 9.11

The complete accounting cycle for a manual accounting system.

In a computer accounting system, posting, trial balance preparation, and interim financial statement preparation occur virtually at the same time. Closing is also different, as you will see in Section 9.6.

Formal financial statements use adjusted balances. Interim financial statements are quickly produced by accounting software and normally use unadjusted balances.

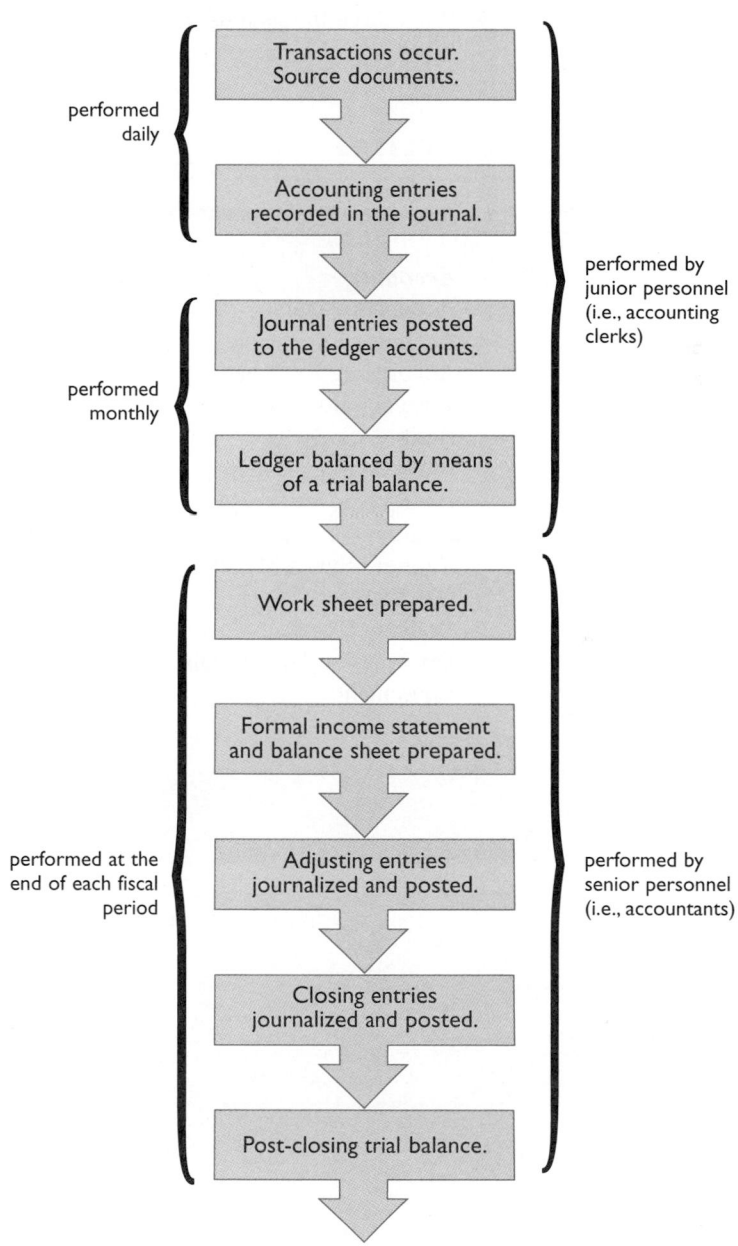

Section 9.3   Review Questions

1. Explain the time period concept.
2. What does the final stage of the accounting cycle involve?
3. What is a real account?
4. What is a nominal account?
5. What are nominal accounts also called?
6. Which accounts in the ledger are the nominal accounts?
7. Why are "old" balances cleared out of the nominal accounts?
8. Explain what is meant by "closing an account."
9. What three things must be done at the end of the accounting period?
10. What steps have been added to the accounting cycle in this chapter?

Section 9.3   Exercises

1. A list of accounts appears below. **Indicate which of these are nominal accounts.**

Accounts

Accounts Payable	Insurance Expense
Accounts Receivable	Land
Advertising Expense	Legal Expense
Automobiles	Mortgage Payable
Bank	Postage Expense
Bank Charges Expense	Rent Expense
Bank Loan	Revenue from Commissions
Building	Salaries Expense
Capital—Sylvia Magill	Sales
Car Expense	Supplies
Delivery Expense	Supplies Expense
Drawings—Sylvia Magill	Telephone Expense
Equipment	Wages Expense

2. A simplified ledger appears below and in your Workbook.

Bank		Bank Loan		S. Mosar, Capital		S. Mosar, Drawings	
100			300		740	750	

Accounts Receivable		Accounts Payable		Advertising Revenue		Sales Revenue	
200			150		1750		450

Supplies				Bank Charges		Miscellaneous Exp.	
50				20		5	

Equipment				Printing Expense		Rent Expense	
1050				500		250	

				Telephone Expense		Utilities Expense	
				25		40	

				Wages Expense	
				400	

A. Calculate the total assets, total liabilities, and owner's equity. Prove the accuracy of your figures.

B. By stroking out and/or changing balances in your Workbook, show what the account balances would be after the closing entries were completed.

3. Workbook Exercise: Complete a chart showing the steps in the accounting cycle for a business using a manual accounting system.

4. **Complete each of the following statements by writing in your Workbook the appropriate word or phrase from the list below.**

A. Accounting is _____ in nature.

B. The _____ states that financial reporting is done in equal periods of time.

C. Asset and liability accounts are considered to be _____ accounts.

D. _____ have their balances continue on into the succeeding fiscal period.

E. Revenue, expense, and drawings accounts are considered to be _____ accounts.

F. The balances in _____ do not continue into the _____ fiscal period.

G. Another name for a nominal account is a _____.

H. Nominal accounts begin each fiscal period with _____.

I. The process of removing the "old" balances from the nominal accounts is known as _____.

J. _____ means to cause it to have no balance.

K. During a fiscal period, the Capital account shows _____.

L. Changes in equity during a fiscal period (except for additional investments by the owner) are contained in _____ accounts.

M. At the end of the fiscal period, the ledger is brought up to date by _____.

N. One of the final steps in the accounting cycle is to bring the Capital account _____ and to _____ the nominal accounts.

O. The final step in the accounting cycle is _____.

List of Words or Phrases

a nil balance	nominal accounts
close out	real
closing an account	real accounts
closing the accounts	revenue, expense, and drawings
cyclical	temporary equity account
next	the balance at the beginning of the period
journalizing and posting the adjusting entries	the post-closing trial balance
nominal	time period concept
	up to date

9.4 | Journalizing and Posting the Closing Entries

You have just studied the objectives of the closing entries. Now you will learn how to achieve those objectives.

The source of the data for the closing entries is the work sheet. All of the necessary figures for the closing entries exist in one place on the work sheet. To explain the closing entry process, let us continue with the work sheet and the ledger for Global Logistics, which you worked with in Section 9.2.

There is no single way that closing entries must be recorded. This text uses a four-step approach to the closing entries. Shown below, in Figure 9.12, is the work sheet for Global Logistics. The figures for the four closing steps are clearly identified.

FIGURE 9.12

Completed work sheet for Global Logistics.

Global Logistics	Work Sheet						Year Ended Dec. 31, 20-4	
ACCOUNTS	TRIAL BALANCE		ADJUSTMENTS		INCOME STATEMENT		BALANCE SHEET	
	DR	CR	DR	CR	DR	CR	DR	CR
Bank	520 51						520 51	
Accounts Receivable	18475 –						18475 –	
Supplies	1 480 90			① 95490			526 –	
Prepaid Insurance	6564 –			② 2494 –			4070 –	
Furniture & Equipment	4196 –						4196 –	
Automotive Equipment	54600 –						54600 –	
Accounts Payable		2510 –		③ 626 –				3136 –
GST Payable		1240 –						1240 –
GST Recoverable	720 –						720 –	
Bank Loan		25000 –						25000 –
P. Marshall, Capital		28895 42						28895 42
P. Marshall, Drawings	42000 –						42000 –	
Shipping Revenue		213821 –				213821 –		
Bank Charges Expense	3500 –				3500 –			
Miscellaneous Expense	1951 65		③ 85 –		2036 65			
Rent Expense	24000 –				24000 –			
Telephone Expense	1800 –		③ 45 –		1845 –			
Truck Expense	41951 16		③ 496 –		42447 16			
Utilities Expense	3750 –				3750 –			
Wages Expense	65957 20				65957 20			
	271466 42	271466 42						
Supplies Expense			① 95490		95490			
Insurance Expense			② 2494 –		2494 –			
			407490	407490	146984 91	213821 –	125107 51	58271 42
Net Income					66836 09			66836 09
					213821 –	213821 –	125107 51	125107 51

Closing Entry 4: the figure for the fourth closing entry

Closing Entry 2: the figures for the second closing entry

Closing Entry 1: the figures for the first closing entry

Closing Entry 3: the figure for the third closing entry

Closing Entry No. 1

The first closing entry transfers the balances in the revenue account(s) to a new nominal account called Income Summary. The figures for this closing entry are found in the Income Statement section credit column of the work sheet, as outlined in Figure 9.12 on page 327. Use all of the highlighted figures, down to and including the subtotals, to formulate your entry.

Because revenue accounts have credit balances, debit entries are needed to close them out. Knowing this will help you work out the first closing entry for Global Logistics, which appears below in Figure 9.13.

FIGURE 9.13

The first closing entry for Global Logistics.

		Closing Entries			
Dec.	31	Shipping Revenue	213 8 2 1 —		
		Income Summary			213 8 2 1 —

Closing Entry No. 2

The second closing entry transfers the balances in the expense accounts to the Income Summary account. The figures for this closing entry are found in the Income Statement section debit column of the work sheet as outlined in Figure 9.12 on page 327. Use all of the highlighted figures down to and including the subtotals, and no others.

Because expense accounts have debit balances, credit entries are needed to close them out. Understanding this will help you work out the second closing entry for Global Logistics, which appears below in Figure 9.14.

FIGURE 9.14

The second closing entry for Global Logistics.

	31	Income Summary	146 9 8 4 91	
		Bank Charges Expense		3 5 00 —
		Miscellaneous Expense		2 0 3 6 65
		Rent Expense		24 0 0 0 —
		Telephone Expense		1 8 45 —
		Truck Expense		42 4 4 7 16
		Utilities Expense		3 7 50 —
		Wages Expense		65 9 5 7 20
		Supplies Expense		9 5 4 90
		Insurance Expense		2 4 94 —

The ledger of Global Logistics after posting the first and second closing entries is shown below in Figure 9.15.

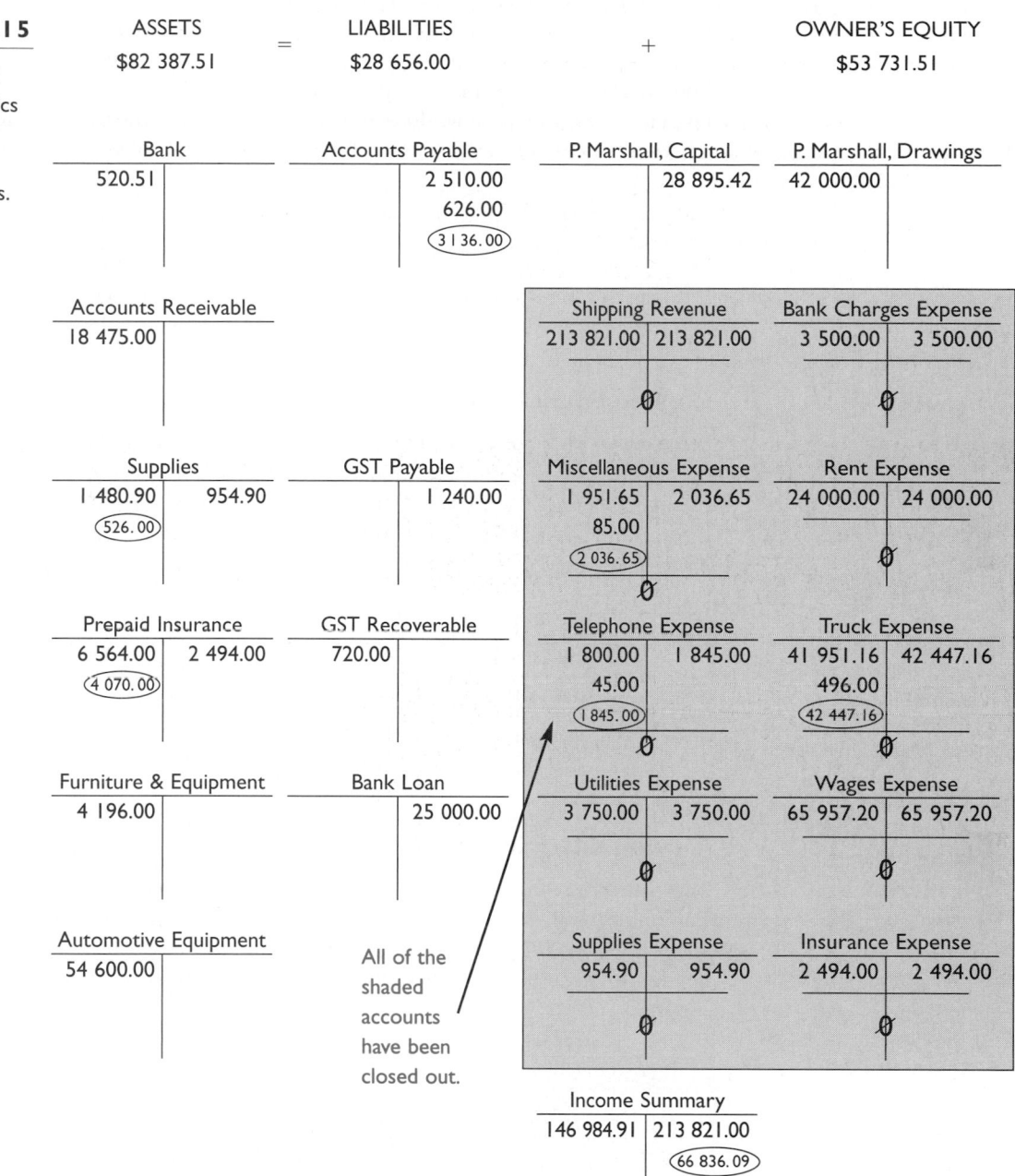

FIGURE 9.15

The ledger of Global Logistics after posting the first two closing entries.

ASSETS	=	LIABILITIES	+	OWNER'S EQUITY
$82 387.51		$28 656.00		$53 731.51

Bank
520.51

Accounts Payable
2 510.00
626.00
(3 136.00)

P. Marshall, Capital
28 895.42

P. Marshall, Drawings
42 000.00

Accounts Receivable
18 475.00

Shipping Revenue
213 821.00 | 213 821.00
Ø

Bank Charges Expense
3 500.00 | 3 500.00
Ø

Supplies
1 480.90 | 954.90
(526.00)

GST Payable
1 240.00

Miscellaneous Expense
1 951.65 | 2 036.65
85.00
(2 036.65)
Ø

Rent Expense
24 000.00 | 24 000.00
Ø

Prepaid Insurance
6 564.00 | 2 494.00
(4 070.00)

GST Recoverable
720.00

Telephone Expense
1 800.00 | 1 845.00
45.00
(1 845.00)
Ø

Truck Expense
41 951.16 | 42 447.16
496.00
(42 447.16)
Ø

Furniture & Equipment
4 196.00

Bank Loan
25 000.00

Utilities Expense
3 750.00 | 3 750.00
Ø

Wages Expense
65 957.20 | 65 957.20
Ø

Automotive Equipment
54 600.00

All of the shaded accounts have been closed out.

Supplies Expense
954.90 | 954.90
Ø

Insurance Expense
2 494.00 | 2 494.00
Ø

Income Summary
146 984.91 | 213 821.00
(66 836.09)

The equity section of the ledger is considerably changed at this point. All of the revenue and expense accounts now have nil balances. They have been closed out. Only three accounts in the equity section have a balance. Observe that the accounting equation still balances with the total of the equity section remaining at $53 731.51. Ignoring the accounts with nil balances, the equity section appears as follows:

P. Marshall, Capital	P. Marshall, Drawings	Income Summary	
28 895.42	42 000.00	146 984.91	213 821.00
			(66 836.09)

The balance in the Income Summary account represents either the amount of net income or the amount of net loss. It will be closed out to the owner's Capital account.

The Income Summary account for Global Logistics now contains the following:

- the total revenues of $213 821.00 on the credit side;
- the total expenses of $146 984.91 on the debit side;
- the account balance of $66 836.09 credit, which is the net income figure.

If a loss had been suffered, the debit side of the account would have been greater than the credit side, and the account would have a debit balance.

Closing Entry No. 3

The third closing entry transfers the balance in the Income Summary account to the owner's Capital account. The amount is easily picked up from the work sheet. If the Income Summary account has a credit balance, it will take a debit entry to close it. If the account has a debit balance, it will take a credit entry to close it. The third closing entry for Global Logistics appears below in Figure 9.16.

FIGURE 9.16

The third closing entry for Global Logistics.

	31	Income Summary		66 8 3 6 09	
		P. Marshall, Capital			66 8 3 6 09

Some students use the acronym REID to remember the four closing entries:
Revenue
Expense
Income
Drawings

Closing Entry No. 4

The fourth closing entry transfers the balance of the Drawings account to the Capital account. Again, the figure for this entry is easily picked up from the work sheet. Because the Drawings account always has a debit balance, a credit entry is needed to close it. The fourth closing entry for Global Logistics appears below in Figure 9.17.

FIGURE 9.17

The fourth closing entry for Global Logistics.

	31	P. Marshall, Capital		42 0 0 0 –	
		P. Marshall, Drawings			42 0 0 0 –

FIGURE **9.18**

The ledger of Global Logistics after all four closing entries have been posted.

The ledger for Global Logistics, with all four closing entries posted, appears in Figure 9.18 below. The objectives of the closing entries have been achieved. The Capital account shows the true balance, and the nominal accounts are cleared and ready for the next fiscal period.

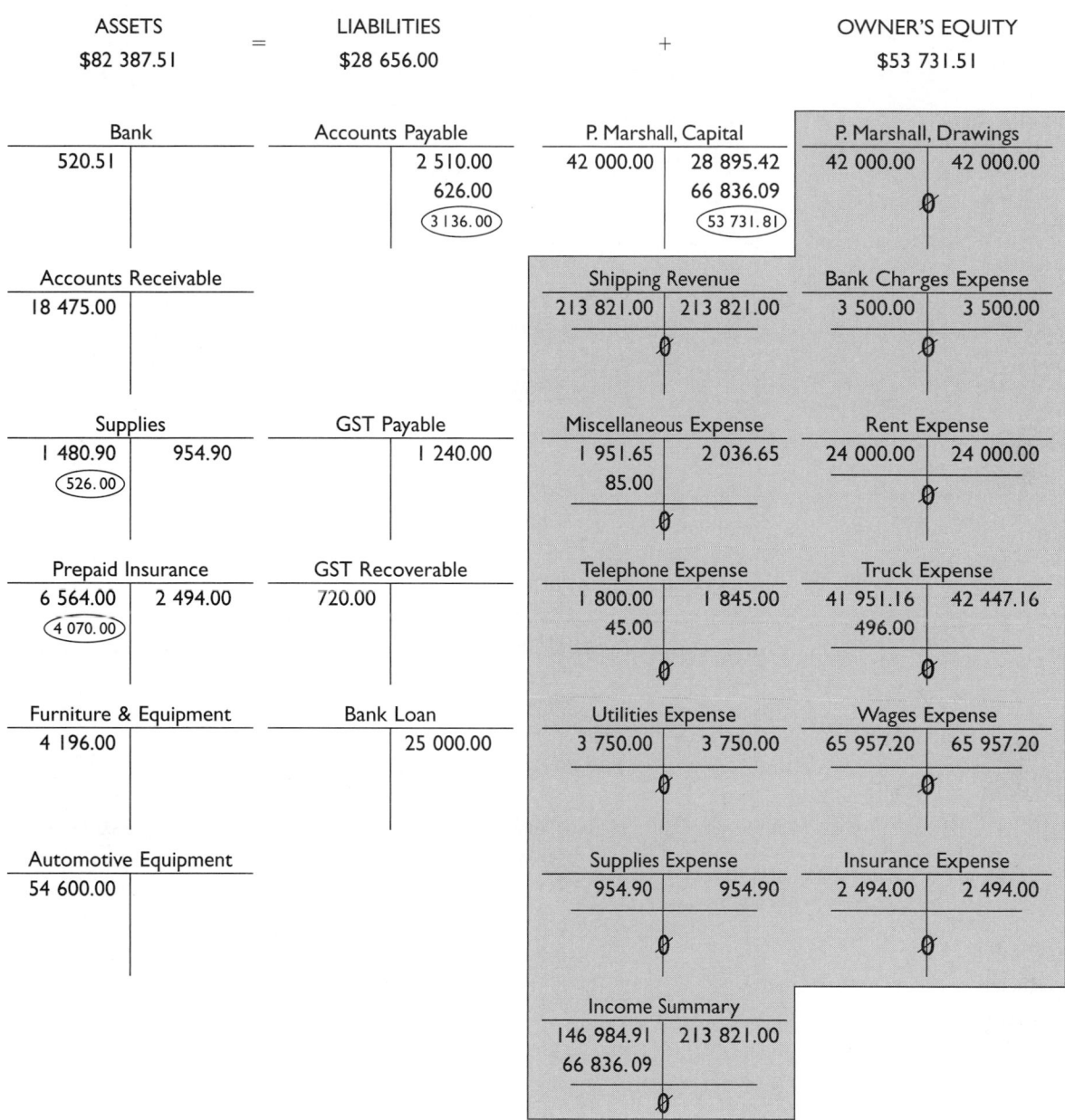

ASSETS	=	LIABILITIES	+	OWNER'S EQUITY
$82 387.51		$28 656.00		$53 731.51

Bank
520.51

Accounts Payable
2 510.00
626.00
(3 136.00)

P. Marshall, Capital
42 000.00 | 28 895.42
| 66 836.09
| (53 731.81)

P. Marshall, Drawings
42 000.00 | 42 000.00
| Ø

Accounts Receivable
18 475.00

Shipping Revenue
213 821.00 | 213 821.00
| Ø

Bank Charges Expense
3 500.00 | 3 500.00
| Ø

Supplies
1 480.90 | 954.90
(526.00)

GST Payable
| 1 240.00

Miscellaneous Expense
1 951.65 | 2 036.65
85.00 |
| Ø

Rent Expense
24 000.00 | 24 000.00
| Ø

Prepaid Insurance
6 564.00 | 2 494.00
(4 070.00)

GST Recoverable
720.00

Telephone Expense
1 800.00 | 1 845.00
45.00 |
| Ø

Truck Expense
41 951.16 | 42 447.16
496.00 |
| Ø

Furniture & Equipment
4 196.00

Bank Loan
| 25 000.00

Utilities Expense
3 750.00 | 3 750.00
| Ø

Wages Expense
65 957.20 | 65 957.20
| Ø

Automotive Equipment
54 600.00

Supplies Expense
954.90 | 954.90
| Ø

Insurance Expense
2 494.00 | 2 494.00
| Ø

Income Summary
146 984.91 | 213 821.00
66 836.09 |
| Ø

All of the shaded accounts have been closed out.

FIGURE 9.19

FIGURE 9.19

The general journal with all of the adjusting and closing journal entries journalized.

DATE		PARTICULARS	P.R.	DEBIT	CREDIT
		GENERAL JOURNAL			PAGE ___
		Adjusting Entries			
20-4					
Dec.	31	Supplies Expense		9 5 4 90	
		Supplies			9 5 4 90
	31	Insurance Expense		2 4 9 4 —	
		Prepaid Insurance			2 4 9 4 —
	31	Miscellaneous Expense		8 5 —	
		Telephone Expense		4 5 —	
		Truck Expense		4 9 6 —	
		Accounts Payable			6 2 6 —
		Closing Entries			
	31	Shipping Revenue		2 1 3 8 2 1 —	
		Income Summary			2 1 3 8 2 1 —
	31	Income Summary		1 4 6 9 8 4 91	
		Bank Charges Expense			3 5 0 0 —
		Miscellaneous Expense			2 0 3 6 65
		Rent Expense			2 4 0 0 0 —
		Telephone Expense			1 8 4 5 —
		Truck Expense			4 2 4 4 7 16
		Utilities Expense			3 7 5 0 —
		Wages Expense			6 5 9 5 7 20
		Supplies Expense			9 5 4 90
		Insurance Expense			2 4 9 4 —
	31	Income Summary		6 6 8 3 6 09	
		P. Marshall, Capital			6 6 8 3 6 09
	31	P. Marshall, Capital		4 2 0 0 0 —	
		P. Marshall, Drawings			4 2 0 0 0 —

Closing Entries—Summary

The four closing entries do the following:

1. close out the revenue account(s) to the Income Summary account;
2. close out the expense accounts to the Income Summary account;
3. close out the Income Summary account to the Capital account;
4. close out the Drawings account to the Capital account.

Post-Closing Trial Balance

The accuracy of the ledger must be checked after you have finished journalizing and posting the adjusting and closing entries. This is done by taking off the post-closing trial balance.

The post-closing trial balance for Global Logistics is shown below in Figure 9.20.

FIGURE 9.20

The post-closing trial balance for the ledger of Global Logistics.

GLOBAL LOGISTICS POST-CLOSING TRIAL BALANCE DECEMBER 31, 20-4		
	DR	CR
Bank	$ 520.51	
Accounts Receivable	18 475.00	
Supplies	526.00	
Prepaid Insurance	4 070.00	
Furniture & Equipment	4 196.00	
Automotive Equipment	54 600.00	
Accounts Payable		$ 3 136.00
GST Payable		1 240.00
GST Recoverable	720.00	
Bank Loan		25 000.00
P. Marshall, Capital		53 731.81
	$83 107.51	$83 107.51

Uses of the Work Sheet

In sections 9.2 and 9.4 you have expanded your use of the work sheet and you should realize now that a work sheet is beneficial in the following ways:

1. A work sheet provides a method of organizing the figures for the financial statements. It contains all of the up-to-date figures for the statements in one convenient place.
2. A work sheet lets the accountant see the effect of adjusting entries before they are recorded in the accounts. Accountants sometimes have a choice in how to handle an adjustment.
3. A work sheet proves the arithmetic accuracy of the figures before they are used in the financial statements.
4. A work sheet is the source for all of the information for recording the adjusting and the closing entries.

Section 9.4   Review Questions

1. What is the normal source of the information for the closing entries?
2. Explain exactly how to obtain the information for the first closing entry.
3. Explain exactly how to obtain the information for the second closing entry.
4. In what new account are the revenues and expenses summarized?
5. What does the balance in the Income Summary account represent (before it is closed out)?
6. What is the purpose of a post-closing trial balance?
7. Why is a post-closing trial balance more brief than a regular trial balance?
8. Give the four uses of a work sheet.

Section 9.4   Exercises

1. Shown below is the completed work sheet for Dr. E. Santala of Cornwall, Ontario. **In your Workbook, journalize the adjusting and closing entries for Dr. Santala.**

Dr. E. Santala, Dentist	Work Sheet						Year Ended Dec. 31, 20-4	
ACCOUNTS	TRIAL BALANCE		ADJUSTMENTS		INCOME STATEMENT		BALANCE SHEET	
	DR	CR	DR	CR	DR	CR	DR	CR
Bank	13 060 10						13 060 10	
Accounts Receivable	37 490 –						37 490 –	
Supplies	10 350 –			①7 250 –			3 100 –	
Prepaid Insurance	5 906 –			②4 050 –			1 856 –	
Equipment	64 434 17						64 434 17	
Investment – Bonds	100 000 –						100 000 –	
Accounts Payable		3 315 –						3 315 –
GST Payable		1 050 –						1 050 –
GST Recoverable	690 –						690 –	
E. Santala, Capital		204 315 77						204 315 77
E. Santala, Drawings	80 000 –						80 000 –	
Fees Earned		180 374 –				180 374 –		
Interest Earned		7 500 –		③2 500 –		10 000 –		
Bank Charges Expense	170 –				170 –			
Miscellaneous Expense	1 436 50				1 436 50			
Rent Expense	30 000 –				30 000 –			
Telephone Expense	2 759 –				2 759 –			
Utilities Expense	2 957 –				2 957 –			
Wages & Salaries Expense	47 302 –				47 302 –			
	396 554 77	396 554 77						
Supplies Expense			①7 250 –		7 250 –			
Insurance Expense			②4 050 –		4 050 –			
Bond Interest Receivable			③2 500 –				2 500 –	
			13 800 –	13 800 –	95 924 50	190 374 –	303 130 27	208 680 77
Net Income					94 449 50			94 449 50
					190 374 –	190 374 –	303 130 27	303 130 27

2. Shown below is the completed work sheet for R. Tompko, who operates a barber shop in Milton, Ontario.

In your Workbook:

A. Explain why there are two adjustments to the supplies account.

B. Journalize the adjusting and closing entries in the general journal provided.

C. Post the adjusting and closing entries in the general ledger provided.

D. Take off a post-closing trial balance.

Golden Tresses Hair Stylists	Work Sheet						Year Ended Dec. 31, 20-	
ACCOUNTS	TRIAL BALANCE		ADJUSTMENTS		INCOME STATEMENT		BALANCE SHEET	
	DR	CR	DR	CR	DR	CR	DR	CR
Bank	790 –						790 –	
Supplies	2755 –		①800 –	②1055 –			2500 –	
Prepaid Insurance	2450 –			③1625 –			825 –	
Equipment	17005 –						17005 –	
Accounts Payable		1075 –		①800 –				1875 –
GST Payable		580 –						580 –
GST Recoverable	365 –						365 –	
R. Tompko, Capital		9342 –						9342 –
R. Tompko, Drawings	42000 –						42000 –	
Revenue		98370 –				98370 –		
Advertising Expense	1200 –				1200 –			
Bank Charges Expense	96 –				96 –			
Supplies Used Expense	6950 –		②1055 –		8005 –			
Miscellaneous Expense	1902 –				1902 –			
Rent Expense	6000 –				6000 –			
Utilities Expense	2104 –				2104 –			
Wages Expense	25750 –				25750 –			
	109367 –	109367 –						
Insurance Expense			③1625 –		1625 –			
			3480 –	3480 –	46682 –	98370 –	63485 –	11797 –
Net Income					51688 –			51688 –
					98370 –	98370 –	63485 –	63485 –

3. Indicate whether each of the following statements is true or false by placing a "T" or an "F" in the space indicated in your Workbook. Explain the reason for each "F" response in the space provided.

a. Journalizing and posting the adjusting and closing entries is a routine task that can be done by any knowledgeable accounting clerk.

b. All of the data required to journalize the adjusting and closing entries can be found on the work sheet.

c. It can be assumed that all adjustments have been thought of once the work sheet is completed.

d. The adjusting entries must be journalized and posted to bring the ledger into agreement with the figures on the financial statements.

e. An explanation is needed for each individual adjusting entry being journalized.

f. The adjusting and closing entries in the journal are dated as of the end of the fiscal period.

g. The closing entries can be processed only by using the four-step method.

h. The figures for the first closing entry are taken from the income statement section, debit column, of the work sheet.

i. Because revenue accounts have debit balances, credit entries are needed to close them out.

j. The second closing entry transfers the balances in the expense accounts to the Income Summary account.

k. When the adjusting entries and the first two closing entries are journalized and posted, all but three of the accounts in the equity section of the ledger will have nil balances.

l. A loss has occurred if the Income Summary account has a credit balance before it is closed out.

m. The first two entries in the Income Summary account are the same as the subtotals of the income statement section of the work sheet.

n. The Income Summary account is not closed out if a loss occurs.

9.5 | Adjusting for Depreciation

Earlier in this chapter, you learned about three simple adjustments and how they affect the statements and the books of account. Each adjustment for supplies, insurance, and late invoices changes the totals on both the balances sheet and income statement. You will see that the adjustment for fixed assets, referred to as depreciation, has a similiar effect.

The Nature of Depreciation

Assets that are bought for business use to produce revenue over several fiscal periods, are known as "fixed assets." Assets of this type are also known as "long-lived assets," "capital equipment," and "plant and equipment."

With the exception of land, every fixed asset is expected to be used up in the course of time and activity. Thus, the asset decreases or depreciates in value. **Depreciation** refers to an allowance made for the decrease in value of an asset over time.

The following example shows how depreciation works: Assume that a person purchases a new van at a cost of $24 000 in order to begin a delivery business. After operating for five years, the business is closed down. As part of closing down the business, the owner sells the van (now used) for $1 500. Over the five-year period, the van cost the business $24 000 − $1 500 which is $22 500. Clearly, the van was needed to carry on the business; the "van expense" helps produce revenue in the five different fiscal periods.

The $22 500 cost of the van cannot be ignored. It is part of the true profit picture of the business. Theoretically, the $22 500 must be considered an expense of the business at the rate of $4 500 ($22 500/5 yrs.) for each of the five years. The profit picture of the company over its five-year life might then look like this:

	20-1	20-2	20-3	20-4	20-5
Revenues	$57 560	$65 250	$68 354	$65 270	$59 230
Expenses					
Depreciation — Van	$ 4 500	$ 4 500	$ 4 500	$ 4 500	$ 4 500
Other Expenses	36 750	38 256	39 954	42 570	45 320
Total Expenses	$41 250	$42 756	$44 454	$47 070	$49 820
Net Income	$16 310	$22 494	$23 900	$18 200	$ 9 410

The schedule shows that the $22 500 net cost of the van has been spread evenly over its five-year life. This is generally how depreciation works. Each year that the company benefited from the van's use has been charged with $4 500, an equal portion of its cost. Depreciation can be thought of as allocating a part of the cost of an asset as an expense for each accounting period during which the business uses that asset. Depreciation meets the requirement of the Matching Principle and helps accountants report net income fairly.

Calculating Depreciation

It is not possible to calculate depreciation exactly until the end of the asset's life. Only then can you say how many years it was used and determine its final worth. But accountants and business people cannot wait until then. The depreciation must be included on every year-end income statement. So depreciation must be estimated while the asset is still in use.

Methods of Depreciation

The two most common methods of calculating depreciation are the straight-line method and the declining-balance method.

Straight-Line Depreciation

The simplest way of estimating depreciation is the straight-line method. The **straight-line method of depreciation** divides up the net cost of the asset equally over the years of the asset's life. For this method, the following formula is used:

$$\text{Straight-line depreciation for one year} = \frac{\text{Original cost of asset} - \text{Estimated salvage value}}{\text{Estimated number of periods in the life of the asset}}$$

The following two examples show how the calculation works.

1. Tip Top Trucking purchased a truck for $78 000 on January 1, 20-2. It estimated that the truck would be used for six years, and at the end of that time, could be sold for $7 800. (The $7 800 is the salvage value and is an estimated amount.)
    Applying the formula to these data gives the following calculation:

$$\text{Estimated annual depreciation} = \frac{\$78\ 000 - \$7\ 800}{6} = \$11\ 700$$

This gives an estimated annual depreciation figure of $11 700 for the truck. The figure is the same each year.

2. Tip Top Trucking purchased $5 120 of furniture on January 1, 20-2. The company estimated that the furniture would be used for 10 years, at which time it would have a value of $500.

Applying the formula to these data gives the following calculation:

$$\text{Estimated annual depreciation} \quad = \quad \frac{\$5\ 120 \quad - \quad \$500}{10} \quad = \quad \$462$$

This gives an estimated annual depreciation figure of $462 for the furniture. The figure is the same each year.

Adjusting for Depreciation

Some beginning accounting students have no difficulty handling the adjusting entries for supplies and insurance, but do have difficulties with the adjusting entries for depreciation. Perhaps this is so because there is an extra concept involved with the adjustment for depreciation. Before this additional concept is introduced, you will treat depreciation just like any other adjustment you have dealt with in this chapter. To learn how to make the adjustment for depreciation, follow the example below. Tip Top Trucking purchased the truck set up in the Truck account on January 1, 20-2.

In simplified T-account form, the balances are:

Truck		Depreciation Expense — Truck	
20-2		20-2	
Dec. 31 78 000		Dec. 31 0̸	

Previously, on page 337, the calculation of depreciation for this truck came to $11 700 each year. This is the amount of value that is "used" in one year. It can also be regarded as the expense of using the truck for one year.

The basic adjusting entry for depreciation of the truck is one that does two things. It reduces the value of the truck by the amount of $11 700, and it sets up the Depreciation Expense account for the same amount. For Tip Top Trucking, these two objectives are accomplished by the adjusting entry shown below:

	DR	CR
Depreciation Expense — Truck	11 700	
Truck		11 700

The effect that this adjusting entry has on the accounts is shown below:

Truck		Depreciation Expense — Truck	
20-2		20-2	
Dec. 31 78 000		Dec. 31 0̸	
	11 700		11 700
66 300		11 700	

The two accounts shown above now give a more accurate picture. The balance in the Truck account is reduced to show that one year of its useful life has expired. And, the Depreciation Expense account now shows a balance of $ 11 700, a one-year portion of the cost of the truck. This was all done to meet the requirements of the Matching Principle.

The adjusting entry for depreciation is not journalized at this time, but it is recorded first on the work sheet just like the other adjustments.

Accumulated Depreciation Account

Although the accounting practice above is sound, it would only be used by a small business. For larger businesses or businesses using computerized accounting systems, a variation of the above system is used. This is done because, in many cases, people who use the balance sheet require additional information. In this example, if you were to look at the balance sheet for the data shown for Tip Top Trucking, you would see the item Truck at $66 300. But the information doesn't tell you how old the truck is, if the business will have to purchase a new truck soon, or if costly breakdowns are bound to happen in the near future due to the age of the truck.

The following balance sheet presentation provides more useful information.

Fixed Assets		
Truck	$78 000	
Less: Accumulated Depreciation	11 700	$66 300

This presentation is clearer because the fixed asset section contains more information. For example, you can tell that the truck is fairly new because its net remaining value is close to its original value. The truck is probably still covered by the manufacturer's warranty.

To provide the data for the balance sheet presentation above, the adjusting entry for depreciation expense debits the account Depreciation Expense as before, but the credit is made to a new account called Accumulated Depreciation. The required adjusting entry is as follows:

	DR	CR
Depreciation Expense — Truck	11 700	
Accumulated Depreciation — Truck		11 700

After the first year's depreciation is entered, the three accounts are as shown in simplified T-account form below. The balances are:

Truck		Accumulated Depreciation — Truck		Depreciation Expense — Truck	
20-2			20-2	20-2	
Dec. 31 78 000			Dec. 31 11 700	Dec. 31 11 700	

These two accounts together show the net
book value of the truck – $66 300.

An accumulated depreciation account is know as a valuation or contra account. A **contra account** is one that is displayed alongside an associated account and has a balance that is opposite to the account it is associated with. The normal balance for Truck is a debit; the normal balance for Accumulated Depreciation—Truck is a credit.

Accumulated depreciation is also known as a **valuation account**. A valuation account is one that is used, together with an asset account, to show the true net value of the asset. Observe how Truck and Accumulated Depreciation—Truck show the original cost of the asset, the total depreciation that has been charged as an expense, and, taken together, the net book value of the asset.

The first contra account you learned was GST Recoverable, which is a contra account for GST Payable.

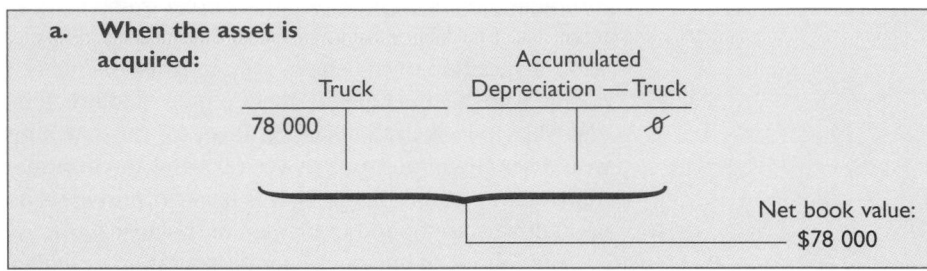

Net book value is the cost of an asset less accumulated depreciation. It is also known as the undepreciated capital cost.

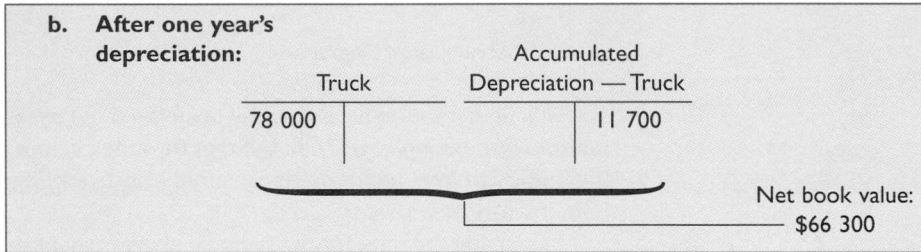

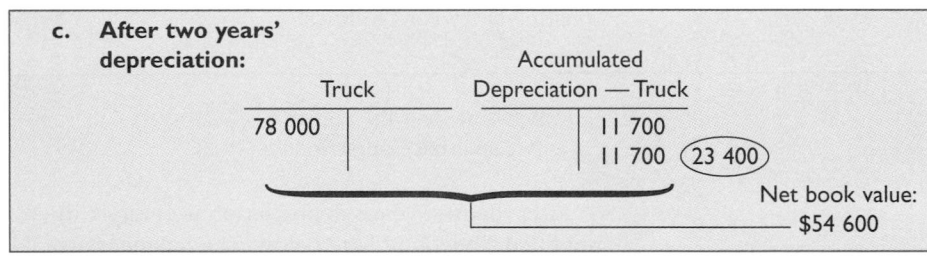

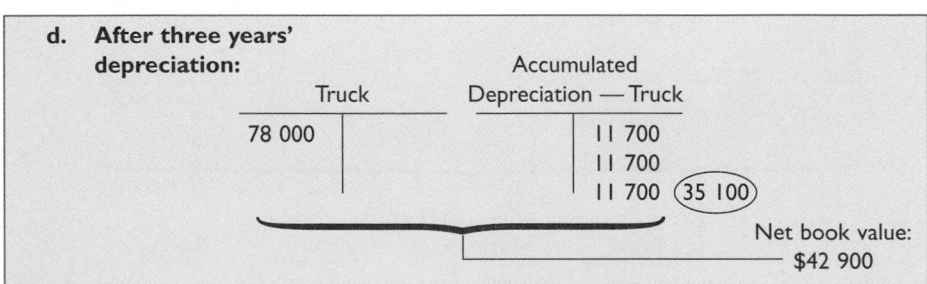

The Adjusting Entry for Depreciation

To summarize, the adjusting entry for depreciation:

1. records the depreciation for the period in a depreciation expense account;
2. increases the appropriate accumulated depreciation account for the asset. This reduces the net book value of the asset.

The basic adjusting entry for depreciation is:

	DR	CR
Depreciation Expense	$$$$	
Accumulated Depreciation (Asset)		$$$$

FIGURE 9.21

The partially completed work sheet for Tip Top Trucking, with the adjusting entries and extensions for prepaid expenses and late-arriving invoices already entered.

As you will recall, adjusting entries are first recorded on the work sheet. To demonstrate how to handle the adjusting entries for this chapter, the work sheet of Tip Top Trucking is used. This work sheet is shown in Figure 9.21 below. The adjusting entries for prepaid expenses and late-arriving invoices have already been entered.

Two adjusting entries for depreciation are required for Tip Top Trucking because there are two fixed assets on the trial balance. The depreciation figures for these two items were calculated previously on pages 337 and 338. They are, for Truck, $11 700; and for Furniture, $462.

Tip Top Trucking	Work Sheet						Year Ended Dec. 31, 20-4	
ACCOUNTS	**TRIAL BALANCE**		**ADJUSTMENTS**		**INCOME STATEMENT**		**BALANCE SHEET**	
	DR	CR	DR	CR	DR	CR	DR	CR
Bank	1 575 07							
Accounts Receivable	25 590 40							
Supplies	1 725 50			① 1 200 50			525 —	
Prepaid Insurance	3 895 —			② 2 647 —			1 248 —	
Furniture	5 120 —							
Acc. Dep. – Furniture		924 —						
Truck	78 000 —							
Acc. Dep. – Truck		23 400 —						
Accounts Payable		4 731 15		③ 643 50				5 374 65
GST Payable		1 340 —						
GST Recoverable	851 —							
Loan Payable		25 000 —						
R. Hansen, Capital		39 916 64						
R. Hansen, Drawings	48 000 —							
Trucking Revenue		226 742 90						
Automotive Expense	52 631 12		③ 516 —		53 147 12			
Interest Expense	2 500 —							
Miscellaneous Expense	1 974 —		③ 127 50		2 101 50			
Rent Expense	24 000 —							
Telephone Expense	2 165 —							
Utilities Expense	3 820 —							
Wages Expense	70 207 60							
	322 054 69	322 054 69						
Supplies Expense			① 1 200 50		1 200 50			
Insurance Expense			② 2 647 —		2 647 —			

Note the two new accumulated depreciation accounts on the work sheet above. You can tell from their balances that two years' depreciation has already been charged. The adjusting entries to record the depreciation for Tip Top Trucking are:

	DR	CR
1. Depreciation Expense—Truck	$11 700	
Accumulated Depreciation—Truck		$11 700
2. Depreciation Expense—Furniture	$ 462	
Accumulated Depreciation—Furniture		$462

You can see these entries recorded (coded 4) on the work sheet for Tip Top Trucking in Figure 9.22 below.

FIGURE 9.22

Work sheet for Tip Top Trucking with adjusting entries for depreciation added. After entering the adjustments for depreciation, the rest of the work sheet is completed in the usual way.

Tip Top Trucking	Work Sheet						Year Ended Dec. 31, 20-4	
ACCOUNTS	TRIAL BALANCE		ADJUSTMENTS		INCOME STATEMENT		BALANCE SHEET	
	DR	CR	DR	CR	DR	CR	DR	CR
Bank	1575 07						1575 07	
Accounts Receivable	2559 040						2559 040	
Supplies	1725 50			① 1200 50			525 –	
Prepaid Insurance	3895 –			② 2647 –			1248 –	
Furniture	5120 –						5120 –	
Acc. Dep. – Furniture		924 –		④ 462 –				1386 –
Truck	78000 –			④			78000 –	
Acc. Dep. – Truck		23400 –		11700 –				35100 –
Accounts Payable		4731 15		③ 643 50				5374 65
GST Payable		1340 –						1340 –
GST Recoverable	851 –						851 –	
Loan Payable		25000 –						25000 –
R. Hansen, Capital		39916 64						39916 64
R. Hansen, Drawings	48000 –						48000 –	
Trucking Revenue		22674 290				22674 290		
Automotive Expense	52631 12		③ 516 –		53147 12			
Interest Expense	2500 –				2500 –			
Miscellaneous Expense	1974 –		③ 127 50		2101 50			
Rent Expense	24000 –				24000 –			
Telephone Expense	2165 –				2165 –			
Utilities Expense	3820 –				3820 –			
Wages Expense	70207 60				70207 60			
	322054 69	322054 69						
Supplies Expense			① 1200 50		1200 50			
Insurance Expense			② 2647 –		2647 –			
Depreciation Expense – Truck			④ 11700 –		11700 –			
Depreciation Expense – Furniture			④ 462 –		462 –			
			16653 –	16653 –	173950 72	22674 290	160909 47	108117 29
Net Income					52792 18			52792 18
					22674 290	22674 290	160909 47	160909 47

Depreciation on the Financial Statements

The financial statements for Tip Top Trucking appear below and on page 344 in Figures 9.23 and 9.24. On these statements, you will see:

1. depreciation expense on the income statement;
2. accumulated depreciation deducted from its respective fixed asset account on the balance sheet.

The data for these statements came from the work sheet shown in Figure 9.22 on page 342.

Depreciation accounts have nil balances throughout the year. Therefore, they would not show up on the regular trial balance and must be added near the bottom of the accounts column.

FIGURE 9.23

The income statement for Tip Top Trucking, showing the depreciation expenses.

TIP TOP TRUCKING		
INCOME STATEMENT		
YEAR ENDED DECEMBER 31, 20-4		
Revenue		
Trucking Revenue		$226 742.90
Operating Expenses		
Automotive Expense	$53 147.12	
Interest Expense	2 500.00	
Miscellaneous Expense	2 101.50	
Rent Expense	24 000.00	
Telephone Expense	2 165.00	
Utilities Expense	3 820.00	
Wages Expense	70 207.60	
Supplies Expense	1 200.50	
Insurance Expense	2 647.00	
Depreciation Expense — Furniture	462.00	
Depreciation Expense — Truck	11 700.00	
Total Expenses		173 950.72
Net Income		$ 52 792.18

TIP TOP TRUCKING
BALANCE SHEET
DECEMBER 31, 20-4

ASSETS

Current Assets			
Bank		$ 1 575.07	
Accounts Receivable		25 590.40	
Supplies		525.00	
Prepaid Insurance		1 248.00	$28 938.47
Fixed Assets			
Furniture and Equipment	$ 5 120.00		
Less Accumulated Depreciation	1 386.00	$ 3 734.00	
Truck	$78 000.00		
Less Accumulated Depreciation	35 100.00	42 900.00	46 634.00
Total Assets			$75 572.47

LIABILITIES AND OWNER'S EQUITY

Current Liabilities			
Accounts Payable		$ 5 374.65	
GST Payable	$ 1 340.00		
Less GST Recoverable	851.00	489.00	$ 5 863.65
Long-Term Liability			
Loan Payable			25 000.00
R. Hansen, Capital			
Balance, January 1		$39 916.64	
Net Income	$52 792.18		
Drawings	48 000.00		
Increase in Capital		4 792.18	
Balance, December 31			44 708.82
Total Liabilities and Owner's Equity			$75 572.47

Other Methods for Calculating Depreciation

You have learned the straight-line method of calculating depreciation, which effectively meets the requirements of the Matching Principle. That is, the straight-line method spreads out the cost of fixed assets so that net income is reported fairly each year. As you work with depreciation, you may encounter a variety of situations that will affect your calculations. Some of these are outlined below.

Depreciation for Part Year

The previous calculations were for a full year. Sometimes an asset is used for only part of a year, making further calculation necessary. This can happen if the asset is purchased or disposed of during the year. It may also happen if the fiscal period being reported on is shorter than one year.

Consider the following example. The Edwards Company purchases a building on May 1, 20-3 for $120 000. The building is expected to be used for 30 years, after which it will be worth $30 000. The Edwards Company prepares quarterly financial statements (that is, it issues statements every three months).

The annual depreciation for the above building is ($120 000 − $30 000)/30, which is $3 000. The monthly depreciation is $3 000/12, or $250. However, in the first statement period after the purchase of the asset, it had been in use for only two months. Therefore, depreciation for only two months can be charged to this period. This amount is $500.

Declining-Balance Depreciation

There is more than one way of calculating depreciation. The declining-balance method is common because the government of Canada requires a variation of it on statements that are submitted for income tax purposes. A company that does not use the declining-balance method must modify the financial statement that it sends to the government.

The declining-balance method of depreciation calculates the annual depreciation by multiplying the remaining undepreciated cost of the asset by a fixed percentage. In the first year, the undepreciated cost is equal to the purchase price (capital cost). Some of the percentage figures set by the government are shown in the table below.

Canada Customs and Revenue Agency refers to Depreciation as Capital Cost Allowance.

Canada Customs and Revenue Agency Rates of Capital Cost Allowance (Depreciation)		
Class	Description	Rate
3	Buildings of brick, stone, or cement	5%
6	Buildings of frame, log, or stucco	10%
8	Office furniture and equipment	20%
10	Automobiles, trucks, tractors, computer equipment	30%
12	Computer software (except systems software)	100%

To see how declining-balance depreciation is calculated, assume that computers are purchased on January 1, 20-1 for $22 000. This is the initial capital cost figure. The table above shows the rate to be used is 30 per cent.

Year 1

For the 20-1 fiscal year, the depreciation = $22 000 × 30% = $6 600

Summary:	Original cost before depreciation	$22 000
	Less depreciation for 20-1	6 600
	Undepreciated cost (net book value) at end of 20-1	$15 400

Year 2

For the 20-2 fiscal year, the depreciation = $15 400 × 30% = $4 620

Summary:	Undepreciated cost after first year 15 400	$15 400
	Less depreciation for 20-2	4 620
	Undepreciated cost (net book value) at end of 20-2	$10 780

Year 3

For the 20-3 fiscal year, the depreciation = $10 780 × 30% = $3 234

Summary:	Undepreciated cost after second year	$10 780
	Less depreciation for 20-3	3 234
	Undepreciated cost (net book value) at end of 20-3	$ 7 546

The annual calculations continue in this way until the computers are scrapped.

Comparison of the Two Methods of Depreciation

The two schedules below show how the depreciation for the above asset would be calculated under the straight-line and the declining-balance methods. Assume that the computers were expected to last for eight years and have an ending value of $2 000.

Straight-line method		
Year	Depreciation Expense	Undepreciated Cost
Original cost		$22 000
1	$2 500	19 500
2	2 500	17 000
3	2 500	14 500
4	2 500	12 000
5	2 500	9 500
6	2 500	7 000
7	2 500	4 500
8	2 500	2 000

Declining-balance method		
Year	Depreciation Expense	Undepreciated Cost
Original cost		$22 000
1	$6 600	15 400
2	4 620	10 780
3	3 234	7 546
4	2 264	5 282
5	1 585	3 697
6	1 109	2 588
7	776	1 812
8	544	1 268

The straight-line method produces depreciation figures that are the same each year. Over the estimated life of the asset, its book value is gradually reduced until it reaches the estimated final value. Only one calculation is necessary.

The declining-balance method produces depreciation figures that are larger in the early years and smaller in the later years. The estimated final value is ignored when using this method, making a new calculation necessary every year.

Taxation Regulations

Accountants specialize in understanding rules and regulations regarding taxation. Taxation is a challenging area of study because accounting procedures are often detailed, complex, and subject to change. For example, you know that Canada Customs and Revenue Agency (CCRA) requires businesses to use the declining-balance method when calculating depreciation, but the agency adds more rules than you have learned so far.

One such depreciation rule relates to when an asset is purchased part of the way through the year. The length of time an asset is owned in its first year is ignored by the CCRA. Instead, CCRA generally allows 50% of the asset's cost to be eligible for depreciation in its first year of use, regardless of the month it was purchased. CCRA refers to this as the "50% rule."

If the 50% rule were applied to the $22 000 purchase of computers described on page 345, the depreciation in Year One would change from $6 600 to $3 300 ([$22 000 × 50%] × 30%). You might initially think this is unfair to the business, but remember that it does not matter when the computers were purchased. If they were purchased with just a few weeks left in the fiscal year, CRA would still allow a depreciation claim of $3 300. In fact, the 50% rule simplifies work for the company's accountants because they do not have to factor in the length of time each new asset was owned. The calculations below show that the impact of the 50% rule is minimized over time.

Declining-balance method		
Year	Depreciation	Undepreciated Cost
Original cost		$22 000
1	$6 600	15 400
2	4 620	10 780
3	3 234	7 546
4	2 264	5 282
5	1 585	3 698
6	1 109	2 588
7	776	1 812
8	544	1 268

Declining-balance method with the 50% rule		
Year	Depreciation	Undepreciated Cost
Original cost		$22 000
1	$3 300	18 700
2	5 610	13 090
3	3 927	9 163
4	2 749	6 414
5	1 924	4 490
6	1 347	3 143
7	943	2 200
8	660	1 540

In this case, the depreciation expense under the 50% rule is smaller in the first year but larger in all subsequent years. Graphically, the three variations you have learned for calculating depreciation are summarized in the depreciation graph below.

At this stage you do not have to learn the details of taxation accounting. (In fact, unless otherwise stated, the 50% rule will be ignored for the exercises in this text.) But you should be able to understand some conclusions drawn from this illustration.

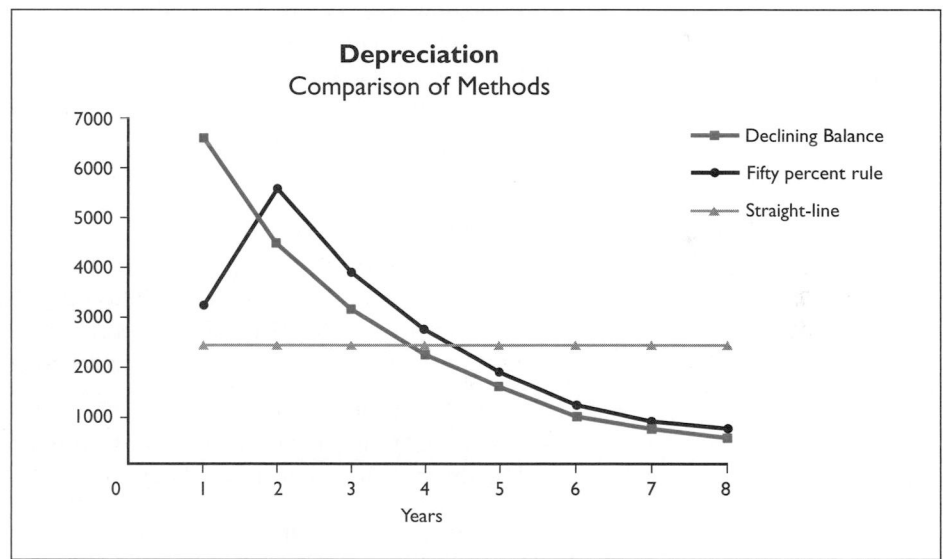

1. The first-year effect that the 50% rule has on the declining-balance method of depreciation will be made up over time.
2. When compared to straight-line depreciation, declining balance methods produce higher amounts of depreciation expense in the early years of the life of the asset.
3. The straight-line method produces a consistent debit to Depreciation Expense, and this amount is higher than the amounts produced by declining balance methods in the later years in the life of the asset.

Perhaps these conclusions have caused you to ask some questions. For example, is the business pleased with the declining-balance method, or would it prefer the straight-line calculations for its tax calculations? How does the declining-balance method benefit the interests of government? Can a business use the 50% rule to its advantage? Wondering about these questions indicates a high-level of curiosity, and curiosity is essential to your becoming a successful student of accounting.

Section 9.5   Review Questions

1. Define "depreciation."
2. Why is it not possible to make a precise calculation of depreciation until the end of the asset's useful life?
3. What is the simplest depreciation method?
4. Give the formula for calculating straight-line depreciation.
5. How is depreciation for partial years handled when straight-line depreciation is used?
6. Give the basic adjusting entry for depreciation.
7. How is a depreciable asset represented in the ledger accounts?
8. What is a contra account?
9. What depreciation method is required by Canada Customs and Revenue Agency for income tax purposes?
10. Describe how to calculate declining-balance depreciation.
11. Why is taxation a challenging area of study?
12. Under Canada Customs and Revenue Agency rules, how much of an asset's cost can be used for calculating its first-year depreciation?
13. How can the 50% rule simplify an accountant's work?

Section 9.5   Exercises

1. **In your Workbook, for each of the following situations, allocate the total cost to the proper fiscal periods. Assume that the company commenced business on January 1, 20-1 and has a fiscal year-end of December 31.**

   A. A truck was purchased on January 1, 20-1 for $18 000. It was expected to last for five full years, at the end of which it would have a trade-in value of $3 000. Use the straight-line method of depreciation.

20-1	20-2	20-3	20-4	20-5

   B. A used vehicle was bought on November 1, 20-1 for $5 800. It was expected to last for four full years, at the end of which it would have a resale value of $1 000. Use the straight-line method of depreciation.

20-1	20-2	20-3	20-4	20-5

C. A building was purchased on May 1, 20-2 for the sum of $113 000. It was expected to last for 25 years, at which time it would have a resale value of $5 000. Use the straight-line method of depreciation.

20-1	20-2	20-3	20-4	20-5

D. A new machine was bought on January 1, 20-1 for $54 000. It is depreciated using the declining-balance method at the rate of 20 per cent.

20-1	20-2	20-3	20-4	20-5

E. A new building was bought on July 1, 20-1 for $282 000. It is depreciated using the declining-balance method at the rate of 5 per cent.

20-1	20-2	20-3	20-4	20-5

2. A company purchases computer equipment costing $100 000, which it expects to last for seven years and to have a salvage value of $5 500.

A. **For the use of management, prepare a depreciation schedule for the first five years of the asset's life showing depreciation calculated on a straight-line basis.**

B. **Prepare a depreciation schedule for the first five years of the asset's life showing depreciation calculated on a declining-balance basis at the rate of 30 per cent.**

C. **Using the amounts from Year 3 of your schedules, prepare the adjusting entry required by the straight-line method of depreciation. Repeat for the declining-balance method. Which adjusting entry saves the company the most money? Why?**

3. On pages 336–337, a van costing $22 500 is depreciated for five years, and the net income is calculated for the years 20-1 through 20-5. For this exercise assume the entire cost of the van was counted as an expense in the year 20-1.

A. **Under the above assumption, calculate the net incomes for each of the five years. Write your answers in the spaces provided in your Workbook.**

B. **To compare the two different sets of net income, complete a bar chart in the space provided in your Workbook.**

C. **Which year misrepresents net income most dramatically? Are the net incomes for the other years overstated or understated? In which year would the least amount of tax be paid?**

4. **This exercise appears in your Workbook.**
   The simplified general ledger of Shahid Company of Abbotsford, British Columbia, at the end of its annual fiscal period appears below.

   A. **Using the additional information that is provided, record the year-end adjusting entries directly in the T-accounts.**

   B. **Prepare an adjusted trial balance.**

Bank		Accounts Receivable		Supplies	
400		8 285		1 900	

Prepaid Insurance		Land		Buildings	
1 800		50 000		70 000	

Accum. Depr. Buildings		Equipment		Accum. Depr. Equipment	
	6 750	96 500			24 000

Accounts Payable		J. Salk, Capital		J. Salk, Drawings	
	3 200		144 985	30 000	

Revenue		Bank Charges Expense		Delivery Expense	
	140 700	450		1 500	

Miscellaneous Expense		Telephone Expense		Utilities Expense	
490		390		1 300	

Wages Expense		Supplies Expense		Insurance Expense	
56 620					

Depreciation Exp.—Buildings		Depreciation Exp.—Equipment	

Additional Information

1. Inventory of supplies at the year-end is $850.
2. Unexpired insurance at the year-end is $625.
3. Depreciation is calculated on a straight-line basis. The building is expected to last 40 years, after which it will be worth $25 000. The equipment is expected to last 15 years, after which it will be worth $6 500. Ignore the 50% rule.

5. The simplified trial balance for Viera Associates at December 31, 20—, after a fiscal period of one year, is given below, along with some additional information. **Complete the work sheet for Viera Associates.**

VIEIRA ASSOCIATES TRIAL BALANCE DECEMBER 31, 20—		
	DR	CR
Bank	$ 5 080.20	
Accounts Receivable	17 491.00	
Supplies	2 635.00	
Prepaid Insurance	1 800.00	
Equipment	10 200.00	
Accumulated Depreciation—Equipment		$ 6 022.08
Automobiles	32 500.00	
Accumulated Depreciation—Automobiles		16 575.00
Accounts Payable		4 802.50
GST Payable		940.20
GST Recoverable	516.80	
C. Vieira, Capital		21 821.04
C. Vieira, Drawings	48 000.00	
Consulting Fees		154 326.00
Automobile Expense	32 756.04	
General Expense	1 575.00	
Rent Expense	10 000.00	
Telephone Expense	1 567.00	
Wages Expense	40 365.78	
	$204 486.82	$204 486.82

Additional Information

1. Supplies on hand at December 31 amounted to $1 035.00.
2. Prepaid insurance at December 31 amounted to $820.00.
3. Depreciation is calculated using the declining-balance method at Canada Customs and Revenue Agency's prescribed rates. Ignore the 50% rule.

6. A new company purchased $60 000 of office furniture on its first day of business.

   A. Prepare the adjusting entries required for the first two years under a true declining-balance method of depreciation.

   B. Prepare the adjusting entries required for the first two years if Canada Customs and Revenue Agency's 50% rule is used.

7. Workbook Exercise: Calculating depreciation with the 50% rule in effect.

9.6 | Adjusting and Closing Accounts with Simply Accounting

An eight-column work sheet uses just one page to show the entire year-end picture of a business's account balances and financial statements. Accountants have long appreciated this "synoptic" perspective. In fact, some accounting software programs continue to provide a work sheet option so accountants can perform year-end procedures that are similar to those in a manual system. Simply Accounting does not provide a work sheet option. Instead, an accountant determines the necessary adjustments—perhaps with T-accounts and a pencil—and enters the adjustments as journal entries. For the closing entries, most of the work is done by the software.

Adjusting and closing functions proceed so quickly with Simply Accounting, there is no need for you to practise using them at this time. (You will have the opportunity to adjust and close accounts when you complete the Summary Exercises. Nevertheless, even without a hands-on computer session, you will increase your understanding of adjusting and closing concepts by carefully examining the illustrations and text explanations that follow.

The work sheet, income statement, and balance sheet for Tip Top Trucking were shown in Figures 9.22, 9.23, and 9.24 on pages 342–344. If Simply Accounting were the accounting system used by Tip Top Trucking, the first step to take at year-end would be to calculate and journalize the adjusting entries. Using the same data from the work sheet on page 342, the adjusting entries would look like those shown in Figure 9.25.

FIGURE 9.25

The adjusting entries for Tip Top Trucking using Simply Accounting.

General Journal Display

File   Options   Help

12/31/04 to 12/31/04

			Debits	Credits
12/31/04	J1	worksheet, To adjust the supplies account		
		5080 Supplies Expense	1,200.50	-
		1100 Supplies	-	1,200.50
12/31/04	J2	worksheet, To adjust for insurance used		
		5090 Insurance Expense	2,647.00	-
		1150 Prepaid Insurance	-	2,647.00
12/31/04	J3	worksheet, To adjust for late invoices		
		5005 Automotive Expense	516.00	-
		5030 Miscellaneous Expense	127.50	-
		2010 Accounts Payable	-	643.50
12/31/04	J4	worksheet, To adjust for depreciation		
		5100 Depreciation Expense--Furniture	462.00	-
		5110 Depreciation Expense--Truck	11,700.00	-
		1555 Acc. Depreciation--Furniture	-	462.00
		1650 Acc. Depreciation--Truck	-	11,700.00
			16,653.00	16,653.00

When the adjusting entries are posted, the year-end income statement in Simply Accounting would appear as in Figure 9.26. Compare it to the one shown in Figure 9.23 on page 343.

on page 343.

FIGURE 9.26

The year-end income statement for Tip Top Trucking.

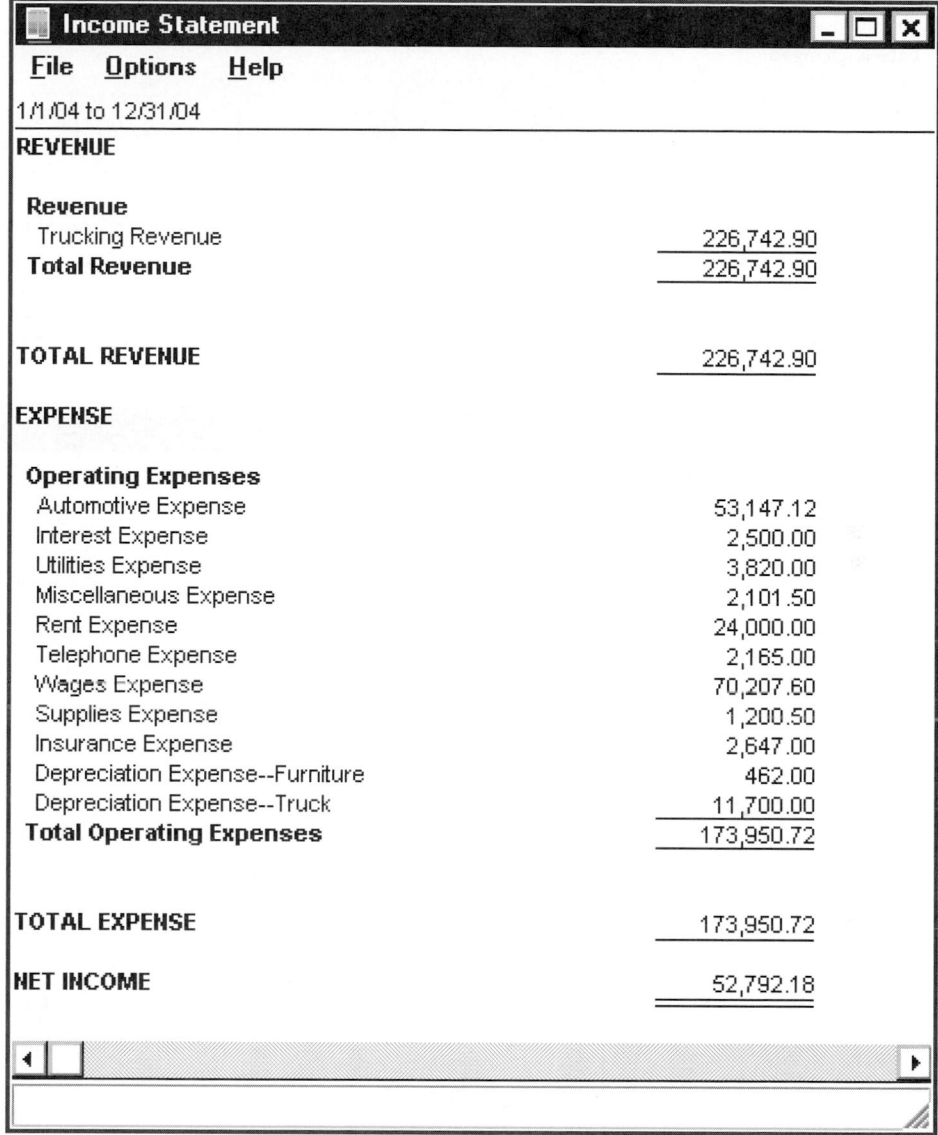

Income Statement		
File Options Help		
1/1/04 to 12/31/04		
REVENUE		
Revenue		
Trucking Revenue		226,742.90
Total Revenue		226,742.90
TOTAL REVENUE		226,742.90
EXPENSE		
Operating Expenses		
Automotive Expense		53,147.12
Interest Expense		2,500.00
Utilities Expense		3,820.00
Miscellaneous Expense		2,101.50
Rent Expense		24,000.00
Telephone Expense		2,165.00
Wages Expense		70,207.60
Supplies Expense		1,200.50
Insurance Expense		2,647.00
Depreciation Expense--Furniture		462.00
Depreciation Expense--Truck		11,700.00
Total Operating Expenses		173,950.72
TOTAL EXPENSE		173,950.72
NET INCOME		52,792.18

After year-end statements and reports are printed and the computer files are backed up, the accountant is ready to close the accounts. First, the owner's capital account needs to be designated as the one that will receive the net income or net loss amount at the end of the year. (This is accomplished by a simple menu selection.) Then, the accountant changes the Session date to the first day of the new fiscal year (January 1, 2005). A warning similar to the one shown in figure 9.27 is given.

FIGURE 9.27

Simply Accounting's warning screen that Revenue and Expense accounts will be closed if the date is changed.

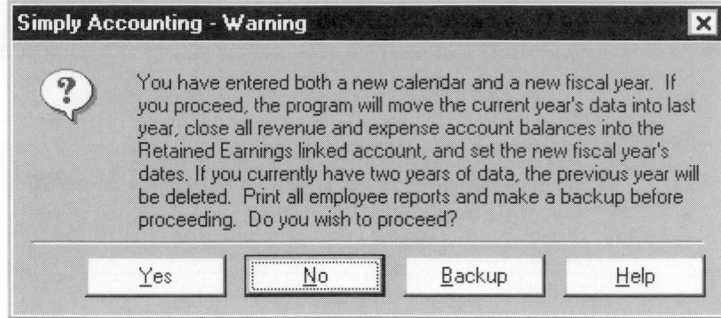

Notice that the above warning advises that revenue and expense account balances will be closed to the Retained Earnings account (capital). When the accountant clicks the Yes button, all but one step of the closing process will be accomplished. If the accountant were to display the trial balance immediately after clicking the Yes button, it would look like Figure 9.28.

FIGURE 9.28

The trial balance January 1, 20-5 showing all revenue and expense accounts reset to zero.

Trial Balance

File   Options   Help

As At 1/1/05		Debits	Credits
1010	Bank	1,575.07	-
1050	Accounts Receivable	25,590.40	-
1100	Supplies	525.00	-
1150	Prepaid Insurance	1,248.00	-
1550	Furniture	5,120.00	-
1555	Acc. Depreciation--Furniture	-	1,386.00
1600	Truck	78,000.00	-
1650	Acc. Depreciation--Truck	-	35,100.00
2010	Accounts Payable	-	5,374.65
2020	GST Payable	-	1,340.00
2025	GST Recoverable	851.00	-
2550	Loan Payable	-	25,000.00
3010	R. Hansen, Capital	-	92,708.82
3050	R. Hansen, Drawings	48,000.00	-
4010	Trucking Revenue	-	0.00
5005	Automotive Expense	0.00	-
5010	Interest Expense	0.00	-
5020	Utilities Expense	0.00	-
5030	Miscellaneous Expense	0.00	-
5040	Rent Expense	0.00	-
5050	Telephone Expense	0.00	-
5060	Wages Expense	0.00	-
5080	Supplies Expense	0.00	-
5090	Insurance Expense	0.00	-
5100	Depreciation Expense--Furniture	0.00	-
5110	Depreciation Expense--Truck	0.00	-
		160,909.47	160,909.47

Double-click to display All Transactions Report for current account.

When the date is changed to the first day of the new fiscal year, Simply Accounting performs the first three closing entries you read about on pages 329–330. That is, the software program closed the revenue and expense accounts, and then transferred the net income ($52 792.18) to the capital account. The program did the first three steps of closing without the aid of the Income Summary account and journal entries.

Drawings is the one item that the "automatic" closing process of Simply Accounting missed for the Tip Top Trucking example. The balance of $48 000 in R. Hansen, Drawings belongs to the previous year and must be closed. The senior accountant would therefore debit R. Hansen, Capital $48 000 and credit R. Hansen, Drawings $48 000. The four steps of closing would then be complete. A summary of the effect of closing on the equity section of the balance sheet is shown in Figure 9.29.

FIGURE 9.29

The equity section of Tip Top Trucking before and after closing.

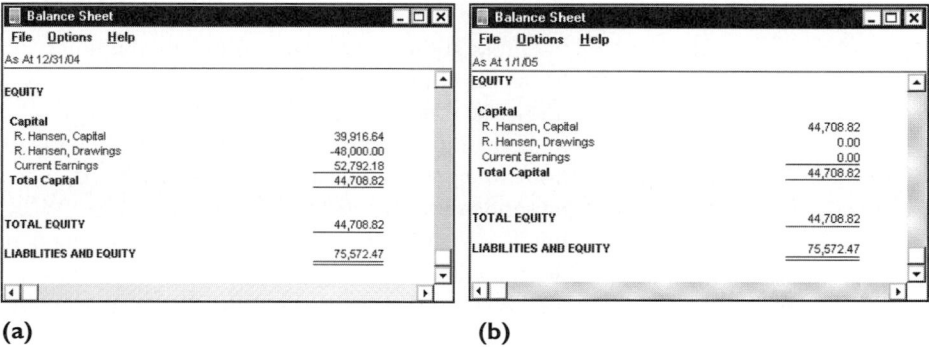

(a)   (b)

Notice that the balances of drawings and current earnings (net income) were transferred to the capital account.

Section 9.6   Review Questions

1. When using Simply Accounting, what is the first step an accountant would take at year-end?
2. List three other duties the accountant would perform after step one above but before advancing the Session date.
3. When the senior accountant does advance the Session date to the first day of a new fiscal year, what steps of the closing process does Simply Accounting perform?
4. For Tip Top Trucking, what additional closing step did the senior accountant have to take?

Section 9.6   Exercise

1. Figure 9.11 on page 323 is a chart showing the accounting cycle for a manual accounting system. In your workbook, re-draw this chart for a computer accounting system.

Challenge Exercise

2. Accountants often use spreadsheets to complete work sheets for their employer or clients. In your workbook, you will find an exercise for developing a spreadsheet model for an eight-column work sheet that can be used time and time again.

CHAPTER 9 Summary

CHAPTER HIGHLIGHTS

After you have completed Chapter 9, you should:

- understand why adjusting entries are necessary;
- be able to make the adjusting entries for supplies, prepaid insurance, late-arriving invoices, and depreciation;
- be able to use eight-column work sheets;
- know which accounts are nominal and which accounts are real;
- understand the purpose of nominal accounts and why they must be cleared;
- understand the purpose of the Income Summary account;
- know the complete accounting cycle;
- know the four benefits of the work sheet;
- be able to journalize and post the adjusting and closing entries;
- know the purpose of the post-closing trial balance;
- understand the purpose of contra accounts;
- know the difference between straight-line and declining-balance methods of depreciation;
- describe how accounting software deals with adjusting and closing concepts.

ACCOUNTING TERMS

adjusting entry
audit
closing an account
contra account
declining-balance method of depreciation
depreciation
Income Summary account

nominal account
post-closing trial balance
prepaid expense
real account
straight-line method of depreciation
valuation account

CHAPTER 9 Review Exercises

① The senior accountant for Koo Graphics discovered that the company's accounting clerk had a different method of recording the purchase of automobile insurance. Specifically, when one-year policies were purchased on July 1, the clerk debited Insurance Expense $7 200 and credited Bank $7 200.

A. Has the clerk done anything seriously wrong? Explain.

B. Use the T-accounts in your workbook to calculate the December 31 year-end adjustment for insurance. Journalize the adjusting entry.

2 During 20-1, its first year of operation, Magna Company purchased $2 852.12 of office supplies. At the end of 20-1, the office supplies on hand were valued at $1 325.60.

During 20-2, Magna Company purchased $2 956.75 of office supplies. At the end of 20-2, the office supplies on hand were valued at $1 500.50.

In the Supplies account and the Supplies Expense account provided in your Workbook, show in logical order the effect of:

A. the office supplies purchased;

B. the supplies expense adjusting entries;

C. the supplies expense closing entries.

Assume purchases of supplies are debited to the Supplies account.

---

3 **Use T-accounts and prepaid insurance listings to help you with this exercise.**

During its first year of operation, Aztec Computers purchased the following insurance policy:

	Company	Policy Date	Term	Premium
20-1	National	March 1	1 year	$240

A. Calculate the prepaid insurance at the end of 20-1.

B. Calculate the insurance expense for 20-1.

C. Give the adjusting entry for insurance used in 20-1.

During its second year of operation, Aztec Computers purchased the additional insurance policies shown below:

	Company	Policy Date	Term	Premium
20-2	National	Mar. 1	1 year	$ 600
	Regal	Sept. 1	1 year	1 440
	Standard	Nov. 1	1 year	120

D. What is the balance in the Prepaid Insurance account at the end of 20-2 before any adjusting entry?

E. Calculate the value of prepaid insurance at the end of 20-2.

F. What is the insurance expense for 20-2?

G. Give the adjusting entry for insurance used in 20-2.

H. Prove the insurance expense figure for 20-2 by calculating it in another way.

4 The work sheet for J. Soo and Associates is shown below, with the trial balance figures already entered.

A. Using the additional information given below, complete an eight-column work sheet in your Workbook.

Work Sheet			J. Soo and Associates					Year Ended Dec. 31, 20–5	
ACCOUNTS	TRIAL BALANCE		ADJUSTMENTS		INCOME STATEMENT		BALANCE SHEET		
	DR	CR	DR	CR	DR	CR	DR	CR
Bank	2 160 –							
Accounts Receivable	11 500 –							
Supplies	1 950 –							
Prepaid Insurance	624 –							
Equipment	9 200 –							
Automobile	18 350 –							
Accounts Payable		5 920 –						
GST Payable		310 –						
GST Recoverable	340 –							
J.Soo, Capital		36 662 –						
J.Soo, Drawings	7 500 –							
Commissions		35 650 –						
Car Expense	3 214 –							
Miscellaneous Expense	902 –							
Rent Expense	6 000 –							
Utilities Expense	1 563 –							
Wages Expense	15 239 –							
	78 542 –	78 542 –						

B. Journalize the adjusting entries in a two-column general journal.

C. Post the adjusting entries to the T-account ledger provided in the Workbook and take off an adjusted trial balance.

Optional

D. Prepare an income statement and a balance sheet.

Additional Information

- The value of the supplies on hand at the year-end was $640.
- The prepaid insurance at the year-end was calculated to be $260.
- Late-arriving invoices pertaining to the 20-3 fiscal period were for:

Car Expense	$ 50
Miscellaneous Expense	65
Total	$ 115

5 From the trial balance and the additional information shown below, complete the work sheet in the Workbook for Karen Millette owner of a real estate business in Gimli, Manitoba, for the year ended September 30, 20-4. Ignore GST and PST.

KAREN MILLETTE, REAL ESTATE
TRIAL BALANCE
SEPTEMBER 30, 20-4

Bank	$ 3 800	
Accounts Receivable	10 900	
Supplies	500	
Prepaid Insurance	1 000	
Land	50 000	
Building	70 000	
Accum. Dep. — Building		$ 6 825
Furniture and Equipment	15 000	
Accum. Dep. — Furniture and Equipment		5 400
Automotive Equipment	17 000	
Accum. Dep. — Automotive Equipment		8 670
Accounts Payable		400
Bank Loan		100 000
Karen Millette, Capital		35 005
Karen Millette, Drawings	30 000	
Commissions Revenue		96 600
Advertising Expense	4 700	
Bank Charges	8 100	
Car Expense	8 000	
Commissions Expense	18 000	
Miscellaneous Expense	200	
Postage Expense	600	
Telephone Expense	900	
Utilities Expense	2 200	
Wages Expense	12 000	
	$252 900	$252 900

Additional Information

- The supplies inventory at September 30 is $200.
- The prepaid insurance schedule shows a value of $300 for prepaid insurance.
- Depreciation is calculated using the declining-balance method at Canada's Custom and Revenue Agency's prescribed rates. Assume that the building is made of brick. Ignore the 50% rule.

6 Tom Michaud is in the plastering business under the name of Tom's Plastering. **From the following trial balance and the additional information shown below, prepare the work sheet and the financial statements in your Workbook for Tom's Plastering for the year ended October 31, 20-1.**

TOM'S PLASTERING
TRIAL BALANCE
OCTOBER 31, 20-1

	DR	CR
Bank	$ 1 412.01	
Accounts Receivable	7 545.00	
Supplies	1 416.70	
Small Tools	1 903.00	
Prepaid Insurance	2 107.80	
Equipment	9 500.00	
Accumulated Depreciation — Equipment		$ 3 200.00
Truck	19 500.00	
Accumulated Depreciation — Truck		8 000.00
Accounts Payable		2 407.35
GST Payable		702.00
GST Recoverable	480.00	
Bank Loan		10 000.00
Tom Michaud, Capital		17 510.28
Tom Michaud, Drawings	35 534.00	
Revenue		120 365.00
Bank Interest and Charges	1 325.15	
Materials Used	25 369.20	
Miscellaneous Expense	756.32	
Rent Expense	6 000.00	
Telephone Expense	864.32	
Truck Expense	8 325.40	
Utilities Expense	4 563.26	
Wages Expense	35 582.47	
	$162 184.63	$162 184.63

Additional Information

- Late bills pertaining to the 20-1 year were as follows:

Supplies	$ 56.20
Miscellaneous Expense	26.85
Truck Expense	563.85
Total	$646.90

- Office supplies on hand at October 31 are valued at $360.
- Unexpired insurance at October 31 is calculated at $510.95.
- Depreciation is calculated using the straight-line method. All assets were on hand for the entire year.

   The equipment cost $9 500 and was expected to last for 10 years. It was estimated that it would be worth $1 500 at the end of that time.

   The truck cost $19 500 and was expected to last for 5 years. It was estimated that it would be worth $3 500 at the end of that time.

- The small tools at October 31 are valued at $350. The tools represented by the difference between the $350 figure and the trial balance figure have been lost, stolen, or used up.
- Of the $25 369.20 shown on the trial balance under Materials Used, $2 850 is still on hand and unused.

Comprehensive Exercises

1. The general ledger trial balance of the Oakville Journal, after a fiscal period of one year, is given below. Additional information is also provided on page 362.

	DR	CR
OAKVILLE JOURNAL		
TRIAL BALANCE		
DECEMBER 31, 20-8		
Bank	$ 2 000.00	
Accounts Receivable	15 317.20	
Supplies and Materials	23 795.16	
Prepaid Insurance	4 200.00	
Land	75 000.00	
Buildings	105 000.00	
Accum. Dep. — Buildings		$ 7 500.00
Equipment	95 700.00	
Accum. Dep. — Equipment		22 710.00
Automotive Equipment	75 325.00	
Accum. Dep. — Automotive Equipment		30 000.00
Accounts Payable		9 216.42
GST Payable		1 280.00
GST Recoverable	750.00	
Bank Loan		100 000.00
Mortgage Payable		110 000.00
R. Lucht, Capital		61 148.91
R. Lucht, Drawings	50 000.00	
Revenue — Advertising		218 946.00
Revenue — Circulation		91 315.00
Bank Interest and Charges Expense	12 150.00	
Building Maintenance Expense	3 220.00	
Car Expense	4 960.50	
Miscellaneous Expense	5 940.13	
Mortgage Interest Expense	5 500.00	
Postage Expense	1 240.00	
Office Salaries Expense	34 319.15	
Sales Promotions Expense	2 750.00	
Telephone Expense	2 946.00	
Truck Expense	26 334.19	
Utilities Expense	11 350.00	
Wages Expense	94 319.00	
	$652 116.33	$652 116.33

With the additional information below, complete the following activities in your Workbook:

A. Complete the work sheet.

B. Prepare the income statement and the balance sheet for 20-8.

C. Journalize the adjusting and closing entries.

D. Post the adjusting and closing entries in the T-accounts provided. Ignore dates.

E. Take off a post-closing trial balance.

Additional Information

- Late bills arriving in January 20-9 that pertain to the 20-8 fiscal period are as follows:

Supplies and Materials	$ 509.60
Car Expense	200.00
Truck Expense	746.20
Miscellaneous Expense	35.00
Total	$1 490.80

- The value of materials and supplies at the year-end amounted to $8 013.56.
- The value of unexpired insurance at the year-end amounted to $1 325.00.
- Depreciation is calculated on a straight-line basis.

    Buildings: cost, $105 000.00; estimated terminal value, $5 000.00; estimated life, 40 years.

    Equipment: cost, $95 700.00; estimated terminal value, $20 000.00; estimated life, 10 years.

    Automotive Equipment: cost, $75 325.00; estimated terminal value, $5 325.00; estimated life, 7 years.

---

2. **Given the following limited information, prepare the closing entries for O. Como.**

O. COMO BALANCE SHEET NOVEMBER 30, 20—			
Assets			
Bank			$100
Accounts Receivable			300
Supplies			70
Total Assets			$470
Liabilities			
Accounts Payable			$150
Owner's Equity			
Balance November 1		$170	
Net Income	$650		
Drawings	500		
Increase in Equity		150	
Balance November 30			320
Total Liabilities and Owner's Equity			$470

O. COMO INCOME STATEMENT MONTH ENDED NOVEMBER 30,20—		
Revenue		$1 800
Expenses		
General Expense	$ 50	
Utilities	100	
Wages	1 000	
		$1 150
Net Income		$ 650

Questions for Further Thought

Briefly answer the following questions.

1. Explain why the time period concept pertains more to the income statement than to the balance sheet.

2. The Bank account is ongoing or continuous in nature. Explain.

3. Is the owner's Capital account a nominal account? Explain.

4. Suppose that the nominal accounts are not closed out at the end of a fiscal period. Explain how this affects account data for the next fiscal period.

5. Assume that the accounts are updated and closed out at the end of an accounting period. For how long will the account balances remain accurate?

6. Usually, the owner's Capital account is up to date only on the last day of the fiscal period. Why does this not create a problem for the users of the financial data?

7. What would be the best first step toward balancing a post-closing trial balance that did not balance?

8. During the first years of an asset's life, which method of depreciation is more beneficial to a business— straight-line or declining balance? Taking your answer into account, why do you think Canada Customs and Revenue Agency requires businesses to use the declining-balance method?

Case Studies

CASE 1

A Balancing Act

Piran, a student in accounting, comes to you, his teacher, with the following difficulty. After a great deal of time and effort, Piran has failed to balance the post-closing trial balance, and has become quite frustrated. "Everything was going fine," he says. "My balance sheet balanced. My income statement agreed. I just can't figure it out." Piran's balance sheet, income statement, and post-closing trial balance are given below and on page 365.

BALANCE SHEET

Assets

Bank	$ 1 301	
Accounts Receivable	7 406	
Supplies	385	
Land	21 900	
Buildings	75 382	
Equipment	19 462	
Total Assets		$125 836

Liabilities

Bank Loan	$12 000	
Accounts Payable	5 726	
Mortgage Payable	52 672	
Total Liabilities		$ 70 398

Owner's Equity

Beginning Balance		$71 314	
Net Loss	$ 876		
Drawings	$15 000		
Decrease in Equity		15 876	
Ending Balance			55 438
Total Liabilities and Owner's Equity			$125 836

INCOME STATEMENT

Revenue		$19 462
Expenses		
Advertising	$ 3 902	
Delivery	3 764	
Wages	12 000	
Utilities	672	$20 338
Net Loss		$ 876

POST-CLOSING TRIAL BALANCE

Bank	$ 1 301	
Account Receivable	7 406	
Supplies	385	
Land	21 900	
Buildings	75 382	
Equipment	19 462	
Bank Loan		$ 12 000
Accounts Payable		5 726
Mortgage Payable		52 672
Owner's Equity		57 190
	$125 836	$127 588

Questions

1. How can you tell quickly which figure(s) on the post-closing trial balance are probably the incorrect ones?
2. Which figure(s) are wrong in this trial balance?
3. Explain what error or errors Piran has made.

CASE 2

A Mix-Up in Year-End Accounting

Alicia Lee is a self-employed public accountant in Dartmouth, Nova Scotia. She performs a variety of accounting services for a number of clients within a 300 kilometre radius of her office. Currently, she happens to be working in a small town about 120 kilometres from home.

While there, Alicia receives a telephone call from her office regarding a problem with the work of another client in the town where she is working. Before returning home, Alicia pays a visit to this other client, Academy of Music, to provide assistance.

Academy of Music does its own accounting up to the trial balance stage. Alicia does the year-end accounting. She has recently provided Academy of Music with a set of financial statements and a list of adjusting and closing entries for the client to journalize and post. The client takes off the post-closing trial balance.

The accounting clerk for Academy of Music sensed that something was wrong with the list of adjusting and closing entries. He decided not to process them until he talked to Alicia. Alicia has to work with data available in the client's office because all of her working papers are at her office. To prepare to study the situation, she gathers the four documents shown on pages 366 through 368.

ACADEMY OF MUSIC
BALANCE SHEET
DECEMBER 31, 20-2

Assets

Current Assets		
Bank	$ 3 750	
Accounts Receivable	18 184	
Supplies	300	
Prepaid Insurance	630	$22 864
Plant and Equipment		
Equipment	$22 375	
Automobile	18 012	40 387
Total Assets		$63 251

Liabilities and Owner's Equity

Current Liability		
Accounts Payable		$5 085
F. Oke, Capital		
Balance January 1	$51 098	
Net Income	$34 068	
Drawings	27 000	
Increase in Capital	7 068	
Balance December 31		58 166
Total Liabilities and Owner's Equity		$63 251

ACADEMY OF MUSIC
INCOME STATEMENT
YEAR ENDED DECEMBER 31, 20–2

Revenue		
Fees Earned		$95 300
Operating Expenses		
Bank Charges Expense	$ 102	
Car Expense	16 222	
Miscellaneous Expense	370	
Rent Expense	6 000	
Telephone Expense	500	
Utilities Expense	3 825	
Wages Expense	28 375	
Supplies Expense	650	
Insurance Expense	1 420	
Depreciation — Equipment	2 000	
Depreciation — Automobile	1 768	
		61 232
Net Income		$34 068

ACADEMY OF MUSIC
ADJUSTING AND CLOSING ENTRIES
DECEMBER 31, 20–2
(provided by Alicia Lee)

	DR	CR
Adjusting Entries		
Supplies Used	810	
Supplies		810
Insurance Used	1 080	
Prepaid Insurance		1 080
Car Expense	210	
Miscellaneous Expense	160	
Accounts Payable		370
Closing Entries		
Fees Earned	81 316	
Income Summary		81 316
Income Summary	51 672	
Bank Charges Expense		1 120
Car Expense		13 280
Miscellaneous Expense		215
Rent Expense		5 400
Telephone Expense		400
Utilities Expense		3 307
Wages Expense		25 060
Supplies Expense		810
Insurance Expense		1 080
Income Summary	25 388	
F. Oke, Capital		25 388
F. Oke, Capital	20 000	
F. Oke, Drawings		20 000

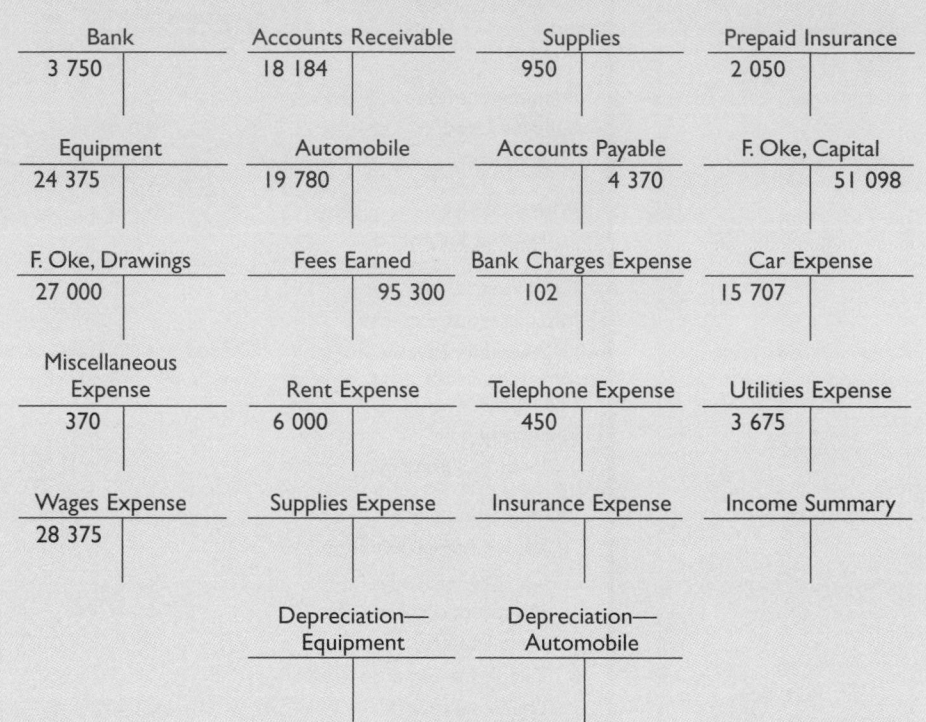

ACADEMY OF MUSIC
UNADJUSTED GENERAL LEDGER
December 31, 20–2

Bank	Accounts Receivable	Supplies	Prepaid Insurance
3 750	18 184	950	2 050

Equipment	Automobile	Accounts Payable	F. Oke, Capital
24 375	19 780	4 370	51 098

F. Oke, Drawings	Fees Earned	Bank Charges Expense	Car Expense
27 000	95 300	102	15 707

Miscellaneous Expense	Rent Expense	Telephone Expense	Utilities Expense
370	6 000	450	3 675

Wages Expense	Supplies Expense	Insurance Expense	Income Summary
28 375			

Depreciation— Equipment	Depreciation— Automobile

Questions

1. How can Alicia tell if something is wrong?
2. Is the list of adjusting and closing entries the correct one? Explain.
3. Does the list supplied have anything to do with Academy of Music? Explain.
4. Give the most likely explanation for the error.
5. Work out the adjusting entries from the information that you have available. Start to prepare a new list of the correct adjusting and closing entries. (You can do this by restructuring the work sheet, starting with the Balance Sheet and Income Statement columns and working backwards.)
6. Work out the closing entries and complete a correct list of adjusting and closing entries.

CASE 3
Challenge

Can You Meet This Deadline?

Stetsko and Company performs all of its own accounting up to the trial balance stage. Then Lu and Company, a firm of chartered accountants from the big city, prepares the adjusting entries and the financial statements.

You are an auditor with Lu and Company and have just completed the financial statements for Stetsko. You have just driven 800 kilometres to deliver these statements for an important business meeting that day and to begin some other audit work.

When you open your files, you find that your working papers have been tampered with. Most important, the balance sheet, the work sheet, and the list of adjusting entries for Stetsko are missing. Only the income statement is present.

The important meeting is only two hours away. Working only with the client's pre-adjustment trial balance and the income statement, which are shown below and on page 370, prepare an up-to-date balance sheet in time for the meeting. In addition, prepare a list of the adjusting entries that would have been on the work sheet. (Note: To really "get into" this case, set a clock for two hours from the time you begin working on it.)

STETSKO AND COMPANY
PRE-ADJUSTED TRIAL BALANCE
JUNE 30, 20—

	DR	CR
Bank	$ 4 172.50	
Accounts Receivable	27 421.00	
Supplies	1 365.00	
Prepaid Insurance	2 280.00	
Furniture and Equipment	12 596.00	
Accum. Dep. — Furniture and Equipment		$ 2 500.00
Automotive Equipment	24 800.00	
Accum. Dep. — Automotive Equipment		6 500.00
Accounts Payable		6 521.92
Bank Loan		20 000.00
Sales Tax Payable		560.00
I. Stetsko, Capital		25 558.20
I. Stetsko, Drawings	15 000.00	
Sales		58 072.50
Bank Charges Expense	1 132.10	
Automotive Expense	4 547.52	
Miscellaneous Expense	761.50	
Rent Expense	2 600.00	
Telephone Expense	1 712.00	
Wages Expense	21 325.00	
	$119 712.62	$119 712.62

```
                        STETSKO AND COMPANY
                          INCOME STATEMENT
                     SIX MONTHS ENDED JUNE 30, 20—

Revenue
    Sales                                                      $58 072.50
Operating Expenses
    Automotive Expense                        $  4 997.52
    Bank Charges Expense                         I 132.10
    Depreciation — Furniture and Equipment         500.00
    Depreciation — Automotive Equipment         I 250.00
    Insurance Expense                           I 580.00
    Miscellaneous Expense                         851.50
    Rent Expense                                2 600.00
    Supplies Expense                              955.00
    Telephone Expense                           I 822.00
    Wages Expense                              21 325.00        37 013.12
    Net Income                                                $21 059.38
```

CASE 4

Co-operative Learning

A Better Way of Depreciating a Truck?

The company you work for depreciates its trucks using the declining-balance method at Canada Customs and Revenue Agency's prescribed rates. Your boss suggests to you that this does not fairly charge the cost of the truck to the years of its use. It is her opinion that the cost of the truck should be charged over the years on the basis of actual use — that is, on the basis of kilometres travelled. This could be called a "distance-used" method. You agree that it is worth considering, and decide to make a comparison.

In your investigation, you select one truck that was recently sold and for which you have full and complete records. The truck was bought on January 1, 20-1 at a cost of $35 000, had no major repairs, and lasted until December 31, 20-8, at which time it was sold for $3 500. Your records also show that the truck travelled the distances in the following table:

Year	Distance
20-1	21 468 km
20-2	35 698 km
20-3	42 654 km
20-4	45 965 km
20-5	40 365 km
20-6	35 632 km
20-7	27 526 km
20-8	16 201 km
Total	265 509 km

Questions

1. Working in pairs, prepare two depreciation schedules for the above truck to compare the declining-balance method with the distance-used method. One partner is to prepare each schedule. With the distance-used method, the depreciation for the first year is calculated as follows: 21 468/265 509 × (35 000 − 3 500).

2. Discuss the merits of your boss's proposal. You and your partner are to prepare a memo to your boss, using the memo form found in the Skills Appendix, explaining your views based on your findings.

Career

David Yan / Bank and Investment Team Manager

David Yan had taken both accounting and economics courses by the time he graduated from Eric Hamber Secondary School in 1985. His graduation write-up in the school's yearbook describes him as "an avid sports fan who possesses a keen ability at picking winners." His future plans included enrolling in the Commerce faculty at the University of British Columbia and acquiring the ability to perform a reverse somersault slam-dunk on the basketball court.

While David failed to achieve his basketball dreams, he did graduate on the Dean's Honours list from the faculty of Commerce at U.B.C. While working to obtain his bachelor's degree, David gained part-time employment at Canada Trust. He entered their management trainee program after university and enjoyed a number of successful years with that organization. Then, in 1993, David became a manager with the Toronto Dominion Bank. The TD branch that David managed turned out to be just blocks away from his former high school—Eric Hamber Secondary School.

David's teachers remembered him as a lively person with the ability to motivate fellow students. He also maintained a positive outlook in almost all circumstances. For example, when a student/staff softball game he organized resulted in a crushing defeat for the students, David remained cheerful. In fact, he often joked about the event and used it as a tool for enhancing good relations with the staff. Years later, David offered to become actively involved in the life of the school. With so many agreeable memories, it is little wonder that teachers welcomed the chance to work with him again.

David provided many volunteer services to Eric Hamber Secondary during his six years as a Toronto Dominion Bank manager. His list of contributions includes speaking to Career and Personal Planning 12 classes, hosting career preparation students at his branch, helping to organize a multi-year homecoming celebration for former Hamber students, conducting seminars for teachers about financial planning and management, and presenting a nine-hour business and economics program to grade 10 students. David's dedication and energy provided an exemplary model of how the business community can play a role in education.

In the year 2000, David moved to the main office of the Toronto Dominion Bank in Vancouver to manage the Private Client Centre. This Centre deals with clients who have a high net worth and who desire specialized service and expertise in dealing with wealth management. The Private Client Centre offers private banking, investment counselling, brokerage services, estate planning, trust management, and more.

Besides coordinating and managing the operations, David's initial role at the Centre was to mesh a staff of professionals from different disciplines into a cohesive unit. Now, David is enjoying an increasing role in recruiting new clients.

What skills and personality traits are important in a career path like David's? When asked, David mentioned that being gregarious and motivated helps. And, he added, one must be willing to take the initiative when dealing with potential customers and with colleagues.

Discussion

1. How did David prepare for his career in high school? In university?
2. What evidence is there that David was a good academic student?
3. Who benefited from the volunteer services David gave to Eric Hamber Secondary School? Explain each of your answers.

DAVID YAN
David is an avid sports fan which explains his keen ability at picking winners; just ask Sweetness. Infamous for his kamakazi slide checks (on and off the court) and his long cold stares, this grad fears nothing. His long nights at school studying for history and algebra tests exemplify his dedication to school. Future plans include Commerce at U.B.C. and a reverse somersault slamdunk (just like Gus). LONG LIVE LIVERPOOL!

4. This article gives you a glimpse into David's personality. Make a list of his other personal characteristics that you can determine from this career profile.

5. How did the personality traits you listed above help David in his role as a bank manager and as manager of the Private Client Centre.

Research

6. Arrange a brief interview with the manager of a local bank or credit union. Ask for a summary of his or her job activities. Then make a list of the personality traits that the manager thinks are important for the job. Compare the list to the one you made for David Yan. Comment on the two lists, taking note of the common factors, as well as the differences.

10

Cash Control
and Banking

The word "cash" can be used in both a narrow and a broad sense. In its narrow sense, cash means dollar bills and coins. In its broad sense, cash also includes cheques, bank balances, and other items such as credit card vouchers or money orders — anything that can be deposited in a bank account.

Cash in this broad sense is vital to a business. The principal objective of a business is to earn a profit. This profit must eventually be converted into cash. A business needs cash to pay its bills, to meet its expenses, to reward its owners, and so on. Much of accounting, then, is concerned with receiving, paying, and safeguarding cash.

10.1 | Payment Systems

Wise business owners take a keen interest in how cash flows into and out of their businesses. Customers use different ways to pay a business. Likewise, a business uses different methods to pay its vendors, employees, and service providers. For simplicity, both cash receipts and cash payments are referred to as payment systems in this section of the text. Cash receipts are incoming payments from others; cash payments are outgoing payments to others.

A **payment system** provides a method for people to exchange one value for another. For example, buying a car with a cheque or cash means both parties exchange something of value. In Canada, methods of payment are changing as technology changes. Descriptions of the main payment systems—cash, cheques, credit cards, debit cards, and direct transfers—are listed below.

Cash

Cash usually consists of dollar bills and coins. Cash is a popular way to make payments. However, even though the volume of cash transactions is large, the value of individual transactions tends to be small.

One reason why the volume of cash transactions is large is because they can be made so easily. Buyers and sellers meet face to face, and value is immediately traded from one to the other. These simple transactions have the added feature of privacy since even the names of the buyers and sellers are unimportant.

Two factors that limit the value of individual cash transactions are portability and security. Carrying a large number of bills and coins is awkward and risky. When a business must make a large cash transaction, it often hires a security company to transport the bills and coins.

Cheques

There are methods of making payments other than by using bills and coins. These types of payments are referred to as **non-cash transactions**. Cheques are presently the most common form of non-cash transactions in Canada. Paying by cheque transfers money (or value) from one individual's bank account to another individual's bank account. Unlike paying with coins and bills, the exchange of money is delayed. For example, when you accept a cheque from someone, it will probably pass through these stages:

1. You will either cash the cheque or deposit it in your bank account. In either case, the bank will require that you endorse the cheque by signing it on the reverse side. By endorsing the cheque, you are legally contracting to guarantee the cheque should anything go wrong with it. Endorsement is discussed more fully on page 386.
2. The bank gives you cash, or credits your account for the amount of the cheque.
3. Your bank then forwards the cheque through the bank clearinghouse to the bank of the person who issued the cheque.
4. The issuer's bank attempts to deduct the amount of the cheque from the issuer's bank account. The deduction will be made if the balance in his or her account is large enough to cover the cheque.

In addition to a delay in exchanging money, you are likely aware of another difference between paying by cheque and paying with cash. That is, paying by cheque cannot be anonymous. Names are known and supporting identification may be needed.

Cheques carry the risk of being rejected by the issuer's bank. If the balance in the issuer's account is not large enough, the bank stamps the cheque "Not Sufficient Funds" (NSF) and sends it back to your bank. The cheque has now been "dishonoured"; in common speech, it has "bounced." An **NSF cheque** is one that was not cashed when presented to the issuer's bank because there were not sufficient funds in the issuer's bank account to cover the amount of the cheque. You will learn how to do the accounting for NSF cheques in Section 10.4.

Credit Cards

FIGURE 10.1

VISA and MasterCard
statistics for Canada.

A person with a credit card has a pre-arranged spending limit with the issuer of the card. (Typical card issuers are banks, department stores, or oil companies.) Bank credit cards like VISA and MasterCard are widely used. Among the facts that Figure 10.1 below reveals is that Canadians held nearly 38 million of these cards in 1999 and owed 28.2 billion dollars.

Credit Card Statistics—VISA and MasterCard								
	A	B	C	D	E	F	G	H
As at Fiscal Year Ending Oct. 31	Number of Cards in Circulation[1] (Millions)	Net Retail Volume[2] (Billions)	Outstanding Dollars[1] (Billions)	Net Dollar Volume[2][4] (Billions)	Average Sale	Reported Lost or Stolen[2]	Number of Cards Fraudulently Used[2]	$ Amount of Fraudulent Accounts written off (Millions)
1977	8.2	$ 3.6	$ 1.38	$ 4.0	$30.46	—	—	—
1978	9.0	$ 4.9	$ 1.84	$ 5.4	$32.50	—	—	—
1979	9.9	$ 6.6	$ 2.35	$ 7.3	$35.72	—	—	—
1980	10.8	$ 8.8	$ 2.87	$ 9.4	$39.47	—	—	—
1981	12.0	$10.6	$ 3.40	$ 11.5	$42.43	—	—	—
1982	11.6	$13.8	$ 3.72	$ 13.4	$50.30	259,028	—	$ 15.88
1983	12.1	$14.8	$ 3.73	$ 14.9	$49.88	275,754	19,200	$ 17.39
1984	13.1	$16.9	$ 4.42	$ 17.1	$52.05	299,152	21,332	$ 16.79
1985	14.0	$19.4	$ 5.06	$ 20.4	$51.90	330,380	21,026	$ 17.54
1986	15.5	$23.0	$ 5.76	$ 23.6	$55.15	378,239	22,326	$ 18.61
1987	17.6	$26.4	$ 6.76	$ 26.9	$58.52	108,571	23,913	$ 15.78
1988	19.4	$30.3	$ 7.84	$ 31.2	$61.90	460,348	25,773	$ 15.63
1989	20.4	$36.1	$ 9.30	$ 36.9	$66.00	522,204	30,919	$ 19.20
1990	23.2	$38.6	$10.80	$ 42.5	$67.22	520,716	32,851	$ 28.90
1991	24.3	$40.4	$11.19	$ 44.0	$67.40	623,946	53,968	$ 44.60
1992	24.4	$43.1	$11.40	$ 46.9	$69.30	650,088	61,234	$ 63.50
1993	25.0	$47.9	$13.20	$ 52.8	$70.50	674,988	63,442	$ 75.20
1994	27.5	$55.1	$15.40	$ 61.1	$72.40	731,052	63,635	$ 70.60
1995	28.8	$61.3	$17.44	$ 68.1	$74.51	648,824	66,109	$ 72.64
1996	30.2	$67.7	$18.70	$ 75.1	$77.80	794,996	77,740	$ 83.60
1997	31.9	$76.0	$20.50	$ 84.3	$82.50	858,625	89,982	$ 88.08
1998	35.3	$84.1	$23.90	$ 93.9	$89.96	895,817	126,384	$104.80
1999	37.7	$94.3	$28.20	$106.0	$90.35	823,934	132,836	$134.10

Source: Canadian Bankers Association

(1) As at last day of fiscal year end.

(2) Reported total to fiscal year end.

(3) Percentage of outstandings as at year end.

(4) Equals total of Net Retail Volume (sales) and cash advance volume.

Credit card transactions involve three parties: the holder of the card, the vendor, and the issuer of the card (a bank, for example). A person who holds a bank credit card can make a purchase from any business that accepts the card. The business receives payment from the bank, usually within the same business day. The holder of the card who made the purchase repays the bank at some later time. If the holder of the card pays within a specified time period, no interest is charged on the purchase.

Did you know that the most common place for credit card theft is the workplace? Cars are the second most likely place your card will be stolen. *Source: Safeguarding Your Money*

People who use credit cards find them safe and convenient. The business costs of lost, stolen, and fraudulent cards, however, are enormous. By studying Figure 10.1 again, you will discover that over 134 million dollars was lost in 1999 from illegal use of VISA and MasterCard credit cards. While these costs affect all parties involved in credit card transactions, they are primarily an expense of the institutions that issue the cards.

Debit Cards

Canadians use debit cards more frequently each year. In 1994, the number of debit card transactions amounted to about 5 per cent of all non-cash transactions. By 1998, that number had soared to approximately 28 per cent.

The main growth in the popularity of debit cards is due to the convenience of **point of sale** (POS) terminals. These machines help take money directly from the cardholder's bank account and transfer it to the business's bank account. The electronic backbone of the transfer is the *Interac* network, an organization managed by a group of Canadian financial institutions.

When a customer wishes to make a purchase using a debit card, the cashier enters the sale, passes the customer's card through a POS terminal or register, and waits while the customer enters data using the number pad. The customer agrees to the amount of the sale, selects the account to be debited, and enters a personal identification number. If the customer's bank account has enough funds available to cover the sale, the transaction is completed. A POS terminal and a card reader are shown in Figure 10.2.

The debit card gets its name from the fact that the bank will reduce the customer's bank account at the time the transaction is made.

FIGURE 10.2

A Point of Sale terminal and a card reader.

Direct Transfers

Transfers from one bank account to another can happen without cheques and debit cards. Very often, they happen electronically at pre-set times. Mortgage payments, insurance payments, and charitable donations are examples of items that you can authorize your bank to take out of your account at regular intervals (debits). You may also receive amounts into your account electronically, such as your weekly pay or deposits from investments (credits).

Other popular methods of direct transfers include electronic systems for individuals and businesses to make payments within Canada and internationally. Telephone banking provides access to your accounts for electronic transfers and bill payments. Additionally, the growth of the Internet allows the general public to make payments online. Figure 10.3 shows the computer screen seen by a customer about to pay a telephone bill. The transaction is taking place at the website of the customer's bank. The icon at the bottom left-hand corner of the figure looks like a lock. This means the website has a high level of security in order to prevent unauthorized individuals from gaining access to private information.

FIGURE 10.3

Paying a bill on the
Internet.

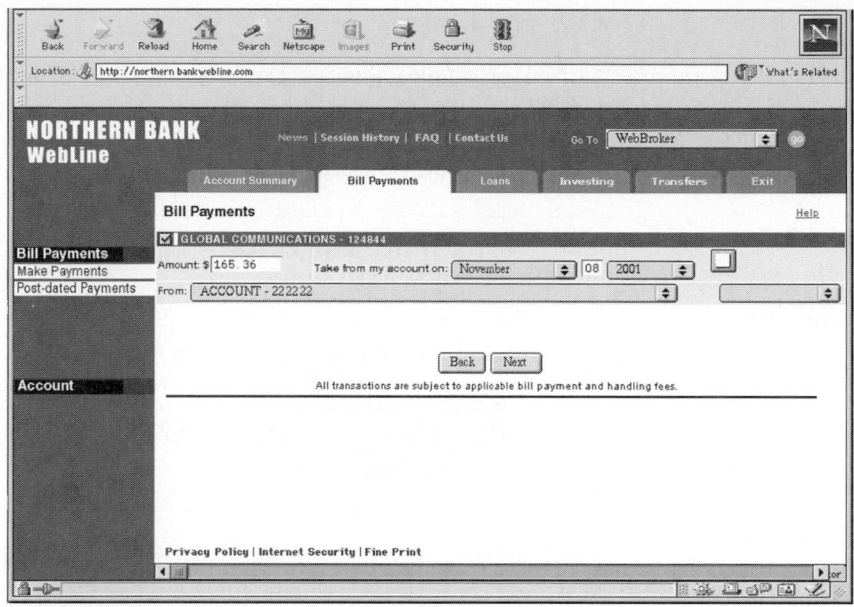

Comparison of Methods

The two tables in Figure 10.4 allow you to compare the methods Canadians use to make payments. (Payments with cash alone are excluded from these figures since precise data for coin and bill transactions are not available.)

The top table in Figure 10.4 reveals how many times each method of payment is used (volume). The bottom table reveals dollar amounts (value). Interesting conclusions can be made from the two sets of data. For example, from the 1998 figures you can determine that while the quantity of debit and credit card transactions is close to the number of cheque transactions, their combined value is less than 1% of the total cheque value. Exercise 3 on page 380 allows you to further analyze the data in Figure 10.1.

FIGURE 10.4

Payment methods
in Canada.

Cashless Payment Systems **Volume** of Transactions (in millions)					
	1994	1995	1996	1997	1998
Cheques issued	2,022.8	1,941.5	1,850.9	1,736.3	1,690.0
Credit card payments	784.1	846.5	903.5	956.8	1,008.8
Debit card payments	185.2	393.8	676.5	1,003.9	1,355.4
Other	454.1	542.3	642.1	710.1	825.7
Total	**3,446.2**	**3,724.1**	**4,073.0**	**4,407.1**	**4,879.9**

Cashless Payment Systems **Value** of Transactions (in billions of Canadian dollars)					
	1994	1995	1996	1997	1998
Cheques issued	25,159.9	20,339.3	15,959.0	18,589.7	19,250.5
Credit card payments	61.6	68.5	76.4	85.7	98.6
Debit card payments	9.4	18.8	30.2	44.3	58.5
Other	242.5	283.7	331.5	450.1	547.4
Total	**25,473.4**	**20,710.3**	**16,397.1**	**19,169.8**	**19,955.0**

Source: Bank for International Settlements, Bank of Canada

For more recent data on
the use of cheques, credit
cards and debit cards,
visit www.pearsoned.ca/
accounting1

Case Application

The Mattress Shop is a business with several outlets in the Greater Vancouver area of British Columbia. Foam mattresses and foam specialty products account for the bulk of their retail sales. The pie chart in Figure 10.5 shows how customers pay for the foam products. The percentages indicate the respective portions of total sales (value).

FIGURE 10.5

Sources of contributions to total cash sales.

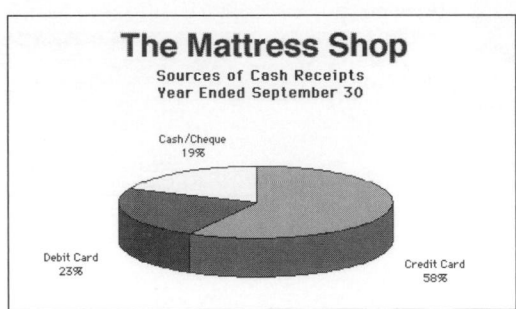

Note that the percentages for The Mattress Shop are quite different than the totals shown in Figure 10.4. From a national perspective, cheques have the highest dollar value of payments. From The Mattress Shop's experience, more "cash" is received from customers purchasing with credit cards. You can conclude from this that how a particular business receives payment for goods largely depends on what a business sells and to whom it sells to (retail customers, businesses, governments, and so on). You will perform additional analysis of The Mattress Shop's cash receipts when you complete Exercise 4 on page 380.

Section 10.1   **Review Questions**

1. Using the broad sense of the word, identify four items included in the definition of cash.
2. What is the function of a payment system?
3. Give two reasons why transactions with coins and bills tend to be for amounts of small value.
4. What is a non-cash transaction?
5. What is the most common form of non-cash transaction in Canada?
6. Explain why the actual exchange of value is delayed when cheques are used for payments.
7. Why would a cheque be rejected by a bank?
8. What is an NSF cheque?
9. Why is the word "bounced" used for NSF cheques?
10. What two advantages do customers get from using credit cards?
11. When would interest be charged against the holder of a credit card?
12. In point form, list the steps a customer takes when making a purchase with a debit card.
13. What is the name of the organization that manages the electronic network for debit card purchases?
14. List three examples of direct transfers.
15. Canadians now use credit and debit cards almost as much as cheques. Comment on the accuracy of this statement.

Section 10.1   **Exercises**

1. **Complete the following in your Workbook:**

   A. Record three things you already knew about debit and credit cards. Include your personal experiences or those of friends and relatives.

   B. List three things you would like to know about debit and credit cards.

   C. Find a partner. Share your two lists with him or her. Record your partner's lists in the space provided in your workbook.

   D. Be prepared to share items from your lists with the class.

2. **Complete each of the following statements by writing in your Workbook the appropriate word or phrase from the list below. A word or phrase may be used once, more than once, or not at all.**

   A. _____ usually consists of dollar bills and coins.

   B. Of the payment systems covered in the text, _____ take the longest time to transfer money from one party to another.

   C. To overcome the lack of portability of cash, _____ are used.

   D. Websites must be _____ to ensure payment information remains private.

   E. A pre-set limit for the amount a person can purchase is a feature of _____.

   F. The _____ symbol indicates that debit cards may used for purchases.

   G. Transactions with _____ are made frequently but typically have small dollar values.

   H. Of the three most common non-cash payment systems, _____ are experiencing the most rapid growth in use.

   I. Using _____ is the payment system that provides the greatest annual dollar value.

   J. When making a payment with _____ , you need not provide personal identification.

   K. Monthly mortgage payments are examples of _____ .

   L. The number of debit and credit card transactions are close to the frequency of _____ .

   List of Words or Phrases

cash	Interac
cheques	large-value transfers
credit cards	MasterCard
debit cards	non-cash transactions
direct transfers	secured
electronic	VISA

3. **In Figure 10.1 on page 375, you will find statistics about how Canadians use bank credit cards (VISA and MasterCard). Refer to that data when answering the following in your Workbook.**

Part A

a. What is the dollar difference between the amount of bank cards in circulation in 1977 and 1999?

b. What is the percentage increase of cards for the same period? (*Hint: Take your answer from question a above and divide by the 1977 figure.*)

c. Why are the yearly amounts of columns B and D different? (*Read the footnotes in Figure 10.1 carefully.*)

d. What do you suppose a cash advance from a credit card is? Calculate the amount of cash advances for 1999.

e. Cardholders must pay interest on the amounts in column C. Calculate the percentage increase in column C from 1977 to 1999. (*Hint: Refer to the procedure in questions a and b above.*) Is there any year in which the amounts in Column C have declined?

f. Calculate the percentage increases in columns F, G, and H from 1995 to 1999. Are there any years in this time frame that the amounts in F, G, and H decreased?

Part B

a. Write two to three paragraphs about the trends and problems of credit card use in Canada. In your paragraphs, refer to three pieces of information you discovered in Part A above. Also include at least one finding that you discovered on your own.

4. Ruth Bruinooge is the senior accountant for The Mattress Shop in Vancouver, B.C. She wants to know if there are any significant patterns in how their customers use cash, credit cards, and debit cards. After entering data into a spreadsheet, you produce the following graph:

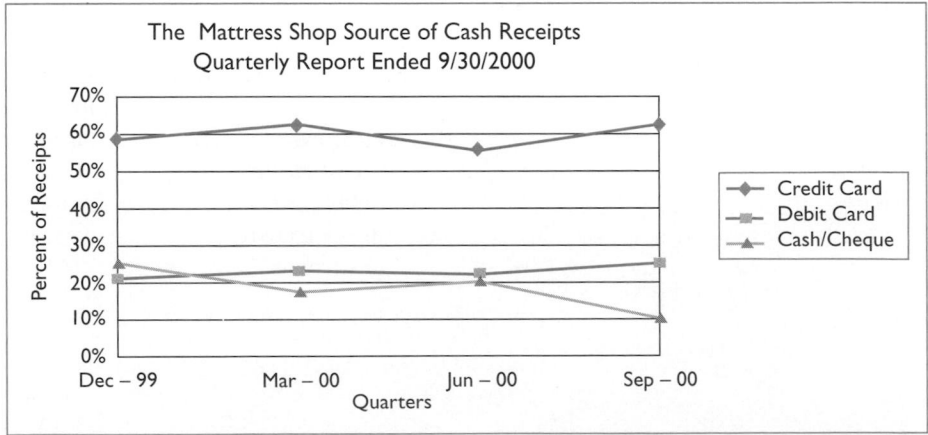

Required

In your workbook, you will find a form that simulates an e-mail window. Assuming you are a new employee in the accounting department of The Mattress Shop, compose an e-mail for Ms. Bruinooge to satisfy her curiosity about customer payment methods. In addition to your own observations, pay attention to:

a) The relationship between cash and credit cards use throughout the year.
b) The trend of debit card use.

For tips on writing e-mail correspondence, refer to the Student Skills Appendix.

10.2 | Accounting for Cash Receipts

A large part of business banking concerns the "cash receipts." The **cash receipts** of a business are the funds taken in from business operations and include all items considered to be money—including cheques, money orders, credit card slips, debit card transfers, bills, and coins. These funds must be carefully controlled and safeguarded. This section covers some important aspects to consider when accounting for cash receipts.

1. Mail Receipts

A business that sells on credit usually receives payment from its customers in the form of cheques sent by mail. Each business day, the clerk in charge of the mail separates out any cheques received and prepares a listing of them. The clerk then gives the cheques to the accounting department for deposit in the bank. The accounting department uses this list to prepare the cash receipt list or cash receipts daily summary you previously saw in chapter 6 on page 171.

The mail clerk is usually someone who does not work in the accounting department. Having an independent person sort and total the cheques helps to ensure that the funds received will be handled and recorded properly. If cheques from customers paying their accounts totalled $4 700, the accounting entry would be:

	DR	CR
Bank	4 700–	
Accounts Receivable		4 700–

2. Over-the-Counter Sales

Some small businesses sell some goods over the counter and place the money received in a drawer or cash box. It is customary for a business of this type to use sales slips to record its cash receipts. There are at least two copies of a slip for each sale, and they are prenumbered to ensure that all slips can be accounted for. This is a simple but effective accounting technique for controlling cash. The total of the cash received for one day should match the total of the sales slips.

3. Cash Register Receipts

When you go shopping, you will see a variety of cash registers. Some of these cash registers are called point-of-sale terminals. A **point-of-sale terminal** is an electronic cash register or debit card terminal connected to a central computer that is the heart of a sophisticated information system. This information system includes connections for credit and debit card transactions.

Cash registers can also be of the "stand-alone" variety, meaning that they are not connected to a central computer. Even stand-alone cash registers have many valuable features. Today's cashier may never have to make a mental or manual calculation. Prices, sales taxes, discounts, and change computations can all be handled automatically, reducing the possibility of error. As well, a number of calculations are made automatically as transactions occur, building up totals to be printed out later.

At the end of a business day, cash register receipts are deposited in the business's bank account. These receipts may include cheques, debit card and credit card slips, all of which are counted as part of the total cash deposit.

Electronic receipts at cash registers come from online debit and credit card transactions. When a customer purchases with a debit card, the deposit in the merchant's account appears to be made instantly. In reality, individual transactions are accumulated in a batch and deposited at a later time. This procedure saves processing costs.

The added purchasing convenience of debit and credit cards helps a business increase its sales. These features are not free of charge. For example, a bank takes a discount (a percentage) off each credit card sale. The percentage charged will vary with the volume of sales. Generally, a large business pays a smaller percentage per sale than a small business. Although bank rates and plans vary, a charge of 2 to 3 percent is common. At the end of the month, the journal entry for credit card use might look like the following:

	DR	CR
Credit Card Discount Expense	200	
Bank		200

An accountant might choose to accumulate all bank service charges—including fees for debit and credit cards—in one account.

Presently, debit card charges are calculated on the number of transactions rather than the dollar value of each sale. For example, a business might pay 15 cents each time a customer pays with a debit card.

Preparing Cash Proofs

Whether a business uses a point-of-sale terminal, or whether its employees fill out sales slips by hand, it must have a system of verifying the accuracy of cash receipts each day. To prove that cash receipts amounts are correct in a system using a cash register, someone must count the cash received. Then, someone must compare the total of the cash counted with the total shown by the cash register. The two totals should be the same. Consider the following example:

a) A business starts the day with $75. This amount is called the **change fund** or **float** and consists of small bills and coins. This fund is used to make change for customers. It is placed in the cash drawer of the cash register at the beginning of each business day. At the close of the day, small bills and coins equalling the amount of the float are taken from the cash register drawer and put safely away. This is the float for the next business day.

The float is created in the first place by issuing and cashing a cheque made out to Cash. The accounting entry for the transaction is:

	DR	CR
Cash Float	75.00	
Bank		75.00

b) At the end of the day, the cash register tape reveals the following totals:

Cash Sales	$2300.00
PST	184.00
GST	161.00

c) Someone counts the cash in the register and arrives at a total of $2 720.00 This amount includes the cash float.

d) A different person fills out a cash proof form, which is customized to suit the nature of the business. (See Figure 10.6) A **cash proof** is an accounting procedure that compares cash receipts *according to source documents* against cash receipts *according to a physical count*.

FIGURE 10.6

A completed cash proof form

```
Cash Proof
                        Date November 3, 20–
Cash Register Tape Totals
     Cash Sales        $    2300 00
     PST                      184 00
     GST                      161 00
     Receipts per tape       2645 00

Cash Received
     Cash Count        $    2720 00
     Less: Change Fund        75 00
     Actual Cash Received    2645 00

CASH SHORT OR OVER     $       Ø
```

The cash counted is $2 720. Since the cashier began the day with $75, the actual cash received on November 3 is $2 645. The cash register tape totals match the actual cash received. The cashier can be assured that he or she made no mistakes giving out change.

The journal entry for the day's receipts is as follows:

	DR	CR
Bank	2 645.00	
Sales		2 300.00
PST Payable		184.00
GST Payable		161.00

More details can be added to preparing cash proofs. For example, a business may deposit credit card slips, accept payments on account, and so on. Yet, the fundamental procedures of preparing a cash proof remain the same:

1) Record the total of the cash received as revealed by cash register tapes, sales slips, or other source documents.
2) Compare the total above with an actual count of cash, remembering to factor in the float.

Cash Short or Over

Regardless of how sophisticated the cash register is or how carefully sales slips are filled out, people make errors when dealing with cash. For example, sooner or later a cashier will give out either too much or too little change. When this happens, the totals on the cash proof form will not agree.

Using the same cash register tape totals as in Figure 10.6, suppose that the cash count at the end of the day was $2 700 instead of $2 720. The cash proof form would then be prepared as follows:

FIGURE 10.7

A completed cash proof form showing a shortage.

Cash Proof		
	Date November 3, 20–	
Cash Register Tape Totals		
Cash Sales	$	2300 00
PST		184 00
GST		161 00
Receipts per tape		2645 00
Cash Received		
Cash Count	$	2700 00
Less: Change Fund		75 00
Actual Cash Received		2625 00
CASH SHORT OR OVER	$	20 00

The cash register tape indicates sales of $2 645 on November 3. The actual cash counted is $20 less than the tape indicates. A cash shortage is said to exist because the actual cash received is less than the source documents indicate.

What caused the cash shortage? There could be several reasons. For instance, perhaps the cashier gave $20 extra to a customer when making change, and the customer did not inform the cashier of the error. A few businesses require cashiers to make up shortages out of their own pockets, but most retail stores accept errors as part of doing business.

Accounting for a cash shortage is straightforward. For the situation shown in Figure 10.7, the journal entry is:

	Dr.	Cr.
Bank	2625.00	
Cash Short or Over	**20.00**	
Sales		2300.00
PST Payable		184.00
GST Payable		161.00

Notice that credit amounts have not changed and that the debit to Bank must be $2 625 because that is the actual amount of cash received. To make debits equal credits, the accountant simply creates an account and names it **Cash Short or Over.** As the name suggests, this account will receive entries for both shortages and overages.

An **overage** occurs when more cash is received than the source documents indicate. Imagine that on the next business day, the cash proof is as follows:

Cash Proof

Date November 4, 20–

Cash Register Tape Totals

Cash Sales	$	2800 00
PST		224 00
GST		196 00
Receipts per tape		3220 00

Cash Received

Cash Count	$	3300 00
Less: Change Fund		75 00
Actual Cash Received		3225 00

CASH SHORT OR (OVER) $ 5 00

This time, there is $5 more in the cash register drawer than the tape shows there should be. The accounting entry required is shown below:

	Dr.	Cr.
Bank	3 225.00	
Sales		2 800.00
PST Payable		224.00
GST Payable		196.00
Cash Short or Over		**5.00**

If the amounts from the November 3rd and November 4th cash proofs were posted to the Cash Short or Over account, the balance would be as shown below:

Cash Short or Over

Nov. 3	20.00	Nov. 4	5.00
	(15.00)		

At any particular time, the balance in this account represents either a shortage (expense, debit) or an overage (income, credit) depending on the type of balance in the account. The account is placed in the expense section of the chart of accounts because it is usual for the account to end up with a debit balance. This is because customers who have been given too little change are more likely to complain than those who have been given too much change.

The Current Bank Account

Business bank accounts usually involve more work for the bank's employees. For example, checking the coins and currency in a business's deposit can be quite time-consuming. People in business are expected to use a type of bank account known as the current account. A **current bank account** is designed especially for use by business owners. The principal features of a current bank account are outlined below.

- No interest is earned.
- There is a small minimum charge for each monthly statement period.
- A bank statement is provided each month.

- The paid cheques are returned to the depositor each month along with the bank statement.
- Books of duplicate deposit slips are provided free of charge.

There may be slight variations of these features from one bank to another and from time to time.

Preparing the Business Deposit

During the business day, the day's receipts are prepared for deposit. It is best to make the deposit as soon as possible to avoid having a large amount of money on the premises. However, the nature of some businesses makes them unable to complete this task until after banking hours. They must then use the night depository service.

The person preparing the deposit must keep the following in mind:

1. Bills must be sorted by denomination for ease of counting.
2. Coins are to be rolled and placed in a wrapper by denomination when there are sufficient quantities.
3. Banks require that the depositor endorse (that is, guarantee) each cheque by signing it on the reverse side. Businesses endorse all cheques *for deposit only* as shown in Figure 10.9 below. Usually, a business has an approved rubber stamp with which to make the endorsements. The endorsement shown in Figure 10.9 is a **restrictive endorsement**. A restrictive endorsement places conditions on the cashing or depositing of the cheque. The cheque below could only be deposited into the account of Tech Industries Limited; nothing else could happen to it. If the cheque was lost or stolen, it could not be cashed. If, on the other hand, a cheque is endorsed in blank—that is, with just a signature—it could possibly be cashed by anyone who happened to get hold of it.

FIGURE 10.9

A restrictive endorsement on the back of a cheque.

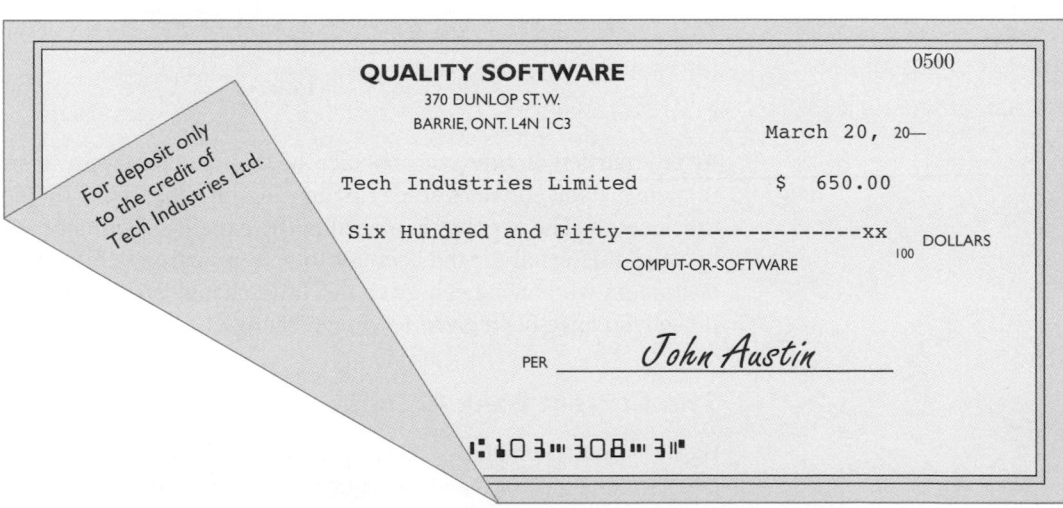

4. The completed deposit slip must agree with the cash proofs and the accounting entries.
5. A duplicate deposit slip, stamped by the bank, must be obtained as the company's receipt for the deposit. The bank retains the original. If a night depository is used, the bank will mail out the receipted duplicate deposit slip. A completed deposit slip is shown in Figure 10.10 on page 387.

FIGURE 10.10

A completed deposit slip
for a business.

						1031716 (6/00)

COMPANY NAME   ☐ CAD   ACCOUNT NUMBER
                             ☐ USD

COL. A	PARTICULARS	AMOUNT	COL. B	PARTICULARS		AMOUNT
1			8			
2			9			
3			10			
4			11			
5			12			
6			13			
7			14			
			CHEQUE SUB-TOTAL (COLS. A + B) (CARRY FORWARD)			

Scotiabank™   **BUSINESS ACCOUNT DEPOSIT**

					X 5	

COMPANY NAME   ☐ CAD
                                               ☐ USD

| | | | | | X 10 | |
| | | | | | X 20 | |

DATE

ITEMS	NO. OF ITEMS	AMOUNT	X 50	
CHEQUES SUB–TOTAL (BROUGHT FORWARD)			X 100	
			X	

DEPOSITED BY

U.S. CHEQUES			U.S. CASH	
VISA			FLD 4 TOTAL CASH	
FLD 3 TOTAL NO. OF ITEMS ▶			FLD 5 COIN	
SUB–TOTAL			SUB-TOTAL (BROUGHT FORWARD)	

ACCOUNT NUMBER

U.S. EXCHANGE   PLUS MINUS

(DEP)   **TOTAL DEPOSIT**

(FLD 2) SERIAL NUMBER   (FLD 3) TOTAL NO. OF ITEMS   (FLD 4) TOTAL CASH   (FLD 5) COIN   (TELLER)

™ Trademark of The Bank of Nova Scotia.

Section 10.2   **Review Questions**

1. Name the most common types of cash receipts of a business that sells on credit.
2. What is the usual reason a business would receive "mail" receipts?
3. What is the difference between a stand-alone cash register and a point-of-sale terminal?
4. When a customer buys an item with a debit card, a deposit is instantly made in the merchant's account. True or False? Explain.
5. For credit card purchases, banks charge businesses a percentage of the total sale. How does this method differ when a debit card is used?
6. Describe what the "float" is.
7. What is a cash proof?
8. What are the two fundamental procedures one must follow when preparing a cash proof?

9. Why are there cash overages or cash shortages?
10. Which is the more common—cash overage or cash shortage? Explain.
11. Who uses a current bank account?
12. When a business deposit is prepared, what must be done with the coins?
13. How is a cheque endorsed for a business deposit?
14. What is meant by a "restrictive" endorsement?

Section 10.2   **Exercises**

1. **Complete each of the following statements by writing in your Workbook the appropriate word or phrase from the list below. Not all words or phrases are used as answers.**

   A. The _____ of a business represent the money taken in from business operations.
   B. It is customary for a business that _____ to receive payment from its customers by way of cheques through the mail.
   C. Cheques received in the mail are _____ by the mail clerk before being deposited in the bank.
   D. Sales slips are _____ to ensure that all slips are accounted for.
   E. At the end of a business day, cash register receipts are _____ in the business's bank account.
   F. An electronic cash register that is connected to a central computer is known as a _____.
   G. A small quantity of money used to start the cash register activity for the day is known as a _____.
   H. An overage produces a _____ in the Cash Short and Over account.
   I. A shortage produces a _____ in the Cash Short and Over account.
   J. Cash _____ are more common than cash _____.
   K. Businesses are required by the banks to use a _____.
   L. Cheques received by a business are endorsed _____ before being deposited.

   List of Words or Phrases

balanced	for deposit only
cash float	Internet
cash receipts	listed
cash sales	overages
credit	point-of-sale terminal
current bank account	prenumbered
debit	sells on credit
deposited	shortages

2. A business's cash receipts data for two days were as follows:

   A. On February 27, the cash register tape showed cash receipts for the day to be $980.15. The cash float at the start of the day was $50.00. The total cash counted (including float) at the end of the day was $1 005.15.
   B. On February 28, the cash register tape showed cash receipts to be $856.35. The float remained at $50.00. The total cash counted (including float) was $910.85.

Required

a) **Using the forms in your workbook, prepare cash proofs and journal entries for February 27 and February 28.**

b) **Post the journals entries to the T-account provided. Is the balance debit or credit? Would this be the normal type of balance in the account? Why?**

---

3. A business uses sales slips (or vouchers) to keep track of cash receipts. Using the information given below, perform the following:

A. **Complete the Cash Proof using the form provided in your Workbook. The business does not accept credit card transactions.**

B. **Record the journal entry for the day's transactions in the general journal provided. Date it April 16.**

Vouchers for the Day (sorted)

Cash Sales

Voucher	Sale	GST	PST	Total
No. 57	$315.00	$22.05	$25.20	$362.25
No. 59	392.00	27.44	31.36	450.80
No. 61	740.00	51.80	59.20	851.00
No. 64	375.00	26.25	30.00	431.25
No. 67	374.00	26.18	29.92	430.10

Charge Sales

Voucher	Sale	GST	PST	Total
No. 58	$206.00	$14.42	$16.48	$236.90
No. 62	310.00	21.70	24.80	356.50
No. 63	216.00	15.12	17.28	248.40

Cash Refunds

Voucher	Sale	GST	PST	Total
No. 60	$102.00	$ 7.14	$ 8.16	$117.30
No. 65	208.00	14.56	16.64	239.20

Returns for Credit

Voucher	Sale	GST	PST	Total
No. 66	$ 58.00	$ 4.06	$ 4.64	$ 66.70
No. 68	214.00	14.98	17.12	246.10

Cash in Drawer, after Removing Change Fund

Bills		Coins	
$5 × 29		1¢ × 263	
$10 × 80		5¢ × 251	
$20 × 23		10¢ × 311	
$50 × 6		25¢ × 652	
		$1.00 × 187	
		$2.00 × 19	

---

4. **Assume that the Cash Short or Over account is posted daily as in the account on page 384. Examine the account and answer the questions that follow.**

A. On how many days was there a cash shortage?

B. On how many days was there a cash overage?

C. Is the net result for the month an overage or a shortage?

D. Does this account as it stands represent an expense or an income?

No. 5850	Cash Short or Over						
Date	Particulars	P.R.	Debit	Credit	DR CR	Balance
July 20— 3			10 —			
4			2 —			
7				5 —		
10			20 —			
11				1 —		
12			5 —			
14				50		
17				1 50		
18			2 —			
20			1 —			
24			10 —			
25				75		
26			3 —			
27			10 —			
28			5 —			
31			1 —		Dr	60 25

5. At the end of a business day, Joanne Adamson is responsible for preparing the night deposit for Marks and Associates. The deposit is to be made up from the currency and VISA slips and cheques shown below.

1. **Prepare the deposit on the form provided in the Workbook for June 10, 20—. Use account no. 756210.**
2. **Make the deposit agree with the accounting entry figure of $8 978.29.**

Currency

Bills			Coin		
$5	×	42	1¢	×	151
$10	×	78	5¢	×	86
$20	×	101	10¢	×	158
$50	×	22	25¢	×	141
$100	×	8	$1.00	×	57
			$2.00	×	85

VISA Slips

James	$109.14
Carter	83.46
Paracy	483.64
DeCorte	102.72
Hill	24.61
Melnyk	630.23
Thrower	85.60

Cheques

Thompson	$362.73
Meyer	55.64
Bogard	911.64
Geyer	155.50
Metsopoulis	228.98
Morris	189.95
Savela	334.91
Webb	25.68

10.3 | Accounting for Cash Payments

Credit terms are an essential part of business trade. When businesses buy goods and services from other businesses on credit, accounts payable are created. To clear or reduce accounts payable, businesses usually write cheques, which is one of the reasons why cheques remain the dominant payment system in Canada.

A sample of a cheque written to reduce an account payable is shown in Chapter 6, Figure 6.9 on page 170. In a manual system, the business either keeps a copy of the cheque, or it records vital data on a cheque stub. The cheque copy or stub is then used by the accounting department to make the accounting entry. Later, the bank pays the cheque and issues a bank statement that will help the accounting department verify the accuracy of all cheques written.

Cheques take time to prepare. A business owner may assign the task of preparing cheques for signature to an accounting clerk. The clerk fills in necessary data but leaves the cheque unsigned. The owner can then sign the cheque at his or her convenience.

Preparing cheques for signature is a procedure handled well by accounting software. For example, an accounting clerk may use a software package, such as Simply Accounting, to record the debits and credits for a payment on account. After the entry is prepared, the clerk instructs the software program to print the cheque for signature and post the entry.

Electronic Payments

On page 377, you saw that a business can receive payment over the Internet. It follows, then, that it can also make payments over the Internet.

Observe Figure 10.11 and notice that a company is preparing to pay three bills: a telephone bill, a utilities bill, and a vendor.

FIGURE 10.11

Payments made using the Internet.

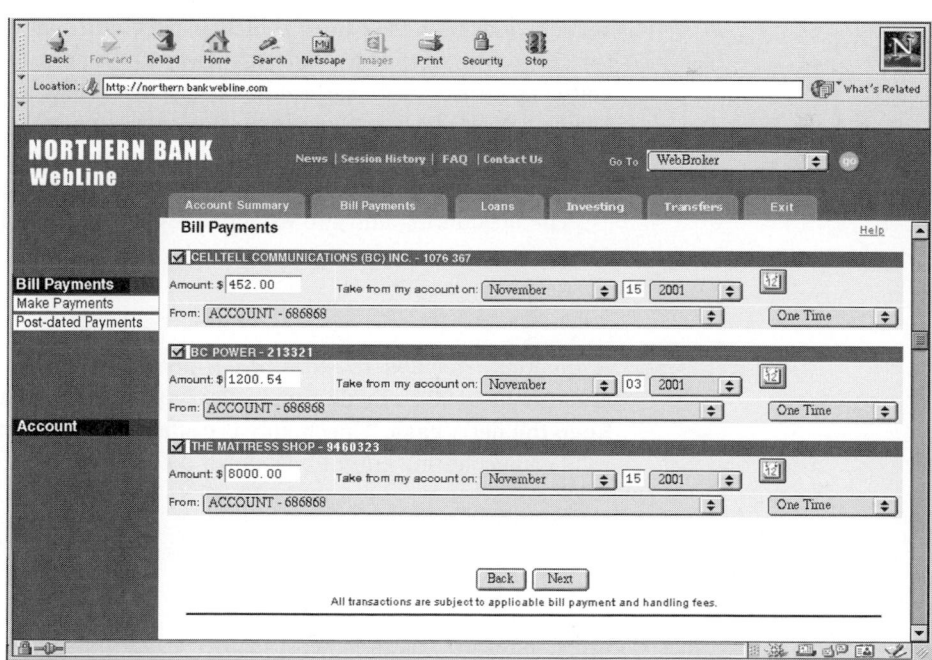

Cheques can also be post-dated by writing in a date at sometime in the future. The cheques cannot be cashed until the future date is reached.

In addition to entering amounts, the business has specified the date it wants the payments to be made — November 3 and November 15. The $452.00 for the telephone bill and the $8000.00 for the loan payment will not be transferred from the business's current account until November 3 and November 15 respectively. These are called post-dated payments and are a convenient way for a business to organize its bill-paying procedure.

Petty Cash

Even though the most common way of paying for expenditures is by cheque, it is not always convenient to do so. Payment in cash is often expected. Consider the following transactions:

- The custodian needs some electrical fuses. During her lunch hour, she purchases some electrical fuses from the hardware store with her own money. She then submits the cash register slip to the accounting department so that she may be repaid.
- Two salaried employees are asked to work overtime in order to complete a special job. They are each given $12 for supper money.
- A courier company delivers a parcel for which charges of $12.50 must be paid immediately.

The usual way to pay for small expenditures of this type is with cash from a petty cash fund. A petty cash fund is a small quantity of cash, usually no more than $200, that is kept in the office for small expenditures.

Establishing a Petty Cash Fund

To establish a petty cash fund, a small sum ($100 to $200) is withdrawn from the bank account and put in the care of someone in the office. More precisely, a cheque is issued (usually made out to Petty Cash) and given to the person selected to be in charge of the petty cash. This person cashes the cheque and brings the money (in the form of small bills and coins) back to the office to be kept in a metal cash box (with a lock). This is known as the imprest system. The **imprest method for petty cash** is a system for handling small expenditures in which a certain amount of cash is entrusted to an individual.

An imprest is a cash advance.

The accounting entry to establish a petty cash fund is shown by the following example:

TRANSACTION

A business decides to establish a petty cash fund of $100. A cheque in the amount of $100 is made out to Petty Cash and given to the person chosen to keep the petty cash. The cheque is cashed and the money put in a petty cash box.

The accounting entry to establish the petty cash fund is the following:

	DR	CR
Petty Cash	$100	
Bank		$100

When this accounting entry is posted, the petty cash box will contain $100 in cash and will be in agreement with the Petty Cash account.

Operating the Petty Cash Fund

The keeper of the petty cash fund is authorized to make small payments out of the fund as necessary. Every amount paid out of the fund must be replaced by a bill or voucher for the expenditure (submitted by the person receiving the money). If a bill is not available, the recipient of the money must fill out a petty cash voucher such as the one shown in Figure 10.12 below. A **petty cash voucher** is a form that is filled out when money is paid out of the petty cash fund and no bill for the expenditure is available.

The bill or petty cash voucher is then placed in the box. A supply of unused petty cash vouchers (also known as petty cash slips) is kept with the petty cash fund.

At any time, the total of the bills, vouchers, and cash in the petty cash box should be equal to the amount of the petty cash fund. The keeper of the fund is responsible for seeing that this is so.

FIGURE 10.12

A petty cash voucher.

PETTY CASH VOUCHER
DATE   March 15, 20–
AMOUNT   12.00 + GST .84 Total 12.84
PAID TO   Holmes Hardware
EXPLANATION   2 extension
cords for janitors
SIGNATURE   P. Watts
Received by
CHARGE TO A/C   #590
Miscellaneous Exp.

Accounting for this aspect of petty cash is easy because no accounting entries are made. It is one of those accounting situations in which it is convenient to allow the records to become temporarily inexact.

Replenishing the Petty Cash Fund

The cash in the petty cash box decreases as bills and vouchers are paid. A point is reached when there may not be enough cash in the fund to pay for the next bill or voucher presented. To prevent this, a minimum dollar amount is usually placed on the fund. When this minimum amount for the petty cash fund is reached, the fund must be replenished. **Replenishing petty cash** is the procedure by which the petty cash fund is renewed when it reaches a predetermined minimum amount.

To show the accounting for replenishing petty cash, let us work with a petty cash fund of $100 with a minimum amount of $10. Assume that the contents of the petty cash box are:

Cash	$ 5.11
Bills and vouchers	94.89
Total	$100.00

Assume further that the bills and vouchers contained in the petty cash box are the following:

No.	Account Charged	Amount	GST	Total
1	Miscellaneous Expense	$12.00	$.84	$12.84
2	Postage	10.00	.70	10.70
3	Miscellaneous Expense	12.50	.88	13.38
4	Building Maintenance	11.00	.77	11.77
5	Donations	5.00	—	5.00
6	Building Maintenance	4.50	.32	4.82
7	Truck Expense	15.00	1.05	16.05
8	Miscellaneous Expense	5.00	.35	5.35
9	Postage	5.00	.35	5.35
10	Supplies	9.00	.63	9.63
		$89.00	$5.89	$94.89

The petty cash fund must be replenished because the petty cash box contains less cash than the lower limit of $10. The steps to be followed are:

Step 1 The keeper of the fund prepares a summary by account of the charges from the bills and vouchers in the box. There is no definite form in which the summary must be prepared. The summary might be drawn up like the one in Figure 10.13 below. The bills and vouchers from which the summary is prepared must be attached to the summary.

FIGURE 10.13

A summary of charges from a petty cash fund.

Petty Cash Fund	
Summary of Charges	
October 2, 20–	
Building Maintenance	15 50
Donations	5 00
Miscellaneous Expense	29 50
Postage	15 00
Supplies	9 00
Truck Expense	15 00
GST Recoverable	5 89
	94 89

Step 2 The petty cashier submits the summary, together with the bills and vouchers, to the person or department that issues cheques.

Step 3 A cheque, usually made out to Petty Cash for an amount equal to the total on the summary (in this case $94.89), is given in exchange for the vouchers. The summary and the supporting documents together are accepted as the source document for the cheque.

Step 4 The cheque is cashed by the petty cashier and the money is added to the total ($5.11) in the petty cash box. The fund is then restored to its original amount of $100 and is then ready to begin another cycle.

Step 5   An accounting entry must be made for the cheque that was issued to replenish the petty cash. In our example, the accounting entry is:

	DR	CR
Building Maintenance	15.50	
Donations	5.00	
Miscellaneous Expense	29.50	
Postage	15.00	
Supplies	9.00	
Truck Expense	15.00	
GST Recoverable	5.89	
Bank		94.89
	Debits taken	Credit taken
	from summary	from cheque

We have seen that only two accounting entries are involved in petty cash transactions:

1. the entry to establish the fund (a similar entry is used to increase the fund);
2. the entry to replenish the fund.

Section 10.3   Review Questions

1. What is the most common method of paying off an accounts payable?
2. What is meant by "preparing a cheque for signature"?
3. What is a post-dated payment?
4. What is the purpose of a petty cash fund?
5. When is a petty cash voucher used?
6. Describe the contents of the petty cash box.
7. How can the contents of the petty cash box be checked for correctness?
8. When is the petty cash fund replenished?
9. What happens to the vouchers in the petty cash box?

Section 10.3   Exercises

1. On January 15, Kendra Wah issues a cheque in the amount of $200 to establish a petty cash fund. **Give the accounting entry in general journal form to establish the petty cash fund**. You will find a form in the Workbook.

2. On February 20, Seneca Sales Company issues a cheque to increase the petty cash fund from $100 to $150. **Give the accounting entry in general journal form to increase the petty cash fund**. You will find a form in the Workbook.

3. On March 16, after a bill of $13.01 is paid, the contents of a petty cash fund with a lower limit of $10 are as follows:

Cash	$2.05		
Bills and Vouchers	*Amount*	*GST*	*Total*
Supplies	$10.00	$.70	$10.70
Miscellaneous Expense	6.04	.42	6.46
Miscellaneous Expense	1.25	.09	1.34
Sales Promotion	8.50	.60	9.10
Building Maintenance	10.50	.74	11.24
C. Parkes, Drawings	12.00	—	12.00
Car Expense	8.17	.57	8.74
Postage	8.50	.60	9.10
Miscellaneous Expense	2.05	.14	2.19
Postage	9.00	.63	9.63
Miscellaneous Expense	4.15	.29	4.44
Building Maintenance	12.16	.85	13.01

A. Prepare the summary of charges necessary to replenish the fund.

B. In general journal form, write out the accounting entry necessary to replenish the fund.

You will find forms in the Workbook.

---

4. On June 10, 20—, a petty cash fund with a lower limit of $12 is in the following condition:

Cash	$0.61		
Bills and Vouchers	*Amount*	*GST*	*Total*
Delivery Expense	$15.00	$1.05	$16.05
Wages	10.00	—	10.00
Office Expense	15.02	1.05	16.07
Supplies	10.75	.75	11.50
Advertising	12.00	.84	12.84
Supplies	11.79	.83	12.62
Advertising	15.00	1.05	16.05
Wages	12.50	—	12.50
Office Expense	12.14	.85	12.99
P. Martin, Drawings	10.00	—	10.00
Office Expense	4.20	.29	4.49
Office Expense	2.00	.14	2.14
Supplies	11.35	.79	12.14

A. Prepare the summary of charges necessary to replenish the fund.

B. In general journal form, write out the required accounting entry to replenish the fund.

You will find forms in the Workbook.

---

5. Indicate whether each of the following statements is true or false by placing a "T" or an "F" in the space indicated in your Workbook. Explain the reason for each "F" response in the space provided.

A. The amount in the Petty Cash account in the general ledger must never change.

B. A petty cash voucher must be prepared for every payment out of the fund.

C. The petty cash fund is used for the purpose of cutting down on the number of cheques issued.

D. The accounting entry to replenish the petty cash fund is made by the keeper of the fund.

E. The petty cash box is locked and put away in a safe place outside business hours.
F. The keeper of the petty cash fund must never borrow from it.
G. The petty cash summary is organized by general ledger accounts.
H. A payment out of petty cash can be charged only to an expense account or an asset account.
I. If an auditor were to check the petty cash fund, the procedure would be to total all of the cash and vouchers in the box and check this total against the balance in the Petty Cash account.

10.4 | Accounting Controls for Cash

Every business establishes some type of accounting system or set of procedures. The owner of a business should take the time and effort to establish a good system that has strong "internal control."

Internal Control

An accounting system that promotes employee honesty, accuracy, and efficiency is considered to have good internal control. **Internal control** is the set of accounting procedures established to protect the assets from theft and waste, ensure accurate accounting data, encourage efficiency, and adhere to company policies.

No internal control is necessary in a small business where the owner functions alone. But as the business grows and employees are hired, accounting controls become a factor in managing the business. Where there are a large number of employees, a good system of internal control is essential. A business should not take chances about its employees' honesty and dedication. Neither should it expose its employees to unnecessary temptation. The business should take whatever steps it can to protect itself and its employees.

A good system of internal control can be quite involved and highly detailed. Some fundamental rules of good internal control are:

1. Where possible, two different people should be processing and preparing accounting documents independently of each other, and their work must agree.
2. The person who records transactions or prepares accounting records should not also control or handle the physical assets.
3. All assets should be kept in a safe place. Two authorized persons should be present when negotiable assets are dealt with. (Negotiable assets are the ones that can easily be converted to cash.)
4. Only a few key employees should be allowed to approve and authorize transactions.
5. An independent public accountant should periodically carry out an audit to ensure that the accounting system is being followed correctly. If weaknesses are found, the system should be improved.
6. Responsibilities should be clearly established. It should be easy to tell who is responsible for errors or missing assets.

Procedures for the Control of Cash

Internal control affects all aspects of a business but is especially needed for cash. Cash is the single item most likely to be stolen outright by employees. Cash is also the item most likely to be embezzled (secretly stolen) with the help of falsified accounting records. Cash has no special marks to identify it and is easily exchanged for other goods or services.

The following are internal control measures specially designed to protect the cash of a business.

1. **Separate duties.** In general, the same people should not handle the cash and keep the records for the cash. For example, the person who opens the mail and prepares the daily list of mail receipts should not be a member of the accounting department. If this procedure is followed, a theft can take place only if two or more employees decide to act together. (This is known as collusion.) However, a mail clerk who acted alone could be caught easily. Suppose that the mail clerk managed to cash a customer's cheque for personal use. The customer's account would not be credited with the amount of the cheque and there would eventually be a complaint. An investigation would point to the mail clerk who had access to the cheque.

2. **Deposit funds daily.** The total cash receipts for the day should be deposited by the end of that day. This keeps the amount of cash in the office to a minimum. Theft is both prevented and discouraged. Banks provide a night depository system for the benefit of businesses that take in cash outside banking hours.

3. **Deposit funds intact.** The cash receipts of each business day should be deposited intact. Cash received during the day should not be available for making payments or for borrowing by employees. (Note: Sometimes it is necessary to pay a cash refund out of a cash register. This procedure would be supported by evidence from the cash register tape.)

4. **Make all payments by cheque or electronic transfer of funds.** Except for petty cash expenditures and cash refunds, payments are made by cheque or electronic transfer of funds. When this procedure is followed, and all cash receipts are deposited intact, the records prepared by the company will correspond to the records prepared by the bank. It is then possible to compare one against the other. This control technique, known as the bank reconciliation, is described below.

5. **Endorse cheques "For Deposit Only."** Then each cheque can only be credited to the business's bank account and cannot be cashed in any other way.

6. **Prepare deposit slips in duplicate.** The deposit slip shows the details of the deposit. It is useful if any question arises regarding the deposit. The teller should stamp a duplicate of the deposit slip and the business should retain it as a receipt.

7. **Reconcile bank accounts monthly.** As mentioned above, the company's and the bank's records can be compared or "reconciled." If a company has more than one bank account, each one should be reconciled monthly.

Bank Reconciliation

Since both the bank and the business keep a record of cash, you might expect the month-end balance shown by the bank statement to agree with the month-end balance shown by the general ledger Bank account. But this rarely happens.

Usually, the bank statement balance differs from the Bank account balance in the general ledger. How, then, can the accounting department be certain that either record is correct? The accuracy of both balances is proven by a process known as the bank reconciliation. A **bank reconciliation** is a routine procedure to determine why the balance on deposit in the bank does not agree with the balance of cash shown by the books of the company. The procedure involves a thorough investigation of the two sets of records and ends only after all causes of the difference are uncovered. The process is completed by the preparation of a bank reconciliation statement. A **bank reconciliation statement** is a statement showing the causes for the difference between the bank balance as shown by the bank and the bank balance as shown in the general ledger of the depositor.

Steps in Preparing a Bank Reconciliation Statement

The steps in preparing a bank reconciliation statement are outlined below.

Step 1 Have the following records available:
   a. the bank statement and related data received from the bank;
   b. the bank reconciliation statement for the previous month;
   c. a printout of the general ledger Bank account. (*Note: Journals may be needed if the ledger account shows posted totals instead of each individual debit or credit affecting Bank.*)

Step 2 Write a proper heading, then divide the page down the middle. Write "Bank's Record" on one side, "Company's Record" on the other side.

Step 3 Enter the ending balance from the bank statement on the side of the page headed Bank's Record. Enter the ending balance from the general ledger Bank account on the side of the page headed Company's Record.

If you were doing a bank reconciliation for Boxwell and Company, your work at this stage would look like Figure 10.14 below. Notice that the bank thinks the business has $1,204.90 on March 31, while Boxwell and Company thinks it has $1,157.76.

FIGURE 10.14

Early stages of a bank reconciliation statement.

Boxwell and Company
Bank Reconciliation
March 31, 20–

Bank's Record		**Company's Record**	
Balance on statement	$ 1204.90	Balance in ledger	$ 1157.76

Step 4 Search for and identify all of the "discrepancy items"; that is, the items causing the two balances to differ. Finding these is the most difficult and the most important part of the reconciliation. It involves an item-by-item comparison of the bank's record with the business's records. Locating the discrepancy items involves a well-organized and skillful search. The discrepancy items for Boxwell and Company are described on page 401.

Step 5 Record the discrepancy items on the reconciliation statement, adding or subtracting them as necessary until the two balances are shown to be equal.

A cheque that is cashed by the bank is referred to as a cancelled cheque.

To list the discrepancy items for Boxwell and Company, we will start with the Bank's Record. The discrepancy items that occur most frequently are outstanding cheques. An **outstanding cheque** is a cheque that is issued and recorded by the company, but not yet cashed by the bank. Recall that when a cheque is issued by a business, it is recorded promptly in the books of the business. But it is not recorded in the records of the bank until it is presented to them for payment. In many cases, this may be after several days or even weeks have passed.

Another common discrepancy item is the late deposit. A **late deposit** is a deposit that is made and entered in the books of the business on the last day (usually) of the period covered by the bank statement, but which does not appear on the statement because of a processing delay at the bank.

The outstanding cheques and late deposit for Boxwell and Company are recorded as shown in Figure 10.15.

FIGURE 10.15

The partial bank reconciliation statement for Boxwell and Company after recording outstanding cheques and late deposits.

Boxwell and Company
Bank Reconciliation
March 31, 20–

Bank's Record			Company's Record	
Balance on statement		$ 1 204.90	Balance in ledger	$ 1 157.76
Deduct:				
Outstanding cheques				
#602	$ 60.00			
#705	72.40			
#709	51.90			
#710	200.00			
#711	2.75	387.05		
		$ 817.85		
Add:				
Late deposit		300.51		
Adjusted Balance		$ 1 118.36		

Each discrepancy item represents an increase or decrease to the bank's March 31 balance of $1 204.90. Common sense should tell you which it is. Just decide what effect the item has on the prior balance and add or subtract accordingly. For example, when an outstanding cheque finally arrives at the branch, the bank will pay it and reduce the bank balance. When the bank learns of the late deposit, it will increase the bank balance.

Notice the two totals for cash. They still do not agree ($ 1 118.36 ≠ 1 157.76). You must now record discrepancy items that affect the balance of cash in the ledger. Usually, these items are identified on the bank statement as debit memos or credit memos. Common debit memos are interest charges, service charges, and other authorized deductions from the business's account. Interest earned is a typical credit memo.

The discrepancy items affecting Boxwell and Company's ledger account balance of cash are shown in the Company's Record section of Figure 10.16.

The two balances of cash now agree. The true balance of cash on March 31, 20— is $1 118.36. As it turned out, neither the bank nor the company made mistakes when computing their bank balances. When the bank arrived at a total of $1 204.90 on March 31, it made entries unknown to the business (i.e., the two debit memos.) Similarly, when the business produced a March 31st total of $1 157.76, it made entries unknown to the bank (i.e., the cheque and deposit.) When the bank statement arrives at the business, all the "unknown" entries can be discovered and the two cash amounts reconciled.

Handling Errors

What if the typical discrepancy items are revealed and recorded, but the two cash totals still do not agree? For example, suppose the ledger side for Boxwell and Company showed a March 31st balance of $1,082.36. All else being the same, the reconciliation statement would look like Figure 10.17.

FIGURE 10.16

The completed reconciliation statement for Boxwell and Company.

Boxwell and Company
Bank Reconciliation
March 31, 20–

Bank's Record			**Company's Record**		
Balance on statement		$ 1 204.90	Balance in ledger		$ 1 157.76
Deduct:			*Deduct Debit memos:*		
Outstanding cheques			Interest Charges	$ 25.90	
#602	$ 60.00		Service Charges	13.50	39.40
#705	72.40				
#709	51.90				
#710	200.00				
#711	2.75	387.05			
		$ 817.85			
Add:					
Late deposit		300.51			
Adjusted Balance		$ 1 118.36	Adjusted Balance		$ 1 118.36

FIGURE 10.17

The reconciliation statement for Boxwell
and Company showing an error of $36.00.

Boxwell and Company
Bank Reconciliation
March 31, 20–

Bank's Record			**Company's Record**		
Balance on statement		$ 1 204.90	Balance in ledger		$ 1 121.76
Deduct:			*Deduct Debit memos:*		
Outstanding cheques			Interest Charges	$ 25.90	
#602	$ 60.00		Service Charges	13.50	39.40
#705	72.40				1 082.36
#709	51.90				
#710	200.00				
#711	2.75	387.05			
		$ 817.85			
Add:					
Late deposit		300.51			
		$ 1 118.36	Out of balance by $36.00		$ 1 082.36

There is a difference of $36.00 between the two balances of cash. Either the bank or
the business has made an error. To discover it, you need to examine how the discrepancy items in Figure 10.17 were discovered in the first place.

Identifying Discrepancy Items

A methodical approach for comparing bank and business records will reveal the discrepancy items described above and any errors that may exist. The following suggestions will be helpful to you in making such a comparison.

1. The bank records must be compared item by item with the business's records.
   When individual items are found to correspond exactly, mark them with a

coloured pen or pencil. These items are said to be cleared. **After this is done, the items with no marks beside them are the discrepancy items.**

2. When comparing the records, it is important to deal with items from the previous reconciliation statement. Most of those items will be cleared up during the current month. However, there are usually a few that do not get cleared up in the current month and must be carried forward to the new reconciliation statement. For example, consider a cheque that was outstanding on the reconciliation statement for February 28. This cheque would be outstanding as of March 31 if it was not cashed during the month of March. It would have to go on the reconciliation statement for March 31. On the other hand, if the cheque was cashed during the month of March, it would no longer be an outstanding cheque and would be marked off as being cleared.

3. If the two final totals on the reconciliation statement are not equal, **repeat the item-by-item comparisons**. This time, use a different coloured pen or a different checkmark to clear items. Be careful to examine dollar amounts precisely when clearing items.

Both the bank and the business can make errors when recording account entries. For example, a $520 cheque correctly written by the business may be entered as $52 by the bank. When preparing its bank reconciliation statement, a business would discover this error and contact the bank.

In the case of Boxwell and Company, suppose your item-by-item comparison revealed cheque #703 for the purchase of supplies was correctly written for $48. But when the accounting clerk did the journal entry, he mistakenly entered the amount as $84.

Errors can either increase or decrease the prior balance. You must think through each situation. For Boxwell and Company, the reconciliation statement would now look like the one shown in Figure 10.18.

FIGURE 10.18

A bank reconciliation statement with provision for an error.

Boxwell and Company
Bank Reconciliation
March 31, 20–

Bank's Record			**Company's Record**		
Balance on statement		$ 1 204.90	Balance in ledger		$ 1 121.76
Deduct:			*Deduct Debit memos:*		
Outstanding cheques			Interest Charges	$ 25.90	
#602	$ 60.00		Service Charges	13.50	39.40
#705	72.40				1 082.36
#709	51.90		*Add:*		
#710	200.00		Error in journalizing cheque		
#711	2.75	387.05	#703 for supplies. Was		
		$ 817.85	entered as $84. Should have		
Add:			been $48. Difference $36		36.00
Late deposit		300.51			
Adjusted Balance		$ 1 118.36	Adjusted Balance		$ 1 118.36

Bringing the Accounts Up to Date

By now, you can identify the main outcome of bank reconciliation. That is, the ledger account for Bank is brought up to date. (Bringing the Bank account up to date includes the correction of errors, should they exist.) Simply preparing the bank reconciliation statement, however, does not bring the Bank account up to date. If discrepancy items appear, the process is incomplete until journal entries are made.

Only the discrepancy items on the company's side of the reconciliation statement require journal entries. For the reconciliation statement in Figure 10.18 on page 402, the following two journal entries are necessary:

		DR	CR
Mar 31	Bank Service Charges	13.50	
	Interest Expense	25.90	
	Bank		39.40
	To record bank charges for March		
31	Bank	36.00	
	Supplies		36.00
	To correct error in journalizing cheque #703		

Special Considerations for Bank Reconciliation

Two types of cheques deserve special mention in a discussion of discrepancy items: certified cheques and NSF cheques. A **certified cheque** is one for which the bank takes the funds out of the issuer's account in advance. It puts these funds in a special account to honour the cheque when it is presented. A certified cheque is clearly marked as being certified. The person to whom the cheque is issued is guaranteed that the cheque has sufficient cash backing it.

When preparing a bank reconciliation statement, a certified cheque will not appear as a discrepancy item even if it is outstanding. (That is, it has been written but not cashed.) Both the bank and the business know about the certified cheque before it is cashed, and both have deducted it from their cash balances.

In section 10.1 you learned what an NSF cheque is. NSF cheques demand attention when reconciling a bank account. For example, when a credit customer pays with a cheque, the business deposits it and makes a journal entry similar to the following:

		DR	CR
May 5	Bank	150.00	
	A/R—Roy Walters		150.00

If the cheque is returned as NSF, it is worthless and the bank deducts the amount of the cheque from the business's account. If this happens near the end of the month, the amount will appear as a discrepancy item. This forces the business to make a journal entry opposite to the one recorded when the cheque was first deposited:

		DR	CR
May 31	A/R—Roy Walters	150.00	
	Bank		150.00

The business now informs Mr. Walters that he once again owes the business $150. Additional amounts may be applied against his account to cover the extra costs the bank may have charged the business for processing the NSF cheque.

Personal Bank Reconciliation

Individuals, as well as businesses, should reconcile their bank accounts regularly. Neither a person nor a business can be certain of the accuracy of bank records unless they are reconciled. A reconciliation for a personal account is simpler than

To view a step-by-step demonstration for preparing a bank reconciliation statement, visit www.pearsoned.ca/accounting1

one for a business. Usually, there are fewer transactions, and only the one personal record (the personal record book) to compare with the bank statement. Still, it is a task requiring care and perseverance.

Section 10.4   Review Questions

1. Define "internal control."
2. Why is internal control unnecessary for a one-person business?
3. When does internal control become necessary?
4. Describe what is meant by "separation of duties" with respect to internal control.
5. What is the purpose of having an independent audit?
6. Why should responsibilities be firmly established?
7. Why is cash control extremely important?
8. Explain what is meant by the phrase "depositing funds intact."
9. What is a bank reconciliation?
10. Why is a bank reconciliation necessary?
11. What is a discrepancy item?
12. What is an outstanding cheque?
13. What is a late deposit?
14. What does it mean to bring the accounts up to date, with respect to a bank reconciliation?
15. In Figure 10.18 on page 402, cheque 602 seems to be an outstanding cheque that appeared on a previous reconciliation statement. What indications are there in Figure 10.18 that would lead one to this conclusion?

Section 10.4   Exercises

1. **Analyze the following mini-cases and prepare a brief written evaluation of each. Consider the following questions to help prepare your evaluations.**

   Is there dishonesty or theft?
   Is there income tax evasion?
   Are there poor hiring practices?
   Who benefits? the owner? the employee?
   Who loses? the owner? the public?
   Are there weaknesses in internal control?
   Are there strengths in internal control?
   What steps could be taken to improve the system?

   A. The Doggie Salon is a very small family operation in the business of washing and grooming dogs. The work is done for cash and the money is collected when the dog is picked up. There is no paper work. The owner pockets the cash.
   B. Andy Tran is negotiating with a contractor to have his driveway paved. After a price is unofficially agreed upon, Andy tells the contractor that the job is hers if she is willing to take cash under the table at a 15 per cent discount. The contractor agrees because she needs the work.
   C. Kladis Gozzard drives a delivery van for Excel Electrical Supply. She is allowed to take the van home at night so that she can make deliveries on her way to and from work. Kladis usually manages to slip some materials for her-

self into the van. She drops these off at her home, where she either uses them herself or sells them to others.

D. Sasha Gerdes has a position of authority with the Exact Company. She arranges for a major repair to be performed on her home and for the repair bill to be sent to her employer. Sasha intercepts the bill when it arrives, approves it for payment, and has it processed through the company.

E. Kashif Rasheed has a responsible position with Apex Company. He arranges with a supplier of goods to the company to charge a higher than normal price for them. Kashif later approves these inflated bills for payment. Kashif receives a percentage of the total bill in cash from the supplier.

F. Wellington Sand and Gravel is engaged by Crown Road Builders to deliver loads of stone to the site of a road building project. The stone costs $1 000 a load. Jim Cox, supervisor at the site, signs for each load as it is received. The signed slips form the basis for the invoice sent by Wellington Sand and Gravel to Crown Road Builders. Jim Cox has a friend who is building a house not far from the job site. The house needs a lot of stone for the large driveway, basement, and garage. Jim diverts a number of loads from the job site to the home of his friend, and signs for them as if they had been delivered to the project. Jim is rewarded by his friend for the favour.

G. Valley Ridge is a ski resort with an extensive network of cross-country ski trails. The fee for cross-country skiing is $15 per day, paid at the main chalet. Many people do not bother to pay for the cross-country skiing but merely drive to remote sections of the course and enter and exit freely.

H. A friend of yours works as a waitress in a local restaurant. One evening, you are dining at the restaurant at a time when your friend is on duty. You suggest to her that it would be nice if you could have a free dinner. Your friend replies that she would surely be caught.

I. Geoff Lake is the accounts receivable clerk for a large company. On many occasions, customers come personally to the company to pay their accounts in cash. Geoff, who is often short of money, keeps the cash for his own use with the intention of paying it back later. He is far behind in paying back the money.

J. Stephanie Chabot is a roofing contractor. She has a hired crew that does all of the roofing. Stephanie makes the contacts and does the estimating. She never loses any materials. Her workers find it impossible to work for anyone else without Stephanie's knowledge.

K. Armin and Ashley own a butcher shop and grocery store. Whenever they need food for their family, they just take it home out of the store. There is no bookkeeping involved.

L. Andre Tremblay is a carpenter. He is building a new bathroom in his home and requires some plumbing work. Andrew Carmichael is a plumber. He is building an addition onto his house and needs some carpentry work. The two men agree to exchange services free of charge.

---

2. The personal chequing account record and the bank statement for the account of Paul Swartz for the month of June are shown on page 406. Paul Swartz's bank reconciliation statement for May is also shown.

a. From these records, using the form in the Workbook, reconcile the bank account of Paul Swartz as of June 30.

b. State what entry or entries are necessary to bring the personal record to the true bank balance.

A. Paul Swartz's previous reconciliation.

Paul Swartz
Bank Reconciliation
May 31, 20–

Personal Record		Bank Statement		
Latest balance	1 200.75	Latest balance		1 450.75
		Deduct:		
		Outstanding cheques		
		#44	100–	
		#45	150–	250–
True balance	1 200.75	True balance		1 200.75

B. Paul Swartz's personal record.

CHEQUE NO.	DATE	CHEQUE ISSUED TO	AMOUNT OF CHEQUE		√	AMOUNT OF DEPOSIT		BALANCE FORWARD 1 200 75	
46	20– Jun. 2	Rowlands Garage	237	50				963	25
47	4	Joanne's Clothes	92	50				870	75
48	9	Provincial Treasurer	9	–				861	75
49	15	Rockway Gardens	7	73				854	02
50	20	The Examiner	5	50				848	52
51	20	Daily Times	6	30				842	22
	27	Salary				1740	–	2582	22
52	30	Marigold Apartments	875	–				1707	22

C. Bank statement sent to Paul Swartz.

GENERAL BANK

STATEMENT OF ACCOUNT WITH   PAUL SWARTZ

CHEQUES		DEPOSITS	DATE		BALANCE
Balance forward			May	31	1 450.75
100.00			June	1	1 350.75
150.00			June	4	1 200.75
237.50			June	9	963.25
92.50	9.00		June	16	861.75
7.73			June	20	854.02
		1 740.00	June	27	2 594.02
5.50			June	30	2 588.52
S.C. 1.75			June	30	2 586.77
S.C Service Charge					

3. **Answer the following questions about J.C. Waters's bank reconciliation statement as shown below.**

J.C. WATERS
BANK RECONCILIATION STATEMENT
MARCH 31, 19—

Balance per bank statement		$2 046.75
Add late deposit, March 31		271.50
		$2 318.25
Less outstanding cheques		
#418	$ 62.80	
#522	103.40	
#523	41.90	208.10
True balance		$2 110.15
Balance per Cash account		$2 186.85
Less bank charges	$ 5.40	
NSF cheque — Walker	71.30	76.70
True balance		$2 110.15

a. Does the $2 046.75 represent the bank balance at the beginning or at the end of the month?

b. Why do you think the March 31 deposit was not included in the bank balance?

c. How does Waters know that there are three cheques outstanding? Why are they subtracted?

d. Is $2 186.85 the cash balance at the beginning or at the end of the month?

e. What is an NSF cheque? Why is it subtracted from the balance per books?

f. A certified cheque for $200 payable to R. Smit is still outstanding. Why is it not part of the outstanding cheques on the bank reconciliation statement?

4. **From the following records, prepare the bank reconciliation statement for the current bank account of Wagner and Wagner as of April 30, 20—. Record all the necessary journal entries. Forms are in your workbook.**

Wagner and Wagner
Bank Reconciliation
March 31, 20–

Bank's Record			Company's Record		
Balance on statement		$943.80	Balance in ledger		$367.08
Deduct:			Deduct Debit memos:		
Outstanding cheques			Interest Charges	$50.00	
#1431	$ 54.25		Service Charges	12.00	62.00
#1433	138.60				
#1435	56.53				
#1437	195.82				
#1439	270.30				
#1440	141.72	857.22			
		$ 86.58			
Add:					
Bank Error	2.00				
Late Deposit	216.50	218.50			
		$305.08			$305.08

Ledger Account

Bank   #1010

Date		Particulars	Dr	Cr	Balance
20–					
March	31				367.08
April	1	deposit	410.00		777.08
	1	#1441		431.02	346.06
	1	Interest Charges		50.00	296.06
	1	Service Charges		12.00	284.06
	4	deposit	216.50		500.56
	4	#1442		61.21	439.35
	8	deposit	658.20		1,097.55
	10	#1443		423.39	674.16
	10	deposit	171.41		845.57
	15	#1444		118.30	727.27
	20	#1445		380.53	346.74
	27	#1446		82.85	263.89
	30	deposit	94.00		357.89

April Bank Statement

DESCRIPTION	DEBITS	CREDITS	DATE		BALANCE
BALANCE FORWARD			MAR	31	943.80
DEPOSIT		216.50	APR	1	1,160.30
DEPOSIT		410.00		1	1,570.30
#1431	54.25			2	1,516.05
#1441	431.02			2	1,085.03
CM ENCODING ERROR		2.00		2	1,087.03
#1437	195.82			3	891.21
DEPOSIT		216.50		4	1,107.71
#1433	138.60			5	969.11
DEPOSIT		658.20		8	1,627.31
DM NSF CHEQUE	250.00			9	1,377.31
DEPOSIT		171.41		10	1,548.72
#1444	118.30			20	1,430.42
#1439	270.30			21	1,160.12
#1440	141.72			23	1,018.40
#1443	423.39			27	595.01
DM LOAN INTEREST	36.00			30	559.01
DM SERVICE CHANGE	5.60			30	553.41

10.5 | Using Computers for Bank Reconciliation

Completing the important process of bank reconciliation seems to be straightforward. In reality, it can be a time-consuming task. Consider a large business that writes hundreds of cheques per month and makes numerous deposits. Getting the bank's balance of cash to agree with the ledger's is demanding, especially if the accounting clerk makes errors identifying discrepancy items.

Computers can make the demands of bank reconciliation easier, but the steps required are essentially the same as the ones you used when you reconciled accounts in the previous section. To get an idea of the similarities between the methods, examine Figure 10.19 on page 410, which shows an account reconciliation for Simply Accounting.

The account being reconciled in Figure 10.19 is #1010 Bank. The accounting clerk took the first step in the reconciliation process by entering one number—an "End Balance" of $44 582.89. This refers to the final balance on the May 31st bank statement. Simply Accounting reproduces the ledger details for the Bank account and shows them in the first six columns. The software can now compare the bank statement balance with the ledger account balance.

You will have an opportunity to use Simply Accounting for bank reconciliation if you do the summary exercise "Sunshell Designs".

Each time the accounting clerk identifies an item that appears on both the statement from the bank and in the six columns that show ledger account data, he clicks the "C" column. Simply Accounting then changes the status of the item to "Cleared." If the clerk works systematically, the "unresolved" balance will approach zero. In this case, you can see the attempt at reconciliation is still out by $244.60. The clerk will click the circle beside the word "Expense." When he enters the amount for service charges and loan interest, the unresolved amount will be zero.

FIGURE 10.19

A bank reconciliation
window in Simply
Accounting.

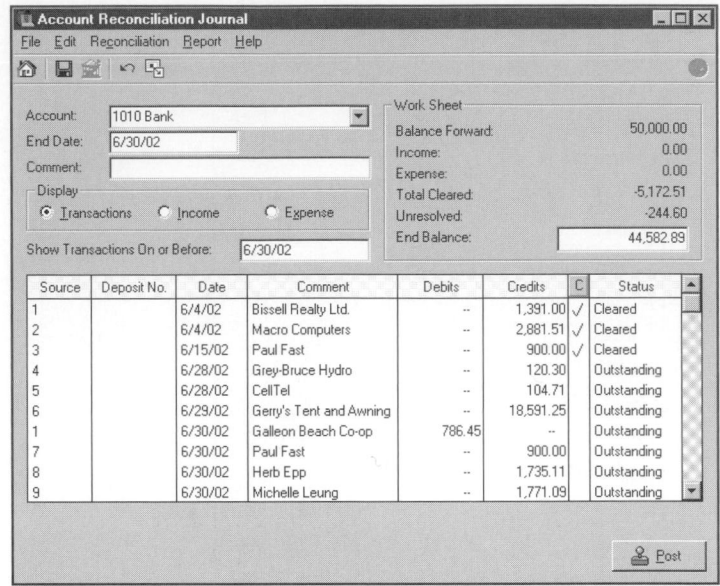

Using accounting software to reconcile the Bank account proceeds quickly. No calculations are necessary because all numerical tasks are left to the computer. When the unresolved balance is zero, Simply Accounting even prompts the clerk to bring the account up to date. The software then helps the clerk journalize and post the proper amounts.

With the increase in popularity of online banking, accounting software goes even further in speeding bank reconciliation. Now, discrepancy items can be identified electronically. Figure 10.20 shows an online bank statement. The account holder is about to click the download button. This action will save the bank statement data in a format that Simply Accounting uses to identify discrepancy items. The clerk no longer needs to search the bank statement and Bank account in the ledger item by item.

FIGURE 10.20

Downloading a bank
statement from an
online bank.

Online banks download
statement data in for-
mats other than Simply
Accounting, including formats that can be used by
spreadsheet software.

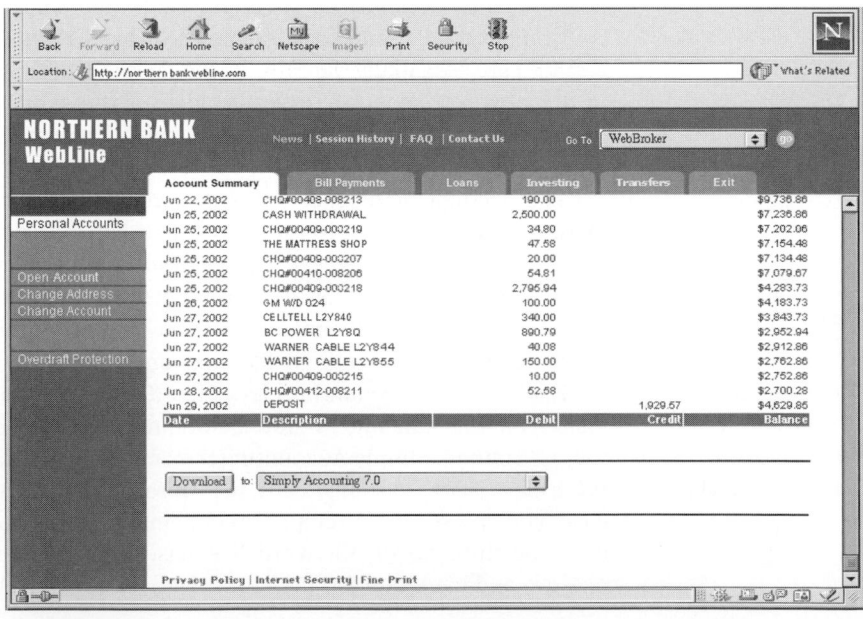

Section 10.5   Review Questions

1. When using Simply Accounting for bank reconciliation, what does marking an item as "cleared" mean?
2. What must the accounting clerk do once the unresolved balance reaches zero?
3. What significant advantage does online banking have for the bank reconciliation process?

Section 10.5   Exercises

1. **Load the spreadsheet model named reconcile.xls into your computer. Information in this model is for Proctor and Kemp, which is shown in Exercise 2 on page 414. The raw data are arranged in side-by-side sections. The sections contain the following:**

   a) data downloaded from the company's online bank;
   b) the outstanding cheques from the previous month's reconciliation statement;
   c) the company's ledger account data, exported from Simply Accounting.

   ### Required
   1. In the side-by-side data sections, delete the amounts that appear in both the bank's records and the company records. (This is similar to marking them as cleared.)
   2. Copy the amounts that remain and paste them into the bank reconciliation model for Proctor and Kemp. This model appears beside and below the data sections.

Communicate It

You are employed by Boxwell and Company. After working with your bank reconciliation spreadsheet model for some time, you are unable to get the May 31 statement balanced. Finally, after examining the returned cheques, you find that bank personnel have made an encoding error. They mistakenly entered cheque #751 for $31.09 as $31.90. Prepare a business letter dated June 4 to inform them of their error and to outline the action you want taken. Use the business letter format found in the Skills Appendix.

CHAPTER 10 Summary

CHAPTER HIGHLIGHTS

Now that you have completed Chapter 10, you should:

- be able to identify the advantages and disadvantages of the various methods of payment in Canada;
- be able to compare trends in cheque, credit card, and debit card use;
- appreciate the role of technology in Canada's payment systems;
- be able to prove the cash and prepare the bank deposit;
- be able to account for cash shortages or overages;
- know the features of a current bank account;
- know the purpose of a petty cash fund;
- know how to establish, operate, and replenish a petty cash fund;
- know the accounting entries for establishing and for replenishing a petty cash fund;
- understand the need for accounting controls over expenditures;
- understand the meaning of internal control;
- know the specific control features associated with cash;
- be able to reconcile a bank statement for a business or an individual;
- be able to perform the accounting entries that result from a bank reconciliation;
- understand how accounting software makes bank reconciliation easier

ACCOUNTING TERMS

bank reconciliation	NSF cheque
bank reconciliation statement	outstanding cheque
cash proof	payment system
cash short or over	petty cash fund
change fund	petty cash voucher
current bank account	point-of-sale terminal
float	purchase order
imprest method for petty cash	replenishing petty cash
internal control	restrictive endorsement
late deposit	

CHAPTER 10 Review Exercises

Using Your Knowledge

1 You keep the petty cash fund for Graphic Art Supplies. Since the fund is very low, you are in the process of preparing the petty cash summary to be used to obtain a cheque to replenish the fund.

A listing of the vouchers in the petty cash box, giving a description of the nature of the payment for each appears below. Below right is the chart of accounts for Graphic Art Supplies.

Prepare the petty cash summary for the purpose of obtaining the replenishing cheque.

Petty Cash Vouchers	Amount	GST	Total	Chart of Accounts
1. Gas receipt	$39.00	$2.73	$41.73	101 Bank
2. Paint for building	13.50	.95	14.45	105 Accounts Receivable
3. New broom for janitor	12.75	.89	13.64	110 Merchandise Inventory
4. Printer Cartridge	32.87	2.30	35.17	115 Supplies
5. Supper money for employee	7.50	.53	8.03	120 Equipment
6. Postage stamps	15.00	1.05	16.05	125 Automobile
7. New window pane	20.00	1.40	21.40	201 Bank Loan
8. Fax charge	10.50	.74	11.24	205 Accounts Payable
9. Payment to student for cleaning up the grounds	10.50	—	10.50	305 Judi Mavar, Capital
10. Mileage to employee for using personal car for business	17.50	—	17.50	310 Judi Mavar, Drawings / 405 Sales
11. Coffee and doughnuts brought in for a business meeting	24.35	1.70	26.05	505 Purchases
12. Parking receipt of owner	7.00	.49	7.49	510 Freight-in
13. Supper money for employee	7.50	—	7.50	515 Advertising
14. Postage for parcel delivery	15.00	1.05	16.05	520 Bank Charges
				525 Building Maintenance
				530 Car Expense
				535 Delivery Expense
				540 Donations Expense
				545 Light and Heat Expense
				550 Miscellaneous Expense
				555 Telephone Expense
				560 Wages Expense

2 Shown below and on pages 415 and 416 are all of the records that you will need to reconcile the current bank account of Proctor & Kemp at July 31, 20—.

A. Bank reconciliation statement for the previous month's end, shown below.

Proctor & Kemp					
Bank Reconciliation Statement					
June 30, 20 –					
Balance per bank statement	1 40 6 03	Balance per general ledger			7 7 3 28
Add late deposit	5 5 1 00	Deduct bank charge not entered in books of company			
	1 95 7 03				
Deduct outstanding cheques		(1) Service charge	16.50		
# 083	5.10	(2) Loan interest	33.50		5 0 00
780	71.03				
828	400.00				
846	96.02				
852	123.50				
860	15.00				
871	16.01				
873	17.50				
881	33.60				
886	121.47				
889	60.00				
890	170.00				
891	31.94				
892	27.61				
894	13.82				
898	12.50				
899	18.65	1 23 3 75			
Adjusted balance	7 23 28	Adjusted balance			7 23 28

B. A listing of cash receipts for July.

$ 262.75
312.70
274.19
161.40
700.20
265.92
400.61
396.21
316.40
$3 090.38

C. July general journal entry affecting "Bank."

	DR	CR
Bank	$5.10	
Miscellaneous Income		$5.10
To cancel outstanding cheque		
No. 083, issued June 20—		

D. A listing of cash payments for July.

Explanation	Chq. No.	Bank Credit
	900	$ 100.00
	901	171.31
	902	142.19
Loan interest, June		33.50
Service charge, June		16.50
	903	16.41
	904	17.50
	905	10.00
	906	12.40
	907	19.61
	908	31.40
	909	76.39
	910	65.20
	911	500.00
	912	216.75
	914	8.21
	915	2.60
	916	9.40
	917	50.00
	918	50.00
	919	33.19
	920	29.33
	921	65.00
	922	25.00
	923	25.00
	924	419.63
	925	372.60
	926	900.00
		$3 419.12

E. Partial general ledger Bank account.

BANK							No. 101
Date		Particulars	P.R.	Debit	Credit	Balance	DR CR
20– June 30 July 31 31 31		Total cash receipts Total cash payments	CR14 CP18 J9	3090.38 5.10	3419.12	773.28 449.64	DR DR

F. July bank statement.

(Note: Normally, the bank returns all of the "paid" (cancelled) cheques to the business along with the bank statement. This cannot be done in a textbook. Instead, on the bank statement in parentheses beside each amount in the Cheques column is either an explanation of the charge or the cheque number.)

Cheques				Deposits	Date	Balance
					June 30	1 406.03
18.65	(899)	31.94	(891)	551.00	July 2	1 906.44
121.47	(886)				3	1 784.97
100.00	(900)	96.02	(846)	262.75	5	1 851.70
12.50	(898)				5	1 839.20
71.03	(780)	27.61	(892)		6	1 740.56
142.19	(902)				6	1 598.37
400.00	(828)			312.70	8	1 511.07
15.00	(860)	13.82	(894)		9	1 482.25
16.01	(871)	171.31	(901)		10	1 294.93
17.50	(904)				10	1 277.43
10.00	(905)			274.19	11	1 541.62
500.00	(911)				12	1 041.62
33.60	(NSF cheque of R.C. Jones)			161.40	15	1 169.42
50.00	(913)				16	1 119.42
170.00	(890)	12.40	(906)		17	937.02
76.39	(909)				19	860.63
31.40	(908)			700.20	22	1 529.43
9.40	(916)	19.61	(907)		23	1 500.42
2.60	(915)				23	1 497.82
				265.92	25	1 763.74
33.19	(919)			400.61	26	2 131.16
17.50	(873)				27	2 113.66
50.00	(917)			396.21	30	2 459.87
25.00	(922)	419.63	(924)		31	2 015.24
165.00	(VISA discount fee)				31	1 850.24
29.00	(Interest on loan)				31	1 821.24
12.60	(Service charge)				31	1 808.64

Reconcile the bank account and make the necessary accounting entries in the books of the company. Cheque no. 913 is for supplies. You will find forms in the Workbook.

3 **Workbook Exercise: Additional bank reconciliation exercise.**

Cases for Further Thought

Briefly answer the following questions.

1. For emergency use only, you acquired a card that permits you to use the automatic tellers for your bank. You have never had to use the service until now, when you find yourself out of town and without money. However, you cannot remember your personal identification number, which is necessary to operate the machines. When seeking help from a nearby bank branch, you are told that there is no way for them to help you get your number. Comment on this predicament.

2. PQ Company has a petty cash fund, but it is not under any one employee's control. Why is this undesirable?

3. The auditor of a company, when checking the petty cash fund, finds a number of employees' i.o.u.'s in the fund. However, the fund totals correctly with the i.o.u.'s included. What course of action should the auditor take?

4. You control the petty cash fund for a company. An employee presents you with a legitimate bill to be paid from the fund, but there is not enough cash in the fund to pay it. What will you do?

5. You accepted a cheque for a debt from a friend because you knew with certainty that sufficient funds were in the bank to cover it. However, there were not sufficient funds in the account when you presented the cheque for payment five days later. How could this be possible?

6. You are about to write a cheque for $4 500 to pay for a new computer. While you are waiting, another customer pays for an identical purchase with a bank credit card. You know that the merchant will receive only about $4 365 for the credit card sale because of the amount the business is charged by the credit card company. You offer the merchant a cheque for $4 365. Will the merchant accept your offer? Comment on this.

7. Bill Wallingford, a local business person, neither rolls coins nor arranges currency by denomination when he is making up his daily deposit. Assuming that the bank accepts Bill's deposit in this state, what effect will Bill's behaviour have on the bank teller and the people in the line-up behind him?

Case Studies

CASE 1

Cola Profits Go Flat

Recent college graduate Kris Falusi was extremely pleased with his recent career choice as a management trainee with a large movie theatre chain called Showtime Cinemas Incorporated. His first assignment was to investigate the quickly shrinking profit margins of the snack bar at the local Showtime theatre.

The manager suspected that the profits from soft drink and popcorn sales were declining rapidly. Yet he observed just as many people ordering large colas and jumbo containers of popcorn as always. He urged Kris to investigate this problem immediately with the goal of restoring profits to their previous level.

Kris started by interviewing the snack bar employees. Within days, he discovered the cause of the shrinking profits. He uncovered a scheme so effective that it allowed three part-time snack bar employees to steal as much as $60 per evening and still balance their cash register.

Impossible? No. Here's how the scheme worked:

In order to verify the cash register sales figures for soft drinks and popcorn, the manager of the snack bar routinely matched the number of drink and popcorn containers used with the amount of cash on hand. For instance, if 100 popcorn containers were used during a shift and each large order of popcorn sells for $3.00, the cash register should contain $300 in cash under the heading "Popcorn."

The dishonest employees simply reused discarded containers retrieved from the theatre aisles during intermission. These containers were refilled and resold, allowing employees to bypass the cash register and keep the sales revenue for themselves while still balancing cash register totals with the number of new cups used.

Kris discovered that some employees stole as much as several hundred dollars per month using this method.

Questions

1. Prepare a list of cash controls Kris could use to prevent such theft in the future.
2. What action should Kris take against the dishonest employees? Why?
3. Cash control experts believe not only that effective cash controls must be used, but also that employees must see them being used. Explain this statement.

CASE 2

Service Charges: Are They Always Fair?

Sarah Leung and her husband Irwin have two bank accounts: a savings account and a chequing account. Each of the two accounts is a joint account, meaning that either of the partners can independently use the accounts in all respects.

The two partners keep a personal record of each account and do attempt to keep them up to date. However, it is not always easy to do this, particularly with the chequing account, which gets a lot of use. Both partners cannot have the personal register at the same time, which would let them make the appropriate updating entries. Still, each one often needs to write a cheque at a time when the other partner has the register. When this happens, the one without the register tries to remember to make a note of the cheque or cheques written. These notes are supposed to bring the register up to date as quickly as possible.

In theory this sounds simple enough, but it does not always work in practice. During one particular Christmas rush, neither Sarah nor Irwin took the register at a time when both were writing lots of cheques. And because they were either tired or busy or distracted, they failed to update the register for several days. Each assumed that there was plenty of money in the account.

However, on this occasion, the balance in the chequing account was overspent and the account was overdrawn. This means that the balance in the account became a minus balance. In effect, this is a bank loan. In such a case, the bank takes action to cover the overdraft. It looks to see if there are any funds available in other accounts owned by the same depositor. If there are, it transfers sufficient funds to cover the overdraft, allowing the cheque to be honoured. The Leungs had a healthy balance in their savings account and the transfer was made. The bank charged $3.50 for the service.

Unfortunately, in this case, the Leungs had written several cheques and each one put the account into a new overdraft position. Each time, the bank followed the same procedure, including the $3.50 service charge. Since there were 14 such cheques, the total charge was $49.00.

The Leungs did not learn of the overdraft situation until they received their bank statement in the mail. When they saw what had happened, they were annoyed.

Questions

1. In your opinion, why were the Leungs annoyed?
2. In your opinion, were the Leungs justified in being annoyed? Explain.
3. Why do you think the bank acted in the manner it did?
4. What can the Leungs do to ensure that their personal register is kept up to date in the future? Explain.
5. Are there other means for the Leungs to pay for their purchases that might prevent this situation from occurring? Explain.

CASE 3

Challenge

Trials of a Young Entrepreneur

Garn Mennell, a student, started up a summer business as a small contractor. Garn was regarded as being "handy with tools" and was proficient at building decks and garages and re-roofing houses.

The funds with which to start his business came from the following sources: a recent inheritance of $5 000, a low-interest loan of $10 000 from his brother, and a $3 000 non-interest-bearing loan from a chartered bank (part of a government program to help youth employment). With these funds, Garn purchased a used truck for $7 000, ladders and equipment for $1 000, and other tools for $500. The remaining funds were placed in a business bank account.

Garn was quite good at attending to the numerous details associated with starting up a new business. As well, he did a thorough job of looking after the banking records and of obtaining and filing vouchers for all expenditures. He also designed first-rate estimating sheets and contracts to help him in pricing and ensuring a solid legal base for each job. However, Garn had absolutely no knowledge of accounting, and he completely neglected this aspect of running the business.

During the first season of business, Garn was able to get a number of jobs, but not enough to keep him busy all of the time. He bought construction materials on credit and was able to pay his trade debts when they became due. At the end of the season, he had no trade debts, had repaid the bank loan, and had paid back one-half of the principal (but no interest) on the loan from his brother. He was satisfied that things were going well. He had lots of spending money, was enjoying himself thoroughly, and had a truck to drive around in. As well, he took pleasure in owning his own business and could hold his head high among his friends.

The second season was much the same as the first except that jobs were fewer. Although Garn's work was of good quality, he was not very good at acquiring new business. He felt awkward about knocking on doors looking for work and relied on newspaper advertisements and the Yellow Pages. As a consequence, Garn had fewer contracts and was able to enjoy more free time along with his status as a businessman. Toward the end of the season, however, he began to suspect that all was not well. He was beginning to experience difficulty in paying his trade bills on time, and this made him uneasy. At the end of the season, he was concerned enough to ask the help of a family friend who was an accountant. The first suggestion he received was to make a list of the assets and liabilities of the business, which he did. The list showed the following:

Assets		Liabilities	
Bank balance	$150	Bank loan	$2 000
Truck (market value)	5 500	Loan from brother	5 000
Total	$5 650	Two years' interest	950
		Trade debts	2 000
		Total	$9 950

For two seasons, Garn had been confident that he was operating a profitable business. He was absolutely certain that he had made a profit on every job. But now he was shaken by the picture presented by the list of assets and liabilities.

Questions

1. How much cash did Garn have in the bank to begin with, after purchasing the major assets?
2. What is Garn's present equity figure?
3. Is it possible to determine Garn's profit or loss? Explain.
4. Is it possible to determine how much money Garn withdrew for personal use? Explain.
5. How could the above situation develop without Garn's being aware of it?
6. Outline briefly the reasons for Garn's predicament.
7. What is meant by "spending capital"?
8. What is the best course of action for Garn to take now?

CASE 4

Group Discussion

The Good Life on Plastic Money

Pol and Andrea Rossetti grew up during the age of credit cards. It is not surprising, then, that they have lots of them. Pol, in particular, likes to show off his wallet full of credit cards. They include Sears, The Bay, Canadian Tire, TD/Canada Trust Visa, Citibank MasterCard, Esso, Petro Canada, American Express, Royal Bank Visa, CIBC Aerogold Visa, and Diners Club.

Pol and Andrea saw no reason to worry about using credit cards. They were both university graduates with high-paying jobs and lots of common sense and ability. But they also liked the good life and denied themselves very little. They bought an expensive house with fine furnishings. They ate out two or three times a week. They loved to travel and took at least one overseas vacation a year.

When they were in their twenties and living in an apartment, their lifestyle was easy to maintain. They found no difficulty in making payments on time and avoided any interest charges.

When they were in their thirties (with two children) and living in their nice home, their use of credit cards changed. They seemed to lose sight of the "account balance" amount and could see only the figure for the "minimum payment required." In most cases, this was the amount that they paid.

Now, Pol and Andrea are in their forties. To their surprise, they often have difficulty paying even the minimum. Several times now, they have received letters from creditors requesting them to reduce the balance of their account. Without really understanding it all, Pol and Andrea have realized that they are in a financial hole and need help. For assistance, they turn to the Metropolitan Credit Counselling Service.

Questions

1. Explain the chain of circumstances that led up to the situation in which Pol and Andrea find themselves.
2. In your opinion, how common is Pol's and Andrea's situation? Explain.
3. When credit limits are established in order to keep spending within reason, how can a situation like Pol's and Andea's develop?
4. What will the advice of the credit counselling service probably be? Explain fully.
5. Will Pol and Andrea be able to continue their lifestyle?

Career

Janice Fukakusa / Executive Vice President, Personal & Commercial Banking, Royal Bank

Although Janice Fukakusa earned a BA degree in political science from the University of Toronto in 1976, she soon realized that she would need more than that to progress in the business career that she desired. After completing her MBA (Master of Business Administration) at night school, she obtained her CA (Chartered Accountant) designation while working for Price Waterhouse, a large accounting firm.

Another of the designations she earned while working at Price Waterhouse was that of Chartered Business Valuator (CBV). The chartered business valuator evaluates businesses for purchase or sale. "In addition, the CBV course teaches you to do financial planning for a company," Janice explains, "that is, to determine how, when, where, and why a company should borrow or spend money." The objective is to ensure as profitable a future as possible for the company.

It is interesting to compare the work of the valuator with that of the auditor. Whereas the valuator looks at what the company should do with its money in the future, the auditor checks back on how, where, when, and why a company spent its money in the recent past.

Janice joined the Royal Bank in 1985, where she has held various positions in corporate banking, account management, corporate finance, treasury, strategic development, and corporate functions. One interesting project was the financial restructuring and computerization of the Royal Bank's British operations, for which she travelled to London, England. "Before automation, it took five days to integrate information; with the automated general ledger, we can integrate financial reports much more quickly," she says proudly.

In 1999, Janice was appointed executive vice-president of Personal & Commercial Banking. In this area, Janice is responsible for specialized services including: commercial markets, special loans, specialized financial products, and private equity.

Prior to moving to her current department, Janice was working in corporate finance. This meant that, among other duties, she gave advice to large-size business clients. These large businesses sometimes raise funds for their projects by issuing stocks and bonds for investors to buy.

Janice recommends to students that they try to get summer jobs in offices, particularly in accounting-related areas like bookkeeping.

How should a student who is interested in a career in banking proceed? "It's a definite competitive advantage if a job applicant already has confidence and experience in dealing with people and numbers." She also suggests that the student who wants to aim high in banking should obtain a chartered accountancy designation first. "In fact, we are now looking for CA's when we are hiring. The MBA [Master of Business Administration], although a valuable degree for some banking purposes, doesn't give the depth of accounting training that is necessary in today's complex banking world."

Janice emphasizes that banks offer a steady and rewarding career path to those who obtain the right credentials and have a desire to achieve.

Discussion

1. What does a chartered business valuator (CBV) do?
2. What two types of confidence and experience does Janice Fukakusa think the student who is interested in a career in banking should have? Why do you think that she considers them important?
3. What additional degree does Janice think that the ambitious student should attain? Why?

Research and Writing Question

4. In the profile, you were told that large businesses raise funds by issuing stocks and bonds. Find out what corporate stocks and corporate bonds are. Write a short report of a couple of paragraphs describing what corporate stocks are, what corporate bonds are, and what some of the basic differences between the two are. Use the memo report form that you will find in the Skills Appendix.

Accounting for a Merchandising Business

So far, we have studied only service businesses. These are the businesses that sell services rather than goods. Now, however, you are ready to study accounting for the merchandising business. A **merchandising business** is a business that buys goods and sells them at a profit.

There are different categories of merchandising business. A **wholesaler** is a merchandising business that buys goods from manufacturers and sells to retailers. A **retailer** is a merchandising business that buys goods from wholesalers and manufacturers and sells to the public.

11.1 Merchandise Inventory

Businesses that buy goods for the purpose of selling them at a profit are dealing in merchandise. The quantity of merchandise on hand is known as **merchandise inventory** or stock-in-trade.

The type of merchandise included in inventory varies from business to business. For instance, the merchandise inventory of a lumber company consists of various types and sizes of wood products. The merchandise inventory of a food retailer consists of a variety of food commodities. The merchandise inventory of an automobile dealer consists of new and used cars as well as replacement parts.

Supplies are bought in order to be used in a business. Merchandise is bought in order to be sold.

423

Two Aspects of Merchandise Inventory

Figure 11.1 below shows the two aspects of merchandise inventory—goods sold and goods not sold. Assume that a business had goods worth $120 000 available for sale during a fiscal period, and that goods worth $25 000 were still on hand (unsold) at the end of the period.

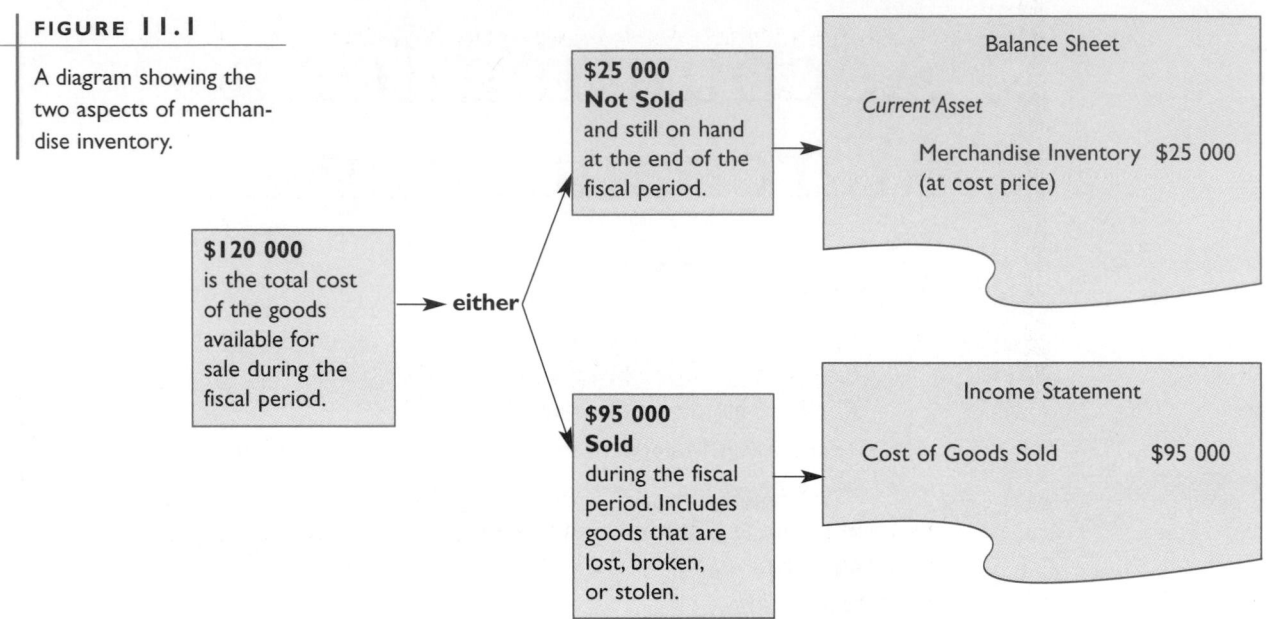

Periodic Inventory System

Over the years, accounting for inventory has been done most commonly by the periodic system. It has been the popular choice because it is inexpensive. The **periodic inventory system** is one in which the cost of the inventory sold is determined only at the end of each fiscal period. This usually means once a year. Businesses that use this method do not keep up-to-date inventory records nor do they calculate the cost of goods sold between statement dates.

Another system, the perpetual inventory system (described in Section 11.5), has become more common in recent years because of the increased use of computers in business.

The Inventory Cycle

Merchandise is generally sold fairly quickly in a successful business. The business has to renew its stock regularly in order to have sufficient quantities on hand. Merchandise moves in and out of the business in a regular pattern, as shown in the following steps.

1. There is inventory at the beginning of the accounting period.
2. Merchandise is sold and moves out more or less continually during the accounting period.
3. Merchandise is replaced by the purchase of new stock from time to time.

4. The inventory at the end of the accounting period is more or less the same as at the beginning.

The simplified data below show that the typical pattern holds true whether we are speaking in terms of units or dollars.

	Units	Dollars
Beginning inventory	1 700	$ 42 500
Merchandise purchased	5 500	143 000
Total goods available for sale	7 200	$185 500
Merchandise sold	5 800	149 100
Ending inventory	1 400	$ 36 400

These data can be shown in the form of an equation as follows:

$$\underset{\$42\ 500}{\underset{\text{beginning inventory}}{\text{Cost of}}} + \underset{\$143\ 000}{\underset{\text{merchandise purchased}}{\text{Cost of}}} - \underset{\$149\ 100}{\underset{\text{merchandise sold}}{\text{Cost of}}} = \underset{\$36\ 400}{\underset{\text{ending inventory}}{\text{Cost of}}}$$

Merchandise Inventory and the Financial Statements

When the periodic inventory system is used, no effort is made during the fiscal period to find out either the figure for the cost of the goods sold or the figure for the goods on hand (unsold). This creates a problem at statement time because the statements cannot be prepared without these two figures.

Physical Inventory

When the periodic inventory system is used, it is necessary at statement time to take a physical inventory. A **physical inventory** is a procedure by which the unsold goods of a merchandising business are counted and valued (at cost price). This ending inventory figure is significant in three respects:

1. It is an important current asset on the balance sheet.
2. It is needed to calculate the cost of goods sold figure for the income statement.
3. It will be used as the beginning inventory figure for the next accounting period.

Merchandise Inventory on the Balance Sheet

A merchandising business buys goods to sell to its customers. Therefore, it keeps a stock of goods on hand. This inventory of goods usually has a large dollar value and must be included as an asset on the balance sheet. Merchandise inventory is listed as a current asset because it will normally be sold and converted into cash within one year. It is listed at its cost price, and not its selling price, in accordance with the cost principle. Merchandise inventory on a simplified balance sheet is shown in Figure 11.2 on page 426.

EASTPORT HARDWARE
BALANCE SHEET
JUNE 30, 20—

Assets

Current Assets

Bank	$ 1 205	
Accounts Receivable	18 305	
Merchandise Inventory	42 582	
Supplies	3 526	
Prepaid Insurance	3 564	$ 69 182

Plant and Equipment

Store Equipment	$ 25 658	
Delivery Equipment	18 350	44 008
		$ 113 190

Cost of Goods Sold on the Income Statement

You have seen that the inventory that *was not sold* belongs on the balance sheet. Similarly, the cost of the inventory that *was sold*, known as the **cost of goods sold**, belongs on the income statement.

An item that is sold for $100 may have cost around $75. This leaves a profit of $25 before deducting other expenses. Clearly, the cost of any item sold is a very significant expense. The total cost of all of the items sold is usually the biggest expense figure for a merchandising business.

When the periodic inventory method is used, no attempt is made to have the cost of goods sold figure available during the period. It has to be obtained by a calculation when the income statement is prepared. This calculation is based on the inventory equation shown to you previously:

$$\text{Cost of beginning inventory} + \text{Cost of merchandise purchased} - \text{Cost of merchandise sold} = \text{Cost of ending inventory}$$

A simple mathematical rearrangement of this equation gives the cost of goods sold formula. It is this formula that is used to calculate the cost of goods sold figure for the periodic inventory system.

$$\textbf{Cost of beginning inventory} + \textbf{Cost of merchandise purchased} - \textbf{Cost of ending inventory} = \textbf{Cost of merchandise sold}$$

To calculate the cost of goods sold, three figures are needed to substitute for the terms in the formula. These are:

1. the beginning inventory figure, which is last year's ending inventory figure;
2. the merchandise purchased figure, which is accumulated during the period in an account called Purchases (you will read about this in the next section);
3. the ending inventory figure, which is obtained by taking a physical inventory— by counting and valuing the entire inventory.

These data are presented on the income statement as shown in Figure 11.3 below. Observe the special Cost of Goods Sold section.

FIGURE 11.3

A simple income state-
ment for a merchandising
business.

Gross profit = Selling price
− Cost of goods sold

EASTERN TRADING COMPANY INCOME STATEMENT YEAR ENDED DECEMBER 31, 20–		
Revenue		
Sales		$231 967
Cost of Goods Sold		
Inventory, January 1	$ 55 325	
Purchases	120 402	
Cost of Goods Available for Sale	$175 727	
Less Inventory, December 31	57 350	
Cost of Goods Sold		118 377
Gross Profit		$113 590
Operating Expenses		
Bank Charges Expense	$ 375	
Building Maintenance Expense	875	
Car Expense	2 507	
Depreciation Expense	1 075	
Miscellaneous Expense	275	
Rent Expense	12 000	
Telephone Expense	957	
Utilities Expense	1 850	
Wages Expense	36 587	
Total Operating Expenses		56 501
Net Income		$ 57 089

Observe the following:

1. The cost of goods sold figure is considered to be so significant that the statement is prepared in two stages.
2. The first stage determines the gross profit. The **gross profit** is the difference between the selling price and the cost price of the goods sold. It can also be seen as the profit figure before deducting other expenses. The gross profit is a figure that the merchant will watch carefully. It is important to have enough gross profit to cover expenses and leave a sufficient net profit or, as we usually call it, net income. Most companies try to reach a specific target gross profit percentage.
3. The cost of goods sold calculation is shown on the statement.
4. The Expenses section is now headed *Operating Expenses*.

Limitation of the Periodic Inventory System

When the periodic inventory system is used, accurate financial statements cannot be obtained unless a physical inventory is taken. This is a time-consuming procedure that often makes it necessary to interrupt business operations for a day or two. At the same time, the periodic system is relatively easy to manage throughout the year. This is important for small businesses, such as drugstores and hardware stores, that have to keep track of inventories made up of a large number of different items. However, improvements in the quality and cost of computerized accounting systems are influencing more and more businesses away from the periodic system.

Section 11.1   Review Questions

1. Describe a service business.
2. Describe a merchandising business.
3. Define the terms "wholesaler" and "retailer."
4. Describe the merchandise inventory of a drugstore.
5. Give another name for merchandise inventory.
6. What has happened to the goods available for sale that are not on hand?
7. Where is merchandise inventory listed on the balance sheet?
8. Explain the importance of the cost of goods sold figure.
9. Explain the meaning of gross profit.
10. What types of businesses use the periodic inventory system?
11. Explain why a small variety store would choose to use the periodic inventory system.
12. Give the four steps in the inventory cycle.
13. Give the cost of goods sold formula.
14. Why is it necessary to take a physical inventory when using the periodic inventory system?
15. Describe a limitation of the periodic inventory system.

Section 11.1   Exercises

1. **Workbook Exercise: Completing the chart below by filling in the blank spaces for selling prices, cost prices, and gross profits.**

	Selling price	Cost price	Gross profit	Cost of goods sold as a % of selling price	Gross profit as a % of selling price
Easy	$ 250	$	$ 100	%	%
	$	$ 85	$ 40	%	%
	$ 80	$ 56	$	%	%
	$	$ 75	$ 75	%	%
	$ 300	$ 195	$	%	%
	$ 225	$	$ 63	%	%
More difficult	$	$ 54	$	%	40 %
	$ 500	$	$	70 %	%
	$ 200	$	$	65 %	%
	$	$ 120	$	%	52 %

2. The chart shown below also appears in the Workbook.

    A. Complete the chart by filling in the missing figures.

	Year 1	Year 2	Year 3
Beginning inventory	100 units	units	units
Merchandise purchased	units	900 units	units
Goods available for sale	800 units	units	units
Merchandise sold	units	1 000 units	800 units
Ending inventory	300 units	units	50 units

    B. If the units cost $5 each throughout Year 3, work out the Cost of Goods Sold section of the income statement.

3. For each of the following, calculate the cost of goods sold and the gross profit.

	Sales	Beginning Inventory	Purchases	Ending Inventory
1.	$125 000	32 000	74 250	33 500
2.	$750 585	85 600	410 360	88 300
3.	$288 635	65 550	110 357	60 548
4.	$174 000	33 800	82 640	33 500
5.	$255 324	48 500	150 650	50 300

4. Given below are some accounts and their balances for a merchandising business, as well as the ending inventory figure. **From this data, calculate the cost of goods sold figure.**

The ending inventory figure is $15 600.

Accounts	Balances
Bank	$ 1 500
Accounts Receivable	22 450
Merchandise Inventory	14 500
Supplies	1 300
Automobile	18 000
Equipment	22 000
Accounts Payable	4 532
T. Lao, Capital	77 558
T. Lao, Drawings	12 000
Sales	82 600
Purchases	41 300
Advertising	1 100
Car Expense	5 500
Rent Expense	9 000
Utilities Expense	2 150
Wages Expense	13 890

5. Given below is a simple trial balance and the ending inventory figure for London Retailers after a fiscal period of one month. GST and PST are ignored.

LONDON RETAILERS
TRIAL BALANCE
JUNE 30, 20—

	Debit	Credit
Bank	$ 3 000	
Accounts Receivable	29 350	
Merchandise Inventory	24 500	
Supplies	1 250	
Automobile	17 500	
Accumulated Depreciation — Automobile		$ 3 500
Equipment	35 000	
Accumulated Depreciation — Equipment		6 000
Accounts Payable		7 222
T. Wilkes, Capital		70 028
T. Wilkes, Drawings	5 000	
Sales		55 325
Purchases	18 575	
Advertising Expense	500	
Car Expense	750	
Rent Expense	1 000	
Utilities Expense	900	
Wages Expense	4 750	
	$142 075	$142 075

Given that the ending inventory figure is $25 350, answer the following:

1. Give the beginning inventory figure.
2. Give the selling price of the goods sold.
3. Calculate the cost price of the goods sold.
4. Calculate the gross profit.
5. Calculate the total operating expenses.
6. Calculate the net income.

11.2 | Accounting Procedures for a Merchandising Business

So far, you have learned the following facts about the periodic inventory system for a merchandising business:

- The final inventory figure must be included on the balance sheet as a current asset.
- The cost of goods sold figure must be included on the income statement.
- Neither the inventory figure nor the cost of goods sold figure is known during the accounting period.
- The cost of goods sold figure can be calculated by means of the formula developed in the previous section.

Now you will learn about the accounts that are needed to do the accounting for the cost of goods sold and merchandise inventory.

The Merchandise Inventory Account

Under the periodic inventory system, the merchandise inventory of a business is kept in two accounts. One of these is the Merchandise Inventory account. It shows the inventory figure as of the beginning of the accounting period.

At the fiscal year-end, the inventory is counted and valued at cost price to arrive at the merchandise inventory grand total for the financial statements. The inventory account is adjusted to equal the updated figure. This becomes the beginning inventory figure for the next fiscal period. This periodic inventory adjustment is the only accounting entry made to the Merchandise Inventory account.

You will now find a Merchandise Inventory account appearing in the assets section in most of your trial balances. Remember that the account represents the balance that was updated at the end of the preceding fiscal period. For your purposes, the balance of the Merchandise Inventory account represents the beginning inventory for the current period.

The Purchases Account

Purchases is the other account where the merchandise inventory of a business is kept. The merchandise purchased during the fiscal period is collected in the Purchases account. "Purchases" is a short version of "Purchases of Merchandise for Resale." The Purchases account is found in the expense section of the ledger. Some accountants place it as the first account in that section. If merchandise for resale is purchased for cash, the accounting entry (at the cost price) is:

	DR	CR
Purchases	$$$$	
GST Recoverable	$$$$	
Bank		$$$$

If merchandise for resale is purchased on account, the accounting entry (at the cost price) is:

	DR	CR
Purchases	$$$$	
GST Recoverable	$$$$	
Accounts Payable		$$$$

Be sure you understand that it is the purchase of merchandise inventory that is being discussed here. Other items purchased are handled in the usual way. For example, if a tire company buys office supplies, Office Supplies is debited. However, if a tire company buys tires for sale to its customers, Purchases is debited.

The Sales Account

The revenue account for a merchandising business is called "Sales." If goods are sold for cash, the basic accounting entry (at the selling price) is:

	DR	CR
Bank	$$$$	
GST Payable		$$$$
PST Payable		$$$$
Sales		$$$$

If goods are sold on account, the basic accounting entry (at the selling price) is:

	DR	CR
Accounts Receivable	$$$$	
GST Payable		$$$$
PST Payable		$$$$
Sales		$$$$

When a business sells goods, the physical inventory is reduced. However, no accounting entries are made to record this decrease in inventory when the periodic system is used. It is easier to allow the inventory to be inexact during the fiscal period and to correct it at the end. You will be shown how to do this later in the chapter.

The Freight-in Account

*The Freight-in account is for the expense of shipping **in** goods for sale.*

*The Delivery Expense account is for the expense of shipping **out** goods that have been sold.*

Freight on incoming merchandise is considered to be one of the costs of the goods. The Freight-in account is used to accumulate any transportation charges on incoming goods.

These charges are kept separate from transportation charges on outgoing goods, which are recorded in Delivery Expense. Freight-in is accumulated separately because it is a cost related to the goods purchased and must be included in the calculation of the cost of goods sold. The Freight-in account is usually placed right after the Purchases account in the ledger.

On page 426, you learned a formula for calculating the cost of goods sold. To factor in the Freight-in account, a minor adjustment is made to the formula, as shown below.

Beginning Inventory + Purchases − Ending Inventory = Cost of Goods Sold

Beginning Inventory + (Purchases + Freight-in) − Ending Inventory = Cost of Goods Sold

The charges for freight-in and for delivery expense are usually found on invoices from trucking companies, railways, or other transportation companies. If a business has its own trucks, these charges may be found on bills related to the running of the equipment, such as bills for gasoline, oil, and repairs.

Duty refers to the special charges imposed by the government on certain goods imported from a foreign country. If any duty is being charged, it is handled in the same way as freight-in and debited to a Duty account.

Section 11.2   Review Questions

1. Why is the final inventory figure included on the balance sheet?
2. How is the cost of goods sold figure determined for inclusion on the income statement?
3. In what two accounts in the general ledger is merchandise inventory recorded?
4. What does the balance in the Merchandise Inventory account represent during the fiscal period?
5. What prices are used to value the merchandise inventory?
6. What is the account title "Purchases" a short version of?
7. Give the accounting entry for the purchase of merchandise for resale on account.
8. Give the accounting entry for the purchase of a delivery truck for cash.
9. What is the revenue account usually called in the ledger of a merchandising company?
10. If the periodic inventory system is used, what accounting step is ignored when a sale is made?
11. What charges are recorded in the Freight-in account?

Section 11.2   Exercises

1. **Journalize the following transactions in two-column general journal form for Excel TV and Stereo:**

Transactions

December

1   Received an invoice, No. 435, from Paramount Manufacturing for a shipment of television sets, $3 045.00 plus GST of $213.15, total $3 258.15.

2   Received an invoice, No. B616, from Murray Transport Company for transportation charges on the above shipment of television sets, $435.00 plus GST of $30.45, total $465.45.

3   Received an invoice, No. 7042, from Swiss Stationers for a shipment of office forms and supplies to be used in the business, $236.00 plus GST of $16.52, total $252.52.

4   Issued Sales Invoice, No. 789, to W. Purbhoo for stereo speakers and electronic parts, $417.00 plus GST of $29.19 and PST of $33.36, total $479.55.

5   Issued Cash Sales Slip, No. 143, for the cash sale of merchandise from the store, $92.00 plus GST of $6.44 and PST of $7.36, total $105.80.

6   Received an invoice, No. 902, from Haniko Electric for a shipment of electronic parts, $2 678.00 plus GST of $187.46, total $2 865.46.

2. **In your Workbook, complete each of the following statements by inserting in the spaces provided the most appropriate word or phrase from the list given below.**

A. The final inventory figure appears on the _____ and on the _____.

B. Neither the _____ nor the _____ is known during the accounting period.

C. The cost of goods sold figure is _____ using a _____.

D. Merchandise inventory is kept in two accounts. These are _____ and _____.

E. The _____ normally shows the merchandise inventory figure as of the _____.

F. At the fiscal year-end, the inventory is counted and valued at _____.

G. The Merchandise Inventory account is adjusted _____.

H. The _____ is the only accounting entry made to the Merchandise Inventory account.

I. Merchandise purchased during the fiscal period is debited to the _____.

J. The "Purchases" account is a short form of _____.

K. If merchandise is purchased on account, the account debited is _____.

L. If a tire company purchases office supplies, the account debited is _____.

M. For a merchandising business, the sales account is the _____.

N. When a business using the periodic inventory system sells goods, there is no accounting entry to record the _____.

O. The Freight-in account is used to accumulate _____.

List of Words or Phrases

at the end of the fiscal period	inventory figure
balance sheet	merchandise inventory
beginning of the fiscal period	Merchandise Inventory account
calculated	office supplies
cost of goods sold figure	purchases
cost prices	Purchases account
decrease in inventory	purchases of merchandise for resale
formula	Revenue account
income statement	transportation charges on incoming goods
inventory adjustment	

3. **Complete the following chart in your Workbook.**

Opening Inventory	Purchases	Freight-in	Closing Inventory	Cost of Goods Sold
$20 000	40 000	5 000	25 000	
$29 000	50 000	1 000	30 000	
$12 000		1 000	15 000	50 000
	90 000	8 000	39 000	101 000
$50 000	100 000		60 000	100 000
$75 000	200 000	5 000		200 000

11.3 | **Work Sheet for a Merchandising Business**

As you already know, the figures for the financial statements are obtained from a completed work sheet. Therefore, you must learn to handle three new merchandising accounts on the work sheet.

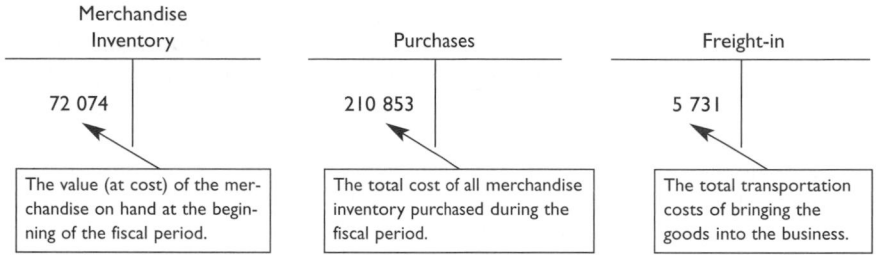

Merchandise Inventory	Purchases	Freight-in
72 074	210 853	5 731
The value (at cost) of the merchandise on hand at the beginning of the fiscal period.	The total cost of all merchandise inventory purchased during the fiscal period.	The total transportation costs of bringing the goods into the business.

You will see these new accounts on the partial work sheet in Figure 11.4 below. Notice the three-step procedure used by the accountant who prepared the work sheet. First, the beginning inventory was extended to the debit column of the income statement. In the second step, ending inventory—obtained by a physical count—was entered in both the credit column of the income statement and in the debit column of the balance sheet. And third, the amounts for Freight-in and Purchases were transferred to the debit column of the income statement.

The third step shown below is not out of the ordinary. But consider how Merchandise Inventory was treated in the first and second steps. Why did the accountant transfer an asset to the income statement? And why is the year-end count of inventory entered in both the income statement and balance sheet sections of the work sheet? Figure 11.5 on page 436 shows you the answers.

Figure 11.5 on page 436

FIGURE 11.4

Partial work sheet showing how Merchandise Inventory, Purchases, and Freight-in are handled on a work sheet.

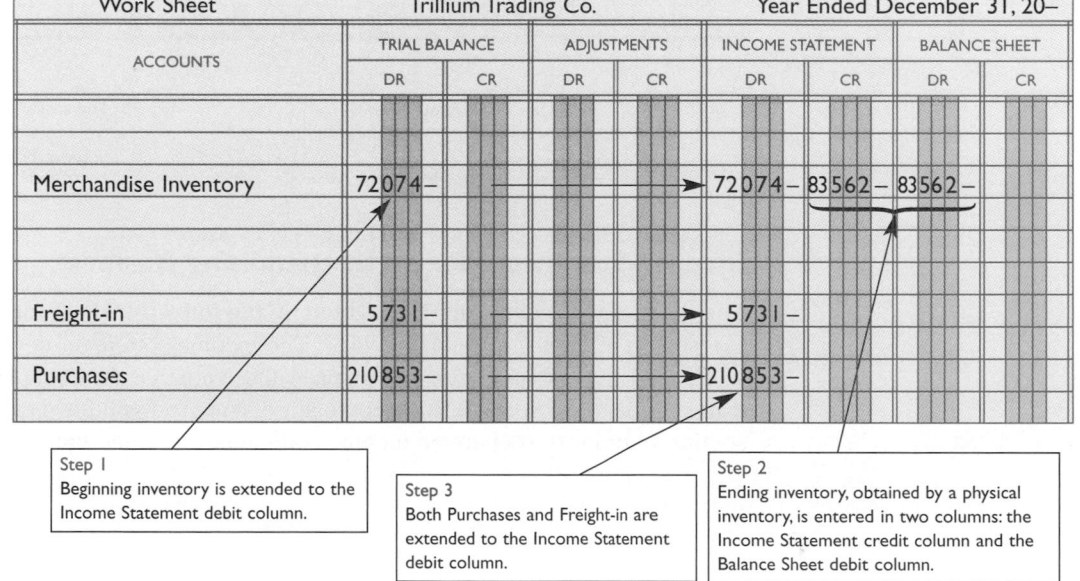

Work Sheet	Trillium Trading Co.				Year Ended December 31, 20–			
	TRIAL BALANCE		ADJUSTMENTS		INCOME STATEMENT		BALANCE SHEET	
ACCOUNTS	DR	CR	DR	CR	DR	CR	DR	CR
Merchandise Inventory	72074–				72074–	83562–	83562–	
Freight-in	5731–				5731–			
Purchases	210853–				210853–			

Step 1
Beginning inventory is extended to the Income Statement debit column.

Step 3
Both Purchases and Freight-in are extended to the Income Statement debit column.

Step 2
Ending inventory, obtained by a physical inventory, is entered in two columns: the Income Statement credit column and the Balance Sheet debit column.

The three steps the accountant took with the merchandising accounts were needed to get all the amounts in the cost of goods formula on the work sheet. Recall that the formula is stated as:

Beginning Inventory + (Purchases + Freight-in) − Ending Inventory = Cost of Goods Sold

In the income section of the work sheet, you can see the cost of goods formula expressed in debits and credits. Beginning inventory, purchases, and freight-in represent costs and are shown as debits, while ending inventory is shown as a credit, because it represents a deduction in the calculation. Ending inventory represents goods purchased but not sold. The higher the ending inventory, the lower the cost of goods sold.

Without the amounts displayed in Figure 11.5, it would be impossible to prepare an income statement using the work sheet alone. Also, by entering the ending inventory in the debit column of the balance sheet, the Merchandise Inventory account is brought up to date at the end of the year.

FIGURE 11.5

Partial work sheet explaining how Merchandise Inventory, Freight-in, and Purchases are related to the financial statements.

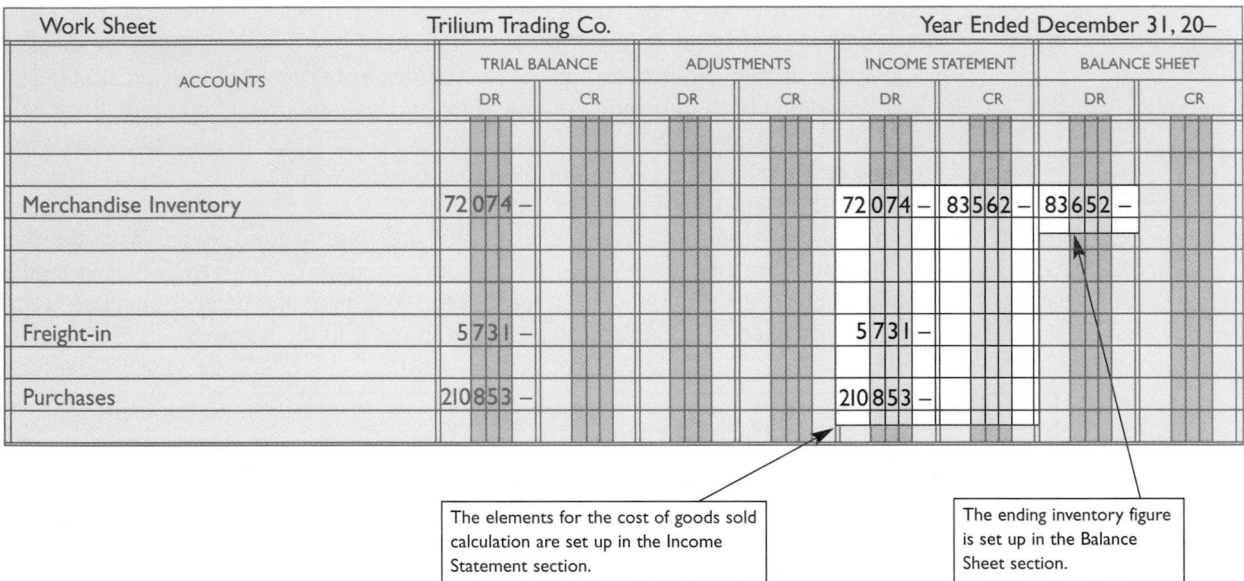

The elements for the cost of goods sold calculation are set up in the Income Statement section.

The ending inventory figure is set up in the Balance Sheet section.

Income Statement for a Merchandising Business

The three new accounts are highlighted on the full work sheet for Trillium Trading Co. shown in Figure 11.6 on page 437. The income statement developed from this work sheet appears in Figure 11.7 on page 438. Note that the Cost of Goods Sold section is a major addition to the income statement. You will have to master this new section in order to prepare an income statement for a merchandising business.

FIGURE 11.6

The full work sheet for
Trillium Trading Co.

ACCOUNTS	TRIAL BALANCE DR	TRIAL BALANCE CR	ADJUSTMENTS DR	ADJUSTMENTS CR	INCOME STATEMENT DR	INCOME STATEMENT CR	BALANCE SHEET DR	BALANCE SHEET CR
Work Sheet — Trillium Trading Co. — Year Ended December 31, 20—								
Bank	4 072 –						4 072 –	
Accounts Receivable	25 690 –						25 690 –	
Merchandise Inventory	72 074 –				72 074 –	83 562 –	83 562 –	
Supplies	2 840 –			2 560 –			280 –	
Prepaid Insurance	4 242 –			2 915 –			1 327 –	
Equipment	24 316 –						24 316 –	
Accum. Deprec.—Equipment		8 754 –		3 112 –				11 866 –
Automobiles	37 416 –						37 416 –	
Accum. Deprec.—Automobiles		19 082 –		5 500 –				24 582 –
Accounts Payable		12 780 –		565 –				13 345 –
GST Payable		2 200 –						2 200 –
GST Recoverable	1 650 –						1 650 –	
PST Payable		2 500 –						2 500 –
Bank Loan		10 000 –						10 000 –
R. Kehoe, Capital		97 228 –						97 228 –
R. Kehoe, Drawings	40 000 –						40 000 –	
Sales		377 508 –				377 508 –		
Advertising Expense	1 141 –				1 141 –			
Bank Charges Expense	2 651 –				2 651 –			
Car Expense	4 749 –		250 –		4 999 –			
Delivery Expense	1 377 –				1 377 –			
Freight-in	5 731 –				5 731 –			
Miscellaneous Expense	1 507 –		315 –		1 822 –			
Purchases	210 853 –				210 853 –			
Rent Expense	12 000 –				12 000 –			
Salaries Expense	24 000 –				24 000 –			
Telephone Expense	1 850 –				1 850 –			
Utilities Expense	3 673 –				3 673 –			
Wages Expense	48 220 –				48 220 –			
	530 052 –	530 052 –						
Supplies Expense			2 560 –		2 560 –			
Insurance Expense			2 915 –		2 915 –			
Depreciation Expense—Automobile			5 500 –		5 500 –			
Depreciation Expense—Equipment			3 112 –		3 112 –			
			14 652 –	14 652 –	404 478 –	461 070 –	218 313 –	161 721 –
Net Income					56 592 –			56 592 –
					461 070 –	461 070 –	218 313 –	218 313 –

TRILLIUM TRADING CO.		
INCOME STATEMENT		
YEAR ENDED DECEMBER 31, 20—		
Revenue		
Sales		$377 508
Cost of Goods Sold		
Merchandise Inventory, January 1	$ 72 074	
Purchases	210 853	
Freight-in	5 731	
Goods Available for Sale	$288 658	
Less Merchandise Inventory, December 31	83 562	205 096
Gross Profit		$172 412
Operating Expenses		
Advertising Expense	$ 1 141	
Bank Charges Expense	2 651	
Car Expense	4 999	
Delivery Expense	1 377	
Depreciation Expense — Automobile	5 500	
Depreciation Expense — Equipment	3 112	
Insurance Used	2 915	
Miscellaneous Expense	1 822	
Rent Expense	12 000	
Salaries Expense	24 000	
Supplies Expense	2 560	
Telephone Expense	1 850	
Utilities Expense	3 673	
Wages Expense	48 220	115 820
Net Income		$ 56 592

Closing Entries for a Merchandising Business

A very interesting result occurs when the closing entry process, described in Chapter 9, is applied to a merchandising business. The process very neatly cancels out the old inventory figure and sets up the new one. In other words, the closing entry process automatically updates the inventory account at the end of the fiscal period.

You can see how this is done by studying the simplified data in Figures 11.8 to 11.10 on pages 439 and 440.

FIGURE 11.8

A simplified work sheet with the figures for the first and second closing entries outlined.

Work Sheet					Lee Company				Year Ended December 31, 20–	
ACCOUNTS	TRIAL BALANCE		ADJUSTMENTS		INCOME STATEMENT		BALANCE SHEET	
	DR	CR	DR	CR	DR	CR	DR	CR
Bank	2 500 –						2 500 –	
Accounts Receivable	12 150 –						12 150 –	
Merchandise Inventory	15 300 –				15 300 –	16 200 –	16 200 –	
B. Lee, Capital		27 880 –						27 880 –
B. Lee, Drawings	10 000 –						10 000 –	
Sales		35 000 –				35 000 –		
Purchases	14 250 –				14 250 –			
Freight-in	2 370 –				2 370 –			
General Expense	416 –				416 –			
Rent Expense	1 200 –				1 200 –			
Wages Expense	4 694 –				4 694 –			
	62 880 –	62 880 –			38 230 –	51 200 –	40 850 –	27 880 –
Net Income					12 970 –			12 970 –
					51 200 –	51 200 –	40 850 –	40 850 –

First closing entry includes ending inventory.

Second closing entry includes beginning inventory.

FIGURE 11.9

The four closing entries, derived from the work sheet, Figure 11.8.

			GENERAL JOURNAL		
			Closing Entries		
20–					
Dec.	31		Merchandise Inventory	16 200 –	
			Sales	35 000 –	
			Income Summary		51 200 –
	31		Income Summary	38 230 –	
			Merchandise Inventory		15 300 –
			Purchases		14 250 –
			Freight-in		2 370 –
			General Expense		416 –
			Rent Expense		1 200 –
			Wages Expense		4 694 –
	31		Income Summary	12 970 –	
			B. Lee, Capital		12 970 –
	31		B. Lee, Capital	10 000 –	
			B. Lee, Drawings		10 000 –

FIGURE 11.10

The general ledger after completing the closing entries. The account balances before the closing entries are entered in black.

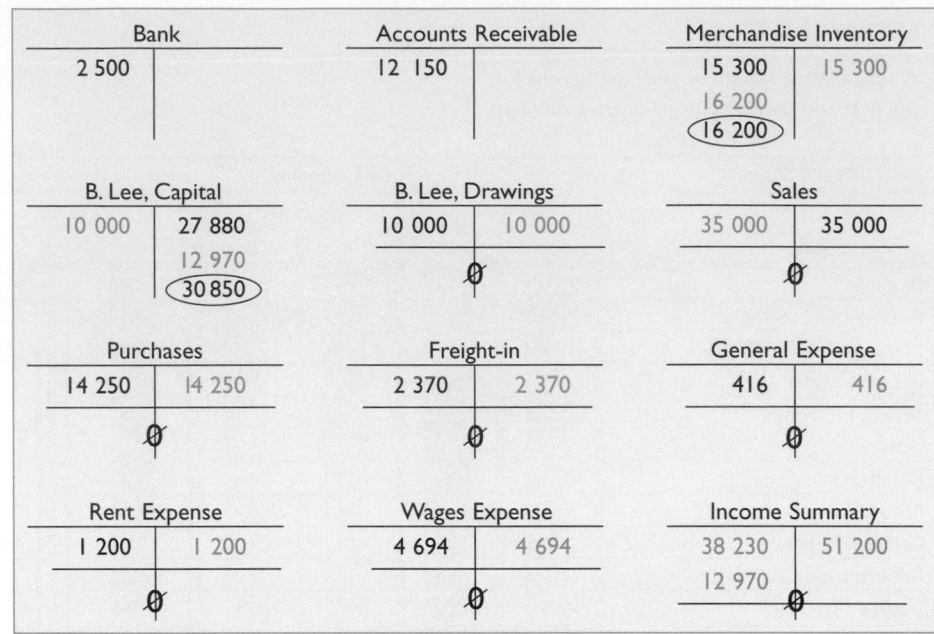

Trial Balance

DR	CR
2 500	30 850
12 150	
16 200	
30 850	30 850

As you can see, the closing entry process has had the following effects:

1. It has closed out all of the equity accounts except Capital.
2. It has updated the Capital account. The new balance is $30 850.
3. It has adjusted the Merchandise Inventory account. The new balance is $16 200. This balance will remain in the account until the next set of closing entries is recorded.

Section 11.3   Review Questions

1. Name the three new accounts that appear on the work sheet of a merchandising company.
2. What does the trial balance figure for Merchandise Inventory represent?
3. What does the trial balance figure for Purchases represent?
4. What important function must be carried out before the work sheet for a merchandising business can be completed?
5. Explain in detail how to extend the Merchandise Inventory line.
6. Explain how to extend the Purchases line.
7. Explain how to extend the Freight-in line.
8. Where are the figures found for the Cost of Goods Sold section of the income statement?

9. Why is the Cost of Goods Sold section of the income statement so important?
10. Is the closing entry process basically the same as it was when first introduced?
11. What must one be careful of when recording the first two closing entries?
12. What new result occurs after processing the first two closing entries?
13. Where is the information for the closing entries found?
14. What is the total effect of all of the closing entries?

Section 11.3   **Exercises**

1. The partially completed work sheet shown below also appears in the Workbook.

  A. **Complete the work sheet.** The ending inventory figure is $43 700.

  B. **Prepare an income statement.**

  C. **Prepare a balance sheet.**

  D. **Journalize the closing entries.**

Work Sheet		Bok Trading Company					Year Ended December 31, 20–	
	TRIAL BALANCE		ADJUSTMENTS		INCOME STATEMENT		BALANCE SHEET	
ACCOUNTS	DR	CR	DR	CR	DR	CR	DR	CR
Bank	500 –							
Accounts Receivable	17 910 –							
Merchandise Inventory	39 600 –							
Supplies	2 500 –			② 1 200 –				
Prepaid Insurance	1 800 –			③ 1 150 –				
Equipment	27 850 –							
Accumulated Deprec—Equip.		5 200 –		④ 2 600 –				
Accounts Payable		7 400 –		① 350 –				
GST Payable		550 –						
GST Recoverable	390 –							
PST Payable		628 –						
R. Bok, Capital		63 712 –						
R. Bok, Drawings	10 000 –							
Sales		94 310 –						
Purchases	41 500 –		① 300 –					
Freight-in	950 –							
Miscellaneous Expense	350 –		① 50 –					
Rent Expense	4 800 –							
Telephone Expense	1 500 –							
Utilities Expense	2 750 –							
Wages Expense	19 400 –							
	171 800 –	171 800 –						
Supplies Expense			② 1 200 –					
Insurance Expense			③ 1 150 –					
Depreciation Expense—Equip.			④ 2 600 –					

2. Shown below is the trial balance for Small Engine Sales and Service at December 31, 20—, the end of an annual fiscal period.

SMALL ENGINE SALES AND SERVICE
TRIAL BALANCE
DECEMBER 31, 20—

	DR	CR
Bank	$ 520	
Accounts Receivable	12 260	
Merchandise Inventory	36 050	
Supplies	1 975	
Parts and Materials	10 350	
Prepaid Insurance	1 150	
Equipment	18 600	
Accumulated Depreciation — Equipment		$ 12 505
Truck	18 000	
Accumulated Depreciation — Truck		14 975
Accounts Payable		5 360
GST Payable		850
GST Recoverable	420	
PST Payable		980
H. Rohr, Capital		29 010
H. Rohr, Drawings	25 000	
Revenue — Sales		80 362
Revenue — Service		66 215
Bank Charges	410	
Freight-in	862	
Miscellaneous Expense	650	
Purchases	52 795	
Rent Expense	3 600	
Telephone Expense	1 250	
Truck Expense	5 825	
Utilities Expense	2 240	
Wages Expense	18 300	
	$210 257	$210 257

A. Complete the work sheet in your Workbook, using the following additional information.
   a. Closing inventory of merchandise—$35 651
   b. Closing inventory of supplies—$350
   c. Closing inventory of parts and materials—$4 560
   d. Unexpired insurance at December 31—$600
   e. Late bills—none.
   f. Depreciation at Canada Customs and Revenue Agency's prescribed rates using declining-balance methods. Round up to the nearest dollar.

See page 345 for CCRA's prescribed rates.

B. Prepare an income statement.
C. Prepare a balance sheet.
D. Journalize the adjusting and closing entries.

    E. Post the adjusting and closing entries to the T-accounts provided in the Workbook.

    F. Take off a post-closing trial balance.

3. Shown below is the completed work sheet for Barbini Stone Products.

    A. Journalize the adjusting and closing entries in the general journal.

    B. Post the adjusting and closing entries to the T-accounts provided in the Workbook.

    C. Take off a post-closing trial balance.

Work Sheet	Barbini Stone Products					Year Ended December 31, 20–		
ACCOUNTS	TRIAL BALANCE		ADJUSTMENTS		INCOME STATEMENT		BALANCE SHEET	
	DR	CR	DR	CR	DR	CR	DR	CR
Bank	3250 –						3250 –	
Accounts Receivable	33930 10						33930 10	
Merchandise Inventory	43700 –				43700 –	40500 –	40500 –	
Supplies	3400 50			② 2104 –			1296 50	
Prepaid Insurance	2090 –			③ 950 –			1140 –	
Land	35000 –						35000 –	
Building	95000 –						95000 –	
Accumulated Depreciation — Building		17620 –		④ 3869 –				21489 –
Equipment	53400 –						53400 –	
Accumulated Depreciation — Equipment		31527 –		⑤ 4375 –				35902 –
Truck	76000 –						76000 –	
Accumulated Depreciation — Truck		57752 –		⑥ 5474 –				63226 –
Accounts Payable		40820 20		① 1135 –				41955 20
GST Payable		1350 –						1350 –
GST Recoverable	720 –						720 –	
PST Payable		1560 –						1560 –
T. Barbini, Capital		159180 05						159180 05
T. Barbini, Drawings	36000 –						36000 –	
Sales		232250 –				232250 –		
Advertising Expense	2570 –		① 100 –		2670 –			
Freight-in	3705 –		① 70 –		3775 –			
Miscellaneous Expense	1750 –		① 25 –		1775 –			
Purchases	80702 50		① 940 –		81642 50			
Telephone Expense	1250 –				1250 –			
Utilities Expense	12316 –				12316 –			
Wages Expense	57275 15				57275 15			
	542059 25	542059 25						
Supplies Expense			② 2104 –		2104 –			
Insurance Expense			③ 950 –		950 –			
Depreciation Expense—Building			④ 3869 –		3869 –			
Depreciation Expense—Equipment			⑤ 4375 –		4375 –			
Depreciation Expense—Truck			⑥ 5474 –		5474 –			
			17907 –	17907 –	221175 65	272750 –	376236 60	324662 25
Net Income					51574 35			51674 35
					272750 –	272750 –	376236 60	376236 60

11.4 # Merchandise Returns and Allowances

When a sale is made on account, the seller issues a sales invoice and makes the appropriate accounting entry. No further action is necessary for most sales transactions, except to ensure that the customer pays the account.

In the Books of the Vendor

Occasionally, however, a correction or a cancellation of a sales invoice is necessary. Consider the sales invoice in Figure 11.11 below.

FIGURE 11.11

The customer's copy of a sales invoice.

Phone	842-9999			P.O. BOX 298
Fax	842-8866	ECHO BAY		Station 8
		VANCOUVER, B.C.		V7C 8P7

MASTHEAD MARINE

SOLD TO: Penticton Marina
4000 Skaha Lake Road
Penticton, B.C.
V2A 6G9

DATE: April 14, 20—
TERMS: 60 days

QUANTITY	PART NO.	DESCRIPTION	PRICE	AMOUNT
2	15-2500	Gusher '25' pump	$315.00	$630.00
8 Pacs.	48-1020	Skyblazer Red Signal		
		Flares	18.50	148.00
				$778.00
		GST		54.46
		Total		$832.46

SALES INVOICE CUSTOMER'S COPY **NO. 8321**

Masthead Marine, the vendor, will make the following accounting entry for this invoice. In this example, there is no provincial sales tax.

	DR	CR
Accounts Receivable	$832.46	
Sales		$778.00
GST Payable		54.46

In T-accounts:

Accounts Receivable (Penticton Marina)	GST Payable	Sales
832.46	54.46	778.00

The purchaser in this transaction is Penticton Marina. Assume that Penticton Marina learns that the Skyblazer flares are defective. Penticton Marina will notify the seller, Masthead Marine, that the flares are defective and are being returned. Penticton Marina will expect its account to be decreased by Masthead Marine.

Credit Invoice

The standard procedure in this situation is for the seller to issue a credit invoice. A credit invoice, or a credit note, is a "minus" invoice issued by the vendor to reverse a charge that was previously made on a regular sales invoice. Credit invoices are used to adjust, correct, or cancel a charge to a customer's account for any of the reasons given below:

- The goods prove to be defective and are returned.
- The goods prove to be less than satisfactory but are kept by the customer. In this case, the customer will be given an allowance (a reduction) off the invoice price.
- An error is made on the sales invoice. In this case, the error will be made right.

FIGURE 11.12

The customer's copy of a credit invoice.

The path of a credit invoice is the same as that of a sales invoice.

Phone 842-9999
Fax 842-9966

ECHO BAY
VANCOUVER, B.C.

P.O. BOX 298
Station 8
V7C 8P7

MASTHEAD MARINE

SOLD TO   Penticton Marina
4000 Skaha Lake Road
Penticton, B.C.
V2A 6G9

DATE   April 16, 20—
TERMS 60 days

The path of a credit invoice is the same as that of a sales invoice.

QUANTITY	PART NO.	DESCRIPTION	PRICE	AMOUNT
8 Pacs.	48-1020	Skyblazer Red Signal Flares (defective merchandise)	$18.50	$148.00
		GST		10.36
		Total		$158.36

The word "credit" is prominently displayed.

SALES INVOICE   CUSTOMER'S COPY   **NO. 841**

In our example, Masthead Marine issues the credit invoice shown in Figure 11.12 on page 445.

A credit invoice has the opposite effect from a regular sales invoice. The customer's account and the sales account will be decreased. Masthead Marine will make the following accounting entry for the credit invoice:

	DR	CR
Sales	$148.00	
GST Payable	10.36	
Accounts Receivable		$158.36

The customer's account receives a credit, just as the term "credit invoice" implies.

After the credit invoice is processed by Masthead Marine, the effect in the accounts is as follows:

Accounts Receivable (Penticton Marina)		GST Payable		Sales	
832.46	158.36	10.36	54.46	148.00	778.00
(674.10)			(44.10)		(630)

The balance in Penticton Marina's account has been correctly reduced to $674.10.

In the Books of the Purchaser

Penticton Marina, the purchaser, will handle the transaction in a similar manner. When the source documents are received, the following accounting entries are made.

When the (purchase) invoice is received:

	DR	CR
Purchases	$778.00	
GST Recoverable	54.46	
Accounts Payable		$832.46

In the accounts:

Purchases		GST Recoverable		Accounts Payable (Masthead Marine)	
778.00		54.46			832.46

The "credit invoice" allows the customer to reduce a liability (or amount owing) by debiting Accounts Payable.

When the credit invoice is received:

	DR	CR
Accounts Payable	$158.36	
Purchases		$148.00
GST Recoverable		10.36

In the accounts:

Purchases		GST Recoverable		Accounts Payable (Masthead Marine)	
778.00	148.00	54.46	10.36	158.36	832.46
(630.00)		(44.10)			(674.10)

Cash Refunds

The cash sale is a common business transaction. However, dissatisfaction can occur with cash sales as well as with charge sales. A customer who has paid cash for merchandise that has to be returned will usually receive a refund. A **cash refund** is the return of money to the buyer from the seller when merchandise is returned.

In principle, the accounting for refunds is similar to that for credit invoices. However, when a refund is given:

- no credit invoices are issued (neither accounts receivable nor accounts payable is affected);
- instead, cash is handed over, or a cheque is issued. The accounting entry to record the transaction affects the Bank account. A refund cheque issued for goods returned requires the following accounting entry:

	DR	CR
Sales	$$$$	
GST Payable	$$$$	
Bank		$$$$

If there was PST on the original transaction, it must be accounted for as well.

Returns and Allowances Accounts

Some businesses, such as large department stores, want detailed information about returns and allowances. They want to know what proportion of their sales was returned by their customers. They also want to know what proportion of their purchases (of merchandise) they returned to their suppliers. Businesses that require this specialized information accumulate it in special "returns and allowances" accounts.

Sales Returns and Allowances Accounts

The accounts in Figure 11.13 below contrast the two different methods of handling returns and allowances for sales.

FIGURE 11.13

Chart showing the two methods of handling sales and returns and allowances.

Where no account for returns and allowances is used	
Sales	
560	2 500
395	2 240
720	3 560
	2 152
	3 852
	2 695
	15 324

Where a separate account for returns and allowances is used			
Sales		Sales Returns and Allowances	
2 500		560	
2 240		395	
3 560		720	
2 152		1 675	
3 852			
2 695			
16 999			

Net book value = 15 324

Take note of the following observations:

- The single account on the left on page 447 produces an account balance that represents the net sales figure. To obtain the returns and allowances figure, one would have to analyze the account.
- The two accounts at the right produce two account balances. One represents the total sales figure. The other represents the total returns and allowances figure.

Purchases Returns and Allowances Accounts

The concept is exactly the same for purchases returns and allowances. Figure 11.14 below contrasts the two different methods of handling returns and allowances for purchases.

FIGURE 11.14

Chart showing the different methods of handling purchases returns and allowances.

The effect here is the same as that for sales on page 447. The two accounts provide information not provided by one account alone.

Sample Transactions Using Returns and Allowances Accounts

Sales Returns and Allowances

TRANSACTION 1   Simplex Company sells $500 of goods to A. Moss. An invoice is issued for the sale on November 12, 20—. PST is added at the rate of 8 per cent. GST is added at the rate of 7 per cent.

The accounting entry to be made by Simplex Company is as follows:

	DR	CR
Accounts Receivable (A. Moss)	$575.00	
Sales		$500.00
PST Payable		40.00
GST Payable		35.00

TRANSACTION 2   Some of the goods sold to A. Moss are defective and are returned. Simplex Company issues a credit invoice for $180 plus PST of $14.40 and GST of $12.60, total $207.00.

The accounting entry to be made by Simplex Company is as follows:

	DR	CR
Sales Returns and Allowances	$180.00	
PST Payable	14.40	
GST Payable	12.60	
Accounts Receivable (A. Moss)		$207.00

The effect of the two transactions in the accounts is shown below:

GST Payable		Accounts Receivable (A. Moss)		PST Payable		Sales	Sales Returns and Allowances
12.60	35.00	575.00	207.00	14.40	40.00	500.00	180.00

Net sales = $320.00

Purchases Returns and Allowances

TRANSACTION 1   On June 12, 20—, Baytown Drug Mart receives a shipment of drugs and the sales invoice for them from Drug Wholesale in the amount of $1 147 plus GST of $80.29, total $1 227.29. There is no provincial sales tax on the purchase transaction.

The accounting entry to be made by Baytown Drug Mart is as follows:

	DR	CR
Purchases	$1 147.00	
GST Recoverable	80.29	
Accounts Payable (Drug Wholesale)		$1 227.29

TRANSACTION 2   On June 14, Baytown Drug Mart notices that a number of packages in the shipment from Drug Wholesale are damaged. The damaged goods are returned for credit, and a credit invoice is received from Drug Wholesale for $438.00 plus GST of $30.66, total $468.66.

The accounting entry to be made by Baytown Drug Mart is as follows:

	DR	CR
Accounts Payable (Drug Wholesale)	$468.66	
Purchases Returns and Allowances		$438.00
GST Recoverable		30.66

The effect of the above entries in the accounts is shown below:

Purchases		Purchases Returns and Allowances		Accounts Payable (Drug Wholesale)		GST Recoverable	
1 147.00			438.00	468.66	1 227.29	80.29	30.66

Net purchases = $709.00

Returns and Allowances on the Income Statement

Both sales returns and allowances and purchases returns and allowances appear on the income statements of companies that use them. They are treated as deductions from sales and from purchases, respectively. Their inclusion on the statement makes the statement slightly more difficult to prepare. The income statement of Trillium Trading Company in Figure 11.15 below shows returns and allowances on the income statement.

FIGURE 11.15

The income statement of Trillium Trading Co. showing returns and allowances.

TRILLIUM TRADING CO. INCOME STATEMENT YEAR ENDED DECEMBER 31, 20—			
Revenue			
Sales		$398 659	
Less Returns and Allowances		21 151	
Net Sales			$377 508
Cost of Goods Sold			
Merchandise Inventory, January 1		$ 72 074	
Purchases	$229 209		
Less Returns and Allowances	18 356		
Net Purchases		210 853	
Freight-in		5 731	
Goods Available for Sale		$288 658	
Less Merchandise Inventory, December 31		83 562	
Cost of Goods Sold			205 096
Gross Profit			$172 412
Operating Expenses			
Advertising Expense		$ 1 141	
Bank Charges Expense		2 651	
Car Expense		4 999	
Delivery Expense		1 377	
Depreciation Expense — Automobiles		5 500	
Depreciation Expense — Equipment		3 112	
Insurance Used		2 915	
Miscellaneous Expense		1 822	
Rent Expense		12 000	
Salaries Expense		24 000	
Supplies Used		2 560	
Telephone Expense		1 850	
Utilities Expense		3 673	
Wages Expense		48 220	115 820
Net Income			$ 56 592

Revised Cost of Goods Sold Formula

To handle all types of business situations, the cost of goods formula is changed slightly. The revised formula shows "Net Cost of Merchandise Purchased." This takes into account the likelihood that there will be some returns and allowances during the period. The formula, in its final form, is as follows:

Cost of beginning inventory	+	Net cost of merchandise purchased	−	Cost of ending inventory	=	Cost of merchandise sold

Section 11.4   Review Questions

1. What form is issued when a sale is made on account?
2. When a sale is made on account and the customer is satisfied, what does the company expect the customer to do?
3. What happens when a customer is dissatisfied with the merchandise?
4. What business form is issued when a customer's account is adjusted downward?
5. Describe how a credit invoice is different from a regular invoice.
6. What is another name for a credit invoice?
7. For what three reasons are credit invoices issued?
8. Using the simplest system studied so far, give the accounting entry for the issuing of a credit invoice. Ignore GST and PST.
9. What is a cash refund?
10. Using the simplest system studied so far, give the accounting entry for a cash refund for merchandise returned by a customer. Ignore GST and PST.
11. Why do some businesses keep "returns and allowances" accounts?
12. Briefly explain the difference between accounting for a business that keeps returns and allowances accounts and one that does not.
13. Using the simplest system studied so far, give the accounting entry for a credit note for $100 for goods returned to a supplier. Ignore GST and PST.
14. Using returns and allowances accounts, give the accounting entry for a credit note for $100 for goods returned to a supplier. Ignore GST and PST.
15. Explain how to handle returns and allowances accounts on the income statement.

Section 11.4   Exercises

1. **Examine the two source documents on page 452 and answer the questions that follow.**

   A. From the point of view of Acadia Equipment and Supply, what source document is document A?

   B. From the point of view of Cornwallis Construction, what source document is document A?

   C. What source document is document B?

   D. Which company is the sender of the documents?

E. Which company is the purchaser?

F. Give the accounting entries for these two documents as if you were the accountant for Acadia Equipment and Supply. Acadia Equipment and Supply does not use returns and allowances accounts.

G. Give the accounting entries for these two documents as if you were the accountant for Cornwallis Construction. Cornwallis Construction does not use returns and allowances accounts.

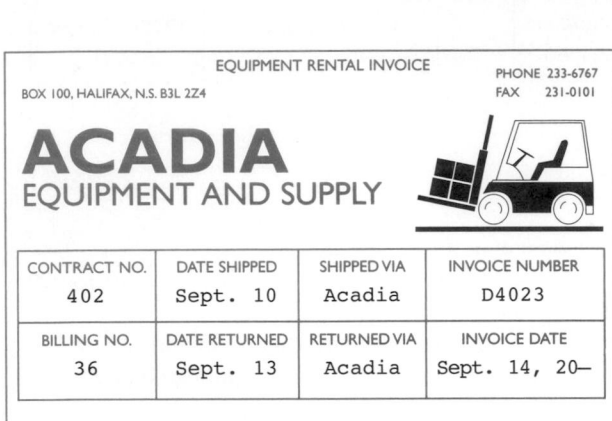

STOCK NO.	DESCRIPTION	NO. DAYS WEEKS, MOS.	RATE	AMOUNT
146	Forklift truck	3 days	$100.00	$300.00
			GST	21.00
				$321.00

Document A

STOCK NO.	DESCRIPTION	NO. DAYS WEEKS, MOS.	RATE	AMOUNT
146	Credit allowed due to malfunction of forklift truck	1/2	$100.00	$50.00
			GST	3.50
				$53.50

Document B

2. **Journalize the following transactions of Copeland's Furniture Mart. Copeland's Furniture Mart does not use returns and allowances accounts.**

A. May 31: Cash sales slip No. 1060 to A. Rosen for sale of goods $155 plus GST of $10.85 and PST of $12.40, total $178.25. Cash received.

B. June 4: Cash refund slip No. 1075 to A. Rosen for return of goods $155 plus GST of $10.85 and PST of $12.40, total $178.25. Cash paid out.

3. Jasper Company does not keep separate accounts for returns and allowances. The Sales account and the Purchases account for Jasper Company for a one-year period are represented below.

Sales								No. 405		
Date		Particulars	PR	Debit		Credit		D/C	Balance	
Dec.	31	For the year	J40			376 462 09				
	31	For the year	J40	47 650 32				C	328 811 77	

Purchases								No. 505		
Date		Particulars	PR	Debit		Credit		D/C	Balance	
Dec.	31	For the year	J40	186 235 32						
	31	For the year	J40			27 356 04		D	158 879 28	

A. **Give the gross sales figure.**

B. **Give the sales returns and allowances figure.**

C. **Give the net sales figure.**

D. **Give the gross purchases figure.**

E. **Give the purchases returns and allowances figure.**

F. **Give the net purchases figure.**

G. **Explain briefly how having separate returns and allowances accounts would help the management of this company.**

4. The latest two income statements for Lief Business Systems show the following sales data. The business does not use returns and allowances accounts.

	20–1	20–2
Net Sales	$207 890.00	$249 468.00

When studying these data, the owner, Mr. Lief, notes with satisfaction the increase in net sales of 20 per cent.

Mr. Lief never looks at the accounts in the ledger. If he did, he would see the following (simplified) data.

ACCOUNT	Sales							No. 400		
Date		Particulars	PR	Debit		Credit		Dr/Cr	Balance	
20–1		Sales for the year				209 300 00		CR	209 300 00	
		Returns and allowances		1 410 00				CR	207 890 00	
		Closing entry		207 890 00					Ө	
20–2		Sales for the year				264 688 00		CR	264 688 00	
		Returns and allowances		15 220 00				CR	249 468 00	
		Closing entry		249 468 00					Ө	

What information is Mr. Lief not receiving? Explain why this information might be important to him.

5. **From the following partial work sheet, prepare the income statement for Island Traders to the point of the gross profit figure.**

Work Sheet	Island Traders		Year Ended December 31, 20—	
			Income Statement	
Accounts			DR	CR
Merchandise Inventory			43 250.40	48 901.25
Sales				102 356.00
Sales Returns and Allowances			4 698.23	
Freight-in			6 235.14	
Purchases			60 258.20	
Purchase Returns and Allowances				9 562.45

11.5 | Sales Discounts

A **cash discount** is a reduction of the amount of a bill if payment is made on or before the discount date stated on the bill. The purpose of a cash discount is to encourage the customer to pay promptly.

Terms of Sale

Every business establishes certain terms of sale with its customers. The phrase **terms of sale** refers to the arrangements made with customers as to when the goods or services are to be paid for and whether a cash discount is offered.

There are various terms of sale. The most common ones are outlined below.

Standard Terms of Sale

1. **C.O.D.** Cash on delivery. The goods must be paid for at the time they are delivered.

2. **On Account or Charge.** The full amount of the invoice is due at the time the invoice is received but a brief time, usually 25 days, is given to make the payment.

3. **30 Days or Net 30.** The full amount of the invoice is due 30 days after the date of the invoice.
   60 Days or Net 60. The full amount of the invoice is due 60 days after the date of the invoice.

4. **2/10,n/30.** This is read as "two per cent, ten, net thirty" or just "two, ten, net thirty." If the bill is paid within 10 days of the invoice date, a cash discount of 2 per cent may be taken. Otherwise, the full amount of the invoice is due 30 days after the invoice date.
   1/15,n/60. If the bill is paid within 15 days of the invoice date, a cash discount of 1 per cent may be taken. Otherwise, the full amount of the invoice is due 60 days after the invoice date.

The terms of sale often depend on the customer's reputation for reliability in paying. A reliable customer of long standing will probably be granted very favourable terms. A new customer, about whom little is known, may be expected to pay cash on delivery, at least for a short time.

The terms of sale are recorded on the sales invoice shown in Figure 11.16 below. Every time a sale is made and an invoice is sent out, the customer is reminded of the terms for payment. Also, the terms are usually recorded on the customer's account card, so that the credit manager, the sales manager, and other interested people may refer to them easily.

Accounting for Cash Discounts

Accounting for a cash discount begins at the time a credit sale is made to a customer and an invoice offering a cash discount is issued. Examine the invoice shown below in Figure 11.16, for which Masthead Marine is the seller and Nanaimo Marina is the buyer.

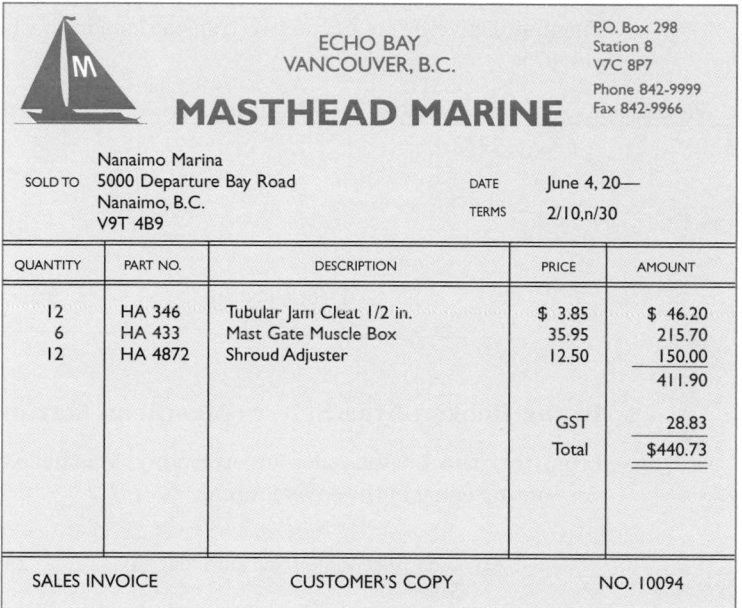

MASTHEAD MARINE

ECHO BAY
VANCOUVER, B.C.

P.O. Box 298
Station 8
V7C 8P7
Phone 842-9999
Fax 842-9966

| SOLD TO | Nanaimo Marina
5000 Departure Bay Road
Nanaimo, B.C.
V9T 4B9 | | DATE | June 4, 20— |
| | | | TERMS | 2/10,n/30 |

QUANTITY	PART NO.	DESCRIPTION	PRICE	AMOUNT
12	HA 346	Tubular Jam Cleat 1/2 in.	$ 3.85	$ 46.20
6	HA 433	Mast Gate Muscle Box	35.95	215.70
12	HA 4872	Shroud Adjuster	12.50	150.00
				411.90
			GST	28.83
			Total	$440.73

SALES INVOICE   CUSTOMER'S COPY   NO. 10094

In the Books of the Buyer (Nanaimo Marina)

The invoice, when received by Nanaimo Marina, becomes a purchase invoice. For this purchase invoice, the following accounting entry is recorded in the purchases journal:

	DR	CR
Purchases	$411.90	
GST Recoverable	28.83	
Accounts Payable (Masthead Marine)		$440.73

In the T-accounts, the effect is:

Purchases	GST Recoverable	Accounts Payable (Masthead Marine)
411.90	28.83	440.73

Someone in the accounting department of Nanaimo Marina will be responsible for checking the purchase invoices to see if any discounts are offered. Where discounts are offered, special treatment is necessary to ensure that payment is made within the discount period.

Discounts Earned are also called "Discounts off Purchases" or "Purchase Discounts."

In this case, the cheque is made out for $431.92. This amount is arrived at by deducting the 2 per cent discount ($8.81) from the amount of the invoice ($440.73). The tear-off portion of the cheque will show that the cheque is in payment of invoice No. 10094, and that a discount of $8.81 had been deducted. The cheque is mailed before the discount date.

From the cheque copy, the following accounting entry is made in the cash payments journal:

	DR	CR
Accounts Payable (Masthead Marine)	$440.73	
Discounts Earned		$ 8.81
Bank		431.92

The cumulative effect of the two transactions in the T-accounts is:

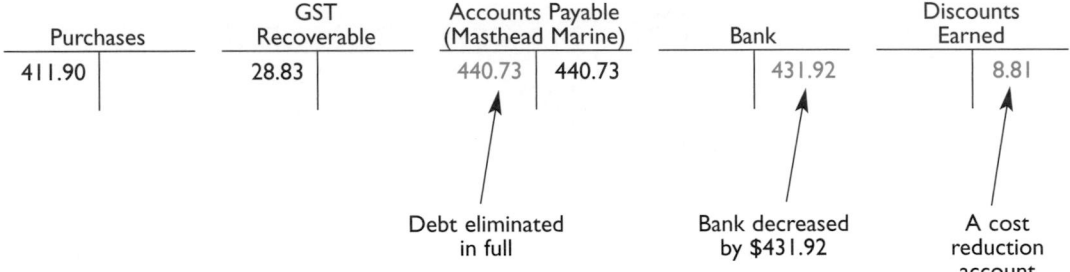

In the Books of the Seller (Masthead Marine)

From the data on the sales invoice copy, Masthead Marine makes the following accounting entry in the sales journal:

	DR	CR
Accounts Receivable (Nanaimo Marina)	$440.73	
Sales		$411.90
GST Payable		28.83

The effect in the T-accounts is:

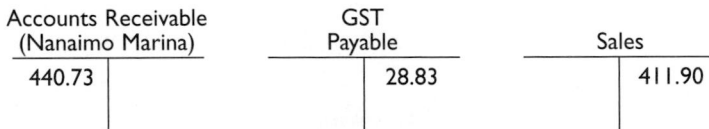

Upon receiving Nanaimo Marina's cheque for $431.92, Masthead Marine includes the cheque on the Daily List of Cash Receipts. A copy of the listing is forwarded to the accounts receivable clerk for posting to the customer's account in the subsidiary ledger. This clerk checks any discounts taken to see that they are calculated correctly and are within the discount period. The customer's account is credited with the gross amount, in this case $440.73.

Discounts Allowed are also
called "Discounts off Sales"
or "Sales Discounts."

From the listing, an accounting entry is also recorded in the cash receipts journal as follows:

	DR	CR
Bank	$431.92	
Discounts Allowed	8.81	
Accounts Receivable (Nanaimo Marina)		$440.73

After this accounting entry, the cumulative effect in the accounts is:

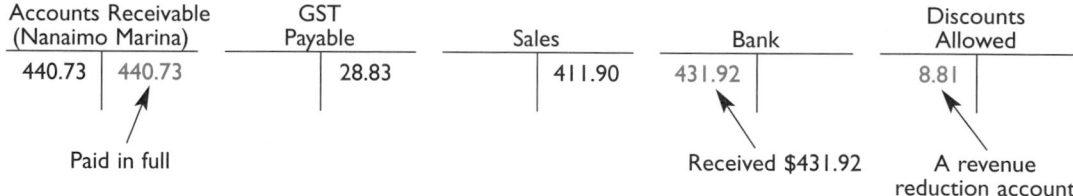

Additional Cash Discounts Facts

1. Occasionally, a customer takes a *late discount*. In other words, the customer takes the discount after the discount period has passed.

   Business people try to be reasonable when faced with this situation. There may be postal delays to consider. No business wants a reputation for being cheap. At the same time, a business does not want to be taken advantage of by its customers.

   If a business decides to disallow a late discount, the usual practice is to cash the customer's deficient cheque and to credit the customer's account with the amount of the cheque only, not the gross amount. This will leave a small balance in the account. It is good business to write a polite letter requesting that the customer make up the deficiency.

2. Every business will try to take advantage of the cash discounts offered by its suppliers. Therefore, entries to the Discounts Earned account can be expected to occur frequently. These entries will normally require a special column when a columnar journal is used.

3. Not all businesses offer cash discounts to their customers. A business that does not offer cash discounts will not have a Discounts Allowed account.

4. Occasionally, an invoice is received on which there is a cash discount and, some time before the discount date, a portion of the goods is returned or an allowance granted. In a case such as this, the usual procedure is to take the discount on the net cost of the goods, that is, the invoice figure less the credit note amount. Also, the discount date is adjusted to start from the date shown on the credit note.

5. Some businesses allow discounts only on the merchandise portion of an invoice, not on the taxes portion. For example, on the invoice in Figure 11.16 on page 455, the discount would be allowed only on the merchandise figure of $411.90 and would amount to $8.24. The vendor who follows this practice usually records the discount amount on the invoice so that there will be no confusion.

Cash Discounts on the Income Statement

There is more than one way of handling cash discounts on the income statement. The method selected depends on the amount of the discounts and the preference of the accountant. If the amounts involved are small, they might be combined into another account such as Miscellaneous Expense. A more formal method is shown in Figure 11.17 below. When the formal method is used, Discounts Allowed and Discounts Earned are treated as deductions from Sales and from Purchases respectively.

FIGURE 11.17

The income statement of Trillium Trading Co., showing discounts allowed and discounts earned.

TRILLIUM TRADING CO.
INCOME STATEMENT
YEAR ENDED DECEMBER 31, 20—

Revenue			
Sales		$403 955	
Less: Returns and Allowances	$ 21 151		
Discounts Allowed	5 296	26 447	
Net Sales			$377 508
Cost of Merchandise Sold			
Inventory, January 1		$ 72 074	
Purchases	$233 567		
Less: Returns and Allowances	$18 356		
Discounts Earned	4 358	22 714	
Net Purchases		210 853	
Freight-in		5 731	
Merchandise Available for Sale		$288 658	
Less: Inventory, December 31		83 562	205 096
Gross Profit			$172 412
Operating Expenses			
Advertising Expense		$ 1 141	
Bank Charges Expense		2 651	
Car Expense		4 999	
Delivery Expense		1 377	
Depreciation Expense — Automobiles		5 500	
Depreciation Expense — Equipment		3 112	
Insurance Used		2 915	
Miscellaneous Expense		1 872	
Rent Expense		12 000	
Salaries Expense		30 340	
Supplies Used		2 560	
Telephone Expense		1 850	
Utilities Expense		3 673	
Wages Expense		48 220	115 820
Net Income			$ 56 592

Section 11.5   **Review Questions**

 1. Define "cash discount."
 2. Define "terms of sale."
 3. Why would a business sell goods C.O.D.?
 4. Why would the buying firm accept C.O.D. as the terms of sale?
 5. What does the term "Net 30" mean?
 6. What does the term "2/10,n/30" mean?
 7. Where would the customer see the terms of sale for a transaction?
 8. Where could the manager of a business see the terms of sale for any customer?
 9. How does a business ensure that cash discounts are taken when available?
10. Which account — Discounts Allowed or Discounts Earned — is associated with a sales transaction?
11. What is another name for Discounts Allowed?
12. What is another name for Discounts Earned?
13. A business may not have an account for Discounts Allowed. Explain why.
14. Assume that there is a sales transaction followed by a sales return, and that there is a discount offered. On what figure is the discount calculated? On what date does the discount period begin?
15. Where does "Discounts Allowed" appear on the income statement?
16. Where does "Discounts Earned" appear on the income statement?

Section 11.5   **Exercises**

 1. **Complete the following schedule by calculating the amount of the payment that is necessary in each case. Where credit notes are involved, assume that the discount period is adjusted to start from the date on the credit note. This chart appears in your Workbook.**

Date of Invoice	Total of Invoice	Terms of Sale	Amount of Credit Note	Date of Credit Note	Date Payment Is Made	Amount of Payment Required
Mar. 12	$ 52.50	2/10,n/30	—	—	Mar. 20	
May 18	47.25	Net 30	—	—	May 27	
Sep. 4	115.50	3/15,n/60	—	—	Oct. 10	
Feb. 6	1 050.00	1/20,n/60	$126.00	Feb. 18	Mar. 6	
Oct. 19	588.00	2/10,n/30	42.00	Nov. 5	Nov. 27	
Aug. 27	882.00	2/15,n/60	168.00	Sep. 7	Sep. 10	

2. Complete the following schedule by calculating the date that payment is required to pick up the discount, and the amount of the payment required. This chart appears in your Workbook.

Date of Invoice	Total of Invoice	Terms of Sale	Amount of Credit Note	Date of Credit Note	Date Payment Is Made	Amount of Payment Required
May 14	$147.00	2/10,n/30	—	—		
Apr. 15	315.00	3/20,n/60	$42.00	May 1		
Jun. 3	220.05	2/10,n/60	78.75	Jun. 20		
Nov. 20	59.25	2/15,n/60	36.75	Dec. 2		

3. **A.** In two-column general journal form, record the accounting entry for the invoice shown below in the books of Circle Supply.

900 Park Street	**Circle◯Supply**		Maple City, SK

SOLD TO   Watson Construction
1500 Randell Road
Maple Creek, SK   S3Y 7N5   INVOICE NUMBER 715

DATE   August 3, 20–   TERMS 2/10,n/30

Quantity	Description	Unit Price	Amount
10 boxes	#10 Woodscrews	$5.50	$55.00
2	Standard Crowbars	4.10	8.20
			63.20
	GST		4.42
			$67.62

B. On August 12, a cheque in the amount of $66.27 is received from Watson Construction. **In two-column general journal form, show the accounting entry to be recorded in the books of Circle Supply.**

C. Watson Construction charges the merchandise shown on the above invoice to an account called Small Tools and Supplies. **Show the journal entries for the above two transactions that will be made in the books of Watson Construction. Use appropriate dates.**

4. **A.** **In the books of Circle Supply, in two-column general journal form, show the accounting entry to be recorded for the invoice below.**

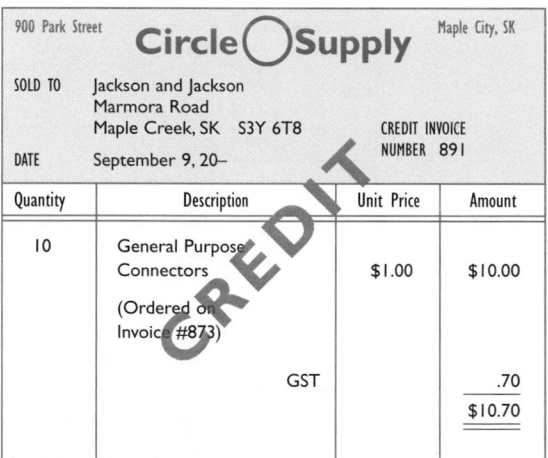

900 Park Street	Circle◯Supply		Maple City, SK

SOLD TO	Jackson and Jackson		
	Marmora Road		
	Maple Creek, SK S3Y 6T8	INVOICE NUMBER 873	
DATE	September 3, 20–	TERMS 2/10,n/30	

Quantity	Description	Unit Price	Amount
100	General Purpose Connectors	$1.00	$100.00
	GST		7.00
			$107.00

B. Some of the goods are found to be inadequate and are returned for credit. The following credit invoice is issued. **Show the accounting entry in general journal form to record this credit invoice in the books of Circle Supply.** Circle Supply does not use a Returns and Allowances account.

900 Park Street	Circle◯Supply		Maple City, SK

SOLD TO	Jackson and Jackson		
	Marmora Road		
	Maple Creek, SK S3Y 6T8	CREDIT INVOICE	
DATE	September 9, 20–	NUMBER 891	

Quantity	Description	Unit Price	Amount
10	General Purpose Connectors	$1.00	$10.00
	(Ordered on Invoice #873)		
	GST		.70
			$10.70

C. On September 19, a cheque is received in full payment of the sales invoice, less the credit invoice, less the cash discount. **Show the accounting entry in general journal form to record the receipt of this cheque.**

D. **Record the accounting entries to be made for the above transactions in the books of Jackson and Jackson. Use appropriate dates.** The goods affect the Supplies account.

Perpetual Inventory

There are many businesses for which the periodic inventory system is not adequate. Competition forces them to use the perpetual inventory system, which provides up-to-the-minute information about the company's stock. This is information that would not be possible if the periodic inventory system were used.

How It Works

The **perpetual inventory system** is one in which a detailed record of items in stock is kept up to date on an ongoing basis. Not many years ago, this was possible for only a few businesses. It took many employees at considerable cost to produce the information on a card file. Additions to the inventory were made from copies of receiving reports, which represented goods coming into the plant. Deductions from the inventory were made from copies of shipping orders, which represented goods going out of the plant. An example of a perpetual inventory card is shown in Figure 11.18 below.

FIGURE 11.18

A card from a perpetual inventory file.

INVENTORY CONTROL CARD

Stock Number	L591		Maximum	500 DOZ.
Description	200 Watt Light Bulbs		Minimum	50 DOZ.
Location: Row	17	Bin 35		

Date	Reference	Unit Cost	Quantity Received	Quantity Shipped	Balance on Hand
20– Nov. 5	Balance Forward				216
11	S.O. 436			100	116
14	S.O. 501			40	76
19	S.O. 530			35	41
21	S.O. 539			20	21
22	R.R. 1074	41 ¢	450		471
25	S.O. 561			75	396

Today, computers are able to do the work far more effectively at a reasonable cost. With a computer system, the inventory records are kept in a computer file. The system is organized numerically with each item being given a unique code. As goods are received from suppliers, receiving reports are made out. Copies of these reports are then sent to the data entry clerk, who enters the items into the inventory. If purchased goods are returned, the appropriate deductions from inventory are made.

The more technically complex part of the system happens in respect to sales. For example, in a store, each cash register is a point-of-sale terminal connected to the store's main computer. As items are sold, the cashier's duties include entering the code numbers and the quantities sold via the cash register keyboard or by means of an electronic scanner. The information is transferred directly to the store's central computer, which is programmed to make the appropriate deductions from the inventory and to make the accounting entries shown below. (Assume that goods that cost $100 are sold for $150.)

	DR	CR	
1. Bank	$172.50		
Sales		$150.00	
PST Payable		12.00	selling price
GST Payable		10.50	
2. Cost of Goods Sold	$100.00		
Merchandise Inventory		$100.00	cost price

Sales returns are generally handled by a separate department, usually the customer service department.

As good as the system is, it doesn't automatically know when goods are lost, stolen, or broken. Therefore, a manual check of the inventory is required. This is usually carried out on a random basis throughout the year. The quantity of individual items on hand is counted and compared with the book inventory shown by the computer. Any differences are adjusted to agree with the quantity counted manually.

Comparing the Perpetual and Periodic Inventory Systems

The transaction above describes a sale of merchandise for $150 under the perpetual inventory system. By examining the two parts of this transaction, you can determine a few of the differences between the periodic and perpetual inventory systems. First, it is important to note that a sale under the perpetual inventory system has two parts. The first part records the receipt of cash (or accounts receivable), the amount of the sale, and the taxes. This is familiar to you.

The second part of the transaction is the cost portion. Inventory has been sold and is no longer owned by the business. The cost of this inventory is recorded by debiting the Cost of Goods Sold account and crediting the Merchandise Inventory account.

Debiting the Cost of Goods Sold account for each sale means that the cost of goods sold formula required by the periodic inventory system is no longer needed. As a result, the Purchases account and the Purchases Returns and Allowances account—important items in the cost of goods sold formula—are unnecessary when the perpetual inventory system is used.

Other important differences between the two inventory systems will become clear to you as you work your way through the following set of transactions. Fifty portable stereo units were sold by Sound Wave Electronics, a wholesaler. The purchaser is Fidelity Sound, a retailer. The units cost Sound Wave Electronics $45 each; they were sold on account to Fidelity Sound for $90.

The set of transactions that follows includes the original sale, a return of goods, a payment on account, and a cash discount for prompt payment. Compare how the journal entries would differ for each business depending on which inventory system it used.

A) Journal Entries for Sound Wave Electronics

1) Sales Invoice
Fifty portable stereos (costings $45 each) are sold to Fidelity Sound for $90; terms 2/10, net 30. Total $4 500, plus GST.

Periodic Inventory System			Perpetual Inventory System		
	Dr	Cr		Dr	Cr
Apr 18 Accounts Receivable	4815.00		Apr 18 Accounts Receivable	4815.00	
Sales		4500.00	Cost of Goods Sold	2250.00	
GST Payable		315.00	Merchandise Inventory		2250.00
			Sales		4500.00
			GST Payable		315.00

Observations
The cost of the sale is accounted for under the perpetual inventory system (50 × $45 = $ 2 250). The cost of the goods that were sold and the Merchandise Inventory account are temporarily ignored under the periodic system.

2) Credit Invoice
Fidelity Sound finds 10 of the portable stereos to be defective and returns them to Sound Wave Electronics.

Periodic Inventory System				Perpetual System			
		Dr	Cr			Dr	Cr
Apr 20	Sales Returns and Allowances	900.00		Apr 20	Sales Returns and Allowances	900.00	
	GST Payable	63.00			GST Payable	63.00	
	Accounts Receivable		963.00		Merchandise Inventory	450.00	
					Cost of Goods Sold		450.00
					Accounts Receivable		963.00

Observations
With the perpetual method, Merchandise Inventory is debited because the stereo units are back in the store. Cost of Goods Sold is reduced because a $900 portion of the sale has been cancelled.

3) Remittance Slip
Fidelity Sound pays the amount owed ($4815 less the return of $963 equals $3 852). Also, prompt payment earns a 2% discount.

Periodic Inventory System				Perpetual Inventory System			
		Dr	Cr			Dr	Cr
Apr 27	Bank	3774.96		Apr 27	Bank	3774.96	
	Sales Discount	77.04			Sales Discount	77.04	
	Accounts Receivable		3852.00		Accounts Receivable		3852.00

Observations
The entries are the same under both systems.

B) Journal Entries for Fidelity Sound

1) Purchase Invoice
Fifty portable stereos are brought from Sound Wave Electronics for $90; terms 2.10, net 30. Total $4500, plus GST.

Periodic Inventory System				Perpetual Inventory System			
		Dr	Cr			Dr	Cr
Apr 18	Purchases	4500.00		Apr 18	Merchandise Inventory	4500.00	
	GST Recoverable	315.00			GST Recoverable	315.00	
	Accounts Payable		4815.00		Accounts Payable		4815.00

Observations
No Purchases account exists under the perpetual inventory system. The Merchandise Inventory account is debited for purchase and credited for sales. Such treatment shows that Merchandise Inventory is updated on an ongoing or "perpetual" basis.

2) Credit Invoice
Fidelity Sound finds 10 of the portable stereos to be defective and returns them to Sound Wave Electronics.

Periodic Inventory System				Perpetual Inventory System			
		Dr	Cr			Dr	Cr
Apr 20	Accounts Payable	963.00		Apr 20	Accounts Payable	963.00	
	Purchase Returns and Allow.		900.00		Merchandise Inventory		900.00
	GST Recoverable		63.00		GST Recoverable		63.00

Observations
The perpetual system decreases the asset account. No record of merchandise returned to suppliers will appear on financial statements.

3) Cheque Copy
Fidelity Sound pays the amount owed ($4815 less the return of $963 equals $3852). Also, prompt payment earns a 2% discount.

Periodic Inventory System				Perpetual Inventory System			
		Dr	Cr			Dr	Cr
Apr 27	Accounts Payable	3852.00		Apr 27	Accounts Payable	3852.00	
	Bank		3774.96		Bank		3774.96
	Purchase Discounts		77.04		Discounts Earned		77.04

Observations
Except for the names of the account titles for discounts, the entries are the same.

Even though transportation charges and purchases discounts affect the cost value of merchandise inventory, GAAPs allow you to accumulate these items in separate accounts rather than charging them to the Merchandise Inventory account.

You may use the preceding set of transactions as a guide for making most of the journal entries you will encounter when you use the perpetual inventory system. Transportation charges were not mentioned, but you should know that they are handled the same way under both inventory systems, That is, continue to debit Freight-in when you encounter transportation charges.

One other transaction you will likely deal with when using the perpetual inventory system occurs when a customer returns defective goods that are so spoiled that they cannot be sold again. Recording the return as a debit to Merchandise Inventory would overstate the asset account because the returned merchandise has no value. To handle such an event, accountants create an expense account and give it a name such as Inventory Shrinkage. If an accounting clerk debited Merchandise Inventory when worthless goods were returned, the following entry would fix the error:

	DR	CR
Inventory Shrinkage	$$$	
Merchandise Inventory		$$$

The entry above can also be used when a physical inventory reveals an over-stated amount in the Merchandise Inventory account. Examples of possible causes for the discrepancy may be theft and damage.

Section 11.6   Review Questions

1. Describe the perpetual inventory system.
2. Before the use of computers, what form did a perpetual inventory system take?
3. Why did only a few businesses keep track of inventory on card files?
4. Name the source document for additions to inventory in a manual system.
5. Name the source document for deductions from inventory in a manual system.
6. In a department store environment, how are the deductions made from the inventory after a sale?
7. Is it necessary to count the inventory when a perpetual system is used? Explain.
8. What is the basic entry for the cost portion of sale when the perpetual inventory system is used?
9. Switching from a periodic system to a perpetual system adds one new account to the ledger and eliminates at least two. Identify these accounts.
10. How are transportation charges handled under both inventory systems?
11. If inventory were lost, stolen, or damaged under a perpetual inventory system, you would credit Merchandise Inventory. What account would you debit?

Section 11.6   Exercises

1. **Complete each of the following statements by writing in your Workbook the appropriate word or phrase from the list on page 466.**

   A. Additions to inventory are usually made from copies of _____.
   B. _____ forces department stores to use the perpetual inventory system.
   C. In a computer inventory system, each inventory item is given a _____.
   D. The _____ inventory system produces up-to-the-minute information that cannot be produced by the _____ inventory system.

E. Deductions from inventory are usually made from copies of _____ or through _____ in a modern store.

F. Any differences between the _____ figures and the actual figures require an _____ to the book figure.

G. Even in a computer inventory system, a _____ of the stock is necessary.

H. A journal entry for a sale under the perpetual inventory system includes a debit to _____ and a credit to _____.

I. When buying inventory, the _____ account is not used with the perpetual inventory system.

J. Spoiled merchandise forces a debit to the _____ account.

List of Words or Phrases

adjustment	merchandise inventory
avoid	periodic
book	perpetual
competition	point-of-sale terminals
cost of goods sold	Purchases
count	receiving reports
damaged inventory	shipping orders
Inventory Shrinkage	unique code

2. Two inventory cards from the perpetual inventory file of Outpost Marine are included in the Workbook. These cards are shown on page 467.

A. From the source documents listed below, choose those that pertain to the two selected inventory items and record the increases or decreases on the cards as if you were the inventory clerk.

B. Assume that the quantities on hand are the latest purchases. Calculate the cost value for these two inventory items for inclusion in a summary for the grand inventory total.

Source Documents			Stock No.	Quantity	Unit Price
March	1	Shipping Order No. 921	730-0320	5	
	1	Shipping Order No. 922	713-3011	6	
	2	Receiving Report No. 630	736-0551	10	5.10
	3	Shipping Order No. 923	714-1018	35	
		Receiving Report No. 631	375-1000	20	10.50
	4	Receiving Report No. 632	931-4014	25	9.05
	5	Shipping Order No. 924	730-0320	15	
	8	Receiving Report No. 633	423-6757	5	25.60
		Shipping Order No. 925	713-3011	10	
	10	Receiving Report No. 634	703-1912	25	.50
	11	Receiving Report No. 635	602-4210	20	1.45
		Shipping Order No. 926	705-1912	15	
	12	Shipping Order No. 927	707-1129	100	
	15	Receiving Report No. 636	713-3011	35	9.40
	18	Receiving Report No. 637	920-0012	24	2.55
	19	Shipping Order No. 928	730-0320	2	
	20	Receiving Report No. 638	640-3121	30	40.25
	23	Shipping Order No. 929	713-3011	15	
	25	Receiving Report No. 639	730-0320	25	16.00
	30	Shipping Order No. 930	730-0320	12	
	31	Shipping Order No. 931	713-3011	20	
		Receiving Report No. 640	715-6745	12	5.20

INVENTORY CONTROL CARD

Stock Number   730-0320   Maximum   30

Description   SCHAEFER CHEEK BLOCK   Minimum   10

Location: Row   16   Bin   3

Date	Reference	Unit Cost	Quantity Received	Quantity Shipped	Balance on Hand
Feb. 20	Forward	15.50			28
26	S.O. 904			5	23

INVENTORY CONTROL CARD

Stock Number   713-3011   Maximum   50

Description   BARTON CAM CLEAT   Minimum   20

Location: Row   20   Bin   14

Date	Reference	Unit Cost	Quantity Received	Quantity Shipped	Balance on Hand
Feb. 24	Forward	9.20			37
26	S.O. 910			10	27

3. **This exercise also appears in your Workbook.**

Shown below are some of the accounts (in T-account form) from the ledger of Master Security Systems. Master Security Systems has a computer accounting system and is able to keep its inventory and cost of goods accounts up to the minute. There is no account for Purchases. Assume that the Bank account has a balance of $40 000.

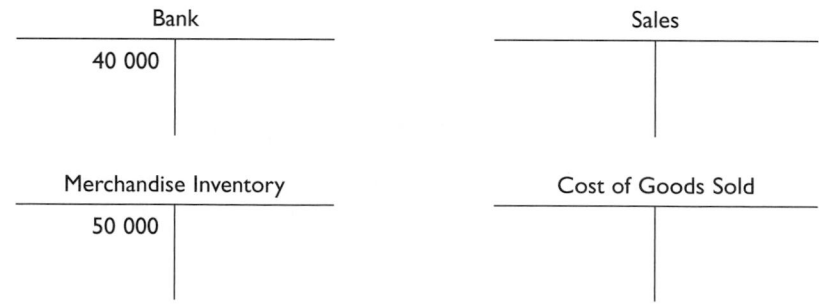

Record the journal entries for the following transactions directly into the ledger accounts. Ignore Freight-in, GST, and PST. When you finish recording the entries, calculate the balance of each account.

TRANSACTIONS

1. Purchased merchandise for cash at a cost of $10 000.
2. Sold goods for cash. The goods, recorded in the inventory at $6 000, are sold for $11 000. *(Note: There are two aspects of this transaction to record.)*
3. Sold goods for cash. The goods, recorded in the inventory at $9 000, are sold for $15 000. *(Note: There are two aspects of this transaction to record.)*
4. Purchased merchandise for cash at a cost of $3 000.

---

4. The following transactions affecting a retail business named Fleet Foot Runners occurred in the month of May:

Purchase Invoice

May 3 Purchased 40 pairs of cross-training running shoes from Lau's Sports Warehouse for $39.95 per pair, terms 2/10, net 30. The amount before taxes was $1 598, plus GST of $111.86, total $1709.86.

Credit Invoice

7 Returned 5 defective pairs of running shoes to Lau's Sports Warehouse and received a full credit for these items.

Cheque Copy

12 Deducted the discount for early payment, paid the full amount owed to Lau's Sports Warehouse.

Cash Register Tape

22 Sold five pairs of the cross-training running shoes at a retail price of $74.95 per pair. Amount of the cash sales was $374.75, plus PST of $29.98, GST of $26.23, total $430.96.

Cash Register Tape

29 Customer returned a pair of the cross-training running shoes after wearing them for one week; customer complained that they did not fit properly. The manager of Fleet Foot Runners granted a full cash refund; however, the runners were worn and damaged and could not be sold again. (Note: This transaction needs two separate journal entries.)

Required

A. Using the perpetual inventory system, journalize the above transactions for Fleet Foot Runners.
B. Using the perpetual inventory system, journalize the transactions dated May 3, 7, and 12 for Lau's Sports Warehouse.

11.7 | # Simply Accounting Inventory Applications

From studying the perpetual inventory system, you can appreciate why it used to present a challenge to accountants. Basically, in addition to recording revenue transactions in the regular way, accounting staff had to debit Cost of Goods Sold and credit Merchandise Inventory each time a sale was made. If a business sold many different items, the task was extremely time-consuming. For example, it would be difficult for a music store to look up the cost value of each CD or cassette tape. Large department and hardware stores faced even greater burdens. For such businesses, the periodic inventory system was clearly the superior solution.

Eventually, sophisticated computer systems streamlined the flow of inventory information for large businesses. Now, even small businesses enjoy the benefits of the perpetual inventory system by using accounting software like Simply Accounting. In this section, you will see how Simply Accounting handles the demands of the perpetual inventory system. And, if you complete the Summary Exercise, you can use the Inventory and Services module of Simply Accounting for a new business named Sunshell Designs.

Sunshell Designs wholesales a product best described as a "beach tent," which protects people from the sun and wind. The beach tents are called sunshells. The business sells two sizes of sunshells to retailers—medium and large—and it supplies the sunshells with or without the purchaser's corporate logo.

Creating Inventory Items

One of the first tasks for the accounting clerk of Sunshell Designs is to use Simply Accounting to create "electronic inventory cards" for each of the four inventory items it has in stock. The information for each item includes the selling prices, which are listed below:

Sunshell—large	$26.50
Sunshell—large with logo	$32.50
Sunshell—medium	$23.50
Sunshell—medium with logo	$29.50

Other critical data Simply Accounting needs at this stage are the ledger accounts that will be affected when an inventory item is sold. These are referred to as linked accounts and are shown in Figure 11.19 below.

FIGURE 11.19

The linked accounts for large sunshells.

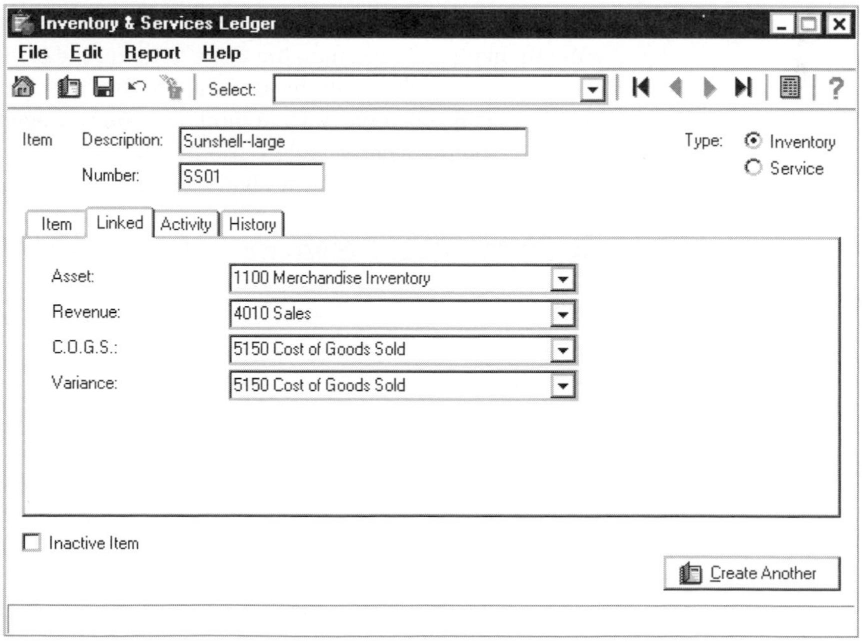

Later, you will see how the linked accounts identified in Figure 11.19 are used by Simply Accounting.

Making Purchases

Sunshell Designs buys its stock from a manufacturer named Gerry's Tent and Awning. The accounting clerk uses Simply Accounting to complete the first purchase invoice. The computer screen would look like Figure 11.20 below.

FIGURE 11.20

The invoice for Sunshell Design's first purchase.

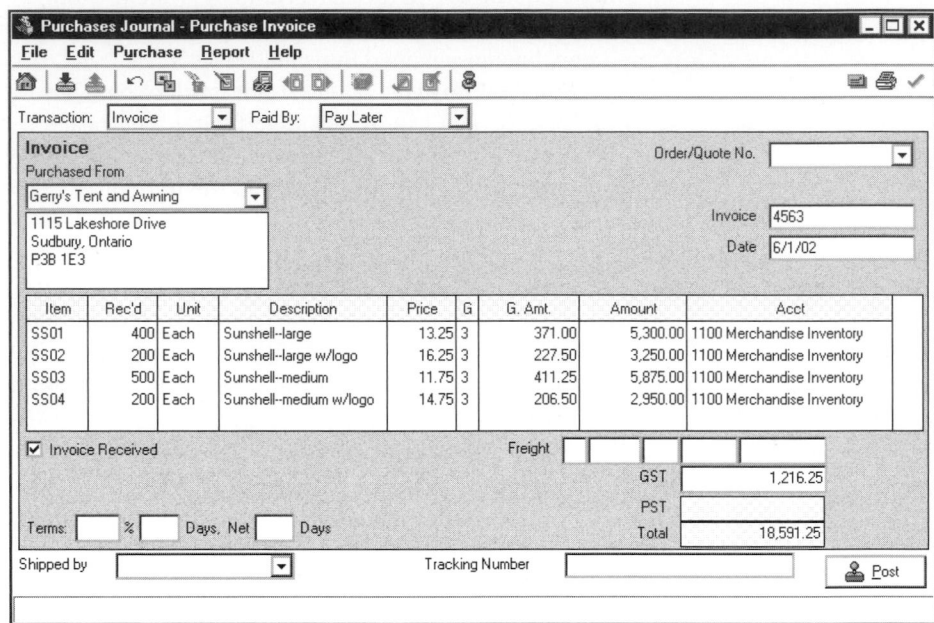

To complete the purchase invoice in Figure 11.20, the accounting clerk enters the stock number in the Item column and the quantity bought in the Rec'd (Received) column. In the next column, the Price column, the clerk enters some very important data. The prices shown in this column are the cost prices Sunshell Designs pays for its merchandise inventory. (In a moment, you will see how Simply Accounting uses this data when a sale is made.) The purchase invoice in Figure 11.20 produces the journal entry shown below in Figure 11.21.

FIGURE 11.21

The journal entry for the first purchase.

Purchases Journal Entry

File Options Help

6/1/02 (J1)

	Debits	Credits	Project
1100 Merchandise Inventory	17,375.00	-	
2150 GST Recoverable	1,216.25	-	
2050 Accounts Payable	-	18,591.25	
	18,591.25	18,591.25	

Making Sales

To enter the first sale, the accounting clerk prepares the sales invoice shown in Figure 11.22.

FIGURE 11.22

The invoice for Sunshell Design's first sale.

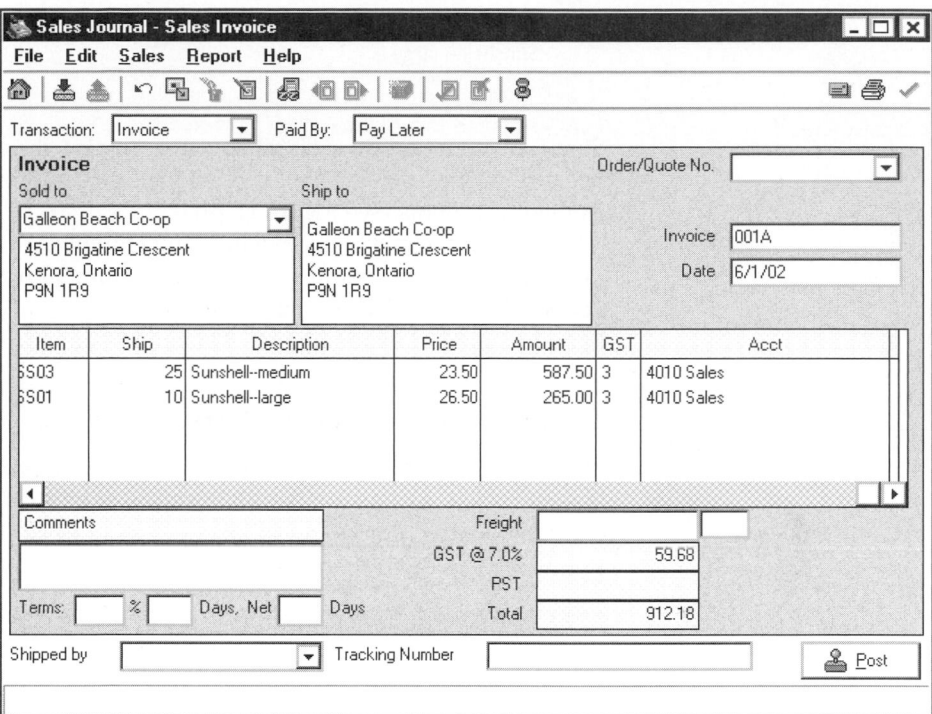

As soon as the accounting clerk enters the item numbers, Simply Accounting retrieves data from the inventory cards and displays the amounts shown in the Price column—$23.50 and $26.50.

The main point of this section comes next. When the accounting clerk clicks the Post button at the bottom-right corner of Figure 11.22, the journal entry seen in Figure 11.23 is processed.

FIGURE 11.23

The journal entry for the first sale.

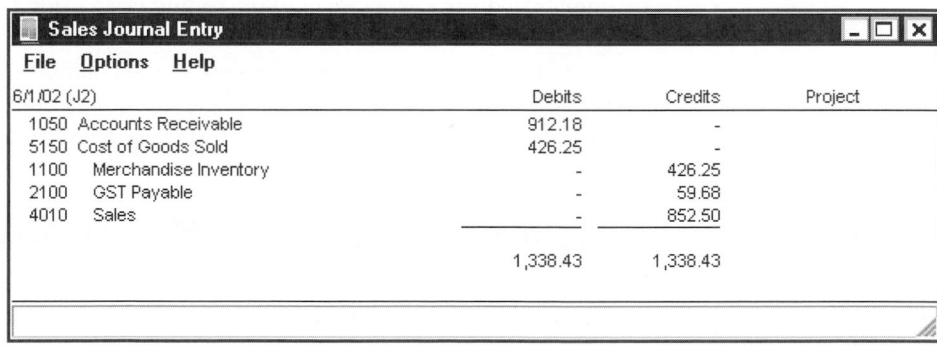

Three of the amounts in Figure 11.23 can be traced back to the sales invoice in Figure 11.22—Accounts Receivable, $912.18; GST $59.68; and Sales, $852.50. What should be apparent to you is that the cost portion of this sale has been produced automatically by the software. Simply Accounting went back to the purchase invoice (Figure 11.20), picked up the cost prices of the medium and large sunshells, and performed the following calculation:

	Quantity	*Cost Price*	*Totals*
Sunshell—medium	25	$11.75	$293.75
Sunshell—large	10	$13.25	$132.50
			$426.25

Simply Accounting then distributed the cost of the sale to the proper accounts because Cost of Goods Sold and Merchandise Inventory were previously identified as linked accounts (see Figure 11.19).

The essential fact to understand is that Simply Accounting does the cost portion of an inventory sale automatically. This feature allows for a huge reduction in the accounting workload and enables even small businesses to take advantage of the benefits provided by the perpetual inventory system.

Displaying Inventory Reports

Many of the advantages that the perpetual inventory system has over the periodic inventory system involve the ability to generate up-to-the-minute reports about inventory status. For example, an accounting clerk using Simply Accounting can easily produce the report shown in Figure 11.24.

FIGURE 11.24

An inventory summary report for Sunshell Designs.

Inventory Synopsis

File Options Help

6/1/02			Price	Quantity	Cost	Value	Margin (%)
Sunshell--large	SS01	Each	26.50	390	13.25	5,167.50	50.00
Sunshell--large w/logo	SS02	Each	32.50	200	16.25	3,250.00	50.00
Sunshell--medium	SS03	Each	23.50	475	11.75	5,581.25	50.00
Sunshell--medium w/l...	SS04	Each	29.50	200	14.75	2,950.00	50.00
						16,948.75	

The report in Figure 11.24 shows selling prices, cost prices, quantities on hand, total cost values, and margins. (The margin column reveals that, after the cost of a sunshell is deducted, 50 percent of the selling price is left to pay for operating expenses and allow for a profit.)

If further investigation is needed, the accounting clerk can produce a detailed report on the activity and status of particular inventory items. For example, Figure 11.25 shows the movement of large sunshells in and out of the business, as well as the current balance on hand. Dollar amounts and invoice references are also displayed.

FIGURE 11.25

Detailed sales activity of large sunshells.

Inventory and Services Transaction Detail Report

File Options Help

Date	Type		Source	Qty In	Qty Out	On Hand	Amount	Balance
Sunshell--large SS01								
Balance forward						0		0.00
6/1/02	PUR	J1	4563	400		400	5,300.00	5,300.00
6/1/02	SAL	J2	001A		10	390	-132.50	5,167.50
Unit of measure: Each				400	10		5,167.50	

Double-click to display the record on this line

Section 11.7   **Review Questions**

1. Why has the perpetual inventory system been a challenge for accountants?
2. When inventory "cards" are created in Simply Accounting, which price is recorded—selling or cost?
3. What are linked accounts?
4. When an accounting clerk prepares a sales invoice and enters a stock item number, Simply Accounting generates an amount in the Price column. Where does Simply Accounting find this amount?
5. When a sales invoice is posted, what asset account is automatically credited by Simply Accounting? What "expense" account is automatically debited?
6. If the selling price of large sunshells were increased to $39.75, what would be the new percent margin? (Refer to Figure 11.24.)

Section 11.7   **Exercises**

1. To use Simply Accounting's Inventory and Services Module for Sunshell Designs, complete the summary exercise. Note: You should first complete the summary exercise for Travel Trailers.

2. To work on a budgeting exercise that involves merchandise inventory, complete Case Study 5 on page 492.

11.8   # Manufacturing Businesses—A Comparison

At this point in your study of accounting, you should have no trouble explaining the major differences between a service business and a merchandising business. You might begin by stating the obvious. That is, the service business earns revenue by selling services; the merchandising business earns revenue by selling goods. The merchandising business, therefore, has an extra expense because it must first buy the goods it sells. This extra expense is called *cost of goods sold*. Since cost of goods sold is a major expense, it is moved to a prominent position on the income statement, as shown below in Figure 11.26.

FIGURE 11.26

A basic comparison of the income statements for a service business and a merchandising business.

Income Statement Service Business	Income Statement Merchandising Business
Fees Earned	Sales
	− Cost of Goods Sold
	= Gross Profit
− Operating Expenses	− Operating Expenses
= Net Income	= Net Income

To complete this comparison, you would also point out that buying goods and then selling them at a higher price makes a slight modification on the balance sheet of a merchandising business. Specifically, the goods purchased for resale appear as a current asset named Merchandise Inventory.

Now that you know about merchandising businesses, you should extend your knowledge to manufacturing firms. Manufacturing accounting is very detailed. If you study accounting in your post-secondary years, you will cover manufacturing accounting in depth. For now, you will keep your comparison of manufacturing accounting to merchandising accounting basic, just like the above comparison for service and merchandising businesses.

Comparing Income Statements

Both merchandising and manufacturing firms earn revenue from selling goods. The essential difference between the two is that the merchandising business buys the goods it sells; the **manufacturing business** makes the goods it sells. This difference, while important, will not affect the basic calculation of net income. For both types of firms, net income is determined by the following calculation.

Sales − Cost of Goods Sold = Gross Profit − Operating Expenses = Net Income

Important distinctions between merchandising and manufacturing firms do appear when you closely examine a particular part of the above calculation. It should be easy for you to guess what part this is. If you remember that one of these firms buys the goods it sells while the other makes the goods it sells, you can expect that significant variations will exist in the cost of goods sold section. A comparison of the two cost of goods sold sections appears below in Figure 11.27.

FIGURE 11.27

Cost of Goods Sold sections of income statements for merchandising and manufacturing firms.

Merchandising Firm	Manufacturing Firm
Cost of Goods Sold Beginning Inventory + Purchases = Cost of Goods Available − Ending Inventory = Cost of Goods Sold	*Cost of Goods Sold* Beginning Finished Goods + Cost of Goods Manufactured = Cost of Goods Available − Ending Inventory of Finished Goods = Cost of Goods Sold

Figure 11.27 shows that the primary difference in calculating cost of goods sold for merchandising and manufacturing firms boils down to the cost of "purchases" versus the "cost of goods manufactured." This seems straightforward. So why is manufacturing accounting so much more detailed than merchandising accounting? The reason is that determining the cost of purchases is simple; it can be obtained from the balances of a few accounts in the ledger. However, determining the cost of goods manufactured is complex.

The manufacturer starts with raw materials and ends with a good ready to be sold. Along the way, a great variety of costs can be attached to the manufacture of that good. It is vital that management knows what these costs are and how they can control them. In fact, management's need to know about costs has created an entire branch of accounting know as cost accounting. **Cost accounting** is a specialized area of accounting that concentrates on determining, controlling, and reporting the costs of doing business. (Note: While many cost accountants find employment in manufacturing companies, their expertise can help the profitability of other type of businesses as well.)

The cost of goods manufactured introduced in Figure 11.27 requires a detailed calculation. Normally, the calculation is too long to fit easily on an income statement. Therefore, a separate manufacturing statement is prepared and only the final amount is reported on the income statement. Consider the manufacturing statement in Figure 11.28 for the business Gerry's Tent and Awning.

FIGURE 11.28

A manufacturing statement that reveals the cost of manufacturing goods in a fiscal period.

Another name for the manufacturing statement is the "schedule of the cost of goods manufactured."

The amount at the bottom of this statement — the cost of goods manufactured — $147 000 gets carried forward to the income statement.

GERRY'S TENT AND AWNING MANUFACTURING STATEMENT YEAR ENDED DECEMBER 31, 20—			
Raw materials			
Opening inventory of raw materials		$30 000	
Raw materials purchased	$60 000		
Freight charges	2 000		
Cost of raw materials purchased		62 000	
Raw materials available for use		$92 000	
Less: ending inventory of raw materials		25 000	
Raw materials used			$ 67 000
Direct labour			42 000
Factory overhead			
Indirect labour		$16 000	
Factory supplies used		1 000	
Municipal taxes		5 000	
Depreciation of factory and equipment		4 000	
Utilities		7 000	
Insurance		8 000	
Total factory overhead costs			41 000
Total manufacturing costs			$150 000
Add: Goods in process inventory, January 1			12 000
Total goods in process during the year			$162 000
Deduct: Goods in process inventory, December 31			15 000
Cost of goods manufactured			$147 000

To understand how to calculate the cost of goods manufactured, observe the three important items shown in boldface: raw materials used, direct labour, and factory overhead. These are three important costs common to manufacturing businesses.

Raw materials are essential components that become part of the finished product. The raw materials for Gerry's Tent and Awning would include nylon fabric, fibreglass poles, and so on. Examine Figure 11.28 again. You can see that calculating the cost of raw materials used is similar to calculating cost of goods sold (Opening inventory, plus purchases, minus ending inventory).

Direct labour represents the wages for those employees who have a specific role in the making of the finished goods. Wages to workers on an assembly line is a good example of direct labour.

Factory overhead includes a range of expenses that support the manufacturing process. These include indirect labour, which is different than direct labour. **Indirect labour** represents wages to workers who support the manufacturing process. One example would be the janitorial staff that cleans the debris from an assembly line. Both assembly line workers and janitorial staff are needed, but the wages of the janitorial staff are not easily associated with the number of units produced each day.

Together, raw materials used, direct labour, and factory overhead represent the manufacturing costs for a fiscal period. However, you must remember that on any given day, including the start and end dates of a fiscal period, there is bound to be unfinished work in the factory. This is called goods in process. **Goods in process** refers to goods that have had some raw materials, direct labour, or overhead applied to them, but that are not yet in their finished states.

To arrive at an amount for the cost of goods manufactured, you must include work in process. Therefore, add the total manufacturing costs (raw materials, direct labour, and factory overhead) to the value of goods in process at the beginning of the year. The answer represents the total goods in process for the year. When you deduct the value of goods still in process at the end of the year, the difference must be the value of finished or manufactured goods. This calculation is seen at the bottom of the statement shown in Figure 11.28.

Comparing Balance Sheets

Remember the earlier statement: "The merchandising business buys the goods it sells; the manufacturing business makes the goods it sells." This explanation of the key difference between merchandising and manufacturing focuses on "goods." It follows, therefore, that the only real difference you will see on the balance sheets of these two types of firms relates to the reporting of goods, otherwise know as inventory.

In the current asset section of the merchandising firm, you will find an account named Merchandise Inventory. This represents the cost value of merchandise on hand. In contrast, the manufacturing business lists three inventory accounts in its current asset section. The first is Finished Goods Inventory, which is comparable to Merchandise Inventory. The other two you have just learned. They can be seen on the manufacturing statement in Figure 11.28, as well as on the balance sheet. They are the Raw Materials Inventory and the Goods in Process Inventory.

Summary

Due to the complexities of manufacturing accounting, some educational institutions delay its introduction until students reach their second year of post-secondary studies. Yet, by being exposed to manufacturing accounting at this time, you benefit in at least two ways. First, you can see how a sound knowledge of merchandise accounting and the cost of goods sold formula can help you understand manufacturing statements. And, second, by recognizing the great variety of costs associated with manufacturing a good, you can begin to appreciate the important role of a cost accountant.

Section 11.8   **Review Questions**

1. What is the major expense that a merchandising business has that a service business does not?
2. What is the essential difference between a merchandising business and a manufacturing business?
3. Describe the differences in calculating the cost of goods sold for merchandising and manufacturing businesses.
4. What is cost accounting?
5. Why is the calculation for the cost of goods manufactured not normally shown on the income statement?
6. Give another name for the manufacturing statement.
7. What three important costs make up the manufacturing costs for a fiscal period?
8. Explain the difference between direct labour and indirect labour.
9. What are goods in process?
10. What is another name for goods in process?
11. Explain mathematically how goods in process and the total manufacturing costs are combined to determine the cost of goods manufactured.
12. Identify the three inventory accounts that may appear on the balance sheet of a manufacturing firm.
13. Give an example of how understanding the cost of goods sold formula helps you with a calculation on the manufacturing statement.

Section 11.8   **Exercises**

1. The manufacturing statement of Codling Company shows the cost of goods manufactured to be $312 000 for the year ended December 31, 20–. Other income statement items for the year are Sales $512 600; Beginning Finished Goods $24 900; and Ending Inventory of Finished Goods $27 800.

   Required:
   Prepare a partial income statement (from sales to gross profit) for Codling Company.

2. Fill in the seven blanks in the manufacturing statement for Cull's Novelties on page 478. This manufacturing statement also appears in your Workbook.

CULL'S NOVELTIES
MANUFACTURING STATEMENT
YEAR ENDED DECEMBER 31, 20—

Raw materials

Opening inventory of raw materials		$42 500	
Raw materials Purchased	$89 600		
Freight charges	6 900		
Cost of raw materials purchased		(1)	
Raw materials available for use		$(2)	
Less: ending inventory of raw materials		(3)	
Raw materials used			$125 300
Direct labour			109 800
Factory overhead			
Indirect labour		$37 000	
Factory supplies used		11 600	
Property taxes		11 800	
Depreciation of factory and equipment		18 900	
Utilities		19 500	
Maintenance		8 000	
Total factory overhead costs			(4)
Total manufacturing costs			$(5)
Add: Goods in process inventory, January 1			22 000
Total goods in process during the year			$(6)
Deduct: Goods in process inventory, December 31			(7)
Cost of goods manufactured			$318 400

3. A list of manufacturing items for Ryder Industries appears below in alphabetical order. From this list, prepare a manufacturing statement for Ryder Industries for the year ended December 31, 20–.

Depreciation of factory and equipment	$11 000
Depreciation of small tools	500
Direct labour	67 800
Ending inventory of raw materials	20 600
Factory supplies used	6 800
Freight charges	2 900
Goods in process inventory, December 31	29 700
Goods in process inventory, January 1	13 300
Indirect labour	13 500
Maintenance and repair	12 500
Opening inventory of raw materials	17 600
Property taxes	7 900
Raw materials Purchased	45 300
Utilities	13 600

4. Use the Internet or library to help you complete the following research tasks:

A. Find a Canadian manufacturing company.

B. Locate the annual report for that company.

C. Print or photocopy the income statement, manufacturing statement, and balance sheet.

D. Make a list of the similarities and differences between the statements of you discovered and the statements shown or referred to in this section.

Note: For help locating annual reports online, visit *www.pearsoned.ca/ accounting1*

CHAPTER 11   Summary

CHAPTER HIGHLIGHTS

Now that you have completed Chapter 11, you should:

- know what is meant by the terms merchandising business, wholesaler, and retailer;
- know what is meant by merchandise inventory or stock-in-trade;
- list merchandise inventory correctly on the balance sheet and on the income statement;
- understand what is meant by gross profit;
- understand the purpose of offering a cash discount;
- know the accounting entries for discounts earned and discounts allowed;
- know how discounts earned and discounts allowed are presented on the income statement;
- know the difference between the periodic and the perpetual inventory systems;
- know the inventory cycle and the cost of goods sold calculation;
- know the accounting entries for 1) the purchase and sale of merchandise inventory, 2) freight-in, and 3) duty;
- understand the accounting entries that affect the Merchandise Inventory account;
- understand the need to take an end-of-period inventory;
- be able to prepare a work sheet for a merchandising business;
- be able to record the closing entries for a merchandising business;
- understand the concept of merchandise returns and allowances;
- be able to identify a credit invoice and to make the accounting entries for a credit invoice issued and a credit invoice received;
- know the accounting entries for a cash refund;
- understand why some businesses use special accounts for returns and allowances;
- know the accounting entries for transactions that affect returns and allowances accounts;
- be able to prepare an income statement that includes returns and allowances accounts;
- know the similarities between a manufacturing business and a merchandising business;
- identify the accounting elements that are particular to a manufacturing business;
- understand how Simply Accounting makes the perpetual inventory system practical for small business.

ACCOUNTING TERMS

cash discount	direct labour
cash refund	duty
C.O.D.	factory overhead
cost accounting	Freight-in account
cost of goods manufactured	goods in process
cost of goods sold	gross profit
credit invoice	indirect labour
credit note	manufacturing business

manufacturing statement
merchandise inventory
merchandise business
periodic inventory system
perpetual inventory system
physical inventory

raw materials
retailer
stock-in-trade
terms of sale
wholesaler

CHAPTER 11   Review Exercises

Using Your Knowledge

1 In a two-column general journal, record the accounting entries for the following selected transactions of Industrial Supply owned by Johnston Lem. Industrial Supply uses the periodic inventory system and does not use returns and allowances accounts. Choose your own account names. Ignore PST.

TRANSACTIONS

May
1   *Sales Invoice*
    No. 501, to Hewitt Construction for the sale of merchandise on account, $656.00 plus GST of $45.92, total $701.92.
5   *Purchase Invoice*
    From EMJ Steel Inc., No. 702, for merchandise for resale, $1 072.14 plus GST of $75.05, total $1 147.19.
8   *Credit Invoice Received*
    From Great Lakes Wood Products, No. 702, allowance for defective goods, $585.00 plus GST of $40.95, total $625.95.
9   *Sales Invoice*
    No. 502, to Northern Contracting, for sale of merchandise on account, $846.00 plus GST of $59.22, total $905.22.
15 *Credit Invoice Issued*
    No. 503, to Precision Instruments, for unsatisfactory goods returned, $600.00 plus GST of $42.00, total $642.00.
19 *Cash Sales Slip*
    No. 12520, to Quality Carpeting, for the cash sale of merchandise, $102.50 plus GST of $7.18, total $109.68.
26 *Purchase Invoice*
    From Pacific Transport, No. 371, for transportation charges on incoming merchandise, $896.50 plus GST of $62.76, total $959.26.

2 Twin-City Electronics is a business owned by J. Hudec. **In a two-column general journal, record the accounting entries for the selected transactions below.** Twin-City Electronics uses returns and allowances accounts.

TRANSACTIONS

June
4   *Sales Invoice*
    No. 14522, to KBM television, for the sale of merchandise, $353.00 plus GST of $24.71, total $377.71; transaction is exempt from PST.
5   *Sales Invoice*
    No. 14523, to R. Willis, for sale of merchandise, $500.00 plus GST of $35.00 and PST of $40.00, total $575.00.
9   *Credit Invoice Issued*
    No. 14524, to Court Street Clinic, regarding defective goods returned, $450.00 plus GST of $31.50 and PST of $36.00, total $517.50.
11 *Cash Sales Slip*
    No. 5602, to W. Yoller, cash sale of merchandise, $425.00 plus GST of $29.75 and PST of $34.00, total $488.75.
12 *Credit Invoice Received*
    From Toshiba Corporation, No. 7654, for defective merchandise returned, $2 478.00 plus GST of $173.46, total $2 651.46.
17 *Purchase Invoice*
    From Harry's Trucking, No. 442, for transportation charges on incoming merchandise, $256.00 plus GST of $17.92, total $273.92.
23 *Credit Invoice Issued*
    No. 14525, to Northland Maintenance, for return of defective merchandise, $575.00 plus GST of $40.25 and PST of $46.00, total $661.25.

30 *Purchase Invoice*
   From Imperial Supply, No. 1205, for merchandise for resale, $530.00, and supplies, $270.00, plus GST of $56.00, total $856.00.

---

③ Indicate whether each of the following statements is true or false by placing a "T" or an "F" in the space indicated in your Workbook. Explain the reason for each "F" response in the space provided.

A. A "wholesaler" is a "merchandiser." Therefore, a "merchandiser" is a "wholesaler."

B. Some of the goods found in the inventory of a hardware store are also goods found in the inventory of a building supply store.

C. Merchandise inventory is on the balance sheet under Prepaid Expenses.

D. The cost of goods sold figure normally includes the cost of goods that are lost, stolen, or broken.

E. The merchandise inventory of a drugstore is calculated by counting all of the goods on hand and multiplying by the selling prices marked on the goods.

F. An item that cost $40 and sold for $80 produced a gross profit of 50 per cent of the selling price.

G. The difference between the selling price and the cost price of the goods for a fiscal period is also the net income figure before any operating expenses are deducted.

H. The goods not sold represent the ending inventory.

I. The goods sold at selling prices represent the revenue figure.

J. The perpetual inventory system has not been commonly used because of the amount of work required to keep track of the many individual items in the inventory.

K. A used car business could easily use the perpetual inventory system because the number of items in its inventory is quite small.

L. XYZ department store uses the periodic inventory system. It must take a physical inventory at least once a year.

M. A perpetual inventory results in a "calculated" inventory figure. The inventory quantities shown on a perpetual inventory listing should be checked by actually inspecting the inventory from time to time. This would make clear whether or not any goods had been stolen.

N. If the beginning inventory was 10 000 units and the ending inventory was 12 000 units, the business sold more units than it purchased.

O. The merchandise inventory figure can be found during the fiscal period from the Merchandise Inventory account.

P. The Purchases account is used to accumulate all purchases during the period.

Q. When a business that uses the periodic inventory system sells goods, no accounting entry is made to reduce the merchandise inventory. If it were made, the entry would be debit Cost of Goods Sold and credit Merchandise Inventory.

R. The Freight-in account is used to accumulate all transportation charges during the fiscal period.

S. Freight-in increases cost of the goods acquired.

T. On the work sheet, the Purchases figure in the trial balance is extended to the Income Statement section, Debit column.

U. On the work sheet, the Merchandise Inventory figure in the trial balance is extended to the Balance Sheet section, Debit column.

V. Both the beginning and the ending inventory figures are shown on the income statement of a merchandising company.

W. The Merchandise Inventory account is automatically adjusted by the closing entries.

X. A credit invoice is issued by the vendor and received by the buyer.

Y. The accounting entry for a credit note issued is either a. or b. below. Ignore taxes.

	DR	CR
a. Accounts Receivable	$$$$	
Sales		$$$$
or		
b. Accounts Receivable	$$$$	
Sales Returns and		$$$$
Allowances		

Z. The best match for Merchandise Inventory on a balance sheet of a manufacturing company is Raw Materials Inventory.

4 From the partial work sheet shown below, prepare an income statement.

Work Sheet Master Security Systems			Year Ended December 31, 20–	
Accounts	Income Statement		Balance Sheet	
	Debit	Credit	Debit	Credit
Bank				
Accounts Receivable				
Merchandise Inventory	45 957.00	43 500.00		
Supplies				
Prepaid Insurance				
Equipment				
Accum. Depreciation — Equipment				
Automobiles				
Accum. Depreciation — Automobiles				
Accounts Payable				
GST Payable				
GST Recoverable				
PST Payable				
Bank Loan				
A. Kiriella, Capital				
A. Kiriella, Drawings				
Sales		229 350.50		
Sales Returns and Allowances	4 092.00			
Purchases	75 316.20			
Purchases Returns and Allowances		7 621.90		
Freight-in	1 592.00			
Advertising Expense	1 585.00			
Bank Charges Expense	2 685.00			
Car Expense	8 356.00			
Delivery Expense	5 695.21			
General Expense	1 632.25			
Rent Expense	12 000.00			
Telephone Expense	1 115.33			
Utilities Expense	3 875.25			
Wages Expense	47 256.32			
Supplies Expense	2 563.00			
Insurance Expense	2 417.00			
Depreciation Expense — Automobiles	7 424.00			
Depreciation Expense — Equipment	6 086.00			
	229 647.56	280 472.40		
Net Income	50 824.84			
	280 472.40	280 472.40		

5 The statement below shows the results of operation for two successive years.

GREEN'S GARDEN CENTRE
INCOME STATEMENT
YEARS ENDED DECEMBER 31, 20–1 AND 20–2

	20-1	20-2
Sales	$100 000	$120 000
Costs of Goods Sold		
Opening Inventory	$ 20 000	$ 25 000
Purchases		
Goods Available for Sale	$	$ 63 000
Less Closing Inventory	25 000	
Cost of Goods Sold	$	$
Gross Profit	$ 65 000	$
Expenses	$	$ 37 000
Net Income	$ 33 000	$ 42 000

A. **In your Workbook, fill in the blanks to complete the statement.**
B. Suppose that, on December 31, 20-1, the merchandise inventory was miscounted. Instead of $25 000 as shown, it was incorrectly counted as $21 000.
   a. **What effect would this understatement have on the net income figure for 20-1?**
   b. **What effect would it have on the net income figure for 20-2?**
C. **What effect, if any, would the above-noted error have on the balance sheet for 20-1?**

6 General Marine is a company that maintains a perpetual inventory that includes several hundred items. Two of the items listed on the February 28 inventory are:

Item	Code	Quantity on Hand
Harken Blocks	460	32
Proctor Tiller Extenders	911	25

A. Shown below are the source documents for inventory items received and inventory items shipped during the month of March. **From this list of source documents, select those that pertain to the two items above and calculate the number of each of the two items on hand at the end of March.**

Date		Source Document	Stock Number	Quantity
March				
	1	Shipping Order	460	8
	2	Shipping Order	911	5
		Receiving Report	551	10
	3	Shipping Order	1018	35
	4	Receiving Report	1000	20
		Receiving Report	4014	25
		Shipping Order	460	10
	8	Receiving Report	6757	5
		Shipping Order	911	8

11	Receiving Report	1912	25
	Receiving Report	4210	20
12	Shipping Order	1912	15
	Shipping Order	1129	100
15	Receiving Report	911	40
18	Receiving Report	112	24
	Shipping Order	460	2
20	Receiving Report	3121	30
23	Shipping Order	911	15
25	Receiving Report	460	30
	Shipping Order	460	15
30	Shipping Order	911	12
31	Receiving Report	6745	12

B. If the price of the items purchased on March 25 was $46 each, calculate the value of item #460 for the inventory.

---

7 The Sutton Hardware Store takes inventory only at the end of the calendar year because of the inconvenience involved. The gross profit of the business is stable and averages 40 per cent of sales. On January 31, at the end of the first month of business, the ledger included the following five account balances:

Merchandise Inventory	$ 51 920
Sales	103 850
Purchases	73 950
Freight-in	1 258
Operating Expenses	22 357

Use the above information to estimate the closing inventory, then prepare a condensed income statement for the month of January.

---

8 The accountant for a small company prepared an income statement that showed a net income figure of $38 525. The company's bank requested an audit of this statement. The errors described below were found by the auditor who checked the books and records:

A. The $4 200 cost of new equipment had been charged to Repair Expense instead of to Equipment. Depreciation on this equipment is for a full year at Canada Customs and Revenue Agency's prescribed rates using the declining-balance method.
B. A $100 credit to Purchases Returns and Allowances was incorrectly credited to Sales Returns and Allowances.
C. Repairs to Automobiles was incorrectly overstated by the amount of $1 500.
D. No adjusting entry for supplies was made. The ledger showed a balance for supplies of $2 850; the supplies counted at the year-end amounted to $840.
E. The ending inventory figure used by the company accountant was $32 650, but there were a number of errors made in arriving at that figure. The auditor revised the ending inventory figure to be $29 350.

Calculate the net income figure that would appear on the audited income statement.

9 Hiram Retail is a family-owned department store in Winnipeg, Manitoba. When the physical inventory was taken at year-end, an entire department was overlooked. As a result, the inventory was understated by $10 000.

Use some hypothetical figures to help you answer the following questions.

A. How will the inventory understatement affect the cost of goods sold?
B. How will the inventory understatement affect the gross profit?
C. How will the inventory understatement affect the net income?
D. How will the inventory understatement affect the balance sheet?
E. What would be your answers to questions 1 to 4 if the $10 000 error had been an inventory overstatement?
F. If you were the manager of a company and were looking for a way to make the profit appear higher, what might you consider doing?
G. If you were the owner of a company and were considering cheating to save on income tax, what might you consider doing?

10 **Give the accounting entries in general journal form for each of the source documents below as they would be made in the books of Circle Supply.** Circle Supply uses Returns and Allowances accounts.

900 Park Street   **Circle ◯ Supply**   Maple City, SK

SOLD TO	G. Baker		
	East Side Road		
	Maple Creek, SK S3Y 4H2	INVOICE NUMBER 802	
DATE	Aug. 9, 20–	TERMS 2/10,n/30	

Quantity	Description	Unit Price	Amount
1 Ctn	#35 Copper Wire	$65.00	$ 65.00
24	Propane Torch Refills	5.95	142.80
			$207.80
	7% GST		14.55
	8% PST		16.62
			$238.97

900 Park Street   **Circle ◯ Supply**   Maple City, SK

SOLD TO	G. Baker		
	East Side Road		
	Maple Creek, SK S3Y 4H2	CREDIT INVOICE	
DATE	Aug. 17, 20–	NUMBER 851	

Quantity	Description	Unit Price	Amount
	Credit to correct price on Propane Torch refills		
24	Propane Torch Refills	$5.95	$142.80
	Should be		
24	Propane Torch Refills	5.35	128.40
			$ 14.40
	7% GST		1.01
	8% PST		1.15
			$ 16.56

CREDIT

G. Baker   No. 1001
EAST SIDE ROAD
MAPLE CREEK, SK S3Y 4H2

AUGUST 26, 20 –

PAY TO THE
ORDER OF _____ Circle Supply _____ $ 217.96

Two Hundred and Seventeen   96 DOLLARS
                             100

CENTENNIAL BANK
MAPLE CITY BRANCH   *G. Baker*

A14 2D004A 054 D0300 3C

IN PAYMENT OF THE FOLLOWING

Invoice #802	$238.97	
Credit Invoice #851	16.56	
	$222.41	
2 per cent discount	4.45	
	$217.96	No. 1001

11 **Prepare an income statement from the following partial work sheet.**

Work Sheet Superior Trading Company	Year Ended December 31, 20–			
	Income Statement		Balance Sheet	
Accounts	Dr	Cr	Dr	Cr
Bank				
Accounts Receivable				
Merchandise Inventory	44 323.40	43 750.00		
Supplies				
Prepaid Insurance				
Equipment				
Automobiles				
Accounts Payable				
GST Payable				
GST Recoverable				
PST Payable				
Bank Loan				
Grace Strom, Capital				
Grace Strom, Drawings				
Sales		207 245.50		
Sales Returns and Allowances	4 102.00			
Purchases	73 219.20			
Purchases Returns and Allowances		5 625.00		
Freight-in	1 501.00			
Advertising Expense	1 426.00			
Bank Charges Expense	2 247.00			
Car Expense	8 135.00			
Delivery Expense	5 535.00			
Depreciation Expense — Automobiles	3 600.00			
Depreciation Expense — Equipment	2 400.00			
Discounts Allowed	3 525.24			
Discounts Earned		1 023.65		
General Expense	1 505.15			
Rent Expense	12 000.00			
Telephone Expense	1 052.25			
Utilities Expense	1 785.25			
Wages Expense	46 056.35			
Supplies Used	2 203.00			
Insurance Used	2 075.00			
	216 690.84	257 644.15		
Net Income	40 953.31			
	257 644.15	257 644.15		

Questions for Further Thought

Briefly answer the following questions.

1. A road building company might have several inventories on hand. These could include office supplies, sand, stone, asphalt, and gasoline. Explain the difference between these inventories and merchandise inventory.

2. The text indicates that merchandise that is lost, broken, or stolen is lumped in with the cost of goods sold. Explain the logic of this.

3. Merchandise inventory on hand at the end of the fiscal period is listed on the balance sheet at its cost price. Indirectly, some inventory is listed on the income statement at its selling price. Explain.

4. Give a logical reason for showing the gross profit separately on the income statement.

5. Having a computer inventory system allows a business to carry a smaller total inventory. Explain why this is possible. What is the advantage of being able to carry a smaller inventory?

6. The text states that the selling prices of goods, but not the cost prices, are marked on the merchandise. Why are the cost prices not marked on the goods?

7. The merchandise sold is listed in two places on the income statement. Explain why this is done.

8. Explain why the closing inventory is valued at its cost price.

9. Explain why freight-in is included in the cost of goods sold calculation.

10. Give a logical reason why a business would close down for a day or two in order to take inventory.

11. Many business people who use the periodic inventory system would rather not bother with taking inventory. However, they do it anyway. Explain why.

12. Assume that a large department store wants to take a quick inventory with some sacrifice of accuracy, to give it a rough idea of its progress. Try to devise a method of shortening the inventory procedure to give a reasonably close result.

13. The method of handling the merchandise inventory on the work sheet may be thought of as a "manipulation" rather than as an "adjustment." Explain.

14. Which financial statement do you think is of the most interest to a banker? Explain your answer.

15. What do you think is the most common error made by students when doing the closing entries for a merchandising business?

16. Explain how the credit note got its name.

17. In purchase transactions where there are returns and allowances involved, it is normal to wait until all of the source documents are received before making payment. Why would this be done?

18. Some businesses refuse to give a refund for merchandise returned. Explain how they handle this type of transaction.

Cases for Further Thought

Briefly answer the following question.

1. Paula Waukey is the owner of a paper products business. Her company makes available a large variety of papers and paper-related products, such as disposable towels, coffee filters, table covers, disposable coffee cups, and so on. Paula's customers could buy more cheaply by dealing directly with the manufacturers of the products. However, they continue to do business with Paula. Explain why Paula's customers choose to do business with her.

Case Studies

CASE 1

Analyzing Income Statements for
Two Merchandising Companies

Shown below are the income statements for two different companies in the furniture business.

INCOME STATEMENTS
YEAR ENDED DECEMBER 31, 20—

	Company A	Company B
Revenue		
Sales	$121 206	$415 072
Cost of Goods Sold	70 704	211 686
Gross Profit	$ 50 502	$203 386
Operating Expenses		
Advertising Expense	—	$ 43 072
Bank Charges Expense	$ 990	5 765
Building Maintenance Expense	140	3 500
Delivery Expense	6 301	22 685
Depreciation Expense	4 102	12 521
Insurance Expense	509	1 532
Licences Expense	120	435
Utilities Expense	1 850	5 775
Miscellaneous Expense	119	717
Rent Expense	4 800	12 000
Telephone Expense	275	716
Wages Expense	10 402	40 307
Total Operating Expenses	$ 29 608	$149 025
Net Income	$ 20 894	$ 54 361

Questions

1. Describe your mental picture of these two companies (large or small, high profile or low profile, etc.) giving specific reasons for your impression.
2. Company B's expenses are much larger than Company A's, yet Company B is able to earn more than twice the net income of Company A. How is this possible?
3. The relationship between the cost price of the goods and the selling price of the goods is crucial in any business. Consider the following analysis for Company A:

| Sales | $121 206 — 100% |
| Cost of Goods Sold | $ 70 704 — 58% |

Company A's goods cost 58 per cent of their selling price.
   a. Calculate this same percentage figure for Company B.
   b. If the figure for Company B were 58 per cent, the same as for Company A, how much lower would Company B's net income be?

CASE 2

Why Have Gross Profits Declined?

Piran Trewin is the owner of Spyhill Ski Shop. His accountant has just handed him the financial statements for the year. The income statement is shown below in condensed form; that is, only the information needed for the case is given.

Piran is upset by this statement, and suggests to his accountant that an error has been made. His accountant assures him that everything was checked and double-checked because of the low net income figure. No error was found.

Piran is particularly troubled by the gross profit figure. The operating expenses appear to be normal. Piran explains that all of his merchandise is marked up 100 per cent and that there have been no special sales needed to move the goods. In other words, Piran feels that the gross profit should be at its normal figure of approximately 50 per cent.

Because he has to be away a great deal, Piran relies heavily on his store manager. In past years, Jill Zaba was the manager and no problems were encountered. A year ago, Jill left for a better position. This year, the store was managed by Jonathon Yeo. This is Jonathon's first job as store manager.

SPYHILL SKI SHOP
INCOME STATEMENT
YEAR ENDED JUNE 30, 20—

Revenue			
Sales		$110 000	100%
Cost of Goods Sold			
Opening Inventory	$ 36 500		
Purchases	67 000		
Cost of Goods Available	$103 500		
Less Closing Inventory	36 000	67 500	61%
Gross Profit		$ 42 500	39%
Operating Expenses		29 000	26%
Net Income		$ 13 500	12%

Questions

1. Assuming that the sales figure is correct, what should the figure for cost of goods sold have been?
2. What is the most likely reason for the high figure for cost of goods sold?
3. Try to show the cost of goods sold section as it would have appeared if there had been no irregularity.
4. Suggest ways in which the owner can prevent any irregularities.

CASE 3

Squeeze Play?

Highway Construction is a firm that builds major roads and highways. Its contracts frequently involve substantial sums of money. Consequently, its accounts receivable and accounts payable are quite sizeable.

Highway Construction obtains large quantities of raw materials, supplies, and services from numerous smaller companies. These are always purchased on credit, and the amounts of money involved are usually considerable. Individual bills of $100 000 or more are not uncommon. At the time of purchase, Highway Construction always agrees to the supplier's terms of sale. These terms usually request payment within 30 days with no discounts.

In road construction, cash inflows are often slow and irregular. As a result, Highway Construction makes no attempt to adhere to the terms laid down by the suppliers. It pays its debts when it own cash position is good. Often, the suppliers have to wait for as long as 90 to 100 days.

Small suppliers can seldom afford to wait 100 days for customers to pay large sums of money. Small suppliers have their own debts to pay and payrolls to meet. Therefore, Lequita Adkins, the chief accountant for Highway Construction, receives many telephone calls urgently requesting immediate payment of overdue accounts.

Lequita is experienced at dealing with these suppliers. Over the years, she has worked out a neat scheme for handling their requests for payment. First, she expresses surprise that the supplier did not know that Highway Construction always takes 90 days to pay its suppliers. Lequita then goes on to say that the only exception to this policy is if a supplier offers a 2 per cent cash discount. The supplier is usually desperate for the money and agrees to the 2 per cent discount, which at the time may seem trivial.

Lequita Adkins claims that she makes money for Highway Construction with this scheme, even if she has to borrow the money at 10 per cent to make the payment. She says that she can back up the claim with calculations.

Questions

1. Is Lequita Adkins a clever business person? Explain.
2. Is Lequita's policy an ethical one?
3. On a bill for $200 000, how much is a 2 per cent discount?
4. Is Lequita correct when she states that she makes money for the company with this scheme? Prove your answer with a calculation.
5. If you were the accountant for Highway Construction, how would you handle the accounts payable situation? Write a paragraph outlining the policy you would adopt.

CASE 4

Challenge

A Scheme To Save Income Tax?

Vince Lyons owns a large and profitable sporting goods business in Corner Brook, Newfoundland. He has recently had a run of bad luck on the stock market, which has left him very short of funds. Unfortunately, he is badly in need of money to pay his income tax, which is almost due.

Vince desperately needs a way to reduce the amount of income tax that he will have to pay. After much searching, he comes up with a scheme that he thinks may work. He describes this scheme to his wife, Monisa, to get her reaction.

Vince explains to Monisa that his income tax is based primarily on the net income of the business. He shows her condensed figures (that is, only those figures needed for understanding the problem) for the current year and the projected figures for next year. These are shown below.

The Actual Figures

	This year's actual figures	Next year's projected figures
Sales	$250 000	$300 000
Cost of Goods Sold:		
Beginning inventory	$ 50 000	$ 60 000
Purchases	147 500	170 000
Goods available for sale	$197 500	$230 000
Less ending inventory	60 000	65 000
Cost of Goods Sold	$137 500	$165 000
Gross Profit	$112 500	$135 000
Expenses	65 000	75 000
Net Income	$ 47 500	$ 60 000

Vince's Proposed Altered Figures

	This year's actual figures (modified)	Next year's projected figures (modified)
Sales	$250 000	$300 000
Cost of Goods Sold:		
Beginning inventory	$ 50 000	$ 40 000
Purchases	147 500	170 000
Goods available for sale	$197 500	$210 000
Less ending inventory	40 000	65 000
Cost of Goods Sold	$157 500	$145 000
Gross Profit	$ 92 500	$155 000
Expenses	65 000	75 000
Net Income	$ 27 500	$ 80 000

Vince proposes to understate this year's ending inventory by $20 000, causing the net income to be understated by the same amount. This way, Vince expects to reduce his tax bill by $7 000.

Vince does not consider this action to be dishonest. He explains to Monisa that an understatement this year will cause an overstatement next year. He shows her the figures as they would appear containing the suggested inventory change. As Vince points out, the net income for the two years is still $107 500, regardless of how it is calculated. Although he will pay less tax this year, he will make it up by paying more next year. Rather than cheating, he is simply postponing tax payment for a while. According to Vince, he will have no problem paying his taxes next year.

Questions

1. Is Vince correct when he claims that the net income for the two years remains the same no matter how it is calculated?
2. Will Vince be breaking the law? Will he be violating any GAAPs?
3. Does the scheme offer a hidden benefit to Vince apart from the $7 000 tax deferral?
4. What dangers do you see in this scheme? Who would be most likely to detect it?

CASE 5

Challenge

Budgeting—How Many Doughnuts will the Grade 12s Eat?

The ability to use spreadsheet models to help make sound decisions is important. Enlai Chu knows this. He is the chairperson of the graduation committee of Hammarskjold High School. Enlai and his committee must decide what merchandise to sell in order to finance this year's graduation activities. After several meetings, the committee has made the following plans.

Background Information

The committee's main purpose is to raise money for the dinner and dance at the end of the year. The total cost of the facilities, meals, and music is $20 000, based on a projected attendance of 300 students.

Students who attend the dinner and dance pay $50 each. The balance of the cost must be met through fundraising.

In addition to the dinner and dance, the committee plans to buy a gift for the school on behalf of the graduating class. The committee also wants to contribute to the school's scholarship fund. Enlai Chu prepared a financial forecast or budget, which is shown in Exhibit A on page 493.

Previous graduation committees washed cars and sold muffins to raise funds. This year's committee does not want to wash cars, and just selling muffins will probably not generate the $6 000 needed. A new fundraising project is needed.

A variety of plans to raise money were suggested. Committee members favour the idea of switching product lines from muffins to doughnuts. They believe doughnuts are more popular than muffins, with the result that the $6 000 could be raised by selling doughnuts alone.

HAMMARSKJOLD HIGH SCHOOL
GRADUATION COMMITTEE BUDGET
SEPTEMBER 30, 20–2 TO JUNE 11, 20–3

Revenue

Ticket Sales	$15 000	
Fundraising	6 000	$21 000

Expenses

Dinner/Dance	$20 000	
Gift to School	500	
Scholarship Fund	500	21 000
Net Income		—

EXHIBIT A   The graduation committee's budget.

Loading a Spreadsheet Model

Assume that you are a member of the graduation committee and that Enlai has given you the task of using a spreadsheet program to help evaluate the doughnut proposal.

Enlai started a spreadsheet model by entering data and a few formulas into a rough work area. A rough work area contains data that can be used in other sections of the spreadsheet called output areas. Output areas are designed specifically for viewing or printing. To closely examine the model of a rough work area shown in Exhibit B below, use your spreadsheet software to load the file named grad.xls.

	A	B	C
1	*Doughnut Proposal*		
2	*Rough Work Area*		
3			
4	1. Cost per dozen		$3.60
5	2. Cost per doughnut		$0.30
6	3. Retail price per doughnut		$0.50
7	4. Estimated daily sales (doz.)		30
8	5. Estimated daily sales (ea.)		360
9	6. Selling days available		
10	(1 per week)		33
11			

EXHIBIT B   The rough work area for the doughnut proposal.

Column C contains raw data (values) and formulas:

1. Cell C4: Doughnuts are purchased by the committee at a cost of $3.60 per dozen.
2. Cell C5 contains the formula =C4/12. This formula calculates the cost of doughnuts at $.30 each.
3. Cell C6: Enlai has suggested a selling price of $.50 for each doughnut.
4. Cell C7: Enlai believes that committee members can sell 30 dozen doughnuts per day.
5. Cell C8 contains the formula =C7*12, which produces the total number of doughnuts sold per day.
6. Cell C10: The committee wants to limit doughnut sales to one day per week. At this rate, Enlai determined that there are 33 selling days between September 30 and the end of the year.

Creating the Output Area

To expand the model, you will build an output area beside and below the rough work area. This way, you can always insert columns and rows in one area without disturbing data in the other.

Starting at cell E11, **enter the labels shown in Exhibit C below**.

	A	B	C	D	E	F	G
1	Doughnut Proposal						
2	Rough Work Area						
3							
4		1. Cost per dozen	$3.60				
5		2. Cost per doughnut	$0.30				
6		3. Retail price per doughnut	$0.50				
7		4. Estimated daily sales (doz.)	30				
8		5. Estimated daily sales (ea.)	360				
9		6. Selling days available					
10		(1 per week)	33				
11					Hammarskjold High School		
12					Projected Profits--Doughnut Sales		
13					September 30, 20-2 to June 11, 20-3		
14							
15				Sales			
16				Cost of Goods Sold			
17				Gross Profit			
18							

EXHIBIT C   Labels for the output area for the doughnut proposal.

Entering Formulas for Budgetary Projections

The formulas start in column F and follow basic logic. For example, the Sales projection is found by multiplying the retail price of each doughnut by the number sold each day by the selling days available ($.50 × 360 × 33 = $5 940). However, to calculate the formula for Sales at cell F15, you will use cell references, not values. In cell language, this means entering =C6*C8*C10. Enter this formula now. *(Note: You will soon see the advantage of using cell references to connect the rough work area to the output area, instead of just keying values in the output area.)*

The formula for Cost of Goods Sold is similar to the one for Sales. **Think about what this formula should be and enter it at F16.** Also, you know that gross profit is the difference between sales and the cost of goods sold, so **enter a formula at F17**, as well.

Adding Percentages

Common-size percentages present a clear picture of the relationship between sales, cost of goods sold, and gross profit. **Prepare formulas for common-size percentages** in column G. (Use absolute cell references, a technique you learned in the spreadsheet section of Chapter 6.) After applying cell formats, your work should look like Exhibit D on page 495.

Analyzing Results

The projected gross profit of $2 376 from doughnut sales is far from the target of $6 000. **Move the cell pointer to cell C7**, which represents the amount of sales per day in dozens. **Change this amount to 40.** The new gross profit should be $3 168. If your model shows a different gross profit, use Exhibit E on page 495 to check your formulas.

	A	B	C	D	E	F	G
1	Doughnut Proposal						
2	Rough Work Area						
3							
4		1. Cost per dozen	$3.60				
5		2. Cost per doughnut	$0.30				
6		3. Retail price per doughnut	$0.50				
7		4. Estimated daily sales (doz.)	30				
8		5. Estimated daily sales (ea.)	360				
9		6. Selling days available					
10		(1 per week)	33				
11					Hammarskjold High School		
12					Projected Profits--Doughnut Sales		
13					September 30, 20-2 to June 11, 20-3		
14							
15				Sales		$5,940.00	100%
16				Cost of Goods Sold		3,564.00	60%
17				Gross Profit		$2,376.00	40%
18							

EXHIBIT D   The completed output area for the doughnut proposal.

	D	E	F	G
11		Hammarskjold High School		
12		Projected Profits--Doughnut Sales		
13		September 30, 20-2 to June 11, 20-3		
14				
15	Sales		=C6*C8*C10	=F15/$F$15
16	Cost of Goods Sold		=C5*C8*C10	=F16/$F$15
17	Gross Profit		=F15-F16	=F17/$F$15
18				

EXHIBIT E   The formulas for the output area for the doughnut proposal.

Changing cell C7 to 40 clearly demonstrates the advantage of using cell references to link the rough work area to the output area. You do not have to edit formulas in the output area to revise the projection of gross profit. When you change values in the rough work area, new forecasts are automatically calculated in the output area.

To experiment, **change the value at cell C7** until you determine how many dozen doughnuts must be sold to earn a gross profit of approximately $6 000. Once you arrive at an answer, **change C7 back to 30**.

Predicting a Break-Even Point

Using the trial-and-error method above, you probably determined that selling 76 dozen doughnuts will reach—and slightly surpass—the fundraising goal of $6 000. This is a useful bit of information, but there is a more efficient way to get it.

Move the cell pointer to row 11 and insert three rows. Then, enter the labels that are highlighted in Exhibit F on page 496.

To have your spreadsheet calculate the number of doughnuts the grad committee needs to sell to reach its goals, enter the following formulas:

- At C11, enter the formula to calculate the profit margin per doughnut. This is simply the retail price minus the cost price, or =C6−C5. The answer is 20 cents.
- At C12, enter the fundraising target of $6 000.
- At C13, you need to develop a formula that calculates how many dozen doughnuts must be sold each day they are on sale in order to raise $6 000. If the committee makes only 20 cents per doughnut, it has to sell 30 000 of them during the school year to make $6 000 (6 000 ÷ .20 = 30 000).

	A	B	C	D	E	F	G
1	*Doughnut Proposal*						
2	*Rough Work Area*						
3							
4		1. Cost per dozen	$3.60				
5		2. Cost per doughnut	$0.30				
6		3. Retail price per doughnut	$0.50				
7		4. Estimated daily sales (doz.)	30				
8		5. Estimated daily sales (ea.)	360				
9		6. Selling days available					
10		(1 per week)	33				
11		7. Profit margin per doughnut					
12		8. Fundraising target					
13		9. Break-even sales (in dozens)					
14					Hammarskjold High School		
15					Projected Profits--Doughnut Sales		
16					September 30, 20-2 to June 11, 20-3		
17							
18				Sales		$5,940.00	100%
19				Cost of Goods Sold		3,564.00	60%
20				Gross Profit		$2,376.00	40%
21							

EXHIBIT F Labels for creating a break-even section for the doughnut proposal.

Since you want to express the number of doughnuts that must be sold per day, divide 30 000 by the number of days the committee will be selling doughnuts (33). The formula is now 6 000 ÷ .20 ÷ 33 = 909.

Now you know that the committee must sell 909 doughnuts per day. To express this in dozens, divide by 12. This revises the formula to 6 000 ÷ .20 ÷ 33 ÷ 12 = 76 dozen (rounded to the nearest dozen).

This formula must be entered using cell references. **At cell C13, enter =C12/C11/C10/12**. If you format cell C13 to show values correct to zero decimal places, the answer will be 76.

Testing the Model

You are now at a stage where you can test your model. Before you start, make sure the gross profit shown in cell F20 is $2 376. If it is not, you probably changed some data in your rough work area. Make sure your model also contains Enlai's original data, which are shown back in Exhibit B on page 493.

Remember, the problem is how to get the projected profit from $2 376 to the target of $6 000. Suppose you think increasing the retail price to $.60 is a good idea. (**Enter .60 at cell C6.**) But you also believe that raising the price will cause the daily sales to decline to 28 dozen. (**Make this change at cell C7.**) In addition, you think you can convince the committee to sell doughnuts on a few extra days. (**Change cell C10 to 40.**) Your spreadsheet model should show the same results as Exhibit G on page 497.

Notice that the gross profit has improved to $4 032. But the break-even point is still too high at 42 dozen per day, because, in your judgment, only about 28 dozen could actually be sold. More decisions will have to be made in order to reach the goal.

	A	B	C	D	E	F	G
1	Doughnut Proposal						
2	Rough Work Area						
3							
4		1. Cost per dozen	$3.60				
5		2. Cost per doughnut	$0.30				
6		3. Retail price per doughnut	$0.60				
7		4. Estimated daily sales (doz.)	28				
8		5. Estimated daily sales (ea.)	336				
9		6. Selling days available					
10		(1 per week)	40				
11		7. Profit margin per doughnut	$0.30				
12		8. Fundraising target	$6,000				
13		9. Break-even sales (in dozens)	42				
14					Hammarskjold High School		
15					Projected Profits--Doughnut Sales		
16					September 30, 20-2 to June 11, 20-3		
17							
18				Sales		$8,064.00	100%
19				Cost of Goods Sold		4,032.00	50%
20				Gross Profit		$4,032.00	50%
21							

EXHIBIT G The model for the doughnut proposal after three values were changed in the rough work area.

Summary

While developing this model, you have learned no new spreadsheet functions or techniques. However, you have applied your spreadsheet skills to a problem that comes up frequently in merchandising: determining the number of sales that would be required to meet a given profit target.

You are now posing "what if?" questions to your spreadsheet model. For example, what if we raise the price? What if the quantity of sales drops? What if we sell more often than one day per week? Posing "what if?" questions is a frequent use to which spreadsheet models are put. The spreadsheet model responds quickly and accurately to your questions. You will use your spreadsheet model to answer more questions when you complete the computer exercises that follow. The answers you get will help you make good decisions.

Evaluating the Doughnut Sales

1. You will now make your own decisions about the doughnut-selling proposal. If Enlai's original amounts are used, you know that the $6 000 target for gross profit is a long way off. Read the following four suggestions as to how the graduation committee can increase its gross profit:

    i)   Reduce the cost of buying doughnuts. The lowest price available is $3.60 per dozen, but the supplier will reduce the cost by $.10 per dozen if more than 40 dozen are purchased at one time.
    ii) Increase the selling price.
    iii) Increase the number of doughnuts sold per day. The school has a population of 1 400 students; the cafeteria does not sell doughnuts or similar snacks.
    iv) Increase the number of days that committee members sell doughnuts. The current proposed schedule is one lunch hour per week, and there are eight members on the committee.

Answer the questions that follow. You may type your responses directly into the grad spreadsheet model and transfer them to a word-processing file later.

Questions

1. How much money per day will the committee save by ordering 40 dozen doughnuts instead of 30?
2. Are the savings calculated in question 1 worthwhile? Explain.
3. How much would you be willing to pay for a doughnut sold during your school lunch hour?
4. Would your answer to question 3 be different if you were part of the graduating class of Hammarskjold High School? Explain.
5. If the committee sets too high a price for its doughnuts, it risks having an additional expense. What is this?
6. What risks are faced if the committee tries to sell too many doughnuts on a given day?
7. What problems might arise as a result of selling doughnuts on too many days during the school year?

After you complete questions 1 through 7, use your spreadsheet model to help you make decisions about the doughnut proposal. Make your changes in the rough work area. Then, in a section below the output area, type your reasons for each change. (You may want to copy and paste these to a word-processing file later.)

Check with your instructor about which parts of the spreadsheet model you should print.

Proposing a New Grad Committee Budget

You have done a good deal of work to evaluate the doughnut proposal. But now you need to help Enlai Chu prepare a new overall budget in a format similar to Exhibit A on page 493. Complete the following activities.

1. Expand the grad spreadsheet model.

   a) Move the cell pointer to an area of your spreadsheet model that is below and to the right of the common-size percentages for doughnut sales. (This would be somewhere around cell H20; the exact location is up to you.) Key in the Grad Committee Budget data shown in Exhibit A on page 493. Use labels, values, formulas, and functions. This data will be referred to as the "overall budget."

   b) Expand your rough work area so that its data can be linked to the overall budget you just entered. For example, the *Ticket Sales* total of $15 000 from Exhibit A is based on 300 students multiplied by a price of $50 each. Therefore, enter both 300 and 50 into separate cells in the rough work area. Then, develop an appropriate formula in your overall budget that links the *Ticket Sales* amount to the work area cells that contain the 300 and 50 amounts.

   c) Use a cell reference to link the gross profit (which appeared in cell F20 in Exhibit G on page 497) to the *Fundraising* amount in the overall budget.

2. Use your expanded spreadsheet model to reconsider your previous decisions about raising funds. Think about what changes you can make to relieve some of the pressure on the selling of doughnuts. (Note: In his campaign speech, Enlai Chu said that he does not favour an increase in the price of the dinner/dance tickets.)

Make any changes in your decisions that you think are appropriate and type the reasons for doing so in an area below the overall budget. (You can copy and past this information to a word-processing file later.)

3. Even if fewer than 300 students attend the dinner and dance, the company renting the facilities to the committee will not reduce its price of $20 000. The committee members believe that the lowest likely attendance figure will be 280. Create a duplicate of the grad file. Then, prepare a new balanced budget in the event that only 280 students buy tickets. Type the reasons for changes you make in an area below the budget.

In this context, a balanced budget refers to one that projects revenues to meet or surpass expenses.

Preparing a Sub-committee Report

You have made decisions that you think are in the best interests of the graduation committee. However, you are only one person. Others will have different opinions and reach different conclusions.

A committee will often form a smaller sub-committee. The members of a sub-committee work together to reach "collective" decisions. Then they present their recommendations to the larger committee.

With two other students, form a "finance subcommittee" of the graduation committee. This sub-committee must reach an agreement or a consensus about all matters concerning the graduation committee's budget.

One other issue must be dealt with. Some graduation committee members claim that it is irresponsible to switch from muffins to doughnuts. They maintain that muffins are more healthful, and that this fact should be more important than financial considerations. To support their position, they claim that good quality muffins can be bought for $4.08 per dozen and that fellow students would buy and enjoy them.

Work with the members of your sub-committee to come up with creative and realistic solutions to the problems faced by the graduation committee. You may want to adapt and expand the grad spreadsheet model to evaluate how beneficial muffin sales might be. Summarize your findings in a written report. (Note: You may want to include one or two pie charts, which are easily created in Excel and copied into word-processing programs.) Also be prepared to give an oral presentation. You will find advice on giving oral presentations in the Skills Appendix.

Modifying Accounting Systems

In Chapter One, you learned that a senior accountant is usually responsible for maintaining the entire accounting system. This responsibility involves a wide range of activities, one of which includes making decisions about how accounting clerks record transactions. Obviously, debits must equal credits for every transaction, but the methods for processing transaction data may vary. Senior accountants tailor accounting systems to fit the size and nature of individual businesses.

So far, the accounting system you have used most often has required you to manually record entries in a general journal, post the debits and credits of each entry to individual accounts, and take off a trial balance. In this chapter, you will learn how to make these manual procedures more efficient. You could argue that there is little sense in making a manual system more efficient because most businesses now use computer technology to meet their accounting needs. While this is true, you will see that key components of computerized systems are based on the manual procedures. By learning various methods of manual accounting, you set a good foundation for understanding computerized accounting systems.

12.1 | Subsidiary Ledger Systems

As a business grows, its ledger grows too, but not all parts grow in the same way. The increase in the number of ledger accounts comes mainly from having more accounts for customers and creditors. The other ledger accounts seldom increase in number; they increase only in the size of their balances. Some large businesses have ledgers that contain many thousands of customers' accounts.

FIGURE 12.1

The growth of a ledger.

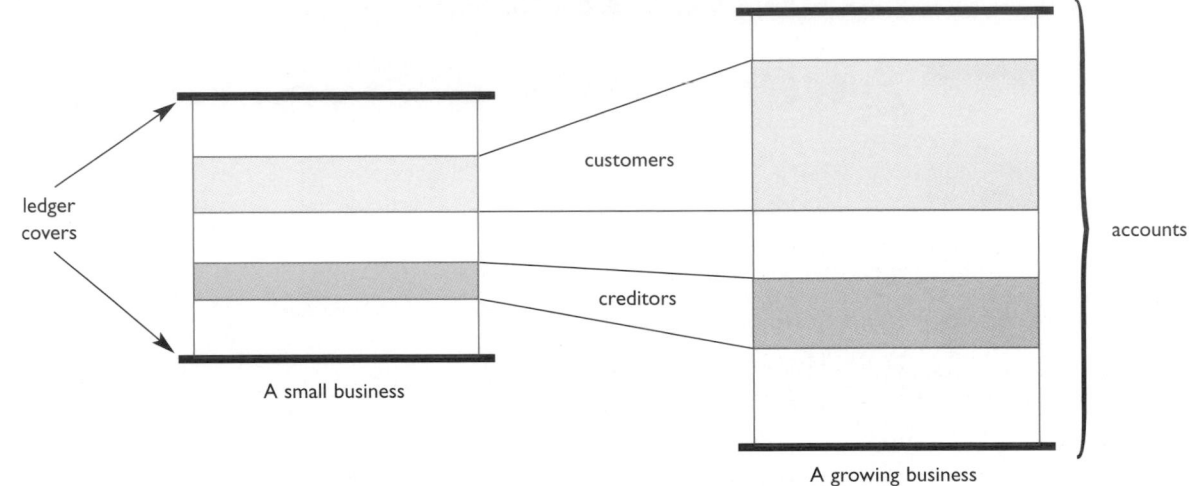

In Chapters 8 and 9, the individual accounts of customers and creditors were not included on the work sheet or on the balance sheet. Instead, the total of the customers' accounts and the total of the creditors' accounts were included. These were called *control* accounts. Individual customers' accounts and the individual creditors' accounts are in a separate ledger, known as *subsidiary ledgers*. The main ledger, now to be called the *general ledger*, contains the control accounts. It makes good business sense to separate these accounts from the rest of the ledger. They can be looked after independently by accounting clerks, making a more efficient accounting system.

To begin the study of subsidiary ledgers, examine the simplified T-accounts ledger in Figure 12.2 on page 503. This is a typical ledger, except that, for the purpose of demonstration, the number of customers' and creditors' accounts is very small.

FIGURE 12.2

A simple ledger with customers' and creditors' accounts highlighted.

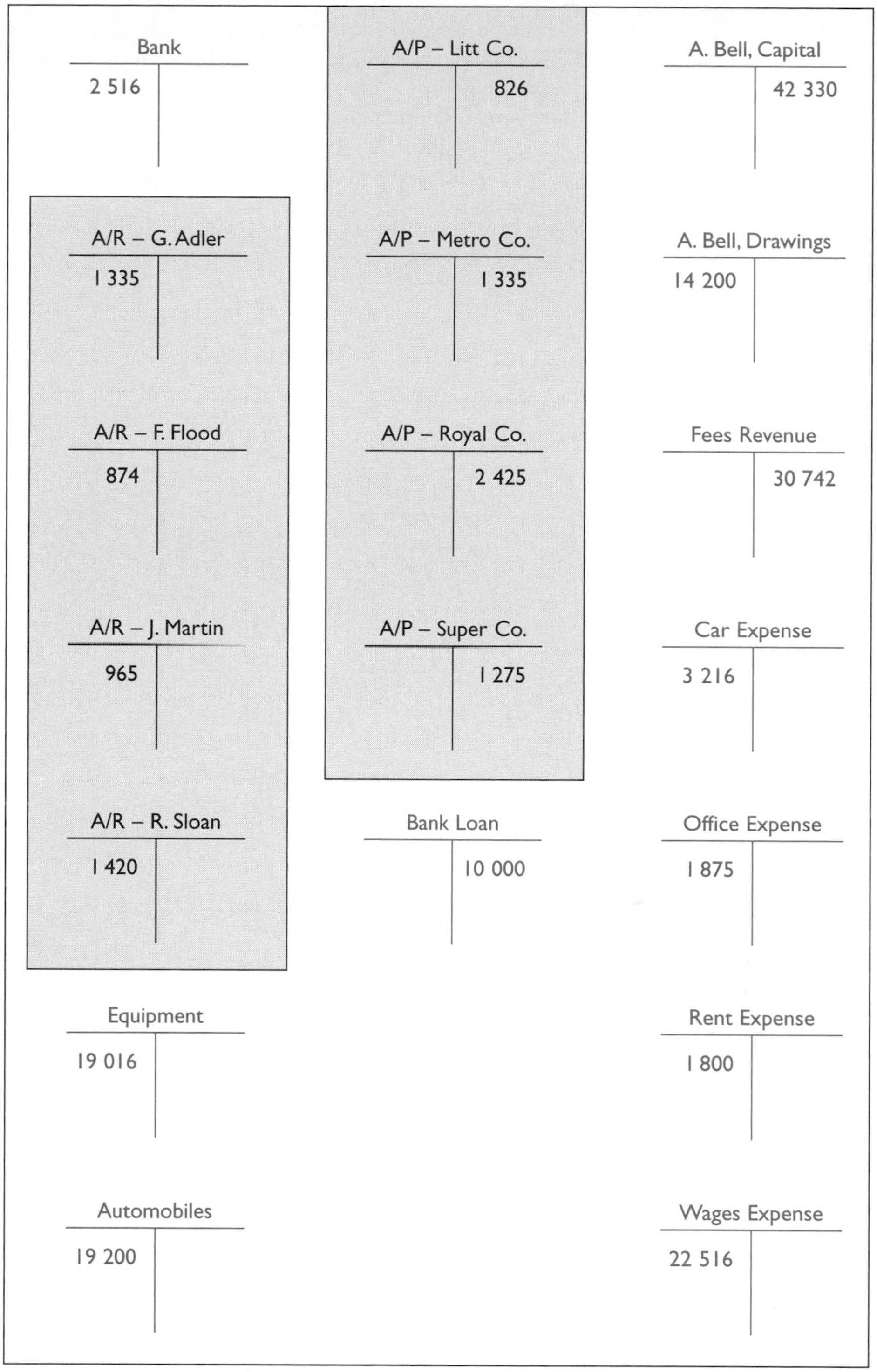

Bank	A/P – Litt Co.	A. Bell, Capital
2 516	826	42 330

A/R – G. Adler	A/P – Metro Co.	A. Bell, Drawings
1 335	1 335	14 200

A/R – F. Flood	A/P – Royal Co.	Fees Revenue
874	2 425	30 742

A/R – J. Martin	A/P – Super Co.	Car Expense
965	1 275	3 216

A/R – R. Sloan	Bank Loan	Office Expense
1 420	10 000	1 875

Equipment		Rent Expense
19 016		1 800

Automobiles		Wages Expense
19 200		22 516

From this ledger, mentally extract all of the accounts of customers (Accounts Receivable) and all those of creditors (Accounts Payable). Set them aside in two separate groups. This is shown in Figure 12.3 below. In each new group, arrange the accounts in alphabetical order.

By definition, a group of accounts is a ledger. Therefore, each of the two new groups of accounts is a ledger. The accounting system now contains three ledgers.

FIGURE 12.3

Creation of new ledgers with general ledger not in balance.

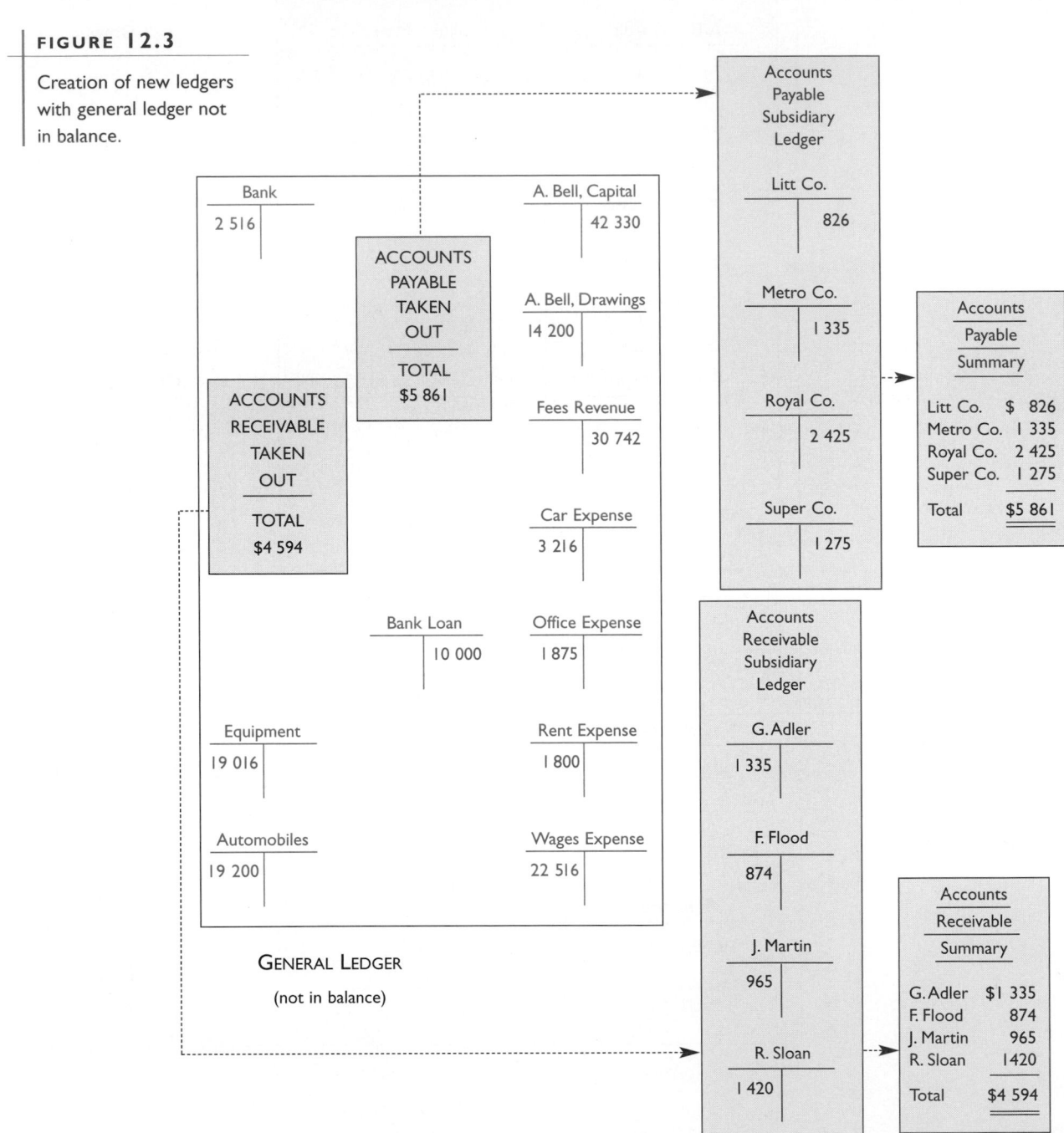

The ledger of customers' accounts is known as the *accounts receivable ledger*. The **accounts receivable ledger** is a book or file containing all of the accounts of customers. The accounts in this ledger normally have debit balances.

The ledger of creditors' accounts is known as the accounts payable ledger. The **accounts payable ledger** is a book or file containing all of the accounts of ordinary creditors. The accounts in this ledger normally have credit balances.

It is necessary for each ledger to have its own identity, now that there are three ledgers in the system. For this reason, the main ledger is called the general ledger. The **general ledger** is the main ledger of a business containing accounts for assets, liabilities, equity, revenues, and expenses.

The changeover to the three-ledger system is not yet completed. Certain accounts were removed from the general ledger in Figure 12.3 on page 504. Therefore, it no longer balances within itself. It cannot be left in this condition. Balancing the general ledger is fundamental to the whole process of accounting.

The next step, therefore, is to open two *control accounts* in the general ledger to replace all of those accounts that were removed from it. The two control accounts are called Accounts Receivable and Accounts Payable. They are shown in Figure 12.4 on page 506.

Notice that the Accounts Receivable account is given a debit balance of $4 594. This debit balance replaces all of the customers' accounts that were removed. Observe also that the Accounts Payable account is given a credit balance of $5 861. This credit balance replaces all of the creditors' accounts that were removed. The final state of the three-ledger system is shown in Figure 12.4 on page 506.

Subsidiary Ledgers

Each of the two new ledgers in our accounting system, the accounts receivable ledger and the accounts payable ledger, is called a *subsidiary ledger*. A **subsidiary ledger** is a separate ledger that contains a number of accounts of a similar type, such as accounts receivable. The accounts in a subsidiary ledger make up the detailed data for one related *control account* in the general ledger. A **control account** is a general ledger account that is related to a subsidiary ledger. The balance in the control account represents the sum of all of the account balances contained in the related subsidiary ledger.

Subsidiary ledgers must be included in the monthly balancing process of a manual system. A subsidiary ledger must agree with its **control account**. The account balances in a subsidiary ledger must be totalled, and that total must agree with the balance of the control account. If it does not, errors exist that must be found and corrected. In the three-ledger system, the financial statements should not be prepared until the three ledgers have all been balanced. Only then can you feel confident that the figures are correct.

The ordinary creditors of a business are its suppliers. These are sometimes called "trade creditors." Their accounts appear in the accounts payable ledger. The bank or the mortgage holder are a different type of liability and do not appear in an accounts payable ledger.

The total of the subsidiary ledger must agree with the total of the control account. That is how a subsidiary ledger is balanced.

FIGURE 12.4

General ledger in balance in a
simple three-ledger system.

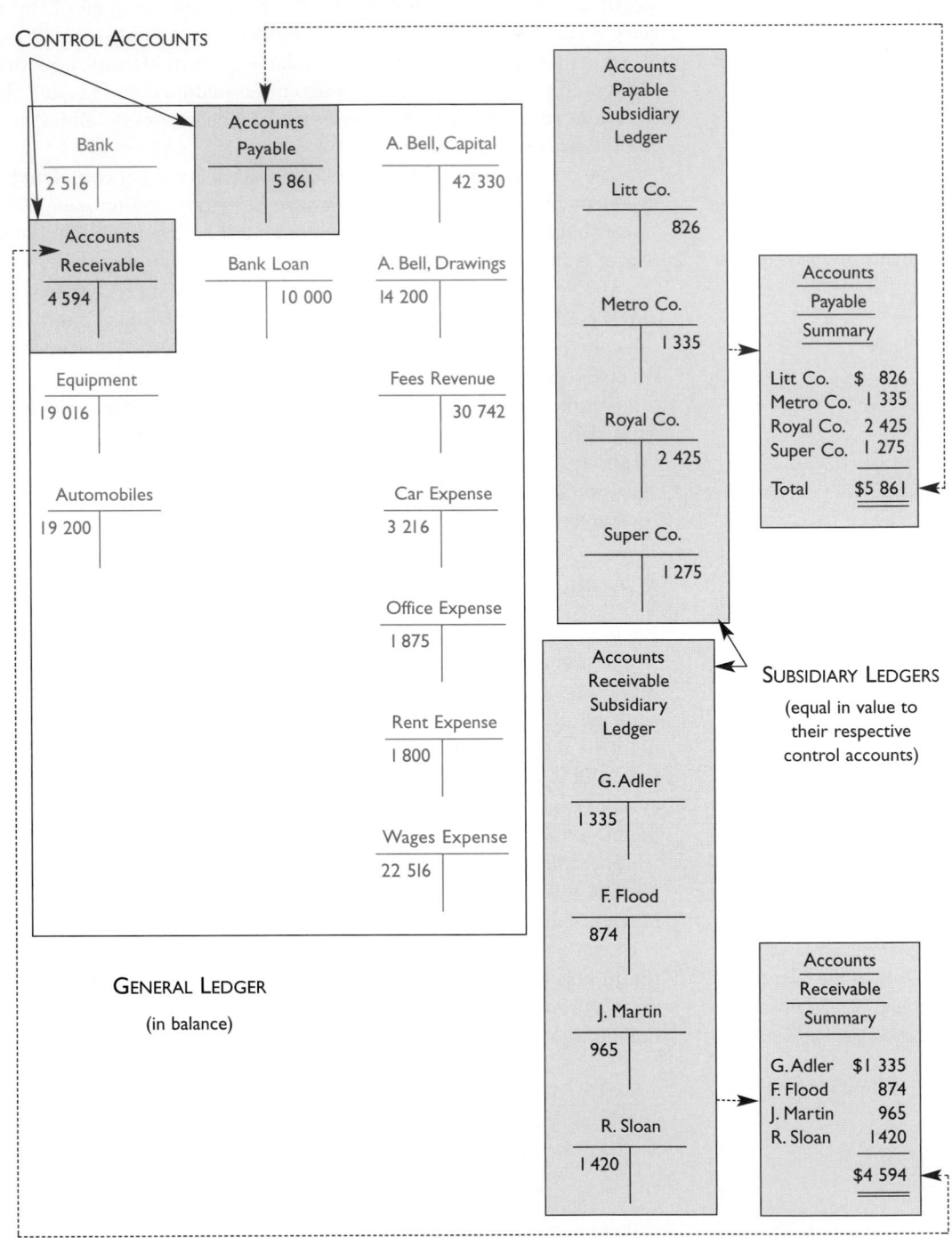

CONTROL ACCOUNTS

Bank		Accounts Payable		A. Bell, Capital	
2 516			5 861		42 330

Accounts Receivable		Bank Loan		A. Bell, Drawings	
4 594			10 000	14 200	

Equipment			Fees Revenue	
19 016				30 742

Automobiles			Car Expense	
19 200			3 216	

Office Expense
1 875

Rent Expense
1 800

Wages Expense
22 516

GENERAL LEDGER

(in balance)

Accounts
Payable
Subsidiary
Ledger

Litt Co.
826

Metro Co.
1 335

Royal Co.
2 425

Super Co.
1 275

Accounts Payable Summary	
Litt Co.	$ 826
Metro Co.	1 335
Royal Co.	2 425
Super Co.	1 275
Total	$5 861

Accounts
Receivable
Subsidiary
Ledger

G. Adler
1 335

F. Flood
874

J. Martin
965

R. Sloan
1 420

SUBSIDIARY LEDGERS

(equal in value to
their respective
control accounts)

Accounts Receivable Summary	
G. Adler	$1 335
F. Flood	874
J. Martin	965
R. Sloan	1420
	$4 594

Bookkeeping for Accounts Receivable

To see how the manual bookkeeping for an accounts receivable ledger is managed, let's look at the jobs of two members of an accounting department—an accounts receivable clerk and a general ledger clerk. (For this example, assume that multiple copies of each source document are made.) The clerks should follow the notes and procedures outlined below to create a subsidiary ledger system.

1. There are two source documents that affect accounts receivable:
   a. *sales invoices;*
   b. *cash receipts daily summaries.*
2. One copy of each source document is forwarded to the *accounts receivable clerk.*
3. The work of the accounts receivable clerk requires:
   a. *for each sales invoice*—a debit entry to a customer's account;
   b. *for each receipt on account*—a credit entry to a customer's account.
4. A copy of each source document is forwarded to the *general ledger clerk.*
5. The work of the general ledger clerk requires an accounting entry for every source document, not just sales invoices and cash receipts on account.
   a. For each sales invoice, the accounting entry is:

	DR	CR
Accounts Receivable	$$$$	
Sales (Revenue)		$$$$
GST Payable		$$$$
PST Payable		$$$$

   b. *For each receipt on account,* the accounting entry is:

	DR	CR
Bank	$$$$	
Accounts Receivable		$$$$

6. In a manual system, the subsidiary ledger is updated daily and balanced with its control account monthly.

Notice the contrast between the procedures in points three and five. The accounts receivable clerk does not make a complete accounting entry. The clerk merely increases a customer's account by a debit entry or decreases a customer's account by a credit entry. The general ledger clerk makes a complete, balanced entry.

Balancing the Ledgers

There are three ledgers to balance in a three-ledger system. The procedure for balancing the general ledger remains the same. However, the subsidiary ledgers must also be balanced. This is usually done by the subsidiary ledger clerk as follows.

A subsidiary ledger must be balanced with its control account as shown in Figure 12.5 on page 508. The procedure is simple:

Step 1   Make sure that the subsidiary ledger and the control account are posted to the same date.

Step 2   Total all of the account balances in the subsidiary ledger.

Step 3   Match the total against the balance of the control account in the general ledger.

FIGURE 12.5

Balancing a subsidiary
ledger with its control
account.

The Accounts Receivable
Summary may also be
referred to as the
Accounts Receivable
Listing or the Accounts
Receivable Trial Balance.

```
         ACCOUNTS RECEIVABLE SUMMARY
                  MAY 31, 20—

         A. Adams                    $ 50
         C. Hussein                    30
         B. Kwan                      100
         S. Smith                      25
         T. Thomas                    175
         W. Wand                       35
         Total                      $415
```

```
              GENERAL LEDGER
              TRIAL BALANCE
               MAY 31, 20—

                            DR          CR
Bank                     $ 200
Accounts Receivable        415
Supplies                   140
Accounts Payable                     $ 635
Capital                                210
Drawings                   400
Revenue Expense                      1 210
Advertising Expense        125
Utilities Expense          325
Wages                      450
                        $2 055      $2 055
```

If the two totals agree, the subsidiary ledger is in balance. If the two do not agree,
the subsidiary ledger is not in balance. This means that there are errors to be found
and corrected somewhere in the ledgers.

Bookkeeping for Accounts Payable

The accounts payable can be handled by a set of procedures similar to those you
learned for accounts receivable.

The highlights of a system for accounts payable are:

1. There are two source documents that affect accounts payable:
   a. *purchase invoices*
   b. *cheque copies—on account only*
2. The accounts payable subsidiary ledger is maintained by the accounts payable
   clerk.

Each purchase invoice goes through a rigorous series of verifying checks before being recorded in the accounts. It is important to ensure that (a) the goods or services were actually ordered, (b) the goods or services are the right ones and were received in good condition, (c) the price on the invoice is the agreed price, and (d) there are no errors or omissions on the invoice.

3. The work of the accounts payable clerk requires:
   a. *for each purchase invoice*—a credit entry to a creditor's account;
   b. *for each cheque copy (on account)*—a debit entry to a creditor's account.
4. The general ledger is maintained by the general ledger clerk.
5. The work of the general ledger clerk requires the making of accounting entries for every source document, not just purchase invoices and cheque copies on account.
   a. *For each purchase invoice*, the accounting entry is:

	DR	CR
An asset or an expense*	$$$$	
GST Recoverable	$$$$	
Accounts Payable		$$$$

   * Which account is affected depends on what was purchased.

   b. *For each cheque copy on account*, the accounting entry is:

	DR	CR
Accounts Payable	$$$$	
Bank		$$$$

6. In a manual system, the subsidiary ledger is updated daily and balanced with its control account monthly.

Non-Routine Entries to Subsidiary Ledgers

You have seen that accounting systems are designed so that the information flows to the office clerks by means of business source documents. However, some transactions do not fit into the regular accounting routine.

For example, suppose that Naomi Kuper, the owner of a business, collects a $200 account in full from a customer, B. Ayotte. Ms. Kuper happens to be short of cash at the time. She keeps the money for her personal use instead of turning it in to the business.

First, Ms. Kuper informs the accounting department of the transaction. She has no wish to deceive anyone. The accountant makes the following accounting entry in the journal:

	DR	CR
N. Kuper, Drawings	$200	
Accounts Receivable		$200

To record the collection by N. Kuper of the account of B. Ayotte Funds were kept by N. Kuper for her personal use.

There is no regular source document for this type of transaction. Without the source document, the accounts receivable clerk will not learn about the transaction in the usual way. The accountant understands this, and will make the entry in the subsidiary ledger personally, or will inform the clerk by means of a written memo. The accountant must attend to this promptly because the subsidiary ledger must be kept up to date.

Locating Errors When a Subsidiary Ledger Does Not Balance

When a subsidiary ledger does not balance, a search for the errors must be made. When looking for errors, remember that for every amount entered in a subsidiary ledger, there must be an equivalent amount entered in the control account, and vice versa.

In your search for errors, there is no need to go back in the accounts beyond the current month. The ledgers are balanced at the end of every month and the trial balances are kept on file as proof. If errors exist in the accounts, they must have been made since they were last balanced.

Subsidiary Ledgers In Simply Accounting

Most businesses large enough to need a subsidiary ledger system use accounting software. Study the following Simply Accounting illustrations carefully. To get a good overview of how sub-ledgers work in accounting software, compare the illustrations to what you have just learned about manual subsidiary ledgers systems. You will have the opportunity to use subsidiary ledgers in Simply Accounting when you complete the summary exercises.

If you worked with Sam's Softball City in the preceding chapters, you recorded all transactions in the General module. The General module contains the general ledger and the general journal. In Figure 12.6 below, the "Accounts" icon represents the general ledger and the "General" icon represents the general journal.

FIGURE 12.6

The Home window of Simply Accounting showing the General module.

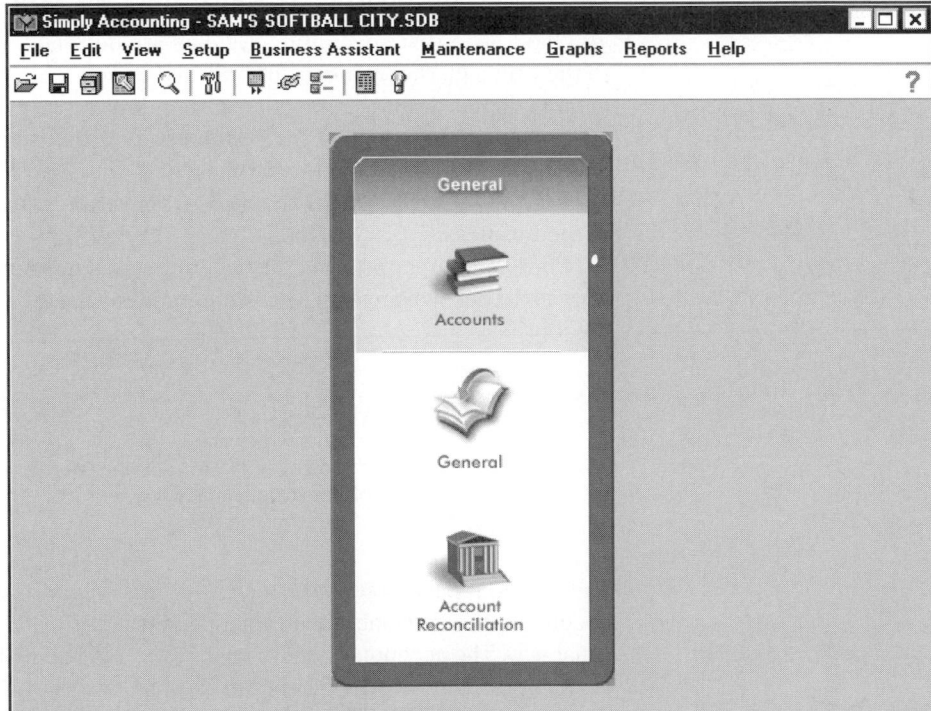

When you select View, Modules from the Home window of Simply Accounting, you will find the two subsidiary ledgers presented in this section. Simply Accounting organizes these ledgers in the Payables and Receivables modules, which are displayed in Figure 12.7.

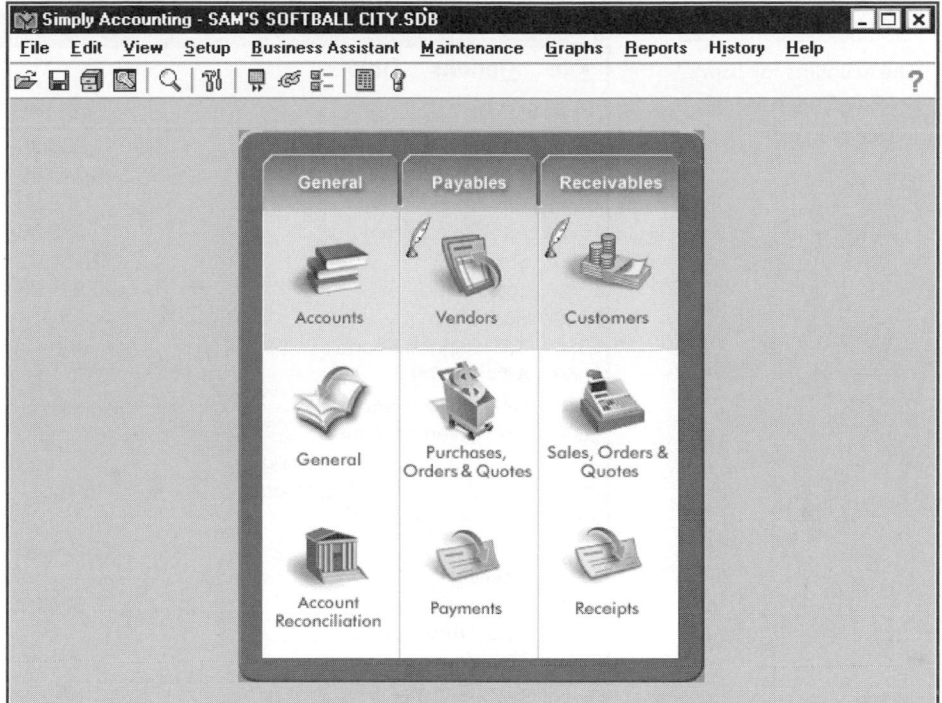

Converting the General Ledger accounts you used for Sam's Softball City is easy. To refresh your memory, the General Ledger accounts after two months of operation are shown in Figure 12.8. Notice that each customer and vendor has their own general ledger account.

FIGURE 12.8

The accounts for Sam's Softball City in a single-ledger system.

Trial Balance

File   Options   Help

As At 5/31/01

		Debits	Credits
1010	Bank	11,266.30	-
1050	A/R--Chatham Steelers	5,243.00	-
1060	A/R--Infield Flyers	0.00	-
1070	A/R--Remdal Red Sox	535.00	-
1200	Supplies	2,484.00	-
1300	Equipment	36,991.08	-
2010	Bank Loan	-	35,000.00
2050	A/P--Cannon Sports	-	0.00
2060	A/P--Cell Tel	-	0.00
2070	A/P--Eastern Electric	-	1,495.86
2080	A/P--Ewert Equipment	-	12,425.50
2090	A/P--Pro Motion Advertising	-	1,444.50
2100	A/P--Sandhu Sporting Goods	-	0.00
2200	GST Payable	-	745.50
2300	GST Recoverable	427.98	-
3010	Opening Capital	-	20,000.00
3050	S. Lucas, Drawings	6,000.00	-
4010	Rental Revenue	-	12,650.00
5010	Advertising Expense	1,350.00	-
5020	Bank Charges	250.00	-
5030	Miscellaneous Expense	48.00	-
5040	Rent Expense	9,000.00	-
5050	Telephone Expense	168.00	-
5060	Utilities Expense	1,398.00	-
5070	Wages Expense	8,600.00	-
		83,761.36	83,761.36

Assume you have the task of setting up the Receivables sub-ledger for Sam's Softball City. To do this, you open the Customers icon (shown in Figure 12.7), select "Create new accounts," and enter basic data for each of the customers—the Chatham Steelers, Infield Flyers, and Remdal Red Sox. When finished, the subsidiary ledger accounts are represented by the icons in Figure 12.9.

FIGURE 12.9

The customers in the Receivables ledger of Sam's Softball City.

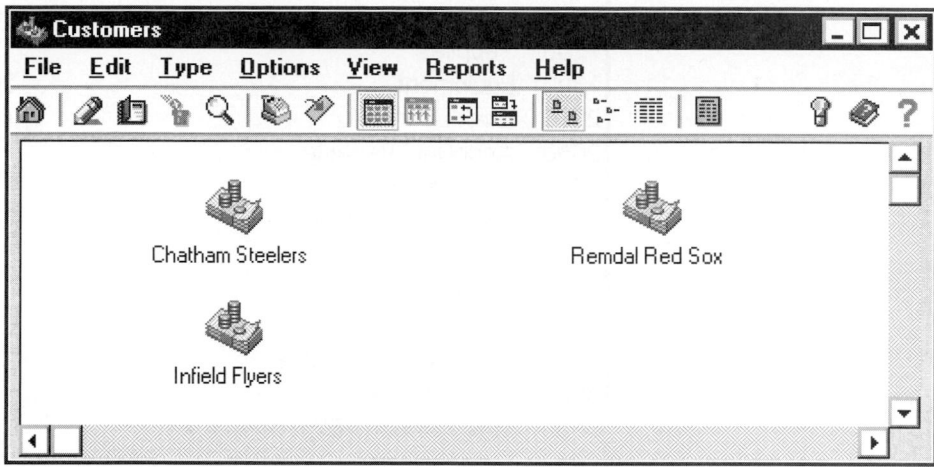

Two invoice amounts owed by the Chatham Steelers and Remdal Red Sox would also be entered. A report that is similar to the manual accounts receivable trial balance shown back on page 508 appears in Figure 12.10 below.

FIGURE 12.10

The accounts receivable summary or trial balance.

Customer Aged Summary					
File Options Help					
As at 5/31/01	Total	Current	31 to 60	61 to 90	91+
Chatham Steelers	5,243.00	5,243.00	-	-	-
Remdal Red Sox	535.00	-	535.00	-	-
	5,778.00	5,243.00	535.00	-	-

Notice that the total amount of accounts receivable is $5 778. The "customer aged summary" above offers a little more information than the manual accounts receivable summary shown on page 508 because it reveals that the Remdal Red Sox are a bit slow in paying the $535 they owe the business.

To set up the Payables module, you follow the same procedures used for the Receivables.

To adjust the General module, all the customer and vendor accounts shown in Figure 12.8 would be deleted from the general ledger. In their place, two control accounts would be created, one for Accounts Receivable and one for Accounts Payable. The balance in each of these control accounts would be the same as the totals in the newly created sub-ledgers. These steps are identical to the requirements of a manual three-ledger system. The modified General Ledger is shown in the trial balance in Figure 12.11. Notice that the balance of Accounts Receivable is the same as the total shown in Figure 12.10.

Trial Balance		
File **Options** **Help**		
As At 5/31/01	Debits	Credits
1010 Bank	11,266.30	-
1050 Accounts Receivable	5,778.00	-
1200 Supplies	2,484.00	-
1300 Equipment	36,991.08	-
2010 Bank Loan	-	35,000.00
2050 Accounts Payable	-	15,365.86
2200 GST Payable	-	745.50
2300 GST Recoverable	427.98	-
3010 Opening Capital	-	20,000.00
3050 S. Lucas, Drawings	6,000.00	-
4010 Rental Revenue	-	12,650.00
5010 Advertising Expense	1,350.00	-
5020 Bank Charges	250.00	-
5030 Miscellaneous Expense	48.00	-
5040 Rent Expense	9,000.00	-
5050 Telephone Expense	168.00	-
5060 Utilities Expense	1,398.00	-
5070 Wages Expense	8,600.00	-
	83,761.36	83,761.36

To link ledgers, choose Setup, Linked Accounts, and the module you wish to link to the general ledger. Then select specific accounts to link from the drop-down menus.

A key advantage of Simply Accounting's three-ledger system comes from "linking" the ledgers. The important result of linking is that when you make a journal entry in a subsidiary ledger, accounts in the General Ledger are automatically updated. For example, suppose Sam's Softball City needed to pay an amount it owed to Pro Motion Advertising. If you were the accounting clerk, you would double-click the Payments icon in the Payables module. After a few more selections, your screen would look like Figure 12.12.

When the Post button is clicked, the subsidiary ledger will no longer show the amount owing to Pro Motion Advertising; invoice 98884 for $1 444.50 has been paid and the subsidiary ledger account will be reduced to zero. More significantly, the journal entry created by clicking the Post button will affect accounts in the general ledger, as shown in Figure 12.13.

FIGURE 12.12

Journal entry data prepared in the Payables module.

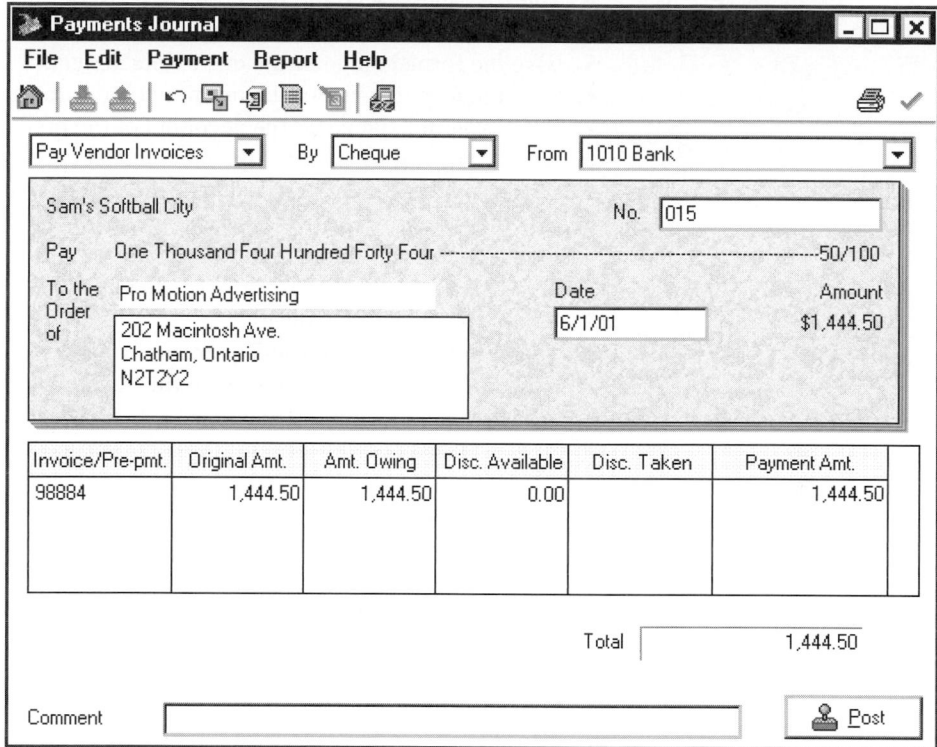

The accounts in the general ledger are updated automatically because they were "linked" when the Payables module was prepared. The benefits of linking are significant because it saves time and allows the General Ledger clerk to perform other accounting duties.

FIGURE 12.13

The General Ledger accounts affected by the journal entry in the Payables module.

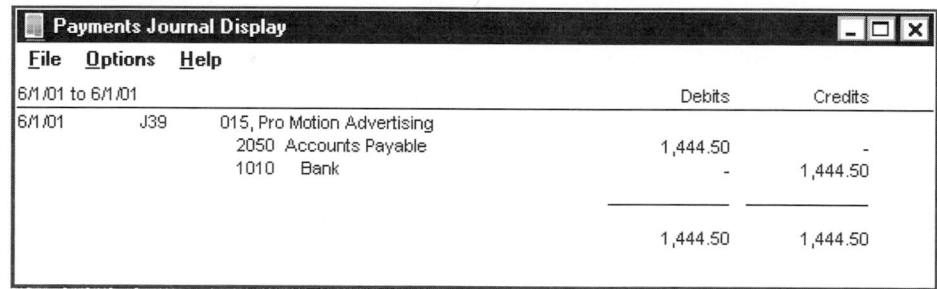

Section 12.1   Review Questions

1. What types of accounts increase in number in a growing business?
2. What usually happens to the other accounts?
3. Which type of employee looks after the accounts receivable accounts in a typical office?
4. The customers' accounts are considered to be a ledger when they are separated from the main ledger. Explain why.
5. Give the formal name of the customers' ledger.
6. Give the formal name of the ordinary creditors' ledger.
7. What type of balance do the accounts of the creditors usually have?
8. What is the formal name of the main ledger?
9. What type of accounts are found in the main ledger?
10. Give the names of the two accounts in the main ledger that replace the accounts of customers and trade creditors.
11. Describe the ledger-balancing process in a three-ledger system.
12. What is a subsidiary ledger?
13. The accounts receivable ledger normally has only accounts with debit balances. How then is it possible to balance this ledger?
14. What are the two source documents that affect accounts receivable?
15. How do the clerks who look after the different ledgers learn about the transactions?
16. Describe the work done by the accounts receivable clerk.
17. Describe the work done by the general ledger clerk.
18. Why is the accounts receivable ledger updated daily?
19. Normally, a subsidiary ledger will not balance with its control account if both ledgers are not posted up to the same point in time. Explain.
20. What has to be done if a subsidiary ledger does not balance with its control accounts? Whose responsibility is it?
21. Describe how to take off a subsidiary ledger trial balance.
22. There is a "control" aspect to the system of subsidiary ledgers and control accounts. Describe this.
23. What are the two source documents that affect accounts payable?
24. If a business is large enough to use a subsidiary ledger system, what else would it likely use?
25. How does linking produce a key advantage in Simply Accounting's subsidiary ledger system?

Section 12.1　　**Exercises**

1. To compare manual subsidiary ledger systems to computerized ledger systems, complete the chart that appears in your Workbook. To guide you, the first two answers are shown below:

SUBSIDIARY LEDGER FEATURES AND REQUIREMENTS	MANUAL SYSTEM	SIMPLY ACCOUNTING
a. Customers and vendors are removed from the general ledger.	✔	✔
b. Copies of source documents are sent to the general ledger clerk.	✔	✔
c. Control accounts are required.		
d. Totals in the subsidiary ledgers must be balanced with general ledger accounts at the end of each month.		
e. Two source documents affect Accounts Receivable.		
f. Produces a report that also indicates the age of invoices.		
g. The general ledger clerk and subsidiary ledger clerks work with copies of the same source document.		
h. Produces reports showing customer and vendor balances.		
i. A journal entry by a subsidiary ledger clerk automatically updates accounts in the general ledger.		
j. Totals in the subsidiary ledgers always balance with the general ledger control accounts.		

2. The simplified trial balance of Proctor's Pet Store in Weyburn, Saskatchewan, is shown below.

PROCTOR'S PET STORE
TRIAL BALANCE
JUNE 30, 20—

Bank	$ 1 150	
A/R – P. Shewchuk	350	
A/R – J. Britt	920	
A/R – C. Powell	1 500	
A/R – D. Zecca	500	
A/R – W. Liu	2 900	
Supplies	1 550	
Equipment	15 037	
A/P – Cleaners' Supply House		$ 900
A/P – Wendall's Store		250
A/P – Arnwell Animal Hospital		1 500
Tracy Proctor, Capital		18 122
Tracy Proctor, Drawings	11 000	
Revenue		29 435
Utilities Expense	2 475	
Miscellaneous Expense	316	
Rent Expense	12 000	
Telephone Expense	509	
	$ 50 207	$ 50 207

A. Calculate the total value of the accounts receivable accounts.

B. Calculate the total value of the accounts payable accounts.

C. T. Proctor changes over to a three-ledger system of accounting, with subsidiary ledgers and control accounts. **Perform the following:**

   a. Show the new general ledger trial balance.

   b. Show the accounts receivable subsidiary ledger listing in alphabetical order and make sure it agrees in total with the general ledger control account.

   c. Show the accounts payable subsidiary ledger listing in alphabetical order and make sure it agrees in total with the general ledger control account.

3. Hans Schmidt operates a repair shop in Acton, Ontario. On December 31, 20—, the trial balance for the business included the following accounts of customers and suppliers:

Customers		Trade Suppliers	
Aho, Armas	$ 95.20 DR	Biltmore Plumbing	$ 215.00 CR
Bobzin, Stan	526.00 DR	Fleming Door Frames	85.00 CR
Cobb, John	1 552.00 DR	Goodrich Rubber	352.00 CR
Dealice, Guido	956.30 CR	Hlady Aluminum	1 565.00 CR
Franzmann, Sheila	1 230.00 DR	Host Rent-a-Car	295.10 CR
Howe, George	29.60 DR	Ideal Woodcraft	75.00 DR
James, Leslie	3 750.00 DR	Imperial Trailers	335.60 CR
Mutz, J.	642.00 DR	KBM Supply	1 525.00 CR
Robbenhaur, M.	1 200.80 DR	Urbanski Tile	743.25 CR
Torma, Mike	175.10 CR		
Wen, William	478.30 DR		

Answer the following questions:

A. What should the balance be in the Accounts Receivable control account?

B. What should the balance be in the Accounts Payable control account?

C. Give the most likely explanation for the credit balances in the list of customers' accounts.

D. Give the most likely explanation for the debit balance in the list of suppliers' accounts.

E. What figure should appear on the balance sheet for accounts receivable? Explain your answer.

F. Would it be proper to transfer the two credit balances from the receivables to the payables, and the one debit balance from the payables to the receivables? Give some points for and against such an action.

G. Suppose that the transfer suggested above was made. What would the balances be in the control accounts?

---

4. Your office duties with Valley Distribution include those of the accounts receivable clerk. You are to post daily to the customers' accounts from the business documents that you receive.

On the morning of each working day, the following business documents arrive on your desk:

a. copies of all sales invoices issued on the previous working day by the sales department.

b. a listing of the day's cash receipts, prepared first thing each morning by the clerk who opens the mail.

A. Set up the accounts receivable ledger as of June 30, 20— from the following detailed trial balance. If you are using the Workbook, the ledger is set up for you.

VALLEY DISTRIBUTION
ACCOUNTS RECEIVABLE TRIAL BALANCE
JUNE 30, 20—

	Inv. No.		
Adams Bros., 12 Mountain Avenue	480	$ 67.20	
	507	94.20	$ 161.40
Cozo & Son, 620 Main Street	512		75.65
A.G. Farmer, 120A Blackwell Court	514		315.62
S.P. Handy, Ltd., 75 Porter Road	484	216.25	
	511	200.22	416.47
R. Mortimer, 60 Hawley Crescent	470	516.25	
	496	621.90	
	505	608.36	1 746.51
Renforth Sales, 192 Dale Place	510		137.62
Vista Limited, 2001 Central Ave.	515		50.00
			$2 903.27

B. Make the entries to the customers' accounts from the following business papers. In the particulars columns, enter invoice numbers. For each invoice, the amount shown is the total, including all taxes.

TRANSACTIONS

July

2   *Invoices*

No. 516, Adams Bros., $59.24.

No. 517, Renforth Sales, $145.50.

Cash Receipts

A.G. Farmer, No. 514, $315.62.

S.P. Handy, Ltd., No. 484, $216.25.

3   *Invoice*

No. 518, Cozo & Son, $75.85.

Cash Receipts

Nil

4   *Invoices*

No. 519, A.G. Farmer, $217.90.

No. 520, The Williams Company, 417 Lake Street, $150.00.

Cash Receipts

Adams Bros., No. 480, $67.20.

R. Mortimer, No. 470 and No. 496, $1 138.15.

5   *Invoices*

No. 521, Vista Limited, $94.95.

No. 522, S.P. Handy, Ltd., $104.16.

No. 523, R. Mortimer, $56.00.

Cash Receipt

Renforth Sales, No. 510, $137.62.

6   *Invoices*

No. 524, Adams Bros., $167.07.

No. 525, The Williams Company, $75.00.

Cash Receipts

Cozo & Son, No. 512, $75.65.

Vista Limited, No. 515, $50.00.

C. Take off a trial balance of the subsidiary ledger as of July 6 and balance the subsidiary ledger with the control account. The senior accountant has arrived at a control figure of $2 048.45.

---

5. On September 30, 20—, the detailed accounts payable trial balance of Magnetic Controls Company was as follows:

MAGNETIC CONTROLS COMPANY
ACCOUNTS PAYABLE TRIAL BALANCE
SEPTEMBER 30, 20—

		Inv. No.			
Daiton Enterprises	106 Fleet Street, Bathurst	516			$ 430.74
Gordon & Associates	7400 King Street, Oakville	B7407			216.92
Henderson Associates	Box 65, Welland	16421	$ 507.00		
		16907	615.00	1 122.00	
Kohler, R.M.	141 Nixon Avenue, Bathurst	615			104.70
North Shore Packaging	1500 Middle Road, Leduc	901			74.87
Orenson & Company	560 The Eastway, Dauphin	1604	$1 046.26		
		1809	516.15	1 562.41	
Riggs, J.B.	75 Baxter Road, Enfield	74621			502.00
Smithers, P.R.	106 Farr Street, Woodstock	74			57.05
Union Advertising	7900 Primeau Avenue,	16352	$ 436.21		
	Markham	17201	702.16		
		17306	518.90	1 657.27	
					$5 727.96

A. **Set up the accounts payable ledger of Magnetic Controls Company.**
   If you are using the Workbook, the ledger is already set up for you.
B. **From the selected business documents listed below, perform the duties of the accounts payable clerk by making the entries to the accounts payable ledger. Record the source document numbers in the subsidiary ledger accounts.** For all purchase invoices, the amount shown is the total, including appropriate taxes.

TRANSACTIONS

October

1   *Purchase Invoices*
        Smithers, P.R., No. 104, $151.89.
        North Shore Packaging, No. 1046, $57.25.
    Cheque Copies
        No. 65720, Union Advertising, on account, $800.00.
        No. 65721, Henderson Associates, Inv. 16421, $507.00.

2   *Purchase Invoices*
        Wrouse & Reid, 14 Kay Street, Sackfield, No. 597G, $316.29.
        Union Advertising, No. 18002, $505.00.
        Orenson & Company, No. 1856, $216.00.
    Cheque Copies
        No. 65772, Daiton Enterprises, Inv. 516, $430.74.
        No. 65723, Orenson & Company, on account, $500.00.

5   *Purchase Invoices*
        Gordon & Associates, No. B7502, $315.20.
        Kohler, R.M., No. 719, $174.90.
        Riggs, J.B., No. 74998, $472.47.
    Cheque Copies
        No. 65734, North Shore Packaging, Inv. 901, $74.87.
        No. 65735, Union Advertising, balance of Inv. 17201, $338.37.

6   *Purchase Invoices*
        Daiton Enterprises, No. 702, $375.62.
        Henderson Associates, No. 17436, $1 746.21.
    Cheque Copy
        No. 65739, Gordon & Associates, Inv. B7407, $216.92.

7   *Purchase Invoices*
        Henderson Associates, No. 17807, $65.25.
        Kohler, R.M., No. 792, $107.64.
        Wrouse & Reid, No. 602B, $392.61.
    Cheque Copies
        No. 65744, Henderson Associates, Inv. 16907, $615.00.
        No. 65745, Orenson & Company, balance of Inv. 1604, $546.26.
        No. 65746, Wrouse & Reid, Inv. 597G, $316.29.
        No. 65747, Smithers, P.R., Inv. 74, $57.05.

C. **Take off an accounts payable ledger trial balance and see that it agrees with the balance of the control account.** The control account figure is $6 221.79.

6. The simplified general ledger and subsidiary ledgers of Blue Bell Company are given below in T-accounts. These accounts are set up for you in the Workbook. Complete the activities below and on page 523.

General Ledger

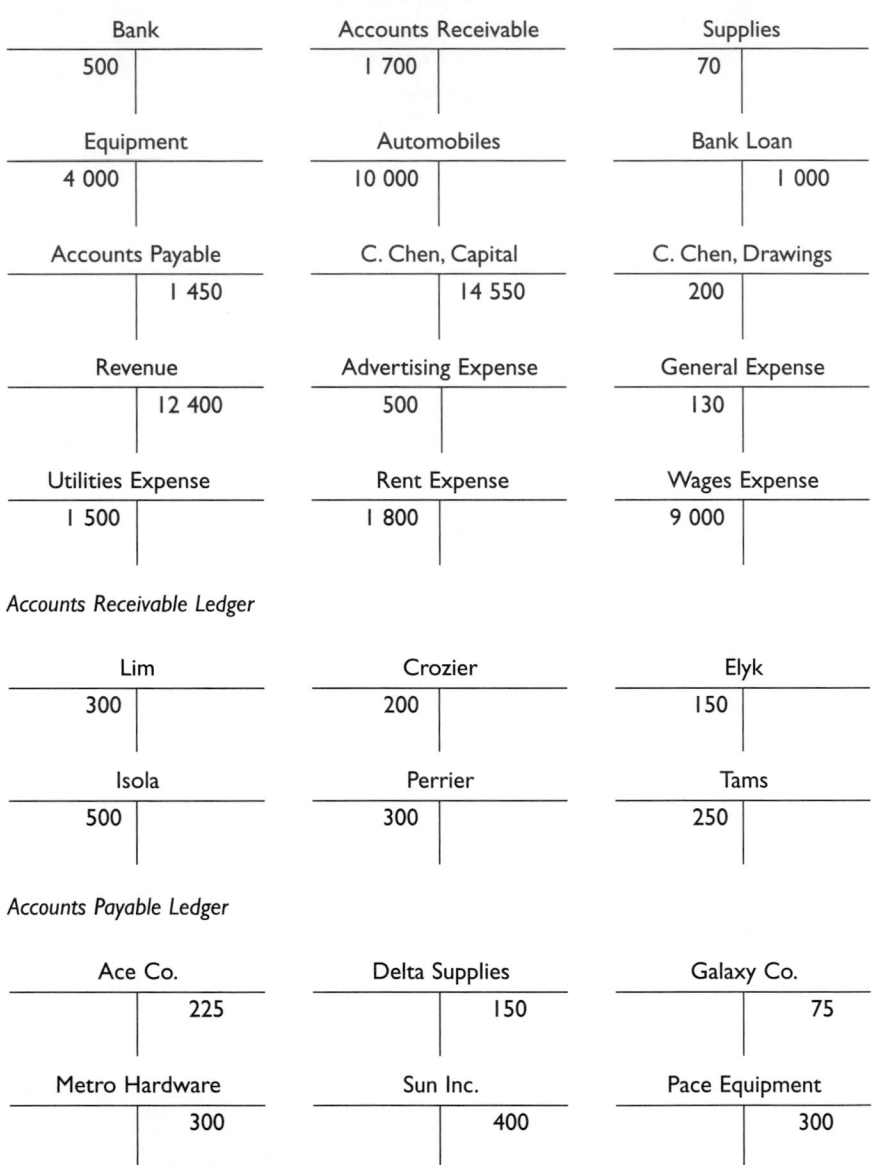

Bank		Accounts Receivable		Supplies	
500		1 700		70	

Equipment		Automobiles		Bank Loan	
4 000		10 000			1 000

Accounts Payable		C. Chen, Capital		C. Chen, Drawings	
	1 450		14 550	200	

Revenue		Advertising Expense		General Expense	
	12 400	500		130	

Utilities Expense		Rent Expense		Wages Expense	
1 500		1 800		9 000	

Accounts Receivable Ledger

Lim		Crozier		Elyk	
300		200		150	

Isola		Perrier		Tams	
500		300		250	

Accounts Payable Ledger

Ace Co.		Delta Supplies		Galaxy Co.	
	225		150		75

Metro Hardware		Sun Inc.		Pace Equipment	
	300		400		300

A. Ensure that the subsidiary ledgers are in balance with their respective control accounts.

B. Perform the duties of the accounts receivable clerk. Select from the source documents shown below those that affect the accounts receivable and make the entries directly to the T-accounts in the subsidiary ledger.

C. **Perform the duties of the accounts payable clerk. Select from the source documents shown below those that affect the accounts payable and make the entries directly to the T-accounts in the subsidiary ledger.**

D. **Perform the duties of the general ledger clerk. Work out the accounting entries for all of the source documents shown below, journalize them in a two-column general journal, and post to the T-accounts in the general ledger. Ignore dates, explanations, PST, and GST.**

Source Documents

No.	Document	Name	Amount	Explanation
1.	Sales invoice	Crozier	$220	Sale on account
2.	Purchase invoice	Ace Co.	150	Advertising
3.	Cash receipt	Elyk	150	On account
4.	Sales invoice	Perrier	175	Sale on account
5.	Purchase invoice	Sun Inc.	130	Supplies
6.	Cash receipt	Isola	300	On account
7.	Sales invoice	Tams	40	Sale on account
8.	Cheque copy	Sun Inc.	400	On account
9.	Purchase invoice	Metro Hardware	350	Utilities
10.	Cash receipt	Perrier	300	On account
11.	Cheque copy	Ace Co.	225	On account
12.	Cheque copy	Pace Equipment	300	On account
13.	Cash sales slip	Winters	175	Cash sale
14.	Cheque copy	Chen	320	Drawings

E. **Balance the three ledgers.**

12.2 | The Synoptic Journal

As a growing business adds customers and vendors, it uses subsidiary ledgers to meet the extra demands placed on its accounting system. Just as the ledger system is modified, the journalizing system can be adjusted to make the accounting process more efficient. One journal system used by small businesses practically eliminates the two-column general journal by recording only non-routine transactions in it. The everyday, routine transactions are entered in a "specialized" journal called the **synoptic journal**. The synoptic journal is a journal with a number of columns to accumulate accounting entries. Most special journals have a number of columns and are known as **multi-columnar journals**.

GST is ignored in this section so that the main topic — the synoptic journal — can be presented more easily. A full synoptic journal requires a wide page, which is not feasible in a textbook. This should in no way interfere with your understanding of the synoptic journal. GST will be picked up again in the next section.

Journalizing in the Synoptic Journal

The synoptic journal is sometimes referred to as the "columnar" journal.

An illustration of a synoptic journal is shown in Figure 12.14 on page 524. Observe the special money column headings for Bank debit, Bank credit, Accounts Receivable debit, Accounts Receivable credit, Accounts Payable debit, Accounts Payable credit, Sales credit, Purchases debit, and PST Payable credit.

FIGURE 12.14

A page from a synoptic journal.

A synoptic journal need not be identical to the one in the illustration. The headings depend to some extent on the nature of the business. For example, a service business would not need a column for purchases. Also, a synoptic journal may be designed with more columns than shown in the illustration.

SYNOPTIC JOURNAL					MONTH OF _____ 20 __									PAGE ___		
DATE	CUSTOMER SUPPLIER	REF NO	BANK		ACCOUNTS RECEIVABLE		ACCOUNTS PAYABLE		SALES	PURCHASES	PST PAYABLE	OTHER ACCOUNTS				
			DR	CR	DR	CR	DR	CR	CR	DR	CR	ACCOUNT	P.R.	DR	CR	

The synoptic journal is used because it has special columns in which to sort items during the journalizing process. This saves time later when entries are posted. The individual items in the special columns are not posted singly. Only the totals of the special columns are posted, so that only one posting is needed for each.

For example, assume that 50 individual amounts have been entered in the Bank debit column of a synoptic journal. It is the total of these 50 amounts, not each separate amount, that is posted. The accounting department saves a good deal of time and effort by posting totals rather than individual amounts.

In theory, one could have a special column for every general ledger account. However, this would make the journal too cumbersome to be practicable. In practice, special columns are set up only for items that occur frequently. A general section, called Other Accounts is provided for other items. Accounts in this section are posted individually.

Journalizing in the synoptic journal is easy. Obtain a sheet of "synoptic" paper and try the following sample entries for Bombay Trading Company.

As stated earlier, GST is ignored in this section.

TRANSACTION 1   May 4: Cash Sales Ticket No. 57: Sale of $256.00 of merchandise for cash, PST of $20.48, total $276.48.

You should have no trouble working out the accounting entry for this transaction which is:

	DR	CR
Bank	$276.48	
Sales		$256.00
PST Payable		20.48

In the synoptic journal, this accounting entry would be recorded as follows:

SYNOPTIC JOURNAL					MONTH OF May 20 –									PAGE 41		
DATE	CUSTOMER SUPPLIER	REF NO	BANK		ACCOUNTS RECEIVABLE		ACCOUNTS PAYABLE		SALES	PURCHASES	PST PAYABLE	OTHER ACCOUNTS				
			DR	CR	DR	CR	DR	CR	CR	DR	CR	ACCOUNT	P.R.	DR	CR	
May 4	Cash Sale	57	276 48						256 –		20 48					

TRANSACTION 2   May 5: Sales Invoice No. 165: Issued to Paul Rogan, sale of $412.00 of merchandise on account, PST of $32.96, total $444.96.

The accounting entry for this transaction is:

	DR	CR
Accounts Receivable (P. Rogan)	$444.96	
Sales		$412.00
PST Payable		32.96

In the synoptic journal, this entry follows the previous entry in the manner shown below. Observe that no explanations are necessary for routine transactions. Also, remember that the postings to the subsidiary ledgers are made directly from source documents.

SYNOPTIC JOURNAL — MONTH OF May 20 — PAGE 41

DATE	CUSTOMER SUPPLIER	REF NO	BANK DR	BANK CR	ACCOUNTS RECEIVABLE DR	ACCOUNTS RECEIVABLE CR	ACCOUNTS PAYABLE DR	ACCOUNTS PAYABLE CR	SALES CR	PURCHASES DR	PST PAYABLE CR	OTHER ACCOUNTS ACCOUNT	P.R.	DR	CR
May 4	Cash Sale	57	276 48						256 —		20 48				
5	P. Rogan	165			444 96				412 —		32 96				

TRANSACTION 3 **May 6: Purchase Invoice: Received from Empire Wholesale for merchandise purchased on account, $816.00.**

The accounting entry for this transaction is:

	DR	CR
Purchases	$816.00	
Accounts Payable (Empire Wholesale)		$816.00

In the synoptic journal, the entry is recorded as shown below:

SYNOPTIC JOURNAL — MONTH OF May 20 — PAGE 41

DATE	CUSTOMER SUPPLIER	REF NO	BANK DR	BANK CR	ACCOUNTS RECEIVABLE DR	ACCOUNTS RECEIVABLE CR	ACCOUNTS PAYABLE DR	ACCOUNTS PAYABLE CR	SALES CR	PURCHASES DR	PST PAYABLE CR	OTHER ACCOUNTS ACCOUNT	P.R.	DR	CR
May 4	Cash Sale	57	276 48						256 —		20 48				
5	P. Rogan	165			444 96				412 —		32 96				
6	Empire Wholesale							816 —		816 —					

TRANSACTION 4 **May 7: Purchase Invoice and Cheque Copy No. 74: For the cash purchase of supplies from Deluxe Stationers, $235.40.**

The accounting entry for this transaction is:

	DR	CR
Supplies	$235.40	
Bank		$235.40

SYNOPTIC JOURNAL — MONTH OF May 20 — PAGE 41

DATE	CUSTOMER SUPPLIER	REF NO	BANK DR	BANK CR	ACCOUNTS RECEIVABLE DR	ACCOUNTS RECEIVABLE CR	ACCOUNTS PAYABLE DR	ACCOUNTS PAYABLE CR	SALES CR	PURCHASES DR	PST PAYABLE CR	OTHER ACCOUNTS ACCOUNT	P.R.	DR	CR
May 4	Cash Sale	57	276 48						256 —		20 48				
5	P. Rogan	165			444 96				412 —		32 96				
6	Empire Wholesale							816 —		816 —					
7	Deluxe Stationers	74		235 40								Supplies		235 40	

The purchase of supplies does not happen frequently. Therefore, there is no special column for Supplies and the item is entered in the Other Accounts section.

TRANSACTION 5   **May 7: Cheque Copy No. 75: Paid the rent for the month to Ryder Realty, $800.00.**

The accounting entry for the transaction is:

	DR	CR
Rent Expense	$800.00	
Bank		$800.00

In the synoptic journal, the accounting entry is recorded as shown below:

SYNOPTIC JOURNAL   MONTH OF ___May___ 20 —   PAGE 41

DATE	CUSTOMER SUPPLIER	REF NO	BANK DR	BANK CR	ACCOUNTS RECEIVABLE DR	ACCOUNTS RECEIVABLE CR	ACCOUNTS PAYABLE DR	ACCOUNTS PAYABLE CR	SALES CR	PURCHASES DR	PST PAYABLE CR	OTHER ACCOUNTS ACCOUNT	P.R.	DR	CR
May 4	Cash Sale	57	276 48						256 –		20 48				
5	P. Rogan	165			444 96				412 –		32 96				
6	Empire Wholesale							816 –		816 –					
7	Deluxe Stationers	74		235 40								Supplies		235 40	
7	Ryder Realty	75		800 –								Rent Exp.		800 –	

Rent Expense is recorded in the Other Accounts section because it is an infrequently occurring item.

Additional Transactions

A number of additional transactions of a routine nature are listed below. Try to journalize them on your own before comparing your work with the synoptic journal entries in Figure 12.15 on pages 528 and 529.

May

10   *Cheque Copy No. 76*
          Issued to A. Baldwin on account, $173.50.
       Cheque Copy No. 77
          Issued to G. English & Co. on account, $500.00.

11   *Cash Receipt*
          Received from R. Mayotte on account, $352.00.
       Cash Receipt
          Received from P. Fuhr on account, $620.00.

13   *Cheque Copy No. 78*
          Issued to M. Cham in payment of wages, $585.00.
       Cheque Copy No. 79
          Issued to D. Adams in payment of wages, $650.00.

14   *Sales Invoice No. 166*
          Issued to M. Delgaty for merchandise sold on account, $196.00 plus $15.68 PST, total $211.68.
       Sales Invoice No. 167
          Issued to Carl Kwan for merchandise sold on account, $240.00 plus $19.20 PST, total $259.20.

17   *Purchase Invoice*
       Received from Continental Railway for freight charges on incoming merchandise, $436.50.

18   *Purchase Invoice*
       Received from Budget Oil for gasoline and oil used in the delivery truck, $262.54.

19   *Cheque Copy No. 80*
       Issued to P. Kerr, the owner, for personal use, $800.00.

20   *Cheque Copy No. 81 together with Purchase Invoice*
       Issued to Ideal Supply in payment of merchandise purchased for cash, $475.00.

21   *Purchase Invoice*
       Received from Circle Supply for supplies purchased on account, $267.50.
       Purchase Invoice
       Received from Deluxe Stationers for the purchase on account of a new office desk at a cost of $1 053.95 and merchandise at a cost of $224.70, total $1 278.65.

24   *Memorandum from Owner*
       To the effect that the company has borrowed $5 000.00 from the bank effective immediately.

26   *Cheque Copy No. 82*
       Issued to Empire Wholesale on account, $400.00.
       Purchase Invoice
       Received from Prairie Manufacturing for the purchase of merchandise on account, $750.00.
       Cash Receipt
       Received from R. Stoddard on account, $300.00.

27   *Cheque Copy No. 83*
       Issued to M. Ejima for wages, $585.00
       Cheque Copy No. 84
       Issued to D. Adams for wages, $650.00.

31   *Sales Invoice No. 168*
       Issued to Purity Company for the sale of merchandise on account, $540.00 plus $43.20 PST, total $583.20.

Balancing the Synoptic Journal

At the bottom of every journal page, and at the end of every month, a procedure called *cross-balancing* is performed on the synoptic journal, or on any columnar journal.

   Cross-balancing is the process of checking the grand total of all of the debit columns against the grand total of all of the credit columns to make sure that the two grand totals agree. The steps in cross-balancing a columnar journal are described below. Refer to Figure 12.15 on pages 528 and 529 as you study these steps.

Step 1   Immediately beneath the last entry on the page, draw a single ruled line across all money columns of the journal.

Step 2   Separately total (foot) each money column and write in the total in small pencil figures just beneath the single ruled line. You will recall that these tiny pencil figures are known as pencil footings or pin totals.

Step 3   Using a printing calculator, separately add all of the pin totals of the debit columns and all of the pin totals of the credit columns. Include all columns of the journal. These two sums should yield the same grand total. The journal is in balance if the two sums are the same. The journal is out of balance if the two sums are not the same. A journal out of balance indicates that at least one error has been made in its preparation. You may not proceed to the posting of the journal until all errors have been located and corrected.

FIGURE 12.15

Synoptic journal with entries for one month.

SYNOPTIC JOURNAL   MONTH OF ____May____ 20 __ —

DATE	CUSTOMER SUPPLIER	REF NO	BANK DR	BANK CR	ACCOUNTS RECEIVABLE DR	ACCOUNTS RECEIVABLE CR	ACCOUNTS PAYABLE DR	ACCOUNTS PAYABLE CR	SAL...
May 4	Cash Sale	57	2 7 6 48						2 5
5	P. Rogan	165			4 4 4 96				4 1
6	Empire Wholesale							8 1 6 —	
7	Deluxe Stationers	74		2 3 5 40					
7	Ryder Realty	75		8 0 0 —					
10	A. Baldwin	76		1 7 3 50			1 7 3 50		
10	English & Co.	77		5 0 0 —			5 0 0 —		
11	R. Mayotte		3 5 2 —			3 5 2 —			
11	P. Fuhr		6 2 0 —			6 2 0 —			
13	M. Cham	78		5 8 5 —					
13	D. Adams	79		6 5 0 —					
14	M. Delgaty	166			2 1 1 68				1 9
14	Carl Kwan	167			2 5 9 20				2 4
17	Continental Railway							4 3 6 50	
18	Budget Oil							2 6 2 54	
19	P. Kerr	80		8 0 0 —					
20	Ideal Supply	81		4 7 5 —					
21	Circle Supply							2 6 7 50	
21	Deluxe Stationers							1 2 7 8 65	
24	Continental Bank		5 0 0 0 —						
26	Empire Wholesale	82		4 0 0 —			4 0 0 —		
26	Prairie Manufacturing							7 5 0 —	
26	R. Stoddard		3 0 0 —			3 0 0 —			
27	M. Ejima	83		5 8 5 —					
27	D. Adams	84		6 5 0 —					
31	Purity Company	168			5 8 3 20				5 4
			6 5 4 8 48	5 8 5 3 90	1 4 9 9 04	1 2 7 2 00	1 0 7 3 50	3 8 1 1 19	1 6 4

Step 4 When the journal is balanced, write in the column totals immediately beneath the pin totals.

Step 5 Draw a double ruled line across all money columns immediately beneath the column totals.

PAGE __41__

HASES		PST PAYABLE		OTHER ACCOUNTS				
R		CR	ACCOUNT	P.R.	DR		CR	
		2 0 48						
		3 2 96						
6 –								
			Supplies		2 3 5 40			
			Rent Exp.		8 0 0 –			
			Wages Exp.		5 8 5 –			
			Wages Exp.		6 5 0 –			
		1 5 68						
		1 9 20						
			Freight-in		4 3 6 50			
			Delivery Exp.		2 6 2 54			
			Drawings		8 0 0 –			
5 –								
			Supplies		2 6 7 50			
4 70			Office Equip.		1 0 5 3 95			
			Bank Loan				5 0 0 0 –	
0 –								
			Wages Exp.		5 8 5 –			
			Wages Exp.		6 5 0 –			
		4 3 20						
5 70		1 3 1 52			6 3 2 5 89		5 0 0 0 00	

Debits 0·	T	Credits 0·	T
6548·48	+	5853·90	+
1499·04	+	1272·00	+
1073·50	+	3811·19	+
2265·70	+	1644·00	+
6325·89	+	131·52	+
		5000·00	+
17712·61	T	17712·61	T

Cross-balancing the synoptic journal

Forwarding in the Synoptic Journal

A new journal page is started at the beginning of each month. Also, during the month, a new page must be started whenever a page is filled up. When a new page is started in any columnar journal during the month, it is customary to start it off with the balanced totals from the bottom of the previous page. The totals at the end of one page are "forwarded" to the next page. This procedure is illustrated in Figure 12.16 below.

FIGURE 12.16

Forwarding in the synoptic journal.

A SYNOPTIC PAGE JUST COMPLETED

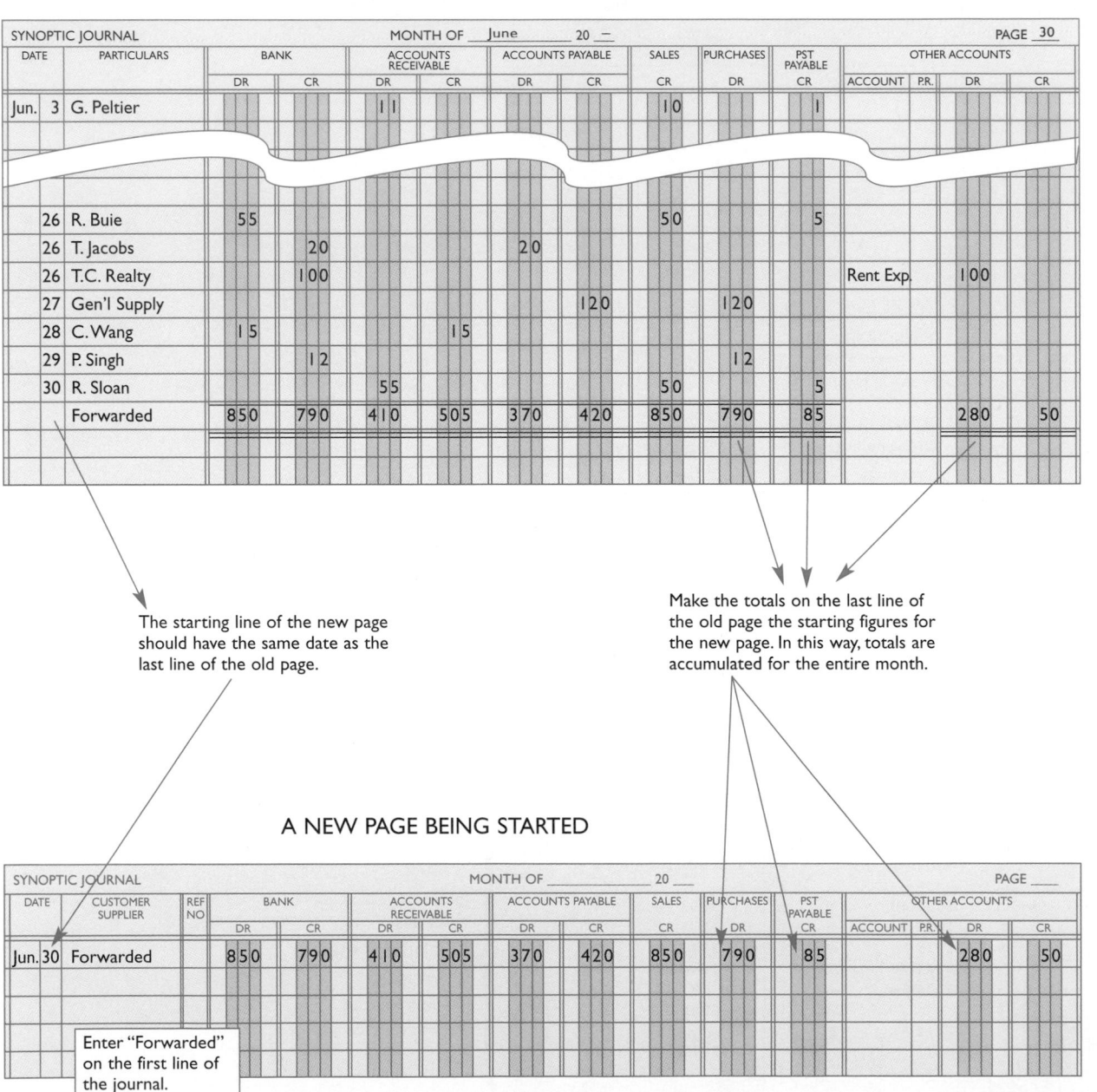

The starting line of the new page should have the same date as the last line of the old page.

Make the totals on the last line of the old page the starting figures for the new page. In this way, totals are accumulated for the entire month.

A NEW PAGE BEING STARTED

Enter "Forwarded" on the first line of the journal.

Posting the Synoptic Journal

Let us recall some facts about posting in general before discussing how to post the synoptic journal. First, posting to the general ledger is done once a month. Therefore, the synoptic journal is posted once a month because it is posted to the general ledger. Second, posting to the subsidiary ledgers is done directly from source documents. The subsidiary ledger posting is done daily by an accounting clerk not involved with the general ledger.

Posting the synoptic journal requires a different procedure because it is a multi-columnar journal. The basic procedure is illustrated in Figure 12.17 below, using a simplified example. Study the example carefully, and observe that:

- the synoptic journal is balanced before posting is begun;
- for each of the "special" columns, the column totals are posted rather than the individual amounts within the columns. By posting only the totals, a great deal of time is saved;
- the Other Accounts section lists items that are generally unrelated. Therefore, the individual amounts contained within the columns in this section have to be posted separately. Posting the Other Accounts section of the synoptic journal is very similar to posting from a two-column general journal.

FIGURE 12.17

Posting the synoptic journal (simplified).

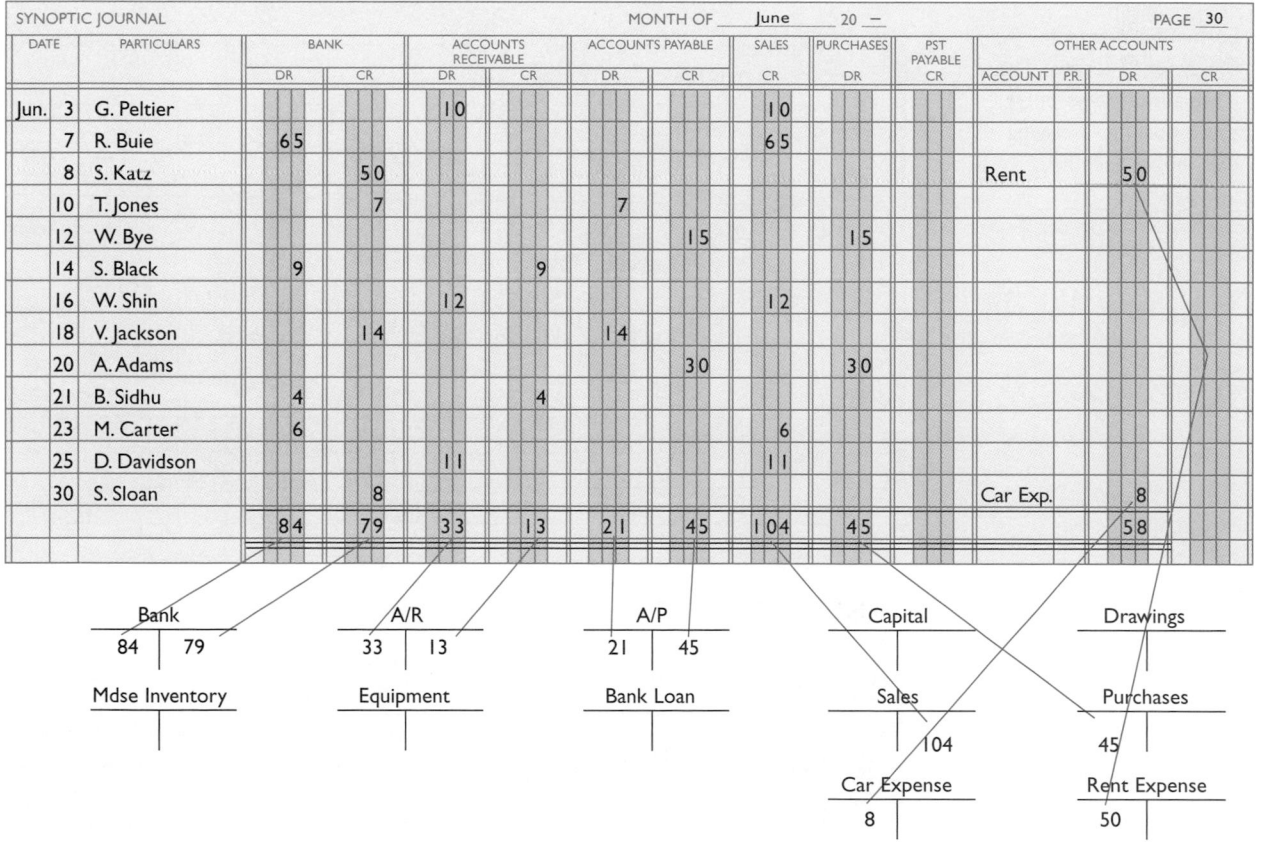

Formal Technique for Posting the Synoptic Journal

Figure 12.18 below and on page 533 shows an example of formal posting from the synoptic journal. Observe the following details:

- the entries in the accounts are dated for the last day of the month;
- "Sn" or "SN" and the journal page number are used in the accounts when cross-referencing;
- the following rules apply when cross-referencing in the journal:

  1. the account number is entered in parentheses immediately beneath the column total being posted;
  2. for items in the Other Accounts section, the account number is entered in the Posting Reference column beside the amount being posted;

- the account balances are not calculated until all of the postings are completed.

The entirely posted synoptic journal appears as shown in Figure 12.19 on pages 534 and 535, with the posting reference numbers entered.

Figure 12.19 on pages 534 and 535

FIGURE 12.18

Formal posting from the synoptic journal. The illustration shows only three postings involving two ledger accounts.

SYNOPTIC JOURNAL (Partial)

DATE		PARTICULARS	REF NO	BANK DR	BANK CR	ACCOUNTS RECEIVA DR	CR
June	1	Cash Sale	58	56 –			
	3	Paul Boxer	169			112 –	
	5	A.O.K. Wholesale	762				
	6	Deluxe Stationers	85		3720		
	7	Ryder Realty (1/2 req.)	86		400 –		
	30	Cannon Company	172			96 –	
				1627 –	255090	628 –	57
				(101)	(101)		

GENERAL LEDGER (Two accounts only)

ACCOUNT	Bank		NO. 101					
DATE		PARTICULARS	P.R.	DEBIT	CREDIT	DR. CR.	BALANCE
Apr.²⁰ 30		Balance brought forward	—			DR	102283
May	31		Sn41	654848			
	31		Sn41		585390	DR	171741
June	30		Sn42	1627 –			
	30		Sn42		255090	DR	79351

Two-Journal System

In a manual system, accounting offices make use of both the synoptic journal and the two-column journal. Typically, the synoptic journal is used by a junior employee to record the routine transactions of the business. The two-column general journal is used by a senior accounting employee to record entries of a non-routine, and usually more complex, nature. The synoptic journal system can therefore be described as a *two-journal system*.

MONTH OF ___June___ 20 _–_   PAGE __42__

OUNTS PAYABLE CR	SALES CR	PURCHASES DR	Supplies DR	OTHER ACCOUNTS ACCOUNT	P.R.	DR	CR
	5 6 –						
	1 1 2 –						
3 1 6 –		3 1 6 –					
			3 7 20				
				Rent Expense	580	4 0 0 –	
	9 6 –						
9 70 1 0 9 4 22	6 8 4 –	7 7 6 –	1 5 3 20			2 3 9 6 22 1 0 0 0 00	
9 70 1 0 9 4 22	6 8 4 –	7 7 6 –	1 5 3 20			2 3 9 6 22 1 0 0 0 00	

ACCOUNT	Rent Expense					NO. 580	
DATE	PARTICULARS	P.R.	DEBIT	CREDIT	DR. CR.	BALANCE	
May 20 31	Balance brought forward	—			DR	4 0 0 0 –	
June 30		Sn42	4 0 0 –		DR	4 4 0 0 –	

FIGURE 12.19

Synoptic journal showing posting references.

SYNOPTIC JOURNAL						
DATE	PARTICULARS	CHQ NO	BANK DR	BANK CR	ACCOUNTS RECEIVA DR	CR
June 1	Cash Sale	58	5 6 –			
3	Paul Boxer	169			1 1 2 –	
5	A.O.K. Wholesale	762				
6	Deluxe Stationers	85		3 7 20		
7	Ryder Realty (1/2 req.)	86		4 0 0 –		
7	S. Tan	87		7 3 50		
9	Codling & Co.	88		4 6 20		
12	S. Jordan		9 6 –			9
12	Y. Shanine		3 7 5 –			3 7
12	A. Esmay	89		3 1 2 –		
12	R. French	90		2 8 5 –		
13	M. Birch	170			2 5 0 –	
15	Y. Rashid	171			1 7 0 –	
18	Continental Transport					
18	Bay Oil					
19	G. Nguyen	91		3 0 0 –		
20	RV Supply	92		3 0 0 –		
20	Square Supplies					
22	Deluxe Stationers					
22	Crescent Bank		1 0 0 0 –			
25	A.O.K. Wholesale	93		2 0 0 –		
27	Lanigan Mfg.					
27	M. Lu		1 0 0 –			1 0
28	A. Esmay	94		3 1 2 –		
29	R. French	95		2 8 5 –		
30	Cannon Company	172			9 6 –	
			1 6 2 7 –	2 5 5 0 90	6 2 8 –	5 7
			(101)	(101)	(105)	(10

MONTH OF **June** 20 —   PAGE **42**

ACCOUNTS PAYABLE DR	ACCOUNTS PAYABLE CR	SALES CR	PURCHASES DR	Supplies DR	OTHER ACCOUNTS ACCOUNT	P.R.	OTHER ACCOUNTS DR	OTHER ACCOUNTS CR
		56 –						
		112 –						
	316 –		316 –					
				3 7 20				
					Rent Expense	580	400 –	
3 50								
6 20								
					Wages Expense	595	312 –	
					Wages Expense	595	285 –	
		250 –						
		170 –						
	87 50				Freight-in	555	87 50	
	64 72				Delivery Exp.	540	64 72	
					Ripley Drwgs	305	300 –	
			300 –					
	46 –			46 –				
	420 –			70 –	Office Equip.	140	350 –	
					Bank Loan	210		1 000 –
0 –								
	160 –		160 –					
					Wages Expense	595	312 –	
					Wages Expense	595	285 –	
		96 –						
9 70	10 94 22	6 84 –	7 76 –	1 53 20			2 396 22	1 000 00
(05)	(205)	(401)	(550)	(125)				

Variations in Journalizing in the Synoptic Journal

1. Debit entries may be entered in Credit columns and credit entries may be entered in Debit columns, but they must be circled, or written in red. This special treatment of an entry indicates that its effect in the column is the opposite to that specified in the column heading. When the column is totalled, the circled item must be subtracted to give the proper total. A refund or a credit invoice would be handled in this way (see Figure 12.20 below).

2. Most accounting entries require only one line in the synoptic journal. However, there are times when two or more lines may be required. This occurs when at least two of the accounts affected by the transaction need to be entered in the Other Accounts section of the journal (see Figure 12.20 below).

FIGURE 12.20

Variations in recording in the synoptic journal.

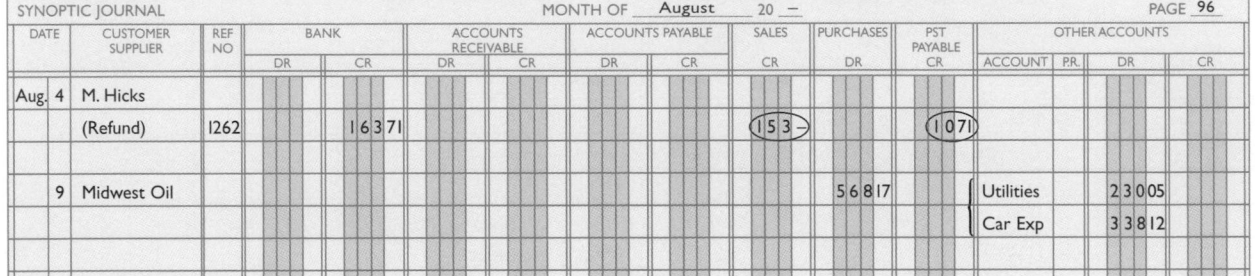

SYNOPTIC JOURNAL																MONTH OF August 20 —								PAGE 96

DATE	CUSTOMER SUPPLIER	REF NO	BANK		ACCOUNTS RECEIVABLE		ACCOUNTS PAYABLE		SALES	PURCHASES	PST PAYABLE	OTHER ACCOUNTS			
			DR	CR	DR	CR	DR	CR	CR	DR	CR	ACCOUNT	P.R.	DR	CR
Aug. 4	M. Hicks														
	(Refund)	1262		1 6 3 71					(1 5 3)		(1 0 71)				
9	Midwest Oil									5 6 8 17		Utilities		2 3 0 05	
												Car Exp		3 3 8 12	

Section 12.2   Review Questions

1. The two-column general journal is mainly used for what type of transaction?
2. For what type of transaction are the specialized journals used?
3. Define "multi-columnar journal."
4. Why does each line of the synoptic journal usually balance?
5. Explain how the synoptic journal saves time when entries are posted.
6. How do accountants determine which items are special columns set up in the synoptic journal?
7. Explain how to balance a synoptic journal.
8. Explain how to forward the synoptic journal.
9. Why is it important to forward in a synoptic journal?
10. Explain how to cross-reference in the synoptic journal.
11. Why is a general journal usually used along with a synoptic journal?
12. Describe how to record a debit entry in a credit column. How is the entry handled when the columns are being totalled?
13. Explain why some accounting entries require more than one line in the synoptic journal.

Section 12.2   **Exercises**

1. **Indicate whether each of the following statements is true or false by entering a "T" or an "F" in the space indicated in your Workbook. Explain the reason for each "F" response in the space provided.**

   a. A non-routine transaction is one that is out of the ordinary.
   b. The synoptic journal is ideally suited to a large company.
   c. A synoptic journal is a multi-columnar journal.
   d. In the synoptic journal, there would be a special column for Sales Tax Payable because it is a frequently occurring item.
   e. The headings in a synoptic journal are always the same as those shown in the textbook.
   f. The main advantage of the synoptic journal is time saved in journalizing transactions.
   g. An advantage of the synoptic journal is that it is not necessary to balance the accounting entry for every transaction.
   h. The synoptic journal is balanced at the end of every month and at the end of every page.
   i. The accuracy of the synoptic journal is checked by cross-balancing.
   j. The synoptic journal should be cross-balanced before the final totals are inked in and the journal ruled off.
   k. It is customary to forward the totals from one page of the synoptic journal to the next.
   l. The total of the Other Accounts debit section is posted as a debit to the general ledger.
   m. The postings from the synoptic journal are dated the last day of the month.
   n. No cross-referencing is necessary when using a synoptic journal.
   o. A two-journal system provides a different route for non-routine transactions.
   p. A debit amount can be entered in a credit column if it is circled.
   q. Every entry in the synoptic journal takes only one line.

2. **On page 19 of the synoptic journal of Donway Distributing, record the transactions listed below for the month of August 20—. Add sales tax of 8 per cent on all sales of merchandise. Ignore GST. Use the following chart of accounts.**

DONWAY DISTRIBUTING
Chart of Accounts

101	Bank	305	A. Orlando, Capital
105	Accounts Receivable	310	A. Orlando, Drawings
110	Merchandise Inventory	405	Sales
115	Supplies	505	Purchases
118	Land	510	Freight-in
120	Building	515	Advertising
121	Accumulated Depreciation — Building	520	Building Maintenance
125	Office Equipment	525	Car Expense
126	Accumulated Depreciation — Office Equipment	530	Interest and Bank Charges
		535	Utilities Expense
201	Accounts Payable	540	Miscellaneous Expense
205	Bank Loan	545	Telephone Expense
210	PST Payable	550	Wages Expense
215	Mortgage Payable		

TRANSACTIONS

August

2   *Cheque Copy No. 702*

To D. Macdonald, for painting the business premises, $856.00.

3   *Sales Invoice No. 210*

To N. Rae, sale of goods on account, $184.00 plus PST.

Cash Receipt

From Viceroy Homes, on account, $150.00.

5   *Cheque Copy No. 703*

To T. Vint, for wages, $290.00.

Cash Sales Slip No. 91

To M. Franci, cash sale of merchandise, $85.00 plus PST.

8   *Cheque Copy No. 704*

To Cash, for cash purchase of postage stamps, $320.00 (cashed by an employee who purchased the stamps).

Sales Invoice No. 211

To Atlas Stores, sale of goods on account, $502.00 plus PST.

9   *Purchase Invoice*

From Diamond Wholesalers, merchandise purchased on account, $925.00.

10   *Purchase Invoice*

From Continental Railway, for freight charges on incoming goods, $315.00.

11   *Cash Sales Slip No. 92*

To J. Vincent, cash sale of merchandise, $150.00 plus PST.

12   *Cheque Copy No. 705*

To Vance Brothers, on account, $300.00.

Cheque Copy No. 706

To T. Vint, for wages, $290.00.

15   *Cheque Copy No. 707*

To Century News, for newspaper advertisement, $42.00.

Cheque Copy No. 708

To A. Orlando, for owner's personal use, $300.00.

18   *Cash Sales Slip No. 93*

To A. Anderson, cash sale of merchandise, $55.00 plus PST.

19   *Cheque Copy No. 709*

To Merry Manufacturing, on account, $500.00.

Cheque Copy No. 710

To T. Vint, for wages, $290.00.

Cash Receipt

From J. Regnault, on account, $200.00.

22   *Cheque Copy No. 711*

To Trade Group, mortgage instalment, $356.75 ($285.20 is debt reduction; $71.55 is interest expense).

Sales Invoice No. 212

To T. Schmidt, sale of goods on account, $170.00 plus PST.

23   *Purchase Invoice*

From Deluxe Oil Company, $240.00 ($180.00 for business use; $60.00 for personal use by owner).

24   *Bank Debit Advice*
         From General Bank, for service charge, $42.00.
25   *Cheque Copy No. 712*
         To A. Orlando, for owner's personal use, $500.00.
26   *Cash Sales Slip No. 94*
         To K. Beka, cash sale of merchandise, $110.00 plus PST.
       Cheque Copy No. 713
         To T. Vint, for wages, $290.00.
29   *Purchase Invoice*
         From Federated Supply, for the purchase of merchandise, $1 240.00.
30   *Cheque Copy No. 714*
         To Public Utilities Commission, for hydro charges for month, $146.00.
31   *Sales Invoice No. 213*
         To Brian Patel, sale of goods on account, $190.00 plus PST.
       Cash Receipt
         From J. Klassen, on account, $400.00.

After recording the transactions, do the following:

A. Cross-balance and rule the journal.

B. Summarize the postings that would be made to the general ledger. List the information in three columns: Account; Debit Amount; Credit Amount. Show that the postings are balanced by totalling the two money columns.

---

3. **This exercise also appears in your Workbook.**
   Shown on page 540, in condensed form, are the synoptic journal and the T-account general ledger of Plastic Products, owned by Jean Webb.

   A. Post the synoptic journal to the general ledger. Ignore dates and cross-references. Use check marks to indicate that postings are completed.

   B. Take off a general ledger trial balance.

SYNOPTIC JOURNAL

SYNOPTIC JOURNAL		BANK		ACCOUNTS RECEIVABLE		ACCOUNTS PAYABLE		SALES	PURCHASES	PST PAYABLE	OTHER ACCOUNTS				MONTH OF June 20 — PAGE 16
DATE	PARTICULARS	DR	CR	DR	CR	DR	CR	CR	DR	CR	ACCOUNT	P.R.	DR	CR	
Jun. 20	Forwarded	1 800	1 450	2 150	1 970	1 270	1 350	1 750	1 460	160					
23	Laine	55						50		5					
23	Moors		60								Rent		60		
24	Park			110				100		10					
25	Reid	80			80										
25	Ruel		250			250									
25	Sacerty		20								Telephone		20		
26	Bass						150		150						
26	Clayton						300		300						
27	Delski		40								Wages		40		
27	Eady						90				Car Exp.		90		
27	Green		70								Freight		70		
27	Hock	400			400										
30	Klaus		230			230									
30	McCoy	88						80		8					
30	Nagy			77				70		7					
30	Perry			44				40		4					
		2 423	2 120	2 381	2 450	1 750	1 890	2 090	1 910	194			280		

GENERAL LEDGER

Bank	Accounts Receivable	Mdse Inventory	Supplies
70	350	900	100

Equipment	Bank Loan	Accounts Payable	PST Payable
2 000	1 000	150	300

J. Webb, Capital	J. Webb, Drawings	Sales	Bank Charges
3 020	500	4 500	40

Car Expense	Freight-in	General Expense	Purchases
500	100	90	2 000

Rent Expense	Telephone Expense	Utilities Expense	Wages Expense
300	50	1 220	750

Comprehensive Exercise

4. Felicia Dunn is the owner of Crest Hardware. She operates it with her husband and with occasional part-time help.

   The books of account consist of a general ledger, two subsidiary ledgers, and a synoptic journal.

   Most of the sales of the business are cash sales. The cash receipts are deposited in the bank on a daily basis. All payments are made by cheque.

   The number of accounts in both subsidiary ledgers is very small. The Dunns grant credit to only a few customers and they buy stock from only a few suppliers. The subsidiary ledger routine is very simple. The postings to the subsidiary ledgers are made directly from the source documents.

   The three ledgers of Crest Hardware are set up in the Workbook from the following trial balances:

GENERAL LEDGER TRIAL BALANCE
JUNE 30, 20—

		DR	CR
101	Bank	$ 12 400.00	
105	Account Receivable	5 365.25	
110	Merchandise Inventory	46 090.20	
115	Supplies	1 395.00	
120	Store Equipment	40 906.00	
121	Accum. Deprec. — Store Equip.		$ 14 726.00
130	Delivery Equipment	39 500.00	
131	Accum. Deprec. — Delivery Equip.		20 145.00
201	Accounts Payable		6 265.35
205	PST Payable		240.00
210	Loan Payable — Federal Finance		8 550.85
301	F. Dunn, Capital		87 952.08
302	F. Dunn, Drawings	6 000.00	
401	Sales		53 714.50
505	Delivery Expense	5 258.00	
510	Freight-in	956.23	
515	General Expense	2 953.10	
520	Purchases	14 120.00	
525	Rent Expense	2 400.00	
530	Wages Expense	14 250.00	
		$191 593.78	$191 593.78

ACCOUNTS RECEIVABLE TRIAL BALANCE
JUNE 30, 20—

R. Lai	Invoice #1407	$2 072.15
G. Langford	Invoice #1431	316.20
R. Potts	Invoice #1436	2 976.90
		$5 365.25

ACCOUNTS PAYABLE TRIAL BALANCE
JUNE 30, 20—

City Hardware Supply	Invoice #1742	$2 742.10
Special Steel Products	Invoice #147	3 523.25
		$6 265.35

A. Record the journal entries for the transactions listed below in the synoptic journal. Use journal page 73. The PST is 8%; ignore GST.

B. Post to the subsidiary ledgers on a daily basis directly from the source documents.

TRANSACTIONS

July

2   *Cash Sales Slip*
> No. 206, $216.00 plus PST.

    Sales Invoice
> No. 1475, to R. Lai, $190.00 plus PST.

    Purchase Invoice
> From City Hardware Supply, No. 1802, for the purchase of merchandise for resale, $1 264.25.

3   *Cash Sales Slip*
> No. 207, $102.00 plus PST.

    Cash Receipt
> From R. Lai, $2 072.15 on account.

6   *Cash Sales Slip*
> No. 208, $350.00 plus PST.

    Cheque Copy
> No. 316, to R. Niosi, wages for part-time help, $175.00.

7   *Cash Sales Slip*
> No. 209, $140.00 plus PST.

    Purchase Invoice
> From City Hardware Supply, No. 1834, for purchase of merchandise for resale, $2 316.25.

    Cheque Copies
> No. 317, to Special Steel Products, $500.00 on account.
> No. 318, to City Hardware Supply, $2 742.10 on account.
> No. 319, to F. Dunn, for owner's personal use, $800.00.

9   *Cash Sales Slip*
> No. 210, $260.00 plus PST.

    Sales Invoice
> No. 1476, to G. Langford, $590.00 plus PST.

12 *Cash Sales Slip*
> No. 211, $40.00 plus PST.

    Purchase Invoice
> From Special Steel Products, No. 192, for merchandise for resale, $375.00.

    Cheque Copy
> No. 320, to J. Sacco, wages for part-time help, $200.00.

13 *Cheque Copy*
> No. 321, to Special Steel Products, on account, $3 023.25.

14 *Cash Sales Slip*
> No. 212, $185.00 plus PST.

    Sales Invoice
> No. 1477, to R. Potts, $321.00 plus PST.

    Purchase Invoice
> From Clix Oil Company, No. 1244, for gasoline and oil used in the delivery truck, $475.00.

Cheque Copy

No. 322, to Provincial Treasurer, paying PST for previous month, $240.00.

16   *Cash Sales Slip*

No. 213, $175.00 plus PST.

Cash Receipt

From G. Langford, $316.20 on account.

17   *Purchase Invoice*

From Joe Jay Transport, No. 344, charges for transportation on incoming merchandise, $375.15.

19   *Cash Sales Slip*

No. 214, $240.00 plus PST.

Cheque Copy

No. 323, to Oak Investments, for the rent for the month, $600.00.

23   *Cash Sales Slip*

No. 215, $89.00 plus PST.

Sales Invoice

No. 1478, to R. Lai, $311.00 plus PST.

Cheque Copies

No. 324, to D. Phin, for part-time wages, $175.00.

No. 325, to Public Utilities, for electricity and water for the month, $176.10.

No. 326, to City Telephone, for telephone bill for the month, $149.00.

24   *Cash Receipt*

From R. Lai, $205.20 on account.

26   *Cheque Copy*

No. 327, to City Hardware Supply, $1 264.25 on account.

28   *Cheque Copy*

No. 328, to F. Dunn, for personal use, $800.00.

C. Balance the synoptic journal.
D. Post the synoptic journal to the general ledger.
E. Balance the general ledger by means of a trial balance.
F. Balance the subsidiary ledgers by means of a trial balance.

12.3 | The Five-Journal System

The synoptic journal described in the previous section is suitable only for a very small business or organization. The reason for this is that only one person at a time can work on it. Most businesses soon grow to a point where more than one person needs to be involved in the journalizing process. Systems using more than one journal were developed for this reason. The five-journal system is a popular choice for medium and large businesses, and its structure forms the basis for several accounting programs.

The **five-journal system** is one in which five separate journals are operated at the same time, with each journal restricted to a particular type of transaction. The basic structure of the five-journal system is illustrated in Figure 12.21 on page 544. As you can see, the accounting entries are channelled from the various source documents into the five separate journals. Each journal is restricted to a particular type of transaction. Each of the journals is posted individually to the general ledger. As before, the subsidiary ledgers are posted independently from separate copies of the source documents.

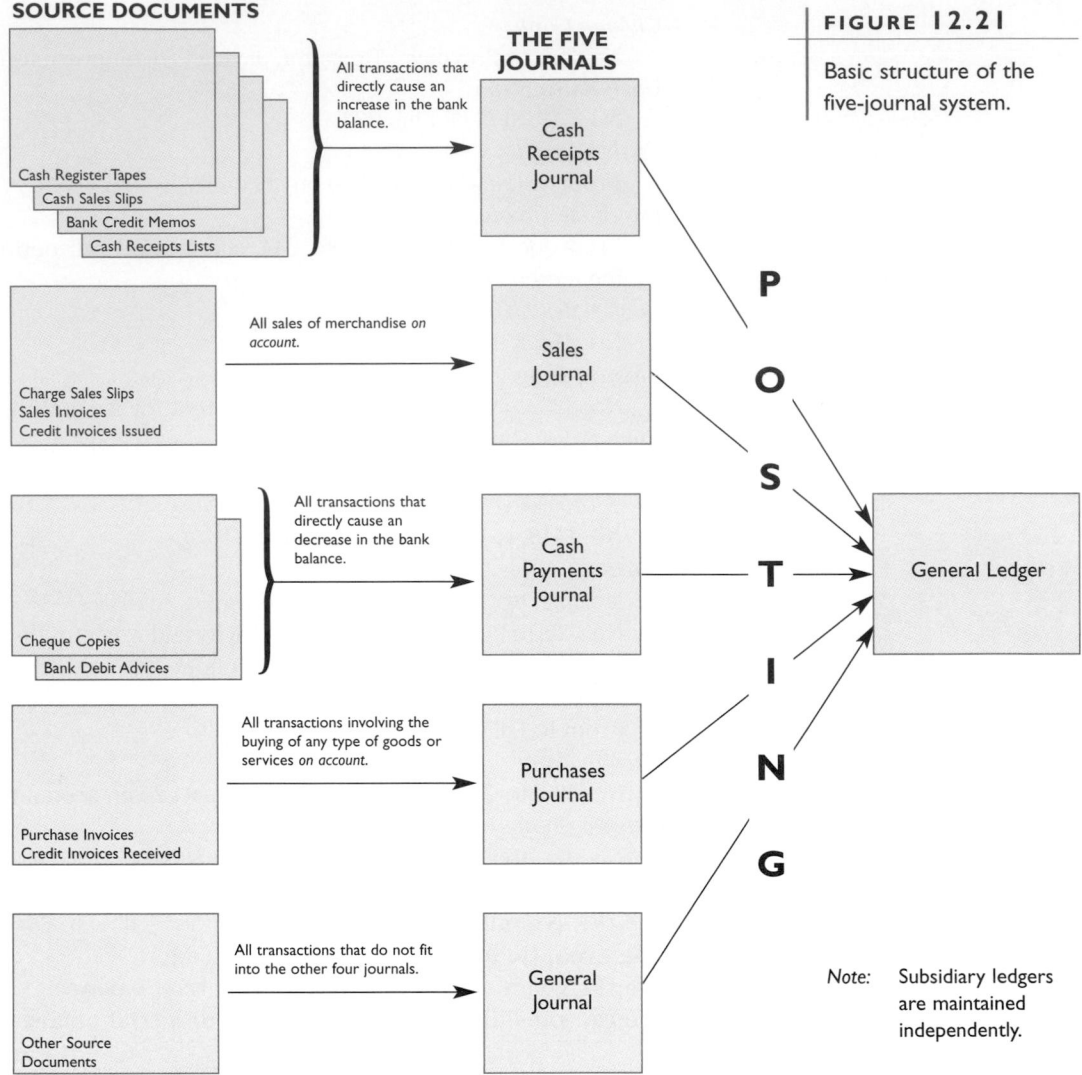

SOURCE DOCUMENTS

Cash Register Tapes
Cash Sales Slips
Bank Credit Memos
Cash Receipts Lists

All transactions that directly cause an increase in the bank balance.

Charge Sales Slips
Sales Invoices
Credit Invoices Issued

All sales of merchandise *on account.*

Cheque Copies
Bank Debit Advices

All transactions that directly cause an decrease in the bank balance.

Purchase Invoices
Credit Invoices Received

All transactions involving the buying of any type of goods or services *on account.*

Other Source Documents

All transactions that do not fit into the other four journals.

THE FIVE JOURNALS

Cash Receipts Journal

Sales Journal

Cash Payments Journal

Purchases Journal

General Journal

P O S T I N G

General Ledger

FIGURE 12.21

Basic structure of the five-journal system.

Note: Subsidiary ledgers are maintained independently.

There are two main advantages to using a number of journals. The first is that doing so allows several people to be involved in the journalizing process at the same time. The second is that it makes the accounting system more efficient by allowing specialization of duties among the staff. The five-journal system inevitably leads to the accounting clerks becoming specialists within the system. Large offices may require a specialist for each journal. Smaller offices often find that one person can handle two journals very well. A natural relationship exists between sales and cash receipts. There is also a natural relationship between purchases and cash payments. These pairs make very effective units of work within the accounting department.

Learning to operate the five-journal system is not going to be difficult for you. You will find no difference in the general journal. Also, each of the new "special" journals is a columnar journal similar in concept to the synoptic journal. The real difference lies in the fact that all of the routine transactions do not go into a single journal. Instead, they are channelled into one of four special journals.

Cash Receipts Journal

The **cash receipts journal** is used to record all transactions that directly increase the bank balance. Every accounting entry in the cash receipts journal involves a debit to Bank. The two most common transactions in the cash receipts journal are "cash sales" and "receipts on account."

A partially completed page from a typical cash receipts journal is shown in Figure 12.22 below. It was prepared from the following source documents.

TRANSACTIONS

February

4   *Cash Sales Slip No. 64*

     Issued to R. Lentz, merchandise $118.00, GST $8.26, PST $9.44, total $135.70.

     Cash Sales Slip No. 65

     Issued to M. Reid, merchandise $78.25, GST $5.48, PST $6.26, total $89.99.

5   *Cash Receipts*

     Received from T. Song on account, $500.00.

     Received from P. Yurick on account, $160.50.

6   *Cash Sales Slip No. 66*

     Issued to G. Ostrum, merchandise $105.00, GST $7.35, PST $8.40, total $120.75.

     Cash Receipt

     Received from K. Pape on account, $106.47.

7   *Bank Credit Advice*

     Received from Centre Bank, for interest earned, $725.00.

8   *Cash Sales Slip No. 67*

     Issued to C. Drew, merchandise $85.25, GST $5.97, PST $6.82, total $98.04.

FIGURE 12.22

A partially completed page of a cash receipts journal.

CASH RECEIPTS JOURNAL   MONTH OF ___Feb.___ 20 _—_   PAGE __16__

DATE		PARTICULARS	OTHER ACCOUNTS CR			GST PAYABLE CR	PST PAYABLE CR	SALES CR	ACCOUNTS RECEIVABLE CR	REF. NO.	BANK DR
			ACCOUNT	P.R.	AMOUNT						
Feb.	4	R. Lentz				8 26	9 44	118 —		64	135 70
	4	M. Reid				5 48	6 26	78 25		65	89 99
	5	F. Song							500 —		500 —
	5	P. Yurick							160 50		160 50
	6	G. Ostrum				7 35	8 40	105 —		66	120 75
	6	K. Pape							106 47		106 47
	7	Centre Bank	Interest Earned		725 —						725 —
	8	C. Drew				5 97	6 82	85 25		67	98 04

Special Considerations

- The cash receipts journal is a columnar journal and follows the rules for all columnar journals.
- Cash sales go into the cash receipts journal. Sales on account go into the sales journal. If a sale is partly for cash and partly on account, it goes into the cash receipts journal.

Sales Journal

The **sales journal** is used to record all transactions involving the sale of merchandise on account. Transactions related to sales on account are the only ones entered in the sales journal. The source documents for entries to the sales journal are sales invoices, credit invoices, and charge sales slips.

A partially completed page from a sales journal is shown in Figure 12.23 below. It was prepared from the following transactions:

TRANSACTIONS

February

5   *Sales Invoice No. 652*

     Issued to R. Rau, merchandise $59.00, GST $4.13, PST $4.72, total $67.85.

     Charge Sales Slip No. 125

     Issued to L. Sauve, merchandise $84.50, GST $5.92, PST $6.76, total $97.18.

6   *Credit Invoice No. 653*

     Issued to C. Myzk for unsatisfactory merchandise returned, merchandise $145.00, GST $10.15, PST $11.60, total $166.75.

     Sales Invoice No. 654

     Issued to R. Halfmoon, merchandise $245.85, GST $17.21, PST $19.67, total $282.73.

7   *Charge Sales Slip No. 126*

     Issued to H. Didyk, merchandise $110.25, GST $7.72, PST $8.82, total $126.79.

8   *Sales Invoice No. 655*

     Issued to A. Han, merchandise $65.00, GST $4.55, PST $5.20, total $74.75.

FIGURE 12.23

A partially completed page of a sales journal.

Circled amounts have the opposite effect (DR or CR) to that which is specified in the column heading.

SALES JOURNAL   MONTH OF __Feb.__   PAGE __22__

DATE		PARTICULARS	GST PAYABLE CR	PST PAYABLE CR	SALES CR	REF. NO.	ACCOUNTS RECEIVABLE DR
20— Feb.	5	R. Rau	4 13	4 72	59 —	652	67 85
	5	L. Sauve	5 92	6 76	84 50	125	97 18
	6	C. Myzk	(10 15)	(11 60)	(145 —)	653	(166 75)
	6	R. Halfmoon	17 21	19 67	245 85	654	282 73
	7	H. Didyk	7 72	8 82	110 25	126	126 79
	8	A. Han	4 55	5 20	65 —	655	74 75

Special Considerations

- Only special columns are used in the sales journal.
- The rules for columnar journals apply to the sales journal.

Cash Payments Journal

The **cash payments journal** is used to record all transactions that directly decrease the bank balance. Every accounting entry in the cash payments journal results in a credit to Bank. The most common type of transaction recorded in the cash payments journal involves the issuing of a cheque. Cheques may be issued for a number of reasons.

Figure 12.24 on page 547 shows a partially completed page of a cash payments journal. The journal was prepared from the following transactions:

TRANSACTIONS

February

3   *Cheque Copies*

   No. 72, issued to Collins Bros. on account, $250.00.

   No. 73, issued to Taylor Company on account, $550.00.

4   *Bank Debit Advice*

   Received from Centre Bank, for bank service charges, $54.65.

   Cheque Copies

   No. 74, issued to B. Sims for wages, $650.21.

   No. 75, issued to C. Tett for wages, $702.35.

5   *Cheque Copies*

   No. 76, issued to D. Wedow, the owner, for personal use, $1 000.00.

   No. 77, issued to Harbour Trade Centre, for the cash purchase of merchandise for resale, $905.65, GST $63.40, total $969.05.

   No. 78, issued to Kyro's Supply, for the cash purchase of supplies, $323.73, GST $22.66, total $346.39.

   No. 79, issued to Superior Engineering, a down payment on the purchase of equipment costing $5 029.00, $1 000.00.

FIGURE 12.24

A partially completed page of a cash payments journal.

CASH PAYMENTS JOURNAL   MONTH OF ___ Feb. ___ 20 __   PAGE __19__

DATE	PARTICULARS	OTHER ACCOUNTS CR			WAGES DR	GST RECOVERABLE DR	PURCHASES DR	ACCOUNTS PAYABLE DR	REF. NO.	BANK CR
		ACCOUNT	P.R.	AMOUNT						
Feb. 3	Collins Bros.							250 —	72	250 —
3	Taylor Company							550 —	73	550 —
4	Centre Bank	Bank Charges		54 65						54 65
4	B. Sims				650 21				74	650 21
4	C. Tett				702 35				75	702 35
5	D. Wedow	Drawings		1 000 —					76	1 000 —
5	Harbour Trade					63 40	905 65		77	969 05
5	Kyro's Supply	Supplies		323 73		22 66			78	346 39

Special Considerations

- The cash payments journal is sometimes called the cash disbursements journal.
- The cash payments journal follows the rules for columnar journals.
- Purchases for cash go into the cash payments journal. Purchases on account go into the purchases journal. A purchase that is partly paid for by cash goes into the cash payments journal.

Purchases Journal

The **purchases journal** is used to record all transactions involving the buying of goods or services on account. Every accounting entry in the purchases journal results in a credit to Accounts Payable. The suppliers' invoices are the source documents for entries in the purchases journal.

A partially completed page of a purchases journal is shown in Figure 12.25 on page 548. The journal was prepared from the following transactions: (Remember that PST is already included in the totals.)

TRANSACTIONS

February

3   *Purchase Invoice*

Received from Williams Equipment, for repairs to warehouse, $562.50, GST $39.38, total $601.88.

4   *Purchase Invoice*

Received from Acklands, for supplies, $762.58, GST $53.38, total $815.96.

Purchase Invoice

Received from Pascoe's, for items charged to miscellaneous expense, $145.36, GST $10.18, total $155.54.

5   *Purchase Invoice*

Received from Reliable Trading, for merchandise for resale, $2 500.00, GST $175.00, total $2 675.00.

Purchase Invoice

Received from Mason & Mason, for merchandise for resale, $1 950.00, GST $136.50, total $2 086.50.

6   *Purchase Invoice*

Received from Grand Trunk Railway, for transportation charges on incoming merchandise, $256.00, GST $17.92, total $273.92.

Purchase Invoice

Received from Hector Oil Company, for gas and oil used in the company automobiles, $315.62, GST $22.09, total $337.71.

FIGURE 12.25

A partially completed page of a purchases journal.

PURCHASES JOURNAL   MONTH OF ____ Feb. ____ 20 __   PAGE _31_

DATE		PARTICULARS	OTHER ACCOUNTS CR			CAR EXPENSE DR	GST RECOVERABLE DR	SUPPLIES DR	PURCHASES DR	REF. NO.	ACCOUNTS PAYABLE CR
			ACCOUNT	P.R.	AMOUNT						
Feb.	3	Williams Equipment	Bldg. Repairs		562 50		39 38			120	601 88
	4	Acklands					53 38	762 58		121	815 96
	4	Pascoe's	Misc. Expense		145 36		10 18			122	155 54
	5	Reliable Trading					175 —		2 500 —	123	2 675 —
	5	Mason & Mason					136 50		1 950 —	124	2 086 50
	6	Grand Trunk Railway	Freight-in		256 —		17 92			125	273 92
	6	Hector Oil Company				315 62	22 09			126	337 71

Special Considerations

- The purchases journal follows the rules for all columnar journals.
- The accountant for a business may file purchase invoices alphabetically or numerically. Where numerical order is used, a reference number must be placed on every purchase invoice received. Examples of these reference numbers may be observed in the second last column of the purchases journal shown above in Figure 12.25.

Posting in the Five-Journal System

Each of the four special journals must be cross-balanced and ruled before they can be posted at the end of each month. The procedure for balancing a columnar journal was learned in the previous section. Basically, you must add the debit column totals, add the credit column totals, and see that the two sums are the same. If the sums are equal, the journal is ruled and ready for posting.

You already know how to post the general journal. You have just learned how to post a columnar journal. This is almost all that you need to know to post in the five-journal system.

Each journal is posted separately. The order in which they are posted does not matter. No attempt to balance the ledger should be made until all five journals have been posted.

There is no change in the way subsidiary ledgers are handled. They are still posted directly from copies of source documents and are balanced against their control accounts monthly.

Cross-Referencing

When several journals are used, it becomes necessary to identify them specifically by means of a code. For example, page 17 of the general journal is identified as GJ17. Each of the several journals is given its own simple code as follows:

Journal	Code
Cash Receipts	CR
Cash Payments	CP
Sales	S
Purchases	P
General	GJ or J
Synoptic	SN

The sample account shown below in Figure 12.26 uses the new coded posting references in an account.

FIGURE 12.26

A ledger account showing the journal codes.

ACCOUNT	Accounts Receivable							NO.	110	
DATE		PARTICULARS	P.R.	DEBIT		CREDIT	DR CR	BALANCE		
Mar. 20– 31		Balance Forwarded	—				Dr	6 4 7 4 07		
31			S67	13 0 4 7 25				19 5 2 1 32		
31			CR74			12 0 9 6 40		7 4 2 4 92		
31			J19			4 2 42	Dr	7 3 8 2 50		

Section 12.3   Review Questions

1. Why is the synoptic journal suitable only for a small business or organization?
2. Describe the five-journal system.
3. Give the two main advantages of using a number of journals.
4. Describe the types of transactions that go in each of the four special journals.
5. What are the two most common transactions that are entered in a cash receipts journal?
6. How do you handle a sale that is partly on account and partly for cash?
7. Why is a "general" section not needed in the sales journal?
8. Every accounting entry in the cash payments journal has one common element. What is it?
9. Give another name for the cash payments journal.
10. What is the source document for all entries in the purchases journal?
11. In what order are the journals posted in a five-journal system?
12. What codes are used for cross-referencing in the five-journal system?
13. What is the general journal used for?

Section 12.3   Exercises

I. A list of transactions appears below. **From this list, select and record those transactions that would be recorded in the cash payments journal. Ignore GST.**

TRANSACTIONS
April

1 The owner, Patricia Sopinka, increased her equity in the business by depositing her personal cheque for $1 000.00 in the business bank account.

2 Issued cheque No. 40 to J. Chekov for the cash purchase of supplies, $155.15.

3 Issued sales invoice No. 70 to M. Kosir. This was for the sale of merchandise of $180.00 plus provincial sales tax of 7 per cent.

5 Received a purchase invoice from Sue Brown Manufacturing for the purchase of merchandise, $791.80.

8 Issued cheque No. 41 to Chong Supply Co. for the cash purchase of merchandise, $342.40.

9 Received a cheque from Carol Padovik on account, $350.00.

10 Issued cheque No. 42 to Municipal Hydro for the cash purchase of electricity for one month, $78.00.

12 Received a purchase invoice from District Supply for the purchase of supplies, $450.47.

15 Issued cheque No. 43 to Sharon Maki Wholesale on account, $750.00.

17 Issued sales invoice No. 71 to Carole's Catering. This was for the sale of merchandise of $250.00 plus PST of 7 per cent.

19 Received a debit memo from the bank for service charges for one month, $54.00.

22 Received a memo from the owner stating that she had collected $200.00 on account from P. Walker but had kept the money for her personal use.

24 Cash sales slip No. 72 was issued for the cash sale of merchandise, $85.00 plus PST of $5.95.

25 Issued cheque No. 44 for the cash payment of the telephone bill for one month, $45.00.

30 Issued cheque No. 45 to Projects Inc. on account, $1 000.00.

Cross-balance the journal.

2. In which of the five journals would each transaction below be recorded?

TRANSACTIONS

a. A cheque is issued to a supplier on account.
b. A purchase invoice is received from a supplier of merchandise.
c. A cheque is received on account from a customer.
d. A cash sale is made to a customer.
e. A sale on account is made to a customer.
f. A cheque is issued to the owner for his personal use.
g. A cheque is issued to pay the wages for the period.
h. A sales invoice is used.
i. A correcting entry is made to transfer a debit amount from the Supplies account to the Miscellaneous Expense account.
j. A cheque is issued to pay for a cash purchase of merchandise.
k. A bank debit advice for a service charge is received.
l. A cheque is issued to a supplier on account.
m. A cheque is issued to pay the monthly rent.
n. A bank debit advice is received with respect to a bad cheque.
o. A bank credit advice is received with respect to interest earned.
p. A new typewriter is purchased and a down payment is required. A cheque is issued.
q. The owner collects a debt from a customer but keeps the money for his personal use.
r. The owner spends a sum of money out of his own pocket for business purposes and is reimbursed by means of a cheque.

3. A. Journalize the transactions shown on page 552 in the five journals of Domino Wholesale Company. The accounts for Domino Wholesale Company are as follows:

Bank	Sales
Accounts Receivable	Purchases
Merchandise Inventory	Freight-in
Supplies	Bank Charges
Equipment	Delivery Expense
Accounts Payable	General Expense
GST Payable	Utilities Expense
GST Recoverable	Postage Expense
PST Payable	Rent Expense
Anna Popov, Capital	Telephone Expense
Anna Popov, Drawings	Wages Expense

B. Balance and rule each of the five journals.

TRANSACTIONS

Date	Source Document	No.	Name	Explanation	Amount	GST	PST	TOTAL
May 1	Cheque copy	75	Morris Company	Rent for May	$425.00	$29.75		$454.75
2	Purchase invoice		Grinnelco	Merchandise	378.00	26.46		404.46
2	Cash receipt		R. Jones	On account	436.80			436.80
4	Cash sales slip	97	A. Racicot	Merchandise sold	70.00	4.90	$5.60	80.50
4	Information memo			An error was discovered in the general ledger. An amount of $30 that had been debited to General Expense should have been debited to Supplies.	30.00			30.00
5	Cheque copy	76	P. Fobert	Wages	275.00			275.00
8	Sales invoice	317	C. Perry	Goods sold	215.00	15.05	17.20	247.25
9	Cash receipt		S. Storey	On account	95.00			95.00
9	Purchase invoice		Wonder Mfg.	Supplies	110.25	7.72		117.97
9	Cheque copy	77	A. Popov	Personal use	300.00			300.00
10	Purchase invoice		Pressed Fittings	Merchandise	435.75	30.50		466.25
10	Sales invoice	318	Mercer Company	Goods sold	190.00	13.30	15.20	218.50
11	Cash receipt		R. Russell	On account	200.00			200.00
12	Purchase invoice		Newday Supplies	Supplies	210.00	14.70		224.70
12	Cheque copy	78	General Supply	On account	125.50			125.50
15	Purchase invoice		Baldwin's	Supplies	78.75	5.51		84.26
15	Sales invoice	319	T. Ward	Goods sold	216.00	15.12	17.28	248.40
16	Credit invoice issued	320	C. Perry	Merchandise returned	70.00	4.90	5.60	80.50
16	Cash receipt		R. Grant	On account	150.00			150.00
17	Cash sales slip	98	P. Fuhrman	Goods sold	65.00	4.55	5.20	74.75
17	Sales invoice	321	B. Adler	Goods sold	195.00	13.65	15.60	224.25
18	Cheque copy	79	Provincial Treasurer	Sales tax for prior month	497.07			497.07
19	Purchase invoice		Continental Railway	Freight-in	96.40	6.75		103.15
19	Sales invoice	322	G. Nolan	Goods sold	110.00	7.70	8.80	126.50
19	Information memo			An error was detected in the accounts receivable ledger. An amount of $62 that should have been credited to J. Walker's account was credited in error to M. Walker's account.	62.00			62.00
22	Cheque copy	80	Bell Canada	Telephone	52.70	3.69		56.39
22	Cheque copy	81	Baldwin's	Cash purchase of supplies	26.25	1.84		28.09
23	Sales invoice	323	W. Phillips	Goods sold	280.00	19.60	22.40	322.00
23	Cash sales slip	99	P. Leonard	Goods sold	190.00	13.30	15.20	218.50
23	Cash sales slip	100	H. Fogh	Goods sold	370.00	25.90	29.60	425.50
24	Credit invoice received		Grinnelco	For merchandise returned	55.00	3.85		58.85
25	Bank debit memo		Western Bank	Bank service charge	34.70			34.70
25	Cheque copy	82	A. Popov	Personal use	300.00			300.00
26	Cheque copy	83	O.K. Welding	On account	150.00			150.00
29	Cheque copy	84	A. Popov	Repaying owner for expenditures that she made for business purposes. Charge: General Expense 35.00 Supplies 110.00	145.00	10.15		155.15
30	Cheque copy	85	S. Tybo	Wages	300.00			300.00
31	Purchase invoice		Jim's Garage	Gas and oil used in the delivery vehicle	187.30	13.11		200.41

Comprehensive Exercise

4. **In your workbook, you will find an exercise for journalizing, posting, and balancing in a five-journal system.**

12.4 | Computer Accounting Systems

If you were responsible for designing a computer accounting system for a business you might be overwhelmed at all the software and hardware options available. To develop an efficient system, you would be wise to start by evaluating the current size and future plans of the business. Consider, for example, a newly formed business named J. Jacobs Wholesale. It is a relatively small business, but it is growing rapidly. All employees in the accounting department have computers at their desks and are "networked" together, as shown in Figure 12.27.

FIGURE 12.27

A local area network suitable for the accounting department of J. Jacobs Wholesale.

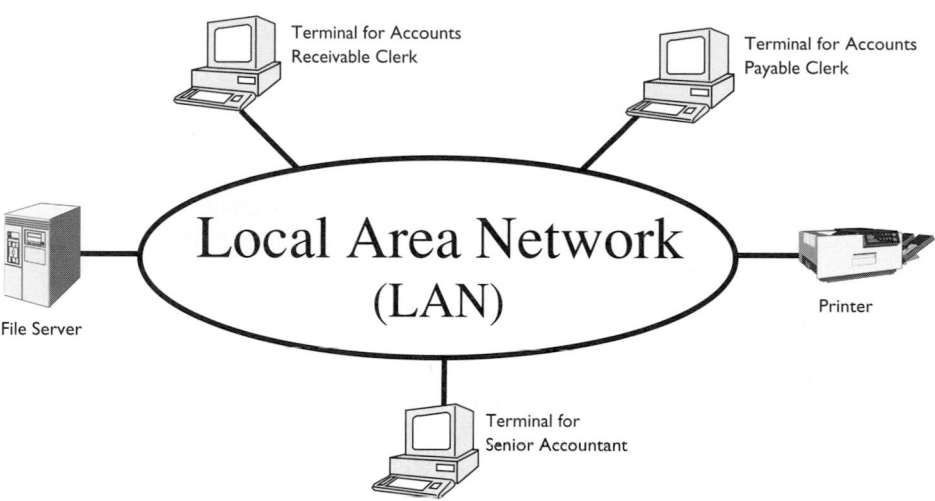

A file server is a computer that delivers programs and files to other computers in the local area network or LAN. Computers in the LAN are "networked" or linked together so users have access to the same files.

Just a few years ago, this company would have used a manual five-journal system. The accounts receivable clerk would have handled the Sales and Cash Receipts Journals, and the accounts payable clerk would have managed the Purchases and Cash Payments Journal. The senior accountant would have taken responsibility for non-routine transactions in the General Journal, including the adjusting entries at the end of the fiscal period. Now, because technology offers so many advantages, a manual five-journal system for this size of company is inappropriate.

Ruling out a manual system still leaves you with a number of decisions to make about the computer accounting system for J. Jacobs Wholesale. Simply Accounting, the software package presented to this point in this text, would be unsuitable because it is a single-user package. Only one person at a time can perform the accounting duties. As you can see from figure 12.27, there are three people in the accounting department who must work on the books at the same time.

However, ACCPAC International, Inc. has a range of products that will satisfy the needs of various sizes of business—from relatively small firms to very large companies. Another product, Simply Accounting Pro, has the look and feel of Simply Accounting but with more features, one of which allows more than one user at a time to work on a business's accounts. Simply Accounting Pro can be structured for up to six users. A three-user pack would be sufficient for J. Jacobs Wholesale. This is a good solution because it provides an inexpensive, yet powerful accounting system that is easily learned by the accounting staff.

If projections for J. Jacobs Wholesale anticipate even more rapid growth in the near future, you might consider choosing a software package with even more capabilities than Simply Accounting Pro. This larger program is known as ACCPAC. (Note: ACCPAC has several different versions; each variation of the software has a slightly different name.)

ACCPAC is packaged by module, and each ledger—Accounts Payable, Accounts Receivable, Payroll, and so on—can be purchased separately as required. Journals for the General Ledger, called source journals, can be designed to operate just like a five-journal system. For J. Jacobs Wholesale, the software source codes and journals are as follows:

ACCPAC

Source Code	Source Journal
GL-GJ	General Journal
GL-CR	Cash Receipts Journal
GL-CP	Cash Payments Journal
GL-SJ	Sales Journal
GL-PJ	Purchases Journal

Batch Processing

Since ACCPAC can meet the needs of very large businesses, it obviously possesses more features than Simply Accounting. The differences in features are not important for you to learn at this time. What is interesting and relevant to the topic of this chapter is the system that ACCPAC uses to process transactions. Simply Accounting uses a direct-posting method. With this method, each source document generates a journal entry. As soon as an accounting clerk finishes entering the data for a single journal entry, he or she posts the data to the accounts.

Conversely, ACCPAC transactions are recorded in groups or batches. A batch of transactions can be any logical combination, such as the cash receipts for a day, the purchases on account for a week, and so on. The logical groupings for J. Jacobs Wholesale would be based on the manual five-journal system you learned in Section 12.3. A batch of transactions would exist for cash receipts, cash payments, purchases, sales, and general journal entries. All cheque copies, for example, would be recorded in a batch that would be very similar to a cash payments journal.

The batch of transactions is usually printed and verified before it is posted. Corrections are easily made to a batch of transactions. When all amounts and totals are verified, the batch is posted as a group. The entire procedure of sorting transaction data into logical groups or batches and then posting them as a group is know as **batch processing**.

ACCPAC provides "General Ledger Data Entry" forms for recording batches. A batch of transactions for J. Jacobs is shown in Figure 12.28.

FIGURE 12.28

A batch of cash payment transactions ready for input.

General Ledger Data Entry Form
G/L Journal Entry
Single Currency

			Date
Prepared by	*LC*		01/24/—
Approved by	*TW*		01/24/—

Batch Number __13__   Batch Description *Cash payments for the week* _____ (Max. of 30 characters)

Date *January 24, 20—*   Period __1__   Year *20—*   Source *GL-CP*

Entry Number   Entry Description   (Max. of 30 characters)

Detail Reference	Detail Description (Max. of 30 characters)	Account	Debit	Credit	Quantity
451A	*Stationery — Fungs*	*1150*	*72.58*		
451B	*GST*	*2150*	*5.08*		
452	*W. Holm Ltd.*	*2010*	*892.00*		
453A	*Computer Warehouse*	*1500*	*1233.90*		
453B	*GST*	*2150*	*86.37*		
454	*Mickey's Manufacturing*	*2010*	*657.83*		
455	*M & M Transport*	*2010*	*170.26*		
	January cheques 451 to 455	*1010*		*3118.02*	
	Totals:		*3118.02*	*3118.02*	

Entry Comment (Max. of 30 characters)

General Ledger Data Entry Form 9 of 10   Filename: GL-JESC.RET

Notice the section in the top-right corner of the form. There is a spot to identify who prepared the batch and who approved it. This is an effective method of accounting control offered by batch processing. One person can prepare a batch, and another can verify it for accuracy. Both of these steps can take place before posting. Instead of using the manual form shown in Figure 12.28, some companies have one person prepare a batch in a spreadsheet while another employee enters the batch in ACCPAC. Printouts from both the spreadsheet and ACCPAC can then be compared against each other before posting. For a real-life example of batch processing, read the case study on page 556.

Section 12.4   **Computer Review Questions**

1. What is the starting point for developing an efficient accounting system?
2. Why would the regular version of Simply Accounting be inappropriate for J. Jacobs Wholesale?
3. Identify one of the chief advantages that Simply Accounting Pro has over the regular version of Simply Accounting.
4. Would a large business choose Simply Accounting Pro or ACCPAC?
5. Describe the direct-posting method of Simply Accounting.
6. In computer accounting, what is a batch? Give an example.
7. Define batch processing.
8. Identify two aspects of batch processing that help establish an effective method of accounting control.

Section 12.4   **Computer Exercises**

1. On pages 557 to 558, you will find transactions for J. Jacobs Wholesale for the last week of January, 20—. Some of the accounting systems you can choose to process these transactions are listed below. Find out which system your teacher wants you to use for the transactions for the end of January.

   A. *ACCPAC Batches (Manual forms)*
   In your workbook, there are General Ledger Data Entry Forms similar to the one shown in Figure 12.28 on page 555. Go through the entries listed on pages 557–558 and prepare one batch of transactions for each of the following: the General Journal, the Cash Receipts Journal, the Cash Payments Journal, the Sales Journal, and the Purchases Journal. Use Figure 12.28 as your guide; each of your finished batches should be similar to this illustration.

   B. *ACCPAC Batches (Computer—spreadsheet forms)*
   Follow the same instructions as above, but instead of using the General Ledger Data Entry Forms in your workbook, use the Excel spreadsheet model prepared for you on disk. The file is named accpac.xls.

   C. *Simply Accounting Pro (Computer—accounting software)*
   This software package is becoming more common in schools because it installs and works well on computer networks. If your school has access to a multi-user version of Simply Accounting Pro, choose a partner. One of you will be responsible for handling the Payables module, the other will manage the Receivables module. (Decide which one of you will process the occasional general journal entry.) Your teacher has access to the computer files for J. Jacobs Wholesale. Print the reports required by your teacher.

   D. *Simply Accounting (Computer—accounting software)*
   You know this is not the best choice for J. Jacobs Wholesale because it is a single-user software package. However, assume that the Accounts Payable clerk and Accounts Receivable clerk are on vacation. You, the senior accountant, will have to do all the transactions listed on pages 557–558. Your teacher has access to the computer files for J. Jacobs Wholesale. Print the reports required by your teacher.

J. JACOBS WHOLESALE
CHART OF ACCOUNTS

1010	Bank	4010	Sales
1050	Accounts Receivable	4050	Sales Returns and Allowances
1100	Merchandise Inventory	4100	Discounts Allowed
1150	Supplies	5010	Purchases
1500	Office Equipment	5050	Purchases Returns and Allowances
1550	Land	5100	Discounts Earned
1600	Buildings	5150	Freight-in
2010	Accounts Payable	5200	Advertising Expense
2050	Bank Loan	5250	Bank Charges Expense
2070	Loan Payable	5300	Insurance Expense
2100	GST Payable	5350	Miscellaneous Expense
2150	GST Recoverable	5400	Office Expense
2500	Mortgage Payable	5450	Telephone Expense
3010	J. Jacobs, Capital	5500	Utilities Expense
3050	J. Jacobs, Drawings	5550	Wages Expense

TRANSACTIONS

January

26   *Cash Receipt*

No. 672, from A. Porter Ltd. on account, total $802.50.

Cheque Copy

No. 456, for supplies purchased from Lion's Supply, $452.08 plus GST of $31.65, total $483.73.

Cheque Copy

No. 457, to Mickey's Manufacturing on account, total $2 527.34.

27   *Cash Receipt*

No. 673, from Torrence Trading Co. on account, total $1 496.93.

Cash Receipt

No. 674, from Don's Cameras in full payment of account, $963.00 less a discount of $18.00, total received $945.00.

Purchase Invoice

No. 07183C, from W. Holm Ltd. for merchandise; terms 2/10,n/30; $2 644.04 plus GST of $185.08, total $2 829.12.

28   *Sales Invoice*

No. B878, to Don's Cameras; terms 2/10,n/30; $1 500.45 plus GST of $105.03, total $1 605.48.

Sales Invoice

No. B879, to Sonja's Price Beaters; terms 2/10,n/30; $853.66 plus GST of $59.76, total $913.42.

Purchase Invoice

No. A4194, from M & M Transport for freight delivery; terms net 30; $178.00 plus GST of $12.46, total $190.46.

Purchase Invoice

No. 266A, from E.G.J. Manufacturing for merchandise; terms 1/10,n/30; $3 000.00 plus GST of $210.00, total $3 210.00.

29   *Cash Receipt*

No. 675, from Young's Gym on account, total $1 806.16.

Cheque Copy

No. 458, for the personal use of the owner, Judy Jacobs, total $3 100.00.

Sales Invoice

No. B880, to Tudor Co.; terms 2/10,n/30; $1 742.05 plus GST of $121.94, total $1 863.99.

Memorandum

The owner took computer paper (Supplies) from the business for her personal use, total $55.00 plus GST of $3.85, total $58.85.

30   *Bank Credit Memo*

Increased the bank loan by $5 000.00.

Cheque Copy

No. 459, to W. Holm Ltd. on account, $1 616.77 less a discount of $30.22, total paid $1 586.55.

Cheque Copy

No. 460, to Computer Warehouse for a modem (Office Equipment), $135.00 plus GST of $9.45, total $144.45.

Sales Invoice

No. B881, to Frank Hurt Ltd.; terms 2/10,n/30; $445.36 plus GST of $31.18, total $476.54.

Purchase Invoice

> No. 30589, from Carlson Advertising for direct-mail advertising; terms n/30; $987.00 plus GST of $69.09, total $1 056.09.

Purchase Invoice

> No. 7312, from Mickey's Manufacturing for merchandise; terms 2/10,n/30; $1 633.00 plus GST of $114.31, total $1 747.31.

31   *Cheque Copy*

> No. 461, to Shantz Supply on account, $583.15.

Cheque Copy

> No. 462, for wages, total $9 009.15.

Memorandum

> The senior accountant advises that a purchase of software earlier in the month was debited to Office Equipment. Since then, she has discovered from a tax bulletin that Canada Customs and Revenue Agency allows software to be claimed immediately as an expense. Change the debit to Office Expense, total $2 280.96.

12.5   Case Application: Modifying Accounting Systems

Doug Reichert has taught business courses in Vancouver, B.C., for over 25 years. For 20 of those years, his students have played the popular board game Monopoly© to wind up their school year. "The students enjoy this class activity more than any other, but it's more than just fun and games," says Mr. Reichert. "Accounting for all the transactions that occur while playing Monopoly© helps students tie course concepts together and apply them to them to an exciting business simulation."

What makes Mr. Reichert's experience with the game especially relevant to concepts covered in this chapter are the ways he has gradually modified the accounting system. "The first time we played, the students used a general journal to record each transaction, a procedure that took a minimum of three lines to cover the debit, credit, and explanation data. The students did not complain about the time it took to journalize because they were having fun. But, when it came time to post, their mood changed dramatically."

Most Monopoly© transactions, with the exception of trading a property for a property, involve receiving or paying cash. For Mr. Reichert's students, this meant pages and pages of general journal entries filled with debits and credits to Bank. Since each Bank entry had to be posted individually, the Bank account typically occupied three to five pages in the ledger by the time posting was finished.

Mr. Reichert soon modified the journalizing system. The methods he adopted borrowed features from the synoptic journal and multi-journal systems you learned in this chapter. Like the synoptic journal, accounts were spread across a page in columns. And, like the five-journal system, entries were channelled into specific journals. For example, all payments were recorded in a cash payments journal, and all receipts were entered in a cash receipts journal.

This system fit the nature of the Monopoly© businesses because classmates worked in pairs. On any given day, one partner took responsibility for the cash payments journal, the other handled the cash receipts journal. The two opposing teams at a game board followed the same routine. Samples of the two special journals appear in Figures 12.29 and 12.30. (Note: In the illustrations, the students have recorded the time in the date column.)

FIGURE 12.29

The Cash Receipts Journal

Names: Phoebe Tsui
Vanessa Lee

CASH RECEIPTS JOURNAL   PAGE 1

DATE		EXPLANATION	BANK DEBIT	RENT REVENUE CREDIT	GOV'T GRANT CREDIT	SPECIAL REVENUE CREDIT	OTHER ACCOUNTS TITLE	P/R	CREDIT	DEBIT
May 3 20—										
11	10	Opening Investment	1 5 0 0				V. Lee, CAPITAL		7 5 0	
							P. Tsui, CAPITAL		7 5 0	
	12	Bank Dividend	5 0			5 0				
	20	Passed Go	2 0 0		2 0 0					
	30	✔	2 0 0		2 0 0					
	32	Xmas Fund	1 0 0			1 0 0				
	46	Vermont©	6	6						
	49	Vermont©	6	6						
	51	✔	2 0 0		2 0 0					
	55	Short Line©	2 5				Travel Revenue		2 5	

FIGURE 12.30

The Cash Payments Journal

Names: Phoebe Tsui
Vanessa Lee

CASH PAYMENTS JOURNAL   PAGE 1

DATE		EXPLANATION	BANK CREDIT	RENT EXPENSE DEBIT	SPECIAL ASSESSMENTS DEBIT	LAND DEBIT	OTHER ACCOUNTS TITLE	P/R	DEBIT	CREDIT
May 3 20—										
11	13	Vermont Ave.©	1 0 0			1 0 0				
	14	St. Charles Ave.©	1 0	1 0						
	15	Water Works©	1 5 0				Utilities		1 5 0	
	20	Tax	1 7 4				Income Tax		1 7 4	
	25	Virginia Ave.©	1 6 0			1 6 0				
	31	Short Line©	2 0 0				Railroads		2 0 0	
	36	✔	5 0				Jail Expense		5 0	
	43	Pay Hospital	1 0 0		1 0 0					
	48	Park Place©	3 5	3 5						
	56	Traded Vermont© for St. James©				1 8 0	Gain on Trade/Land		(8 0)	1 0 0

The two-journal system proved to be much more efficient that the general journal alone. Most entries were written rapidly on one line, bookkeeping duties were divided evenly between the partners, and, most importantly, posting was done quickly. (In the cash receipts journal, only the final total of the Bank column was posted; likewise for the cash payments journal.)

It is interesting to note that other accounting teachers running the Monopoly© simulation at Mr. Reichert's school do not use the exact same journals as those shown in Figures 12.29 and 12.30. Some vary the number and the titles of the special columns. Mr. Reichert sees this diversity as a positive item to discuss with his classes. "Students begin to realize that, as the senior accountants of their Monopoly©

partnership, they have a say in how the journals are organized and what accounts are debited and credited." For example, when students land on the "Luxury Tax"© square, they can choose to either make an entry in the Special Assessments column, or they can create an account called Luxury Tax© and place the entry in the Other Accounts section of the cash payments journal. "They make the choice," says Mr. Reichert, "and this really helps build their confidence." The students soon see that accounting methods can be easily modified to meet the unique needs of different enterprises.

The accounting system for Monopoly© at Mr. Reichert's school continues to evolve. Another teacher, Mike Albrecht, now uses Simply Accounting during game days. "It is a little awkward organizing the playing space in a computer lab because each partnership needs access to a computer, and each board game has three partnerships competing. It can be done, however, and it is worth it. My students don't have to post by hand, and they produce financial statements on demand."

With the efficiency offered by Simply Accounting, Mr. Albrecht's students have plenty of time after playing is done to generate graphs, analyze financial data, and prepare reports. A sample of a chart of accounts that his classes use is shown in Figure 12.31.

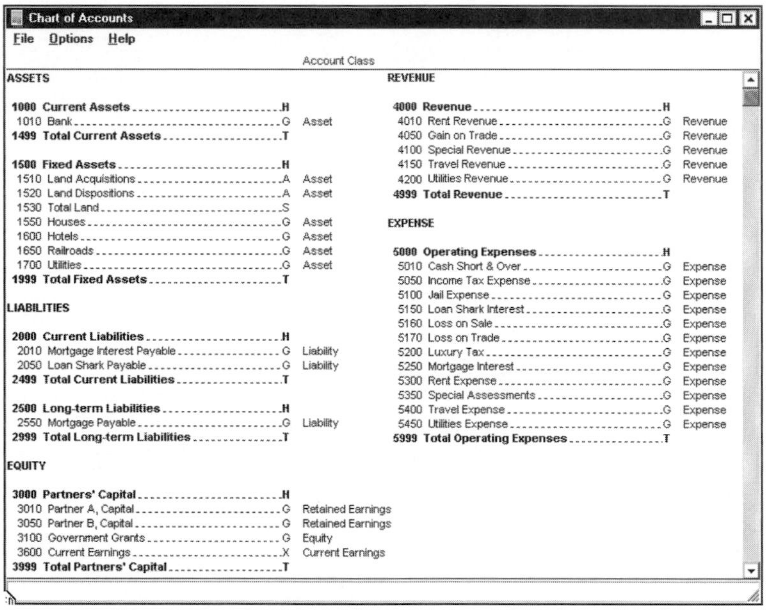

FIGURE 12.31

A chart of accounts in Simply Accounting for the board game Monopoly©.

The Loan Shark Payable and Loan Shark Interest accounts refer to special loans authorized by the teacher to keep a bankrupt team afloat until the game time limit has been reached.

You'll notice that the chart of accounts in Simply Accounting shows some special modifications that accommodate the Monopoly© simulation. For example, Land Acquisitions, Land Dispositions, and Total Land seem unusual. The reason why Mr. Albrecht had his students create this set of accounts is because Simply Accounting does not currently allow an account to be used twice in a single journal entry. This creates a challenge when property is traded. For example, if "Boardwalk" (costing $400) were traded for "Pacific Avenue" (costing $300), Land would receive both a debit and a credit, as illustrated by the following journal entry:

	DR	CR
Land (Pacific Avenue©)	$300	
Loss on Trade	100	
Land (Boardwalk©)		$400

Using Mr. Albrecht's adaptations, the journal entry would be entered in Simply Accounting as follows:

	DR	CR
Land Acquisitions	$300	
Loss on Trade	100	
Land Dispositions		$400

On the balance sheet, a Total Land account calculates the difference between all Land acquired and all Land disposed. The net figure represents the Land owned at the date of the balance sheet, so the accounting objective is achieved, even though it had to be achieved in an indirect manner.

The key point to remember is that accounting systems are flexible. The Monopoly© simulation presented unique challenges to the manual system used by Mr. Reichert and the computer system used by Mr. Albrecht. Yet, in both instances, modifications were made to successfully meet the needs of the "business."

TRANSACTIONS

Listed below are sample Monopoly© transactions for two partners: Nicole Wang and Lou Rivera. In the journals provided in your workbook, record the transactions as though you were one of the partners. Use May 1 for the month and day.

Optional: If you have access to Simply Accounting, use that software to process the Monopoly© transactions below. Your teacher has access to the Simply Accounting files that produced the chart of accounts in Figure 12.31 on page 560.

1. Cash Receipts

    a. Collected $1 500 to start the game. Nicole Wang and Lou Rivera are partners and have an equal claim on assets.

    b. Collected $200 as you pass Go. (Passing Go is considered to be a Government Grant.)

    c. Received $50 for having "guests" stay at your Boardwalk© property.

    d. Received $25 for use of your Short Line Railroad©.

    e. Collected $100 inheritance.

    f. Received $28 from use of your Electric Company©.

    g. You have a short-term cash problem, so you mortgage Electric Company© and receive $75 (as stated on the back of the property card).

    h. Received $10 for a beauty contest. (Use Special Revenues for income received by the Chance© and Community Chest© cards.)

    i. Received $70 from a guest at Park Place©. (That property is part of a monopoly, so the rent is double the usual amount of $35.)

    j. Received $200 from a guest at Boardwalk© where you recently made some improvements by buying one house.

    k. Improvements to Boardwalk© and Park Place© have been scrapped. You liquidate both houses by selling them at a loss to the bank for $200. (The original price of the houses was $400.)

    l. Received $4 from a guest at Baltic Avenue©.

2. Cash Payments

a. Purchased Boardwalk© for $400.
b. Landed on Income Tax and had the choice of paying $200 or 10% of all cash and property. You decided to pay 10%, which amounted to $170.
c. Bought Short Line Railroad© for $200.
d. Purchased Park Place© for $350.
e. Made improvements to your property by buying one house for Boardwalk© and one house for Park Place©. Total cost was $400.
f. Paid $50 to get out of Jail.
g. Paid $25 for use of Reading Railroad©.
h. Paid $18 for a stay at Kentucky Ave.©, which was owned by a competitor.
i. Paid doctor's fee of $50.
j. Bought the Electric Company© for $150.
k. Paid a utilities bill to WaterWorks© for $32.
l. Bought Baltic Avenue© for $60.
m. Paid $22 for a stay at Ventnor Ave©, which was owned by another competitor.
n. Paid the mortgage on the Electric Company© in full. The total payment was $83 ($75 for the mortgage, $8 for interest).

3. Non-cash Trade

a. Traded the Short Line Railroad© (cost value $200) for Mediterranean Ave.© (cost value $60). Either journal may be used. The Cash Payments journal is more convenient.

4. Cash Trade

a. Traded Boardwalk© (cost value $400) for Pacific Ave.© (cost value $300) and $900 cash. If you are using a manual system, you should use the Cash Receipts journal to record this transaction (Hints: Two lines will be necessary; make use of the column at the far right of the journal.)

5. Cash Short and Over

a. The receipts and payments above are for your first day of playing. Total the Bank debits in the cash receipts journal, total the Bank credits in the cash payments journal, and subtract the total Bank credits from the total Bank debits. This is the cash you have according to your journal entries. Write this answer in your workbook in the space beside the title "Cash per Journals."
b. Assume you counted the cash at the end of the day and your total was $1 252. Write this in the space beside "Cash Count" in your workbook. Calculate the difference between the "Cash per Journals" and "Cash Count." As you can see, the cash count is short of the cash per journals. **Make the necessary shortage entry in the Cash Payments journal.** Use the Cash Short and Over account. (Note: If your actual cash counted exceeded the totals from the journals, you would record the overage in the Cash Receipts journal.)

6. Optional

If you are using a manual system, cross-balance the journals, post, and prepare a trial balance. If you are using Simply Accounting, print the income statement and balance sheet.

CHAPTER 12 Summary

CHAPTER 12 Summary

CHAPTER HIGHLIGHTS

Now that you have completed Chapter 12, you should:

- know what a subsidiary ledger is and what a control account is;
- understand the theory of the three-ledger system of accounting;
- know how accounts receivable and accounts payable are presented on a balance sheet;
- understand a simple accounting system for accounts receivable and for accounts payable;
- know the source documents and the accounting entries that affect accounts receivable and accounts payable;
- know how to handle non-routine transactions that affect subsidiary ledgers;
- be able to locate errors in a subsidiary ledger that is out of balance;
- understand the accounting control features of the three-ledger system;
- understand how software is used for subsidiary ledgers.
- understand the advantages of a multi-columnar journal;
- be able to journalize, cross-balance, post, and forward in a synoptic journal;
- know the advantages of the synoptic journal;
- know the variations in journalizing in a columnar journal;
- understand the advantages of the five-journal system;
- be able to journalize and post in the five-journal system;
- understand how accounting systems are adapted to meet the needs of businesses;
- understand the basic concepts of computer journal systems in accounting.

ACCOUNTING TERMS

accounts payable ledger
accounts receivable ledger
cash payments journal
cash receipts journal
control account
cross-balancing
five-journal system

general ledger
multi-columnar journals
purchases journal
sales journal
subsidiary ledger
synoptic journal

CHAPTER 12 Review Exercises

Using Your Knowledge

1 At the end of May, 20—, Ken Nakamoto found that the accounts receivable ledger and its control account were out of balance. His efforts to balance the manual system's ledgers uncovered the errors listed below:

Errors
1. A sales invoice for $600 was posted in the subsidiary ledger as $660.
2. A cash receipt on account for $300 was not posted in the subsidiary ledger.
3. A sales invoice for $500 was missed entirely by the general ledger clerk.
4. The debit entry pertaining to a sales invoice for $800 was posted in the general ledger as a credit.
5. A sales invoice for $550 was not posted in the subsidiary ledger.
6. A sales invoice for $750 was missed entirely, by both the subsidiary ledger clerk and the general ledger clerk.
7. A cash receipt on account for $280 was not posted in the subsidiary ledger.

Given that the subsidiary ledger figure (before balancing) is $32 456:

1. **Determine the correct total for the subsidiary ledger and the control account.**
2. **Calculate the control figure before any corrections were made.**

Ignore GST and PST.

---

2 In your Workbook, complete the chart shown below by placing check marks in the appropriate boxes. Ignore GST and PST.

Source Document	In the Subsidiary Ledger						In the General Ledger										
	Which subsidiary ledger is affected?		Will the account be increased or decreased?		Will the account be debited or credited?		The accounting entry will be										
							Bank		Accounts Receivable		Accounts Payable		Asset or Expense		Revenue	
	A/R	A/P	In-crease	De-crease	Dr	Cr	Dr	Cr	Dr	Cr	Dr	Cr	Dr	Cr	Dr	Cr
purchase invoice																
cash receipt on account																
sales invoice																
cheque copy on account																

Comprehensive Exercises

3 Rachel Bragg is a public accountant in Cornwall, Ontario. On March 31, 20—, her general ledger trial balance is as follows:

R. BRAGG
GENERAL LEDGER TRIAL BALANCE
MARCH 31, 20—

No.				
101	Bank	$ 1 748.00	
105	Accounts Receivable	7 220.00	
110	Supplies	2 750.00	
115	Office Equipment	20 800.00	
116	Accumulated Depreciation — Office Equipment		$ 2 400.00
120	Automobile	29 500.00	
121	Accumulated Depreciation — Automobile		4 800.00
205	Accounts Payable		6 264.70
206	GST Payable		185.00
207	GST Recoverable	102.00	
301	R. Bragg, Capital		47 374.15
302	R. Bragg, Drawings	12 000.00	
401	Fees Income		31 650.00
505	Car Expense	3 295.60	
515	Miscellaneous Expense	375.40	
520	Rent Expense	3 000.00	
525	Telephone Expense	516.15	
510	Utilities Expense	950.20	
530	Wages Expense	10 416.50	
		$92 673.85	$92 673.85

A. Set up the general ledger accounts as of March 31, 20—. If you are using the Workbook, the ledger is already set up for you.

B. Set up the accounts receivable ledger as of March 31, 20—. Ensure that the total of the four accounts is equal to the balance of the control account in the general ledger. If you are using the Workbook, the ledger is already set up for you.

The accounts receivable ledger on March 31, 20— contains the following accounts:

			Inv. No.	
Blue Cab Company	16	Fox Street	74	$1 920.00
Champion Store	175	Main Street	75	750.00
Oasis Restaurant	325	Second Street	76	1 550.00
Village Restaurant	400	Main Street	77	3 000.00
				$7 220.00

C. **Set up the accounts payable ledger as of March 31, 20—. Ensure that the total of the four accounts is equal to the balance of the control account in the general ledger.** If you are using the Workbook, the ledger is already set up for you.

The accounts payable ledger on March 31, 20— contains the following accounts:

M. Ball, Consultant	430	Red Road, Bigtown	$1 515.00
R & R Supply	151	King Street	2 740.00
Stirling Company	46	River Road	759.50
Tom's Garage	705	Victoria Street	1 250.20
			$6 264.70

D. **Each day, you are to perform the duties of both the accounts receivable clerk and the accounts payable clerk. From the list of business transactions shown below, you are to make the entries daily to any customers' or creditors' accounts in the subsidiary ledgers. Although it will be necessary for you to work directly from the list of transactions, try to imagine that you are working directly from the source documents themselves. Also, remember that not all business transactions affect the accounts of customers and creditors.** This business is registered for the GST. The 7 per cent rate is included on the appropriate transactions. The business is PST exempt.

TRANSACTIONS

April

1 *Cheque Copy*

No. 105, to P. Walters for the monthly rent, $1 000.00 plus GST of $70.00, total $1 070.00.

3 *Sales Invoice*

No. 78, to Blue Cab Company, $800.00 plus GST of $56.00, total $856.00.

5 *Cash Receipt*

From Oasis Restaurant, $1 000.00, on account.

8 *Purchase Invoice*

From Tom's Garage, No. 701, for gasoline and oil used in the business automobile, $295.00 plus GST of $20.65, total $315.65.

9 *Cheque Copy*

No. 106, to R. & R. Supply on account, $740.00.

12 *Sales Invoices*

No. 79, to Champion Store, $500.00 plus GST of $35.00, total $535.00.
No. 80, to Village Restaurant, $1 000.00 plus GST of $70.00, total $1 070.00.

15 *Cheque Copy*

No. 107, to Municipal Telephone for service for the month, $75.50 plus GST of $5.29, total $80.79.

15 *Cash Receipt*

From Blue Cab Company, $1 920.00 on account.

19 *Sales Invoice*

No. 81, to Oasis Restaurant, $390.00 plus GST of $27.30, total $417.30.

22 *Purchase Invoice*

From Stirling Company, No. 512, for supplies, $210.00 plus GST of $14.70, total $224.70.

24 *Cheque Copies*

>   No. 108, to M. Ball on account, $1 000.00.
>
>   No. 109, to Stirling Company on account, $759.50.

30 *Cheque Copies*

>   No. 110, to Municipal Hydro for electricity for the month, $90.00 plus GST of $6.30, total $96.30.
>
>   No. 111, to R. Carter, for part-time wages for the month, $300.00.

E. Each day, you are to perform the duties of the junior accountant. Journalize each of the transactions above in the two-column general journal. Do not post to the general ledger accounts until the end of April.

F. As the junior accountant, you are to post the general journal to the general ledger at the end of the month. Then you are to take off a general ledger trial balance. It is your responsibility to see that the ledger balances.

G. As the accounts receivable clerk, you are to take off a trial balance of the accounts receivable ledger as of April 30, 20—. It is your responsibility to see that the accounts receivable ledger balances with the control account.

H. As the accounts payable clerk, you are to take off a trial balance of the accounts payable ledger as of April 30, 20—. It is your responsibility to see that the accounts payable ledger balances with the control account.

---

4 Indicate whether each of the following statements is true or false by placing a "T" or an "F" in the space indicated in your Workbook. Explain the reason for each "F" response in the space provided.

a. The general journal is not normally used if the business has a synoptic journal.

b. There is a special column for every general ledger account in the synoptic journal.

c. The chief disadvantage of the synoptic journal is that you have to post column totals.

d. An accounting entry that takes more than one line cannot be recorded in the synoptic journal.

e. There would be a special column for Rent Expense in the synoptic journal.

f. The synoptic journal is balanced at the end of every page.

g. The date used when formally posting the synoptic journal is the last day of the month.

h. A credit to Sales in the synoptic journal would normally be entered in the Other Accounts credit column.

i. All sales of merchandise are recorded in the sales journal.

j. The cash payments journal is also known as the cash disbursements journal.

k. Additional cash invested in the business by the owner would be recorded in the general journal.

l. A bank debit advice requires an entry in the cash receipts journal.

m. The five-journal system inevitably leads to the clerks becoming specialists within the system.

n. The general ledger would not balance if only four of the five journals were posted.

o. A purchase partly for cash and partly on account would be recorded in the purchases journal.

5 Two columns of a synoptic journal are totalled incorrectly, but the errors offset each other. The total of the Sales column is $2 000 more than it should be, and the total of the Accounts Receivable credit column is $2 000 less than it should be.

A. What will be the effect on the accounts? On the ledger? On income? On total assets?

B. How might the errors be detected?

6 **This exercise is set up for you in the Workbook.**
The combined chart of accounts and general ledger trial balance of Bristol Appliances Company as at December 31, 20— is given below.

No.	Account	Dr	Cr
105	Bank	$ 16 225.85	
110	Accounts Receivable	8 231.70	
115	Supplies	312.50	
120	Merchandise Inventory	37 416.40	
125	Equipment	26 800.00	
126	Accumulated Depreciation — Equipment		$ 12 400.00
130	Truck	22 200.00	
131	Accumulated Depreciation — Truck		8 400.00
205	Accounts Payable		12 358.50
210	Bank Loan		18 000.00
215	PST Payable		360.00
220	GST Payable		315.00
225	GST Recoverable	210.00	
305	S. Scales, Capital		59 562.95
310	S. Scales, Drawings		
405	Sales		
505	Purchases		
510	Delivery Expense		
515	General Expense		
520	Rent Expense		
525	Telephone Expense		
530	Wages Expense		
		$111 396.45	$111 396.45

The accounts receivable ledger trial balance as at December 31, 20— is given below.

ACCOUNTS RECEIVABLE TRIAL BALANCE
DECEMBER 31, 20—

C. Bruk	Invoice No. 325	$ 363.40
M. Howard	296	3 559.25
J. Joss	306	1 048.80
S. Persaud	217	155.25
D. Wilkins	331	3 105.00
		$8 231.70

The accounts payable ledger trial balance as at December 31, 20— is given below.

ACCOUNTS PAYABLE TRIAL BALANCE
DECEMBER 31, 20—

Smith's Service Station		—
Stirling Company	Ref. No. 245	$ 4 815.00
Triangle Electric	4701	4 280.00
Universal Vacuums	6508	1 070.00
Western Electric	246	2 193.50
		$12 358.50

A. Post the subsidiary ledgers on a daily basis directly from the source documents.

B. In the journals of Bristol Appliances Company, record the transactions shown below.

The company uses the five journals shown below.

	Page
Cash Receipts Journal	61
Cash Payments Journal	117
Sales Journal	82
Purchases Journal	74
General Journal	29

*(**Note:** An 8 per cent provincial sales tax and a 7 per cent goods and services tax is to be added to all sales transactions. The business is PST exempt on purchases.)*

TRANSACTIONS

January

1 *Cash Sales Slip*

No. 410, to T. Arthur, $125.00 plus PST plus GST.

Cash Receipts List

From C. Bruk, $363.40, in payment of No. 325.

Cheque Copy

No. 376, to J.C. Brown, for the cash purchase of general expense items, $374.50 including GST of $24.50.

3 *Purchase Invoice*

From Smith's Service Station, No. 1212, $319.93 including GST of $20.93, for gasoline and oil used in the delivery truck.

4 *Sales Invoice*

No. 347, to M. Howard, $310.00 plus PST plus GST.

8 *Memorandum*

An error was discovered in a previous transaction. An amount of $90.00 was debited to Delivery Expense in error. It should have been debited to General Expense.

9 *Cash Sales Slip*

No. 402, to H. McPhee, $800.00 plus PST plus GST.

10 *Purchase Invoice*

From Western Electric, No. 306, $706.20 including GST of $46.20, for the purchase of merchandise.

Cheque Copy

No. 377, to Stirling Company, $749.00 including GST of $49.00, for the cash purchase of merchandise.

15 *Cheque Copies*

No. 378, made out to Cash, $1 200.00, for the wages for the first half of the month.

No. 379, to S. Scales, $300.00, for personal use.

No. 380, to Provincial Treasurer, $360.00, for the PST for the previous month.

Cash Receipts List

From J. Joss, $1 048.80, in payment of No. 306.

From S. Persaud, $155.25, in payment of No. 217.

From D. Wilkins, $3 150.00, in payment of No. 321.

18 *Cheque Copies*

No. 381, to Triangle Electric, $4 280.00, in payment of No. 4701.

No. 382, to Stirling Company, $4 815.00, in payment of No. 245.

No 383, to Western Electric, $2 193.50, in payment of No. 246.

No. 384, to Smith's Service Station, $319.93, in payment of No. 1212.

22 *Sales Invoices*

No. 348, to D. Wilkins, $300.00 plus PST plus GST.

No. 349, to C. Bruk, $1 080.00 plus PST plus GST.

Purchase Invoice

From Triangle Electric, No. 4912, $963.00 including GST of $63.00, for purchase of merchandise.

25 *Cheque Copies*

No. 385, to Bell Canada, $42.80 including GST of $2.80, for the telephone service for the month.

No. 386, to Admirable Company, $567.10 including GST of $37.10, for the cash purchase of merchandise.

No. 387, to Grayson Brothers, $481.50 including GST of $31.50, for the business rent for the month.

31 *Purchase Invoice*

From Universal Vacuums, No. 6722, $1 337.50 including GST of $87.50, for the purchase of merchandise.

Cheque Copies

No. 388, to Local Hydro, $117.70 including GST of $7.70, for the hydro for the month.

No. 389, made out to Cash, $1 350.00, for the wages for the last half of the month.

No. 390, to the Receiver General for Canada, $105.00, for the net GST collected in December.

C. Balance the four special journals and post the five journals to the general ledger.

D. Prepare a general ledger trial balance as of January 31.

E. Prepare subsidiary ledger trial balances as of January 31.

Questions for Further Thought

Briefly answer the following questions.

1. What do the terms "division of labour" and "specialization" have to do with accounts receivable?
2. Subsidiary ledgers are looked after by junior employees. Explain why.
3. Why are subsidiary ledger accounts usually arranged alphabetically?
4. Do all creditors' accounts go in the accounts payable ledger? Explain.
5. Can there be other control accounts besides accounts receivable and accounts payable?
6. Is it enough to show just the total of accounts receivable on the balance sheet? Explain.
7. Subsidiary ledger clerks do not make balanced accounting entries. Explain.
8. You are instructed by the owner that a certain customer has died and that her account will not be collectable. What should be done with the account? What accounting entry or entries should be made?
9. The general ledger clerk receives a copy of every source document. The subsidiary ledger clerks receive copies of only some source documents. Explain why this is so.
10. Pet World and Salon uses a synoptic journal in which no columns for accounts receivable are provided. Give a reason for omitting these columns.
11. In the synoptic journal, there is no column for Sales debit. A debit entry to sales may be entered in the Sales credit column provided that it is circled. How else could the debit entry to Sales be recorded?
12. After cross-balancing the synoptic journal, an accountant found (by good fortune) that one of the totals was incorrect. How then could the journal have cross-balanced?
13. The text states that a natural relationship exists between sales and cash receipts. Explain this statement.
14. There could be more than five journals in an accounting system. Name one other journal that would be a sensible addition to the system.
15. You have just posted the cash payments journal but have not yet done the cash receipts journal. You notice that the Bank account has a credit balance. Is this a problem? Explain.

Cases for Further Thought

Provide a solution to each of the following case studies.

1. Northern Contracting is a small company with fewer than a dozen employees. The formal accounting of Northern Contracting is performed by a public accountant. The owner and his wife do the clerical routines. Why would the public accountant not be expected to perform the clerical routines? Specifically, name the tasks that the owner and his wife would probably have to do themselves.
2. A very small business uses a synoptic journal. This business does not have independent clerks to maintain subsidiary ledgers, nor does it prepare copies of source documents for posting to subsidiary ledgers. Suggest a system of posting to subsidiary ledgers for this business.
3. You are taking over as the accountant for a small company that has been using only a two-column general journal. You have decided to change to a two-journal system including a synoptic journal. How would you go about selecting the headings for the columns?
4. Bob Jarvis, the accountant for Wright Brothers, sets up an accounting system to eliminate the accounts receivable and accounts payable ledgers. All invoices owing to creditors and all invoices due from customers are kept in separate file folders until paid. When invoices are paid, they are removed from the customers' and creditors' files and placed in a file for paid invoices. At the end of the month, the unpaid files are totalled, and these totals agree with the balances in the control accounts in the general ledger.

    What advantages and disadvantages are there to such a system?
5. Shoe store owner D. Mugami made approximately 300 credit sales and 100 credit purchases each month. Mr. Mugami recorded all of these sales and purchases in a general journal. A friend asked him why he did not use a sales journal and a purchases journal. Mr. Mugami replied that he did not understand their use. He believed that they simply divided the work among several people. Since he did his own accounting, he had no need for these special journals.

    Is division of labour the only reason for using special journals? Explain.

Case Studies

Gaining Control over Accounts Receivable

When Mehran Jafari went to work as the chief accountant for Durante Paving Company, he quickly noticed that the system of handling accounts receivable was quite different from any system that he had encountered before. The system was theoretically simple and worked as follows:

a. The production department issued sales invoices and sent them to the accounting department. The accounting department, after making the appropriate accounting entries, filed these invoices in an "unpaid invoices" file, arranged alphabetically by customer.

b. As payments were received from customers, the appropriate invoices were withdrawn from the unpaid file, stamped paid, and filed in a "paid invoices" file.

c. The file of unpaid invoices represented the accounts receivable subsidiary ledger of the company.

Each month, the accounting department prepared a detailed list of the unpaid invoices for the owner. When the owner, Mr. Durante, looked over this list, he always found errors in it, such as an item on the list that he knew had been paid, or an item listed twice and showing slightly different amounts. Mr. Durante was annoyed by these errors, and often accused the accounting department of incompetence. Jafari was also concerned because, since joining the company, he hadn't once been able to balance the subsidiary ledger with the general ledger control account. Jafari launched an investigation to find and overcome the weakness in the system. He found no fault with his own staff members, who performed their duties correctly. But he did find a serious problem with the "unpaid invoices" file. Other employees, particularly engineers and production supervisors, were continually using the file, inserting and removing invoices without notifying the accounting department. These employees claimed that they needed the invoices for reference when discussing charges with customers, renegotiating a price, and so on. The engineering department did not keep its own file of invoices on special numbered forms. The invoices were typed up on ordinary letterhead paper.

Questions

1. Identify the problems with this system of handling accounts receivable. Give examples of specific occurrences that would create errors in the accounts receivable.

2. Suggest changes to the system that would allow the accounting department to gain control over the accounts receivable.

CASE 2

Looking After Number One: Good or Bad?

Joan Webster, the owner of a small business, decides that she should "look after Number One," as she puts it.

Webster has a thorough system of recordkeeping for accounts receivable. She makes certain that every debt is collected on time, and her collection record is extremely good. However, Webster has an entirely different attitude toward accounts payable. "Why," she asks, "should I keep records of how much I owe to others? Let them keep track of how much I owe them. And, if they don't do a thorough job of it, maybe I'll get away without paying for something." She believes that other businesses should control their accounts receivable as she controls hers.

As a result of this policy, Webster's procedure for handling incoming purchase invoices is very casual. After the purchase invoices are received and checked, they are placed in a pile on an office desk. The pile represents the accounts payable of the business, but no accounting entries are made to record them.

The purchase invoices stay in the pile on the desk until a request for payment is made. Then Webster removes the particular invoice in question and authorizes its payment. When the cheque in payment is issued, the purchase invoice is then accounted for as if it were a cash purchase of goods or services. The purchase invoice is filed with the cheque copy.

Questions

1. List the problems with this system. Is Webster's policy a reasonable one? Explain.
2. Would Webster's accounts be useful in providing information for management decisions? Why or why not?
3. When financial statements are prepared, how should the pile of unpaid bills be handled?

CASE 3

A Personalized Synoptic Journal?

Jacques Larose has owned Pinedale Park Campgrounds on beautiful Deerfield Lake for over three years. His financial statements show a good income from cabin and trailer lot rentals since he purchased the park. Over the years, Jacques has been careful to record all bookkeeping transactions in a synoptic journal very similar to the one shown on pages 528 and 529. He has been very satisfied with its speed, ease, and accuracy.

Now, however, he would like to expand his synoptic journal in order to better measure the success of his new snack bar and gasoline pumps. His primary concern is to track the purchases and sales of snack foods and gasoline in order to determine if these two new ventures are worthwhile.

Also, he would like to maintain closer control of his drawings since he seems to be taking cash and snack foods for personal use almost daily. As a result, he finds the "Other Accounts" column filling up rapidly with drawings entries.

While he would like to keep using the synoptic journal, he isn't sure how to rename the columns to suit the needs of his business, so he has come to you for assistance.

Questions

1. Prepare a list of new column headings that Jacques could add to his existing synoptic journal in order to meet the increased requirements of his business. Indicate whether these columns measure debits or credits.
2. When might Jacques be forced to replace the synoptic journal with a different system?

CASE 4

Challenge

No Journal!

Assume that you have just taken a job with Goodwood Construction as a senior accounting clerk. You are somewhat surprised by the accounting system Goodwood uses, described below. In your previous position, you had become accustomed to the traditional five-journal system.

Goodwood does not use a traditional purchases journal or cash payments journal. In fact, Goodwood does not use a journal for these transactions. Here is the system used by Goodwood:

1. When a purchase invoice is received, it is verified in all respects.
2. No entry is made in a journal. Instead, the cheque to pay the purchase invoice is prepared. A simplified example of the type of cheque used is shown below:

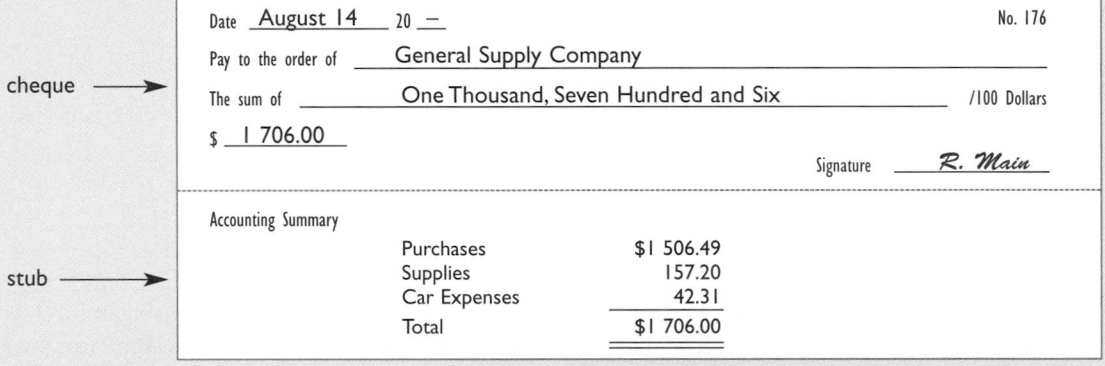

3. The original cheque and the cheque copy are forwarded to the accounting department.
4. The cheque itself is filed temporarily until time for payment arrives. Payment is looked after by another employee.
5. The cheque copies are accumulated by the month in a two-hole binder. This file of cheque copies is used for reference purposes during the month.
6. At the end of the month, the file of cheque copies becomes the basis for one grand accounting entry for all of the cheque copies. The procedure is to go through the file a number of times, each time making an addition to one particular item. For example, all of the purchases might be added the first time through, all of the supplies the second time through, and on the third pass, all of the car expenses. Eventually, all of the individual charges are subtotalled by account. The grand total of all of the individual subtotals, of course, has to balance with the total of

all of the cheques. It is not an easy process because there is a lot of room for making errors. One grand accounting summary is eventually prepared. An example is shown below:

```
                ACCOUNTING SUMMARY
                  CHEQUE COPIES
               MONTH OF AUGUST, 20 –

        Purchases           $25 326.12
        Supplies              2 568.21
        Car Expenses          4 352.78
            —                    $$
            —                    $$
            —                    $$
            —                    $$
            —                    $$
        Total               $42 158.63
        Total Cheques       $42 158.63
```

The above summary is used as the source document for one accounting entry to record all of the cheque copies for the month. The large, compound entry is recorded in the general journal. The entry is made as if all of the cheques were paid even though many of them would still be on hand.

Questions

1. Why would a system like this be used?
2. What difficulties or inconveniences can you see in such a system?
3. How should the cheque copies be filed? Is there a need for more than one file?
4. How should the cheques not issued be dealt with at the month-end? At statement time?
5. Give a name to this system.
6. What is your general impression of the system? Would you adopt it? Give reasons.

Career

My name is Roberta Lei. I am a grade 11 student trying to add as much business experience as I can to my high school education. I believe now is the time to pencil in and rule out some possible career options. I am taking courses in accounting, business computer applications, electronic design and publishing, and career preparation. Midway through my first course in accounting, I ventured out of the school setting for a week of work experience in the accounts payable department of the Hong Kong Shanghai Banking Corporation (HSBC).

Before starting my week at HSBC, I worried about fitting in at a large, downtown office. Did I have any skills that would be valuable to the organization? Would my duties be confined to filing papers and making coffee? After all, my accounting knowledge was not extensive. I had only just completed the chapter on posting—and that experience shook my confidence and my self esteem. My teachers tell me that I am a good student, but transposition errors and careless addition mistakes often seemed to leave my trial balance out of balance. Posting was agony for me. The only benefits I gained from it were the doses of perseverance and tenacity it added to my character.

When I met the accounts payable supervisor at HSBC, he assured me that I would participate in a variety of office activities. I did not have to worry about being unqualified—becoming a fully-trained accounting clerk was not on the list of expectations. Rather, a good outcome of the week is to be able to describe the tasks of the job and how those tasks fit into the overall organization of the business.

The accounts payable department at HSBC uses ACCPAC as its accounting software. It was similar to what I had used at school—Simply Accounting. I enjoyed Simply Accounting because no longer did I have to suffer through posting by hand. My trial balance balanced every time! However, I still made mistakes when I made journal entries.

The accounts payable department of HSBC wrote over $200 000 in cheques during the week I was there. Expenses ranged from coffee supplies, telephone bills, and stationery supplies to legal and consulting fees. At the start of my work experience week, I was curious to see how they could handle such a high volume of transactions without experiencing the frustration and

anxiety I felt when completing relatively simple textbook assignments.

Here is a brief overview of how HSBC organizes its system of managing accounts payable:

1. Purchase invoices are received and coded by one of the four accounting clerks. (Coding means that the appropriate ACCPAC account numbers are assigned to an invoice. For example, if an invoice was for stationery, the ACCPAC code for Office Supplies would be written on the invoice.)
2. After coding, the invoices are passed to another clerk, who sorts them into batches. All the invoices from a particular branch of Grand & Toy is an example of such a batch of transactions.
3. The data entry clerk takes a batch of invoices— for example, from a branch of Grand & Toy—and records them in ACCPAC. The clerk prints the batch and passes the printout and the original invoices to another clerk.
4. The new clerk searches for errors. If some are found, the batch is returned to the data entry clerk and the batch is edited.
5. The corrected batch is passed to the supervisor for further checking.
6. After the supervisor checks the batch, it is passed to the accounts payable manager who performs one final check. If no errors are found, the manager posts the batch and instructs the software to prepare a cheque for the supplier.

During my one-week work experience at HSBC, I helped at all of the stages I have described above. To my amazement, I felt little stress when doing my duties, even though the transactions were numerous, the amounts were large, and the money was real. Perhaps my lack of anxiety was due to the fact that I knew my work would be checked and checked again before it was posted to accounts.

In addition, I quickly felt confident with ACCPAC because of its descriptive icons and user-friendly nature. Preparing a batch listing was easy. I especially appreciated ACCPAC's mini-spreadsheet feature, which acted as an advanced adding machine tape and allowed me to check a batch of transactions before printing it.

Working in the accounts payable department at HSBC enabled me to appreciate the incredible amount of work that goes on for every cheque that is written. It also provided me with additional insight on the accounting cycle. From the receiving of purchase invoices to issuing the final cheques—every step of the way requires meticulous inspection by the staff to ensure the accuracy of the records—and a happy, smiling manager.

I performed other duties during my week with HSBC—organizing reports, distributing mail, and filing cheque copies and personal expenses records in cabinets that spanned the entire length of the office. Working with adults was a rewarding experience. I believe I met my career preparation goals by experiencing some job activities that I found interesting and challenging, as well as discovering some that I would rather avoid in the future. Also, I was able to conclude that one cannot appreciate the ease and comfort of computerized bookkeeping—and understand its benefits—until one has struggled to post by hand!

Questions

1. Explain Roberta's reasons for adding business experience to her high school education.
2. For Roberta, why was posting an agonizing experience?
3. What was one of the main goals of Roberta's career preparation experience?
4. Why did Roberta prefer Simply Accounting over manual bookkeeping?
5. Why did Roberta feel more stress with Simply Accounting than with ACCPAC?
6. Using boxes and arrows, draw a simple flow chart that traces a path that begins with the arrival of a purchase invoice at HSBC to the writing of the cheque needed to pay it.
7. Did Roberta accomplish her career preparations goals? Explain.

Challenge

8. Roberta described an accounting system that HSBC uses for receiving, posting, and paying purchase invoices. Interview someone from the accounting department of a local business and list the steps the business takes from the time it receives an invoice until it prepares the cheque to pay that invoice. Pay attention to the software used (if any) and to the number of people who check the accuracy of journal entry data before it is posted. Compare the accounting system you discover to the one Roberta described for the HSBC.

Business Organizations and Decision-Making

To this point, most of the businesses you have encountered in accounting have had one owner. You may recall that these types of organizations are called sole proprietorships. Sole proprietorships are simple to organize and maintain, but their simplicity can bring limitations to a business. Involving more people in the ownership of a business is a strategy that can expand management expertise and the capital of a business. Two common forms of ownership that involve more than one "owner" are partnerships and corporations.

The study of partnerships and corporations can be complex and is primarily reserved for more senior accounting courses. In this chapter, your goals will be to acquire a basic background of partnerships and corporations and to apply mathematical formulas to aid in decision-making tasks commonly associated with these two forms of ownership. For partnerships, you will learn how to divide the capital among the partners; and, for corporations, you will use business ratios to analyze corporate financial statements.

You will also acquire new spreadsheet and accounting software skills in this chapter. And, as you learn some of these skills, you will see that accountants pay attention to more than just analyzing past results. They also use their expertise to predict, prepare for, and control future events through a process called budgeting.

13.1 | Partnerships

Partnerships are another form of business organization that you will encounter in your accounting studies. The structure of partnerships may be quite simple or quite complex. In the next two sections, you will become familiar with the basic nature of partnerships, and will use a spreadsheet for calculating the net income of the partnership.

A **partnership** is a legal arrangement in which two or more persons (called partners) join together in a business and share in its profits and losses. A company's name often indicates if it is a partnership. Names such as H. Gregg and Sons, Siwicki and Associates, and Lem and Kato are typical.

Each province in Canada has its own Partnership Act to govern the operations of partnerships within its boundaries. There is little difference in the partnership acts of the various provinces.

Partnership Accounts

The main difference between accounting for a partnership and for a sole proprietorship occurs in the capital and drawings accounts. A sole proprietorship is owned by one person. It has one capital account and one drawings account. A partnership is owned by two or more persons. Each of the owners needs a capital account and a drawings account. Therefore, a partnership has more than one capital account and more than one drawings account.

Figure 13.1 offers a simple, graphic comparison of the books for a sole proprietorship and those for a partnership with three partners. Observe that the main difference between the two forms of business organization is reflected in the capital and drawings accounts.

FIGURE 13.1

A comparison of the accounts for a single proprietorship and for a partnership.

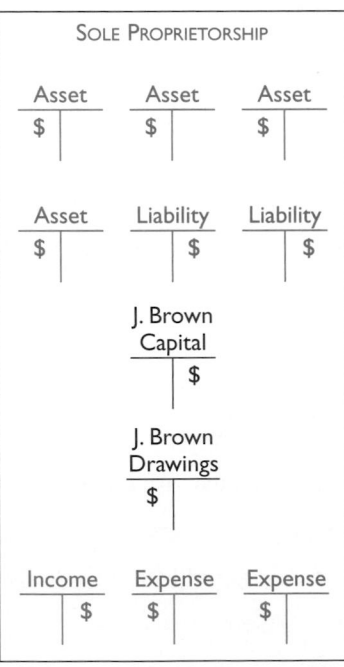

Most of the day-to-day accounting for a partnership is the same as for a sole proprietorship. The one aspect of partnership accounting that is new concerns the partners' capital accounts. The partners' capital accounts represent their respective stakes in the business. They must be maintained accurately and in accordance with the wishes of the partners. Their wishes will be stated in the partnership agreement. You will encounter this new aspect of accounting at the end of the fiscal period. At that time, the partnership net income or net loss is calculated and divided among the partners.

Advantages and Disadvantages of a Partnership

Advantages

1. A partnership lets the business owners bring together greater financial resources than a single proprietorship.
2. A partnership combines the varied abilities of the owners, giving the management team a broader base of skills than that of a single proprietorship.
3. Compared to a corporation, a partnership is simple to organize. It is usually only necessary to register the firm with the provincial government and pay a nominal fee required in the regulations.
4. Partners make decisions without having to involve or report to a wide group of people. This is not the case in many large corporations who have many "owners" or shareholders.
5. A partnership does not pay its own income tax and, therefore, avoids the complication of "double taxation" that corporate shareholders must face. (You will learn about corporate tax in a later section.) Partnership income is treated like the income of a sole proprietorship. That is, partnership income is distributed to the partners who then include it as part of their personal income for taxation purposes.

Disadvantages

1. A partnership has a limited life. If any partner dies, goes bankrupt, or becomes mentally ill, the partnership is terminated by law. The remaining partners must arrange to buy out the departed partner's share of the firm. They must also register a new partnership to carry on the business.
2. Partners have unlimited liability. Every partner is liable for the debts of the partnership. This means that an unpaid creditor may sue any partner personally to recover the money. If the creditor wins the lawsuit, the partner must pay the creditor. The partner may have to sell off personal property, causing financial hardship. This partner in turn has the legal right to recover the money from the other partners. But this may be time-consuming, costly, and inconvenient. Since the creditor will likely choose to sue the partner with the most funds, the other partners may avoid responsibility. In that case the sued partner is an unfortunate victim.
3. Partners have "mutual agency." This means that all of the partners are bound by the actions of any one of them, as long as these actions are within the normal scope of the firm's business activities. If one of the partners happens to make a poor business decision, the others cannot say that they are not responsible.

Limited Partnerships

Mutual agency and unlimited liability may make it difficult for a partnership to attract new capital. For example, suppose Aisha, a wealthy individual, wanted to invest in a partnership but was worried that one of the other partners might enter into a foolish contract, which would bind all the partners (mutual agency). If the unwise contract led to the bankruptcy of the partnership, Aisha's substantial personal assets could be claimed by the partnership's creditors (unlimited liability).

To overcome the obstacles of mutual agency and unlimited liability, a limited partnership could be formed. A **limited partnership** is one where the liability of at least one of the partners is restricted to the amount he or she invests in the business. This arrangement creates two classes of partners: general partners and limited partners. **General partners** have unlimited liability and usually manage the business. **Limited partners** have limited liability and a limited role in daily operations. In the example above, Aisha could invest in the partnership, receive a financial return on her investment, participate in some major decisions, and yet still enjoy the security of protecting her other personal assets. Her financial return and limited role in the business would be outlined in the partnership agreement.

Partnership Agreement

Partnerships are formed for various reasons. This means that there is a variety of ownership situations.

No one should enter into a partnership without first obtaining legal advice. A lawyer will see that the firm is registered, provide professional advice to safeguard the interest of the individual partners, and prepare the partnership agreement. The **partnership agreement** is a legal contract that sets forth the terms and conditions of the partnership. The agreement helps the partners to have harmonious relationships from the very beginning. This means that the partnership has a better chance for success and survival.

The following details are included in a partnership agreement:

1. The firm's name and address.
2. The partners' names and addresses.
3. The date on which the partnership is formed.
4. The nature of the partnership business.
5. The duties of the individual partners and the amount of time that they agree to devote to business activities.
6. The amount of capital to be contributed by each of the partners.
7. The salaries (if any) to be paid to each of the partners.
8. The rate of interest (if any) to be paid on the partners' capital account balances.
9. How net income or net loss will be shared.
10. The procedure to be followed in case the partnership ends suddenly because of the death or bankruptcy of a partner.

Partnership Acts

The Partnership Acts of the various provinces protect, in a general way, persons who have entered into partnerships. The terms of these acts, however, cannot take individual cases into account. In particular, the laws state that **if there is no partnership agreement, profits and losses are to be divided equally**. This may be unfair in many instances. Some partners may have contributed more than others to a business.

Partners who have no agreement are bound by the terms of a provincial partnership act, whether it is fair or not. Thus they have a strong reason for ensuring that there is an effective partnership agreement.

Apportionment of Net Income or Net Loss for a Partnership

In a one-owner business, net income, net loss, and drawings are handled in the accounts in a straightforward manner. In a partnership, the process is more complex. Net income must be properly credited to the individual partners' equity accounts.

The following three factors help you decide how to divide up the net income or net loss.

1. *Salaries*   A partner's share of net income (or net loss) often includes some payment for active involvement in running the business. For example, one partner may help manage the business full time and another may not participate at all. Clearly, the partner who participates should be rewarded for the extra time and effort. This is generally referred to as *salary.*
2. *Interest*   A partner's share of net income (or net loss) may include payment for his or her investment in the business. For example, assume that one partner's investment in the business is $100 000 and another's is $20 000. An agreement to pay interest at, say, 10 per cent would reward the partners with $10 000 and $2 000 respectively. The payment of interest rewards the partners in proportion to how much they have invested.
3. *Income- or loss-sharing ratio*   Individual partners expect to receive extra compensation if they bring special talent, business connections, or experience to the partnership. For example, a partner may have some special ability or family connections that will bring additional business to the company.

These special factors are taken into account when the income- or loss-sharing ratio is decided on. The **income- or loss-sharing ratio** is the percentages in which the net income or net loss is apportioned to the partners, after salaries and interest are deducted.

> **Note:** Salaries and interest are calculated and distributed first when apportioning net income or net loss. Any remaining net income or net loss is then divided in the income- or loss-sharing ratio.

Statement of Distribution of Net Income

Once the net income is known, the amount that goes to each partner can be calculated. The factors involved in the calculation, are listed in the partnership agreement.

To show how the net incomes of the individual partners are calculated, a formal statement is prepared. The **statement of distribution of net income** shows in detail how the net income is apportioned to the partners.

Case 1   *Net income greater than salaries and interest together.*

Morris and Graves are partners. Their capital accounts are $100 000 and $40 000 respectively. Their partnership agreement states the following:

1. Graves is allowed a salary of $22 000, and Morris, a salary of $10 000.
2. Interest is allowed on the balances in the capital accounts at the rate of 10 per cent.
3. After allowing for salaries and interest, the balance of the net income is divided equally.

At December 31, 20—, the end of their fiscal year, the partnership net income was $130 624.16. The net income is divided according to the calculation shown in Figure 13.2 below.

FIGURE 13.2

A rough calculation of the apportionment of net income where the net income is greater than the combined total of salaries and interest.

		Morris	Graves	Total
1.	Allocate salaries to partners:	10 000 –	22 000 –	32 000 –
2.	Allocate interest to partners	10 000 –	4 000 –	14 000 –
	Morris — 10% of $100 000 = $10 000			
	Graves — 10% of $40 000 = $4 000			
	Subtotals	20 000 –	26 000 –	46 000 –
3.	Determine balance of			
	net income:			
	$130 624.16			
	less 46 000.00			
	$ 84 624.16 divided equally	42 312.08	42 312.08	84 624.16
	Totals to Partners	62 312.08	68 312.08	130 624.16

This calculation is presented by means of the formal statement of distribution of net income as shown in Figure 13.3.

FIGURE 13.3

A statement of distribution of net income where the net income is greater than the salaries and interest combined.

MORRIS AND GRAVES
STATEMENT OF DISTRIBUTION OF NET INCOME
YEAR ENDED DECEMBER 31, 20—

	Net Income available for distribution		$130 624.16

	Morris's Share	Graves's Share	Total
Salary allowed to Graves	$10 000.00	$22 000.00	$ 32 000.00
Interest at 10 percent allowed on Capital account balances	10 000.00	4 000.00	14 000.00
Morris: 10% of $100 000 = $10 000			
Graves: 10% of $40 000 = $4 000			
Balance of net income divided equally	42 312.08	42 312.08	84 624.16
Totals	$62 312.08	$68 312.08	$130 624.16

Case 2   Net income less than salaries and interest together.

On June 30, 20—, the partnership of Watts, Cheng, and Lebowitz completed a fiscal year with a net income of $40 152.16. The partnership agreement specifies that net income or net loss is to be allocated according to the following terms.

1. The following salaries are allowed: Watts, $18 000; Cheng, $9 000; Lebowitz, nil.
2. Interest is allowed on capital account balances at eight per cent. The partners' capital account balances are: Watts, $80 000; Cheng, $100 000; Lebowitz, $200 000.

3. The remaining net income or net loss is to be divided as follows: Watts, 25 per cent; Cheng, 25 per cent; Lebowitz, 50 per cent.

The distribution of net income calculation is shown below in Figure 13.4. Note that in this particular case the total of the salaries and interest is greater than the net income figure. This requires special handling when making the calculation.

FIGURE 13.4

A rough calculation of the apportionment of net income where the net income is less than the combined total of salaries and interest.

	Watts	Cheng	Lebowitz	Total
1. Allocate salaries to partners	18 000 –	9 000 –	–	27 000 –
2. Allocate interest to partners	6 400 –	8 000 –	16 000 –	30 400 –
Watts — 8% of $80 000 = $ 6 400				
Cheng — 8% of $100 000 = $ 8 000				
Lebowitz — 8% of $200 000 = $16 000				
Subtotals	24 400 –	17 000 –	16 000 –	57 400 –
3. Deduct Net Income Deficiency				
$57 400.00				
Less 40 152.16				
$17 247.84 divided on				
ratio of 1:1:2	4 311 96	4 311 96	8 623 92	17 247 84
Totals to Partners	20 088 04	12 688 04	7 376 08	40 152 16

This calculation is presented formally on the statement of distribution of net income as shown in Figure 13.5 below.

FIGURE 13.5

A statement of distribution of net income where net income is less than salaries and interest combined.

WATTS, CHENG, AND LEBOWITZ STATEMENT OF DISTRIBUTION OF NET INCOME YEAR ENDED JUNE 30, 20—				
Net Income available for distribution				$40 152.16
	Watts's Share	Cheng's Share	Lebowitz's Share	Total
Salaries allowed to partners	$18 000.00	$9 000.00		$27 000.00
Interest allowed on Capital accounts				
at 8 per cent	6 400.00	8 000.00	16 000.00	30 400.00
Watts: 8% of $80 000 = 6 400				
Cheng: 8% of $100 000 = 8 000				
Lebowitz: 8% of $200 000 = 16 000				
Subtotals	$24 400.00	$17 000.00	$16 000.00	$57 400.00
Deduct: Net Income deficiency				
in ratio of 1:1:2	4 311.96	4 311.96	8 623.92	17 247.84
Total	$20 088.04	$12 688.04	$7 376.08	$40 152.16

Accounting for Salaries, Interest, and Drawings in a Partnership

Salaries and Interest

According to the law, a partner participates in a partnership for a share of the earnings of the business, not for a salary or for interest on investment. Therefore, salaries and interest are only used as mathematical factors when dividing net income. Salaries and interest are used in the calculation at the end of the fiscal period. They are then distributed to the partners as part of their share of the net income. But they are not entered into the accounts as salaries and interest.

Drawings

The partners usually need to receive money from the business during the year. Any such payments are considered to be drawings and are debited to the partners' respective drawings accounts. The partners should know roughly how well the business is doing. They can draw money based on their anticipated share of the profits. In some businesses, the amount of the drawings is fixed by formal agreement.

The partners' drawings accounts and their respective shares of the net income are transferred to their capital accounts as part of the closing entry process.

Financial Statements for a Partnership

Financial statements for a partnership include more than the balance sheet and the income statement. A partnership also requires a statement of distribution of net income, which you have just studied, and a statement of partners' capital, which is described on page 588.

The financial statements of a partnership consist of the following:

Statement No. 1. Balance Sheet
Statement No. 2. Income Statement
Statement No. 3. Statement of Distribution of Net Income
Statement No. 4. Statement of Partners' Capital

The financial statements for a partnership have to be prepared in a certain order. This is because information from one statement is needed to complete another. The statements of a partnership are prepared in the following order:

1. Income Statement
2. Statement of Distribution of Net Income.
3. Statement of Partners' Capital.
4. Balance Sheet.

The preparation of the four statements for a partnership is studied below.

Income Statement (Statement 1)

The income statement is prepared in the usual way from information on the work sheet. Figure 13.6 shows the income statement for Jones, Ross, and Warner.

FIGURE 13.6

The income statement for Jones, Ross, and Warner.

			Statement 1
	JONES, ROSS, AND WARNER		
	INCOME STATEMENT		
	YEAR ENDED DECEMBER 31, 20—		

Income

Sales			$82 940.00
Operating Expenses			
Advertising Expense		$3 000.00	
Automotive Expense		4 702.00	
Depreciation of Automobiles		2 137.50	
Depreciation of Furniture and Equipment		702.00	
General Expense		525.00	
Insurance Expense		484.00	
Rent Expense		2 400.00	
Supplies Expense		625.00	
Telephone Expense		1 290.00	
Utilities Expense		600.00	
Wages Expense		9 536.00	26 001.50
Net Income			$56 938.50

Statement of Distribution of Net Income (Statement 2)

After the net income figure of $56 938.50 is determined, additional information needed to complete the statement is found in the partnership agreement. In this case,

1. G. Ross and A. Warner are to receive annual salaries of $5 000 each.
2. Interest is allowed on capital at the rate of 10 per cent.
3. After allowing for salaries and interest, the balance of net income or net loss is apportioned in the ratio of 2:1:2 to Jones, Ross, and Warner respectively.

You are already familiar with the statement of distribution of net income. For Jones, Ross, and Warner, the statement is shown in Figure 13.17 below.

FIGURE 13.7

The statement of distribution of net income for Jones, Ross, and Warner.

				Statement 2
	JONES, ROSS, AND WARNER			
	STATEMENT OF DISTRIBUTION OF NET INCOME			
	YEAR ENDED DECEMBER 31, 20—			
Net income available for distribution				$56 938.50

	M. Jones	G. Ross	A. Warner	Total
Salaries allowed to partners		$ 5 000.00	$ 5 000.00	$10 000.00
Interest on Capital accounts	$ 1 945.21	1 513.71	2 541.08	6 000.00
M. Jones $19 452.12 at 10%				
G. Ross $15 137.09 at 10%				
A. Warner $25 410.79 at 10%				
Balance of net income divided in ratio of 2:1:2	16 375.40	8 187.70	16 375.40	40 938.50
Total distribution to partners	$18 320.61	$14 701.41	$23 916.48	$56 938.50

Statement of Partners' Capital (Statement 3)

The **statement of partners' capital** shows the changes in the partners' capital accounts for the fiscal period. It is shown on a separate statement because there is not enough room on the balance sheet for more than one proprietor.

The statement begins with the capital account balances carried forward from the previous period's statement. The increases from profits and the decreases from drawings are then summarized. The statement ends with the current end-of-period balances.

The information for this statement is picked up from the work sheet and the statement of distribution of net income. The only exception to this occurs if a partner has increased his or her capital investment with a cash contribution. This piece of information can be picked up from the partner's capital account.

For Jones, Ross, and Warner, the statement of partners' capital is shown in Figure 13.8.

FIGURE 13.8

The statement of partners' capital for Jones, Ross, and Warner.

	M. Jones	G. Ross	A. Warner	Total
				Statement 3
JONES, ROSS, AND WARNER				
STATEMENT OF PARTNERS' CAPITAL				
YEAR ENDED DECEMBER 31, 20—				
Capital Balances January 1	$19 452.12	$15 137.09	$25 410.79	$ 60 000.00
Add: Share of Net Income for Year (Statement 2)	18 320.61	14 701.41	23 916.48	56 938.50
	$37 772.73	$29 838.50	$49 327.27	$116 938.50
Deduct: Drawings for Year	18 500.00	14 000.00	22 396.00	54 896.00
Capital Balances December 31	$19 272.73	$15 838.50	$26 931.27	$ 62 042.50

Balance Sheet (Statement 4)

The balance sheet of a partnership is the same as for a sole proprietorship, except for the equity section. The final capital figures are taken from statement 3, the statement of partners' capital. The balance sheet for Jones, Ross, and Warner appears in Figure 13.9.

FIGURE 13.9

The balance sheet for
Jones, Ross, and Warner.

Statement 4

JONES, ROSS, AND WARNER
BALANCE SHEET
DECEMBER 31, 20—

ASSETS

Current Assets
Petty Cash	$ 100.00	
Bank	3 700.00	
Accounts Receivable	35 403.00	$39 203.00

Prepaid Expenses
Supplies	$ 875.00	
Insurance	416.00	1 291.00

Investment
Property — at cost		20 000.00

Fixed Assets
Furniture and Equipment	$ 7 000.00		
Less Accumulated Depreciation	4 192.00	$ 2 808.00	
Automobiles	$12 000.00		
Less Accumulated Depreciation	7 012.50	4 987.50	7 795.50
			$68 289.50

LIABILITIES

Current Liabilities
Accounts Payable	$ 6 137.00	
Wages Payable	110.00	$6 247.00

PARTNERS' EQUITY

Partners' Capital (Statement 3)
M. Jones	$19 272.73	
G. Ross	15 838.50	
A. Warner	26 931.27	62 042.50
		$68 289.50

Section 13.1   **Review Questions**

1. Define partnership.
2. Give two examples of a partnership name.
3. What is the main difference between the accounts of a partnership and a proprietorship?
4. How many capital accounts does a partnership have?
5. List three advantages of the partnership form of business organization.
6. List three disadvantages of the partnership form of business organization.
7. Explain the purpose of the partnership agreement.
8. In your opinion, what are the three most important items contained in a partnership agreement?
9. Why is it advisable for a partnership to have a formal agreement?
10. Explain, in general, why there is more to the process of handling net income (or loss) and drawings for a partnership than for a sole proprietorship.

11. Three factors affect the calculation of the distribution of net income or net loss to the partners. Name them.
12. How is a partner who puts more time and effort into the business usually rewarded?
13. What is the usual way to reward a partner who has a greater investment in the business?
14. What two items are deducted before net income or net loss is apportioned?
15. After the two items described in question 14 are deducted, what must you do to determine a partner's share of net income or net loss?
16. How is the net income of a partnership calculated?
17. How is net income or net loss apportioned in the absence of a partnership agreement?
18. Give the name of the financial statement that shows the apportionment of net income or net loss.
19. Explain if and how salaries and interest are recorded in the accounts.
20. There are four additional financial statements for a partnership. Name the two new ones introduced in this chapter.
21. Give the order in which to prepare the financial statements of a partnership.
22. Why is there a statement of partners' capital?

Section 13.1 Section Exercises

1. **In your workbook, prepare a list of the most appropriate words or phrases to complete the following statements.** A list of words and phrases is given on page 591.

   a. The partners of a business share in its _____ and _____.
   b. There is a separate _____ account and _____ account for each partner.
   c. You can usually tell if a business is a _____ from its name. You can also tell by examining its _____.
   d. The day-by-day accounting for a partnership is no different than for a _____.
   e. Accounting for the partners' _____ is the principal new aspect of partnership accounting.
   f. The capital accounts of a partnership must be maintained in agreement with the terms of the _____.
   g. Persons may pool their _____ when forming a partnership.
   h. Persons may bring together _____ when forming a partnership.
   i. A partnership is simple to _____.
   j. A partnership is not subject to _____.
   k. According to the law, a partnership is terminated by the _____, _____, or _____ of any partner.
   l. There is no _____ in regards to partnership debts.
   m. _____ means that the partners are legally bound by the actions of any one of them.
   n. The partnership agreement should be worked out with the help of a _____.
   o. The _____ of the various provinces come into play where there is no partnership agreement and a dispute arises.

List of Words or Phrases

capital accounts	incapacity	organize
capital	insolvency	partnership acts
death	lawyer	partnership agreement
different resources	ledger	partnership
double taxation	limited liability	profits
drawings	losses	proprietorship
financial resources	mutual agency	

2. Given below are data extracted from the work sheet of Li and Ahu, who are partners in business.

Li and Ahu	Work Sheet	Year Ended December 31, 20–8	
		Balance Sheet	
Accounts		Debit	Credit
P. Li, Capital			116 240
P. Li, Drawings		38 500	
S. Ahu, Capital			204 760
S. Ahu, Drawings		59 300	
		836 495	736 170
Net Income			100 325
		836 495	836 495

Using the additional information given below, prepare:
A. a statement of distribution of net income,
B. a statement of partners' capital.

Additional Information
- Neither partner receives a salary.
- Interest at 10 per cent is allowed on capital.
- The income-sharing ratio is 2:3 for Li and Ahu respectively.

3. Given below is a simplified work sheet for General Associates, owned in partnership by H. Hacio, J. Jaako, and S. Saasto.

General Associates — Work Sheet — Year Ended December 31, 20–4	Trial Balance		Adjustments		Inc Statement		Bal Sheet	
Accounts	Dr.	Cr.	Dr.	Cr.	Dr.	Cr.	Dr.	Cr.
Bank	500						500	
Mdse. Inventory	8 000				8 000	9 000	9 000	
Equipment	4 000			500			3 500	
Accounts Payable		2 000						2 000
Hacio, Capital		5 000						5 000
Hacio, Drawings	8 000						8 000	
Jaako, Capital		3 000						3 000
Jaako, Drawings	4 000						4 000	
Saasto, Capital		1 000						1 000
Saasto, Drawings	4 000						4 000	
Sales		45 000				45 000		
Purchases	12 000				12 000			
General Expense	500				500			
Rent	2 500				2 500			
Wages	12 500				12 500			
	56 000	56 000						
Deprec. Equip.			500		500			
			500	500	36 000	54 000	29 000	11 000
Net Income					18 000			18 000
					54 000	54 000	29 000	29 000

Using the additional information given below, prepare:
A. a statement of distribution of net income;
B. a statement of partners' capital;
C. a simple balance sheet;

Additional Information
- Interest at 20 per cent is allowed on capital.
- Salaries are given to Jaako, $4 200; Saasto, $4 000.
- The income-sharing ratio is 2:1:1 for Hacio, Jaako, and Saasto respectively.

4. This exercise appears in your Workbook.
Three partnership situations are described below. **For each one, complete the chart to show how you would arrange for the partnership profits to be apportioned.**

1. A and B operate a partnership in which:
— the two partners maintain equal capital account balances,
— both partners work full time in the business,
— neither partner has any special background or experience.

Complete the chart.

Give a salary to a partner or partners?	Y or N?	
If yes, which one(s)?		
Give interest on capital balances?	Y or N?	
Divide balance of net income equally?	Y or N?	
If N, ratio to favour which partner?		

2. A and B form a partnership in which:
  — A invests $200 000 in cash,
    B invests $20 000 in cash.
  — A does not participate at all in running the business,
    B works full time in the business.
  — A has many profitable business connections,
    B has a great deal of experience and talent in the industry.

Complete the chart.

Give a salary to a partner or partners?	Y or N?	
If yes, which one(s)?		
Give interest on capital balances?	Y or N?	
Divide balance of net income equally?	Y or N?	
If N, ratio to favour which partner?		

3. A, B, and C form a partnership in which:
  — A invests $500 000 cash in the business,
    B invests $100 000 cash in the business,
    C makes no financial investment.
  — A and B do not work in the business in any way,
    C works full time in the business.
  — A and B have no experience, talent, or connections,
    C is experienced, talented, and has connections.

Complete the chart.

Give a salary to a partner or partners?	Y or N?	
If yes, which one(s)?		
Give interest on capital balances?	Y or N?	
Divide balance of net income equally?	Y or N?	
If N, ratio to favour which partners?		

5. In your Workbook, for each of the following situations, informally prepare the calculation of apportionment of net income.

	a.		b.		c.		d.			e.		
Partners	A	B	A	B	A	B	A	B	C	A	B	C
Capital account balances	50 000	50 000	25 000	150 000	100 000	100 000	20 000	20 000	25 000	10 000	20 000	80 000
Rate of interest on capital	nil		nil		nil		8%			10%		
Salaries	nil		nil		10 000	25 000	20 000	nil	nil	nil	12 000	8 000
Income- or loss-sharing ratio	3 : 2		capital accounts		1 : 1		4 : 3 : 2			5 : 3 : 1		
Net income or loss	$60 000		$72 800		$90 000		$135 000			$130 000		

13.2

Corporations

A **corporation** is an entity which the law considers to be separate and distinct from its owners. Its capital is divided into shares which are held by shareholders. The corporation is a very common form of business organization. Since most large businesses and industries are corporations, they do more business in terms of dollars than partnerships and proprietorships put together.

You can recognize a corporation by its name. According to the laws of Canada and the provinces, a corporation name must include

1. the word *Limited* (which may be abbreviated "Ltd.") or
2. the word *Incorporated* (which may be abbreviated as "Inc." or "Corp.")

Accounting for corporations, particularly for large companies, can be very complex. This section does not go into advanced or specialized accounting theory. Rather, it explains the basic concepts of accounting for corporations, so that you will be able to interpret their financial statements.

Original Purpose of Corporations

Corporations were originally created to raise large amounts of capital for risky and costly ventures. The easiest way to obtain funds for a risky venture was from many small investors. Each investor was then able to participate with a relatively small amount of money for a share in the anticipated profits. The potential effect of a loss for any one investor was thereby reduced.

For example, assume that a capital investment of $2 000 000 is required to put a new business into operation. This capital would be difficult to raise from only a few people. It is much easier to raise it from a large number of persons. If there were 200 000 contributors they would have to pay only $10 each. Each contributor would receive a **share certificate** (also known as a stock certificate) indicating the amount of that person's share in the venture. A person who owns shares in a company is a **shareholder** or **stockholder**. Each shareholder will share in the company's profits in the same proportion as his or her shares in the company.

Characteristics of Corporations

1. A corporation may have different kinds of shares, as will be explained later. However, only *common shareholders* have voting rights. The controlling owners of a corporation are its **common shareholders**. A small private corporation may have only one shareholder, while a large public corporation usually has many. Each common share in a corporation carries one vote at any shareholders' meeting. For example, a shareholder who owns 50 common shares of a corporation is entitled to 50 votes, whereas one who owns 10 common shares is entitled to 10 votes.

2. An incorporated company is a separate legal entity in the eyes of the law. It is an artificial legal being, separate from those who own it. Even if only one person owns the corporation, it still has a separate legal identity from that person. Its existence continues regardless of anything that may happen to any of its shareholders. A corporation has the following rights and obligations of a real person.

    1. It can buy or sell property in its own name.
    2. It can sue or be sued in its own name.
    3. It can enter into legal contracts in its own name.
    4. It must pay its own income tax.

3. The shareholders are financially liable for any actions of the corporation only up to the fully paid value for their shares. They thus have what is known as **limited liability**. In this respect, the corporation is quite different from the single proprietorship and partnership, where the business owners have *unlimited* liability.

4. For the protection of shareholders and prospective shareholders, corporations are subject to government control. The federal government laws concerning corporations are found in the Canada Business Corporations Act. Each of the provinces has a similar act.

5. Company policy is decided by a committee of the shareholders called a **board of directors**. Directors are elected by the shareholders at the annual meeting. Control of the company is usually in the hands of a few shareholders who have large holdings of the company's shares. They are able to vote themselves in as directors. Directors do not run the day-to-day operations of the company, but they control the affairs of the company by passing by-laws and making major policy decisions.

6. The board of directors passes by-laws to establish the executive positions of a company. These include the positions of president, vice-president(s), (executive) secretary, and treasurer. The daily operations of the company are controlled by these hired company officers, or executives.

7. In theory, to control a corporation one must own 50 per cent of the shares, plus one. In fact, a corporation can be effectively controlled through a much smaller percentage of shares. This is because shares are widely distributed and most shareholders do not participate in policy decisions.

Advantages and Disadvantages of Corporations

Now that you know some of the characteristics of a corporation, it will be helpful to sort them in terms of advantages and disadvantages.

Advantages

Limited Liability

1. In case of a lawsuit or bankruptcy, the liability of shareholders is limited to the amount that they paid for their shares of the company. The personal possessions of the shareholders are protected because the corporation is a separate legal "entity." (Note: Before lending funds to a corporation, a loan grantor might ask for a personal guarantee from a shareholder. If the shareholder agrees, he or she forfeits the right to limited liability.)

Ease of Raising Capital

2. Since there may be many shareholders, large investments of capital can be assembled relatively easily.

Continuity

3. The company continues to exist despite the death, insolvency, or incapacity of any of its shareholders. (It is a separate legal entity.)

Ease of Transferring Ownership.

4. Shares of a company may be easily transferred to other people. This is especially true of public corporations that have their shares traded on a stock market.

No Mutual Agency

5. There is no mutual agency (as there is in partnerships). An individual shareholder with no special status in the company is unable to bind the corporation to a contract.

Tax Considerations

6. Small businesses in Canada pay a relatively low rate of tax—about 23%. If the board of directors decides to keep all profits in the company, this low rate could be advantageous for the shareholders. An accountant specializing in tax should be consulted, however, before deciding whether corporate tax rates are preferable to those for proprietorships or partnerships.

Disadvantages

Lack of Direct Influence

1. Most individual shareholders have no influence in the life of the corporation. The board of directors that controls the corporation is elected by the shareholders at the annual meeting. A shareholder has only one vote per share. Those with the most shares have the most votes. It is this group (called majority shareholders) which controls the corporation because they decide who is to be elected to the board of directors.

Government Regulations

2. Government controls and regulations can be strict, and corporate law is often difficult to read and understand.

Organizational Costs

3. The fees and legal expenses for incorporating a company are more substantial than those required for forming a sole proprietorship or partnership.

Tax Considerations

4. Tax considerations may also be considered a disadvantage, especially in large corporations with good earnings. Since a corporation is a legal entity, it pays its own income tax. When the after-tax profits of the company are distributed to the shareholders, the shareholders are required to include these as income on their personal income tax return. In effect, this is double taxation. (Note: To minimize the amount of double taxation, Canada Customs and Revenue Agency establishes tax credits for shareholders of Canadian companies.)

Public and Private Corporations

Public Corporations

Business corporations can be either public corporations or private corporations. A **public corporation** obtains its capital partly by the sale of shares to the general public. You will find the shares of public corporations traded on various stock exchanges, such as the Toronto Stock Exchange (TSE), the Canadian Venture Exchange (CDNX), and so on.

Corporations that list their shares for trading on a stock market must publish their audited financial statements annually and distribute copies to all shareholders. These publicly traded companies also produce interim financial statements. The common time period for interim statements is every three months (quarterly). These statements and other financial data are readily available on the Internet. Although quarterly financial statements are not audited, they do provide investors with valuable updates on a company's progress.

Private Corporations

A **private corporation** must meet certain special conditions. The number of shareholders cannot exceed 50. The corporation must raise funds privately and is not allowed to advertise the sale of its shares to the public. Most private corporations are small or medium-sized businesses. They have been incorporated by the owners to allow them to retain control of the business while obtaining the benefit of limited liability to protect their personal assets.

Accounts of a Corporation

The accounts of a corporation differ in one major respect from those of a proprietorship or a partnership. The accounts of a proprietorship or partnership have Capital and Drawings accounts. The accounts of a corporation have neither. In their place, the total capital of all of the shareholders together may be recorded in just two accounts: a Capital Stock account and a Retained Earnings account.

The **Capital Stock account** is the capital invested by the shareholders when they purchase company shares.

The **Retained Earnings account** is the capital that comes from company profits which have not yet been paid out to shareholders.

These two new accounts are shown in Figure 13.10 on page 598.

Assets	Liabilities	Equity
Bank	**Accounts Payable**	**Capital Stock**
$$	$$	$$
Accounts Receivable	**Bank Loan**	**Retained Earnings**
$$	$$	$$
Supplies	**Mortgage Payable**	**Revenue**
$$	$$	$$
Buildings		**General Expense**
$$		$$
Equipment		**Utilities Expense**
$$		$$
		Wages
		$$

Simple Balance Sheet of a Corporation

A simplified balance sheet of a corporation is given in Figure 13.11. The illustration shows the two components of the shareholders' equity—Shared Earnings and Retained Earnings.

CROWN INDUSTRIES LIMITED
BALANCE SHEET
JUNE 30, 20—

ASSETS		LIABILITIES	
Current Assets		*Current Liabilities*	
Bank	$ 13 000	Accounts Payable	$ 12 800
Accounts Receivable	25 350	Bank Loan	5 000
Merchandise Inventory	20 742		$ 17 800
	$ 59 092		
		SHAREHOLDERS' EQUITY	
		Share Capital	
		Authorized and Issued	
Fixed Assets		10 000 Common Shares	$100 000
Land	$ 35 000	*Retained Earnings*	51 292
Plant and Equipment	75 000		$151 292
	$110 000		
TOTAL	$169 092	TOTAL	$169 092

Retained Earnings

The Retained Earnings account represents a company's accumulation of profits over the years, less any profits paid out to shareholders. Profits paid out are known as dividends. The Retained Earnings account represents a claim on assets and is similar to the familiar capital account of a sole proprietorship.

The Retained Earnings account is affected by two types of accounting activity.

1. *Net Income or Net Loss*   At the end of each fiscal period, the net income or net loss of a corporation is transferred out of the Income Summary account into the Retained Earnings account. A net income increases the Retained Earnings account and is entered as a credit. A net loss decreases the Retained Earnings account and is entered as a debit.

   If a net income is earned, the accounting entry is:

	DR	CR
Income Summary	$$$$	
Retained Earnings		$$$$

2. *Dividends*   The shareholders of a company are its owners. They expect to receive some of the company's profits in the form of dividends. The directors have the power to declare a dividend. That means they vote a payment to shareholders out of the accumulated net profits in the Retained Earnings account. A dividend declared reduces the credit balance in the Retained Earnings account. The accounting entries for this are explained below.

   Normally, the Retained Earnings account has a credit balance, which is the accumulated net income from years in which a profit was made. It is possible however, for the account to have a debit balance—a state of negative retained earnings. This usually follows a severe loss or a series of losses. A retained earnings account with a debit balance is known as a **deficit**.

Dividends

A **dividend** is an amount paid to the shareholders out of company profits. Each share of the company receives an equal dividend. The amount paid (if any) is decided (declared) by the board of directors at a directors' meeting.

If dividends are paid in cash, the company's total assets figure will be reduced. Accordingly, an equity account must also decrease, and that equity account is Retained Earnings.

Whether a dividend is distributed or not depends on the directors. Only the directors have the power to declare a dividend. They may decide not to declare a dividend, but to use the retained earnings for some other purpose—for example, company expansion. The ordinary shareholder has no direct say in the matter.

Normally, dividends are not declared unless a company is earning satisfactory profits on a regular basis.

Declaring the Dividend

The board of directors meets on an agreed date to decide whether to declare a dividend. If the board of directors declares a dividend, it decides to pay all the shareholders who own shares on a certain future date. These are the shareholders of record. The directors also decide the date when the cheques will be issued. Therefore, there are three important dates associated with dividends.

1. *The date of declaration* This is the day on which the directors meet and vote for the dividend.
2. *The date of record* The shareholders who own the shares on this day will be the ones who receive the dividends. Because company shares may change hands frequently (usually through the stock market), a good system is necessary for keeping stock records up to date and accurate.
3. *The date of payment* This is the date the dividend cheques are to be issued. It is usually a few weeks after the date of record, to give the accounting department time to make the proper calculations and to get the cheques ready for the mail.

Dividends are usually stated at so much a share; for example, a dividend may be $.50 per share for the quarter (a three-month period). Once the board of directors has declared a dividend, the payment becomes a legal obligation of the company. If the company fails to make the payment, the shareholders can sue in the courts. Various provincial and federal laws protect the interests of shareholders.

Dividends may only be declared if the following two requirements can be met.

1. Enough cash is available to make the payment.
2. The credit balance in the Retained Earnings account must be large enough that paying the dividend will not create a deficit.

Accounting for Dividends

Accounting for dividends is usually done in two stages as follows.

1) When the board of directors declares a dividend, the liability is set up in a Dividends Payable account. The Retained Earnings account is reduced by the same amount.

For example, Apex Limited is incorporated with 100 000 shares. Its retained earnings balance is $95 500. On January 10, 20—, the directors of Apex Limited declare a dividend of 50 cents a share to be paid to shareholders of record on January 31. Payment will be made on February 15.

The accounting entry to record the declaration on January 10 is:

	DR	CR
Retained Earnings	$50 000	
Dividends Payable		$50 000

2) On February 15, when the dividend is paid, the accounting entry to record the payment is:

	DR	CR
Dividends Payable	$50 000	
Bank		$50 000

Common Stock (Common Shares)

A corporation's basic class of stock is known as **common stock**. The rights of the holders of common stock include the following:

1. The right to vote at shareholders' meetings. Each share of common stock carries the right to one vote.
2. The right to receive any common dividends in proportion to the number of shares held.
3. The right to share in the assets that remain after creditors have been paid if the corporation is liquidated.

Preferred Stock (Preferred Shares)

A corporation may issue more than one class of stock. Each class of capital stock must be kept in a separate account.

Figure 13.12 shows a simplified general ledger with more than one capital stock account. The accounting entries are the same for each class of stock.

FIGURE 13.12

The general ledger of a corporation showing separate accounts for two classes of shares.

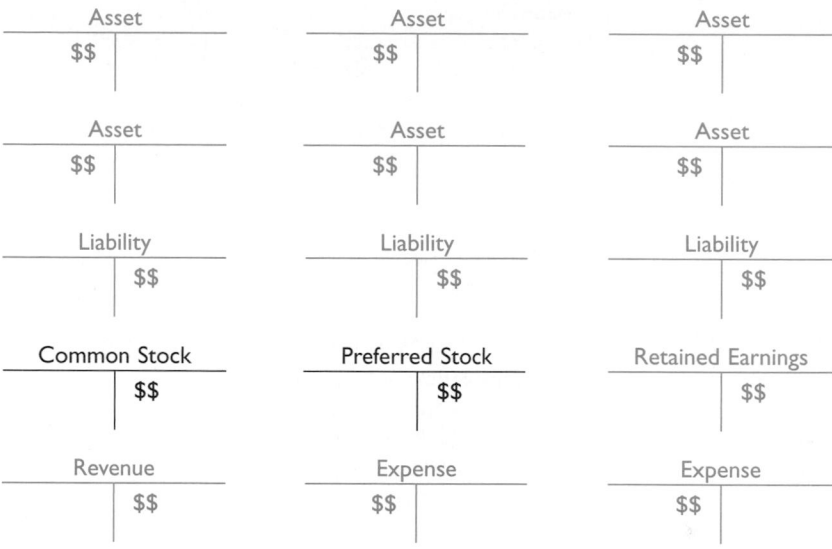

Preferred stock means shares that have a special privilege when it comes to the payment of dividends. A disadvantage of preferred shares is that they normally do not carry voting rights. The common shareholders usually issue preferred stock so that they can acquire additional capital funds from outsiders without having to give up any control of the company.

If a company issues preferred stock, the preferred shareholders receive dividends first, before anything is paid to the common shareholders. Also, if a corporation is liquidated, the preferred shareholders recover their equity before the common shareholders.

Preferred stock can be recognized by the way the company describes it. The following examples show how preferred stock may be described.

Par Value refers to a preset value printed on the preferred share certificate.

1. *8% preferred stock, $100 par value* (a preferred stock with a dividend per share of eight per cent of $100, or $8).
2. *$8 preferred stock, $100 par value* (a preferred stock with a dividend of $8 a share).
3. *$5 preferred stock* (a preferred stock carrying a dividend of $5 a share).

The dividend for preferred shares is limited to a fixed amount. But the amount of a dividend for common shares is limited only by the earning capacity of the company. In a very profitable year it is possible for the common stockholders to receive a very large dividend while the preferred stockholders are restricted to their fixed amount.

Preferred shareholders do not necessarily receive dividends every year. If a corporation is not in a position to pay dividends, then the preferred shareholders may be no better off than the common stockholders.

A simplified balance sheet of a corporation having both preferred and common shares is shown in Figure 13.13.

FIGURE 13.13

A simplified balance sheet showing both preferred and common shares.

DELTA CORPORATION BALANCE SHEET DECEMBER 31, 20–3		
ASSETS		
Bank		$ 1 200
Accounts Receivable		35 236
Supplies		1 800
General Equipment		46 588
Automotive Equipment		20 239
		$105 063
LIABILITIES		
Accounts Payable		$ 12 563
Bank Loan		20 000
		$ 32 563
SHAREHOLDERS' EQUITY		
Capital Stock — Common		
5 000 Shares, no par value	$50 000	
Capital Stock — Preferred $2		
1 000 shares, no par value	10 000	
Retained Earnings	12 500	72 500
		$105 063

Section 13.2   Review Questions

1. Which form of business organization is the most dominant in our economy?
2. In a legal sense, what is special about a corporation?
3. How does one know if a company is a corporation?
4. Explain the original purpose of corporation. Give an example of the benefits to one of the owners.
5. What does the owner of a corporation receive to show that he or she has ownership in the company.
6. What are the owners of a corporation called?
7. Explain what is meant by *limited liability*.
8. Name the federal government act that controls the actions of corporations.
9. How is the board of directors elected?
10. What are the responsibilities of the board of directors?
11. What is the difference between a director and a company officer or executive?
12. Explain the difference between a public and a private corporation.
13. In what major respect do the accounts of a corporation differ from those of a proprietorship?
14. What does the Capital Stock account represent?
15. What does the Retained Earnings account represent?
16. What item causes retained earnings to increase?
17. Is the increase in question 16 above recorded as a debit or a credit to the Retained Earnings account?

18. What two items cause retained earnings to decrease?
19. Are the decreases in question 18 above recorded as debits or credits to the Retained Earnings Account?
20. What type of balance does the Capital Stock account have?
21. What type of balance does the Retained Earnings account usually have?
22. What would cause a negative balance in retained earnings?
23. What is a negative balance of retained earnings called?
24. Explain the basis upon which dividends are distributed to the shareholders.
25. Who decides if there is to be a dividend?
26. Give two reasons why a dividend might not be declared.
27. Explain how a dividend is created.
28. Explain how it is determined who is to receive dividends.
29. Explain why the payment date is a few weeks after the date of record.
30. What can the shareholders do if a declared dividend is not paid?
31. Give the accounting entry (ignore amounts) to record the declaration of a dividend.
32. Give the accounting entry (ignore amounts) to record the payment of a dividend.
33. Give the name for the basic class of stock of a corporation.
34. Give the name for the second class of stock of a corporation.
35. What is the usual advantage associated with preferred stock?

Section 13.2   Exercises

1. **In your Workbook, in a numbered column, write down the word or phrase that corresponds to each of the following definitions.** A list of words and phrases is given below.

   a. A corporation that does not obtain its capital from the general public.
   b. The true owners of a corporation.
   c. A company which by law has an existence separate and distinct from its owners.
   d. The restricted responsibility for the debts of a corporation.
   e. A certificate indicating how much ownership a person has in a corporation.
   f. The group of shareholders who are elected to control the operations of the company.
   g. A person who owns shares in a company.
   h. An amount of earnings declared by the board of directors to be distributed to the shareholders of a corporation in proportion to their holdings of shares.
   i. The day on which the directors meet and vote for the dividend.
   j. The day as of which it is determined who owns the company shares and therefore who is to receive the dividends.
   k. The account used to show the liability for dividends.

List of Words or Phrases

board of directors	date of record
private corporation	dividend
common shareholders	dividend payable
shareholder	share certificate
corporation	limited liability
date of declaration	

2. **This exercise appears in your Workbook.**

A corporation began business on January 1, 20-1. Over the next seven years it made profits and paid out dividends as shown in the chart below.

Complete the Retained Earnings column of the chart.

Year	Profits (Losses)	Dividends Paid	Retained Earnings at Year-end
1	($45 000)	nil	
2	($20 000)	nil	
3	$25 000	nil	
4	$48 000	nil	
5	$110 000	$50 000	
6	$156 000	$100 000	
7	$227 000	$120 000	

Answer the following questions.

A. **Why were no dividends paid in the first three years?**
B. **Could a dividend have been paid in year 4?**
C. **In your opinion, why was a dividend not paid in year 4?**
D. **All of the retained earnings were not paid out in dividends. Give reasons why this would be the case.**

3. Mandrell Limited has 10 000 common shares authorized and issued. The trial balance of the company as of December 31, 20-3, is shown on the next page.

Prepare a simple balance sheet for Mandrell Limited as of December 31.

TRIAL BALANCE
DECEMBER 31, 20-3

	DR	CR
Bank	$ 500.25	
Accounts Receivable	7 858.35	
Merchandise Inventory	25 326.00	
Supplies	450.00	
Land	50 000.00	
Buildings	275 000.00	
Equipment	116 125.40	
Accounts Payable		$ 23 125.60
Bank Loan		50 000.00
Mortgage Payable		212 325.40
Capital Stock (10 000 Common Shares)		100 000.00
Retained Earnings		89 809.00
	$475 260.00	$475 260.00

4. Complete each of the following statements by writing in your Workbook the appropriate word or phrase from the list below.

   a. A dividend is distributed to the _____ in proportion to the number of shares held.
   b. Retained Earnings represents the company's net _____ of earnings.
   c. Only the _____ has the power to declare a dividend.
   d. When dividends are declared they are declared to _____ on a certain date.
   e. A good system is necessary for keeping _____ up to date and accurate.
   f. _____ are usually stated at so much a share.
   g. Once declared, a dividend becomes a _____ of the company.
   h. The Retained Earnings account normally has a _____ balance.
   i. When a dividend is declared, it is set up in a _____ account.
   j. When a dividend is declared, the _____ account is reduced.

List of Words or Phrases

accumulation	legal liability
board of directors	Retained Earnings
credit	shareholders' records
Dividends Payable	shareholders of record
dividends	shareholders

5. **In your Workbook, complete the schedule shown below for a company whose fiscal year ends on December 31.**

Year	Number of Shares Sold	Cumulative Number of Shares Issued	Income for Year	Dividend Declared Dec. 15	Total Dividend for Year	Retained Earnings Dec. 31
1	10 000		$52 500	$1.00		
2	12 000		$50 250	$1.50		
3	12 500		$60 750	$1.60		
4	15 000		$75 200	$1.75		
5	20 000		$95 050	$1.85		

6. Precision Tools Limited is a company incorporated with 220 000 common shares outstanding. On March 1, 20— the board of directors of the company declared a dividend of 25 cents a share to be paid on March 31 to shareholders of record on March 15.

   Answer the following questions in your Workbook.

   A. **Calculate the total dividend to be paid.**
   B. **Journalize the accounting entry to record the declaration of the dividend.**
   C. **Journalize the accounting entry to record the payment of the above dividend.**

7. Regus Corporation is started with authorized capital stock of 10 000 common shares and 100 000 $5 preferred shares.

A. In the T-accounts provided in the Workbook, post the accounting entries for the following transactions for the first year of operation.

TRANSACTIONS
1. The owner pays $20 000 for 10 000 shares of common stock.
2. 10 000 preferred shares are sold to the general public at $50 a share.
3. Land ($100 000) and a building ($200 000) are purchased for cash.
4. A net income of $88 000 is earned for the year. (Debit Other Assets and credit Retained Earnings.)
5. The preferred dividend is declared.

B. Prepare a simple balance sheet for Regus Corporation after transaction 5.

13.3 | Ratio and Percentage Analysis for Corporations

In chapter 8, you worked with percentage changes, trend analysis, and common-size statements. Now you will learn a number of other ratios and percentages that make it easier to interpret the financial statements of a business. Simple calculations can be made for specific aspects of the statements.

These figures are not very meaningful by themselves. They should be used with other pertinent information, and compared with figures for the industry as a whole.

In general, there are two aspects to accounting ratios and percentages — liquidity and profitability. **Liquidity ratios** (also called **solvency ratios**) are used to decide how easily a company can pay its debts. **Profitability percentages** are used to evaluate a company's ability to earn a profit. They are usually compared with the results of other years, other companies, or other investment opportunities.

Several specific ratios are described in this section. The financial statements for Okada Wireless Ltd. that appear on pages 607 and 608 are used for the calculations.

Liquidity ratios determine how easily a company can pay its debts. Profitability percentages are used to evaluate a company's ability to earn a profit.

FIGURE 13.14

The Comparative
Balance Sheet for
Okada Wireless Ltd.

OKADA WIRELESS LTD.
COMPARATIVE BALANCE SHEET
DECEMBER 31, 20-3 AND 20-2

ASSETS	20-3	20-2
Current Assets		
Bank	$ 13 260	$ 8 600
Accounts Receivable	20 320	15 250
Merchandise Inventory	46 900	25 600
Prepaid Expenses	1 800	2 400
Total Current Assets	**$ 82 280**	**$ 51 850**
Fixed Assets		
Land	$220 000	$220 000
Buildings	147 600	156 000
Equipment	103 500	108 500
Total Fixed Assets	**$471 100**	**$484 500**
Total Assets	**$553 380**	**$536 350**
LIABILITIES		
Current Liabilities		
Accounts Payable	$ 35 740	$ 21 640
Bank Loan	25 000	15 000
Total Current Liabilities	**$ 60 740**	**$ 36 640**
Long-Term Liabilities		
Mortgage Payable	$ 245 000	$ 257 000
Total Liabilities	**$305 740**	**$293 640**
SHAREHOLDERS' EQUITY		
Common Stock	$ 100 000	100 000
Retained Earnings	147 640	142 710
Total Shareholders' Equity	**$247 640**	**$242 710**
Total Liabilities and Equity	**$553 380**	**$536 350**

FIGURE 13.15

The Comparative Income Statement for Okada Wireless Ltd.

OKADA WIRELESS LTD. COMPARATIVE INCOME STATEMENT DECEMBER 31, 20-3 AND 20-2		
	20-3	**20-2**
Revenue		
Net Sales	**$338 520**	**$325 600**
Cost of Goods Sold		
Inventory, January 1	$ 25 600	$ 22 240
Net Purchases	201 500	175 480
Goods Available for Sale	$ 227 100	197 720
Less Inventory, December 31	46 900	25 600
Cost of Goods Sold	$ 180 200	$ 172 120
Gross Profit	**$158 320**	**$153 480**
Operating Expenses		
Advertising Expense	$ 16 090	$ 21 640
Car Expense	17 460	19 800
Depreciation Expense	13 400	13 400
Insurance Expense	5 100	4 800
Interest Expense	12 780	13 600
Miscellaneous Expense	600	910
Utilities Expense	5 200	4 750
Supplies Expense	3 400	2 880
Telephone Expense	1 500	1 405
Wages Expense	42 660	36 074
Total Operating Expenses	**$118 190**	**$119 259**
Net Income before taxes	**$ 40 130**	**$ 34 221**
Taxes	9 230	7 871
Net Income after taxes	**$ 30 900**	**$ 26 350**

Current Ratio or Working Capital Ratio

The formula:

$$\text{current ratio} = \frac{\text{total current assets}}{\text{total current liabilities}}$$

The data:

	20-3	**20-2**
Total Current Assets	$82 280	$51 850
Total Current Liabilities	$60 740	$36 640

The computations:

	20-3	**20-2**
current ratio =	$\frac{82\ 280}{60\ 740}$	$\frac{51\ 850}{36\ 640}$

The results:

	20-3	**20-2**
current ratio =	1.35:1	1.42:1

A current ratio or working capital ratio, measures the ability of a business to pay its debts.

Interpretation   The **current ratio** measures a business's ability to pay its debts in the normal course of business operations. This is an important consideration because a business that is unable to pay its debts can be closed down by its creditors.

The general standards for interpreting current ratios are shown in the table below.

Current Ratio	Interpretation
2.5	very good
2.0	good
1.5	fair
1.0	poor*
less than 1.0	precarious

* Except in certain specialized industries such as public utilities.

The current ratio for Okada Wireless Ltd. is not good. Its ability to pay its debts on time is not assured. The company should seek to improve this ratio.

The current ratio is also referred to as the **working capital ratio**. The working capital of a business is found by subtracting the total current liabilities from the total current assets. The working capital for Okada Wireless Ltd. for year 20-3 is $82 280 − $60 740 = $21 540.

Quick Ratio or Acid-Test Ratio

The formula:

$$\text{quick ratio} = \frac{\text{total current assets (less inventory and prepaid expenses)}}{\text{total current liabilities}}$$

The data:

	20-3	20-2
Current Assets		
Bank	$ 13 260	$ 8 600
Accounts Receivable	20 320	15 250
Merchandise Inventory	46 900	25 600
Prepaid Expenses	1 800	2 400
Total Current Assets	$82 280	$51 850
Total Current Liabilities	$60 740	$36 640

The computations:

20-3	20-2
$\text{quick ratio} = \dfrac{\$82\ 280 - \$48\ 700}{\$60\ 740}$	$\dfrac{\$51\ 850 - \$28\ 000}{\$36\ 640}$

The results:

	20-3	20-2
quick ratio =	.55:1	.65:1

Interpretation The calculation of the quick ratio differs from the calculation of the current ratio in that it includes only quick assets, those that can be converted into cash quickly. Therefore, the **quick ratio** or **acid-test ratio** measures a business's ability to pay its debts within a short period of time (say, two months). It would be used by someone who was concerned about whether the business could continue operating. A quick-ratio figure of less than 1 is undesirable, but not uncommon.

A quick ratio measures the ability of a business to pay its debts within a short period of time.

Debt and Equity Percentages

The formulas:

$$\text{debt ratio} = \frac{\text{total liabilities}}{\text{total assets}}$$

$$\text{equity ratio} = \frac{\text{total equity}}{\text{total assets}}$$

The data:

	20-3	20-2
Total Liabilities	$305 740	$293 640
Total Equity	$247 640	$242 710
Total Assets	$553 380	$536 350

The computations:

	20-3	20-2
debt ratio =	$\frac{305\ 740}{553\ 380} \times 100$	$\frac{293\ 640}{536\ 350} \times 100$

	20-3	20-2
equity ratio =	$\frac{247\ 640}{553\ 380} \times 100$	$\frac{242\ 710}{536\ 350} \times 100$

The results:

		20-3	20-2
debt ratio	=	55.2%	54.7%
equity ratio	=	44.8%	45.3%

Interpretation The **debt ratio** shows what proportion of the total assets are financed with borrowed money. The **equity ratio** shows what proportion of the total assets are financed with shareholders' money. The two percentages are *complementary*, which means that they add up to 100.

Creditors and prospective creditors are interested in these two ratios. They like to see a high proportion of shareholders' money in a business. Shareholders with a high stake in the business are strongly committed to its success.

Creditors of Okada Wireless Ltd. have some cause for concern. The amount of debt may be high, based on industry standards. In many cases however, a ratio of 50% is considered adequate.

Rate of Return on Net Sales

The formula:

$$\text{rate of return on net sales} = \frac{\text{net income}}{\text{net sales}} \times 100$$

The data:

	20-3	20-2
Net Income	$30 900	$26 350
Net Sales	$338 520	$325 600

The computations:

	20-3	20-2
return on net sales =	$\dfrac{30\ 900}{338\ 520} \times 100$	$\dfrac{26\ 350}{325\ 600} \times 100$

The rate of return on net sales measures the dollars that remain after expenses have been deducted.

The results:

	20-3	20-2
return on net sales =	9.1%	8.1%

Interpretation   The **rate of return on net sales** measures the dollars that remain after all expenses are deducted from net sales. Comparing this figure with other years gives an indication of how well a company is performing. In the case of Okada Wireless, the rate of return has increased by one percent, which is an encouraging sign.

When evaluating a company, it is important to look at the rate of return figure as well as the net income figure in dollars. As shown by the schedule below, a business can have an increase in net income as measured in dollars and still have a drop in the net income percentage.

	Year 2	Year 1
Sales	$525 000	$500 000
Net Income	$50 500	$50 000
Net Income %	9.6%	10.0%

Rate of Return on Shareholders' Equity

The formula:

$$\text{return on shareholders' equity} = \frac{\text{net income}}{\text{owner's average equity}} \times 100$$

The data:

	20-3	20-2
Net Income	$30 900	$26 350
Beginning Equity	$242 710	$235 980*
Ending Equity	$247 640	$242 710

*Would be picked up from previous year's statement.

The computation:

		20-3		**20-2**	
return on shareholders' equity	=	$\dfrac{30\ 900}{\dfrac{242\ 710 + 247\ 640}{2}} \times 100$		$\dfrac{26\ 350}{\dfrac{235\ 980 + 242\ 710}{2}} \times 100$	

The rate of return on shareholders' equity measures the return-on-investment figures.

The results:

		20-3	**20-2**
return on owner's equity	=	12.6%	11.0%

Interpretation The **rate of return on shareholders' equity** measures how well the business is doing when compared with other investments the shareholders might make using the capital from the business. In particular, the shareholders would be interested in knowing how much the equity could earn in interest if it could be loaned out. However, the capital of a business cannot just be taken out. Buyers must be found first.

The shareholders of Okada Wireless Ltd. would be quite happy with the above return-on-investment figures. They are much higher than current interest rates.

Additional Ratios, Percentages, and Statistics

The following calculations can also be used to evaluate the health of a business.

Collection Period

The formula:

$$\text{collection period} = \frac{\text{accounts receivable}}{\text{average charge sales per day}}$$

The data:

	20-3	**20-2**
Accounts Receivable	$20 320	$15 250
Sales*	$338 520	$325 600

*Assume that all sales are charge sales.

The computations:

		20-3	**20-2**
collection period	=	$\dfrac{20\ 320}{338\ 520 \div 365}$	$\dfrac{15\ 250}{325\ 600 \div 365}$

The results:

		20-3	**20-2**
collection period (in days)	=	22	17

Interpretation   The **collection period** or **accounts receivable turnover** figure gives an indication of how many days' sales are represented by the account receivable. The lower the number, the better it is. The meaning of the figure depends on the business's usual terms of sale and its discount policy. A rule of thumb is that the figure should be less than one and a half times the usual credit period. If a discount for prompt payment is offered, the figure should be lower.

The collection period for Okada Wireless Ltd. became larger in 20–3, but it is well below the normal credit period of 30 days.

Inventory Turnover

The formula:

$$\text{inventory turnover} = \frac{\text{cost of goods sold}}{\text{average merchandise inventory}}$$

Inventory turnover is the number of times a business is able to sell and replace its inventory in one year.

The data:

	20-3	20-2
Cost of Goods Sold	$180 200	$172 120
Beginning Inventory	$ 25 600	$ 22 240
Ending Inventory	$ 46 900	$ 25 600

The computations:

	20-3	20-2
inventory turnover =	$\dfrac{180\ 200}{\dfrac{25\ 600\ +\ 46\ 900}{2}}$	$\dfrac{172\ 120}{\dfrac{22\ 240\ +\ 25\ 600}{2}}$

The results:

		20-3	20-2
inventory turnover	=	5.0	7.2

Interpretation   The **inventory turnover** figure represents the number of times a business has been able to sell and replace its inventory in one year. An inventory turnover of 8.0 means that the business has been able to sell and replace its goods eight times a year or every month and a half. To be most useful, this figure must be compared with those of other years, or with those of other companies in the same line of business. Not all lines of business have the same rate of turnover.

Okada Wireless Ltd. shows a marked decrease in the turnover figure from its first year to its second. Perhaps the company has added new lines of merchandise with higher profit margins. Consequently, the stock may stay in the store longer, but still generates a good net income.

Times Interest Earned Ratio

The formula:

$$\text{times interest earned} = \frac{\text{net income}}{\text{interest expense}}$$

The data:

	20-3	20-2
Net Income	$30 900	$26 350
Interest Expense	$12 780	$13 600

The computations:

		20-3	20-2
times interest earned	=	$\dfrac{\$30\ 900}{\$12\ 780}$	$\dfrac{\$26\ 350}{\$13\ 600}$

The results:

		20-3	20-2
times interest earned	=	2.4	1.9

Some analysts add interest expense to the net income before dividing. Can you say why?

Interpretation   The **times interest earned ratio** measures the company's ability to cover its interest expense. The higher the ratio, the better. The figures for Okada Wireless Ltd. are low, but at least there has been a recent improvement. A company with a low figure (say, 5) has to be concerned about interest charges. Creditors would be very cautious in dealing with a company with a low figure.

Earnings Per Share

The following formula for earnings per share is for a simple capital structure. Assume that Okada Wireless Ltd. has 200 000 common shares outstanding.

The formula:

$$\text{earnings per share} = \dfrac{\text{net income (after tax)}}{\text{number of common shares outstanding}}$$

The data:

	20-3	20-2
Net Income (after tax)	$30 900	$26 350
number of common shares	200 000	200 000

The computations:

		20-3	20-2
earnings per share	=	$\dfrac{\$30\ 900}{200\ 000}$	$\dfrac{\$26\ 350}{200\ 000}$

The results:

		20-3	20-2
earnings per share	=	$0.15	$0.13

Interpretation   The earnings per share figure (EPS) is used to measure the performance of a corporation and its executive officers. Shareholders and prospective investors may use the figure to compare earning power over a number of periods. This helps them determine trends and stability. Shareholders and prospective investors also compare a company's EPS against the same ratio for other companies to evaluate each as a potential investment.

The EPS for Okada Wireless Ltd. appears to be low; however, at least it is a positive number, which indicates that the company is making a profit rather than incurring a loss. Also, the EPS for Okada Wireless improved by 2 cents per share in the past year.

Price Earnings Ratio

The Price Earnings Ratio (P/E ratio) is for public corporations only because a market price is needed for the calculation. Assume that Okada Wireless Ltd. is trading on the Toronto Stock Exchange at $4.50 per share. At the end of last year, assume it was trading at $3.13 per share.

The formula:

$$\text{price earnings ratio} = \frac{\text{market price per share}}{\text{earnings per share}}$$

The data:

	20-3	20-2
market price (assumed)	$4.50	$3.13
earnings per share	$0.15	$0.13

The computations:

	20-3	20-2
price earnings ratio =	$\dfrac{\$4.50}{\$0.15}$	$\dfrac{\$3.13}{\$0.13}$

The results:

	20-3	20-2
price earnings ratio =	29	24

Interpretation   The price earnings ratio tells how outside investors feel about the company. The stock market quotation reflects their confidence in the shares of the company.

The P/E ratio of a company is used to help compare alternative investment opportunities and is of little value by itself. Suppose, for example, that Company A and company B manufacture the same item, are equal in all other ways, and have P/E ratios of 14 and 19 respectively. This is like saying that you can spend $14 to buy a share of Company A that will earn $1, or you can spend $19 for a share of Company B that will earn $1. The $14 stock would seem to be the better buy.

A high P/E ratio indicates high investor confidence. Sometimes, this confidence is justified. Investors may know facts about a company or industry that makes them willing to pay much more per share than a company is earning per share.

Other times, a high P/E ratio may indicate investor overconfidence. Up until the year 2000, P/E ratios for "high-tech" or "dot-com" companies were extremely high. In fact, since most dot-com companies were losing money, P/E ratios could not be calculated. (A Price/Sales ratio was used instead.) Yet investors were still willing to pay substantial amounts for these companies. One leading dot-com company that was barely earning a profit boasted a P/E ratio of 1 760! It is not surprising that the market prices for these stocks fell substantially in 2001.

The P/E ratio for Okada Wireless Ltd. has increased from 24 to 29. Investor confidence in the stock is growing at a rate that is faster than the growth in earnings per share.

Ratio Analysis and Computers

In Canada, corporations dominate the business side of the economy. They own the majority of business assets and are therefore the subject of intense interest and analysis. All companies listed on a stock exchange are public corporations and, as such, are governed by a number of regulations. These regulations include full disclosure of audited financial information. In other words, the public has access to a public corporation's financial statements. This is not true of a private corporation.

In the recent past, if an investor wanted to analyze the statements of a public corporation, a trip to the library to obtain an annual financial report was needed. Now, the Internet provides interested parties fast access to a huge amount of financial data. For example, if you were interested in buying shares in Placer Dome Inc., a large Canadian gold producer, a few minutes on the Internet would supply you with financial statements, share price data, and recent news. All you need to know is the company's trading symbol, and there are search sites to help you find it. In Figure 13.16, the trading symbol for Placer Dome is **PDG.TO**. A few clicks of the mouse will produce some key financial ratios displayed in Figure 13.16 below.

FIGURE 13.16

Financial information available on the Internet.

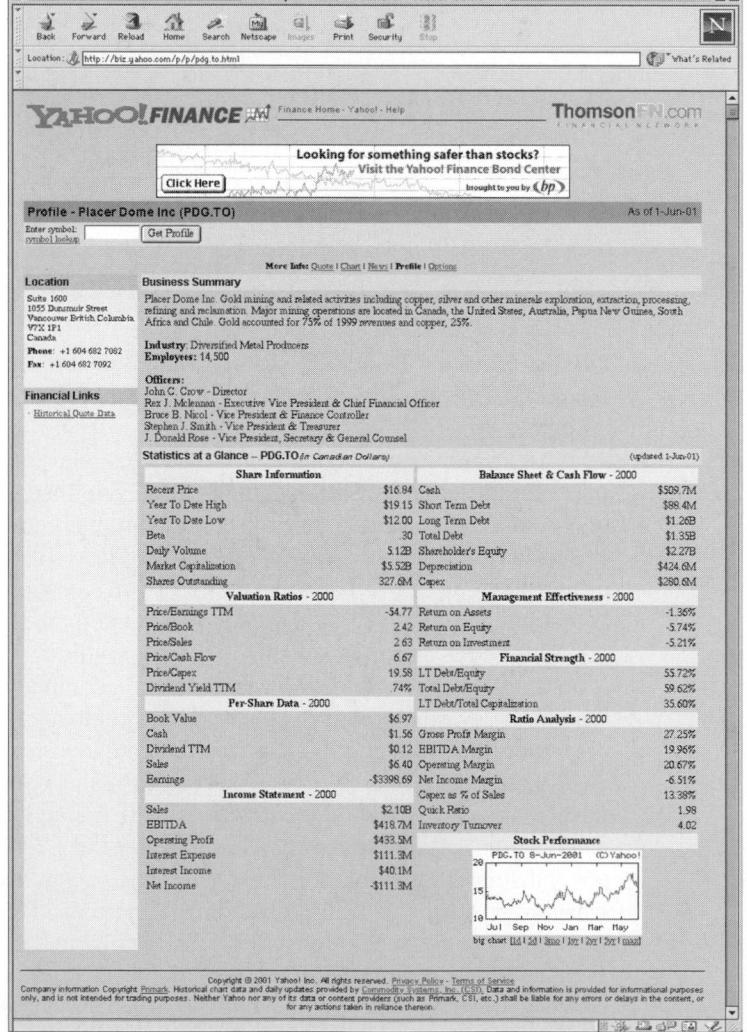

Book value shows how much equity common shareholders have on a per share basis. Investors find it interesting to compare book value with the market price per share.

A Spreadsheet for Financial Analysis

If you did not wish to rely on the Internet for financial analysis, developing a spreadsheet model to perform the repetitive calculations would be beneficial. In Figure 13.17 a spreadsheet model has been prepared for Okada Wireless Ltd.

FIGURE 13.17

A spreadsheet model for analyzing Okada Wireless Ltd.

	A	B	C	D	E
1	OKADA WIRELESS LTD.				
2	Raw Data	20-3	20-2		
3	Current Assets	82 280	51 850		
4	Accounts Receivable	20 320	15 250		
5	Beginning Inventory	25 600	**22 240**	*from previous year	
6	Ending Inventory	46 900	25 600		
7	Prepaid Expenses	1 800	2 400		
8	Total Assets	553 380	536 350		
9	Current Liabilities	60 740	36 640		
10	Total Liabilities	305 740	293 640		
11	Beginning Equity	242 710	**235 980**	*from previous year	
12	Ending Equity	247 640	242 710		
13	Common Shares (number)	200 000	200 000		
14	Market Price (year end)	$4.50	$3.13		
15	Net Sales	338 520	325 600		
16	Credit Sales	338 520	325 600		
17	Cost of Goods Sold	180 200	172 120		
18	Interest Expense	12 780	13 600		
19	Net Income	30 900	26 350		
20					
21					
22	OKADA WIRELESS LTD.				
23	Key Ratios and Statistics	20-3	20-2	Change	
24	Current Ratio	1.35	1.42	-0.06	
25	Quick Ratio	0.55	0.65	-0.10	
26	Collection Period	22	17	5	
27	Inventory Turnover	5.0	7.2	-2.2	
28	Debt Ratio	55.2%	54.7%	0.5%	
29	Equity Ratio	44.8%	45.3%	-0.5%	
30	Times Interest Earned Ratio	2.4	1.9	0.5	
31	Rate Of Return On Net Sales	9.1%	8.1%	1.0%	
32	Rate Of Return On Equity	12.6%	11.0%	1.6%	
33	Earnings Per Share	$0.15	$0.13	0.02	
34	Price/Earnings Ratio	29	24	5	
35					

The top portion of the spreadsheet model is for entering data from the financial statements. The bottom portion contains formulas that have to be entered only once. From that point, they will instantly calculate new results when new data are typed in the top portion of the model. You will enter the ratio analysis formulas in an upcoming spreadsheet exercise.

Section 13.3   **Review Questions**

1. What are the two aspects associated with accounting ratios and percentages?
2. What is the purpose of working out simple ratios and percentages?
3. Explain the purpose served by a liquidity ratio.
4. Explain the purpose served by a profitability percentage.
5. Once ratios and percentages have been calculated, to what must they be compared for a meaningful result?
6. What is the formula for the collection period statistic?

7. What does the collection period statistic mean?
8. How is the inventory turnover calculated?
9. What does the inventory turnover figure mean?
10. Explain the reason for the difference between the turnover figure for a fruit market and the figure for a gift store.
11. How is the times interest earned statistic calculated?
12. What is required of a public corporation that a private corporation does need to do?

Section 13.3   **Section Exercises**

1. The balance sheet and income statement for Saturn Sales Company Ltd. are shown below and on page 619. **Assume that all sales are made on account.**

SATURN SALES COMPANY, LTD.
BALANCE SHEET
DECEMBER 31, 20-5

ASSETS
Current Assets
Bank	$ 3 400	
Accounts Receivable	33 070	
Merchandise Inventory	27 400	$ 63 870

Prepaid Expenses
Supplies		1 500

Plant and Equipment
Land	$ 50 000	
Buildings	125 000	
Equipment	69 000	244 000
Total Assets		$309 370

LIABILITIES AND EQUITY
Current Liabilities
Bank Loan	$ 25 000	
Accounts Payable	17 970	$ 42 970

Long-Term Liability
Mortgage Payable		65 700

Shareholders' Equity
Share Capital	$100 000	
Retained Earnings	100 700	
Total Shareholders' Equity		200 700
Total Liabilities and Equity		$309 370

Calculate the following ratios to one decimal place. Give your opinion as to whether each ratio is poor, fair, good, etc. A schedule is provided in your Workbook.

SATURN SALES COMPANY, LTD.
INCOME STATEMENT
YEAR ENDED DECEMBER 31, 20-5

Revenue

Sales		$343 342

Cost of Goods Sold

Merchandise Inventory, January 1	$ 26 500	
Purchases	226 500	
Merchandise Available for Sale	$253 000	
Less Merchandise Inventory, December 31	27 400	225 600
Gross Profit		$117 742

Operating Expenses

Interest Expense	$ 8 256	
Depreciation of Building	6 250	
Depreciation of Equipment	6 900	
Power Expense	2 800	
Miscellaneous Expense	350	
Telephone Expense	425	
Car Expense	4 940	
Wages Expense	47 815	
Total Operating Expenses		77 736
Net Income before taxes		$ 40 006
Income Taxes		9 201
Net Income		$ 30 805

    a. current ratio
    b. quick ratio
    c. collection period
    d. inventory turnover
    e. rate of return on net sales
    f. rate of return on owner's equity (Ignore the requirement for an average
       equity figure.)
    g. debt ratio
    h. equity ratio
    i. times interest earned

---

2. The following data apply to Calvino Company Ltd.

    a. The collection period is 36.5.
    b. The current ratio is 1.3.
    c. The rate of return on net sales is 12.5.
    d. The debt ratio is 15.

**Use these data to fill in the missing information on the partially completed
financial statements in your Workbook.** You will find copies of these statements on page 620. Ignore income taxes.

CALVINO COMPANY
INCOME STATEMENT
YEAR ENDED DECEMBER 31, 20-8

Revenue

Sales	$170 000
Cost of Goods Sold	
Opening Inventory	
Purchases	$128 500
Goods Available for Sale	
Closing Inventory	
Cost of Goods Sold	$129 000
Gross Profiit	$
Operating Expenses	$
Net Income	$

CALVINO COMPANY
BALANCE SHEET
DECEMBER 31, 20-8

ASSETS

Current Assets

Bank	$ 3 700
Accounts Receivable	
Merchandise Inventory	10 500
Total Current Assets	$
Plant and Equipment	
Land	$ 35 000
Buildings and Equipment	
Total Plant and Equipment	$
Total Assets	$

LIABILITIES AND SHAREHOLDERS' EQUITY

Current Liabilities

Bank Loan	$ 15 000
Accounts Payable	
Total Current Liabilities	$
Shareholders' Equity	
Share Capital	$ 30 000
Retained Earnings	$106 000
Total Shareholders' Equity	$
Total Liabilities and Shareholders' Equity	$

3. Examine Figure 13.16 on page 616.

    A. Identify five ratios/percentages from 13.16 that you learned in this section.

    B. Identify three ratios/percentages that are unknown to you.

    C. Attempt to explain the items identified in part B above.

    D. Based on Figure 13.16, comment on the financial strength of Placer Dome.

4. Create a spreadsheet model that will produce the same results as those shown in Figure 13.17. All cell contents in the bottom portion of the spreadsheet are to be formulas. The first few are done for you below. When you are done, write a business letter to the president of the company, Jiro Okada, on the state of the company. In the letter, make sure you refer to the results of your analysis.

Note that the spreadsheet for Okada Wireless has been set to "show formulas." This setting allows the display of the formulas for cells in Rows 22 and 23. This setting also temporarily affects the format of the spreadsheet. The columns are wider (to show the formulas) and the dollar values are not aligned.

	A	B	C	D
1	OKADA WIRELESS LTD.			
2	Raw Data	20-3	20-2	
3	Current Assets	82280	51850	
4	Accounts Receivable	20320	15250	
5	Beginning Inventory	25600	**22240**	*from previous year
6	Ending Inventory	46900	25600	
7	Prepaid Expenses	1800	2400	
8	Total Assets	553380	536350	
9	Current Liabilities	60740	36640	
10	Total Liabilities	305740	293640	
11	Beginning Equity	242710	**235980**	*from previous year
12	Ending Equity	247640	242710	
13	Common Shares (number)	200000	200000	
14	Market Price (year end)	4.5	3.13	
15	Net Sales	338520	325600	
16	Credit Sales	338520	325600	
17	Cost of Goods Sold	180200	172120	
18	Interest Expense	12780	13600	
19	Net Income	30900	26350	
20				
21				
22	=A1			
23	Key Ratios and Statistics	20-3	20-2	Change
24	Current Ratio	=B3/B9	=C3/C9	=B24-C24
25	Quick Ratio	=(B3-B6-B7)/B9	=(C3-C6-C7)/C9	=B25-C25
26				

5. Shown below side by side are the simplified financial statements of Pluto Company Ltd. and Neptune Company Ltd. These two companies are in the same line of business. Pluto Company is considering expanding its business by purchasing Neptune Company. Neptune Company has been having financial difficulties recently.

    A. Work out all of the key ratios and statistics for the two companies. Assume that all sales are on account. A schedule is provided in your Workbook or you can use the spreadsheet template you created in exercise 4 above.

    B. Comment on any of the above ratios that are unfavourable. Is the situation serious? Can it be overcome? How?

    C. Decide whether Pluto Company should proceed with the purchase of Neptune Company and give evidence to support your opinion.

BALANCE SHEETS
DECEMBER 31, 20—

	Pluto	Neptune
Current Assets		
Bank	$ 5 000	$ 10 000
Accounts Receivable	80 000	72 000
Merchandise Inventory	52 000	40 000
Supplies	1 800	2 500
	$138 800	$124 500
Plant and Equipment		
Land	$ 70 000	—
Buildings	125 000	—
Equipment	85 000	$142 000
Automobiles	62 000	92 000
	$342 000	$234 000
Total Assets	$480 800	$358 500
Current Liabilities		
Bank Loan	$ 30 000	$ 90 000
Accounts Payable	32 000	30 000
	$ 62 000	$120 000
Long-Term Liabilities		
Mortgage Payable	$ 60 000	—
Total Liabilities	$122 000	$120 000
Shareholders' Equity		
Common Stock	$ 20 000	$ 50 000
Retained Earnings	338 800	188 500
Total Shareholders' Equity	$358 800	$238 500
Total Liabilities and Equity	$480 800	$358 500

INCOME STATEMENTS YEAR ENDED DECEMBER 31, 20–		
	Pluto	*Neptune*
Sales	$921 630	$570 000
Cost of Goods Sold		
Beginning Inventory	$ 48 000	$ 42 000
Purchases	609 000	304 100
Goods Available for Sale	$657 000	$346 100
Less Ending Inventory	52 000	40 000
Cost of Goods Sold	$605 000	$306 100
Gross Profit	$316 630	$263 900
Operating Expenses		
Depreciation Expense	$ 33 500	$ 55 000
Gas and Oil Expense	42 600	47 200
Interest Expense	15 000	20 000
Power Expense	7 500	6 000
Miscellaneous Expense	1 900	1 500
Rent Expense		24 000
Telephone Expense	1 500	1 200
Wages Expense	72 000	57 000
Total Operating Expenses	$174 000	$211 900
Net Income before taxes	$142 630	$ 52 000
Taxes	$ 32 805	$ 11 960
Net Income after taxes	$109 825	$ 40 040

13.4 | Partnership Accounting Using Spreadsheets

Spreadsheets offer a large amount of mathematical capabilities—so large, in fact, that you will likely use only a small portion of them at any one time. It is difficult to master all the mathematical functions of a spreadsheet quickly. It is best to be patient, knowing that when an accounting task presents you with a particular mathematical need, you can use a spreadsheet to provide the solution.

For example, suppose you were given the task of apportioning the net income for the partnership of Morris and Graves. You could do this by hand, as shown in Figure 13.2 on page 584. Or, you could use a spreadsheet model similar to the one shown in Figure 13.17 on page 617.

The spreadsheet in Figure 13.17 is straightforward. Rough data pertaining to the partnership is found in the top portion of the spreadsheet, and the distribution of the net income is located in the bottom section. **Load the spreadsheet file named MorrisGraves.xls into your computer**. Labels and formatting have been done for you, but other cell contents have been left blank. You are to use Figure 13.19 as a guide to complete the spreadsheet for Morris and Graves. (Note: Figure 13.19 is the same spreadsheet as Figure 13.18, but it shows the "formulas" for the cell contents rather than the results produced by the formulas.)

To show cell contents, a simple selection to show Formulas is made, usually from the Preferences menu. If you cannot find the selection, use your spreadsheet's help menu.

FIGURE 13.18

A spreadsheet model for apportioning the net income of a partnership.

	A	B	C	D	E	F	G
1		**Morris and Graves**					
2		RAW DATA					
3		Net Income	$130,624				
4		Partner A					
5		Morris's Salary	$10,000				
6		Morris's Capital	$100,000				
7		Interest on Capital	10%				
8							
9		Partner B					
10		Graves's Salary	$22,000				
11		Graves's Capital	$40,000				
12		Interest on Capital	10%				
13							
14							
15							
16							
17			MORRIS AND GRAVES				
18			STATEMENT OF DISTRIBUTION OF NET INCOME				
19			YEAR ENDED DECEMBER 31, 20—				
20							
21		Net Income available for distribution				$130,624	
22				Morris's	Graves's		
23				Share	Share	TOTALS	
24		Salaries allowed to partners		$10,000	$22,000	$32,000	
25		Interest at 10% of capital account balances		10,000	4,000	14,000	
26							
27						$46,000	
28		Balance of income divided equally		42,312	42,312	84,624	
29		Totals		$62,312	$68,312	$130,624	
30							

FIGURE 13.19

A spreadsheet model where the user has opted to show the "formulas" or cell contents.

	A	B	C	D	E	F	G
1		**Morris and Graves**					
2		RAW DATA					
3		Net Income	130624.16				
4		Partner A					
5		Morris's Salary	10000				
6		Morris's Capital	100000				
7		Interest on Capital	0.1				
8							
9		Partner B					
10		Graves's Salary	22000				
11		Graves's Capital	40000				
12		Interest on Capital	0.1				
13							
14							
15							
16							
17			MORRIS AND GRAVES				
18			STATEMENT OF DISTRIBUTION OF NET INCOME				
19			YEAR ENDED DECEMBER 31, 20—				
20							
21		Net Income available for distribution				=C3	
22				Morris's	Graves's		
23				Share	Share	TOTALS	
24		Salaries allowed to partners		=C5	=C10	=D24+E24	
25		Interest at 10% of capital account balances		=C6*C7	=C11*C12	=D25+E25	
26							
27						=SUM(F24:F26)	
28		Balance of income divided equally		=(F21-F27)/2	=(F21-F27)/2	=D28+E28	
29		Totals		=SUM(D24:D28)	=SUM(E24:E28)	=F27+F28	
30							

When "Show Formulas" is selected, certain cell formats are temporarily turned off. You can observe this in column C of the "Raw Data" area of Figure 13.19 where dollar sign, percent, and rounding formats have been suspended.

Adapting the Spreadsheet Model

Suppose the partners, Morris and Graves, are working out a change to their partnership agreement. Graves wants a bonus because she is doing substantially more work on a day-to-day basis. She proposes that once the profit reaches $100 000, a bonus arrangement should come into effect. The proposed bonus schedule is given below:

Morris and Graves
Bonus Schedule

Profit	Bonus Percentage
$100 000 – $149 999	5
$150 000 – $199 999	10
$200 000 – $249 999	15
$250 000 – $299 999	20
$300 000 and over	25

Using the above schedule, you can compute how much Graves would receive if a substantial profit were reached. For example, if the profit were $180 000, you would look up where the $180 000 would fit in the schedule and select the number in the adjacent column—in this case, 10%.

Looking up amounts is a task that spreadsheets can do well. Observe how Figure 13.20 shows the bonus schedule in a format that the spreadsheet can use.

FIGURE 13.20

The spreadsheet model with the bonus schedule and calculations.

	A	B	C	D	E	F	G
1		**Morris and Graves**					
2		RAW DATA					
3		Net Income	$130,624		LOOKUP TABLE		
4		Partner A			**Net Income**	**Bonus %**	
5		Morris's Salary	$10,000		**0**	**0%**	
6		Morris's Capital	$100,000		**100,000**	**5%**	
7		Interest on Capital	10%		**150,000**	**10%**	
8					**200,000**	**15%**	
9		Partner B			**250,000**	**20%**	
10		Graves's Salary	$22,000		**300,000**	**25%**	
11		Graves's Capital	$40,000				
12		Interest on Capital	10%				
13							
14							
15							
16							
17				MORRIS AND GRAVES			
18				STATEMENT OF DISTRIBUTION OF NET INCOME			
19				YEAR ENDED DECEMBER 31, 20—			
20							
21		Net Income available for distribution				$130,624	
22				Morris's	Graves's		
23				Share	Share	TOTALS	
24		Salaries allowed to partners		$10,000	$22,000	$32,000	
25		Interest at 10% of capital account balances		10,000	4,000	14,000	
26		**Bonus Percentage**	**5%**		**6,531**	**6,531**	
27						**$52,531**	
28		Balance of income divided equally		39,046	39,046	78,093	
29		Totals		$59,046	$71,578	$130,624	
30							

One of the spreadsheet functions is a predefined formula. The SUM function is the most familiar to you.

To get your spreadsheet to look like Figure 13.20, type the Lookup Table data in columns E and F. Then type the label, *Bonus Percentage*, at cell B26. (You do not have to use boldface type.)

The key cell is C26. That cell contains a function called a "lookup function." It will perform the same steps you took a few moments ago when you came up with a 10% bonus for a net income of $180 000. Specifically, the lookup function will:

1. Select the net income amount ($130 624, at cell C3);
2. run that number down the first column of the lookup table (E5 to E10);

3. and, after the net income amount runs into a value in column E greater than itself, the function will display the appropriate percentage from the second column of the table (5%).

The lookup function at cell C26 is as typed as follows.

=VLOOKUP(C3,E5:F10,2)

Name of the Function

Arguments are specific values that functions use. Arguments can be numbers, cell references, text, etc.; they are separated by commas.

- VLOOKUP (The V stands for vertical, which means the arrangement of the table of data is taller than it is wide.)

Arguments of the Function
- C3 is the net income
- E5:F10 is the table of data
- 2 stands for the second column of the table, which is where the percentages are found.

Left of the data entry line, where you type formulas, you may see an "=" sign. Clicking this will open a path for you to discover all the functions offered by your spreadsheet.

In your spreadsheet at cell C26, type the lookup function above. Then, enter the appropriate formulas at cells E26 and F26.

Your spreadsheet model is now ready to answer some "what if" questions. The ability to answer such questions makes spreadsheets especially valuable to business owners. For example, what if the partnership earns a net income of $225 000? How then would the net income be distributed? What if the net income is $275 000? How would the figures change? By entering $225 000 at C3, followed by $275 000, your spreadsheet model will instantly provide the answers to these "what if" questions.

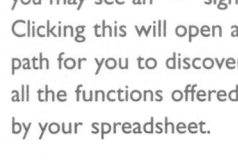

Section 13.4   **Computer Exercises**

1. To consider the proposal from Graves carefully, Morris projected the partnership's net income over the next five years as follows:

Year 1	$195 000
Year 2	$210 000
Year 3	$245 000
Year 4	$275 000
Year 5	$310 000

Required

1. Enter the projection for Year 1 ($195 000) at cell C3. Cells D29 and E29 show how the $195 000 will be split between the partners. In cells C40 and C41, **re-key** the values at D29 and E29. (Note: Don't simply copy and paste D29 and E29; errors will result. If you want to experiment with a variation of copying and pasting, highlight D29 and E29, and choose **Edit**, **Copy**. Then move the cell pointer to Cell C40 and choose **Edit**, **Paste Special**. In the dialogue box that appears, select **Values** and **Transpose**. Examine the contents of C40 and C41 after you press the Enter key. It should be apparent how the spreadsheet responded when you selected Values and Transpose.)

2. Repeat for the remaining years. The answers for the first two years are shown on page 627.

	A	B	C	D	E	F	G	H
17			MORRIS AND GRAVES					
18			STATEMENT OF DISTRIBUTION OF NET INCOME					
19			YEAR ENDED DECEMBER 31, 20—					
20								
21		Net Income available for distribution				$210,000		
22				Morris's	Graves's			
23				Share	Share	TOTALS		
24		Salaries allowed to partners		$10,000	$22,000	$32,000		
25		Interest at 10% of capital account balances		10,000	4,000	14,000		
26		Bonus Percentage	15%		31,500	31,500		
27						$ 77,500		
28		Balance of income divided equally		66,250	66,250	132,500		
29		Totals		$86,250	$123,750	$210,000		
30								
31								
32		Morris's Projections						
33								
34				Year 1	Year 2	Year 3	Year 4	Year 5
35				195,000	210,000	245,000	275,000	310,000
36								
37		Projected Distribution of Net Income						
38								
39				Year 1	Year 2	Year 3	Year 4	Year 5
40			Morris	**84,750**	**86,250**	#####	#####	#####
41			Graves	**110,250**	**123,750**	#####	#####	#####
42								

3. Chart the Projections.

Graphs are very easily done in spreadsheets. One important thing for you to do is to lay out and highlight the data properly so that there are no blank cells between values and labels. For Morris's projections of the distribution of net income, the data in rows 39, 40, and 41 is already in a suitable format. To highlight the data, place the cell pointer at the top left corner of the data (cell B39) and drag the mouse through the projections, as shown below:

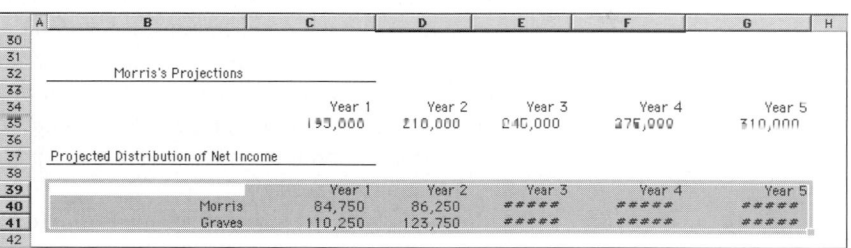

With the data highlighted, simply select the chart icon in Microsoft Excel, choose the type of chart you want, and follow the steps suggested by the software. Try to produce a chart similar to the one that appears below:

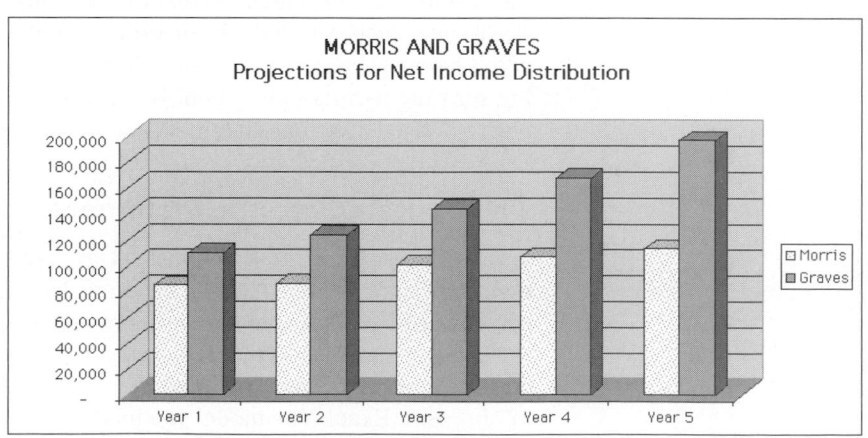

4. Act as an advisor to Morris. Analyze the results from the projections, including what the bar chart reveals. Prepare a business letter to Morris outlining your recommendations. If you are using Microsoft Word, you can copy and paste data, including the chart, from Excel to Word.

Optional

5. Using the same projections from Morris, act as an advisor to Graves. Try preparing a different chart and make recommendations to support her point of view.

13.5 | Budgeting with Spreadsheets and Simply Accounting

After analyzing the financial results of a fiscal period and making appropriate decisions, accountants take measures that help them plan and prepare for future events. A **budget** is a financial plan that involves a forecast of financial figures. The budget that we are most familiar with is a forecast of revenues and expenditures; in other words, a budgeted income statement. All types of organizations, from charities to businesses to governments, budget their revenues and expenses. You have probably heard of annual provincial and federal budgets. Governments carefully estimate how much revenue they expect to generate from taxes and then plan how much will be allocated to each department for spending.

Budgeting can be simple or complex depending on the size of the organization. For example, a large organization may employ a team of accountants to work on a variety of departmental budgets, which then fit into a master budget for the entire organization. A small business might have only one accountant who is in charge of the budgeting process.

Regardless of the size of a business, the following stages of budgeting for a small business are common to the budgeting process in general. First, the accountant goes on a fact-finding mission. Next, the accountant uses the information gathered to make predictions about accounts in the ledger. The third stage ensures an information system is established to provide feedback about the accuracy of budgetary predictions. And, finally, the accountant interprets the feedback and communicates the results to management so that they can make wise and timely decisions.

To introduce you to the basic process of budgeting, you will first prepare a budgeted income statement for Sam's Softball City, a business which has been operating for only two months. Then, you will extend the budgeting process to include both a budgeted income statement and a budgeted balance sheet for a new business.

The Budgeted Income Statement

You will begin by using a spreadsheet to prepare a simple budgeted income statement for Sam's Softball City. Then you will see how Simply Accounting can provide a system of feedback that management can use to make important decisions.

Load the spreadsheet model named *samsbudget.xls* into your computer. The income statement amounts were imported from Simply Accounting and formats were applied in Microsoft Excel. The model you load should look like Figure 13.21 on page 629.

A two-month income
statement for Sam's
Softball City.

	A	B	C
1	Sam's Softball City		
2	Income Statement		
3	Two Months Ended May 31		
4			
5	REVENUE		
6	Rental Revenue	$ 12,650	
7			
8	EXPENSES		
9	Advertising Expense	$ 1,350	
10	Bank Charges	250	
11	Miscellaneous Expense	48	
12	Rent Expense	9,000	
13	Telephone Expense	168	
14	Utilities Expense	1,398	
15	Wages Expense	8,600	
16		20,814	
17			
18	NET INCOME(LOSS)	$ (8,164)	
19			

The figures shown are for two months. Predicting annual figures takes time, effort, and expertise. For now, you will simply multiply amounts in column B by various factors to increase the amounts to annual figures. (The factors to increase the amounts are shown in column C of Figure 13.22 below. For example, the estimate for the annual amount of Rental Revenue will be 10 times greater than what was produced in the first two months. Rent Expense, on the other hand, will be 6 times greater than the May 31 amount).

Move the cell pointer to cell D6. Enter the formula, **=B6*C6**. (Don't worry about the formatting yet.) Highlight cells D6 to D15 and choose Edit, Fill Down. Delete the unwanted results at D7 and D8. To produce the total expenses and net income figures in column D, copy and paste the corresponding cells from column B (B16 and B19) in Column D.

The "Format Pointer"
button gives an even
quicker way to
duplicate formats.

To quickly apply consistent formatting between columns B and D, highlight cells B6 to B18 and choose Edit, Copy. Move the cell pointer to D6 and choose Edit, Paste Special. From the dialogue box that appears, select **Formats**, and press the Enter key. After you add a heading in column D, your work will look like Figure 13.22.

Annual budgeted figures
for Sam's Softball City.

	A	B	C	D	E
1	Sam's Softball City				
2	Income Statement				
3	Two Months Ended May 31		Increase	Annual	
4			Factor	Budget	
5	REVENUE				
6	Rental Revenue	$ 12,650	10	$ 126,500	
7					
8	EXPENSES				
9	Advertising Expense	$ 1,350	7	$ 9,450	
10	Bank Charges	250	6	1,500	
11	Miscellaneous Expense	48	20	960	
12	Rent Expense	9,000	6	54,000	
13	Telephone Expense	168	5	840	
14	Utilities Expense	1,398	6	8,388	
15	Wages Expense	8,600	6	51,600	
16		20,814		126,738	
17					
18	NET INCOME(LOSS)	$ (8,164)		$ (238)	
19					

Budgeting In Simply Accounting

The annual budget income statement you just produced in Excel may turn out to be very accurate. However, you will not be able to verify the accuracy of the projections for 10 more months. If you waited that long, the business would lose the advantages that budgeting offers. On the other hand, if a system of feedback is in place, managers can compare the budgeted figures to actual performance. Then they can take corrective measures to help control and minimize trouble spots. Accounting software like Simply Accounting overcomes the delay by providing regular feedback on how well the business is keeping to its budgeted amounts.

Load the Simply Accounting files named *Sam's Softball City 13*. (The "13" designates the proper files for this chapter.) To prepare these files for budgeting, choose **Setup**, **Settings** and select the **General** tab. Check the box that allows for budgeting revenues and expenses and use the drop down menu to set the "Budget period frequency" to **Monthly**. Click the OK button.

Now you will enter data in the revenue and expense accounts. Open the ledger and double-click the Rental Revenue account. Select the Budget tab and check the box beside the phrase, "Budget this Account."

Next, your preliminary work from Excel will prove useful. In the field next to "Total budgeted amount," enter the annual forecast of revenues, which was calculated in your spreadsheet model at cell D6—$126 500. If you want Simply Accounting to distribute the annual figure evenly to each of the months, press the Allocate button. Your monitor will be similar to Figure 13.23 below.

FIGURE 13.23

Entering budget information in Simply Accounting.

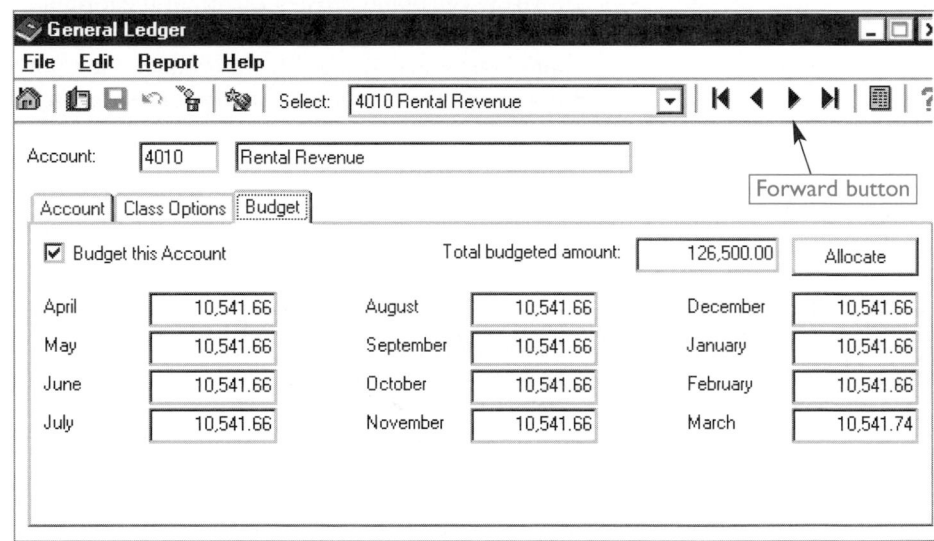

If you are unhappy with any of the amounts produced by pressing the Allocate button, you can change the monthly allocations individually.

Move to the first expense account by pressing the "forward" button next to the account field near the top right of your monitor. Repeat the steps you took for Rental Revenue for each of the expense accounts. Use the annual budgeted amounts from your spreadsheet model (or from Figure 13.22 on page 629).

Displaying Budget Reports

Once the revenue and expense accounts are set up for budgeting, you can choose a few different budgeted income statements. Choose **Reports, Financials, Income Statement**. Then, use the drop-down menu next to "report type" to select Comparison of Actual to Budget (Current). For "report on," use the drop-down menu to select Actual vs. Budget (dollar difference). When you click the OK button, the statement you produce will look like Figure 13.24.

FIGURE 13.24

Comparison of actual and budget figures.

Income Statement				
File Options Help				
Comparison of Actual to Budget April to May	Actual to 5/31/01		Budget	Difference
REVENUE				
Rental Revenue	12,650.00		21,083.32	-8,433.32
	12,650.00		21,083.32	-8,433.32
TOTAL REVENUE	12,650.00		21,083.32	-8,433.32
EXPENSE				
Advertising Expense	1,350.00		1,574.98	-224.98
Bank Charges	250.00		249.98	0.02
Miscellaneous Expense	48.00		159.98	-111.98
Rent Expense	9,000.00		9,000.00	0.00
Telephone Expense	168.00		139.98	28.02
Utilities Expense	1,398.00		1,397.98	0.02
Wages Expense	8,600.00		8,600.00	0.00
	20,814.00		21,122.90	-308.90
TOTAL EXPENSE	20,814.00		21,122.90	-308.90
NET INCOME	-8,164.00		-39.58	-8,124.42

The accountant for Sam's Softball City has completed the first three stages of the budgeting process: information was gathered, predictions were made, and Simply Accounting provided feedback about the predictions in Figure 13.24 above. Now the accountant must interpret the results and communicate with management.

If you were accountant for the business, you would note that the total expenses for the first two months were very close to the budgeted amount (only a $308.90 difference). The revenue situation, however, would alarm you. Rental revenue is $8 433.32 below the expected amount. How would you react? First, you might revise the projection shown in Figure 13.22. Perhaps the forecast of $126 500 is too high for the first year of operations. Or, perhaps the annual target for revenue is reasonable, but a slow start is to be expected and sales should rise soon. If this is the case, you would use Simply Accounting and go to the computer screen shown in Figure 13.23 on page 630. You would then change amounts in the data entry fields for each month, reducing totals for the first part of the year and increasing them in the latter.

If you decide the forecasts are fine, then you must make recommendations to respond to the results in Figure 13.24. Perhaps you think revenue will meet expectations if the budget for advertising expenditures is increased. Since revenue is presently insufficient to provide funds for more advertising, you might recommend that the business increase its demand loan with the bank. No matter what recommendation you offer, this example should help you understand how important budgeting is to controlling and directing business events.

The Budgeted Balance Sheet

Profit projections are important, but managers of a business need to know more. For example, they must know whether there will be enough cash in the business to pay employees in a particular month. Or, they might need to know how much money they must to borrow in order to purchase new computer equipment. Such issues involve assets and liabilities, so it is important for many businesses to extend the budgeting process to include the balance sheet.

Developing a budgeted balance sheet is a complex task in a large organization, but you can get a glimpse of the procedure by looking at a new business that sells just one product. Karissa Lee has the opportunity to import a brand of flavoured lip gloss sticks for teenagers called "Sweet Lips." She would like to sell this product to local retail stores.

Karissa wants a good picture of the potential risks and rewards before starting operations. In addition to forecasting her revenues and expenses, she also wants to know what her financial position will be one year from now. In other words, she wants both a budgeted income statement and a budgeted balance sheet. You will see how she accomplishes these goals by building a spreadsheet model for these budgeted financial statements. Then you will have the chance to build the same model when you complete the computer exercises at the end of this section.

Karissa names the business KLSL Wholesalers. She enters the initial fact-finding stage of budgeting by preparing a list of important details about her business proposal. These appear in the spreadsheet model shown in Figure 13.25 below:

FIGURE 13.25

Rough data and calculations for KLSL Wholesalers.

	A	B	C	D	E	F	G
1			KLSL Wholesalers				
2			Data and Rough Calculations				
3		*Sales and COGS*			*Other Cash Expenses*		
4		1. Projected unit sales	100,000		14. Salaries	$ 35,000	
5		2. Price per unit:	$ 1.00		15. Bank Loan Interest Rate	8%	
6		3. Cost per unit	$ 0.45		16. Other Expenses	$ 6,000	
7		4. Sales	$ 100,000				
8		5. COGS	$ 45,000		*Depreciation*		
9		6. % Sales for Cash	20%		17. Building	$ 45,000	
10		7. % Sales for Credit	80%		18. Salvage Value	$ 5,000	
11					19. Estimated Useful Life	20	
12		*Other Assets*			20. Yearly Depreciation (yrs)	$ 2,000	
13		8. Opening Cash	$ 5,000				
14		9. Year-end A/R (% of credit sales)	10%		21. Equipment	$ 10,000	
15		10. % of Inventory Exceeding Sales	20%		22. Salvage Value	$ 1,000	
16		11. Land	$ 40,000		23. Estimated Useful Life	10	
17					24. Yearly Depreciation (yrs)	$ 450	
18		*Liabilities*					
19		12. Bank Loan	$ 65,000		*Beginning Equity*		
20		13. Year-end A/P (% of purchases)	10%		25. Capital	$ 35,000	
21							
22							

Before you can understand how to build a budget for KLSL Wholesalers, you need to know more about the amounts and percentages shown in Figure 13.25. Some require no explanation. Others come from Karissa's knowledge of the business. Study the information below to understand the data in Figure 13.25.

Sales and Cost of Goods Sold	**Other Cash Expenses**
• **Item 1:** Projected unit sales are 100 000 Sweet Lips. • **Item 2:** The business plans to sell the lip gloss for $1.00 each. • **Item 3:** Each lip gloss costs 45 cents. • **Items 4-5:** These results calculated by a spreadsheet formula. • **Item 6:** Twenty percent of the total sales are expected to be made on a cash sale basis. • **Item 7:** Eighty percent of the total sales are expected to be made on credit.	• **Items 14-16:** Lists other cash expenses such as Salaries, Bank Loan Interest Rate, and Other Expenses.
Other Assets	**Depreciation**
• **Item 8:** Shows the opening cash balance. • **Item 9:** Ten percent of the annual projected credit sales is expected to be owing at the end of the year. • **Item 10:** The business plans to purchase 20 percent more inventory than it will sell in order to build up and maintain merchandise inventory. • **Item 11:** The cost value of land for warehouse.	• **Items 17-19:** Data needed to calculate straight-line depreciation on the building. • **Item 20:** Result calculated by a spreadsheet formula. • **Items 21-24:** Data needed to calculate straight-line depreciation of the equipment.
Liabilities	**Beginning Equity**
• **Item 12:** amount of the demand loan from the bank. The business pays interest (not principal) monthly. • **Item 13:** Ten percent of the projected credit purchases is expected to be owing at the end of the year.	• **Item 25:** Beginning equity figure

Karissa has other sources of income for her livelihood, so she plans to have no drawings in the business's first year.

Karissa uses cell references to the "data and rough calculations" area of the spreadsheet to produce the opening balance sheet, which appears in Figure 13.26 on page 634.

The fact-finding stage of budgeting is over and Karissa is ready to expand and refine her projections so that she can prepare the budgeted statements. Developing the budgeted income statement is relatively easy. To give maximum flexibility when inserting, deleting and changing the widths of rows and columns, Karissa locates the budgeted income statement below and beside the current spreadsheet data. This statement is shown in the bottom right area of Figure 13.27.

Like the opening balance sheet, the budgeted income statement is primarily made up of cell references from the "data and rough calculations" area of the spreadsheet. It also includes a few formulas and a sum function. The budgeted balance sheet for June 30, 20-4, will follow the same pattern, but its formulas will be slightly more complex. This is due to the extra variables that need to be considered when projecting balance sheet items. For example, cash comes into the business from cash sales and the collection of accounts receivable. It goes out of the business

FIGURE 13.26

The opening balance
sheet of KLSL
Wholesalers.

	A	B	C	D	E	F	G
1			KLSL Wholesalers				
2			Data and Rough Calculations				
3		*Sales and COGS*				*Other Cash Expenses*	
4		1. Projected unit sales		100,000	14.	Salaries	$ 35,000
5		2. Price per unit:	$	1.00	15.	Bank Loan Interest Rate	8%
6		3. Cost per unit	$	0.45	16.	Other Expenses	$ 6,000
7		4. Sales	$	100,000			
8		5. COGS	$	45,000		*Depreciation*	
9		6. % Sales for Cash		20%	17.	Building	$ 45,000
10		7. % Sales for Credit		80%	18.	Salvage Value	$ 5,000
11					19.	Estimated Useful Life	20
12		*Other Assets*			20.	Yearly Depreciation (yrs)	$ 2,000
13		8. Opening Cash	$	5,000			
14		9. Year-end A/R (% of credit sales)		10%	21.	Equipment	$ 10,000
15		10. % of Inventory Exceeding Sales		20%	22.	Salvage Value	$ 1,000
16		11. Land	$	40,000	23.	Estimated Useful Life	10
17					24.	Yearly Depreciation (yrs)	$ 450
18		*Liabilities*					
19		12. Bank Loan	$	65,000		*Beginning Equity*	
20		13. Year-end A/P (% of purchases)		10%	25.	Capital	$ 35,000
21							
22							
23			KLSL Wholesalers				
24			Opening Balance Sheet				
25			July 1, 20-3				
26		*Assets*			*Liabilities*		
27		Cash	$ 5,000		Bank Loan		$ 65,000
28		Land	40,000				
29		Building	45,000		*Owner's Equity*		
30		Equipment	10,000		Karissa Lee, Capital		35,000
31			$ 100,000				$ 100,000
32							

In addition to cell references, there are two sum
functions in the opening
balance sheet of KLSL
Wholesalers.

FIGURE 13.27

The budgeted income
statement for KLSL
Wholesalers.

	B	C	D	E	F	G	H	I	J
23		KLSL Wholesalers							
24		Opening Balance Sheet							
25		July 1, 20-3							
26	*Assets*			*Liabilities*					
27	Cash	$ 5,000		Bank Loan	$ 65,000				
28	Land	40,000							
29	Building	45,000		*Owner's Equity*					
30	Equipment	10,000		Karissa Lee, Capital	35,000				
31		$ 100,000			$ 100,000				
32									
33									
34								KLSL Wholesalers	
35								Budgeted Income Statement	
36								Year Ending June 30, 20-4	
37									
38								Sales	$ 100,000
39								Cost of Goods Sold	45,000
40								Gross Profit	$ 55,000
41								Expenses:	
42								Salaries	35,000
43								Depreciation	2,450
44								Interest	5,200
45								Other	6,000
46								Total Expenses	$ 48,650
47									
48								Net Income	$ 6,350
49									
50									

for cash expenses and accounts payable payments. These various inflows and outflows complicate the projected balance of cash, so it is best to prepare a separate
statement of projected cash flows. For KLSL Wholesalers, the projected statement
of cash flow is seen in Figure 13.28. Note the column and row references to visualize its location on the spreadsheet model.

The two most challenging formulas Karissa created when projecting the cash flow
were the ones for the collection of accounts receivable and payable. But even these
were based on the simple logic outlined at the top-left of the spreadsheet model. For
example, to determine how much money would be received from collecting accounts
receivable, first calculate the credit sales ($100 000 × 80% = $80 000). Then, multiply
the credit sales by the percentage of accounts receivable that are expected to be out-

The cash flow projections for KLSL Wholesalers.

In more senior accounting courses, you will discover that accountants are extremely interested in "cash flow." In fact, a *cash flow statement*, sometimes called a *statement of changes in financial position*, is the third prominent financial statement that you will find in the annual report of a company.

	K	L	M	N
50		KLSL Wholesalers		
51		Cash Flow Projections		
52		Year Ending June 30, 20-4		
53				
54		*Opening Balance of Cash*	$ 5,000	
55		*Cash Inflows*		
56		Cash Sales	20,000	
57		Collection of A/R	72,000	
58			$ 92,000	
59		*Cash Outflows*		
60		Salaries	$ 35,000	
61		Other	6,000	
62		Loan Interest	5,200	
63		Payments of A/P	48,600	
64			$ 94,800	
65				
66		Net Cash Flow	$ (2,800)	
67				

standing at year-end ($80 000 × 10% = $8 000). Finding the difference between these two amounts produces the $72 000 you see at cell M57 in Figure 13.28. (Note: To achieve the same answer more directly, you could multiply the credit sales by the complement of projected accounts receivable. That is, $100 000 × 80% × **90%** = $72 000.)

To enter this formula at cell M57, you could key =C7*.8*.9. Using values like .8 and .9 in a cell formula, however, defeats the purpose of the "data and rough calculations" area at the top left of the spreadsheet model. Showing data in that area makes it easy to update the spreadsheet later when new projections are made. Hiding values in cell formulas makes them difficult to find and edit.

Karissa used cell references instead of values and entered the following formula at M57: **=C7*C10*(1–C14)**. This produces the same result as keying =100 000*.80*.90, but using cell references in formulas will be beneficial later.

The cash flow projections show that the business expects cash outflows to exceed cash inflows by $2 800. This means that the opening of cash balance of $5 000 will be reduced to $2 200 on the budgeted balance sheet. The spreadsheet formula for calculating this amount of $2 200 on the balance sheet is now simple, thanks to the statement of cash flow projections. Projections for other asset, liability, and equity accounts require fewer steps and are shown in Figure 13.29 below.

The budgeted balance sheet for KLSL Wholesalers.

	O	P	Q	R	S	T	U
67		KLSL Wholesalers					
68		Budgeted Balance Sheet					
69		June 30, 20-4					
70							
71	*Assets*			*Liabilities*			
72	Cash (see cash flow projections)	$ 2,200		Bank Loan	$ 65,000		
73	Accounts Receivable	8,000		Accounts Payable	5,400		
74	Inventory	9,000				$ 70,400	
75	Land	40,000		*Owner's Equity*			
76	Building (net)	43,000		Karissa Lee, Capital	$ 35,000		
77	Equipment (net)	9,550		Net Income	6,350		
78				Ending Capital		41,350	
79		$ 111,750				$ 111,750	
80							

Adjusting the Budgeted Statements

Karissa now has an idea of what her financial position will look like one year from now. But what if she is not satisfied with the results shown in Figure 13.29? The amount of cash is small ($2 200) and the bank loan remains high at $65 000. She might need to reconsider some of the basic elements of her business venture. For example, perhaps she set the price of Sweet Lips too low. What if she sells them for $1.08 each? If she did that, however, she may have to reduce the estimate of total unit sales, perhaps to 95 000. What impact would these changes have on the budgeted income statement and balance sheet?

The preceding paragraph poses "what if" questions. As you saw earlier in Section 13.4, a well-designed spreadsheet model is good at answering these types of questions. All Karissa has to do is move the cell pointer to the top left of the spreadsheet model. At cell C4, she enters **95 000**; at C5, **1.08**. As soon as she does, a number of cells in her budgeted statements are instantly updated. Some of the new amounts are shown in Figure 13.30 below.

FIGURE 13.30

The budgeted balance sheet after changes are made to the selling price and projected unit sales.

The user has split the spreadsheet window in Figure 13.30 into four panes by dragging the black bars located on the scroll bars. There are now four scroll bars instead of two. Manipulating them allows the user to see remote parts of the spreadsheet in the same computer window.

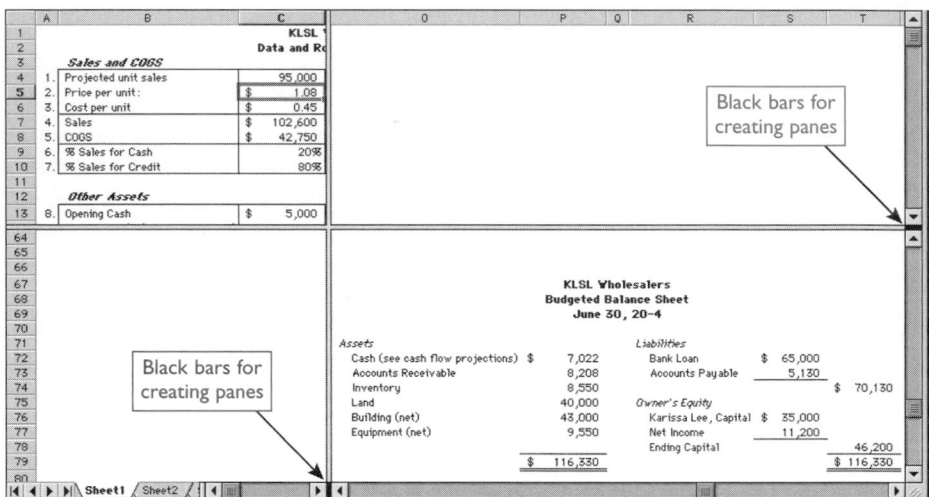

The budgeted balance sheet shows that a combination of a higher selling price and lower unit sales will increase the amount of cash to $7 022 and net income to $11 200. This is critical data for Karissa to analyze. Perhaps she will decide that the new cash and net income amounts are sufficiently attractive for her to proceed with her business plan. She makes this important decision based on the data that was provided by her spreadsheet model.

Other amounts on the budgeted balance sheet changed when new figures were entered in cells C4 and C5. These include the amounts for accounts receivable, inventory, accounts payable, total liabilities, total assets, and total liabilities and equity. Data in the other statements (the budgeted income statement and cash flow projections) were also revised. Karissa could have prepared her first set of budgeted statements by hand. However, with so many calculations affected by the simple revision of the selling price and unit sales projections, you can appreciate how much more labour and time would be involved had she done so. Her spreadsheet model certainly enhances her ability to make quick and effective decisions.

Section 13.5   **Review Questions**

1. What is a budget?
2. What type of budget is most common?
3. In a large organization, what would be the components of a master budget?
4. Identify four stages of budgeting in a small business.
5. How does a system of feedback for budgeting help business managers?
6. Why do the managers of a business need to know more than just profit projections?
7. Identify a third prominent financial statement found in the annual reports of companies?
8. Why is it a good idea to limit the use of values in a spreadsheet formula?
9. What is the advantage of splitting the window of a spreadsheet model into panes?
10. Explain the disadvantages of preparing a budgeted balance sheet by hand.

Section 13.5   **Exercises**

1. Refer to Figure 13.24 on page 631. Budgeting needs to be done with care if it is to be useful. Write a short memo to the owner, Samuel Lucas, explaining what he has forgotten in the budget for Sam's Softball City. (Hint: Refer to Chapter 9 to find some expenses not shown in Figure 13.24.) Also, explain any other concerns to the owner about the budget.

Challenge

2. Load the spreadsheet model named sweetlips.xls. You should see the early stages of the budgeting spreadsheet model that Karissa Lee prepared in this section. It should look like Figure 13.26 on page 634.

   A. Using cell references, formulas, and functions, develop a spreadsheet model just like the one Karissa created in this section. This means you will create a budgeted income statement, a projection of cash flows, and a budgeted balance sheet.

   Hints:
   • Use Figures 13.25 to 13.29 to guide you in choosing the location of the various sections of the spreadsheet model. The text illustrations will also help you apply formats and will help you verify the accuracy of your cell formulas and functions.
   • To help you build your formulas and functions, refer to the 25 points listed on page 633.
   • As you develop the spreadsheet model, you may want to divide your computer window in panes, as shown in Figure 13.30 on page 636.
   • Constructing the proper formula for "Payments of A/P" in the "Cash Flow Projections" section requires care. Use the text explanation on pages 634 and 635 for "Collection of A/R" to help you.

   B. Testing your model.
   Apply the following tests to your spreadsheet model. If your model fails to respond properly, you will have to find and revise problematic cells.

- When done, your balance sheet should look like Figure 13.29 on page 635.
- Split your windows into panes, just like Figure 13.30 on page 636. Change cell C4 to 95 000, C5 to 1.08. The amounts in your budgeted balance sheet should be the same as those shown in Figure 13.30.
- The owner decides the percentage of cash sales is too high. At cell C9, change the projection for cash sales from 20% to 15%. (Credit sales will automatically adjust to 85% because of a pre-existing spreadsheet formula.) Your balance sheet should still balance, and your new totals for Cash and Accounts Receivable should be $6 509 and $8 721 respectively.
- The owner decides that she wants to carry less inventory in the warehouse. Therefore, change cell C15 to 15%. Your spreadsheet model should look like the illustration below. Compare the numbers in the budgeted balance sheet against yours.

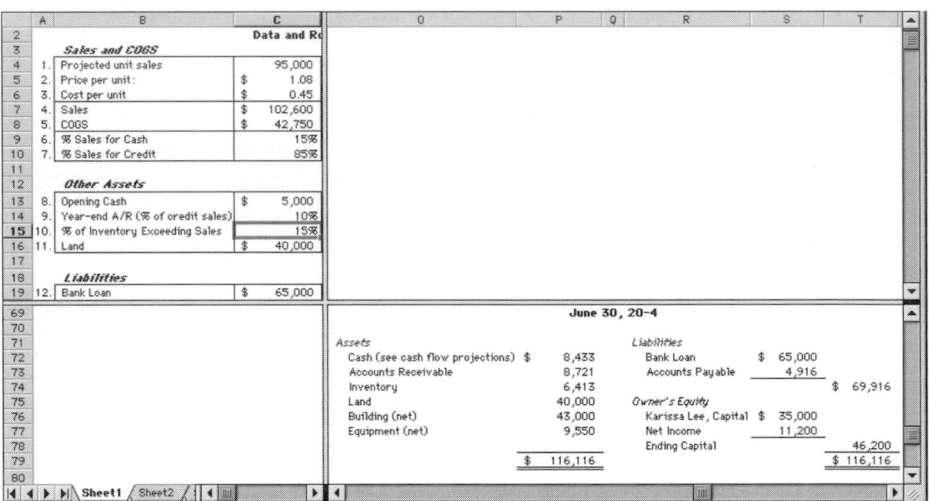

Extra Challenge

3. The spreadsheet model for KLSL Wholesalers responds with a new budgeted balance sheet each time a "what if" question is asked. What if the percentage of cash sales is lower? What if we buy less inventory? What if we increase the unit price to $1.08? What if unit sales drop to 95 000? You now appreciate how a spreadsheet can answer such "what if" questions. Accordingly, this is a good time to enhance your model with a new spreadsheet function called the **IF** function.

The IF function has a familiar structure. That is, it begins with an = sign, followed by the name of the function, followed by the "arguments" it works on, which are contained within brackets. (Arguments can be other functions, formulas, cell references, values, and text.)

To see the IF function at work, suppose Karissa Lee wanted to reach a net income target of $15 000, and that she wanted cells in the "rough data area" to indicate whether the target had been reached. An IF function could be written as follows:

=IF(S83>C6,"Target has been reached by:","Projected profits are below target")

Working from left to right, the function can be explained in parts:

1. **=IF** The name of the function.
2. **S83>C6** The first argument which, in this case, is a formula that describes a mathematical condition. Cell S83 contains the net income amount, and C6 contains 15 000. In ordinary language, the condition is: "if net income is greater than $15 000."
3. **"Target has been reached by:"** The second argument is what the spreadsheet will display in the cell if the condition above **is** met. The argument is a string of text that must be enclosed in quotations. (The quotations will not be displayed in the cell.)
4. **"Projected profits are below target"** The third argument is a string of text that will display if the condition above **is not** met.

Another way to describe the three arguments is a condition, a true response, and a false response. It is important to note that the set of arguments is enclosed in brackets, and that each argument is set apart from the others by commas.

In the adjacent cell, Karissa could enter another IF function, written as follows:

=IF(S83>C6,S83-C6,0)

You should be able to guess what this function will do. If the net income (S83) is greater than $15 000 (C6), the cell will display the difference. If net income does not exceed $15 000, a value of zero will be shown. Mastering the IF function opens a range of possibilities when you are building spreadsheet models.

Refer to the illustration on page 640 to help you interpret the cell references in this example.

Required

A. Make sure your spreadsheet amounts are the same as those shown in the illustration connected to Exercise 2, part B, on page 637.

B. Highlight row 6 and insert about six rows. **From cell B6 to C7, insert the IF function data described above for the net income target of $15 000.** Refer to section B of the illustration on page 640 to guide you. (Note: Be careful about the cell reference to net income; because you had some freedom in choosing the location for sections of your spreadsheet model, S83 may not contain the net income figure you want.)

C. The owner is not happy with the bank loan of $65 000. She decides that the year-end balance of cash should be no more than $5 000. Any extra year-end amount is to be applied against the bank loan in order to reduce interest costs in the following year. **In cells B9 to C10, enter IF function data to calculate the amount to be applied against the bank loan.** And, to finish your spreadsheet model, make small adjustments to the formulas in the Cash and Bank Loan cells in the budgeted balance sheet. Use the illustration on page 640 as your guide.

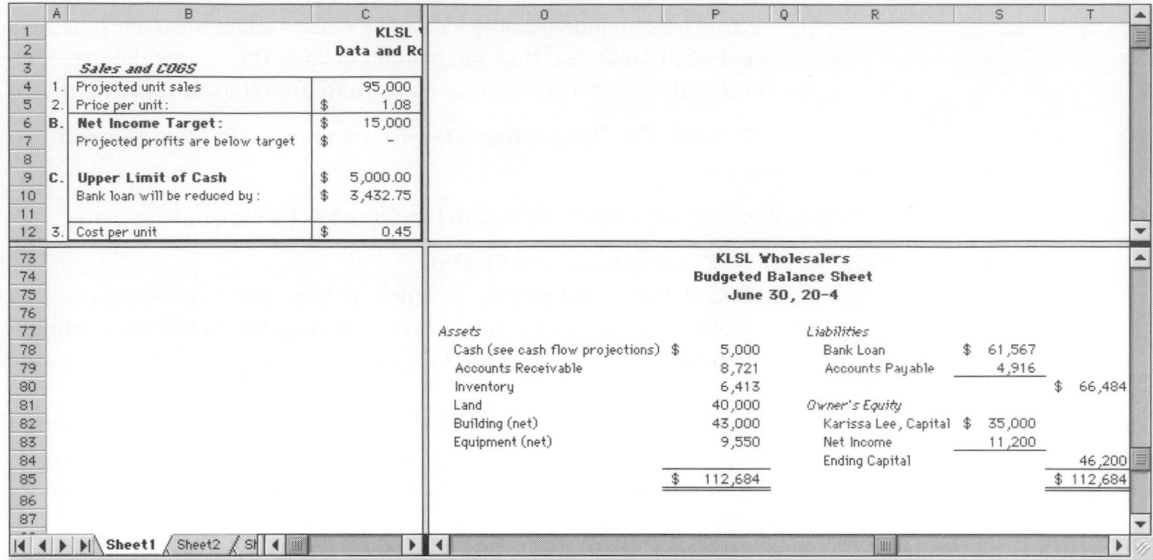

D. Increase the unit price to $1.10. At this price, how many Sweet Lips must be sold in order to reduce the year-end balance of the bank loan by $10 000? (Experiment with the values in cell C4 until you get the answer you want.) What is the net income at this quantity of sales? Keeping the selling price at $1.10 per unit, at what quantity of sales will there be no reduction in the bank loan? What is the net income at this level of sales? At $1.10 per unit, what quantity of sales will produce a net loss?

Section 13.5   Communicate It

Write a business letter to Karissa Lee that recommends a unit price for Sweet Lips and an appropriate target for the quantity of sales. In your letter, refer to the discoveries you made in Part D above. To help your explanations, try copying and pasting budgeted balance sheets into your word-processing program. (Note: If you are using Microsoft Word, try Paste Special under the Edit menu and choose Microsoft Excel Object.) For help with your business letter, refer to the Skills Appendix.

CHAPTER 13 Summary

CHAPTER HIGHLIGHTS

Now that you have completed Chapter 13 you should:

- be able to define "partnership";
- understand how the equity section of a partnership differs from that of a proprietorship;
- know the advantages and disadvantages of a partnership;
- be able to prepare the accounting forms for simple partnership formations;
- be able to perform the calculations to apportion partnership net income or net loss;
- be able to prepare the four financial statements for a partnership;
- develop a spreadsheet to apportion partnership net income or loss;
- understand that a corporation has a number of owners called shareholders;
- understand how the accounts of a corporation differ from those of a sole proprietorship or a partnership;
- know the difference between common and preferred shares;
- be able to give four reasons why a corporation is considered to be a separate legal entity from its owners;
- explain what limited liability means;
- know that a corporation is governed by strict rules and regulations;
- know what a director is and what the board of directors does;
- know the difference between a public corporation and a private corporation;
- understand the items in the equity section of a corporation's ledger and be able to prepare a simple balance sheet for a corporation;
- understand what a dividend is and the three dates associated with dividends;
- be able to calculate a dividend and to prepare the accounting entries for dividends;
- be able to calculate and interpret liquidity ratios and statistics;
- be able to calculate and interpret profitability percentages;
- be able to use a spreadsheet for financial analysis;
- know the role of a master budget in a large organization;
- describe the stages of budgeting for a small business;
- use a spreadsheet and Simply Accounting for budgeting;
- develop a generic spreadsheet model for a budgeted balance sheet.

ACCOUNTING TERMS

acid-test ratio	common shareholder
board of directors	common stock
book value	comparative financial statement
budget	corporation
budgeted balance sheet	current ratio
budgeted income statement	debt ratio
Capital Stock account	deficit
cash flow	dividend
Collection period	earnings per share

equity ratio
income- or loss-sharing ratio
general partner
inventory turnover
limited liability
limited partnership
limited partner
liquidity ratio
master budget
partnership
partnership agreement
price earnings ratio
private corporation

public corporation
quick ratio
rate of return on net sales
rate of return on owner's equity
Retained Earnings account
share certificate
shareholder
statement of partners' capital
statement of distribution of net income
times interest earned ratio
working capital
working capital ratio

CHAPTER 13 Review Exercises

Using Your Knowledge

1. The shareholders' equity of Kingston Investments Limited consists of the following:

Common Stock
Authorized, 5 000 shares; no par value;
issued and fully paid, 5 000 shares;
book value of issued shares, $54 260

Preferred Stock
six per cent cumulative preferred;
par value $25; authorized, issued,
and fully paid; 20 000 shares

Retained Earnings
$157 206

Prepare the Shareholders' Equity section of the balance sheet.

2. The balance sheet of Rollins Limited as of December 31, 20– appears below.
Study the balance sheet and answer the questions that follow.

ROLLINS LIMITED
BALANCE SHEET
DECEMBER 31, 20—

ASSETS		LIABILITIES	
Bank	$ 3 750	Bank Loan	$150 000
Accounts Receivable	42 906	Accounts Payable	49 601
Merchandise Inventory	70 374		$199 601
Plant and Equipment	505 061		
		SHAREHOLDERS' EQUITY	
		Capital Stock	
		25 000 Common Shares	250 000
		Retained Earnings	172 490
	$622 091		$622 091

Answer the following questions in your Workbook.

A. **How much equity was raised by the sale of common shares?**

B. **How much equity was generated by company profits?**

C. **Assuming that all shares were sold for the same price, for how much each were the shares sold?**

D. **Is this company in a good position to pay out dividends? Yes or no? Explain.**

---

3 The issued capital stock of Marwell Limited is as follows:

- No par value common shares, 76 700 shares.
- Six per cent preferred shares, par value $10, 27 500 shares.

A. **Calculate the total dividend on the preferred stock.** (Hint: Determine what will be multiplied by 6 percent.)

B. **Calculate the total dividend on the common stock if the rate is to be 26 cents per share.**

C. **Show the journal entries necessary to record the declaration of both of the above dividends.** Date of declaration is April 12.

D. **Show the journal entries necessary to record the payment of the above dividends.** Date of payment is April 30.

---

4 You are given the following limited information about a company by a client.

Sales (approximate)	$300 000
Long-term debt	nil
Current ratio	1.7
Quick ratio	.8
Collection period	63 days
Inventory turnover	2.9
Debt ratio	.56
Times interest earned	11.2
Net income as a percentage of equity	7.6

Discuss the meanings of these ratios and statistics in a small group. Prepare a report about the company and be ready to present the results of your discussion to the class.

---

5 On the financial statements of Phoenix Company, an inventory turnover figure of 9.1 is shown. This figure is based on the following information:

Cost of goods sold	$100 000
Beginning inventory	$ 10 000
Ending inventory	$ 12 000

The calculation made by the company is:

$$\frac{100\ 000}{\left(\dfrac{10\ 000 + 12\ 000}{2}\right)} = 9.1$$

You, an employee, feel that the average inventory is really much higher. You know that the inventories shown on an end-of-month basis are:

January	$ 10 000
February	11 000
March	13 000
April	15 000
May	17 000
June	20 000
July	22 000
August	23 000
September	20 000
October	15 000
November	14 000
December	12 000
Total	$192 000

The total of $192 000 divided by 12 gives a figure of $16 000. Using this figure in the calculation produces an inventory turnover figure of 6.3.

Is the $16 000 figure the real average inventory? Is the 6.3 the real inventory turnover figure? Explain.

---

6 Choose two companies in the same industry (oil, technology, health, etc.)

A. **Search the Internet until you discover the EPS for each. Write these figures down.**

B. **Explain what the EPS ratio means to an investor who is considering the purchase of stock in one of your two companies.**

---

7 During your research to answer question 6 above, you should be able to find the companies' P/E Ratios.

A. **What does P/E Ratio stand for? How is the ratio calculated?**

B. **Write down the P/E Ratio for each of the two companies.**

C. **Based on the P/E ratio, which company appears to be the better buy? Explain.**

---

8 C. Lemaire, R. Kennedy, B. Henning, and S. Dudley are lawyers in partnership. They have just completed their December 31, 20— fiscal year with a net income figure of $126 040.28. Their partnership agreement stipulates that Lemaire and Kennedy, the senior partners, are to receive salaries of $12 500 before distributing the remainder of net income equally.

Calculate the share of net income for each of the partners. Show your calculations.

9 A. Barnes, W. Doby, and S. Firoz are partners who share income and loss in the ratio of 4:4:3 respectively. Their partnership agreement further stipulates that S. Barnes receives a salary of $10 000 while the others receive none, and that interest is to be allowed at nine per cent on the capital account balances held throughout the year. The capital account balances have been $20 000, $35 000, and $5 500 for A. Barnes, W. Doby, and S. Barnes, respectively.

Prepare a statement of distribution of net income for the year ended April 30, 20—. The net income was $87 199.21.

10 The work sheet for Frame Brothers for an annual fiscal period is shown on page 646. Additional information appears below.

Additional Information
- S. Frame receives a salary of $20 000, G. Frame receives a salary of $16 000.
- S. Frame and G. Frame divide the remainder of net income in the ratio of 2:1 respectively.

A. Prepare the statement of distribution of net income.

B. Prepare the statement of partners' capital.

C. Prepare the balance sheet.

D. Prepare the closing entries.

Frame Brothers — Work Sheet — *Year Ended Dec. 31, 20—*

ACCOUNTS	TRIAL BALANCE DR.	TRIAL BALANCE CR.	ADJUSTMENTS DR.	ADJUSTMENTS CR.	INCOME STATEMENT DR.	INCOME STATEMENT CR.	BALANCE SHEET DR.	BALANCE SHEET CR.
Petty Cash	100 —						100 —	
Bank	625 40						625 40	
Accounts Receivable	18184 32						18184 32	
Merchandise Inventory	54110 —				54110 —	57150 —	57150 —	
Supplies	1480 —			② 830 —			650 —	
Prepaid Insurance	632 —			③ 408 —			224 —	
Furniture & Equipment	38146 —						38146 —	
Accum. Depr. Furn. & Equip.		9814 40	④ 5666 32					15480 72
Automobiles	53285 80						53285 80	
Accum. Depr. Automobiles		22746 24	⑤ 9161 86					31908 10
Bank Loan		10000 —						10000 —
Accounts Payable		11442 30		① 1798 54				13240 84
Sales Tax Payable		2387 40						2387 40
S. Frame, Capital		40000 —						40000 —
S. Frame, Drawings	21166 12						21166 12	
G. Frame, Capital		40000 —						40000 —
G. Frame, Drawings	21133 40						21133 40	
Sales		271405 40				271405 40		
Bank Charges	900 —				900 —			
Miscellaneous Expense	384 40				384 40			
Purchases Expense	94624 40		① 1683 20		96307 60			
Rent Expense	24000 —				24000 —			
Telephone Expense	1200 —		① 115 34		1315 34			
Utilities Expense	1940 40				1940 40			
Wages Expense	75883 50				75883 50			
	407795 74	407795 74						
Supplies Expense			② 830 —		830 —			
Insurance Expense			③ 408 —		408 —			
Deprec. Furn. & Equipment			④ 5666 32		5666 32			
Deprec. Automobiles			⑤ 9161 86		9161 86			
			17864 72	17864 72	270907 42	328555 40	210665 04	153017 06
Net Income					57647 98			57647 98
					328555 40	328555 40	210665 04	210665 04

Problems and Cases for Further Thought

Briefly answer the following questions.

1. Ajax Corporation is a small corporation with authorized capital of 100 000 shares of common stock. The only shareholder is John Smith, who owns all of the 10 000 shares that have been issued. Suggest a way for John Smith to acquire desperately needed cash for the corporation without giving up any control.

2. Limited liability is an advantage for persons willing to invest in business ventures. Give an example of a situation where it could be a disadvantage to someone doing business with a corporation.

3. The text states that a corporation can be effectively controlled without having 50 per cent of the shares plus one, in fact with a much smaller percentage. Explain how this can be true.

4. Suppose a large chemical-producing corporation was responsible for the deaths of many people and was ordered by the courts to pay out several millions in compensation. The shareholders of the corporation are protected by limited liability. How would they be affected?

5. A dividend is *declared* on March 1, 20-2 by the directors of Power Limited. On that date you own 50 shares of Power Limited. You are sure to receive the dividend. True or false? Explain.

6. A company with a high inventory turnover is able to operate on a low per-item profit margin. A company with a low inventory turnover cannot survive on a low margin. Explain why.

7. A company with a high debt ratio probably also has a low figure for times interest earned. Why?

8. The collection period of a company is gradually increasing. What could be causing this? Give two possibilities.

9. The assets of a company are based on their cost prices and, therefore, many of the assets are undervalued, so is the equity because the two are mathematically related. How does this affect the debt/equity ratio? The rate of return on owner's equity?

10. It becomes necessary for you to evaluate two companies very quickly. You decide to use only five ratios. Which five ratios would you select and why?

11. A company with an equity ratio of 8 per cent is seeking to purchase goods from you on credit. Explain the danger of dealing with this company. What could you do to protect yourself?

12. Your banker is concerned about your current ratio, which is calculated from the data below.

Current Assets	
Bank	$ 150
Accounts Receivable	9 052
Merchandise Inventory	22 540
Prepaid Expenses	800
Marketable Securities — at cost	80 000
	$112 542

Current Liabilities	
Accounts Payable	$ 75 256
Bank Loan	100 000
	$175 256

Why is the banker concerned about this current ratio? You are able to show that the marketable securities have a market value of $125 000. How does this change the picture?

13. The current ratio for your company is calculated as follows:

$$\frac{152\ 630}{82\ 603} = 1.8$$

The auditor of your company discovers that $42 000 of obsolete merchandise is included in the inventory figure. How should this be handled? How will it affect the current ratio?

Case Studies

Buy the Shares or the Assets?

Jane Church, the owner of a corporation, has decided to get out of the glass and mirror business. She has put the 10 000 company shares up for sale at the very fair price of $750 000.

Cynthia Pollock is anxious to purchase the business and has made an offer to Jane for the full asking price. However, her offer is for the assets of the business, not for the shares. She is concerned about the fact that the merchandise inventory of $300 000 is shown on the financial statements at $50 000.

Questions

1. What could Jane Church have gained by showing the inventory incorrectly on the financial statements?
2. If the inventory were misrepresented on the financial statements, Cynthia was not responsible for it. Why, then, would she be concerned about it?
3. Why is it to Jane's advantage to sell the shares of the company rather than just the assets?
4. Why is it to Cynthia's advantage to buy the assets of the company and not the shares?

Control of a Corporation

An acquaintance of yours, Mr. Farmer, offers to sell you some shares that he owns in a medium-sized and very profitable company. He acquired these shares some time ago as an investment. Mr. Farmer claims that he is selling them because he needs cash to take advantage of another investment opportunity.

Mr. Farmer shows you the following breakdown of the shareholdings of the company:

Mrs. Allair	30 shares	She is a widow who inherited her shares upon the death of her husband. She has shown no interest whatever in the company affairs, and is quite satisfied that it must be an excellent company because she receives a dividend cheque regularly.
R. Baker	40 shares	He acquired his shares from a third person in settlement of a debt. He attends the company meetings regularly and is highly critical of the management. Whenever he suggests a change, however, he is always voted down.
S. Clarke	65 shares	He is the secretary-treasurer of the company, a position that he held for 15 years. He is also one of the three company directors.
D. Brasseur	100 shares	She is the general manager, president, and a director of the company, which she started 15 years ago.

C. Everett	10 shares	He had his shares given to him. He does not know anything about the company and is not interested. He would be willing to sell his shares for a fair price.
Mrs. Greig	35 shares	Mrs. Greig is a wealthy lady who travels a great deal. She has had no known direct involvement in any affairs of the company. It is not known how she acquired her shares.
H. Moukas	70 shares	He has been the vice-president for the last 10 years, is the brother-in-law of the president, and is also a director.
Mr. Farmer	150 shares	

Mr. Farmer believes that the company could earn substantially higher profits with new management. By acquiring his shares, you would become the shareholder with the largest individual holdings. You would stand a good chance of gaining control of the company by getting the support or acquiring the shares of the four small shareholders.

Mr. Farmer is asking $50 000 for his shares. This is a fair price. You have the management skills, the technical expertise, and the experience to handle the company.

Questions

1. How many shares are there in total?
2. Which shareholders control the corporation? Give their names and the total number of shares held by them.
3. If you were to buy Farmer's shares, who could you count on for sure support?
4. How many additional shares would you need on your side to get certain control?
5. What do you think of your chances of getting the needed shares? Give reasons.
6. What would the controlling shareholders likely do to prevent you from acquiring a controlling interest?
7. Decide on a course of action and give reasons for your answer.

CASE 3

A Problem of Sudden Termination

R. Iwasko and G. Nashimo have been partners in the business of importing goods from Japan and other Pacific countries. Even though the business has been very profitable, the two partners had to draw heavily on their personal resources to get the business started and to cope with rapid growth.

On January 31, 20—, the balance sheet of the business is as shown below. The equity figure of $90 496 does not represent the true worth of the business which is estimated to be in the neighbourhood of $300 000.

On February 1, Nashimo is killed in an automobile accident. Lawyers for the estate of the deceased inform Iwasko that Nashimo's death legally terminates the partnership. Further, the family is taking the legal steps necessary to obtain Nashimo's share of the worth of the business.

Iwasko is fully aware that he will have to comply with the law. However, he has his own future to think about. He hopes to be able to continue to operate the business because it has proven to be profitable and satisfying.

```
                        IWASKO AND NASHIMO
                          BALANCE SHEET
                          JANUARY 31, 20—

                              ASSETS

Current Assets
Cash                                              $    438
Accounts Receivable (net)                           13 072
Merchandise Inventory                              125 000
Prepaid Insurance                                      415
Supplies                                             1 432      $140 357

Plant and Equipment
Land                                              $ 35 000
Buildings                          $145 000
Less Accumulated Depreciation        32 075        112 925
Furniture and Equipment            $ 72 000
Less Accumulated Depreciation        48 456         23 544
Automobiles                        $ 22 473
Less Accumulated Depreciation        15 903          6 570       178 039
                                                                $318 396

                  LIABILITIES AND PARTNERS' EQUITY

Current Liabilities
Accounts Payable                                  $112 500
Bank Loan                                           50 000      $162 500
Mortgage Payable                                                  65 400

Partners' Equity
R. Iwasko, Capital                                $ 45 248
G. Nashimo, Capital                                 45 248        90 496
                                                                $318 396
```

Questions

1. What does partnership law state regarding the death of a partner?
2. What is Nashimo's equity in the business?
3. What is the estimated worth of the business?
4. How much should Nashimo's family get out of the business?
5. What problem does this present for Iwasko?
6. What would be the most straightforward way for Iwasko to resolve the problem suggested in 5 above?
7. Give one undesirable aspect and one desirable aspect of this course of action.
8. Suggest an alternative course of action, one involving participation in the business by Nashimo's family. Give an undesirable aspect of this course of action.
9. What must happen if Iwasko can neither borrow money nor make a deal with Nashimo's family?
10. What additional hardship would this involve?
11. How could insurance be used to avoid difficulties of sudden termination?

CASE 4

Challenge

The Partner You Know or the Shareholder You Don't—Choosing between a Partnership or Corporation

Cheryl, Yvonne, and Beverly Chong are sisters who have created a board game that they hope will be a great success. The game is called *Issues*. It is about the humorous conflicts that commonly arise in male/female relationships. They plan to manufacture the game in Saint John, New Brunswick, and distribute it throughout North America.

Each of the sisters has $200 000 to invest in the business. Before beginning operations, they want to raise $1 200 000 to cover the cost of plant and equipment items and ensure an adequate cash reserve during the start-up phase.

Cheryl, Yvonne, and Beverly have named their business *Sell Dem Board Games* and must soon decide whether it will be a partnership or a corporation. If they form a partnership, the local bank has pre-approved a $600 000 loan at an annual interest of 9%. The bank manager said that if they form a corporation, adjustments to the loan agreement would have to be made.

The sisters are concerned about the interest expense associated with the bank loan. An obvious source of alternative funds is their brother, Jack. Although uninvolved in the creation of the game, Jack's personal net worth is substantial. He thinks their idea is a good one and has offered to invest $600 000 to become a general partner in the business. (He rejected the role of a limited partner because he wants to be involved in the daily operations.)

To determine his share of the annual net income or loss, Jack makes the following proposal. He wants 5 per cent interest on whatever his capital balance is at the start of each year. He says the sisters can receive the same percentage on their capital balances. After interest is allocated to the capital accounts, he suggests the rest of the net income or loss be divided according to each partner's original capital investment (3:1:1:1). Each of the sisters will be allowed to draw $24 000 per year for personal expenses; Jack wants $42 000. He is not in favour of incorporation; and, if the sisters decide to incorporate, Jack is undecided about becoming a shareholder.

The sisters appreciate Jack's financial offer, but they are concerned about bringing him into the business as a partner. Although they love him as a brother, they think his aggressive, take-charge personality might upset the pleasant, cooperative working relationship that the sisters share.

If the sisters incorporate the company, they could become a public corporation and sell shares as a means of raising capital. They have investigated listing a company on the Canadian Venture Exchange (CDNX), a stock exchange that specializes in emerging companies.

Part A

1. Why would the bank manager pre-approve a loan to the sisters if they formed a partnership but not if they formed a corporation?
2. What adjustments do you think would be made to the loan agreement if the sisters formed a corporation?
3. The sisters have prepared budgeted income statements for the first two years of operation. They project a net income in the first year of $66 000 and a net income in the second year of $138 000. Based on these projections and on Jack's proposal, complete the tasks on page 652:

a) Prepare a distribution of partnership income for each of the first two years. The start date is July 1, 20–0. The name of the business is *Sell Dem Board Games*.

b) Prepare a summary of how the partners' capital balances would change over the first two years. Your summary should show the capital balances for July 1, 20-0; June 30, 20-1; and June 30, 20-2. Also include the component percentage for each share of capital.

(Note: You may use a spreadsheet for the above tasks. You can start with a blank spreadsheet file or use the partially prepared model named *chongs.xls*.)

Part A

Sell Dem Board Games — Year 1

Sample Setup

RAW DATA	
Net Income	$ 66 000
Partner A	
Jack's Capital	$600 000
Interest on Capital	5%
Sisters Capital	$200 000
Drawings — Jack	$ 42 000
Drawings — Sisters	$ 24 000

SELL DEM BOARD GAMES
STATEMENT OF DISTRIBUTION OF PROJECTED NET INCOME
YEAR ENDED JUNE 30, 20-1

Net Income available for distribution					$66 000
	Cheryl's Share	Yvonne's Share	Beverly's Share	Jack's Share	TOTALS
Interest at 5% of capital account balance	$ XX	$ XX	$ XX	$ XX	$ XX
Balance of income divided 1:1:1:3	XX	XX	XX	XX	$ XX XX
Total share of net income	$ XX	$ XX	$ XX	$ XX	$ XX
					$ XX

SELL DEM BOARD GAMES
STATEMENT OF OF PARTNERS' CAPITAL
YEAR ENDED JUNE 30, 20-1

	Cheryl's	Yvonne's	Beverly's	Jack's	TOTALS
Capital Balances July 1, 20-0	$200 000	$200 000	$200 000	$600 000	$1 200 000
Add Share of Net Income	XX	XX	XX	XX	XX
	$ XX	$ XX	$ XX	$ XX	$ XX
Deduct Drawings for year	XX	XX	XX	XX	XX
Total Capital	$XX	$XX	$ XX	$ XX	$ XX

Part A

Use the same format for Year 2 calculations. Then prepare the two-year summary below.

Sell Dem Board Games — Year 2

Sample Setup

		SELL DEM BOARD GAMES SUMMARY OF CAPITAL BALANCES JULY 1, 20-0 TO JUNE 30, 20-2				
		Cheryl's	Yvonne's	Beverly's	Jack's	Total Capital
July 1, 20-0 Percent		$200 000 XX%	$200 000 XX%	$200 000 XX%	$600 000 XX%	$1 200 000 XX%
June 30, 20-1 Percent		$XX XX%	$XX XX%	$XX XX%	$XX XX%	$XX XX%
June 30, 20-2 Percent		$XX XX%	$XX XX%	$XX XX%	$XX XX%	$XX 100%

Part B

From investigating the Canadian Venture Exchange website, Cheryl, Beverly, and Yvonne discovered that their business could meet the minimum requirements for forming a public corporation. However, since they had no prior earnings, they would need $750 000 in assets before listing a company on the exchange. This means that the company would need a bank loan of $150 000. Additionally, they discovered that the costs of going public are significant. They include:

CDNX Fees:	$ 6 000
Securities Commissions Fees:	1 500
Sponsorship/Consulting Fees:	8 000
Investment Dealer Fees:	55 000
Accounting Fees:	12 000
Legal Fees	20 000
Total:	$ 102 500

Once listed, the costs of maintaining a public company are about $25 000 more than they would be if it were a private company.

Yvonne proposes that the sisters list the business on the CDNX and issue 550 000 shares to the general public at $1 each. The sisters would each hold 200 000 shares (total 600 00). Once business commences, the company would have 1.2 million dollars in assets ($600 000 from the sisters, $550 000 from the general public, and $150 000 from the bank).

1. The projected net income for the first year as a partnership is $66 000. Adjust this figure if the business incorporates and goes public. You will have to turn the drawings into management salaries and will have to consider interest on the bank loan. Also, for comparative purposes, apply the total cost of going public against the first year's net income. (In reality, the costs of forming the corporate organization are listed as assets—not expenses—since they will benefit many years of the company's life.)

2. Prepare a shareholders' equity section for June 30, 20-1.
3. Adjust the second year's projected net income of $138 000.
4. Prepare a shareholders' equity section for June 30, 20-2.
5. Calculate the share of equity that each sister will have on June 30, 20-2. Compare this amount to the share of equity each sister would have under Jack's partnership proposal.

Part C

1. Prepare a report to Cheryl, Yvonne, and Beverly that communicates the results of your analysis of Jack's partnership proposal and of Yvonne's suggestion of listing the business on the Canadian Venture Exchange. You should use a word processor to prepare your report, which will be more impressive if you include data and charts from a spreadsheet.

Optional

2. Visit the website of the Canadian Venture Exchange (www.cdnx.com) and find a document that lists the benefits and consequences of forming a public corporation. In your report, include some of the points you discover on the website.

CASE 5

Challenge

If you completed the spreadsheet model for Okada Wireless Ltd. (Exercise 4 on page 617) you may adapt it for this exercise.

To Lend or Not To Lend

Part A

In the city of Hamilton, Gary Maw owns the most popular store for stereo and electronic equipment. Gary's store is extremely modest, but the location is ideal. There is good access to Gary's store from anywhere in the city. Gary has built up an excellent reputation for quality merchandise, low prices, and excellent service.

Gary Maw's improving financial position is shown by the comparative financial statements shown on page 655.

Questions

1. **Complete a schedule of key ratios for 20-6, 20-7, and 20-8. Assume that one-half of all sales are credit sales.**
2. **Provide a general statement about this business, giving your opinion of its profitability, efficiency, weaknesses, and so on.**

COMPARATIVE BALANCE SHEET
DECEMBER 31, 20-5, 20-6, 20-7, AND 20-8

	20-5	20-6	20-7	20-8
ASSETS				
Cash	$ 3 040	$ 1 814	$ 8 680	$ 6 180
Accounts Receivable	37 820	39 000	45 500	49 600
Merchandise Inventory	22 200	23 400	25 600	35 000
Store Equipment	11 950	9 950	8 350	7 150
Total Assets	$75 010	$74 164	$88 130	$97 930
LIABILITIES AND EQUITY				
Bank Loan	$20 000	$20 000	$ 30 000	$30 000
Accounts Payable	24 794	25 148	23 714	30 064
Owner's Equity	30 216	29 016	34 416	37 866
Total Liabilities and Equity	$75 010	$74 164	$88 130	$97 930

COMPARATIVE INCOME STATEMENT
YEARS ENDED DECEMBER 31, 20-6, 20-7, AND 20-8

	20-6	20-7	20-8
Sales	$180 000	$210 000	$240 000
Cost of Goods Sold	89 200	100 000	121 550
Gross Profit	$ 90 800	$110 000	$118 450
Operating Expenses			
Depreciation	$ 2 000	$ 1 600	$1 200
Interest	3 000	3 000	4 500
Other Expenses	37 000	45 000	49 300
Total Operating Expenses	$ 42 000	$ 49 600	$ 55 000
Net Income	$ 48 800	$ 60 400	$ 63 450
Drawings	$ 50 000	$ 55 000	$ 60 000

Part B

Gary Maw has learned recently that a national chain of electronics and stereo specialists is opening a branch store within a year in a large new downtown mall. To meet this competition, Gary believes that he will have to restructure his store to provide greater room, variety, and convenience in more modern surroundings.

Gary intends to acquire the empty property next door to his store and to build a modern store with plenty of parking. He has found out the following facts:

1. The property will cost $80 000 and the building $170 000, for a total of $250 000.
2. The bank rate is 12 per cent.
3. The current mortgage rate is 9 per cent, and a mortgage loan in the amount of $210 000 is available if he decides to go ahead.
4. Additional equipment costing $10 000 will be needed.

Gary has no outside savings. He realizes that he will have to obtain an additional bank loan of $50 000. He knows that he will have to reduce his drawings by about half until the new store is firmly established and profitable. He is determined to become much more aggressive in collecting accounts receivable. He intends to do some serious research into advertising.

Gary has had a preliminary discussion with the bank manager about borrowing the additional $50 000. The bank manager wants to see a set of budgeted financial statements for 20-9, as if the expansion had taken place.

3. **Acting as the accountant for Gary Maw, prepare the budgeted income statement. Use the additional information given below.**

   Additional Information
   - Allow for 10 per cent growth in sales (a conservative figure).
   - Assume that the gross profit will be 50 per cent (a conservative figure).
   - Take into account a full year's bank interest on a new, increased bank loan.
   - Take into account a full year's interest on the mortgage.
   - Depreciate the new building at the rate of 5 per cent.
   - Depreciate all of the equipment at the rate of 20 per cent.
   - Other expenses are estimated to be $60 900.

Extra Challenge

4. **Prepare the budgeted balance sheet as at the end of 20-9. Use the additional information given below.**

   Additional Information
   - All but $40 000 of accounts receivable will be collected.
   - All but $30 000 of accounts payable will be paid.
   - Ending merchandise inventory is estimated to be $50 000.
   - Owner withdraws $25 000 for personal use.

5. **Acting as the bank manager, decide whether or not you would grant the increased bank loan. Write a memo to a senior official at your regional headquarters, giving the reasons for your decision. Also include several factors not directly related to accounting that may help you make a decision. Use the memo format that you will find in the Skills Appendix.**

14

Payroll Accounting

The term **payroll** refers to that part of the accounting process that deals with salaries, wages, and commissions paid to employees. Payroll may seem simple to the worker who receives money in return for time and effort. However, it is a complex process, and the person in charge has a great deal of responsibility. The payroll accountant must be well informed about numerous government rules, regulations, and other related matters.

Both federal and provincial governments have passed legislation that greatly affects payroll procedures. Examples include the Income Tax Act, the Employment Insurance Act, the Canada Pension Plan Act, and various provincial hospitalization acts. These acts set out regulations that employers, by law, must follow. The regulations are numerous and often complex, and take a great deal of study. Canada Customs and Revenue Agency supplies booklets outlining all of the federal rules and regulations and makes electronic versions of these booklets available on their website.

The minimum requirements an employer must follow are:

1. to make appropriate payroll deductions from the earnings of employees, according to the regulations;

2. to know what income and other benefits (such as the use of an automobile, travel allowances, etc.) are taxable;

3. to keep up with changes in the regulations;

4. to keep detailed payroll records as required and permit these records to be checked on request;

5. to send to the government, or other agencies, the amounts withheld from the employees, together with the employer's own contribution where required.

This chapter covers only the most basic aspects of payroll preparation.

14.1 | Gross Pay

Gross pay is the amount of an employee's earnings before any deductions are made. There are three different methods of compensating an employee: salaries, wages, and commissions.

Salaries

Salaries are paid to office workers, teachers, supervisors, managers, executives, and many civil servants. A **salary** is a fixed sum of money paid to an employee on a regular basis over a period of time (usually one year). A person on salary is allowed a certain number of sick days without any loss of pay.

Consider the case of Harold Evans, who is employed by Nor-Can Grocers Ltd., a food wholesaler. Mr. Evans receives an annual salary of $62 400 and is paid every two weeks, or biweekly. There are 26 biweekly pay periods in a year. His gross pay for each biweekly pay period is calculated as follows:

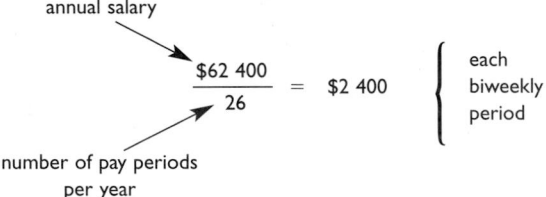

annual salary

$$\frac{\$62\ 400}{26} = \$2\ 400 \quad \left\{ \begin{array}{l} \text{each} \\ \text{biweekly} \\ \text{period} \end{array} \right.$$

number of pay periods per year

> "Biweekly" means every two weeks or 26 times a year. Another possible pay period is "semi-monthly," which means twice a month or 24 times a year.

Wages

Wages are payments to workers for their labour, on an hourly, daily, or weekly basis, or by the piece. Payment by the piece means that the workers are paid according to the quantity of goods they produce (piecework). Some businesses pay a minimum hourly rate plus a piecework bonus for quantities produced over and above a stated amount per day or week.

Time Clocks and Timecards

Timecards may be used by workers who are paid by the hour. A **timecard** is a card on which a time clock records the times that the employee starts and finishes work each day. Timecards are used by the payroll department to calculate the total hours worked by each employee for each pay period.

When a timecard is inserted into a time clock, the clock automatically imprints the time at which the employee is entering or leaving work. This is referred to as "punching in" and "punching out." Time clocks are normally located near the employees' entrance to the plant, and placed so that they can be seen by a supervisor to prevent improper use. A timecard for a one-week period is shown in Figure 14.1 below. The times are automatically printed by the clock in one of six columns: Morning In, Morning Out, Afternoon In, Afternoon Out, Extra In, Extra Out.

FIGURE 14.1

A completed time card.

Time Card

Week Ended   September 14   20 —
Social Ins. No. 603 456 667
Name   Burns, Joseph

| Day | Morning | | Afternoon | | Extra | | Total |
	In	Out	In	Out	In	Out	Hours
M	7:58	12:01	12:59	5:01			8
T	7:56	12:01	12:58	5:02			8
W	8:03	12:00	12:58	5:01			$7\frac{3}{4}$
T	7:58	12:01	12:59	5:01			8
F	7:59	12:01	12:57	5:00	5:57	7:02	8/1
S	7:59	12:02					/4
S							

		Hours	Rate	Earnings
Regular Time		$39\frac{3}{4}$	12.00	477.00
Overtime		5	18.00	90.00
Gross Pay				567.00

Numbers appearing after a slash refer to overtime hours.

Completing the Timecard

At the end of each pay period, the payroll department completes the timecards, for all employees who receive wages. For each card, a payroll clerk must perform the steps outlined below.

Step 1 Calculate the number of hours worked each day. Regular hours and overtime hours are shown separately.

Step 2 Total the number of regular hours.

Step 3 Total the number of overtime hours.

Step 4 Complete the bottom section of the card. There is space provided to multiply the regular hours by the regular rate, and the overtime hours by the overtime rate. Then add the regular earnings and the overtime earnings to obtain the gross pay for the employee.

Rules made by a company must not conflict with legislation passed by government, such as the various Employment Standards Acts in each province.

Notes

The actual rules used in business will vary from company to company. But for the calculations in this text, the rules below are used.

1. The regular work week consists of a five-day week of 8 hours per day for a total of 40 hours. Any additional time worked after 5:00 p.m., or on Saturday or Sunday, is considered overtime.
2. Employees who are late arriving for work are penalized as follows:
    - 15 minutes, if they are late by 1 to 15 minutes;
    - 30 minutes, if they are late by 16 to 30 minutes, and so on.
3. The rate of pay for overtime is one-and-a-half times the regular rate.

Commissions

Commissions are paid to sales representatives. When the sales representative makes a sale, he or she gets a percentage of the dollar value, called a **commission**. In most cases, however, a basic salary is paid, in addition to the commission, to provide the employee with at least a minimum income during difficult periods.

Consider the case of Ann Ferguson, a sales representative for Nor-Can Grocers Ltd., who receives $250 per week and a commission equal to 2.5 per cent of the net sales she makes. During the last two weeks, Ms. Ferguson sold $59 000 worth of merchandise.

Ann Ferguson's pay is calculated as follows:

Basic salary (two weeks $\times$ $250) = $500
Commission (2.5% $\times$ $59 000) = $1475
Total earnings for two weeks = $1975

Section 14.1   **Review Questions**

1. Define "payroll."
2. Why does the person in charge of payroll have a responsible position?
3. Name three pieces of legislation that affect payroll.
4. How does one obtain the details of government regulations regarding payroll?
5. Describe the five most basic payroll requirements imposed on an employer.
6. What is gross pay?
7. What is a salary?
8. What are wages?
9. Explain the purpose of the timecard.
10. Explain the rule to be used in this textbook for determining what constitutes overtime hours.
11. Explain the rule to be used in this textbook in regard to late arrival for work.
12. What is the overtime rate to be used in this text?
13. What are commissions?
14. Why would someone on commission also get a salary?

Section 14.1   **Exercises**

(*Note:* Use the rules set out on page 659–660 where necessary.)

I. Complete the following schedule in your Workbook.

Annual Salary	Payroll Period	Gross Pay Per Period
$39 000	Weekly	
	Weekly	$800
$22 750	Biweekly	
	Biweekly	$1 250
$36 000	Semi-monthly	
	Semi-monthly	$1 800
$30 000	Monthly	
	Monthly	$3 200

2. Phyllis Marshall earns a salary of $35 000 per year. **In the Workbook, calculate the gross pay she would receive for one pay period using each of the payroll periods given.**

Payroll Period	Gross Pay
a. Weekly	
b. Biweekly	
c. Semi-monthly	
d. Monthly	

3. Complete the following schedule in your Workbook.

Total Hours	Regular Rate	Regular Hours	Overtime Hours	Regular Pay	Overtime Pay	Gross Pay
46	$11.50					
43	$14.50					
$44\frac{1}{2}$	$12.00					
54	$21.00					
$47\frac{1}{4}$	$13.75					

4. Grace Fung works in a factory assembling radio components. She is paid $50 a day ($25 for a half day) plus $4 for each component that she completes. **In the Workbook, calculate Grace's gross pay for one week on the basis of the production figures given below.**

Day	Number of Units Completed	Salary	Piecework Earnings	Gross Pay
Monday	10			
Tuesday	9			
Wednesday $\left(\frac{1}{2}\right)$	5			
Thursday	11			
Friday	10			
TOTALS				

5. The timecards for two employees are given below and in your Workbook.

A. Determine and write in the total number of regular hours and overtime hours worked each day for each employee.

B. Calculate and write in the regular and the overtime earnings for each employee.

C. Calculate and write in the gross pay for each employee.

Time Card							
Week Ended July 23 20 —							
Social Ins. No. 642 393 438							
Name Kashim Baksh							
Day	Morning		Afternoon		Extra		Total
	In	Out	In	Out	In	Out	Hours
M	7:58	12:01	12:58	5:01			
T	8:07	12:00	12:57	5:02			
W	7:56	12:03	12:59	5:00			
T	7:59	12:02	1:01	5:03			
F	7:57	12:02	12:59	5:01			
S							
S							
			Hours	Rate		Earnings	
Regular Time				14.00			
Overtime							
Gross Pay							

Time Card							
Week Ended July 23 20 —							
Social Ins. No. 643 461 217							
Name Monica Peterson							
Day	Morning		Afternoon		Extra		Total
	In	Out	In	Out	In	Out	Hours
M	7:58	12:01	1:00	5:02			
T	7:59	12:00	12:58	5:01	5:59	8:55	
W	7:57	12:01	12:59	5:02			
T	7:56	12:01	12:58	5:03			
F	7:59	12:01	12:59	5:01			
S	7:58	12:01					
S							
			Hours	Rate		Earnings	
Regular Time				12.20			
Overtime							
Gross Pay							

6. The Greenfield Real Estate Company pays its salespeople a basic salary of $325 per month plus a 2 per cent commission on their sales. **In your Workbook, complete the schedule shown below.**

Salesperson	Sales for Month	Salary	Commission	Gross Earnings
Mary Hunt	$90 000			
Anna Nasser	$122 000			
Bob Rennie	$75 000			
Fay Savard	$316 000			
Paul Thors	$50 000			
Gloria Lem	$70 000			
Gladys Wilson	$26 000			

14.2 | **Payroll Deductions and Net Pay**

Employees are hired with the understanding that they will be paid a certain amount per hour, week, month, or year. However, certain deductions are made before the employee is actually paid.

As we have seen, Harold Evans receives an annual salary of $62 400, payable every two weeks in equal portions of $2 400. This amount is his gross pay. When Evans receives his cheque, however, it is made out for only $1 530.77. Harold Evans was not shortchanged the difference of $869.23. The $869.23 is the total amount withheld from his pay. The amount that Harold Evans receives, $1 530.77, is his net pay. The net pay is the amount of pay remaining after all deductions have been made.

The payroll equation is:

$$\text{GROSS PAY} - \text{DEDUCTIONS} = \text{NET PAY}$$

For Harold Evans:

$$\$2\ 400.00 - \$869.23 = \$1\ 530.77$$

Typical payroll deductions include:
- Registered Pension Plan
- Union Dues
- Personal Income Taxes
- Canada Pension Plan
- Employment Insurance
- Health Insurance

Payroll Journal

In a manual accounting system, the calculations that are needed in order to arrive at the net pay for Harold Evans are recorded in a special journal. The **payroll journal**, or **payroll register**, is a columnar journal designed especially for recording payroll calculations and figures. The payroll journal used by Nor-Can Grocers Ltd. is shown in Figure 14.2 below. For Harold Evans, the first amount recorded in the journal is his gross pay of $2 400.

FIGURE 14.2

A payroll journal form with gross pay recorded.

Payroll Journal For the two weeks ended Jan. 28 20 —

Employee	Net Claim Code	Earnings Gross	RPP	Union Dues	Taxable Earnings	Federal Tax	Provincial Tax	Total Tax Deduction	CPP	EI	Ext'd Health Insur.	Group Life	Total Deductions	Net Pay
Harold Evans	I	2400 00												

For space considerations, columns for regular and overtime pay have been omitted from this payroll journal example.

Social Insurance Number

An employer must withhold certain amounts from an employee's pay. These deductions include Canada Pension Plan or Quebec Pension Plan contributions, personal income taxes, and employment insurance premiums. To ensure that employees get proper credit for their contributions, the federal government requires all employees to have a social insurance number, recorded on a social insurance card.

The social insurance number system enables Canada to permanently identify every citizen of the country. The government uses the number to direct information correctly to an individual's account or file. Also, the federal government will not pay out any benefits unless the claimant has a social insurance number. A social insurance card, with a nine-digit number, is shown in Figure 14.3 on page 665.

FIGURE 14.3

A social insurance card.

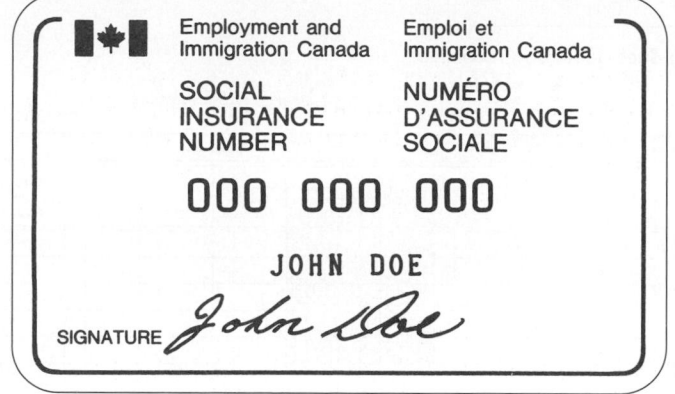

Contributions to a registered pension plan are not subject to income tax. This allows the invested funds to grow much faster. The funds invested in such a plan are taxed when they are withdrawn. This usually happens some time after retirement.

FIGURE 14.4

Payroll journal with RPP deduction recorded.

Registered Pension Plan Deduction

Employees are often enrolled in private "registered" pension plans through their workplaces. A **registered pension plan** (RPP) or a **registered retirement savings plan** (RRSP) is a private pension plan approved by the government for income tax purposes. The amount paid into a registered plan (up to an allowed limit) may be deducted by the employees from their earned income when calculating their income taxes.

Often, both the employee and the employer contribute an amount that is a set percentage of the employee's gross pay. Nor-Can Grocers Ltd. has a registered pension plan. Both the employees and the employer contribute to the plan at the rate of 5 per cent of gross pay.

The deduction for Harold Evans is 5 per cent of $2 400, which is $120. This is recorded in the RPP column of the payroll journal as shown in Figure 14.4 below. The company contributes an equal amount. You will see how the employer's contribution is handled later.

Payroll Journal   For the two weeks ended Jan. 28 20 —

Employee	Net Claim Code	Earnings				Deductions											
		Gross	RPP	Union Dues	Taxable Earnings	Federal Tax	Provincial Tax	Total Tax Deduction	CPP	EI	Ext'd Health Insur.	Group Life		Total Deductions	Net Pay
Harold Evans	1	2400 00	120 00												

Union Dues Deduction

The employees of many businesses are organized in labour unions. Union dues are often deducted by the employer and paid periodically to the union. This obligation of the employer is usually part of the contract negotiated between the employer and the employees' union.

The amount that is deducted from the employees' pay is set by the union. The union to which Harold Evans belongs requires a deduction of $40 each pay period from every union member. Figure 14.5 on page 666 shows this amount recorded correctly in the payroll journal.

FIGURE 14.5

Payroll journal with union dues deduction recorded.

Payroll Journal   For the two weeks ended Jan. 28 20 —

Employee	Net Claim Code	Earnings			Deductions												
		Gross	RPP	Union Dues	Taxable Earnings	Income Tax		Total Tax Deduction	CPP	EI	Ext'd Health Insur.	Group Life		Total Deductions	Net Pay
						Federal Tax	Provincial Tax								
Harold Evans	1	2400 00	120 00	40 00											

Income Tax Deduction

According to Canadian income tax laws, employers must make a deduction from the earnings of each employee for personal income tax. The amount is based on two factors:

1. the total of the employee's personal tax credits;
2. the amount of the employee's taxable earnings.

Personal Tax Credits Return/The Net Claim Code

Tax credits are particular benefits allowed by the government that reduce the amount of tax an individual must pay.

Employees in Canada are accustomed to filling out a Personal Tax Credits Return form known as the TD1. The federal government supplies these forms in order to help employers calculate the amount of tax to withhold from each employee's pay. In 2001, provincial governments added their own versions of TD1s, so certain employees now complete both a federal form and provincial form. The front page of completed federal TD1 form for Harold Evans is shown in Figure 14.6 on page 667. This form is used to determine the employee's net claim code.

Each employee's payroll deduction for income tax is based on the net claim codes and the taxable earnings. The net claim codes vary, depending on the employee's marital status, the number of dependent children, and other factors that governments deem to be tax credits. (A careful examination of Figure 14.6 will give you an idea of these other factors.) Employees complete TD1 forms at the time of hiring, or when an event, such as the birth of a baby, changes their tax status.

Figure 14.6 shows that Harold Evans has no personal tax credits beyond the basic personal amount granted to each employee; that is, $7 412. Once he signs the back of the form, his employer refers to a booklet that contains the chart shown in Figure 14.7 on page 668. This chart is used to determine net claim codes. You can see from Figure 14.7 that Harold Evans' net claim code is 1. You will use this net claim code figure when referring to the income tax deduction tables.

Taxable Earnings

"Remuneration" means any wages, salary, or commission paid to an employee for work done.

Canada Customs and Revenue Agency instructs an employer to first determine the employee's gross remuneration. Then, the employer must subtract certain deductions before determining the tax to withhold. The most common deductions subtracted are:

- contributions to a registered pension plan (RPP);
- union dues;
- contributions to a registered retirement savings plan (RRSP);
- alimony or maintenance payments required by a court order.

FIGURE 14.6

An employee's federal TD1 form (front).

Employees who have no special tax credits complete a federal TD1 form, but they are not required to complete a provincial TD1 form.

The preceding items reduce the amount of earnings subject to tax. After they are subtracted from gross pay, the resulting figure is called taxable earnings. **Taxable earnings** is the amount used to determine how much income tax is to be withheld from the employee. The calculation necessary to obtain the taxable earnings figure for Harold Evans can be seen below.

Gross pay		$2 400
Less: Registered pension plan deduction	$120	
Union dues deduction	40	160
Taxable earnings		$2 240

FIGURE 14.7

A chart to determine federal claim codes.

Total claim amount ($) Montant total de la demande ($)		Claim code Code de demande	Total claim amount ($) Montant total de la demande ($)		Claim code Code de demande
No claim amount / Nul		0	15,632.01 – 17,276.00		7
Minimum – 7,412.00		1	17,276.01 – 18,920.00		8
7,412.01 – 9,056.00		2	18,920.01 – 20,564.00		9
9,056.01 – 10,700.00		3	20,564.01 – 22,208.00		10
10,700.01 – 12,344.00		4	22,208.01 and over / et		X
12,344.01 – 13,988.00		5	Manual calculation is required by the employer Calcul manuel est requis par l'employeur		
13,988.01 – 15,632.00		6	No withholding / Aucune retenue		E

Chart 1 – Tableau 1
Federal claim codes – Codes de demande fédéraux

FIGURE 14.8

Payroll journal showing taxable income.

The taxable earnings figure for Harold Evans is recorded in the payroll journal as shown in Figure 14.8 below.

Payroll Journal — For the two weeks ended Jan. 28 20 —

Employee	Net Claim Code	Earnings Gross	RPP	Union Dues	Taxable Earnings	Federal Tax	Provincial Tax	Total Tax Deduction	CPP	EI	Ext'd Health Insur.	Group Life	Total Deductions	Net Pay
Harold Evans	1	2400 00	120 00	40 00	2240 00									

Employee Income Tax Deductions

Canada Customs and Revenue Agency provides deduction tables for employers who use a manual system to calculate payroll.. The tables are in booklet and electronic form. The electronic versions of the deduction tables are quickly and easily obtained from CCRA's website.

To collect income tax from employment income, CCRA does not wait until the end of the year for an employee to send in the tax owing. Instead, the employer deducts funds from each pay cheque the employee receives and then remits the tax to the government.

An income tax return is a detailed report, filed by April 30th, that determines the precise amount of tax that each person was obliged to pay in the preceding year.

The amount of tax deducted from each pay cheque is actually an estimate of how much the employee owes. One important factor supporting the estimate is the TD1 form that you just read about. After the end of the calendar year, the employee completes an income tax return by April 30th. Since the income tax return is more detailed than the TD1 form, it will likely reveal a number items that further affect the employee's tax status.

When the employee completes an income tax return, he or she discovers if the total amount of tax the employer deducted in the previous year was too high or too low. If more money was deducted than necessary, the government sends a refund. If the amount of tax deducted was too low, the employee makes up the difference by including a payment with the tax return.

Income Tax Tables

Prior to 2001, the amount of income tax to be deducted from an employee's pay was determined from federal income tax tables. Provincial income tax was determined as a percentage of the basic federal income tax. For example, if an employee owed a net federal tax of $4 000, and the provincial tax rate was set at 50% of the federal tax, the provincial government would be owed $2 000 (50% × $4 000). The total tax paid by the employee would be $6 000 ($4 000 + $2 000).

Now, provincial income tax is determined by the **tax on income (TONI) method**. The **tax on income method** is a calculation that applies provincial tax percentages on income instead of on federal tax. Under this method, provinces set their own tax rates and personal tax credit amounts, which may not correspond to the federal amounts.

The reason this tax detail is mentioned in this text is because it changes the way an employer deducts income tax from an employee's pay. Now, two income tax deduction tables must be used—a federal tax deduction table and a provincial tax deduction table. Pages from these two tables are shown pages 679 and 680 respectively. The employer uses the tables to determine two different income tax deduction amounts. The two amounts are added together to produce a total deduction for income tax.

FIGURE 14.9

A section of the **federal** income tax tables showing the deduction for Harold Evans.

To find the federal portion of the income tax deduction for Harold Evans, use the Tax Table 3 on page 679. (Notice that this table is for biweekly pay periods.) The column along the left side shows the biweekly pay brackets. Along the top are 11 column headings representing the net claim codes.

The amount to deduct for income tax is found where the correct "pay category" line intersects with the correct "net claim code" column. Referring back to Figure 14.8 will remind you that Harold Evans's taxable earnings are $2 240. On the federal tax table, $2 240 falls with the pay category of 2218 − 2242. His net claim code is 1. Figure 14.9 shows that the figure at the intersection of this row and column is $359.40.

The procedure illustrated in Figure 14.9 is repeated to discover the provincial portion of the income tax deduction. Using the provincial tax deduction shown on Table 4 on page 680, the correct pay category for the taxable earnings of $2 240 is 2226 − 2250. Assuming the net claim code is 1, the income tax deduction is $149.50, as illustrated in Figure 14.10 on page 670.

Ontario
Federal tax deductions only
Effective January 1, 2001
Biweekly (26 pay periods a year)

Pay / Rémunération		Federal claim codes/Co				
		0	1	2	3	4
From De	Less than Moins de					Dedu Reten
1834. -	1858	320.55	274.95	269.90	259.75	249.65
1858. -	1882	325.85	280.20	275.15	265.05	254.95
1882. -	1906	331.10	285.50	280.45	270.30	260.20
1906. -	1930	336.40	290.80	285.70	275.60	265.50
1930. -	1954	341.65	296.05	291.00	280.90	270.75
1954. -	1978	346.95	301.35	296.30	286.15	276.05
1978. -	2002	352.25	306.60	301.55	291.45	281.35
2002. -	2026	357.50	311.90	306.85	296.70	286.60
2026. -	2050	362.80	317.20	312.10	302.00	291.90
2050. -	2074	368.05	322.45	317.40	307.30	297.15
2074. -	2098	373.35	327.75	322.70	312.55	302.45
2098. -	2122	378.65	333.00	327.95	317.85	307.75
2122. -	2146	383.90	338.30	333.25	323.10	313.00
2146. -	2170	389.20	343.60	338.50	328.40	318.30
2170. -	2194	394.45	348.85	343.80	333.70	323.55
2194. -	2218	399.75	354.15	349.10	338.95	328.85
2218. -	2242	405.05	359.40	354.35	344.25	334.15
2242. -	2266	410.30	364.70	359.65	349.50	339.40
2266. -	2290	415.60	370.00	364.90	354.80	344.70
2290. -	2314	420.85	375.25	370.20	360.10	349.95

For Harold Evans, the federal and provincial claim codes are the same. For simplicity, this text will assume most provincial net claim codes are identical to federal net claim codes.

Ontario
Provincial tax deductions only
Effective January 1, 2001
Biweekly (26 pay periods a year)

Rete

Aux deux semair

Pay Rémunération		Provincial claim codes/Codes de demande p						
		0	1	2	3	4	5	6
From De	Less than Moins de		Deduct from each pay Retenez sur chaque paie					
1938. -	1962	138.80	120.75	118.85	115.05	111.25	107.40	103.60
1962. -	1986	141.45	123.00	121.10	117.25	113.45	109.65	105.80
1986. -	2010	144.10	125.20	123.30	119.50	115.65	111.85	108.05
2010. -	2034	146.80	127.45	125.50	121.70	117.90	114.05	110.25
2034. -	2058	149.45	129.65	127.75	123.90	120.10	116.30	112.45
2058. -	2082	152.10	131.85	129.95	126.15	122.30	118.50	114.70
2082. -	2106	154.75	134.10	132.15	128.35	124.55	120.70	116.90
2106. -	2130	157.40	136.30	134.40	130.55	126.75	122.95	119.15
2130. -	2154	160.10	138.85	136.60	132.80	128.95	125.15	121.35
2154. -	2178	162.75	141.50	139.20	135.00	131.20	127.40	123.55
2178. -	2202	165.40	144.15	141.85	137.30	133.40	129.60	125.80
2202. -	2226	168.05	146.80	144.55	139.95	135.65	131.80	128.00
2226. -	2250	170.75	149.50	147.20	142.60	138.05	134.05	130.20
2250. -	2274	173.40	152.15	149.85	145.25	140.70	136.25	132.45
2274. -	2298	176.05	154.80	152.50	147.95	143.35	138.75	134.65

The two tax deduction amounts—$359.40 and $149.50—are recorded in the payroll journal. The sum of these two deductions—$508.90—is also recorded in the journal, and it is this total deduction that Harold Evans will see when he receives his pay cheque. The payroll journal completed to this stage is shown below in Figure 14.11.

Payroll Journal

For the two weeks ended Jan. 28 20 —

Employee	Net Claim Code	Earnings				Deductions											
		Gross	RPP	Union Dues	Taxable Earnings	Income Tax			CPP	EI	Ext'd Health Insur.	Group Life		Total Deductions	Net Pay	
						Federal Tax	Provincial Tax	Total Tax Deduction								
Harold Evans	1	2400 00	120 00	40 00	2240 00	359 40	149 50	508 90								

Canada Pension Plan Deduction

The federal government instituted a pension plan for Canadian workers that became effective January 1, 1966. This plan is called the Quebec Pension Plan in Quebec and the **Canada Pension Plan** (CPP) in the rest of the country.

The Employers' Guide to Payroll Deductions provides many details about the plan. In particular, it states:

Employers must deduct the required Canada Pension Plan contributions from the remuneration of every employee who meets all three of the following criteria:

- the employee is eighteen years old and has not reached seventy years of age;
- the employee is employed in pensionable employment during the year; and
- the employee is not receiving a Canada or a Quebec Pension Plan retirement or disability pension.

Employee Contributions

Tables for determining CPP deductions are also provided in booklets and in electronic form. Again, CCRA's website is the best source for the electronic versions. Some pages of the CPP tables are included at the end of this section.

Gross pay is used in the CPP tables, not taxable earnings.

To determine the deduction for an employee, refer to the tables for the proper pay period (weekly, biweekly, etc.) and look down the column headed "Pay Rémunération" until you find the bracket containing the employee's gross pay figure. Observe the CPP deduction figure in the shaded column to the right. Figure 14.12 below shows how to find the CPP deduction for Harold Evans, whose gross pay is $2 400.

FIGURE 14.12

A section from the CPP tables showing the deduction figure for Harold Evans.

Canada Pension Plan Contributions
Biweekly (26 pay periods a year)   **Aux**

Pay Rémunération			Pay Rémunération		
From - De	To - À		From - De	To - À	
1513.10 -	1523.09	59.49	2233.10 -	2243.09	90.45
1523.10 -	1533.09	59.92	2243.10 -	2253.09	90.88
1533.10 -	1543.09	60.35	2253.10 -	2263.09	91.31
1543.10 -	1553.09	60.78	2263.10 -	2273.09	91.74
1553.10 -	1563.09	61.21	2273.10 -	2283.09	92.17
1563.10 -	1573.09	61.64	2283.10 -	2293.09	92.60
1573.10 -	1583.09	62.07	2293.10 -	2303.09	93.03
1583.10 -	1593.09	62.50	2303.10 -	2313.09	93.46
1593.10 -	1603.09	62.93	2313.10 -	2323.09	93.89
1603.10 -	1613.09	63.36	2323.10 -	2333.09	94.32
1613.10 -	1623.09	63.79	2333.10 -	2343.09	94.75
1623.10 -	1633.09	64.22	2343.10 -	2353.09	95.18
1633.10 -	1643.09	64.65	2353.10 -	2363.09	95.61
1643.10 -	1653.09	65.08	2363.10 -	2373.09	96.04
1653.10 -	1663.09	65.51	2373.10 -	2383.09	96.47
1663.10 -	1673.09	65.94	2383.10 -	2393.09	96.90
1673.10 -	1683.00	66.37	2393.10 -	2403.09	97.33
1683.10 -	1693.09	66.80	2403.10 -	2413.09	97.76

FIGURE 14.13

Payroll journal with CPP deduction recorded.

The CPP deduction for Harold Evans is $97.33. It is recorded in the CPP column of the payroll journal, as shown in Figure 14.13 below.

Payroll Journal   For the two weeks ended Jan. 28 20 —

Employee	Net Claim Code	Earnings					Deductions												
		Gross	RPP	Union Dues	Taxable Earnings	Income Tax			CPP	EI		Ext'd Health Insur.	Group Life		Total Deductions	Net Pay			
						Federal Tax	Provincial Tax	Total Tax Deduction											
Harold Evans	1	2400 00	120 00	40 00	2240 00	359 40	149 50	508 90	97 33										

There is an upper limit on the amount of CPP to be paid in one year. The limit for each year is shown at the bottom of the CPP tables. By referring to the bottom of Table 1 on page 676, you can see the limit for the year 2001 was $1 496.40. It is the employer's responsibility to keep track of the total deducted for every employee. Once the maximum is reached, no further deductions are to be made in that calendar year.

Employer's Contribution

Every employer is also required to make a contribution on behalf of the employees that is equal to the total of the contributions of the employees. You will be shown how to do this in a later section.

Employment Insurance Deduction

In Canada, employed workers pay a portion of their earnings into an **employment insurance** (EI) fund. If a worker who has made sufficient contributions to the fund becomes unemployed while willing and able to accept employment, that worker is entitled to receive payments out of the fund.

Employee Contributions

The EI premium deductions are similar to income tax and CPP deductions in the way they are treated when preparing the payroll. Money for EI premiums is deducted from the employee's pay cheque, and the tables to determine the deductions are provided by CCRA. One feature that sets the EI tables apart is that there is only one set which is used for all payroll periods (monthly, biweekly, etc.)

A mathematical examination of the tables shows that, in 2001, it cost an employee $2.25 to insure $100 of earnings. (To verify this, divide any CPP premium in Figure 14.4 by the corresponding remuneration—$54 divided by $2 400, for example. The result will be 2.25% or $2.25 per $100.) The most an employee can insure is $39 000. The amount of employment income that is insured is referred to as **insurable earnings**.

The annual maximum amount of insurable earnings is printed at the bottom of each page in the tables, as are the maximum premiums. The maximum premiums for 2001 are $877.50, or 2.25% of $39 000. Once an employee's premiums reach this total, no further deductions are made until the next calendar year.

Harold Evans's deduction figure is found in Figure 14.14 below. Notice that his gross pay of $2 400 is used in the "Insurable Earnings/Rémunération assurable" column.

FIGURE 14.14

A section of the EI tables showing the deduction for Harold Evans.

Employment Insurance Premiums   **Cotisation**

Insurable Earnings Rémunération assurable			Insurable Earnings Rémunération assurable			Insurable Earnings Rémunération assurable		
From - De	To - À		From - De	To - À		From - De	To - À	
2304.23 -	2304.66	51.85	2336.23 -	2336.66	52.57	2368.23 -	2368.66	53.29
2304.67 -	2305.11	51.86	2336.67 -	2337.11	52.58	2368.67 -	2369.11	53.30
2305.12 -	2305.55	51.87	2337.12 -	2337.55	52.59	2369.12 -	2369.55	53.31
2305.56 -	2305.99	51.88	2337.56 -	2337.99	52.60	2369.56 -	2369.99	53.32
2331.78 -	2332.22	52.47	2363.78 -	2364.22	53.19	2395.78 -	2396.22	53.91
2332.23 -	2332.66	52.48	2364.23 -	2364.66	53.20	2396.23 -	2396.66	53.92
2332.67 -	2333.11	52.49	2364.67 -	2365.11	53.21	2396.67 -	2397.11	53.93
2333.12 -	2333.55	52.50	2365.12 -	2365.55	53.22	2397.12 -	2397.55	53.94
2333.56 -	2333.99	52.51	2365.56 -	2365.99	53.23	2397.56 -	2397.99	53.95
2334.00 -	2334.44	52.52	2366.00 -	2366.44	53.24	2398.00 -	2398.44	53.96
2334.45 -	2334.88	52.53	2366.45 -	2366.88	53.25	2398.45 -	2398.88	53.97
2334.89 -	2335.33	52.54	2366.89 -	2367.33	53.26	2398.89 -	2399.33	53.98
2335.34 -	2335.77	52.55	2367.34 -	2367.77	53.27	2399.34 -	2399.77	53.99
2335.78 -	2336.22	52.56	2367.78 -	2368.22	53.28	2399.78 -	2400.22	54.00

FIGURE 14.15

Payroll journal with EI
deduction recorded.

The EI deduction for Harold Evans is $54.00. This deduction is recorded in the EI column of the payroll journal as shown in Figure 14.15 below.

Payroll Journal

For the two weeks ended Jan. 28 20 —

Employee	Net Claim Code	Earnings			Deductions												
						Income Tax											
		Gross	RPP	Union Dues	Taxable Earnings	Federal Tax	Provincial Tax	Total Tax Deduction	CPP	EI	Ext'd Health Insur.	Group Life		Total Deductions	Net Pay
Harold Evans	1	2400 00	120 00	40 00	2240 00	359 40	149 50	508 90	97 33	54 00					

Employer's Contribution

The employer is also required to contribute to the EI fund. The employer's contribution is 1.4 times that contributed by the employees. You will see how the employer's contribution is handled in a later section.

Health Insurance Deduction

Basic Health Coverage

There is a variety of provincial health plans that provide basic health care to residents. In the province of Ontario, where Nor-Can Grocers Ltd. is located, residents receive basic health care coverage free under the **Employer Health Tax** program. Therefore, in Ontario there are no payroll deductions from the employees' remuneration for basic health care. The health tax program in Ontario is paid for by contributions made by the employers.

Extended Health Coverage

In recent years, private insurance companies have developed plans that provide additional benefits not included in the basic provincial health plans. Examples of additional benefits are semi-private care, prescription drugs, dental health, and extra benefits in out-of-country care. Many employees choose to enroll in these private health plans, for which a premium is charged. The premium for a single person is less than that for a married person or for one who has dependent children. The rates to be used in this text for extended health care are given below. For Nor-Can Grocers Ltd.'s plan, the employees pay the full premium.

BIWEEKLY EXTENDED HEALTH INSURANCE RATES	
1. Single person	$12.00
2. Married person	$24.00

For Harold Evans, who is married, the biweekly premium is $24.00. Figure 14.16 on page 674 shows this amount recorded properly in the payroll journal.

FIGURE 14.16

Payroll journal with health insurance deduction recorded.

Payroll Journal — For the two weeks ended Jan. 28 20 —

Employee	Net Claim Code	Earnings: Gross	Deductions: RPP	Union Dues	Income Tax: Taxable Earnings	Federal Tax	Provincial Tax	Total Tax Deduction	CPP	EI	Ext'd Health Insur.	Group Life		Total Deductions	Net Pay
Harold Evans	1	2400 00	120 00	40 00	2240 00	359 40	149 50	508 90	97 33	54 00	24 00				

Group Life Insurance Deduction

Some firms make it possible for their employees to enroll in a group life insurance plan. Premiums for this plan are handled as payroll deductions. Premiums are negotiated between the insurance company, the employees' group, and the company. Usually, the premium depends on the amount of insurance coverage selected.

For the purposes of this text, the insurance premium rate is as shown below. The maximum coverage is $100 000. The employees pay the full premium.

> GROUP LIFE INSURANCE
> BIWEEKLY PREMIUM RATE
>
> **$0.50 for each $1 000 of coverage**

FIGURE 14.17

Payroll journal with group life deduction recorded.

Harold Evans has $50 000 of group life insurance coverage. His premium is $\$0.50 \times 50 = \$25.00$. Figure 14.17 below shows this amount recorded correctly in the payroll journal.

Payroll Journal — For the two weeks ended Jan. 28 20 —

Employee	Net Claim Code	Earnings: Gross	Deductions: RPP	Union Dues	Income Tax: Taxable Earnings	Federal Tax	Provincial Tax	Total Tax Deduction	CPP	EI	Ext'd Health Insur.	Group Life		Total Deductions	Net Pay
Harold Evans	1	2400 00	120 00	40 00	2240 00	359 40	149 50	508 90	97 33	54 00	24 00	25 00			

Life and accident insurance pays claims if the employee dies or is injured in an accident. Disability insurance provides an income if the employee develops a serious illness and cannot work.

Other Deductions

Other deductions may be made from an employee's earnings if authority is granted by the employee. They are handled in a manner similar to those deductions already discussed. Some of these other deductions include the United Way, Canada Savings Bonds, and disability insurance.

Calculating Net Pay

FIGURE 14.18

Payroll journal showing total deductions and net pay.

At this point, the last deduction has been made for Harold Evans. There are two steps remaining. First, the deductions are totalled and the total is entered in the column headed Total Deductions. Second, the total deductions figure ($869.23) is subtracted from the gross pay figure ($2 400), giving the net pay figure ($822.15). The net pay figure is entered in the Net Pay column. These two final amounts, Total Deductions and Net Pay, are shown entered in the payroll journal in Figure 14.18 below.

Payroll Journal   For the two weeks ended Jan. 28 20 —

Employee	Net Claim Code	Earnings			Deductions											
		Gross	RPP	Union Dues	Taxable Earnings	Federal Tax	Provincial Tax	Total Tax Deduction	CPP	EI	Ext'd Health Insur.	Group Life		Total Deductions	Net Pay
Harold Evans	1	2400 00	120 00	40 00	2240 00	359 40	149 50	508 90	97 33	54 00	24 00	25 00		869 23	1530 77

Completing the Payroll Journal

FIGURE 14.19

A completed payroll journal.

The procedure that has been discussed and illustrated for Harold Evans is repeated for each of the employees in the company. One line of the payroll journal is used for each employee. All of the payroll details for every employee are entered in the journal. The final step in preparing the payroll journal is adding all of the money columns and cross-balancing the journal. The completed payroll journal for Nor-Can Grocers Ltd. is shown in Figure 14.19 below.

Payroll Journal   For the two weeks ended Jan. 28 20 —

Employee	Net Claim Code	Earnings			Deductions											
		Gross	RPP	Union Dues	Taxable Earnings	Federal Tax	Provincial Tax	Total Tax Deduction	CPP	EI	Ext'd Health Insur.	Group Life		Total Deductions	Net Pay
Harold Evans	1	2400 00	120 00	40 00	2240 00	359 40	149 50	508 90	97 33	54 00	24 00	25 00		869 23	1530 77
Ronald Leung	4	2100 00	105 00	40 00	1955 00	276 05	111 25	387 30	84 43	47 25	24 00	10 00		697 98	1402 02
Robert Funston	2	2500 00	125 00	40 00	2335 00	375 50	157 85	533 35	101 63	56 25	24 00	50 00		930 23	1569 77
Denise Murray	1	2300 00	115 00	40 00	2145 00	338 30	138 85	477 15	93 03	51 75	12 00	20 00		808 93	1491 07
Lee Williams	5	2400 00	120 00	40 00	2240 00	324 00	134 05	458 05	97 33	54 00	24 00	50 00		843 38	1556 62
		11700 00	585 00	200 00				2364 75	473 75	263 25	108 00	155 00		4149 75	7550 25

Proving the Accuracy of the Payroll Journal

To prove the accuracy of the payroll journal, ensure that:

Step 1   the sum of all of the Deductions columns = the Total Deductions column;

Step 2   the Gross Earnings column − the Total Deductions column = the Net Pay column.

Canada Pension Plan Contributions
Biweekly (26 pay periods a year)

Cotisations au Régime de pensions du Canada
Aux deux semaines (26 périodes de paie par année)

Pay Rémunération From - De	To - À		Pay Rémunération From - De	To - À		Pay Rémunération From - De	To - À		Pay Rémunération From - De	To - À	
1513.10	1523.09	59.49	2233.10	2243.09	90.45	2953.10	2963.09	121.41	3673.10	3683.09	152.37
1523.10	1533.09	59.92	2243.10	2253.09	90.88	2963.10	2973.09	121.84	3683.10	3693.09	152.80
1533.10	1543.09	60.35	2253.10	2263.09	91.31	2973.10	2983.09	122.27	3693.10	3703.09	153.23
1543.10	1553.09	60.78	2263.10	2273.09	91.74	2983.10	2993.09	122.70	3703.10	3713.09	153.66
1553.10	1563.09	61.21	2273.10	2283.09	92.17	2993.10	3003.09	123.13	3713.10	3723.09	154.09
1563.10	1573.09	61.64	2283.10	2293.09	92.60	3003.10	3013.09	123.56	3723.10	3733.09	154.52
1573.10	1583.09	62.07	2293.10	2303.09	93.03	3013.10	3023.09	123.99	3733.10	3743.09	154.95
1583.10	1593.09	62.50	2303.10	2313.09	93.46	3023.10	3033.09	124.42	3743.10	3753.09	155.38
1593.10	1603.09	62.93	2313.10	2323.09	93.89	3033.10	3043.09	124.85	3753.10	3763.09	155.81
1603.10	1613.09	63.36	2323.10	2333.09	94.32	3043.10	3053.09	125.28	3763.10	3773.09	156.24
1613.10	1623.09	63.79	2333.10	2343.09	94.75	3053.10	3063.09	125.71	3773.10	3783.09	156.67
1623.10	1633.09	64.22	2343.10	2353.09	95.18	3063.10	3073.09	126.14	3783.10	3793.09	157.10
1633.10	1643.09	64.65	2353.10	2363.09	95.61	3073.10	3083.09	126.57	3793.10	3803.09	157.53
1643.10	1653.09	65.08	2363.10	2373.09	96.04	3083.10	3093.09	127.00	3803.10	3813.09	157.96
1653.10	1663.09	65.51	2373.10	2383.09	96.47	3093.10	3103.09	127.43	3813.10	3823.09	158.39
1663.10	1673.09	65.94	2383.10	2393.09	96.90	3103.10	3113.09	127.86	3823.10	3833.09	158.82
1673.10	1683.09	66.37	2393.10	2403.09	97.33	3113.10	3123.09	128.29	3833.10	3843.09	159.25
1683.10	1693.09	66.80	2403.10	2413.09	97.76	3123.10	3133.09	128.72	3843.10	3853.09	159.68
1693.10	1703.09	67.23	2413.10	2423.09	98.19	3133.10	3143.09	129.15	3853.10	3863.09	160.11
1703.10	1713.09	67.66	2423.10	2433.09	98.62	3143.10	3153.09	129.58	3863.10	3873.09	160.54
1713.10	1723.09	68.09	2433.10	2443.09	99.05	3153.10	3163.09	130.01	3873.10	3883.09	160.97
1723.10	1733.09	68.52	2443.10	2453.09	99.48	3163.10	3173.09	130.44	3883.10	3893.09	161.40
1733.10	1743.09	68.95	2453.10	2463.09	99.91	3173.10	3183.09	130.87	3893.10	3903.09	161.83
1743.10	1753.09	69.38	2463.10	2473.09	100.34	3183.10	3193.09	131.30	3903.10	3913.09	162.26
1753.10	1763.09	69.81	2473.10	2483.09	100.77	3193.10	3203.09	131.73	3913.10	3923.09	162.69
1763.10	1773.09	70.24	2483.10	2493.09	101.20	3203.10	3213.09	132.16	3923.10	3933.09	163.12
1773.10	1783.09	70.67	2493.10	2503.09	101.63	3213.10	3223.09	132.59	3933.10	3943.09	163.55
1783.10	1793.09	71.10	2503.10	2513.09	102.06	3223.10	3233.09	133.02	3943.10	3953.09	163.98
1793.10	1803.09	71.53	2513.10	2523.09	102.49	3233.10	3243.09	133.45	3953.10	3963.09	164.41
1803.10	1813.09	71.96	2523.10	2533.09	102.92	3243.10	3253.09	133.88	3963.10	3973.09	164.84
1813.10	1823.09	72.39	2533.10	2543.09	103.35	3253.10	3263.09	134.31	3973.10	3983.09	165.27
1823.10	1833.09	72.82	2543.10	2553.09	103.78	3263.10	3273.09	134.74	3983.10	3993.09	165.70
1833.10	1843.09	73.25	2553.10	2563.09	104.21	3273.10	3283.09	135.17	3993.10	4003.09	166.13
1843.10	1853.09	73.68	2563.10	2573.09	104.64	3283.10	3293.09	135.60	4003.10	4013.09	166.56
1853.10	1863.09	74.11	2573.10	2583.09	105.07	3293.10	3303.09	136.03	4013.10	4023.09	166.99
1863.10	1873.09	74.54	2583.10	2593.09	105.50	3303.10	3313.09	136.46	4023.10	4033.09	167.42
1873.10	1883.09	74.97	2593.10	2603.09	105.93	3313.10	3323.09	136.89	4033.10	4043.09	167.85
1883.10	1893.09	75.40	2603.10	2613.09	106.36	3323.10	3333.09	137.32	4043.10	4053.09	168.28
1893.10	1903.09	75.83	2613.10	2623.09	106.79	3333.10	3343.09	137.75	4053.10	4063.09	168.71
1903.10	1913.09	76.26	2623.10	2633.09	107.22	3343.10	3353.09	138.18	4063.10	4073.09	169.14
1913.10	1923.09	76.69	2633.10	2643.09	107.65	3353.10	3363.09	138.61	4073.10	4083.09	169.57
1923.10	1933.09	77.12	2643.10	2653.09	108.08	3363.10	3373.09	139.04	4083.10	4093.09	170.00
1933.10	1943.09	77.55	2653.10	2663.09	108.51	3373.10	3383.09	139.47	4093.10	4103.09	170.43
1943.10	1953.09	77.98	2663.10	2673.09	108.94	3383.10	3393.09	139.90	4103.10	4113.09	170.86
1953.10	1963.09	78.41	2673.10	2683.09	109.37	3393.10	3403.09	140.33	4113.10	4123.09	171.29
1963.10	1973.09	78.84	2683.10	2693.09	109.80	3403.10	3413.09	140.76	4123.10	4133.09	171.72
1973.10	1983.09	79.27	2693.10	2703.09	110.23	3413.10	3423.09	141.19	4133.10	4143.09	172.15
1983.10	1993.09	79.70	2703.10	2713.09	110.66	3423.10	3433.09	141.62	4143.10	4153.09	172.58
1993.10	2003.09	80.13	2713.10	2723.09	111.09	3433.10	3443.09	142.05	4153.10	4163.09	173.01
2003.10	2013.09	80.56	2723.10	2733.09	111.52	3443.10	3453.09	142.48	4163.10	4173.09	173.44
2013.10	2023.09	80.99	2733.10	2743.09	111.95	3453.10	3463.09	142.91	4173.10	4183.09	173.87
2023.10	2033.09	81.42	2743.10	2753.09	112.38	3463.10	3473.09	143.34	4183.10	4193.09	174.30
2033.10	2043.09	81.85	2753.10	2763.09	112.81	3473.10	3483.09	143.77	4193.10	4203.09	174.73
2043.10	2053.09	82.28	2763.10	2773.09	113.24	3483.10	3493.09	144.20	4203.10	4213.09	175.16
2053.10	2063.09	82.71	2773.10	2783.09	113.67	3493.10	3503.09	144.63	4213.10	4223.09	175.59
2063.10	2073.09	83.14	2783.10	2793.09	114.10	3503.10	3513.09	145.06	4223.10	4233.09	176.02
2073.10	2083.09	83.57	2793.10	2803.09	114.53	3513.10	3523.09	145.49	4233.10	4243.09	176.45
2083.10	2093.09	84.00	2803.10	2813.09	114.96	3523.10	3533.09	145.92	4243.10	4253.09	176.88
2093.10	2103.09	84.43	2813.10	2823.09	115.39	3533.10	3543.09	146.35	4253.10	4263.09	177.31
2103.10	2113.09	84.86	2823.10	2833.09	115.82	3543.10	3553.09	146.78	4263.10	4273.09	177.74
2113.10	2123.09	85.29	2833.10	2843.09	116.25	3553.10	3563.09	147.21	4273.10	4283.09	178.17
2123.10	2133.09	85.72	2843.10	2853.09	116.68	3563.10	3573.09	147.64	4283.10	4293.09	178.60
2133.10	2143.09	86.15	2853.10	2863.09	117.11	3573.10	3583.09	148.07	4293.10	4303.09	179.03
2143.10	2153.09	86.58	2863.10	2873.09	117.54	3583.10	3593.09	148.50	4303.10	4313.09	179.46
2153.10	2163.09	87.01	2873.10	2883.09	117.97	3593.10	3603.09	148.93	4313.10	4323.09	179.89
2163.10	2173.09	87.44	2883.10	2893.09	118.40	3603.10	3613.09	149.36	4323.10	4333.09	180.32
2173.10	2183.09	87.87	2893.10	2903.09	118.83	3613.10	3623.09	149.79	4333.10	4343.09	180.75
2183.10	2193.09	88.30	2903.10	2913.09	119.26	3623.10	3633.09	150.22	4343.10	4353.09	181.18
2193.10	2203.09	88.73	2913.10	2923.09	119.69	3633.10	3643.09	150.65	4353.10	4363.09	181.61
2203.10	2213.09	89.16	2923.10	2933.09	120.12	3643.10	3653.09	151.08	4363.10	4373.09	182.04
2213.10	2223.09	89.59	2933.10	2943.09	120.55	3653.10	3663.09	151.51	4373.10	4383.09	182.47
2223.10	2233.09	90.02	2943.10	2953.09	120.98	3663.10	3673.09	151.94	4383.10	4393.09 *	182.90

B-32 Employee's maximum CPP contribution for the year 2001 is $1496.40
* If the earnings are above this amount, follow the calculation method shown in publication T4001, *Payroll Deductions - Basic Information*.

La cotisation maximale de l'employé au RPC pour l'année 2001 est de 1496,40 $
* Si la rémunération dépasse ce montant, consultez la méthode de calcul qui se trouve dans la publication T4001, *Renseignements de base sur les retenues sur la paie*.

TABLE 1 Canada Pension Plan contributions schedule.

Employment Insurance Premiums / Cotisations à l'assurance-emploi

Insurable Earnings Rémunération assurable From - De	To - À		Insurable Earnings Rémunération assurable From - De	To - À		Insurable Earnings Rémunération assurable From - De	To - À		Insurable Earnings Rémunération assurable From - De	To - À	
2176.23	2176.66	48.97	2208.23	2208.66	49.69	2240.23	2240.66	50.41	2272.23	2272.66	51.13
2176.67	2177.11	48.98	2208.67	2209.11	49.70	2240.67	2241.11	50.42	2272.67	2273.11	51.14
2177.12	2177.55	48.99	2209.12	2209.55	49.71	2241.12	2241.55	50.43	2273.12	2273.55	51.15
2177.56	2177.99	49.00	2209.56	2209.99	49.72	2241.56	2241.99	50.44	2273.56	2273.99	51.16
2178.00	2178.44	49.01	2210.00	2210.44	49.73	2242.00	2242.44	50.45	2274.00	2274.44	51.17
2178.45	2178.88	49.02	2210.45	2210.88	49.74	2242.45	2242.88	50.46	2274.45	2274.88	51.18
2178.89	2179.33	49.03	2210.89	2211.33	49.75	2242.89	2243.33	50.47	2274.89	2275.33	51.19
2179.34	2179.77	49.04	2211.34	2211.77	49.76	2243.34	2243.77	50.48	2275.34	2275.77	51.20
2179.78	2180.22	49.05	2211.78	2212.22	49.77	2243.78	2244.22	50.49	2275.78	2276.22	51.21
2180.23	2180.66	49.06	2212.23	2212.66	49.78	2244.23	2244.66	50.50	2276.23	2276.66	51.22
2180.67	2181.11	49.07	2212.67	2213.11	49.79	2244.67	2245.11	50.51	2276.67	2277.11	51.23
2181.12	2181.55	49.08	2213.12	2213.55	49.80	2245.12	2245.55	50.52	2277.12	2277.55	51.24
2181.56	2181.99	49.09	2213.56	2213.99	49.81	2245.56	2245.99	50.53	2277.56	2277.99	51.25
2182.00	2182.44	49.10	2214.00	2214.44	49.82	2246.00	2246.44	50.54	2278.00	2278.44	51.26
2182.45	2182.88	49.11	2214.45	2214.88	49.83	2246.45	2246.88	50.55	2278.45	2278.88	51.27
2182.89	2183.33	49.12	2214.89	2215.33	49.84	2246.89	2247.33	50.56	2278.89	2279.33	51.28
2183.34	2183.77	49.13	2215.34	2215.77	49.85	2247.34	2247.77	50.57	2279.34	2279.77	51.29
2183.78	2184.22	49.14	2215.78	2216.22	49.86	2247.78	2248.22	50.58	2279.78	2280.22	51.30
2184.23	2184.66	49.15	2216.23	2216.66	49.87	2248.23	2248.66	50.59	2280.23	2280.66	51.31
2184.67	2185.11	49.16	2216.67	2217.11	49.88	2248.67	2249.11	50.60	2280.67	2281.11	51.32
2185.12	2185.55	49.17	2217.12	2217.55	49.89	2249.12	2249.55	50.61	2281.12	2281.55	51.33
2185.56	2185.99	49.18	2217.56	2217.99	49.90	2249.56	2249.99	50.62	2281.56	2281.99	51.34
2186.00	2186.44	49.19	2218.00	2218.44	49.91	2250.00	2250.44	50.63	2282.00	2282.44	51.35
2186.45	2186.88	49.20	2218.45	2218.88	49.92	2250.45	2250.88	50.64	2282.45	2282.88	51.36
2186.89	2187.33	49.21	2218.89	2219.33	49.93	2250.89	2251.33	50.65	2282.89	2283.33	51.37
2187.34	2187.77	49.22	2219.34	2219.77	49.94	2251.34	2251.77	50.66	2283.34	2283.77	51.38
2187.78	2188.22	49.23	2219.78	2220.22	49.95	2251.78	2252.22	50.67	2283.78	2284.22	51.39
2188.23	2188.66	49.24	2220.23	2220.66	49.96	2252.23	2252.66	50.68	2284.23	2284.66	51.40
2188.67	2189.11	49.25	2220.67	2221.11	49.97	2252.67	2253.11	50.69	2284.67	2285.11	51.41
2189.12	2189.55	49.26	2221.12	2221.55	49.98	2253.12	2253.55	50.70	2285.12	2285.55	51.42
2189.56	2189.99	49.27	2221.56	2221.99	49.99	2253.56	2253.99	50.71	2285.56	2285.99	51.43
2190.00	2190.44	49.28	2222.00	2222.44	50.00	2254.00	2254.44	50.72	2286.00	2286.44	51.44
2190.45	2190.88	49.29	2222.45	2222.88	50.01	2254.45	2254.88	50.73	2286.45	2286.88	51.45
2190.89	2191.33	49.30	2222.89	2223.33	50.02	2254.89	2255.33	50.74	2286.89	2287.33	51.46
2191.34	2191.77	49.31	2223.34	2223.77	50.03	2255.34	2255.77	50.75	2287.34	2287.77	51.47
2191.78	2192.22	49.32	2223.78	2224.22	50.04	2255.78	2256.22	50.76	2287.78	2288.22	51.48
2192.23	2192.66	49.33	2224.23	2224.66	50.05	2256.23	2256.66	50.77	2288.23	2288.66	51.49
2192.67	2193.11	49.34	2224.67	2225.11	50.06	2256.67	2257.11	50.78	2288.67	2289.11	51.50
2193.12	2193.55	49.35	2225.12	2225.55	50.07	2257.12	2257.55	50.79	2289.12	2289.55	51.51
2193.56	2194.00	49.36	2225.56	2225.99	50.08	2257.56	2257.99	50.80	2289.56	2289.99	51.52
2194.01	2194.44	49.37	2226.00	2226.44	50.09	2258.00	2258.44	50.81	2290.00	2290.44	51.53
2194.45	2194.88	49.38	2226.45	2226.88	50.10	2258.45	2258.88	50.82	2290.45	2290.88	51.54
2194.89	2195.33	49.39	2226.89	2227.33	50.11	2258.89	2259.33	50.83	2290.89	2291.33	51.55
2195.34	2195.77	49.40	2227.34	2227.77	50.12	2259.34	2259.77	50.84	2291.34	2291.77	51.56
2195.78	2196.22	49.41	2227.78	2228.22	50.13	2259.78	2260.22	50.85	2291.78	2292.22	51.57
2196.23	2196.66	49.42	2228.23	2228.66	50.14	2260.23	2260.66	50.86	2292.23	2292.66	51.58
2196.67	2197.11	49.43	2228.67	2229.11	50.15	2260.67	2261.11	50.87	2292.67	2293.11	51.59
2197.12	2197.55	49.44	2229.12	2229.55	50.16	2261.12	2261.55	50.88	2293.12	2293.55	51.60
2197.56	2197.99	49.45	2229.56	2229.99	50.17	2261.56	2261.99	50.89	2293.56	2294.00	51.61
2198.00	2198.44	49.46	2230.00	2230.44	50.18	2262.00	2262.44	50.90	2294.01	2294.44	51.62
2198.45	2198.88	49.47	2230.45	2230.88	50.19	2262.45	2262.88	50.91	2294.45	2294.88	51.63
2198.89	2199.33	49.48	2230.89	2231.33	50.20	2262.89	2263.33	50.92	2294.89	2295.33	51.64
2199.34	2199.77	49.49	2231.34	2231.77	50.21	2263.34	2263.77	50.93	2295.34	2295.77	51.65
2199.78	2200.22	49.50	2231.78	2232.22	50.22	2263.78	2264.22	50.94	2295.78	2296.22	51.66
2200.23	2200.66	49.51	2232.23	2232.66	50.23	2264.23	2264.66	50.95	2296.23	2296.66	51.67
2200.67	2201.11	49.52	2232.67	2233.11	50.24	2264.67	2265.11	50.96	2296.67	2297.11	51.68
2201.12	2201.55	49.53	2233.12	2233.55	50.25	2265.12	2265.55	50.97	2297.12	2297.55	51.69
2201.56	2201.99	49.54	2233.56	2233.99	50.26	2265.56	2265.99	50.98	2297.56	2297.99	51.70
2202.00	2202.44	49.55	2234.00	2234.44	50.27	2266.00	2266.44	50.99	2298.00	2298.44	51.71
2202.45	2202.88	49.56	2234.45	2234.88	50.28	2266.45	2266.88	51.00	2298.45	2298.88	51.72
2202.89	2203.33	49.57	2234.89	2235.33	50.29	2266.89	2267.33	51.01	2298.89	2299.33	51.73
2203.34	2203.77	49.58	2235.34	2235.77	50.30	2267.34	2267.77	51.02	2299.34	2299.77	51.74
2203.78	2204.22	49.59	2235.78	2236.22	50.31	2267.78	2268.22	51.03	2299.78	2300.22	51.75
2204.23	2204.66	49.60	2236.23	2236.66	50.32	2268.23	2268.66	51.04	2300.23	2300.66	51.76
2204.67	2205.11	49.61	2236.67	2237.11	50.33	2268.67	2269.11	51.05	2300.67	2301.11	51.77
2205.12	2205.55	49.62	2237.12	2237.55	50.34	2269.12	2269.55	51.06	2301.12	2301.55	51.78
2205.56	2205.99	49.63	2237.56	2237.99	50.35	2269.56	2269.99	51.07	2301.56	2302.00	51.79
2206.00	2206.44	49.64	2238.00	2238.44	50.36	2270.00	2270.44	51.08	2302.01	2302.44	51.80
2206.45	2206.88	49.65	2238.45	2238.88	50.37	2270.45	2270.88	51.09	2302.45	2302.88	51.81
2206.89	2207.33	49.66	2238.89	2239.33	50.38	2270.89	2271.33	51.10	2302.89	2303.33	51.82
2207.34	2207.77	49.67	2239.34	2239.77	50.39	2271.34	2271.77	51.11	2303.34	2303.77	51.83
2207.78	2208.22	49.68	2239.78	2240.22	50.40	2271.78	2272.22	51.12	2303.78	2304.22	51.84

C-18 Yearly maximum insurable earnings are $39,000
Yearly maximum employee premiums are $877.50

Le maximum annuel de la rémunération assurable est de 39 000 $
La cotisation maximale annuelle de l'employé est de 877.50 $

TABLE 2   Employment insurance premiums schedule.

Employment Insurance Premiums — Cotisations à l'assurance-emploi

Insurable Earnings Rémunération assurable			Insurable Earnings Rémunération assurable			Insurable Earnings Rémunération assurable			Insurable Earnings Rémunération assurable		
From - De	To - À		From - De	To - À		From - De	To - À		From - De	To - À	
2304.23	2304.66	51.85	2336.23	2336.66	52.57	2368.23	2368.66	53.29	2400.23	2400.66	54.01
2304.67	2305.11	51.86	2336.67	2337.11	52.58	2368.67	2369.11	53.30	2400.67	2401.11	54.02
2305.12	2305.55	51.87	2337.12	2337.55	52.59	2369.12	2369.55	53.31	2401.12	2401.55	54.03
2305.56	2305.99	51.88	2337.56	2337.99	52.60	2369.56	2369.99	53.32	2401.56	2402.00	54.04
2306.00	2306.44	51.89	2338.00	2338.44	52.61	2370.00	2370.44	53.33	2402.01	2402.44	54.05
2306.45	2306.88	51.90	2338.45	2338.88	52.62	2370.45	2370.88	53.34	2402.45	2402.88	54.06
2306.89	2307.33	51.91	2338.89	2339.33	52.63	2370.89	2371.33	53.35	2402.89	2403.33	54.07
2307.34	2307.77	51.92	2339.34	2339.77	52.64	2371.34	2371.77	53.36	2403.34	2403.77	54.08
2307.78	2308.22	51.93	2339.78	2340.22	52.65	2371.78	2372.22	53.37	2403.78	2404.22	54.09
2308.23	2308.66	51.94	2340.23	2340.66	52.66	2372.23	2372.66	53.38	2404.23	2404.66	54.10
2308.67	2309.11	51.95	2340.67	2341.11	52.67	2372.67	2373.11	53.39	2404.67	2405.11	54.11
2309.12	2309.55	51.96	2341.12	2341.55	52.68	2373.12	2373.55	53.40	2405.12	2405.55	54.12
2309.56	2309.99	51.97	2341.56	2341.99	52.69	2373.56	2373.99	53.41	2405.56	2405.99	54.13
2310.00	2310.44	51.98	2342.00	2342.44	52.70	2374.00	2374.44	53.42	2406.00	2406.44	54.14
2310.45	2310.88	51.99	2342.45	2342.88	52.71	2374.45	2374.88	53.43	2406.45	2406.88	54.15
2310.89	2311.33	52.00	2342.89	2343.33	52.72	2374.89	2375.33	53.44	2406.89	2407.33	54.16
2311.34	2311.77	52.01	2343.34	2343.77	52.73	2375.34	2375.77	53.45	2407.34	2407.77	54.17
2311.78	2312.22	52.02	2343.78	2344.22	52.74	2375.78	2376.22	53.46	2407.78	2408.22	54.18
2312.23	2312.66	52.03	2344.23	2344.66	52.75	2376.23	2376.66	53.47	2408.23	2408.66	54.19
2312.67	2313.11	52.04	2344.67	2345.11	52.76	2376.67	2377.11	53.48	2408.67	2409.11	54.20
2313.12	2313.55	52.05	2345.12	2345.55	52.77	2377.12	2377.55	53.49	2409.12	2409.55	54.21
2313.56	2313.99	52.06	2345.56	2345.99	52.78	2377.56	2377.99	53.50	2409.56	2409.99	54.22
2314.00	2314.44	52.07	2346.00	2346.44	52.79	2378.00	2378.44	53.51	2410.00	2410.44	54.23
2314.45	2314.88	52.08	2346.45	2346.88	52.80	2378.45	2378.88	53.52	2410.45	2410.88	54.24
2314.89	2315.33	52.09	2346.89	2347.33	52.81	2378.89	2379.33	53.53	2410.89	2411.33	54.25
2315.34	2315.77	52.10	2347.34	2347.77	52.82	2379.34	2379.77	53.54	2411.34	2411.77	54.26
2315.78	2316.22	52.11	2347.78	2348.22	52.83	2379.78	2380.22	53.55	2411.78	2412.22	54.27
2316.23	2316.66	52.12	2348.23	2348.66	52.84	2380.23	2380.66	53.56	2412.23	2412.66	54.28
2316.67	2317.11	52.13	2348.67	2349.11	52.85	2380.67	2381.11	53.57	2412.67	2413.11	54.29
2317.12	2317.55	52.14	2349.12	2349.55	52.86	2381.12	2381.55	53.58	2413.12	2413.55	54.30
2317.56	2317.99	52.15	2349.56	2349.99	52.87	2381.56	2381.99	53.59	2413.56	2413.99	54.31
2318.00	2318.44	52.16	2350.00	2350.44	52.88	2382.00	2382.44	53.60	2414.00	2414.44	54.32
2318.45	2318.88	52.17	2350.45	2350.88	52.89	2382.45	2382.88	53.61	2414.45	2414.88	54.33
2318.89	2319.33	52.18	2350.89	2351.33	52.90	2382.89	2383.33	53.62	2414.89	2415.33	54.34
2319.34	2319.77	52.19	2351.34	2351.77	52.91	2383.34	2383.77	53.63	2415.34	2415.77	54.35
2319.78	2320.22	52.20	2351.78	2352.22	52.92	2383.78	2384.22	53.64	2415.78	2416.22	54.36
2320.23	2320.66	52.21	2352.23	2352.66	52.93	2384.23	2384.66	53.65	2416.23	2416.66	54.37
2320.67	2321.11	52.22	2352.67	2353.11	52.94	2384.67	2385.11	53.66	2416.67	2417.11	54.38
2321.12	2321.55	52.23	2353.12	2353.55	52.95	2385.12	2385.55	53.67	2417.12	2417.55	54.39
2321.56	2321.99	52.24	2353.56	2353.99	52.96	2385.56	2385.99	53.68	2417.56	2417.99	54.40
2322.00	2322.44	52.25	2354.00	2354.44	52.97	2386.00	2386.44	53.69	2418.00	2418.44	54.41
2322.45	2322.88	52.26	2354.45	2354.88	52.98	2386.45	2386.88	53.70	2418.45	2418.88	54.42
2322.89	2323.33	52.27	2354.89	2355.33	52.99	2386.89	2387.33	53.71	2418.89	2419.33	54.43
2323.34	2323.77	52.28	2355.34	2355.77	53.00	2387.34	2387.77	53.72	2419.34	2419.77	54.44
2323.78	2324.22	52.29	2355.78	2356.22	53.01	2387.78	2388.22	53.73	2419.78	2420.22	54.45
2324.23	2324.66	52.30	2356.23	2356.66	53.02	2388.23	2388.66	53.74	2420.23	2420.66	54.46
2324.67	2325.11	52.31	2356.67	2357.11	53.03	2388.67	2389.11	53.75	2420.67	2421.11	54.47
2325.12	2325.55	52.32	2357.12	2357.55	53.04	2389.12	2389.55	53.76	2421.12	2421.55	54.48
2325.56	2325.99	52.33	2357.56	2357.99	53.05	2389.56	2389.99	53.77	2421.56	2421.99	54.49
2326.00	2326.44	52.34	2358.00	2358.44	53.06	2390.00	2390.44	53.78	2422.00	2422.44	54.50
2326.45	2326.88	52.35	2358.45	2358.88	53.07	2390.45	2390.88	53.79	2422.45	2422.88	54.51
2326.89	2327.33	52.36	2358.89	2359.33	53.08	2390.89	2391.33	53.80	2422.89	2423.33	54.52
2327.34	2327.77	52.37	2359.34	2359.77	53.09	2391.34	2391.77	53.81	2423.34	2423.77	54.53
2327.78	2328.22	52.38	2359.78	2360.22	53.10	2391.78	2392.22	53.82	2423.78	2424.22	54.54
2328.23	2328.66	52.39	2360.23	2360.66	53.11	2392.23	2392.66	53.83	2424.23	2424.66	54.55
2328.67	2329.11	52.40	2360.67	2361.11	53.12	2392.67	2393.11	53.84	2424.67	2425.11	54.56
2329.12	2329.55	52.41	2361.12	2361.55	53.13	2393.12	2393.55	53.85	2425.12	2425.55	54.57
2329.56	2329.99	52.42	2361.56	2361.99	53.14	2393.56	2394.00	53.86	2425.56	2425.99	54.58
2330.00	2330.44	52.43	2362.00	2362.44	53.15	2394.01	2394.44	53.87	2426.00	2426.44	54.59
2330.45	2330.88	52.44	2362.45	2362.88	53.16	2394.45	2394.88	53.88	2426.45	2426.88	54.60
2330.89	2331.33	52.45	2362.89	2363.33	53.17	2394.89	2395.33	53.89	2426.89	2427.33	54.61
2331.34	2331.77	52.46	2363.34	2363.77	53.18	2395.34	2395.77	53.90	2427.34	2427.77	54.62
2331.78	2332.22	52.47	2363.78	2364.22	53.19	2395.78	2396.22	53.91	2427.78	2428.22	54.63
2332.23	2332.66	52.48	2364.23	2364.66	53.20	2396.23	2396.66	53.92	2428.23	2428.66	54.64
2332.67	2333.11	52.49	2364.67	2365.11	53.21	2396.67	2397.11	53.93	2428.67	2429.11	54.65
2333.12	2333.55	52.50	2365.12	2365.55	53.22	2397.12	2397.55	53.94	2429.12	2429.55	54.66
2333.56	2333.99	52.51	2365.56	2365.99	53.23	2397.56	2397.99	53.95	2429.56	2429.99	54.67
2334.00	2334.44	52.52	2366.00	2366.44	53.24	2398.00	2398.44	53.96	2430.00	2430.44	54.68
2334.45	2334.88	52.53	2366.45	2366.88	53.25	2398.45	2398.88	53.97	2430.45	2430.88	54.69
2334.89	2335.33	52.54	2366.89	2367.33	53.26	2398.89	2399.33	53.98	2430.89	2431.33	54.70
2335.34	2335.77	52.55	2367.34	2367.77	53.27	2399.34	2399.77	53.99	2431.34	2431.77	54.71
2335.78	2336.22	52.56	2367.78	2368.22	53.28	2399.78	2400.22	54.00	2431.78	2432.22	54.72

Yearly maximum insurable earnings are $39,000 — Le maximum annuel de la rémunération assurable est de 39 000 $
Yearly maximum employee premiums are $877.50 — La cotisation maximale annuelle de l'employé est de 877.50 $ **C-19**

TABLE 2 (cont'd)   Employment insurance premiums schedule.

Ontario
Federal tax deductions only
Effective January 1, 2001
Biweekly (26 pay periods a year)

Ontario
Retenues d'impôt fédéral seulement
En vigueur le 1er janvier 2001
Aux deux semaines (26 périodes de paie par année)

Pay / Rémunération		Federal claim codes/Codes de demande fédéraux										
		0	1	2	3	4	5	6	7	8	9	10
From De	Less than Moins de		Deduct from each pay / Retenez sur chaque paie									
1834. -	1858	320.55	274.95	269.90	259.75	249.65	239.55	229.40	219.30	209.20	199.05	188.95
1858. -	1882	325.85	280.20	275.15	265.05	254.95	244.80	234.70	224.55	214.45	204.35	194.20
1882. -	1906	331.10	285.50	280.45	270.30	260.20	250.10	239.95	229.85	219.75	209.60	199.50
1906. -	1930	336.40	290.80	285.70	275.60	265.50	255.35	245.25	235.15	225.00	214.90	204.80
1930. -	1954	341.65	296.05	291.00	280.90	270.75	260.65	250.55	240.40	230.30	220.20	210.05
1954. -	1978	346.95	301.35	296.30	286.15	276.05	265.95	255.80	245.70	235.60	225.45	215.35
1978. -	2002	352.25	306.60	301.55	291.45	281.35	271.20	261.10	250.95	240.85	230.75	220.60
2002. -	2026	357.50	311.90	306.85	296.70	286.60	276.50	266.35	256.25	246.15	236.00	225.90
2026. -	2050	362.80	317.20	312.10	302.00	291.90	281.75	271.65	261.55	251.40	241.30	231.20
2050. -	2074	368.05	322.45	317.40	307.30	297.15	287.05	276.95	266.80	256.70	246.60	236.45
2074. -	2098	373.35	327.75	322.70	312.55	302.45	292.35	282.20	272.10	262.00	251.85	241.75
2098. -	2122	378.65	333.00	327.95	317.85	307.75	297.60	287.50	277.35	267.25	257.15	247.00
2122. -	2146	383.90	338.30	333.25	323.10	313.00	302.90	292.75	282.65	272.55	262.40	252.30
2146. -	2170	389.20	343.60	338.50	328.40	318.30	308.15	298.05	287.95	277.80	267.70	257.60
2170. -	2194	394.45	348.85	343.80	333.70	323.55	313.45	303.35	293.20	283.10	273.00	262.85
2194. -	2218	399.75	354.15	349.10	338.95	328.85	318.75	308.60	298.50	288.40	278.25	268.15
2218. -	2242	405.05	359.40	354.35	344.25	334.15	324.00	313.90	303.75	293.65	283.55	273.40
2242. -	2266	410.30	364.70	359.65	349.50	339.40	329.30	319.15	309.05	298.95	288.80	278.70
2266. -	2290	415.60	370.00	364.90	354.80	344.70	334.55	324.45	314.35	304.20	294.10	284.00
2290. -	2314	420.85	375.25	370.20	360.10	349.95	339.85	329.75	319.60	309.50	299.40	289.25
2314. -	2338	426.15	380.55	375.50	365.35	355.25	345.15	335.00	324.90	314.80	304.65	294.55
2338. -	2362	431.45	385.80	380.75	370.65	360.55	350.40	340.30	330.15	320.05	309.95	299.80
2362. -	2386	437.00	391.40	386.35	376.25	366.10	356.00	345.90	335.75	325.65	315.50	305.40
2386. -	2410	443.25	397.65	392.60	382.45	372.35	362.25	352.10	342.00	331.90	321.75	311.65
2410. -	2434	449.50	403.90	398.85	388.70	378.60	368.45	358.35	348.25	338.10	328.00	317.90
2434. -	2458	455.75	410.10	405.05	394.95	384.85	374.70	364.60	354.50	344.35	334.25	324.10
2458. -	2482	462.00	416.35	411.30	401.20	391.05	380.95	370.85	360.70	350.60	340.50	330.35
2482. -	2506	468.20	422.60	417.55	407.45	397.30	387.20	377.10	366.95	356.85	346.70	336.60
2506. -	2530	474.45	428.85	423.80	413.65	403.55	393.45	383.30	373.20	363.10	352.95	342.85
2530. -	2554	480.70	435.10	430.05	419.90	409.80	399.65	389.55	379.45	369.30	359.20	349.10
2554. -	2578	486.95	441.30	436.25	426.15	416.05	405.90	395.80	385.70	375.55	365.45	355.30
2578. -	2602	493.20	447.55	442.50	432.40	422.25	412.15	402.05	391.90	381.80	371.70	361.55
2602. -	2626	499.40	453.80	448.75	438.65	428.50	418.40	408.30	398.15	388.05	377.90	367.80
2626. -	2650	505.65	460.05	455.00	444.85	434.75	424.65	414.50	404.40	394.30	384.15	374.05
2650. -	2674	511.90	466.30	461.25	451.10	441.00	430.85	420.75	410.65	400.50	390.40	380.30
2674. -	2698	518.15	472.50	467.45	457.35	447.25	437.10	427.00	416.90	406.75	396.65	386.50
2698. -	2722	524.40	478.75	473.70	463.60	453.45	443.35	433.25	423.10	413.00	402.90	392.75
2722. -	2746	530.60	485.00	479.95	469.85	459.70	449.60	439.50	429.35	419.25	409.10	399.00
2746. -	2770	536.85	491.25	486.20	476.05	465.95	455.85	445.70	435.60	425.50	415.35	405.25
2770. -	2794	543.10	497.50	492.45	482.30	472.20	462.05	451.95	441.85	431.70	421.60	411.50
2794. -	2818	549.35	503.70	498.65	488.55	478.45	468.30	458.20	448.10	437.95	427.85	417.70
2818. -	2842	555.60	509.95	504.90	494.80	484.65	474.55	464.45	454.30	444.20	434.10	423.95
2842. -	2866	561.80	516.20	511.15	501.05	490.90	480.80	470.70	460.55	450.45	440.30	430.20
2866. -	2890	568.05	522.45	517.40	507.25	497.15	487.05	476.90	466.80	456.70	446.55	436.45
2890. -	2914	574.30	528.70	523.65	513.50	503.40	493.25	483.15	473.05	462.90	452.80	442.70
2914. -	2938	580.55	534.90	529.85	519.75	509.65	499.50	489.40	479.30	469.15	459.05	448.90
2938. -	2962	586.80	541.15	536.10	526.00	515.85	505.75	495.65	485.50	475.40	465.30	455.15
2962. -	2986	593.00	547.40	542.35	532.25	522.10	512.00	501.90	491.75	481.65	471.50	461.40
2986. -	3010	599.25	553.65	548.60	538.45	528.35	518.25	508.10	498.00	487.90	477.75	467.65
3010. -	3034	605.50	559.90	554.85	544.70	534.60	524.45	514.35	504.25	494.10	484.00	473.90
3034. -	3058	611.75	566.10	561.05	550.95	540.85	530.70	520.60	510.50	500.35	490.25	480.10
3058. -	3082	618.00	572.35	567.30	557.20	547.05	536.95	526.85	516.70	506.60	496.50	486.35
3082. -	3106	624.20	578.60	573.55	563.45	553.30	543.20	533.10	522.95	512.85	502.70	492.60
3106. -	3130	630.45	584.85	579.80	569.65	559.55	549.45	539.30	529.20	519.10	508.95	498.85
3130. -	3154	636.70	591.10	586.05	575.90	565.80	555.65	545.55	535.45	525.30	515.20	505.10

This table is available on diskette (TOD).   D-10   Vous pouvez obtenir cette table sur disquette (TSD).

TABLE 3   Biweekly federal tax deductions schedule.

Ontario
Provincial tax deductions only
Effective January 1, 2001
Biweekly (26 pay periods a year)

Ontario
Retenues d'impôt provincial seulement
En vigueur le 1er janvier 2001
Aux deux semaines (26 périodes de paie par année)

Pay / Rémunération		Provincial claim codes/Codes de demande provinciaux										
From De / Less than Moins de		0	1	2	3	4	5	6	7	8	9	10
		Deduct from each pay / Retenez sur chaque paie										
1938. -	1962	138.80	120.75	118.85	115.05	111.25	107.40	103.60	99.80	95.95	92.15	88.35
1962. -	1986	141.45	123.00	121.10	117.25	113.45	109.65	105.80	102.00	98.20	94.35	90.55
1986. -	2010	144.10	125.20	123.30	119.50	115.65	111.85	108.05	104.20	100.40	96.60	92.80
2010. -	2034	146.80	127.45	125.50	121.70	117.90	114.05	110.25	106.45	102.65	98.80	95.00
2034. -	2058	149.45	129.65	127.75	123.90	120.10	116.30	112.45	108.65	104.85	101.05	97.20
2058. -	2082	152.10	131.85	129.95	126.15	122.30	118.50	114.70	110.90	107.05	103.25	99.45
2082. -	2106	154.75	134.10	132.15	128.35	124.55	120.70	116.90	113.10	109.30	105.45	101.65
2106. -	2130	157.40	136.30	134.40	130.55	126.75	122.95	119.15	115.30	111.50	107.70	103.85
2130. -	2154	160.10	138.85	136.60	132.80	128.95	125.15	121.35	117.55	113.70	109.90	106.10
2154. -	2178	162.75	141.50	139.20	135.00	131.20	127.40	123.55	119.75	115.95	112.10	108.30
2178. -	2202	165.40	144.15	141.85	137.30	133.40	129.60	125.80	121.95	118.15	114.35	110.50
2202. -	2226	168.05	146.80	144.55	139.95	135.65	131.80	128.00	124.20	120.35	116.55	112.75
2226. -	2250	170.75	149.50	147.20	142.60	138.05	134.05	130.20	126.40	122.60	118.75	114.95
2250. -	2274	173.40	152.15	149.85	145.25	140.70	136.25	132.45	128.60	124.80	121.00	117.15
2274. -	2298	176.05	154.80	152.50	147.95	143.35	138.75	134.65	130.85	127.00	123.20	119.40
2298. -	2322	178.70	157.45	155.15	150.60	146.00	141.45	136.85	133.05	129.25	125.40	121.60
2322. -	2346	181.80	160.10	157.85	153.25	148.65	144.10	139.50	135.25	131.45	127.65	123.80
2346. -	2370	185.25	162.80	160.50	155.90	151.35	146.75	142.20	137.60	133.65	129.85	126.05
2370. -	2394	189.10	165.70	163.45	158.85	154.30	149.70	145.10	140.55	136.10	132.30	128.50
2394. -	2418	193.30	168.95	166.65	162.05	157.50	152.90	148.35	143.75	139.20	135.00	131.15
2418. -	2442	197.45	172.15	169.85	165.30	160.70	156.15	151.55	146.95	142.40	137.80	133.85
2442. -	2466	201.65	175.35	173.10	168.50	163.90	159.35	154.75	150.20	145.60	141.05	136.55
2466. -	2490	205.80	178.60	176.30	171.70	167.15	162.55	158.00	153.40	148.80	144.25	139.65
2490. -	2514	210.00	182.35	179.50	174.95	170.35	165.75	161.20	156.60	152.05	147.45	142.90
2514. -	2538	214.15	186.55	183.55	178.15	173.55	169.00	164.40	159.85	155.25	150.65	146.10
2538. -	2562	218.35	190.70	187.75	181.80	176.80	172.20	167.60	163.05	158.45	153.90	149.30
2562. -	2586	222.50	194.90	191.90	185.95	180.00	175.40	170.85	166.25	161.70	157.10	152.50
2586. -	2610	226.70	199.10	196.10	190.15	184.20	178.65	174.05	169.45	164.90	160.30	155.75
2610. -	2634	230.90	203.25	200.30	194.35	188.40	182.40	177.25	172.70	168.10	163.55	158.95
2634. -	2658	235.05	207.45	204.45	198.50	192.55	186.60	180.65	175.90	171.30	166.75	162.15
2658. -	2682	239.25	211.60	208.65	202.70	196.75	190.80	184.85	179.10	174.55	169.95	165.40
2682. -	2706	243.40	215.80	212.80	206.85	200.90	194.95	189.00	183.05	177.75	173.15	168.60
2706. -	2730	247.60	219.95	217.00	211.05	205.10	199.15	193.20	187.25	181.30	176.40	171.80
2730. -	2754	251.75	224.15	221.15	215.20	209.25	203.30	197.35	191.40	185.45	179.60	175.00
2754. -	2778	255.95	228.35	225.35	219.40	213.45	207.50	201.55	195.60	189.65	183.70	178.25
2778. -	2802	260.15	232.50	229.55	223.60	217.60	211.65	205.70	199.75	193.80	187.85	181.90
2802. -	2826	264.30	236.70	233.70	227.75	221.80	215.85	209.90	203.95	198.00	192.05	186.10
2826. -	2850	268.50	240.85	237.90	231.95	226.00	220.05	214.10	208.15	202.15	196.20	190.25
2850. -	2874	272.65	245.05	242.05	236.10	230.15	224.20	218.25	212.30	206.35	200.40	194.45
2874. -	2898	276.85	249.20	246.25	240.30	234.35	228.40	222.45	216.50	210.55	204.60	198.65
2898. -	2922	281.00	253.40	250.40	244.45	238.50	232.55	226.60	220.65	214.70	208.75	202.80
2922. -	2946	285.20	257.55	254.60	248.65	242.70	236.75	230.80	224.85	218.90	212.95	207.00
2946. -	2970	289.40	261.75	258.80	252.80	246.85	240.90	234.95	229.00	223.05	217.10	211.15
2970. -	2994	293.55	265.95	262.95	257.00	251.05	245.10	239.15	233.20	227.25	221.30	215.35
2994. -	3018	297.75	270.10	267.15	261.20	255.25	249.30	243.35	237.35	231.40	225.45	219.50
3018. -	3042	301.90	274.30	271.30	265.35	259.40	253.45	247.50	241.55	235.60	229.65	223.70
3042. -	3066	306.10	278.45	275.50	269.55	263.60	257.65	251.70	245.75	239.80	233.85	227.85
3066. -	3090	310.25	282.65	279.65	273.70	267.75	261.80	255.85	249.90	243.95	238.00	232.05
3090. -	3114	314.45	286.80	283.85	277.90	271.95	266.00	260.05	254.10	248.15	242.20	236.25
3114. -	3138	318.65	291.00	288.00	282.05	276.10	270.15	264.20	258.25	252.30	246.35	240.40
3138. -	3162	322.80	295.20	292.20	286.25	280.30	274.35	268.40	262.45	256.50	250.55	244.60
3162. -	3186	327.00	299.35	296.40	290.45	284.50	278.55	272.55	266.60	260.65	254.70	248.75
3186. -	3210	331.15	303.55	300.55	294.60	288.65	282.70	276.75	270.80	264.85	258.90	252.95
3210. -	3234	335.35	307.70	304.75	298.80	292.85	286.90	280.95	275.00	269.05	263.05	257.10
3234. -	3258	339.50	311.90	308.90	302.95	297.00	291.05	285.10	279.15	273.20	267.25	261.30

This table is available on diskette (TOD).   E-10   Vous pouvez obtenir cette table sur disquette (TSD).

TABLE 4   Biweekly provincial tax deductions schedule.

Section 14.2   Review Questions

1. What is gross pay?
2. What is net pay?
3. What is the payroll equation?
4. Where are the payroll calculations made?
5. Explain the purpose of the social insurance number.
6. What is an RPP?
7. Where does one encounter the net claim amount?
8. Where is the net claim code used?
9. On what two things does the income tax deduction depend?
10. What is a TD1 form?
11. Explain how taxable earnings are determined.
12. What is the purpose of an income tax return?
13. Explain why a person might get a refund by filing an income tax return.
14. Explain why it is slightly more difficult to determine the deduction for income tax now that the provinces use the TONI method.
15. Explain how to find the deduction figure for the CPP.
16. How much does it cost an employee to insure $100 of earnings against unemployment.
17. Where does a person see the maximum deduction figure for unemployment insurance?
18. Explain how to complete the payroll journal.
19. Describe how to test the accuracy of the payroll journal.

Section 14.2   Exercises

1. **A. In your Workbook, complete the schedule that appears below. Use Tables 1, 2, 3, and 4, starting on page 676, where necessary.**

   B. For Y. Van Del, how many deductions for CPP will be made during the year? What will be the amount of the final deduction?

Employee	Biweekly Gross Pay	CPP Deduction	EI Deduction	RPP (5%) Deduction
F. Mazur	$2 180			
C. Koch	$2 200			
P. Parsons	$2 350			
G. Vittelli	$2 270			
Y. Van Del	$2 430			

2. **In your Workbook, complete the line shown below.** J. Bell is married, does not belong to a union, and has $100 000 of group life insurance coverage and full extended health insurance coverage. The rate of RPP contribution is 5 per cent.

Payroll Journal   For the two weeks ended June 10 20 —

| Employee | Net Claim Code | Earnings | | | | Deductions | | | | | | | | | | | |
		Regular	Extra	Gross	RPP	Union Due	Taxable Earnings	Tax Deduction	CPP	EI	Health Insur.	Ext'd Group Life		Total Deductions	Net Pay
							Income Tax								
J. Bell	8	2310 –		2310 –											

3. **A.** **Complete the following payroll journal in your workbook. Take note of the different net claim codes. Total and prove the accuracy of your journal.**
B. **Explain why A. Vroom and C. Huang have the same gross pay but not the same net pay.**

Payroll Journal   For the two weeks ended February 15, 20 —

| Employee | Net Claim Codes | | Earnings | Deductions | | | | | | | | | | | |
	Fed.	Prov.	Gross	RPP 6.00%	Union Dues	Taxable Earnings	Federal Tax	Provincial Tax	Total Tax Deduction	CPP	EI	Ext'd Health Insur.	Total Deductions	Net Pay
							Income Tax							
A. Vroom	10	10	2150 00		60 00							36 00		
C. Huang	1	1	2150 00		60 00							18 00		
R. Leidel	3	4	2300 00		60 00							36 00		
S. Tan	2	2	2375 00		60 00							36 00		
R. Morris	4	5	2425 00		60 00							36 00		
Totals														

4. **Complete each of the following statements by writing in your Workbook the appropriate word or phrase from the list on page 683.**

   a. An amount kept back from an employee's gross pay is known as a _____.
   b. The amount of pay remaining after all deductions have been made is known as _____.
   c. Payroll calculations are summarized in a book known as the _____.
   d. Keeping back an amount from an employee's pay is called _____ it.
   e. Certain payroll deductions are made on behalf of the federal government. The _____ system is used to keep track of all of these deductions for all citizens of the country.
   f. The deductions in question e. above are for _____, _____, and _____.
   g. To assist employers in making the deductions in question f. above, the government provides _____.
   h. The CPP deduction and the EI deduction are based on the _____ figure.

i.   For the CPP, there is a _____ figure after which no further deductions will be made for the year.
j.   Employers, as well as employees, must _____ to the CPP and EI funds.
k.   A payroll made every two weeks is known as a _____ payroll.
l.   A private pension plan that is approved by the government is known as a _____ pension plan.
m.   An employee fills out a TD1 form in order to determine the _____.
n.   The _____ is based on the figure arrived at in question m. above.
o.   The deduction for income tax is not based on gross earnings. It is based on _____ earnings.

List of Words or Phrases

biweekly	net claim amount
Canada Pension Plan	net claim code
columnar	net pay
contribute	payroll deduction
deduction tables	payroll journal
employment insurance	registered
gross pay	social insurance number
income tax	taxable
maximum	withholding

14.3 | Recording the Payroll

Once the payroll journal has been prepared and balanced, the payroll is almost ready to be journalized. Before it is, other aspects of payroll must be considered. For example, employers are required to contribute to certain federal and provincial government plans. Employers often refer to these obligations as "payroll taxes." The Canada Pension Plan and Employment Insurance fund are examples of payroll taxes, and each represents an expense to the business.

The business may agree to other payroll expenses as part of the employment contract with its employees. A retirement plan, for instance, is a substantial benefit that makes a business appealing to employees. A business might therefore think it wise to contribute to such a plan in order to attract and reward qualified staff. For Nor-Can Grocers Ltd., the following aspects of payroll must be taken into account:

1.   the totals from the payroll journal;
2.   the *employer's* contribution to the CPP;
3.   the *employer's* contribution to the EI fund;
4.   the *employer's* contribution to the RPP.

The accounting entries to record each of the above four aspects of payroll are explained on pages 683–685.

The Accounting Entries

1. The Totals from the Payroll Journal

Figure 14.20 on page 684 shows the totals taken from the payroll journal of Nor-Can Grocers Ltd., recorded in the form of a general journal entry.

FIGURE 14.20

Totals from the payroll journal recorded in the general journal.

		GENERAL JOURNAL				PAGE 43	
DATE		PARTICULARS	PR	DEBIT		CREDIT	
20– Jan.	28	Salaries Expense		11700 –			The gross pay
		Reg. Pension Plan Payable				585 –	
		Union Dues Payable				200 –	
		Employees' Income Tax Payable				2364 75	
		Canada Pension Plan Payable				473 75	
		Employment Insurance Payable				263 25	
		Extended Health Insurance Payable				108 –	
		Group Life Insurance Payable				155 –	
		Salaries Payable				7550 25	
		To record payroll totals for Jan. 28, 20–					

Each of the credit items is a column total and represents a liability to be paid in the near future.

2. The Employer's Contribution to the Canada Pension Plan

Every employer is also required to make a contribution to the Canada Pension Plan on behalf of their employees that is equal to the contributions deducted from their pay. The payroll journal for Nor-Can Grocers Ltd. above shows that the employees contributed $473.75 through payroll deductions. The employer must contribute an equal amount. Figure 14.21 below shows the accounting entry for this recorded in the general journal. Observe the two aspects of this accounting entry:

1. There is an expense because the business has to pay out of its own funds.
2. There is a liability because the business owes the money. It has not been paid yet.

FIGURE 14.21

General journal entry to record employer's CPP contribution.

Jan.	28	Canada Pension Plan Expense		473 75			
		Canada Pension Plan Payable				473 75	
		Employer's CPP contribution					

3. The Employer's Contribution to Employment Insurance

For their contribution to the Employment Insurance fund, employers are instructed to calculate their EI premium at 1.4 times the employees' premium. The payroll journal for Nor-Can Grocers Ltd. shows that the employees contributed $263.25 through payroll deductions. The employer must contribute this amount multiplied by 1.4; that is, $263.25 \times 1.4 = \$368.55$. Figure 14.22 below shows the accounting entry for this recorded in the general journal. Note the two aspects: the expense and the liability.

FIGURE 14.22

General journal entry to record employer's EI contribution.

Jan.	28	Employment Insurance Expense		368 55			
		Employment Insurance Payable				368 55	
		Employer's EI contribution					

4. The Employer's Contribution to the Registered Pension Plan

The agreement between Nor-Can Grocers Ltd. and its employees states that both the employees and the employer shall contribute equally to the RPP. The payroll journal for Nor-Can Grocers Ltd. shows that the employees paid $585 to the RPP through payroll deductions. The employer, therefore, is liable for an equal amount. Figure 14.23 below shows the accounting entry for this recorded in the general journal.

FIGURE 14.23

General journal entry for employer's RPP contribution.

Jan.	28	Registered Pension Plan Expense	585 –	
		Registered Pension Plan Payable		585 –
		Employer's RPP contribution		

The Effect in the Accounts

Each of the four accounting entries starting on page 683 is posted to the accounts in the general ledger. Figure 14.24 below shows the effect of these four accounting entries in the accounts involved.

FIGURE 14.24

General ledger accounts with payroll entries recorded.

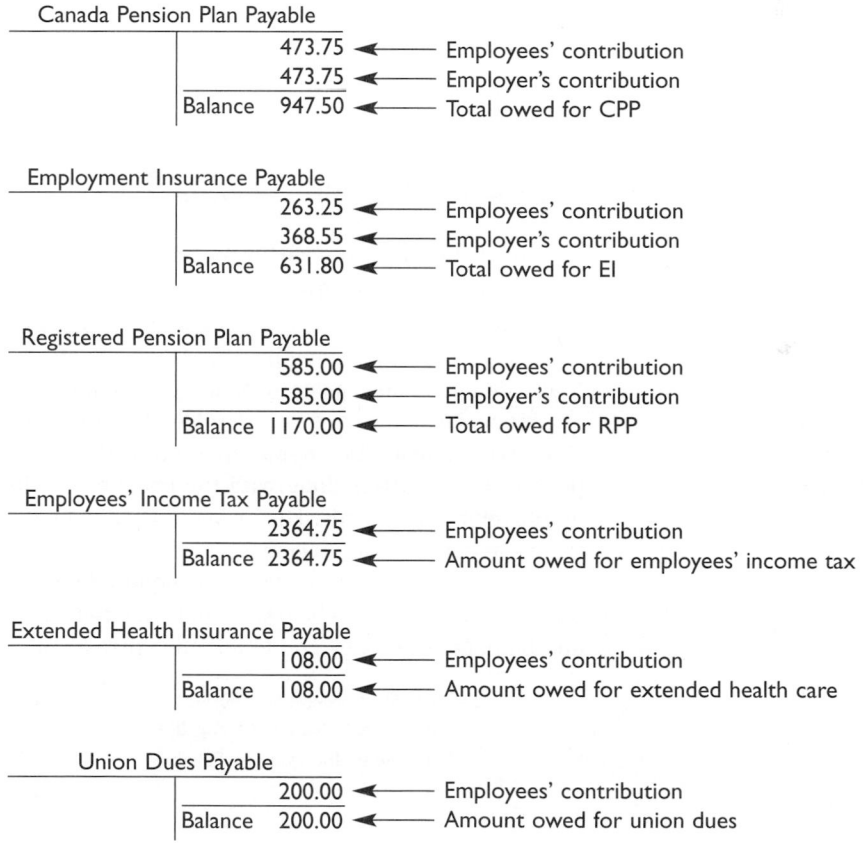

LIABILITY ACCOUNTS

Canada Pension Plan Payable
| | 473.75 ◄——— Employees' contribution
| | 473.75 ◄——— Employer's contribution
| Balance | 947.50 ◄——— Total owed for CPP

Employment Insurance Payable
| | 263.25 ◄——— Employees' contribution
| | 368.55 ◄——— Employer's contribution
| Balance | 631.80 ◄——— Total owed for EI

Registered Pension Plan Payable
| | 585.00 ◄——— Employees' contribution
| | 585.00 ◄——— Employer's contribution
| Balance | 1170.00 ◄——— Total owed for RPP

Employees' Income Tax Payable
| | 2364.75 ◄——— Employees' contribution
| Balance | 2364.75 ◄——— Amount owed for employees' income tax

Extended Health Insurance Payable
| | 108.00 ◄——— Employees' contribution
| Balance | 108.00 ◄——— Amount owed for extended health care

Union Dues Payable
| | 200.00 ◄——— Employees' contribution
| Balance | 200.00 ◄——— Amount owed for union dues

continued

FIGURE 14.24

(continued)

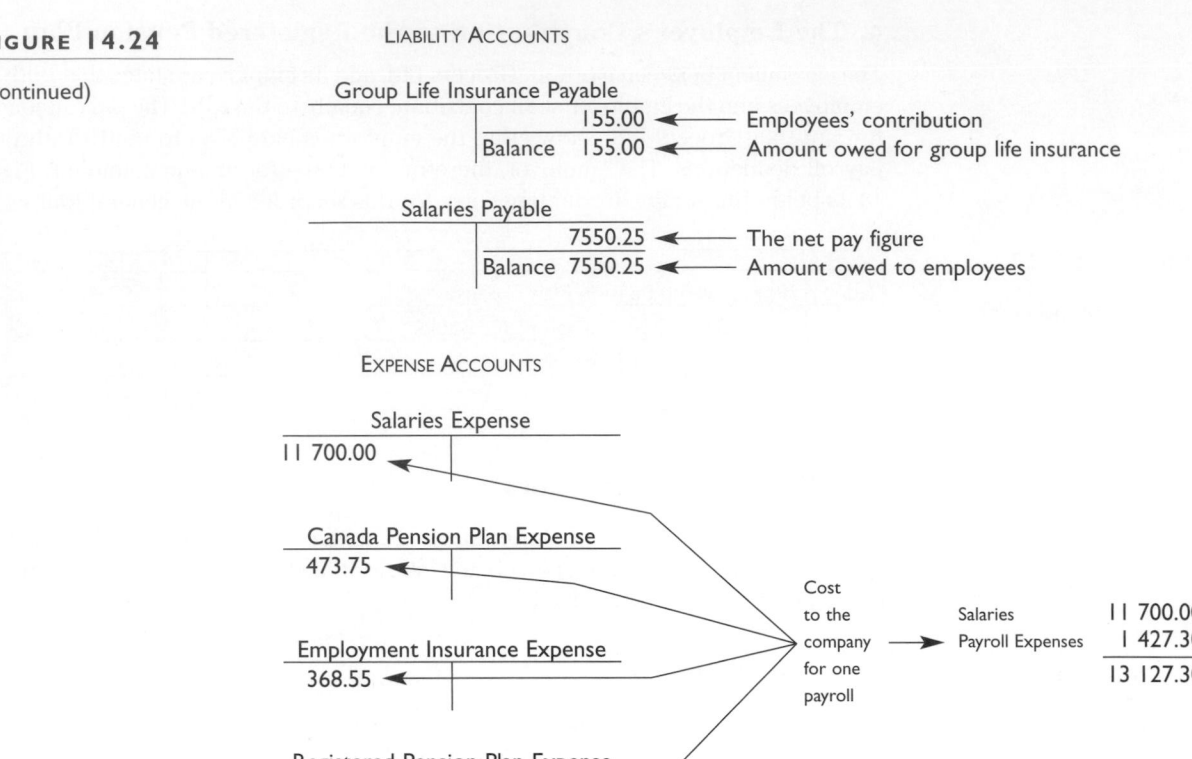

LIABILITY ACCOUNTS

Group Life Insurance Payable
| | 155.00 ◄──── Employees' contribution
| Balance | 155.00 ◄──── Amount owed for group life insurance

Salaries Payable
| | 7550.25 ◄──── The net pay figure
| Balance | 7550.25 ◄──── Amount owed to employees

EXPENSE ACCOUNTS

Salaries Expense
11 700.00 ◄

Canada Pension Plan Expense
473.75 ◄

Employment Insurance Expense
368.55 ◄

Registered Pension Plan Expense
585.00 ◄

Cost to the company for one payroll ──►

Salaries	11 700.00
Payroll Expenses	1 427.30
	13 127.30

Payment of Payroll Liabilities

To the Federal Government

The amounts withheld from employees for the federal government in any month are to be paid by the 15th day of the following month. For example, deductions made in August are due by September 15. This regulation applies to the Canada Pension Plan, unemployment insurance, and personal income taxes.

A special two-part form, PD7AR (Tax Deduction — Canada Pension Plan — Employment Insurance Remittance Return), accompanies the payment. The upper portion is submitted along with the cheque. The lower portion is retained for the employer's own records. The payment may be made at a branch of a bank or sent to the appropriate taxation centre.

To determine the amount of the cheque, add the balances *for the month just ended* for the accounts shown below. Assume that the amounts shown below are the month-end balances (i.e. They are double the corresponding balances from Figure 14.24.).

Cheques sent to the Government of Canada are made out to the Receiver General.

Canada Pension Plan Payable	$1 895.00
Employment Insurance Payable	1 263.60
Employees' Income Tax Payable	4 729.50
Total	$7 888.10

One cheque is drawn for the combined amount of $7 888.10 and is paid to the Receiver General. The accounting entry to record the payment is:

	DR	CR
Canada Pension Plan Payable	$1 895.00	
Employment Insurance Payable	1 263.60	
Employees' Income Tax Payable	4 729.50	
Bank		$7 888.10

Other Payroll Taxes and Deductions

Details concerning payroll taxes and payroll deductions can change whenever there is a change in policy or a new agreement with employees. If you worked in a payroll department, you would likely encounter various payroll items not covered in this chapter (e.g., workers' compensation programs, provincial health plans, charitable donations, and so on). However, even if you met with an unfamiliar payroll requirement, you should be able to categorize it and have a general idea of how to deal with it.

For example, in Ontario, a program called the Employer's Health Tax (EHT) requires private sector employers with annual payrolls of over $400 000 to contribute to the Ontario Health Insurance Plan—a plan which benefits employees. You should be able to recognize this as a payroll tax (just like CPP and EI). Accordingly, once the amount of EHT is determined, you know you would have to debit an expense account and credit a liability account. Then, a few weeks after the payroll is prepared, a cheque would be remitted to provincial government to clear the liability.

Likewise, if the employees of your company agreed to contribute to a charity through a payroll plan, you should be able to understand that this would be treated like any other payroll deduction. That is, pay would be withheld from employees and a liability account created. The liability account would receive the credit that would have otherwise been credited to Bank. Within a few weeks of the payroll period, a cheque would be written to the charity to clear the liability.

Section 14.3   Review Questions

1. List four aspects of payroll that require accounting entries.
2. Not all of the columns in the payroll journal are used to work out the accounting entry. Explain why.
3. How is the employer's share of CPP calculated?
4. How is the employer's share of EI calculated?
5. If the deduction from employees for EI is $100, how much will the employer have to pay?
6. Explain why there are liability accounts involved in payroll.
7. Explain why there is more than one expense account involved in payroll.
8. To whom is the cheque to the federal government made out?
9. Explain how the amount of the cheque to the federal government is calculated.
10. What form is prepared to accompany the cheque noted in question 9?
11. When is the cheque to the federal government due?

Section 14.3   **Exercises**

1. The illustration below shows the final column totals from the payroll of Hudson Fisheries for the semi-monthly pay period ended October 15.

> **A. Given that the employer matches the employees' contributions for RPP, prepare the general journal entries to record this payroll.**

Payroll Journal   For the 1/2 month ended October 15 20 —

Employee	Net Claim Code	Regular	Extra	Gross	RPP	Union Dues	Taxable Earnings	Tax Deduction	CPP	UI	Ext'd Health Insce.	Group Life		Total Deductions	Net Pay
			Earnings				Income Tax					Deductions			
TOTALS		9965 –	3225 90	13190 90	659 54	168 –	12363 36	2554 44	180 52	186 86	181 –	317 –		4247 36	8943 54

> **B. Post the journal entries for the above payroll to the T-accounts provided in the Workbook.**
>
> **C. Journalize and post the accounting entry to pay the employees.**
>
> **D. Given that the payroll for the next period is identical to the one above, post the second payroll for October to the T-accounts (all entries).**
>
> **E. Journalize and post the accounting entry to pay the employees.**
>
> **F. Answer the following questions.**
> > **a. How much is owed to the federal government for the month of October?**
> >
> > **b. How much is owed to the health insurance agency for the month of October?**
> >
> > **c. Give the accounting entry for the payment in question a. above.**
> >
> > **d. Give the accounting entry for the payment in question b. above.**

---

2. Examine the following T-accounts and answer the questions below.

CPP Payable		EI Payable		Employer's Income Tax Payable	
	185.12	Feb	265.35	Feb	502.36
	185.12		371.49	Mar 502.36	
Mar 370.24		Mar 636.84			525.24
	190.40		268.20	Apr 525.25	
	190.40		375.48		
Apr 380.80		Apr 643.68			

> **A.** How is the $371.49 amount of the EI Payable account calculated? _____
>
> **B.** In the CPP Payable account, why does the $185.12 appear twice? _____
>
> **C.** What is the length of the pay period? _____
>
> **D.** What amount was remitted to the federal government in March? _____

3. **Briefly answer each of the questions appearing below.**

   A. The first pay period in February ends on the 14th. One of the payroll journal entries is the following:

	DR	CR
CPP Expense	$184.00	
CPP Payable		$184.00

   How much was deducted from the employees' pay for the CPP?

   B. In this same pay period, the journal entry for employment insurance is the following:

	DR	CR
EI Expense	$212.80	
EI Payable		$212.80

   How much was deducted from the employees' pay for employment insurance?

   C. Assume that the payroll data for the second pay period in February are the same as the first. What will be the balances at the end of the month in each of the following accounts?

   a. Employment Insurance Expense
   b. Employment Insurance Payable
   c. Canada Pension Plan Expense
   d. Canada Pension Plan Payable

   D. Using the group life insurance rates given in the text at page 674, calculate the insurance coverage for an employee from whom a payroll deduction of $37.50 was made in the second pay period.

14.4 | Basic Payroll Records

You are aware by now of the importance of written records in the accounting process. There are a number of important records produced by the payroll department. Three of these are:

1. the payroll journal;
2. the payroll cheque;
3. the employee's earnings record.

Payroll Journal

The completed payroll journal was shown in Figure 14.18 on page 675. It is prepared for each pay period and used to accumulate all of the figures for each pay period. Some businesses use the payroll journal as a book of original entry. Certain column totals are posted directly from the payroll journal to the general ledger. When a computer system is used, accounting software can easily generate reports that contain typical payroll journal data.

Payroll Cheques

FIGURE 14.25

A payroll cheque for Harold Evans.

Most businesses pay their employees by cheque or electronic funds transfer. A summary that shows the employee's gross pay, the various deductions, and the net pay accompanies each payment. When a payroll cheque is used, this summary is often attached as a tear-off portion. A payroll cheque is shown in Figure 14.25 below.

NAME Harold Evans

Regular Earnings	Extra Earnings	GROSS PAY	RPP	UNION DUES	Income Tax	CPP	EI	HEALTH INSCE	GROUP LIFE		TOTAL DEDUC.	NET PAY
2400.00		2400.00	120.00	40.00	508.90	97.33	54.00	24.00	25.00		869.23	1530.77

DETACH AND RETAIN THIS STATEMENT
OF YOUR EARNINGS AND DEDUCTIONS
FOLD BEFORE DETACHING

NOR-CAN GROCERS LTD.
400 Collier St., Barrie, ON L4M 3W3

PAYROLL 1371

Date Jan. 28 20–

PAY TO THE ORDER OF Harold Evans $1530.77

THE SUM OF One Thousand, five hundred, thirty and 77/100 Dollars

NOR-CAN GROCERS LIMITED

NATIONAL BANK OF CANADA

Les Williams

0:162410000400: 04550000083003000

Employee's Earnings Record

FIGURE 14.26

An earnings record form for Harold Evans.

The employer must keep track of many details with respect to each employee's earnings. The employee's **earnings record** form is used to accumulate payroll details every payday, individually by employee. This form is illustrated in Figure 14.26 below.

NAME Evans, Harold J. SIN 430 837 013 EXEMPTION CODE 1 DATE OF BIRTH April 28, 1968
ADDRESS MARITAL STATUS M DEPENDANTS 0 DEPARTMENT

2000 5th St.
Barrie, ON
L4M 4Y8

PHONE
1-705
444-4444

DATE	STANDARD EARNINGS			STANDARD DEDUCTIONS						
Jan. 4	2400		2400	120–	40–	508.90	97.33	54–	24–	25–

DATE STARTED: April 18, 1993

DATE LEFT:

		1	2	3	4	5	6	7	8	9	10	11	12	13	14	15	16
		NET	EARNINGS			DEDUCTIONS											INSURED
		CLAIM					Union				Health	Group	TOTAL	NET	CHQ	CPP	EARNINGS
DATE	EMPLOYEE	CODE	REGULAR	EXTRA	GROSS	RPP	Dues	Tax	CPP	EI	Insce	Life	DEDUC'S	PAY	NO	TO DATE	TO DATE
1/14	Evans HJ	1	2400–	–	2400–	120–	40–	508.90	97.33	54–	24–	25–	869.23	1530.77	001	97.33	2400–
1/28	Evans HJ	1	2400–	–	2400–	120–	40–	508.90	97.33	54–	24–	25–	869.23	1530.77	006	194.66	4800–
2/11	Evans HJ	1	2400–	–	2400–	120–	40–	508.90	97.33	54–	24–	25–	869.23	1530.77	011	291.99	7 200–

At the end of the calendar year, the column totals of the employee's earnings record provide the information necessary for the T4 slips. A **T4 slip** must be prepared for every employee, and represents a summary of the employee's earnings and deductions for one year. This form is required for income tax purposes. Copies of each employee's T4 slip are sent to Revenue Canada and copies are given to the employee.

A T4 slip is shown in Figure 14.27 on page 691.

FIGURE 14.27

A T4 slip for Harold Evans.

Employer's name – Nom de l'employeur			
Nor Can Grocers Ltd.			

Canada Customs and Revenue Agency   Agence des douanes et du revenu du Canada

T4
STATEMENT OF REMUNERATION PAID
ÉTAT DE LA RÉMUNÉRATION PAYÉE

Year / Année 2001

VOID ANNULÉ ☐

Employment income – line 101 Revenus d'emploi – ligne 101	Income tax deducted – line 437 Impôt sur le revenu retenu – ligne 437
14 62 400 00	22 13 231 40

Business Number Numéro d'entreprise

54   15 363 1891   2T110 1

Province of employment Province d'emploi	Employee's CPP contributions – line 308 Cotisations de l'employé au RPC – ligne 308	EI insurable earnings Gains assurables d'AE
10 ON	16 1496 40	24 39 000 00

Social insurance number Numéro d'assurance sociale

12   430 837 013

Exempt – Exemption CPP - QPP / EI
28 ☐ ☐
RPC - RRQ / AE

Employment Code Code d'emploi
29   17

Employee's QPP contributions – line 308 Cotisations de l'employé au RRQ – ligne 308	CPP/QPP pensionable earnings Gains donnant droit à pension - RPC/RRQ
17	26

Employee's name and address – Nom et adresse de l'employé

Last name – Nom de famille	First name – Prénom	Initials - Initiales
EVANS	Harold	J.

2000 5th Street
Barrie, ON
L4M 4Y8

Employee's EI premiums – line 312 Cotisations de l'employé à l'AE – ligne 312	Union dues – line 212 Cotisations syndicales – ligne 212
18 877 50	44 1040 00

RPP contributions – line 207 Cotisations à un RPA – ligne 207	Charitable donations – Schedule 9 Dons de bienfaisance – Annexe 9
20 3120 00	46

Pension adjustment – line 206 Facteur d'équivalence – ligne 206	RPP or DPSP registration number N° d'agrément d'un RPA ou d'un RPDB
52	50 0228481

Other information (see the back) Autres renseignements (voir au verso)

35	314 00	40	603 79
Box – Case	Amount – Montant	Box – Case	Amount – Montant

Box – Case	Amount – Montant	Box – Case	Amount – Montant	Box – Case	Amount – Montant	Box – Case	Amount – Montant

T4 (00)

For recipient. Attach to your income tax return.   **2**

Section 14.4   Review Questions

1. Name the three important payroll records discussed in this section.
2. How do employees who are paid by cheque learn of the details of their pay?
3. What is an employee's earnings record?
4. What is the purpose of the employee's earnings record?
5. What is the purpose of the T4 slip?
6. Name the three parties that would obtain copies of the T4 slip.

Section 14.4   Exercises

1. Mary Watson started work with the Empire Company of Medicine Hat, Alberta, on January 1 at a salary of $2 180 for every two weeks. Mary received two $100 pay raises during the year. The first took place after 20 weeks. The second took place after 30 weeks. Part of Mary's employee's earnings record card is shown on page 692.

Date	Employee	Net Claim Code	Reg	Extra	Gross	Pension	Union	Income Tax	CPP	EI	Health Insce	United Appeal	Net Pay
			Earnings			Deductions							
Jan 14	Mary Watson	4	2180.00		2180.00	109.00	50.00	404.50	87.87	49.05	24.00	5.00	1450.58
June 3	Mary Watson	4	2280.00		2280.00	114.00	50.00	434.50	92.17	51.30	24.00	5.00	1509.03
Aug 12	Mary Watson	4	2380.00		2380.00	119.00	50.00	464.50	96.47	53.55	24.00	5.00	1567.48

A. Calculate the following yearly totals for Mary Watson:
   a. gross pay
   b. Canada Pension Plan
   c. employment insurance
   d. registered pension plan
   e. income tax

B. For which pay period was the last CPP deduction for the year made? What was the amount of this last deduction?

C. For which pay period was the last E.I. deduction for the year made? What was the amount of this last deduction?

---

2. Given below is a simplified employee's earnings record for Carol Mann for the period from January 1 to December 31, 20—. Carol Mann is paid monthly.

   A. From this record, determine the figures that would be entered on the T4 slip in the following boxes.
      a. Box 14   Employment Income Before Deductions
      b. Box 16   Employee's Canada Pension Plan Contributions
      c. Box 18   Employee's EI Premiums
      d. Box 20   Registered Pension Plan Contributions
      e. Box 22   Income Tax Deducted

   B. Explain the CPP deductions for September.

   C. Explain why the EI deduction did not increase when Carol received a salary increase in September.

NAME Carol Mann S.I.N. 723 852 487							
Date	Gross Pay	CPP	EI	RPP	Inc Tax	Other	Net Pay
Jan 31	3 500.00	137.82	78.75	175.00	777.70	125.56	2 205.17
Feb 28	3 500.00	137.82	78.75	175.00	777.70	125.56	2 205.17
Mar 31	3 500.00	137.82	78.75	175.00	777.70	125.56	2 205.17
Apr 30	3 500.00	137.82	78.75	175.00	777.70	125.56	2 205.17
May 31	3 500.00	137.82	78.75	175.00	777.70	125.56	2 205.17
Jun 30	3 500.00	137.82	78.75	175.00	777.70	125.56	2 205.17
Jul 31	3 500.00	137.82	78.75	175.00	777.70	125.56	2 205.17
Aug 31	3 500.00	137.82	78.75	175.00	777.70	125.56	2 205.17
Sep 30	4 000.00	159.32	90.00	200.00	973.25	125.56	2 451.87
Oct 31	4 000.00	159.32	90.00	200.00	973.25	125.56	2 451.87
Nov 30	4 000.00	75.20	67.50	200.00	973.25	125.56	2 558.49
Dec 31	4 000.00	—	—	200.00	973.25	125.56	2 701.19

14.5 | **Using a Computer for Payroll**

To complete the payroll journal for Nor-Can Grocers Ltd., you used tables from a government booklet to determine deductions for income tax, CPP, and EI. Preparing payroll from these tables gave you a good understanding of the nature of deductions. However, if you worked in the payroll department of an actual business, you would likely use a computer to complete the payroll tasks you performed for Nor-Can Grocers.

Tables on Diskette

Canada Customs and Revenue Agency provides a computer program that may be used instead of the deduction tables that are printed in booklet form. The electronic version is called Tables on Diskette (TOD). A program that utilizes these electronic tables is named WinTOD. You may download it free of charge at CCRA's website (www.ccra-adrc.gc.ca).

WinTOD is an uncomplicated program that acts as a simple payroll calculator. The data entry screen for Harold Evans is shown in Figure 14.30 below:

FIGURE 14.28

Payroll data for Harold Evans entered in WinTOD.

Regular Salary1		_ □ X
Employee's name (optional)	Harold Evans	
Pay period ending date (optional)	2001-01-28	YYYY-MM-DD
Province of Employment	Ontario	▼
Pay Period	Biweekly payments (26)	▼
Gross income for the pay period	2400.00	☐
Deductions to determine taxable income	160.00	☐
Requested additional tax deduction	49.00	
Year to date CPP deducted (optional)	0.00	☐ Exempt CPP
Year to date EI deducted (optional)	0.00	☐ Exempt EI
Federal claim code from TD1	Claim code 1	▼
Provincial claim code from TD1 (prov)	Claim code 1	▼
	View Deductions	

The first four fields of data in Figure 14.28 identify the employee, the pay period, province, and how many times per year the employee is paid. After Harold Evans' salary of $2 400 is entered, the user selects the box next to "Deductions to determine taxable income." A new window appears and will be similar to Figure 14.29 on page 694.

The $120 and $40 amounts are the contributions Harold Evans makes to his company pension plan and union. These amounts are subtracted from his gross pay to determine his taxable income. Back at the data entry screen in Figure 14.28, a total of $160 is shown.

FIGURE 14.29

The deductions to determine taxable income.

The asterisks in Figure 14.29 designate items that have to be deducted at source. A "deduction at source" is a phrase used to describe money that is withheld from the employee's paycheque.

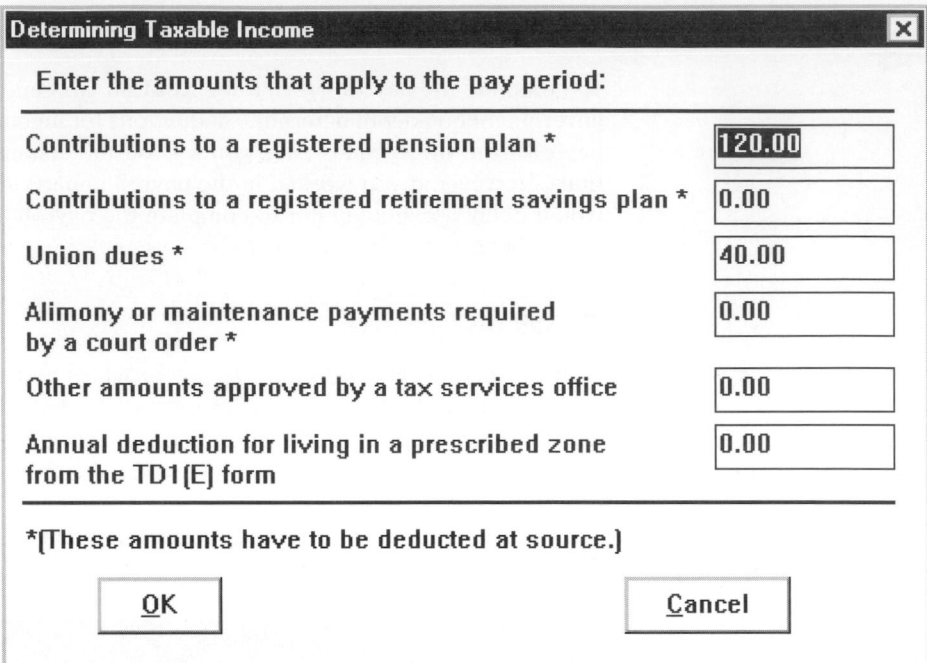

The additional tax deduction in Figure 14.28 is $49, which is the sum of the Harold Evans' health insurance and group life insurance premiums. After the federal and provincial claim codes are selected, the "View Deductions" button is pressed to show Figure 14.30 below:

FIGURE 14.30

WinTOD's calculation of net pay for Harold Evans.

Payroll Deductions for Regular Salary

Employee's name (optional)	Harold Evans		
Pay period ending date (optional)	2001-01-28		
Gross salary (or pension income) for the pay period			2400.00
EI insurable earnings for the pay period			2400.00
Taxable income for the pay period			2240.00
Canada Pension Plan (CPP) deductions		97.41	
Employment Insurance (EI) deductions		54.00	
Deductions for federal tax	361.60		
Deductions for provincial tax	149.70		
Total Tax	511.30	511.30	
Requested additional tax deduction		49.00	
Total Deductions		711.71	711.71
Net pay amount			1528.29
Federal claim code from the TD1(E)	Claim code 1		
Provincial claim code from the TD1(E)	Claim code 1		
Employer's pay period	Biweekly payments (26)		
Province of employment	Ontario		

Print Screen   Cancel   OK

Figure 14.30 summarizes Harold Evans deductions and calculates his net pay. If you compare the net pay shown above with the one displayed in the manual payroll journal back above, you will notice a slight discrepancy in the net pay results.

This happens because WinTOD uses precise mathematical formulas to calculate deductions, while the CCRA booklets use "to and from" salary ranges for looking up deductions. Harold Evans will be unconcerned about the discrepancy because the amounts are small, and they will be cleared up when he files his personal tax return by April 30th of the following year.

An accountant using WinTOD can print the data shown in Figure 14.30 to help with the preparation of paycheques. While WinTOD is fast and more convenient than using the deduction booklets, it does not store and accumulate payroll data for each employee. To meet the many demands of payroll, businesses prefer to use accounting software.

Simply Accounting's Payroll Module

Since you have already completed payroll journals and other payroll tasks by hand, you will appreciate how efficiently accounting software handles the same duties. Load the Simply Accounting files named *Nor-Can Grocers* into your computer. You will enter the payroll data for Harold Evans on January 14, 2001, the first payroll of the year for Nor-Can Grocers Ltd.

Creating a Payroll Ledger Card

Begin by opening the Employees icon in the Payroll module. You will receive a message that there are no employees on file, so you need to click the Create button. Start a payroll ledger card for Harold Evans by entering the personal data shown in Figure 14.31.

FIGURE 14.31

Personal data for the payroll ledger card of Harold Evans.

The illustrations in this section are from Simply Accounting, Version 8.5. If you are using a different version, your screen will look different, but the principles will be the same.

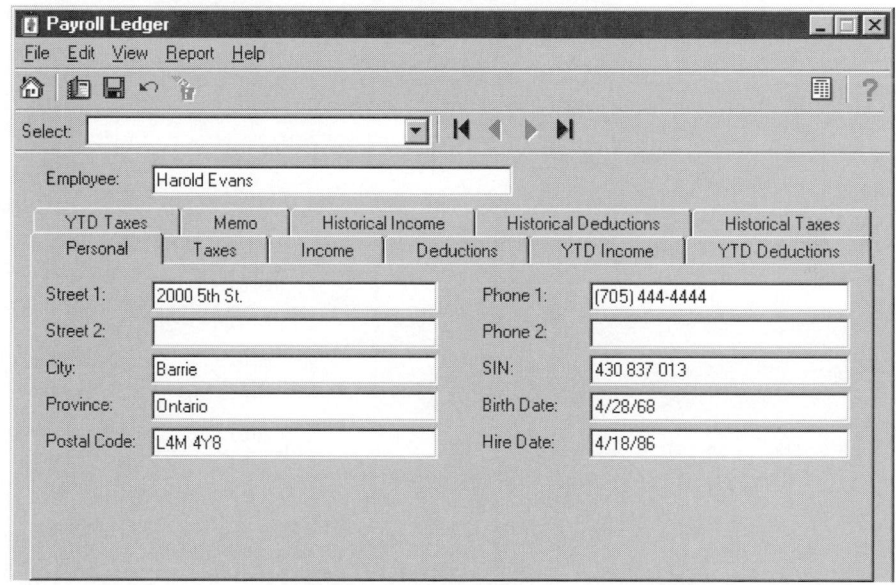

In Figure 14.31, there are eleven "tabs" for entering data. When you click a tab, a new group of data fields appears. For example, when you click the "Taxes" tab, you will see a screen similar to Figure 14.32 on page 696. Enter the data shown in Figure 14.32.

After you enter the data shown in Figure 14.32, click the Income tab and enter **2 400** in the "Salary Per Period" field and **26** in the "Pay Periods Per Year" field. You may leave the other fields in the Income section as they are.

FIGURE 14.32

Data fields under the Taxes tab of the payroll ledger card.

Versions other than Simply Accounting 8.5 will not show a field for the Provincial Claim.

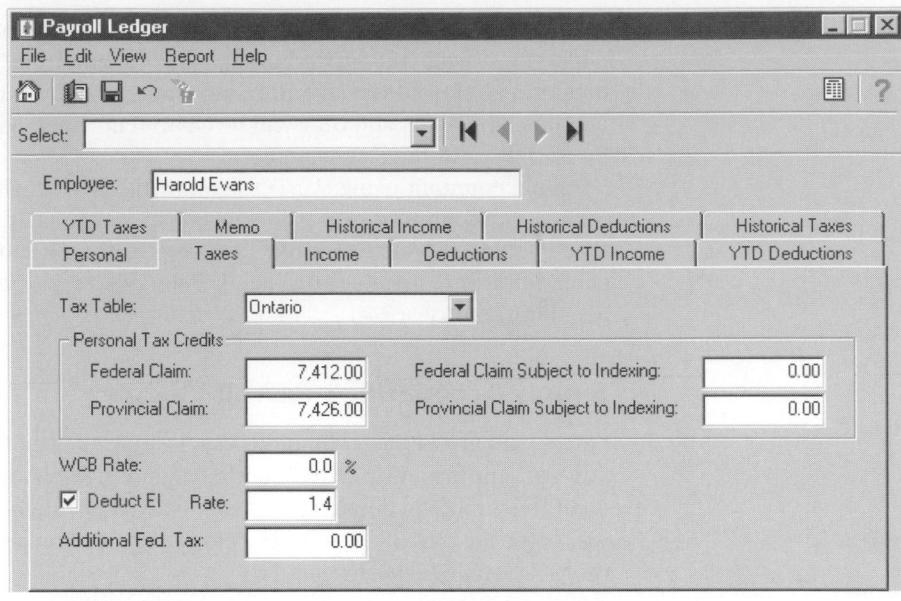

Click the Deductions tab and enter the amounts shown in Figure 14.33. Notice that Harold Evans's deductions for Health Insurance ($24) and Group Life ($25) have been summed and entered as $49 in the "Health/GL" field.

FIGURE 14.33

Deductions from Harold Evans's pay.

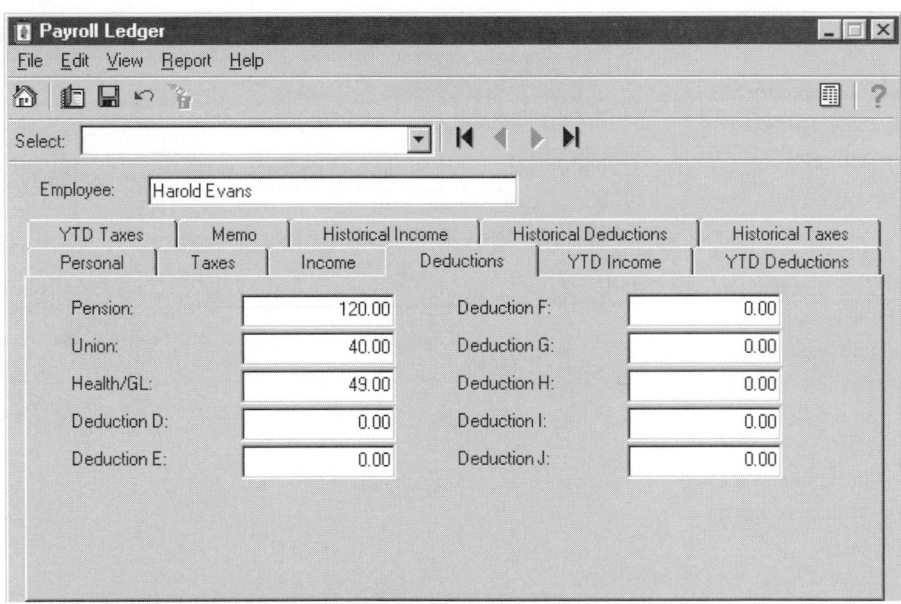

The other tabs in the payroll ledger card for Harold Evans deal with historical and year-to-date (YTD) information. Since the January 14th payroll is the first payroll of the year for Nor-Can Grocers Ltd., you do not need to complete the historical and YTD sections of the ledger card. Therefore, press the Create Another button and return to the Home window of Simply Accounting.

Linking Accounts

A key benefit of using the Payroll module of Simply Accounting is that the software will automatically generate a payroll journal entry that will affect ledger accounts in the General module. Before Simply Accounting can do this however, you must identify the general ledger accounts you want to receive debits or credits when a payroll is prepared. In other words, you must establish a link between the Payroll module and the General module.

From the Home window, choose Setup, System Settings, Linked Accounts, Payroll. There are two general ledger accounts to identify under the Income tab—Bank and Salaries Expense. Enter these accounts in the fields shown in Figure 14.34 below.

FIGURE 14.34

General ledger accounts under the Income tab of Payroll Linked Accounts.

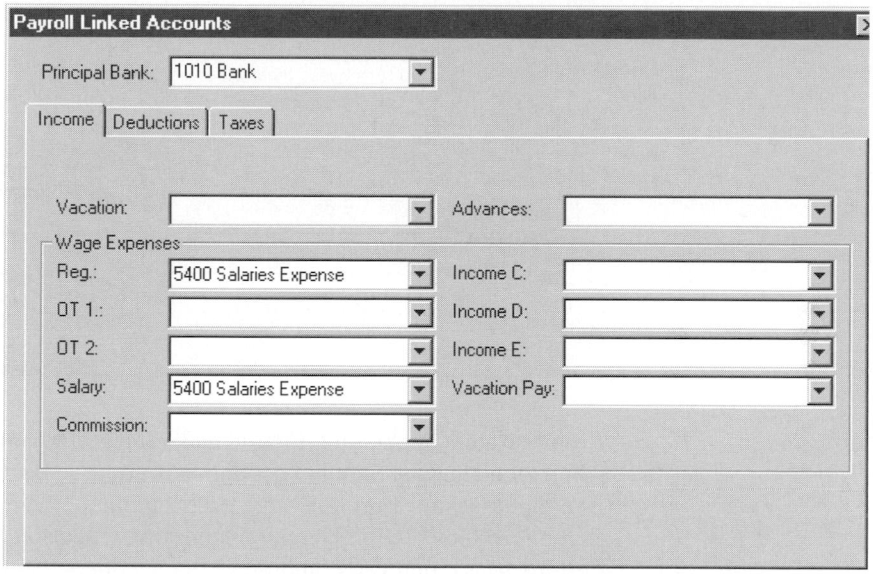

Click the Deductions tab and use Figure 14.35 below to link payable accounts to some of the "at-source" deductions.

FIGURE 14.35

Linked accounts for some of Harold Evans's deductions.

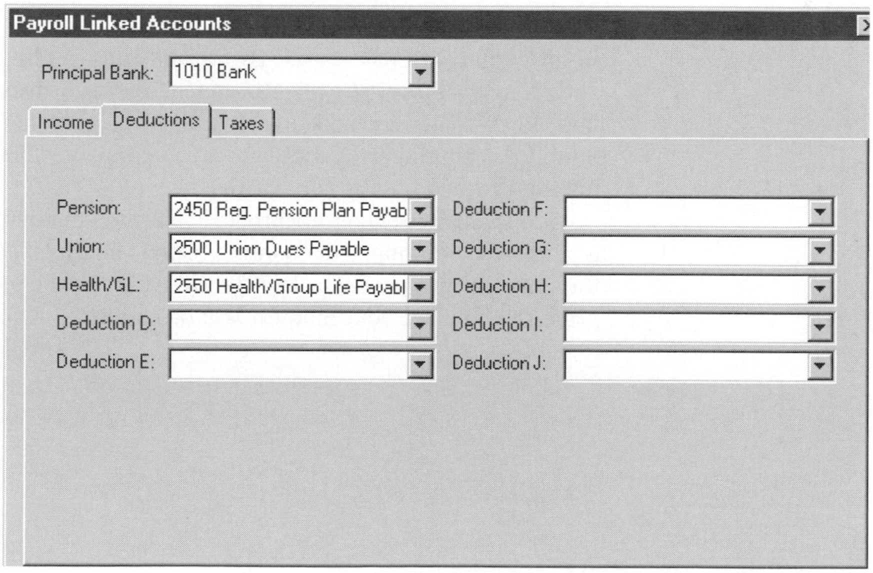

The most interesting tab in "Payroll Linked Accounts" is the Taxes tab. It has two distinct sections: one for payables and one for expenses. Click the Taxes tab and enter the accounts shown in Figure 14.36.

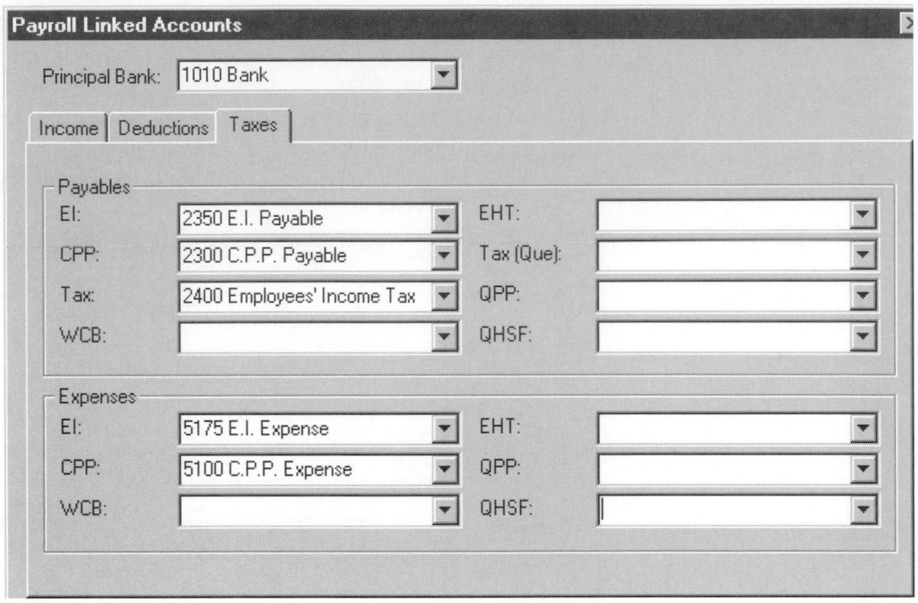

FIGURE 14.36

General ledger accounts under the Taxes tab of Payroll Linked Accounts.

From carefully examining Figure 14.36 and using your knowledge of payroll, you can anticipate what Simply Accounting is about to do. It will calculate the three government taxes for Harold Evans and accumulate them in the three accounts shown in the Payables section. Simply Accounting will also calculate the Nor-Can's contributions to E.I. and C.P.P. and debit the accounts shown in Expenses section. (The credit portions on Nor-Can's contributions will be distributed to E.I. Payable and C.P.P. Payable.) Click OK when you are done.

Making Journal Entries

Before you try to pay Harold Evans on January 14th, return to the Home window and choose **History**, **Enter Historical Information**, **Payroll**. If you made a mistake when you linked accounts, it will show up at this stage. If you made no errors, Simply Accounting will advise you to backup your files. Ignore this advice by pressing the Proceed button.

Preparing a cheque for Harold Evans and completing the payroll journal entries is very easy in Simply Accounting. Open the Paycheques icon—which represents the Payroll journal—and select Harold Evans as the payee of the cheque. When you press the Tab key, your monitor will be similar to Figure 14.37 on page 699.

A payroll cheque for
Harold Evans.

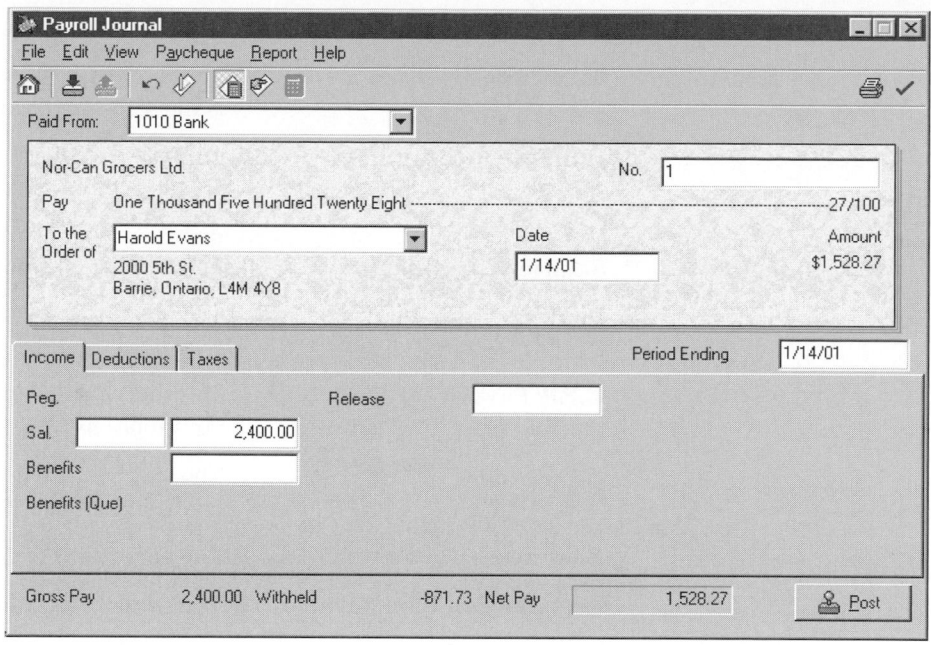

The payroll calculations have been made for you. A summary of gross pay, amounts withheld, and net pay appear at the bottom of Figure 14.37. If you need more details about the amounts withheld, you can click the Deductions and Taxes tabs.

Simply Accounting has prepared more than the payroll cheque. Choose **Report, Display Payroll Journal Entry**. Your monitor should look similar to Figure 14.38 below.

FIGURE 14.38

The payroll journal entry
for Harold Evans.

Payroll calculations can
vary slightly because
tax tables are subject
to change. Businesses
using Simply Accounting
regularly update the
tax tables. The amounts
shown on your monitor
may have been deter-
mined by different
tax tables.

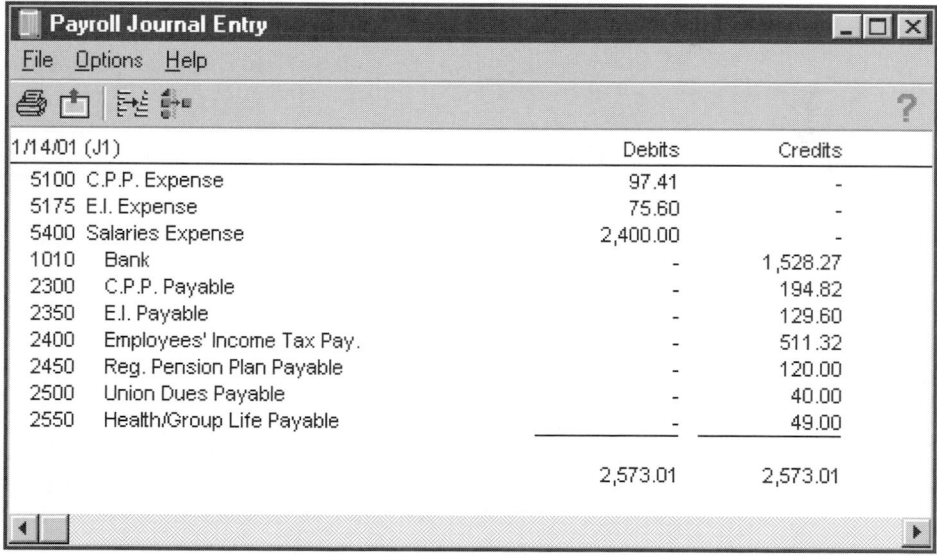

A brief analysis of the accounts and amounts in Figure 14.38 is helpful:

C.P.P. Expense	This is the employer's contribution; the amount is the same as Harold Evans's contribution.
E.I. Expense	This is the employer's contribution; the amount is 1.4 times more than Harold Evans's contribution of $54.00.
Salaries Expense	The amount of gross pay.
Bank	The amount of the cheque written to Harold Evans.
C.P.P. Payable	The sum of the employer's and employee's contributions ($97.41 + $97.41).
E.I. Payable	The sum of the employer's and employee's contributions ($75.60 + $54.00).
Employees' Income Tax Pay.	The employee's tax deduction.
Reg. Pension Plan Payable	The employee's contribution.
Union Dues Payable	The employee's contribution.
Health/Group Life Payable	The employee's contribution.

Opening the payroll journal, selecting an employee to be paid, and pressing the Post button is almost all you need to do to prepare a payroll in Simply Accounting. For Nor-Can Grocers Ltd., one payroll item has been missed. Recall that Nor-Can agreed to contribute to the employees' Registered Pension Plan. Simply Accounting did not recognize this contribution in the journal entry displayed in Figure 14.38. A separate entry must be made in the General journal. You will do this when you complete Computer Exercise 1 below. For now, close the window that looks like Figure 14.38 and post the entry generated by Harold Evans's paycheque.

Section 14.5 — Computer Exercises

1. Complete the January 14th payroll.

    A. You have already journalized and posted the January 14th payroll journal entry for Harold Evans. Now, repeat all the steps you took for Harold Evans to process the payroll for the rest of Nor-Can's employees. The details you need to create payroll ledger cards for each employee in Simply Accounting are listed on page 701.

    B. Use the General journal to record Nor-Can's contributions to the employees' registered pension plan. Total employee RPP deductions amounted to $585. Recall that Nor-Can Grocers Ltd. contributes an amount equal to that contributed by the employees.

Employee	Ronald Leung		Employee	Robert Funston
Street	9 Irish Lane		Street	18 Byron Cres.
City	Barrie		City	Barrie
Province	Ontario		Province	Ontario
Postal	L4M 6H8		Postal	L4N 6G6
Phone	(705) 444-4829		Phone	(705) 444-7740
SIN	469 244 420		SIN	462 331 265
Birth date	11/03/55		Birth date	5/27/72
Hire date	12/27/70		Hire date	3/13/88
Tax Table	Ontario		Tax Table	Ontario
Federal Claim	$11 300		Federal Claim	$9 000
Salary	$2 100		Salary	$2 500
Pay Periods	26		Pay Periods	26
RPP	$105		RPP	$125
Union Dues	$40		Union Dues	$40
Health/GL	$34		Health/GL	$74

If you are using Simply Accounting, Version 8.5 or higher, enter the same amounts for federal and provincial claim codes—except for Denise Murray. For her, use a provincial amount of $7 426.

Employee	Denise Murray		Employee	Lee Williams
Street	517 Big Bay Point		Street	30 Drury Lane
City	Barrie		City	Barrie
Province	Ontario		Province	Ontario
Postal	L4N 3Z6		Postal	L4M 3C6
Phone	(705) 435-8934		Phone	(705) 435-7112
SIN	581 311 263		SIN	493 212 435
Birth date	3/26/84		Birth date	5/11/68
Hire date	10/06/99		Hire date	8/15/93
Tax Table	Ontario		Tax Table	Ontario
Fed./Prov. Claim	$7 412/$7 426		Federal Claim	$13 988
Salary	$2 300		Salary	$2 400
Pay Periods	26		Pay Periods	26
RPP	$115		RPP	$120
Union Dues	$40		Union Dues	$40
Health/GL	$32		Health/GL	$74

2. Complete the January 28th payroll.

A. You will be able to process the January 28th payroll very quickly. Change the session date to 01-28-01. Then open the Paycheques icon, prepare a cheque for each employee, and post the associated payroll journal entry. (Note: There are no changes in the payroll figures; each employee is to receive the same amount as in the period ended January 14, 2001.)

B. Use the General journal to record Nor-Can's contributions to the employees' registered pension plan. The amounts will be the same as the January 14th payroll.

C. Add your name to the company information (Setup, System Settings, Company Information) and print the reports required by your teacher.

3. Figure 14.30 on page 694 shows the results of calculating Harold Evans' payroll deductions using WinTOD. The amounts shown in Figure 14.30 used payroll tables for the year 2001.

    A. Go to website for Canada Customs and Revenue Agency (www.ccra-adrc.gc.ca) and search for a copy of the current payroll tables. (If you are using your home computer, you may download a copy of WinTOD or a "pdf" version of the tables.) Using the same salary data for Harold Evans as found in the text, calculate the current deduction for C.P.P. and E.I. How have the amounts changed over the years? Is the employer's contribution more or less than it was in 2001? What conclusions can you reach about trends in the C.P.P. and E.I. programs?

Section 14.5   Communicate It

Assume you are the accountant in charge of payroll for a company named C & G Associates. Employee Ted Ayles has just advised you that his personal tax exemptions have increased by $2 600. You determine that this will cause his net claim code to go from 2 to 4.

    Ted is not sure if he wants you to officially change his net claim code because he believes that having a lower code will mean that he will receive a bigger tax refund in April of each year.

    Write an e-mail that explains net claim codes to Ted. Make sure he understands the effect that a higher code number will have on his take-home pay. Also include a comment about Ted's reason for wishing to leave his net claim code unchanged. Would he really get a bigger tax refund and, if so, is this a sound idea?

CHAPTER 14 Summary

CHAPTER HIGHLIGHTS

Now that you have completed Chapter 14, you should:

- understand the nature of accounting for payroll;
- be able to determine common payroll deductions and read government tables of deductions for income tax, employment insurance, and the Canada Pension Plan;
- understand the purpose of the TD1 form;
- know how to determine the employer's contribution for employment insurance, and Canada Pension Plan;
- know how to prepare basic payroll records: the payroll, the payroll cheque and the employee's earnings record;
- know the accounting entries to record a complete payroll;
- understand that employees' deductions out of payroll, and the employer's obligatory contributions, are to be remitted to the appropriate government department or other organization;
- understand how the T4 slip is prepared from the employee's earnings record;
- know how to complete a simple payroll using a computer accounting program.

ACCOUNTING TERMS

Canada Pension Plan (CPP)
commission
employee's earnings record
employment insurance (EI)
gross pay
net claim code
net pay
payroll

payroll register
registered pension plan (RPP)
salary
taxable earnings
timecard
T4 slip
wages
payroll journal

CHAPTER 14 Review Exercises

Using Your Knowledge

1 A blank payroll journal for this exercise appears in the Workbook.

A. Prepare the payroll journal from the data given below for the two weeks ending August 12, 20—. Use the rates and rules given in the text at pages 659–660 if not stated otherwise.

a.

Employee	Hours Worked Wk. 1	Hours Worked Wk. 2	Net Claim Code	Hourly Rate	Ext'd Health Insurance Coverage	Life Insurance Coverage
Axelson, A.	40	48	9	$25.00	Family	$ 50 000
Jones, P.	40	44	1	26.00	Single	100 000
Koehler, M.	40	40	3	29.00	Family	50 000
Yamada, S.	46	46	5	24.00	Family	100 000
Sauve, R.	40	40	4	28.50	Single	75 000

b. Each employee is enrolled in the registered pension plan with contributions set at 4 per cent of the gross pay. The employer matches the employees' contributions.

c. Union dues are set at $18.00 for each employee per pay period.

B. Total the columns of the payroll journal and perform the steps to ensure its accuracy.

C. Journalize the accounting entries as outlined in Section 14.3.

---

2 A blank payroll journal for this exercise appears in the Workbook.

A. Prepare the payroll journal from the data given below for the two weeks ending January 20, 20—. Use the rates and rules given in the text at pages 659–660 except where stated otherwise.

a. Each of the employees listed below is employed by Mason Trading Company. All employees are paid every two weeks. Those in the warehouse are paid on an hourly basis. The salespeople are paid a salary plus commission.

For the warehouse workers, a regular work week is 40 hours. These workers belong to the CAW union and pay union dues of $20 each pay period. Overtime is paid at the rate of time and a half.

The salespeople are paid a basic salary of $1 000 per pay period. They also receive a commission of 2 per cent of their sales for the period. Salespeople do not belong to the union.

Employee	Net Claim Code	Hours	Hourly Rate	Net Sales	Ext'd Health Insurance Status	Group Life Insurance Coverage
Cower, I.	4	80	$28.00		Single	$100 000
Durand, D.	6	84	26.00		Married	100 000
Hansen, W.	8	85	26.00		Married	50 000
Kuchma, E.	2	86	26.00		Single	75 000
Milani, M.	5			$65 000	Married	100 000
Nyman, G.	3			69 500	Married	90 000
Sutherland, T.	9			61 000	Married	80 000

    b. The employee rate of contribution to the registered pension plan is 5 per cent of gross pay. The employer contributes one and a half times the amount paid by the employees.

    c. Group life insurance is paid for entirely by the employees at the rate of 35 cents for each $1 000 of coverage.

B. Complete and balance the payroll journal.

C. Journalize the accounting entries to record the aspects of the payroll covered in Section 14.3.

Comprehensive Exercises

3   Karen Paquette of Carman, Manitoba, has been in business for several years. Given on page 706 are selected ledger accounts for her business. Shown in these accounts are all of the accounting entries affecting payroll for the month of February.

Answer the following questions regarding the accounting entries:

    a. What is the total cost related to payroll for the month of February?
    b. Explain the credit entry of $3 050 in the bank account.
    c. What is the length of the payroll period?
    d. Explain the debit entry of $250 in the Extended Health Insurance Payable account.
    e. To what extent does the employer contribute to the employees' pension fund?
    f. How often is payment made by the company for extended health insurance?
    g. Give the amount of the cheque that will be sent to the federal government in March.

Bank	
8 225	
3 050	
8 680	
250	
2 010	

CPP Payable	
740	190
	190
	200
	200

Wages Expense	
10 000	
10 500	

EI Payable	
920	210
	294
	230
	322

CPP Expense	
190	
200	

RPP Payable	
2 010	500
	500
	505
	505

EI Expense	
294	
322	

Income Tax Payable	
1 390	750
	760

RPP Expense	
500	
505	

Employer Health Tax is a payroll tax payable to the government of Ontario.

Extended Health Insurance Payable	
250	125
	125

Employer Health Tax Expense	
122	
128	

Employer Health Tax Payable	
	122
	128

Payroll Payable	
8 225	8 225
8 680	8 680

4 Shown below are the summary figures for the first four payrolls for Precision Company. These are followed by additional information.

Payroll Summaries

Pay Date	Gross Pay	CPP	EI	RPP	Income Tax	Ext'd Health	Union Dues	Net Pay
Jan 14	$5 700	$ 98	$101	$285	$560	$75	$50	$4 531
Jan 28	5 400	90	97	270	520	75	50	4 298
Feb 11	5 800	99	103	290	570	75	50	4 613
Feb 25	5 900	100	105	295	580	75	50	4 695

Additional Information

- Use the rules set out in the chapter. Round off to the nearest dollar where necessary.
- The company matches the RPP contribution.
- Payment for extended health insurance is made on the 15th of the following month.
- Payments for RPP and union dues are made at the end of every second month.
- Assume that the bank balance always has sufficient funds on hand to make the payments.
- The accounts needed for this exercise are those shown below. They are set up for you in the Workbook.

    Bank
    Canada Pension Plan Payable
    Employment Insurance Payable
    Registered Pension Plan Payable
    Employees' Income Tax Payable
    Extended Health Insurance Payable
    Union Dues Payable
    Payroll Payable
    Wages Expense
    Canada Pension Plan Expense
    Employment Insurance Expense
    Registered Pension Plan Expense

A. Record all accounting entries for these four payrolls for the period from January 1 to March 15. Record these entries directly into the T-accounts in your Workbook without using a journal. Record the entries in their correct order.

B. Calculate the total expense of these four payrolls. Show that this total expense figure is equal to the total paid out in cash.

Questions for Further Thought

Briefly answer each of the following questions.

1. In the government booklet for the Canada Pension Plan, there is a summary of types of employment and benefits that are subject to CPP contributions. What steps would you take to resolve a doubt you had about a certain kind of employment?

2. Give one definite advantage of being paid a) by the hour; b) by salary; c) by commission.

3. Usually there is at least a one-week delay in paying employees. What do you think is the reason for this?

4. From the employee's point of view, are payroll deductions simply a loss of money? Explain.

5. With insurance in general, the greater the risk you represent, the more you pay. For example, if you have a number of speeding convictions, your car insurance premium increases. In some cases, your insurance might be cancelled. In view of the above, is it right to regard employment insurance as "insurance"? Explain.

6. Why do you think registered pension plans have been set up when the Canada Pension Plan already exists?

7. Income taxes are deducted on an estimated basis from each pay during the year. How does the government eventually get the right amount from each person?

8. Management and unions are often adversaries. Why would management agree to deduct dues for the benefit of a union that it may consider to be an opponent?

Cases for Further Thought

Briefly answer the following questions.

1. Matt Cook's T4 slip indicates that his employer has withheld $5 260 for income tax from his earnings for the year. When Matt prepares his income tax return, he discovers that the total tax he has to pay is only $4 830. How can this happen?

2. Maxwell Company's payroll is due to be paid this afternoon. The payroll amounts to $22 565, but Maxwell Company has only $14 275 in its general bank account. Should Maxwell Company be concerned about this, and, if so, to what degree? Explain. What steps should Maxwell Company be taking in regard to this situation?

Case Studies

Wage Increases — What's Fair?

The following salaries and wages are paid by the Magic Tape Company.

Employee		*Salary or Wage*
General Manager:	P. Sanderson	$80 000
Plant Workers:	M. Bailey	18 000
	B. Dorst	19 000
	N. Gehrals	28 000
	V. Ripley	35 000

The owner of the company, P. Epps, grants a 10 per cent pay raise to the plant employees to cover a 10 per cent rise in the cost of living. Sanderson, the general manager, argues that what applies to the plant employees also applies to him, and he puts in a request for a 10 per cent pay increase as well.

Questions

1. Comment on Sanderson's request, using some simple calculations or figures.
2. Are percentages a fair way to compare earnings? If you think so, defend your position in a short paragraph. If you think not, suggest an alternative and explain why you think your alternative is fairer.

Wage Increases — How Much Can Be Offered?

You are the proprietor of Brite Cleaners. The following data are extracted from your most recent income statement:

Revenue:	Cleaning	$134 900
	Storage	5 974
	Tailoring	30 500
		$171 374
Expense:	Rent	$4 800
	Delivery	2 930
	Wages	104 300
	Supplies Used	3 250
	General Expense	1 975
	Depreciation	7 560
	Power	4 250
		$129 065
	Net Income	$ 42 309

The employees have requested a 20 per cent increase in wages.

Questions

1. Assuming that no other expense is affected, how much would the wage increase cost the company?
2. Can you grant this request and still make a profit, in light of the above statement?
3. How much would the net income be if the increase were granted?
4. You want to make at least $30 000 per year from the business, and you expect an increase of $5 000 in revenue for the coming year. Calculate the maximum increase that you can grant to your employees, expressed in dollars and as a percentage. Assume that there is no increase in other expenses.

CASE 3

Challenge

A Profit-Sharing Proposal

A.

You are the accountant for Sayers & Company, a successful and growing company. The company has just completed its sixth fiscal year of operation. Its income statement for 20-1 is shown below in abbreviated form.

Sayers & Company
Income Statement
Year Ended December 31, 20–1
(Figures in thousands)

Revenue		$2 000
Operating Expenses		
Wages	$ 400	
Other Expenses	1 280	
Total Expenses		1 680
Net Income		$ 320

The company is currently engaged in wage negotiations with its union. There have been persistent difficulties between the union and the company, resulting in one strike and several other disruptions. At present, the union is demanding a 10 per cent wage increase retroactive to the beginning of the 20-1 year.

The owner is frustrated by the confrontations between union and management. She hopes to eliminate them by introducing a plan that would tie employees' wages to company profits.

She makes the following proposal to the employees.

> Sayers & Company
> Profit-Sharing Plan
>
> Item 1.   The employees will terminate their connection with the union.
> Item 2.   There will be no more wage negotiations.
> Item 3.   The total wages figure for every fiscal year will be fixed — at 60 per cent of the income-before-wages figure (net income plus wages).
> Item 4.   The plan will be retroactive to January 1, 20–1.
> Item 5.   The plan is expected to foster harmony, increase productivity, and keep the number of employees to a minimum. It is to the employees' benefit to keep their numbers as low as they can.

Questions

1. From the income statement above, calculate the wages as a percentage of the income-before-wages figure.
2. Prepare a revised income statement for 20-1 on the basis of the owner's profit-sharing formula.
3. **a.** Give the increase in wages for 20-1 if the employees accept the profit-sharing proposal.
   b. Calculate the percentage wage increase for 20-1.
4. Explain the employer's claim that the employees will benefit if they keep their numbers down.

B.

As part of the discussions with the employees, the owner reveals the company's forecasts for the next three years. These are as follows:

	20-2	*20-3*	*20-4*
Revenue	$2 100	$2 200	$2 500
Other Expenses (excluding wages)	1 320	1 400	1 580

Questions

5. Using the above data, prepare a schedule showing the projected income statements side by side for the years 20-1, 20-2, 20-3, and 20-4 on the assumption that the profit-sharing plan is accepted.
6. In light of the projected data, show the percentage wage increases for 20-2, 20-3, and 20-4. This is done by using the following calculation:

$$\frac{\text{increase in wages for the year}}{\text{wages figure for prior year}} \times 100$$

7. Calculate the average percentage increase for the three years 20-2, 20-3, and 20-4.
8. In terms of wage increases only, explain why employees should or should not accept the profit-sharing proposal.

C.

Assume the employees accepted the owner's profit-sharing proposal. Also, assume that the years 20-2, 20-3, and 20-4 have been concluded and that the actual figures for these years are now known. Some of these figures (in thousands) are given below:

	20-2	20-3	20-4
Revenue	$2 150	$2 280	$2 350
Other Expenses	1 320	1 390	1 400

Questions

9. Complete a side-by-side schedule of the income statements for the years 20-1, 20-2, 20-3, and 20-4 on the basis of the actual data.

10. Comparing these data with the projected data worked out previously, give your opinion regarding whether the profit-sharing plan has been a financial success. Consider both the employees' and the employer's point of view. In your analysis, include a calculation of the average percentage increase in wages for 20-2, 20-3, and 20-4.

11. Investigate some of the benefits that unions provide workers. What advantages might the employees have foregone in accepting the proposal?

SUMMARY EXERCISES —
Overview

The summary exercises that follow allow you to reinforce and develop your accounting skills, especially those that relate to accounting software. Read the following descriptions for each of these three exercises.

1) Kalley's Database Developments (Part 2)

The instructions for this exercise are designed for Simply Accounting and are found in your workbook. The accounting tasks are similar those required by Travel Trailers, so it is best to complete Chapter 12 prior to attempting this exercise. Also, completing the two Simply Accounting exercises in Chapter 7, including Part 1 of Kalley's Database Developments, is recommended.

The Simply Accounting activities you will perform are:

- creating customers and vendors;
- using the General, Payables, and Receivables modules;
- Bank reconciliation;
- preparing the adjusting and closing "entries" with Simply Accounting.

2) Travel Trailers

You will use two subsidiary ledgers when you complete this exercise—the Accounts Receivable ledger and the Accounts Payable ledger. Travel Trailers is designed for manual accounting using a five-journal system, so completing Chapter 12 is advisable.

You may decide to use Simply Accounting to complete the accounting requirements for Travel Trailers. Instructions for Simply Accounting are given where needed, and occur more frequently in the early stages of the exercise. There are two Simply Accounting exercises in Chapter 7 you should complete before doing Travel Trailers — Sam's Softball City and Kalley's Database Developments.

The Simply Accounting activities you will do for Travel Trailers are:

- using the General, Payables, and Receivables modules to process transactions;
- creating special invoices for discounts, returns, and allowances;
- and printing the financial statements, along with some special reports for the subsidiary modules.

For the purposes of comparing accounting systems, you may want to try Travel Trailers using the five-journal system, and then complete the transactions using Simply Accounting.

3) Sunshell Designs

This exercise has two sections. The first introduces you to working with Simply Accounting's Inventory module. The second give you the opportunity to try the Project module, where you allocate revenues and expenses to different parts of the business to see which is more profitable. When you complete Sunshell Designs, you will have used every one of Simply Accounting's six accounting modules.

The Simply Accounting activities you will perform are:

Section I

- using the General, Payables, and Receivables modules;
- creating inventory items;
- using the Inventory module;
- preparing payroll cheques (basic — Chapter 14 helpful but not required);
- completing a bank reconciliation.

Section II

- all the activities in Section I and;
- using the Project module to distribute revenue and expenses between branches.

SUMMARY EXERCISE —
Travel Trailers

Travel Trailers is a business owned and operated by Charles Fowler. The business earns its income from the selling and servicing of recreational vehicles. All sales and service transactions are subject to a 7 per cent goods and services tax (GST) and to an 8 per cent provincial sales tax (PST). Ignore PST on purchases.

Travel Trailers offers a 2 per cent cash discount on all sales on account if payment is made in full within 20 days of the invoice date.

Travel Trailers has a financing arrangement with Federated Finance Company for the sale of its major items, travel trailers, and mobile homes. When these units are sold on credit, Federated Finance pays Travel Trailers in full and takes on the responsibility of collecting from the customer. Thus, Travel Trailers receives payment in full for each unit sold and is able to treat the transaction as a cash sale.

❶ If you are using a manual system, set up the general ledger of Travel Trailers as of May 31, 20— from the following combined chart of accounts and general ledger trial balance. If you are using the Workbook, the ledger is set up for you.

TRAVEL TRAILERS
GENERAL LEDGER TRIAL BALANCE
MAY 31, 20—

101 Bank	$ 11 751.75	
110 Accounts Receivable	2 719.75	
115 Merchandise Inventory	125 423.00	
120 Supplies	1 151.00	
125 Prepaid Insurance	2 650.00	
130 Equipment	34 472.00	
131 Accumulated Depreciation — Equip.		$ 6 000.00
140 Truck	38 000.00	
141 Accumulated Depreciation — Truck		16 000.00
201 Accounts Payable		21 386.09
205 Bank Loan		120 000.00
210 PST Payable		3 030.78
212 GST Payable		2 651.90
215 GST Recoverable	1 629.28	
305 C. Fowler, Capital		40 245.76
310 C. Fowler, Drawings	15 000.00	
405 Sales		189 423.51
407 Discounts Earned		1 034.20

(Note: Trial balance continued on next page.)

501 Discounts Allowed	357.00	
505 Purchases	96 581.75	
510 Freight-in	1 174.72	
515 Bank Charges and Interest Expense	4 516.50	
520 Delivery Expense	5 650.20	
522 Depreciation of Equipment		
523 Depreciation of Truck		
525 Insurance Expense		
530 Utilities Expense	4 350.40	
535 Miscellaneous Expense	994.58	
540 Rent Expense	6 250.00	
545 Supplies Expense		
550 Telephone Expense	1 376.20	
555 Wages Expense	45 724.11	
	$399 772.24	$399 772.24

598 Income Summary

② **Set up the accounts receivable ledger of Travel Trailers as of May 31, 20—from the following information.** If you are using the Workbook, the ledger is already set up for you.

Customer	Address	Invoice	Date	Amount
B. Fraser	15 Gray St., London, ON N6A 4T9	634	May 10	$ 402.50
W. Hoyle	49 First St., Winnipeg, MB R3B 2H9	635	May 12	86.25
A. Newman	250 Fort Road, Fort Erie, ON L2A 4H1	629	Apr. 30	287.50
Schell Brothers	96 Garrison Ave., Halifax, NS B3H 2B5	633	May 4	1 161.50
N. Thompson	20 Wilson Ave., Red Deer, AB T4N 3Y3	630	May 1	684.25
L. Walker	4 Dennis Ave., Acton, ON L7J 2M6	631	May 2	97.75
			Total	$2 719.75

③ **Set up the accounts payable ledger of Travel Trailers as of May 31, 20—from the following information.** If you are using the Workbook, the ledger is already set up for you.

Supplier	Address	Ref. No.	Terms	Amount
Double-G Industries	17 LaSalle St., Hull, QUE J8X 4H6	420	Net 30	$11 315.25
Maynard's Delivery	49 Mill St., Barrie, ON L4M 4Y2			nil
Modern Mobile Homes	680 Gray Rd., Wesleyville, NF A0G 4R0	2213	Net 30	2 247.00
National Hardware	64 Venture St., Alymer, ON N5H 1H5	2309	Net 30	2 982.09
Parker Manufacturing	10 Bergen St., Kamloops, BC V2C 2A9			nil
Windsor Manufacturing	47 Armstrong Ave, Nanaimo, BC V9R 5T5	404	Net 30	4 841.75
			Total	$21 386.09

Travel Trailers uses five journals in its manual accounting system, as shown on page 718.

Sales Journal Page 19

Date	Particulars	PST Payable CR	GST Payable CR	Sales CR	Ref. No.	A/R DR

Purchases Journal Page 74

Date	Particulars	Other Accounts DR			GST Rec'ble DR	Freight-In DR	Supplies DR	Pchs's DR	Ref. No.	A/P CR
		Account	PR	Amount						

Cash Receipts Journal Page 37

Date	Particulars	Other Accounts CR			GST Payable CR	PST Payable CR	Sales CR	A/R CR	Ref. No.	Bank DR
		Account	PR	Amount						

Cash Payments Journal Page 84

Date	Particulars	Other Accounts DR			GST Rec'ble DR	Wages DR	Drawings DR	A/P DR	Ref. No.	Bank CR
		Account	PR	Amount						

General Journal Page 5

Date	Particulars	PR	Debit	Credit

4 **Journalize the following transactions for June. Use the journal page numbers shown. Post to the subsidiary ledgers daily directly from the source documents. Assume that Travel Trailers is exempt from paying PST on its purchases. Sales and purchase discounts are calculated on the total amount, including taxes.**

Load the Simply Accounting files named *Travel Trailers.SDB*. The Home window on page 718 appears showing the three modules you will be using: General, Payables, and Receivables. Double click the Vendors and Customers icons to get an idea of who sells to and buys from Travel Trailers.

If you are using a computer, the icon above alerts you to instructions and information that will help you use Simply Accounting for the Travel Trailers exercise. If you are using a manual system, skip the computer instructions and go on to the next transaction.

TRANSACTIONS

June

1   *Sales Invoice*

No. 636, to A. Newman, for repairs to trailer, $590.00 plus GST $41.30 plus PST $47.20, total $678.50.

Open the Sales (Orders & Quotes) Journal and enter the data in the illustration below. Notice that it looks like an invoice. If your monitor shows a different number of columns, you can change this by choosing the Customize icon located just above the invoice field. (Then select from the various tabs and options.) Column widths can be changed by dragging the vertical lines in the column headings.

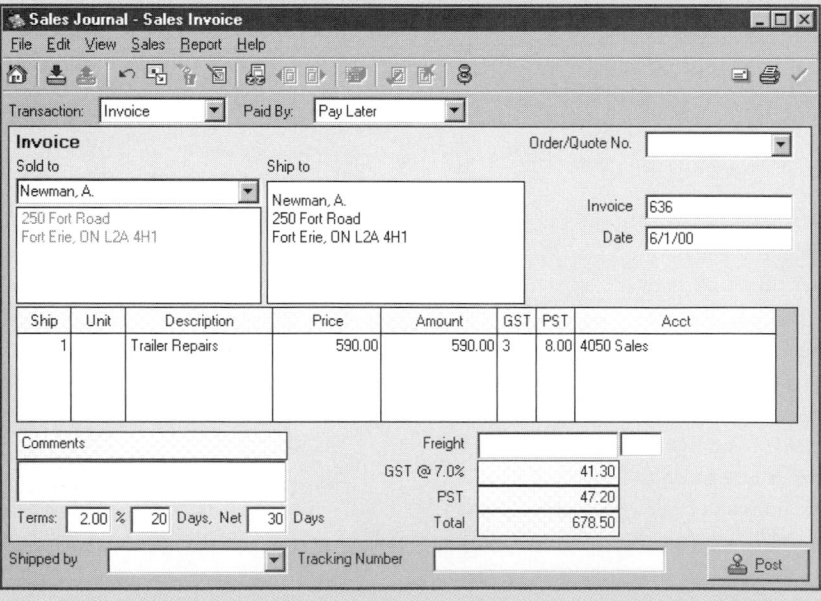

Notes and Tips
- Select the customer from the drop-down menu in the Sold To field.
- The invoice number appears automatically. (Your teacher may want you to add your initials.)
- Always ensure the default date matches what you intend.
- Use the Tab key to move from field to field.
- The "3" in the GST field is a special code. Press Enter while the cursor is in that field to see the other codes.
- Enter 8 in the PST field, which stands for 8 per cent.
- Press Enter in the Account field to select an account from the drop-down list.
- Notice that Simply Accounting calculates the invoice totals and enters the credit terms.
- Important. You can tell if you are on the right track by comparing the totals produced by Simply Accounting to the transaction data in the text. Nevertheless, before posting, check each journal entry by choosing **Report**, **Display Sales Journal Entry**. Making this selection for the above sales invoice will produce the journal entry below. Verify it as the entry you want, and then post the transaction.

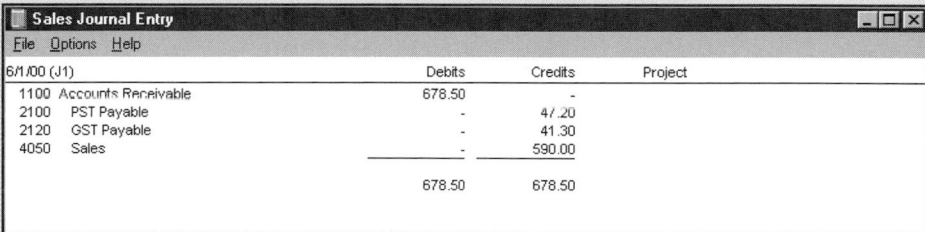

Sales Journal Entry			
File Options Help			
6/1/00 (J1)	Debits	Credits	Project
1100 Accounts Receivable	678.50	-	
2100 PST Payable	-	47.20	
2120 GST Payable	-	41.30	
4050 Sales	-	590.00	
	678.50	678.50	

1   *Cheque Copy*

No. 755, to General Real Estate, for the rent for June, $1 250.00 plus GST $87.50, total $1 337.50.

You have a few options when you want to make a credit to Bank. For example, you could use the General Journal, the Purchases (Orders and Quotes) Journal, or the Payments Journal. For Travel Trailers, use the Payments Journal each time the source document is a *Cheque Copy*. For the rent, the entry in the Payments Journal appears on page 720.

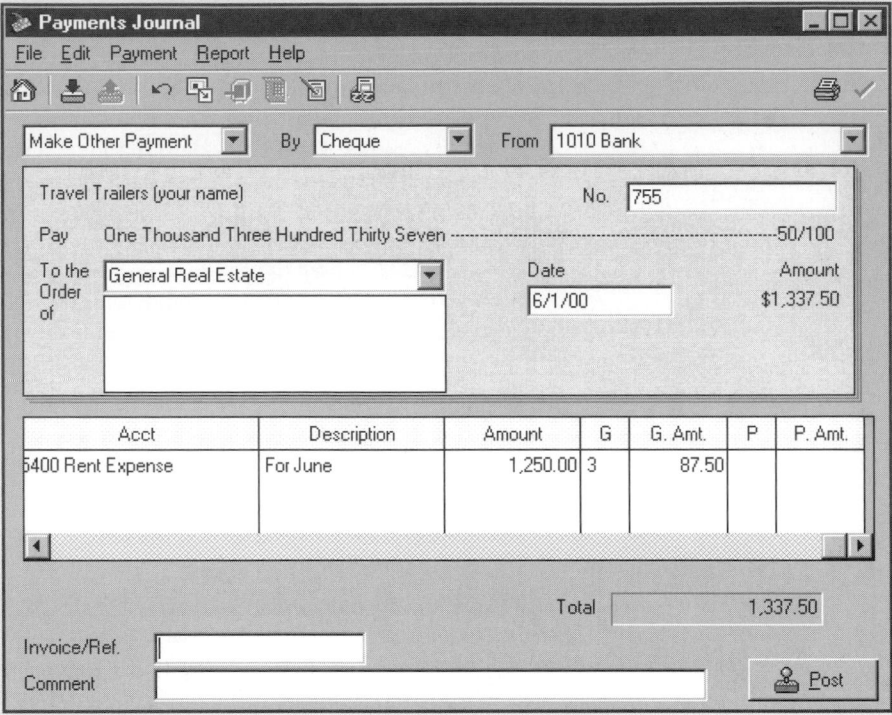

Notes and Tips

- Use the drop-down menu to select "Make Other Payment" in the field at the top-left corner.
- Enter the cheque number. When the software asks you if you want to have your subsequent cheques re-numbered, click OK.
- Key General Real Estate. When the software asks you if you want to add General Real Estate to your list of payees, click "Quick Add."
- The G field is for the GST code, which is 3.
- Check the entry by choosing Report, Display Payments Journal Entry.

2 *Sales Invoice*
  No. 637, to L. Walker, for trailer parts, $900.00 plus GST $63.00 plus PST $72.00, total $1 035.00.

You have done a sales invoice before, so proceed as you did for invoice 636. Do your best to avoid posting mistakes. Checking the journal entry (Report, Display Journal Entry) before posting will minimize your errors. If you do post incorrect data, see the advice at the end of this exercise.

2 *Cheque Copy*
  No. 756, to Double-G Industries, on account, $5 000.00.
3 *Purchase Invoices*
  From Parker Manufacturing, No. 40, for supplies, $236.00 plus GST $16.52, total $252.52; terms 2/10,n/30.
  From Double-G Industries, No. 472, for trailer parts, $1 475.00 plus GST $103.25, total $1 578.25; terms net 30.

You need no new advice for cheque copy no. 756. Use the Purchases Journal for the both of the above purchase invoices. The Simply Accounting data for the invoice from Parker Manufacturing is shown below.

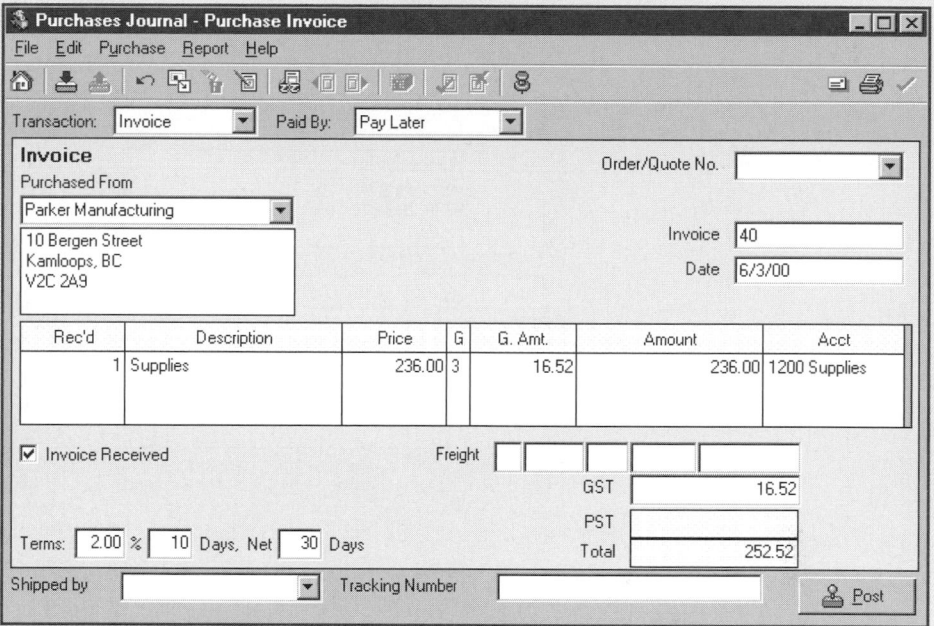

Notes and Tips

- Entering 1 in the Rec'd column, 236.00 in the Price column, and 3 in the G column will give Simply Accounting enough data to compute the other amounts shown above.
- Important: Enter the credit terms near the bottom left of the screen (2/10;n/30). Identifying the credit terms offered by this vendor will help you deal with discounts later.

4   *Cash Receipts List*
   From W. Hoyle, invoice 635 on account, $86.25.

Use the Receipts Journal for this customer's payment of her account. Pressing the Tab key in the Payment Amt. Field will enter the amount shown.

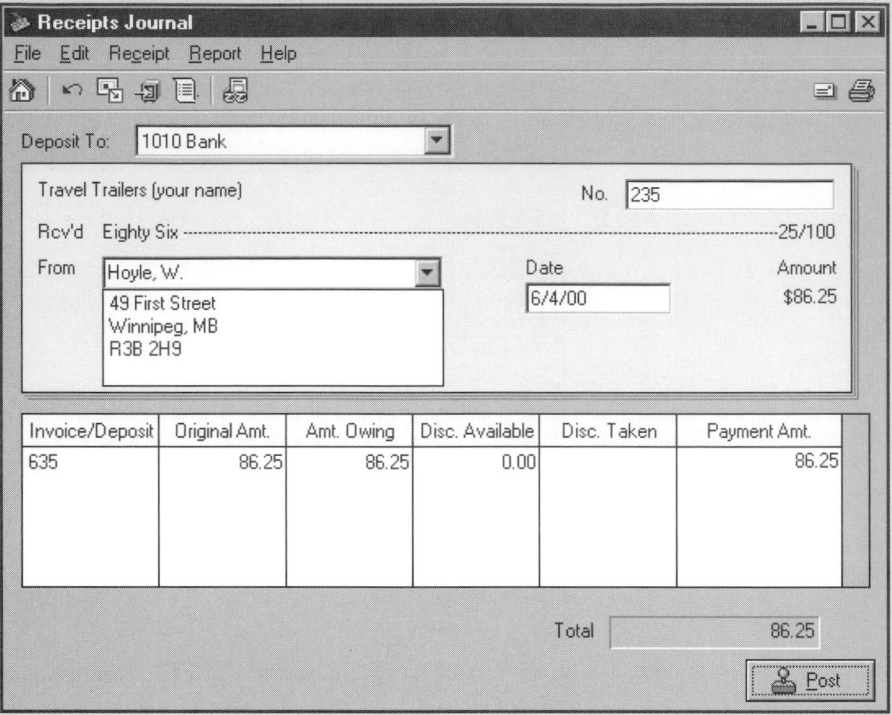

4 *Cash Sales Receipt*

From Federated Finance Company, No. 7042, for the sale of a trailer, selling price, $12 700.00 plus GST $889.00 plus PST $1 016.00, total $14 605.00.

Use the Sales Journal for this transaction. Be sure to follow the notes and tips that appear below the illustration.

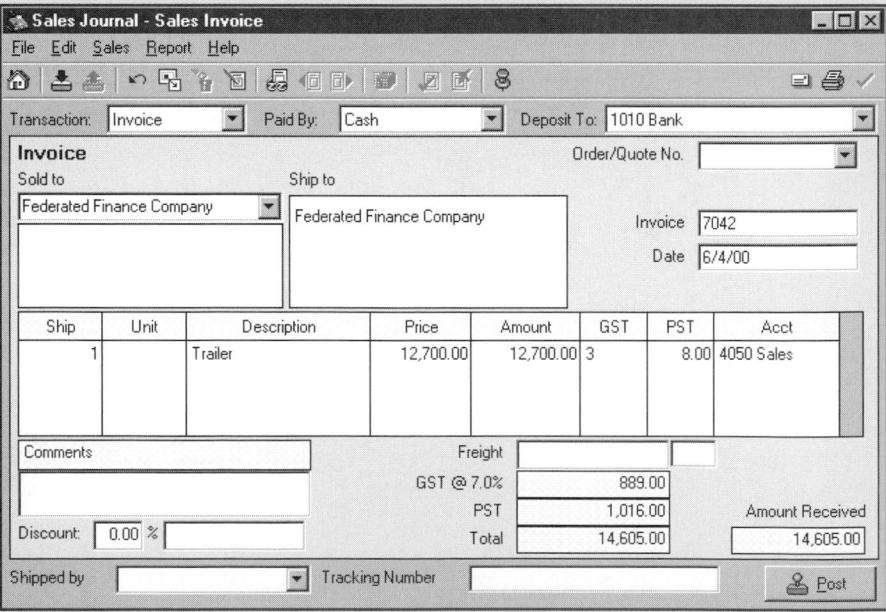

Notes and Tips
- Enter Cash in the Paid By field.
- Key Federated Finance Company in the Sold To field. (Use the "Quick Add" button when prompted to do so.)
- Key 7042 in the Invoice field.
- Enter the invoice data. Be very careful to enter 0 in the Discount field. When you check the journal entry, it should look like the one below.

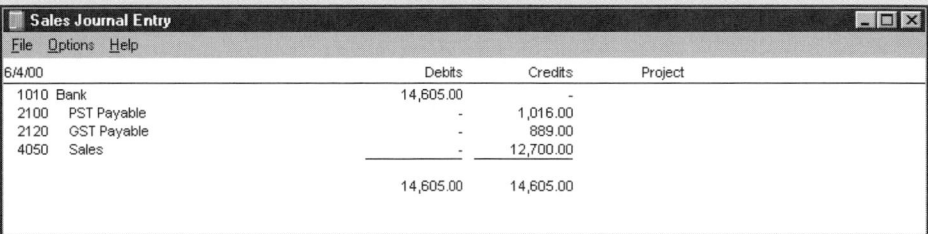

6/4/00		Debits	Credits	Project
1010	Bank	14,605.00	-	
2100	PST Payable	-	1,016.00	
2120	GST Payable	-	889.00	
4050	Sales	-	12,700.00	
		14,605.00	14,605.00	

- When you click the Post button, decline the software's offer to change the numbering sequence of the invoices.

4   *Bank Debit Advice*
     From Central Bank, for interest on bank loan for May, $1 200.00.

For most of the remaining transactions, you decide which journal to use. If there is no source document number provided in the text, key your initials into Simply Accounting's source document fields.

5   *Cheque Copies*
     No. 757, to C. Fowler, for personal use, $1 000.00.
     No. 758, made out to Cash, for the wages for the week, $2 178.50.

5   *Sales Invoice*
     No. 638, to N. Thompson, for trailer repairs and parts, $1 370.00 plus GST $95.90 plus PST $109.60, total $1 575.50.

8   *Cheque Copy*
     No. 759, to J.C. Pat Supply, for the cash purchase of supplies, $243.50, and miscellaneous expense items, $135.25; total $378.75 plus GST $26.51; total $405.26.

In the Payments Journal, if you use a row for the supplies and a row for the miscellaneous expense items, Simply Accounting's calculation of GST will be off by one cent. You decide how to overcome this issue.

8   *Memorandum*
     Correction required: $56.20 of Miscellaneous Expense had been debited to Freight-in in error.

9   *Cash Receipts List*
     From A. Newman, on account, $287.50.

9   *Purchase Invoices*

      From Windsor Manufacturing, No. 452, for trailer parts, $1 452.00 plus GST $101.64, total $1 553.64; terms net 30.

      From Maynard's Delivery, No. 64, for transportation charges on incoming merchandise, $217.50 plus GST $15.23, total $232.73; terms 2/10,n/30.

10   *Bank Debit Advice*

      From Central Bank, bank loan reduced by agreement with C. Fowler, $10 000.00.

10   *Sales Invoice*

      No. 639, to B. Fraser, for trailer parts, $450 plus GST $31.50 plus PST $36.00, total $517.50.

10   *Cash Receipts List*

      From Schell Brothers, on account, $1 161.50.

      From B. Fraser, on account, $402.50.

      From N. Thompson, on account, $684.25.

      From Federated Finance Company, No. 7043, for the sale of a trailer, $14 500.00 plus GST $1 015.00 plus PST $1 160.00, total $16 675.00.

10   *Cheque Copies*

      No. 760, to Modern Mobile Homes, payment in full of account, $2 247.00.

      No. 761, to Double-G Industries, on account, $5 000.00.

10   *Purchase Invoice*

      From Windsor Manufacturing, No. 481, for a new trailer, $14 500.00 plus GST $1 015.00, total $15 515.00; terms net 30.

11   *Sales Invoice*

      No. 640, to Schell Brothers, for trailer parts and service, $1 700.00 plus GST $119.00 plus PST $136.00, total $1 955.00.

11   *Cheque Copies*

      No. 762, to C. Fowler, for personal use, $500.00.

      No. 763, made out to Cash, for the wages for the week, $2 042.75.

      No. 764, to Parker Manufacturing, paying Invoice No. 40 less the 2 per cent discount, total $247.47.

Processing purchase discounts is easy in Simply Accounting if you remembered to enter the credit terms in the original purchase invoice. Pressing the Tab key will accept the various default amounts shown in the illustration on page 725.

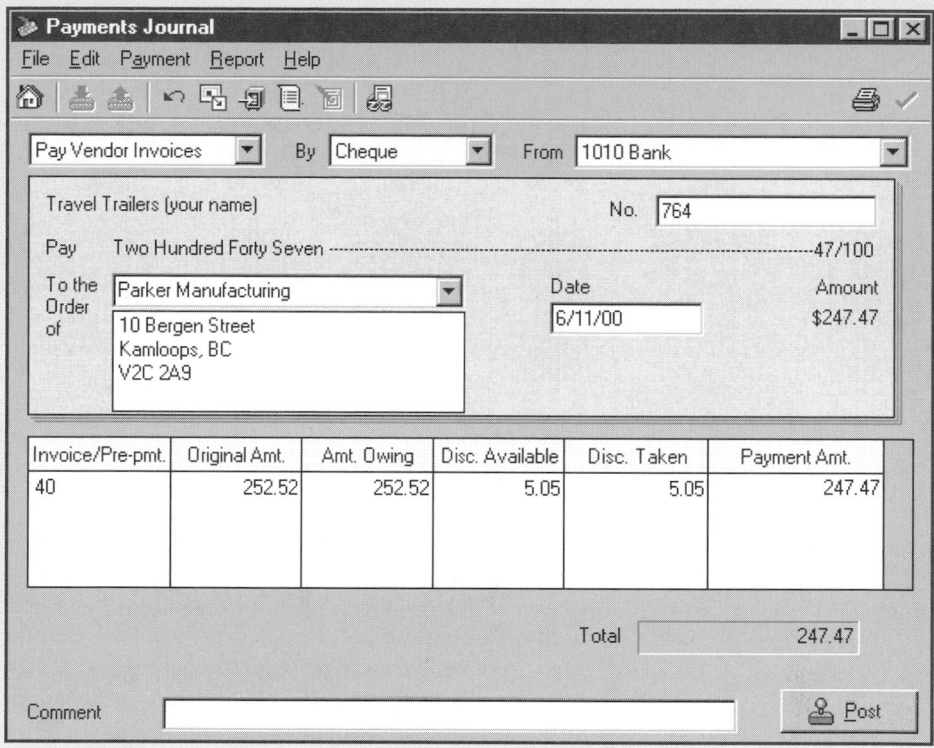

Notes and Tips

- If you forgot to enter the credit terms, try the editing procedure explained at the end of this exercise. Or, before using the Payments Journal above, you can enter a "negative" purchase invoice for the amount of the discount. (Simply use the Purchases Journal and use negative numbers for the amounts. The account to select is Discounts Earned.)

Checking the journal entry for the above data will produce the following result.

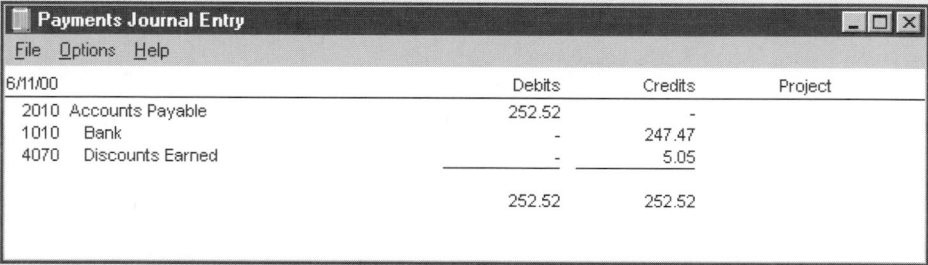

11 *Cheque Copy*

No. 765, to Craighurst Garage, cash payment for repairs to delivery truck, $420.00 plus GST $29.40, total $449.40.

15 *Cash Receipts List*

From Federated Finance Company, No. 7044, for the sale of a trailer, $15 000.00 plus GST $1 050.00 plus PST $1 200.00, total $17 250.00.

15   *Cheque Copies*

No. 766, to Provincial Treasurer, paying the provincial sales tax for May, $3 030.78.

No. 767, to Windsor Manufacturing, on account, $15 000.00.

16   *Purchase Invoices*

From Maynard's Delivery, No. 82, for transportation charges on incoming goods, $197.10 plus GST $13.80, total $210.90, terms 2/10,n/30.

From National Hardware, No. 2412, for trailer parts, $279.72 plus GST $19.58, total $299.30; terms net 30.

From Double-G Industries, No. 515, for a new trailer, $19 094.40 plus GST $1 336.61; total $20 431.01; terms net 30.

From Windsor Manufacturing, No. 499, for trailer parts, $283.50 plus GST $19.85, total $303.35; terms net 30.

17   *Sales Invoice*

No. 641, to W. Hoyle, for trailer servicing, $1 100.00 plus GST $77.00 plus PST $88.00, total $1 265.00.

17   *Cheque Copy*

No. 768, to Emerald Store, for the cash purchase of miscellaneous expense items, $145.80 plus GST $10.21, total $156.01.

18   *Cheque Copies*

No. 769, to C. Fowler, owner's personal use, $1 200.00.

No. 770, to National Hardware, on account, $2 982.09.

No. 771, to Maynard's Delivery, paying Invoice No. 64 less the 2 per cent discount, total $228.08.

18   *Credit Invoice Issued*

No. 69, to L. Walker, to cancel Invoice No. 631, $85.00 plus GST $5.95 plus PST $6.80, total $97.75.

The credit invoice above and the one that follows can be handled in a two-step process. First, in either the Sales or Purchases Journal, enter a negative invoice (using minus signs before the amounts) and post. Second, open either the Receipts or Payments Journal and accept the default amounts that appear for the negative invoice you just posted. Finish by posting the receipt or payment.

The main decision you make is before you take the first step. You will need to decide if you want to record a negative sale or a negative purchase.

19   *Credit Invoice Received*

From Double-G Industries, No. 600, for a 10 per cent price adjustment on Invoice No. 515, $1 909.44 plus GST $133.66, total $2 043.10.

19   *Purchase Invoice*

From National Hardware, No. 2480, for trailer parts, $409.50 plus GST $28.67, total $438.17; terms net 30.

19   *Cheque Copy*

No. 772, made out to Cash, for the wages for the week, $2 040.00.

22   *Sales Invoice*

No. 642, to L. Walker, for trailer parts and service, $290.00 plus GST $20.30 plus PST $23.20, total $333.50.

22   *Purchase Invoice*

From Parker Manufacturing, No. 140, for trailer parts, $367.20 plus GST $25.70, total $392.90; terms 2/10,n/30.

24   *Cash Receipts List*

From Federated Finance Company, No. 7045, for the sale of a trailer, $18 500.00 plus GST $1 295.00 plus PST $1 480.00, total $21 275.00.

25   *Cheque Copies*

No. 773, to C. Fowler, for personal use, $350.00.

No. 774, to Maynard's Delivery, paying Invoice No. 82 less the 2 per cent discount, total $206.68.

No. 775, to Humber Fuels, cash payment for fuel and oil for the delivery truck, $399.00 plus GST $27.93, total $426.93.

26   *Bank Debit Advice*

From Central Bank, bank loan reduced by agreement with C. Fowler, $15 000.00.

26   *Sales Invoice*

No. 643, to A. Newman, for trailer repairs, $236.00 plus GST $16.52 plus PST $18.88, total $271.40.

27   *Cash Receipts List*

From N. Thompson, in payment of Invoice No. 638 less the cash discount, $1 543.99.

28   *Cheque Copies*

No. 776, to Windsor Manufacturing, on account, total $2 213.74.

No. 777, made out to Cash, for the wages for the week, $2 452.00.

No. 778, to City Hydro, for the hydro for the month, $495.80 plus GST $34.71, total $530.51.

No. 779, to Bell Canada, for telephone for the month, $202.00 plus GST $14.14, total $216.14.

29   *Cash Receipts List*

From Schell Brothers, in payment of Invoice No. 640 less the cash discount, total $1 915.90.

29   *Purchase Invoice*

From National Hardware, No. 2561, for supplies, $930.00 plus GST $65.10, total $995.10; terms net 30.

30   *Sales Invoice*

No. 644, to W. Hoyle, for trailer servicing, $230.00 plus GST $16.10 plus PST $18.40, total $264.50.

30   *Cheque Copy*

No. 780, Receiver General, paying the net GST for the month of May, $2 651.90 less $1 629.28, total $1 022.62.

30   *Cash Receipts List*

From B. Fraser, in payment of Invoice No. 639 less the cash discount, total $507.15.

⑤ Balance the four columnar journals.

⑥ Post the five journals to the general ledger.

⑦ Balance the general ledger as of June 30.

⑧ Balance the subsidiary ledgers as of June 30.

⑨ Prepare an eight-column work sheet using the additional information below:

1. Supplies on hand at June 30 — $1 300.00.
2. Prepaid insurance as of June 30 — $1 599.00.
3. Late purchase invoices as of June 30:

   Purchases $740.00

   Miscellaneous Expense $102.00
4. Merchandise inventory at June 30 — $136 120.00.
5. Depreciation is calculated using the straight-line method. (Remember that the statement period is half a year.)

   Truck: Cost, $38 000.00; estimated life, 9 years; estimated terminal value, $2 000.00.

   Equipment: Cost, $34 472.00; estimated life, 10 years; estimated terminal value, $4 472.00.

Prepare the adjusting entries in the General Journal. Do not do the closing entries.

⑩ Prepare an income statement (six-month fiscal period) and a balance sheet as of June 30.

Check with your teacher to determine which reports and statements you should print. Be aware that there are detailed reports about the customers and vendors of Travel Trailers.

⑪ Journalize and post the adjusting and the closing entries.

⑫ Take off a post-closing trial balance.

Correcting Posted Errors

You learned how to correct general journal entries in Chapter 7 when you completed Sam's Softball City. Sometimes this required you to prepare and post two new entries (the undo/redo method), and other times you could fix your problem with just one journal entry.

Adjusting and Looking Up Invoices Icons

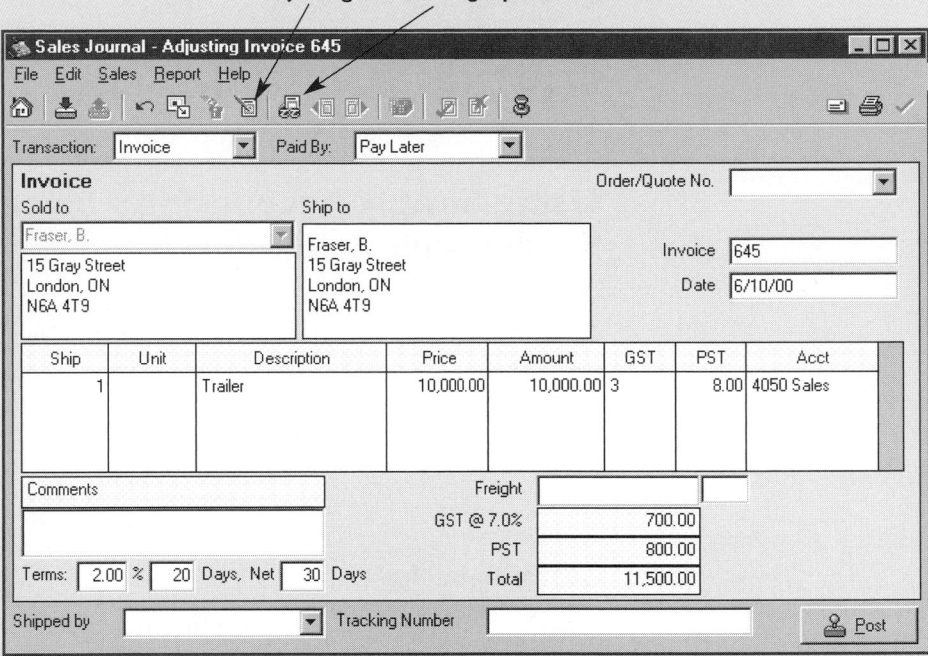

Simply Accounting does have an automatic adjusting feature that you can use for Travel Trailers. For example, suppose you journalized a sale to B. Fraser on June 10 for $1 000 before taxes. Soon after, you realize the amount should have been for $10 000.

To correct the problem, you enter the Sales journal and click the icon for looking up an invoice (see above). After you select the erroneous invoice, press the "adjust invoice" icon (see above) and change the amount of the sale from $1 000 to $10 000. Your work would look like the following.

When you post the entry above, Simply Accounting does the undo/redo method by processing two new journal entries for you automatically. These are identified as J13 and J14 in the following illustration. (J12 is the erroneous entry.)

All Journal Entries Display				_ □ ×
File Options Help				
6/10/00 to 6/10/00			Debits	Credits
6/10/00	J12	645, Fraser, B.		
		1100 Accounts Receivable	1,150.00	-
		2100 PST Payable	-	80.00
		2120 GST Payable	-	70.00
		4050 Sales	-	1,000.00
6/10/00	J13	ADJ645, Reversing J12. Correction is J14.		
		2100 PST Payable	80.00	-
		2120 GST Payable	70.00	-
		4050 Sales	1,000.00	-
		1100 Accounts Receivable	-	1,150.00
6/10/00	J14	645, Fraser, B.		
		1100 Accounts Receivable	11,500.00	-
		2100 PST Payable	-	800.00
		2120 GST Payable	-	700.00
		4050 Sales	-	10,000.00

SUMMARY EXERCISE —
Sunshell Designs

Using Simply Accounting's Inventory and Services Module

Two methods of keeping track of inventory were described in Chapter 11: the periodic inventory system and the perpetual system. When accounting is done manually, the periodic system is usually selected because it requires less work and expense. However, computers eliminate the extra accounting tasks required by the more informative perpetual inventory system. As a result, the perpetual system is gaining in popularity. You will use the perpetual inventory system in this exercise as you work with the *INVENTORY* and Services module of Simply Accounting.

Business Background

Paul Fast is a professional engineer. In his spare time, he designed a mini-tent made of nylon and folding fibreglass rods. The purpose of this product is to provide protection from the sun, wind, and blowing sand. Paul expects it to be used by regular visitors to beaches, lakes, or similar locations. He chose "Sunshell" as a name for the product and formed a business called Sunshell Designs to market it.

June is the first month of operations. The opening balance sheet of Sunshell Designs appears in Figure 1 below:

FIGURE 1

The opening balance sheet for Sunshell Designs.

Sunshell Designs
Balance Sheet
May 31, 20–2

Assets		Liabilities	
Bank	$50 000.00	Bank Loan	$30 000.00
Supplies	1 250.67	Accounts Payable	907.55
Equipment	975.88		
Furniture	1 369.54	Owner's Equity	
		S. Kalley, Capital	22 688.54
	$53 596.09		$53 596.09

Paul Fast intends to sell sunshells to department stores and retail outlets. The sunshells are manufactured by Gerry's Tent and Awning in Sudbury, Ontario. The first purchase invoice from Gerry's Tent and Awning is shown in Figure 2 on page 732.

Preparing the INVENTORY Module

Use Simply Accounting to load the *Sunshell.SDB* file. Three modules have already been set up: the GENERAL, the Payables, and the Receivables. You may wish to display the reports of these modules in order to get an idea of the accounts, customers, and vendors that Sunshell Designs has established.

FIGURE 2

Sunshell Design's first
purchase of inventory.

A sunshell with an
enhanced logo is
identified by "w/logo."

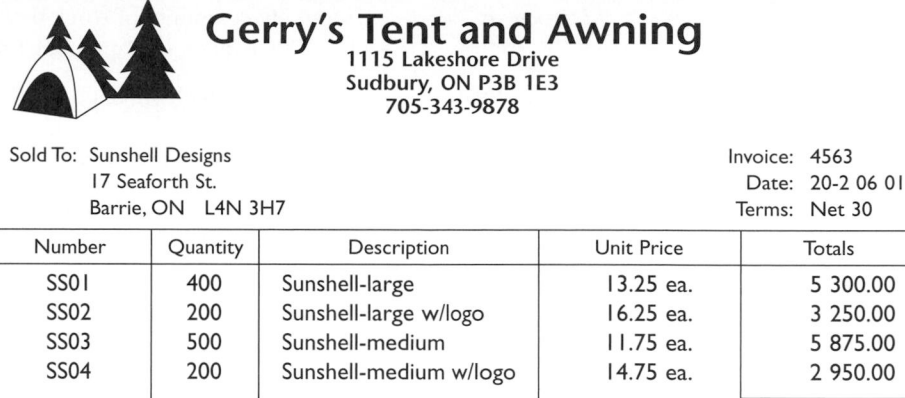

Gerry's Tent and Awning
1115 Lakeshore Drive
Sudbury, ON P3B 1E3
705-343-9878

Sold To: Sunshell Designs
          17 Seaforth St.
          Barrie, ON   L4N 3H7

Invoice: 4563
Date: 20-2 06 01
Terms: Net 30

Number	Quantity	Description	Unit Price	Totals
SS01	400	Sunshell-large	13.25 ea.	5 300.00
SS02	200	Sunshell-large w/logo	16.25 ea.	3 250.00
SS03	500	Sunshell-medium	11.75 ea.	5 875.00
SS04	200	Sunshell-medium w/logo	14.75 ea.	2 950.00
			Sub-total	17 375.00
			GST	1 216.25
GST#899321265			Amount Owed	18 591.25

Before using the Inventory module, you must create electronic inventory cards.
Most of the data for the first card can be obtained from the purchase invoice displayed in Figure 2 above.

Open the Inventory and Services icon and click the Create button. The first inventory item is *Sunshell-large*. Enter the information shown in Figure 3 below.

FIGURE 3

The electronic inventory
card for Sunshell-large.

The meanings of the fields shown in Figure 3 are as follows:

Item   The name and number of the new product (Sunshell-large, SS01)

Unit of Measure   The unit by which this product is sold. "Each" means that the
                    product is sold individually. Other examples of units are box,
                    carton, dozen, and so on.

Minimum Level   The smallest amount of stock that the business wants to keep on hand. When quantities approach this number, it is time to re-order.

Selling Price   The price at which Sunshell Designs will sell this product. (***Note:*** *This information is not on the purchase invoice shown in Figure 2. Sunshell Designs plans to sell this item for $26.50.*)

When you finish entering the data in Figure 3, you must link the Inventory module to the General ledger. Click the "Linked" tab, which you can see in Figure 3, and enter the accounts shown in Figure 4.

FIGURE 4

The Linked tab showing the General Ledger accounts related to the Inventory module.

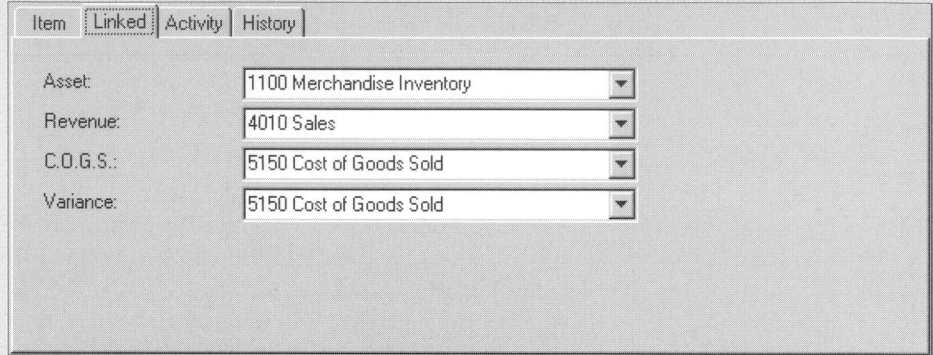

An explanation of each of the accounts in Figure 4 is given below.

Asset   The asset account that will be affected when these sunshells are bought and sold (Merchandise Inventory).

Revenue   The revenue account that will be credited when these sunshells are sold (Sales).

C.O.G.S.   The expense account that will be debited when these sunshells are sold (Cost of Goods Sold).

Variance   A special account some businesses use to gather amounts if inventory levels go below zero. This is not an issue for Sunshell Designs, so Cost of Goods Sold is entered.

After linking the accounts, click the "Create Another" button. **Then, create inventory cards for the remaining three items shown on the invoice in Figure 2 on page 732.** To do this, you need to know the selling prices of the remaining inventory items. They are:

1) Sunshell-large w/logo, $32.50;
2) Sunshell-medium, $23.50; and
3) Sunshell-medium w/logo, $29.50.

Enter 100 in the Minimum Level field for each item. When you have completed the last ledger card and have returned to Simply Accounting's Home window, double-click the Inventory and Services icon to see the subsidiary ledger you have created.

As a final step, return to the Home window and choose Setup, Linked Accounts, Inventory Items. In the Adjustment Write-off field, select the Inventory Shrinkage account. This expense account is often used to receive amounts when inventory is lost, stolen, or damaged.

Recording Purchases

You can now journalize the first purchase of merchandise from Gerry's Tent and Awning. Even though this transaction involves the purchase of inventory, do not make the entry in the Inventory module. Instead, open the Purchases journal and enter the data shown in Figure 5.

FIGURE 5

Data from the first invoice entered in the Purchases journal.

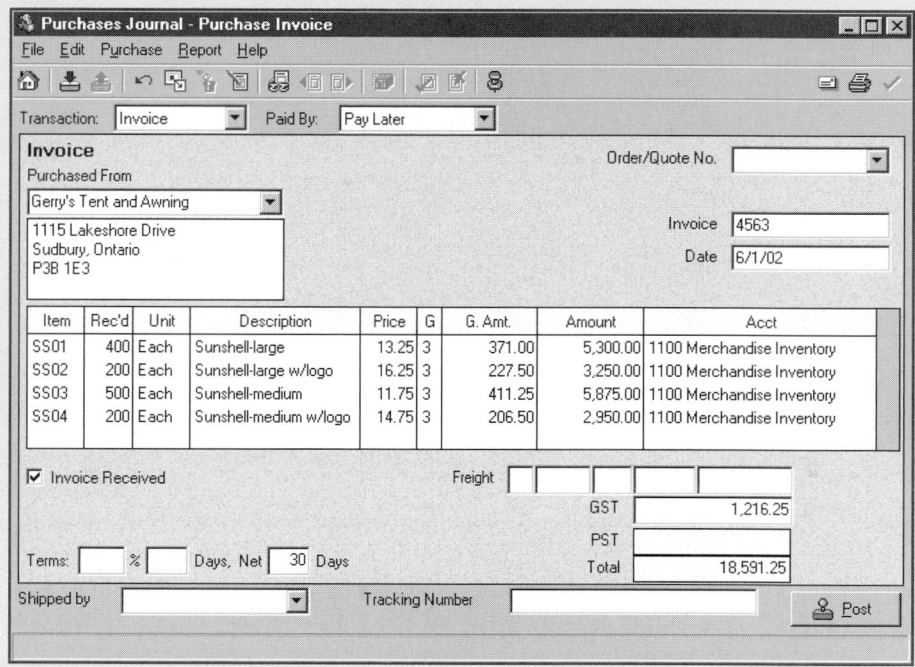

Notes and Tips

It is assumed that you completed the exercise for either Travel Trailers or Kalley's Database Developments and know how to use the Payables and Receivables modules. Therefore, you should need little help to get your monitor to look like Figure 5 above. However, the following advice may be useful.

- Press Enter while the cursor is in the Item field in order to select from the list of inventory items. Alternatively, you can key the item numbers; use upper-case letters.
- Enter the quantities received and the prices. Be aware that these are the cost prices; it is extremely important that you enter them accurately.
- If you have a different number of columns showing in your invoice, use the Customize button (located just above the Transaction field) to make adjustments.

Before you post, check the journal entry, which should look like Figure 6 below.

FIGURE 6

The journal entry for the first purchase.

Purchases Journal Entry

File   Options   Help

6/1/02 (J1)

	Debits	Credits	Project
1100 Merchandise Inventory	17,375.00	-	
2150 GST Recoverable	1,216.25	-	
2050 Accounts Payable	-	18,591.25	
	18,591.25	18,591.25	

Notice that Merchandise Inventory is debited for this transaction. If you were using the periodic inventory system, Purchases would have been debited. Post when you are sure your work is correct.

Recording Sales

In Chapter 11, you learned that the perpetual inventory system has two parts to each sale. The first is very familiar to you:

	DR	CR
Accounts Receivable (or Bank)	$$$$$	
Sales		$$$$$
GST Payable		$$$$

You have had less experience with the second part of the sales transaction, which is the cost portion.

	DR	CR
Cost of Goods Sold	$$$$$	
Merchandise Inventory		$$$$$

The debit to Cost of Goods Sold represents the business's cost of buying the merchandise it sold. The credit to Merchandise Inventory is made because stock leaves the store and merchandise inventory is reduced. Simply Accounting will automatically generate the cost portion of a sales transaction for you.

On June 1, Sunshell Designs made its first sale to Galleon Beach Co-op in Kenora, Ontario. The partial invoice appears below in Figure 7:

FIGURE 7

A partial invoice for the first sale made by Sunshell Designs.

Sales Invoice 001 to Galleon Beach Co-op, June 1, 20-2

Number	Quantity	Description	Unit Price	Totals
SS03	25	Sunshell-medium	23.50 ea.	587.50
SS01	10	Sunshell-large	26.50 ea.	265.00
			Sub-total	852.50
			GST	59.68
			Amount Owed	912.18

Use the Sales Journal to record the invoice data in Figure 7. When you are done, your monitor will look similar to Figure 8 on page 736. (With Simply Accounting, it will be more convenient to number sales invoices with one digit instead of the three that appear on Sunshell's source document.)

FIGURE 8

The journal entry screen for sales on account.

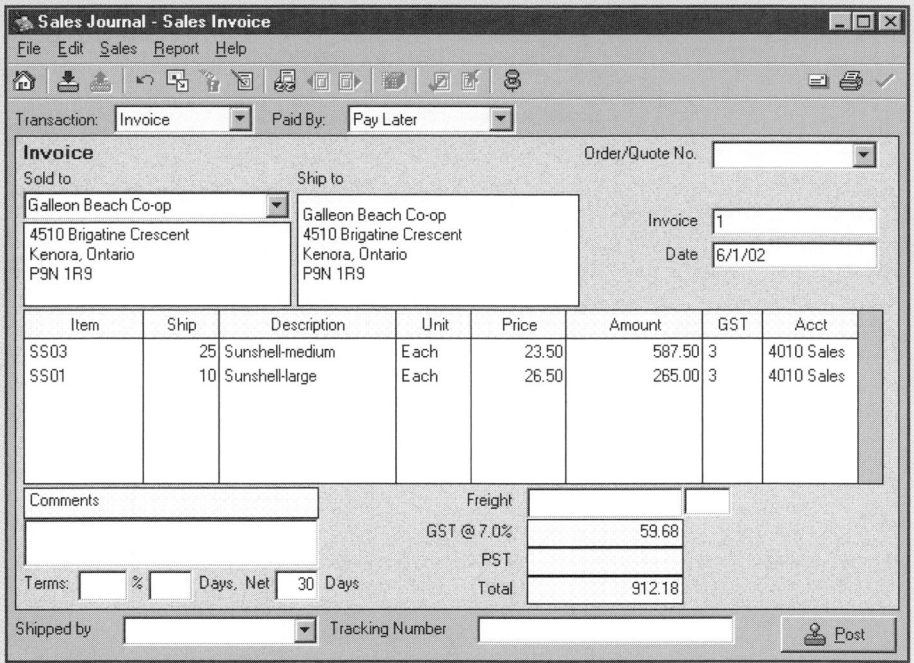

When you check the journal entry, your monitor will display the information in Figure 9.

FIGURE 9

The journal entry for the first sale of merchandise.

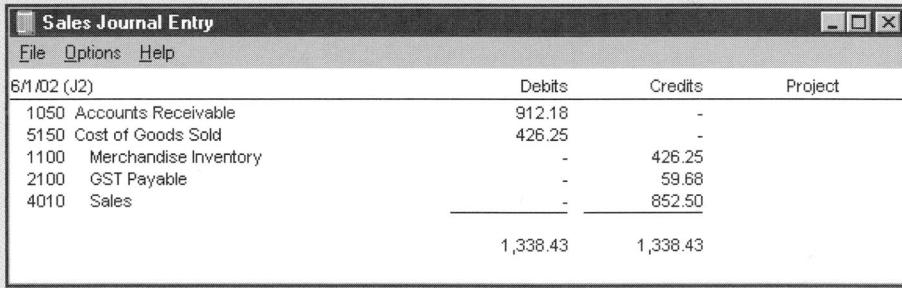

If you compare the above two illustrations, can you determine what amount appears in Figure 9 that you did not enter when preparing the data in Figure 8? The answer is $426.25, which is debited to Cost of Goods Sold and credited to Merchandise Inventory. This is the cost portion of the sale transaction under the perpetual inventory system. It is generated automatically. Simply Accounting used the linking data in the Inventory module to select the proper accounts. Then the software program calculated the average cost of the sunshells (using data on the purchase invoice from Gerry's Tent and Awning) and multiplied by the quantity sold.

Notice that Simply Accounting "sandwiches" the cost portion of the transaction between the sale portion. Post this journal entry when you are sure it is correct.

Recording Sales Returns

On June 4, five of the medium sunshells sold to Galleon Beach Co-op were returned. They had been damaged in transport. To journalize, you first need to enter a negative sales invoice.

Enter −5 in the ship field and add a notation to the source document number. Your monitor will look like Figure 10 below.

FIGURE 10

The journal entry screen for a sales return (a credit invoice).

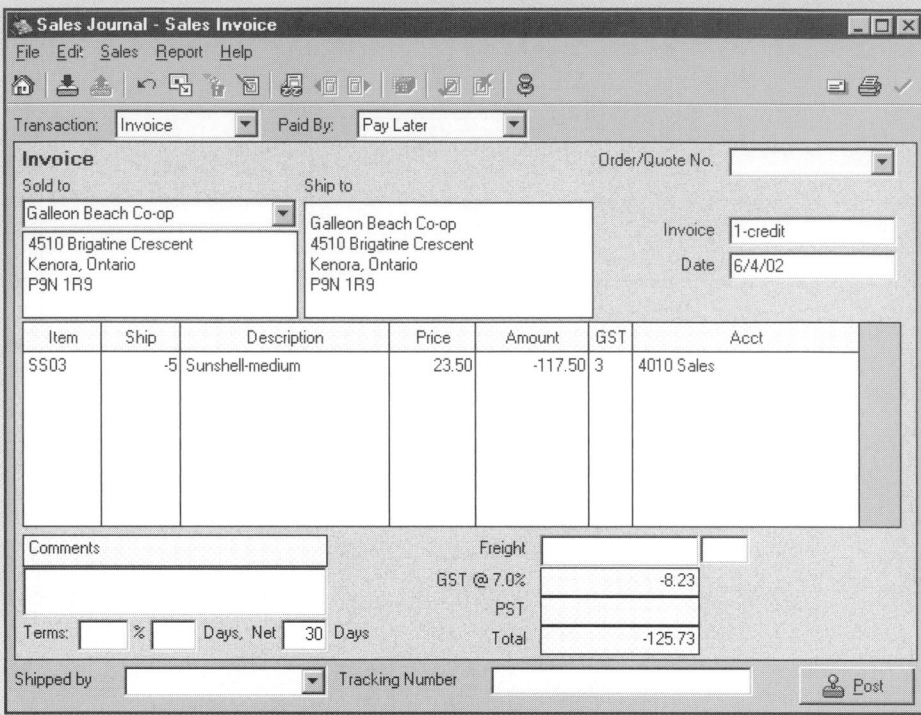

The journal entry produced by the credit invoice is shown in Figure 11.

FIGURE 11

The journal entry for a credit invoice.

Sales Journal Entry

File Options Help

6/4/02 (J3)	Debits	Credits	Project
1100 Merchandise Inventory	58.75	-	
2100 GST Payable	8.23	-	
4010 Sales	117.50	-	
1050 Accounts Receivable	-	125.73	
5150 Cost of Goods Sold	-	58.75	
	184.48	184.48	

Sunshell Designs has chosen to record returns in its Sales account rather than in a Sales Returns and Allowances account.

You must post the journal entry shown in Figure 11. Be aware that this entry creates an issue. The merchandise inventory coming back into the store is damaged and has no value. The journal entry in Figure 11, however, increases Merchandise Inventory by $58.75. Clearly, this overstates that asset account and an adjustment must be made.

To make the necessary adjustment, open the Adjustments journal in the Inventory module and enter the data shown in Figure 12 on page 738.

FIGURE 12

Adjusting the merchandise inventory because the returned goods cannot be sold again.

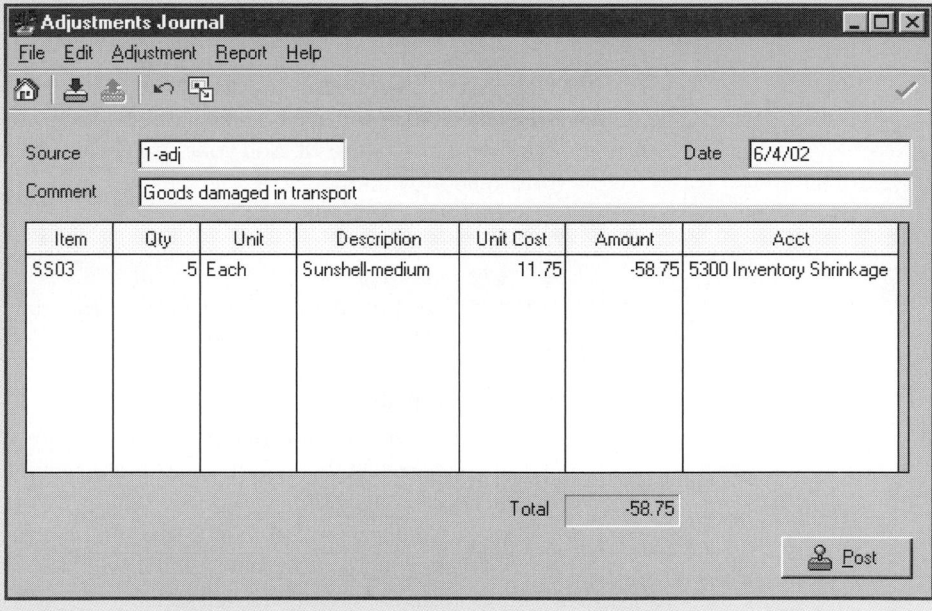

The data above will reduce the merchandise inventory by $58.75. Notice that an account other than Cost of Goods Sold will be debited because the sunshells were, in fact, not sold but damaged. The journal entry produced by the data in Figure 12 is the last one shown in the summary of the first four journal entries displayed in Figure 13 below.

FIGURE 13

A summary of the first four journal entries for Sunshell Designs.

```
All Journal Entries Display                                    _ □ ×
File  Options  Help
6/1/02 to 6/4/02                                    Debits      Credits
6/1/02     J1      4563, Gerry's Tent and Awning
                   1100  Merchandise Inventory     17,375.00        -
                   2150  GST Recoverable            1,216.25        -
                   2050    Accounts Payable              -      18,591.25

6/1/02     J2      1, Galleon Beach Co-op
                   1050  Accounts Receivable          912.18        -
                   5150  Cost of Goods Sold           426.25        -
                   1100    Merchandise Inventory          -        426.25
                   2100    GST Payable                    -         59.68
                   4010    Sales                          -        852.50

6/4/02     J3      1-credit, Galleon Beach Co-op
                   1100  Merchandise Inventory         58.75        -
                   2100  GST Payable                    8.23        -
                   4010  Sales                        117.50        -
                   1050    Accounts Receivable            -        125.73
                   5150    Cost of Goods Sold             -         58.75

6/4/02     J4      1-adj, Goods damaged in transport
                   5300  Inventory Shrinkage           58.75        -
                   1100    Merchandise Inventory          -         58.75

                                               20,172.91    20,172.91
```

Computer Exercises

Use Simply Accounting to record the rest of June's transactions for Sunshell Designs. Before you start, make sure you have completed the four transactions that appear in Figure 13. Add your name where indicated in the Setup, Company Information window.

June

4   *Cheque Copy*

No. 001, to Bissell Realty Ltd. for the monthly rent, $1 300.00 plus GST of $91.00, total $1 391.00.

Notes and Tips

*   Use the Payments Journal and choose Make Other Payment in the top-left field. Key Bissell Realty Ltd. and press the Quick Add button when prompted.
*   Since this transaction will occur monthly, press the icon beside the house icon and below the Edit menu. You will be prompted to save this transaction as a "recurring transaction," which will save you time when you make the entry again in subsequent months.

4   *Purchase Invoice*

No. 683C, from Simcoe Supplies for office supplies, $436.49 plus GST of $30.55, total $467.04. Terms net 30. (Ignore PST.)

Notes and Tips

*   For purchase invoices, keying 1 in the "Rec'd" column and the cost ($436.49) in the "Price" column will help Simply Accounting extend and total the invoice for you.

5   *Cheque Copy*

No. 002, to Macro Computers for a computer system, $2 693.00 plus GST of 188.51, total $2 881.51. (Use Quick Add when prompted.)

5   *Purchase Invoice*

No. 5129, to Running Bear Transport for delivery of goods received on June 1 from Gerry's Tent and Awning, $182.00 plus GST of $12.74, total $194.74. Terms 30 days.

5   *Sales Invoice*

No. 002, to Scugog Novelty appear below.

Number	Quantity	Description	Unit Price	Totals
SS01	5	Sunshell-large	26.50	132.50
SS03	10	Sunshell-medium	23.50	235.00
SS04	5	Sunshell-medium w/logo	29.50	147.50
			Sub-total	515.00
			GST	36.05
			Amount Owed	551.05

12　*Owner's Memo*

Four sunshells (one of each type) were given away for promotional purposes. Total cost value of the stock was $56.00.

Notes and Tips
- Use the Adjustments Journal in the Inventory module.
- Use your initials in the Source field.
- Enter negative numbers in the "Qty" field.
- Think about which account would be most appropriate for the debit amount of $56.00.

12　*Sales Invoice*

No. 003, to Georgina Resorts. Details appear below.

Number	Quantity	Description	Unit Price	Totals
SS01	15	Sunshell-large	26.50	397.50
SS03	30	Sunshell-medium	23.50	705.00
			Sub-total	1 102.50
			GST	77.18
			Amount Owed	1179.68

15　*Cheque Copy*

No. 003, to Paul Fast, the owner, for his personal use, total $900.00.

16　*Sales Invoice*

No. 004, to Stevens Department Stores. Details appear below.

Number	Quantity	Description	Unit Price	Totals
SS01	50	Sunshell-large	26.50	1 325.00
SS03	75	Sunshell-medium	23.50	1 762.50
SS04	25	Sunshell-medium w/logo	29.50	737.50
			Sub-total	3 825.00
			GST	267.75
			Amount Owed	4 092.75

19　*Credit Invoice*

No. CM002, from Scugog Novelty. They returned one large sunshell in damaged condition. The sunshell cannot be repaired. Details appear below.

Number	Quantity	Description	Unit Price	Totals
SS01	1	Sunshell-large	26.50	26.50
			Sub-total	26.50
			GST	1.86
			Amount Owed	28.36

Remember, this is a "minus" invoice.

Notes and Tips
- After you journalize and post the "negative" sales invoice on page 739, think about the extra step required, then take it.

22   *Sales Invoice*

No. 005, to Ajax Department Stores. Details appear below.

Number	Quantity	Description	Unit Price	Totals
SS01	35	Sunshell-large	26.50	927.50
SS03	35	Sunshell-medium	23.50	822.50
			Sub-total	1 750.00
			GST	122.50
			Amount Owed	1 872.50

22   *Owner's Memo*

Paul Fast, the owner, took two large sunshells home for his personal use. Total cost value $26.50.

Notes and Tips
- The Adjustments journal can handle the reduction in inventory, but what are you going to do with the GST the business was entitled to recover when it first bought these two large sunshells?

28   *Cheque Copy*

No. 004, to the Grey-Bruce Hydro for the monthly utilities bill, $112.43 plus GST of $7.87, total $120.30.

28   *Cheque Copy*

No. 005, to Bell Canada for the monthly telephone bill, $97.86 plus GST of $6.85, total $104.71.

29   *Cheque Copy*

No. 006, to Gerry's Tent and Awning for invoice 4563, total $18 519.25.

Notes and Tips
- In the top-left field of the Payments Journal, switch the selection to "Pay Vendor Invoices." Press the Tab key repeatedly to quickly select the defaults shown.

30   *Remittance Advice*

Remittance slip No. 001, from Galleon Beach Co-op for payment of invoice 001, less the return, total $786.45.

30   *Sales Invoice*

No. 006A, to Galleon Beach Co-op. Details appear below.

Number	Quantity	Description	Unit Price	Totals
SS01	10	Sunshell-largre	26.50	265.00
SS03	25	Sunshell-medium	23.50	587.50
			Sub-total	852.50
			GST	59.68
			Amount Owed	912.18

30   *Cheque Copy*

   No. 007, to Paul Fast, the owner, for his personal use, total $900.00.

30   *Cheque Copies*

   Paid the two employees, Herb Epp and Michelle Leung, their wages for the month. Use the Payroll Journal to prepare cheque 008 for Herb Epp and 009 for Michelle Leung.

Notes and Tips

- Even if you have not yet completed Chapter 14 covering payroll, you can still use the Payroll journal to prepare these cheques. Since the payroll cards for the employees have already been entered, processing the cheques is easy.

   Open the Paycheques icon in the Payroll module. Select Herb Epp and press the Tab key. You should see payroll calculations automatically made at the bottom of the screen. Choose *Report, Display Payroll Journal Entry* to see what Simply Accounting has done. It should look similar to the illustration below.

Payroll Journal Entry				‌_ □ ✕
File Options Help			
6/30/02 (J25)	Debits	Credits	Project
5110 C.P.P. Expense	74.43	-	
5210 E.I. Expense	73.92	-	
5600 Wages Expense	2,200.00	-	
1010 Bank	-	1,735.11	
2410 C.P.P. Payable	-	148.86	
2420 E.I. Payable	-	126.72	
2430 Employees' Inc. Tax Payable	-	337.66	
	2,348.35	2,348.35	

- Do not be concerned if your screen shows slightly different amounts than those in the above illustration. This happens because you may be using a different version of Simply Accounting's payroll tax tables. (Businesses update their tax tables at least once per year.)
- Post the transaction for Herb Epp and repeat for Michelle Leung (cheque 009).

30   *Bank Statement*

The bank statement from the Georgian Bay Bank arrived today and is shown below.

Bank Statement
June 29, 20-2

Description	Debits	Credits	Date		Balance
			May	29	50,000.00
#001	1,391.00		Jun	5	48,609.00
#002	2,881.51			6	45,727.49
#003	900.00			17	44,827.49
DM Loan Interest	232.98			29	44,594.51
DM Service Charge	11.62			29	44,582.89

Notes and Tips
- When the Bank account was created, it was set up for reconciliation. This means all the transactions affecting Bank were stored and are available for use by the Account Reconciliation Journal of Simply Accounting. Open the Account Reconciliation icon located in the General module.
- Select 1010 Bank and enter the ending balance of cash from the bank statement ($44,582.89) in the field on the right side your screen.
- Determine which of the cheques have been paid by the bank and indicate this by clicking the "C" column next to the amount of the cleared cheque. Your monitor should look like the illustration below.

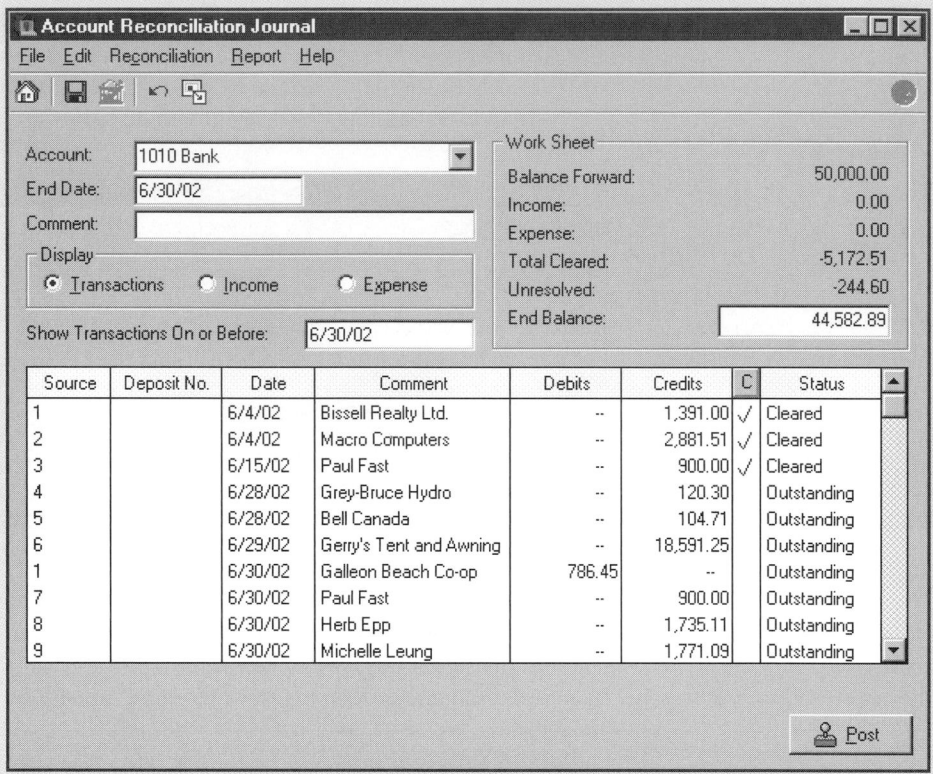

- Notice that there is an unresolved balance of $244.60. This is due to the bank deducting service charges and interest on June 29. Sunshell Designs learned of this deduction when it received the statement. To reconcile the Bank account and record the journal entries for service charges and interest, click the Expense circle located just above the date for transactions. It will be easy for you to record the expenses. (Use your initials for the source document reference.) When you are done, check the journal entries created, which should look like those on page 743.

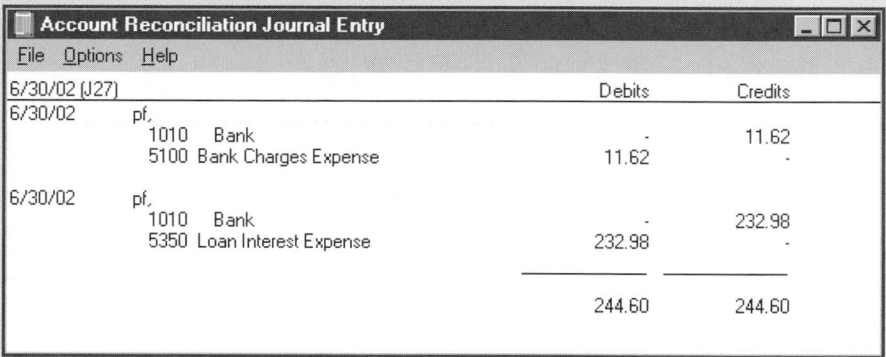

2 **Print the income statement for June and the balance sheet as of June 30.**

Extending Your Computer Knowledge

Make the selections necessary to view the Inventory and Services Detail Report. Use this report to help you answer the following questions:

1 Which inventory item had the highest sales (in terms of units sold)?

2 If the current pace of sales continues, in what month will Sunshell Designs have to reorder the item identified in question 1?

3 Which inventory item had the lowest unit sales?

4 What can be done to increase the sales of the item identified in question 3? (Write some specific suggestions.)

Communicate It

Paul Fast is concerned that your accounting work is in error. The percentages in the above report show each inventory item at a 50 per cent margin. Yet Paul knows he doubled all cost amounts to arrive at retail prices. He believes, therefore, that the margins should be 100 per cent.

Write Paul a letter to clear up the misunderstanding. To help state your case, you should view another version of the *Inventory and Services Detail* report.

First, however, choose Setup, Settings and click the Inventory and Services tab. Change the profit evaluation from margin to markup. Examine the figures the new report shows and determine how Simply Accounting calculates the percentages. Refer to this new report in your explanation to Paul.

Using Simply Accounting's Project Module

A business may have numerous activities and locations that contribute to its overall net income. These separate activities or locations are sometimes called *profit centres*. It is important to assess the profit made by each branch of a firm separately. To help with this assessment, they can use a computer module that assigns revenues and costs to different parts of a business. In this section, we will look at the Project module of Simply Accounting.

Business Background

Paul Fast was satisfied with the volume of sunshells he sold to retailers in the first month of operations. Sensing that the demand for his products was high, he opened a small retail location in Wasaga Beach, Ontario. At this new outlet, he hopes to earn higher profits by selling sunshells at retail prices.

He rented a small beachfront store and transferred an employee, Michelle Leung, to manage the retail operations. To record and evaluate the revenues and costs of the Wasaga Beach location, you will use the Project module of Simply Accounting.

Preparing the Project Module

The Project module is not for making journal entries. Rather, it merely organizes and displays the information that you have entered in other modules.

Paul Fast wants the accounting data of this business broken down into branches: one for the wholesale operations in Barrie, Ontario, and one for the retail operations in Wasaga Beach. The two branches may be referred to as the two profit centres of the business.

Load the file you used for Sunshell Designs in the month of June (Sunshell.SDB). Make necessary corrections before you carry on with July's transactions.

From the Home window of Simply Accounting, choose View, Modules, Project. Now that you can see the Project module icon, open the program and click the Create button. Call the first project Wasaga and accept the default date. There are no revenues and expenses to carry over. Call the second project Barrie. (You could carry over June's revenues and expenses for Barrie, but this is not necessary for the purposes of the exercise.)

To make some changes to the system settings of the Project module, choose Setup, Settings from the Home window. Click the Project tab and make the three important selections below.

1) Allocate Payroll Transactions by **Amount**;
2) Allocate Other Transactions by **Amount**; and
3) **Warn** if allocation is not complete.

There is not much more to setting up the Project module. One change you should make is to the name of the module. Perhaps "project" does not fit the business. Two branches are what really exist: the Barrie branch (wholesale) and the Wasaga branch (retail). Therefore, choose Setup, Names and change the project title to Branch. You will notice the effect of this change when you return to the Home window.

Entering Transactions

Now that you have created two profit centres, the way you record revenues and expense transactions in the other modules will be slightly different. From now on, you must indicate the branch to which each revenue and expense transaction belongs. For example, the first entry for July is as follows:

July

1   *Cheque Copy*

> No. 010, to Bissell Realty Ltd., for rent in Barrie, $1 300 plus GST of $91, total $1 391.

Notes and Tips

- Open the Payments Journal and enter the above transaction. (You can quickly do this by presssing the "recall recurring transaction" button and change the date.)
- Although you established the Project/Branch module, you have to customize each journal to show the Allocation column. Click the Customize Journal button (see Figure 14 below) and make the appropriate selection. This column allows you to allocate revenues and expenses to each branch. (You can change column widths by dragging the vertical lines in the column headings.)
- Once you can see the "Allo" column, double-click it, press Enter in the Branch column, and follow the prompts to allocate the entire rent payment to the Barrie branch. A check mark will appear in the "Allo" when you are done. Your monitor should look like Figure 14 below.

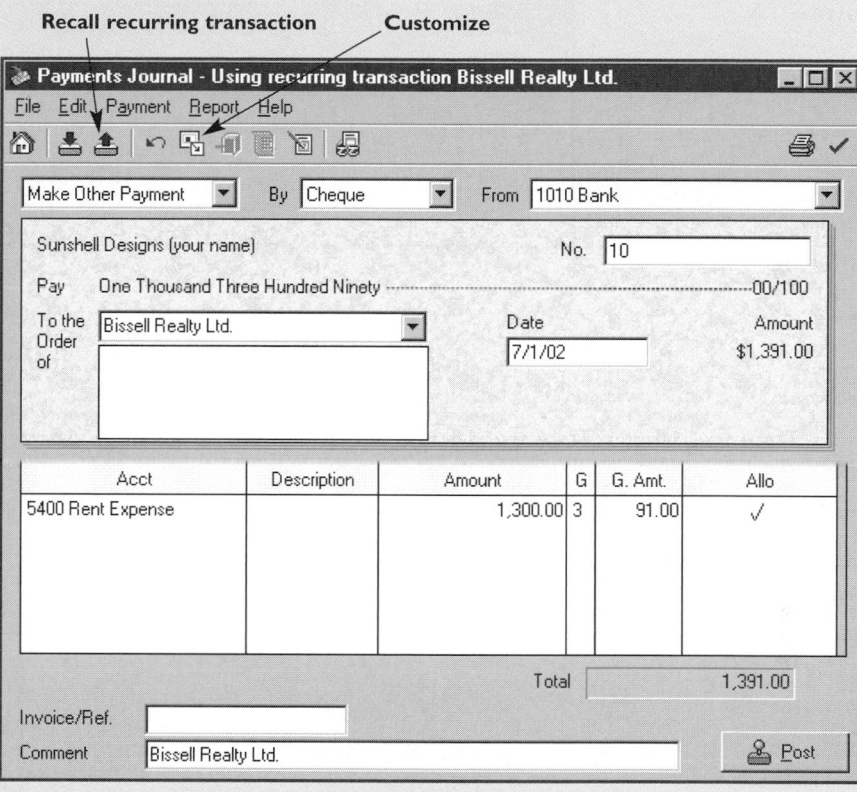

FIGURE 14

The allocated rent payment to Bissell Realty.

- Be sure to check each journal entry before posting. When you select Report, Display Payments Journal Entry, your monitor will look like Figure 15. Post the entry when done.

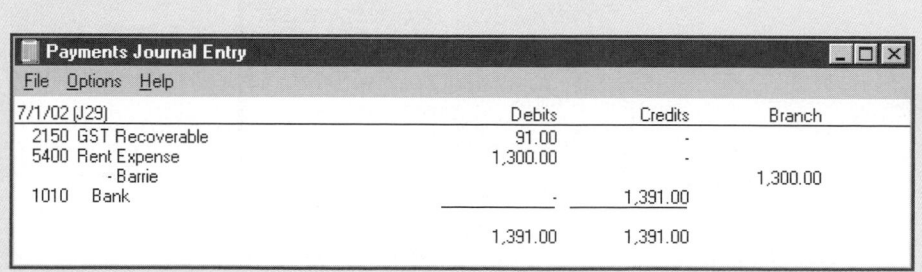

FIGURE 15

The journal entry that shows the entire rent expense amount being allocated to the Barrie branch.

When you double click on the "Allo" column and the cursor is in the Branch field, try keying W before pressing the enter key. This will speed your work.

The second entry of the month is the rent payment for the retail location at Wasaga Beach, Ontario. The details are as follows:

July
1   *Cheque Copy*
       No. 011, to Wildwood Realty Ltd., for rent in Wasaga Beach, $600 plus GST of $42, total $642.

Notes and Tips
- In the Payments Journal, key Wildwood Realty Ltd. and press the Quick Add button. Allocate the entire amount to the Wasaga branch. Your journal entry should look like Figure 16 below before you post it.

FIGURE 16

The rent expense amount allocated to the Wasaga branch.

Payments Journal Entry				
File Options Help				
7/1/02 (J30)		Debits	Credits	Branch
2150 GST Recoverable		42.00	-	
5400 Rent Expense		600.00	-	
- Wasaga				600.00
1010 Bank		-	642.00	
		642.00	642.00	

Reporting Capabilities

You need to allocate all of the remaining revenue and expense transactions in July to the proper branch. At the end of the month, you will see the benefit of your efforts. In addition to viewing the overall income statement, you will get a good idea of the profitability of each branch. The reporting capabilities of Simply Accounting are illustrated in Figure 17 below:

FIGURE 17

The income statements of Sunshell Designs showing the overall statement at the top and the branch statements at the bottom.

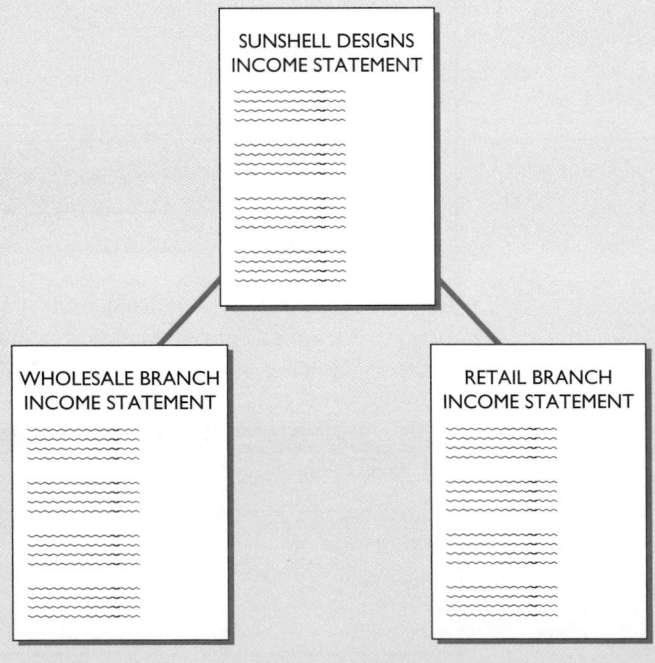

Computer Exercises

❶ Complete July's accounting activities for Sunshell Designs. Allocate each revenue and expense transaction to the correct branch.

July 2   *Owner's Memo*

Create inventory ledger cards for the Wasaga branch. The numbers, names, and selling prices are listed below.

1) RSS01, Sunshell-large-R, $39.75;
2) RSS02, Sunshell-large w/logo-R, $48.75;
2) RSS03, Sunshell-medium-R, $35.25; and
3) RSS04, Sunshell-medium w/logo-R, $44.25.

Notes and Tips
- You created inventory cards when you first started Sunshell Designs. Refer to page 732 to refresh your memory. The minimum level for each is 30. You should be able to handle the linking requirements on your own.
- There is no transaction required for this memo from the owner.

July
2   *Purchase Invoice*
     No. 5119, from Gerry's Tent and Awning. Details appear below.

Number	Quantity	Description	Unit Price	Totals
RSS01	75	Sunshell-large-R	26.50	993.75
RSS02	75	Sunshell-large w/logo-R	23.50	1,218.75
RSS03	75	Sunshell-medium-R	11.75	881.25
RSS04	75	Sunshell-medium w/logo-R	14.75	1,106.25
			Sub-total	4,200.00
			GST	294.00
			Amount Owed	4,494.00

You must make decisions about allocating revenues and expenses in July's transactions.

Notes and Tips
- Since the above transaction involves assets and liabilities, you do not have to allocate amounts to the Wasaga branch. Only revenues and expenses are to be allocated.

3   *Purchase Invoice*
     No. 6234, from Running Bear Transport for delivering the sunshells to the Wasaga Beach store, $83.00 plus GST of $5.81, total $88.81.
3   *Sales Invoice*
     No. 007, to Georgina Resorts. Details appear on page 749.

Number	Quantity	Description	Unit Price	Totals
SS01	10	Sunshell-large	26.50	265.00
SS03	20	Sunshell-medium	23.50	470.00
			Sub-total	735.00
			GST	51.45
			Amount Owed	786.45

3   *Purchase Invoice*

No. 812C, from Simcoe Supplies for office supplies for the Wasaga Beach store, $163.00 plus GST of $11.41, total $174.41. Ignore the PST on this purchase. Terms net 30 days.

3   *Owner's Memo*

Four sunshell (one of each type) were used for promotional purposes at the Wasaga Beach store. Total cost value of the stock was $56.00.

4   *Purchase Invoice*

No. 332, from Big Bay Supply Co. for a cash register for the Wasaga Beach Store, $812.00 plus GST of $56.84, total $868.84. Ignore the PST on this purchase. Use the Quick Add feature for this new vendor. Terms n30.

4   *Remittance Advice*

No. 002, from Scugog Novelty in payment of invoice 002, less the return on June 19, total $522.69.

4   *Cash Sales Summary*

No. 001-R, for the partial week of sales in Wasaga Beach. Details appear below.

WEEKLY SUMMARY OF CASH SALES				
Number	Quantity	Inventory Items	Retail Price	Totals
RSS01	1	Sunshell-large ret	39.75	39.75
RSS02	1	Sunshell-large w/logo ret	48.75	48.75
RSS03	3	Sunshell-medium ret	35.25	105.75
RSS04	2	Sunshell-medium w/logo ret	44.25	88.50
			Total Sales	282.75
			PST Charged	22.62
			GST Charged	19.79
			Total Cash Collected	325.16

Notes and Tips

PST is collected from customers at Wasaga Beach.

- This is the summary of the cash sales from the Wasaga branch. In order to get your screen to look like the illustration below, you will have to press the Customize Journal button and add the PST and Allocation columns.
- This is a cash sale. Make the correct selection in the "Paid by" field.
- Use the Invoice number shown in the illustration.
- Since this transaction involves revenues and expenses, you will have to allocate each row of the invoice to the Wasaga branch. (Double-click in the "Allo" column and follow the prompts.)

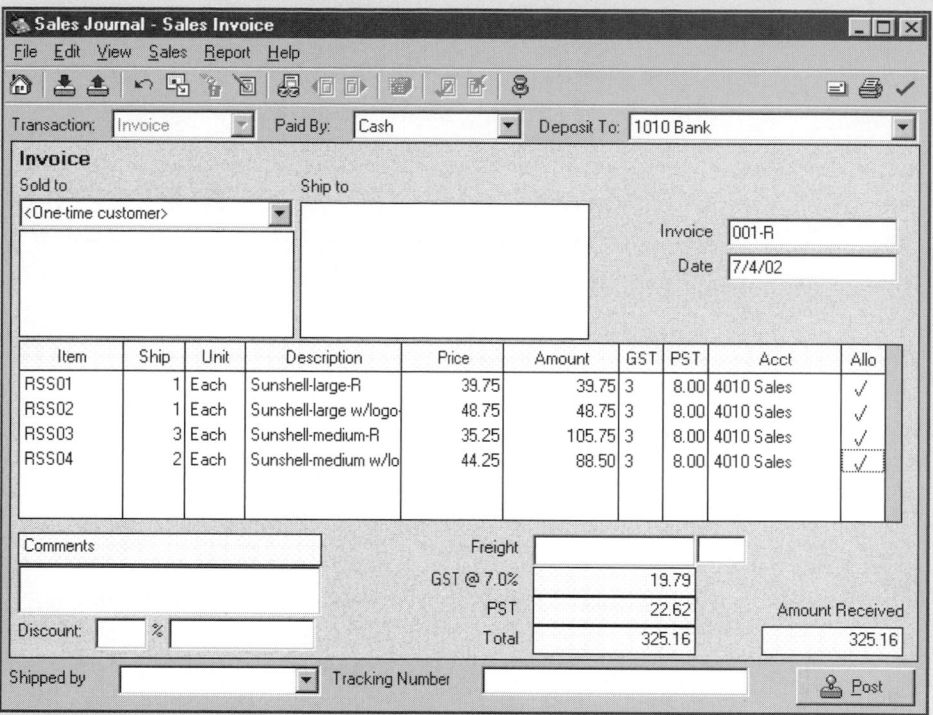

- Check the journal entry before posting, it should look like the illustration below.

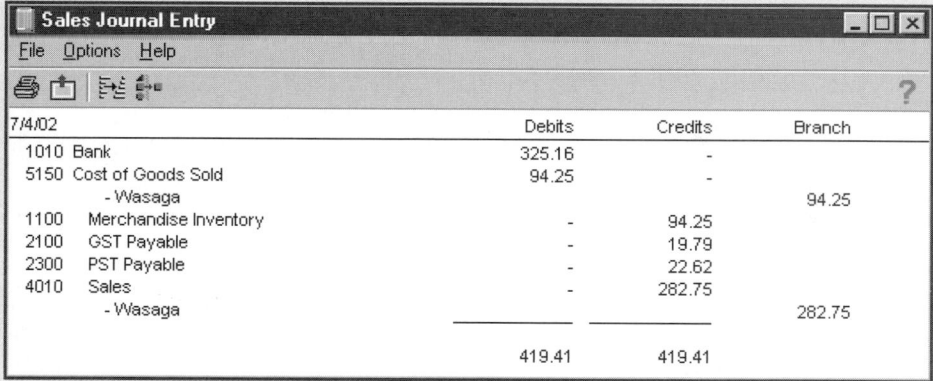

10 *Cheque Copy*

No. 012, to Simcoe Supplies in payment of invoice 683C, total $467.04.

10 *Cheque Copy*

No. 013, to Running Bear Transport in payment of invoice 5129, total $194.74.

11 *Cash Sales Summary*

No. 002-R, for the second week of sales in Wasaga Beach. Details appear below.

WEEKLY SUMMARY OF CASH SALES				
Number	Quantity	Inventory Items	Retail Price	Totals
RSS01	1	Sunshell-large ret	39.75	39.75
RSS02	0	Sunshell-large w/logo ret	48.75	0.00
RSS03	4	Sunshell-medium ret	35.25	141.00
RSS04	2	Sunshell-medium w/logo ret	44.25	88.50
			Total Sales	269.25
			PST Charged	21.54
			GST Charged	18.85
			Total Cash Collected	309.64

15 *Cheque Copy*

No. 014, to the Receiver General for June 30 payroll liabilities. Check your June 30 trial balance and write one cheque to clear the amounts in three payroll liability accounts.

15 *Cheque Copy*

No. 015, to Paul Fast, the owner, for his personal use, total $900.00.

18 *Sales Invoice*

No. 008, to a new customer. Sights and Sounds Ltd., 355 Beatty Ave., Owen Sound, ON N4K 6S3 705-749-2643. Use the Full Add feature instead of Quick Add to insert this business into the Receivables module. Then enter the invoice details below. Also, Paul Fast is unhappy with the cash flow of his new business and wants his customers to pay more promptly. To add incentive, he is now offering credit terms of 2/10, net 30. Choose Setup, Settings, and the Receivables tab. Enter the new credit terms, which will now appear by default on all sales invoices. (Make sure Sights and Sounds Ltd. is offered these terms on invoice 008.)

Number	Quantity	Description	Unit Price	Totals
SS01	10	Sunshell-large	26.50	265.00
SS02	5	Sunshell-large w/logo	32.50	162.50
SS03	20	Sunshell-medium	23.50	470.00
SS04	15	Sunshell-medium w/logo	29.50	442.50
			Sub-total	1 340.00
			GST	93.80
			Amount Owed	1 433.80

18 *Remittance Advice*

No. 003R, from Stevens Department Store in payment of invoice 004, total $4 092.75.

18 *Cash Sales Summary*

No. 003-R, for the third week of sales in Wasaga Beach. Details appear on page 752.

WEEKLY SUMMARY OF CASH SALES				
Number	Quantity	Inventory Items	Retail Price	Totals
RSS01	3	Sunshell-large ret	39.75	119.25
RSS02	2	Sunshell-large w/logo ret	48.75	97.50
RSS03	5	Sunshell-medium ret	35.25	176.25
RSS04	1	Sunshell-medium w/logo ret	44.25	44.25
			Total Sales	437.25
			PST Charged	34.98
			GST Charged	30.61
			Total Cash Collected	502.84

24   *Sales Invoice*

No. 009, to Scugog Novelty. Details appear below.

Number	Quantity	Description	Unit Price	Totals
SS01	10	Sunshell-large	26.50	265.00
SS03	10	Sunshell-medium	23.50	235.00
SS04	5	Sunshell-medium w/logo	29.50	147.50
			Sub-total	647.50
			GST	45.33
			Amount Owed	692.83

25   *Cash Sales Summary*

No. 004-R, for the fourth week of sales in Wasaga Beach. Details appear below.

WEEKLY SUMMARY OF CASH SALES				
Number	Quantity	Inventory Items	Retail Price	Totals
RSS01	1	Sunshell-large ret	39.75	39.75
RSS02	0	Sunshell-large w/logo ret	48.75	0.00
RSS03	5	Sunshell-medium ret	35.25	176.25
RSS04	1	Sunshell-medium w/logo ret	44.25	44.25
			Total Sales	260.25
			PST Charged	20.82
			GST Charged	18.22
			Total Cash Collected	299.29

27   *Remittance Advice*

No. 004-R, from Sights and Sounds Ltd. in payment of invoice 008, $1 433.80 less discount of $28.68, total received $1 405.12.

28   *Cheque Copy*

No. 016, to the Grey-Bruce Hydro for the monthly utilities bill, $186.42 plus GST of $13.05, total $199.47. (***Note:*** *Of the total expense, $84.03 belongs to the Wasaga Beach location.*)

28   *Cheque Copy*

No. 017, to Bell Canada for the monthly telephone bill, $158.97 plus GST of $11.13, total $170.10. (***Note:*** *Of the total expense, $52.09 belongs to the Wasaga Beach location.*)

31 *Cash Sales Summary*

No. 005-R, for the fifth week of sales in Wasaga Beach. Details appear below.

WEEKLY SUMMARY OF CASH SALES				
Number	Quantity	Inventory Items	Retail Price	Totals
RSS01	0	Sunshell-large ret	39.75	0.00
RSS02	0	Sunshell-large w/logo ret	48.75	0.00
RSS03	3	Sunshell-medium ret	35.25	105.75
RSS04	1	Sunshell-medium w/logo ret	44.25	44.25
			Total Sales	150.00
			PST Charged	12.00
			GST Charged	10.50
			Total Cash Collected	172.50

31 *Sales Invoice*

No. 010, to a new customer. Best Retail Stores, 1151 Mervyn Rd., Peterborough, ON K9J 7K9. Use the Full Add feature. Details appear below.

Number	Quantity	Description	Unit Price	Totals
SS03	150	Sunshell-medium	23.50	3 525.00
			Sub-total	3 525.00
			GST	246.75
			Amount Owed	3 771.75

31 *Purchase Invoice*

No. 5223, from Gerry's Tent and Awning. Details appear below.

Number	Quantity	Description	Unit Price	Totals
SS03	400	Sunshell-medium	11.75 ea.	4 700.00
			Sub-total	4 700.00
			GST	329.00
			Amount Owed	5 029.00

31 *Cheque Copy*

No. 018, to Paul Fast, the owner, for his personal use, total $900.00.

31 *Cheque Copies*

Paid the two employees, Herb Epp and Michelle Leung, their wages for the month. Use the Payroll Journal to prepare cheque 019 for Herb Epp and 020 for Michelle Leung. Remember that Michelle is the employee at the Wasaga branch; Herb works in Barrie. To allocate in the Payroll Journal, choose Paycheque, Allocate.

31   *Bank Statement*

The bank statement from the Georgian Bay Bank arrived today and is shown below. Use it along with the Account Reconciliation Journal to reconcile the Bank account and to make the necessary journal entries. Allocate 10 percent of the bank expenses to the Wasaga branch.

Bank Statement
June 29, 20-2

Description	Debits	Credits	Date		Balance
			Jun	30	44,582.89
#005	104.71			30	44,478.18
#004	120.30			30	44,357.88
Dep		786.45		30	45,144.33
#007	900.00		Jul	2	44,244.33
#008	1,735.11			2	42,509.22
#006	18,591.25			2	23,917.97
#010	1,391.00			3	22,526.97
#011	642.00			4	21,884.97
Dep		522.69		4	22,407.66
Dep		325.16		4	22,732.82
#013	194.74			10	22,538.08
#009	1,771.09			10	20,766.99
Dep		309.64		10	21,076.63
#014	1,244.43			17	19,832.20
Dep		4,092.75		18	23,924.95
Dep		502.84		18	24,427.79
Dep		299.29		25	24,727.08
Dep		1,405.12		27	26,132.20
DM Loan Interest	187.50			30	25,944.70
DM Service Charge	38.95			30	25,905.75

2 In addition to printing the income statement for July, you are to print the Branch Income Detail reports. Under the Reports menu, you can easily make the selections for producing these summaries of revenues and expenses for the month of July.

3 When you see the Branch Income Detail reports, export them to a Microsoft Excel file by choosing File, Export and selecting the proper file format (.xls). In Microsoft Excel, re-format the data into common-size income statements.

Communicate It

Paul Fast believes that his profits should be much higher at the centre in Wasaga Beach because he can sell sunshells there at retail prices. Are his beliefs accurate? Analyze the spreadsheet files you exported from Simply Accounting and communicate your findings to Mr. Fast in a short report. If you wish, use the memo report form found in the Skills Appendix.

Generally Accepted Accounting Principles, Concepts, and Conventions (GAAPs)

The generally accepted accounting principles, concepts, and conventions are listed in the order in which they are taught.

The Business Entity Concept

The business entity concept provides that the accounting for a business or organization be kept separate from the personal affairs of its owner, or from any other business or organization. This means that the owner of a business should not place any personal assets on the business balance sheet. The balance sheet of the business must reflect the financial position of the business alone. Also, when transactions of the business are recorded, any personal expenditures of the owner are charged to the owner and are not allowed to affect the operating results of the business.

The Continuing Concern Concept
(or The Going Concern Concept)

The continuing concern concept assumes that a business will continue to operate, unless it is known that it will not. The dollar values associated with a business that is alive and well are straightforward. For example, a supply of envelopes with the company's name printed on them would be valued at their cost price. This would not be the case if the company were going out of business. In that case, the envelopes would be difficult to sell because the company's name is on them. When a company is going out of business, the values of the assets usually suffer because they have to be sold under unfavourable circumstances. The values of such assets often cannot be determined until they are actually sold.

The Principle of Conservatism

The principle of conservatism provides that accounting for a business should be fair and reasonable. Accountants are required in their work to make evaluations and estimates, to deliver opinions, and to select procedures. They should do this in such a way that assets or profits are neither overstated nor understated.

The Objectivity Principle

The objectivity principle states that accounting will be recorded on the basis of objective evidence. Objective evidence means that different people looking at the evidence will arrive at the same values for the transaction. Simply put, this means that transactions will be based on fact and not on personal opinion or feelings.

The source document for a transaction is almost always the best objective evidence available. The source document shows the amount agreed to by the buyer and the seller, who are usually independent and unrelated to each other.

The Revenue Recognition Convention

The revenue recognition convention states that revenue be recorded in the accounts (recognized) at the time the transaction is completed. Usually, this just means recording revenue when the bill for it is sent to the customer. If it is a cash transaction, the revenue is recorded when the sale is completed and the cash received.

It is not always quite so simple. Think of the building of a large project such as an office tower. It takes a construction company a number of years to complete such a project. The company does not wait until the project is entirely completed before it sends its bill. Periodically, it bills for the amount of work completed and receives payments as the work progresses. Revenue is taken into the accounts on this periodic basis.

It is important to take revenue into the accounts properly. If this is not done, the income statements of the company will be incorrect and the readers of the financial statements misinformed.

The Time Period Concept

The time period concept provides that accounting take place over specific time periods known as fiscal periods. These fiscal periods are of equal length, and are used when measuring the financial progress of a business.

The Matching Principle

The matching principle is an extension of the revenue recognition convention. The matching principle states that each expense item related to revenue earned must be recorded in the same accounting period as the revenue it helped to earn. If this is not done, the financial statements will not measure the results of operations fairly.

The Cost Principle

The cost principle states that the accounting for purchases must be at the cost price to the purchaser. This is the figure that appears on the source document for the transaction in almost all cases. There is no place for guesswork or wishful thinking when accounting for purchases.

The value recorded in the accounts for an asset is not changed later if the market value of the asset changes. It would take an entirely new transaction based on new objective evidence to change the original value of an asset.

There are times when the above type of objective evidence is not available. For example, a building could be received as a gift. In such a case, the transaction would be recorded at fair market value which must be determined by some independent means.

The Consistency Principle

The consistency principle requires that a business must use the same accounting methods and procedures from period to period. When they change a method from one period to another they must explain the change clearly on the financial statements. The readers of financial statements have the right to assume that consistency has been applied unless they are notified of some change in procedure.

The consistency principle prevents people from changing methods for the sole purpose of manipulating figures on the financial statements.

The Materiality Principle

The materiality principle requires accountants to include in a firm's financial statements any information that could be considered material (or important) to the users of that financial information. For it to be acceptable not to include information in the financial statements, it must be such that neither the net income nor the financial position of the firm are impacted in any significant way. Excluding particular information must not lead statement users to make decisions different from what they would make were they to have that information.

The Full Disclosure Principle

The full disclosure principle states that all information needed for a full understanding of a company's financial statements must be included with the financial statements. Some items may not affect the ledger accounts directly. These would be included in the form of accompanying notes. Examples of such items are outstanding lawsuits, tax disputes, and company takeovers.

Skills Appendix

Tips for Writing a Business Letter

A business letter should strive to be three things: clear, concise, and courteous. Here are some ideas to help you write business letters that achieve these objectives.

Purpose

Ask yourself before you begin the letter, "Why am I writing this letter? What is my goal?" You should be able to sum up your goal in one sentence. For example, your goal might be something like the ones listed below:

- to persuade an office manager to hire you as a summer assistant while her employees are on vacation;
- to persuade a business owner to sponsor a student in the Students' Marathon for the United Appeal;
- to explain that generally accepted accounting principles require asset values to be determined from source documents rather than from personal opinion (see, for example, Case 2 — question 3 on page 114).

Every sentence in the letter, other than personal greetings, should contribute in some way to the goal you have stated. The person receiving your letter will appreciate the trouble you have taken to make your purpose in writing clear and will probably be more favourably impressed with what you have to say.

Concise

Some people think that, because what they have to say is important, they should take many extra sentences to say it. But how does the person who receives the letter feel about having to wade through unnecessary paragraphs?

On the other hand, necessary information must not be left out of a business letter just to keep it short. A business letter should be concise, that is, it should say what needs to be said in an economical way. Most business letters are one or two pages long. If your letters are longer than that, go through and ask yourself why each sentence is necessary. Certain sentences may not be necessary. Or you may find that you started to say things that should be saved for a separate document. For example, in an application letter, you may have started to tell the personnel manager things about yourself that should be in your résumé.

Clear

Sometimes, when people are unsure of what they want to say, they pad their letters with words that sound important but don't actually contribute to their message. For example, consider the following sentence:

> With regard to your verbal communication in our recent interaction, the matter has been given due consideration by this writer and in all actuality, policy changes may indeed be indicated in the foreseeable future.

The communication would be much better if the writer had just said,

> I have thought over what you told me during our recent discussion. I agree that we should change our policy.

Remember, the primary purpose of a business letter is always effective communication.

Courteous

Courtesy in a business letter is not primarily a matter of formal rules or language. There could never be enough rules to cover every situation we might encounter. Rather, we should ask ourselves, "How would I want to be told this information if someone else had to tell it to me?" Thinking about our communications in this way helps us write letters that other people are prepared to receive, even if we cannot always tell them what they want to hear.

Format for a Business Letter

There are certain formats and conventions that are used in preparing a standard business letter. Examples of these are listed below and a typical business letter format is also illustrated in Figure A1 on the following page. When asked to write a letter as part of an assignment from this textbook, you may use the format described and illustrated here.

The format illustrated here is called the full block format; it is simple to learn and very common in business.

FIGURE A1

Sample format for a business letter.

A business
letter is
single-spaced.
One blank
line separates
paragraphs.

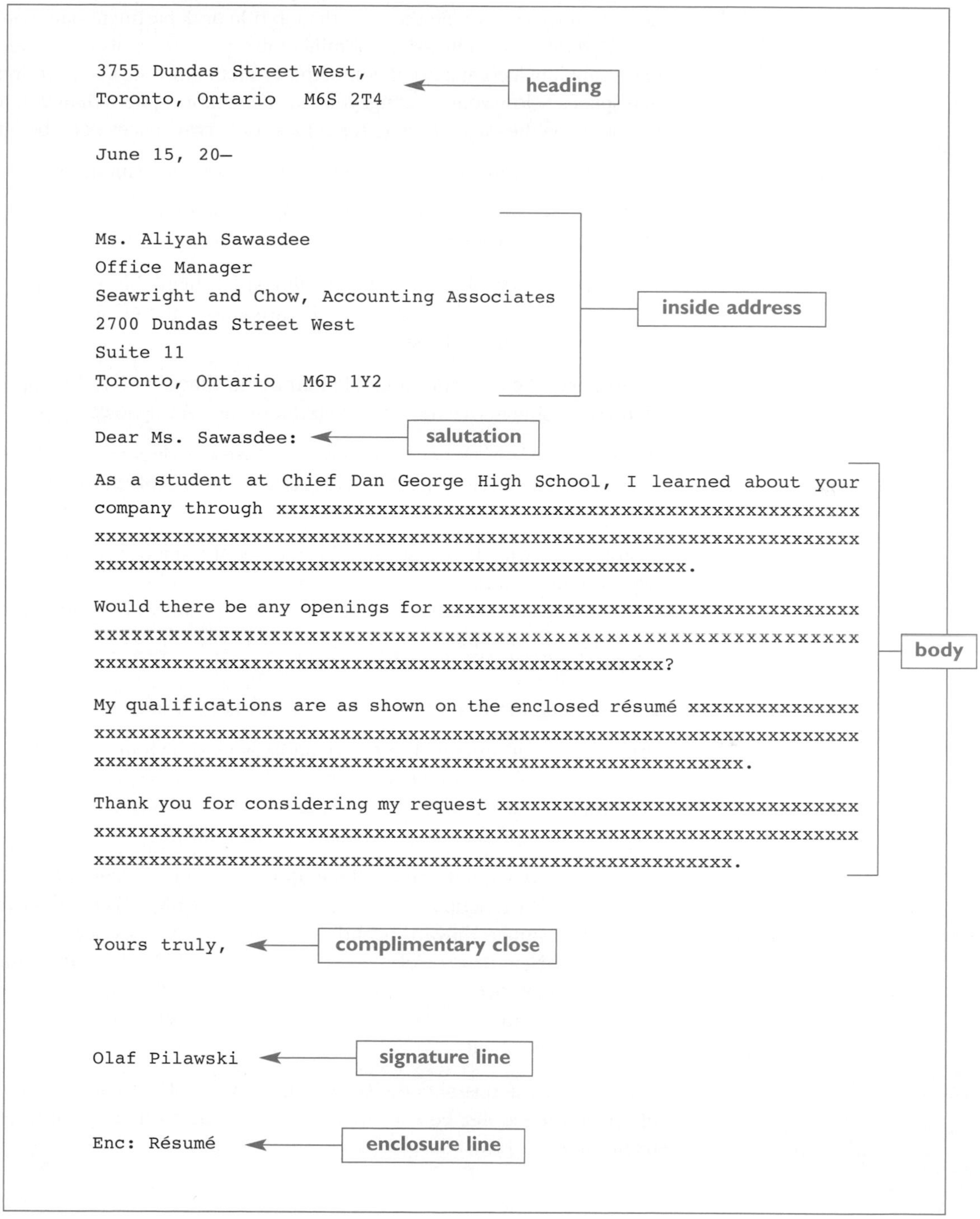

```
    3755 Dundas Street West,          ←    heading
    Toronto, Ontario   M6S 2T4

    June 15, 20—


    Ms. Aliyah Sawasdee
    Office Manager
    Seawright and Chow, Accounting Associates    ——    inside address
    2700 Dundas Street West
    Suite 11
    Toronto, Ontario   M6P 1Y2

    Dear Ms. Sawasdee:  ←    salutation

    As a student at Chief Dan George High School, I learned about your
    company through xxxxxxxxxxxxxxxxxxxxxxxxxxxxxxxxxxxxxxxxxxxxxx
    xxxxxxxxxxxxxxxxxxxxxxxxxxxxxxxxxxxxxxxxxxxxxxxxxxxxxxxxxxxxxx
    xxxxxxxxxxxxxxxxxxxxxxxxxxxxxxxxxxxxxxxxxxxxxxxx.

    Would there be any openings for xxxxxxxxxxxxxxxxxxxxxxxxxxxxxxxx
    xxxxxxxxxxxxxxxxxxxxxxxxxxxxxxxxxxxxxxxxxxxxxxxxxxxxxxxxxxxxxx
    xxxxxxxxxxxxxxxxxxxxxxxxxxxxxxxxxxxxxxxxxxxxxxx?           ——    body

    My qualifications are as shown on the enclosed résumé xxxxxxxxxxxxxxx
    xxxxxxxxxxxxxxxxxxxxxxxxxxxxxxxxxxxxxxxxxxxxxxxxxxxxxxxxxxxxxx
    xxxxxxxxxxxxxxxxxxxxxxxxxxxxxxxxxxxxxxxxxxxxxxxxxxxx.

    Thank you for considering my request xxxxxxxxxxxxxxxxxxxxxxxxxxxxx
    xxxxxxxxxxxxxxxxxxxxxxxxxxxxxxxxxxxxxxxxxxxxxxxxxxxxxxxxxxxxxx
    xxxxxxxxxxxxxxxxxxxxxxxxxxxxxxxxxxxxxxxxxxxxxxxxxxxx.


    Yours truly,  ←    complimentary close



    Olaf Pilawski  ←    signature line


    Enc: Résumé  ←    enclosure line
```

The full block letter format aligns all parts with the left margin.

Additional Notes on the Format of the Business Letter

Inside Address   In most situations, if you do not know the name of the person to whom the letter should be addressed, phone and find out. But in some cases, that is not practical; you should then use the job title or department name only, for example, *The Registrar* (the admissions administrator of a university), or *Customer Service* (a department of a company). If your letter is short, start the inside address at least three line spaces below your heading; you may need more spaces than that to centre the letter nicely on the page. If the letter is long, only two spaces need be left.

Salutation   Leave one line space blank before the salutation.

Body   Leave one line space blank before beginning the body. It is usual to leave a blank space between the paragraphs.

Complimentary Close   Leave one line space blank before typing the complimentary close. *Yours truly*, and *Sincerely*, are among the most commonly used complimentary closes in business.

Signature   Leave approximately four blank spaces before typing your name. Then sign your name above the typed version in the four spaces.

Enclosure Line   When you have enclosed a document with the letter, your résumé, for example, type the abbreviation *Enc.* below your typed signature on the page. If you state what the enclosure is, use the following format: *Enc: Résumé*

Copy Notation   If you are sending a copy of the letter to someone other than the person named in the inside address, place the notation cc: at the margin below the enclosure line, leave two spaces and type in the name of the person who will receive the copy, for example, *cc: Loukah Aziz, Director of Sales*

Preparing an Envelope for a Business Letter

Prepare the address and the return address as shown in Figure A2 on the following page. Don't abbreviate the street name. Provinces may be shown with full name or in an abbreviated form. When using the abbreviated form, use the standard two-letter abbreviations preferred by Canada Post, as follows:

NF	Newfoundland and Labrador	MB	Manitoba
NS	Nova Scotia	SK	Saskatchewan
PE	Prince Edward Island	AB	Alberta
NB	New Brunswick	BC	British Columbia
PQ	Quebec	YT	Yukon Territory
ON	Ontario	NT	Northwest Territories
NU	Nunavut		

Always give the postal code its own line if possible. If you cannot do that because of space limitations, be sure that it is separated by a space of at least two spaces from the rest of the address.

FIGURE A2

Standard form for address of business envelope.

```
Olaf Pilawski
3755 Dundas Street West
Toronto, Ontario
M6S 2T4


                    Ms. Aliyah Sawasdee
                    Office Manager
                    Seawright and Chow, Accounting Associates
                    2700 Dundas Street West
                    Suite 111
                    Toronto, Ontario  M6P 1Y2
```

Notice that you do not need to place a comma at the end of each line when preparing the address on an envelope for a business letter.

A business letter is folded in thirds before being placed in a long envelope, usually a No. 9 or No. 10. Figure A3 below shows how the folding and inserting should be done.

FIGURE A3

Folding and inserting a business letter.

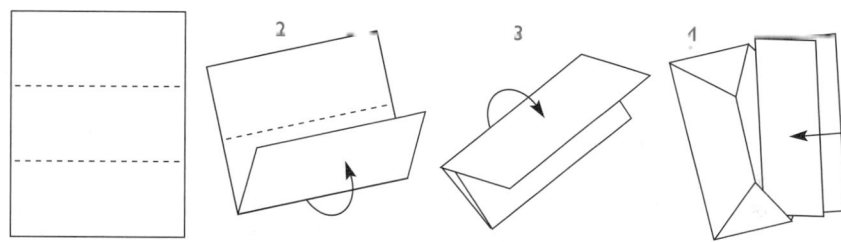

If the letter introduces a long document that is being sent in a 9 × 12 manila envelope, the letter should not be folded in thirds but rather attached to the document it introduces.

Tips for Writing Memos

A memo is less formal than a letter. It is usually written within an organization or to someone with whom you are already dealing. For example, a student who has a summer job in an office might receive a memo from the supervisor asking for suggestions for saving and recycling paper, as part of the firm's environment awareness campaign. The form of the memo might look like Figure A4 on the following page.

The simple way that the memo is set up is intended to save time. Most memos are short and factual. (If the memo is lengthy, it should be organized in a report format.)

Use the memo form if you are asked to write a memo as part of an assignment.

Sample memo format.

```
To:      Olaf Pilawski
From:    Etta Leacock
Re:      Employee Suggestions for Company Environment Awareness Campaign
Date:    July 13, 19—
```

Olaf, as you probably know, xxxxxxxxxxxxxxxxxxxxxxxxxxxxxxxxxxxxxxxxxxxxxxxx
xxxxxxxxxxxxxxxxxxxxxxxxxxxxxxxxxxxxxxxxxxxxxxxxxxxxxxxxxxxxxxxxxxxxxxxxxxxx
xxxxxxxxxxxxxxxxxxxxxxxxxxxxxxxxxxxxxxxxxxxxxxxxxxxxxxxxxxx.

Could you please provide me with xxxxxxxxxxxxxxxxxxxxxxxxxxxxxxxxxxxxxxxxxxxx
xxxxxxxxxxxxxxxxxxxxxxxxxxxxxxxxxxxxxxxxxxxxxxxxxxxxxxxxxxxxxxxxxxxxxxxxxxxx
xxxxxxxxxxxxxxxxxxxxxxxxxxxxxxxxxxxxxxxxxxxxxxxxxxxxxx by July 20?

I would be most interested to hear whether you think that xxxxxxxxxxxxxxxxxxxxxxx
xxxxxxxxxxxxxxxxxxxxxxxxxxxxxxxxxxxxxxxxxxxxxxxxxxxxxxxxxxxxxxxxxxxxxxxxxxxx
xxxxxxxxxxxxxxxxxxxxxxxxxxxxxxxxxxxxxxxxxxxxx!

Etta

E-mail Advice

The electronic version of the memo is e-mail, a form of communication familiar to most of us. Since you likely use e-mail now, and will continue to do so, developing good habits is advantageous. Keep in mind the following points.

Subject Line   Always include one. Make it short but meaningful. If it is vague, the recipient might delete the message without reading it.

Brevity   Keep your e-mails brief. Long e-mails take time to compose and read. Both senders and receivers appreciate short messages. If you have a number of points, each with specific purpose, try dividing the points into separate e-mail messages.

Replying   When responding to an e-mail, you may want to refer to portions of the sender's text. However, try to avoid overloading your response with lengthy copies of previous e-mails.

Promptness   Attempt to reply to your e-mails as soon as you read them, otherwise, they may tend to pile up. The key to staying current is to keep your replies brief.

Identification   Take advantage of the "signature" features of e-mail software. A signature contains identifying information that allows recipients to contact you (e.g., phone, fax, address, and so on).

Discretion   Keep the tone of your e-mail correspondence pleasant and business-like. Resist including anything that you might regret later. Remember that e-mail messages may be published to a large number of people.

Tips for Giving an Oral Report

In business and in non-profit organizations, you may be asked to report to a group of co-workers or colleagues on a subject about which you have some information. You may also be given an assignment in this accounting course which would require you to speak to a group of fellow students. Here are some tips that may help you prepare to give an oral report:

1. Many people are nervous about speaking up in front of others. This is quite normal. Remember that the people who are listening to you are not sitting there in order to make you feel nervous; they are there only to hear what you have to say. It will be their turn to speak some time, so they should be sympathetic to your uneasiness.

2. After you have done your research, it is a good idea to write down the main points you want to make on a small card, to remind yourself of them while you are talking. It is usually not a good idea to write out everything you have to say and attempt to read it out loud. If you are looking at the page instead of at your listeners, they will not be as interested in your presentation.

3. If you mix up something from the card, do not allow the mix-up to throw you off; remember that only you know what is written on the card anyway! You can change the order of your points, correct yourself, or return to something you missed without causing any serious problems.

4. Look at different people in the group as you are talking. They will be more interested in your comments when they see that you are interested in them.

5. When you finish your report, be sure to ask if there are any questions. This will help ensure that you have covered everything and that your listeners understand what you are saying.

6. It is a good idea to have a plan for ending your presentation. Usually, in the classroom, your teacher will close off the presentation when you are done by thanking you. But what if you are to speak to a small group where there is no teacher or chairperson present? Before you begin, ask another student to introduce your presentation, let you know when you are running out of time, and get up and thank you when you are finished. These steps will help to ensure a smooth presentation.

How to Solve a Case Study

What is a case study?

A *case* or *case study* is a problem taken from the business world to be used as a learning tool by students. It requires students to analyze and find solutions to situations that accountants and business people commonly deal with. Case studies allow the students to apply the theory learned in class and to practise their decision-making skills.

Common concerns about cases

Some students feel frustrated by the limited information available in most cases. They often feel that a valid solution to a problem is difficult without additional data. Real life situations, however, seldom provide us with as much information as we would like and, as a result, reasonable assumptions must often be made in order to arrive at a solution. As well, the problems outlined in case studies seldom result in "perfect" or "ideal" solutions, such as those found in mathematics or sciences. Even the most polished solution to a business problem will feature disadvantages, risks, and compromises.

Steps for Solving a Case Study

How is the solution to a case study presented? In both the business world and in a school setting, the solution to a case study should be carefully prepared, factual, and to the point. A common method of organizing the information for a case study report will follow these steps:

1. State the problem.

The first step towards any effective solution is to define the problem clearly. Be careful to determine the *main* problem and to avoid being distracted by less important issues or by the effects of problems. For example, in a case about dishonest employees, would the fact that an employee is dishonest be the manager's main problem or the poor cash controls and sloppy accounting procedures that allowed theft to occur? Clearly, *as a manager*, the manager should focus on the inadequate cash controls.

When explaining the main problem, avoid vague phrases such as "weak management" or "poor planning." These comments are far too general to lead to an effective solution. Always state the problem in specific terms, such as "The manager made a mistake when she permitted...," making it clear what you think the mistake was.

After dealing with the main problem, other less important problems can also be discussed in terms of their effect on the company, its customers, and its employees.

2. List the solutions.

Almost every problem can be solved in different ways. The student's job is to examine several possible solutions and to weigh the advantages and disadvantages of each in order to arrive at the very best method of solving the problem. On the other hand, do not wait for a "perfect" solution, because even the best ideas will involve risks and compromises.

3. Determine the best solution.

Choose the best solution after carefully considering the strengths and weaknesses of all the possible solutions listed. Clearly justify your choice by explaining how the needs of the firm are met to the greatest extent possible by the solution you have adopted. Sometimes you will be asked to prepare a memo, letter, or report explaining your solution.

4. Explain how your proposed solution might be implemented.

Simple case study solutions may end with the best solution, but more complex cases require this final step. The word "implemented" simply describes how the solution will be put into effect to solve the main problems of the case study. This section of the memo, letter, or report may feature the steps required to carry out the recommended solution successfully. It should also anticipate problems that might lead to failure.

Glossary —
Accounting Terms

A

Account   A specially ruled page used to record financial changes. There is one account for each different item affecting the financial position. All of the accounts together form the ledger.

Account balance   The value of an account showing the dollar amount and an indication as to whether it is a debit or a credit value.

Account form of balance sheet   A balance sheet which presents the information in a horizontal format, the assets being shown to the left and the liabilities and equity being shown to the right. *Contrast* Report form of balance sheet.

Account title   The name of the item for which an account is prepared, entered at the top of the account page.

Accountability   The obligation of management (or another group or person) to supply evidence, usually periodic, of its action or performance as required by custom, regulation, or agreement.

Accountant   A professional person who develops and maintains the accounting systems, interprets the data and prepares reports; supervises the work of accounting employees and participates in management decisions.

Accounting   The process of gathering and preparing financial information about a business or other organization in a form that provides accurate and useful records and enables decisions to be made.

Accounting clerk   An employee who ensures that transactions are properly recorded and that supporting documents are present and correct. Carries out routine calculations and banking transactions.

Accounting cycle   The total set of accounting procedures that must be carried out during each fiscal period.

Accounting entry   All the changes in the accounts caused by one business transaction, expressed in terms of debits and credits. For each accounting entry, the total of the debit amounts will equal the total of the credit amounts.

Accounting period   The period of time over which the earnings of a business are measured. *Same as* Fiscal period.

Accounts payable   The money that a business owes to its creditors. This money is a liability of the business.

Accounts payable ledger   A book or file containing all the accounts of ordinary creditors representing amounts owed to them by the business.

Accounts receivable   The money that is owed to a business by its customers. This money is considered an asset of the business.

Accounts receivable aging schedule   A detailed breakdown of customers' accounts showing how long they have been unpaid.

Accounts receivable ledger   A book or file containing all the accounts of debtors (customers) representing amounts owed by them to the business.

Accounts receivable turnover   The number of days it takes a business to collect an account receivable. *Same as* Collection period.

Account title   The account name.

Accrued expense   An expense incurred during an accounting period for which payment is not due until a later accounting period. This results from the purchase of services which at the time of accounting have only been partly performed, are not yet billable, and have not been paid for.

Acid-test ratio   The ratio of current assets, excluding inventory, to current liabilities. *Same as* Quick ratio.

Adjusting entry   An entry made before finalizing the books for the period to apportion amounts of revenue or expense to the proper accounting periods or operating divisions. For example, the apportioning of wages between accounting periods when the current period ends between two paydays.

Asset   Anything owned that has a dollar value. *Contrast* Liability.

Audit   An examination of the accounting records and internal controls of a business in order to be able to express an opinion about the business's financial position and results of operation.

Auditing   The process of conducting an audit. *See* Audit.

B

Balance column account   The most commonly used type of account, in which there are three money columns, one for the debit amounts, one for the credit amounts, and one for the amount of the balance. *Same as* Three-column account.

Balance sheet A statement showing the financial position (the assets, liabilities, and capital) of an individual, company, or other organization on a certain date.

Balance sheet – account form Information on the balance sheet presented in a side-by-side or horizontal format.

Balance sheet – report form Information on the balance sheet presented in a one-above-the-other or vertical format.

Bank credit advice A business form by means of which a bank informs a depositor that an increase has been made in the bank account and the reason for the increase.

Bank debit advice A business form by means of which a bank informs a depositor that a decrease has been made in the bank account and the reason for the decrease.

Bank deposit An amount of money or its equivalent placed in a bank account.

Bank reconciliation A routine procedure to find out the reasons for a discrepancy between the balance on deposit as shown by the bank and the balance on deposit as show by the depositor.

Bank reconciliation statement A statement showing the differences between a bank account as reflected in the books of the bank and the same account as reflected in the books of the depositor.

Board of directors A group of people selected by the shareholders who decide on policies for a corporation.

Book of original entry Any journal; that is, the book that contains the first, or original, record of each transaction. *Same as* Journal.

Bookkeeper An employee who ensures that transactions are properly recorded and that supporting documents are present and correct. Carries out routine calculations and banking transactions. *Same as* Accounting clerk.

Book value The figure that indicates how much equity common shareholders have on a per share basis.

Budget A plan that contains a forecast of financial figures for a company or department.

Budgeted balance sheet A plan that provides information on the financial position of the company, at a future date, based on revenue and expense forecasts.

Budgeted income statement A financial plan that includes the forecast of revenues and expenses for the company within a set period of time.

Business entity concept *See* GAAP Appendix.

Business transaction A financial event that changes the values in certain accounts and therefore affects the financial position of the business.

C

Canada Pension Plan (CPP)   A pension plan instituted by the federal government for Canadian workers.

Capital   The difference between the total assets and total liabilities of a business. *Same as* Net worth, Owner's equity.

Capital Stock account   The capital invested by the shareholders when they purchase company shares.

Cash discount   A reduction that may be taken in the amount of a bill provided that the full amount is paid within the discount period shown on the bill.

Cash flow   The pattern of revenue and expenses of a business; determines the availablity of cash in the business to meet expenses.

Cash payments journal   A special columnar journal used to record all transactions that directly cause a decrease in the bank balance.

Cash proof   An accounting procedure that compares cash receipts, according to the source documents, against cash receipts according to a physical count.

Cash receipts   These are the funds taken in from business operations and include all items considered to be money—cheques, money orders, credit card slips, debit card transfers, bills, and coin.

Cash receipts daily summary   A business paper, prepared daily, that lists the monies received by a business from customers on account and other sources.

Cash receipts journal   A special columnar journal in which are recorded the accounting entries for all transactions that directly cause an increase in the bank balance.

Cash refund   The return of money to the buyer by the seller in respect to deficient goods that were paid for and later returned.

Cash sales slip   A business form showing the details of a transaction in which goods or services are sold to a customer for cash.

Cash short or over   The amount of money by which the business's cash receipts for the day are more or less than what they should be.

Certified cheque   A cheque for which the bank takes the funds out of the payer's account in advance, and puts them aside to honour the cheque when it is presented by the payee.

Change fund   A small quantity of bills and coins, usually between fifty and one hundred dollars, placed in the drawer of a cash register at the beginning of the day for the purpose of making change for customers. *Same as* Float.

Chart of accounts   A list of the accounts of a business and their numbers, arranged according to their order in the ledger.

Cheque copy   A copy of a cheque, used as the source document for a payment made by cheque.

Classified balance sheet   *See* Classified financial statement.

Classified financial statement A financial statement in which data are grouped according to major categories.

Closing an account   To cause an account to have a nil balance by means of a journal entry.

C.O.D. (Cash on delivery)   A term of sale whereby goods must be paid for at the time they are delivered.

Collection period   The ratio of accounts receivable to charge sales for the year, multiplied by 365. It indicates the average number of days it takes the business to collect an account receivable. *Same as* Accounts receivable turnover.

Commission   An amount paid periodically to a salesperson or an agent calculated as a percentage of the amount of goods or services sold by that person.

Common shareholder   The controlling owners of a corporation.

Common-size financial statement   A financial statement that shows individual items as percentages of a selected figure, known as the base figure.

Common stock   A corporation's basic class of stock.

Comparative financial statement   A financial statement that compares income statements or balance sheets by presenting the figures for successive years side by side, along with the amount of change.

Consistency principle   *See* GAAP Appendix.

Contra account   An account that must be considered along with a given asset account to show the true book value of the asset account. *Same as* Valuation account.

Continuing concern concept   *See* GAAP Appendix.

Control account   A general ledger account, the balance of which represents the sum of the balances in the accounts contained in a subsidiary ledger.

Corporation   A corporation is a special form of business that is owned by shareholders. *Same as* limited company.

Correcting journal entry   An accounting entry to rectify the effect of an error.

Cost accounting   A specialized area of accounting that concentrates on determining, controlling, and reporting the costs of doing business.

Cost of goods sold   The total cost of goods sold during an accounting period.

Cost of goods manufactured   Total costs of raw materials, direct labour, and factory overhead in a fiscal period.

Cost principle   *See* GAAP Appendix.

Credit   To record an amount on the right-hand side of an account. *Contrast* Debit.

Credit invoice   A business form issued by a vendor to reverse a charge that has been made on a regular sales invoice. The reason for the reversal is explained in detail on the invoice. *Same as* Credit note.

Credit note   A business form issued by a vendor to reverse a charge that has been made on a regular sales invoice. The reason for the reversal is explained in detail on the note. *Same as* Credit invoice.

Creditor   Anyone who is owed money by the business. *Contrast* Debtor.

Cross balancing   The procedure whereby the total of all the debits in a journal is checked against the total of all the credits in the journal to make sure that the two totals agree.

Cross-referencing   Part of the posting sequence in which the journal page number for a given entry is recorded in the appropriate account, and the account number, in turn, is recorded on the journal page.

Current asset   Unrestricted cash, an asset that will be converted into cash within one year, or an asset that will be used up within one year.

Current bank account   A type of deposit account offered by the bank specifically to meet the needs of businesses.

Current liability   A short-term debt, payment of which is expected to occur within one year.

Current ratio   The ratio of current assets to current liabilities. *Same as* Working capital ratio.

Customer's statement of account   A record of a customer's account for a one-month period, showing purchases made during the period, payments received during the period, and the unpaid balance remaining. Statements of account are usually sent out each month by a business to its customers.

D

Daily interest savings account   A bank account that offers fairly high interest, calculated on a daily basis, on fluctuating savings. Cheques cannot be used with this account.

Debit   To record an amount on the left-hand side of an account. *Contrast* Credit.

Debt ratio   The ratio of the total liabilities of a business to the total assets. This measures the proportion of total assets acquired through borrowed money. The debt ratio is complementary to the equity ratio. *See* Equity ratio.

Debtor   Anyone who owes money to the business. *Contrast* Creditor.

Decimal point error   A mistake caused by misplacing the decimal point in an amount.

Declining balance method of depreciation   A method of calculating the annual depreciation of an asset as a fixed percentage of the remaining value of the asset. Under this method, the asset's annual depreciation becomes progressively smaller. The percentages to be used are determined by government regulation. *Contrast* Straight-line method of depreciation.

Deficit   An account with a debit balance; a business loss.

Delivery expense   Transportation charges on outgoing merchandise. *Contrast* Freight-in.

Depreciation   The decrease in value of a fixed asset over time. For accounting purposes, this decrease is calculated according to a mathematical formula.

Detailed audit tape   In a cash register, a paper tape that provides a continuous record of all transactions that occur on a business day and can be accessed only by authorized persons. *Same as* Audit strip.

Direct labour   An expense that has a direct link in making finished goods, for example, workers on an assembly line.

Discrepancy item   An item arising out of a transaction that has not been recorded equally in both the bank statement and the records of the depositor. *See* Bank reconciliation.

Dividend   Amount paid to shareholders out of the company's profits.

Double entry system of accounting   The system of accounting in general use in which every transaction is recorded both as a debit in one or more accounts and as a credit in one or more accounts. Under this system, the total of the debit entries equals the total of the credit entries.

Doubtful account   An account receivable that may not be collectible.

Doubtful debt   *Same as* Doubtful account.

Drawings   A decrease in owner's equity resulting from a personal withdrawal of funds or other assets by the owner.

Dual purpose sales slip   A business form showing the details of a transaction in which goods or services are sold either for cash or on account.

Duty   Special charges imposed by the government of a country on certain goods imported from a foreign country.

E

Earnings per share   A dollar amount assigned to a company share calculated to measure the performance of that company and its executive officers.

Employee's earnings record   A form used to provide a cumulative record of all the payroll data during a calendar year for a particular employee. One is prepared for each employee.

Employment Insurance (EI)   A fund that employed workers pay into. Unemployed workers who have contributed to this fund are entitled to receive payments out of the fund while unemployed.

Equity ratio   The ratio of the total equity to the total assets of a business. This measures the proportion of total assets acquired by invested capital. The equity ratio is complementary to the debt ratio. *See* Debt ratio.

Expense A decrease in equity resulting from the costs of the materials and services used to produce the revenue. *Contrast* Income, Revenue.

F

Factory overhead Costs that include a range of expenses that support the manufacturing process.

Financial analysis The analysis of the income statement and the balance sheet in order to arrive at an understanding of financial position. *See below.*

Financial position The status of a business, as represented by the assets, liabilities, and owner's equity.

Fiscal period The period of time over which earnings are measured. *Same as* Accounting period.

Five-journal system An accounting system in which five journals are kept in process at the same time, each one recording transactions of a particular type.

Fixed asset A long-term asset held for its usefulness in producing goods or services. *Same as* Plant and Equipment.

Float A small quantity of bills and coins, usually between fifty and one hundred dollars placed in the drawer of a cash register at the beginning of the day for the purpose of making change for customers. *Same as* Change fund.

Forwarding The process of continuing an account or journal on a new page by carrying forward all relevant information from the completed page.

Freight-in Transportation charges on incoming merchandise. *Contrast* Delivery expense.

Full disclosure principle *See* GAAP Appendix.

Fundamental accounting equation The equation that states that total assets minus total liabilities are equal to owner's equity.
A − L = OE.

G

GAAP *See* Generally accepted accounting principles.

General ledger A book or file containing all the accounts of the business other than those in the subsidiary ledgers. The general ledger accounts represent the complete financial position of the business.

General partner Co-owner of a company with unlimited liability and very little protection for their assets. A general partner would have direct management responsibility for the company.

Generally accepted accounting principles Guidelines established by professional accountants to be followed in the preparation of accounting records and financial statements.

Going concern concept   *See* GAAP Appendix.

Goods and services tax (GST)   In Canada, a value-added tax collected by the seller of most goods and services and remitted to the federal government.

Goods in process   Goods that have had some raw materials, direct labour, or factory overhead applied to them, but that are not yet in a finished state.

Goodwill   An intangible asset of a business that has a value in excess of the sum of its net assets.

Gross pay   Earnings before deductions.

Gross profit   In a trading business, the excess of net sales over the cost of goods sold.

GST   *See* Goods and Services Tax.

H

Harmonized sales tax   A tax, collected in the provinces of New Brunswick, Nova Scotia, and Newfoundland, that is a combined provincial sales tax and the goods and services tax. It is charged on the same items as the goods and services tax.

HST   *See* Harmonized Sales Tax

I

Imprest method   The method of handling petty cash in which the removal of monies is only recorded in the accounts at the time when the fund is replenished.

In balance   A state in which the total value of all the accounts (or columns in a journal) with debit balances is equal to the total value of all the accounts (or columns in a journal) with credit balances. *Contrast* Out of balance.

Income   An increase in equity resulting from the proceeds of the sale of goods or services. *Same as* Revenue. *Contrast* Expense.

Income sharing ratio   The percentage of net income apportioned to the partners, after salaries and interest. *Contrast* loss-sharing ratio.

Income statement   A financial statement that summarizes the items of revenue and expense, and shows the net income or net loss of a business, for a given fiscal period.

Income summary account   The temporary account to which the total revenues and the total expenses are transferred during the closing process. The balance of the account represents the net income or the net loss for the period and is transferred to the owner's capital account as part of the closing process.

Indirect labour   An account that represents wages to workers who support the manufacturing process, for example, janitorial staff.

Input tax credit   Goods and services tax paid on purchases by a business which is not a final consumer. The business subtracts this from the GST collected from customers and remits the balance to the federal government.

Insiders   The owners, managers, and executive group of a company who have access to company information not available to others. *Contrast* Outsiders.

Internal control   The plan of organization and all the coordinated methods used to protect assets, ensure accurate, reliable accounting data, encourage efficiency, and assure adherence to company policies.

Inventory turnover   For a trading business, the cost of goods sold figure divided by the average merchandise inventory. This represents the number of times the business has been able to sell its inventory in a year.

J

Journal   A specially ruled book in which accounting entries are recorded in the order in which they occur. A transaction is recorded in the journal before it is recorded in the ledger. *Same as* Book of original entry.

Journal entry   An accounting entry in the journal.

Journalizing   The process of recording entries in the journal.

L

Late deposit   A deposit that is made on the last day (usually) of the period covered by the bank statement but does not appear on the bank statement until the following period.

Ledger   A group or file of accounts that can be stored as pages in a book, as cards in a tray, as tape on a reel, or magnetically on disk. *See* Account.

Liability   A debt of an individual, business, or other organization. *Contrast* Asset.

Limited company   *See* Corporation.

Limited liability   Restricted responsibility for a business's debts; based on the amount the owners have invested in the business.

Limited partners   Co-owners of a company whose liability is restricted to their investments in the company, and who also have a limited role in the operation of the company.

Limited partnership   An arrangement where at least one of the owners' liability is restricted to the amount they have invested in the company.

Liquidation   The sale of the assets of a business for cash.

Liquidity   The ease with which an asset can be converted into cash.

Liquidity ratio   One of a number of ratios or numbers calculated by formula and used to help assess the ability of a company to pay its debts. *Same as* Solvency ratio.

Long-term liability   A liability which, in the ordinary course of business, will not be paid within one year.

Loss-sharing ratio   The percentage of net loss apportioned to the partners, after salaries and interest. *Contrast* Income-sharing ratio.

M

Manufacturing business   A business that buys raw materials which it converts into new products and sells to earn a profit.

Manufacturing statement   Accounting form that shows the cost of manufacturing goods in a fiscal period.

Master budget   A formal financial plan a business uses to measure performance and control costs.

Matching principle   *See* GAAP Appendix.

Materiality principle   *See* GAAP Appendix.

Merchandise inventory   The goods handled by a merchandising business. *Same as* Stock-in-trade.

Merchandising business   A business that buys goods to resell them at a profit.

Multi-columnar journal   A journal containing a number of columns in which items of a similar nature are grouped during the recording phase. Its purpose is to reduce the labour of posting.

N

Net claim code   A code that indicates the employee's marital status, number of dependent children and other factors that the government considers to be tax credits; income tax deductions are based on this code.

Net income   The difference between total revenues and total expenses if the revenues are greater than the expenses. *Contrast* Net loss.

Net loss   The difference between total revenues and total expenses if the expenses are greater than the revenues. *Contrast* Net income.

Net pay   Earnings after deductions.

Net worth   The difference between the total assets and total liabilities of a business. *Same as* Capital, Owner's equity.

Nominal account   An account with a balance that does not carry into the next fiscal period, for example, Revenue, Expense, and Drawings accounts.

Non-profit organization   A non-profit organization carries on activities to meet certain needs within society and not for profit. Examples are churches, service clubs, recreational clubs (such as community hockey league) or organizations (such as the cancer society.)

NSF cheque   A cheque that was not cashed when presented to the issuer's bank because there were not sufficient funds in the issuer's bank account to cover the amount of the cheque.

O

Objectivity principle *See* GAAP Appendix.

On account An item purchased or sold that is not paid for at the time; money received or paid to reduce an amount owed.

Opening an account The process of setting up a new account in the ledger.

Opening entry The first accounting entry in the general journal, the entry that records the beginning financial position of a business, thereby opening the books of account.

Out of balance A state in which the total value of all the accounts (or columns in a journal) with debit balances does not equal the total value of all the accounts (or columns in a journal) with credit balances. *Contrast* In balance.

Outsiders A company's bankers and other creditors, prospective investors, shareholders, government agencies such as Revenue Canada, and others who do not have access to company information as do insiders. *Contrast* Insiders.

Outstanding cheque A cheque that is issued and recorded, but not cashed, during the period covered by a bank statement, and therefore is not recorded on the bank statement. *See* Discrepancy item.

Owner's equity The difference between the total assets and total liabilities of a business. *Same as* Capital, Net worth.

P

Partnership A form of business in which more than one person shares in the ownership and operation of a business.

Partnership agreement A legal contract that sets forth the terms and conditions of the partnership.

Payment system A method that people use to exchange one value for another.

Payment on account Money paid to a creditor to reduce the balance owed to that creditor.

Payroll The total process of calculating and preparing the employees' earnings.

Payroll journal A columnar page on which are recorded the details for calculating individual net pays of employees as well as the total payroll figures for the period. *Same as* Payroll register.

Payroll register A columnar page on which are recorded the details for calculating individual net pays of employees as well as the total payroll figures for the period. *Same as* Payroll journal.

Pencil footings Tiny pencil-figure totals used in accounts and journals. *Same as* Pin totals.

Percentage analysis Turning the figures on a financial statement into percentages of one base figure, usually the net income (income statement) or assets (balance sheet). The results are used in analyzing financial statements.

Periodic inventory method   A method of accounting for merchandise inventory in which the cost of the inventory sold is determined only at the end of an accounting period. *Contrast* Perpetual inventory method.

Perpetual inventory method   A method of accounting for merchandise inventory in which the record of items in stock is kept up to date on a daily basis. *Contrast* Periodic inventory method.

Personal chequing account   A bank account that pays no interest on the account balance, designed for those who write a lot of personal cheques.

Petty cash fund   A small quantity of cash, usually no more than $200, that is kept in the office for small expenditures.

Petty cash voucher   A form that is filled out when money is removed from the petty cash fund and no bill for the expenditure is available.

Physical inventory   The procedure by which the unsold goods of a merchandising business are counted and valued at the end of a fiscal period.

Pin totals   Tiny pencil-figure totals used in accounts and journals. *Same as* Pencil footings.

Plant and equipment   Long-term assets such as trucks, held for their usefulness in producing goods or services, and not normally for sale. *Same as* Fixed assets.

Point of sale summary   A document that provides information to the business on sales at that location for that day.

Point-of-sale terminal   An electronic cash register that is connected to and is able to interact with a central computer.

Post-closing trial balance   The trial balance that is taken after the closing entries have been posted.

Posting   The process of transferring the accounting entries from the journal to the ledger.

Preferred stock   Shares in a corporation that have a special privilege for first payment of dividends.

Prepaid expense   An expense, other than for inventory, with benefits that extend into the future, paid for in advance.

Price earnings ratio   The ratio between the market price of a share to the earnings per share. It reflects the amount of confidence the public has in the stock.

Principle of conservatism   *See* GAAP Appendix.

Private corporation   A small or medium-sized business that raises funds privately. Cannot exceed 50 shareholders and cannot advertise the sale of its shares.

Producing business   A business which produces materials directly from natural sources; a farm, for instance, or a fishery.

Profitability percentage One of a number of percentages calculated by formula and used to help assess the company's ability to earn a profit.

Provincial sales tax A percentage based tax, established by the provincial government, on the price of goods sold to a customer.

Proving the cash The process of counting the cash receipts at the end of the day and comparing the total of the book figure for total cash receipts for the day as determined by the company records.

Public accountant An accountant who offers services professionally to the general public.

Public accounting The profession of the public accountant who offers a variety of accounting services to the public for a fee.

Public corporation A company that obtains its capital partly by shares sold to the general public. Shares of these public corporations are listed on the stock exchanges.

Purchase invoice The name given to a supplier's sales invoice in the office of the purchaser. *See* Sales invoice.

Purchase on account A purchase that is not paid for at the time it is made; also called a purchase on credit.

Purchase order A business form initiated by the Purchasing Department authorizing the supplier to ship certain goods or to perform certain services as detailed on the form, and to send a bill for these goods or services.

Purchases journal A special columnar journal in which are recorded the accounting entries for all transactions involving the buying of goods or services on account.

Pure savings account A bank account which pays a high interest rate and allows no cheques to be written. Used mainly for savings.

Q

Quick ratio The ratio of current assets, excluding inventory, to current liabilities. *Same as* Acid-test ratio.

R

Rate of return on net sales The ratio of net earnings to net sales, expressed as a percentage, used comparatively to measure the net income performance of a company.

Rate of return on owner's equity The ratio of net earnings to average owner's equity, expressed as a percentage, used to evaluate the company's performance relative to other investment opportunities such as government bonds.

Raw materials Essential components that become part of a finished product.

Real accounts An account the balance of which is not closed out at the end of the fiscal period but which is carried forward into the succeeding period.

Receipt on account   Money received from a debtor to reduce the balance owed by that debtor.

Receiving report   A business form initiated by the Receiving Department that contains detailed information about goods received from suppliers.

Registered pension plan   A private pension plan, registered and approved by the government, for which contributions, up to a given maximum, may be deducted when calculating taxable income. *Same as* Registered retirement savings plan.

Registered retirement savings plan (RRSP)   A private pension plan, registered and approved by the government, for which contributions, up to a given maximum, may be deducted when calculating taxable income. *Same as* Registered pension plan.

Remittance advice   The tear-off portion of a cheque, or a separate business form accompanying a cheque, which explains what the cheque is for.

Replenishing petty cash   The procedure whereby the petty cash fund is renewed when it reaches a lower limit.

Report form of balance sheet   A balance sheet which presents the information in a vertical format, the assets section being presented above the liabilities and equity section. *Contrast* Account form of balance sheet.

Restrictive endorsement   One that places a condition on the cashing or depositing of a cheque.

Retained Earnings account   The capital that comes from company profits which have not yet been paid to shareholders.

Retail sales tax   A percentage tax based on and added to the price of goods sold to a customer.

Retailer   A merchandising business that buys goods from wholesalers and manufacturers and sells them to the general public with a view to making a profit.

Revenue   An increase in equity resulting from the proceeds of the sale of goods or services. *Same as* Income. *Contrast* Expense.

Revenue recognition convention   *See* GAAP Appendix.

Reversing entry   An entry made at the beginning of an accounting period to cancel an adjusting entry made at the end of the prior accounting period. Made as part of the process for recording revenues and expenses in their proper accounting period.

S

Salary   A fixed amount paid regularly to an employee for services, regardless of the number of hours worked. Salary is usually set at a certain amount per week, per month, or per year, and is paid weekly, half-monthly, or monthly.

Sale on account   A sale for which no money is received at the time it is made; also known as a sale for credit.

Sales invoice   A business form, prepared whenever goods or services are sold on account, showing a description of goods or services, the price, and other information. *See* Purchase invoice.

Sales journal   A special columnar journal in which are recorded the accounting entries for all sales of merchandise on account.

Service business   A business that sell a service, not a product.

Share certificate   A document that indicates the amount of the person's share in the venture. Also known as a stock certificate.

Shareholder   A person who owns shares in a company. Also known as a stockholder.

Sole proprietorship   A business enterprise, the equity of which belongs entirely to one person.

Solvency ratio   One of a number of ratios or numbers calculated by formula and used to help access the company's ability to pay its debts. *Same as* Liquidity ratio.

Source document   A business paper, such as an invoice, that is the original record of a transaction and that provides the information needed when accounting for the transaction.

Statement of account   A detailed record of a customer's account, usually for a period of one month.

Statement of distribution of net income   A document that shows how the income is divided among the partners.

Statement of partners' capital   A document that shows the changes in the partners' capital accounts for the fiscal period.

Stock-in-trade   The goods handled by a merchandising business. *Same as* Merchandise inventory.

Straight-line method of depreciation   A method of calculating the depreciation of an asset whereby the depreciation is apportioned equally to each year of the asset's life. *Contrast* Declining-balance method of depreciation.

Subsidiary ledger   A separate ledger that contains a number of accounts of a similar type, such as the accounts receivable ledger or the accounts payable ledger. The accounts in a subsidiary ledger make up the detailed information in respect to one particular control account in the general ledger.

Synoptic journal   A multi-columned journal with a number of selected special columns and two general columns. The special columns are used to record the more frequently occurring items; the two general columns are used to record the less frequently occurring items. Each of the special columns is reserved for a specific type of entry as indicated in the column heading. At posting time, the totals of the special columns and not the individual items contained in the columns are posted to the general ledger.

T

T4 slip   A formal document prepared by employers for all employees showing payroll data for the year, such as total gross pay and total income tax deducted, which is used to work out an individual's income tax return.

Taking off a trial balance   The process of comparing the total value of the debit accounts in a ledger with the total value of the credit accounts in a ledger. *See* Trial balance.

Taxable earnings   These equal the employee's pay after the premiums for Canada Pension Plan, employment insurance, and any registered pension plan have been deducted from the gross pay.

Temporary account   An account that accumulates data for only one fiscal period at a time. Revenue, expense, and drawings accounts are temporary. *Same as* Nominal account.

Terms of sale   The conditions agreed to at the time of sale, between the buyer and the seller, in respect to the length of time allowed for payment and whether a cash discount can be taken.

Three-column account   The most commonly used type of account, in which there are three money columns, one for the debit amounts, one for the credit amounts, and one for the amount of the balance. *Same as* Balance column account.

Timecard   A card that records the times that an employee starts and finishes work each day. A timecard is usually for a one- or two-week period.

Times interest earned ratio   The number arrived at by formula to show the company's ability to cover its interest expense out of net earnings.

Time period concept   *See* GAAP Appendix.

Total personal exemption   An amount made up of several items, limited by regulation, the total of which may be deducted from earnings for income tax purposes.

Transaction   *See* Business transaction.

Transaction log   A document generated by a point-of-sale terminal that contains detailed information about each transaction.

Transposition error   A mistake caused by the interchanging of digits when transferring figures from one place to another. The trial balance difference that results from such an error is always exactly divisible by 9.

Trend analysis   A document that presents financial data in percentages, for a number of periods, so that tendencies can be seen that are not evident when looking at the dollar figures alone.

Trial balance   A special listing of all the account balances in a ledger, the purpose of which is to see if the dollar value of the accounts with debit balances is equal to the dollar value of the accounts with credit balances. *See* Taking off a trial balance.

Two-column general journal   A simple journal with two money columns, one for the debit amounts and one for the credit amounts.

V

Valuation account   An account that must be considered along with a given asset account to show the true value of the asset account. *Same as* Contra account.

Value-added tax   A tax which government levies at each stage in the production/distribution chain as value is added to the product.

Voucher   A business document that establishes the validity of accounting records.

Voucher jacket   A file folder, containing all the information and documents belonging to a single purchase order.

Voucher system   A rigid set of procedures by which the documents supporting all expenditure transactions must be verified before any payments are authorized.

W

Wages   An amount paid periodically to an employee based on the number of hours worked or the quantity of goods produced. Wages are usually paid on a weekly or biweekly basis.

Wholesaler   A merchandising business that buys goods from manufacturers and other suppliers and sells them to retailers with a view to making a profit.

Work sheet   An informal business form prepared in pencil on columnar bookkeeping paper, used to organize and plan the information for the financial statements.

Working capital   The difference between the current assets and the current liabilities of a business.

Working capital ratio   A measure of a business's ability to pay its debts by the ratio of current assets to current liabilities. *Same as* Current ratio.

Glossary —
Computer Terms

ABS function   A spreadsheet function that ensures that the results of cell calculations will be shown as absolute values, which means that they will not be shown as negative numbers.

absolute cell reference   A cell reference that does not change when copied to a new location. Both the row and column references are preceded by a dollar sign ($C$20, for example).

batch processing   A method in computer accounting that requires clerks to enter transactions as a group. The group can be any logical combination, such as the cash receipts for a day, the credit purchases for a week, and so on.

cell   The intersection of a column and a row on a spreadsheet. Information is located in a cell.

cell contents   The data that is typed into a cell. Examples are labels, values, formulas, cell references, and functions.

cell displays   The data that is shown at each cell in a grid. Cell displays often differ from cell contents because they include the results of formulas, functions, and cell references.

cell protection   A feature of many spreadsheet programs that prevents the accidental erasure of cell contents.

cell reference   A way of reproducing the data from one cell into another. The = or + sign together with the cell location (=A9, for example) is entered in the new cell. Any data in A9 will be reproduced automatically into the new cell and will change when the data in A9 changes.

defaults   Selections that automatically appear in software; they are designed by programmers to save computer users time and effort. For example, a program may format to two decimal places without input from the user.

directory   A portion of a computer disk that is set up to store a specific set of files. A directory is similar in concept to a file folder.

electronic spreadsheet   Software designed to perform a variety of mathematical tasks.

file server   A computer that delivers programs and files to other computers in a LAN.

format   The appearance of the spreadsheet. For example, the figures may or may not have dollar signs; columns may be widened or narrowed as needed.

formula   A mathematical operation performed by a spreadsheet that usually involves cells (=A1+A2, for example).

formula bar   The toolbar that indicates the formula that is being applied to the data

function   Detailed formula built into the program of a spreadsheet.

function prefix   *See* **prefix symbol**.

IF function   A spreadsheet function that can make simple decisions about what will be displayed in a cell. Hence, it is categorized as a logical function.

label   On a spreadsheet, a word or other symbol which is not used in mathematical calculation. *See* **value**.

LAN (local area network)   A computer work area with computers, printers, and file servers wired together.

linked accounts   Accounting software program feature in which changes in one module will automatically update information in other modules.

mixed cell reference   A cell reference, part of which changes when copied to a new location and part of which does not. *See also* **absolute cell reference**; **relative cell reference**.

prefix symbol   A symbol that begins a formula, function, or cell reference. It enables the spreadsheet to distinguish these items from labels. Examples of prefix symbols include = and @.

relative cell reference   A cell reference that will change when copied to a new location.

scrolling   Moving the cursor or cell pointer around on the screen, bringing new columns and rows into view.

software modules   Separate components of a computer program. With accounting software, some modules are similar in concept to subsidiary ledgers.

spreadsheet   A software program designed to perform a large assortment of mathematical tasks, including calculating, organizing, and presenting data

value   On a spreadsheet, a number or amount. Values can be manipulated using mathematical formulas. *See* **label**.

What if?   A phrase often associated with spreadsheets because it highlights their usefulness in helping accountants make decisions. For example, when the accountant changes one value, the spreadsheet updates all dependent calculations instantly. This enables the accountant to provide immediate answers to the question "What if?"

Index

Credits

The publisher has made every reasonable effort to trace the ownership of material in this book to make full acknowledgement for its use. If any errors or omissions have occurred, they will be corrected in future editions, providing written notification has been received by the publisher.

Page 14 Courtesy of Jeff Cox

Pages 32, 36, 65, 145, 195, 196, 197, 288, 627 © 2001 Microsoft Corporation." All rights reserved." Terms of use last updated August 29, 2001.

Page 46 Courtesy of Julia Stavreff, C.A.

Page 76 Courtesy of Larry Lancefield, CA, IFA, CFE

Page 115 Courtesy of Melanie Appleyard

Page 207 Courtesy of Phil Quackenbush

Page 249 Courtesy of Fred Branch

Page 301 Courtesy of Lilian Goh

Page 371 Courtesy of David Yan

Page 422 Courtesy of Janice Fukakusa

Page 176 Courtesy of NCR Canada Ltd.

Page 558–562 MONOPOLY ® and © 2001 Hasbro, Inc. Used with permission.

Page 576 Courtesy of Roberta Lei

Page 616 Browser: © 2000 Yahoo! Inc. All rights reserved. Screen content: Courtesy of Thomson Financial/First Call

Pages: 186, 188, 665, 667, 668, 669,670, 671, 672, 676, 677, 678, 679, 680, 691, 693, 694 Canada Customs & Revenue Agency. Reproduced with permission of the Minister of Public Works and Government Services Canada, 2001

Pages 104–106, 108, 141–143, 227–230, 232–234, 283–289, 352–355, 469–472, 510–515, 560, 629–631, 695–699, Summary Exercises – pages 713–754 courtesy of ACCPAC International